SANDINO'S NATION

Sandino's Nation

Ernesto Cardenal and Sergio Ramírez Writing Nicaragua, 1940–2012

STEPHEN HENIGHAN

McGill-Queen's University Press
Montreal & Kingston • London • Ithaca

ISBN 978-0-7735-4314-0 (cloth)
ISBN 978-0-7735-4315-7 (paper)
ISBN 978-0-7735-8242-2 (ePDF)
ISBN 978-0-7735-8243-9 (ePUB)

Legal deposit second quarter 2014
Bibliothèque nationale du Québec

Printed in Canada on acid-free paper that is 100% ancient forest free (100% post-consumer recycled), processed chlorine free

This book has been published with the help of a grant from the Canadian Federation for the Humanities and Social Sciences, through the Awards to Scholarly Publications Program, using funds provided by the Social Sciences and Humanities Research Council of Canada. Funding has also been received from the University of Guelph's Vice-President of Research and Internationalization and the University of Guelph's School of Languages and Literatures.

McGill-Queen's University Press acknowledges the support of the Canada Council for the Arts for our publishing program. We also acknowledge the financial support of the Government of Canada through the Canada Book Fund for our publishing activities.

Library and Archives Canada Cataloguing in Publication

Henighan, Stephen, 1960–, author
Sandino's nation: Ernesto Cardenal and Sergio Ramírez writing Nicaragua, 1940–2012/Stephen Henighan.

Includes bibliographical references and index.
Issued in print and electronic formats.
ISBN 978-0-7735-4314-0 (bound). – ISBN 978-0-7735-4315-7 (pbk.). – ISBN 978-0-7735-8242-2 (ePDF). – ISBN 978-0-7735-8243-9 (ePUB).

1. Cardenal, Ernesto – Criticism and interpretation. 2. Ramírez, Sergio, 1942– – Criticism and interpretation. 3. Authors, Nicaraguan – 20th century. 4. Nicaragua – History – Revolution, 1979 – Literature and the revolution. 5. Politics and literature – Nicaragua. 6. Nicaragua – History – 20th century. I. Title.

PQ7519.C34Z85 2014 861'.64 C2013-908242-5
C2013-908243-3

This book was typeset by Interscript in 10/13 Sabon.

Contents

Acknowledgments vii

Abbreviations xi

Citation System xiii

1 Priest and Politician as Arbiters of Sandino's Nation 3

2 Nicaraguan History to 1979 21

3 Cardenal: The Contemplative's Poetry (1940–68) 45

4 Ramírez: From Student Activist to Exiled Writer (1956–75) 118

5 Cardenal: The First Incursion into Prose (1970–75) 194

6 Nicaraguan History, 1979–90 225

7 Ramírez: Towards the Novelist as Vice-President (1976–89) 239

8 Cardenal: The Revolutionary Poet (1969–89) 340

9 Nicaraguan History after 1990 426

10 Ramírez: The Politician as Writer after the Revolution (1990–2006) 443

11 Cardenal: The Poet as Memoirist, the Nation as Relic (1990–2006) 563

12 Ortega's Nation: Two Dissident Writers Face Globalization (2007–12) 627

Notes 689

Bibliography 711

Index 735

Acknowledgments

This book, more than any other that I have written, owes much to other people. To undertake my initial research, I relied on a three-year Standard Research Grant from the Social Sciences and Humanities Research Council of Canada. I'm grateful to Donna Pennee, Alan Filewod, and Jacqueline Murray for advice on preparing my grant application, and to Daniel Chouinard, Gordana Yovanovich, and Stephanie Nutting for assistance in revising my teaching schedule once the grant had been obtained.

I am equally grateful to the Friends of the Princeton Library for a grant that allowed me to consult the Sergio Ramírez Papers. Without this opportunity, my research for this book would not have been complete. I owe a large debt to the attentive, efficient and welcoming staff of the Rare Books and Manuscripts Department at Princeton's Firestone Library. For their help and cooperation, I also thank the staffs of the McLaughlin Library at the University of Guelph, particularly Paul Stack and Heather Martin; the British Library, London; the Bodleian Library, University of Oxford; and the Taylorian Institution Library, Oxford, where I spent months reading and taking notes, and where particular thanks are due to John Wainwright and Helen Buchanan. My research in Oxford was rendered more congenial by the hospitality I received at Wadham College, where I thank Robin Fiddian for securing me a temporary membership to the Senior Common Room, and Cliff Davies for support and hospitality.

In Managua, I thank Ernesto Cardenal and Sergio Ramírez for taking time from their busy schedules to speak to me, and their respective assistants, Luz Marina Acosta and Betty de Solis, for facilitating these interviews. In Guelph, I'm indebted to Padraig O'Cleirigh for his biblical expertise, to my graduate students Lisa Bellstedt and Maca Suazo Flores for their illuminating engagement with Nicaraguan literature, and to my late colleague

Nora Cerbatov and her executor, Kris Inwood, for giving me access to the collection of Sandinista literature in her library. Christopher GoGwilt's perceptions, during a brief but incisive conversation in Manhattan, revealed to me how a book could be made of this material. On the conference circuit, I'm grateful to Aurora Camacho de Schmidt for discussing her meetings with Ernesto Cardenal with me in San José, Costa Rica, and Jeffrey L. Gould for providing useful secondary reading suggestions in Toronto.

I would like to thank my research assistants. The late Sebastián Suárez, my research assistant in the summer of 2001, when the shape of this project had not yet become clear, collected a treasure trove of material that, when I rediscovered it a decade later, helped me to revive a book that I had abandoned. I thank Sebastián for this posthumous gift, as I thank Jaqueline Dubon, my research assistant in the summer of 2012, for her meticulousness and determination, and her ability to combine hard work with curiosity and enthusiasm. I'm indebted to the School of Languages and Literatures at the University of Guelph for funding these assistantships. I thank Lidia Valencia Fourcans for additional research on this project.

I'm grateful to Edwin Williamson, Jacqueline Rattray, Fiona J. Mackintosh, Irene Blayer, Rafael Montano, Norman Cheadle, Sophie Lavoie, and Berenice Villagómez, among others, for offering me fora in which to present early versions of this material at: Université Laval, Quebec; Brock University, St Catharines, Ontario; Université du Québec à Montréal; Universidad Centroamericana, San José, Costa Rica; University of Manitoba, Winnipeg; University of Edinburgh; University of Oxford; University of Western Ontario, London; York University, Toronto; University of Saskatchewan, Saskatoon; University of British Columbia, Vancouver; Carleton University, Ottawa, Concordia University, Montreal; University of Toronto; and Princeton University. Sections have been published in different form in the *Modern Language Review*, the *Bulletin of Hispanic* Studies, the *Bulletin of Spanish Studies*, the *Revista Canadiense de Estudios Hispánicos,* and *Latin American Narratives and Cultural Identity: Selected Readings* (New York: Peter Lang 2004), edited by Irene Maria F. Blayer and Mark Cronlund Anderson. Grateful acknowledgment is made to the editors for permission to reprint, as it is to the Firestone Library at Princeton University for permission to cite from its manuscript collection. For permission to reproduce photographs, I thank Sergio Ramírez, Luz Marina Acosta, Chris Vail, Pedro Meyer and Zone Zero, and Jorge Colón Torres. Every effort has been made to contact copyright holders.

This book would not have been published without substantial financial assistance. In addition to McGill University and Queen's University, I am in the debt of the Social Sciences and Humanities Research Council of Canada for an Aid to Scholarly Publications Program grant. I thank Kevin Hall, Vice-President Research and Internationalization at the University of Guelph, for his timely financial support, and Ruediger Mueller for taking the initiative to ensure that the School of Languages and Literatures, University of Guelph, matched Dr Hall's generosity. I thank Mark Abley at McGill-Queen's for his enthusiasm for this book and his expert guidance in navigating the strange isles of scholarly book publication. I'm grateful to Ryan Van Huijstee for welcoming this book to the MQUP fold, Curtis Fahey for his engaged and encouraging copy editing, and Barry Levely for a map of Nicaragua. I also thank the anonymous academic assessors of my manuscript for their very useful suggestions. My most enduring debt is to Ana Lorena Leija, who has been "patient, very patient" with my habit of diverting conversations to the subject of Cardenal and Ramírez. I am particularly in her debt for the skill and patience with which she debugged a snarled Word file of this book.

Decades before I imagined this book, my obsession with Nicaragua was nourished at Swarthmore College by the members of the Latin American Studies Group and other Nicaragua enthusiasts. I thank Michele Besso, Thomas Bossert, Jonathan Conning, Wendy Hoben, Hugh Lacey, Donna Mullarkey, Brad Roth, Kenneth E. Sharpe, and Max Yarowsky for helping to shape and encourage my thinking about the Nicaraguan Revolution.

Abbreviations

AEU	Asociación de Estudiantes Universitarios (University Students' Association) [Guatemala]
AMNLAE	Asociación de Mujeres Nicaragüenses Luisa Amanda Espinoza (Luisa Amanda Espinoza Association of Nicaraguan Women)
ASTC	Asociación Sandinista de Trabajadores de la Cultura (Sandinista Association of Culture Workers)
CEPAL/ECLA	Comisión Económica para América Latina/Economic Commission for Latin America [Chile]
CIA	Central Intelligence Agency [United States]
COSEP	Consejo Superior de la Empresa Privada (High Council of Private Enterprise)
CSUCA	Consejo Superior Universitario Centroamericano (Governing Council of Central American Universities)
CUSO	Canadian University Services Overseas
DAAD	Deutscher Akademischer Austauschdienst (German Academic Foreign Exchange Service)
DEA	Drug Enforcement Agency [United States]
DGSE	Dirección General de Seguridad del Estado (Department of State Security)
EDUCA	Editorial Universitaria Centroamericana (Central American University Press)
ELN	Ejército de Liberación Nacional (National Liberation Army) [Colombia]
EPS	Ejército Popular Sandinista (Sandinista People's Army)
EU	European Union

EZLN	Ejército Zapatista de Liberación Nacional (Zapatista National Liberation Front) [Mexico]
FER	Frente Estudiantil Revolucionario (Revolutionary Student Front)
FMLN	Frente Farabundo Martí de Liberación Nacional (Farabundo Marti National Liberation Front) [El Salvador]
FSLN	Frente Sandinista de Liberación Nacional (Sandinista Front for National Liberation)
GN	Guardia Nacional (National Guard)
GPP	Guerra Populàr Prolongada (Prolonged People's War)
ISI	Import-Substitution Industrialization
JGRN	Junta de Gobierno de Reconstrucción Nacional (Governing Junta of National Reconstruction)
MRS	Movimiento de Renovación Sandinista (Sandinista Renewal Movement)
NAFTA	North American Free Trade Agreement
NATO	North Atlantic Treaty Organization
OAS	Organization of American States
PEN	Poets Essayists Novelists
PRI	Partido Revolucionario Institucional (Party of Revolutionary Institutions) [Mexico]
PSN	Partido Socialista Nicaragüense (Nicaraguan Socialist Party)
SMP	Ley del Servicio Militar Patriótico (Patriotic Military Service Law)
TP	Tendencia Proletaria (Proletarian Tendency)
UCA	Universidad Centroamericana (Central American University) [Managua]
UMAP	Unidad Militar de Ayuda a la Produccion (Military Unit for Assisting in Production) [Cuba]
UNAM	Universidad Nacional Autónoma de México (National Autonomous University of Mexico)
UNAN	Universidad Nacional Autónoma de Nicaragua (National Autonomous University of Nicaragua)
UNAP	Unión Nacional de Acción Popular (National Union for People's Action)
UNICEF	United Nations International Children's Emergency Fund/ United Nations Children's Fund
UNO	Unión Nacional Opositora (National Opposition Union)
USAID	United States Agency for International Development

Citation System

For reference purposes, works by Ernesto Cardenal and Sergio Ramírez will be indicated in the text using the abbreviations below.

English translations of titles of works in Spanish or other languages, enclosed in parentheses, will follow the title of each work the first time it appears. An italicized English title refers to an existing translation; a non-italicized title indicates a literal rendering of the title of a work that had not been translated into English at the time this book was written.

Subsequent references to the work will use the English title where a translation exists and the original title where there is no translation. Where a published English translation is extant, English versions of quotes are from the translation; in other cases, translations are by the author.

This book uses the Spanish naming system. Many figures discussed use two surnames; the first is the paternal surname and the second the maternal surname. When only one surname is mentioned, or when names are alphabetized, as in the Bibliography or the Index, the first, paternal surname takes precedence.

WORKS BY ERNESTO CARDENAL

AG	*Los años de Granada*
AL	*Abide in Love*
AN	*Antología nueva*
AOP	*Apocalypse and Other Poems*
AT	*Antología*
CANC	*Cántico Cósmico*
COSC	*Cosmic Canticle*
EC	*En Cuba*
ED	*El estrecho dudoso*

ESI	*Evangelio de Solentiname I*
ESII	*Evangelio de Solentiname II*
FV	*Flights of Victory*
GOLD	*Los ovnis de oro. Poemas indios/Golden UFOs. The Indian Poems*
GS1	*The Gospel in Solentiname 1*
GS2	*The Gospel in Solentiname 2*
GS3	*The Gospel in Solentiname 3*
GS4	*The Gospel in Solentiname 4*
GT	*Gethsemani, Ky.*
HIA	*Homenaje a los indios americanos*
IC	*In Cuba*
IE	*Las ínsulas extrañas. Memorias 2*
MMOP	*Marilyn Monroe and Other Poems*
OMM	*Oración por Marilyn Monroe y otros poemas*
OO	*Los ovnis de oro*
OS	*The Origin of Species and Other Poems*
PL	*Pluriverse: New and Selected Poems*
PS	*Psalms*
PT	*Pasajero de tránsito*
RP	*La revolución perdida: Memorias 3*
SA	*Salmos*
SDR	*La santidad de la revolución*
TNO	*Telescopio en la noche oscura*
TV	*Tata Vasco*
UIEC	*Unpublished interview with the author*
VA	*Vida en el amor*
VP	*Vida perdida: Memorias*
VPL	*Versos del pluriverso*
VV	*Vuelos de victoria*
WWN	*With Walker in Nicaragua and Other Early Poems*
ZHOD	*Zero Hour and Other Documentary Poems*

WORKS BY SERGIO RAMÍREZ

AF	*Las armas del futuro*
AM	*Adiós muchachos: una memoria de la revolución sandinista*
AMM	*Adiós Muchachos: A Memoir of the Sandinista Revolution*
AO	*El alba de oro: La historia viva de Nicaragua*

BM	*Un baile de máscaras*
BMF	*Biografía Mariano Fiallos*
BV	*Balcanes y volcanes y otros ensayos y trabajos*
CA	*Confesión de amor*
CATM	*Charles Atlas también muere*
CC	*Cuentos completos*
CD	*Castigo Divino*
CLM	*El cielo llora por mí*
CS	*Clave de sol*
CYC	*Catalina y Catalina*
DTT	*De Tropeles y Tropelías*
EN	*Estás en Nicaragua*
EP	*La edad presente es de lucha*
HFT	*Hatful of Tigers: Reflections on Art, Culture and Politics*
LF	*La Fugitiva*
LIC	*Lección inaugural del curso 1969–1970: La juventud y la nueva Nicaragua*
MBS	*Margarita, How Beautiful the Sea*
MLM	*Margarita, está linda la mar*
MUM	*Mil y una muertes*
MV	*Mentiras verdaderas*
NC	*Nuevos cuentos*
OC	*Oficios compartidos*
PDCN	*La problemática del derecho constitucional nicaragüense*
PVS	*El pensamiento vivo de Sandino*
RA	*El reino animal*
SF	*Seguimos de frente*
SLT	*Señor de los tristes*
SNM	*Sombras nada más*
SRP	Sergio Ramírez Papers (Princeton University)
STO	*Stories*
TBF	*To Bury Our Fathers*
TDMS	*¿Te dio miedo la sangre?*
TDPO	*A Thousand Deaths Plus One*
TF	*Tiempo de fulgor*
TO	*Tambor olvidado*
UISR	Unpublished interview with the author

SANDINO'S NATION

HONDURAS
SEGOVIA MOUNTAINS
Ocotal
Estelí
Matagalpa
Corinto
León
Lake Managua
NICARAGUA
Managua
Masaya
Masatepe
Granada
Lake Nicaragua
Bluefields
Caribbean Sea
Pacific Ocean
Rivas
San Juan del Sur
Solentiname Archipelago
San Carlos
San Juan River
San Juan del Norte
N
0 25 50 Kilometres
0 25 50 Miles
COSTA RICA

1

Priest and Politician as Arbiters of Sandino's Nation

INTRODUCTION

When the author of this study was an adolescent, he heard a radio talk-show host disparage Bianca Jagger, the then-wife of British rock star Mick Jagger, as "the world's only known Nicaraguan." He laughed, as did his buddies on the school bus where the radio was playing, and, once the bus arrived at his rural Canadian high school, repeated the joke to friends. A few years later, when the adolescent had become a student in the United States, he found that the daily coverage of the Nicaraguan Revolution in the *New York Times* evaluated not only the revolutionary regime's policies but also its personalities, some of whom were well-known writers. In much of the Western world during the 1980s, readers of newspapers and serious literature, along with viewers of television news reports, became familiar with names such as Daniel Ortega, Tomás Borge, Edén Pastora, Sergio Ramírez, Ernesto Cardenal, Violeta Chamorro, Gioconda Belli, Arturo J. Cruz, Carlos Fonseca Amador, and Anastasio Somoza. News reports even included background information on Augusto César Sandino, the nationalist hero who fought a guerrilla war against the US Marines from 1927 to 1933. Now, it seemed, there were many "known Nicaraguans." What had changed?

How a nation is perceived by the outside world differs from how it perceives itself. Yet the two dynamics can be related: a nation's crises or rearticulations of its identity participate in earning it attention from other nations. This book studies the construction of Nicaraguan national identity during the three central periods of the country's recent history – before, during, and after the 1979–90 Revolution – through a close reading of the work of its two best-known and most prolific modern authors, Ernesto Cardenal and Sergio Ramírez, both of whom were also pivotal figures in the Sandinista

Ernesto Cardenal and Sergio Ramírez, San José, Costa Rica, 1971 (courtesy of Sergio Ramírez)

Revolution. (Chapters 2, 6, and 9 summarize the interpretation of Nicaraguan history that guides my analysis.) Though this book mixes literary and historical analysis, and is written by someone who holds degrees in both literature and political science, it does not aim to contribute to the branch of academic writing known as cultural studies. My readings, though informed by literary and cultural theory, assert the value of paying close attention to a literary text and how it works, both as an activity of inherent aesthetic and moral value, and as a revealing method of understanding the cultural and historical conditions that gave birth to the work. In recent years I have read too many monographs by colleagues whose enthusiasm for cultural studies has led them to substitute for serious scholarship superficial, ideologically mandated, often inaccurate generalizations about material that they lack the professional training to evaluate; an almost inevitable corollary of this approach seems to be neglect of the literary work, or its misrepresentation through selective, tendentious readings of its contents. In the twenty-first century, when "cultural studies" has become a buzzword employed by MBA-inspired university administrators to close down language programs, such as those where students might read Nicaraguan literature in the original Spanish, and replace them with survey courses in English that do not offer students first-hand engagement with another language or literature, it is no longer possible to claim – as some scholars did in the 1990s – that cultural studies is a politically progressive movement. While a few individual cultural studies scholars no doubt view themselves as knights of the left, this delusion withers on examination of the ends the "cultural studies" slogan serves in the university context: obliteration of smaller programs offering specialized knowledge of, and intimate communication with, cultures other than one's own; the promotion of huge classes and "efficient processing" of large student numbers, objectification of and distance from the "other," homogenization and uniformity; "credentialling" instead of education. This book, therefore, will attempt to study Nicaraguan culture, both literary and otherwise, in a way that avoids the pitfalls of cultural studies.

APPROACHES TO THE NICARAGUAN NATION

A strongly literary approach is particularly appropriate in the Nicaraguan case because, as will be argued in the chapters that follow, literacy and literature played a pivotal role in reimagining the nation during the 1970s and 1980s. After 1990, the erosion of this privileged position, in which writing was both valuable in itself and much more than words on a page, provoked a crisis as the imperative to construct the nation yielded to the question of how to imagine oneself (and how to survive economically, whether as a labourer, a professional, or an artist) in the context of emerging transnational structures. This crisis is explored in chapters 9 to 12. In my pinpointing of 1990 as a watershed, I am influenced by the classification of E.J. Hobsbawm in *Age of Extremes: The Short Twentieth Century, 1914–1991*. Latin America's, and particularly Central America's, embroilment in the Cold War meant that the end of this "century" was felt as such in Central America, with an immediacy equivalent to the way in which it was felt in other Cold War theatres, such as Central Europe or Southern Africa. This is evident in events such as the defeat of the Sandinistas in the 1990 elections and the 1992 settlement of the long-running civil war in El Salvador. In broader terms, I take the early 1990s to be a recognizable point of transition after which individual and community life is shaped by accelerated forms of globalization. Among the traits of this accelerated globalization – a term I use to reflect the fact that globalization of one kind or another has been going on for centuries – I would list the disappearance of the Soviet Union and the battles of the First Gulf War, two events in 1991 that consolidated the position of the United States as the planet's hegemonic military power; the dissolution or declining importance of transnational alliances based on ideology, such as the Warsaw Pact and the North Atlantic Treaty Organization

(NATO), and their displacement by trading blocks such as the European Union (EU), consolidated in 1992, or the North American Free Trade Agreement (NAFTA), which came into effect in 1994; the digitalization of commerce; the unchallenged predominance of neo-liberal economic ideas and, concomitantly, the widening dissemination of individualistic liberal social ideas, particularly as related to lifestyles and sexuality; the spread, during the early 1990s, of email and portable personal computers; the replacement of local or national businesses with transnational chains; and the increasing prevalence of ethnic, regional, or gender identities, rather than national identity, as primary forms of personal identification.

History did not end, as Francis Fukuyama had predicted in an early moment of post-Cold War euphoria, but it did become more diaphanous and difficult to pin down. The influence of the past on the present did not vanish, but it grew less deterministic and obvious. The retreat of diachronic history, the evaporation of the sensation of living inside a national chronology, sapped traditional structures of authority of their vitality. Authority figures who were archetypes of Spanish American society, such as the politically outspoken priest or the writer-politician – the archetypes embodied, respectively, by Ernesto Cardenal and Sergio Ramírez – no longer commanded axiomatic authority in the public sphere. This erosion of patriarchy and patriarchal authority was one form taken by the weakening of national identity.

This study makes substantial use of Benedict Anderson's definition of the nation as the imagined community of a literate bourgeoisie. While Anderson's ideas are not entirely congruent with the Nicaraguan case, where the virtual absence of a credible bourgeoisie relegated the nation-building enterprise to an alliance of peasants, rural artisans, and renegade oligarchical youth, and where, contrary to Anderson's portrait of nationalism as a product of secularization, the Catholic religion played a significant role in concentrating national feeling, the fact that his theory is developed through Spanish American examples makes it an apt point of reference. Yet, despite its value, Anderson's *Imagined Communities*, first published in 1983, provides limited guidance, even in its revised 1991 edition, in how to theorize the nation under accelerated globalization. Here, it seems, we are still groping for clarity: a groping to which this study attempts to contribute.

Anderson's depiction of the evolution of national consciousness collects its evidence from the larger nations of South America. Owing to historical factors that are discussed in chapter 2 and elsewhere, Central American nationhood, and Central American literature, belong to a particular regional history that does not always match "Latin American" norms derived from the study of larger countries that articulated their nationalism through the struggle against Spain in the Wars of Independence in the early nineteenth century – wars in which Central America remained on the sidelines. In spite of centuries of marginalization and periodic bouts of outright genocide – in Nicaragua in the sixteenth century, in El Salvador in the early 1930s, in Guatemala in the early 1980s – the heritage of the indigenous civilizations – Mayan in Guatemala and Honduras, Náhuat in Nicaragua – is an integral feature of Central American culture which, as Arturo Arias points out, is received differently and with more weight than is the case in some other Latin American cultures. Even today, the Central American nations, as tiny as they are, remain remarkably different from one another: to drive across the border from Guatemala to El Salvador, or from Nicaragua to Costa Rica, is to enter a distinct physical, social, and mental environment. In spite of these discrete identities, it is impossible to deny the existence of a common regional history, from the Liberal-versus-Conservative strife of the nineteenth century to the capitalist-versus-Marxist struggles of the 1980s, both of which engulfed the isthmus in its entirety. This history has created certain common cultural features and a literature with recognizable regional traits. Much of this study concentrates on the specificities of Nicaraguan history and Nicaraguan literature; these need to be understood, however, as existing within a common Central American frame: a context that is particularly evident in chapters 4, 7, and 10, which are devoted to the writing of Sergio Ramírez, whose work reflects a strong sense of Central American identity and a consciousness of parallel developments in neighbouring countries.

One of the benefits of writing about Nicaragua is that the activism of the 1980s –when the author made his own first visit to the country – has left a legacy of mid-career scholars who became fascinated with Nicaragua at an early stage of their intellectual development, and whose substantial publications give anyone undertaking a book such as this a head start that would not be available if one were researching other smaller Spanish American nations. It is a pleasure to stand on these scholars' shoulders. My debt to Roger Lancaster's writing on Nicaraguan machismo is obvious in my analysis of the erosion of patriarchy, as my debt to Arturo Arias, who has pioneered the study of Central American literature as a distinctive field, is in my textual readings. Jeffrey L. Gould's and Elizabeth Dore's respective work on the elimination of the category of the indigenous and the installation of a "mestizo norm" in the western half of Nicaragua is an essential prelude to my analysis of the ways in which Cardenal and Ramírez construct the nation. I am also indebted to a score of other scholars, cited in the pages that follow, who have published valuable research on individual works by Cardenal or Ramírez. One of my most important intellectual debts is to

Michel Gobat's *Confronting the American Dream: Nicaragua under US Imperial Rule*. By illuminating the elite anti-Americanism of the Conservative oligarchy of Granada, Gobat's book helped to clear up contradictions that had confused me since the early 1980s, when, as a student, I puzzled over how it was possible for radical figures such as Ernesto and Fernando Cardenal to come from the heart of what the Nicaraguans I met described as the Conservative part of the country.

This vision of Granada Conservatives as an alienated, suppressed, would-be governing class changed not only my understanding of the career of Ernesto Cardenal but also my perception of 1970s and 1980s Sandinismo. After reading Gobat's work, it is difficult not to see the Frente Sandinista de Liberación Nacional (FSLN; Sandinista Front for National Liberation), which coalesced as a broad-based alliance around 1975, as a coming-together of ostracized Conservative oligarchs and their children with Sergio Ramírez's *Ventana* movement of professionals from Liberal families who were radicalized during their studies in León, along with insurgents such as Tomás Borge and Daniel Ortega who came from poor or lower-middle-class families that were not strongly identified with either Conservative or Liberal traditions. This three-way union, even more than the much-cited reconciliation of the FSLN's three ideological tendencies (see chapter 2), now came into focus as the origin of the Sandinista government. It is telling that, after the split in the FSLN in late 1994 and early 1995 (see chapter 9), it was overwhelmingly those who had not belonged to either Conservative or Liberal traditions prior to their conversion to Sandinismo who remained loyal to the FSLN. In light of this development, it is possible, even during the years of Sandinista government, to detect in retrospect the Conservative or Liberal underlay beneath the Sandinista veneer in many of the movement's most prominent members. While one needs to guard against unwarranted applications of hindsight, it is clear that the political cultures of origin of prominent Sandinistas played a more decisive role in guiding their various conceptualizations of the Nicaraguan nation than was admitted at the time.

PRIEST AND POLITICIAN

The pairing of Ernesto Cardenal and Sergio Ramírez and their writing offers an expansive vision of the constructions of Nicaraguan nationality that came together to form Sandinismo. Though both lived abroad for extended periods during the decades prior to the Revolution, and though from 1980 onward the two men were neighbours in the Pancasán district of Managua and after 1995 both were involved in the Movimiento de Renovación

Sandinista (MRS; Sandinista Renewal Movement), in many respects they embody distinct, even opposing, threads within the Sandinista fabric: the Conservative versus the Liberal; the revolutionary radical versus the social democrat; the devout Catholic versus the agnostic of evangelical Protestant background; the white descendant of European immigrants versus the mestizo who feels close to his Náhuat roots; the urbanite who isolated himself in rural retreats versus the man from a village who lived his adult life in large urban centres; the member of the foreign-educated elite versus the professional who studied at local and national institutions; the poet versus the prose writer; the celibate versus the family man; and, above all, the priest versus the politician. Each writer adopted Sandino's example as the template for the nation, yet here, too, divergences arose. Ramírez's Sandino was an exemplary rural mestizo who fought for a nation defined by the union of the indigenous with the Hispanic: almost, at times, a brown-skinned racial nationalist; Cardenal's Sandino, by contrast, was a Christ-figure at the national level, a man whose sacrifice permeated the soil of the homeland and whose lesson of martyrdom helped to mediate the discrepancies between religious and revolutionary discourses and set an example for the self-sacrifice of the young guerrillas and militiamen of the 1970s and 1980s. Each of these Sandinos has come to the fore at different times in modern Sandinismo. Their articulations by Cardenal and Ramírez, like other aspects of the two writers' production, sprang from the ways in which each, respectively, took over, exploited, and revised the long-standing Spanish American archetypes of the revolutionary priest and the multifaceted builder of the nation who is at once writer, politician, educator, and lawmaker.

The revolutionary priest is one of the central archetypes of Latin American patriarchy. The Catholic Church, which traditionally collaborated in maintaining divisions of social class, ethnicity, and race by ministering to the wealthy and assuring the poor that the Gospel message of "blessed are the meek" meant that they would inherit the kingdom of heaven in the next life, draws on the authority of an omnipotent God. The revolutionary priest redirects this authority by invoking Scripture to assert that God abhors injustice. His rhetoric insists on the possibility of constructing the kingdom of heaven on earth. The content of this terrestrial Utopia has varied over time; between 1959 and 1990, the Utopia imagined by the revolutionary priest was influenced by Marxism, or might be explicitly Marxist.

The first priest ordained in the New World was Fray Bartolomé de Las Casas (1483–1566), the son of a wealthy merchant from Seville. Having taken orders on the island of Hispaniola (later the Dominican Republic and Haiti) in 1510, he became Latin America's first priest in the revolutionary tradition. In December 1511 Las Casas attended a sermon in Santo Domingo in which the Spanish Dominican priest Antonio de Montesinos warned his flock that they were committing mortal sin by exploiting the indigenous people (Fox, 2007: 63). Montesinos's sermon changed the young priest's life. As bishop of Guatemala and Chiapas, Las Casas denounced the brutality of the Spanish conquest of the New World, decrying the massacres of indigenous people. His polemical pamphlet, *Brevísima relación de la destrucción de las Indias* (1542; *The Devastation of the Indies: A Brief Account*), pioneered the inversion of authority that underlies the revolutionary priest's rhetorical strategies. Las Casas associates the indigenous people with Christian imagery, asserting that "su comida es tal que la de los sanctos padres en el desierto" (*Brevísima*, 12; "their repasts are such [as] the food of the holy fathers in the desert" [*Devastation*, 38]) and describing them as "ovejas mansas" (*Brevísima*, 13; "this sheepfold" [*Devastation*, 39]); the Spanish conquistadors, on the other hand, are "como lobos y tigres y leones crudelísimos de muchos días hambrientos" (*Brevísima*, 13; "like ravening beasts, wolves, tigers or lions that had been starved for many days" [*Devastation*, 39]) and are referred to caustically as those "que se llaman cristianos" (*Brevísima*, 15; "who called themselves Christians" [*Devastation*, 67]). Las Casas's activism led to changes in Spanish colonial policy, such as Las Leyes Nuevas (New Laws) of 1543, which attempted to eliminate the drafting of unpaid indigenous labour through the system known as the *encomienda*, and the establishment of commissions of enquiry into abuses committed by conquistadors. Las Casas, however, died a defeated man. *De thesauris*, his final futile protestation that the colonization of the Americas was against God's will, was published in 1562, four years before his death, at a time when the rate at which land was being allotted to Spanish settlers was accelerating. A statue of Las Casas in Antigua Guatemala continues to attract the homage of devout Maya; the Ejército Zapatista de Liberación Nacional (EZLN; Zapatista Army for National Liberation) chose to launch its armed struggle for indigenous rights on 1 January 1994, in the Chiapas city of San Cristóbal de Las Casas, which bears the priest's name.

By the nineteenth century, the focus of the revolutionary priest's activism had become the emerging Spanish American nation. The prototype of the patriarchal revolutionary priest in this Romantic tradition is Father Miguel Hidalgo (1752–1811), who is commemorated in Mexico each September as "the father of the nation." In September 1810 Hidalgo, whose personal connections bridged the gap between wealthy European-descended Mexicans impatient with the colonial regime and the rural, mainly indigenous poor, gave a speech calling for a general uprising. In Edwin Williamson's summation, "Hidalgo's aims were sweeping but unfocused: abolition of the Indian tribute, the return of Indian lands and death to all Spaniards" (Williamson 1992: 215). His speech, popularly known as the "Grito de Dolores" ("Shout of Pain"), ignited a peasant revolt that led, by way of a lengthy armed conflict, to Mexican independence. Like Las Casas, Hidalgo presented himself as the protector of indigenous Americans. Even after his capture and execution in 1811, his adoption of the dark-skinned Virgin of Guadelupe as the emblem of the independence movement continued to lend the insurgency a religious and cultural coherence that enabled it to fend off the condemnation of "the higher levels of the clergy [who] hurled anathemas and excommunications upon the insurgents, raising fears among the general population" (Guedea 2000: 289). After Hidalgo's death, a mestizo (or mulatto – accounts vary) priest, Father José María Morelos, became the leader of the independence forces until his capture and execution in 1815. Moving one step beyond Las Casas, Hidalgo and Morelos enshrined Scripture's opposition to injustice in the symbol of a brown-skinned Virgin who wept for the poor. The Virgin of Guadelupe, who for a majority of modern Mexicans remains their most immediate emotional connection to the Catholic Church, provided the Mexican state with a tacit foundation of respect for the poor and the indigenous past. This legacy, promoted by two revolutionary priests, is an ideological counterweight, built into Mexican national discourse, to the injustice, racism, and corruption that has characterized the country since independence. In the twentieth century, Hidalgo himself became a potent ideological symbol when the painter José Clemente Orozco (1883–1949) created an enormous mural portrait of a torch-bearing Hidalgo giving his "Shout of Pain" speech at the top of the interior staircase of the state government house in Guadalajara. The wretched masses of the poor, preparing to rise up as they hear Hidalgo's words, make explicit the relevance of the nineteenth-century priest's quest for justice and national autonomy to the ideological struggles of the twentieth century.

In the post-1959 era, the revolutionary priest, by definition, works for national liberation through the creation of a socialist Utopia that attempts to implement divine justice on earth. Camilo Torres, the Colombian priest who influenced Ernesto Cardenal, died fighting with guerrillas of the Cuban-inspired Ejército Nacional de Liberación (ELN; National Liberation Army), having argued, in Cardenal's words, that "que la revolución fuera con violencia o sin violencia no dependía del pueblo sino de la clase dirigente. Y ya desde fray Bartolomé de Las Casas la lucha armada había quedado justificada, cuando él dijo que los naturales de América tenían derecho 'de hacernos guerra justísima y lo tendrían hasta el día del juicio'" (*IE*, 68; "whether the revolution occurred with or without violence did not depend on the people but rather on the governing class. And so since Fray Bartolomé de Las Casas armed struggle has been justified, when he said that the natives of the Americas had the right 'to make a very just war on us and they would have it until Judgment Day'"). The advent of liberation theology, developed in the 1960s and 1970s by theologians such as the Peruvian Gustavo Gutiérrez and the Brazilian Leonardo Boff, and expressed in the church's "preferential option for the poor," as articulated at the conferences of Latin American bishops in Medellín, Colombia, in 1968 and Puebla, Mexico, in 1979, condoned, and even encouraged, radical secular commitments: "By starting from the reality of poverty and injustice in Latin America, the new theologians hoped to bring the church back to earth, to face the facts and do something about them ... What the Latin-American theologians find particularly attractive in [Karl] Marx is his suggestion of the relationship between experience and theory – that if man has sufficient understanding of his reality he can improve that reality and himself, and that this new situation in turn influences and educates him" (Lernoux 1980: 30).

The election, in 1978, of the militantly anti-Communist Polish Pope John Paul II, who appeared to encourage the liberation theologians during his first visit to Latin America to attend the Puebla conference (Lernoux 1980: 425–32), then turned sharply against them, curtailed official support for left-wing, and even mildly liberal, political activism among priests. Yet, in spite of Vatican reprisals against progressive priests – ranging from Leonardo Boff, who in 1985 was condemned to a year of silence, to the fourth-term Massachusetts Democratic Congressman Father Robert Drinan, whom Pope John Paul II obliged to leave politics in 1980, to Cardenal himself, and his brother Fernando Cardenal, who in 1985 lost the right to administer the sacraments (a privilege that Fernando Cardenal later recovered with the support of the Jesuit Order) – the tradition of the revolutionary priest has become ingrained as an enduring, albeit dissident, tendency within Catholicism. The Haitian priest Jean-Bertrand Aristide, who was restored to lay status by Vatican dispensation in 1996, was twice elected president of his country on the strength of a rhetoric influenced by liberation theology. During his first presidential term (February–September 1991 and October 1994–February 1996, interrupted by a coup that forced him into exile in the United States), Aristide remained a priest; his second term (February 2001–February 2004, which also ended in a coup, this time organized by the United States) was conducted as a lay person. In 2008 the "barefoot" Paraguayan priest Fernando Lugo, who was converted to liberation theology during five years as a missionary in Ecuador, was elected president of his country after negotiating a suspension of his priesthood with John Paul II's successor, Pope Benedict XVI (Lugo was also forced out of office, in 2012, by a constitutional coup). As Cardinal Josef Ratzinger, Benedict had directed John Paul II's campaign against Latin American liberation theology; he was responsible for the interrogation and formal silencing of his former doctoral student Leonardo Boff, who was forced by Ratzinger and John Paul II to leave the Catholic Church after he refused to resign his editorship of the magazine *Vozes* in 1991 and announced his intention of attending the environmentalist Earth Summit in Rio de Janeiro in 1992, a meeting that the church opposed.[1]

The democratic processes that brought Aristide, and particularly Lugo, to power in the post-Cold War environment coexist with a depletion of the liberation theology priest's patriarchal authority. The revolutionary priest's function as avenging arbiter of the implementation of God's will in an unjust world is diminished in a democratic environment by the need to submit to the sound-bite strategies of electoral politics in order to win the support of the "average voter." In this sense, the participation of the liberation theology-influenced priests Ernesto Cardenal, Fernando Cardenal, Miguel D'Escoto Brockmann, and Edgardo Parrales in the Sandinista government may be read as the final instalment in the tradition founded by Fray Bartolomé de Las Casas. Even in the 1980s, the position of the revolutionary priest had become ambiguous. This was particularly true of Ernesto Cardenal, in part because of his role as one of the Nicaraguan government's travelling ambassadors and in part because of the amalgam of self-consciously "revolutionary" elements with which he assembled his personal appearance: the impetuousness of the revolutionary beret tempered by the long white hair of a prophet and the beard and glasses of an intellectual; the plain white Nicaraguan peasant shirt offset by proletarian blue jeans and hippie sandals. This self-consciously constructed appearance was rendered even more ambiguous by the fact that Cardenal, unlike most of his predecessors in the tradition founded by Las Casas, was also an artist: one of Latin America's foremost poets in addition to an accomplished sculptor.

Cardenal's complex identity as a contemplative radical – a gentle, introverted man who inspired young people to pick up guns, a member of the white elite who lived with peasants and helped to resuscitate moribund indigenous traditions, a Marxist revolutionary with a Bible in his hand, a bohemian reinterpreter of the Gospels, a spiritual recluse skilled at manipulating the secular world to his advantage, a poet of the concrete and the material who distrusted metaphors yet was capable of bending language like a politician, a throwback to the past who was acclaimed as a harbinger of the future – destabilized many assumptions, provoking contradictory reactions in those who met him. Thomas Merton considered that "he was one of the rare vocations we have had [in the Gethsemani Monastery in Kentucky] who certainly and manifestly combined the gifts of a contemplative with those of an artist" (Merton 1981: 323). Lawrence Ferlinghetti noticed "that angelic smile of his … there seemed to be something childlike and eternal about him" (Ferlinghetti 1984: 6). To Spanish American student radicals of the 1970s and 1980s, Cardenal was a paradox: a religious man who inspired the allegiance of a generation that was shedding religious belief. As Roberto Bolaño recalled: "La lectura de Cardenal nos fascinaba a nosotros precisamente, que éramos lascivos y pecadores y no íbamos nunca a misa … cada día que pasaba éramos más pecadores, y en ese afán nos ayudaba, por no decir nos alentaba, la poesía de Ernesto Cardenal" (Bolaño 2004: 168; "We were fascinated by reading Cardenal precisely because we were lascivious and sinners and never went to Mass … with each day that passed we were worse sinners and to that end we were aided, not to say encouraged, by the poetry of Ernesto Cardenal"). Bolaño wrote a poem entitled "Ernesto Cardenal y yo" ("Ernesto Cardenal and I") in which he imagines asking the priest whether homosexuals, prostitutes, and sadomasochists will be welcome "En el Reino de los Cielos/que es el comunismo" (*Los perros románticos*, 18; "In the Kingdom of Heaven/which is Communism") and receives an affirmative response. Graham Greene, on the other hand, who met Cardenal shortly prior to the triumph of the Sandinista Revolution, was more skeptical: "I thought him perhaps a trifle consciously charismatic with his white beard and his flowing white hair and the blue beret on top, and he seemed a little conscious of his own romantic character as a priest, a Communist and a refugee from Somoza, who had destroyed his monastery on an island in the Great Lake" (Greene 1984: 137). Yet Stephen Kinzer, Nicaragua correspondent for the *New York Times* during the 1980s, emphasized that Cardenal "did much to spread the Sandinista mystique around the world" (Kinzer 2008). Salman Rushdie, though a supporter of the Sandinista government, confessed to "my difficulties with the Minister of Culture, Ernesto Cardenal … he claimed, heart-freezingly, that Nicaragua was the 'first nation on earth to have nationalized poetry'" (Rushdie 1987: xviii). The most extreme reaction was that of Mario Vargas Llosa, who by way of the anonymous autobiographical narrator of his novel *Historia de Mayta* (1984; *The Real Life of Alejandro Mayta*) claimed: "Aún conservo vivo la impresión de insinceridad e histrionismo que me dio. Desde entonces, evito conocer a escritores que me gustan para que no me pase con ellos lo que con el poeta Cardenal, al que, cada vez que intento leer, del texto mismo se levanta, como un ácido que lo degrada, el recuerdo del hombre que lo escribió" (*Historia*, 92; "I still have a vivid impression of his insincerity and his histrionics. Ever since then, I've tried to avoid meeting the writers I like, so that the same thing that happened with the poet Cardenal doesn't happen with them. Every time I try to read him, something like acid flows out of the book and ruins it – the memory of the man who wrote it" [*Real Life*, 80]). By contrast, in 2008 Fidel Castro, who was no longer a political ally of Cardenal's (since Cuba was supporting the official FSLN, from which Cardenal was estranged), recalled his personality with approbation, particularly when compared to Sandinista leaders who had soiled their ideals after 1990: "I perceived in Father Ernesto Cardenal, unlike others in the Nicaraguan leadership, an image of sacrifice and privations resembling that of a medieval monk. He was a true prototype of purity" (Castro 2008). The poet and political activist Margaret Randall, who shared this view, was disconcerted by Cardenal's "enthusiasm for scarcity" and equated it with "the concept of voluntary poverty espoused by certain Catholic saints" (Randall 2009: 200).

Politics, as Cardenal has pointed out, is theatre; the public figure, of necessity, must diverge from the private universe of the writer. The "man" who writes the poems is constructed on the page, through his delineation of a world in which a problematized male identity and the recuperation of national history support and illuminate each other. This world is delineated by Sergio Ramírez, by contrast, through the coexistence of different, sometimes apparently opposing, functions in the same individual.

The archetype with which Ramírez is associated is of more recent vintage, having arisen with the Wars of Independence at the beginning of the nineteenth century. In the aftermath of the independence struggle, the new Latin American nations were characterized by the prominence of literary intellectuals who were drafted into multiple functions in the nation-building effort. The Mexican historian Jorge G. Castañeda maintains that, "partly as a result of the weakness of representative institutions, key intellectuals occupied a decisive space in many Latin societies ... Nation building was incomplete and in the vacuum created by these absences, the intellectual stood out" (Castañeda 1993: 177). These figures were nearly always associated with Liberalism, though, as Edwin Williamson notes, their reforming zeal was often attenuated by a residual nostalgia for the hierarchical structures of eighteenth-century neo-classicism against which the independence movements had rebelled, and by a concern for order in the chaos of the early nineteenth century (Williamson 1992: 287). This tendency is exemplified by the Argentine Romantic poet Esteban Echeverría (1805–51) and his friend

Domingo Faustino Sarmiento (1811–88), author of *Facundo: Civilización y barbarie* (1845; Civilization and Barbarism), one of the touchstones of nineteenth-century Liberal-Conservative debate about the nature of the Spanish American nation, and still a controversial work today. Sarmiento was also a prominent educational reformer and, later, as president of Argentina from 1868 to 1874, "created the institutions of a centralized nation state" (Williamson 1992: 277). Andrés Bello (1781–1865), who began his career as a pre-independence Romantic poet devoted to singing the natural wonders of Venezuela, then, after independence, moved to conservative Chile, where he founded the national university, wrote the first grammar of the Spanish language composed in the Americas and created the country's legal code (which became the model for other Spanish American legal codes). Bello's career illustrates the tension between the struggle for freedom and the quest for order that attended the national-building efforts of early-nineteenth-century organic intellectuals.

Countries such as Argentina, Chile, Venezuela, and Mexico had substantial urban and middle-class populations. Central America's exclusion from the Wars of Independence, and its lack of a nation-building bourgeoisie, or even of large urban centres (with the debatable exception of Guatemala City), meant that figures such as those mentioned above were not a decisive feature of life in the isthmus during the nineteenth century; one could even argue that their appearance was delayed until the 1970s. Aware that his own career is often understood in these terms, Sergio Ramírez notes: "Aquí en el siglo XIX el intelectual, el poeta, el jurista, el periodista, el militar, el revolucionario era la misma persona" (*UISR*; "here, in the nineteenth century, the intellectual, the poet, the lawyer, the journalist, the soldier, the revolutionary, were the same person"). However, he sees his own assumption of such multiple responsibilities in the late twentieth century as an aberration caused by "las circunstancias de la revolución" (*UISR*; "the circumstances of the revolution"). The year 1990, when voters defeated both a government of Marxist-influenced literary intellectuals in Nicaragua and the presidential candidacy of a neo-liberal novelist, Mario Vargas Llosa, in Peru, appears to have brought this chapter to a close. The organic intellectual has been dispersed into his component parts by the individualistic, information-drenched societies of accelerated globalization.

For Castañeda, the organic intellectual is a post-independence offshoot, in a secular context, of the tradition of religious activism that was founded by Fray Bartolomé de Las Casas. Intellectuals, initially religious in orientation and later also secular, "have through their writings, teachings, speeches, and other activities systematically substituted for innumerable institutions and social actors" (Castañeda 1993: 178). In Western Europe and the United States, where, as Ramírez observes, "se dio la temprana división del trabajo" (*UISR*; "the division of labour occurred early"), the religious figure's engagement with social issues is understood better than is that of the writer who is also a politician. For this reason, Ramírez's presence in the Sandinista government was less of an international *cause célèbre* than that of Cardenal; it was more of a source of puzzlement. For US news organizations who portrayed the Sandinistas as Soviet proxies, it was easy to suppress the awkward fact that the vice-president was someone who sounded like a social democrat and was known to be an internationally respected intellectual, and to focus on figures who evoked familiar Latin American revolutionary imagery, such as Cardenal or long-time guerrilla comandante Tomás Borge. After the first flush of Somoza's overthrow, when Ramírez was profiled in the *New York Times* and *Time* magazine (see chapter 4), he received disproportionately little coverage. One of the rare attempts to assess his position was that of the eloquent but insular anti-Sandinista journalist Shirley Christian. Writing prior to Ramírez's election as vice-president, Christian claimed:

> Only one person who was not on the Sandinista National Directorate proved capable of making a significant place for himself in the power structure. He was Sergio Ramírez … Ramírez was named "counselor" to [Daniel] Ortega. But it was not clear whether he exerted real influence on policy or merely tried to interpret National Directorate decisions and make them palatable. A man with a hulking frame, brooding eyes, and a soft voice, he was a talented enigma and perhaps the only real politician in the Sandinista leadership. Friends said he went through periods of severe emotional crisis in the early years of the new government, some having to do with the education of his children under the new order. But his skill with words made Ramírez indispensable to the Sandinistas. He could make tough and totalitarian positions sound mild and logical. He could explain and justify radical policies in a framework of Western liberal theory. He could deflect criticism and turn it back against the questioner. But what he himself thought almost no one knew. (Christian 1985: 190)

Christian may exaggerate the "enigmatic" aspects of Ramírez's personality. Her own ideologically distorted interpretation of Sandinismo makes it impossible for her to conceive of a radical nationalist intellectual who is not a "totalitarian" belonging in such a government. In fact, Ramírez's speeches of the early 1980s are clear in their statements of his beliefs and analysis of

Nicaraguan history; intellectuals from other parts of Latin America recognized in him the writer-politician of the Spanish American historical tradition. For this reason, Mario Vargas Llosa, though sharing some of Christian's ideology, took a far more sanguine view of Ramírez's contradictions, describing him as "un hombre culto ... con fino sentido del humor" ("a civilized man ... with a refined sense of humour") and noting, in a mild vein, that "Los adversarios de Sergio Ramírez dicen que, en público, extrema su radicalismo para no perder posiciones entre sus compañeros sandinistas, pero que, en el fondo, es uno de los más moderados del régimem" (*Contra viento y marea III*, 251; "Sergio Ramírez's adversaries say that in public he exaggerates his radicalism so as not to lose ground among his revolutionary compañeros, but that deep down he is one of the most moderate members of the regime"). The multiple identities inherent in Ramírez's position were also evident to other Latin American writers. After accompanying Ramírez on a trip to the Nicaraguan countryside, Julio Cortázar wrote: "Pienso en sus cuentos, en su novela cuyo título pregunta: *¿Te dio miedo la sangre?*, y mientras lo oigo discutir problemas de ganadería con sus compañeros veo como en un reflejo múltiple algo que me sigue asombrando, la casi inconcebible coincidencia en tantos dirigentes 'nicas' del estadista, el combatiente y el intelectual" (*Papeles inesperados*, 342–3; "I think of his short stories, of his novel *To Bury Our Fathers* and while I listen to him discussing problems of livestock farming with his *compañeros* I see as though in a multiple reflection something that continues to astonish me: the almost unimaginable convergence in so many 'Nica' leaders of the statesman, the intellectual and the combatant"). The resuscitation of this early-nineteenth-century archetype that had been seen as fading from Latin American life cast a particular spell on intellectuals such as Cortázar and the Mexican writer Carlos Fuentes, whose fascination with Ramírez's personality and multiple roles, and with the emergence of such a figure from a modest rural background, led to a long friendship between the two men. Fuentes characterized Ramírez as "Franco y reservado. Cándido y sagaz. Directo y calculador. Libérrimo y disciplinado. Devoto de su mujer, sus hijos, sus amigos. Intransigente con sus enemigos. Elocuente en el foro. Discreto en la intimidad. Firme en sus creencias éticas. Flexible en su acción política. Religioso en su dedicación literaria" ("Prólogo," *Una vida por la palabra*, 11; "Frank and reserved. Ingenuous and wise. Freewheeling and disciplined. Devoted to his wife, his children, his friends. Intransigent with his enemies. Eloquent at the podium. Discreet in private. Firm in his ethical beliefs. Flexible in his political action. Religious in his dedication to literature").

Literature, with its ability to fuse the spirituality of the eternal with the pungent evocation of the moment, was the religion that Ernesto Cardenal and Sergio Ramírez shared. More than socialism or Christianity or Sandinismo, writing enabled them to maintain their focus on their experiences as Nicaraguans through all stages of their careers: each time that they suffered political setbacks, they returned to literature. The international audience for their writing increased during the 1980s as a result of global curiosity about events in Nicaragua. In this atmosphere of fervour and crisis, their portrayals of the nation acquired fresh authority. Yet both Cardenal and Ramírez depicted their homeland, imagined its history, people, and identity, throughout their lives: before the Revolution of 1979–90, during it, and after it had ended. The breadth and consistency of their respective literary endeavours has not been adequately addressed by scholarly criticism.

Starting with two books on Cardenal published in Spanish in 1975 (see chapter 8), critical attention focused on Nicaraguan literature as the product of a revolutionary dynamic. This interest resulted in a spate of research articles on both writers that began in the early 1980s and petered out around 1993. Yet this Revolution-driven focus on their careers has limitations. The works that received the most extensive critical attention were those that became widely available in the heat of the Revolution, primarily Cardenal's collection of short poems about Sandinista Nicaragua, *Vuelos de Victoria* (1984; *Flights of Victory*) and Ramírez's novel *¿Te dio miedo la sangre?* (1977; *To Bury Our Fathers*). The perspective from the heart of the Revolution influenced the selection of earlier works by these authors that critics chose to study. Hence Cardenal's *Hora 0* (1960; *Zero Hour*) was widely studied because it spoke of Sandino and appeared, somewhat deceptively, to be a clear forerunner to *Flights of Victory* and the Nicaraguan Revolution. *El estrecho dudoso* (1966; *The Doubtful Strait*), by contrast, was ignored, even though it is one of Cardenal's most ambitious and accomplished works, because its Conservative, Catholic outlook did not appear to be consistent with the utterances of the revolutionary poet and Sandinista minister of culture. Ramírez's short story "Charles Atlas también muere" ("Charles Atlas Also Dies"), with its anti-imperialist commentary, was widely anthologized, yet his first novel, *Tiempo de fulgor* (1970; A Season of Light), which is set in the late nineteenth century and reflects a Liberal ideological vision, was not translated or published internationally.

The two writers' evolutions from their respective Conservative and Liberal origins to Sandinista positions were not addressed by this partial view. During the Revolution, fragments of each writer's oeuvre were hauled into the light for public examination outside the context of their respective creative trajectories. The ambitious books that each writer published towards the end of the Sandinista years, Cardenal's *Cántico cósmico* (1989; *Cosmic Canticle*) and Ramírez's *Castigo Divino* (1988; Divine Punishment), though they have come to be seen, over time, as their most important works, have received surprisingly scanty critical attention: by the time these books began to circulate internationally, the revolution was over and the academic appeal of studying Sandinista literature had diminished. Though three or four good articles were published on *Castigo Divino*, the book's remarkable intricacy demands a more extensive treatment. By the same token, some of the more politically engaged work of the 1980s, such as Ramírez's speeches and essays from this period, have been consigned to the dust-heap of Cold War history; yet, like the revelatory essays on Central American culture that he wrote in Berlin in the 1970s, many of these 1980s essays present vigorous analyses of Nicaraguan history which, while propelled by the radicalism of the moment, stand up to scrutiny today and do not deserve to be discarded as propaganda from a half-forgotten regime.

Neither writer's later work has received sufficient critical attention. Ramírez's late major novel, *Sombras nada más* (2002; Only Shadows Remain), though highly regarded within Spanish America, has received little diffusion or critical attention in other languages; the same is true of the engaging postmodern novel *Mil y una muertes* (2004; *A Thousand Deaths Plus One*) and of Ramírez's later short stories. Cardenal's memoirs, a massive, uneven work, yet one that is highly revealing of both his own development and that of Nicaraguan society and Latin American revolutionary culture, has been the object of no critical attention at all beyond a handful of book reviews, nor has his post-revolution poetry been adequately considered.

The purpose of this study, therefore, is twofold: to trace the evolution of the depiction of the Nicaraguan nation in the literary work of Ernesto Cardenal and Sergio Ramírez from their earliest publications to the years after the re-election of Daniel Ortega and the FSLN in November 2006, as a way of assessing the different images and imaginary communities that have cohered around ideas of Nicaraguanness, the male Spanish American intellectual, and his ever more uneasy patriarchal authority as would-be arbiter of the nation; and, by stacking up close readings of the two authors' works in chronological order, to restore their books to the times and circumstances that created them, re-evaluating the two men's massive literary output and achievement in ways that illuminate both its full artistic depth and its thematic and stylistic development.

2

Nicaraguan History to 1979

EARLY HISTORY

The struggle for national integration is central to Nicaraguan history. Located in the heart of Central America, the country is divided between a heavily populated Pacific Coast of volcanoes, crater lakes, and moderately productive agricultural land, and a sprawling, sparsely inhabited Atlantic Coast region dominated by dense jungle, fast-flowing rivers, and salt-water lagoons that make both agriculture and transportation arduous. Contemporary Nicaragua remains the only region in Central America where it is not possible to drive between the Pacific and the Atlantic oceans.

From the beginning of history until the early twentieth century, the two halves of the country, in addition to being settled by people of different ethnic backgrounds who spoke languages that were not mutually comprehensible, were governed by different regimes. During the Classical period of Mayan civilization in Central America (250–900 CE), Nicaragua remained peripheral to the Mayan urban centres situated in present-day southern Mexico, Guatemala, and Honduras; but the western half of the country, populated by the Chorotega people, who spoke a language called Mangue, was influenced by the theocratic, authoritarian precepts of Mayan culture. The population remained small, however, until large-scale immigration from Mexico began to settle the Pacific Coast around the year 1000. These peoples, who spoke variants of the Aztec language of Náhuatl, which they used as a lingua franca, subjugated and gradually assimilated the Chorotegas. They developed a hierarchical, slaveholding agricultural society whose staple food was corn. It was a society rooted in unquestioning obedience to rigid concepts of religious duty. During roughly the same period, the eastern fringe of the country was settled by the Sumu, descendants of the advanced

Chibcha culture of Colombia. The Sumu, who had a strong warrior tradition, adapted to the jungle by becoming hunters and fishermen in the bush and on the rivers. Over time, weaker Sumu groups were pushed into the less desirable inland territories and diverged in culture and language from the people on the coast.

The first encounter with Europeans occurred in 1502, when Christopher Columbus landed on the Atlantic Coast. Nicaragua's population, which was probably between 600,000 and one million people at the time of contact, shrank to 30,000 by 1545 and 8,000 by 1578 (Smith 1993: 37). The population decline was precipitated by lack of immunity to European diseases, as occurred elsewhere in the Americas, but also reflected a conscious resistance to colonized status. According to contemporary reports, the indigenous people killed their own children and abstained from sex to avoid producing slaves, whom the Spaniards transported to work in mines in Hispaniola (ibid.: 37, 52). Paving the way from the authoritarian traditions of his Náhuat-descended predecessors to the ruling family cliques of later Nicaraguan history, the governor, Pedro Arias de Ávila, who became known as Pedrarias Dávila, imposed tyrannical rule, executed competing conquistadors, and bequeathed his power to his son-in-law, Rodrigo de Contreras, who instituted a reign of terror from 1534 to 1544. Located far from Mexico City, the capital of the Viceroyalty of New Spain, to which all of Central America, known as the Kingdom of Guatemala, was officially subordinated under the Spanish colonial system, "Nicaragua remained a semi-autonomous, self-governing unit" (ibid.: 53–4). The Nicaraguan economy depended on the kidnapping of indigenous people to work in Spanish mines in Hispaniola and later Peru, or in their drafting, through the feudal *encomienda* or the successor system of *repartimiento*, to work in mines or on plantations within Nicaragua. Attempts to implement the New Laws, fought for by Fray Bartolomé de Las Casas, were "obstructed by the Spanish settlers" (ibid.: 56).

From the sixteenth century until Central America gained independence in 1821, local Spaniards on the Pacific Coast exploited the indigenous population through labour drafts, debt slavery, peonage, and confiscation of land and property. The colonial administration's efforts to intervene, motivated by fears that population decrease would lead to the disappearance of a labour force, proved fruitless. By the late eighteenth century, indigenous community and family structures had disintegrated as a consequence of men either fleeing labour drafts or leaving their families to search for wage labour; the institution of marriage had almost disappeared, and most children were orphans. Spaniards' casual liaisons, concubinage with, or rape of, indigenous women, created a modest mestizo population at the same time that the social and economic disadvantages associated with indigenous identity led many Nicaraguans to repudiate their Náhuat-Chorotega heritage. As Elizabeth Dore writes of a village in eighteenth-century Nicaragua: "After centuries of population crisis and social dislocation, cultural markers of Indianness were weak" (Dore 2006: 41). The crisis of indigenous culture laid the foundation for the later "creation of a mythical history that suppressed the existence of Indians in the twentieth century" (Gould 1998: 59) by insisting that Nicaragua was a uniformly mestizo nation. At the same time, the destruction of the family unit became an enduring trait of Nicaraguan society, and a characteristic that differentiated the country from many other Spanish American cultures: even today "the majority of families are matriarchal" (White and Calderón 2008: 55). As late as 1979, 34 per cent of households were headed by a single mother (Lancaster 1992: 17), a figure that rose dramatically among poorer families, which were also those with a more marked, if generally unacknowledged, indigenous heritage.

Spanish colonialism was a short-lived phenomenon on Nicaragua's Atlantic Coast. Local resistance to enslavement, and the repeated incursions of pirates from England, France, and Holland, drove the last Spanish mission out of the Atlantic Coast in 1610. By 1580, the port of Bluefields had become a meeting point where "buccaneers could rest, recuperate and replenish their ships' stores" (Smith 1993: 41) before returning to the Caribbean to plunder Spanish galleons. During the seventeenth century, large numbers of African slaves either escaped to, or were shipwrecked on, Nicaragua's Atlantic Coast. They intermarried with coastal Sumu; by the late seventeenth century, a new ethnic group, the Miskito, distinct in language, customs, and physical appearance from both the coastal Sumu and their inland cousins, had emerged from this fusion. By the end of the century, the Miskito had become the dominant culture of the Atlantic Coast, driving out, assimilating, or annihilating competing coastal cultures.

Miskito dominance depended on connivance with pirates and smugglers, most of whom, as England tightened its hold on the Caribbean, were English-speaking. In order to finance their British-influenced customs, which "required expensive uniforms for the kings and admirals and governors, and firearms, English clothes and especially rum for the whole tribe" (Floyd 1967: 64), the Miskito staged repeated raids on Costa Rica and exacted tribute from the Sumu, Rama, and other indigenous groups. By the eighteenth century, the Miskito were receiving formal backing from the British Navy. In 1740 an official British protectorate, responsible to the governor of Jamaica, was established on the "Miskito Coast." In 1780 Miskito forces joined an unsuccessful British expedition to expel Spain from western

Nicaragua in the hope of establishing a British canal across the isthmus. The Treaty of Paris, in 1783, obliged the British to leave the Nicaraguan coast for British Honduras (now Belize). The Spanish, however, were unable to re-establish their authority, and power devolved upon the Miskito king.

After Central America gained independence from Spain in 1821, Jamaican traders, including both creolized whites and those of mixed race, poured into the region in search of mahogany. The Miskito king retained formal power, but, under a system of increasingly overt British domination, his offspring were educated in Jamaica or England. The growing presence of US business interests in Central America in the second half of the nineteenth century forced the British to barter away part of their authority in the Treaty of Managua in 1860; one of the consequences of this treaty was to separate the Miskito royal family from the territory where most of the Miskito population lived. German Moravian missionaries, who arrived on the coast in 1849 and began preaching in Miskito in 1860, filled the vacuum. They developed a written form of the Miskito language and succeeded in establishing Protestant Christianity as a unifying feature in Miskito culture, creating another rift with the Catholic, Spanish-speaking Pacific Coast. In the years after 1860 the Miskito lost power, in spite of remaining the majority population on the Atlantic Coast, as US investment in lumber, bananas, and rubber opened the way for English-speaking merchants of Jamaican descent to act as middlemen and become the region's dominant power.

At the time of the Central American Federation's independence from Spain in 1821, Nicaragua's population was 190,000, growing by mid-century to 290,000 (Booth 1982: 13). The majority of the country's inhabitants lived in or around the cities of León, Granada, Managua, and Masaya, all of which were located close to the Pacific Coast. The elites, who were of Spanish or lightly mixed ancestry, were divided between trade-oriented, often free-thinking Liberals and agriculture-based, more devout Conservatives. In 1823 the Liberals withdrew Central America from the Conservative-dominated Mexican Empire, attempting to consolidate their gains by repressing local Conservatives. Conservative reprisals ignited a civil war that caused the Central American Federation to splinter into the five republics of Costa Rica, Nicaragua, El Salvador, Honduras, and Guatemala.

Nicaraguan independence in 1838 occurred in an atmosphere of economic crisis and continuing violence between Liberals, based in León, and Conservatives, based in Granada. Both groups saw an opportunity for profit and prosperity in building a maritime transportation route across the country, extending the thoroughfare offered by the San Juan River and Lake Nicaragua to the Pacific Ocean. The United States, Great Britain, and France all commissioned studies to build a canal system across Central America via

Nicaragua. The British, by virtue of their de facto control of the Atlantic Coast, had the upper hand. The British consul to Central America, Frederick Chatfield, who styled himself virtual ruler of the country, ordered the British Navy to blockade Nicaragua in 1842 and 1844. To placate the British, the Conservative government was obliged to turn over Nicaragua's tobacco industry to two British nationals; in 1848 British forces, assisted by Miskito troops, occupied the Atlantic Coast towns of Greytown and San Juan del Norte. Invoking the Monroe Doctrine of 1823, which promised to quash incursions from outside the hemisphere, the Nicaraguan politicians Pablo Buitrago and José Guerrero wrote to US President James Polk and Secretary of State James Buchanan asking for support against the British. In 1850, after military skirmishes between British and American forces, which culminated in the US bombardment and burning of Greytown, Washington and London signed the Clayton-Bulwer Treaty "which provided (without consulting Nicaragua) for joint US-British control of any transisthmian canal" (Booth 1982: 17).

As Britain's involvement in the Crimean War sapped its resources for overseas adventures and the California Gold Rush boosted the expansion and wealth of the United States, control of Nicaragua slipped into US hands, where it would remain, almost without interruption, until 1979. In 1849 the Conservative government granted the US financier Cornelius Vanderbilt a concession to establish a transit route, by riverboat and stagecoach, across Nicaragua. As it was quicker for East Coast Americans hoping to find wealth in California to travel by way of Nicaragua than to make the gruelling trek across the US prairies, the route became so profitable that financiers Cornelius Garrison and Charles Morgan prised the business away from Vanderbilt. Conflict between the Liberals, backed by Garrison, and the Conservatives, supported by Vanderbilt, escalated. In 1853 Nicaraguan President Fruto Chamorro called a conference to ratify changes to the constitution that would ensconce the Conservatives in power. The Liberal response to the institutionalization of Conservative rule was to recruit US mercenaries to attack the Conservative stronghold of Granada in 1851 and 1853. When these attacks failed, the US businessman Byron Cole was contracted to hire William Walker, a professional filibuster from Tennessee who had invaded and occupied the Mexican state of Sonora, to complete the job.

FROM WILLIAM WALKER TO ANASTASIO SOMOZA GARCÍA

In October 1855 Walker, a strong believer in Manifest Destiny who saw an opportunity for wealth in the land grants he had been promised in return for his services, led fifty-seven Californians in an assault on Granada. They captured the city and held prominent Conservative families hostage. Betraying the Liberals, who had invited him into the country, Walker appointed a Conservative, Patricio Rivas, as his puppet president. The United States recognized the Rivas administration. Costa Rica, fearing that this was the first step in a US occupation of all of Central America, declared war on Walker. The Costa Rican president, Juan Rafael Mora, denounced Walker as "the scum of all the earth" (Colby 2011: 35). Costa Rican troops defeated Walker in two decisive battles, the first inside Costa Rica and the second at Rivas, in southwestern Nicaragua, before withdrawing because of a cholera epidemic. Walker returned to Granada and on 29 June 1856 ran a presidential election in which he "openly concocted the results and in July declared himself the new president of Nicaragua" (Smith 1993: 73). President Walker declared Nicaragua's official language to be English and initiated a massive expropriation of agricultural land belonging to Conservative families. He reinstated slavery and aligned the country with the slaveholding states of the southern United States, which, eager to bolster their numbers, began to regard the other Central American nations with a hungry eye. In the first two months after Walker became president, more than two thousand Americans arrived in Nicaragua to take up land grants and reproduce the slaveholding plantation society of the Deep South. President Walker declared: "With the negro-slave as his companion, the white man would become fixed to the soil; and they together would destroy the power of the mixed race which is the bane of the country" (Colby 2011: 8).

This threat inspired Costa Rica, El Salvador, Honduras, and Guatemala, assisted behind the scenes by an outraged Cornelius Vanderbilt, and by the British government, which continued to try to thwart US dominance in Central America, to unite in a military campaign to drive out Walker. The first blow, however, was struck by Nicaraguans themselves. Fighting with bows and arrows and hurling rocks, Nicaraguan irregulars defeated Walker's forces in a battle at San Jacinto on 14 September 1856. This battle has been interpreted as the first coalescing of a Nicaraguan national consciousness, and the point of origin of a tradition of resistance to the incessant foreign invasions that have defined the country's history: 14 September is a national holiday in Nicaragua. Andrés Castro, a tailor too poor to own a weapon, who is reputed to have killed a Yankee filibuster during the battle by hurling a boulder at his head, is one of Nicaragua's national heroes. San Jacinto, however, may have been an anomaly; in fact, most Nicaraguans avoided the war or expressed admiration for the US culture Walker claimed to exemplify: "If an astounding 3.5 per cent of Costa Rica's population went to war, only about half a per cent of all Nicaraguans participated in what they would later celebrate as their nation's foundational event" (Gobat 2005: 39).

As the war progressed, Charles Morgan and Cornelius Garrison sent boatloads of US mercenaries to support Walker and his faltering, cholera-wracked army. In reprisal, Cornelius Vanderbilt supplied the allied Central American forces with weapons and military advisers. In January 1857 the Costa Ricans captured the San Juan River, cutting off transportation across the country and marooning the besieged Walker in Rivas. On 1 May 1857 Walker surrendered and was evacuated by the US Navy. He returned to the United States a hero but would not renounce his Manifest Destiny to rule Central America. In 1860, during a subsequent filibustering adventure, he was captured by the British and turned over to the government of Honduras, which executed him by firing squad. While it is debatable whether the Walker intervention forged a nascent national consciousness among ordinary Nicaraguans, it is evident that, partly in reaction to Walker, and partly as a result of accepting Walker's view that Nicaragua's Manifest Destiny was to be the site of a canal system that would be at the core of US-dominated global commerce, Nicaragua's elite became more unified.

Walker's campaign, notably his attempt to burn Granada to the ground during his retreat from the city in 1856, instilled an innate anti-Americanism in the great Conservative families; at the same time, they imitated the United States. Ideological differences between Liberals and Conservatives dwindled as the latter accepted the free-trading precepts of the former group; both profited from the late-nineteenth-century coffee boom. Communally held indigenous *ejido* lands were expropriated and privatized. In Mexico and Guatemala, this was a Liberal policy; in Nicaragua, it was implemented by the Conservative President Pedro Joaquín Chamorro Alfaro. The abolition of the *ejido* was the final blow in the destruction of indigenous identity in the Pacific Coast areas of Nicaragua, consolidating the myth of a mestizo nation. As Dore writes of Diriomo, near Granada: "After the demise of common property and the indigenous community, little by little ethnic distinctions within the pueblo were forgotten and Diriomeños considered themselves simply Nicaraguan peasants" (Dore 2006: 69). Thirty years of relative peace ensued as the United States was consumed by civil war and internal economic problems; coffee, which supplanted the proposed canal as the route to integration into the world economy, attracted entrepreneurial European immigrants. By 1890, the population had risen to 423,000. The Liberals, pushing for greater industrialization to break the dependence on coffee, took power in 1893 under the ambitious President José Santos Zelaya.

Zelaya, who dreamed of a united Central America, began by unifying the Atlantic and Pacific regions of Nicaragua. He centralized power in Managua, subordinating the warring strongholds of León and Granada, and built a national army. As a Liberal, he supported foreign investment. His rule was initially well received by the United States, which saw in Zelaya's drive to assert Nicaraguan sovereignty over the Atlantic Coast the possibility of ousting the Anglo-Miskito alliance that impeded the expansion of US business interests. In 1894 Zelaya ordered Nicaraguan troops to land at Bluefields on their way to a border skirmish with Honduras. British Marines landed in reprisal but were forced to withdraw when US Marines landed to support Zelaya. A Declaration of Reincorporation was signed, integrating the Atlantic Coast into Nicaragua as the Department of Zelaya. The mayor of Bluefields, a US citizen, witnessed the document.

Zelaya separated church and state, founded free public schools, and banned English and Miskito, the two most widely spoken languages on the coast, as mediums of instruction. He undertook lengthy negotiations with the United States to secure a guarantee of Nicaraguan sovereignty in return for granting the United States an exclusive concession for a transisthmian canal. His policy began to unravel in 1903 when Theodore Roosevelt invaded northern Colombia and hewed out the new country of Panama for the purpose of building a canal. At the same time, Conservatives, angry about the rise of mestizos to positions of social prominence under Zelaya's regime and frustrated by the increasing competition posed by immigrant German traders, threatened an uprising. Zelaya executed alleged Conservative plotters, prompting a violent revolt by the Conservative strongman General Emiliano Chamorro.

US hostility to Zelaya mounted as, furious with the US decision to build the canal through Panama, the president explored Japanese and British sources of finance for a competing canal through Nicaragua. In 1907 Zelaya was forced to accept US-Mexican mediation when General Chamorro joined forces with the Honduran army to invade northern Nicaragua. In October 1909 the US secretary of state, Philander Knox, who had business interests on the Atlantic Coast, where Zelaya's imposition of Spanish-speaking mestizo administrators was unpopular, fomented an uprising with assistance from the Guatemalan dictator Manuel Estrada Cabrera. Mercenaries from New Orleans were recruited to join the rebel forces; when two American mercenaries were captured and executed, the United States forced Zelaya to resign as president. The former foreign minister, José Madriz, became president and continued the war. Nicaraguan forces recaptured Bluefields. In retaliation, US Marines invaded the Atlantic Coast and forced Madriz to resign. The Conservative Juan Estrada replaced Madriz, but, when his cabinet complained that he was allowing excessive US interference in Nicaraguan affairs, he, too, was forced to resign. His vice-president, Adolfo Díaz, a former accountant in the La Luz and Los Angeles Mining Company, in which Philander Knox had a substantial interest, became president on 5 May 1911.

Díaz paid "compensation" to US businesses and Conservative families for their "suffering" under Zelaya's rule. The Chamorro family received more than $500,000. The payments bankrupted the country and destroyed the currency. US economists took over Nicaragua's finances and created a new currency, the córdoba, and a new National Bank of Nicaragua, which they incorporated in Connecticut. A retired US military officer became chief customs collector; Brown Brothers of New York were put in control of establishing coffee prices and operating the country's railroads and steamships, which they allowed to decay. The contents of Nicaragua's national treasury were siphoned into Brown Brothers accounts in New York. When Philander Knox visited Nicaragua on 5 March 1912 he was greeted by violent demonstrations; the president of the Constituent Assembly, the US-educated Conservative Ignacio Suárez, welcomed Knox with a speech in which he said, "Your visit … has awakened fears and misgivings" (Gobat 2005: 82). Conservative anti-Americanism, whose origins lay in Walker's invasion, revived, even though many Conservatives continued to collaborate with US business interests.

As the Díaz administration lost credibility, the Constituent Assembly named General Luis Mena president. When the United States refused to recognize Mena, he staged an uprising. The revolt spread as Benjamín Zeledón, a Liberal coffee grower, attacked the government in protest against US control of coffee prices. A panicked Díaz, fighting on two fronts, asked US President William Howard Taft for assistance. Taft sent twenty-seven hundred Marines. Mena surrendered, but Zeledón, outnumbered and poorly armed, fought to the death. US Marines "paraded the rebel leader's corpse, lashed to the back of a horse, before the public" (Booth 1982: 31). Among those who witnessed this humiliation was a seventeen-year-old boy named Augusto César Sandino.

The crushing of the two uprisings consolidated the rule of the US occupation forces. The US insisted that General Emiliano Chamorro be named ambassador to Washington. Chamorro negotiated the Chamorro-Bryan Treaty, signed in 1914 and ratified in 1916, which legalized de facto US rule of Nicaragua. In return for three million dollars, deposited in the New York banks that held the country's debts, Nicaragua granted the United States perpetual tax-free rights over any canal system built in the country. Nicaragua renounced the right to collaborate with other countries on a canal, gave the United States a ninety-nine-year lease on the Corn Islands on the Atlantic Coast, established a US naval base, which would operate under

US law, in the Gulf of Fonseca, and withdrew from the Central American Court of Justice, a decision that "torpedoed an incipient Central American unification movement" (Booth 1982: 35). The Chamorro-Bryan Treaty became so notorious in Latin America that forty-five years later, when General Chamorro's great-nephew (and Ernesto Cardenal's cousin), the journalist Pedro Joaquín Chamorro Cardenal, visited Cuba, Che Guevara "greeted him coldly with the words, 'Pedro Joaquín Chamorro, as in the Chamorro-Bryant [*sic*] Treaty?'" (Gobat 2005: 132).

The main beneficiary of the agreement was General Chamorro: when he returned to Nicaragua in 1916 to run for president, US Marines ensured that he was the only candidate by preventing either Liberals or dissident Conservatives from campaigning. In 1921 General Chamorro was succeeded as president by his uncle, Diego Manuel Chamorro. When the older Chamorro died in office in 1923, the Conservative Party split over his succession. The US State Department decided that the most effective way to unite Nicaragua's elites was through a coalition government. The ticket of Conservative President Carlos Solórzano and Liberal Vice-President Juan Bautista Sacasa, which defeated the resurgent General Emiliano Chamorro in national elections in 1924, fell apart when the government's US financial adviser, Dr Jeremiah Jenks, objected to Solórzano's attempt to replace the US directors of the National Bank of Nicaragua with Nicaraguan citizens. The US Marines withdrew from the country. In October 1925 General Chamorro staged a coup and began re-Americanizing the National Bank. Sporadic Liberal revolts in support of Sacasa flared up throughout 1926. In May US Marines landed at Bluefields to put down a pro-Sacasa revolt; by 1927, they had also occupied the Pacific Coast. US naval commander Admiral Julian L. Latimer ordered Sacasa to throw "700 tons of war materials into the sea" (Smith 1993: 90). Sacasa complied, but one of his soldiers, Augusto César Sandino, salvaged some of the weapons and fled to the mountainous northern region of the Segovias to fight a guerrilla war against US occupation.

In August 1926 a young Liberal named Anastasio Somoza García had "captured" his undefended hometown of San Marcos. Forced out of the country by General Chamorro, Somoza, having learned fluent English in Philadelphia, returned as an interpreter for the Liberal General José María Moncada (who may have been Somoza's biological father). The appearance of Somoza and Sandino, who embodied divergent renegade tendencies in the shattered Liberal Party, presaged the eclipse of the Chamorro family, and of Conservative power. The struggle between Somocismo and Sandinismo would dominate Nicaraguan politics into the twenty-first century.

In May 1927 US envoy Henry L. Stimson imposed a peace treaty on the feuding Liberals and Conservatives. Through this treaty, "the US military secured the right not only to run Nicaraguan elections but to establish and lead a native armed force – the Guardia Nacional [GN] de Nicaragua that was to become the main guarantor of the democratic process" (Gobat 2005: 205). The treaty returned Adolfo Díaz to the presidency but offered the Liberal Moncada the chance of becoming president in 1928 if he cooperated with the Americans; Sandino was offered the governorship of Jinotega. In a letter to Moncada, Sandino replied, "Yo no me vendo ni me rindo" (*PVS*, 85; "I will neither sell out nor surrender"). Sandino insisted on the necessity of a war of national liberation. In words that foreshadow Fidel Castro's "La historia me absolverá" ("History Will Absolve Me") speech in 1953, Sandino said: "Seeing that the United States of North America, lacking any right except that with which brute force endows it, would deprive us of our country and our liberty, I have accepted its unjust challenge, leaving to History the responsibility for my actions" (Smith 1993: 93). Sandino retreated to a remote village. Major Harold Clifton Pierce and fifty US Marines were sent to arrest him. They failed miserably. After a series of battles, Sandino took over most of the Segovias. The town of Jícaro, renamed Ciudad Sandino, became his capital. The US marine force swelled to twelve hundred, then twenty-eight hundred, troops but could not make serious inroads into the Sandinistas' control of the mountains.

Sandinista ideology was nationalist, Panamerican, and egalitarian; it rejected Communist Party orthodoxy as represented by the Salvadoran leader Farabundo Martí. Influenced by the Mexican Revolution's resuscitation of the indigenous past, Sandino, the illegitimate son of a minor landowner and his indigenous servant, became the first prominent Nicaraguan in centuries to acknowledge with pride his indigenous heritage: "Soy nicaragüense y me siento orgulloso de que en mis venas circule, más que cualquier [otra], la sangre india americana" (*PVS*, 87; "I am Nicaraguan and I feel proud that in my veins flows, more than any other, the blood of the American Indian").

On 16 July 1927 Sandino staged a carefully executed multi-prong attack on the town of Ocotal, which had been occupied by the US Marines and the GN, who had built an air strip there. The first stage of the attack was to blow up the US air strip. The Marines, backed up by a US air strike launched from Managua – "the first organized dive-bombing attack in history" (Macaulay 1967: 81) – inflicted heavy casualties on the Sandinistas and local civilians, but Sandino's show of force made him a legend throughout the Americas. Prominent figures such as the Peruvian politician Víctor Raúl Haya de la Torre, the Mexican philosopher and cabinet minister José

Vasconcelos, and the Chilean poet Gabriela Mistral, who would later become the first Latin American to win the Nobel Prize for Literature, declared their support for Sandino (ibid.: 84). While US Secretary of State Frank B. Kellogg condemned Sandino as a "common outlaw" (ibid.: 83) and the Liberal elite feared his radicalism, "the Granada-based Conservative oligarchy did not share the fears of most other elite Nicaraguans" (Gobat 2005: 232). Conservatives were waging a "culture wars" campaign against the short-skirted, lipstick-wearing "modern woman" influenced by US popular culture; although rich, they disdained the "materialism" of US social norms. Fearing the erosion of the Catholic religion in the wake of an influx of Protestant missionaries, the prominent Catholic couple Salvador and Isabel "la Católica" Cardenal (who were Ernesto Cardenal's grandparents) launched a high-profile, sometimes violent campaign against US Protestant missionaries (Gobat 2005: 322). Perceiving the United States as a threat to Conservative values, the great families of Granada longed for an end to the occupation. Not even Sandino's adoption of the symbols of the hated Mexican Revolution, such as the red-and-black flag, stemmed the Conservatives' courting of the insurgency.

The United States, meanwhile, was overstretched in Nicaragua. US strategists wanted to withdraw troops from the Segovias in order to send them to China. To limit US casualties, the GN was sent into the front lines; the Marines were assigned to non-combat roles. When Moncada became president in 1928, he planned to create a national army. US President Herbert Hoover vetoed the project, ordering Moncada to beef up the US-controlled GN. On 31 December 1930 Sandinista guerrillas ambushed ten US Marines, killing eight and wounding two: public opinion in the United States demanded that the Marines come home. On 13 February 1931 Henry Stimson, now US secretary of state, reduced the Marine contingent to five hundred men and announced that the United States would withdraw completely after the 1932 Nicaraguan elections. The public mood in the US, even prior to these events, may be judged by words spoken by the character of Jason Compson, the struggling cotton farmer in William Faulkner's novel *The Sound and the Fury* (1929): "Work like hell all day every day, send them your money … and them up there in Washington spending fifty thousand dollars a day keeping an army in Nicaragua or some place" (292).

In the Segovias, the Sandinistas founded cooperatives and created a state within a state. Yet the new society was not the personalistic imposition of an authoritarian leader, as is evident from the fact that both the war and Sandinista social policies were sustained during 1929, when Sandino spent most of the year in Mexico campaigning for international support. The new society of the Segovias was created by local peasants seeking "political autonomy and social justice" (Gobat 2005: 235). Nicaraguans elsewhere in the country, however, saw the Sandinistas as predominantly a Segovian phenomenon. In spite of the international support Sandino attracted, and the discreet approval of Granada Conservatives, Sandinismo failed to connect with the broader population's welling hatred of the United States. On 25 October 1931 six thousand placard-waving demonstrators in Managua marched against the US occupation, yet none of the placards mentioned Sandino (ibid.: 237). Nonetheless, as coffee prices fell with the deepening of the global economic Depression, and hardship grew throughout Nicaragua, the Sandinista insurgency began to spread. Throughout 1931 Sandinista guerrillas attacked US-owned mines and banana plantations on the Atlantic Coast with impunity; by early 1932 a Sandinista cell "was operating in the south of the country around Rivas" (Smith 1993: 97).

As the Sandinistas tested the limits of their territorial and ideological gains, and the Conservatives retreated into an impotent hostility that loathed the United States as the bearer of an inherently corrupt modernity, the collaborationist wing of the Liberal Party was developing the authoritarian political culture that would sustain it over the next seven decades. The GN, whose importance grew as the US Marines prepared to leave, became the public embodiment of the Liberal Party. Sandino's crushing defeat of the GN at La Pelona on 28 October 1932 raised questions about the unit's ability to maintain "order" once the Marines were gone. A vigorous public debate ensued concerning who should be named the GN's leader. Anastasio Somoza García, an undistinguished soldier who had worked as a "boxing referee, baseball umpire, electrical meter reader, and privy inspector" (Macaulay 1967: 237) before becoming Moncada's interpreter, impressed Secretary of State Stimson with his physical size and his flawless American English; the attractive young wife of the aging US ambassador, Matthew Hanna, pushed very hard for Somoza, apparently because she was having an affair with him (Booth 1982: 46; Macaulay 1967: 237). When Sacasa (who was Somoza's wife's uncle) won the 1932 elections, he appointed Somoza head of the GN.

As soon as the Americans withdrew from Nicaragua on 1 January 1933, Sandino, who as recently as 28 December 1932 had fought a pitched battle against government forces, ended his military campaign. Conservatives in Congress pushed for recognition of Sandino as a general who had engaged in a "patriotic" struggle, while Liberals insisted that Sandino be denounced as a "bandit" (Gobat 2005: 248). On 2 February 1933 Sandino flew to Managua, where Somoza drove him to the presidential palace "passing the cheering crowds lining the streets, who were proclaiming Sandino a national hero" (Smith 1993: 99). Sandino and Sacasa negotiated a peace agreement guaranteeing Nicaragua's financial independence, a review of the Chamorro-Bryan Treaty, amnesty for the Sandinistas in return for disarmament, the elimination of the word "bandit," in reference to Sandino, from all government documents, and a land grant along the Coco River, where the Sandinistas would found cooperatives and develop locally produced food to replace imports. Sacasa, however, could not control the GN. Somoza's men staged repeated raids on the cooperative on the Coco River, where the disarmed Sandinistas were planting their crops. For the next year, Sandino and Sacasa negotiated over the constitutional status of the GN. On 23 February 1934 Sacasa and Sandino dined at the presidential palace in Managua. As Sandino left the palace for his brother's Managua home, his car was surrounded by National Guardsmen, who dragged Sandino, his brother, and two of his generals to an abandoned air field and murdered them; the next morning, the Guard entered the Sandinista cooperative on the Coco River and murdered three hundred men, women, and children.

THE SOMOZA DICTATORSHIP

The murder of Sandino and his followers was an attempt to extirpate the Sandinista traditions of national autonomy and social justice from the fabric of Nicaraguan culture, leaving the Liberals dominant and the Conservatives in thrall to a vanishing past. It was a virtual coup d'état by Somoza against his wife's uncle. From Sandino's assassination until the triumph of the Sandinista Revolution on 19 July 1979, the Somoza family ruled Nicaragua. The Somozas yielded the presidency to collaborators and puppets for limited periods, but they always maintained tight control on the economy and the GN. Anastasio Somoza García allowed Sacasa to languish in the presidency, with little effective control, until 6 June 1936. When he resigned, Somoza became president. As his power depended on the loyalty of the GN, the force began to absorb an ever larger proportion of the national budget, in the form of new equipment, pay raises, and, from 1939 onward, training by US military advisers. Franklin D. Roosevelt's "Good Neighbour Policy" – support for tyrants who were loyal to the United States as a means of avoiding the high costs of foreign intervention – ensured a steady flow of material and personnel to keep the Somozas in charge. Roosevelt, who is reputed to have said, "Somoza's a son of a bitch, but he's ours" (Macaulay 1967: 258), built a US-staffed military academy in Nicaragua and invited Somoza to address the US Congress. During the 1940s, General Emiliano Chamorro staged various unsuccessful uprisings against Somoza, "each followed by a wave of anti-Conservative repression" (Booth 1982: 63). Conservative hatred of Somoza stemmed from outrage that the old oligarchy's role as the country's rulers had been usurped, accentuated by a prejudice that Somoza was unfit to rule because he was not from a well-known family, was comparatively dark-skinned, and many of his cronies and deputies were mestizos (Vilas 1992: 312–13).

Somoza restructured the Liberal Party, the unions, and, eventually, the national economy to promote his power and prosperity and that of his family. As cotton prices rose in the post-1945 period, small farmers were removed from their land to facilitate the creation of enormous cotton plantations run by prominent Liberals and some old Conservative landowners. Displaced people flowed into the cities, increasing the gap between rich and poor. Somoza earned millions of dollars per year by charging "presidential commissions" to both foreign and local businesses in return for concessions to mine gold, cut timber, and extract rubber. He introduced restrictions on the importation of certain products, particularly those dominated by Conservative interests, then smuggled these items into the country and sold them at inflated prices in stores he owned. Somoza named himself director of Nicaragua's banks and railroads, receiving a hefty salary from each institution for his "services." By 1944, only eight years after formally taking power, Somoza owned fifty-one cattle ranches and forty-six coffee plantations. The Somozas replaced the Chamorros as Nicaragua's most powerful family, with Somoza's sons, uncles, and cousins running major institutions. By 1947, four of the eight wealthiest Nicaraguans were members of the Somoza family, another was Somoza's business partner, and a sixth was the chief of the GN.

A rising demand for technical trades and professions enlarged the middle class, yet the number of poor and unemployed grew rapidly throughout the 1940s and 1950s. In 1947 the elderly Leonardo Argüello, elected president as a Somoza puppet in order to appease the United States, which was reluctant to support another presidential term for Somoza, surprised his masters by trying to dismantle the Somocista state and exile Somoza and his West Point-educated son, Anastasio Somoza Debayle. Somoza García woke up Argüello at three in the morning, told him he was no longer president, and sent him into exile in Mexico. Somoza's uncle, Víctor Román y Reyes, took over as president. In the ensuing wave of repression, many anti-Somocistas were murdered, hundreds were imprisoned, and thirty thousand people fled into exile in Costa Rica.

In 1950 the Chamorro family allowed itself to be bought off with lucrative public appointments and a guarantee of one-third of the seats in Congress for the Conservative Party. Somoza exploited Cold War anti-Communism to consolidate his rule. In 1954 he allowed the Central Intelligence Agency (CIA) to use his private estates as a training location for the mercenary army created by the United States to overthrow the democratically elected president of Guatemala, Jacobo Arbenz. With a population of fewer than two million people, Nicaragua had the highest number of graduates (nearly three thousand) of any country in Latin America of the notorious School of the Americas, run by the United States in the Panama Canal Zone to teach "security techniques," notably torture. A clumsy attempt to assassinate Somoza, organized by young Conservatives disaffected by their elders' collaboration with the regime, took place in April 1954. The leader, Adolfo Báez Bone, was killed, as were dozens of innocent peasants who happened to live near where the incident occurred. On 21 September 1956 a young poet, Rigoberto López Pérez, slipped into a Liberal Party celebration in León and shot Anastasio Somoza García four times. US President Dwight Eisenhower had American doctors rushed to the hospital in the Panama Canal Zone where Somoza was being treated, but the dictator died a week later. Shocked, the United States expressed strong support for the new government of Somoza's "clever" son, Luis Somoza Debayle, who was later succeeded by his more brutal brother, Anastasio Somoza Debayle, known as Tacho II, who also ran the GN. Among the three thousand people imprisoned on suspicion of collaboration with López Pérez (who may have acted unaided) was Pedro Joaquín Chamorro Cardenal, now editor of the Conservative newspaper *La Prensa*, who, in spite of his powerful family connections, underwent weeks of torture. Chamorro was eventually released into internal exile and, accompanied by his wife, Violeta Barrios de Chamorro, escaped to Costa Rica. In May and June 1959 Chamorro and Luis Cardenal led the Rebellion of Olama y los Mollejones, a "Social Christian" guerrilla uprising against Somoza; all of their one hundred guerrillas were said to be from wealthy Conservative families who were relatives of the Chamorros and the Cardenals. The young men were captured. Fearing the wrath of the Conservative oligarchy, Somoza did not dare to execute them. After a year in prison, Chamorro was exiled to the United States, ending the last significant Conservative insurgency against the Liberal dictatorship. From this point on, the revolutionary initiative passed to a modified form of Sandinismo.

The repression unleashed in the wake of Somoza García's assassination stimulated the revival of Sandinista traditions. The two-year imprisonment of the León law student Tomás Borge Martínez, suspected of being an accomplice of López Pérez, became the catalyst for student activism: "El 13 de octubre [de 1958] los estudiantes reunidos en asamblea decretaron un paro general de dos días … a favor de la libertad de Borge" (*BFM*, 157; "On October 13 [1958] the students gathered in assembly declared a general strike of two days … in support of Borge's freedom"). Borge was released into internal exile, then fled the country. Anti-Somoza activism radicalized the traditionally Liberal student life of León; after the triumph of the Cuban Revolution in January 1959, students sought a specifically Nicaraguan revolutionary ideology. On 23 July 1959 the GN opened fire on a demonstration, killing four students. From this point on, León became a centre for clandestine activity against the dictatorship. With young people from both Liberal and Conservative backgrounds searching for alternative allegiances, more than sixty attempted insurgencies occurred between 1956 and 1960. The GN easily dispatched these neophytes, yet in some cases the students were joined by aging veterans of Sandino's army, resulting in the transmission of Sandinista concepts of national autonomy and social justice to a younger generation.

Carlos Fonseca Amador, whose father, Fausto Amador, was Somoza's business manager, was absorbed in the study of the life of Sandino and travelled often to Cuba, where he befriended the legendary guerrilla Tania (Tamara Bunke), who would later die during Che Guevara's Bolivian campaign. Fonseca wrote articles in which he mingled quotes from Sandino with Cuban reformulations of Marxist social analysis. This emerging ideology became the basis of a new movement, reputed to have been founded in Tegucigalpa, Honduras, in July 1961 by Fonseca, Borge, and Silvio Mayorga under the tutelage of Colonel Santos López, who had fought with Sandino. Fonseca insisted that the movement adopt the name Frente Sandinista de Liberación Nacional, combining the Sandinista heritage with the concept of "national liberation," which, exemplified by the Cuban Revolution, was gaining popularity among young people throughout Latin America. As Tomás Borge reflected:

> Se juntan, de este modo, dos generaciones de nicaragüenses sellados por la presencia histórica del pensamiento Sandinista … Las viejas y nuevas generaciones sandinistas se buscaron en medio de las tinieblas hasta detectarse en el momento político y económico justo. Los viejos sandinistas nos trasmitieron sus experiencias que cayeron en un terreno hambriento de semillas y nuevas perspectivas. En verdad lo que ocurrió fue un desplazamiento del conocimiento escrito sobre la lucha de Sandino a la carne, los huesos y las palabras de los veteranos sobrevivientes. (Borge, *Carlos, el amanecer ya no es una tentación*, 26–7; And so, two generations of Nicaraguans came together, linked by the historic presence of Sandinista thought … The old and new generations of

> Sandinistas sought each other out in those dark times and found one another at the precise political moment. The old Sandinistas passed on their experiences, and we nurtured them in fields hungry for seeds and new perspectives. What was really taking place was the transference of all that which had been written about Sandino's struggle to the flesh, bones and words of the surviving veterans. [*Carlos, the Dawn Is No Longer beyond Our Reach*, 35–6])

In an apparent paradox, Borge, whose enthusiasm to undertake revolutionary adventures was fired by his adolescent reading of the German writer of romances of the US Wild West, Karl May (Borge, *paciencia*, 14; *Patient*, 10), and who himself engaged in an uneven career as a writer, maintains that the move to revolutionary action depended on a "transference of all that which had been written." The statement underscores a tension in Sandinista ideology between the belief in the genesis of an autonomous national literature as the precondition for the reimagining of the colonized nation-space as an independent country, and the obsession with guerrilla warfare, death, and heroic martyrdom. This strain of Sandinismo, impatient with writing the nation, perceives the revolutionary lineage as existing in blood and bone and the rural oral tradition.

The FSLN was slow in making its presence felt. In 1963 it robbed banks to gather funding, took over a radio station, and fought against the GN along the Coco River, experiencing heavy casualties. These defeats persuaded Carlos Fonseca of the need to establish networks of rural and urban support among trade unions, students, teachers, and peasants. The Nicaraguan economy was booming in the 1960s, with foreign investment, encouraged by John F. Kennedy's Alliance for Progress, flooding into the country. Nicaragua had the highest economic growth rate in Central America, yet, as the Somoza family appropriated more and more of the country's land and businesses, the number of poor people continued to increase. In August 1966 René Schick, a Somoza crony who had been acting as puppet president, died in office. The Conservative strongman Fernando Agüero united various opposition parties to run against Anastasio Somoza Debayle for president in elections scheduled for February 1967. On 22 January 1967, sixty thousand people marched against Somoza in Managua. When Agüero called on the crowd to rise against the dictator, the GN opened fire, killing forty people and wounding more than one hundred. The next month, Somoza easily defeated Agüero for president. In April, the tactically astute Luis Somoza died of a heart attack, leaving Tacho II as president, head of the GN, and proprietor of the Somoza economic empire. In August the FSLN, mistakenly believing that the country was ripe for a general uprising, launched an invasion from Honduras. Engaging the GN in combat at Pancasán, the Sandinistas and their peasant supporters suffered a decisive defeat. Many Sandinistas, including Silvio Mayorga, one of the FSLN's three founders, were killed. Just prior to the battle in which Mayorga and twelve other Sandinistas died, Carlos Fonseca recalled a young guerrilla named Daniel Ortega from Pancasán to the urban environment he knew best, sparing Ortega from almost certain death. Later that year, Ortega, whose two brothers had also joined the Sandinistas, was sentenced to fourteen years in prison for robbing a Managua bank to raise funds for the FSLN (Morris 2010: 42–3). For Somoza, Pancasán was a pyrrhic victory: the battle made Nicaraguans aware of the Sandinistas as a force fighting to overthrow the dictatorship. They "favourably contrasted this approach to that of middle-class parliamentary organisations ... whose futile attempts to try to win rigged elections had caused loss of life and further repression without any concomitant gains and without offering any alternative political programme to that of the Somocista governments" (Smith 1993: 118–19).

Seizing on the momentum created by Pancasán, Fonseca devoted the next three years to reorganizing and integrating the FSLN's urban support networks. The process slowed when the Costa Rican government arrested and imprisoned Fonseca for much of 1969–70, yet the organizing continued. In late 1969, in the hills around Matagalpa, the FSLN, supported by local peasants, succeeded in establishing a guerrilla base which, for the first time, inflicted losses on the GN and resisted efforts to dislodge it. In order to unify the country's elites, long-time US Ambassador Turner Shelton – who did not speak Spanish and whose face appeared on the Nicaraguan 20-córdoba note – brokered a deal that rewrote the constitution, replaced Somoza as president with a three-man committee, including Fernando Agüero, and gave the Conservatives more seats in Congress. The main consequence of this arrangement was to discredit the Conservative Party as a viable alternative to Somoza, who, Nicaraguans were aware, retained control of the economy and the GN even though he was no longer president.

After 1970 world prices for Nicaragua's agricultural products fell, and economic hardship increased. The GN's assaults on rural areas believed to be sympathetic to the Sandinistas increased the peasants' hatred of the dictatorship. The Sandinistas' now efficient urban organizations coordinated marches, demonstrations, and occupations of churches. In both the cities and the countryside, a Sandinista culture, deriving from the FSLN's 1969 "Historic Program," took shape in organizations in which workers, peasants, and young people participated. This culture, which opposed the worship of consumerism and US power promoted by Somoza, revolved around the promise of land reform, civil rights and a mixed economy, literacy, poetry and study, anti-racism, an activist clergy, equality between women and men, duty, self-sacrifice, and the veneration of Sandinista martyrs.

The confrontation between the country's two cultures came to a head on 23 December 1972, when one of the worst earthquakes in modern Central American history destroyed Managua. More than 20,000 people died in the earthquake and three-quarters of the capital's population was left homeless. In the chaos, the GN's command chain disintegrated. Guardsmen looted ruined homes. Somoza called in six hundred US Marines, who patrolled the capital until the GN could be reorganized, "leaving an indelible impression of US troops storming through the devastated streets, shouting orders in English to a bewildered population and incinerating corpses with flame-throwers" (Black 1983: 148). The earthquake drove a wedge between Somoza and his supporters among the middle class and the elite. Almost $200 million in international aid poured into the country; most of it ended up in the pockets of Somoza or the GN. Guardsmen set up shops amid the rubble, where they sold at inflated prices the food and medicine that had been donated by relief organizations. Somoza ensured that most of the profits from rebuilding the city accrued to his benefit. He created new construction companies that threw up cheap housing and reaped huge profits; he repaved the city streets with paving-stones from his own factory rather than the traditional tarmac, and drove elite competitors out of business.

In the aftermath of the earthquake, *La Prensa* editor Pedro Joaquín Chamorro set up a dissident Conservative party, which called for a boycott of the 1974 elections. Amid demonstrations and protests, the Sandinistas competed with elite figures who had broken with the Liberal and Conservative parties to channel popular discontent. On 27 December 1974 the Sandinistas seized the initiative when the suave, quadrilingual Comandante Eduardo Contreras Escobar, known as both "Marcos" and "Comandante Cero" (Commander Zero), and the rural guerrilla Germán Pomares took thirty members of the elite hostage at a Christmas party at the house of Somoza's former minister of agriculture. US Ambassador Shelton had left only ten minutes before Contreras and Pomares entered the party. The hostages included Somoza's brother-in-law, his cousin, his foreign minister, the head of ESSO Nicaragua, and two ambassadors. After tense negotiations, Somoza was forced to pay a ransom of one million dollars, publish an FSLN manifesto in the official media, release more than a dozen Sandinista prisoners, including Daniel Ortega, and provide a plane to fly the prisoners and hostage takers to Cuba.

The release of imprisoned leaders complicated the internal politics of Sandinismo. In 1975 the movement split into two rival tendencies, the Guerra Popular Prolongada (GPP; Prolonged People's War) led by Tomás Borge, which emphasized a "Vietnamese" strategy of a long war of attrition conducted from the mountains, and the Tendencia Proletaria (TP; Proletarian Tendency), led by Jaime Wheelock Román, a young Chilean-educated Marxist intellectual from a wealthy landowning family, which emphasized "organizing and propagandizing in factories and poor neighborhoods" (Booth 1982: 143) in order to instill class consciousness in the workers and prepare the ground for a Marxist revolution. Carlos Fonseca tried to mediate between the two groups.

During the negotiations, a third group, the Terceristas (Third Wayers), emerged. This was a broader, looser, less ideological coalition led by Daniel Ortega, his brothers Humberto and Camilo, Edén Pastora, and the Mexican-born Víctor Tirado. These leaders, some of whom had been expelled from the GPP by Borge, adopted a strategy originally proposed by Eduardo Contreras: they opened up the movement to Christians and non-socialists and tried to form alliances with disenchanted sectors of the middle classes.[1] Unimpeded by an ideological program dictating the need to wait for ideal conditions, the Terceristas took the military initiative as popular hatred of the regime, fuelled by the increasingly brutal acts of repression committed by the GN, spilled into the streets. In November 1976 the Guard killed Eduardo Contreras and Roberto Huembes, one of the leaders of the Proletarian Tendency, in Managua, and Carlos Fonseca in the northern mountains, on consecutive days. Fonseca's body was taken to a chapel, where his hands were cut off and flown by helicopter to Managua to prove to Somoza that he was dead (Zimmermann 2000: 203). Claiming to have destroyed the FSLN, Somoza asked the United States for economic assistance.

The CIA believed Somoza's claims, leading US President Jimmy Carter in early 1977 to decide he could pressure Somoza to improve his human-rights record without risking a resurgence of guerrilla activity. As soon as Somoza lifted state-of-siege legislation, the Carter administration gave him $2.5 million in military aid, with $12 million in economic aid promised to follow. In the relaxed political environment, demonstrations and occupations of churches and schools became rampant. In October 1977 the Terceristas launched simultaneous attacks, albeit disorganized and unsuccessful, on Ocotal, San Carlos, Masaya, and the GN headquarters in Managua. At the same time, in Costa Rica, a group of twelve prominent Nicaraguans, including numerous business leaders, Father Fernando Cardenal, Father Miguel d'Escoto Brockmann, and Sergio Ramírez, collectively known as "Los Doce"

("The Twelve"), issued a statement declaring that the Sandinistas must be part of any eventual political solution. The declaration struck a blow against Carter's attempt to foment "Somocismo without Somoza": saving the dictatorship by exiling the dictator. As spontaneous popular uprisings occurred throughout the country, the three factions of the Sandinistas patched up their differences in order to take advantage of a welling mass movement for which they were the only credible potential leaders. From fewer than twenty guerrillas in 1961 and barely one hundred in 1970, the FSLN began to grow rapidly as idealistic young people thronged to join the Revolution. In early 1978 the three tendencies combined accounted for nearly one thousand fighters; by late 1978, the Terceristas alone could field two thousand fighters, more than one-quarter of them young women.

In a telling intersection of Conservative and Sandinista sentiment, which had first coincided in the 1920s, fifty thousand people flooded into the streets on 10 January 1978 to protest the assassination of Pedro Joaquín Chamorro Cardenal. In retaliation for an article in *La Prensa* exposing the operations of Plasmaferesis – a business run by Somoza's son, Anastasio Somoza Portocarrero, and a crony named Cornelio Hüeck, which sold the blood of poor Nicaraguans to the United States for huge profits – the company's owners arranged for Chamorro to be shot on his way to work. The assassination of Chamorro, which his cousin and best friend Ernesto Cardenal, who had been travelling in the Middle East, learned about from a copy of *Time* magazine in the Madrid airport, led thirty thousand people to descend on Plasmaferesis and destroy the factory. The Nicaraguan elite, shocked by the killing of a member of its own class, called for a general strike. In Monimbó, an indigenous suburb of Masaya, a Mass in memory of Chamorro was attacked by the GN. Fighting with stones and homemade weapons, the indigenous people drove the guardsmen out of Monimbó, barricaded the suburb, and declared it a liberated zone. The neighbourhood held out for two weeks against a GN siege. The Guard retook Monimbó in house-to-house fighting that killed two hundred people, including Tercerista leader Camilo Ortega, the youngest and most ideologically flexible of the three Ortega brothers. In response, US President Carter cut off military aid to Somoza. When Somoza made minor concessions, such as allowing The Twelve to return to Nicaragua, Carter restored the aid and wrote Somoza a letter whose congratulatory tone disgusted all levels of Nicaraguan society, persuading even moderate reformers that the United States would never abandon Somoza and that their only hope lay with the Sandinistas. Somoza, however, who distrusted Carter, began to look elsewhere for support, purchasing weapons from Israel. As Carter planned a coup d'état to achieve his strategy of "Somocismo without Somoza," the Sandinistas realized they must pre-empt a change of government that might defuse the revolution.

On 23 August 1978 a commando led by Edén Pastora (who had assumed Eduardo Contreras's designation as Comandante Cero), Hugo Torres Jiménez (Comandante Uno), and Dora María Téllez (Comandante Dos) disguised themselves as National Guardsmen, entered the National Palace, occupied the Chamber of Deputies, and kidnapped the entire Congress. Over two and a half days, Téllez, a twenty-two-year-old medical student, negotiated with Somoza over the phone. She obtained $500,000, the release of sixty Sandinista prisoners, including Tomás Borge, who had been captured by the GN in 1976, and safe passage out of the country. Thousands of people cheered the assault team and the prisoners on their way to the airport. Paradoxically, the hostage taking bought Somoza time to forestall the coup being planned by the United States. Eighty-five National Guardsmen were arrested for alleged complicity in Jimmy Carter's plot to eliminate Somoza.

On 28 August the Terceristas collaborated with representatives of big business in a general strike that closed 75 per cent of the businesses in Managua. The war grew increasingly bloody as the desperate GN began strafing and napalming towns and villages, vandalizing hospitals and churches, engaging in mass killings of schoolchildren, and attacking the Red Cross. As casualty figures climbed into the thousands, attempts at international mediation failed yet had the result of publicizing Nicaragua's appalling human-rights record around the world.

From January 1979, prominent Somocistas began to discreetly leave the country. The institutions of the Liberal Somocista state disintegrated. Somoza's decision to bow to the International Monetary Fund by devaluing the córdoba by 40 per cent drove more poor people into the Sandinista ranks. From May to July 1979 battles pitting "ordinary people, some very young, against well-armed, well-trained troops with a literal licence to kill" (Smith 1993: 128) raged as control of cities such as Estelí, León, and Masaya passed back and forth between the GN and the Sandinistas. The death toll between mid-1977 and mid-1979 is estimated at forty thousand to fifty thousand people (Booth 1982: 181) in a national population of barely three million. Israel made a desperate attempt to save Anastasio Somoza Debayle by dispatching to Nicaragua a ship crammed with weapons and ammunition; yet on 14 June 1979 Jimmy Carter, unable to countenance further slaughter, ordered US forces to oblige the Israeli ship to turn back on the high seas (*AM*, 253). In a last-ditch effort to preserve the Somocista state, Carter sent the Argentine-raised State Department Latin American expert William Bowdler to propose a transitional plan that would exclude the

Sandinistas from power. On 17 July 1979 the Sandinistas took power in León, declaring the city the provisional capital: Somoza fled to Miami, taking with him the exhumed remains of his father and brother. On the morning of 18 July, as Daniel Ortega was handing out the first land-reform certificates on a hacienda outside León, the only surviving film image of Augusto César Sandino, which showed him taking off his hat, appeared again and again on television screens across Nicaragua (*AM*, 265).

The virtual presence of Sandino signalled a fundamental realignment of Nicaraguan nationality. The Liberal ideology of capitalist modernization became the creed of an exiled opposition; the Conservative ideology of Catholic corporatism split, with some Conservatives finding a new expression of their beliefs in the nationalism, liberation theology, and society of revolutionary duty fomented by Sandinismo, while other Conservatives became the voice of the internal opposition. For the first time since 1502, Nicaraguan territory was not governed at the behest of foreigners; the weak, neo-colonial state, bent to US and British will since 1838, yielded to the revolutionary nation. The vocabulary of Sandinista ideology, in its revised, Marxist-influenced form, would become the language through which Nicaraguan nationality was defined. What Beverley and Zimmerman write of literary politics was also true of politics writ large: "The Sandinista counterculture that had very gradually developed in the 1960s, maintained in the schools, churches, and small journals during the lowest ebb of the movement, would come in the 1970s to redefine the whole sphere of literature, so that even non-Marxist and nonrevolutionary writers were co-opted or reread in relation to the insurrectionary project of the Frente" (Beverley and Zimmerman 1990: 78). The "insurrectionary project," shaped to a significant extent by its literary culture, would become the measure of the nation.

3

Cardenal: The Contemplative's Poetry (1940–68)

ERNESTO CARDENAL: BIOGRAPHY

Ernesto Cardenal Martínez was born in the Conservative stronghold of Granada in 1925. His family, of mixed Basque, German Jewish, and English ancestry, were wealthy Catholic merchants, descendants of a sea pilot named Lorenzo Cardenal, of Basque and possibly also Sephardic Jewish descent (*SLT*, 199), who arrived in Nicaragua from northern Spain in the early nineteenth century. Lorenzo's son, and the author's great-grandfather, Pedro Cardenal, was foreign minister in the first Conservative government after the defeat of William Walker. Cardenal's maternal great-grandfather, a German Jew from Poland named Johannes Jakob Teufel, came to Nicaragua in order to travel to the California Gold Rush, was captured in a battle between Liberals and Conservatives, and remained in the country, adopting the name Jacobo Martínez in honour of the man who spared him from the firing squad. After his release, Martínez married into the Somoza family: Bernabé Somoza, a famous nineteenth-century bandit, was Cardenal's great-great uncle and Anastasio Somoza García's grandfather (*VP*, 418). Cardenal's coeval first cousin, Pedro Joaquín Chamorro Cardenal, also lived near to the grandiose Casa de los Leones, the largest colonial mansion in Granada's central square, which belonged to Cardenal's grandparents and where young Ernesto often resided. Cardenal was closely related to the two most important Nicaraguan poets of the generation preceding his, Pablo Antonio Cuadra Cardenal (1912–2002), a cousin on his father's side, and José Coronel Urtecho (1906–94), an uncle on his mother's side; both were Conservative nationalists who were drawn to avant-garde literary forms. They would later be instrumental in Cardenal's explorations of the work of Ezra Pound.

Ernesto Cardenal, Managua, 1951 (courtesy of Luz Marina Acosta)

When Cardenal was five years old, his grandfather sent his father, Rodolfo Cardenal, to León to manage the family store in that city where, in the past, houses owned by the Conservative Cardenal family had been sacked by Liberal supporters. Cardenal grew up with an acute awareness of Nicaragua's political divisions, and a nascent religious vocation. When his brother became ill, he promised God that he would become a priest if his brother recovered: "Y como se sanó quedé con la perfecta y serena convicción de que iba a serlo" (*VP*, 408; "And since he recovered I was left with the perfect, peaceful conviction that I was going to become one").

Cardenal began reading poetry at an early age, particularly that of Rubén Darío, and of his older cousin, Pablo Antonio Cuadra; he kept notebooks in which he wrote about the history of León. When Cardenal was twelve, his family moved to Managua. He and his brother were sent to study at the Colegio Centroamericano, facing Lake Nicaragua on the outskirts of Granada. There he was taught by Jesuit priests; his classmates were members of the Conservative elite, many of them close relatives. Immersion in this environment consolidated Cardenal's Conservative Catholic opposition to the Somoza dictatorship. In his teens, he began writing poetry about his search for God and his relations with young women. After graduating from the Colegio Centroamericano at the age of eighteen, Cardenal studied briefly in Managua, then travelled to Mexico City to begin a degree at the Universidad Nacional Autónoma de México (UNAM; National Autonomous University of Mexico), where, against his family's wishes, he devoted himself to literature. At UNAM Cardenal came into contact with Mexico City's vigorous literary culture, spending time with the Nicaraguan poet Ernesto Mejía Sánchez, the Guatemalan short-story writer Augusto Monterroso, and the Mexican writers Octavio Paz and Rosario Castellanos, among others.

During these years, Cardenal continued to write poetry, and to feel torn between his longing for marriage and his desire to devote his life to God. A first collection, *Carmen y otros poemas* (Carmen and Other Poems), centring on the emotional aftermath of unrequited love, was circulated privately in the mid-1940s. Cardenal published poems in Mexican literary magazines and began to establish a reputation when a long poem, "La ciudad deshabitada" ("The Abandoned City"), inspired by the disillusionment of his first Platonic love affair, appeared in the Mexican magazine *Cuadernos Americanos*. He graduated from UNAM in 1946 with a thesis entitled "Ansías y lengua de la nueva poesía nicaragüense" ("Longings and Language of the New Nicaraguan Poetry") which was published in Madrid in 1949 as the introduction to the anthology *Nueva poesía nicaragüense* (New Nicaraguan Poetry), edited by Orlando Cuadra Downing.

In 1948 Cardenal entered the master's program in American literature at Columbia University in New York. There he was introduced to the work of the US Trappist Thomas Merton, who had also studied at Columbia. Cardenal became fascinated by Merton's dual identity as monk and poet. At Columbia, he studied with literary critics such as Lionel Trilling and Mark Van Doren; the latter had been influential in Merton's conversion to Catholicism and had also taught the poets John Berryman and Allen Ginsberg. In spite of his later claim that his English was not good enough to grasp the subtleties of discussion in these seminars, Cardenal completed his MA. The writers he read during this period, particularly Ezra Pound but also T.S. Eliot, William Carlos Williams, and Walt Whitman, stimulated a rapid evolution in his poetic technique. The work of Pound, in particular, contributed to Cardenal's development of Exteriorism, the technique that sustained his best-known subsequent poetry. Paul Borgeson argues that "los dos años en Columbia son el período de más rápida evolución en la carrera de Cardenal" (Borgeson 1984: 31; "the two years at Columbia were the period of most rapid evolution in Cardenal's career").

After graduation, Cardenal travelled in France, Switzerland, Italy, and Spain, sometimes alone and at other times in the company of Pablo Antonio Cuadra or the young poet Carlos Martínez Rivas. He made a pilgrimage to the Balearic Isles, where he knocked on the door of the English poet Robert Graves and was invited in for lunch. Like other young men rebelling against the Liberal dictatorship of Somoza, Cardenal and Cuadra sought in the Fascist Spain of General Francisco Franco a restitution of Catholic corporatist values. This position made them bitterly unpopular with dissident Spanish intellectuals. Juan Goytisolo, for example, recalled visiting Madrid in 1950:

> Las características políticas de un gobierno autoritario como el de Franco habían atraído lógicamente a un puñado de intelectuales y universitarios simpatizantes de ellas; algunos disfrutaban incluso de becas oficiales y se erigían en defensores del nebuloso ideal falangista: poetas como Ernesto Cardenal y Pablo Antonio Cuadra profesaban devoción a la figura inmarchita de José Antonio [Primo de Rivera], antes de convertirse religiosamente, como el primero, al ideal revolucionario y sucumbir al hechizo de líderes carismáticos como Castro y Guevara. (Goytisolo 1985: 181; The political characteristics of an authoritarian government like Franco's had naturally attracted a handful of intellectuals and university students who were sympathetic toward them; some even enjoyed official scholarships and set themselves up as defenders of nebulous Falangist ideals: poets like Ernesto Cardenal and Pablo Antonio Cuadra worshipped the unblemished figure of José Antonio [founder of the Spanish Falangists], before undergoing religious conversion as the first did to revolutionary ideals yielding to the spell of charismatic leaders like Castro and Guevara. [*Forbidden Territory*, 153–4])

Goytisolo's rage leads him into imprecision: Cardenal never met Guevara, who died in 1967, three years before Cardenal's decade-long coolness towards the Cuban Revolution began to warm into support. Yet Madrid, where Cardenal later claimed to have done more drinking than studying, did not provide him with answers. He returned to Nicaragua at the age of twenty-five uncertain about his future, torn between religious commitment and the desire for marriage, hating Somoza and his dictatorship, and longing to write poetry. He sculpted in clay at the School of Fine Arts in Managua. His sculptures won awards, and he had his first international exhibition in Washington, D.C., in 1956. With his relative Reynaldo Téfel (a descendant of the brother of Cardenal's great-grandfather Teufel), he ran a small bookstore, Nuestro Tiempo (Our Time), which became a centre of literary and political debate.

Cardenal also published limited-edition poetry collections under the imprint El Hilo Azul (The Blue Thread); he contributed political articles to *La Prensa* and literary articles to the *Revista Conservadora* (Conservative Review), and frequented Conservative intellectual circles. He joined relatives from the Chamorro and Téfel families in forming a small centre-right nationalist opposition party, the Unión Nacional de Acción Popular (UNAP; National Union for People's Action). He began to write short poems that he disseminated anonymously in mimeograph and that became underground favourites as far away as Peru and Chile. The authorship of these "epigrams," many of them critical of the Somoza dictatorship, was a subject of speculation. In 1954 Cardenal became involved in Alfredo Báez Bone's April Conspiracy to assassinate Anastasio Somoza García. After the conspiracy failed, and many of his fellow conspirators were murdered by the GN, Cardenal spent months in hiding.

In 1955, at the age of thirty, having been permitted to resume normal life, Cardenal fell in love with an eighteen-year-old fine arts student named Ileana. After a tortured courtship, she rejected him, choosing to marry a Somocista diplomat. On 2 June 1956, while standing in his bookstore listening to the din of the wedding procession, attended by Somoza and his entourage, on Roosevelt Avenue, Cardenal experienced a moment of religious ecstasy that decided his fate. After vowing to devote himself to a contemplative life, he travelled to the United States in 1957 to enter the Gethsemani Monastery in Kentucky. He chose this monastery with the aim of having Thomas Merton as his tutor, a goal in which he was successful. During the more than two years that Cardenal spent in the monastery, he and Merton developed a close intellectual and personal complicity. They planned to found a contemplative community together in Nicaragua. Merton encouraged Cardenal to study indigenous American cultures. The books with which he supplied Cardenal provided the background for the influential poems Cardenal later would write on indigenous themes. Merton also played a pivotal role in Cardenal's political evolution, instilling in him what he described as the notion "que un contemplativo debía estar siempre comprometido con su pueblo, y con los problemas sociales y políticos de su lugar" ("Un contemplativo," 46; "a contemplative should always be committed to his people, and to the social and political problems of his place"). Finally, Merton encouraged Cardenal, who left Gethsemani in 1959, to study for the priesthood. Cardenal's departure was officially due to frail health; yet the realization that, having completed the two years of his novitiate, he would no longer have the right to speak to Merton other than by way of hand signals may have influenced his decision. Between Cardenal's departure and Merton's death in 1968, the two men maintained an impassioned correspondence, planning religious communities and arranging to rendezvous in Mexico and later in Nicaragua – plans that never came to fruition. Dom James Fox, the abbott of Gethsemani, tried to curtail communication between Merton and Cardenal, "intent on putting an end to an epistolary friendship which was becoming too hot to handle" (Letson 1990: 94).

Cardenal's first two books of poetry, *Epigramas* (1960) and *Hora 0* (1960; *Zero Hour and Other Documentary Poems*), were published shortly after his arrival at the Benedictine monastery in Cuernavaca, Mexico. A third book, *Gethsemani, Ky.* (1960), containing poems written in the US monastery, appeared a few months later. Cardenal and his friend Ernesto Mejía Sánchez edited an anthology of *Poesía revolucionaria nicaragüense* (1961; Nicaraguan Revolutionary Poetry), which they made repeated efforts to smuggle into Nicaragua. During his two years in Mexico, Cardenal underwent psychoanalysis to cure stomach problems that had contributed to his departure from Gethsemani; he also became acquainted with US Beat poets who were living in Mexico. Through one of these poets, he met the activist Margaret Randall, who in 1970 would help to introduce Cardenal to Cuba, and would later write books about the role of women and Christians in the Nicaraguan Revolution. The 1959 "Social Christian" Rebellion of Olama y los Mollejones, led by his cousin and best friend Pedro Joaquín Chamorro, rather than the Cuban Revolution, which had come to power four months earlier, captured Cardenal's idea of revolution at this time. Not even the assurances of the Catholic Cuban poet Cintio Vitier, whom Cardenal met in Mexico, that one could be a Catholic in revolutionary Cuba softened Cardenal's opposition to what he perceived as Castro's atheistic Communism.

In late 1961 Cardenal entered the Seminario de Cristo Sacerdote (Seminary of Christ the Priest), located in the mountains of the Department of Antioquia in Colombia, to complete his training. He was allowed to continue sculpting and to maintain his correspondence with Thomas Merton, in which they refined their vision of the religious community Cardenal would found once he was ordained. Both men agreed that the community must be rooted in the mixed indigenous and Latin roots of Spanish America. As his troubles with Rome diminished the likelihood of his being able to join Cardenal in the community's foundation, Merton wrote: "I know we will always be united in prayer" (Letson 1990: 97). During his time in Antioquia, Cardenal studied the religious beliefs of the indigenous cultures of Colombia and Venezuela, and wrote his *Salmos* (1964; *Psalms*), prayers that allude to the contemporary political world. He came into contact with liberation theology through one of its early exponents, the Colombian priest Camilo Torres. Having entered politics at the head of a mass movement, Torres was obliged to ask Rome to restore him to lay status. The director of the seminary forbade the novices from speaking to Torres, yet Cardenal made a clandestine appointment with Torres in Bogotá to plead with him not to abandon the principle of non-violence. Torres failed to appear for the meeting and soon afterwards Cardenal was granted permission to return to Nicaragua for ordination. He was ordained a priest in Managua on 15 August 1965 by the bishop of Chontales and Río San Juan, whose jurisdiction included the Solentiname archipelago at the isolated southern extremity of Lake Nicaragua, where Cardenal planned to found his contemplative community. In October, Cardenal returned to the United States to visit Merton, persuading him to write a letter in which he petitioned Pope Paul VI to be allowed to leave Gethsemani in order to join Solentiname. Merton's letter was never sent, but he continued to express effusive enthusiasm for Cardenal's project. With money donated by relatives, and with Rome's approval, Cardenal purchased an old farm near a half-completed church on the island of Mancarrón in the Solentiname archipelago. On a high spit of land at the end of the island, surrounded on three sides by water (and which afforded exceptional views of the heavens at night), he established a religious community on 13 February 1966.

The eleven years that Cardenal spent in Solentiname consolidated his religious vocation and his literary reputation, and, as time passed, made him known as a controversial and increasingly radical theologian. The monastery was unconventional from the outset in its acceptance of a married couple as founding members, and in its dedication to studying indigenous cultures. The members wore the traditional Nicaraguan peasant shirt, the *cotona*, rather than a habit. After visiting, Robert Pring-Mill wrote: "There is scant ritual and no written constitution ('The first rule is that there are no formal rules,' Cardenal says), but I felt the presence of a deep spirituality. There is a good deal of meditation and a great amount of hard work – agriculture, fishing, handicrafts" (Pring-Mill 1975: 7–8). Cardenal encouraged the peasants to develop their artistic abilities by painting the local landscape. He accumulated a library of five hundred thousand volumes (Letson 1990: 102) and continued to write prolifically. Prior to establishing himself in Solentiname, Cardenal had published in Colombia *Oración por Marilyn Monroe y otros poemas* (1965; *Marilyn Monroe and Other Poems*), which expressed a Mertonian critique of materialism that bordered on a loathing of the secular world. His book-length poem, *El estrecho dudoso* (1966; *The Doubtful Strait*), recounted the story of the Spanish conquest of Central America, and Nicaragua in particular, in ways that suggested parallels between the authoritarianism of the sixteenth century and that of the present.

Cardenal conceived the Solentiname community as a utopian microcosm of a potential future Nicaragua: "At first, Cardenal argued on a Mertonian basis that a community constructed according to Christian principles – including nonviolence and community of goods – would infect by example the world surrounding it without needing to resort to armed struggle" (Beverley and Zimmerman 1990: 67). Over time, this position grew more difficult to sustain. The Battle of Pancasán in 1967 and the death of Thomas Merton in suspicious circumstances in Bangkok in 1968, while campaigning against the Vietnam War, pushed Cardenal towards a more overt identification with the revolutionary left. Taking stock of his religious commitment, he published a prose work, *Vida en el amor* (1970; *Abide in Love*), based on his meditations in Gethsemani, and began working on *El Evangelio en Solentiname* (1975; *The Gospel in Solentiname*), based on recordings of Mass in Solentiname, during which the peasants reinterpreted the Gospels in terms of their daily lives.

In 1970 Cardenal accepted Cintio Vitier's invitation to travel to Cuba to serve as a juror for the Casa de las Américas Prize. Having initially intended to make only a short visit to the country, Cardenal spent three months travelling in Cuba and spoke to hundreds of people. He returned to Havana the next year to interview Fidel Castro. Cardenal's travelogue, *En Cuba* (1972; *In Cuba*), announced his conversion to socialism. While the portrait of revolutionary society in the book is not uncritical, Cardenal inexorably reaches the conclusion that in Cuba the closest approximation to Christian values is represented by the revolutionary government, while the Catholic Church has lost its sympathy for the poor. *In Cuba* was widely read in Latin America. Published just as many of the intellectuals who had rallied to Fidel Castro's side during the 1960s broke with the regime over the imprisonment and "self-criticism" of the once-privileged poet Heberto Padilla, Cardenal's book played an important role in sustaining support for Castro among Latin

American intellectuals and students in the face of public denunciations by influential former allies such as Mario Vargas Llosa and Carlos Fuentes.

Cardenal's new stance altered his approach to Nicaragua's problems. In spite of his growing theological radicalization, he maintained his adherence to non-violence, responding to Carlos Fonseca's invitation to join the FSLN by giving the Sandinista leader a biography of Gandhi. Yet readings in Solentiname now included, in addition to the Bible, "discursos de Fidel, de [Salvador] Allende, el Che, Mao ... No dejaba de ser eso prolongación de la Biblia" (*IE*, 213; "speeches of Fidel, of [Salvador] Allende, Che, Mao ... This continued to be an extension of the Bible"). Cardenal's poetry, like his growing contact with liberation theologians elsewhere in Latin America, reflected his attempt to fuse Christianity and Marxism. He travelled to Chile to visit the Marxist President Salvador Allende, and to Peru to discuss with the "military radical" President Juan Velasco Alvarado the possibility of a visit to that country by Fidel Castro; his meetings with activist priests in Chile persuaded him that a fusion of Christianity and Marxism was possible. Intimations of this shift in perspective are evident in *Homenaje a los indios americanos* (Homage to the American Indians), a book Cardenal had been working on since the early 1960s and published in three different editions between 1969 and 1972. After the earthquake in Managua in the latter year, Cardenal published two long poems, "Canto Nacional" ("Nicaraguan Canto"), in which a resurrected Augusto César Sandino becomes a modern Sandinista guerrilla, and *Oráculo sobre Managua* (*Oracle over Managua*) – "Cardenal's most crucial work of transition" (Beverley and Zimmerman 1990: 3) – in which the young guerrilla poet Leonel Rugama, who gave up his life for the cause, is portrayed as a Christ figure.

The radicalization of Cardenal's poetry developed in tandem with a more politically committed vision of the role of art in society. In 1976, influenced by the Costa Rican poet Mayra Jiménez, Cardenal established poetry workshops for the young people of Solentiname. The act of recreating the world around them in verse accelerated the young peasants' political radicalization. In 1976 Cardenal secretly joined the FSLN, supporting the Tercerista faction; he began to travel abroad to raise money for the movement. The young people of the community, having undertaken military training, resolved that in order to put into practice their religious beliefs and artistic vision, they must engage in armed struggle. On 12 October 1977, while Cardenal was out of the country (but with his knowledge), the young people of Solentiname participated in a Sandinista attack, planned by Humberto Ortega, on the GN barracks in San Carlos, near the Costa Rican border. The Guard repelled the assault with air support. The guerrillas were wounded or killed or fled to Costa Rica; those who returned to Solentiname were arrested by the GN, tortured, and murdered. The Guard razed every building in the Solentiname community except for the church, which was converted into a barracks. Declared a wanted man by Somoza, Cardenal published an open letter, which circulated widely in Latin America, "Lo que fue Solentiname" ("What Was Solentiname"), in which he indicated that the members of his community had chosen armed struggle out of their love of God.

From 1977 until the Sandinista triumph in 1979, Cardenal, based in Costa Rica, travelled throughout Europe and the Americas, giving talks and readings to raise funds for the Sandinistas. Returning to the country as the Revolution triumphed, he was named minister of culture in the new government. His initiatives in this portfolio included establishing workshops where older indigenous people taught almost-forgotten arts and crafts to young people, and an expansion of the training in "naive" landscape painting that had been pioneered in Solentiname. These two projects regenerated and consolidated the artisanal styles most visible in contemporary Nicaraguan markets. By far Cardenal's most controversial project was his creation of a national network of poetry workshops under the direction of Mayra Jiménez.

From the beginning of the Sandinista government, competition over the direction to be taken by Sandinista literary policy arose between the Ministry of Culture, run by Cardenal and his deputy, the poet Daisy Zamora, and the Asociación Sandinista de Trabajadores de la Cultura (ASTC; Sandinista Cultural Workers' Association), run by the poet Rosario Murillo, who had been Pedro Joaquín Chamorro's personal assistant at *La Prensa* and was the life-partner of Daniel Ortega. Murillo controlled the literary tabloid *Ventana*. Cardenal's ministry was committed to making art accessible to the masses while Murillo defended the interests of professional artists who objected to seeing the meagre budget for literary activity squandered on semi-literate workers and peasants, and claimed to fear the replacement of art by pamphleteering. Cardenal's foreign readings and speaking engagements, which led to his spending roughly half of each year outside the country – trips he professed to find boring but viewed as his duty to the Revolution – left the ministry vulnerable to attack.

The poetry workshops were initially highly successful, spreading throughout the country in the wake of the 1980–81 literacy campaign. Soldiers, peasants, and urban youth participated in more than seventy weekly workshops. Workshop poems were published in mimeographed literary journals in order to break down the distinction between amateur and professional writers; there was also an official journal of workshop poetry, *Poesía Libre* (Free Poetry), edited by Cardenal's protégé, the Masaya poet Julio Valle-Castillo. Following seven rules established by Cardenal, the poems produced in these workshops were concrete and Exteriorist and eschewed the use of metaphors or rhyme.[1] The movement spawned literary contests and a national radio show.

However, Murillo's astute manipulation of *Ventana*, her access to Daniel Ortega, and overt hostility to a haughty foreigner, Mayra Jiménez, playing a dominant role in an area as sensitive as the new Nicaraguan culture, compounded by the accusation that the poetry workshops were producing propaganda or mechanical imitations of Cardenal's own poetry, coalesced to undermine support for the project. In September 1982, as a result of a campaign launched by Rosario Murillo, who "le hizo la guerra y no descansó hasta que la destituyeran" (*RP*, 343; "waged war on her, and would not rest until she was dismissed"), Daisy Zamora was forced to resign as deputy minister of culture. Daniel Ortega named Francisco Lacayo, an efficient, diplomatic bureaucrat, as Zamora's replacement. Lacayo attempted a reconciliation between the Ministry of Culture and the ASTC. He, too, became the object of a defamation campaign orchestrated by Murillo, and was forced to resign. Ortega declined to name a third deputy minister, "tal vez para evitar conflictos con [Rosario Murillo]" (*RP*, 343; "perhaps to avoid conflicts with [Rosario Murillo]"); the poet Vidaluz Meneses became Cardenal's unofficial assistant and replacement during his absences from the country. By 1983, Mayra Jiménez had been forced to return to Costa Rica, Rosario Murillo's *Ventana* had begun denouncing Julio Valle-Castillo, and the number of poetry workshops had dropped to about thirty. The workshops were placed under the responsibility of regional centres where, although technically programs of the Ministry of Culture, they answered to local Sandinista activists who were often more loyal to the ASTC. Cardenal's influence on the poetry being produced in the workshops waned.

During Pope John Paul II's controversial visit to Nicaragua in 1983, the sight of Cardenal among the delegation greeting him at the airport caused the Pope to rush forward, shouting at Cardenal, "You must regularize your situation!" Cardenal dropped to his knees, while the pope wagged an admonishing finger at him in television pictures that were broadcast around the world. This global notoriety multiplied Cardenal's invitations to read, speak, and raise funds in other countries. In 1984 he published *Vuelos de Víctoria* (*Flights of Victory*), short poems written during the last days of the struggle against Somoza and the early days of the Revolution.

Increasingly marginalized after 1985, when Pope John Paul II suspended his right to administer the sacraments, Cardenal devoted more time to his own writing. He returned to indigenous themes in *Quetzalcóatl* (1986) and *Los Ovnis de Oro* (1988; *Golden UFOs. The Indian Poems*), his collected indigenous poems. The projects he undertook as minister of culture during this period, such as the creation of a museum of Latin American art and the establishment of an annual international book fare in Managua, were initially promising but collapsed for lack of funding. In 1988, during the *compactación* – the rationalization caused by the Contra War's drain on the economy (see chapter 6) – Rosario Murillo argued successfully for the dissolution of both the Ministry of Culture and the ASTC, and their replacement by an Institute of Culture under her direction. Murillo's action shocked activists on both sides of the debate between the ASTC and the Ministry of Culture, provoking open criticism from writers such as Gioconda Belli and disillusionment among Murillo's ASTC followers. Cardenal was on an official visit to Japan when he received a phone call telling him that he was no longer minister of culture. He was later given a face-saving ceremonial title. Freed from official duties but in poor health, he retreated to Solentiname to complete his epic poem *Cántico Cósmico* (1989; *Cosmic Canticle*), which fused religious, scientific, and historical interpretations of human life. In a show of solidarity, the Cuban government awarded Cardenal the Haydée Santamaría Medal.

The Sandinista electoral defeat of February 1990 was a shock for Cardenal, who was even more surprised than other Sandinistas that the people could reject the Revolution. He considered returning to Solentiname but finally decided to remain in Managua. Prior to the Sandinistas' departure from office, Cardenal's gargantuan steel sculpture of Augusto César Sandino in silhouette was mounted on the Tiscapa Mound, the former site of Somoza's presidential palace, from where it is visible over much of Managua. With the help of German friends, Cardenal launched the art gallery and cultural centre, Casa de los Tres Mundos (House of the Three Worlds), in Granada; he maintained an office and displayed some of his own sculptures in Galeria los Dos Mundos (The Two Worlds Gallery) in Managua. In 1993 Cardenal published his mystical poem *Telescopio en la noche oscura* ("Telescope in the Dark Night"), which recounts his 1956 religious conversion.

In late 1994, as a serious split emerged in the Sandinista Front, Cardenal was the first well-known figure to resign from the FSLN. He later became a supporter of Sergio Ramírez's Movimiento de Renovación Sandinista. Cardenal abandoned poetry for a decade in order to write his memoirs, which appeared in three large volumes: *Vida perdida* (1999; Lost Life), *Las ínsulas extrañas* (2002; The Strange Isles), and *La revolución perdida* (2004; The Lost Revolution). In 2004 he announced that he would write more verse, and in 2005 a new volume of poems, *Versos del Pluriverso* (Verses from the Pluriverse), appeared. That same year, Cardenal was nominated for the Nobel Prize for Literature. In 2006 he campaigned for Herty Lewites and, after Lewites's death, Edmundo Jarquín as president on the MRS ticket. He continued to travel selectively to give readings and interviews, and to participate in Nicaraguan cultural events such as the Granada Poetry Festival. In Managua, Cardenal devoted increasing amounts of his time to running poetry workshops for children suffering from cancer (López-Baralt 2012: 198–9). In 2009 he edited an anthology of the children's poetry, *Me gustan los poemas y me gusta la vida* (I Like Poems and I Like Life). Cardenal was awarded the Zacatecas International Prize in Mexico in 2008 and the Pablo Neruda Poetry Prize in Chile in 2009; that year he published a new collection of poems, *Pasajero de Tránsito* (Passenger in Transit). In 2010 he was again nominated for the Nobel Prize.

In early 2011 Cardenal undertook an extensive reading tour of the United States to promote new English translations of his poems. Later in the year he travelled to Mexico to read from a new poem, *Tata Vasco*, that was published as an independent volume; he also published a new book of theological essays, *Este mundo y otro* (This World and Another). In January 2012 he made a return visit to Solentiname, widely covered in the media, in the company of intellectuals, politicians, and academics to celebrate his eighty-seventh birthday and attend the liberation-theology "Misa Campesina" ("Peasant Mass"), performed by Carlos and Luis Mejía Godoy in the island's recently reconstructed church (González 2012). The next month, it was announced that the 2013 Granada Poetry Festival would be dedicated to Cardenal. In May 2012 Cardenal was named the winner of the Queen Sofía Poetry Prize, the most important prize for Spanish-language poetry, for his lifetime production. The choice was not unanimous as some jury members raised objections for "motivos extraliterarios" ("extra-literary motives"), which commentators interpreted as meaning that "la política ... jugó en su contra" ("El Reina Sofía" 2012; "politics ... worked against him").

Politics continued to play a significant role in Cardenal's life. In 2008, while attending the inauguration of Fernando Lugo as president of Paraguay, Cardenal denounced the corruption of President Daniel Ortega, accusing him of running a family dynasty reminiscent of that of the Somozas. Upon returning to Nicaragua, Cardenal was accused of defaming a German businessman; this case had already been dismissed in 2005, but a pro-Ortega judge found Cardenal guilty and ordered him to pay a fine of 20,000 córdobas (about 700 Euros). When he refused to pay, his bank accounts were frozen and he was sentenced to a prison term. As Nicaraguan law forbids imprisoning people over the age of eighty, Cardenal retained his freedom. He travelled in Europe and Latin America to publicize his persecution. More than sixty writers and intellectuals, including José Saramago, Mario Vargas

Llosa, Eduardo Galeano, Mario Benedetti, and Laura Restrepo, signed a petition protesting Cardenal's sentence. In November 2012 Cardenal's presence in Spain, where he received the Queen Sofia Poetry Prize from the queen's hands, and where, according to the Madrid newspaper *El País*, his arrival was greeted with a "homenaje y reconocimientos de una estrella de rock" (Morales 2012; "homage and recognitions of a rock star"), caused Daniel Ortega to make a last-minute decision to withdraw Nicaragua from the Ibero-American Summit in Cádiz (González 2012). Once again, as he had been for most of his life, Ernesto Cardenal was a symbol of political opposition to the government of Nicaragua.

CARDENAL'S YOUTHFUL POETRY

The momentum towards a poetry that harmonizes the vastness of the universe and the infinite nature of divine love with the concrete conditions of daily life, particularly the quest for social justice within the framework of the nation-state, understood as the product of a specific sequence of historical events, is discernible from the beginning of Ernesto Cardenal's poetic career. One of his first poems, "La casa de Cristo" ("The House of Christ"), written at the age of fifteen in 1940, addresses this dilemma with striking directness. Cardenal turned naturally in his early poems to the subject of his relationship with deity; but, in a concern that foreshadowed his later work, he longed to anchor Christ in his immediate surroundings:

> Muéstrame dónde vives y en qué casa
> O dime por lo menos en qué calle
> Qué vía he de seguir para que te halle
> Y qué casa o qué parque hay por tu casa.
> (Borgeson 1984: 22; Show me where you live and in which house/Or tell me at least on which street/Which path I should follow to find you/And which house or what park is near your house.)

The formal qualities of this verse – hendecasyllabic lines, rhyming in a pattern of ABBA – display the heritage of Rubén Darío's *modernismo*. Even at this early stage, however, the oracular tones of religious diction with its imperative verb forms ("Show me") are evident. (The second verse opens with "Give me" and the final line with "But give me"). The search for Christ's house is a conceit: "casa" may be understood in a spiritual, rather than a literal, sense. Having established this conceit, Cardenal worries at it with dogged disingenuousness, insisting that he must know Christ's surname, the block where he lives, the park closest to his house. The tension presages the poet's future efforts to fuse spiritual and secular life.

The poems of *Carmen*, written in Granada and Mexico City in his late teens, are addressed to the young woman, Carmen Chamorro Benard, with whom he experienced his first great romantic passion when he was eighteen and she was fourteen. The poet's vision of this unattainable young woman eventually merges with a nostalgic vision of the city of Granada. A strain particularly evident in the *Carmen* poems is the merging, in the poetic speaker's mind, of love for a very young woman with universal love. Where "La casa de Cristo" tries to render deity in everyday terms, "Inmortal amor" ("Immortal Love"), one of the longest poems in *Carmen*, reverses the trope by expressing the poet's carnal longings in spiritual, even ethereal terms:

> Tu cuerpo
> es otro cuerpo mío más lejano
> donde yo me refugio huyendo de la muerte,
> la muerte que de niño me persigue …
> Tú no morirás nunca!
> (*Obra primogénita*, 97–8; Your body/is another body of mine more remote/where I seek shelter escaping from death/the death that has been pursuing me since I was a child …/You will never die!)

The love-object becomes not so much another human being to be understood or explored as an extension of the poet that is blessed with immortality. The experience of love runs close to that of religious ecstacy: of discovering within oneself a component that is immortal. Cardenal was less in love with Carmen than with a metaphysical need to bathe in love; his mentor Coronel Urtecho referred to this as Cardenal's "enamoramiento del amor" (Arellano 1974: 165; "infatuation with love"). Yet, if Cardenal's love for young women was curiously immaterial in its obsessions, his love for God and the universe was obstinately materialistic.

In writing about love, Cardenal, like other young male poets of his generation, adopted motifs from Pablo Neruda. This is evident in his use of a natural imagery that did not arise from his experience. Hence, the Nicaraguan, raised in an arid landscape of volcanoes and crater lakes, could write in a poem called "Mejor Morirse" ("Better to Die"): "Quisiera desbordarme como un río/salir lejos de mí, furiosamente/como el agua de los locos manantiales" (*Obra primogénita*, 99; "I want to overflow like a river/get away from myself, fiercely/like the water of the crazy/wild springs"). Neruda, product of the verdant mountains of southern Chile and their coursing rivers, came by such imagery naturally: he would later open his *Canto General* (1950) with a sonorous reference to "ríos, ríos arteriales" (105; "rivers, arterial rivers" [*Canto General*] [English], 13). Cardenal's use of "springs," a favourite Neruda trope, is not accompanied by the delight in sexuality that throbs through Neruda's *Veinte poemas de amor y una canción desesperada* (1924; *Twenty Love Poems and a Song of Despair*), in lines such as "Mi cuerpo de labriego salvaje te socava" (35; "My rough peasant's body digs in you" [*Twenty Love Poems*, 3]), even though Neruda's book astonished the adolescent Cardenal as "lo que no se había visto nunca en lengua castellana" (*AG*, 93; "what had not ever been seen in the Spanish language"). Nerudian tropes persist in "La ciudad deshabitada," the most ambitious of the *Carmen* poems.

Most of the early poems about Carmen do not go far beyond rather tame observations of her hair and eyes as somewhat disappointing outposts on the road to eternal love. In "La ciudad deshabitada," an enormously lush, self-consciously tropical poem written in Mexico City in 1946, Cardenal evokes Carmen by opposition, through an anguished description of the city from which she is now absent. The recurring image of Carmen's breasts as a forbidden fruit, whose enjoyment the poetic speaker will now be denied, structures the first two-thirds of the poem in post-Nerudian lines such as, "Corolas fosforescentes, toda la noche sus pechos charla y charla/tumultuosos y tibios en lo oscuro un corazón" (*Obra primogénita*, 116; "Phosphorescent corollas, the whole night her breasts/warm and tumultuous in the darkness, a heart babbles and babbles"). In other lines, the images of breasts combine with Neruda-like river imagery: "Creí que rodearía el paraíso con tres tumultuousos ríos de carne/y en su pecho bebería los lirios atolondrados de la infancia" (*Obra primogénita*, 117; "I thought I would surround paradise with three tumultuous rivers of flesh/and at her breast I would drink the impetuous lilies of childhood"). These lines, hinting at Cardenal's semi-conscious awareness of an infantile strain that suffuses his presentation of his infatuation with this fourteen-year-old, illustrate Neruda's poor fit as a model. An intimation of the poet Cardenal would later become appears only in the penultimate stanza, where Granada ceases to be an anguished vacancy, provoking an almost Oedipal search for the mother, and begins to be described in terms of its history. The conquistador Francisco Hernández de Córdoba, the city's founder, is depicted as saying that Granada "será mi mujer para siempre" (*Obra primogénita*, 120; "will be my wife forever"). Cardenal evokes this line in order to make the connection between the city and his lost would-be wife; but the reference leads to a later poem about Hernández de Córdoba, in which Cardenal's trademark mythologization of a dissident reading of national history begins to emerge.

It soon became clear that Neruda's carnal, verbally ebullient poetic temperament was not a viable model for the devout, mystically inclined Cardenal. For this reason, and because of their support, at this time, for opposite sides in the Spanish Civil War (*AG*, 95), the Chilean's influence on the young Nicaraguan was not enduring. Even so, in interviews during his years as minister of culture, Cardenal would stress the influence of Neruda, an exemplary Latin American of impeccable revolutionary credentials, mentioning only selectively the later, far more formative and aesthetically enduring, if politically inopportune, influence of the American Fascist sympathizer Ezra Pound. During a press conference given at the Ministry of Culture in Managua in 1981, for example, Cardenal responded to a question about his favourite poets by saying: "Para mí la influencia más determinante al comienzo de mi carrera literaria fue Neruda" (Press Conferences; "For me the most decisive influence at the beginning of my literary career was Neruda"). When speaking in the United States, however, Cardenal made no effort to conceal the importance to his poetic practice of poets such as Walt Whitman, Carl Sandburg, and, particularly, Pound. In a press conference in New York, on 30 November 1983, Cardenal responded to a question about the Nicaraguan poetry workshops by stating: "En realidad las técnicas para escribir poesía que les damos a los obreros y los campesinos están tomadas de Ezra Pound" (Press Conferences; "In fact the techniques that we give the workers and peasants to write poetry are taken from Ezra Pound").

Pound's influence, although absorbed by Cardenal from the late 1940s onward, did not shape his work in obvious ways for almost a decade. The impact of Neruda's combination of romanticized love and insurgent politics was more immediate. This influence persists in the *Epigramas* (Epigrams), but here, for the first time, Cardenal is speaking in a voice that is unmistakably his own. During his days in Mexico he had devised a very personal method for writing. He wrote at night: "apagada la luz, construía los poemas mentalmente como una oración y luego la encendía para trasladar al papel su inspirada fecundidad" (Arellano 1974: 167; "with the lights out, he constructed the poems mentally, like a prayer, and then he would turn the light on to transfer his inspired creativity to paper"). Originality of voice, particularly his distinctive oracular tone, now accompanied this original method of composition. For the first time, Cardenal's inimitable fusion of the quotidian and the eternal, reflected through the prism of national politics and history, becomes discernible. It is at its most pithy in an epigram such as the following: "Me contaron que estabas enamorada de otro/y entonces fui a mi cuarto/y escribí ese artículo contra el Gobierno/por el que estoy preso" (*AN*, 10; "They told me you were in love with another man/and then I went off to my room/and wrote that article against the Government/that landed me in jail" [*AOP*, 7]). This poem exemplifies the transition from the early epigrams, particularly those addressed to "Claudia," which express the bitterness of romantic disappointment, to those that are dominated by political themes; it makes explicit the link between private and public acts. Here the particulars of Nicaraguan history do not come into play; this short poem could have been the work of a young man in any one of a dozen countries in the Americas.

In the later poems, explicit references to the dictatorship of Anastasio Somoza García as the force that shapes the poet's reality insist on the particularity of Nicaraguan experience, although the emphasis is still on the dictator as ogre rather than on the systemic forces that have put him in power. In one epigram, the poet, hearing sirens at night, imagines scenes of upheaval; he realizes: "No es incendio ni muerte:/Es Somoza que pasa" (*AN*, 11; "It's neither a fire nor death:/Just the Dictator flashing by" [*AOP*, 10]). One of only two epigrams to bear a title (the other is "Epitafio para Joaquín Pasos" ["Epitaph for Joaquín Pasos"]), the caustic monologue "Somoza desveliza la estatua de Somoza en el Estadio Somoza" (13; "Somoza Unveils the Statue of Somoza in the Somoza Stadium") portrays the dictator as deriving his greatest pleasure from reminding the population of his omnipresence in their lives.

If these epigrams set in place one pole of Cardenal's creative vision – individual experience, as shaped by the concrete historical context of the nation – they also include glimpses of the vital second pole: the infinite nature of love, divinity, and the universe, presented through the evocation of scientific descriptions of the cosmos. In a striking anticipation of *Cosmic Canticle*, the penultimate epigram employs cosmic metaphors to express the emotional distance between an estranged couple:

> Ileana: la distancia es tiempo, y el tiempo vuela.
> A 200 millones de millas por hora el universo
> se está expandiendo hacia la Nada
> Y tú estás lejos de mí como a millones de años.
> (*AN*, 14; Ileana: distance is time, and time flies./At 200 million miles an hour the universe/is expanding towards nothingness/And you are millions of years away from me. [*AOP*, 18])

This poem, which opens with a reference to the Andromeda galaxy, strains against the relatively simple metaphor of outer space as a symbol of emotional distance towards the metaphysical complexity that Cardenal would achieve thirty years later. The observation that the universe is expanding towards "nothingness," and that space and time are the same, betrays a deeper anguish than that of mere romantic disappointment. They hint at the difficult task of coordinating emotional, historical, and spiritual concerns.

Yet, in terms of Cardenal's immediate development, the epigrams are significant because they provide a bridge from laments for unrequited love to broader national concerns. Indeed, the Canadian poet Dionne Brand, in her response to the epigrams, "Epigrams to Ernesto Cardenal in Defense of Claudia," interprets even the early epigrams as being less about romantic entanglements than the seductions of the flashy Americanized culture dangled before the Nicaraguan bourgeoisie by the Somoza dictatorship: "some Claudias are sold to companies/some Claudias sell to street corners/even debasement has its uptown/even debasement has its hierarchy" (Brand 1983: 25). This reading would explain the outsized bitterness that appears in the early epigrams, a bitterness that sometimes seems more proportionate to the anger one expresses at a corrupt social order than to that directed at an inconstant young woman. To read in lines such as "De estos cines, Claudia, de estas fiestas/de estas carreras de caballos/no quedará nada para la posteridad/sino los versos de Ernesto Cardenal para Claudia" (*AN*, 10; "Of all these movies, Claudia, of these parties/of these horse races/nothing will be left for posterity/except the verses of Ernesto Cardenal to Claudia" [*AOP*, 6]) the threat of a revolution that will annihilate the corrupt party-going, horse-racing set that collaborated with Somoza (particularly since, at the time he wrote the epigrams, Cardenal's political ideas were reactionary rather than revolutionary) would be stretching the textual evidence. Read as a sequence, however, the epigrams follow the arc of Cardenal's evolution from a poet of love lost to a writer beginning to find ways to analyze, reconstruct, and mythologize the history of one of the most downtrodden nations of the Americas.

Cardenal's point of access to Nicaraguan history was his family's home city of Granada. His first significant achievement in the field of the historical narrative poem, "Con Walker en Nicaragua" ("With Walker in Nicaragua"), was written in late 1950, shortly after his return from Europe. In 1952 this poem was awarded a prize in Nicaragua. Approaching his homeland through the eyes of Clinton Rollins, one of William Walker's filibusters, who recalls his adventures fifty years later, in the first decade of the twentieth century, the poem employs a diction that represents a modulation from the lyricism of the poems about Carmen and Claudia into the anti-lyrical, Exteriorist voice of the later works. The narrator presents himself as a plain-spoken American: "yo, Clinton Rollins, sin pretensión literaria/me entretengo en escribir mis memorias" (*AT*, 20; "I, Clinton Rollins, attempting no literary style,/pass the time by penning my memories" [*WWN*, 43]). Nicaragua is viewed from an outsider's perspective (much as Cardenal must have seen it, returning at the age of twenty-five, after having been absent for seven years), which emphasizes "sus lagos azules entre montes azules bajo el cielo azul" (*AT*, 22; "its blue lakes amid blue mountains under a blue sky" [*WWN*, 47]). Even though there are descriptions of Rivas and León, the poem closes in on two central themes: the serene, enigmatic, cruel personality of William Walker, and the city of Granada.

At this point, Walker is presented not, as he would be later, as a manifestation of a consistent project of US imperialism, but rather as a natural calamity that befell the city. From the beginning, Walker is, in the tradition of the US western, a mysterious stranger: "Ninguno fue su amigo/Y no recuerdo haberlo visto jamás sonreír" (23; "Nobody was his friend/And I don't remember ever having seen him smile" [*WWN*, 47]). Delivering death sentences to captured Nicaraguans in his high-pitched voice – "la voz de una mujer no era más suave que la suya" (23; "And a woman's voice was hardly softer than his" [*WWN*, 47]) – he defies traditional definitions of masculinity, and even of humanity. His fiancée, who died of yellow fever in Nashville, was a deaf mute, a detail that contributes to the portrait of Walker as beyond the reach of human communication. When members of a wealthy Granada family, the Corrals, beseech him to commute the death sentence he has passed against one of its members, he complies by decreeing that the man will no longer be shot at noon, but at 2 P.M. The historical material, though abundant, does not ruffle the poem's lyrical, nostalgic voice; the reader can see Cardenal taking the first steps towards his later Exteriorist mode by including historical anecdotes, without yet integrating diverse discourses into the poem's language. One of the rare exceptions is the inclusion, in block capitals, of the notice "AQUI FUE GRANADA / HERE WAS GRANADA" (31; *WWN*, 62), posted in the central square after the filibusters' attempt to burn the city. The poem also cites the words that are often given as Walker's final utterance when he was about to be executed in Honduras in 1860, "el Presidente de Nicaragua, es nicaragüense" (35; "the President of Nicaragua, is a Nicaraguan" [*WWN*, 71]). Here the line appears as the crowning evidence of Walker's megalomania; when it returns in Cardenal's next major work, *Zero Hour*, the line is explicitly linked to a history of US imperial domination.

"With Walker in Nicaragua" concentrates on a city rather than a country. The narrator, Rollins, recreates a nineteenth-century Granada that is probably not very different from that of Cardenal's infancy: "Granada despertaba cada mañana con campanas/y pregones de vendedores en las calles" (*AT*, 26; "Granada would awake each morning with bells/and cries of vendors in the streets" [*WWN*, 53]). Rollins evokes typical scenes, exotic to his foreign eyes: "las lavanderas semidesnudas lavaban cantando/y los hombres dando de beber o bañando a sus caballos" (*AT*, 26; "half-naked washerwomen washed laundry singing, while men would be watering or bathing their horses" [*WWN*, 53]). Granada's particularity – the exceptional devoutness of its inhabitants, its grand colonial square and location next to Lake Nicaragua – take precedence over any assumption of a national identity. This is not merely a reflection of Cardenal's outlook in 1950 but also an accurate description of how Granada's residents perceived themselves in 1855. Nevertheless, Cardenal writes "With Walker in Nicaragua" as a Granada Conservative. The rebellion against Walker is attributed to the filibuster's attempt to obliterate a beloved city, rather than to the coalescing of a national consciousness. Rollins says of the city's residents,

Amaban a Granada como a una mujer.
Todavía asoman las lágrimas a sus ojos
cuando recuerdan la pérdida de su querida Granada
la ciudad de los Chamorros ...
  Donde una vez hubo amor.
(*AT*, 31; They loved Granada like a woman./Even today tears well up in their eyes/when they remember the loss of their dear Granada/the town of the Chamorros .../Where once there was love. [*WWN*, 63])

The equation of Granada with a woman and the line "Where once there was love" – an anachronistic allusion to Cardenal's love for Carmen Chamorro (*AG*, 212) – illustrate the poem's provenance as the work of a young poet who, while striving to develop a broader scope through the assimilation of history and the foreign voices to which he had been exposed overseas, remained influenced by the lyrical legacy of Darío and Neruda and the parochialism of Conservative Granada. The poem portrays both Walker and Granada in ways that are memorable, yet these two themes are not integrated into an analysis of the power relationships that connect them, as Cardenal's verse would do once he fell under stronger nationalist and Marxist influences. Cardenal's next major narrative poem, *Zero Hour*, enabled him to break out into a national, and even Central American, vision, through the employment of a layered, discursively heterogeneous language that incorporated the lessons of Ezra Pound.

ZERO HOUR: A CONSERVATIVE NATIONAL EPIC

One of the major achievements of Cardenal's career, *Zero Hour* mingles imagery gleaned from Modernist poetry with explanations of the economics of the political subjugation of Central American nationhood. It presents for the first time the story of Augusto César Sandino's life and death as the founding myth of Nicaraguan national consciousness. *Zero Hour* opens with a nocturnal portrait of Central America and its notorious dictators of the 1930s and 1940s. By way of a patchwork of incursions into economics, history, religion, even personal memoir, the poem refines its focus to concentrate on the trajectory of Nicaragua. The procedure suggests that one of the preconditions of writing the nation for a Central American author is to distinguish Central American experience (and, by extension, Central American literariness) from the dominant discourses of South America and Mexico, into which Central American writing is often assimilated for both critical and commercial purposes. Arturo Arias argues: "When we study Central American literature, we also engage in a fascinating exercise of cultural translation, because this literature resists appropriation by South American literature and by the literatures of foreign countries of the diaspora" (Arias 2007: xiv).

Cardenal, who had studied in Mexico and would publish *Zero Hour* there, reacts against the self-confident, highly articulated myths of Mexican nationalism, as well as against the crushing of Nicaraguan nationality by the Somoza dictatorship. The first step in forging a Nicaraguan national mythology is an engagement with the interconnected fates of the five original Central American republics: Guatemala, Honduras, El Salvador, Nicaragua, and Costa Rica. The lyrical introduction soon modulates into intimations of the sinister political fate that has befallen the first four of these five republics:

> Noches tropicales de Centroamérica,
> con lagunas y volcanes bajo la luna
> y luces de palacios presidenciales,
> cuarteles y tristes toques de queda.
> (*AN*, 15; Tropical nights in Central America,/with moonlight lagoons and volcanoes/and lights from presidential palaces,/barracks and sad curfew warnings. [*ZHOD*, 1])

The only human source of light in the otherwise moonlit night comes from the presidential palaces: the population resides in darkness. The opening verse itemizes the oppressive acts committed by the four dictatorships on this night. The overview portrait of Central America culminates in Nicaragua. Yet the focus on Nicaraguanness must be earned by examining the web of oppressive economic relations that have gutted all of these nations of their distinctive, albeit closely related, national cultures.

The transition between the lyrical opening verse and the three pages of deliberately anti-lyrical descriptions of corporate manipulation that follow is a verse from the Bible: "Centinela! Qué hora es de la noche?/Centinela! Qué hora es de la noche?" (15; "Watchman! What hour is it of the night?/ Watchman! What hour is it of the night?" [*ZHOD*, 1]). This passage, from chapter 21 of the Book of Isaiah, relates the moment in which a night watchman receives the news of the fall of Babylon and the divine destruction of its graven images. Verses 11 and 12 speak of the chariot-driver who brings the news:

> He calleth to me out of Se-ir
> Watchman, what of the night?
> Watchman, what of the night?
>
> The watchman said, The
> morning cometh, and also the
> night: if ye will inquire, inquire
> ye: return, come. (Holy Bible, 605)

This reference presages the analysis of Somocismo as the product of an avaricious economic system, a corrupt Babylon ripe for destruction by moral righteousness. The chariot-driver's query, more explicit in the Spanish version ("What hour is it?"), posits Somocismo's inevitable destruction in terms of a cyclical conception of time. The watchman's response that both morning and night come in their time insists on this cyclical framework, which Cardenal develops later through imagery alluding to the seasons.

The section on the economic impact of the United Fruit Company, which follows this transition, is cast in a language deliberately shorn of metaphors. This uncompromising passage is the first clear signal in Cardenal's work of the dramatic change in his poetry that occurred in the late 1950s, as his absorption of Pound and other Modernists became palpable. The clustering of natural metaphors that Cardenal's love poetry had borrowed from

Neruda disappears. The aesthetic transformation of his verse coincided with the incorporation of an economic analysis. The poem makes this explicit in a language that insists on facts, figures, research, and direct quotation, and eschews lyricism or metaphors.

> La condición era que la Compañía construyera el Ferrocarril,
> pero la Compañía no lo construía,
> porque las mulas en Honduras eran más baratas que el Ferrocarril,
> y "un Dibutado más bbarato que una mula"
>   – como decía Zemurray –
> aunque seguía disfrutando de las exenciones de impuestos
> y los 175.000 acres de subvención para la Compañía
> con la obligación de pagar a la nación por cada milla
> que no construyera, pero no pagaba nada a la nación
> aunque no construía ninguna milla (Carías es el dictador
> que más millas de línea férrea no construyó)
> y después de todo el ferrocarril de mierda no era
> de ningún beneficio para la nación
> porque era un ferrocarril entre dos plantaciones
> y no entre Trujillo y Tegucigalpa.
>
> (*AN*, 16–17; The condition was that the Company build the Railroad,/ but the Company wasn't building it,/because in Honduras mules were cheaper than the Railroad,/and "a Gongressman was chipper than a mule,"/as Zemurray used to say,/even though he continued to enjoy tax exemptions/and a grant of 175,000 acres for the Company, with the obligation to pay the nation for each mile/that he didn't build, but he didn't pay anything to the nation/even though he didn't build a single mile (Carías is the dictator/who didn't build the greatest number of miles of railroad)/and after all, that shitty railroad was/of no use at all to the nation/because it was a railroad between two plantations/and not between the cities of Trujillo and Tegucigalpa. [*ZHOD*, 2])

The statement of corporate corruption, and the complicity of dictatorial governments in deforming their nations, is made in a language that combines factual precision with a conversational tone that allows the register to range into sarcasm and profanity. The political lesson is leavened with humour in the parody of the stuttering Spanish of Sam Zemurray, president of the United Fruit Company, when he states that a Honduran congressman is cheaper to "buy" than a mule, and in the observation that Carías Andino is the dictator who did not build the most miles of railway line. The example of railway lines joining banana plantations (or mines with ports), rather than linking cities, was a favourite dependency-theory illustration of the metropolis's distortion of the physical landscape of the periphery.[2] Cardenal's plain, engaged language renders the machinations of transnational corporations comprehensible to readers of many different levels of sophistication. Any vestige of an attempt to use language to create a self-contained universe removed from daily reality – the legacy of the *modernismo* of the earlier Nicaraguan poet Rubén Darío – is nullified by the open expression of anger in a line such as "that shitty railroad was/of no use at all to the nation."

The most striking feature of this passage, only a small section of which is cited above, is its documentary use of quotations from communiqués and direct historical research, and its avoidance of metaphor. As Donald Shaw observes, imagery is scarce even in the poem's more lyrical opening passage: "En 17 versos cruciales (puesto que su función es introducir el tema de 'Hora 0') hay sólo tres ejemplos de lengua figurada" (Shaw 1993: 174; "In 17 crucial lines (since their function is to introduce the theme of *Zero Hour*) there are only 3 examples of figurative language"). The three-page description of the United Fruit Company's practices in Central America, however, announces a shift in Cardenal's aesthetic to the Exteriorism he developed in response to the readings of Ezra Pound made by him and Coronel Urtecho (already collaborating on their *Antología de la poesía norteamericana* [Anthology of United States Poetry], which was published in Madrid in 1963). Gonzalez and Treece point out that Cardenal "took to heart Ezra Pound's injunction to let no form of language or expression be alien to poetry" (Gonzalez and Treece 1992: 288). The entire range of public utterance finds its way into *Zero Hour*. The debt of the second section to Pound's cantos, particularly Canto XXXI, which, is about the genesis of the US independence movement, is impossible to overlook. The origins of Cardenal's descriptions of the injustice built into the structures of the banana industry in Central America echo Pound's account of the impact of the tobacco industry on the eighteenth-century United States:

> Their tobacco, 9 millions, delivered in port of France;
> 6 millions to manufacture
> on which the king takes thirty million
> that cost 25 odd to collect
> so that in all it costs 72 million livres to the
> consumer …
> persuaded (I am) in this branch of the revenue
> the collection absorbs too much. (*Cantos*, 46)

Much of Canto XXXI consists of quotes from letters exchanged by Thomas Jefferson, John Adams, and Benjamin Franklin, in a tone that presages the citations, later in *Zero Hour*, from Sandino, Somoza, Moncada, and US Ambassador Henry Lane. Cardenal's poem exemplifies the characterization of Exteriorism as a collage form intended to suppress all elements of subjectivity. Borgeson cites Cardenal's own description of Exteriorism:

> Pound ha enseñado que la poesía puede ser tan amplia como la prosa y que en ella caben relatos, cuentos, ensayos, reflexiones filosóficas, tratados de economía, denuncias políticas, anécdotas y se pueden incluir también en ella, como en un *collage*, textos de otros autores, recortes de periódicos, cartas, fragmentos de conversaciones y estadísticas, chistes, en fin, todo lo que cabe en la prosa cabe también en esta poesía exteriorista. (Borgeson 1984: 100; Pound has shown that poetry can be as inclusive as prose, and that within it fit tales, short stories, essays, philosophical reflections, economic treatises, policy reports, anecdotes, and it can also include, as in a collage, books from other authors, newspaper clippings, letters, fragments of conversations/talks and statistics, jokes; well, everything included in prose can also be included in this Exteriorist poetry.)

The notion that poetry can be as inclusive as prose suggests that, running against the grain of the modern era, in which the epic poem's prerogative of defining national, regional, or universal identity has been usurped by prose narrative, Exteriorist collage offers a route back to poetry's universalist vocation. As soon as poetry claims to represent more than the individual consciousness, however, the issue arises of the ideology underlying such representations. Various critics have itemized Cardenal's technical debt to Pound. Borgeson maintains that "cuando Pound describió la poesía que él esperaba fuera escrito en el futuro, adelantó una caracterización del verso de Cardenal" (Borgeson 1984: 35; "when Pound described the poetry that he hoped to see written in the future, he provided an advance description of Cardenal's verse"); Veiravé repeats the three precepts developed by the Imagist movement that Pound helped to found in 1912 (Veiravé 1975: 96).[3] Yet this depiction of Cardenal's verse as the programmatic extension of Pound's poetry overlooks the ideological discrepancies between the anti-Semitic propagandist of Mussolini's Italy and the Nicaraguan candidate for ordination who was a close associate of Thomas Merton and would later become ideologically aligned with Fidel Castro. More problematically, such characterizations of Cardenal's development skirt the evolution of Cardenal's politics from a holdover nineteenth-century Conservatism to a revolutionary Marxism inspired by liberation theology.

The first of these questions is addressed by Steven White in his meticulous assessment of the impact of United States poetry on Cardenal's aesthetics. White pushes beyond formal and technical questions to explore the ideological relationship between Pound and Cardenal:

> Pound chose to single out the Jews and specific financiers. Pound attacked the abuse of capitalism, not the system itself (see Pound's Canto XLV); nor, as an elitist, did Pound view his as being a struggle against hierarchy. Unlike Cardenal, whose poetry manifests the ways that social being determines consciousness, Pound remained convinced that each individual's consciousness determines being. Nevertheless (and this is important common ground), both poets are acutely aware of how political and economic developments have the power to condition all aspects of life. Furthermore, both poets realize that solutions to the exploitative situation in which humanity finds itself must be, above all, *ethical*. (White 1993: 170)

White points out that during the 1930s, Cardenal's mentors, José Coronel Urtecho, and Pablo Antonio Cuadra, were, in fact, advocates of the Fascism of Mussolini and Franco. Their quest for "order," and their reaction against a Liberal dictatorship, made them fellow travellers of Pound not only in their aesthetics but also in their political ideology. Cardenal makes clear in *Los años de Granada* (2002; The Years in Granada) that as a young man he shared this outlook (see chapter 11). Only after the epiphany of his visit to Cuba in 1970 does he identify himself as a socialist. For this reason, one has to ask whether the ideology of *Zero Hour* can be described as being diametrically opposed to that of Pound. Cardenal's preference for a poetry in which, as White puts it, "social being determines consciousness," does not necessarily constitute an overt articulation of left-wing principles; rather, it may be simply that Cardenal comes from Spanish America, where social class traditionally has been an immutable feature of the individual's existence and hence a determinant of consciousness, whereas Pound, as a citizen of the United States, was raised with a national mythology of individualistic personal reinvention.

The dependency-theory analysis popular in Mexico, where Octavio Paz, with whom Cardenal had been acquainted since 1943 or 1944, had analyzed the country's national myths in the lyrical, Marxist-influenced essay *El laberinto de la soledad* (1950; *The Labyrinth of Solitude*), may have informed Cardenal's perspective; but there is no evidence that he shared the socialist reading of the relations between metropolis and periphery. If Pound, as White would have it, is an elitist, Cardenal is something even more daunting: a member of a hereditary elite. His anger at railway lines that join banana plantations rather than cities, although it does draw attention to the exploitation of the workers ("Pero el negro tiene siete hijos/Y uno qué va a hacer. Uno tiene que comer/Y se tienen que aceptar sus condiciones de pago" (*AN*, 17; "But the black worker has seven children./And what can you do? You've got to eat,/and you've got to accept what they offer to pay" [*ZHOD*, 3]), may still be interpreted as the reactionary wrath of a local ruling class that has been separated from its customary privileges by transnational agro-business. In this sense, Cardenal's ideological development, as exemplified in *Zero Hour*, corresponds to Gobat's analysis of Catholic Conservatism's reaction to the US military occupation of Nicaragua in the 1920s as the point of origin of the 1979 Sandinista Revolution: "Conservative oligarchs continued to valorize an inward-looking, agrarian-based nationalism constructed against US domination and Americanization. This valorization perhaps explains why, in the 1950s, elite Conservatives responded to the deepening of US influence in their country's affairs by reembracing the figure of Sandino. In doing so, however, they made sure to champion a sanitized (i.e. anticommunist) image of the nationalist martyr" (Gobat 2005: 276–7).

This is precisely Cardenal's response to the web of international capitalism that has sapped the authority of national elites. One of the poem's most striking passages arises in the image of "Y los bananos pudriéndose en los vagones de ferrocarril" (*AN*, 18; "And the bananas rotting in the railroad cars" [*ZHOD*, 3]) at company instructions, in order to decrease supply and keep prices high, which captures the impotence of national agrarian elites before transnational capitalism. Closing with the evocation of "las tierras agotadas/que no le servían ni a Guatemala ni a Honduras" (*AN*, 18; "the exhausted lands/that were now of no use either to Guatemala or Honduras" [*ZHOD*, 4]), the section illustrates the interwoven fates of the Central American nations and suggests the shared dimensions of a distinctively Central American dilemma, in what Arias would characterize as "resistance" to assimilation by South American or Mexican discourses. Having described the fates of Honduras, Guatemala, and Costa Rica under United Fruit Company hegemony, the section leaves two questions hanging: What of Nicaragua? And what response can be mounted to this national debasement? The figure of Sandino answers both questions. The third section of the poem opens: "Había un nicaragüense en el extranjero" (*AN*, 19; "There was a Nicaraguan abroad" [*ZHOD*, 4]). Like the author himself, Sandino takes stock of his Nicaraguanness while working in Mexico. He returns to

Nicaragua to launch his insurgency against the US occupation. By doing so, he becomes an alternate nexus of light in the dark nights of Central America, a counterpoint to the glow from the presidential palaces:

> Qué es aquella luz allá lejos? Es una estrella?
> Es la luz de Sandino en la montaña negra.
> Allá están él y sus hombres junto a la fogata roja
> con sus rifles al hombro y envueltos en sus colchas,
> fumando o cantando canciones tristes del norte,
> los hombres sin moverse y moviéndose sus sombras.
> (*AN*, 21; What's that light way off there? Is it a star?/It's Sandino's light shining in the black mountain./There they are, he and his men, beside the red bonfire/with rifles slung and wrapped in their blankets,/smoking or singing sad songs from the North, the men motionless and their shadows in motion. [*ZHOD*, 7])

The fact that the men's shadows move even when they themselves are still – an effect of the fire – anticipates the clustering of shadows at the poem's conclusion, which evokes the martyred protagonists of national sovereignty as a presence that the lights of Somoza's presidential palace cannot dispel. The passage cited above establishes the image of Sandino's campfire in the hills – "the red bonfire" – as an alternate centre around which Nicaraguans gather. Sandino's insurgency creates a dissident pattern of light and shadow, opposed to that imposed by the dictator's palace and his GN. The poem embraces Sandino's capacity to unite the nation in the struggle against the US Marines, even though the narrative voice identifies Sandino as belonging to a social class less privileged than that of the narrator: "Y Sandino no era inteligente ni era culto/ pero salió inteligente de la montaña./'En la montaña todo enseña' decía Sandino' (*AN*, 21; "And Sandino wasn't intelligent or cultured./But he turned out to have mountain intelligence./'In the mountain everything is a teacher,' Sandino used to say" [*ZHOD*, 7]). The nation itself is the best teacher: it will elevate and instruct humble people such as Sandino who collaborate in the construction of national sovereignty rather than selling their souls to the alienated culture imposed by Somocismo. Even though these passages foreshadow the praise of the mountains as the fountain of wisdom that will become a staple of guerrilla discourse both in Nicaragua – for example, in Omar Cabezas's bestseller *La montaña es algo más que una inmensa estepa verde* (1982; *Fire from the Mountain. The Making of a Sandinista*) – and in Cuba and elsewhere, the content of the "learning" that takes place in the mountains, at this point, is strictly nationalist in orientation.

The third section of *Zero Hour* concludes with the description of Somoza's assassination of Sandino after the latter's guerillas have turned in their arms. This passage emphasizes that, even though the assassin, Somoza, is Nicaraguan, Sandino's assassination is the product of the beggaring of Nicaraguan sovereignty by imperialist forces. The use of untranslated English dialogue highlights the cultural colonization on which Somocismo is based. White demonstrates that Cardenal adopted the account of Sandino's murder almost word for word from a travel book, *Sailing South American Skies*, published in 1936 by the US journalist James Saxon Childers, who had visited Nicaragua a short time after Sandino's death. The passages cited by White also enable the reader to see that Cardenal has suppressed details that do not contribute to the Sandino myth, such as Childers's description of the rebel leader begging for his life in front of the firing squad (White 1993: 174). White concludes that "at the very least, the resemblance between these two texts raises questions about Cardenal's compartmentalization of ethics in terms of his attempt to use original poetry as a way of creating an inspiring ethical identity" (ibid.: 175). At the level of nationalist discourse, the irony that arises – although the narrator, arguably, does not see it as such – is that only an elite narrator, schooled in English, can gain access to the source material necessary to enshrine Sandino as a saint of Nicaraguan nationhood. In essence, the oppressed masses need the Conservative elite because, between the two branches of the Nicaraguan establishment capable of reading English (the other being the Liberal Somoza and his family), only Conservative nationalists will use this knowledge to resuscitate the suppressed history of Sandino's martyrdom and peasant resistance to foreign occupation.

The tension between local nationalist discourse and an alienated discourse dependent on categories defined by the English language comes to a head in the verses that follow Sandino's assassination. In the wake of the hero's death, the narrative point-of-view pulls back to survey the nation in the early morning hours of the next day. Couched in a self-consciously Nicaraguan language, this verse evokes the most traditional aspects of the nation, such as indigenous peoples and wildlife. The natural landscape appears to mourn Sandino's death ("el pájaro pronuncia la misma palabra triste" (*AN*, 25; "The bird utters/the same sad word" [*ZHOD*, 10]), while the telegraphs transmitting the morning's news fail to note that anything is wrong. The contrast in language is explicit in the use of indigenous-derived vocabulary and references to traditional local trades:

Es hora en que el lucero nistoyolero de Chontales
levanta a las inditas a hacer nistoyol,
y salen el chiclero, el maderero y el raicillero

con los platanales todavía plateados por la luna,
con el grito del coyotesolo el perico melero
y el chiflido de la lechuza a la luz de la luna.
(*AN*, 24; It's the hour when the corn-mush star of Chontales/gets the little Indian girls up to make corn mush,/and out come the chicle-seller, the wood-seller, and the root-seller,/with the banana groves still silvered by the moon,/with the cry of the coyote and the honey bear/and the hooting of the owl in the moonlight. [*ZHOD*, 10])

By clustering regional expressions such as "nistoyolero," "chiclero," and "coyotesolo," Cardenal erects a linguistic barricade against foreign invasion. It is telling that the narrator does not allude to the oppressive conditions in which the little Indian girls live, merely insisting on the distinctive culture implied by their presence. By contrast, those occupying the presidential palace awake

con las manos y las caras como manchadas de sangre

"I did it," dijo después Somoza.
"I did it, for the good of Nicaragua."

Y William Walker dijo cuando lo iban a matar:
"El presidente de Nicaragua es nicaragüense."
(*AN*, 25; with hands and faces as though stained with blood./"I did it," Somoza said afterward./"I did it, for the good of Nicaragua."/And William Walker said, when they were going to execute him: "The President of Nicaragua is a Nicaraguan." [*ZHOD*, 11])

The use of English, and the reference to Walker, underline the moment of Sandino's assassination as being, in terms of the cyclical conception of time invoked by the quote from Isaiah, the nadir of Nicaraguan nationhood. Somoza is as much a foreign invader as was the Tennessee filibuster when he occupied the president's office; in fact, Somoza, the colonized sellout, may be worse: his words are cited in English while Walker, ironically, is depicted as speaking in Spanish. Both assert that "Nicaraguanness" is a meaningless category: that anyone who occupies the president's office is Nicaraguan regardless of whether or not he is aware of, or works to further, the country's interests.

The fourth section, making increasing reference to cyclical time, evokes an era of death: "En abril, en Nicaragua, los campos están secos./Es el mes de las quemas de los campos" (25; "In April, in Nicaragua, the fields are dry./It's the month of brushburning" [*ZHOD*, 11]). By contrast, "En mayo llegan las primeras lluvias./La hierba tierna renace de las cenizas" (26; "In May come the first rains./The tender grass is reborn from the ashes" [*ZHOD*, 11]). The description of this rebirth epitomizes the tension in Cardenal's relationship with the English poetic tradition. The reference to the burned fields in April alludes to the opening lines of T.S. Eliot's *The Waste Land* (1922): "April is the cruellest month, breeding/Lilacs out of the dead land ..." (5). For Eliot, April's rains and the germination of the flowers make it "cruel" because the rebirth it heralds is illusory. In his Modernist, post–First World War disillusionment, Eliot provocatively inverts one of the founding lines of the English poetic tradition, the opening of Geoffrey Chaucer's *The Canterbury Tales*, which celebrates the spring rains and the return of the flowers: "Whan that Aprill with his shoures soote/The droghte of March hath perced to the roote ..." (Chaucer 1963: 237). Cardenal marks off Nicaraguan difference through the use of a subordinate clause. April may be the season of the spring rains in England, but "in Nicaragua" the cycles are different: "En mayo/florecen los malinches en las calles de Managua./Pero abril en Nicaragua es el mes de la muerte" (*AN*, 26; "In May/the malinches blossom in the streets of Managua./But April in Nicaragua is the month of death" [*ZHOD*, 11]).

The reiteration of the distinctive rhythms of Nicaraguan life and history occasions the first insertion of the narrator as participant and witness, in the description of the 1954 April Rebellion of Adolfo Báez Bone: "Yo estuve con ellos en la rebelión de abril/y aprendí a manejar una ametrelladora Rising/Y Adolfo Báez Bone era mi amigo" (*AN*, 26; "I was with them in the April rebellion/and I learned to handle a Rising machine gun./And Adolfo Báez Bone was my friend" [*ZHOD*, 11]). Báez Bone's death, after being captured by Somoza, whom he tried to assassinate, is incarnated by the ashes in the burned fields.[4] Nicaraguanness, having been emptied of content by Somoza, regains meaning through Báez Bone's heroic sacrifice, which recapitulates the sacrifice made by Sandino. Cardenal's response to the vacancy at the heart of a Nicaraguan culture blighted by ersatz materialism is to enshrine suppressed elements of national history, particularly the example of patriotic sacrifice. The most problematic aspect of his art is its debt to English-language culture, which, through the poetic innovations of Pound and Eliot, or Childers's journalistic writings, becomes an enabling discourse that makes possible the creation of Cardenal's poetry: art that displaces, through its literary superiority – a Modernist assumption – the weapons and tawdry, demeaning popular culture "MADE IN U.S.A." (*AN*, 27; *ZHOD*, 12) imported into Nicaragua by Somoza.

Cardenal's verse does not advertise its debt to English-speaking sources precisely because its goal is to restore a lost (or imagined) past of Nicaraguan independence and cultural autonomy. The April Rebellion was explicitly Conservative in its aims. Báez Bone was a retired military officer; Pablo Leal, the oligarch who notoriously had his tongue pulled out by Somoza's torturers prior to being murdered, was the father of a girl whom Cardenal had courted as a young man. In the first volume of his memoirs, Cardenal recalls Leal as a man "que yo hubiera querido tener por suegro cuando fuimos compañeros de conspiración" (*VP*, 36–7; "that I would have liked to have as father-in-law when we were co-conspirators"). The claim the poem makes for the conspiracy's leader, Báez Bone, as the essence of the nation is even more explicit than that made for Sandino:

> Porque a veces nace un hombre en una tierra
>   que es esa tierra
> Y la tierra en que es enterrado ese hombre
>   es ese hombre.
> Y los hombres que después nacen en esa tierra
>   son ese hombre.
> Y Adolfo Báez Bone era ese hombre.
> (*AN*, 26; Because at times a man is born in a land/and he is that land./ And the land in which that man is buried/is that man./And the men who afterward are born in that land/are that man/And Adolfo Báez Bone was that man. [*ZHOD*, 12])

This citation represents the first appearance of what would become a powerful motif in Cardenal's later poetry: the body of the dead martyr saturating the earth in which he is buried with the political ideals that inspired his martyrdom. The man and "la tierra" – understood as both the soil and the nation – become intermingled. In poems from the 1980s, such as "En la tumba del guerrillero" ("In the Tomb of the Guerrilla Fighter"), this motif acquires a mystical dimension, fusing socialist concepts of duty with Christian belief in eternal life. The promise of eternal redemption through martyrdom and perpetual presence in national history, the filter through which the individual perceives the infinitely larger trajectory of eternity, originates in the eulogy to Báez Bone, who is the protagonist of an uprising whose ideology is not Marxist, but Conservative.

This fact problematizes readings of *Zero Hour* and, arguably, the understanding of Cardenal's later poetry. Beverley and Zimmerman, for example, perceive in Cardenal's work a "metonymic figural chain," which they describe as follows: "The interplay of anticipations, partial affinities, and identifications this sets up (e.g., in *Hora o* Christ-Sandino, Sandino-Báez Bone, Sandino-the Cuban-inspired guerrilla of the late 1950s) is meant to generate relational patterns suggesting the linkage of all things past, present and future in an ever-expanding associative web, centered on Sandino and the possibility of the revolutionary transformation of Nicaraguan society" (Beverley and Zimmerman 1990: 71). This interpretation reads Cardenal's later poetry and political stances back into *Zero Hour*, which, in fact, does not argue for a "revolutionary transformation of Nicaraguan society" but rather for the restoration of a lost past. Within the textual boundaries of *Zero Hour*, the "figural chain" halts at Báez Bone; the rebirth that is promised – and it is crucial that Cardenal uses the verb "renacer" ("to be reborn") and not the noun "revolución," of which he would later become so fond – depends on Báez's inheritance of the tradition of Sandino: a tradition that is not perceived as socialist or revolutionary.

In this regard, Gobat's statement that the Sandino revived by the Conservative elite during the 1950s was "sanitized," in the sense of not being Communist, needs to be placed in perspective. Sandino's goals were above all nationalistic; the transformation of Nicaraguan society, he believed, would occur once national sovereignty had been secured. The proof of this is his decision to suspend armed struggle as soon as the US Marines withdrew from Nicaragua. Beverley and Zimmerman's contention that the poem's conclusion links Báez Bone to "the Cuban-inspired guerrilla of the late 1950s" overreaches the available evidence. *Zero Hour* was published in 1960, but it was conceived and written "en etapas entre 1954 y 1956, con posterioridad a la 'conspiración de abril'" (Borgeson 1984: 45; "by stages between 1954 and 1956, after the 'April conspiracy'"), reaching completion *before* Fidel Castro launched his guerrilla struggle in the Sierra Maestra in January 1957 (Matthews 1975: 79). The untrained imitators of Castro who sprang up (and were just as quickly put down by the GN) in 1958 and 1959 (Smith 1993: 116) did not enjoy the confidence of Conservatives such as Cardenal. At this time, Carlos Fonseca (whom Cardenal would not meet until 1968)[5] was only beginning to develop his fusion of Sandino's nationalistic self-sacrifice with Cuban-oriented Marxist theory that would create the ideology of modern Sandinismo. The rebellion to which *Zero Hour* looks forward is Pedro Joaquín Chamorro's Conservative, Christian guerrilla insurgency in 1959, the most serious assault on the Somoza dictatorship during an era in which FSLN had not yet been founded. For these reasons, the most persuasive summary of *Zero Hour*'s significance is that of Gobat: "The best-known Conservative exaltation of Sandino's anti-US struggle was

Ernesto Cardenal's poem 'Hora cero' [*sic*], which was written in 1956" (Gobat 2005: 323).

In the closing verses of the fourth section of *Zero Hour* a new element obtrudes: the testimonial tradition. The narrator, in hiding, describes the torture and murder of his *compañeros* by the younger Somoza, while upstairs the older Somoza is throwing a party for the US ambassador, Mr Whelan. The presence of the ambassador in the presidential palace reinforces the parallel with the night of Sandino's death and emphasizes the poem's cyclical portrayal of time. This passage sees the author, anticipating his later studies for the priesthood, adopt the testimonial voice that has been the prerogative of socially engaged Latin American priests since the time of Fray Bartolomé de Las Casas. These verses anticipate the Testimonio writing, marked by eyewitness descriptions of human-rights abuses, that would dominate Central American literature in the 1980s:

Caras en la oscuridad
    Las caras ensangrentadas.
Adolfo Báez Bone; Pablo Leal sin lengua;
Luis Gabuardi mi compañero de clase al que quemaron vivo
y murió gritando *¡Muera Somoza!*
(*AN*, 29; Faces in the darkness./Blood-covered faces./Adolfo Báez Bone; Pablo Leal without a tongue;/my classmate Luis Gabuardi whom they burned alive/and he died shouting Death to Somoza! [*ZHOD*, 15])

Gabuardi's fate is a harbinger of one of the most notorious passages in later Testimonio literature, Rigoberta Menchú's account of the purported burning alive of her brother by the Guatemalan military.[6] Cardenal, however, writes his testimonial not from a subaltern position, such as that of Menchú, but rather from that of the witness invested with authority by virtue of his hierarchical privileges. The defection of the priest from his traditional role in upholding the patriarchal order, one of the phenomena that would expose the fissures in Latin America patriarchy during the 1960s, is prefigured in Cardenal's account of the deaths of Báez Bone, Leal, and Gabuardi. In developing the images with which the poem closes, Cardenal arrogates to himself his hereditary right as an oligarch to define the state of Nicaraguan nationality. The closing passages invert the opening image of the presidential palaces as the most conspicuous sources of light in the darkness of the Central American night, maintaining: "Cuando anochece en Nicaragua la Casa Presidencial/se llena de sombras" (*AN*, 29; "When night falls in Nicaragua the Presidential Mansion/fills with shadows"

[*ZHOD*, 15]). The repetition of the "en Nicaragua," employed earlier to mark off local reality from the cosmopolitan sources of the author's poetic technique, serves here to evoke the specifics of local history, arguably asserting a Nicaraguan distinctness within the shared history of Central America. This vision embraces anonymous martyrs of the Revolution, notorious massacres not alluded to earlier in the poem such as that of the members of Sandino's commune on the Coco River, then a rising chain of heroic public martyrs, culminating in "la gran sombra, la del gran crimen/la sombra de Augusto César Sandino" (*AN*, 30; "the great shadow, the one of the great crime,/the shadow of Augusto César Sandino" [*ZHOD*, 15]).

The final couplet links this history of self-sacrifice on behalf of the nation to the cyclical patterns established by the citation from the Bible and the inversions of motifs borrowed from anglophone Modernism: "Pero el héroe nace cuando muere/y la hierba verde renace de los carbones" (*AN*, 30; "But the hero is born when he dies/and green grass is reborn from the ashes" [*ZHOD*, 15]). Aspects of later Sandinista ideology may be discerned in embryonic form in these lines. The idea that only a conflagration will enable the nation to blossom anew is implicit in the image of grass being reborn from ashes, even though at this stage Cardenal is seeking restoration of a (possibly imaginary) status quo ante rather than revolution. As noted, *Zero Hour* prefigures the worship of guerrillas who have given their lives for the cause as eternal presences. The line anticipates, for example, Tomás Borge's response when, as a prisoner of the Somoza dictatorship, he was told that Carlos Fonseca had died: "Carlos Fonseca es de los muertos que nunca mueren" (Borge 1982: 62; "Carlos Fonseca is one of the dead who never die" [*Carlos, the Dawn*, 87]).[7]

The most surprising feature of *Zero Hour* is that for almost a decade it was an anomaly in Cardenal's poetic production. Often presented as the beginning of his aesthetic and ideological evolution and the inevitable forerunner of poems such as "Nicaraguan Canto," *Oracle over Managua*, and *Cosmic Canticle*,[8] this poem remained marginal to his work of the 1960s. After 1963, when the FSLN, blending the inheritance of Sandino with a harder, more Marxist edge, announced its presence, the Conservative vision of national rebirth forged by Cardenal in *Zero Hour* lost currency among young Nicaraguans. Pedro Joaquín Chamorro and Luis Cardenal's 1959 uprising was the last anti-Somoza insurgency led by the Conservative elite. Writing of his reaction to this rebellion, which he followed closely from Mexico, Cardenal states:

> [Pedro Joaquín] tenía una equivocación de términos, no de fondo. Porque realmente creía en una auténtica revolución, pero le llamaba "social

> cristiana," como si eso hubiera sido posible. Contraponiéndola a la marxista. Ese error yo lo compartía con él entonces, y también Reynaldo Téfel, nuestro ideólogo, y otros amigos. Pero yo abandoné después ese error, y también Reynaldo. Pedro persistió en él ... Yo aprendería después de Cuba que no hay revoluciones cristianas ni ateas; sólo hay revolución verdadera y revolución falsa. (*VP*, 335; [Pedro Joaquín] was mistaken in his terms, not his content. He really believed in an authentic revolution, but he called it "Social Christian," as if this could have been possible. Counterpointing it with the Marxist one. I shared this error with him then, as did Reynaldo Téfel, our ideologist, and other friends. But later I put this error behind me, and Reynaldo did, too. Pedro persisted in this mistake ... After Cuba I would learn that revolutions are not Christian or atheist: there is only authentic revolution and false revolution.)

KEEPING THE FAITH: THE EARLY 1960S

As long as Cardenal persisted in the "error" of assessing revolutionary movements on the basis of their adherence to Christianity, it was difficult, in the environment of 1960s Latin America, for him to find a convincing voice in which to address the definition of Nicaraguan nationhood. Suspicious of Fidel Castro's atheism, he remained on the margins of the decade's revolutionary currents. The Exteriorism he had deployed with such success in *Zero Hour* yielded to nature poetry, explorations of liberation theology, Mertonian critiques of materialism, and investigations of indigenous American cultures. These were the years when Cardenal was studying for the priesthood in Mexico and Colombia, researching indigenous America, and beginning to plan his community in Solentiname, where he hoped that Thomas Merton would join him. His next book, *Gethsemani, Ky.*, published a few months after *Zero Hour*, is a predominantly pastoral collection, based on notes taken in the Trappist monastery in Kentucky (where Cardenal was forbidden to write poetry but was allowed to take notes in prose on his experiences). The poems evoke the natural world of rural Kentucky and reflect on the separation between the contemplative monk and the fast-paced commercial activity of the United States. Recurrent references to the highway and railway line that pass within earshot of the monk-poet's cell counterpoint these divergent philosophies of life. The poems are precise, conversational, and more lyrical than most of Cardenal's verse; in contrast to *Zero Hour*, they do not create collages of elements drawn from a multiplicity of discourses. Occasional references to Nicaragua appear, such as: "Todas las tardes el 'Louisville & Nashville'/por estos campos de Kentucky pasa cantando/y me parece que oigo el trencito de Nicaragua/ cuando va bordeando el Lago de Managua" (*GT*, 8; "Every evening the L&N/goes singing through these Kentucky fields/and I seem to hear the little train at home/in Nicaragua, when it borders the Managua Lake" [*Pluriverse*, 66]). These references tend to be nostalgic, expressing a yearning for a homeland from which the poet's monastic life has separated him. The attempt to imagine the shape of Nicaraguan nationhood dwindles in these quiet, often affecting poems to simple longing for the past, even though that past was lived under a dictatorship. The first of only two explicit allusions to Somoza extracts the dictator from his political context, forcefully expressed in *Zero Hour* as, "Esclavo de los extranjeros/ y tirano de su pueblo/impuesto por la intervención/y mantenido por la no intervención" (*AN*, 28–9; "A slave to foreigners/and a tyrant to his people/imposed by intervention/and kept in power by nonintervention" [*ZHOD*, 14]), recasting his relationship with the homeland in the softer light of the tyranny that can arise from love.

> Ha venido la primavera con su olor a Nicaragua:
> un olor a tierra recién llovida, y un olor a calor,
> a flores, a raíces desenterradas, y a hojas mojadas
> (y he oído el mugido de un ganado lejano …)
> ¿O es el olor del amor? Pero ese amor no es el tuyo.
> Amor a la patria era el del dictador – El dictador
> gordo, con su traje sport y su sombrero tejano –
> El fue quien amó la tierra y la robó y la poseyó.
> Y en esta tierra está ahora el dictador embalsamado
> mientras que a tí el amor te ha llevado al destierro.
> (*GT*, 5; Spring has come with its smell of Nicaragua:/smell of earth recently rained on, and smell of heat,/of flowers, of disinterred roots, wet leaves/(and I have heard the lowing of distant cattle …)/– or is it the smell of love? But this love/is not yours. Love of country, is the Dictator's love/the fat Dictator with his sports clothes and panama hat:/He was the one who loved the country, stole it,/and possessed it. In that earth he lies embalmed:/while love has taken you away to a strange land. [*Pluriverse*, 65])

This passage reflects indirectly Cardenal's ecstatic surrender to God's love, provoked by listening to the dictator's motorcade rolling down Roosevelt Avenue on 2 June 1956. In light of these lines, Cardenal's experience of submitting himself to God's love may be seen as a sign of his definitive acceptance of the fact that the dictator has stripped him of the patriarchal authority that would accrue to him if his social class were to reassume its traditional role of governing the country. As he comments in his memoirs: "Y así yo deseaba ... que cayera el gobierno porque en ese caso yo tendría algo que ver con cualquier otro gobierno que hubiera" (*VP*, 24–5; "And so I wished ... the fall of the government because in that case I would have something to do with any other government that might come to power"). Somocismo has usurped his hereditary privileges. The line "stole it/and possessed it" refers denotatively to the Nicaraguan "tierra" but at a connotative level embraces also the young woman Ileana, whom Somoza vicariously robbed and possessed when his subordinate married her. Stripped of his *hombría*, the poet reconciles himself to his impotence in the temporal realm by aligning himself with the greatest of all patriarchal authorities, God himself. One of the ironies of Cardenal's capitulation to the inevitability of Anastasio Somoza García's omnipotence is that three months later, on 21 September 1956, the dictator was assassinated. His sons would maintain the dictatorship for twenty-three more years, but the image of the dictator as a quasi-divine power was broken. At the same time, Somoza García's assassination enabled him to infringe on the elite territory of martyrdom, until that time the privilege of opposition figures such as Sandino and Báez Bone. By entering the Nicaraguan soil as a murdered corpse, Somoza García gained the privilege of radiating his essence through the clay of the homeland, making it his. The Somoza dictatorship's occupation not only of the political space of the nation but also, through its murdered patriarch, of the spiritual realm of the nation's soil pushes the opposition poet into an exile that is, literally, an un-earthing, a separation from the dictator-saturated soil of the homeland.

The sparing references to Somoza in *Gethsemani, Ky.* are detached from any analysis of economic imperialism. This analysis, having been appropriated by the atheistic Castroite left, falls outside the more restricted creative range of Cardenal's work of the early 1960s. The elements that predominate are the elaboration of a spirituality consistent with the quest for justice on earth, which he would develop further in *Salmos* (1964; *Psalms*), and a continuation of the criticism of the Americanized popular culture of the Liberal Somocista elite, which, in *Oración por Marilyn Monroe y otros poemas* (*Marilyn Monroe and Other Poems*), he would parlay into a broader depiction, influenced by Thomas Merton, of that culture, not merely as an undesirable import into Nicaragua but as the dominant trait of a fallen world. The dictator's cultural alienation is evident in the description of him "with his sports clothes and panama hat." The fact that this alienated essence is that which first "possessed" the Nicaraguan earth and now, in death, permeates it necessitates the poet's "destierro." Cardenal's exile, of course, is not only from the nation but from political debate about the nation: while the hyper-masculine dictator activates his love through possession, the poet's contemplative, exiled love is of a more passive, internalized variety that eschews the secular realm.

In the best-known poem of this generally neglected book, "2AM," the dictator's evil, shorn of its history in foreign military occupation, is portrayed through allusions to universal culture. The opening image of a Managua church "llena de demonios" (*GT*, 19; "filled with demons") where a late-night Mass is taking place presages the return of Somoza from the dead. At the same time, the narrator is aware of his own transgressions: night is "la hora de mis parrandas" ("the time when I went out partying") and the first two of the poem's three verses both conclude with a line from Psalm 51, which appears in boldface in the book's first edition and in italics in most subsequent printings of the poem: "*Y mi pecado está siempre delante de mí*" (*GT*, 19; "And my sin is always before me"). The references to Somoza are animated by allusions to despotic rulers of antiquity such as Og, a legendary giant best known for having been overthrown, Sehon, King of the Amorites, who was slain by Moses, and Caiaphas, the treacherous priest who conspired with Pontius Pilate in the death of Jesus of Nazareth. It is notable that the first two are dictators whose power was terminated by righteous intervention whereas the current dictator's palace – presumably this reference is to Luis Somoza Debayle, although the poem does not distinguish between father and son, referring to both as "Somoza" – is equated with Caiaphas's house. This house "está llena de gente" (*GT*, 19; "is full of people"), and the people present, like others in the nocturnal urban environment, are preparing to commit sinful acts:

> Es la hora en que se reúnen los Consejos de Guerra
> y los técnicos de tortura bajan a las prisiones.
> La hora de los policías secretos y de los espías,
> cuando los ladrones y los adúlteros rondan las casas
> y se ocultan los cadáveres. – Un cuerpo cae al agua.
> (*GT*, 19; It is the hour when the Councils of War meet/and the experts in torture go down to the prisons./The time of the secret police and spies,/when the thieves and the adulterers patrol the houses/and the corpses are hidden. – A body falls into the water.)

The most notable feature of this description is the way in which the dictator's evil, characterized by his use of torturers and secret police, is conceived not in political terms but rather as the most salient example of a broad range of human activities that religious morality would classify under the general category of "evil," such as murder, thievery, and adultery. Evil is omnipresent in the cold darkness, but its very ubiquity (which includes the narrator and his debauchery) undercuts the possibility of political analysis. An almost indiscriminate painting of existence as infected by evil neutralizes human agency. The poem's conclusion suggests that the only available recourse is to continue praying: "Y la iglesia está helada, como llena de demonios/mientras seguimos en la noche recitando los salmos" (*GT*, 19; "And the church is cold, as if filled with demons/while we continue reciting the psalms at night").

Gethsemani, Ky. reflects Cardenal's difficulty in establishing a viable creative approach to national experience that will build on, or develop beyond, the Conservative Catholic vision of rebirth expressed in *Zero Hour*. This obstacle prompts a retreat from depictions of the nation. The reference to the psalms as the sole defence against an evil world that concludes "2AM" anticipates Cardenal's next collection, *Psalms*, both in its subject matter and in its ideological stances. "Mi libro de salmos lo hice estando en el seminario," Cardenal writes (*IE*, 61; "I wrote my book of psalms while in the seminary"), dating the book's composition to his early years in Colombia, where he lived from late 1961 until early 1965. His arrival in the country having stimulated his research into indigenous cultures, he had begun to write "poesía indígena" ("indigenous poetry") concurrently with the psalms (Promis Ojeda, "Espíritu y Materia," 18), but this project took nearly a decade to complete. The *Psalms* belong to the period prior to the activism of the Colombian priest Camilo Torres, whose death in the ranks of the Ejército de Liberación Nacional (ELN; National Liberation Army) began to persuade Cardenal that "la lucha revolucionaria era una lucha cristiana y sacerdotal" (*IE*, 66; "the revolutionary struggle was a Christian and priestly struggle"). The Cardenal who writes *Psalms* is seeking redress from a world of poverty and cruelty in a just, interventionist God. He has not yet taken the next step, which would sanction individual or collective action to reverse injustice in the temporal sphere. One partial consequence of this quietism is that *Psalms* is the only book in Cardenal's career prior to 2011 in which the word "Nicaragua" does not appear. There are no invocations of national history, or the Somoza dictatorship, with the exception of one reference to the National Guard by its initials, "G.N." (*SA*, 15, *PS*, 45). In light of Cardenal's subsequent development, *Psalms* may be read as a last-ditch effort to exhort religious authority, or even deity itself, to intervene in the secular world by laying bare, in accessible contemporary language, the underlying radicalism of many of the psalms habitually read during Mass.

Cardenal's versions of these psalms verge on proposing a pact whereby, if God combats injustice on earth, the poet promises to reward divine justice with eternal praise. One of the best-known of Cardenal's psalms is his rewriting of Psalm 7:

> Líbrame Señor
> de la S.S. de la N.K.V.D. de la F.B.I. de la G.N.
>
> Líbrame de sus Consejos de Guerra
> de la rabia de sus jueces y sus guardias
>
> Tú eres quien juzga a las grandes potencias
> Tú eres el juez que juzga a los Ministros de Justicia
> y a las Cortes Supremas de Justicia
>
> Defiéndeme Señor del proceso falso!
> Defiende a los exiliados y los deportados
> los acusados de espionaje y de sabotaje
>
> Las armas del Señor son más terribles
> que las armas nucleares!
> Los que purgan a otros serán a su vez purgados
>
> Pero yo cantaré a ti porque eres justo
> te cantaré en mis salmos
> En mis poemas.
> (*SA*, 15; Free me Lord/from the S.S. and the N.K.V.D. from the F.B.I. and the G.N./Free me from war councils and their vicious regimen/You are the judge of all judges/You judge the ministers of justice/You are the energy from which all justice is/Defend me then from falsity/the exiled, the lonely, the deported/the accused of espionage and found guilty/and to forced labour transported/But the weapons of God more powerful are/and 'sub specie aeternitas' accurate/ than the judgment of those judges whose judgement will occur/I will celebrate you in my singing/Where you sit in your seat in the high court of no thing. [*PS*, 45])

Cardenal updates the threats to life enumerated in the original psalm, where, in the Spanish edition, the speaker pleads with God to "líbrame de mis perseguidores, sálvame./No sea que me atrapen como un león, y me arrastren sin que nadie me salve" (*Biblia*, 977; "save me from all them that persecute me, and deliver me;/Lest he tear my soul like a lion, rending it in pieces, while there is none to deliver" [*Holy Bible*, 499]). In the contemporary world, the danger of being trapped like a lion has been replaced by councils of war, corrupt judges and courts, and, above all, bureaucratic oppressors whose alienation from the populace is incarnated in their being identified by acronyms. Cardenal apportions blame equally across ideologies, naming the Nazi SS, Stalin's secret police, the American FBI, and Somoza's GN as oppressive forces. The simple language includes, in the midst of ardent supplication, occasional bursts of humour, such as the pun that allows the poet to claim that the "arms" of the Lord are more terrifying than nuclear "arms." Like Cardenal's version, the biblical psalm concludes with the supplicant promising faith and adherence in return for God's protection: "Yo alabaré al Señor por su justicia y cantaré al Nombre del Altísimo" (*Biblia*, 978; "I will praise the LORD according to his righteousness; and will sing praise to the name of the LORD most high" [*Holy Bible*, 500]). The final line of Cardenal's version, however, includes the extra commitment to praise God in his own poems, insisting on the additional benefits and authority that accrue from a poet's religious devotion.

Thomas Merton praised Cardenal for making evident to monks and priests who mechanically chanted the psalms the radicalism inherent in their words: "Qué pocos son los monjes que piensan en el verdadero sentido de los salmos. Si los sacerdotes supieran lo que están recitando a diario" (*IE*, 61–2; "Few are the monks who think about the true meaning of the psalms. If priests knew what they are reciting every day!"). Yet, while expressing the spirit of the original psalms in a contemporary idiom, Cardenal's versions do not refer to specific incidents in the modern world. They depend primarily on general references to injustice, propaganda, and torture. The sole modern historical reality invoked in unmistakable terms by the *Psalms* is the Holocaust of European Jewry committed by Nazi Germany. Cardenal's "Salmo 21," for example, reports: "Me tatuaron un número/Me han fotografiado entre las alambradas/y se pueden contar como en una radiografía todos mis huesos/Me han quitado toda identificación/Me han llevado desnudo a la cámara de gas" (*SA*, 31; "They have tattooed me/and marked me with a number/They have photographed me behind the barbed wire/All my bones can be counted/as on an X-ray film/They have stripped me of my identity/They have led me naked to the gas-chamber" [*PS*, 25]). The apparent point of departure for this evocation of the inmates of the Nazi death camps is the line in the original Psalm 21 that reads: "Con tanto mirarme y observarme pudieron contar todos mis huesos" (*Biblia*, 989; "I may tell all my bones: they look and stare upon me" [*Holy Bible*, 505]). The poem adds modern technology in the metaphor of the X-ray and the reference to poison gas, yet the threat suffered by the speaker of the biblical version is not explicitly that of incarceration, but of having had his hands and feet tortured by "una banda de malvados" (989; "the assembly of the wicked" [*Holy Bible*, 505]). Other, more fleeting references to the destruction of European Jewry appear elsewhere in the *Psalms*, reflecting Cardenal's awareness of his own Jewish heritage and that "tenemos un 12% de sangre judía, lo que en tiempo de Hitler era suficiente para ir a un campo de concentración" (*VP*, 417; "we have 12% Jewish blood, which in the time of Hitler was enough to go to a concentration camp").

In modernizing the vocabulary of the biblical psalms, Cardenal took a decisive step in developing the lexicon of astrophysics that would become central in his later work. In the biblical version, Psalm 150 is a hymn of praise to God, beginning and ending with a cry of "¡Aleluya!" The psalm lists the instruments with which one may praise God, including "mandolinas y flautas ... platillos sonoros" (*Biblia*, 1095; "stringed instruments and organs ... loud cymbals" [*Holy Bible*, 559]). It also instructs the faithful: "alábenlo en el firmamento de su poder" (1095; "praise him in the firmament of his power" [559]). In updating the reference to the firmament, Cardenal spins out a chain of modern cosmological references that foreshadow his later Exteriorist interleafing of citations from texts by physicists with devout, lyrical, or mystical descriptions of the cosmos.

> Alabad al Señor en el cosmos
>   Su santuario
> de un radio de 100.000 millones de años luz
> Alabadle por las estrellas
> y los espacios inter-estelares
> alabadle por los átomos
> y los vacíos inter-atómicos.
> (*SA*, 67; Praise the Lord in his cosmos/Praise him in his sanctuary/Praise him with a radio-signal/100,000 million light-years away/Praise him in the stars/in inter-stellar space/Praise him in the galaxies/in inter-galactic space/Praise him in atoms/in inter-atomic space. [*PS*, 79])

Where the Latin American Bible uses the "ustedes" form of the commands, the habitual second-person plural form in the Americas, Cardenal employs the Peninsular "vosotros," which, while presuming greater intimacy between poet and reader, nonetheless has an archaic, ritual sound to the Latin American ear that would appear to be at odds with Cardenal's goal of rewriting the psalms in an accessible modern idiom. The "vosotros" may be read as a vestigial retention of formal, hierarchical aspects of religious observance: as a conflicted modernizer hedging his bets. At the same time, the remainder of Cardenal's rewriting of Psalm 150 shamelessly hybridizes and breaks down hierarchies in its listing of the instruments with which God may be praised. These include such deliberately discordant pairings as "los espirituales de los negros/y la 5a de Beethoven" and "guitarrras y marimbas" y "toca-discos" (*SA*, 67; "soul-music and Beethoven's fifth," "marimbas and guitars," "high-fi systems" [*PS*, 79]). The cultural diversity proposed by Cardenal – another distinctive trait of modern life – occurs in the absence of the boundaries of a national framework. The rewriting of Psalm 129, for example, which Cardenal entitles "Clamo en la noche en la cámara de tortura" ("I Cry Out at Night in the Torture Chamber"), offers a generalized evocation of the sites of modern oppression such as prisons and concentration camps; likewise, the rewriting of Psalm 130 speaks of a country governed by a "Primer Ministro" (61; "Prime Minister") in the British parliamentary tradition, eschewing the republican context of Latin America. *Psalms* charts the disappearance of the nation that begins with Cardenal's abdication from involvement in Nicaraguan national politics after the loss of Ileana and continues with his physical exile, for most of the period between 1957 and 1965, and his deepening immersion in theology as he completed his training for the priesthood.

Marilyn Monroe and Other Poems, published in Colombia in 1965, negotiates Cardenal's fraught re-engagement with the secular world. The national framework required to anchor this critique in the specific details of history is absent. With the exception of the title poem, this is an unfocused book that gives full rein to Cardenal's combined Conservative and Mertonian rejection of the modern world without delineating a clear context for action, or even an analysis. The book suffers from a relativism that presents negative forces as undifferentiated in their origins, and sometimes even in their effects. Drenched in disenchantment, the poetic voice indulges in a rejection of the secular universe that becomes facile: it is as though a Mertonian critique of consumerism had been applied without a Mertonian awareness of imperialism. The Merton who on 15 March 1968, four months before his death, would write to Cardenal, "I would be ashamed to be in a Latin American country and to be known as a North American" (Letson 1990: 99), has not yet become evident in Cardenal's poetic consciousness, nor has Cardenal rediscovered the engagement with national history, in whose absence his verse wandered across a spectrum of voices during the years after *Zero Hour*.

In an echo of the *Psalms*, the title poem is divided into three sections – short opening and closing stanzas, and a central passage consisting of three long verses – each of which is headed by the word "Señor" (*OMM*, 9, 10, 12; *MMOP*, 75, 76, 77). The poem shares with those of *Psalms* the structure of a prayer; the verbs are either in the second-person imperative ("recibe a esta muchacha"; "accept this girl" [*MMOP*, 75]) or are conjugated with a capitalized "Tú" ("Tú conoces su verdadero nombre" [*OMM*, 9]; "You know her real name" [*MMOP*, 75]). Rather than providing a modern context in which to imagine traditional prayers, this poem takes the further step of using religious morality as a tool with which to assess the modern world. The exploitation of Marilyn Monroe's body by Hollywood is conceived in terms of "el Hijo del Hombre con un látigo en la mano/expulsando a los mercaderes de la 20th Century-Fox [*sic*]/que hicieron de Tu casa de oración una cueva de ladrones" (*OMM*, 10; "the Son of Man stands whip in hand/driving out the money-changers of 20th-Century Fox/who made your house of prayer a den of thieves" [*MMOP*, 75]). The "house of prayer" is the temple of the dead actress's body; the film industry's desecration of this temple is conceived, above all, as an outrage against religious morality. Defilements such as this are endemic to a fallen world described as "este mundo contaminado de pecados y radioactividad" (*OMM*, 10; "this world contaminated equally by radioactivity and sin" [*MMOP*, 76]).

Metaphors such as these depict technological modernity as the accomplice of the ubiquitous human evil evoked in "2AM." The denunciation of evil, in its commercialized secular guise, takes precedence over concern for the dignity of the young woman who became Marilyn Monroe. The poet pleads for divine mercy for this "shopgirl" who "Como toda empleadita de tienda/soñó ser estrella de cine" (*OMM*, 11; "like any other shopgirl/dreamed of being a star" [*MMOP*, 76]). While recognizing that this young woman was exploited from early childhood – "la huerfanita violada a los 9 años" (*OMM*, 9; "the orphan raped at nine" [*MMOP*, 75]) – the poem concentrates its denunciation on the existential inauthenticity of a life lived within the ambit of secular commercialism: "su vida fue irreal como un sueño que un psiquiatra interpreta y archiva" (*OMM*, 11; "her life was as unreal as a dream an analyst reads and files" [*MMOP*, 76]). Psychiatry, like the ersatz dreams of Hollywood, is an illness of modernity, a symptom of the individual's surrender to narcissism. By contrast, the poem asserts that "Tú conoces nuestros sueños mejor que los psiquiatras" (*OMM*, 9; "You know our dreams better than all psychiatrists" [*MMOP*, 75]). Marilyn Monroe serves as a potent symbol of the modern individual's lack of connection to that which is enduring and eternal. She is depicted riding on a yacht, dancing in Rio, and meeting royalty, but in the end "la película terminó sin el beso final" (*OMM*, 11; "The film ended without the final kiss" [*MMOP*, 76]). A life devoted to the material world, the poem maintains, is doomed to dissatisfaction. The ironic tone, intended to dismiss the triviality of the world Monroe inhabited, spills over, to a certain extent, onto the actress herself: not having resisted these temptations, she, too, becomes part of the problem that the poem scorns. The possibility of redemption persists, however, in the familiar image of the actress lying dead in a Los Angeles hotel room with her hand on a telephone. Like the poems of *Psalms*, "Oration for Marilyn Monroe" concludes with an exhortation to God to mend that which is broken in the world: "contesta Tú el teléfono!" (*OMM*, 12; "Lord, answer that phone" [*MMOP*, 77]).

By addressing modern society in explicit terms (as opposed to the more generalized references in the *Psalms*), "Oration for Marilyn Monroe" makes the plea for divine intervention in the secular world even more pointed. No longer protected by the conventions of the psalm, Cardenal's religious ideology transmutes into a disdain of the secular world in all its forms. This tendency emerges more strongly in the other poems in the collection. "DC-7B," which describes a plane crash, mocks the impotence of modern technology before the enduring power of nature. The poem opens with the ironic line, "¿No estaba todo bajo control?" (*OMM*, 15; "Wasn't everything under control?"). The second stanza gives this gibe an intonation of unalloyed condemnation by repeating these words without interrogation marks: "No estaba todo bajo control" (*OMM*, 15; "Everything wasn't under control"). This line introduces the description of the accident. More insistently than in "Marilyn Monroe," the human beings involved appear as little more than automatons numbed by worldly vices: "van fumando o leyendo 'Life' o 'Vogue'" (*OMM*, 15; "they are smoking or reading *Life* or *Vogue*"). Their death is not a tragedy but an illustration of the folly of secularism. References to the two magazines –both of which retail glamorous images to the detriment of words – are repeated until they became a hollow mantra of vacancy. The image of the waters of the ocean contaminated by "gasolina de avión mezclada con sangre" (*OMM*, 16; "airplane fuel mixed with blood") emphasizes the adulteration of humanity through its blending with the products of technology.

The ironies of the other poems in the collection are at a similar level of obviousness. Because these poems only oppose, without offering alternative models, the impression conveyed is of an angry monk peering out from between the bars of his cell at a world that revolts him. "'Los paraísos más económicos del Caribe ...'" ("'The Most Affordable Paradises in the

Caribbean …'") mocks the convention of the Caribbean vacation. In light of Cardenal's later development, it is notable that here his wrath is directed at the insincere language of the advertising that promotes these holiday packages, but ignores the colonized history and poverty of islands such as Antigua, St Lucia, and Tobago. Vestiges of the Exteriorism of *Zero Hour* recur in this poem, in the form of citations from both the diaries of Christopher Columbus (the islands are "fermosas y verdes" [*OMM*, 19; "beautiful and green"]) and from tourist brochures ("un perfecto paraíso"; "a perfect paradise"); but the layering of discourses is cursory and the poetry it creates culminates in embittered put-downs rather than resonant images. In spite of having been written in Colombia, nearly all of these poems address themes revolving around the business or film world of the United States. Cardenal's experience of the United States, divided between graduate studies in upper Manhattan and two years in a monk's cell, did not prepare him to render US life with convincing detail. His criticisms, based on stereotypes, are facile. Nor are these criticisms directed at US government policy: imperialism and foreign interventionism emerge unscathed from this broad attack on the entire secular world.

The absence of a critique of the political implications of commercial culture becomes most obvious in "Managua 6:30 PM," the sole poem set in Nicaragua. The poem, which uses the English rather than the Spanish form of writing the time, cites evidence of foreign domination of the Managua skyline in a voice that is sanguine because it is unfocused. The first stanza opens with the claim that "son dulces los neones," (*OMM*, 47; "neon lights are gentle" [*MMOP*, 73]). Yet, having scorned the commercial world in the United States, the poet cannot maintain the contradiction of exalting it in Nicaragua. The poem ends in an awkward compromise:

> Las crueldades de esas luces no las defiendo
> Y si he de dar un testimonio sobre mi época
> es éste: Fue bárbara y primitiva
> pero poética.
> (*OMM*, 47–8; I do not defend the cruelties behind these lights/And if I am to give a verdict on my age/it is this: Barbarous and primitive it was/but yet poetic. [*MMOP*, 73])

The most striking feature of this declaration is its assumption that "my age" is undifferentiated from one nation to another. The subordinate clause that bracketed off "in Nicaragua," in *Zero Hour*, parlaying this exceptionalism into a mythologization of national history, has disappeared. The poet can no longer read the commercial signs as an extension of Nicaragua's history because by 1965 this history, with Augusto César Sandino's martyrdom as its axis, has become the property of the Marxist-influenced, Cuban-aided FSLN.

Cardenal's religious opposition to modern life reaches a crescendo in the volume's concluding poem, "Apocalipsis" ("Apocalypse"). Histrionic in tone, this ten-page denunciation of a world divided between two evil ideologies is the least successful longer poem of Cardenal's career. Its limitations underline the urgent need for renovation in his poetic vision. A series of fearsome rhetorical questions interrogates the legitimacy of money; this anti-capitalist harangue, however, quickly transmutes into an equally ferocious denunciation of Communism:

> ... Pero
> no creáis tampoco que en el Estado Comunista Perfecto
> las parábolas de Cristo ya estarán anticuadas
> y Lucas 16, 9 ya no tendrá validez
> y ya no serán INJUSTAS las riquezas
> y ya no tendréis la obligación de repartir las riquezas!
> (*OMM*, 51; ... Yet/do not think that in the perfect Communist State/Christ's parables will have lost relevance or Luke 16.9 have lost validity/and riches will be no longer UNJUST /or that you will no longer have a duty to distribute them. [*MMOP*, 74])

"Apocalypse" makes clear that, unable to identify with any secular tendency at the end of eight years of meditation, Cardenal and his poetry have reached a point of aesthetic crisis. The Exteriorism he developed with such striking effect in *Zero Hour* no longer generates the same resonance in the absence of an allegiance to some aspect of the contemporary world. "Apocalypse" rehashes mechanisms from Exteriorism – there are capitalized references to US government organizations and pseudo-scientific allusions to Strontium 90 and Carbon 14 – without anchoring them in the citations from other texts, whether historical or scientific, which might enlarge the poem's expressive range. No mingling of discourses occurs; one hears only the shriek of the Christian who inhabits a world that repels him. The subsequent pages of the poem describe a nuclear war in which New York, Moscow, London, and Beijing are destroyed, as are "todos los museos y las bibliotecas/y todas las bellezas de la tierra" (*OMM*, 56; "all museums and all libraries/and all the beauties of the earth" [*MMOP*, 88]). The poem's imagery is glaringly obvious: a destructive "Máquina" ("Machine") that resembles "a un oso o a un águila" (*OMM*, 57; "a bear or an eagle" [*MMOP*,

89]). Nuclear weapons, in this poem, incarnate a merging of all of the vices of the secular world; the "Machine," for example, has as a brain "un computador que calculaba el nú-/mero de la Bestia" (*OMM*, 57; "a computer programmed to give the Number/of the Beast" [*MMOP*, 89]). Later verses decry the division of the world into "2 bloques/– Gog y Magog – " (*OMM*, 60; "two blocks [Gog and Magog]" [*MMOP*, 91]), named after legendary kingdoms of antiquity.

These verses also scorn the pretensions of atheistic revolutionaries such as Fidel Castro. Cardenal writes of the Beast that "sus cuernos son líderes revolucionarios que aún no/son dictadores/pero lo serán después" (*OMM*, 60; "the horns which you saw are revolutionary/leaders/who are not dictators yet but will be" [*MMOP*, 91]). The line breaks in the Spanish text, setting off "son dictadores" ("are dictators"), stresses Cardenal's warning about the Latin American left. The poem's solution to commercialism comes from outside the secular realm. After the nuclear holocaust, a human unity arises "y esa unión de hombres era una Persona" (*OMM*, 61; "and in their union were one Person" [*MMOP*, 92]). Lacking a terrestrial context in which to express this renewed humanity – the world having been destroyed – the human spirit is reborn in the "wedding" of two cells that is transmitted as an intergalactic song.

This forced ending nevertheless represents a crucial turning point in Cardenal's work. In literally embryonic form, these lines herald the emergence of the language of intergalactic communion that would become central, twenty years later, to *Cosmic Canticle*. The first cell in this rebirth is described as "como una Esposa esperando al Esposo" ("like a Bride awaiting the Bridegroom" [*MMOP*, 92]); later we are told that this cell "celebró … su/Fiesta de Bodas" (*OMM*, 61; "as the Earth had rejoiced when the first cell divided [at its wedding celebration]" [*MMOP*, 92]). Cardenal discovers here the imagery that later will enable him to express his mystical vision of universal love. The rebirth of the earth is expressed through the use of the Poundian word "canticle": "y había un Cántico Nuevo/y todos los demás planetas oyeron cantar/a la Tierra/y era un canto de amor" (*OMM*, 61; "And there was a New Canticle/and all other inhabited planets heard the earth/singing that song of love" [*MMOP*, 92]).

Later Cardenal would confront the problem of how to anchor this vision of the human spirit permeating the universe with a message of rebirth and love, in the Poundian form of the canticle. Ultimately, he had no recourse but to return to his core material, Nicaragua and the terrible history of its struggle for nationhood, where he would eventually find a compelling metaphor for rebirth in the Sandinista Revolution. This required a dramatic political evolution on Cardenal's part, an evolution for which his return to Nicaragua was the initial catalyst. After a long absence, his engagement with national realities through daily life among peasants and radical Christians in Solentiname brought about a shift in his perspective. By the time that *Marilyn Monroe and Other Poems* was in press in Colombia, Cardenal was already on his way back to Nicaragua to be ordained. Having been driven out of Nicaragua by Anastasio Somoza García's symbolic usurpation of his manhood and dominion over the Nicaraguan "tierra," relegating the poet to what he termed "la castración del celibato" (*IE*, 30; "the castration of celibacy"), he returned eight years later, after this crushing of his masculine authority had plunged him into religious conversion – an event he characterized as "una entrega voluntaria. Una decisión que yo hice y pude no hacer" (*IE*, 31; "a voluntary surrender. A decision that I made and that I could have not made"). Though his ambitions for secular power had been thwarted by the dictatorship, he now wielded, as a priest, an authority that surpassed that of the secular realm. Ordination liberated Cardenal from the reactionary posture of the Conservative oligarch sidelined by decades of Liberal dictatorship. It freed him to participate in Nicaraguan daily life, to reimagine his nation's history. The priesthood did not make Cardenal a Sandinista, but without his investiture it is difficult to imagine him returning to live in Nicaragua in the mid-1960s, or playing a prominent role in the revolutionary movement.

THE NATION IN HISTORY: *THE DOUBTFUL STRAIT*

At the time of his return to Nicaragua, Cardenal's creative engagement was restricted to Latin America's remote past, in two projects he was working on simultaneously: his poems on indigenous topics, and his book-length epic of the Spanish conquest of Central America, *El estrecho dudoso* (*The Doubtful Strait*). An early version of the latter work helped to finance Cardenal's downpayment on Solentiname: "unos amigos sin que yo me diera cuenta lo metieron a un concurso con ese propósito, y ganó" (*IE*, 98; "without telling me, some friends sent it to a contest for that purpose, and it won"). Finally published in 1966, *The Doubtful Strait* had occupied Cardenal since about 1960, illustrating the ways in which his creative estrangement from the secular world during the 1960s coexisted with a considered contemplation of the early history of Central America. The poem's origins go back to Cardenal's years in Mexico: "After a year and a half at the Benedictine monastery in Cuernavaca, Cardenal went to Nicaragua for a vacation and stayed at José Coronel Urtecho's farm on the San Juan River ... It is [Coronel] who ... advis[ed] him to attempt a historical poem about Nicaragua because, he said, Nicaragua's history provided so much rich material for a poem" (Williams 1995: xi).

Written in an even more uncompromising Exteriorist style than *Zero Hour*, *The Doubtful Strait* creates a montage of sixteenth-century narratives, some famous and others obscure, assimilated into a central thread that revolves around the dictatorial family rule of Nicaragua's first colonial governor, Pedrarias Dávila and his son-in-law, Rodrigo de Contreras. Austerely anti-lyrical – a trait that alienated some readers, who claimed it was not poetry (Williams 1995: xi) – the book pushes Cardenal's reworking of Ezra Pound's tenets about enlarging the possibilities of poetry one step further than *Zero Hour*. The poem is divided into Poundian Cantos, in which the historical materials that Cardenal collected in Mexico, Nicaragua, and elsewhere are blended into the narration without acknowledgments, quotation marks, or other indications – except for archaic syntax and spelling – that they stem from other texts. Cardenal challenges the barriers between literary genres by adopting the techniques developed by Pound to fend off the novel's dominance as the most popular form of literature with the reading public. Williams suggests that "to 'beat the novelists at their own game,' Pound set out to expand the boundaries of poetic content and language by reviving a purportedly exhausted genre – the epic. His models included the Homeric tale and the Renaissance epic, which shared an emphasis on generic heterogeneity and comprehensiveness" (ibid.: xiv). The diverse sources of the poem's narrative become contending ideologies that illustrate the jostling for power in the isthmus during the sixteenth century. White stresses this point when he asserts that, in *The Doubtful Strait*, Cardenal "is attempting to gather the elements (isolated fragments that do not reflect but *are themselves* the 'complex of ideas' of which Pound speaks) that condition a particular period in Nicaraguan history" (White 1993: 172; emphasis in original).

The "strait" of the title is the potential route for a canal across Central America, an obsession that first entered the Western imagination as a result of the fortuitous geography of Nicaragua, which enabled early travellers to follow the San Juan River and Lake Nicaragua most of the way from the Caribbean Sea to the Pacific Ocean. The poem's other central theme is the formation, internal quarrels, and ultimate destruction of Central America's first non-indigenous governing elites, by implication and occasional ironic reference, as a way of understanding the dictatorships of the twentieth century and forecasting their demise. The poem analyzes Central American history from "outside" and from "above." *The Doubtful Strait* assembles voices in documentary style, but these are not subaltern voices. The testimonies are written, not spoken, a fact that, in the sixteenth-century context, classifies them as expressions of a colonial elite. Cardenal re-engages with the history of his region and nation as an elite Conservative attempting to plumb how Central America's elites were formed.

In spite of the compellingly novelistic narration, and the striking dramatization of the interrelationships among many of the most famous explorers, conquistadors, and priests – Christopher Columbus, Pedro de Alvarado, Balboa, Cortés, Pizarro, Bartolomé de Las Casas – *The Doubtful Strait* has not received substantial attention either from critics interested in Cardenal's adaptation of the techniques of Ezra Pound (White concentrates on *Zero Hour*) or from academics who read Cardenal as a political poet (Borgeson's book-length study deals extremely briefly with *The Doubtful Strait*). The approach from "outside" and "above" is not congruent with later perceptions of Cardenal's identity as a revolutionary poet. Williams stresses those moments when the subaltern voices of indigenous leaders are heard, maintaining that "once their words have been uttered, their voices heard and their actions heeded, their representation moves beyond an othering-type of discourse to their portrayal as agents of their own destiny" (Williams 1995: xxii). This may be true, although the space accorded to indigenous voices is limited; the humanity of the native peoples serves as an ironic counterweight to the prevailing slaughter and barbarism perpetrated by Europeans. As Williams herself signals, irony is a prevailing motif; the poem's opening lines are: "'El país es bello'/le había dicho a Colón Toscanelli" (*ED*, 2; "'The country is beautiful'/Toscanelli had told Columbus" [3]). These two lines, set off in a separate stanza, counterpoint the ugliness that is to follow. Brutal events are treated less with outright condemnation than with a harsh irony. This irony is the mark of a writer who condemns what he sees from within an elite which, although marginalized, is a descendant of those whose genesis the poem describes. The contradictions between the Europeans' self-image as Christian civilizers and their genocidal and fratricidal violence are underscored, but the voice, reined in by the political neutrality that stemmed from Cardenal's alienation from secular forces of both the left and the right during the 1960s, and by what Williams terms "the poem's narrow Christian framework" (Williams 1995: xxii) – a pattern that traces the destruction of an ancestral Eden, a descent into sin and misery and eventual redemption – concentrates on a mostly unadorned narration of the conquerors' actions. The stance that generates the poem's irony, in other words, also contributes to its prosaic tone, depriving it of the rabble-rousing lyricism that appears in the final section of *Zero Hour.*

As in *Zero Hour*, Cardenal approaches the history of Nicaragua by marking off Central American difference. The origins of Central America's peculiar forms of authoritarianism, exemplified in Nicaragua by Pedrarias Dávila in the sixteenth century and the Somozas in the twentieth century, lie in outsiders' avarice, particularly their desire to find a shortcut to the riches of Asia. Like *Zero Hour*, *The Doubtful Strait* closes in on Nicaraguan themes from the broader canvas of the exploitation and domination of Central America (and Mexico). The poem's ironies stem in large part from the conquistadors' geographical, cosmological, and ideological delusions, from their greed and fondness for creating legends and seeing portents, which the poem reports in non-judgmental fashion. The opening Canto, for example, describes Central America's geographical location as it was understood by early European explorers, namely as the gateway to China. Toscanelli's words to Columbus – cited in quotation marks, in contrast to many other documents assimilated into the narration – specify that "de la isla Antilla hasta la de Cipango/se cuentan veinte y seis espacios/Los templos y los palacios están cubiertos de oro" (*ED*, 2; "from the island of Antilla to the island of Cipango/the intervals number twenty-six./The temples and palaces are faced with gold" [3]).

The Cantos are connected by the tissue of the conquistadors' conflicts and explorations: each Canto takes up a theme or an action that has been announced in an earlier Canto. In this way a distinctive Central American history unfolds, resistant, as Arturo Arias notes, to dominant Peninsular or South American discourses (though in this case somewhat integrated into Mexican discourses). Characters such as Pedro de Alvarado and Pedrarias Dávila recur in various Cantos, lending texture to Cardenal's portrait of an emerging oligarchical class. Canto IV, for example, opens with a report of a harangue delivered naked by the young indigenous leader Panquiaco. It is typical of the poem's reliance on documents, and the way in which it eschews traditional dramatic devices, that the reader is not told who the audience is for this speech, although it is clearly a group of Spaniards: "Pero si tanta sed de oro tenéis/que querráis desasosegar y aun matar a los que lo tienen/yo os mostraré una tierra donde saciaréis esa sed" (*ED*, 16; "But if you have such a thirst for gold/that you should want to molest and even kill those who have it/I will show you a land in which to quench this thirst" [17]). This leads to detailed instructions on the route to the Pacific Ocean, complete with the promise that this ocean contains "carabelas" (*ED*, 16; "ships" [17]) like those of the Spaniards, and that the country beyond it has "más oro" (*ED*, 16; "more gold" [17]). Only at this point is the principal listener identified: "Cuando oyó hablar del otro mar Balboa lo abrazó de alegría" (*ED*, 16; "When Balboa heard him talk of the other sea he embraced him for joy" [17]). The narrative does not introduce Vasco Núñez de Balboa, credited with being the first European to see the Pacific Ocean, or give his full name, depending on a reader who either is familiar with the main figures of the conquest or, more dynamically, one who is willing to construct (or reconstruct) a vision of the region's history through immersion in Cardenal's collage.

The second half of Canto IV narrates Balboa's arrival at the shore of the Pacific. Having verified that the water is tidal and salinated, Balboa claims the ocean for the kings of Castile. Canto IV concludes with one of the few moments in *The Doubtful Strait* in which the reader perceives an authorial presence employing imagery to create unity: "El sol se hundió en el mar como un doblón de oro./Y salió la luna" (*ED*, 18; "Like a gold doubloon the sun sank in the sea./And the moon appeared" [19]). The sun, setting in the sea, confirms that the Spaniards are looking west towards Asia; the image of the gold doubloon transmits the Spaniards' gold-besotted mentality that sees coinage and precious metals everywhere.

In spite of his lust for wealth, Balboa is portrayed as the germ of the entrepreneurial bourgeoisie that is crushed before it can take root. In a foretaste of the later division between the agriculturally based Conservatives, who claim a relationship with the Nicaraguan "tierra," and Liberals, who are commercially oriented, depicted as agents of outside interests and, according to this outlook, alienated from the land they inhabit, the explorer and builder Balboa is described favourably by contrast with the usurper Pedrarias Dávila, who seizes wealth created by others and hoards it among members of his family. When Dávila, the Spanish governor, arrives in the territory that will become Nicaragua:

> envió a uno de sus oficiales a preguntar por Balboa.
> "Veislo allí," le dijeron. Creyó que bromeaban.
> Balboa estaba en camisa, con camisa de algodón
> y alpargatas, ayudando a poner el techo de una casa
> y bañado de sudor.
> (*ED*, 20; he sent one of his officials to ask for Balboa./"There he is," they told him. He thought they were joking./Balboa was in shirtsleeves, wearing a cotton shirt/and rope sandals, helping to put a roof on a house/and soaked in sweat. [21])

The vision of Balboa flouting the behaviour of the "hijosdalgos" (*ED*, 20; "noblemen" [21]), who came to the colonies in search of instant elevation to a sybaritic ruling class, in his sweat-drenched investment in building the colony house by house, serves as a provocation to Pedrarias Dávila, the ancestor of Central American Liberalism: "Comenzó la lucha sorda de Pedrarias por eliminar a Balboa" (*ED*, 20; "Pedrarias began a secret struggle to eliminate Balboa" [21]). Pedrarias invents a pretext to cut off Balboa's head. The Canto closes with a legendary anecdote of the kind that the poem reports without commentary, in which Balboa's horse eats a flyer posted by Pedrarias to demonstrate his commitment to "democracy," and with the observation that "las noas de Balboa quedaron solas,/en la mar del sur" (*ED*, 22; "Balboa's ships lay abandoned/in the South Sea" [23]), an indication of the waste of constructive investment caused by this crime.

The institutionalization of the ideological rift in the oligarchy that will later develop into the split between Liberalism and Conservatism begins in Canto IX. Pedrarias, based in Panama, sends Francisco Hernández de Córdoba to "pacificar/las tierras de Nicaragua" (*ED*, 52; "pacify/the lands of Nicaragua" [53]). The opening stanza presents this land first as the "Estrecho Dudoso" (*ED*, 52; "the Doubtful Strait" [53]) – in quotation marks – and only afterwards as Nicaragua. The conquistador founds Granada and León, the two cities that would become the axes of Nicaragua's economy, and of the Conservative and Liberal wings of the national elite respectively. Each city is situated close to a lake (León was later moved inland) and a volcano; each consists of a square, a church, and a fort. Hernández de Córdoba's itemization of the customs of the indigenous people of León concludes with the fact that they worship an aged female goddess who lives in the Masaya volcano and who disappeared "cuando llegaron los cristianos" (*ED*, 54; "when the Christians arrived" [55]). The poem includes in an ironic parenthesis an account of the democratic forms of governance that predominated prior to the arrival of the Spaniards:

> (No se gobernaban por caciques ni por señor ni jefe
> sino por un consejo de ancianos elegidos por votos
> y éstos elegían un capitán general para la guerra
> y cuando moría o lo mataban en la guerra elegían otro
> – y a veces ellos mismos lo mataban
> si era perjudicial para la república –
> y se reunían en la plaza a la sombra de una ceiba:
> aquel consejo de ancianos elegidos por votos.)
> (*ED*, 54; [They were not governed by caciques nor by a lord or chief/ rather by a council of elders elected by votes/and these elders chose an overall war captain/and when he died or was killed in battle they chose another/– and sometimes they killed him themselves/if he was doing

harm to the republic –/and they met in the square under the shade of a ceiba:/that council of elders was elected by votes.] [55])

This passage is crucial in defining Cardenal's evolving political and social vision. It illustrates the importance of his study of indigenous cultures in precipitating his gradual evolution from a Conservative to a revolutionary posture. The democracy of the indigenous peoples contains one feature that dissents from modern democratic ideas: the right to kill a bad "captain." Cardenal's anachronistic insertion of the word "republic," which was not part of the sixteenth-century political lexicon, slants this account by making the assassination of a tyrant part of democratic practice. The justification of the assassination of Anastasio Somoza García would have been obvious to Nicaraguan readers, even though this claim was at odds with Cardenal's stated position of Gandhian non-violence (*IE*, 223). The indigenous people – both noble savages and primitives whose culture was smashed four centuries ago – serve as a flexible vehicle for smuggling into the text this anti-Somocista statement.

The contrast between indigenous democracy and the murderous political culture introduced by the Spaniards is underlined in the concluding stanzas of Canto IX, when Pedrarias comes to Nicaragua to supervise Hernández de Córdoba's decapitation, once again on trumped-up charges. The description emphasizes Hernández de Córdoba's role as a builder ("Fue enterrado en la iglesia que él levantó,/en la ciudad que él fundó, entre el lago y Momotombo" [*ED*, 54]; "He was buried in the church he had raised,/in the city he had founded, between the lake and Momotombo" [55]). Lines such as these demonstrate that Cardenal does not condemn colonization. Colonizers who spread Christianity and build new cities, as Balboa and Hernández de Córdoba do, are seen in a positive light. The deciding factor is the nation: its history, its political culture, the nature of the traditions and institutions inculcated by its historical experience. The indigenous cultures are objects of curiosity, and often of admiration, but ultimately the poem's concerns draft them into the Conservative-Liberal debate as monitors of the greater compatibility of Conservative traditions with the good of the Nicaraguan nation. After Hernández de Córdoba's execution, for example, "salía fuego del Momotombo día y noche" (*ED*, 54; "fire came out of Momotombo day and night" [55]). Both nature and the portents valued by indigenous culture protest the murder of the founder of León, legitimizing anger against the tradition Pedrarias Dávila represents.

Hernández de Córdoba's execution opens the door to Canto X's evocation of the authoritarian governor, "el primer 'promotor del progreso' en Nicaragua/y el primer Dictador" (*ED*, 56; "the first 'promoter of progress' in Nicaragua/and the first Dictator" [57]). The capitalized final word makes explicit Pedrarias Dávila's role as the forerunner of the Somozas. Cardenal discredits Pedrarias's claim to having created "progress" in order to refute the identical claim made by Somoza. The weapon, again, is irony, which takes the form of a sarcastic elaboration that echoes each of the grandiose achievements attributed to the governor:

> introdujo los chanchos en Nicaragua, sí es cierto ...
> (pero ganado de él)
> y el primer 'promotor del comercio' en Nicaragua
> (de indios y negros)
> a Panamá y al Perú
> (en los barcos de él).
> (*ED*, 56; he introduced pigs into Nicaragua, yes it's true/.../[but his own livestock]/and the first "promoter of business" in Nicaragua/[of Indians and negroes]/to Panama and to Peru/[in his own ships]. [57])

The parallels with the Somoza family, and its monopolistic absorption of the Nicaraguan economy, are obvious. A lengthy itemization of some of the governor's properties concludes with the statement: "¡Dulces nombres en los áridos documentos comerciales/de la COLECCIÓN SOMOZA!" (*ED*, 58; "Sweet names in the arid commercial documents/in the Somoza Collection!" [59]). This is one of the few lines in the poem that gives a document's source. The irony of the material on Pedrarias Dávila being contained in an archive assembled under the Somoza government is too overwhelming to pass without notice. Williams describes the Colección Somoza as "a multi-volume compilation of archival documents on the history of Nicaragua from the arrival of the Spaniards to this continent, ... edited by Andrés Vega-Bolaños in the 1950s" (Williams 1995: 177). The original compiler of much of the material contained in this archive, Antonio de Herrera, although mentioned only briefly, serves as one of the poem's models for the role of the chronicler of national history. De Herrera responds to attempts to silence him with the words: "NON DEBE EL CORONISTA DEJAR FASCER SU OFICIO" (*ED*, 58; "THE CHRONICLER MUST NOT FAIL TO DO HIS DUTY" [59]). The use of block capitals (along with archaic spelling) in this injunction justifies Cardenal's own labours. The repetition of these words, again in capitals, at the close of Canto X underlines the significance of narrating the history of Pedrarias Dávila's regime, making more acute the resonance between past and present. This Canto's account of Pedrarias Dávila's self-glorification insists on the fact that these local events are consequences of a larger structural pattern: the occidental world's quest for a canal across Central America to heighten the profitability of commerce with Asia:

Los indios preguntaron al Demonio
(¿a los brujos? ¿a las brujas? ¿a la Vieja del Volcán?)
cómo se verían libres de los españoles
    y el Demonio les contestó:
Que él podía libertarlos de los españoles
"haciendo que los dos mares se juntaran
    (¿y el Canal de Nicaragua?)
pero entonces perecerían los españoles
(¿y el canal Norteamericano en Nicaragua?)
juntamente con los indios."
(*ED*, 60; The Indians asked the Demon/(male witches? female witches? the Old Woman of the Volcano?)/and the Demon replied:/That he could free them from the Spaniards/"causing the two seas to come together/ (the Nicaraguan Canal?)/but then the Spaniards would perish/(the North American [*sic*] Canal in Nicaragua?)/along with the Indians." [61])

The narrator's attitude is here at its most ironically ambiguous, reporting the chronicler's assertion that the indigenous people have turned to the devil, then interrogating it by questioning what has happened to their traditional gods, such as the old woman in the volcano. The demonic prophecy that both Spaniards and Indians will disappear if the two oceans are joined, with its obtrusive reference to the United States, a country that would not come into existence for nearly two hundred and fifty years, is even more conspicuous than the allusion to the Somoza Collection. The narrator's interrogation – "¿y el canal Norteamericano en Nicaragua?"– with its shift in preposition, from "de" ("of") the first time the canal is mentioned to "en" – assuming a foreign entity implanted in Nicaraguan soil – suggests that both founding ethnicities of the Nicaraguan nation would vanish under such a regime.

At the end of Canto X Pedrarias Dávila dies at the age of ninety and is buried in the cathedral alongside Hernández de Córdoba, an image that enshrines Nicaragua's divisive ideological duality – the constructive Conservative and the avaricious Liberal – in the literal foundations of the nation. An earthquake later destroyed León, allegedly causing the original site to be engulfed by the lake.[9] The Canto closes with a statement that "la capital de Nicaragua está allí spectral/bajo el agua" (60; "The capital of Nicaragua lies there, spectre-like/beneath the water" [61]), an image that suggests the inchoate quality of a nation that has been unable to consolidate its identity. The underlying reasons for this spectral quality, however, reside in the imposition of external perceptions on the Nicaraguan nation-space.

Consistent with the poem's oscillation between events driven by global economics and politics and those with a local focus, the national yields to the transnational at the beginning of Canto XIII as one of the poem's central figures, Pedro de Alvarado, makes his dramatic entrance: "Corrió Pedro de Alvarado por la tierra como un rayo" (*ED*, 74; "Pedro de Alvarado tore through the land like a bolt of lightning" [75]). Alvarado, a blond conquistador who is remembered as the most violent of Hernán Cortés's lieutenants during the conquest of Mexico in 1519–21, and who in 1524 became conqueror of Guatemala, wreaking almost unimaginable bloodshed in his campaign to annihilate the country's powerful Mayan cultures, is accorded a large amount of space in the poem. There are two reasons for the extensive narration of Alvarado's deeds. The first stems from Cardenal's awareness of Nicaraguan identity and history as representative of regional Central American patterns. Guatemala, Central America's largest nation, containing roughly half of the region's population, acted as the seat of government for the isthmus during the colonial era, and was the source of the region's political culture. The second reason lies in the poem's Christian patterning. In metaphorical terms, the arrival of Europeans is an expulsion from Eden: both for the indigenous people, who lose their paradise, and for the Spaniards themselves, who are subjected to the secular temptations of gold, the slave trade, and limitless power, which they prove unable to resist. Pedrarias Dávila's regime in Nicaragua represents a descent into sin. Alvarado's entrance marks the poem's moral nadir: an era of utter darkness, from which the region is eventually redeemed.

Depicted as a nearly Satanic figure, Alvarado dominates Cantos XIII, XV, and XVI in the poem's structure of twenty-five Cantos. The key figure of the central section, he is associated with images of both lightning and blackness. Even within Canto XIII, however, a movement towards redemption begins when Alvarado founds the city of Santiago de Quauhtemalan, the forerunner of present-day Antigua Guatemala. Canto XIII closes with a respectful narration of the construction of the city: "Comenzaron a hacer las casas./A traer los horcones para los postes./Caña y lodo para las paredes,/y heno para los techos" (80; "They began to build houses./To bring wooden beams for supports./Mud and cane for the walls/and straw for the roofs" [81]). The image of houses' roofs under construction recalls the positive depiction of Balboa as a builder in Canto V. The two volcanoes, Agua and Fuego, instill intimations of a natural balance. Cardenal's religious patterning, which requires a first glimmer of light to appear during this period of moral disaster, and his Conservative respect for those who invest in and develop their nations, conspire to soften the conclusion of the appropriately numbered Canto XIII, the poem's structural midpoint.

Canto XIV, which describes the new city that will become the capital of Central America for most of the next three hundred years, represents a change in the poem's tone. The opening line – "El día del apóstol Santiago amaneció sereno y claro" (*ED*, 82; "The day of James the Apostle the dawn was clear and serene" [83]) – presages a harmony of religion and good administration that permits the indigenous cultures to flourish within an overarching Christian framework. This Canto relates the city's construction, beginning with its streets, its central square, and its cathedral. A judicious administration distributes land among the settlers and creates an ordered civil and religious life: "Y el Cabildo estableció el precio del puerco,/el precio del huevo (un real de oro),/el orden de la procesión del Santísimo Sacramento/el día del Corpus" (*ED*, 82; "And the Council established the price of pork,/the price of eggs (one golden real),/the order of the procession of the Most Blessed Sacramen t/ the day of Corpus" [83]). The passage goes on to list each of the professions and its place in the procession, exemplifying the inclusive tendency of Latin American corporatism, in which each individual occupies a niche that contributes to the proper functioning of the whole. The reference to sound regulation of the price of pork stands in contrast to Pedrarias Dávila's introduction of pigs to fortify his private monopoly. The founding of Santiago, Guatemala, characterized by orderly administration and a cultural syncretism expressive of Spanish American identity, represents a recovery of the Eden destroyed by the conquistadors' cruelty: "Corrían arroyos medicinales en los prados/Fuentes de claras linfas en las vegas/En alegres campiñas pastaban las vacadas" (*ED*, 84; "Medicinal streams flowed in the meadows./Clear water springs on the lowlands./In merry fields herds of cattle grazed" [85]). Canto XIV closes with a description of the integration of the Mayan Festival of the Volcano into the calendar of royal festivals, in such a way that colonists and Maya each have their place in this ritual:

y entran a la plaza dos compañías de caballería
y después entran marchando dos de infantería
y se tienden por toda la plaza de armas.
Y después entran los indios desnudos
con sus maztlates y embijados,
con plumas de guacamayos y pericos

y con arcas y flechas
y después de ellos vienen muchos instrumentos
y trompetas, y tras ellos otros danzando
con danzas bien ordenadas y vistosas:
Es *la danza del Volcán* ...
(*ED*, 85–6; and two companies of knights enter the square/and two of infantry march in/and cover the entire parade square./And then naked Indians enter/with their maztlates and vermilion paint/with macaw and parakeet feathers/and with bows and arrows,/and after them come many instruments/and trumpets, and behind them others dancing/with very attractive and orderly dances: This is the dance of the Volcano ... [87])

The integration of the two cultures tames the savagery of each. The cavalry, rather than slaughtering indigenous people, marches in disciplined formation; the Maya, their nakedness and picturesque feathers now part of a national, rather than a purely local, ethnic, celebration, appear in "orderly dances." Cardenal's argument for the superiority of an ideology of cultural collaboration is clear. Yet his Conservative variant on this ideology does not elevate racial and cultural *mestizaje*, in imitation of the ideology that emerged in Mexico in the 1920s; rather, Cardenal emphasizes the way in which the respective components of the fabric of the new nation – the Catholic Spaniards and the animistic Maya – each finds its authentic expression through shared submission to a culture of order and duty.

Alvarado's rootless evil brings to a close the Edenic phase in the history of Santiago de Guatemala. When, after a disastrous failed invasion of Peru, he dies in a minor skirmish in northern Mexico, his widow, who succeeds him as governor, berates God for having allowed Alvarado to die. One of the poem's principle narrative techniques, that of extravagant enumeration, reappears:

Doña Beatriz mandó pintar todo el palacio de negro
por dentro y por fuera, salones, patios, cocinas
corredores, caballerizas, ranchos, excusados,
y hasta los tejados,
todo pintado de negro,
y con cortinas negras,
porque el Adelantado había muerto en Muchitilic
que quiere decir "Todo Negro" ...
Y la Catedral estaba también cubierta de paños negros

y toda la ciudad enlutada ...
(*ED*, 94; Dona Beatriz ordered the whole palace to be painted black/within and without, rooms, patios, kitchens,/corridors. stables, huts, latrines/and even the roofing,/all painted black,/with black curtains,/because the Adelantado had died in Muchitiltic/which means "All Black" .../And the Cathedral was also covered in black draperies/and the whole city in mourning ... [95])

The city's assumption of blackness becomes an identification with Alvarado's evil. The decision to drape the cathedral in black, combined with Doña Beatriz's statement – presented in italics to stress its status as a direct citation from source material – "*que ya Dios no la podía hazer mas mal/ del que la avia hecho*" (*ED*, 94; "*that now Godde could do her no greater harme/then he had allready done her*" [95]) – constitutes a defiance of sacred authority that upsets the balance between the secular and religious, European and American, worlds depicted in Canto XIV. In contrast to the opening line of the earlier Canto, which describes the clear sky over the city, here, as soon as Doña Beatriz accepts the governorship and signs the Council book as "*La sin ventura*" (emphasis in original), "el cielo de Guatemala se nubló" (*ED*, 96; "Hapless," "And above Guatemala the sky clouded over" [97]).

The historical event of the eruption of the Agua volcano, which flooded the city, prompting its removal from its original site, appears as retaliation by divine wrath against the population's excessive mourning for the evil Alvarado. The narrator writes of the mudslide unleashed by the volcanic eruption: "y aquel río de tierra y agua y árboles y piedras/fue corriendo hacia la casa del Adelantado Pedro de Alvarado" (*ED*, 96; "and that river of earth and water and trees and rocks/came rushing toward the house of Adelantado Pedro de Alvarado" [97]). The technique of extravagant itemization is prolonged in the narration of the damage wreaked by the eruption, with many of the lines beginning with "and" as a way of underlining the magnitude of the destruction. The city that has wrapped itself in blackness drowns in blackness and is set upon by dark, demonic portents. Doña Beatriz and her daughter are caught in a rising tide of "agua negra" (*ED*, 98; "black water" [99]) before being crushed when the walls of the Oratory fall on them; "La noche estaba oscurísima, no se veían los rostros" (*ED*, 98; "The night was exceedingly dark, you could not see faces" [99]); and finally, "una vaca negra con solo un cuerno" (*ED*, 98; "a black cow with a single horn" [99]) is seen at the doors of Doña Beatriz's palace.

The account of the volcanic eruption does not end with the death and implicit damnation of Doña Beatriz, however, but insists on the lasting harm done to the community. In documentary style, the narrator lists the victims of the mudslide, in a stanza six of whose eleven lines begin with either "murió" ("she/he died") or "murieron" ("they died"): "Murió Robles, el sastre, y su mujer/Murió la mujer de Francisco López ... " (*ED*, 100; "Robles the tailor and his wife died./The wife of Francisco López died ... " [101]). Order is restored only when a procession marches through the streets singing the litanies. The bishop orders the people to "quitar el luto de las iglesias" (*ED*, 100; "the mourning to be removed from the churches" [101]), putting an end to the official mourning for the bloody conquistador. The restoration of religious authority, like the account of the deaths caused by the eruption, makes no mention of indigenous people. Their absence, combined with the image of "el Volcán de Agua ... descabezado" (*ED*, 100; "Volcán de Agua ... decapitated" [101]), throws into relief that the harmony of Canto XIV has been disrupted, and the order that has returned to the city is a fallen state, in which "natural" elements, such as volcanoes and indigenous people, are no longer integrated into a hierarchical chain of authority.

Canto XVII, which portrays the indigenous leader Lempira's failed uprising in Honduras in 1535–37 as a proto-nationalist insurgency vitiated by its ethnic focus, and Canto XVIII, which depicts the appearance of Fray Bartolomé de Las Casas, bishop of Guatemala and Chiapas, at the court of Castille to condemn the conquistadors' brutality and argue for changes in colonial policy, address both the debilitated state of indigenous culture and its need for enlightened stewardship in order to be successfully integrated into the emerging space of the nation. In fact, Las Casas and his opponent from the Vatican, Juan Ginés de Sepúlveda, engaged in a sophisticated theological and philosophical debate, studded with classical and scriptural citations, concerning the appropriate religious definition of the form of humanity represented by indigenous Americans.[10] The words Cardenal puts in Las Casas's mouth, however, come from his brilliant polemical pamphlet *The Devastation of the Indies* (see chapter 1). Although the narrative does not detail the legislative response to Las Casas's pleas, the fact that his words are followed by "un gran silencio" (*ED*, 114; "a long silence" [115]) hints at his success.

This Canto and that which follows underline the poem's Christian ideology. Canto XIX opens with the conquistadors laughing at Las Casas's assertion that the message of Christ is the only weapon needed to pacify the indigenous people: "decían que si 'con palabras y con persuaciones'/reducía a los indios al gremio de la iglesia .../ellos dejarían las armas" (*ED*, 116; "and said that if 'with words and persuasions'/he brought the Indians into the society of the church .../they would lay down their arms" [117]). They set Fray Bartolomé the challenge of taming the province of Tuzulutlán

("Land of War"). In one of the few sequences in *The Doubtful Strait* from which narrative irony is absent, the Maya marvel at the virtue of the priests, who are innocent of the negative traits of other Spaniards:

vestidos de blanco y negro,
cortados los cabellos en forma de guirnalda
y que no comían carne ni querían oro ni mantas ni plumas
ni cacao
Que no eran casados
ni tenían pecado porque no trataban con mujeres,
Que cantaban día y noche las alabanzas de Dios.
(*ED*, 118; dressed in black and white,/their hair cut in the shape of a garland/and that they ate no meat and wanted neither gold nor cloaks nor feathers/nor cocoa./That they were not married/nor had any sin because they had no dealings with women./That day and night they sang the praises of God. [119])

The passage betrays a monastic will-to-power that presents the devout life as the model for integrating indigenous people and their cultures into the national fabric. It sets in place religious morality as a major feature of the ideology that will replace monopolistic dictatorship; the success of this morality is demonstrated when Fray Bartolomé journeys to Tuzulutlán. He both evangelizes the Maya and urges them to modernize their economic arrangements. The Mayan cacique, invited to Santiago to view commercial wealth, displays his adherence to monastic anti-materialism: "le habían ofrecido cosas de valor/y nada quiso recibir/sino tan sólo una pintura de Nuestra Señora" (*ED*, 120; "[they] had offered him things of value,/and he would accept nothing/except a painting of Our Lady" [121]). Having won over the cacique to Christian beliefs, Las Casas is able to rename the "Land of War" Vera Paz ("True Peace").

The poem's concluding Cantos build towards the overthrow of the Pedrarias tyranny. The success of Las Casas's religious morality in winning indigenous support for an integrative modernizing project in the administrative centre of colonial Central America begins the process of isolating the family of the tyrannical governor. This is achieved, in part, through appeals to the imperial centre in Castile, which discredit the governor and his family, although, significantly, the initiative that finally overthrows the tyranny arises from the local level.

Canto XX, employing the technique of exhaustive itemization, reinforces the image of Central America as a potential Eden. In a passage that extends over more than two hundred lines of the poem, the Spanish historian Gonzalo

Fernández de Oviedo, who became a specialist in the natural history of the Americas, describes the birds, plants, and fruit of Central America. This extensive itemization, again with many lines beginning with the word "and," succeeds in conveying the richness and diversity of the tropical flora and fauna. The Canto's final stanza, however, returns to the social and political world, opening with: "Él tenía una casa en el Darién" (*ED*, 130; "He had a house in Darién" [131]). The phrase is repeated in the sixth line of this sixteen-line stanza, the repetition serving as a catalyst for the elaboration of the house's virtues ("con muchos aposentos/altos y bajos, y con un huerto de muchos naranjos/dulces y agrios" (*ED*, 130; "with many rooms/upstairs and below, and with an orchard with many sweet and bitter/orange trees" [131]), which are described through the balancing of adjectives in apposition, such as "upstairs and below" and "sweet and bitter," suggesting the idyllic equilibrium of the life lived by the historian in this place. This lost Eden prepares the ground for the Canto's climactic condemnation of Pedrarias:

> Pero ahora el Darién se despobló. Lo despobló Pedrarias
> alegando que era malsano (porque lo fundó Balboa su yerno).
> Y su casa se está destruyendo, en un pueblo despoblado.
> Todos los vecinos se han estado yendo. Ya no queda nadie
> en Santa María la Antigua del Darién, donde está su casa.
> (*ED*, 130; But now Darién has become deserted. Pedrarias drove the people away/alleging that it was unhealthy (because Balboa, his son-in-law, founded it)./And his house is falling into ruin, in a deserted town./All the neighbors have been leaving. Now no one is left/in Santa Maria la Antigua del Darién, where he has his house. [131])

The Eden proposed by Cardenal in this Canto is not that of nature in its virgin state but of settlements developing in Christian-influenced harmony with nature. The image of Balboa, the builder, returns: his murder, like the murder of Sandino in *Zero Hour*, is the Cain-like betrayal that ruptures the social order. The historian's crumbling house symbolizes the corruption of the project of the civilization and evangelization of the Americas.

However, prior to marshalling the forces that will overthrow Pedrarias, who is responsible for this corruption, Cardenal includes a final digression on the role of the chronicler of history. Canto XXI returns to Santiago de Guatemala, where Bernal Díaz del Castillo, one of the last survivors of Hernán Cortés's 1519–21 conquest of Mexico, lives in straitened financial circumstances. Aware of the fantasy versions of the conquest that have been published by writers in Spain, Díaz – who is never identified by name in this

Canto, although his name does appear in Canto VIII – resolves to "escribir la 'Verdadera Historia.'/Las cosas que él vió y oyó, y las batallas/en las que él estuvo peleando" (*ED*, 134; "write the 'True Story.'/The things he saw and heard, and the battles,/in which he himself fought" [135]). As in the account of Las Casas's appearance at the Court of Castille, where the archbishop emphasizes that he is recounting events that "han visto mis ojos" (*ED*, 112; "my eyes have seen" [113]), and in the emphasis placed on the historical chronicler in Canto X, the value of Díaz del Castillo's work lies in its description of "the things he saw and heard." Díaz gains the confidence to continue writing in spite of his awareness of his defects as a prose stylist. Elegance, the poem insists, in an unmistakable defence of its own anti-lyrical language, lies not in stylistic flourishes but in the expression of the truth:

> y empieza otra vez a escribir, sin elegancia,
> sin policía, sin razones hermoseadas ni retórica,
> según el común hablar de Castilla la Vieja.
> Porque el agraciado componer es decir la verdad …
> Su historia si se imprime verán que es verdadera.
> (*ED*, 140–2; and starts writing again, without elegance,/without
> propriety, without beautified arguments or rhetoric,/according to
> the common speech of Castilla la Vieja./Because graceful composition
> is the telling of the truth …/His history if it is printed they will see
> is truthful. [141–3])

Truth, expressed in accessible, oral language, gives writing value, particularly when this truth reinscribes verities that have been obscured by the lies or propaganda of those in power: this credo sets in place one of the pillars of Cardenal's own *obra*.

The importance that Cardenal lends the notion of the witness to events, although it anticipates 1980s Testimonio, rests on different assumptions. Cardenal's witnesses are not subalterns: figures such as Las Casas and Fernández de Oviedo occupy important positions; Díaz del Castillo's status is less exalted, yet he is literate and has a house and a soldier's pension. Like Cardenal himself, his witnesses are people of substance who dissent from the ruling power. The roots of Cardenal's conception of witness lie in Catholic confession, where truth is also of prime importance. The events recorded transcend the person who records them; it may be for this reason that, in Canto XXI, Díaz del Castillo is referred to only as "un viejo regidor. Un viejo conquistador" (*ED*, 132; "an old alderman. An old conquistador" [133]), or "El viejo" (*ED*, 140; "The old man" [141]). His role as chronicler supersedes his importance as an individual. The key to his authority is his intimate personal knowledge of the milieu he describes – an argument for Cardenal's own return to Nicaragua after eight years abroad.

The final three Cantos narrate the overthrow of the Pedrarias-Contreras dynasty. The brief Canto XXII, which precedes them, serves as a farewell to events in the larger Mesoamerican setting. The Canto describes a sermon given by Fray Bartolomé de Las Casas to other "frailes" (*ED*, 144; "friars" [145]) on a ship off the coast of the Yucatán Peninsula on 1 January 1545. Las Casas condemns the initial colonization of the region, marked by massacres and mass enslavement of the indigenous people. These abuses are portrayed as a missed opportunity: "se pudieran hacer grandes ciudades de españoles/y vivir allí como en un paraíso terrenal" (*ED*, 144; "it was possible to make large cities of Spaniards/and to live there as in an earthly paradise" [145]). Again, colonization's evil is not in its essence but in the manner of its implementation. The Canto closes with the comment "esperaron a que amaneciera" (*ED*, 146; "waited for day to break" [147]), which may be read as a hope for an awakening from the long night of brutality into a Christian treatment of the indigenous people.

The fall of the dictatorship established by Pedrarias Dávila and maintained by his son-in-law Rodrigo de Contreras, who grooms his own sons to succeed him, begins with elite testimonies of discontent. Canto XXIII, the only one in the poem that uses exclusively archaic orthography and syntax, consists of documents directed to the Royal Audiencia in Granada in which well-off – since literate – residents of Nicaragua appeal for retribution against these abuses. The itemization of these crimes, particularly the economic monopoly of the colony by Contreras ("tiene más de la tercera parte de la provincial/(él y su mujer y sus hijos)" (*ED*, 154; "he holds more than the third part of the province/[he and his wife and his sons]" [155]), and his involvement in criminal activities, such as the slave trade of Nicaraguan indigenous people to Peru, tighten the parallel with the Somozas. The narrator underlines this point by following up a twelve-line itemization of the towns owned by Rodrigo de Contreras with a parenthetical reference to the source of these documents: ("Véase COLECCIÓN SOMOZA") (*ED*, 154; "[Cf. SOMOZA COLLECTION]" [155]).

The statements of citizens of the colony are followed by a petition by Bartolomé de Las Casas and Antonio de Valdivieso on behalf of the colony's indigenous people, who are "las mas myserables y mas opresas y agraviadas afligidas/y desamparadas personas que mas ynjustiçias padezcan" (*ED*, 156; "the most miserable & most opressed & injured & afflicted/& helpless people who most injustices suffer" [157]). The miserable state of the indigenous people appears as the culmination of the list of charges against Contreras. The response to this litany of abuse and misery, delivered by the

Audiencia in the stanza's final line, is "que no ha lugar" (*ED*, 158; "the petition is denied" [159]). Being located in Nicaragua, the Audiencia is subject to the Dávila-Contreras regime.

The counterpart to the misery of the dispossessed colonists expressed in Canto XXIII is the misery of the indigenous people, expressed on their behalf in Canto XXIV by the activist Bishop Antonio de Valdivieso. Writing in duplicate to confound official censorship, Valdivieso defies his fear of assassination in order to tell the truth: "Los agravios de los indios son cotidianos" (*ED*, 160; "Affronts to the Indians occur daily" [161]). In a motif that can be read as a program set by Cardenal for himself on his return to Nicaragua, the priest who writes the truth about the dictatorship becomes the catalyst for the uprising that leads to the overthrow of the regime: "Por las cartas del obispo Valdivieso/habían perdido la Gobernación y los indios" (*ED*, 162; "Because of bishop Valdivieso's letters/they'd lost the Governorship and the Indians" [163]). The more powerful Audiencia de los Confines in Guatemala, which has authority over all of Central America (known as the "Kingdom of Guatemala"), removes Rodrigo de Contreras from office. He departs for Spain to negotiate his reinstatement. His sons, Hernando and Pedro, in a parallel with the behaviour of Anastasio Somoza García's sons, Anastasio and Luis, in the aftermath of their father's assassination, launch a campaign of violent retribution. Hernando Contreras organizes a gang of thugs to stab Bishop de Valdivieso. The scene describing the bishop's death reinforces the contrast between the governor's avaricious sons and the priest's devotion through the use, in part, of the kind of supernatural portents that appear earlier in the poem:

> Después abrieron dos cofres:
> uno de oro y plata, el otro de escrituras.
> El obispo en su charco de sangre besaba un crucifijo.
> Su mano ensangrentada quedó pintada en la pared.
> Siempre quedó la sangre viva y roja, dicen,
> como si acabara de salir de sus venas.
> (*ED*, 162; Then they opened two coffers:/one of gold and silver, the other deeds./The bishop in his pool of blood was kissing the crucifix./His bloodied handprint was left on the wall./The blood stayed bright and red, they say,/as though it had just left his veins. [163])

The murderers' shortsightedness is illustrated by the fact that they steal the dying bishop's gold and silver but leave behind his writings, which will live on to condemn them. The image of Valdivieso's blood remaining bright on the wall, like the earlier scenes that depend on portents, represent a cross-pollination from Cardenal's concurrent composition of *Homenaje a los indios americanos* (Homage to the American Indians). These touches infuse the poem with an aesthetic that is lightly culturally hybridized, leavening the otherwise remorseless Christian Conservativism that dictates its outlook and patterning. Nevertheless, the martyr whose death provides the inspiration to bring down the regime is a priest. In the 1950s, when Cardenal wrote *Zero Hour*, the figure of Sandino was still in play and available to be drafted into a Conservative epic. By the mid-1960s, when he was completing *The Doubtful Strait*, Sandino's self-sacrifice, now appropriated by the FSLN, could no longer be made congruent with Conservative resistance to dictatorship. By contrast, Cardenal's re-established male authority as a priest gave him access to figures such as Valdivieso and Bartolomé de Las Casas.

In a parallel to the brutal excesses of Anastasio Somoza Debayle, which exceeded even those of his father, Hernando Contreras succumbs to megalomania, elevating himself from "Maestre de Campo" ("Field Master") to "General" to "Príncipe" (*ED,* 164; "Prince" [165]). As the brothers set off on their final rampage of looting and destruction, the narrator draws attention to the fact that their mother, Doña María de Peñalosa, is "la viuda de Balboa" (*ED,* 164; "Balboa's widow" [165]). Pedrarias Dávila's daughter, forcibly married to Balboa while still in Spain, arrived in the Americas as the widow of a man she had never met, married Rodrigo de Contreras, and gave birth to the final generation of the dynasty. The narrator suggests her possible complicity in the bloody uprising staged by her sons: "ella estaba en el plan?" (*ED*, 164; "was she in on the plan?" [165]).

Mentioned near the beginning of the poem (Canto V), but introduced as a character only at the end (Canto XXIV), Doña María serves as a vehicle to extend the image of Balboa, the secular martyr and representative of the values of Conservative industriousness, to the poem's conclusion, where it dovetails with the images of the religious martyr, Valdivieso, and the crusading religious authority, Las Casas, to forge an alternative governing morality to the rapine and self-enrichment of the Pedrarias-Contreras dynasty (and, by extension, the Liberal tyranny of the Somozas). The poem's conclusion reinforces the values of Catholic Conservatism. The outrage that finally dooms Hernando Contreras in his rampage to lay waste to the colony from whose governorship his father has been expelled is his disdain for royal authority. His followers

> recorrían las calles gritando LIBERTAD
> VIVA EL PRÍNCIPE CONTRERAS
> ¡A LA MIERDA EL REY!
> y tomaban las armas y los caballos que hallaban

y los llevaban a la plaza. Llevaron al obispo,
Bermejo lo sentó en la picota, y lo iba a matar.
Saquearon las tiendas. Abrieron la cárcel real
y sacaron a los presos. Cogieron la plata del Rey.
(*ED*, 166; others ran through the streets shouting FREEDOM / LONG LIVE PRINCE CONTRERAS / TO HELL WITH THE KING / and they seized what weapons and horses they found/and brought them into the square. They brought the bishop along,/Bermejo sat him in the pillory, and was going to kill him./They ransacked the shops. They opened the royal jail/and released the prisoners. They stole the King's silver. [167])

The desecration of royal authority and religious authority merges. The poem consolidates a vision similar to that of Las Casas, determined that the proper implementation of the colonization and evangelization of the Americas will produce a just social order. The paradise evoked at the poem's outset has been definitively lost; the task that remains, the administration of a fallen world, requires adherence to the principles of stern yet humane government, and an activist clergy. Hernando Contreras's men tell the people that "sólo queremos tomar la hacienda del Rey" (*ED*, 168; "we wish to seize the property of the King" [169]); yet when they reach Panama City they discover that "Panamá ya estaba alzada por el Rey" (168; "Panama had now rebelled in support of the King" [169]). The triumph of royalist forces, who drive Contreras into the mangrove swamps, cut off his head and "y la pusieron en una picota/en una jaula de hierro, en la plaza de Panamá" (*ED*, 168; "and they placed it in a pillory/in an iron cage, in the square in Panama" [169]), brings about the end of the dictatorship.

The narrator does not treat sympathetically the fact that the Contreras brothers "repartían las barras de plata a todo mundo" (*ED*, 166; "handed out bars of silver to everyone" [167]); the order to be established will be corporatist, not socialist. This order's triumph is made clear in the brief concluding Canto, where the city of León, cleansed of the crimes of the past, is founded for a second time. The eruption of the Momotombo volcano drowns the original city, damned by its violation of religious order. The final lines of the poem depict this city sinking beneath the waters of the lake: "la ciudad *maldita*/con la mano de sangre en el muro todavía pintada/se iba hundiendo/y hundiendo/en el agua" (*ED*, 170; "the *accursed* city/with the bloodied hand still painted on the wall/was sinking slowly/down down/into the water" [171]). The emphasis on downward movement implied in the repetition of the verb "hundiendo" ("sinking") – conveyed by "down down" in the English translation – suggests the symbolic descent into Hell of the Pedrarias-Contreras dynasty and its works, epitomized by the bloody imprint of Validivieso's hand on the wall.

Echoing Canto XIV's depiction of an idyll of order in Santiago de Guatemala, the poem's penultimate stanza narrates the re-foundation of León according to principles of geometrical symmetry and unyielding royal and religious authority:

> Pusieron la cruz donde iba a estar la Catedral
> y el Alcalde con el cordel y el cuadrante trazó la plaza,
> y le puso horca y cuchillo en nombre del Rey
> y trazó las calles rectas en el campo.
> El lugar de Nuestra Señora de la Merced
> San Francisco
>   La Yglesia de San Sebastián.
> (*ED*, 170; They planted the cross where the Cathedral was going to be/and designated the site of execution in the King's name/and traced out the straight streets in the field,/the place of Our Lady of Mercy/ San Francisco./The Church of Saint Sebastián. [171])

The overthrow of the dictatorship culminates in the construction of a church. No mention is made of whether the conditions of the poor or the indigenous people improve under this new order, the assumption being that order is an end in itself. This outcome makes it difficult, in this case, to interpret the eruption of the volcano as a hybridized portent stemming in part from indigenous precepts; it appears, rather, to be simply a sign of the wrath of God.

This description of the city's second foundation, in which it is difficult to detect any ironic undertones, establishes the parameters of the society that will succeed that of the dynasty: a society that, in the long term, will be governed by the Catholic Conservatives from whom Cardenal is descended. The inclusion of the "the site of execution" among the elements of the new city emphasizes the enforcement of order through stern punishment. By returning to the first half of the sixteenth century in *The Doubtful Strait*, Cardenal located an environment in which his Conservative Christian principles became a viable means of creatively navigating the secular world, sparing him from the mean-spirited denigration of *Marilyn Monroe and Other Poems*. This epic did not solve his problem of how to engage the contemporary world; yet the particular ways in which Cardenal developed the techniques he had derived from Ezra Pound in *The Doubtful Strait*, turning poetry into semi-novelistic narrative and eschewing the lyricism that characterizes passages of his previous Poundian poem, *Zero Hour*, presaged another development in his writing: the shift towards prose in the early 1970s. Borgeson goes so far as to contend that *The Doubtful Strait* is a disguised Latin American Boom novel:

> Cardenal hace en la poesía lo que la crítica ha aplaudido en la novela de las últimas dos décadas: su empleo diestro de la historicidad y la creación ficticia (el marco poético encarnado en la voz que narra, y los juicios éticos) es la misma función de historia y ficción en autores como Carpentier, García Márquez y Fuentes, y gran parte de los novelistas y cuentistas de lo real maravilloso en general. (Borgeson 1984: 56; Cardenal does in poetry what critics have praised in the novel of the last two decades: in his skilful use of historical and fictional creation (the poetic framework, and the ethical judgments, embodied in the narrative voice) he performs the same role as that played by history and fiction in writers like Carpentier, García Márquez and Fuentes, and many of the novelists and short story writers of the marvellous real in general.)

Borgeson's grasp of the Boom's aesthetics is unreliable: "lo real maravilloso" ("the marvellous real") of Alejo Carpentier is a phenomenon distinct from, and earlier than, "el realismo mágico" ("magic realism') of García Márquez.[11] However, his insight that *The Doubtful Strait* marked an incursion into prose-like verse in order to repair and mythologize the shattered husk of Nicaraguan nationhood is accurate, and suggests a telling pattern in Cardenal's career. Twice in his life, at moments of acute ideological crisis, Cardenal abandoned poetry in order to work out in prose the contours of his vision of the nation. The first such moment, to which *The Doubtful Strait* is a precursor, occurs in the early 1970s, as a consequence of his return to Nicaragua to establish the community at Solentiname at a time when the Sandinista struggle against the Somoza dictatorship was intensifying. Only after publishing *Abide in Love* and *In Cuba* does Cardenal begin to write new poetry; the two-volume prose work *The Gospel in Solentiname* follows shortly thereafter. Through these works, Cardenal negotiates his abdication from the values of Catholic Conservatism in favour of an increasingly mystical version of Catholic Marxism that would liberate him to write his poetry of the 1970s and 1980s. An analogous moment occurs after the Sandinista electoral defeat in 1990, when a twelve-year gap (1993–2005) intervened between volumes of poetry as Cardenal devoted himself to his memoirs. The latter interval enabled Cardenal to adjust to the end of his commitment to the FSLN; his first series of prose publications signalled the beginning of this climactic period of his creative life.

4

Ramírez: From Student Activist to Exiled Writer (1956–75)

SERGIO RAMÍREZ: BIOGRAPHY

Sergio Ramírez Mercado was born in 1942 in Masatepe, a town of six thousand people due south of Masaya, between Lake Nicaragua and the Pacific Coast. Standing in the shadow of the Masaya Volcano, Masatepe lies within a few kilometres of the birthplaces of both Augusto César Sandino and Anastasio Somoza García. In contrast to nearby Granada, Masatepe was characterized by deep loyalty to the Liberal Party.

Sergio Ramírez's childhood took place in a rural environment where the consolidation of the Somoza dictatorship was not questioned.[1] He grew up as the second of five children in a single-storey building on the corner of Masatepe's main square that included both the family residence and the hardware store owned by his father, Pedro Ramírez, who was Masatepe's Liberal, pro-Somoza mayor. The Ramírezes were a rowdy clan known for their tall stature, non-stop music making, and love of unbridled gossip, the latter of which honed the future novelist's sense of story. Pedro Ramírez, who was partly deaf, was the only member of the family who was not a practising musician.

Unlike Ernesto Cardenal, who traced his ancestry to nineteenth-century European immigrants, Ramírez came from a rural mestizo culture. His mother, Luisa Mercado, was the first woman in Masatepe to earn a high school diploma; she became director of the local secondary school at a time when women were not normally considered for such positions. Luisa's family, of largely indigenous descent, had adopted a severe work ethic and a strong sense of individual self-improvement as a result of having been converted to the Baptist faith by missionaries from Alabama. The young Sergio was influenced by the disciplined example of his maternal grandfather,

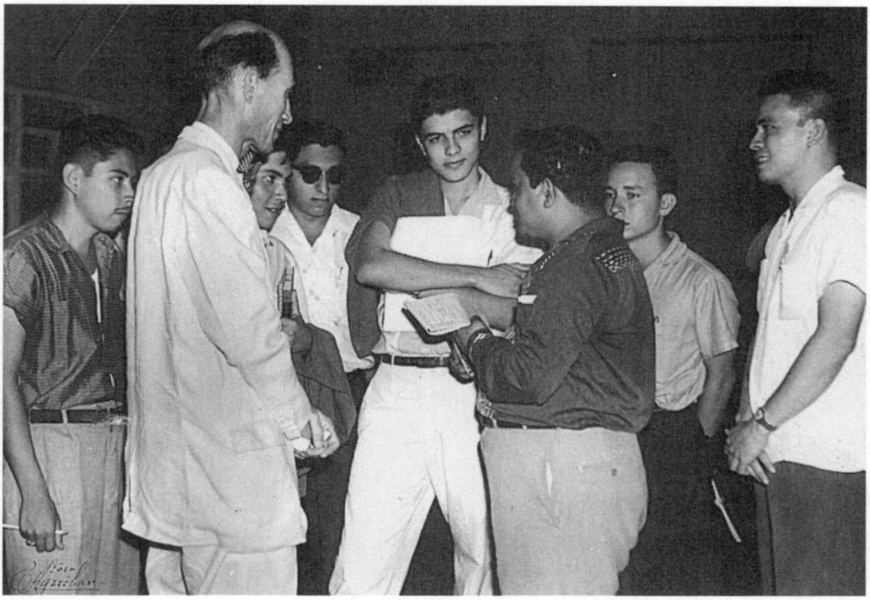

Sergio Ramírez, as a student leader at the National Autonomous University of Nicaragua, is interviewed by *La Prensa*, 1960. Mariano Fiallos Gil stands on his left. (Courtesy of Sergio Ramírez)

Teófilo Mercado. Born in the poorest, most indigenous neighbourhood of Masatepe, Teófilo rose to become one of the town's wealthiest men. Drenched in the positivist ideals that had infused Liberalism with its crusading zeal in late-nineteenth-century Spanish America, he was convinced that the Catholic religion encouraged sloth and backwardness. Even though Sergio Ramírez grew up with exposure to both the Catholic and Protestant religions, his mother's Protestant ethos emerged more strongly in his personality. His maternal grandmother took him to evangelical Protestant services, even though officially he was being brought up as a Catholic. Sergio soon gathered that his parents were, in fact, discreet agnostics who had decided to conform with the religious expectations of their community. As a student, he ceased to attend Mass.

Ramírez's divided religious heritage was not matched in the political realm. Both the Ramírezes and the Mercados supported the Liberal Party. As a child, Sergio met Luis Somoza Debayle, who visited his father at home. At the age of fourteen, he accompanied his family to an estate owned by Anastasio Somoza García, where his mother invited the dictator to attend that year's graduation ceremony at her high school – an invitation that Somoza accepted and fulfilled only weeks prior to being assassinated.

In spite of his identification with the governing party, in a family dedicated to non-stop socializing, the young Sergio Ramírez was a misfit. Six feet two inches tall at the age of twelve, in a country where many adults barely surpassed the five-foot mark, and cross-eyed, he was introverted, withdrawn, and unpopular. The influence of his mother, who "repudiaba las impertinencias, el sentimentalismo, la lágrima fácil" ("repudiated the impertinence, sentimentality, easy tears") of the Ramírez family, forged a personality in which "ganó ella en mi carácter, porque me cuesta mostrar mis emociones" (Cherem 2004b: 63; "she prevailed in my character, because I have difficulty showing my emotions"). The circumstances of his education compounded his introversion. Luisa Mercado sent her son to a girls' school because of the presence of a teacher whom she respected; by the time Ramírez transferred to the boys' school at the age of ten, he was an outcast. He was sent to Managua to attend a school for sons of the National Guard. Lodging with distant relatives, Ramírez explored the city, sat in cinemas, and neglected his studies. As a result of his poor grades, he was recalled to Masatepe and enrolled in the school of which his mother was the director.

Ramírez's absorption in literature deepened at this time: an aunt lent him Argentine translations of nineteenth-century French writers such as Victor Hugo and Alexandre Dumas; his mother, who was his high school literature teacher, taught the works of Federico García Lorca, Pablo Neruda, and classical Spanish poets. At the age of twelve Ramírez won a short story contest for adults organized by a Managua radio station; at fourteen, having become the projectionist in the town's cinema, he published his first newspaper article and wrote a fantasy about local Masatepe customs that Pablo Antonio Cuadra published in the literary supplement of *La Prensa*, under the impression that it was the work of an indigenous elder.

When Ramírez graduated from high school at the age of sixteen, he was taken by his father, whose own education had been limited to four years of primary school, to the Liberal stronghold of León and enrolled in the law school of the Universidad Nacional Autónoma de Nicaragua (UNAN; National Autonomous University of Nicaragua). In León, Ramírez underwent a rapid political radicalization. In his first term, the start of classes was delayed as a result of the rebellion of Olama y los Mollejones. Shortly after the suppression of this Conservative uprising, the GN boasted that it had killed Carlos Fonseca Amador, a recent UNAN alumnus; it later emerged that, in spite of being shot through the lung, Fonseca had escaped. Unaware of his survival, UNAN students held protests in commemoration of Fonseca's life. Ramírez recalls: "De repente y sin mayor conciencia, ni hacerme reflexiones, yo también estaba en las calles. Comencé a pertenecer a otro mundo, a una nueva realidad de protesta constante en la que los estudiantes somocistas eran pésimamente mal vistos" (Cherem 2004b: 74; "Suddenly, and without any greater awareness or deep thought, I, too, was in the streets. I started to belong to another world, a new reality of constant protest in which Somocista students were disdained"). The event that confirmed Ramírez's break with Liberalism was the massacre of 23 July 1959. At a corner of Plaza Jerez, León's central square, a student protest was blocked by armed members of the GN, who had closed off the street and set up a machine gun on a tripod. The GN opened fire on the crowd, killing four students and wounding seventy. Ramírez threw himself into a doorway. Later, when he visited the morgue, he found two close friends among the dead: "Ese fue el día que mi vida cambió para siempre ... éramos adolescentes, llegados de pueblos como el mío, y no sabíamos nada de radicalismos políticos, pero ahora habíamos abierto de golpe los ojos. Me di cuenta que vivíamos en una dictadura que me era totalmente desconocida" (ibid.: 78, 80; "That was the day my life changed forever ... we were teenagers, from villages like mine, and knew nothing of political radicalisms, but now we had suddenly opened our eyes. I realized that we lived in a dictatorship that was totally unknown to me").

The massacre not only changed Ramírez's political orientation; it filled him with the urge to create a new culture for his country. In the aftermath of the massacre, Ramírez became a political leader, participating in an occupation of UNAN. He emerged from this experience convinced that the only viable future for Nicaragua lay in armed struggle. His conclusions were representative of those of a generation that was converting León from a Liberal bastion into the breeding ground of Sandinismo. The students' radicalization, a product of the conjunction of oppressive local conditions and continental euphoria at the triumph of Fidel Castro's revolution in Cuba, was tempered by the UNAN rector. Mariano Fiallos Gil was a strong believer in humanistic learning and democratic debate. In his biography of Fiallos, Ramírez would describe his mentor as a man who, "como Voltaire, encontraba en el dogma el peor enemigo de la condición humana" (*BMF*, 14; "like Voltaire, found in dogma the worst enemy of the human condition"). As the students fought the dictatorship, the rector, who described himself as an apostle of "humanismo beligerante" (Cherem 2004b: 87; "belligerent humanism"), engaged in a political struggle to consolidate UNAN's legal autonomy from the government. The granting of this status – which would eliminate political interference in the appointment of professors, the definition of the curriculum, or the allocation of the budget – had been one of Fiallos's conditions for accepting from Luis Somoza Debayle the job of modernizing Nicaragua's academically decrepit national university. Having achieved the goal of legal autonomy in 1958, Fiallos began creating a professionalized university, with a rigorous curriculum and full-time faculty rather than doctors or lawyers who gave lectures in their spare time to young men who were under little obligation to study. Students like Ramírez were the first cohort to benefit from this disciplined educational structure. They became known as the Generación de la Autonomía (Autonomy Generation); yet sombre political events would skew the meaning of this label, giving it a veneer of political radicalism the rector had not envisaged. The Autonomy Generation were the first group of university students in Nicaraguan history to benefit from a liberal, secular, humanist education; in a striking paradox, they would lay the foundations for a thriving armed socialist revolutionary movement.

In 1959 UNAN had fewer than one thousand students, a startlingly low figure given that Nicaragua at this time counted nearly two hundred thousand young people of university age (*BFM*, 119).[2] The rector urged his charges to modernize their country's culture. In late 1959 Fiallos told Ramírez and his close friend Fernando Gordillo that they must create a new school of thought for Nicaragua; he encouraged them to found a literary journal. The first issue of *Ventana* (Window) appeared in early 1960. The nineteen issues published by Ramírez and Gordillo over the next five years reflected an aesthetic influenced by the US Beat movement and the ideals of political commitment expressed by French Existentialism; they insisted on the centrality of national problems. *Ventana* contested the elitist vanguardism and Catholic anti-materialism of the Vanguardistas (Avant-Gardists), led by Pablo Antonio Cuadra, and their protégés, the Generación Traicionada (Betrayed Generation), reproaching them for criticizing the glitz of New York and Hollywood rather than the poverty of Nicaragua. The *Ventana* manifesto, released by Ramírez, Gordillo, and Alfonso Robles in February 1960, insisted: "Sabemos que los frijoles son más importantes que los chicles" ("We know that refried beans are more essential than chewing gum") and "la poesía es la voz del pueblo" (Borge, *impaciencia*, 235–6; "poetry is the voice of the people" [*The Patient Impatience*, 234–5]).

In their inaugural editorial, Ramírez and Gordillo stressed the significance of literature as a "front": "en verdad que entre la Juventud Universitaria existen muchachos que bien formarían un círculo, que sería nuestro frente Literario" (*SRP*, box 7, folder 14; "in truth among the youth of the university there exist many young men who would form a circle, which would be our literary front"). Over time, some aspects of the competing literary movements began to overlap: *Ventana* published some poems by writers of older generations. Yet the magazine was important as the nucleus around which a new generation of radicalized, anti-Somoza young people coalesced. In his analysis of class formation in Nicaragua, Carlos M. Vilas contends:

> When focusing on the initial stages of Sandinismo in the early sixties, special attention must be given to the *Ventana* group ... The magazine brought together a large group of students, young professionals and literary figures ... Lacking any explicit political identity beyond a shared dislike for Somoza and Somocismo, many of them had been active a few years earlier in the student movement ... With few exceptions the more active members of the *Ventana* group were of a middle class or petty bourgeois orientation with a liberal approach to society and politics. A decade and a half later many of them would hold key positions in the Sandinista government. (Villas 1992: 321)

Finding himself at the core of this group, Ramírez discovered that "vivía yo un ardor impaciente por escribir" (Cherem 2004b: 90; "I lived with an impatient ardour to write"). He began writing poems longhand and publishing them in *Ventana*. The poems soon became short stories. As he was sharing a student room with four other young men, where "no había ninguna oportunidad ni para leer y mucho menos para escribir" (Ríos 2012; "there was no chance to read, let alone write"), and did not own a typewriter, Ramírez would sit with the UNAN's secretaries and write on an unoccupied typewriter, impervious to people who peeped over his shoulder: "escribir para mí era un acto público" (ibid.; "for me, writing was a public act").

The national subject matter of Ramírez's fiction reflected his political commitment, even though his droll, ironic voice was reminiscent of the family storytellers in Masatepe. Ramírez's first months in León sealed the dualities in his personality. He was absorbed into revolutionary political activism at the same time that he came under the influence of the democratic, humanistic Mariano Fiallos. This political initiation created the persona that foreign commentators later would view as contradictory: a man who spoke in the vocabulary of a European social democrat while he served as a leader of one of the most potent movements of Third World Marxism. The second duality that defined Ramírez's personality, that of the artist who was also a politician, sprang from the fact that the need to write and the urge to overthrow the dictatorship took root in him in the same instant: the moment when the GN opened fire on the students in July 1959. Not only were literary and political impulses not incompatible in Ramírez, they were inseparable. After the massacre, he began to read world literature in a systematic way. In addition to editing *Ventana*, he also became one of the founders of the Frente Estudiantil Revolucionario (FER; Revolutionary Student Front). Founded a year prior to the formal creation of the FSLN in 1961, the FER – "radical, heavily influenced by Marxism, and closely linked to the FSLN" (Booth 1982: 111) – would supplant the dominant Christian Democratic student organizations of UNAN and the Universidad Centroamericana (UCA; Central American University) by the late 1960s. It would serve as a conduit for recruiting students into the underground. Two of Ramírez's closest comrades in the FER, Francisco Buitrago and Jorge Navarro, died in combat as Sandinista guerrillas.

In 1962 Carlos Fonseca made a clandestine visit to León. He asked to meet Ramírez and told him that the cultural work of *Ventana* was a vital facet of the Nicaraguan Revolution. Mariano Fiallos had named Ramírez head of public relations for the university; for the last two years of his degree, he acted as the rector's personal secretary. Ramírez would accompany Fiallos to meetings in Managua; during long taxi rides, he absorbed the rector's liberal ideas. The rector urged Ramírez to view himself as a writer first, and not to allow work or politics to prevent him from writing. With Fiallos's help, Ramírez published his first book, a privately financed edition of short stories entitled *Cuentos* (Short Stories), in 1963. Produced by a commercial printer in Managua, the book was circulated by Ramírez's friends; his fiancée, Gertrudis Guerrero, sold copies door-to-door in León.

Ramírez remained in León for a few months after becoming the first member of either the Ramírez or the Mercado families to earn a university degree. He continued to edit *Ventana* and work for Fiallos. His prominence in student politics and university administration broadened the circles in which he moved. In 1962 he was able to travel to a student conference at Université Laval in Quebec City, stopping off in New York on the way back. Yet by 1963 it was clear that his days in León were numbered: his collaborator on *Ventana*, Fernando Gordillo, had been struck by an incurable immune disease, Myastenia gravis, from which he would die in 1967; Mariano Fiallos, although only in his late fifties, was also in declining health; and Ramírez and Gertrudis Guerrero were planning to marry.

Ramírez's romantic life had followed the conventional pattern for a young man of his milieu. As an unsociable adolescent in Masatepe, he had been adopted by a group of older boys who had introduced him at the town's two brothels. In León, at the age of seventeen, he looked out the window of the law faculty, saw a fourteen-year-old girl walking to school in her tartan uniform skirt, and became fascinated by her. Gertrudis Guerrero's family, millionaire bankers in her grandfather's generation, had lost their fortune. Abandoned by her father, Gertrudis and her five siblings had moved with their mother to her grandmother's house. Known as a beauty – Gioconda Belli recalled the adolescent Gertrudis and her sisters as "bellas y esplendorosas" (*El País*, 190; "beautiful and resplendent" [*The Country under My Skin*, 140]) – Gertrudis already had a fiancé, whom Ramírez gradually displaced. They married on 16 July 1964, drove to Costa Rica for their honeymoon, and settled there. Ramírez credits the influence of his wife, and later his daughters, with modernizing his perception of gender relations which, at the age of twenty-one, remained "machista" (Cherem 2004b: 269). The family would live in Costa Rica and West Germany for the next fourteen years, an exile that provided Ramírez with an asset shared by no other Sandinista leader: extended experience of daily life in democratic societies.[3]

Ramírez was encouraged to leave Nicaragua by Mariano Fiallos, who warned him that life in a provincial society under a dictatorship would suffocate him. Carlos Tünnermann Bernheim, who had taught Ramírez law, had been named director of the Consejo Superior Universitario Centroamericano (CSUCA; Governing Council of Central American Universities), an organization based in Costa Rica that coordinated policy among the universities of the isthmus. He invited Ramírez to become CSUCA's public-relations officer, the same role he had occupied at UNAN. The job required Ramírez to travel throughout Central America. Still in his early twenties, he became a well-known figure in intellectual and academic circles. He began to perceive Nicaragua's terrible history through a regional prism: "me volví muy centroamericano" (Cherem 2004b: 93; "I became very Central American"). From this point on, the culture of Central America was one of Ramírez's primary preoccupations.

Yet only three months after his arrival in San José, whose bookstores, cinemas, theatres, and general air of civility contrasted favourably with Nicaragua, even if a certain spontaneous exuberance was lacking, another upheaval occurred in his life when Mariano Fiallos died of kidney disease at the age of fifty-seven. After a vigorous campaign in León, which drew Ramírez back to Nicaragua, Carlos Tünnermann became the new rector of UNAN. Tünnermann's departure from Costa Rica shook up the administrative structure of CSUCA: Ramírez was promoted to director of international programs, a position where he dealt with the Ford Foundation, the United States Agency for International Development (USAID), and other international-aid organizations, such as Canadian University Services Overseas (CUSO) (McFarlane 1989: 156–7). In the summer of 1966 he took an intensive English course at the University of Kansas; putting the language to regular use, and reading widely, he soon became fluent.

The decade that followed Ramírez's move to Costa Rica saw a precipitous ascent in his public and literary career. His position as an academic administrator assisted him in publishing his subsequent books with university presses. In addition to fiction and essays, Ramírez made incursions into the field of Testimonio. His second book, a memoir of his relationship with Mariano Fiallos, entitled *Mis días con el rector* (My Days with the Rector), was published by the UNAN press in 1965; four years later, the same publisher released a new collection of Ramírez's short stories, *Nuevos Cuentos* (New Stories). By this time, Ramírez's importance in CSUCA had increased. In 1966, at the age of twenty-four, he became assistant secretary general; in 1968 he was promoted to acting secretary general. His position as head of the organization was confirmed in 1970 by a vote of the rectors of the five Central American universities. That same year, Ramírez published his first novel, *Tiempo de fulgor* (A Season of Light). In 1971 he published a formal biography, *Biografía Mariano Fiallos*. In 1973 the short story collection *De tropeles y tropelías* (On Mobs and Outrages) became his most widely read work to date, winning a literary prize in Venezuela.

Ramírez's position provided him with high-level administrative and political experience. It was his responsibility to negotiate disputes between universities and national governments, particularly campus invasions by Central American militaries. Yet at the age of thirty he found that his career had reached an impasse. In 1968, with the help of a bank loan, he had founded the Editorial Universitaria Centroamericana (EDUCA; Central American University Press), a bold publishing initiative that aimed to make the region-wide distribution of canonical works of Central American literature – most of which were habitually unavailable or out of print – a reliable feature of intellectual life. In its first two years, EDUCA published seventy titles that sold more than 300,000 copies (*SRP*, box 24, folder 10). The company created a cultural revolution in Central America by making it possible for students or general readers to purchase the most important works of the region's literature at reasonable prices in any of the six republics. EDUCA became so successful that it soon paid off its loan and earned a profit. Works by major figures of Central American literature such as Rubén Darío, Salarrué, and Miguel Ángel Asturias were published alongside those of important contemporary writers such as Augusto Monterroso, Pablo Antonio Cuadra, and Ernesto Cardenal.

The triumph of EDUCA and his position as secretary general of CSUCA provided Ramírez with professional and financial success. He drove a Volvo and travelled widely, making his first trip to Germany and Austria, two destinations key to his later career, in October 1970 (*SRP*, box 39, folder 1); his three young children, Sergio, María, and Dorel, received private educations. Yet both his political and literary ambitions were frustrated. Ramírez met regularly with opponents of the Somoza regime who passed through Costa Rica, such as Carlos Fonseca, Ernesto Cardenal, and the future guerrilla comandante Edén Pastora, yet "el Frente Sandinista me parecía entonces aislado de la sociedad, sin posibilidades políticas ni futuro; sus militantes clandestinos eran valientes pero dogmáticos, una guerrilla entregada al sacrificio pero ajena a la realidad del país" (Cherem 2004b: 102; "the Sandinista Front struck me then as isolated from society, without political possibilities or a future; its clandestine members were brave but dogmatic, a guerrilla army devoted to sacrifice but alien to the reality of the country").

In spite of the reputation earned by his short stories, Ramírez found that his professional career did not allow him time for the ambitious novels he dreamed of writing. The tension inherent in his dual identity as writer and politician came to a head in late 1972 when he received two conflicting offers to go abroad. The Deutscher Akademischer Austauschdienst (DAAD; German Academic Foreign Exchange Service) offered him a grant for a two-year residence in West Berlin to write a novel. The Ford Foundation, which had been impressed by its dealings with the young administrator, had offered in 1969 to support Ramírez through a master's degree in public administration at Stanford University. After a lengthy correspondence and two deferred admissions on account of insufficient funding, Ramírez was scheduled to begin his studies at Stanford in September 1972 (*SRP*, box 43, folders 3–5). At this point, he recalled, "tomé una decisión fundamental en mi vida: quería ser escritor, no burócrata internacional" (Cherem 2004b: 106; "I took a crucial decision in my life: I wanted to be a writer, not an international bureaucrat").

Having sold his Volvo to finance the trip to Germany (he donated half of the proceeds to Edén Pastora and Ernesto Cardenal to organize anti-Somoza activities) (Cherem 2004b: 105), Ramírez moved his family into an aging apartment block in the Wilmersdorf district of West Berlin. While he was in Germany, EDUCA published two books he had prepared prior to his departure: an anthology entitled *El cuento centroamericano* (1974; The Central American Short Story), the first such anthology ever published and the result of months of ransacking libraries for works by forgotten writers; and the influential critical edition *El pensamiento vivo de Sandino* (1974; The Living Thought of Sandino), which consolidated his position among supporters of the FSLN. In Berlin, he learned to speak good German. In later life he would translate into Spanish short fiction by Heinrich Böll, as well as Hermann Schulz's Nicaraguan travel book *Ein Land wie Pulver und Honig* (1978; A Country like Powder and Honey). During his stay in Germany, Ramírez wrote a column called "Ventana" for the San José newspaper *La Nación* and produced two important essays: "El muchacho de Niquinohomo" ("The Boy from Niquinohomo"), a short biography of Augusto César Sandino that was included in subsequent editions of *El pensamiento vivo de Sandino*; and "Balcanes y volcanes" ("Balkans and Volcanoes"), on the formation of Central American culture, which would not be published in Central America until 1983. Crucially, Ramírez also completed the novel *¿Te dio miedo la sangre?* (*To Bury Our Fathers*) during his time in Berlin.

At the end of his stay in Germany, he received an offer to become film-scriptwriter-in-residence at the newly completed Centre Georges-Pompidou in Paris; but the television news of 27 December 1974, announcing Eduardo Contreras's raid on the Somocista Christmas party, alerted him that the FSLN was overcoming its univocal faith in the rural guerrilla and bringing the war to the cities and the bourgeoisie. Perceiving for the first time the possibility of overthrowing the dictatorship, Ramírez decided to return to Central America. Prior to his departure from Berlin, he did detailed research into the holdings of the Somoza family and, anonymously, produced a list of the Somozas' properties entitled "From A to Z." He sent the list to Carlos Tünnermann, then living in Washington, D.C., as a Guggenheim Fellow, who, with the help of the Maryknoll priest Father Miguel d'Escoto Brockmann, leaked it to the investigative journalist Jack Anderson (*SRP*, box 39, folders 5–6). Anderson published the list in his column, which was syndicated in more than three hundred newspapers around the world. The column enraged the Somozas and increased their international isolation.

When Ramírez returned to Nicaragua with his family, he was strip-searched at the airport and detained for three hours. Unable to find work in Managua, he returned to Costa Rica, where the secretary general of CSUCA offered him the job of managing EDUCA. Initially disappointed not to be in Nicaragua, he soon discovered that, during his absence, San José had filled with plotting, exiled Sandinistas. He was recruited into the FSLN, although his membership remained secret; in meetings with Humberto Ortega, he associated himself with the Tercerista faction. He began recruiting prominent members of the bourgeoisie into a potential provisional government.

Even as Ramírez was absorbed by political activity, his literary reputation continued to grow. A new selection of his short stories, *Charles Atlas también muere* (Charles Atlas Also Dies), was published in Mexico in 1976; the same year, he published another anthology, *El cuento nicaragüense* (The

Nicaraguan Short Story), in Managua. In 1977 EDUCA published *Hombre del Caribe* (Man of the Caribbean), a Testimonio Ramírez had collected and edited of the life of Abelardo Cuadra, a National Guardsman who had fought against Sandino, then rebelled against Somoza and been imprisoned and exiled. Also in 1977, *To Bury Our Fathers* was published by Monte Ávila in Caracas; the novel was a finalist for the Rómulo Gallegos Prize, a Spanish edition was published in Barcelona, and translations followed into German, Dutch, Norwegian, Portuguese, Russian, English, Slovenian, and Bulgarian. His life engulfed by politics, Ramírez was unable to capitalize on this literary triumph. He did not publish another novel for more than a decade.

Ramírez travelled in Latin America, taking advantage of his literary contacts, such as Gabriel García Márquez and Julio Cortázar, to arrange meetings with sympathetic governments for the little-known Terceristas. In May 1977 he organized a meeting of prominent Nicaraguan businessmen, priests, and academics in a San José hotel. This group, which became The Twelve, cemented the discontented upper bourgeoisie's links with the Sandinistas. On 5 July 1978, defying an order for their arrest, The Twelve returned to Nicaragua on a plane provided by Panamanian President Omar Torrijos. They were met at the airport by more than two hundred thousand supporters. Ramírez and the others tried to use their presence in the country to force Somoza to introduce reforms. After the attack on the National Palace on 22 August 1978 led by Edén Pastora and Dora María Téllez, The Twelve went underground, fearing for their lives. They eventually took refuge in the Mexican Embassy and, after pressure from US President Jimmy Carter, were granted safe conduct out of the country on 18 December 1978.

In early 1979 Ramírez travelled to various capitals to emphasize the solidarity of the upper bourgeoisie, represented by The Twelve, with the FSLN, and to secure diplomatic recognition for the opposition. As the Sandinista military advance became unstoppable, the Carter administration held a series of panicked meetings in Washington, D.C., San José, and Panama City to try to ensure that Sandinistas would not form a majority in the junta that succeeded Somoza. Ramírez took the leading role in negotiating the conditions for US acquiescence to the transfer of power. A US diplomat – probably William Bowdler – told *Time* magazine: "During the negotiations we had with the junta, Ramírez came out as the strong man. He behaved in a tough manner and struck us as the kind of leftist liberal who has little sympathy for the US and its policy in Central America" ("Downfall," 1979: 35).

In spite of these sentiments, *Time*, like other media outlets, identified Ramírez as "the dominant figure in Nicaragua's government" ("Downfall," 1979: 35). The US media in particular, unaware that Ramírez was a member of the FSLN, pinned its hopes on him as an alternative to the Sandinistas. On 18 July 1979 Ramírez joined much of the Sandinista leadership on the night flight to León, described in Ernesto Cardenal's poem "Luces" ("Lights"), to take command of the nation. Ramírez was soon absorbed in the tasks of reorganizing the ruined country. Although not a member of the National Directorate, Ramírez participated in the lengthy policy discussions that characterized the nine comandantes' meetings:

> Sus decisiones, muchas de ellas claves en la situación de guerra que vivíamos, largamente meditadas y discutidas por largas horas, representaban el fruto de una especie de sabiduría colectiva y del equilibrio; pero ese estilo de debate no se extendió nunca ni al resto de las estructuras del FSLN, ni al sistema político que tratábamos de implantar. (*AM*, 66; Many of its decisions were critical in the context of war we were experiencing. They were meditated at length and discussed for long hours, representing the fruit of a kind of collective and balanced knowledge. However, that style of debate never extended to the rest of the FSLN's structures, nor to the political system we were trying to establish. [*AMM*, 40])

Ramírez also took an interest in cultural policy, founding the publishing company Editorial Nueva Nicaragua, which printed cheap editions of books by both literary writers such as Ramírez himself and Ernesto Cardenal and by guerrilla leaders such as Tomás Borge and Omar Cabezas. As a civilian who did not wear combat fatigues, and a recognized figure of moderation, Ramírez represented Nicaragua abroad on dozens of occasions, making more than twenty diplomatic trips to Western Europe, visiting the United Nations, the White House, the Vatican, many Latin American capitals, cities in the socialist world, such as Warsaw, Moscow, and Pyongyang, North Korea, and Maputo, Mozambique, and other states open to providing Nicaragua with aid, such as Yugoslavia, Iran, Iraq, Algeria, and Libya. After March 1981, when the junta was reduced to three members, Ramírez's collaboration with Daniel Ortega tightened:

> Entraba en cualquier momento a mi despacho, y yo al suyo, discutíamos con franqueza acerca del rumbo de la revolución, si debía o no ser más democrática, nos reíamos siempre de las críticas de aquellos de la vieja guardia que se quejaban de que los terceristas los habíamos marginado, que nos habíamos apoderado del gobierno y que nos habíamos aliado con la burguesía ... Y mientras viajábamos de un punto a otro del país,

> hablábamos de música – él me aficionó a los Tigres del Norte – y de literatura – yo le daba a leer libros, y él también a mí ... (Cherem 2004b: 162–3; He would come into my office whenever he felt like it, and I into his, we debated openly about the direction of the revolution, whether or not it should be more democratic, we always used to laugh about the criticism of the members of the old guard who complained that we, the Terceristas, had marginalized them, that we had seized control of the government and that we had allied ourselves with the bourgeoisie ... and as we travelled from one end of the country to another, we talked about music – he made me fond of the Tigres del Norte – and about literature – I gave him books to read, as he did to me.)

As the FSLN National Directorate assumed more power, it became clear that Daniel Ortega, not Ramírez, was the country's leader. The Sandinista slate for the November 1984 elections featured Ortega for president and Ramírez for vice-president. After the elections, and his formal installation as Nicaragua's vice-president in 1985, Ramírez's responsibilities increased. The years in government tested his relationship with his family. As they reached adolescence, his children, who had returned to Nicaragua speaking to each other in German, went to live in remote villages to cut coffee and teach peasants to read; his two eldest children, Sergio and María, did military service. His son went into battle against the US-backed Contras and later studied engineering and economics in East Germany.

Political commitment also dispersed Ramírez's literary career. Most of the books he published during the 1980s were collections of public speeches: *La edad presente es de lucha* (The Present Age Is One of Struggle) (with Julio Cortázar) and *El alba de oro* (The Golden Dawn) in 1983, *Seguimos de frente* (Forward We Go) in 1985, and *Las armas del futuro* (The Weapons of the Future) in 1987. The important long essay he had written in Germany, together with shorter works on literary topics, appeared as *Balcanes y volcanes y otros ensayos y trabajos* (Balkans and Volcanoes and Other Essays and Works). Ramírez participated in two Testimonios during these years: a personal account of Julio Cortázar's links to Nicaragua, *Estás en Nicaragua* (1985; *Hatful of Tigers*), and the life story of a well-known Sandinista guerrilla: *La marca del Zorro: hazañas del comandante Francisco Rivera Quintero, contadas a Sergio Ramírez* (1989; The Mark of Zorro: Deeds of Comandante Francisco Rivera Quintero as Told to Sergio Ramírez). Foreign newspaper articles on Nicaragua often referred to the fact that the vice-president was "a novelist," yet Ramírez was frustrated that he had still written only two novels. After visiting Nicaragua in July 1986, Salman Rushdie wrote of him: "For many years, he said, he had felt a bit of a fraud when people called him a novelist. 'I wrote [*To Bury Our Fathers*] so long ago, and since then it has been mostly political work. I felt as if I were living on my old capital.' But now he was writing a new novel, working every day, for two hours, early in the morning" (Rushdie 1987: 127). The result, *Castigo Divino* (1988; Divine Punishment), judged by most critics to be his best work and one of the major Latin American novels of his generation, was set in 1930s León. *Castigo Divino* was awarded a prize for murder mysteries in Spain, was translated into French, Dutch, Russian, and Japanese, and, with 30,000 copies sold in Nicaragua, became the best- selling novel in the history of the country's publishing industry. The novel's royalties created a fund, which Ramírez administered, to aid Nicaraguans who suffered long-term disabilities in the Contra War.

The stream of celebrities who visited Nicaragua during the Revolution broadened Ramírez's contacts in political and literary circles. Fidel Castro and future Brazilan President Luís Ignácio "Lula" da Silva forged a long-term alliance after meeting over dinner at Ramírez's house. Ramírez deepened his friendships with Julio Cortázar and Gabriel García Márquez (who, like Mario Vargas Llosa, Carlos Fuentes, Günter Grass, Harold Pinter and Lady Antonia Fraser, Noam Chomsky, the Brazilian singer Chico Buarque de Holanda, and many others, stayed with the Ramírez family during their visits to Nicaragua); he met Salman Rushdie, with whom he would remain in touch. Carlos Fuentes later became an intimate friend and an influential advocate for Ramírez's literary career. It would be years, however, before these contacts were of use to him. Politics continued to throttle his writing. As he had explained to the Cuban writer Miguel Barnet in the early months of the Revolution: "Me he entregado a esta tarea con amor y dedicación, y asumiéndola con sensibilidad de escritor: es un oficio que sigo considerando mío, a pesar de que tengo el presentimiento de que ya nunca podré volver a él; la revolución, es una madre demasiado inflexible con sus hijos" (*SRP*, box 47, folder 7; "I've submitted to this task with love and dedication, taking it on with the sensibility of a writer: it's a profession I continue to consider mine, even though I have the premonition that I'll never be able to return to it; the revolution is a mother who is too inflexible with her children").

The 1990 election, where the huge crowds that greeted Ortega and Ramírez as they campaigned belied a war-weariness that would lead to electoral defeat, exhausted and demoralized him. The years around 1990 were among the most difficult of Ramírez's life. His older sister, Luisa, died of cancer in 1989; his younger brother, Rogelio, died of a diabetic attack in 1992, while on a diplomatic mission to South Korea. The shock of the sudden, unexpected end of the Nicaraguan Revolution, to which he had devoted himself for fifteen years, was one of the greatest emotional crises of his life. He described the morning after the defeat as "la más triste de mi vida" (*CA*, 148; "the saddest of my life"). Defeat also brought the loss of his power and vice-presidential privileges; in its aftermath, Ramírez found himself trapped. He became head of the Bancada Sandinista – the Sandinista members (including his daughter María) elected in the 1990 elections, who held one-third of the seats in the National Assembly. Political manoeuvring consumed his life. He played a key role in increasing the National Assembly's influence and revising the constitution, yet the defeated FSLN was riven with tensions. He founded *El Semanario* (The Weekly), which accepted opinion articles from Nicaraguans of all political persuasions; he taught a creative writing course at UCA. His literary career suffered a blow when, during the recession of the early 1990s, two of the world's most influential publishers, Piper in Germany and Random House in the United States, cancelled publication of *Castigo Divino* after the novel had been translated and announced in their catalogues. Ramírez's literary career in English never recovered from this setback.[4]

The first book that Ramírez published after 1990, a collection of personal essays entitled *Confesión de amor* (1992; Confession of Love), reflected on the experience of the Revolution and discreetly positioned him for a run at the presidency in 1996. Colombian television filmed *Castigo Divino* as a mini-series: the first work by a Nicaraguan to reach the screen. Yet the Nicaraguan broadcast was almost cancelled when descendants of historical figures on whom some characters were based threatened legal action; giving up his parliamentary immunity, Ramírez offered to meet the plaintiff in court (Otis 1992). Embroiled in scandal – the mini-series was finally broadcast– he published a slender collection of short stories, *Clave de Sol* (1992; A-Major). He was named a Chevalier de l'Ordre des Arts et des Lettres by the government of France in 1993. A book of essays on his double identity as writer and politician, *Oficios compartidos* (1994; Shared Trades), appeared the next year. Also in 1994, a volume of Ramírez's collected short stories was issued by the press of UNAM. He started a new novel; but the internal crisis of Sandinismo, as it struggled to find its identity in a post-Cold War world, took over his life.

As the leader of the FSLN's "renovationist" tendency, which argued that Sandinismo must adapt to post-1989 realities by becoming more democratic and less patriarchal, Ramírez found himself in conflict with Daniel Ortega. Underlying the ideological struggle was the tension about which of the two men would be the FSLN presidential candidate in 1996. Internal Sandinista polls showed that Ramírez was the Sandinista most trusted by the population and the only FSLN candidate who would defeat any of the potential Liberal challengers in a presidential election (*SRP*, box 72, folders 4, 9). In January 1994, during the week in which his mother died, Ramírez became the object of attacks in Sandinista media outlets; in January 1995, when these attacks were extended to his daughter, María Ramírez, he resigned from the FSLN. The majority of the FSLN members of the National Assembly, in addition to historic guerrilla comandantes such as Henry Ruíz and Luis Carrión, and nearly all of the prominent women in the party, followed him.[5] Later that year, Ramírez's fourth novel, *Un baile de máscaras* (A Dance of Masks), was published. Set in Masatepe during the twenty-four hours preceding his own birth, it represented an escape from politics into the rural world of his childhood. The novel was a watershed in Ramírez's career: the first of his works to be published by Alfaguara, the Madrid-based conglomerate that in the 1990s became the dominant force in global Spanish-language publishing. Even though *Un baile de máscaras* was published by Alfaguara's Mexico City subsidiary, the company label provided international distribution at a level that Ramírez's fiction had not received before. In 1998 *Un baile de máscaras* would win the Laure Bataillon Prize for the best translated book published in France.

In May 1995 Ramírez founded the Sandinista Renewal Movement to promote his social-democratic vision and serve as a platform for his 1996 presidential campaign. In a nation in crisis, divided between the polarizing figures of Daniel Ortega and the former Somoza official Arnoldo Alemán, the constituency for moderate solutions had evaporated. The support of foreign dignitaries, such as Felipe González of Spain and Carlos Andrés Pérez of Venezuela, failed to help. In spite of visiting every corner of Nicaragua and walking eight hundred kilometres on foot to meet the voters (Cherem 2004b: 241), Ramírez came sixth in the presidential race with 1.3 per cent of the vote (Close 1999: 176). This result was both a political and a personal disaster. Even prior to the campaign, Ramírez had written to an overseas friend: "Hemos tenido muy serias dificultades económicas" (*SRP*, box 38, folder 9; "We've had very serious economic difficulties"); by the end of the campaign, Ramírez was facing more than US$500,000 in personal debt. He sold the vice-presidential mansion that he had bought from the state, moved his family into the adjoining garden house, and sold off the paintings that had been given to him by famous Latin American artists. Resigning as head of the MRS, he spent six years paying off his debts. His political contacts helped him find consulting work, and his literary friends found him speaking opportunities. He held visiting professorships at the University of Maryland

(1999–2000), the Free University of Berlin (2001), and the Instituto Tecnológico de Monterrey (2002) in Mexico. In spite of his financial problems, he had finally achieved the position of having no full-time job other than that of writer.

In 1997 Alfaguara Mexico published a new *Cuentos completos* (Complete Short Stories) with an introduction by the Uruguayan writer Mario Benedetti. A pivotal moment in Ramírez's literary career occurred in 1998, when the initial Alfaguara Prize was split between Eliseo Alberto's novel *Caracol Beach* and *Margarita, está linda la mar* (*Margarita, How Beautiful the Sea*), Ramírez's post-modern reconstruction of the 1956 assassination of Anastasio Somoza García. The head of the Alfaguara jury, Carlos Fuentes, insisted that both winners be awarded the full prize money: $175,000. The sales of this novel, which became an international success, made a substantial contribution to defraying Ramírez's debts. In Cuba, *Margarita, How Beautiful the Sea* was awarded the first annual José María Arguedas Prize; at a dinner in 2001, after the launch of the novel's Cuban edition, Ramírez had what would turn out to be his final meeting with his former close associate Fidel Castro (Cherem 2004b: 176–7). The publication in 1999 of *Adiós muchachos: Memoria de la revolución sandinista* (*Adios Muchachos: A Memoir of the Sandinista Revolution*) consolidated Ramírez's reputation and confirmed his estrangement from politics. In 2001 he published two new books: a short-story collection, *Catalina y Catalina*, and a collection of his lectures, *Mentiras verdaderas* (True Lies). His next novel, *Sombras nada más* (2002; Only Shadows Remain), a reflection on power and commitment set during the days preceding the Sandinista triumph in 1979, became a major international success.

Ramírez developed a growing interest in new technologies. In 2004 he founded *Carátula* (Front Cover), an online journal of Central American literature, which attracted a following of more than 20,000 hits per issue. He served as the magazine's director, assembling an editorial team of young people in their twenties and thirties. His personal website was sophisticated and updated regularly; he experimented with blogging, publishing a collection of his blogs, *Cuando todos hablamos* (2008; When We All Speak), and established active profiles on social-networking sites such as Facebook and Twitter. Ramírez contributed opinion columns to newspapers throughout the Spanish-speaking world and in 2009 made the transition to front-line reporting with a series of feature articles on post-earthquake Haiti for the Madrid newspaper *El País*. In 2007 he was awarded the Order of Merit, First Class, the highest award granted by the Federal Republic of Germany; in 2008 he received a Guggenheim Fellowship to complete his next novel.

The next year he was one of the seventeen public figures named to the Latin American Commission on Drugs and Democracy founded by the ex-presidents of Brazil, Mexico, and Colombia; as a result of this experience, Ramírez became an outspoken advocate of the decriminalization of drugs. In the fall 2009 semester, he was Robert F. Kennedy Professor of Latin American Studies at Harvard University.

During the first decade of the new millennium, Ramírez wrote three new novels: *Mil y una muertes* (2004; *A Thousand Deaths Plus One*), which mingles scenes from his own life with the quest for a nineteenth-century photographer, *El cielo llora por mí* (2008; The Heavens Weep for Me), a detective story set in Managua, and *La Fugitiva* (2011; The Fugitive), a fictionalization of the life of a Costa Rican woman writer. He continued to write short stories, publishing the collection *El reino animal* (The Animal Kingdom) in 2006 and receiving a Rockefeller Foundation Fellowship to complete a new short-story collection during a residence at the Bellagio Center in Italy in 2011. His early works were reprinted in Nicaragua in editions designed for use in the schools. New talks and essays were collected in the volumes *El viejo arte de mentir* (2004; The Old Art of Lying) and *Señor de los tristes* (2006; Knight of the Sad Countenance). The most important non-fiction work he published during this decade was *Tambor olvidado* (2007; Forgotten Drum), a bold polemic that asserts that the myth of "mestizo Nicaragua" is a falsification of the country's triple heritage that suppressed the African element that is omnipresent, if unacknowledged, in Nicaraguan culture.

As had been true throughout his career, Ramírez remained both a close observer of Nicaraguan culture and a promoter of a shared Central American identity. In 2012 he published anthologies of Central American short stories and poems respectively, entitled *Puertos abiertos* (Open Ports) and *Puertas abiertas* (Open Doors). The month-long celebrations in Nicaragua to mark his seventieth birthday in August 2012 were sufficiently elaborate to be publicized with an official logo developed by a public-relations firm. During these celebrations Ramírez published a collection of his newspaper columns over four decades, *Historias para ser contadas: artículos reunidos* (Stories To Be Told: Collected Articles), and an essay collection, *La manzana de oro: ensayos literarios* (The Golden Apple: Literary Essays).

Ramírez's work reached a growing audience – in 2011 he was awarded the prestigious Premio Iberoamericano de Letras José Donoso in Chile – yet, even as he asserted that he was "only a writer," for Nicaraguans, other Central Americans, and many international observers of Nicaragua, he would always be the spokesman of the moderate wing of the Nicaraguan

Revolution. In a 2008 interview given in Granada, Spain, he described "Vice-Presidente" as "ese título indeleble que ya nunca me va a abandonar, porque han pasado después de mí 15 ó 10 personas ocupando ese cargo, pero yo sigo siendo 'el vicepresidente'" (Rodríguez Moya 2009: 118; "that indelible title that will never leave me, because since me ten or fifteen people have occupied that position, but I'm still the 'Vice President'").[6] From his position of authority, as the country's first and eternal modern vice-presidential figure, Ramírez warned in vain against the re-election of Daniel Ortega in 2006 and 2011. In 2008, when the proposed publication of a new edition of the poems of Carlos Martínez Rivas, to which Ramírez had written an introduction, became the centre of a political controversy, he participated in a march against the Ortega regime. His identity as a writer, the way in which his fiction was received and interpreted, continued to emerge from his having been the country's revolutionary vice-president: the writer and the politician remained inseparable.

YOUTHFUL WORKS

Ramírez's first publication was a guest column entitled "Todavía hay más piedras para un Andrés Castro" ("There Are Still More Stones for an Andrés Castro"), published in *La Prensa* on 14 September 1956 to celebrate the hundredth anniversary of the Battle of San Jacinto. Though a patriotic political article, it includes fantastic elements appropriate to fiction. The body of the piece consists of a chorus of voices in which the stones of Nicaragua relate the events of the battle in overwrought, pseudo-nineteenth-century diction. The piece leaves no doubt as to the patriotic message it propounds: "Y si otro Walker quisiera su bota terrible y fiera en Nicaragua poner, yo aquí siempre tengo piedras para cualquier Andrés Castro que quiera partir el cráneo de cualquier invasor altanero" (*SRP*, box 15, folder 1; "And if another Walker elected to place his terrible, savage boot in Nicaragua, here I have stones for any Andrés Castro who might want to split the skull of a haughty invader"). The striking feature of this article is that a rural youth – Ramírez had just turned fourteen – from a Liberal village should express the outlook of Conservative nationalism in a language that persuaded *La Prensa*, the house organ of Conservatism, to publish it. While the divisions between Liberals and Conservatives were sometimes porous,[7] the article nevertheless foreshadows the anti-dictatorial nationalism Ramírez would promote as a student.

The protagonist of Ramírez's first published short story, "El Estudiante" ("The Student"), which was written for the inaugural issue of *Ventana* and later appeared as the opening story in *Cuentos*, also features a protagonist from a Conservative family. Though it reflects a Modernist quest for unity, "El Estudiante" signals Ramírez's determination to capture the reality of his society. As the unnamed protagonist arrives by bus in León, where he is enrolled in university, his first glance out the window brings home both the length of his country's history and the oppressive dictatorship under which it slumbers: "dos Guardias Nacionales metieron a empujones a un hombre a una casa enorme, que parece que en un tiempo fué iglesia" ("Estudiante," 3; "two National Guardsmen pushed a man into an enormous house, which looked as though it had once been a church"). A taxi driver, noticing the ring that identifies the protagonist as a high school graduate, asks him, "¿Taxi, bachiller?" (3; "Taxi, graduate?"). Later, when the student realizes that his father's failure to pay his board is due to his having been imprisoned for participating in the rebellion of Olama y los Mollejones, he pawns the ring and his other possessions to make the trip back to his village. As he steps out onto the street, the taxi driver repeats his offer. This time, though, the student cannot accept the privileged status accorded him: "El anillo ya no estaba allí. Se subió a la acera, apretó fuertemente los noventa pesos y el carro se perdió lentamente a la vuelta de la esquina" (4; "The ring was no longer there. The student stepped onto the sidewalk, clutched the ninety pesos and the car disappeared slowly around the corner"). The student's certainties disappear as the car vanishes.

Of the early stories collected in *Cuentos* (1963), Ramírez suppressed the first four; he kept the remaining six stories and added "Son de pascuas" ("Christmas Music"), a later story that appeared in an anthology in 1964 (*SRP*, box 42, folder 3), for the *Cuentos completos* issued by Alfaguara in 1997; the same stories were collected, under his full name, Sergio Ramírez Mercado, in a cheap edition for Nicaraguan students (complete with true and false comprehension questions) entitled *Primeros cuentos* (First Stories), published in Managua in 2004.

Irony is a dominant trait of Ramírez's style from the beginning of his career. In the early stories, his irony is a reflection of the paralysis of an intellectual living under a dictatorship; it is rooted in the perceived impotence of traditional literary culture to effect social change. The first and longest surviving story from *Cuentos*, "Félis Conclóris," establishes a parallel between the intellectual's absorption in words and the failure to challenge social injustice. The narrator, whose voice initially has a pontificating tone, follows the excitement generated in the national press by the return to his small, impoverished country of a world-famous philologist. The philologist, who is credited with deriving new Latin names for cats and insects and presenting them at scientific conferences in Japan, Cambodia, and Borneo, is the first citizen of his country to have won the "Oxsen Prize." No one knows what this prize is, but everyone assumes it must be significant. The narrator's dissent from the attention lavished on his famous compatriot is firm but insistent; he reads the newspapers while composing the text of a speech he is due to give to a peasant organization, and questions the relevance of a "tipo que sabe mucha gramática" ("a guy who knows a lot of grammar") to a country where "el 67% de la gente no goza del placer de leer y escribir, el 71% tiene un ingreso anual de $93 y el 58% no tiene letrinas en casa" (*CC*, 20; "67% of people do not enjoy the pleasure of reading and writing, 71% have an annual income of $93, and 58% have no toilets at home"). The narrator criticizes not only the lavishing of attention on activities that are extraneous to the nation's problems, but the vacancy of fame itself: "El genio adquiere una nueva personalidad vacía por dentro pero fantásticamente colocada por fuera" (24; "Genius acquires a new personality that is empty on the inside but fantastically well set up on the outside"). Fame is inseparable from forgetting and is one of the state's tools for distracting attention from "sus grandes defectos y errores" (25; "its great defects and errors"). Greeted as a conquering hero when he lands at the airport, the philologist promises to repay his country by inventing the most beautiful word in the language.

This reference to beautiful language sharpens Ramírez's critique, as a member of the Autonomy Generation, of the aesthetic priorities of the Vanguardistas and the Betrayed Generation. The description of the genius's return visit anticipates the triumphal returns of Rubén Darío (who was accused of ingratiating himself with dictators) to Nicaragua in 1907 and 1916 in *Margarita, How Beautiful the Sea*. The complicity of an exclusive immersion in language with the continuation of the dictatorship is made evident when the government agrees to spend public funds on an order of "libros rarísimos en el extranjero para buscar entre ellos piezas de la nueva palabra" (30; "extremely rare books from abroad to search among them for pieces of the new word"). The announcement of the word is delayed; the philologist is interned in a sanatorium. Reduced to cutting dictionary pages into paper birds and muttering gibberish, he is soon forgotten; the country's problems persist. The final paragraphs underline the tale's ironies with a heavy-handedness that suggests a critique of the narrator himself: "Como ven, esta singular historia nada produjo para nuestra economía nacional" (33; "As you can see, this particular story did nothing for our national economy"). The narrator's utilitarian attitude, like the philologist's aesthetic escapism, is an inadequate response to dictatorship. The story's final words are the name of the political party to which the narrator belongs and on whose behalf he is going to speak to the peasants, the "partido de Acción Radical Popular" ("Party of People's Radical Action"). These words of unmistakable political intent stand in contrast to the philologist's Latinate circumlocutions; but the narrator's one-dimensional political commitment condemns him to an isolation that is hardly less desolate.

Like Ernesto Cardenal's youthful epigrams, Ramírez's first stories are dominated by the suffocating presence of the Somoza regime. Even at this early stage of his career, however, Ramírez demonstrates an awareness that dictatorship is not merely the exercise of political power; it is a force that strips a nation of its cultural references and self-respect. This theme would become more prevalent in Ramírez's fiction in the 1970s, particularly in *Charles Atlas también muere*. It makes its first appearance in "El hallazgo" ("The Discovery"), the story of a barman who becomes a well-known local character because of his resemblance to the American movie star "G.P": "G.P. para los parroquianos por fuera y G.P. para él por dentro" (*CC*, 35; "G.P. for his customers on the outside and G.P. for himself on the inside"). The barman's emotional dependence on his identification with the famous actor eliminates his ability to perceive or address the drab reality of his life: "él estaba seguro de que pasaba encima de toda la gente con su aureola de G.P." (36; "he was sure he floated above everybody else with his aura of G.P."). As he ages, he clings to the distinction conferred on him by his looks, even though the men who patronize the bar cease to identify him with the Hollywood actor: "Y fue hallando que todo iba olvidándose, cuando más necesitaba ser G.P. y ser G.P. para los demás" (37; "And he was finding that all was being forgotten, just when he most needed to feel like G.P. and to be G.P. for others"). He begins to rely on strangers, who have not visited the bar before, to note his resemblance to the actor. His sense of self is crushed when one of these strangers tells him that he resembles someone he knows, yet the resemblance turns out to be with an old drinking buddy. In this moment of epiphany, as his internal G.P. begins "hundiendo y hundiendo sin remedio" (39; "sinking and sinking without hope"), the barman is finally able to utter the Hollywood actor's full name – Gregory Peck – and to recognize that he works in a "cochino bar" (39; "filthy bar"). Like the philologist, the barman is revealed to be empty inside, rendered vacant by cultural subservience. The story's ending may be more optimistic than it seems: the barman's decision to show off his movie star smile one last time implies a recognition that he will have to construct a new identity based on the actual conditions of his life.

The exploration of cultural alienation coexists in these apprentice stories with short, mordant pieces about political power and its consequences.

Stories such as "Los graneros del rey" ("The King's Granaries"), in which a king increases a country's prosperity but refuses to distribute the wealth among the people (an obvious allusion to the Nicaraguan economy during the 1960s), and "La banda del presidente" ("The President's Gang"), in which an entire government resigns and the population unmasks the "General" who claims to have taken over as a local actor, are allegorical. Yet, even so, the reader feels Ramírez working his way towards an increasingly sharp-eyed evocation of Nicaraguan life as he not only satirizes the myths of power but traces the consequences of dictatorship in daily life. While in "Tumulto" ("Tumult"), an anecdote about an incident in a crowded market, the descriptions do not always include telling details, the final two stories, "El poder" ("Power") and "Son de pascuas," provide pungent descriptions of provincial Nicaraguan life. In these stories Ramírez develops his distinctive vision, mixing tropical yarn spinning, biting observation, and an acute awareness of the ironies of power.

"El poder" focuses not on the dictator himself but on a *cacique* or local boss, the kind of well-connected, favour-dispensing man of the people who has served as a pillar to many governments. In his hometown, Don Fulgencio dominates public life: "siete años seguidos Juez Local y Líder del Partido, conocedor pulgada a pulgada del terreno que pisaba, de los rostros de los amigos, de la edad de los hijos de los amigos hábiles para inscribirse y votar, de sus debilidades y pequeñas necesidades, de sus entusiasmos y padrino de muchos hijos de correligionarios" (*CC*, 57; "seven years straight local judge and Leader of the Party, the man who knew inch by inch the ground he trod, the faces of friends, the ages of the children of friends eligible to register and vote, their weaknesses and small needs, their enthusiasms, and godfather of many children of coreligionists"). The reader sees Don Fulgencio dispensing justice, but, as he closes the town hall early to receive the minister of finance, who is due to visit, his secretary asks him what power is really like. This secretary "sentía como todos el poder del Juez pero no sabía cómo era" (*CC*, 60; "felt like all others the Judge's power but did not know what it was like"). Don Fulgencio promises to show the secretary the nature of power. The minister's visit is a farce. He jumps out of his chauffeur-driven minivan and urges Don Fulgencio to hand over "las cositas" ("the stuff"), explaining that he is in a hurry to get to Managua. When Don Fulgencio invites the minister's wife to come into his house to rest, she refuses. The "stuff" that Don Fulgencio delivers to the minister's chauffeur – apparently a payoff to retain his position as local leader of the governing party – is derisory: "las cajas de plátanos, el saco de elotes, papayas, naranjas, las cabezas de bananos" ("boxes of bananas, a sack of corn, papayas, oranges, tops of banana trees"). After giving him a few "palmadas grotescas en la espalda" (*CC*, 61; "grotesque slaps on the back") and assuring him that the party is aware that he is doing a good job, the minister drives away, revealing Don Fulgencio as the small-town irrelevance that he is. The restrained narrative voice allows the ironies to stand without comment. The secretary, watching the dust rise behind the departing van, promises himself that he, too, will someday wield power just like the judge. The humour lays bare the mediocrity bred by an authoritarian system, and how it perpetuates itself, more effectively than any denunciation.

The final story that Ramírez conserved from his early production has a more sinister air. Escaping the realm of politicians in which Ramírez was raised, his father having occupied a position somewhat analogous to that of Don Fulgencio, "Son de pascuas" dramatizes the effects of social injustice on ordinary people. Paradoxically, it is also the first of Ramírez's stories to include lush descriptions of the landscape in which he grew up. These descriptions, which mention Masatepe and the surrounding villages by name, enumerate the tropical vegetation in resolutely Nicaraguan vocabulary. The voice of the young woman whose telephone call constitutes the narrative action of this brief story is portrayed passing through "los chagüites, en la espesura de maderos, chilamates, ojoches, tigüilotes, guachapilines" (*CC*, 63; "the flooded fields, the dense woods, the chilamate trees, the macadamia-nut trees, the dragonfruit berries, the tigüilote trees, the crotolaria bushes"). This Náhuatl-derived vocabulary – so resolutely local that even readers from neighbouring Central American countries might not recognize all the words – insists on Nicaraguan cultural specificity.

The story unfolds against a background of Christmas celebrations, complete with parades and fireworks. The combination of these two elements – indigenous vocabulary and rural Hispanic Catholicism – incarnate the mestizo culture of the countryside. Yet this evocation is stripped of potential nostalgia by the story of a young woman who comes to the village telegraph office in order to phone her estranged husband, a private in the GN, to tell him that their youngest daughter is dying of croup. The young woman, a trapeze artist in a visiting circus, urges the Guardsman to visit his daughter before she dies. Against the background of the vegetation through which her call is transmitted and the telephone operator's distraction as he goes outside to watch the fireworks, she repeats to her ex that he has a duty to his daughter: "¿Qué no es tu hija?" (*CC*, 63; "Isn't she your daughter?"). The narrative point of view, which does not allow the reader to hear the husband's replies, accentuates the tension between the festive atmosphere and the woman's despair. The young woman, who is known for her deft execution of a trapeze manoeuvre known as "el pase de la muerte" (64; "the death show"), is interrupted when her older daughter comes to tell her that the younger daughter has died. In a tiny, telling detail, the older daughter is wearing new shoes, an observation that suggests that the mother's financial circumstances may not be as dire as they seem. On hearing of the younger daughter's death, the mother pauses. The story closes with the telephone operator telling her the price of her call: a sign that the world is already moving on without the little girl. "Son de pascuas," dated December 1963, is a very poised, disciplined, and sympathetic story to have been written by a twenty-one-year-old writer.

Ramírez's law thesis, *La problemática del derecho constitucional nicaragüense* (The Situation of Nicaraguan Constitutional Law), presented and printed in 1964, depicts constitutions as a way of characterizing the nation, but one that is always trampled by violence. Hence, Nicaragua's constitutions are both crucial to understanding the country's essence and meaningless in terms of policy implementation. In his survey of the nation's constitutions, Ramírez minimizes the Spanish inheritance and draws a sharp line between South America's successful struggle for independence at the beginning of the nineteenth century, and the experience of Central America, where there was no struggle against Spain and, he asserts, no authentic attainment of sovereignty: "La independencia estaba sólo en el Acta" (*PDCN*, 21; "Independence existed only on paper"). His residual Liberalism is evident in the credit he gives the Zelaya government, at least in its early years, for having tried to match constitutional clauses to the nation's realities: "Como se puede ver, muchas de las actuales instituciones constitucionales, toman su raíz en esta de 1893, en un sentido estructural. Su parte orgánica, se adecuó a las necesidades del país y a sus proyecciones en el futuro de una manera certera" (*PDCN*, 63; "As can be seen, many of the current constitutional institutions took root, in a structural sense, in 1893. Their organic part adjusted itself accurately to the country's needs and their future trajectories"). He notes, however, Zelaya's corruption of Liberal principles as he strayed towards dictatorship; merely recounting this story, in 1964, was a discreet way of evoking the Somoza regime.

Ramírez notes that most constitutional guarantees in Nicaragua "no se han cumplido y permanecen como letra muerta" (*PDCN*, 77; "have not been implemented and remain empty verbiage"). This was a failing that Mariano Fiallos hoped to remedy by establishing UNAN as a legally autonomous institution, a microcosm of fairness and democracy that was independent of the state yet would serve as an example to it. Ramírez had the opportunity to develop the implications of UNAN's autonomy for conceptions of Nicaraguan nationhood when he returned to León to address the incoming class at the beginning of the 1969–70 academic year. The talk he gave was published as a pamphlet, *Lección inaugural del curso 1969–1970: La juventud y la nueva Nicaragua* (The Inaugural Lecture for the Class of 1969–1970: Youth and the New Nicaragua). In this talk, Ramírez does not hesitate to depict autonomy as the seed of a new future for the nation: "La primera chispa de un cambio futuro, es pues, la autonomía. Y es muy cierto que su conquista es el hecho cultural más importante en la historia del país, desde la firma del acta de independencia de 1821" (*LIC*, 18; "The first spark of a future change is autonomy. And it is very clear that its achievement is the most important cultural fact in the history of the country since the signing of the act of independence"). This bold claim illustrates the extent to which for Ramírez and other followers of Mariano Fiallos, the university, with its democratic self-government and open intellectual enquiry, is a microcosm of the future nation, as the Solentiname community is for Ernesto Cardenal and his (far more isolated) followers. While these two microcosms may represent different philosophies –one secular and democratic, the other devout and radical – and certainly had different histories (UNAN was the traditional training ground of Nicaragua's tiny middle class), in the context of the 1960s, the autonomous university harboured nearly as much militant radicalism as Cardenal's commune. Ramírez's speech cites Frantz Fanon; his praise of liberalism veers into a promise of far more profound changes. He speaks of Nicaraguan society as being characterized by "una enajenación total: la enajenación entre sí de dos mundos distanciados, el uno subyacente y el otro que comienza a nacer sobre él" (*LIC*, 9; "a total alienation: the mutual alienation of two worlds that are distanced from each other, one the underlying base and the other which is beginning to be born"). The liberal language yields to the assumptions of a powerful Marxist underlay. Ramírez describes the change he anticipates as encompassing an ambience

> de transformación de estructuras, de actitudes, de tendencias de la sociedad … de un diálogo perpetuo entre los hombres, colocados todos en una base cultural común y a partir de la cual sea posible desarrollar las cualidades intrínsecas del individuo a plenitud, su propia potencia creativa y a la par, … del anulamiento del individualismo practicante que es causa primera de la enajenación, para conseguir un nuevo ser que se coloque como juez de su propio destino y de su propia libertad humana, sin que nada de lo humano le sea ajeno. (*LIC*, 10; of the transformation of structures, of social trends … of a permanent dialogue between men who are all located on a common cultural base from which it

may be possible to develop and fully realize the individual's intrinsic qualities, his creative potential and, at the same time ... to nullify the prevailimg individualism that is the prime cause of alienation, to create a new being who may take his place as the judge of his own destiny and human liberty without anything human being alien to him.)

The final words of this paragraph may pay homage to Mariano Fiallos's favourite quote from Voltaire, yet the declaration's language is replete with Marxist terminology and analysis. The notion that a cultural base generates the superstructure of lived experience, the quest to eliminate "alienation" (which Marx associated with meaningless labour but which here refers to life under Somocismo), and the idea that the eradication of alienation will produce a "new being" – an echo of the Cuban "New Man," softened to make it acceptable in a public talk under a dictatorship – all illustrate the infiltration of revolutionary Marxist concepts and language into the classical liberalism in whose name Fiallos had consolidated UNAN's autonomy. As Ramírez continued to experiment with writing the nation in his fiction, he wrote it, also, in far less coded and ambiguous terms, in his talks and essays.

THE WIDENING FOCUS: *NUEVOS CUENTOS* AND *TIEMPO DE FULGOR*

When Ramírez brought copies of *Cuentos* home to Masatepe, his father told him that now he must write a novel (Cherem 2004b: 97). At first, Ramírez continued to expand his range in the shorter form, including in *Nuevos Cuentos* (1969), which is dedicated to his father and which includes most of the stories that would appear in the internationally published *Charles Atlas también muere* (1976). The limited distribution of the UNAN press meant that stories such as "Nicaragua es blanca" ("Nicaragua Is White"), "El Centerfielder," and "El asedio" ("The Siege"), which have gone on to be widely anthologized, did not receive international distribution until the publication of *Charles Atlas también muere*. These three stories conclude the UNAN collection, which opens with "Bendito – Escondido" ("Hide – and Seek"), a slight piece of local colour that revolves around the consequences of a theft, and "Un lecho de bauxita en Weipa" ("A Bed of Bauxite in Weipa").

The latter is the longest story in the collection, at over twenty pages, and is Ramírez's first extensive experiment with the shifting narrative viewpoints that he would employ in *To Bury Our Fathers*. As the German critic Andrea Rausse maintains, Ramírez "findet hier Erzählungstrukturen, die für die Form seiner Romane wichtig werden und die er dort weiter ausbaut"

(Rausse 1995: 64; "finds here narrative structures that would become important for his novels and which he would develop further there"). This story stands out from the others in the collection not only by virtue of its length and narrative complexity, but also because it is the only story that is not immersed in the oppression, alienation, and violence of Nicaraguan society. In spite of this, the theme of cultural alienation obtrudes on what begins as a tale of marital infidelity.

The protagonist, Walter, lives in Costa Rica. He completed his high school and undergraduate education in New Orleans, graduating from Loyola University. Though brought up as a Catholic, Walter has become interested in Moravian Protestantism and attends courses on religion. While his wife, Julie, is on vacation, he meets Marylin, a prostitute from the Atlantic Coast, who sparks his memories of a girl of the same name with whom he fell in love as a young man in New Orleans. In a sequence of fifteen sections, six of which consist of dense interior monologues, whose speakers' identities are signposted by the repetition of key motifs, Walter evokes the education of the Marylin he knew, Marylin recalls her own upbringing, and a nondramatized third-person narrator recounts Walter's interactions with Julie, and with his best friend, Harry. It is not always easy to decipher who is speaking in the interior monologues. Walter's fantasies about how his relationship with the love of his youth might have played out in the future includes the possibility of "haciendo el amor en un lecho de bauxita en Weipa frente al terso y delicado mar de Timor" (*NC*, 30; " us making love on a bed of bauxite in Weipa by the side of the polished, precious Timor Sea" [*STO*, 42]). This reference to a northern Australian resort town is only one of a multitude of allusions made by Walter to exotic spots around the world. Though the text at no point draws attention to this affinity, both Walter and Marylin are outsiders: he as a gringo in San José, she having grown up as a light-skinned mestiza of partly German Moravian descent among Afro-Caribbeans on Central America's Atlantic Coast: "Bailando en dancings de negros, bebiendo con ellos, acostándome con ellos, la rara, la blanca, la extraña en esos barrios con casas de barandales de madera y tiestos de flores" (*NC*, 37; "Dancing in black men's clubs, drinking, going to bed with them, me, the queer one, the white girl, the stranger in their neighborhoods, with their wooden verandas, their window boxes" [*STO*, 50]).

Marylin is the story's discreet connection to Nicaragua: though she has come to San José from Puerto Limón, on Costa Rica's Atlantic Coast, until the age of fifteen she lived in Puerto Cabezas. Located in Nicaragua's remote northeast and insulated from the depredations of Somocismo, this town prompts no political commentary. Nevertheless, the fact that the story's

Nicaraguan character is a prostitute carries an implicit charge that finally overrides the mournful tale of Walter's nostalgia for his lost youth and his confusions over whether he has betrayed his wife by seeing Marylin – whether he actually commits adultery is left unclear – or whether he betrayed his ideals by substituting a stable marriage for his passion for the first Marylin in his life.

"A Bed of Bauxite in Weipa" is a proto-novel, written in a more intimate, elegiac tone than is customary in Ramírez's short stories. It uses experimental techniques that he had not, at this point, mastered. The three stories that close the collection represent the maturation of Ramírez's early voice and technique. The delusions of the Nicaraguan bourgeoisie are captured with caustic effectiveness, yet an underlying seam of despair is also discernible. "Nicaragua Is White" revolves around the Nicaraguan bourgeoisie's desperate hope that it will snow at Christmas in Managua, relieving them of the burden of tropical identity and ushering them into the "normality" that they see on television. The bourgeoisie's alienation is traced to late-nineteenth-century positivism: the meteorologist who detects evidence of snow flurries advancing towards Nicaragua studied in Germany "becado por el gobierno del General José Santos Zelaya" (*NC*, 48; on "a grant from General José Santos Zelaya's government" [*STO*, 58]). The pseudo-erudite voice satirizes the pretensions to scientific precision of weather forecasting. The meteorologist's instruments, all of them imported, have pompous names, yet his office, located on the poor eastern side of Managua, resembles "un kiosco de refrescos" (*NC*, 49; "a refreshment kiosk" [*STO*, 59)].

The confluence of this pseudo-scientific mentality with personalistic rule becomes evident when the meteorologist insists that his duty demands him to inform the president in person of the arrival of snow, even though it is the middle of the night. The president's initial reaction is that the meteorologist is a madman who should be condemned to a diet of bread and water. This phrase conjures up the anachronistic atmosphere of the kind of ruler produced by cultural alienation: the presidential aide is described as standing in front of "la reproducción del cuadro de David, la coronación de Napoleón" (*NC*, 51; "past the print of David's *The Coronation of Napoleon*" [*STO*, 61]). The president refuses at first to believe that the meterologist is capable of having deduced that snow is coming; it emerges that the US government has also predicted snow in Nicaragua, but the information is regarded as a state secret. Two generations of colonized Nicaraguans confront each other, neither of them taking seriously the other's form of colonial knowledge: the meteorologist, who trained in Europe "antes de la primera guerra mundial" (*NC*, 54; "before the First World War" [*STO*, 64]), belongs to a generation in thrall to nineteenth-century European positivism, while the president is a loyal servant of the United States, which he sees as the sole source of progress and verifiable information.

The meteorologist is ordered to keep quiet about his discovery: the president cannot allow this form of knowledge to upstage his Yankee masters: "Mirá, esta cuestión es de política internacional, y eso lo manejo yo. Entonces, quedamos en que oficialmente fueron los Estados Unidos los que descubrieron que va a caer nieve" (*NC*, 54; "Look, this is a question of international relations, and they're for me to deal with. So, let's say that officially it was the United States who discovered that it's going to snow" [*STO*, 64]). Yet when the snow fails to fall on Managua, the meteorologist, rather than the Americans, is blamed for the error. He explains that in fact snow is falling on Nicaragua, but that it is the impoverished peasants of the northern mountains, rather than the president and his wealthy cohorts in Managua, upon whom this symbol of progress has been bestowed. The fact that snow is not merely a symbol but an active climatological phenomenon becomes evident when some peasants freeze to death. Others, however, feel that "parece que estuviéramos en el cine" (*NC*, 59; "it's like being in the movies" [*STO*, 69]).

The two remaining stories, "The Centerfielder" and "The Siege," are models of terse storytelling. "The Centerfielder" is one of a number of stories that Ramírez would write using Nicaragua's national sport as a metaphor.[8] The anecdote of a Nicaraguan team that disgraced itself at an international baseball competition in Cuba in the 1940s, which recurs in *To Bury Our Fathers*, provides the background to the central character, a middle-aged man named "Matraca" ("Rattle") Parrales who during his youth in the 1940s was an outfielder famous for his spectacular throws to home plate. The story, set in the 1960s, finds Parrales in jail, where he is being interrogated as a possible accomplice in the crimes of his son, a Sandinista guerrilla who has been killed. The National Guardsmen remember that "eras medio famoso con ese tiro a home que tenías" (*NC*, 66; "you made quite a name for yourself with that arm of yours" [*STO*, 22]). In interior monologues that are adroitly integrated into the forward action, Parrales, who realizes that he is about to be executed, recalls his triumphs on the diamond. In spite of the story's harsh realism, its structure depends on a Borgesian motif of the private dream that takes over reality. As he is led across the prison patio to the interrogation room, Parrales imagines the space as a venue for a baseball game. He sees himself chasing a fly ball, then vaulting the wall and escaping.

At the story's conclusion, the captain who orders the Guardsmen to execute him suggests the same scenario as the justification for why Parrales was "shot while trying to escape": "inventate cualquier babosada; que estaba jugando con los otros presos, que estaba de centerfielder, que le llegó un batazo contra el muro, que aprovechó para subirse al almendro, que se saltó la tapia, que corriendo en el solar del rastro lo tiramos" (*NC*, 70; "make up anything you like. Say he was playing with the other prisoners, that he was centerfielder and chased a hit down to the wall, then climbed up an almond tree and jumped over the wall. Put down that we shot him as he was escaping across the slaughterhouse yard" [*STO*, 26]).

In contrast to "Nicaragua Is White," the foreign cultural acquisition in "The Centerfielder" is portrayed not as a source of alienation but rather as part of a domestic popular culture shared by the prisoner and his interrogators. Unlike the bourgeoisie, who flaunt foreign cultural traits as banners of distinction without fully engaging with them, working-class Nicaraguans assimilate cultural imports such as baseball. The irony that victim and executioner share the same dream accentuates the tragedy that they are on different sides.

The most moving and surprising of the stories in *Nuevos Cuentos* is the concluding piece, "The Siege." Septimio and Avelino are middle-aged homosexuals who live together in a small town. Their house is subjected to constant assault by a gang of adolescents who break the windows and climb on the roof. This brutality is encouraged by the machista attitudes of the authorities: even though the dictatorship is not mentioned, its patriarchal structure is projected onto daily life. The town's National Guard captain warns Septimio that "dicen que ustedes viven juntos, que no salen de la quinta, cosas que no son de hombres. Yo solo les advierto. Indecencia no permito yo en este pueblo" (*NC*, 78; "word has it that you two have set up house together, that you never leave the place, that you don't behave like men. I'm only here to warn you. I won't have any indecency in this town" [*STO*, 32]). It is not homosexuality that authorizes the young men to harass and brutalize Septimio and Avelino, but the fact that the couple "don't behave like men" and hence propagate "indecency." As Roger Lancaster points out with reference to this story, "by definition, the men harassing them are behaving like men." He goes on to argue that "violence, force and coercion are distributed differently, elaborated variously, in different power systems" (Lancaster 1992: 247). Hence Septimio and Avelino, though terrorized, are not "gay-bashed" as might occur in an English-speaking society. Their crime is not the arousal of "homosexual panic" (ibid.: 248) in other men, but rather their failure to conform to the predominant definition of masculinity, which categorizes a man as one who commits physical penetration. Lancaster argues that both Septimio and Avelino are what Nicaraguans refer to as "cochones": men who adopt "the passive role in anal intercourse" (ibid.: 238). Their identification with the female is symbolized by their having begun to live together after the deaths of their respective mothers.

In contrast to the proto-macho Somoza, who presides over society at large, an enormous angel, which is described as "era del tamaño de un hombre" (*NC*, 76; "a life-sized plaster figure" [*STO*, 30]), reigns over the second-floor room where Septimio and Avelino share a bed. The arrival by train of this angel, which Avelino inherited from his mother, consecrates the men's decision to live together. The fact that she is the same size as a man suggests that the angel has displaced patriarchal authority within the home. As the emanation of the maternal, female spirit, the angel establishes in the house a realm that is not permeated by patriarchy. This, in symbolic terms, is what provokes the attacks of the town's young men. As befits a societal force, these attackers are neither seen nor named. In the final scene, Avelino reveals to Septimio that the young men "me llevaron al monte, me arrastraron" (*NC*, 81; "took me off into the bushes" [*STO*, 35)]. Responding to his definition, within the terms of their society, as a representative of the female, the members of the gang have treated him as they treat women, by raping him.

The subtlety, economy, and emotional force with which this story of fewer than ten pages is developed marks it as one of Ramírez's major achievements in the short form. The fact that in 1968 a Nicaraguan writer in his mid-twenties should have written a story that shows this degree of sympathy for homosexual male characters remains striking.

Ramírez's first novel, *Tiempo de fulgor* (A Season of Light), written in San José, Costa Rica, in 1967 and 1968 and published by Editorial Universitaria in Guatemala City in 1970, presents both a mythologized history of León and a very discreet commentary on Ramírez's own experiences as a student in the city. The late-nineteenth-century setting sidesteps the Somozas, whose rule channels the themes of Ramírez's early short stories; instead, the tradition of Central American Liberalism in which Ramírez was raised comes to the fore. At the same time, the book showcases a battle of style and manner: the short stories' mordant tone proving unsustainable at novel length, the voices of Juan Rulfo and Gabriel García Márquez, the two most prominent Modernists[9] to dramatize rural Spanish American subject matter, dominate Ramírez's prose.

When read in light of Ramírez's subsequent career, the most striking feature of *Tiempo de fulgor* is the absence of a clearly defined vision of the Nicaragua, or of national history. It is as though, having gone into exile, Ramírez had conceded the country to the Somozas. The novel's intense focus on the city of León obscures, rather than illuminates, the contours of the

Nicaraguan nation. Vilas's observation that in the 1960s members of the *Ventana* group were "lacking any explicit political identity beyond a shared dislike for Somoza and Somocismo" (Vilas 1992: 321) dovetails with Ramírez's comment that during this time he saw the Sandinistas as alien to the life of the country. Lacking an alternative program, Ramírez falls back on the creed with which he was raised, moving the novel's setting backwards in time to the boom years of Central American Liberalism when presidents such as Zelaya in Nicaragua were modernizing their nations and men such as Ramírez's grandfather, Teófilo Mercado, were lifted up by Liberalism's drive to free the individual from religious and social strictures. Echoing Ramírez's own description of his outlook at this time, *Tiempo de fulgor* is "muy centroamericano" ("very Central American").

The novel opens with an extravagant description of the pealing of church bells over the rooftops of León – "infinito golpe de piedra en Catedral y son sonámbulo y lejano en Laborío, floración tintineante de la Merced, golpe de cristal en San Juan" (*TF*, 1; "an endless striking on stone in the Cathedral and a distant, sleepwalking sound in Laborío, the tinkling flowering of the Merced, a crystalline striking in San Juan") – that is an obvious homage to, and parody of, the famous onomatopoeic description of ringing church bells that opens *El señor presidente* (1946; *The President*) by the Guatemalan novelist Miguel Ángel Asturias, who was awarded the Nobel Prize for Literature during the time that Ramírez was writing *Tiempo de fulgor* (*señor presidente*, 115; *The President*, 7). The opening allusion to Asturias establishes the novel as an emanation of a Central American, rather than of a particular national, tradition. The Nicaraguan nation having been despoiled by the Somoza dictatorship, Ramírez wraps the setting of his first novel in a region and an ideology.

In the novel, Ramírez pits an idealized, arguably renewed form of the Liberals' belief system against that of their nineteenth century rivals, the Conservatives. Andrés Rosales, the sickly, introverted young man from the countryside who comes to León to register for medical school, encounters great, but corrupt, families. Though thumbnail summaries of this novel tend to describe it as being about Andrés's apprenticeship, in fact this "protagonist" plays a minor role. His arrival in the city, his memories of an adolescence marked by illness, and his initial encounters with the doctors and hospital in León where he is to receive his medical training are evoked with clarity. The novel opens, though, with a murder committed in a brothel by Don Glauco María, the dissipated figure who symbolizes the decadence of León's great families. Andrés appears only in the second chapter; once the narrator becomes immersed in the family histories of the competing

Sepúlveda and Contreras clans, the young man virtually disappears until the eleventh of the twelve chapters – whereupon he disappears definitively, drowning in the Pacific Ocean.

The contrast between the two great families who incarnate the differences between Liberalism and Conservatism dominate the text. The novel's conclusion echoes the incest that closes García Márquez's *Cien años de soledad* (1967; *One Hundred Years of Solitude*), which, Ramírez reports, "caí en mis manos ya avanzada la escritura" (Cherem 2004b: 98; "fell into my hands when I was already at an advanced point in the writing") and which later he would come to see as an extremely dangerous literary influence, a "veneno" ("poison"; ibid.). In *Tiempo de fulgor* incestuousness carries a particular ideological charge in the debate between Liberalism and Conservatism. It is not a coincidence that the family that epitomizes the latter ideology has the surname Contreras, which enters Nicaraguan history with the tyrannical Rodrigo de Contreras, who ruled the country as governor from 1534 to 1544.

The tone of the novel is earnest and intense, its narrative voice imitating those of the novels of the Spanish American Boom that had been published earlier in the decade by writers such as José Donoso and Mario Vargas Llosa. The only points at which the ironic voice of the short stories recurs is in the descriptions of the pretensions and ultra-piety of the Contreras clan. They claim to be direct descendants of a cousin of the Virgin Mary; they initiate proceedings before the royal courts in Spain "para que su nobleza de sangre fuera reconocida" (*TF*, 73; "so that the nobility of their blood might be recognized"). This obsession with "purity" leads them into endogenous marriages: "Y Bienvenido casó con Salvadora Contreras su sobrina a la que dejó cinco hijos mongólicos y su corazón en un vaso de alcohol, después que lo fusilaron detrás de la iglesia del Laborío, acto para el que mandó a pedir su taburete de cuero y murió sentado" (*TF*, 74; "And Bienvenido married Salvadora Contreras, his niece, to whom he left five children with Down's Syndrome and his heart in a glass of alcohol after he was executed by firing squad behind the Laborío church, an act for which he requested his leather stool and died sitting up").

Such extravagant details, displaying stubborn but obtuse male pride, and related in long, chronicle-like sentences, make for virtual copies of the prose of García Márquez. Yet where the Colombian revels in hyper-masculinity, and dramatizes incest as a lurking fear in a village where everyone is distantly related, Ramírez mocks machismo and presents the Contreras clan's incest as a failure of Conservative ideology. The fall of the dynasty is sealed by Juan Félix Contreras, who returns to León from ten years working in

Germany to find that the great family has dispersed. They no longer all live in the same neighbourhood and no longer dominate business and church activities. Rather than learning the lessons of diversity from his experience abroad, Juan Félix steps back into the archaic role of the provincial patriarch. He visits the surviving Contreras families, interrogates them as to how they are related, and constructs a family tree in order to identify the perfect wife of "pure" Contreras blood. The only qualified candidate – both a Contreras and a virgin – turns out to be Aura Estela Contreras, who has been reduced to working as a municipal clerk. Proclaiming that he will restore the family grandeur, Juan Félix holds a pompous wedding, which the rest of León ignores, and announces that he and his wife will live in chastity for five years while he builds up the family fortune. Once this period has elapsed, and after asking his wife's permission to perform the sexual act, he sets about engendering a son, whom he plans to name Enmanuel. When Aura Estela hemorrhages while giving birth, "Juan Félix no titubeó en responder al preguntársele que a quién salvaba, si a su esposa o a su hijo, que a su hijo, pues era como la iglesia mandaba y entonces con un fórceps arrancaron de la entraña agónica a una niña" (81; "Juan Félix did not hesitate to respond when asked whom they should save, whether his wife or his son, of course his son since it was what the Church decreed, and then with a forceps they pulled from the dying woman's womb a little girl"). The inevitable revelation, held off until the final word of a sentence that runs for more than half a paragraph, lampoons Juan Félix's patriarchal assumptions. His daughter, Aurora Regina, whose name suggests that she will be the queen of a new dawn, marries the violent, dissolute Don Glauco María, descended from the Mendiolas, a family related to the Contreras clan "por la rama de la Virgen María" (75; "by the branch of the Virgin Mary"). Their only child, José Rosendo, drowns in the Pacific (a fate that Andrés replicates), putting an end to the dynasty.

The incest theme, the imitations of García Márquez's phrasing, and the criticisms of Conservative social exclusivity and extreme Catholic religiosity are traits that might be expected in a first novel written in the late 1960s by a young writer from a Liberal Nicaraguan family. The most unexpected characteristic of *Tiempo de fulgor* is its corrosive satire of Latin American patriarchy. The origins of this aspect of Ramírez's vision are difficult to trace. His mother was a powerful force in his upbringing, but the same could be said of García Márquez and Mario Vargas Llosa, the two most potent influences on Spanish American writers of Ramírez's generation; and these two writers, in spite of their radical stances on matters of literary style and politics, upheld traditional Spanish American gender assumptions.

As Diana Sorensen argues, both the fiction and the public and private relations of the novelists of the Boom "were organized around the dominant fictions of masculinity and, therefore, of the patriarchal order" (Sorensen 2007: 149). Ramírez takes the opposite approach, presenting active, entrepreneurial womanhood as a trait of Liberalism. (The historical record does not support this characterization.) In part, this tendency in the novel may be read as a response to the Somozas' merging of Liberalism with extreme patriarchal behaviour. To refute the Somozas, one must refute patriarchy. A strong-but-traditional female figure, such as Úrsula Buendía in *One Hundred Years of Solitude*, who exercises her matriarchal authority from within the confines of immemorial family structures, would not suffice to discredit the Somocista ethos, or renew Liberalism in a form that might enable it to become an alternative (in spite of the contradiction that, with the Somozas, the Liberal Party was in power). Assumptions such as these appear to underlie Ramírez's creation of the Liberal Sepúlveda family, who not only refute the Conservative habit of imtermarriage but are defined by ambitious women of lower-class origins.

Simultaneously epitomizing and ridiculing the dualism of Spanish American "virgin or whore" definitions of femininity, the Sepúlvedas are descended not from the Virgin Mary but from a sixteenth-century prostitute. In contrast to the Contreras family, the Sepúlvedas are exogamous in their reproductive choices and matrilinear; their descent is charted "por línea directa y natural de mujeres y se perdía como una hebra íngrima en la maraña de varones que las poseyeron" (*TF*, 35; "by direct, illegitimate female descent and was lost like a solitary thread in the web of men who had possessed them"). They have their children with men of all social classes, from pirates to priests; though race is not mentioned, the implication is that the Sepúlvedas are mestizos while the Contreras family claims to be white. As Henry Cohen points out, the contrast that Ramírez establishes between outward-looking women and inward-gazing men coincides with one aspect of García Márquez's vision: "The attribution of diversity to females and closedness and sameness to the male Buendías suggests the matrilineal exogamy vs. patriarchal endogamy opposition in Ramírez's book, where such a split has class historical implications" (Cohen 1991: 49). In García Márquez's novel, male desire feeds the urge to break the incest taboo, which the Buendía women try, not always successfully, to uphold. In *Tiempo de fulgor*, exogamy nurtures individual vigour and social progress.

The Sepúlveda genealogy contains more gaps and omissions than does that of the Contrerases, as some of its members "se perdieron por el mundo rodando fortuna" (*TF*, 36; "were lost in the world seeking their fortunes"). Their adventurous openness engenders not merely more varied descendants but also financial prosperity. When Andrés Rosales enters the hospital where he is to undertake his medical training, he learns that it was built with funds donated by Doña Adoración Villalta, a matrilinear descendant of the Sepúlvedas: "una gran dama, con un pecado secreto que expió con diezmos y limosnas" (35; "a great lady, with a secret sin for which she atoned with tithes and alms"). The depiction of the Sepúlvedas' accumulation of wealth is uncritical, reflecting the novel's Liberal, Protestant-influenced vision of self-improvement that leads to social progress through charitable works. This stands in contrast to the Contrerases, who may donate to their church but do not build institutions that benefit the community, and who, in an implicit reference to the Somozas, impoverish the public sphere as they enrich themselves. In this way, even the more pernicious positivist strand that emerged in Spanish American Liberalism in the latter years of the nineteenth century (Williamson 1992: 298–300) is presented as laudable. Cohen is correct to contend that "the Sepúlveda women are also associated with social Darwinism" (Cohen 1991: 46).

By the time of Andrés's arrival in León, the Sepúlvedas are also in decline, having made the fatal mistake of intermarrying with the Contrerases' cousins, the Mendiolas. Don Glauco María, the two lineages' terminal patriarch, is the Sepúlvedas' "primer varón después de siglos de mujeres" (*TF*, 37; "first man after generations of women"). As soon as the Sepúlveda line becomes male, it lapses into the sin of incest. Don Glauco María marries Rosendo Mendiola, who is not only a distant relative but, fatally, a descendant of the cousins of the Virgin Mary. Glauco María bears a strong resemblance to Miguel Páramo, the patriarch's son and end of the family line in Juan Rulfo's *Pedro Páramo* (1955), the strongest literary influence on Ramírez at the time he started writing *Tiempo de fulgor*. "La influencia de Rulfo es palpable en este libro primerizo," Ramírez concedes (Cherem 2004b: 98; "Rulfo's influence is palpable in this apprentice book"). Like Miguel Páramo, Glauco María is a womanizer and a murderer. And like Miguel (Rulfo 1955: 87–93), Glauco "cayó sin sentido de su caballo" (*TF*, 96; "fell senseless from his horse"), though unlike Rulfo's character he does not die from his fall. His name unites that of the Greek god Glaucus, who jumps into the sea and is transformed into an aquatic deity (a fate that foreshadows the drowning deaths of his son José Rosendo and of Andrés Rosales) with the name of the Virgin. The persistent portrayal of the inheritance of the Virgin Mary as lethal suggests that for Ramírez, at least at this early stage of his career, Liberalism is contiguous with his maternal grandfather's Protestant disdain of Catholic sloth. Catholicism and decadence slide close to being synonyms.

The stylistic debt to Rulfo is evident in the interior monologues that are interspersed with the novel's third-person narration. The monologues, which are attributed to a variety of characters, and are often obtrusive or obscure, are this first novel's least successful stylistic feature. Paradoxically, they are most poetic when they are most imitative of Rulfo. The opening scene in the brothel includes the interior monologues of a young girl from the countryside who has been brought to León and seduced into prostitution. These monologues contain the first mention of the seaside house of the Contreras family, where José Rosendo will drown. The parallel drowning death of Andrés may appear arbitrary, yet, as clotted and derivative as *Tiempo de fulgor* may be, it is worked out with the same fiendish intelligence that would structure Ramírez's later novels. Andrés may be a cipher, but he is a significant cipher. When Glauco María returns to León after José Rosendo's death, he sends a letter saying that "quisiera conocer ... al amigo que vive con ustedes en la casa y que según me dicen se parece a mi Rosendo fallecido" (*TF*, 96; "I would like to meet the friend who lives with you in the house and according to what they tell me, looks like my late Rosendo"). The resemblance between Andrés and José Rosendo insinuates that Andrés, whose parentage is obscure, may be an illegitimate child of Glauco María who was raised in the countryside. In this way, Andrés turns out to be the final descendant of the collapsing dynasties of León. The affair that Andrés appears to be having with Aurora, his landlady, while Glauco María is away in Honduras, has incestuous overtones in Andrés's extreme attachment to his mother, which, as Cohen suggests (Cohen 1991: 52), he transfers to Aurora; yet the uncertainty over his paternity also leaves open the possibility that this final disastrous relationship, like the relationship between Aureliano Babilonia and Amaranta Úrsula that closes *One Hundred Years of Solitude*, is incestuous.

The borrowings from Rulfo and García Márquez (and probably also from Carlos Fuentes's *Aura* [1962] and *Cambio de piel* [1967; *A Change of Skin*], in interior monologues narrated in the second person singular), are inflated with a self-conscious extravagance. By contrast, the writing becomes rapt, clear, and painfully revealing in the scene where Andrés describes the terror with which he performs his assigned vivisections in the morgue:

> yo espero que el profesor dé a mis espaldas la señal de que ha terminado el juego, de que no serán los míos un día esos brazos que yo mutilo, esos

> huesos que asierro, los ojos que me miran desorbitados no serán mis ojos mirando desde la losa, porque yo no quiero morir sino quedarme para siempre en su regazo, madre y que mi cabeza descanse al suave contacto de sus piernas y sentir cómo pasa sus manos en mi pelo, porque esas manos largas me protegen de la morgue y de la muerte. (*TF*, 100; I wait for the professor to give the signal behind my back that the game is over, that it won't one day be my arms that I mutilate, my bones that I saw through, my eyes that look at me wide open from the slab, because I do not want to die, but rather to remain forever on your lap, Mother, and may my head rest on the soft touch of your lap and may I feel how you run your hands through my hair, because those long hands protect me from the morgue and death.)

Here the long sentences, descended from the prose of William Faulkner, via García Márquez, communicate an intimate personal vision. Whether this perception is fuelled by a meditation on the death of Fernando Gordillo, which occurred while Ramírez was writing the novel, or a recollection of his visit to the morgue after the 23 July 1959 massacre, it conveys human feeling and an original way of seeing to a degree not present elsewhere in the novel. An integral part of the book's vision is Andrés's impotence before the weight of history: his drowning coincides with the death of the Contreras matriarch, Casilda, who expires "con el rosario entre los dedos" (*TF*, 118; "with her rosary between her fingers"). Don Glauco María's brutality is the novel's only hint of the future advent of the Somozas; yet the commentary on the paralysis bequeathed to younger generations by the collapse of Central American Liberalism is evident. In contrast to constructions of the nation as a betrayed mother, who nevertheless bears responsibility for her own betrayal, found in Mexican depictions of the figure of La Malinche,[10] Ramírez portrays isthmian Liberalism as an ample lap that promises solace from the ravages of Conservative patriarchy.

RESPONSES TO DICTATORSHIP: MARIANO FIALLOS, CHARLES ATLAS, AND THE TORTURE STATE

In his next book, a biography of his mentor, Mariano Fiallos Gil, Ramírez attempts to move beyond the exile's paralysis by tracing the constructive steps that may be taken, even under a dictatorship, to implant responsive, independent civil-society institutions and begin the work of building a different ethos and social structure. *Biografía Mariano Fiallos* (1972) sketches the full trajectory of the UNAN rector's life, yet more than half of this three-hundred-page book is devoted to Fiallos's struggle, between 1957 and 1964, to secure and institutionalize the university's administrative independence from the regime. The university becomes a microcosmic counter-nation where alternative values are incubated for future implementation in civil society. As Fiallos himself argued in a speech given in Managua in July 1961: "Siempre las universidades andan del brazo de los hombres que buscan la libertad" (Fiallos Gil, 14; "Universities always walk arm-in-arm with men who seek freedom").

The biography portrays a Fiallos who, born in León in 1907, is carried by his abilities into government service in Managua as deputy minister of education under Anastasio Somoza García. As a result of this appointment, Fiallos becomes tainted by controversial actions, including a dubious diplomatic mission to Guatemala to try to persuade the democratically elected president (and educator) Juan José Arévalo to formally recognize the Somoza government in spite of the electoral fraud that had allowed the Nicaraguan dictator to cling to power. Fiallos's government career ends badly, with exile in the United States, where he remains marginalized by his limited English and struggles with poor health. After his return home, he makes arduous and ultimately successful attempts to earn a living in agriculture. By his late forties he has become a rural recluse who contributes occasional liberal-minded opinion pieces to newspapers. The assassination of Somoza García, leading to the presidency of the more cerebral Luis Somoza Debayle, opens the door to Fiallos's resumption of a public career and, crucially, to his return to the city of León, portrayed as a Liberal (and more importantly, a liberal) island in the late 1950s sea of Central American dictatorial rule. Ramírez stresses the Central American context, and the malevolent influence of US President Dwight Eisenhower "quien patrocinó a lo largo de sus dos períodos de gobierno, un franco apoyo a las dictaduras militares" (*BMF*, 105; "who, throughout his two terms of government, openly sponsored support for military dictatorships"). Fiallos's identity as a Liberal made him an acceptable choice for the post of rector of UNAN.

The detailed narration of the Autonomy Generation, in which Fiallos retains the support of both the rebellious students and the brutal Somozas, even in the wake of catastrophic events such as the July 1959 massacre, becomes a way of distinguishing an authentic liberalism – which depends on classical liberal principles – from the word's debased use in the title of the party of the dictatorship. The key divergence between these two liberalisms lies in the emphasis placed by humanistic thought on the concept of freedom. For Fiallos, many of Nicaraguan society's weaknesses, particularly in the areas of culture and the sciences, could be overcome if young people undergoing higher education were permitted freedom of thought. As he wrote in *La Prensa* in the midst of the battle over UNAN's autonomy: "La Universidad no se halla bajo régimen militar y por tanto a nadie, ni a catedráticos ni a estudiantes se les prohibe deliberar. Todo lo contrario, se les estimula a deliberar, a pensar, a criticar, a analizar, porque todo se halla en función del pensamiento y del ejercicio de los valores espirituales" (*BMF*, 211; "The university is not under military rule and therefore no one, neither professors nor students, is forbidden to discuss. On the contrary, they are encouraged to discuss, think, criticize, analyze, because everything is based on thought and the exercise of spiritual values").

The country may be under military rule, but the university, Fiallos asserts, is exempt from this yoke. It is telling that he wrote these words in response to government criticisms of the students' protests at revelations that the Somozas had permitted the CIA to use Nicaraguan territory to train Cuban exiles and mercenaries for the failed Bay of Pigs invasion. The point that would eventually lead Fiallos's protégés in the Autonomy Generation to abandon his liberal precepts – "Malversamos sus enseñanzas, aceptando un presupuesto ideológico dogmático" (Cherem 2004b: 88; "We misused his teachings, accepting a dogmatic ideological proposal"), Ramírez would later regret – was the divergence over US imperialism. By 1963, "por primera vez se estaban planteando antagonismos entre la dirigencia estudiantil oficial y el Rector" (*BMF*, 251; "for the first time antagonism was arising between the official student leadership and the Rector"). Fiallos belonged to a generation of Central American Liberals who regarded the United States as an exemplary democracy. In spite of Franklin D. Roosevelt's reviled "Good Neighbour Policy," which provided unblinking support for the bloodiest dictators of the 1930s, the New Deal impressed Central American Liberals; both the dictators and their opponents applauded the naming of major boulevards in Managua and Guatemala City after FDR. Fiallos tended to see US misdeeds in Central America as oversights, inconsistencies in a democratic culture that, if pointed out, would be corrected. He attributed the origins of Central American Liberalism to US influence, emphasizing that the first constitution of the United Provinces of Central America in 1824 had imitated the constitution of the United States. The freedom that Fiallos saw as being promised by US-influenced liberalism included not only freedom of thought and free enterprise but also the "libertad de las clases desheredadas de nuestra sociedad" (Fiallos Gil 1961: 27; "freedom for the disinherited classes of our society"). Like his students, Fiallos understood that US interventions in Central America had consolidated regimes that made the poor become more impoverished and more numerous; unlike his students, he believed that "me basta invocar a los grandes constructores de la nación norteamericana y pedirle a sus paisanos políticos de hoy que honren la memoria de los próceres y que se esfuercen por ser inteligentes" (ibid.; "it is enough for me to invoke the great builders of the US nation and ask of their fellow politicians today that they honour the memory of the heroes and endeavour to be intelligent"). By the early 1960s, requesting that US policies in Central America "be intelligent" was, in all likelihood, asking too much. In the Cold War environment, the violent implementation of ideology, typified by actions such as the overthrow of the democratic government of Guatemala in 1954 and the Bay of Pigs invasion in 1961, bludgeoned local liberal idealism. Revolutionary nationalisms, influenced by the example of Cuba, took liberalism's place.

In this context, Ramírez's attempt to rehabilitate Liberalism, in a novel published as late as 1970, underlines the anomaly of the Nicaraguan situation. The opposition between two wings of the Spanish American middle and upper classes, the devout, agrarian, Spanish-influenced Conservatives and the anti-clerical, urban, French-influenced Liberals, who, as the nineteenth century advanced, shared a growing number of economic interests and social outlooks, had broken down in most of Spanish America by the early twentieth century. In South America, only geographically fragmented Colombia retained these archaic names for the two largest political parties (as it does to this day) (Hylton 2006: 15–30). The ominous events of the Spanish-American War of 1898, which signalled the decisive entry of the United States into Spanish America and the Caribbean as a hegemonic power, combined with the Mexican Revolution of 1910–20, which forged a distinctive Spanish American nationalist discourse based on radical reformist policies and the recognition of indigenous peoples and rural mestizo communities as the nation's cultural foundations, had skewed the terms of political debate. Writing of the 1920s, Edwin Williamson remarks on the "plethora of ideologies that competed to occupy the vacuum left by the strange death of Latin American liberalism" (Williamson 1992: 328). Anti-Americanism became a potent force among the bourgeoisie, who feared that US intervention would vitiate their control of local institutions and natural resources; populist movements channelled the demands of the newly politicized rural and working-class masses; church-going Conservatives, adopting a "modernizationist" perspective, became the new apostles of the free market, even as both former Liberals and former Conservatives veered towards an advocacy of "corporatist" structures in which capitalist activity was directed by an authoritarian state.

Yet the confidence bred in elites in the larger countries of South America during the 1930s, when an economically wounded United States withdrew from the region, giving national authorities free rein to run their own economies, exploit natural resources, and develop internal markets, created a mood in which, during the 1940s, "the ideals of the nineteenth-century liberals revived ... The times favored the democratic concepts professed by the middle class. Governments out of step with them toppled" (Burns and Charlip 2002: 241). These were the years of the reformist Popular Front governments in Chile, of the best years of the Mexican Partido Revolucionario Institucional (PRI; Party of Revolutionary Institutions), under presidents Lázaro Cárdenas and Miguel Alemán, and of liberal presidents such as José Bustamante in Peru. Above all, from the Nicaraguan perspective, they were the years in which Guatemala, Central America's most populous and traditionally its most influential nation, replaced the long dictatorship of Jorge Ubico with a liberal government made up of schoolteachers and shopkeepers (Schlesinger and Kinzer 1982: 25–35). This event in particular threw into relief the chasm between the Liberal banner flown by the Nicaraguan dictatorship and the reality of liberal policies in the rest of Spanish America. Elsewhere, as Burns and Charlip recount, liberalism dissolved dictatorships; in Nicaragua the dictatorship was Liberal.

By the early 1970s, the young Liberal intellectuals from the *Ventana* group had been in a state of paralysis for more than ten years. As the critical references to US President Eisenhower in *Biografía Mariano Fiallos* make clear, younger Liberals were not blind to the role of the United States in establishing and sustaining Nicaragua's long dictatorship; but to systematize criticisms of US intervention into a theory of nationalist resistance to imperialism would be to join the tiny, ideologically dogmatic guerrilla bands of Tomás Borge and Henry Ruíz, secluded in the northern mountains from the bulk of the population, who lived in the cities of the Pacific Coast. *Tiempo de fulgor* is both a lament for the wane of Liberalism and a vindication of the creed's values; *Biografía Mariano Fiallos*, paradoxically, since it deals with events that were barely a decade old, reads even more like a homage to the past. Like the Granada Conservatives whom they opposed, León Liberals were relegated by the Somoza dictatorship to a posture of hurtful, wronged nostalgia for their former glory. Unlike the generation of Mariano Fiallos, who had entered government in the 1940s assuming a congruency between official Liberalism and liberal ideas, the *Ventana* generation knew that they could neither collaborate with the Somoza regime nor change it from within. When Ramírez confronted the present – which, as a member of *Ventana*, hence an opponent of the aesthetic escapism of the Betrayed Generation, he could not avoid doing – his only recourse was irony. Living in Costa Rica, where a brief civil war in the 1940s had led to the institutionalization of one of the world's most peaceful democracies, sharpened this ironic stance with regard to Nicaragua.

Ramírez was already honing his vision of the neutered, culturally colonized Nicaraguan bourgeoisie to a cutting edge in two short stories written after *Tiempo de fulgor*, "Charles Atlas también muere" ("Charles Atlas Also Dies") and "A Jackie, con nuestro corazón" ("To Jackie with All Our Heart"), written in 1970 and 1971 respectively. Both of these stories are narrated in the first person by men who have betrayed the cultural authenticity of Nicaraguan society. The former is probably Ramírez's best-known, most widely reprinted short story: it has appeared in many anthologies in numerous languages; in 1974 a theatrical adaptation was staged in Mexico. The narrator's obsession with Charles Atlas, a figure of US popular culture who is familiar in many countries, resonates well beyond Nicaragua. As Ramírez himself recalls: "Charles Atlas era un mito en América Latina" (Cherem 2004b: 100; "Charles Atlas was a myth in Latin America"). As an adolescent in Masatepe, Ramírez read the ads featuring the story of a ninety-seven-pound weakling having sand kicked in his face and learning to bulk up and confront the bullies; he longed to have thirty dollars – "yo no podía ni soñar con esa cantidad de dinero" (ibid.; "I couldn't even dream of that kind of money") – to send away for the Charles Atlas course.

The story's unnamed narrator carries a reverence for US popular culture to the point of open betrayal of his neighbours. A telegraph operator in the Segovias during the US occupation, small of stature, like Sandino, he reaps the material rewards offered by US popular culture – cigars, girlie magazines, English lessons, and finally the Charles Atlas course – by acting as an informer. His mentor, the US Marine Captain Hatfield, "me presentó una lista de los vecinos de San Fernando, en la que marqué a todos los que me parecían sospechosos ...; al día siguiente los llevaron presos" (*CATM*, 12; "gave me a list of the inhabitants of San Fernando and asked me to mark all those I thought might be involved ... The next day they were all marched off" [*STO*, 2]).

The first paragraph describes the narrator's departure for New York on a cultural exchange that will see him visit US sports clubs and the Charles Atlas corporation, and concludes with the information that, three days after his departure, Captain Hatfield was killed "en un asalto de los sandinistas a Puerto Cabezas" (*CATM*, 11; "in a Sandinista attack on Puerto Cabezas" [*STO*, 1]). The Charles Atlas course, and his English lessons, convert the narrator into "un hombre nuevo" (*CATM*, 14; "a new man" [*STO*, 4]), a phrase that is used ironically to signal the opposite of Che Guevara's ideal of the selfless revolutionary. The narrator is the self-centred, colonized, pumped-up product of US popular culture, who, having betrayed his neighbours, has his photograph taken with the diplomatic and military representatives of the US occupation. As Brad Perri argues, the story "investigates the Nicaraguan body as the site of US cultural colonization. The body constitutes the primary way in which the Nicaraguan performs his identity" (Perri 1999: 36). The narrator's body is "a US export" (ibid.: 37), developed under the tutelage of Captain Hatfield; having been stripped of his culture, he is nothing more than a body. When, at the prodding of his girlfriend, the narrator recognizes himself in a statue of the Greek god Atlas, this mythological identification only tightens his connection with US popular culture, which purports to embody the cumulative heritage of Western civilization.

The narrator's undoing lies in his determination to be accepted at the core of this civilization. To make real the myths he has allowed to mould his body, he must meet Charles Atlas. His host in New York, Mr William Rideout, Jr of the Charles Atlas Corporation, tries to deter him by insisting that "Charles Atlas no existe ... Inventamos este producto en el siglo pasado y Charles Atlas es una marca de fábrica como cualquier otra ... como el rostro afeitado de las cuchillas Gilette" (*CATM*, 21; "Charles Atlas doesn't exist ... We invented our product in the last century, and Charles Atlas is a trademark like any other, like ... the clean-shaven face on Gillette razorblades" [*STO*, 9]). The narrator overcomes this setback by demonstrating that he has mastered colonial mimicry. Exploiting the colonizer's language to his advantage, he threatens to report to "Washington" that he has not been allowed the promised meeting with Charles Atlas: "Washington es una palabra mágica, me aleccionaba el Capitán Hatfield USMC; úsala en un apuro, y si acaso no te sirve, echa mano de la otra que sí es infalible: Departamento de Estado" (*CATM*, 22; "Washington is a magic word, Captain Hatfield USMC had taught me. Use it when you're in a tight spot, and if by any chance that doesn't work, hit them with the other, the State Department: that's a knockout" [*STO*, 10]).

The narrator must resort to the second, more powerful word before he is granted his interview with Charles Atlas; and even this is conceded only on the condition that after the interview he leave the country immediately and discuss his experiences with no one. Expecting to encounter a muscle-bound figure in trunks, he discovers the decrepit body of a 100-year-old man, smelling of medicine, hidden under bedcovers, and afflicted with cancer of the jaw, who rambles in a semi-coherent fashion and finally dies in front of him.

This revelation of the rotting corruption at the heart of US imperial mythology shatters the protagonist's certainties: "en ese momento deseé con toda mi alma no haber insistido" (*CATM*, 27; "I wished with all my heart I hadn't started this" [*STO*, 14]). During the 1980s, the depiction of the ancient, incipiently senile Atlas was often read as a prefiguration of Ronald Reagan. As Pavón points out, the shock the narrator has experienced leaves him only two options: "o aceptar que la realidad es la realidad, o negarla y, al mismo tiempo, negarse a sí mismo" (Pavón 1977: 85; "either accept that reality is reality, or deny it and, at the same time, deny himself"). He chooses the latter course, maintaining his colonized stance and continuing to negate Nicaraguan identity.

The most bracing revelation the narrator must face, however, is the discovery that Charles Atlas, too, is a colonized body: a foreigner who has discarded his culture in order to incarnate the American Dream. Like the narrator, Atlas has had the experience of having his girlfriend point out his resemblance to statues of the Greek god. Having repudiated his culture to the point of giving up his name, he has proceeded farther along the course on which the narrator has embarked: "nací en Calabria en 1827 y mi nombre era Angelino Siciliano ... un nombre como el mío no es muy popular aquí, hay mucho prejuicio. ¿Por qué no habré de llamarme Atlas? Y también cambié el Angelino por Charles. Después vino la gloria" (*CATM*, 29; "I was born in Calabria in 1827. My real name is Angelo Siciliano ... you're not going to get ahead with a name like yours, people here are too prejudiced. Why not call yourself Atlas? And I also changed Angelino for Charles. Then came my days of glory" [*STO*, 16]). Yet this example is not a happy one. On his deathbed, Charles Atlas feels nostalgia for the culture he has relinquished. Like any good Italian boy, he remembers his mama. His final words are: "Recuerdo Calabria ... Calabria y mi madre con el rostro enrojecido por las llamas del horno, cantando ... Una canción ..." (*CATM*, 30; "I remember Calabria ... Calabria, and my mother singing, her face ruddy from the flames of the oven ... A song ..." [*STO*, 16]). As Charles Atlas expires in the attempt to recover his culture by remembering his mother's Calabrian songs, the narrator must confront his own disorientation: "Yo había perdido la noción de todas las cosas" (*CATM*, 30; "I had lost all notion of what was going on" (*STO*, 16)). He returns to Nicaragua. Maintaining his body in superb condition, he boasts that even in old age he could have children, "Si quisiera" (*CATM*, 31; "If I wanted to" [*STO*, 17]). Physically potent yet culturally barren, he has nothing to transmit to subsequent generations; his very un-Central American lack of desire for children attests to the way in which he has been neutered by cultural alienation.

The narrator of "Charles Atlas Also Dies" is a man of modest social background. If he represents the way that cultural colonization is experienced by the masses, the other story that Ramírez wrote during this period, "To Jackie with All Our Heart," is representative of the cultural inauthenticity of the upper classes. The undercurrent of emotional investment that lends "Charles Atlas" its sadness appears to stem from Ramírez's own adolescent experience as a rural Nicaraguan of modest background who longed to be "un fortachón" (Cherem 2004b: 100; "a strongman"). By contrast, the narrator of "To Jackie with All Our Heart" belongs to the Managua upper classes, of which Ramírez at this time had little personal experience. The tone is more satirical and less forgiving. A member of the Virginian Country Club, the narrator identifies himself in the opening sentence as belonging to "nuestros mejores círculos y lo que se llama la sociedad nicaragüense" (*CATM*, 101; "our smartest circles. What passes for high society" [*STO*, 71]). The name of his club is the first of numerous organizations, including both social clubs and US corporations, whose English titles spatter the pages of the Spanish original.

The story revolves around the Somocista elite's gushing response to a rumour that Jacqueline Kennedy Onassis may visit Nicaragua. The cultural alienation of this group affords Ramírez material for savage social satire. The narrator speaks to his gringo diplomat friend Ralph in "uno de los dos idiomas oficiales del *Virginian* (el otro es el español)" (*CATM*, 104; "one of the two official languages used in Virginia [*sic*] [the second being Spanish]" [*STO*, 57]). Ralph, who has served in Argentina and Mexico, clearly has no particular investment in Nicaragua, a fact that the narrator does not perceive because he, too, lacks any sense of his nation's worth. The story functions on a motif of spiralling exaggeration, as the elite's plans for hosting Jacqueline Kennedy Onassis during her visit become more and more extravagant. In order to "evitarle el bochorno de la ciudad, la suciedad, el calor, la gente del pueblo que le acosaría" (*CATM*, 109; "spare her the noise and bustle of the city with its dirt and heat, and the common people who would be sure to mob her" [*STO*, 78]), the narrator suggests to the country club that they receive Ms Onassis on a yacht. The decision to abandon Nicaraguan soil for a point offshore encapsulates the story's criticism of the elite's derision of their homeland. This derision is evident, too, in their profligate use of public finances. Resolving that a yacht is not good enough for such an eminent personage, they bankrupt themselves to purchase the *Queen Elizabeth* in order to receive Ms Onassis. They imagine that with the purchase "repercutería hasta en los Estados Unidos, nos inscribirían con letras de oro en los anales del *jet-set*, ya para siempre; la revista *Time* tendría que poner nuestros nombres en su afamada sección 'People' e incluso, quién me decía que no, el mío aparecería, al morir yo algún día, en la sección 'Milestones,' del magazine" (*CATM*, 113; "We would make news in the United States itself, where our names would be etched in gilt for ever more in the annals of the jet-set; *Time* magazine would have to mention us in its celebrated 'People' section, and perhaps, when my time was up, my own name would appear among its 'Milestones'" [*STO*, 81–2]). The final word – "magazine" – appearing in English in the Spanish text, underlines the narrator's cultural alienation. He and his fellow club members, as is clear, stake their claim to relevance within a US framework. When Ms. Onassis fails to appear in Nicaragua, the narrator remains stranded off the coast in the *Queen Elizabeth*, unable to return to the mainland lest he be ridiculed for making lavish preparations in vain. This fear seals his separation from his country. The story concludes with his declaration that, unless Jackie appears, "yo por lo menos, nunca jamás regresaría" (*CATM*, 118; "I for one will never go back" [*STO*, 85]).

"To Jackie with All Our Heart" illustrates Ramírez's growing impatience with his country's governing classes in the early 1970s. His asperity altered the dominant mode of his short fiction from realism to fantasy and satire. The quest for an appropriate literary mould for his perceptions found a resonant model when he was befriended by the older Guatemalan writer Augusto Monterroso (Arias 2007: 7), who had been living in exile in Mexico City since the US coup against President Jacobo Arbenz.[11] The master of the short-short story, often with a biting conclusion, Monterroso was a strong influence on Ramírez's next book of fiction, *De Tropeles y tropelías* (1973), and would later be instrumental in persuading Joaquín Moritz to publish *Charles Atlas también muere* (*SRP*, box 37, folder 23).

Awarded a prize in a literary contest organized by a Venezuelan magazine two years prior to its publication in book form by a university press in San Salvador, *De Tropeles y tropelías* is an explicit attack on dictatorial brutality. Though neither Nicaragua nor the Somoza family is mentioned by name, it is obvious that they are the targets of this satire. Similarly, the republic where the stories take place is not identified, but, as "De las delicias de la posteridad" ("On the Delights of Posterity") makes clear, it is one of the "países de Centroamérica" (*DTT*, 15; "Central American countries"). The stories are very short, none of them longer than two pages. As in "Félis Conclóris," Ramírez employs erudite language to contain dictatorial savagery that would overwhelm the boundaries of literary art if it were narrated according to the tenets of realism. This slender book is divided into two parts; the first consists of a series of ironically restrained pseudo-essays, their titles and surface tone reminiscent of those of Francis Bacon. These essays are "on" a variety of topics relevant to life in a dictatorship, such as the stench of corpses, the pleasures of homemade bombs, and how to amuse a bored dictator. The second half of the book consists of a phony legal code for a nation under dictatorial rule; it includes 124 brief articles spread over fourteen sections devoted to topics such as private property, the sex trade, and the extraction of confessions. While the stories of the first half are reminiscent of the work of Monterroso, the second part of the book displays a sly Cortazarian sense of humour; the encyclopedic qualities of the short stories of Jorge Luis Borges are present throughout the volume.

The opening section is bracketed by two short essays on the properties of dreams. The first essay, in a Borgesian voice, alludes to sages and scholars of centuries past. Some of these scholarly references are obvious spoofs: a book on Jewish philosophy, for example, is stated as having been published in Munich in 1933, suggesting that it may be Nazi propaganda. The central proposition of the scholars cited by the narrator is that, if many people dream the same dream at the same time, it becomes reality: an idea reminiscent of the extreme idealism that Borges absorbed from the work of Bishop Berkeley and Baruch Spinoza and that he expresses in essays such as "Una nueva refutación del tiempo" (Borges 1980: 284–300; "A New Refutation of Time"). The concept also evokes one of Monterroso's most famous (and certainly his shortest) story, which in its entirety reads: "Cuando despertó, el dinosaurio todavía estaba allí" (Monterroso 1959: 73; "When he awoke, the dinosaur was still there" [Monterroso 1995: 42]). The relevance of this fantasy of dreams transmuting into reality to a political opposition hoping to rid a country of a long-standing dictatorship is obvious; yet, the narrator reports, "aunque el experimento comenzó a efectuarse hace mucho tiempo, no ha sido posible obtener ningún resultado" (*DTT*, 3; "although the experiment began to take place a long time ago, it has not been possible to obtain any results"). Maimonides gives the reason for this failure: it will work only if the dictator, too, is asleep: "Y los tiranos nunca duermen" (3; "And tyrants never sleep"). This ominous conclusion prepares the ground for the succeeding essays on the characteristics of life under a protracted despotism; it also debunks mere idealism as a viable response to sustained brutality.

The theme of dictatorship and Ramírez's borrowings from other writers are linked: the inhibitions and constraints imposed by dictatorial rule stunt a young author's efforts to find his voice by roaming freely through his national reality. The wit and polish of *De Tropeles y tropelías* cannot fail to bely a certain juvenile quality: there is a sense of a brilliant observer poking fun at offensive realities that he does not have the authority to confront or dramatize in detail. Futility and repetition become central themes in stories such as "Del proceso del león" ("On the Lion's Trial") in which, by eating a political prisoner, a lion becomes a political prisoner himself. Borges uses this technique of *mise-en-abîme*, in which characters and situations are projected into loops of infinite repetition, to make philosophical points about the unknowable nature of the universe and the impossibility of imagining time. Ramírez adapts the technique to the depiction of the dynamics of a dictatorship that feels endless. The blame for the tyranny's persistence is apportioned across the national and international spectrum. The Organization of American States (OAS) is ridiculed for insisting that the lion, rather than the dictator, be put on trial after the prisoner is devoured. Nicaraguan readers will be aware that the story alludes to a punishment refined by the Somozas, who "incarcerated prisoners, for months in some cases, in barred cages open to the weather, next to lions and panthers, in the garden of the presidential residence" (Booth 1982: 72). In Ramírez's tale, the lion is condemned to death. Unlike many political prisoners, though, he has his sentence commuted and is allowed to wander the streets. When he encounters one of the witnesses who testified against him, "lo devoró, lo cual provocó un nuevo consejo de guerra y así sucesivamente" (*DTT*, 5; "he devoured him, which caused a new council of war and so on"). This concluding sentence, promising an infinite repetition of the trial of the lion, suggests that the dictatorship, also, is unending.

In a complementary vein, the emperor's-clothes-like "Del hedor de los cadáveres" ("On the Stench of Corpses") satirizes the elite complicity that buttresses the regime. When the dictator's mother dies, His Excellency announces that she will continue to accompany him to public events. The dictator's flunkies become adept at dressing the rotting corpse for public occasions. The deceased great lady even seems to take an interest in the conversation of high-society figures such the "Nuncio Apostólico de Su Santidad" (*DTT*, 7; "The Apostolic Nuncio of His Holiness"), a jab at the Catholic hierarchy's collaboration with tyranny. The dictator's courtiers and allies, overcome by the foul odour, "tragaban el vómito por el terror de ofender al mandatario" (7; "swallowed their vomit for fear of offending the head of state"). The satire of a subservient elite's self-abasement reaches a climax when, just as the dictator's mother has been reduced to a skeleton with "el carmín sobre los huesos de los labios descarnados" (7; "the scarlet lipstick on the bones of the fleshless lips"), the dictator's wife also dies. Fortunately, the narrator notes, the nation's dignitaries are now "perfectamente acostumbrados al olor de la carroña y a los gusanos que tranquilamente se arrastraban por sus platos y subían por sus copas" (7; "perfectly accustomed to the smell of carrion and to the worms that quietly crawled on their dishes and climbed on their drinks"). This grotesque humiliation of the elite brings with it the perversion of national identity and, ultimately, the evaporation of the nation itself.

De Tropeles y tropelías builds towards a vision of annihilation; the book's overriding criticism of the dictatorship has less to do with the massacres and tortures committed by the regime than with its erosion of national autonomy to the point where the idea of nationhood is no longer credible. To use Benedict Anderson's terms, there is no longer an "imagined community" shared by a literate bourgeoisie that believes itself to have characteristics in common. When the literate classes have been suborned into ignoring the national interest and feigning a separation from the masses, the nation vanishes. This theme recurs with greater frequency as the book advances. In "Del olvido eterno" ("On Being Forgotten Forever"), the tyrant offends a great power, which orders that his tiny republic be erased from all atlases; where it once stood, "los cartógrafos imperiales pintaran nada más que el mar azul" (19; "the imperial cartographers painted nothing more than the blue sea"). As a result, the country is soon forgotten. A nation that is not present in the world, that has no cultural identification, does not exist.

The penultimate story, "De los atributos de la nación" ("On the Characteristics of the Nation"), appears to derive from a boast that is often attributed to Anastasio Somoza Debayle (though it is difficult to document): "¡Nicaragua es mi finca!" ("Nicaragua is my farm!"). This story opens with the dictator being informed that the entire national territory is now his personal property: a satiric extrapolation of the kleptomaniac tendencies of Somocismo. This event leads to a discussion of whether the space that was once defined as the nation should be referred to as a country or an hacienda, and the conclusion that "cualesquiera de los dos nombres pudiese ser usado indistintamente" (21; "either of the two names could be used interchangeably"). The final story, "De las propiedades del sueño (II)" ("On the Properties of Dreams (II)"), which appears to have been added after the 1972 Managua earthquake, portrays the dictator dreaming that "los sabios norteamericanos" (22; "United States scholars") have invented a machine that will generate earthquakes at will. He imagines the great advantages of destroying his country: how his political enemies will be crushed when the walls of their prisons collapse, how he will build an idealized country, which will be entirely his private property, out of the ruins to replace the current mediocre reality, and particularly how "la ayuda norteamericana siempre generosa" (22; "ever-generous US aid") will provide him with opportunities to enrich himself to a previously unforeseen extent by embezzling foreign assistance. Ramírez's sharpening political engagement is evident in the shift from the earlier stories, where the dictator's foreign allies were described as "una potencia amiga" (19; "a friendly power"). The United States is now mentioned by name, even though Nicaragua is not. This story signals the shift in Ramírez's public position towards the United States, indicating his adoption of an overt anti-imperialist stance.

The legal code that comprises the second half of *De Tropeles y tropelías* offers a somewhat heavier form of satire. If it is less entertaining than the short stories, it is revealing of the contours of Ramírez's emerging anti-dictatorial ideology. In a parody of legal language, the code lays out the dictatorship's paranoia concerning foreign ideologies, of which the most feared is Communism, and the foreign races that may carry this contagion and so must be banned from entering the republic in order to prevent its contamination. The focus of this satire is less any actual trait of Somocismo than residual prejudices that are current among the Nicaraguan bourgeoisie, most of which stem from late-nineteenth-century Spanish American positivism. The pseudo-scientific detail with which the prohibitions are described parodies this creed. In the farcically lengthy enumeration of banned races, one finds, for example, not simply people of African descent but "negros australes, negros boreales, negros cimarrones, negros de Jamaica o caribises" (*DTT*, 36; "Southern blacks, Northern blacks, maroon blacks, Jamaican blacks or Carib Indians"). The vicious humour of this prohibition pivots on the bourgeoisie's obliviousness to their own nation, whose vast Atlantic Coast region, home to a long-standing Afro-Caribbean population, makes a mockery of the goal of keeping out African-descended people.

The code illustrates a broadening of Ramírez's critique beyond the assertion, implicit in *Tiempo de fulgor*, that a once-vigorous Liberal tradition has become decadent. The attack, not merely on Somocismo, but on an entire bourgeois class, reflects a radicalization of his analysis. If this radicalization is not yet evident in his political stance at the time of the book's publication, it is nevertheless profound and enduring. The legal code may conclude with an itemization of the worst abuses of the Somoza regime, but it does not stop there. Section XIII is entitled "De los medios de la justa confesión" ("On the Means Used to Obtain a Fair Confession"). It presents torture techniques employed by Somocismo as legal norms, codified in a language whose notary-like fussiness both obscures and throws into relief the horrific acts that it is authorizing. Article 112 b) reads:

> Se le aplicará en el cuerpo, en orden descendiente (de cabeza a pies, con énfasis en los órganos genitales) un cabo metálico conectado a pilas electroliticas de corriente alterna, con potencial no superior a los

> 500 watts de potencia; o con cabos eléctricos de alambre desnudo conectados a los sienes, plantas de los pies y palmas de la mano del reo. (*DTT*, 43; That on the body, in descending order [from head to feet, with emphasis on the genital organs] a metallic head connected to electrolytic batteries of alternating current will be applied, whose power will not exceed 500 watts of power, or with heads of exposed electric wire attached to the temples, the soles of the feet and the palms of the defendant's hands.)

The degree of horror increases as this section of the code progresses, precisely because the language retains its legal objectivity. Article 115 c), for example, prescribes the following method of obtaining a confession from a prisoner: "Utilizar a su madre o esposa en actos sexuales con terceros para obligarlo a confesar" (*DTT*, 45; "Use his mother or wife in sexual acts with others to make him confess"). The joke behind this article lies in the fact that, since these things are already done, it is only logical to inscribe them in the legal code.

The code also exemplifies Ramírez's opposition to dictatorship as a manifestation of patriarchal machismo, an unusual posture at the time among the Latin American left, which worshipped revolutionaries such as Fidel Castro or Che Guevara, who matched in machismo and homophobia the dictators against whom they struggled. Article 24 outlines extravagant punishments for male homosexuality, which include stripping gay couples naked, greasing them, and parading them through the streets "no importando quien fuere de entreambos el hechor activo o pasivo" (29; "no matter which of them was the active and which the passive perpetrator"). This final clause ridicules the Nicaraguan prejudice that the "active" male homosexual partner is less deserving of censure than he who is "passive," since the former is still "behaving like a man" (Lancaster 1992: 236–7). The hysteria inspired by male homosexuality, as opposed to the widespread belief that lesbianism is not "real," or is less of an offence to religious morality since it usually does not require penetration, is satirized in the brief succeeding clause: "Si el comercio denunciado fuese de mujer a mujer, se les reprenderá en privado" (*DTT*, 29; "If the intercourse denounced be between woman and woman, they will be scolded in private").

THE REHABILITATION OF SANDINO AND CENTRAL AMERICAN CULTURE

The criticisms of Nicaraguan attitudes made by Ramírez in *De Tropeles y tropelías* extend well beyond an attack on the Somoza dictatorship. Yet it was the book's anti-Somocista stance that attracted public attention and placed Ramírez in the category of a public enemy of the regime. As *De Tropeles y tropelías* was being printed at the Editorial Universitaria in San Salvador, the university campus was invaded by the Salvadoran military, which burned a large part of the initial print run. A second printing was banned in Nicaragua and had to be smuggled into the country. These events, building on the monstrous extortion of foreign aid after the 1972 earthquake, which had hardened many urban Nicaraguans' opposition to the Somoza regime, convinced Ramírez that sufficient support for Sandinismo existed in the cities that it would now be possible for the Sandinistas to make alliances with the bourgeoisie. He had long been convinced that only armed struggle would overthrow the dictatorship, yet he disagreed with Sandinista leader Carlos Fonseca over tactics, believing, like many on the Latin American left, that the defeat and killing of Che Guevara in Bolivia in 1967 had demonstrated the inefficacy of rural guerrilla voluntarism[12] as a way of overthrowing a government (Cherem 2004b: 103). On the other hand, Ramírez shared Fonseca's conviction that one of the keys to generating a positive image of Nicaraguan nationhood lay in the rehabilitation of the figure of Augusto César Sandino. Reviled by official propaganda as a minor bandit, Sandino had been forgotten by much of the Nicaraguan population. Ramírez himself had grown up almost unaware of Sandino, even though he was related to him: his great-aunt, América Tiffer, had been the revolutionary's stepmother. Only in university, where pamphlets about Sandino circulated among the students, had Ramírez become aware of Sandino's achievements.

Between 1966 and 1969, Carlos Fonseca made clandestine visits to San José. These visits had conspiratorial purposes but also allowed Fonseca to spend time in the National Library of Costa Rica researching the life of his literary idol, Rubén Darío (*EN*, 23). The two men, whose wives, Gertrudis Guerrero and María Haydée Terán, had been friends in León, and who shared the experience of having been friends of Fernando Gordillo and protégés of Mariano Fiallos Gil (Zimmermann 2000: 48), albeit at different times, socialized and discussed the prospects for overthrowing Somoza. While Fonseca was imprisoned in Costa Rica in 1969–70, the Ramírezes sent him food and books published by EDUCA (Cherem 2004b: 102). In October 1970 a Sandinista commando hijacked a Costa Rican plane and held two United Fruit Company executives hostage until the Costa Rican government agreed to release Fonseca, Humberto Ortega, and other Sandinistas from prison. Fonseca spent most of the next five years in Cuba, where he devoted much of his time to "researching and writing his analysis of Augusto César

Sandino's role in the struggle for national identity and self-determination in Nicaragua" (Zimmermann 2000: 143). Fonseca sent Sandinistas into archives in a variety of countries to copy and take notes from newspaper articles and books in an attempt to recover the full chronology of Sandino's military campaigns against the US Marines. During this same period, Ramírez was working on *El pensamiento vivo de Sandino* (1974). In addition to doing archival research to recover copies of the revolutionary's writings and statements, he travelled to Mexico to visit the places where Sandino had lived as a migrant worker.

These two Sandinos, both constructed in the early 1970s, and arising from the conversations that Ramírez and Fonseca had held in the late 1960s, were complementary. The absence of any hostility towards Ramírez's interpretation of Sandino on the part of the sometimes doctrinaire Fonseca is evident in the complicit terms in which he continued to write to Ramírez after his secret return to Nicaragua in 1975 (Cherem 2004b: 121).[13] Yet, while they share characteristics, Fonseca's Sandino and Ramírez's Sandino are not the same; the differences between them reflect the emerging discrepancy between the respective visions of the Nicaraguan nation proposed by Fonseca and by the Tercerista tendency that would emerge in 1975.

Published by EDUCA in 1974, *El pensamiento vivo de Sandino*, a collection of Sandino's letters and communiqués arranged in such a way as to create a loose autobiography, became Ramírez's most popular book to date. At the time the Sandinistas overthrew the Somoza dictatorship in 1979, the EDUCA edition was about to go into its sixth printing; editions had been published in other Spanish-speaking countries, and translations had appeared in German, Italian, and Swedish. After the Revolution, Ramírez edited an expanded two-volume edition of Sandino's writings that was published in Managua in 1984 under the shortened title *El pensamiento vivo*; this became the basis for further translations, notably that of Robert Edgar Conrad into English, which altered the book's contents considerably and excluded Ramírez's essay.

Ramírez's interpretation of Sandino's significance for contemporary Nicaraguans appears in "El muchacho de Niquinohomo," an introduction that he was asked to write for the book's German translation and that was incorporated into Spanish-language editions published after 1975. This essay makes explicit the radicalization of Ramírez's analysis that is implicit in the scathing portraits of the Nicaraguan bourgeoisie in his short stories of this period. The obstacle to fully realized Nicaraguan nationhood is no longer simply a thuggish tyrant but the entire compliant, culturally alienated bourgeoisie, both Liberal and Conservative, that sells out the nation in return for scraps from the Somozas' table and an ersatz imitation of US materialist culture. Sandino becomes an exemplary figure because he struggles against the humiliation of the Nicaraguan nation by the US Marines, as a result of which "Nicaragua apareció a los ojos del mundo como un protectorado norteamericano durante un cuarto de siglo y continuó siendo, aunque sin tropas de ocupación, protectorado norteamericano después" (*PVS*, xxvi; "Nicaragua appeared in the eyes of the world as a US protectorate for a quarter of a century and continued, although without occupation troops, to be a US protectorate afterwards"). The latter clause makes clear that Sandino's struggle has not ended.

The final sentence of Ramírez's essay reiterates this call to action, underlining that the purpose of Sandino's life, including his decision to become a martyr, was to create a life that "pudieran ser recobradas como ejemplo en el futuro latinoamericano" (*PVS*, lxix; "could be recovered as an example in the Latin American future"). This continental vocation is the root of the pride Nicaraguans should feel when contemplating Sandino's life. Their country is the site of "la primera guerra de guerrillas librada en el continente americano" (*PVS*, xxxvi; "the first guerrilla war waged on the American continent"). As such, Sandino's campaign is both a "guerra nacional" (lviii; "national war") and a triumph of international anti-imperialist action. Sandino's struggle attracted volunteers from other Latin American countries and, in a foreshadowing of events during the 1980s, inspired the creation of solidarity committees "en New York, en Los Angeles, en Chicago, en Detroit" (xlix).

In concert with Carlos Fonseca, who in a 1970 interview had suggested that Nicaraguan nationality was a credential that must be earned and that the Somozas, among others, could not be considered Nicaraguan (Zimmermann 2000: 149), Ramírez depicts Sandino as having achieved the laurel of Nicaraguanness. In his description of Sandino's arrival in Managua on 2 February 1934, he writes:

> La gente lo aclama tumultuosamente en el aeropuerto y en las calles, todo el mundo quiere conocer a aquel hombre, tan pequeño de estatura y tan sencillo, que había cumplido una hazaña tan increíble. Para muchos, ese general de los humildes en cuyo rostro de muchacho se pintaban las huellas de las durezas de su lucha, había conquistado un derecho que los políticos entregados a los intereses de la compañías yankis nunca habían tenido en cuenta: *el de la nacionalidad, el de poder llamarse nicaragüenses, centroamericanos, latinoamericanos, el derecho de no ser colonos de un imperio*. (*PVS*, lxi, original emphasis; The people acclaimed him tumultuously at the airport and on the streets,

everyone wanted to meet that man, so small in stature and so modest, who had achieved such an incredible feat. For many, that general of the humble in whose boyish face were painted the marks of the hardships of his struggle, had conquered a right that the politicians subjugated to the interests of the Yankee companies had never considered: *that of nationality, that of being able to be called Nicaraguan, Central American, Latin American, the right to not be colonial subjects of an empire.*)

If Nicaraguan nationality, construed as part of a complex of Latin American identities, is the supreme prize conquered for Nicaraguans by Sandino, this is precisely what is lacking at the beginning of his campaign. The catalyst for Sandino's insurgency in this version is the contempt shown towards Nicaraguans by other Spanish Americans. As a worker in the oilfields of Tampico, Mexico, Sandino reads newspaper articles about the US intervention in Nicaragua. A Mexican co-worker taunts him with the words, "Todos ustedes los nicaragüenses no son más que unos vendepatrias" (*PVS*, xxvii; "All you Nicaraguans are nothing but traitors"). Yet, if the impulse behind Sandino's struggle is primarily nationalistic, it has class implications. "El muchacho de Niquinohomo" offers glimpses of a Marxist-influenced language of class analysis that is beginning to adulterate Ramírez's liberalism: Liberal and Conservative leaders are rebuked and equated with one another because they "solo defienden los intereses de dominio de su clase" (xxvi; "defend only the interests of the dominance of their class"); President Zelaya is criticized for believing that the route to progress is by way of "capitalismo mundial en expansión" (xv; "an expanding global capitalism"); the Marxist concept of "praxis" (lxviii) is evoked to capture Sandino's fusion of theory and action. Though light, such touches indicate the socialist patina that Ramírez's language was acquiring amid the political strife of the 1970s. Ramírez has no hesitation in referring to the United States as an "imperio" (lxi; "empire"). When he draws attention to the fact that Sandino was born in the year that Cuba's national hero, José Martí, died fighting for his country's independence (x, xix), he domesticates this Marxist vocabulary (and the Cuban Revolution, with which this reference establishes an implicit parallel) as an expression of nationalism. Fonseca's cocktail of nationalism and Marxism contained a stronger dose of the latter ingredient, yet, in this respect, the two writers' portraits of Sandino are congruent.

Matilde Zimmermann suggests that some of Carlos Fonseca's writings about Sandino "reveal a personal identification with his subject" (Zimmermann 2000: 146). The same is also true of Ramírez. Fonseca identified Sandino as a Liberal who had the perspicacity to understand the corruption of

Nicaraguan Liberalism: "Sandino es el único de los Generales liberales que comprende los móviles de la intervención y la naturaleza entreguista de los burgueses liberales" (Fonseca 1984: 12; "Sandino is the only one of the liberal Generals who understood the motives of the intervention and the subservient nature of the liberal bourgeoisie"). Ramírez devotes more than a third of his essay to establishing the historical background to Sandino's struggle: the guerrilla is introduced only on page twenty-five of a sixty-nine-page article. This background is necessary in part because Ramírez is writing in exile for an international audience, but also because the facts of Nicaraguan history are not available to most Nicaraguans. One of the central chores Sandinista intellectuals such as Fonseca, Ramírez, Jaime Wheelock, and others set themselves during the early 1970s was to recover an accurate chronology of Nicaraguan history, which had been suppressed by years of US intervention and Somocista propaganda; the rehabilitation of Sandino is the most vital element of this project.

Ramírez draws attention to Sandino's status as a dissident from Liberalism: the same position towards which he himself was evolving. He remarks: "Una ironía del destino haría que en un pequeño radio territorial que no alcanzaría diez kilómetros, nacieran Sandino en Niquinohomo, y en otros pequeños poblados más hacia el sur, José María Moncada en Masatepe y Anastasio Somoza en San Marcos" (*PVS*, xxviii; "An irony of fate would decree that within a small geographical radius of less than ten kilometres, Sandino was born in Niquinohomo, and in other small towns further south, José María Moncada was born in Masetepe and Anastasio Somoza in San Marcos"). Ramírez, too, was born within this ten-kilometre radius. Like Fonseca, who believed that the most important legacy of Sandino's life was not his writings, as pithy and telling as these might be, but the example of his actions, which would assist the current generation in their struggle to "change the present and the future" (Zimmermann 2000: 145), Ramírez insists: "No debe perderse la perspectiva de que cada una de las ideas expresadas por Sandino está en alguna medida respaldada por su lucha; hay una correspondencia directa entre su pensamiento y su acción" (*PVS*, iv; "We must not lose sight of the fact that each of the ideas expressed by Sandino is to some extent supported by his struggle; there is a direct correspondence between his thought and his action").

This assertion reflects Fonseca's thinking so directly that it is difficult not to believe that it is a product of the two men's conversations. One studies Sandino's life to fill a gap in Nicaraguan history and recover a sense of national self-respect; but these processes are merely a prelude to concrete action. Both Fonseca and Ramírez dismiss Sandino's adherence to the creed of theosophy as unworthy of mention. Ramírez's portrait suggests that Sandino's resonance as a Nicaraguan everyman was facilitated by his birth in the "Departamento de Masaya, el más densamente poblado de la república" (*PVS*, xxviii; "Department of Masaya, the most densely populated of the republic"). Fonseca, in his pamphlet *Sandino, guerrillero proletario* (Sandino, Proletarian Guerrilla), which was issued by the Editorial Universitaria in León in 1972, also portrays Sandino as a man of the people; both authors, driven by the need to restore national dignity, praise Sandino as the hero of all Nicaraguans. In so doing, they reject the hidebound class analyses of the pro-Moscow Communist Party, the Partido Socialista Nicaragüense (PSN; Nicaraguan Socialist Party),[14] which condemned both Sandino and Fonseca as bourgeois adventurers who should have waited until the socialist consciousness of the masses was ripe before attempting to foment revolution.

Yet ideological fissures are perceptible between the two writers' positions. Though Fonseca states in the first sentence of his essay that Sandino is "el héroe guerrillero nicaragüense cuyo nombre ha pasado a ser símbolo de la ya secular lucha de los pueblos de la América Latina contra el imperialismo yanqui" (Fonseca 1982: 368; "the Nicaraguan guerrilla hero whose name has become a symbol of the secular struggle of the peoples of Latin America against Yankee imperialism"), his Sandino, as his essay's title makes clear, is an exemplary proletarian. Fonseca describes Sandino as an "obrero de procedencia campesina que combatió con las armas contra los invasores norteamericanos en Nicaragua" (ibid.: 368; "worker of peasant origin who fought with arms against the United States invaders in Nicaragua"). The "worker" characterization is not consistent with Sandino's origins as an illegitimate child fathered by a minor landowner with one of the young women who brought in the harvest in his fields. Sandino grew up on his father's hacienda, albeit with fewer privileges than the children who had been born in wedlock (Ramírez's great-aunt Tiffer made young Augusto eat in the kitchen). In another divergence from Ramírez's interpretation, Fonseca's Che Guevara-influenced voluntarism depended on an assumption that peasants are innately rebellious. This questionable assertion, paradoxically, did not stem from socialist beliefs but from a nationalist pride in "las tradiciones combativas del pueblo nicaragüense" ("the combative traditions of the Nicaraguan people"). As described in his long essay, "Notas sobre la montaña y algunos otros temas" ("Notes on the Mountains and Some Other Themes"), completed less than a month before his death in battle in 1976, Fonseca thought that these combative traditions persisted with greater vigour in rural areas because "el campesino está en menor grado expuesto a la penetración ideológica actual, que el enemigo desata a través de los medios de comunicación" (ibid.: 137; "the peasant is less exposed to the contemporary ideological invasion that the enemy unleashes through the media"). This status of the mountains as a refuge from the Yankefied falsehoods of the mass media and a place of contact with authentic Nicaraguan culture, untainted by Yankee-subjugated modernity, was one of the reasons that Fonseca believed that participation in rural guerrilla warfare would forge a "New Man." Not only must the guerrilla learn to sacrifice and think of others – essential preparation for building a socialist society, as Che Guevara had claimed – but, giving Guevarist ideology a stronger nationalist twist, Fonseca foresaw the guerrilla recovering Nicaraguan national traditions which, in urban areas, had been buried or eroded by Somocismo. Foremost among these, was the forgotten legacy of Augusto César Sandino.

Since *Sandino, guerrillero proletario* was published in 1972, while Ramírez was assembling *El pensamiento vivo de Sandino* in San José, it is virtually certain that he read Fonseca's pamphlet. "El muchacho de Niquinohomo" displays considerable research that is not present in Fonseca's essay, particularly on the international ramifications of Sandino's insurgency. Ramírez devotes more space than does Fonseca to analysing Sandino's literary style: "aquel lenguaje que nunca sería ni retórico ni gratuito, cargado de pasión pero también cargado de verdad" (*PVS*, xxxvii; "that language that would never be either rhetorical or cheap, full of passion but also full of truth"). The biggest difference between the two Sandinos may be the submerged yet vital question of race.

The "proletarianism" of Fonseca's Sandino erases his racial heritage. Fonseca does cite the famous line where Sandino vaunts the fact that "soy nicaragüense y me siento orgulloso de que en mis venas circule, más que cualquier otra, la sangre india americana" (Fonseca 1982: 372; "I am Nicaraguan and I am proud that in my veins circulates, more than any other, American Indian blood"), yet the phrase appears in the middle of a citation that is two-thirds of a page in length and Fonseca does not comment on this aspect of Sandino's declaration, stressing instead his subject's military bravery. Ramírez, though he does not quote this line in his essay (it does appear in the documents collected in *El pensamiento vivo de Sandino*), creates a Sandino – and, above all, a Sandinismo – that is implicitly mestizo.

Fonseca tended to skirt the left-wing mestizo nationalism that had been pioneered by the Mexican Revolution and that would become a significant ideological thread in the Sandinismo of the 1980s. Just as the Cuban Revolution was Fonseca's beacon in the darkness (Zimmermann 2000: 9), so the ideology of the Mexican Revolution had provided Sandino with illumination (Hodges 1986: 92–3). Fonseca's discomfort with mestizo nationalism is probably connected to his own background. He drew attention to the correspondence between his family history and that of Sandino: born in 1936, Fonseca was the illegitimate son of a seamstress of peasant background and a wealthy young man, married with children, who was at that time an accountant at an American-owned mine and would later become a close business collaborator of the Somozas. But Fonseca was born in Matagalpa, on the edge of the Segovia Mountains. Unlike Sandino's mother, who was of largely indigenous ancestry, Fonseca's mother came from the mountain village of San Rafael del Norte, where, for historical reasons that remain obscure, some of the peasants have light skin and blue eyes. A lanky man well over six feet tall, with startling pale skin that made him stand out in any Nicaraguan crowd, he was described by Margaret Randall as "exceptionally tall for a Central American, his piercing blue eyes were magnified by the thick round lenses of his wire-framed glasses" (Randall 1992: 203). Fonseca was a poor ambassador for his compatriots' identification with their Náhuat-Chorotega heritage. His theory of the innate rebelliousness of the peasant, bolstered by a strong belief in the revolutionary spirit of the people of the region where he was born, served as a form of compensation for his anomalous appearance. Fonseca once harangued Ernesto Cardenal to move his religious community from Solentiname, which was in a zone of southern Nicaragua that Fonseca associated with "el mercantilismo, y el imperialismo" ("mercantilism and imperialism"), to the northern mountains "que había sido siempre la zona de la resistencia" (*IE*, 223; "that had always been the zone of resistance").

By contrast, Ramírez's decision to emphasize Sandino's birth (like his own) in the Department of Masaya associates the national hero not with a proletarian class but with a mestizo culture. Nicaraguan readers would be aware that Masaya is not only the most densely populated department in the country, but is also well known for communities such as Monimbó, the indigenous suburb of Masaya, which in 1978 would become a bulwark of indigenous resistence to Somoza, and that this department typifies Nicaraguan *mestizaje*. In *Sandino, guerrillero proletario*, Fonseca identifies Sandino's fellow guerrillas as "procedentes de la población campesina" (Fonseca 1982: 373; "coming from the peasant population"); he praises Sandino's lieutenant, "el jefe guerrillero Pedro Altamirano" (ibid.: 383; "the guerrilla leader Pedro Altamirano"), for having resumed the guerrilla war in the mountains after the murder of Sandino, continuing to fight until 1939, when he was tracked down and killed. In both statements, Fonseca deracializes the guerrilla fighters. Ramírez adopts a different stance, identifying Altamirano as an "indígena de Jinotega que aprendió a leer y escribir durante la campaña" (*PVS*, xliv; "Indian from Jinotega who learned to read and write during the campaign"). He is careful to involve Nicaraguans of all ethnicities, including the Miskitos of the Atlantic Coast, in Sandino's struggle, praising "la ayuda de los indígenas zambos[15] y mosquitos que pueblan la zona; soldados sandinistas durante la guerra posterior, esos indígenas formarían una eficiente aunque primitiva marina de guerra con sus piquantes, llevando por el río guerrilleros, municiones y alimentos" (*PVS*, xxxii; "the help of the zambo and Miskito Indians that inhabit the area; Sandinista soldiers during the subsequent war, these Indians would form a primitive but efficient navy, carrying guerrillas, ammunition and food down the river in their *piquante* boats"). Racial inclusiveness meshes with a regional inclusiveness that makes the Atlantic and Pacific coasts and the northern mountains equal contributors in a national project of ridding the country of the Yankee invader. Whereas Fonseca seeks "emancipación nacional" ("national liberation"), which will be won by the "masas populares" (Fonseca 1982: 384; "popular masses"), Ramírez refers to Sandino not as a proletarian but as "un artesano que dejó sus herramientas para pasar directamente al combate" (*PVS*, lxvii; "a craftsman who left his tools to go directly into combat"). His rural middle-class, mixed-race nationalism struggles above all for the recovery of a dignified, existentially authentic sense of Nicaraguan identity that will contribute within a continental spectrum to "el futuro latinoamericano" (*PVS*, lxix; "the Latin American future"). The two writers agree that the oppression of the Nicaraguan people, and the shattering of Nicaraguan national identity, are direct consequences of US imperialism. The theorization of this phenomenon, and its impact on the culture of Central America, would become one of Ramírez's central preoccupations during his years in Berlin.[16]

The publication of *El pensamiento vivo de Sandino* was crucial to confirming the relevance of Ramírez who, like other members of the *Ventana* group, had been in political limbo for more than a decade, to the Sandinista-led opposition. By the early 1970s, the FSLN leadership, realizing that the seizure of power in Nicaragua by a government led by Carlos Fonseca and Tomás Borge would provoke immediate US reprisals, possibly including a military invasion, was exploring options for a broad-based junta that could present an ideologically acceptable face to Washington and the world. Ramírez appears to have been sounded out on this possibility at an early stage (*IE*, 222). Even though he did not change his mind about the Sandinistas' prospects until Eduardo Contreras's December 1974 Christmas Party raid, his analysis was shifting in a more radical direction. His move to Berlin, where he saw Nicaragua's problems from an international perspective, accelerated this process. There, for the first time, he wrote a substantial work of fiction that dramatized the society of Somocista Nicaragua: *To Bury Our Fathers*, which would be published after his return to Central America. Emboldened by distance, and also by contact with an international community of Latin Americans exiled in Europe, such as the Colombian literary critic Carlos Rincón, who lived in East Berlin, and the Chilean writer Antonio Skármeta, who spent his exile in West Berlin, he began to employ the socialist-influenced analytical tools developed by Latin American social science. Like many writers before him, particularly Latin Americans in Paris in the 1920s and 1930s, Ramírez honed his continental intellectual and political vocation by living in a cosmopolitan European city.[17] A lightly fictionalized novella-length memoir of this period, entitled "Vallejo," which Ramírez began in 1974, completed in 1992–93, and included in his collection *Catalina y Catalina* (2001), provides a tongue-in-cheek picture of the antics of the Latin American community in Berlin. Though structural problems make this piece less successful than Ramírez's best work, it is eloquent about the ways in which exile communities educate individuals from one Latin American country about the cultures and problems of other countries in the region, and, at the same time, oblige them to engage with aspects of their own identities that they might be programmed to ignore at home.

The plot revolves around an erratic Peruvian exile named Vallejo (a tongue-in-cheek allusion to the poet César Vallejo), a would-be composer of classical music who dreams of putting on an opera in Berlin and insists that the autobiographical narrator write him a libretto with indigenous themes. Vallejo is convinced that, as a Central American, the narrator will make use of the sacred Mayan text the *Popol Vuh*, which Ramírez (who gives this narrator his own name) confesses that he hasn't read because *indigenismo* does not interest him. The irony of the narrator's lack of awareness of indigenous cultures emerges in a scene where he becomes irritated that Vallejo's interruptions are preventing him from finishing his novel. He reflects that his wife refers to his outbursts of anger as moments when his Mercado side – the character of his mother's family– emerges: "Y 'salírseme el Mercado,' Mercado mi apellido por la rama materna, era lo mismo que salírseme el indio" (*CYC*, 171; "And to have 'the Mercado come out in me' – Mercado is my last name from my mother's side – is the same as having the Indian come out in me"). This reflection prompts a digression on the subject of the narrator's hair, one of the more conspicuous physical traits of his indigenous heritage, and how, when he was a child, it was "indómito al peine" (171; "could not be tamed by the comb").

The dilemma of the Latin American artist in European exile develops through the contrast between the narrator, who is writing a novel set under a dictatorship that remains in power, and for whom it is increasingly difficult to return to his country, and Vallejo, whose native Peru is ruled by the left-wing regime of General Juan Velasco Alvarado, which enhances its legitimacy through a glorification of Peru's Incan-descended culture and would welcome back an exile of Vallejo's political and cultural inclinations. Yet Vallejo refuses to return home "hasta que haya brillado lo suficiente en Europa" (*CYC*, 181; "until he has become famous enough in Europe"). The story, which opens by stressing that the narrator is a "proviciano del trópico" (165; "provincial from the tropics") who lacks previous experience of great cities, rifles through the many different forms that can be taken by exile culture: stereotyped folklore, radical politics, or, more promisingly, the fusion of Latin American themes with European cultural forms.

The first of these options is incarnated by the Chilean exiles who throng Berlin in the aftermath of the September 1973 military coup against the government of Salvador Allende: "en aquellos tiempos casi todos los chilenos exiliados en Berlin escogían como primer oficio el de músicos vestidos de negro tipo Quilapayún, con tamborcitos, tamborones, vihuelas y quenas" (189–90; "in those days almost all of the Chilean exiles in Berlin chose as their primary profession that of musicians dressed in black, like the group Quilapayún, with little drums, big drums, vihuelas and Andean reed flutes"). The narrator submits to this self-objectification at the urging of Vallejo, who, in a moment when the narrator's grant has run out, offers him payment for participating in a demonstration of Latin American culture. In front of an audience of retired Siemens workers, "Leí en alemán apenas cuatro páginas sobre Miguel Ángel Asturias" (*CYC*, 189; "I read in German a mere four pages on Miguel Ángel Asturias"). The allusion to the greatest Central American novelist, who defined his vision of Latin America in Europe, is cast in a comic light owing to the narrator's inability to communicate effectively in his "alemán tropical" (189; "tropical German"). The inevitable trivialization of cultural references when they are separated from their original context is underlined in the fleeting descriptions of Latin American political life in mid-1970s Berlin. The narrator complains about eating soggy spaghetti

> aquellas masas informes que alguno de los estudiantes latinos en Berlín conseguía cuando yo era el invitado de honor de sus encuentros dominicales en el apartamento de cualquiera de ellos, espaguetis o pizzas medio crudas o medio quemadas, algún remedo con comida criolla y siempre cerveza tibia entre discusiones interminables y generalmente a gritos sobre el destino de América Latina, Cuba sí, yankis no, el Che Guevara,

> uno, dos, tres, Vietnam es la consigna, Salvador Allende mucho más temprano que más tarde se abrirán las grandes avenidas ... y la revolución autóctona del general Velasco Alvarado, que ya empezaba a cuartearse. (*CYC*, 182–3; those shapeless blobs that some of the Latino students in Berlin produced when I was the guest of honour at the Sunday meetings at their apartments, spaghetti or pizza half-baked or half-burned, some poor imitation of a typical Latin American dish, and always warm beer between endless discussions and usually shouts about the fate of Latin America, Cuba yes, Yankees no, Che Guevara, one, two, three, Vietnam is the watchword, Salvador Allende much earlier than later, the great avenues will open ... and the autochthonous revolution of General Velasco Alvarado, which was beginning to crack.)

This satire of early 1970s left-wing discourse – extending to an uncharacteristically sloppy misquoting of Allende's final speech (in which he spoke of "alamedas" ["boulevards"], not "avenidas" ["avenues"])[18] – is a reminder that "Vallejo" was completed in the disillusioned aftermath of the Sandinistas' electoral defeat of 1990. Contemporary evidence, such as the socialist language of "El muchacho de Niquinohomo," suggests that, at the time, Ramírez shared many of these students' opinions; in fact, he appears to have acted as a political mentor to some of them. One National Guard officer later accused Ramírez of being his son's "mentor comunista" ("Communist mentor"; Cherem 2004b: 119).[19]

"Vallejo" discounts the options of taking refuge in a folkloric cultural identity, or in the histrionic excesses of exile politics, in favour of pursuing a hybridization of Latin American and European cultures. The character of Vallejo, though sometimes a figure of fun, speaks flawless German and Italian, cooks tasty spaghetti, and engages the narrator in credible debates about the balance between European and indigenous elements that should be sought by Latin American art. As "El muchacho de Niquinohomo" indicates, Ramírez himself had at this time adopted in discreet form the role of an advocate for cultural and ethnic mixing as a key element of a resuscitated Nicaraguan national culture. The narrator agrees to write a libretto on Mayan themes (which, in a structural miscalculation, is included as a ten-page appendix to the novella). Vallejo invites him to an audience with the director of the Deutsche Oper. This time, however, Vallejo fails to appear for the meeting. He disappears, thereby signalling that "esa primavera de 1974 había llegado a su fin" (*CYC*, 199; "that spring of 1974 had come to an end"). The nostalgic tone draws the curtain on a more idealistic time, yet, while the political party chat and popular art of the early 1970s no longer convince, the effort to define Central American culture is spared this affectionate derision. The strongest evidence of the sharpening of Ramírez's analysis during his years in Berlin can be seen in "Balcanes y volcanes" ("Balkans and Volcanoes"), the heavily documented, almost book-length essay to which he devoted the summer and fall of 1973, just prior to his meeting with the character who inspired "Vallejo."

Written as Ramírez's contribution to an anthology of extended essays published in Mexico in 1975 under the title *Centroamérica hoy* (Central America Today), "Balcanes y volcanes" reprised the experience of Miguel Ángel Asturias, who defined his vision of Guatemala by researching Mayan culture at the Sorbonne (Henighan 1999a: 44–50). Ramírez agreed to write the essay after discovering a rich cache of materials on Central America at the Instituto Iberoamericano in Steglitz. In this suburban Berlin archive, his ideas diverged definitively from the Liberal precepts of his youth. Ramírez's analysis of Central America's cultural malaises reflects the dependency-theory approach that dominated Latin American social science during the 1970s; indeed, "Balcanes y volcanes" represents one of the most striking applications of dependency theory to the analysis of culture. Inspired by the Argentine economist Raúl Prebisch and elaborated by the Chilean-based Comisión Económica para América Latina (CEPAL or ECLA; Economic Commission for Latin America), dependency theory posited that the world was divided into a metropolis and a periphery; that the metropolis acquired raw materials from the periphery and sold them back to the periphery as high-priced manufactured goods, resulting in ever-declining terms of trade for peripheral nations; that these nations' economies, social structures, and cultures were conditioned by their relationship, over time, with the metropolis; and that this relationship constituted what dependency theorists, in an adaptation of Marx's terminology for the dynamic that separated capitalist from worker, labelled "the international division of labour." To break this cycle, dependency theory proposed the introduction of high tariff barriers to stimulate local production, a procedure referred to as import-substitution industrialization (ISI) (Prebisch 1967: 95–107). Prebisch began to publish his findings in the 1940s; many of his policy proposals were implemented by Latin American governments in the 1950s. The measures had short-term, limited success in enlarging the Latin American middle class and expanding internal markets, leading ECLA to posit that there was an "easy stage" and a "hard stage" of ISI. By the 1960s and 1970s, most nations that had adopted ISI policies –Chile and Argentina were conspicuous examples – were confronting the intractable "hard stage": the replacement not merely of imported low-tech items such as textiles but of the products of heavy industry and high technology. Economies that had generated new middle classes now could not expand rapidly enough to find employment for their children, who were being educated at universities that had been massively enlarged during the 1950s and 1960s. Jorge Castañeda characterizes the outlook of the students who embraced the revolutionary option during the 1960s and 1970s as that of the offspring of parents who had been lifted into the middle class by ISI policies: "Over a span of twenty years, millions of Latin American students entered a university system seeking answers to the questions their parents had never known well enough to ask. They found most of the satisfactory responses in the teachings, writings, and preachings of the social scientists ... The Latin American social scientist ... provided a coherent, all-encompassing explanation for the status quo – what later become known as dependency theory – and a blueprint for a better world" (Casteñeda 1993: 192–3). Ramírez, though five to ten years older than most of these students, came from a similar background.

The originality of "Balcanes y volcanes" lies in its application of dependency-theory analysis to culture, and to the particular case of Central America. The cultural initiatives Ramírez would champion as vice-president of Nicaragua in the 1980s reflected the understanding of Central America's cultural impasse expressed in this essay. The first sentence presents the evolution of Central American culture as a succession of responses to "aquellas épocas en que un modelo de dependencia hace crisis y es sustituido por otro" (*BV*, 13; "those periods when one model of dependency enters into crisis and is replaced by another"). In conformity with dependency theory's assertion that peripheral cultures are shaped over time by the dominance of the metropolis, and with the importance that the ideas of Prebisch and his colleagues accord to this chronological dimension, Ramírez depicts Central American cultural processes as having acquired their definitive form during the late-nineteenth-century coffee boom: a time when Liberal dominance propelled Central America into the global market economy. This event, Ramírez contends, broke the cultural unity imposed by the Spanish conquest in the sixteenth century and confirmed the "papel asignado a Centroamérica en la división internacional del trabajo" (13; "role assigned to Central America in the international division of labour"). The Liberal boom years, cast as nearly a golden age of endeavour and openness in *Tiempo de fulgor*, are subjected to merciless scrutiny in "Balcanes y volcanes." They emerge as the crucial juncture when the isthmus was subjected to imperialist suzerainty and its culture was skewed by pseudo-scientific positivist discourse. Ramírez describes this transitional moment in historical perspective, stressing the vital lack of a bourgeoisie capable of undertaking the role of nation building. Where dependency theory criticized larger Latin American nations for developing only a "comprador" bourgeoisie – that is, a bourgeoisie unable to fulfill its nation-building role on account of its subservience to foreign capital – Ramírez contends that Central America failed to develop a bourgeoisie at all. The legacy of the coffee boom was the failure to institutionalize either the region or its constituent nations in a way that would break a pernicious legacy in which the legal nation was a fiction divorced from the nation of daily customs. As a result, the rift between provincial yet Europeanized oligarchies (such as the Conservative families of Granada "que habían gobernado en forma de patriciado al país" [*BV*, 61; "who had ruled the country in a patrician way"]) and impoverished peasant populations, which lived outside the republican norms guaranteed by enlightened but ignored constitutions, impeded the flourishing of national cultures. The absence of a substantial bourgeoisie, particularly one with nation-building proclivities, deprived Central America of a dynamic force capable of mediating between the oligarchy that aped European customs and the indigenous cultural influences of the masses.

Ramírez mocks the hodgepodge of medieval, Renaissance, baroque, neoclassical, and art nouveau styles combined at random by governing classes oblivious to their respective significances. He notes:

> Las posibilidades de creación de una cultura nacional, se niegan constantemente a lo largo de este proceso formativo del estado político en Centroamérica, no sólo porque la estructura imposibilita la realización de este proyecto, como sería por ejemplo a través de la educación, sino también porque ni las apropriaciones e imitaciones de la élite serán lo suficientemente reales, creativas o vitales para irradiar un estilo nacional de cultura y porque el mundo subyacente, marcado por los signos pasivos de la dominación, tampoco permitirá ser irradiado. (*BV*, 42; The possibilities of creating a national culture were perpetually denied throughout the formative process of the political state in Central America, not only because social structures made it impossible to carry out this project, as for example through education, but also because the appropriations and imitations of the elite were not sufficiently authentic, creative or vital to irradiate a national cultural style, and because the world of the underlings, scarred by passive signs of domination, would not permit it to be irradiated.)

Since the cultures of the indigenous peoples are oppressed to the point of being unable to participate in a national discourse, the culture of the elites is artificial, failing to incorporate a creative blend of European and local styles that might have evolved into a sequence of national cultures. The potential indigenous contribution to national identity is locked in an oral culture that does not enter the realm of print, where cultural discourse occurs. Like the elite, the indigenous peoples promote a culture that is a product of the Spanish Conquest. Drawing on Aldous Huxley's observations of Guatemala, Ramírez maintains that many styles of dress regarded as "traditionally" Mayan or Náhuat are in fact late-medieval Spanish fashions that were adopted by indigenous elites as a sign of prestige in the sixteenth century and have become frozen in time as banners of aboriginal identity.

"Balcanes y volcanes" is not an anti-Somoza tract. It displays a deep historical focus and integrates a wide range of learning gathered from different branches of knowledge and from the histories of the five original Central American republics. Its core concerns are cultural, and particularly literary. Ramírez argues that Central America has a truncated literature that was born later than that of other regions of the Americas and whose origins, therefore, are in contemporary forms, having been largely silent during periods when other literatures were characterized by neo-classicism, Romanticism, realism, or naturalism. Emerging at the turn of the twentieth century, the literature of Central America was born as a bifurcated form of expression, on the one hand displaying the *costumbrismo* (writing about local customs) of a writer such as the Salvadoran Salarrué, and on the other the escapist vanguardism of Rubén Darío. The elite's base in rural life, reinforced by an international division of labour that assigns Central America the role of agricultural producer, thwarts the development of cities as sites of cosmopolitan cultural expression, as occurred in Mexico and South America. The absence of a national bourgeoisie condemns the region's greatest writer of the period, Darío, to develop in exile, in Valparaíso, Chile, Buenos Aires, Madrid, and finally Paris: "Sólo por medio de este exilio podrá fundar por primera vez un arte nacional centroamericano e incorporarlo con distintos signos al proceso" (*BV*, 52; "Only through this exile may he establish for the first time a Central American national art and incorporate it through different signs into the process"). Managua, at the time of Darío's upbringing, was a fishing village with a few bureaucrats; León, where he grew up, provided barely more artistic sustenance. The official national culture, as represented by the objects Nicaragua chose to send to the Central American Exhibition in Guatemala in 1897, consisted of religious artifacts and mediocre landscape paintings of Rome. It was inevitable that Darío would depart for countries like Chile and Argentina that had formed national bourgeoisies.

This decision had severe consequences for subsequent literary expression, as the consecration of Darío's work by foreign audiences instilled an assumption that literary value was achieved by bypassing local material and seeking the approbation of taste makers in the metropolis (even while asserting national sovereignty). The literature created by those who defined themselves as the rebellious young writers of these comprador provincial elites dependent on the international agricultural markets would be "nacionalista, antiburgués, católico, y más tarde reaccionario" (*BV*, 61; "nationalist, anti-bourgeois, Catholic, and later reactionary"). As Ramírez concedes, this list contains terms that in larger countries would be in contradiction with each other; yet it is an apt description of the intellectual environment in which Ernesto Cardenal was raised, or the outlook of writers such as José Coronel Urtecho and the Betrayed Generation.

In spite of these explicit allusions to the literary culture of Granada, the most striking difference between "Balcanes y volcanes" and "El muchacho de Niquinohomo" is the absence of an assertion of Nicaraguan particularity. While Sandino's example has continental resonance, the experience of 1920s and 1930s Sandinismo is portrayed in the earlier essay as the unique, defining feature of Nicaragua's national trajectory. "Balcanes y volcanes," by contrast, concentrates on the similarities among Central American nations rather than the differences. One of the constants experienced by writers in the five republics during the first half of the twentieth century was the failure to professionalize their vocation. In contrast to Buenos Aires or Mexico City (or even Lima or Bogotá), the Central American milieu suffers not only from a small population, but from one in which the presence of middle-class people, the traditional consumers of literature, is negligible. The consequence of a society divided between oligarchs and peasants is that the writer is condemned to write in his "rato libre" (*BV*, 82; "spare time"), and that rather than anticipating a response to his work from a bourgeoisie concerned about national issues, the writer self-consciously writes for "posterity" – a tendency that promotes aesthetically conservative art detached from local realities – because he exists in a country devoid of literary institutions: "sin lectores, sin librerías, sin editores, sin periódicos, sin revistas, sin crítica" (*BV*, 82; "without readers, without bookstores, without publishers, without newspapers, without magazines, without criticism").

The opportunity to break this provincial suffocation came in 1944 when revolts led by tiny but determined middle classes occurred simultaneously in four of the five Central American republics. In Nicaragua and Honduras the revolts failed; in Guatemala and El Salvador they succeeded. In Costa Rica, where the revolt was delayed, it had the most significant long-term effects, abolishing the military and institutionalizing a bourgeois democracy. The most concentrated effort to break the patterns of the past, though, occurred in Guatemala. Ramírez recalls that the effervescent culture of the Guatemalan Revolution produced substantial writers such as Luis Cardoza y Aragón, Mario Monteforte Toledo, and Augusto Monterroso, all of whom would spend decades in exile in Mexico after the 1954 coup. Above all, the Revolution freed Miguel Ángel Asturias to release *The President* (1946) and *Hombres de maíz* (1949; *Men of Maize*), novels he had been working on for decades but would have been unable to publish under the dictatorships that preceded the 1944 revolt. Ramírez describes the techniques of the former work as Surrealist[20] and hence "una gran novedad en la región a estas alturas" (*BV*, 89; "a great novelty in the region at this point"); but he reserves his greatest praise for the latter novel, which is characterized by "una ruptura desde el lenguaje, que ya no ocupa la función de ser instrumento de colonización interna, de despojo folklórico, de suplantación, de acercamiento paternal y romántico, sino una reivindicación del hombre a partir del lenguaje, en cuanto hombre y no en cuanto indio" (*BV*, 90; "a breaking away, from the roots of literary language, which no longer occupies the function of being an instrument of internal colonization, of folkloric dispossession, of the supplanting of traditional cultures, of paternalistic and Romantic outreach, but a vindication of man from within language, as man and not as Indian").

The advent of transcendent modern artists at the level of Asturias and the painter Carlos Mérida, who are rooted in their own culture and make that culture modern through their engagement with the materials of their art, was a temporary phenomenon that was crushed by US imperialism. Yet the attention that Ramírez devotes to the decade-long flourishing of Guatemalan culture between 1944 and 1954 suggests that he sees this period as a model for what Nicaraguan culture might become after the overthrow of Somoza. The impression that this parallel made on him is evident in his decision to set scenes of *To Bury Our Fathers* (1977), the novel he was just beginning to write, among Nicaraguan exiles in Guatemala after the overthrow of the democratic government, establishing an implicit counterpoint between the two nations' experiences.

Ramírez devotes the final section of "Balcanes y volcanes," entitled "Veni, vidi, vici," to the US campaign, from the late 1940s to the present, to eradicate the sprouts of the national identities that began to emerge in Central America after 1944. The allusion to Julius Cesar foreshadows a clear-eyed analysis of imperialism. In *Biografía Mariano Fiallos* Ramírez had already characterized US President Dwight Eisenhower as the ally of dictators. This assertion sets the stage for his analysis of the instruments of 1960s US domination in Latin America, such as John F. Kennedy's Alliance for Progress, as attempts to destroy positive conceptions of nationality. The argument that the Alliance "willingly accepted military governments in Latin America, particularly if these regimes replaced reform-liberal governments that threatened to pass destabilizing economic measures" (LaFeber 1980: 247), is not uncommon. Ramírez's contribution, drawn from his personal experience of collaborating with USAID in Costa Rica, lies in his detailed analysis of the tactics employed by the United States to erase Central American national identities by linking a discourse of economic freedom to tight integration with US corporate interests: "Entre muchos ejemplos bastaría citar el programa regional de textos educativos para primaria de la USAID/ROCAP, que suministra los libros de lectura a todas las escuelas de la región, preparados bajo asesoría técnica norteamericana y que de acuerdo con denuncias de educadores costarricenses, estarían diseñados entre otras cosas para borrar toda idea de nacionalidad" (*BV*, 96; "Among many examples it would be sufficient to mention USAID's regional program of school textbooks for primary schools, which provides reading materials to all schools in the region, prepared under US technical assistance. According to complaints from Costa Rican educators, they are designed, among other things, to erase the whole idea of nationality"). The servile adoption of US cultural models by the compliant comprador bourgeoisie is depicted as the twentieth-century counterpart to the European artifacts imported or mimicked by Central America's nineteenth-century elites: "Como antes también, al llenarse las ciudades de América Latina de bulevares parisienses y templos griegos, Centroamérica tuvo también su ración de civilización, ahora … se levantarán las funginosas apariciones del *american* [sic] *way of life, grocery stores, supermarkets, department stores, coffee shops, boutiques, discotheques, ten cents*, que no dejarán pronto, como los góticos falsos, de adquirir una patina rural" (*BV*, 99; "As in the past, when the cities of Latin America filled up with Parisian boulevards and Greek temples, Central America also had its share of civilization, now … we are set to witness the appearance of the American Way of Life, grocery stores, supermarkets, department stores, coffee shops, boutiques, discos, five-and-tens, which, like the pseudo-Gothic styles, will soon acquire a rural veneer").

The final pages of "Balcanes y volcanes" are marked by the contrast between a precise, often empirically based, analysis and an increasingly caustic tone. As Ramírez's account approaches present-day consumerism, a palpable anger emerges. His trenchant assessment of Central American culture cannot conceal an ever more pungent partisan engagement. Beneath the celebration of consumption, he finds a highly stratified society and the displacement of indigenous peoples, whom the market economy wrenches from their traditional lands and converts into migrant labourers in other regions of the isthmus. In this way, both of the components required to create an authentic blended culture – a conscious, self-respecting bourgeoisie and strong, engaged rural, indigenous, or African-descended populations – have been debilitated; collaboration between them within a national prism is impossible. The essay closes with a survey of the shattered, largely exile-based cultural production of late 1960s Central America that circles again around the 1954 coup in Guatemala as the moment when the hope of a regional cultural renaissance was smashed, leading to the early 1970s crisis of a "cultura dispersa, mutilada y bajo acecho" (*BV*, 109; "dispersed culture, mutilated and under siege"). A quote from Frantz Fanon makes revolutionary social change the necessary precondition for substantial cultural achievement: "Porque, como recuerda Fanon, sólo el restablecimiento de la nación dará vida, en el sentido más biológico del término, a la cultura nacional" (109; "Because, as Fanon points out, only the reestablishment of the nation will give life, in the most biological sense of the term, to the national culture").

Like the act of compiling *El pensamiento vivo de Sandino*, this phrase implies a commitment to revolutionary change. Yet the most significant immediate consequence of "El muchacho de Niquinohomo" and "Balcanes y volcanes," beyond their political impact, was to overcome the obstacles that were preventing Ramírez from developing as a novelist. Unlike writers raised in cities, where the dramatic complexity of relations between different levels of society is evident, Ramírez had grown up in a rural area in a tiny nation renowned for its poets but barren of a novelistic tradition. In their chapter on literature in *Culture and Customs of Nicaragua* (2008), Steven F. White and Esthela Calderón muster only a few travel writers, the essays on Nicaraguan customs of Pablo Antonio Cuadra, and Rubén Darío's *modernista* fables at the turn of the century as contributors to a prose tradition. They identify no worthwhile prose fiction prior to that of Ramírez (77–93). Ramírez himself has stated: "No hubo en el pasado novelistas ni cuentistas. A lo más, poetas que escribieron o que han escrito novelas y cuentos. Te citaría a Fernando Silva y a Lizandro Chávez" (*AO*, 305; "In the past there were neither novelists nor storytellers. At best, poets who wrote or have written novels and stories. I would mention to you Fernando Silva and Lizandro Chávez"). The first recognized Nicaraguan novel, *Cosmapa* by José Román, was published only in 1944; the first novel by a Nicaraguan (living in exile in Mexico) to receive critical recognition as a literary work, *Trágame tierra* (May the Earth Swallow Me) by Lizandro Chávez Alfaro, appeared in 1969, just one year prior to Ramírez's own first novel. (Chávez would publish two more novels before his death in Managua in 2006.)

As the first professional novelist in his country's long history, Ramírez inherited no motifs or traditions; he was deprived of the experience of developing as a writer by "misreading," as Harold Bloom would put it (Bloom 1973: 5–14), his national predecessors. The Americanized governing family's derision of the nation's culture, pervasive censorship, and Ramírez's own family's absorption into the political apparatus of the dictatorship, all conspired against the development of a lucid vision of Nicaraguan life. Before he could dramatize his society, Ramírez needed to create it. The two long essays he wrote during his first months in Berlin established Sandino's campaign against the US Marines as the essential background to contemporary events. They placed Nicaragua's dilemma, and the problems inherent in being a Nicaraguan writer, in the context of the five Central American republics' fraught, dependent culture. Both essays confirmed cultural and racial *mestizaje* as the glue of national solidarity; "Balcanes y volcanes" stressed the importance of affinities with neighbouring nations with analogous histories, such as Guatemala.[21] (Costa Rica, in spite of his long residence there, was too historically and temperamentally different from Nicaragua to offer imaginative sustenance.) The essays confirmed the Somoza dictatorship, conceived as an extension of the US occupation, as the defining factor in shaping Nicaraguan society and the central strand in any future novel about the country, a theme that would not be dispersed by irony but must be confronted directly and addressed from a perspective capable of tracing the dictatorship's repercussions in a range of lives over decades. All of these elements were poured into *To Bury Our Fathers*, enabling Ramírez to bypass the historical nostalgia and obvious borrowings from other rural Latin American writers of Modernist ambitions such as Rulfo, Asturias, and García Márquez that had characterized *Tiempo de fulgor*. The result of these essays was to permit Ramírez to emerge as a vital artist of the Latin American present. By burrowing deeper into his national and regional culture, he supplied his art with a scope and breadth of perception that had been lacking in his earlier fiction. By creating this palette, he released himself from the cage of impotent irony.

The essays represented the culmination of the long evolution away from Liberalism that had started on the day in 1959 when the National Guard opened fire on the students. In these essays, Ramírez argued his way towards an overt identification with Sandinismo; he also made himself into an indispensable asset to the FSLN. The mid-1970s, when Nicaragua was poised on the brink of transformative change, was an interlude when other writers, including those who already belonged to the FSLN, such as Carlos Fonseca and Jaime Wheelock, also paused to work out their understanding of the country's history in essay form. In literary terms, the most significant of these essayists was a writer who was consciously separating himself from a Conservative, rather than a Liberal, heritage: Ernesto Cardenal.

5

Cardenal: The First Incursion into Prose (1970–75)

ECSTATIC DIALECTICS: *ABIDE IN LOVE*

Cardenal's first book of prose, *Vida en el amor* (*Abide in Love*), appeared in 1970. It is a work of theological reflection, in the style of Thomas Merton's influential *The New Man* (1961), although less learned and metaphysically precise than Merton's work. Cardenal's book is whimsical, mystical, and, in a discreet way, more obviously personal than that of Merton. Like the poems of *Gethsemani, Ky.*, *Abide in Love* emerged from the notebooks Cardenal kept during his apprenticeship in the Trappist monastery in Kentucky. During the 1960s, Cardenal divided the material in the notebooks into three categories: that which could be rewritten as poems; that which could serve as "un testimonio autobiográfico de aquellos días" (*VP*, 314; "an autobiographical testament of those days"), and which, more than three decades later, would appear as the eighth chapter of the first volume of his memoirs; and that which would be combined with earlier writings on mystical topics in *Abide in Love*. In Cardenal's words: "De esas mismas libretas también saqué los principales pasajes de tema místico, algunos escritos en Nicaragua después de mi conversión, pero la mayoría en la Trapa, y ellos forman *Vida en el amor*" (*VP*, 314; "From those same notebooks I also drew the main passages of a mystical nature, some written in Nicaragua after my conversion, but the majority in the monastery, and they comprise *Abide in Love*").

The book's lengthy gestation is evident from the fact that, although published in 1970, it includes a prologue by Thomas Merton, written in January 1966. Read in light of Cardenal's subsequent development, the prologue seems to presage, and even authorize, the fusion of materialist dialectic and mystical Christianity that would become the hallmark of Cardenal's poetry and thought after his conversion to Sandinismo. Merton writes: "The metaphysical structure of love is in a certain sense dialectic. Love demands conflict; it nourishes itself by conflict and emerges purified from conflict. But once love attains its authentic purity in the fire of conflict, it causes the conflict to disappear and with it disappears the contradiction" (Merton 1995: xxi–xxii).

The broad compatibility of Merton's vision of love as a force that arises from dialectical conflict, and finally resolves or synthesizes the contradictions that set off that conflict, with Marxist materialist dialects – particularly when these are somewhat loosely conceived in a project whose overriding impulse is nationalistic, as was the case with Sandinismo – is evident. Cardenal's absorption of Merton's influence develops on two fronts: a revolutionary dialectic, which becomes more pronounced in later works, and a gender dialectic that responds to Cardenal's contradictory feelings about devoting himself to a chaste, contemplative religious life. Since his contemplative life's point of origin – his conversion on 2 June 1956 – is inseparable from his symbolic emasculation by the dictatorship, which stole his would-be fiancée, deprived him of the ability to conduct a political career, and consigned him to exile from his homeland and internment in a private, religious sphere of activity that corresponded more closely to traditional female, than male, roles, the pursuit of divine love is fraught with gender anxiety. In *Abide in Love*, Cardenal writes: "El alma es mujer, y a veces en la presencia de Él el alma se vuelve un poco coqueta, sabiéndose amada y consciente de sus encantos y de su dominio sobre el amado, y a veces se vuelve también un poco tiránica sabiéndolo rendido y sabiéndose dominadora, pero sabiéndose también totalmente rendida y dominada" (*VA*, 81–2; "The soul is feminine, and sometimes in His presence the soul becomes a little flirtatious, knowing that it is loved and conscious of its charms and of its power over the Beloved, and sometimes it also becomes a little tyrannical knowing that He is captivated and knowing of its dominance, but feeling as well entirely captivated and dominated").[1]

This explicitly gendered conception of the soul's relationship to the deity reproduces traditionalist conceptions of the male-female dialectic that portray the man as dominating and the woman as alluring yet destined ultimately to be subjugated by male power. If "the soul is feminine," then the religious contemplative, who lives through his soul, is feminized. Not only does the monk or priest forego the defining male activity of sexual relations with women, but he lives through his surrender to the masculine power of God. Here a new dialectical field emerges, between the gendered and the political facets of Cardenal's absorption of Merton's mysticism. While ordination conferred on Cardenal a position within the Nicaraguan social hierarchy from which to engage with national politics, which the Liberal dictatorship had denied him, the mere fact of being publicly identified as a priest, a symbolic castrato, a pacifist monk in his island retreat, exhorted him to act in the public, political world to redeem himself from this withdrawal from the traditional coordinates of upper-class Spanish American masculinity.

Cardenal's political engagement arises as a form of compensation for his frocked pseudo-femininity; by striking back against the dictatorship, he reclaims his masculinity through his attempted reclamation of the stolen Nicaraguan nation. He is authorized to do this by Merton who, as a gringo, belongs to the society of the dictator's masters; the Merton-Cardenal correspondence channels some of this emotional energy, the relationship between mentor (Merton) and novice (Cardenal) reproducing the interaction between the deity and the "flirtatious" soul in a bond which, if not overtly homoerotic, became a conduit for emotional energy displaced from the sexual relations with women that both men had enjoyed prior to committing themselves to religious life.[2] Like the soul seeking God's love and attention, Cardenal is constantly trying to inveigle Merton to come and live with him in a religious community in Nicaragua, while Merton, like God, remains admired, authoritative, ubiquitous, but impossible to pin down, travelling incessantly, vowing that he is present in spirit in Solentiname, and promising some day to appear there in human form. On 21 July 1968, on his way to Japan on the trip that would end with his death in Bangkok, Merton wrote: "I may get to Nicaragua for a few weeks with you" (Letson 1999: 99). His elusiveness suggests that Cardenal's position was very much that of the coquettish soul pining for the attention of a loving but evanescent deity. Letson, commenting on the conclusion of their correspondence, writes: "Clearly, Merton has shoes hot to travel, but decidedly cool to travel to Nicaragua. A tragic final chapter, this, to what seemed destined to be so fortunate a tale" (ibid.).

While the relationship with Merton is replete with ecstatic overtones, Cardenal's depiction of the bond between an implicitly masculine God and an explicitly feminine soul is far more overt in its use of metaphors freighted with parallels to physical love: "Dios está loco de amor, y su comportamiento por lo tanto es imprevisible. En cualquier momento el Amante puede cometer un disparate porque como todo el que ama, no razona. Está borracho de amor" (*VA*, 43; "God is crazed with love, and God's behavior is therefore unpredictable. God may do something silly at any time, because, like any lover, God does not reason. God is drunk with love" [*AL*, 20]). This vision of God as a lover who may "do something silly" flies in the face of traditional conceptions of the deity as all-knowing and infallible. In Cardenal's dialectic, the active passion of God overwhelms the passive surrender of the feminized soul of the believer in an encounter that contains an almost physical sensuality. God and the believer are a couple like "dos enamorados" (*VA*, 98; "two lovers" [*AL*, 69]). At various points, Cardenal invokes the Song of Songs to characterize this couple's union, as, for example, when he writes: "La juventud es la edad de entregarse a Dios, porque es la edad de las ilusiones y del amor – del amor del hombre a la mujer, y de la primavera y del Cantar de los Cantares – y la entrega a Dios es una entrega de amor" (*VA*, 103; "Youth is the time to surrender to God, for it is the time of illusions and love – of the love of man for woman, and of the spring and the Song of Songs – and surrendering to God is a loving surrender"). Love, in Cardenal's depiction, always craves union, and the union requires that the two beings who will unite be defined in gendered terms: "el amor busca siempre la unión, la identificación del amado con la amada" (*VA*, 135; "For love always seeks union, the identification of the lover and the beloved" [*AL*, 107]). Since a feminine God is, in this context, unimaginable, the believer who seeks God must assume feminine gendering; the deeper the union with God, the more feminized the believer becomes. A monk or priest, having subjected his life to God's will, is permanently gendered as feminine.

Abide in Love, though drenched in Merton's influence, also begins the crucial work of laying the symbolic foundations of Cardenal's public personality, and establishing his capacity to influence others. His sensual, gendered vision of divine love may be the most original facet of his construction of his creative universe, but it is one of the strands that is most difficult to transmit to others. Other motifs that would become dominant in Cardenal's later poetry appear in these reflections in inchoate form. The first of these is opposition to the Somoza dictatorship. Even though the tone and subject matter of *Abide in Love* allow little space for political statement, Cardenal grapples with the question of how a God who is "crazed with love" approaches a man like Anastasio or Luis Somoza Debayle. He finds an instructive parallel in the words of Joan of Arc: "Cuando preguntaron a Juana de Arco en el proceso si Dios amaba a los ingleses, contestó: 'Dios no ama a los ingleses *en Francia*.' Y ése es el misterio de la vocación de todos nosotros. Dios quiere también a un dictador de Nicaragua, pero no lo quiere dictador de Nicaragua" (*VA*, 146; "When they asked St. Joan of Arc at her trial whether God loved the English, she replied: 'God does not love the English in France.' And this is the mystery of our vocation. God also loves the man who is a dictator of Nicaragua, but he does not want him to be the dictator of Nicaragua" [*AL*, 118]). The dictator is the supreme egotist, he who does not submerge himself in union with another but does entirely as he wishes. Sin, in Cardenal's definition, resides in being a slave of one's desires: "Y cuando un hombre así, con su voluntad gobernada, gobierna un pueblo, entonces ese pueblo es gobernado por una dictadura" (*VA*, 119; "And when a man like this, who does not control his will, governs a people, then that people is governed by a dictatorship").

This formulation enables Cardenal to explain dictatorship within a framework of omnipresent divine love. More central to the imagery of his later poetry, however, are the first intimations of socialist thought to appear in Cardenal's *obra*. The vision of love as union annihilates possessive individualism: "La vida en Dios es comunitaria y *comunista* y cada una de las Tres Divinas Personas se da totalmente a las otras, y no hay en ellos 'mío' ni 'tuyo' aunque sí existe en ellas el Yo y el Tú" (*VA*, 124; "God's life is communitarian and communistic, and each of the three divine persons gives himself totally to the others. In the Trinity there is no 'mine' or 'thine,' even though there is an 'I' and a 'Thou'" [*AL*, 95–6]). The word "comunista," italicized in its first appearance in his work, arises in the unexpected context of a discussion of the holy trinity. It is conceived as a form of self-abnegation, although one that does not erase individual identity or subjectivity. This "communism" makes no explicit reference to the economic or political realm; at most, it is theological and metaphysical, although its relevance to the organization of a community such as that which Cardenal founded in Solentiname is obvious.

A second important aspect of Cardenal's creative vision, his use of cosmic and scientific imagery to describe divine union, puts in only a fleeting appearance in *Abide in Love*. The book closes with a discussion of resurrection. Here, too, Cardenal's views are theologically unorthodox. He maintains: "Resucitaremos con todos los cuerpos y con todas las edades, o mejor dicho resucitará un solo cuerpo con muchas edades, en el que todos seremos carne de otros y en el que estaremos todos unos dentro de otros como el feto está dentro de la madre" (*VA*, 185–6; "We shall rise with all bodies and all ages. In it we shall all be flesh of others and within one another as the foetus is in its mother" [*AL*, 159]). This passage adumbrates and foreshadows the Sandinista culture of martyr-worship, in which the proliferation of monuments and homages to dead guerrillas seemed at times to make the dead more present than the living. Cardenal was instrumental in developing this culture. One of his contributions was to convert the Latin American left's traditional cry of "¡Presente!" – meant to recognize dead comrades – into a species of materialist mysticism where the bodies of the dead diffuse through the soil of the nation. In so doing, their material essence transmutes into a spiritual omnipresence that presages a Judgment Day that "será la destrucción de la injusticia en la tierra ... no vemos a los dioses pero creemos que son inmortales/... y lo mismo sucede con los que han muerto por su pueblo" (*CANC*, 454; "will be the destruction of injustice on earth ... we cannot see the gods yet believe them to be immortal/... the same goes for those who have died for their people" [*COSC*, 377–8]). In *Cántico Cósmico* (*Cosmic Canticle*) the dovetailing of the spiritual and physical presence of those who have given their lives for the homeland is supported by a blend of Catholic mysticism and the evocation of the Second Law of Thermodynamics, according to which energy never dies. Hence the body of the guerrilla, "haciéndose suave tierra, humus otra vez/junto con el humus de todos los demás humanos" (*CANC*, 454; "becoming soft earth, humus once again/together with the humus of all the other human beings" [*COSC*, 378]), participates in a form of perpetual resurrection that is simultaneously physical and spiritual.

This ongoing resurrection forges the autonomous, socialist, Catholic nation whose soil extends the image of the religious resurrection of the flesh that Cardenal posits in *Abide in Love* when he writes that in the resurrection "we shall all be flesh of others." In a similar vein, the book's concluding assertion that "todo el cosmos es canto, y canto coral y canto de fiesta, y de fiesta de bodas ..." (*VA*, 189; "The whole universe is a song, a choral chant, a festive song of the wedding feast" [*AL*, 163]) presages the portrait of the dance of the spheres in *Cosmic Canticle*, a dance that is not only gendered but also intensely sensualized. The later poem perceives the cosmos as consisting of binaries whose union makes "Toda cosa coito/Todo el cosmos cópula" (*CANC*, 28; "Each thing coitus/The entire cosmos copulation" [*COSC*, 25]). *Abide in Love* lays the foundation for this vision by closing with a paraphrase of the Bible's statement (John 3: 29) that "el que tiene la esposa es el esposo" (*VA*, 189; "He who has the bride is the bridegroom" [*AL*, 164]). This gendered vision of the infinite implies a gendering of all that is present in creation; the union that Cardenal praises closes with an evocation of singing – a forerunner of the two choruses in *Cosmic Canticle*. *Abide in Love* ends with the assertion that "y nuestro canto, junto con el coro de los astros y el de los átomos, es el mismo del coro de los ángeles" (*VA*, 189; "And our song, together with the chorus of stars and atoms is the same as the angels' chorus" [*AL*, 164]). The fusion of cosmic singing and a gendered relationship with deity would develop in the later poetry.

ISLAND TO ISLAND: *IN CUBA*

A second crucial plank of Cardenal's creative and political personality during the 1980s was set in place with his conversion to socialism after his three-month trip to Cuba in 1970. A product of Cardenal's long-standing friendship with the Catholic Cuban poet Cintio Vitier, who had been trying to persuade Cardenal since the early 1960s that it was possible to live a Catholic life under a Communist revolution, this trip was so controversial that it was preceded by negotiations among the Vatican, the Somoza regime, and the Nicaraguan church hierarchy that became bogged down in debates over the correct interpretation of an ambiguous letter from the Vatican, written in Latin. Cardenal was finally denied permission to make the trip, then decided to go anyway (*IE*, 259). His experiences in Cuba resulted in another fusion that became central to his vision: the fusion of Catholicism and Marxism. It enabled him to overcome a misunderstanding that was common within Cuba: "en una cosa coincidían en Cuba católicos y comunistas, y era un error: que un católico no podía ser comunista porque el comunista tenía que ser ateo. Yo mismo participé en ese error" (*IE*, 260; "on one point Catholics and Communists were in agreement, and it was a mistake: that a Catholic could not be a Communist because the Communist must be an atheist. I myself participated in that mistake").

En Cuba (*In Cuba*) became a bestseller in Latin America, making Cardenal's name known well beyond the circles of those who were acquainted with his poetry. It does not, however, relate the experience of the author's conversion to socialism. The book contains no moment analogous to 2 June 1956. Dedicated "al pueblo cubano/y a Fidel" (*EC*, 7; "To the Cuban People/and to Fidel [*IC*, xii]), the travelogue seems to have been written by an author who accepts the superiority of the socialist system as a given, and whose central preoccupation is to forge a new kind of Catholic immune to traditional Catholic anti-Communism. The argument Cardenal makes is less about the most appropriate form of government for Latin America than about the appropriate political orientation for a devout Catholic.

Blending oral history with a postmodern collage of citations from the Cuban press, posters glimpsed in the streets of Havana, poems and song lyrics, political speeches and many notebook jottings, the book employs some of the same Poundian techniques found in *Zero Hour* and *The Doubtful Strait*. Where the Exteriorism of Cardenal's longer poems creates a text that is anti-lyrical and narrative driven, the application of these strategies to a prose work produces a surface that is more fragmented and episodic than conventional prose reportage. The book is printed with double-spacing between paragraphs or lines of dialogue, which heightens the scattered effect. The chapters, though short, often touch on two or three different subjects, whose connections are implicit or intuitive. In its insistence on allowing the reader to hear Cuban voices speaking, *In Cuba*, together with Elena Poniatowska's *Hasta no verte, Jesús mío* (1969; *Here's to You, Jesusa!*) and

La noche de Tlatelolco (1971; *Massacre in Mexico*), is the forerunner of the Testimonio writing of the 1980s. At the same time, the force of Cardenal's conversion is palpable in the book's pages; as Gerald Martin writes, "of the many writers and thinkers who have written Cuban diaries since 1959, [Cardenal's] may well be the most passionate and illuminating" (Martin 1989: 391).

The Cuba portrayed by Cardenal is a place of spontaneity and effervescent debates about social organization, where oppressive acts occasionally occur but can always be corrected once recognized. Cardenal records accusations against the regime made by his informants, then produces other informants who explain why the original informants cannot possibly be telling the truth. The figure of Fidel Castro, a kind of hyperactive Don Quixote, at once naive, brilliant, crusading, and irrepressible, who puts in appearances everywhere in the country at all hours of the night and day, arguing, discussing, correcting, refining, or reforming the structures of his revolution, is at the book's core. The book culminates in Cardenal's compelling twenty-page narration of a Castro speech, followed, after a brief closing chapter, by an epilogue that consists of an interview Cardenal conducted with Castro a year after his first visit to Cuba, during a late-night drive through Havana in a small car with El Comandante and two young soldiers.

The interview unites the book's two dominant threads – Cardenal's exploration of the role of the devout Catholic in a revolutionary society and his fascination with the figure of Castro – through a conversation between the two men about religion and the prospects for revolution in Latin America. Beneath the book's apparently haphazard surface lies a quest narrative in which Cardenal must solve the puzzle of how to be at once a Catholic and a revolutionary. The numerous interviews with Cuban Catholics of different backgrounds, who have adopted a variety of stances vis-à-vis the revolutionary government, ranging from total allegiance to ambivalence to hostility and open dissidence, build towards the conclusion that adherence to Christian principles demands commitment to socialist revolution. Arriving at this conclusion grants Cardenal personal access to Castro, who, as the embodiment of revolutionary masculinity, is the cure for his emasculation by the Somoza dictatorship. Cardenal's acceptance of the Revolution as a Catholic phenomenon permits him to restore his masculinity, shattered by the marginalization of his once-dominant social class, and called into question by the chastity inherent in his vocation. The hereditary Conservative may be impotent in a Nicaragua divided between a Liberal dictatorship and a Marxist guerrilla insurgency, the priest's vestments and sexual abstinence may impugn his *hombría*, but the revolutionary priest, anointed in his advocacy of the armed struggle by the proto-macho Fidel Castro, possesses a virility that his brethren must respect.

Cardenal's quest may be inspired by personal motives, as the political engagement of most individuals is ultimately driven by the need to repair imbalances in their private lives, but he downplays this aspect of his journey through Cuban Catholicism, stressing repeatedly the potential Pan-American significance of an alliance between Catholics and socialists. A revolutionary socialism united with the Catholic Church would be unstoppable; a revolutionary movement that is rejected by Catholics, on the other hand, is doomed to remain marginalized.[3] This point emerges with particular clarity during Cardenal's conversation with the Cuban foreign minister, Raúl Roa. Occurring in the final section, when Cardenal has begun to consolidate his ideas about the relationship between Catholicism and revolution, this pivotal scene sees Cardenal relinquish the observer status he has maintained for most of the book. Having listened to dozens of voices, the majority of them belonging to Catholics, Cardenal begins to propound his own ideas:

> Yo le dije [a Roa] que como sacerdote y como revolucionario deseaba que desapareciera el conflicto que había habido en Cuba entre la Revolución y la Iglesia, y que deseaba que la Iglesia fuera revolucionaria. Esto era bueno para la Revolución y para la Iglesia. Para la Iglesia, porque era el retorno a las esencias evangélicas del cristianismo primitivo. Para la Revolución, porque aceleraría grandemente el proceso revolucionario de América Latina. La revolución en América Latina no se hará sin la Iglesia. Y también no se hará sin Cuba. Cuba es un modelo para América Latina, pero la revolución sería más fácil en América Latina si también existiera el modelo de la Iglesia revolucionaria en Cuba. (*EC*, 301; I told him that as a priest and as a revolutionary I wanted to see the conflict between the Revolution and the Church in Cuba disappear, and that I wanted the Church to be revolutionary. This would be good for the revolution and good for the Church. For the Church, because it was a return to the evangelical substance of primitive Christianity. For the revolution, because it would greatly accelerate the revolutionary processes in Latin America. Revolution in Latin America will not occur without the Church. And it will not be made without Cuba. Cuba is a model for Latin America, but revolution in Latin America would be easier if there were also the model of a revolutionary Church in Cuba. [*IC*, 272])

Roa objects to Cardenal's ideas, stating that the revolutionary government does not wish to create a national church in Cuba, nor does it wish to be responsible for dividing Latin American Catholicism. Cardenal insists that the promotion of a progressive church, such as that which already exists in circles influenced by liberation theology, particularly in Colombia and Brazil, need not entail doing either of these things: "Se trata de importar a Cuba la revolución de la Iglesia de América Latina" (*EC*, 302; "I'm talking about importing to Cuba the revolution of the Latin American Church" [*IC*, 273]). With this statement, Cardenal arrogates to himself a force capable of strengthening the Cuban Revolution. This conversation represents the book's ideological climax in the sense that it completes the forging of his revolutionary identity. He is rewarded by the foreign finister's response: "Me dijo Roa que yo debía hablar con Fidel" (*EC*, 302; "Roa told me I should talk with Fidel" [*IC*, 273]). Although this meeting does not occur for another seventy pages, from this point on, Cardenal acts as an authority figure. The conversation with Roa is followed by a scene in which a group of young Cubans, recognizing Cardenal by his beard, ask him whether he thinks a Christian should be integrated into the Revolution. When he tells them that Christians should participate in all revolutionary tasks, "Brincaron de alegría ... palmotearon, se abrazaron" (*EC*, 302; "they jumped with joy ... they clapped their hands and hugged one another" [*IC*, 273]).

By bringing together Cuba's socialist revolution and the revolution in the Catholic Church that was occurring elsewhere in Latin America in the post-Medellín environment, Cardenal outlines the culture that might be promoted by a future revolutionary government of Nicaragua, and with which he is already beginning to experiment in Solentiname. Roa's initial words to Cardenal anticipate the Sandinista culture of mystical nationalism, Christianity, and revolutionary self-sacrifice that would begin to cohere later in the 1970s: "La Revolución es también un fenómeno religioso. Hemos tenido días muy difíciles. Sin este elemento religioso y místico que ha tenido esta Revolución, ella no habría sido posible" (*EC*, 301; "The revolution is also a religious phenomenon. We have had some very difficult times. Without the Revolution's religious and mystical element it would not have survived" [*IC*, 272]). Mysticism of the sort Cardenal is developing in Solentiname becomes, in this portrait, a vital element in sustaining the Revolution. In order to acquire the authority to promote this mystical vision, however, he must touch the core of the Revolution: Fidel Castro.

In Cuba opens, curiously, with the same scene that opens the first volume of Cardenal's memoirs, *Vida perdida*, published twenty-seven years later: his memories of the first time he landed in Cuba, changing planes in Havana in 1957 on his way to Kentucky to enter Gethsemani: "Era la Cuba de Batista. Una prima que había estado en Cuba me había contado hacía poco que un muchacho peleaba en las montañas y que se llamaba Fidel Castro"

(*EC*, 9; "It was Batista's Cuba. A cousin of mine who had been in Cuba had told me shortly before that a young man was fighting in the mountains and that his name was Fidel Castro" [*IC*, 1]). The opening two paragraphs establish the identification of the Revolution with the figure of Fidel Castro, and underline Cardenal's central preoccupation concerning his visit: "Llevaba cierta prevención, sobre todo por la cuestión religiosa" (9; "I had some reservations, especially because of the religious question" [*IC*, 9]). Cardenal's parallel exploration of Cuban Catholicism and Fidel's revolutionary manhood structures the collage of scenes that follow.

Fidel's identity as the incarnation of the Revolution, the eternal guerrilla, is established early in the book by Ernesto, one of Cardenal's informants: "Para Fidel la guerrilla en la Sierra Maestra no ha terminado. Él dice que todavía usa barba y vestido de campaña porque todavía está haciendo la guerra" (*EC*, 77; "For Fidel the guerrilla warfare of the Sierra Maestra has not ended. He says he still wears a beard and a uniform because he is still waging war" [*IC*, 64]). An official of Casa de las Américas tells Cardenal: "Es divertido cómo Fidel está siempre contra los dirigentes y a favor del pueblo ... Yo creo que Fidel aún no se ha hecho a la idea de que ahora él es la máxima autoridad" (*EC*, 131; "It's amusing how Fidel is always against the leaders and in favor of the people ... I don't think that Fidel has got used to the idea that he is now the supreme authority" [*IC*, 112]). Cardenal's host Cintio Vitier asserts that "Fidel es el jefe de la oposición en Cuba" (*EC*, 131; "Fidel is the leader of the opposition in Cuba" [*IC*, 112]). Related anecdotes show the country's leader continuing to use guerrilla tactics to solve its problems and rectify abuses. A young poet tells Cardenal of Fidel's reaction to learning of the abuse of prisoners in the Unidad Militar de Ayuda a la Producción (UMAP; Military Unit for Assisting in Production) concentration camps that he would later close down:

> Una noche asaltó una posta de guardia y la capturó y se metió dentro, como que fuera preso, para ver qué trato les daban. Se acostó en una hamaca. Los presos dormían en hamacas. Los despertaban golpeándolos con sables; o si no, les cortaban las cuerdas de la hamaca. Cuando él que los despertaba levantó el sable, se encontró con la cara de Fidel Castro, casi se muere. (30; One night he broke into the camp and lay down in one of the hammocks to see what kind of treatment a prisoner gets. The prisoners slept in hammocks. They were waked with saber whacks if they didn't get up. The guards would cut their hammock cords. When one guard raised his saber he found himself staring at Fidel; he almost dropped dead. [*IC*, 20])

The poet, who worked as a camp guard, recounts similar "break-ins" by Fidel at other camps; El Comandante is portrayed conspiring with everyone from bus drivers to students to improve their treatment by their superiors. Cardenal's account emphasizes the suppleness, avoidance of encrusted bureaucracy, and potential for quick reform afforded by such procedures; it overlooks the shortcomings of personalistic rule even of such an unorthodox variety.

Cardenal absorbs Castro's behaviour as a model of revolutionary Latin American masculinity. As part of this identification, he problematizes Castro's role as a Soviet ally in order to establish his rootedness in Catholic Latin America. An anonymous exchange of dialogue emphasizes Fidel's debt to José Martí (1853–95), the original protagonist of Cuban independence: "Leía mucho a Martí. Creo que tendrá más influencia martiana que marxista" (*EC*, 86; "He read Martí a lot. I think he probably has had more Martían than Marxist influence" [*IC*, 72]). This statement, which by analogy would counsel a Nicaraguan to pay more attention to Sandino than to Marx, is supplemented by the information that, far from wishing to imitate the Soviet-dominated nations of Eastern Europe, Fidel has criticized them for their "materialización vulgar de la conciencia de los hombres" (*EC*, 188–9; "vulgar materialization of the conscience of man" [*IC*, 167]), decrying the way in which these societies corrupt young Cubans who study in them.

Cardenal further distances Cuba from Soviet Communism through a dissection of the speech in which Castro, very controversially, supported the Soviet invasion of Czechoslovakia that crushed the Prague Spring of 1968. Many, particularly in the West, interpret this speech as the end of the creative, original phase of the Cuban Revolution and the beginning of an era of subservience to the Soviet Union.[4] The speech is often seen as foreshadowing the "Quinquineo Gris" (Five Grey Years), the period of doctrinaire retrenchment between the Padilla Case in 1971 (see chapter 3), which cost Castro the support of many foreign intellectuals, and November 1975, when his unilateral decision to intervene in Angola initiated a new period of idealism and relative foreign-policy independence from the Soviet Union. José Lezama Lima, whose fiction and poetry were banned for more than twenty years after his death in 1976 (his rehabilitation was completed in 2008, when his house in Havana was opened as a museum), but who appears in *In Cuba* as a supporter of the Revolution, summarizes Fidel's speech on Czechoslovakia for Cardenal: "Envió antes emisarios para saber si los checos estaban dispuestos a pelear o no. Los informes fueron que no iban a pelear. Era locura que Cuba peleara por ellos … En ese discurso defendiendo la invasión, Fidel, sin embargo, también atacó a la Unión Soviética, a

Yugoslavia a la que llamó falsamente socialista, al régimen liberal de Checoslovaquia y al anterior régimen stalinista; y al único país que defendió fue a Vietnam" (*EC*, 214; "He had sent emissaries to find out if the Czechs were ready to fight and learned that they were not. If would have been madness for Cuba to fight for them ... In that speech defending the invasion, Fidel nevertheless also attacked the Soviet Union and Yugoslavia, which he called pseudosocialist, and the liberal regime in Czechoslovakia, and the former Stalinist regime. The only country he defended was Vietnam" [*IC*, 192]).

In a crossover between the parallel tensions that animate *In Cuba*, the narrative pays progressively more attention to the fate of Catholics within the Revolution even as the book builds towards the climax of Fidel's speech on the national holiday of 26 July, the anniversary of Castro's assault on the Moncada barracks in Santiago in 1953. Fidel's capacity to reimagine Cuban national identity, to sculpt the revolutionary nation, stems from his mastery of words. As one of Cardenal's informants states, Fidel is a compulsive speaker, just as his forerunner José Martí was a compulsive writer. Yet Fidel's passion for the spoken word does not imply a disdain for literary culture. On the contrary, Fidel is portrayed as being fanatically committed to the correct interpretation of the written text, almost as though it were religious scripture. After his 26 July speech he rushes to the office of the official newspaper, *Granma,* where he spends hours revising the proofs of the speech: "se está allí hasta la madrugada. Él mismo corrige las pruebas, quiere cerciorarse que no haya errores" (336; "[he] stays there until dawn. He corrects the proofs himself, he wants to make sure there are no errors" [*IC*, 302]).

The Revolution, meanwhile, is defined by its successful literacy program and its diffusion of literary culture through all levels of society. Books are abundant and, at a price of either seventy-five centavos or one peso, affordable for all. Cardenal learns that a 10,000-copy print run of an anthology of his poems has sold out in a week; Gabriel García Márquez's *One Hundred Years of Solitude* (1967), which at this early stage of its career had sold 500,000 copies in the rest of Spanish America, has sold 80,000 copies in Cuba. The Revolution has built bookstores and libraries everywhere: "Hay librerías en las montañas, donde los libros son llevados en mulas. Hay bibliotecas en las granjas colectivas, en las fábricas, los cuarteles, las cárceles" (*EC*, 91; "There are bookstores even in the mountains, where the books are carried on muleback. There are libraries on the collective farms, in factories, barracks, jails" [*IC*, 76]). In a precursor of the poetry workshops that Cardenal would later found in Nicaragua, the government has established Talleres Literarios, where ordinary people learn to write poetry. Cardenal discovers that his aesthetic has become a model for many of these workshop poets, who tell him: "El realismo socialista de los rusos es una mierda ... los poetas han encontrado su verdadero realismo socialista en el 'exteriorismo' de la poesía nicaragüense. Los poetas cubanos con este 'exteriorismo' pueden escribir ahora sobre el Moncada, las colas, la zafra, las playas, las películas, la vida, la muerte, Vietnam, la voz de Fidel en el radio" (*EC*, 235; "The socialist realism of the Russians was so much shit ... The poets also have found their socialist realism in the 'externalism' of Nicaraguan poetry. Cuban poets with this 'externalism' can now write about Moncada, waiting in line, the harvest, beaches, films, life, death, Vietnam, Fidel's voice on the radio" [*IC*, 212]).

This legitimization of his own procedures integrates Cardenal into the Revolution, just as, in the book's later sections, he advises Cuban Catholics to integrate. One of the book's pivotal scenes occurs when Cardenal reconstructs an incident in which Fidel demonstrates simultaneously his allegiance to textual veracity and his open-mindedness on religious matters. On 13 March 1962 Fidel presided over a commemorative service at the University of Havana for José Antonio Echeverría, a Catholic student leader who died in 1957 in an attack on Batista's presidential palace. A hero to Catholic progressives, José Antonio left behind a political testament, which was read aloud at the memorial service. The master of ceremonies, however, omitted the lines where José Antonio spoke of his religious faith. Fidel leaps in to correct the host: "¿Seremos nosotros, compañero, seremos, compañeros, tan cobardes y seremos tan manco mentales, que vengamos aquí a leer el testamento de José Antonio Echeverría y tengamos la cobardía, la miseria moral, de suprimir tres líneas?" (*EC*, 209; "Can we, comrades, can we, comrades, be so cowardly and can we be such mental cripples that we come here to read Jose Antonio's will and we have the cowardice, the moral misery, to suppress three lines?" [*IC*, 187]). The detail with which Cardenal reconstructs this incident, which occurred nearly a decade prior to his arrival in Cuba, underlines its importance to his construction of the revolutionary nation as an entity that respects both the written text and the would-be revolutionary's religious commitment.

In his linguistic dexterity, his immersion in literary culture, and his determination to employ his learning to teach and improve the people, Fidel incarnates the successful fusion of the literary intellectual and the guerrilla adumbrated by Régis Debray.[5] On 26 July, when Fidel begins speaking, "empieza a decir datos y números. Escuetamente, como un profesor dando su clase" (*EC*, 338; "he began to quote data and figures. Without any frills, like a teacher in class" [*IC*, 305]). Cintio Vitier tells Cardenal that the peasants and workers lack the attention span to listen to the full four hours of

Fidel's speech, and that sometimes they do not understand his educated language; yet, by continuing to listen, even if intermittently, they contribute to their own education. Castro's ability to educate the peasants and workers, to reimagine the policies and contours of the nation, stems from his extraordinary command of the Spanish language. During the July 26 speech, Cardenal observes:

> No va leyendo, excepto cuando los números (y a veces éstos los dice de memoria). El discurso es improvisado y espontáneo pero las palabras le fluyen con facilidad asombrosa. La vocalización es clarísima, cada palabra recalcada en todas sus letras; y la sintáxis siempre es impecable, y aunque a veces los párrafos son largos ninguna frase queda mal construída, nunca tartamudea ni vacila, y a veces hay digresiones, paréntesis dentro de paréntesis, parece que ya se le ha ido la onda, pero regresa después a la idea inicial y ata todos los cabos sueltos y cierra perfectamente la oración. (*EC*, 339–40; Fidel did not read his speech, except when there were figures (some of which he knew by heart). The speech was improvised and spontaneous, but the words flowed with amazing ease. His enunciation was very clear, each word stressed, each letter, always with impeccable syntax, and although at times the paragraphs were long, no sentence was badly constructed, never a stammer or a failing voice; at times there were digressions, parentheses within parentheses, and it sounded as though he had lost track, but he came back to the initial idea, tied all the loose ends together, and ended the sentence perfectly. [*IC*, 306])

The principal subject of the speech is the failure to achieve the ten-million-ton sugar cane harvest that the government had announced as a national crusade. Fidel, accepting responsibility for the failure, offers to resign; the people shout: "¡NO! ¡NO! ¡NO!¡NO!" (*EC*, 344; *IC*, 311). After the speech, Cintio Vitier stresses that all of Fidel's closest friends – Frank País, Abel Santamaría, Camilo Cienfuegos, Che Guevara – are dead: "Ahora ha quedado solo. Bueno, tiene el pueblo" (*EC*, 354; "So now he is alone. But he has the people with him" [*IC*, 320]). The analogy with Cardenal's own decision to renounce his private life in order to devote himself to the peasants of Solentiname is evident; even though the parallel is not perfect – Castro has lost his friends, not his family life – the implicit affinity heightens Cardenal's desire to speak with Castro.

The Cubans' respect for the written word is put to the test at the book's conclusion. Since the Mexican authorities confiscate papers carried by travellers arriving from Cuba, Cardenal decides to leave the notebooks from his trip at Casa de las Américas to be sent to him later: "Allí iba todo lo que yo había oído, bueno y malo … 'Padre, esto es un horror,' 'Peor que lo de Batista,' '¡Tenemos 11 años de estar aguantando ese hombre!' … Un amigo me dijo en México: 'Despídete de esos apuntes, nunca te llegarán.' Me llegaron todos los apuntes" (*EC*, 358; "In the notebooks was all that I had heard, both good and bad … 'Father, this is horrible,' 'Worse than what we had under Batista,' 'We've been putting up with this man for eleven years!' … In Mexico a friend said: 'Say good-by to those notes, they'll never get to you.' All the notes reached me" [*IC*, 323–4]).

The conversation with Fidel Castro that serves as the book's epilogue completes the construction of Cardenal's revolutionary masculinity through the Cuban leader's acknowledgeent of the priest's own literary-based recreation of Nicaraguan nationhood. Cardenal obtains the interview by virtue of his writing. When he enters the car, Fidel tells him: "Recibí su papelito … Su mensaje iba al grano; estaba escrito en estilo revolucionario" (*EC*, 360; "I received your note … Your message was right to the point; it was written in revolutionary style" [*IC*, 325]). The conversation confirms the correctness of the hypothesis of a Marxist-Christian alliance that Cardenal has been pursuing. Castro interrupts Cardenal's account of the left-wing priests he has met in Chile by saying: "Mire usted: la filosofía marxista y el cristiano coinciden en 90%. ¿Verdad?" (*EC*, 360; "Look: Marxist philosophy and Christianity coincide ninety per cent of the time. Right?" [*IC*, 326]). He confirms Cardenal's perception of the mainstream Catholic Church in Cuba: "Era la religión de los ricos. Lo verdaderamente popular aquí eran las religiones africanas. También estaban más vinculados con el pueblo los protestantes" (*EC*, 361; "It was the religion of the rich. What was really popular here was the African religions. And the Protestants too had more ties with the people" [*IC*, 326]).

Pursuing the fusion of religion and revolution, Fidel tells Cardenal how, during his years in the Sierra Maestra, he and the guerrilla priest Padre Guillermo Sardiñas baptized more than one hundred children. Foreshadowing later events in Nicaragua, Castro advises Cardenal that the inclusion of a religious component in revolutionary rhetoric, while not essential to establishing a socialist government, can be very useful in the aftermath of a successful revolutionary struggle: "Para ahorrar ciertos conflitos. Y para animar a los sacrificios que exige el socialismo" (*EC*, 362; "To avoid certain conflicts. And to encourage the sacrifices that socialism demands" [*IC*, 328]). The conversation reaches its climax when Fidel says: "Mire, todas las condiciones de un sacerdote, son las cualidades necesarias en un buen revolucionario"

(*EC*, 364; "Look, all the qualities that make a priest are the qualities needed in a good revolutionary" [*IC*, 330]). This line, which Cardenal echoes by saying, "De un buen sacerdote" (*EC*, 364; "a good priest" [*IC*, 330]), confirms his induction into revolutionary culture. The final moments of the conversation are dedicated to Nicaragua, as Castro asks about Sandino. His last words – and the book's last line of dialogue – are, "Tal vez les caigo un día de estos por su isla …" (*EC*, 367; "Perhaps I'll drop in on them [*sic*] one day at your island …" [*IC*, 333]).[6] This line completes the reconstruction, in revolutionary form, of Cardenal's masculinity. Having had his claim to the Nicaraguan nation shattered by the Somoza dictatorship's usurpation of his elite assumptions, Cardenal has now reconstructed his own model nation-space, the islands of Solentiname, a microcosmic counter-nation that he has forged in the image of his patriarchal, intellectual, creative, religious, and eventually, revolutionary values. The death in 1968 of his model of progressive contemplative masculinity, Thomas Merton, is compensated, in this 1971 conversation, by the advent of a new masculine model in the shape of Fidel Castro. Where Merton made repeated but not entirely credible assertions of his desire to visit Solentiname, Castro offers a throw-away sentence that is more significant because it recognizes Cardenal as a revolutionary equal, a dominant socialist male like Castro: each man governs an insurgent island. *In Cuba*'s denouement seals Cardenal's reconstructed identity.

BUILDING A REVOLUTIONARY CHURCH: *THE GOSPEL IN SOLENTINAME*

Michel Gobat stresses that many Nicaraguans "from Conservative oligarchic families such as the Cuadras, Chamorros, Cardenals, Vivas, Argüellos, Arellanos, Guzmáns and Lacayos" (Gobat 2005: 275) underwent the transformation from reactionary oligarch to revolutionary stalwart. These Conservatives, alienated by decades of US support for a Liberal dictatorship that had eroded their privileges and their self-respect, transmuted their values of national sovereignty, religious duty, an agrarian economy, and a culture of rights and responsibilities, in opposition to rampant commercialism and egotistic individualism, into a Sandinista ideology of national self-definition, mystical liberation theology, land reform, and a culture of revolutionary duty. Gobat explains that prominent Conservatives "served the Sandinista regime by heading the Ministries of Finance, Domestic Commerce, Foreign Trade, Industry, Budget and Planning, Culture and Education, as well as at the Central Bank, the National Development Bank, and the Supreme Court. In addition, elite Conservatives were appointed as vice ministers of the interior, finance, foreign affairs, and agricultural development and agrarian reform. Nearly all of these high-ranking officials remained loyal to the Sandinista Revolution until the bitter end (ibid.)."

Cardenal's conversion presages this pattern. His case is particularly salient not only because of his achievement as a poet but also because his adoption of revolutionary values blazed the trail for other Conservatives. Above all, Cardenal's extreme religiosity required the elaboration of an ideology that would reconcile elite Conservatism with revolutionary values. The primary obstacle to this reconciliation was the nature of Conservatives' Catholicism. The transformation of Cardenal's religious commitment, as put into practice in Solentiname, was a crucial component in developing the distinctive ideology of Sandinismo, with its blend of bourgeois nationalism, Marxism, and Catholic mysticism, and rendering it equally attractive to alienated Conservative oligarchs, rebellious urban youth, and devout, disenfranchised peasants.

By the time of his arrival in Cuba, Cardenal's practice of Catholicism, like that of many Latin American clergy influenced by the 1968 Medellín Conference, was straining against the restrictions of the "Church of the rich." He had already contributed an article to a small Communist newspaper despised by the Sandinistas, "deseando contribuir al diálogo de cristianos y marxistas que comenzaba a existir en otras partes" (*IE*, 205; "wishing to contribute to the dialogue between Christians and Marxists that started to exist in other places"). When he is invited to preach in a Catholic church in Havana whose congregation consists of upper-class white Cubans opposed to the Revolution, he hesitates: "Aquí me veía en una situación extraña: mi predicación que siempre había sido subversiva, aquí resultaba demasiado oficial" (*EC*, 122; "Here I saw myself in a strange situation: my preaching, which had always been subversive, here turned out to be too official-sounding" [*IC*, 104]). After his sermon, in which he thanks God that there are no longer rich people in Cuba, the congregation surrounds him with its complaints about the revolutionary government, claiming that "los dirigentes comunistas son ahora los nuevos ricos" (*EC*, 123; "the communist leaders now are the new rich" [*IC*, 105]).

This chapter of *In Cuba* introduces into the text all the most dire allegations that are levelled against Fidel Castro's regime, particularly with regard to its treatment of the Catholic Church. The rest of the book discredits these allegations one by one. Cardenal's inexorable approach to Fidel Castro over the course of the text is rendered feasible by his progressive deconstruction of traditional Catholic anti-Communism, and his discovery of Catholics who have found common ground, or even total identification, between

Catholicism and Marxism. Two chapters, positioned shortly before the meeting with Raúl Roa at which Cardenal expresses his newly formulated convictions, mention "rehabilitated" religious activists. One anti-Castro Catholic activist, who tells Cardenal that he was beaten in prison, adds that "quiero que sepa: ya no se hace eso. En la granja de rehabilitación lo pasamos bien" (*EC*, 291; "I want you to know that they don't do that anymore. On the rehabilitation farm they treated us well" [*IC*, 263]). The former dissident goes on to say that the racial and class prejudices and lack of understanding of the problems of the poor majority displayed by the other pro-Batista prisoners he met during his incarceration have turned him into a supporter of the Revolution.

This emphasis on Catholic integration into a diverse revolutionary society reaches a crescendo in the chapter that immediately precedes Cardenal's account of Fidel's 26 July speech. Entitled "Tres amigos" ("Three Friends"), the chapter mingles the verbal testimonies of three twenty-five-year-old Cubans, one Catholic, one Protestant, and one Marxist, who are best friends and revolutionary comrades. The Catholic, a former enemy of the regime, has undergone a political conversion in the UMAP camps as a result of seeing rural poverty for the first time and realizing that "para vivir mi fe debía cambiar de vida" (*EC*, 326; "to live my faith, I must change my life" [*IC*, 294]). His statement that "Creo que es una gran gracias de Dios estar viviendo en Cuba actualmente" (328; "I believe it is a great gift of God to be living in Cuba right now" [*IC*, 296]) concludes Cardenal's religious quest.

Between this statement and the account of Fidel's speech, Cardenal includes a brief relation of his lunch with Cintio Vitier and his family. The meal represents a kind of sacramental fusion of Catholic and Marxist values: Cardenal performs a Mass and the family, like others in Cuba at this time, celebrates Christmas on 26 July, with both traditional Cuban "lechón" (suckling pig), provided by the state, and socialist wine from Romania; the servant sits at the table with the family and is addressed as "compañera" (*EC*, 332; *IC*, 297); Vitier's sons, though educated under the Revolution, take communion; and Cardenal refers to the Castro speech they will hear later as "una larga liturgia de la Palabra" (*EC*, 332; "a long liturgy of the Word" [*IC*, 297]).

Cardenal's integration into these values as a Catholic authorizes him to speak as a revolutionary, liberating the voice that expresses itself in the flurry of poetry he published in 1972 and 1973. The theological underpinnings of his new position are worked through in his two-volume prose work, *El Evangelio en Solentiname* (1975; *The Gospel in Solentiname*).[7] Here, too, however, the moment of ideological conversion is absent. Internal evidence in the book's dialogues, in which the peasants comment on passages from the Gospels, suggests that the earliest commentaries are from 1972, after Cardenal's conversion. In his remarks on the first biblical passage discussed, John 1: 1–18, Cardenal tells his flock: "Y al robo se le llama propiedad privada" (*ESI*, 15; "And robbery is called private property" [*GS1*, 11]).

Starting in 1967, the weekly Masses Cardenal held in the little church in Solentiname included a dialogic component, consisting of commentaries on the scriptural passages under discussion. Cardenal recalls of the dialogues: "Primero, yo empecé recogiéndolos en mi memoria, hasta donde me era posible. Después, con más sentido práctico, usamos grabadora" (*ESI*, 9; "I first began collecting them in my mind, insofar as I could. Later, with more common sense, we used a tape recorder" [*GS1*, vii]). In addition to the inner circle of Cardenal's community – the Colombian poet William Agudelo and his wife and family, and the young men from the islands who in 1977 would take up arms as Sandinista guerrillas – peasants from the surrounding area attended the Masses on a more or less regular basis; at least 20 per cent of the population of the Solentiname archipelago attended the Masses at some point (Reed 2008: 281). As Cardenal's community became well known, visitors to this remote region began to flock to the services. These included Father Fernando Cardenal, radical clergy from elsewhere in Latin America, wandering hippies and truth seekers, academics such as the University of Oxford professor Robert Pring-Mill, bankers and businessmen, and prominent cultural figures, including the singer Carlos Mejía Godoy and the writers Sergio Ramírez and Julio Cortázar. The dialogues altered the perceptions of the poor people who participated in them, enabling them to overcome traditional peasant fatalism and begin to see themselves as agents of their own destiny. In Reed's summary: "This meant that familiar beliefs such as 'God made us poor and we don't need to change' and 'Christ came to teach us how to suffer' increasingly fell to the background and new ones such as 'God has seen our suffering and He is on our side' and 'Christ fought for the freedom of the poor; therefore we must follow His example' ascended to the foreground" (ibid.: 292).

This assumption of the lessons of the Gospels as a guide to interpreting daily life changed not only the peasants but also Cardenal. *The Gospel in Solentiname* represents the culmination of his religious evolution. In the late 1950s Thomas Merton's criticisms of consumer society and sympathy for indigenous peoples suggested a means of bridging two discrete components of Cardenal's identity: his Conservative Catholicism and his opposition to the Somoza dictatorship. Cardenal's presence in Colombia during the rise of Camilo Torres's mass movement for change instilled in him the ideal of the revolutionary Latin American priest who speaks on behalf of the poor, even though he disagreed at this time with Torres's decision to adopt armed struggle. The broader post-Medellín environment of the late 1960s sanctioned Cardenal's application of the Gospels to daily life, particularly in the case of the poor, but so did more local events such as the establishment of the first Christian Base Communities (including Solentiname) in Nicaragua in 1966, and the Pastoral Encounter "that took place in Managua in early 1969, where several hundred progressive Church functionaries (both priests and bishops) and the religious met to reflect on Nicaragua's situation in light of the resolutions from both Vatican II and Medellín" (Reed 2008: 278–9). In this context, Cardenal's evolution towards a posture where he was susceptible to embracing socialism during his trip to Cuba in 1970 may be seen as a product of continental and national trends as well as individual circumstances. Life in Solentiname, including both the physical labour he undertook and his formalized Sunday exchanges with the peasants, educated him about the realities of his own country, preparing the ground for his political conversion. In the aftermath of the trip, the Masses in Solentiname enabled him to increase his stature as a figure of authority on the revolutionary left by refining his language and revolutionary praxis. It was through his dialogues with the peasants that Cardenal honed his own consciousness, advanced his political agenda, consolidated his microcosmic counter-nation, confirmed his patriarchal authority in its revolutionary variant, and eventually provided the FSLN with concrete assistance by transforming passive, poorly educated peasant youths into committed young guerrillas.

The peasants' readings of the Gospels stem from their life experience, yet the commentaries exemplify the yoking of the local and the universal; the national context, with rare exceptions, emerges by implication. By the time Julio Cortázar visited the community in 1976, only a year prior to the assault on the San Carlos barracks, he found the island's residents discussing Jesus's arrest in the garden in Matthew 26: 36–56:

> como si hablaran de ellos mismos, de la amenaza que les cayera en la noche o en pleno día, esa vida en permanente incertidumbre de las islas y de la tierra firme y de toda Nicaragua y no solamente de toda Nicaragua sino de casi toda América Latina, vida rodeada de miedo y de muerte, vida de Guatemala y vida del Salvador, vida de la Argentina y de Bolivia, vida de Chile y de Santo Domingo, vida del Paraguay, vida de Brasil y de Colombia. (*Alguien*, 82; as if they were talking about themselves, about the threat of being pounced on at night or in broad daylight, that life of permanent uncertainty on the islands and on the

mainland and in all of Nicaragua and, yes, almost all of Latin America, a life surrounded by fear and death, life in Guatemala and life in El Salvador, life in Argentina and Bolivia, life in Chile and Santo Domingo, life in Paraguay, life in Brazil and Colombia. [*A Change of Light*, 122])

The continental applicability of the peasants' identification of their circumstances with those described in the Bible manifests itself as a revolutionary version of the "Good News" of Christianity. When a visiting student from Puerto Rico complains that Jesus of Nazareth was simply a Jewish nationalist, Cardenal responds: "Jesús todo el tiempo fue consciente de que su misión personal sólo estaba circunscrita a Israel, pero después de la resurrección encargó a los apóstoles que anunciaran la buena nueva a todos los pueblos de la tierra" (*ESI*, 242; "Jesus was always conscious that his personal mission was limited only to Israel, but after the resurrection he charged the apostles to announce the Good News to all the peoples of the earth" [*GS2*, 212]). Implicit in this response is a strong parallel with the Cuban Revolution and the role of Che Guevara in spreading its version of the "Good News," and also with the pioneering role of a potential future revolution in Nicaragua. This parallel becomes more explicit as the dialogues continue. In the final dialogues of Volume II, both Augusto César Sandino and Che Guevara are equated with Jesus of Nazareth, their respective self-sacrifices depicted as religious and socialist in equal proportions. Sergio Ramírez, visiting Solentiname with Cortázar, suggests: "Jesús ha elegido su método de lucha, que es su muerte ... esa muerte él la ha venido preparando, como una forma de acción ... Y creo que Sandino también ha elegido su muerte como un método de lucha" (*ESII*, 263; "Jesus has chosen his way of struggling, which is his death ... that death he has been gradually preparing, as a form of action ... And I believe that Sandino also has already chosen his death as a way of struggling" [*GS4*, 194–5]).

Statements such as these, issuing from a highly influential, rather secular, figure such as Ramírez, illustrate the centrality of the cult of martyrdom to Sandinista ideology. Rooted in liberation theology's commitment to the impoverished masses (and arguably also deriving from the ancestor-worship of Náhuat culture), the veneration of the dead enshrines self-sacrifice as an ideal, promising aspiring young guerrillas that death in combat will lead to eternal presence in future revolutionary society. In one of the final dialogues of Volume II, a discussion of the account of the resurrection in Matthew 28: 1–10, Cardenal preaches to his flock: "La revolución no tiene sentido si no hay resurrección" (*ESII*, 294; "The revolution makes no sense unless there's a resurrection" [*GS4*, 249]). When Esperanza, a young member of the community (and the wife of the future Sandinista captain Bosco Centeno), recalls that Che Guevara told his comrades in Bolivia that if they wished to see him after his death, they need only go to Cuba, where they would find his presence ubiquitous, Cardenal reiterates: "Les habría dicho: Vayan a Cuba, allí me verán; a Cuba, y al resto del mundo. Así les dijo Cristo: Vayan a Galilea y al resto del mundo, allí me verán. También: Vayan a Solentiname ... allí me verán" (*SII*, 294; "He had probably told them: 'Go to Cuba, you'll see me there; to Cuba, and to the rest of the world.' So Christ said to them: 'Go to Galilee and to the rest of the world, there you will see me.' Also: 'Go to Solentiname, there you will see me'" [*GS4*, 250]). The striking feature of this construction of the revolutionary nation is that, at first glance, it appears to skirt the customary emphasis on Nicaragua's history of foreign intervention and the drive to fortify the particularities of the national culture in favour of a sweeping equivalency of times and places, in which Solentiname, the nascent form of the future Nicaraguan nation, gains legitimacy not from its development of primitive painting, poetry workshops, or other expressions of the suppressed Nicaraguan national identity, but rather from being an inheritor of a culture of sacrificing oneself to make a revolution that extends from ancient Galilee to Cuba and Bolivia. As Cortázar points out, the problems faced by Latin American nations during the 1970s, particularly violent dictatorship, did resemble each other. Nonetheless, a contradiction emerges between the nationalist thrust of Sandinista ideology, with its insistence on Nicaraguan specificity, and Sandinismo's commitment to socialist internationalism, here expressed in terms of religious imagery. Christian ideology, whether in a conservative, liberal, or radical variant, elides national boundaries in its striving for a community that is universal; other monotheisms do the same. As Benedict Anderson writes of the imaginary case of a Berber and a Malay meeting in Mecca: "'Why is this man doing what I am doing, uttering the same words that I am uttering, even though we can not talk to one another?' There is only one answer, once one has learnt it: 'Because *we* ... are Muslims'" (Anderson 1983: 54).

The Chileans, Peruvians, Puerto Ricans, Italians, citizens of the United States, Great Britain, Canada, and other countries who came to Mass in Solentiname incarnate this sort of transnational community united by shared rituals. However, Cardenal also employs religious ideology to usher illiterate peasants, disconnected from the nation by poverty, neglect, and geographical remoteness, into what Anderson would term the Nicaraguan "imagined community," which stands in opposition to timeless religious affiliation. The imagined community is based on a shared sense of chronology enshrined in print, defined either by a distinctive national language (Finnish, for example) or by a unique national trajectory within a community of nations that share a language (the case of Nicaragua). By exploiting what Anderson refers to as "a well-known doubleness in Spanish-American nationalism, its alternating grand stretch and particular localism" (Anderson 1983: 62), Cardenal's decision to publish the dialogues that take place during his Masses endows them with the continental resonance observed by Cortázar while also serving the purpose of converting illiterate masses into adherents to a bourgeois vision of shared national chronology: that is, the notion that all Nicaraguans share historical symbols, such as Sandino's self-sacrifice, and that through Nicaraguanness, as expressed in writing, they can understand their lives, their oppression, and what they need to do *as a people* to remedy their poor living conditions, social inequalities, and trampled national identity. Both Christian and Marxist discourses, however, insist that this national liberation movement gains strength from its integration into a succession of such movements stretching from Galilee to Bolivia. Hence when Masses refer to events whose relevance is more local than the basic facts that any literate Spanish American could be expected to know about Nicaragua (the Somoza dictatorship, Sandino's insurgency, the resurgence of guerrilla activity in the 1960s), Cardenal provides explanations directed at the non-Nicaraguan reader. The visit of the brother of a well-known Sandinista martyr, for example, prompts Cardenal to state: "En Nicaragua todos conocen el nombre de David Tejada: el joven del Frente Sandinista de Liberación Nacional que fue matado brutalmente en la cárcel y después arrojado al cráter de lava hirviendo del volcán Masaya" (*ESII*, 273; "In Nicaragua everybody knows the name of David Tejada, the young man from the Sandinista National Liberation Front who was brutally murdered in prison and then thrown into the boiling lava of the crater of the Masaya volcano" [*GS4*, 212]). Such explanations of conditions "in Nicaragua," which reach for continental connections, may seem like a paradoxical means of integrating the marginalized into the imagined community of the nation.

The centrality of print to the endeavour of reimagining the nation is evident in Cardenal's decision to offer poetry workshops for the peasants, organized by the Costa Rican writer Mayra Jiménez, who arrived in Solentiname in 1976 (Craven 2002: 125), and who, after the Revolution, would organize the workshop program of the Ministry of Culture. The culminating stage of the "nationalization" of Solentiname's young people, and the act that prepares them for their decision to undergo military training, is to begin to write. Writing marks the passage from the universal community of radical Christians to the national community, defined by the Sandinista drive to reshape the Nicaraguan nation.

At the conclusion of the second volume of the dialogues, Cardenal equates Lake Nicaragua where Solentiname is located with "el lago de Galilea" (*ESII*, 300; "the Sea of Galilee" [*GS4*, 261]). The reception of this imagery by the peasants is made clear when Esperanza summarizes the life of Jesus of Nazareth: "Él es un guerrillero. Lo han matado por la liberación. Todos los que van a luchar por la liberación, a morir por ella y a resucitar son sus hermanos" (*ESII*, 295; "He's a guerrilla fighter. They've killed him because he fought for freedom. Everybody who goes to fight for freedom, to die for it and to rise again, they're all his brothers and sisters" [*GS4*, 252]). This raises the stakes of the fusion of Catholicism and Marxism to a point not even imagined by most previous applications of the Gospels to the daily life of the poor, suggesting that in order to follow the example of Christ, one must die for the Revolution and be reborn in the memory of the people in the future revolutionary state. In a foreshadowing of the engaged mysticism of *Cosmic Canticle*, Cardenal goes so far as to tell his congregation: "la revolución va a ser también para los muertos, para toda la humanidad que ha muerto antes sin poder ver la revolución" (*ESII*, 296; "the revolution is going to be for the dead, too, for all of humanity that has died without being able to see the revolution" [*GS4*, 254]). While this statement may be read as symbolic, the peasants receive it in a literal way. Óscar responds: "Cuando se cree la sociedad nueva, va a ser como ver salir de los sepulcros al montón de carajos" (*ESII*, 296; "When the new society is created, it's going to be like seeing a bunch of bastards rise up out of the tombs" [*GS4*, 254]). Just as the Bible stories that the residents of Solentiname comment on build to the climax of Christ's crucifixion and resurrection, so the exploratory commentaries of Volume I yield to increasingly committed, ideologized, and militant interpretations of the Gospels in Volume II. The first volume concludes with Cardenal thanking the peasants for helping him to understand that the mere existence of their community constitutes "una experiencia del reino" (*ESI*, 261; "an experience of the kingdom" [*GS2*, 250]); the second volume concludes with a virtual battle cry that urges the young people in the congregation to fight for the socialist-Christian "kingdom" of the future.

Like many dialogues, starting with *The Republic* of Plato, in which the vigorous discussion of the first two sections yields to passively received lessons from Socrates in the later chapters, this one becomes less dialogic, and more teleological, as it progresses. The conservative peasant Pancho, who argues against the community's radical reinterpretation of the Gospels, virtually disappears from the latter half of the dialogues. By the end, armed struggle has become an axiomatic rite of the religiously devout. When Cardenal concludes the volume by explaining that "Amen" is a Hebrew word meaning, "Yes," the implications of this affirmation are obvious. Speaking of the Gospels, Cardenal sums up: "Es la comunidad que estaba comentándolo y que ha dicho 'Sí.' Esta es nuestra respuesta a la palabra de Jesús …" (*ESII*, 305; "It's the community that was commenting on it and that has said 'Yes.' This is our response to the word of Jesus …" [*GS4*, 270]). The community's "Yes" to the Gospels takes the form of the assault on the San Carlos barracks.

Through the dialogues, the imagistic language of religious texts transforms perceptions and engenders acts that influence the course of history. Reed concludes: "Religious language, in this historical case, proved to be *the* arena of struggle and the dialogues based on them *the* vehicle through which the discussants assigned revolutionary meanings to it" (Reed 2008: 294; emphasis in original). As Régis Debray maintains, religion and revolution are both faiths of the book (Debray 1996: 153), sharing a reliance on written language to construct descriptions of the present and promises for the future; even though the Solentiname dialogues are spoken, they originate in biblical texts and return to text in the published book. While the spoken exchanges are blown away by "el viento del lago" (*ESI*, 9; "the wind of the lake" [*GS1*, viii]), the written version, its increasingly unequivocal message of revolutionary commitment clearly delineated in the progression of the commentaries, travels. The published dialogues become themselves a sacred text, a possible alternative to reading the original scriptures. They both contribute to the "imagined community" of print-enshrined Nicaraguanness – a counter-hegemonic literature issuing from Cardenal's microcosmic counter-nation – and pursue an internationalist vocation. As Antidio Cabal, the Venezuelan husband of Mayra Jiménez, states when visiting a Solentiname Mass: "No sé cuántos ejemplares se habrán vendido del primer tomo de *El Evangelio en Solentiname*, pero les doy este dato: en Venezuela cuando me vine se hablan de mil. Son mil personas que reciben la comunicación de lo que aquí se está haciendo. Es una misa que se multiplica después …" (*ESII*, 128; "I don't know how many copies have been sold of the first volume of *The Gospel in Solentiname*, but I'll give you this fact: In Venezuela, when I came here, they had sold a thousand copies. That's a thousand people getting the message about what's being done here. It's a Mass that afterwards multiplies …" [*GS3*, 248]).

The immediate outcome of this "multiplication" of the Masses is the recruitment of Sandinista guerrillas in Nicaragua and supporters abroad. From the outset, the dialogues are animated by a stern anti-materialism. In

Volume I, which Cardenal opens by defining private property as theft, his brother Fernando, reporting to the community on the 1972 Managua earthquake, scorns people who are disconsolate as a result of having lost luxurious homes: "La ruina moral de estas personas fue muy grande ... Lo mismo pasará cuando llegue la revolución, con todos aquellos que han edificado su vida sobre bases falsas" (*ESI*, 207; "The moral ruin of those people was also very great ... The same thing will happen when the revolution comes, with all those who have built their lives on false bases" [*GS2*, 140]). Over the course of the dialogues, anti-materialism transmutes by stages into community and sharing, which in turn grows into an active endorsement of Marxist principles in their 1970s Latin American revolutionary expression.

This transition requires a transformation in the identities of peasant youths and a consolidation of Cardenal's identity as a revolutionary priest. A striking expression of the evolution of the members of the congregation occurs in the response of Elbis (sometimes written "Elvis") Chavarría, a young man barely out of adolescence who would be tortured and murdered by the GN after the San Carlos attack, and whose life and death became a central trope in Cardenal's poetry of the 1980s. Elbis's response to a discussion of John 3: 1–21 at the opening of Volume II of the dialogues charts the course that he and others will follow. Responding to a discussion of the theme of rebirth, Elbis says: "Es el cambio del egoísmo al amor; y de una sociedad basada en el egoísmo a una sociedad basada en el amor. O sea el reino de Dios. Para una sociedad nueva se necesita una humanidad nueva, como nacida de nuevo. Sólo el hombre que se ha transformado, el hombre nuevo, puede entrar al reino" (*ESII*, 17; "It's the change from selfishness to love, and from a society based on selfishness to a society based on love, which means the kingdom of God. For a new society we need a new humanity, like born again. Only somebody who's been transformed, somebody new, can enter the kingdom" [*GS3*, 15]). This succinct presentation epitomizes the peasant's progression from Christian "love" to the militant New Man of Latin American socialism, here presented as the sole category of individual capable of entering the kingdom of heaven. Chavarría's sincere, if simple, formulation of this development recapitulates the stages through which the printed dialogues pass; it exemplifies the peasants' reception of Cardenal's message that improving their living conditions is possible but that this will require a "new humanity," forged in socialist revolution, which will enter "the kingdom," a supple concept that embraces both the new socialist society and, since the revolution will revive in a quasi-literal sense those who died in its name, the hybridized socialist-Catholic heaven. This understanding propelled the young people of Solentiname towards self-sacrifice, and would later prove influential in recruiting thousands of young Nicaraguans into the ranks of the Sandinista guerrillas.

A key assumption of the Solentiname strain of liberation theology, however, is that the Christian does not become less Christian by absorbing Marxist principles. In a discussion of Matthew 13: 31–5, Cardenal's longtime poetic mentor, José Coronel Urtecho, who actively supported the dictatorship in the 1950s and 1960s, then converted to Sandinismo in the 1970s, articulates the relationship between Christianity and Marxism in a formulation that would become highly influential during the years of revolutionary government. Cardenal, significantly, presents Coronel's speech as directed at him:

> El poeta Coronel, dirigiéndose a mí: A propósito de cristianismo y comunismo, se me ocurrieron la otra vez unas ideas sobre este tema y había pensado comunicártelas, y las diré aquí ahora a toda la comunidad. Es esto: El comunismo no puede absorber el cristianismo sin dejar de ser plenamente comunismo y convertirse en cristianismo, mientras el cristianismo puede absorber el comunismo (marxismo-leninismo) y seguir siendo cristianismo y hasta más plenamente. Dicho de otra manera, el comunista no puede convertirse al cristianismo sin dejar de ser exclusivamente comunista y volverse cristiano, mientras el cristiano puede volverse comunista (marxista-leninista) y ser aún más cristiano. (*ESI*, 167; CORONEL, turning to me: "With regard to Christianity and Communism, some thoughts on the subject occurred to me recently and I intended to tell them to you, and I'll tell them now to the whole community. Here they are: Communism cannot absorb Christianity without ceasing to be completely Communist and changing into Christianity, whereas Christianity can absorb Communism (Marxism-Leninism) and continue to be Christianity and even be more Christian. To put it another way, the Communist cannot become a convert to Christianity without ceasing to be exclusively Communist and becoming a Christian, whereas a Christian can become a Communist (Marxist-Leninist) and be even more of a Christian." [*GS*2, 60-61])

The notion that, since Marxism may exist within Christianity but the reverse is not true, the Christian Marxist cannot, by definition, lapse into dogmatic Communism, would animate the later Sandinista quest for a "space" within the doctrinal edifice of the Catholic Church. Conor Cruise O'Brien, commenting on a publication summarizing discussion at a conference on Christian Marxism held at the Universidad Centroamericana in Managua in

September 1979, two months after the Revolution, noted: "The pamphlet goes on with some brilliance to explain the double position of the revolutionary Christians, within the revolution, and within the Church. They don't want to divide *either* the revolution *or* the Church, but to be an integral part of both" (O'Brien 1988: 92).

The diffusion of these ideas throughout Nicaragua, the rest of Latin America, and abroad was facilitated by Cardenal's consolidation of his image as the epitome of the revolutionary priest. The continental success of *In Cuba*, published in Buenos Aires by Carlos Lohlé, and the same company's reissue of Cardenal's *Psalms*, helped to spread this image, which was reflected by critical books such as Alfredo Veiravé's *Ernesto Cardenal, poeta de la liberación latinoamericana* (Poet of Latin American Liberation), published in Buenos Aires in 1975, and José Luis González-Balado's *Ernesto Cardenal. Poeta Revolucionario Monje* (Poet Revolutionary Monk), aimed at a more general readership, published in Salamanca in 1978. *The Gospel in Solentiname* was a crucial building block in Cardenal's self-construction as a Catholic counterpart of Fidel Castro defending a smaller, even more threatened, radical island. In the dialogues, Cardenal repeats and elaborates on a key citation from his conversation with Castro at the conclusion of *In Cuba*, intervening in his congregation's discussion of marriage to equate priestly celibacy with revolutionary commitment:

> San Pablo encontraba que era preferible el celibato para estar más libres para trabajar por el reino. Este es también el caso de muchos revolucionarios, que también han tenido que renunciar al matrimonio por esa causa. El Che ha dicho que los revolucionarios de vanguardia deben tener un amor al pueblo que sea "único, indivisible," y que por tanto deben privarse de "la pequeña dosis de cariño cotidiano" que disfruta el hombre común. Esto me recuerda una frase que me dijo Fidel, cuando yo conversé con él en Cuba: que el Che había sido "como un sacerdote," por su entrega y su espíritu de sacrificio. También me dijo en esa ocasión: "Mire: todas las cualidades de un sacerdote, son las condiciones necesarias de un buen revolucionario." Creo que una de las principales cualidades en las que él estaba pensando era el celibato. (*ESII*, 95;
> Saint Paul found that celibacy was preferable so as to be freer to work for the kingdom. This is also the case of many revolutionaries, even non-Christians, who also have had to give up marriage for that cause. Che has said that revolutionaries in the vanguard must have a love for the people that is "unique, indivisible," and that therefore they must deprive themselves of the "little dose of daily affection" enjoyed by the common

person. This reminds me of a remark of Fidel, when I was talking with him in Cuba: that Che had been "like a priest," through his devotion and his spirit of sacrifice. He also told me on that occasion: "Look: all the qualities of a priest are the qualities needed to make a good revolutionary." I think one of the main qualities he was thinking of was celibacy. [*GS3*, 176–7])

Proceeding from the same flexible definition of "kingdom" – a blending of Catholic and Marxist concepts of paradise – this passage conflates St Paul with Che Guevara, Fidel Castro, and, by implication, Cardenal himself. Celibacy becomes a condition for preserving the revolutionary's patriarchal authority, like that of the priest: both remain above the fray of secular society, formed by the interaction of men with women. Yet the assumption that Fidel's comment was a reference to celibacy is, as Cardenal admits, speculation on his part. He omits the rejoinder which in *In Cuba* he reports having made to Fidel: "a good priest" (*IC*, 330). This reply may have been a response to the Cuban context, where many priests opposed the Revolution; in Solentiname, where religion and revolution have merged, it is no longer necessary. Crucially, this passage enables Cardenal to redefine his own celibacy. No longer "la castración del celibato" (*IE*, 30; "the castration of celibacy"), as he had perceived it during his seminary studies in Colombia, celibacy takes on resonances of revolution, armed struggle, and masculine self-assertion. The conflation of priestly with revolutionary self-abnegation enables Cardenal to command a practical authority not normally accorded men not perceived as virile in a society of traditional gender divisions such as that of rural Nicaragua. Cardenal's Masses criticize the harshness of these inequalities, as, for example during the discussion of the adulterous woman in John 8: 1–11, where members of the community denounce the double standard regarding adultery instilled by Latin American "machismo" (*ESII*, 43; *GS3*, 70). Cardenal responds to the congregation by evoking a passage from the Apocrypha where Jesus says, "en el reino de los cielos 'los hombres serán como las mujeres, y las mujeres como los hombres,'" (43; "in the kingdom of heaven 'men will be like women, and women like men'" [*GS3*, 71]). His attack on the perception of the priest as "castrated" is double-pronged: he attributes to his own condition the robust potency associated with the revolutionary, while he also suggests that paradise will be a realm of less obdurate gender divisions.

Cardenal's self-reinvention, like that of the peasants, takes place within the context of a brutally patriarchal society that had been governed for more than forty years by the proto-macho figure of the violent dictator.

When his religious community receives a visit from a group of Managua business people, including one of Cardenal's cousins (a former priest turned businessman), who have purchased a tract of land on Solentiname as an investment, the social classes revert to their customary roles. The peasants fall silent, while Cardenal and a visiting representative of the Communist Youth of Costa Rica debate the visitors, who oppose the community's reinterpretation of the Gospels with arguments such as: "Hay quienes realizan trabajos más importantes, porque tienen mejor formación intelectual, y ésos deben ser pagados mejor que los que tienen una formación intelectual inferior" (*ESII*, 113; "There are some people who carry out more important tasks, because they have better intellectual training, and they should be paid better than those who have an inferior intellectual training" [*GS3*, 215]). The unresolvable disagreements presage the conflagration to come; the course of the debate, in which Cardenal and the Costa Rican student increasingly speak on behalf of the poor, underscores the poet's assumption, within the context of a Marxist-influenced war of national liberation, of the patriarchal authority invested in the priest. Cardenal extends traditional patriarchy as a way of enforcing a model for democratization. By virtue of this paradox, the timeless, borderless universe of the great religions serves, ironically in terms of the framework established by Benedict Anderson, as a means of entry into the explicitly chronological time of the nation.

The Somoza government's destruction of Solentiname and the works of art stored there in 1977 marked the end of the community, dispersing its survivors underground or into exile. But this catastrophe, crucially, became the point of origin of the development of "the Solentiname model of cultural democratization on a national level" (Beverley and Zimmerman 1990: 95) that would undergird the "imagined community" of revolutionary Nicaragua. In "Lo que fue Solentiname" ("What Was Solentiname"), the widely reprinted open letter that he issued from exile in Costa Rica in the wake of the community's destruction, Cardenal wrote: "No pienso en la reconstrucción de nuestra pequeña comunidad de Solentiname. Pienso en la tarea mucho más importante que tendremos todos, que es la reconstrucción del país entero" (González-Balado 1978: 216; "I'm not thinking about the reconstruction of our small community of Solentiname. I'm thinking about the much more important task that we will all have, which is the reconstruction of the entire country"). By "reconstruction" Cardenal means both the physical rebuilding of a country ravaged by war and the reimagining of the Nicaraguan nation and its history. Cardenal's own poetry would make a vital contribution to the latter project.

6

Nicaraguan History, 1979–90

THE SANDINISTA REVOLUTION: THE FIRST FIVE YEARS

In the government that replaced the Somocista state on 19 July 1979, the disciplined, top-down structures developed by the FSLN during nearly two decades of clandestine activity coexisted with a broad-based junta that included both those who had participated in the armed struggle and civilian opponents of the dictatorship. The disjuncture between these structures was incarnated by a dual-track government in which the junta soon became a façade. The Junta de Gobierno de Reconstrucción Nacional (JGRN; Governing Junta for National Reconstruction), the country's official government, consisted of Comandante Daniel Ortega of the FSLN; Sergio Ramírez (who had kept his FSLN membership secret); Moisés Hassan, a Palestinian-Nicaraguan who had earned a PHD in mathematics in the United States and then organized opposition to the dictatorship in poor neighbourhoods of Managua, and who was also a secret Sandinista; Violeta Barrios de Chamorro, the widow of Pedro Joaquín Chamorro, who represented the values of Nicaraguan Conservatism; and Alfonso Robelo, a millionaire industrialist of Liberal antecedents, who during the late 1970s had been instrumental in coordinating the business class's expressions of opposition to Somoza. Since the FSLN held a majority on the JGRN – though this fact was not made public – the junta approved all decisions made by the National Directorate. Over the first three years of the new government, policy flowed more and more directly from the latter body.

The composition of the National Directorate was a compromise among the three tendencies into which the FSLN had split in 1975. It consisted of nine guerrilla comandantes: Daniel Ortega, Humberto Ortega, and Víctor Tirado from the Terceristas; Jaime Wheelock, Carlos Núñez, and Luis

Carrión from the Proletarian Tendency; and Tomás Borge, Henry Ruíz, and Bayardo Arce from the Prolonged People's War. Sergio Ramírez also participated in meetings of this group. Daniel Ortega, as the only official member of both of the country's governing bodies, soon became the most powerful figure in Nicaraguan politics.

The parallel governments of the JGRN and the National Directorate interacted with ministries whose jurisdictions often overlapped with those of the ruling bodies. Some members of the National Directorate were also cabinet ministers, such as Tomás Borge, minister of the interior, and Jaime Wheelock, who was minister of agriculture. Other cabinet posts were held by Sandinistas who were not members of the National Directorate: Father Miguel d'Escoto Brockmann was foreign minister, Father Fernando Cardenal was minister of education (a post that included responsibility for the National Literacy Crusade), Father Ernesto Cardenal was minister of culture, and Comandante Dora María Téllez was minister of health. Other guerrilla leaders were granted the title of "comandante" but given less significant administrative responsibilities. The most problematic such case was that of Edén Pastora, whose photograph had been published around the world after his raid on the National Palace, and who had been campaigning for a prominent position in government even before the dictatorship had fallen (Morris 2010: 102–3).

By contrast, the JGRN, the National Directorate, and the ministries shared the liability of being staffed by faceless leaders whose names were unfamiliar to the average Nicaraguan, even among those who identified as Sandinistas: "The young men and women who fought the National Guard in the insurrections of 1978 and 1979 considered themselves Sandinistas, but many knew only a few basic facts about the FSLN: its colors were the black and red of Sandino, its leader was Carlos Fonseca, it was serious about taking power, and it fought on the side of workers and peasants" (Zimmermann 2000: 3). Yet, while most of the Sandinista leaders were not well known to the public, some of their surnames were. The proliferation of members of Conservative oligarchical families in the new government raised eyebrows among some Sandinista supporters. On learning the composition of the new regime, one peasant from Estelí who had fought as a Sandinista guerrilla observed: "This is the second Conservative revolution." A popular joke at the time claimed that "León put up the dead, Granada put up the Ministers" (Vilas 1992: 324).

The only FSLN leaders who had popular followings were Tomás Borge, known to the public as an associate of Carlos Fonseca who had been imprisoned and tortured by the National Guard, and Sergio Ramírez, whose name and face had become familiar during his activism with The Twelve. The Sandinista leaders who commanded authority among the population, including Sandino himself, Carlos Fonseca, Eduardo Contreras, and insurgents who had claimed admiring constituencies in particular regions of the country, such as Germán Pomares and the Spanish guerrilla priest Father Gaspar García Lavinia, were all dead. FSLN leaders found themselves in the position of needing to underscore their connections with the dead in order sustain their legitimacy among the living. This practical requirement merged with the quasi-religious Sandinista worship of the martyrs who had made the Revolution possible, and with the radical Catholicism of liberation theology, to forge a culture of constant praise and appreciation of the dead. Legitimacy devolved on guerrillas "from the catacombs," as the popular expression went, who embodied the struggles of the martyrs, and was siphoned away from civilians or other leaders who had not been affiliated with those who had died to make the Revolution.

The day after taking power, the revolutionary government expropriated all property belonging to the Somoza family, revoked the existing constitution, and formally dissolved the GN. During the next month, the financial system and foreign trade were nationalized, the death penalty was abolished, and a bill of rights, known as the Estatuto de Derechos y Garantía de los Nicaragüenses (Statute of Rights and Guarantees of the Nicaraguans), was passed. During the last week of August 1979, the guerrilla forces were regrouped into the Ejército Popular Sandinista (EPS; Sandinista People's Army), under the command of Humberto Ortega, natural resources were placed under control of the state, university education was made free, a law was introduced to combat unemployment, and strict rent controls were imposed.

During 1980, relations with the Carter administration in the United States remained peaceful. Carter approved $30 million in credits to Nicaragua "to stimulate private enterprise" (Booth 1982: 196); he offered another $70 million to assist in the reconstruction of the war-ravaged country, but this money, contingent on a reformulation of the JGRN to eliminate its pro-FSLN majority, was never delivered (*AM*, 143). Even so, by September, Carter had promised and begun to send $75 million in economic aid. The main source of tension between Nicaragua and the United States was FSLN shipments of weapons to the guerrillas of the Frente Farabundo Martí de Liberación Nacional (FMLN; Farabundo Martí National Liberation Front) in neighbouring El Salvador in preparation for their 1980 offensive. These shipments were intermittent and of debatable importance, yet most of the comandantes regarded support for the Salvadoran guerrillas as a revolutionary duty that they refused to give up, even at the risk of provoking US hostility. The bellicose rhetoric of Ronald Reagan, who defeated Jimmy Carter in the November 1980 US elections, made this threat much more acute.

In early 1980 laws were introduced to protect consumers and reduce the prices of basic foodstuffs. At the end of March, the National Literacy Crusade was launched. Truckloads of high school and university students, some of them as young as ten or eleven, were driven to remote villages to live with the peasants in primitive conditions and teach their hosts to read and write. The Literacy Crusade, often regarded as the most successful such campaign in history, reduced Nicaragua's illiteracy rate from an estimated 55 per cent to 12 per cent in a matter of months. Through this experience, a generation of comparatively privileged urban young people developed an intimate knowledge of and sensitivity to the lives of the rural poor.

In April 1980 Violeta Chamorro and Alfonso Robelo resigned from the JGRN. They were replaced later that year by Rafael Córdoba Rivas, the head of the Conservative Party, and a Conservative banker, Arturo J. Cruz, who, in spite of having lived for most of his life in the United States, had been a member of The Twelve. In September an Argentine guerrilla commando assassinated Anastasio Somoza Debayle in Paraguay, where he had gone into exile, eliminating the possibility of a return of the Somozas. When Ronald Reagan was elected president of the United States, the business organization Consejo Superior de la Empresa Privada (COSEP; High Council of Private Enterprise) withdrew its collaboration with the government, alleging that Nicaragua had become a single-party state. One of Reagan's first acts as president was to cancel the delivery of the final $15 million in economic aid authorized by Jimmy Carter. In March 1981 Reagan opened training camps in Florida to prepare former National Guardsmen and mercenaries to launch attacks on Nicaragua. That month the JGRN was reduced to three members, its importance dwindling, as Arturo Cruz was named ambassador to the United States and Moisés Hassan was given a cabinet post. Agricultural and land reform accelerated, as new incentives were provided to small- and medium-sized farmers, and laws were passed to create agricultural cooperatives out of expropriated properties that had been abandoned by Somocistas who had fled to Miami.

The Reagan administration pressured the Inter-American Development Bank to withhold loans to Nicaragua. When the bank approved $500 million in credits to the destroyed country, the United States used its veto to cancel the loan. In spite of such obstacles, Sandinista investment in the public sector continued. By 1981, the number of primary school teachers in Nicaragua had tripled (Dunkerley 1988: 301); for the first time in the country's history, most children were attending school. In February 1982, as seventy thousand young people, many of them former participants in the National Literacy Crusade, fanned out across the country to innoculate the entire population against polio in a campaign that eradicated the disease, Ronald Reagan approved $19 million in covert aid to a group of former National Guardsmen and mercenaries, who came to be known as Contras.

The spectre of war accelerated the FSLN's efforts to extend its effective authority throughout the national territory. The remote, sparsely populated Atlantic Coast beckoned as a potential Contra haven: this region had not participated in the uprising against Somoza, and, as under Zelaya's administration, its Miskito, Sumu, Rama, and Afro-Caribbean inhabitants were suspicious of "Spaniards" sent from the Pacific Coast to administer them. Attempts to implement the National Literacy Crusade in Spanish were received by the peoples of the region as a policy of cultural assimilation. In February 1982 the FSLN removed eight thousand Miskito from their homes along the Honduran border, resettling them into the interior regions of the Atlantic Coast. The Nicaraguan Episcopal Conference denounced this displacement. Under the command of leaders such as Steadman Fagoth and Brooklyn Rivera, the Miskito went into open revolt, the Rivera faction joining forces with Edén Pastora, who had turned against the Revolution and was attacking it from Costa Rica in an offensive hostile to both the Sandinistas and the US-backed forces in Honduras. During 1982, approximately ninety-five Miskito died in combat against Sandinista troops (Blachman, LeoGrande, and Sharpe 1986: 104) and ten thousand more fled to Honduras (Dunkerley 1988: 314), where some, under the command of Fagoth, allied themselves with the Contras.

Yet, in spite of lurid accounts of "genocide" that circulated in even mainstream US newspapers, the FSLN, its negotiating team led by Comandante Luis Carrión, a passionate Christian, found common ground with the Miskito, recognizing their right to inhabit and administer their traditional lands, continuing the literacy campaign in the four languages of the Atlantic Coast, and arming the Miskito to provide for their own defence against the Contras. By 1986, more than ten thousand Miskito had returned to their ancestral homes and Nicaragua had introduced a regional autonomy project that was praised by indigenous leaders throughout the Americas for harmonizing aboriginal rights with national integration (Smith 1993: 238–40). The Miskito insurgency came to an end. As one Miskito leader put it: "We were fighting for the rights of Indians. Once the Sandinistas agreed to recognize our rights, there was no reason to fight anymore" (Wallace 1986: 50). These concessions were an important step in the official recognition of indigenous identities in Nicaragua, a cultural movement that would grow in coming decades and challenge the myth of the "mestizo nation." The proof that the rift between the FSLN and the Atlantic Coast had healed came in the 1990 election, when the region returned a strong majority for the Sandinistas.

During 1982 and 1983, Reagan administration officials became more open in expressing their desire to reverse the Nicaraguan Revolution by military force. In spite of a unanimous vote of the US Congress on 8 December 1982 to prohibit the Pentagon or the CIA from arming or training the Contras, money continued to flow to training camps in Honduras. The United States vetoed loan after loan from the Inter-American Development Bank, cut Nicaragua's sugar quota, and provided $5 million in direct aid to anti-Sandinista Managua businessmen and conservative elements in the Catholic Church. In order to keep "western sources of finance available" (Dunkerley 1988: 298), the FSLN had agreed in January 1980 to assume Somoza's bloated national debt; this made economic austerity even more severe as the costs of the US economic blockade and fighting the Contra war increased. Gasoline rationing went into effect. In March 1983 Pope John Paul II visited Managua. In a homily to 700,000 people, modelled on those he had delivered in Communist Poland, John Paul II urged the population to reject the Sandinistas. When he refused to say a Mass for young Nicaraguans who had died fighting the Contras, the crowd responded by chanting "¡Queremos la paz!" ("We want peace!") The Pope repeatedly shouted, "¡Silencio!" ("Silence!") at the crowd (*AM*, 197); in a gesture that insulted many devout Nicaraguans, he refused to consecrate the sacrifice of the martyrs.

In the month of the pope's visit, between fourteen hundred and two thousand Contras crossed the Honduran border with the goal of capturing the town of Jalapa, declaring it a liberated zone and receiving US recognition for a provisional government (LeoGrande 1998: 309). Reagan administration officials boasted that the Contras would be ruling in Managua by Christmas. Yet, for the first time in nearly 130 years of US incursions into Nicaragua, the invaders were repelled before they could establish a foothold. Over the decade of the 1980s, as the number of Contras grew and the weapons and training provided to them by their US military handlers in Honduras became more fearsome, they failed again and again to capture a single town. The campaign against the Contras consolidated a shared allegiance to Nicaraguan nationality and succeeded in "maintaining the impetus of nationalism to a far higher degree than otherwise would have been the case" (Dunkerley 1988: 321). This occurred in spite of hardening Sandinista hostility to the internal opposition, manifested in unpopular policies such as censoring the now US-funded Conservative newspaper *La Prensa*, which was edited by

Javier Chamorro Cardenal (its Sandinista rival, *Barricada*, was edited by his cousin, Carlos Fernando Chamorro, who was Violeta Chamorro's son; the editorially independent left-wing daily *El Nuevo Diario* was edited by Xavier Chamorro Cardenal, Pedro Joaquín Chamorro's brother).

Terrible economic austerity, the rigid top-down control that had gripped many of the popular organizations set up after 1979, the split in the Catholic Church between pro-Sandinista liberation theologians and the arch-conservative archbishop of Managua, Miguel Obando y Bravo, and the gradual erosion of the social and economic gains that had been made by peasants, small farmers, and most urban workers during the first four years of the Revolution, all added to the FSLN's difficulties without actually threatening the regime. However, the Contra War did represent a long-term threat to Sandinista legitimacy. In response to the first attempted invasion, and after a public debate that lasted six months, on 6 October 1983 the Council of State promulgated the Ley del Servicio Militar Patriótico (SMP; Patriotic Military Service Law) – two years' mandatory military service for young men – in order to supply the EPS with a steady flow of new recruits to fight the Contras. The SMP became by far the most unpopular Sandinista policy, with many young men fleeing the country to escape being sent into the front lines; some of these young men ended up joining the Contras.

In April 1983 the United Nations Children's Fund (UNICEF) declared Nicaragua an international model in the field of public health. Diplomatic initiatives to end the Contra war intensified as Nicaragua circumvented US opposition to win a seat on the United Nations Security Council, which in May passed a resolution against foreign intervention in Central America. In open defiance of the UN resolution, the United States undertook military manoeuvres in Honduras from August 1983 to January 1984. Called Big Pine II, this operation's purpose was to simulate a US invasion of Nicaragua. Bringing together "nineteen ships, over two hundred jet fighters, and twenty thousand personnel" (LeoGrande 1998: 317), these exercises represented the largest US military presence ever assembled in Central America. On 10 October 1983 a specially trained CIA commando unit, operating from a ship in international waters, attacked Nicaragua in speedboats and helicopters, blowing up the country's oil supplies at Corinto; three days later, CIA frogmen blew up the oil pipeline at Puerto Sandino. In February 1984 the CIA mined Nicaragua's ports.

The Reagan administration's disregard for international law alienated governments throughout Europe and the Americas, which, even in the context of Cold War conflict, were baffled that the United States should feel threatened by an underdeveloped country of barely three million people.

Many nations offered aid to Nicaragua. Even the newly elected Progressive Conservative prime minister of Canada, Brian Mulroney, who developed a close personal relationship with the Reagans, not only refused to help the Contras but made Sandinista Nicaragua the largest Central American recipient of Canadian foreign aid (McFarlane 1989: 190). From 1983, Mexico, Colombia, Venezuela, and Panama, under the name of the Contadora Group, pursued regional peace negotiations; the Reagan administration treated this process with derision. Reagan's propaganda machine insisted that Nicaragua was "a Soviet beachhead" on the mainland of the Americas.

In fact, Soviet assistance, though highlighted by the US media, was restrained. Relations with Moscow remained distant: Soviet commentators never used the word "socialist" when referring to Nicaragua, an omission that telegraphed the absence of a strong commitment to the FSLN; in addition to withholding MiG fighters requested by the Sandinistas, the Soviet Union refused to send Nicaragua M-72 tanks, which it supplied even to non-socialist countries, such as Syria. Soviet economic aid to Nicaragua was fitful and consisted mainly of bilateral trade credits (Gilbert 1988: 170). The Kremlin's most substantial contribution to the FSLN government consisted of wheat shipments that were vital in alleviating the shortage of bread. Sandinista leaders had strong emotional ties to Cuba and numerous Cuban advisers were present in Nicaragua, yet, with multiple opposition parties, an outspoken Catholic hierarchy, an influential private sector, and free movement in and out of the country, the Nicaraguan Revolution was infinitely more pluralistic than that of Fidel Castro: Cuba was seen as an inspiration, but not necessarily as a model.

FROM THE 1984 ELECTIONS TO THE 1990 ELECTIONS

In a quest to bolster their international legitimacy, and open the doors to more European and South American aid to offset their growing debt, the Sandinistas advanced national elections, originally scheduled for 1985, to two days before the US elections in November 1984 "so that a reelected Reagan ... would have a harder time justifying an attack on Nicaragua" (LeoGrande 1998: 370). The FSLN ticket of Daniel Ortega for president and Sergio Ramírez for vice-president confronted Clemente Guido of the renamed Democratic Conservative Party and Virgilio Godoy of Somoza's old party, the Liberals. With 75 per cent of eligible voters participating, Ortega won 67 per cent of the vote, Guido 14 per cent, and Godoy 10 per cent; the FSLN won 61 out of 96 seats in the National Assembly.

The election was judged to be fair by international observers and the Latin American and European media. The conservative British news magazine *The Economist* ranked it as "maybe as good a test of opinion as a Mexican election, though not as fair as a Costa Rican one" ("Half-Step" 1984). By contrast, a decade later Mexican historian Jorge Castañeda wrote of the election that "by Latin American and certainly by Nicaraguan standards it was a shining example … If the same tough standards the Sandinistas were being obliged to abide by had been applied to Mexican elections, for example, the PRI [Partido Revolucionario Institucional] would have been removed from power years ago" (Castañeda 1993: 345). Yet, rather than covering the election, the US media followed Arturo Cruz, who had resigned as Nicaraguan ambassador to Washington, as he explained again and again to the television cameras that he was not running for president. Cruz was being paid a salary of $7,000 a month by the Reagan administration, which, according to one of its senior officials, had instructed him "either not to enter the race, or, if he did, to withdraw before the election, claiming the conditions were unfair" (Morris 2010: 151). After the elections, US Secretary of State George Schultz denounced "Sham elections on the Soviet model" (LeoGrande 1998: 375). As Brad Roth writes, this propaganda campaign was successful in obscuring Central American realities from the US public: "In subsequent years, the US media would allow Administration spokespersons and supporters to make uncontradicted references to Nicaragua's government as unelected, and to compare Nicaragua unfavorably to 'the four Central American democracies' to which it was an alleged menace" (Roth 1999: 353). Anti-Nicaraguan paranoia became rampant in the United States, expressed in Hollywood scare movies such as *Red Dawn* (1984), in which Patrick Swayze fights off a combined Nicaraguan-Soviet invasion of the US Midwest. Films that took the opposite view, such as Edward Pressman and Alex Cox's *Walker* (1987), sank at the box office.

The next four years were consumed by US congressional debates over Contra funding and meetings of the Contadora Group. Not even the peace agreements that were signed, such as Esquipulas II in 1987, succeeded in halting the fighting. In 1986 Reagan received $100 million from Congress and a second $100 million from the Senate to fund the Contras; this figure did not include money funnelled to the Contras through backdoor methods, contributions from private donors, or aid from states ideologically sympathetic to the Contras, primarily Israel and Saudi Arabia. By the end of 1986, the Contras had killed fourteen thousand Nicaraguans and kidnapped many more; the EPS had killed seventeen thousand Contras (Dunkerley 1988:

325).[1] On 25 June 1986 the International Court of Justice in The Hague found the United States guilty of being an aggressor state and ordered it to pay indemnity to Nicaragua for all damages caused by the Contras and the CIA. The United States ignored the judgment. Nicaragua made repeated efforts to open a direct dialogue with the United States, which the Reagan administration spurned, insisting that the FSLN must recognize the Contras as a legitimate opposition. The capture of a US citizen, Eugene Hasenfus, whose C-123 cargo plane, loaded with weapons for the Contras, was shot down over southern Nicaragua by a nineteen-year-old with a hand-held missile, reinforced the Sandinista position that the Contras were not a legitimate political force. The capture of Hasenfus led to the revelations of the Iran-Contra scandal, which would cripple Contra support in Washington (Kinzer 1991: 311–23).

Economic conditions in Nicaragua worsened. Soft drinks and alcohol were heavily taxed; sugar, oil, rice, and powdered milk were rationed. In 1987 Costa Rican President Óscar Arias was awarded the Nobel Peace Prize for negotiating the Esquipulas II peace agreement. The United States responded with a campaign to discredit Arias, cancelling an aid package for Costa Rica, and sending Arias's political enemies at home $433,000 to be used to attack him (LeoGrande 1998: 528). Yet, in spite of US hostility, both sides needed to implement Arias's peace agreement: the Contras had been defeated militarily by the EPS, and in Nicaragua inflation was out of control; in October 1988 Hurricane Joan, which left one hundred and eighty thousand Nicaraguans homeless, would make the economic crisis even more acute.

As part of a process known as *la compactación* ("the compression"), Nicaragua's currency was reformed to curb inflation, and many government services, and even whole departments, were eliminated. The FSLN agreed to negotiate with the Contras, naming Humberto Ortega as chief negotiator. In a surprise military operation, the EPS crossed the border into Honduras and destroyed Contra training camps. The United States responded by landing troops in Honduras, provoking a crisis at the UN Security Council. The two countries engaged in tit-for-tat expulsions of diplomats. In early 1989 the córdoba was repeatedly devalued and more cuts were made to services. The new US president, George H.W. Bush, continued to send money to the Contras even as they were supposedly dismantling their bases in Honduras to comply with the Esquipulas peace agreement. At the same time, Bush administration officials brought together fourteen of the twenty-two opposition parties in Nicaragua, ranging from the Communist Party to the far right, into a coalition known as Unión Nacional Opositora (UNO; National

Opposition Union). Influenced by the success of Corazon Aquino in the Philippines, they installed Violeta Chamorro as the coalition's presidential candidate and funded Chamorro's campaign at a higher cost-per-vote than that of Bush's own campaign for the presidency of the United States (Morris 2010: 161). In violation of both US and Nicaraguan law, the Bush administration gave UNO $9 million in campaign funds and provided generous funding for exiled Nicaraguans, including ex-National Guardsmen, to return to Nicaragua to campaign in the election, scheduled for 25 February 1990. As a famous widow, dressed in white by her US image makers, Chamorro embodied the cost of the war. Fidel Castro warned the FSLN that conducting an election during a war was tantamount to asking people to vote for continued conflict. Daniel Ortega and Sergio Ramírez, heeding Castro's advice, suggested rescinding the SMP; but Humberto Ortega, fearing that such a move would prompt mass desertions from the EPS and enable the Contras to capture Nicaraguan territory, opposed this concession.

On 20 December 1989, in the last military act of the Cold War, the United States invaded Panama. With shocking brutality, the US Army murdered four thousand Panamanian civilians and set fire to large sections of Panama City. US troops surrounded the Nicaraguan Embassy and violated the Nicaraguan ambassador's diplomatic immunity by ransacking his official residence (Donnelly 1991: 307–8). In retaliation, the EPS surrounded the US Embassy in Managua with antiquated Soviet tanks. Many Nicaraguans viewed the invasion of Panama with foreboding, seeing in it a warning of the fate that awaited Nicaragua if it re-elected the FSLN; this, indeed, appeared to be Bush's intention. The US president's warnings to Nicaraguan voters that a victory for the FSLN, no matter how democratic or legitimate, would result in renewed war, had a substantial impact on the Nicaraguan electorate. Polling showed that voters preferred Daniel Ortega to Violeta Chamorro in every area except one: the ability to bring peace.

On 21 February 1990, the fifty-sixth anniversary of the murder of Sandino, Daniel Ortega and Sergio Ramírez held a rally in Managua. It was the largest mass meeting in Nicaraguan history; not even Pope John Paul II had attracted such a large crowd. Ortega's failure to announce the withdrawal of the SMP, as it had been rumoured he would do, appears to have sent some of the cheering Sandinista supporters home disappointed. The more than fifteen hundred foreign news agencies that were present in Nicaragua, making this one of the most hotly covered elections in history, conducted non-stop polling. Every poll predicted an Ortega victory; the titanic rally seemed to confirm this. Yet on election day, in a result that startled observers and participants, Violeta Chamorro won 55 per cent of the vote and Ortega

42 per cent. The chief election observer, former US President Jimmy Carter, realized what was happening from his initial sampling of the ballots (*AM*, 279) and prepared to negotiate the first peaceful transfer of power between political rivals in Nicaraguan history. Analysis of the results later showed that, though the FSLN had won among soldiers, bureaucrats, and students and had been highly competitive among professionals and skilled workers, the "pivotal voters turned out to be the poor, especially the poorest of the poor, living in Nicaragua's most impoverished and least accessible places" (Anderson and Dodd 2005: 113). It had not been feasible to poll these people, who had borne the brunt of the Contra War. Everyone had assumed they were Sandinista supporters, but they voted en masse for the widow in white who said she would stop the war. Many poor peasants, who had been forced to join cooperatives when they had expected to be granted private plots of land, were disenchanted with the FSLN, a factor that had led young men from poor peasant families in northern Nicaragua to join the Contras and their parents to vote UNO (Saldaña-Portillo 2003: 125–47; Dore 2006: 6). The votes of the rural poor combined with those of the large families of the Conservative oligarchy, thrilled at the prospect of seeing a Chamorro in power for the first time since the 1920s, to make Doña Violeta the first democratically elected woman president in Latin America.

Like many revolutionaries before them, and in spite of the monstrous setbacks they had suffered at the hands of US aggression and their own ideological rigidity, the Sandinistas were victims of their own success. They had placed the poor at the core of the Nicaraguan imagination, urged the poor to stand up for their rights, and now the poor had become autonomous actors. The vote of the country's most deprived and oppressed people for a "reactionary" candidate would torment many Sandinistas for years to come, yet for the first time these deprived people had not feared to make their demands heard in public.

After Daniel Ortega's concession speech at 6AM on 26 February, Nicaragua fell silent. No one celebrated this victory. Other accounts corroborate that of Gioconda Belli:

> La gente no celebró en las calles la victoria de la UNO … Por el contrario, en los días que siguieron al domingo electoral una atmósfera de luto cayó sobre la ciudad. Parecía Semana Santa, como si toda la población se hubiese marchado … Creo que al dar la victoria a Violeta, el pueblo intercambió el poder de sentirse protagonistas, por la paz, aunque viniera de la burguesía, pero alguna intuición tendrían de que otra vez se verían relegados a ser simplemente "los pobres," ya no

> "las masas populares" que el sandinismo había exaltado. Quienes organizaron celebraciones en esos días fueron la gente de mi clase que recuperaba sus privilegios, los exiliados de Miami, fiestas privadas, no en las calles o las plazas. (Belli 2001: 395–6; People didn't celebrate in the streets the victory of the UNO ... On the contrary – in the days following Election Sunday, the city was enveloped in an air of mourning. The streets looked the same as when everybody left for the holidays at the height of the summer months ... Personally, I think people granted Violeta her electoral victory conscious that they were exchanging their sense of power for peace. They must have sensed that once again they would be relegated to being the "poor people," and not the "popular masses" the Sandinistas had championed. Violeta's victory was celebrated by the upper classes, the Miami exiles, the people [from my social class] who would now regain their old privileges, and they held their parties behind closed doors, not in the streets or the plazas. [Belli 2002: 356])

The era of mass meetings, of defining the nation in the street, had ended. Belli's contention that the vote of the poor to get rid of the Sandinistas was their last act as "protagonists" of the national destiny may sound spiteful, yet, in strictly political terms, subsequent events would bear out this analysis. The poor would remain a rhetorical touchstone in Nicaraguan politics, but, after 1990, serious efforts to improve their living standards stagnated for a decade and a half. In symbolic terms, Nicaragua faced a conundrum: the only definition of national autonomy that existed was inscribed in the culture of Sandinismo. As Alma Guillermoprieto wrote in the election's aftermath: "Nicaragua was not a state until the Sandinistas made it one" (Guillermoprieto 1994: 38). The archaic Conservative vision of devout, Catholic, obedient, hierarchical, agrarian Nicaragua, which had predominated from the 1850s until the late 1920s, failed to connect with the reality of the 1990s, however much some Conservatives, including Violeta Chamorro herself, may have believed otherwise. The Somocista vision of progress through Americanization, though touted by many of the men who surrounded Doña Violeta, contained no positive vision of Nicaraguan people or their culture. Affirmative symbols of national identity other than Sandino were scarce for Nicaraguan mestizos. Those who claimed other heritages began to find meaning in indigenous or Afro-Caribbean identities, which became more strongly articulated after 1990; those who rejected the Nicaraguan Revolution, in some cases retrospectively, immersed themselves in a traditionalist Catholicism (liberation theology dwindled, though it remained powerful in certain neighbourhoods). Young people who grew up after 1990 and had not experienced the Revolution tended to regard it as a period of national disaster.

Yet the more integrated, if paradoxically more openly culturally diverse, Nicaragua inherited by post-1990 governments had cohered around the Sandinista ideals of national autonomy, self-sacrifice, and justice for the poor. With the exception of Pablo Antonio Cuadra, all of Nicaragua's writers and musicians, like most of the country's visual artists, had devoted their works to developing, enriching, and articulating this culture. Nothing illustrated this more clearly than Ernesto Cardenal's eighteen-metre-high sculpture of Augusto César Sandino in silhouette, which was erected on the Tiscapa Mound during the transition from the FSLN to the Chamorro government. This work consecrates both Sandino and modern Sandinismo's debt to the revolutionary example of Cuba, where the epicentre of the nation is the seventeen-metre-high statue of José Martí in Havana's Plaza de la Revolución (Revolution Square). Cardenal's statue is a visual echo of this structure. At a denotative level, the Managua sculpture pays homage to Sandino; at a connotative level, it ensconces the FSLN of the 1970s and 1980s, forged from Carlos Fonseca's fusion of Sandino's example with the ideology of the Cuban Revolution, as the heart of the Nicaraguan nation. In spite of the ideological divergence of post-1990 governments from this vision, the sculpture remained intact, dominating the capital from nearly every angle. All quests for Nicaraguanness led back to Sandino's nation.

7

Ramírez: Towards the Novelist as Vice-President (1976–89)

THE BOOM IN NICARAGUA: *TO BURY OUR FATHERS*

When Ramírez returned to Central America in the summer of 1975, his creative and intellectual energy concentrated on the obsequiousness of the Nicaraguan bourgeoisie. It was the bourgeoisie that, by failing to institutionalize the nation, had allowed a single family to rule for four decades. The central theme of his new collection of short stories, *Charles Atlas también muere* (1976; Charles Atlas Also Dies), was how the hypocrisy and self-abasement of the upper echelons of the bourgeoisie had facilitated violations of the nation-space and the suppression of the national culture. Published in Mexico City and including the title piece and "To Jackie with All Our Heart," in addition to "The Centerfielder," "The Siege," "A Bauxite Bed in Weipa," and "Nicaragua Is White" from the poorly distributed, carelessly printed *Nuevos Cuentos* (New Stories), this collection became Ramírez's first internationally distributed title.

In spite of his FSLN commitments, Ramírez also found time to edit the memoirs of Abelardo Cuadra, a one-time National Guardsman. Cuadra's Testimonio, *Hombre del Caribe* (1977; Man of the Caribbean), contained an eye-witness account of Sandino's execution; the impression this scene made on Ramírez not only stimulated his mental reformulation of Nicaraguan history but would inspire his description of the execution of Oliverio Castañeda in his novel *Castigo Divino* (1988; Divine Punishment). Cuadra, who belonged to the first generation of National Guardsmen, trained by the US Marines, exemplified not the "grupos hegemónicos debilitados" (Cuadra 1977: 14; "weakened hegemonic groups") but rather middle sectors that were absorbed into the dictatorship's repressive apparatus. For Ramírez, Cuadra and his brothers "representan también esa alegre aspiración de los

Sergio Ramírez as a member of the Governing Junta for National Reconstruction, 1981 (copyright holder unidentifiable)

sectores medios dentro del clima ideológico creado por el peso político y cultural de la intervención, de participar en la creación de un aparato supuestamente modernizador y gozar de sus beneficios" (Cuadra, 17; "also represent the joyful aspiration of the middle class, within the ideological climate created by the political and cultural burden of the intervention, to participate in the creation of a supposedly modernizing social force and enjoy its benefits"). Having plumbed the perfidy of the upper classes and the collaborationism of the middle sectors, Ramírez was now prepared to try to capture all of Nicaraguan society in a novel.

¿Te dio miedo la sangre? (*To Bury Our Fathers*), written in Berlin between October 1973 and May 1975,[1] and first published in Caracas in 1977, established Ramírez as a significant novelist. The first internationally published novel by a Central American writer since the death of the Guatemalan Nobel Laureate Miguel Ángel Asturias in 1974, it had a cultural significance that surpassed its substantial literary impact. At a time when political strife both in Nicaragua, and increasingly in El Salvador and Guatemala, was beginning to focus the world's attention on Central America, *To Bury Our Fathers* was a powerful piece of cultural capital that lent status and intellectual heft to the Nicaraguan opposition and later to the FSLN government. The book's complexity, its multiple editions in different countries and languages, ushered Nicaragua into the Latin American literary Boom.

In purely generational terms, this assessment may seem contradictory. The five writers customarily identified as the core of the Boom – Julio Cortázar, José Donoso, Gabriel García Márquez, Carlos Fuentes, and Mario Vargas Llosa – were born in 1914, 1924, 1927, 1928, and 1936 respectively. Ramírez, born in 1942, belonged to the same generation as writers who were identified with the Post-Boom, such as Luisa Valenzuela (born 1938), Antonio Skármeta (1940), Gustavo Sainz (1940), Cristina Peri Rossi (1941), or Isabel Allende (1942). Yet, in aesthetic terms, Ramírez's brooding novel had little in common with the approachable, upbeat populism of Allende, Sainz, or Skármeta, or the post-modern deconstructions of male power that are found in the work of Peri Rossi or Valenzuela. At a time when the Post-Boom was defining itself against the Boom's "total novel" (Shaw 1994: 222–3), Ramírez wrote a totalizing novel of his country's history. In a trait that is reminiscent of the Boom, the novel's female characters conform to sexually objectified roles: they are prostitutes, beauty queens, or circus performers. Like the novels of Vargas Llosa and García Márquez, *To Bury Our Fathers* is immersed in the labyrinths of patriarchal power, pitting rebellious bravado against tyrannical oppression and sons against fathers in a manner that recalls Colonel Aureliano Buendía's uprisings in *One Hundred Years of Solitude*, or Santiago Zavala's revolt against his father in Vargas Llosa's *Conversación en La Catedral* (1969; *Conversation in The Cathedral*). In stylistic terms, the novel suffers from none of the derivative imitations of Asturias, Rulfo, or García Márquez that mar *Tiempo de fulgor*: the fluid, post-Faulknerian sentences, in which multiple subordinate clauses are reined in by an absence of bombast, very close scrutiny of Nicaraguan reality, and a judicious, Modernist incorporation of regional vocabulary into the creation of layered literary effects, hone a voice that is unmistakably Ramírez's own.

At a structural level, however, *To Bury Our Fathers* is drenched in the influence of Vargas Llosa, particularly in those twin summits of narrative complexity in the modern Spanish American novel, *La casa verde* (1965; *The Green House*) and *Conversation in The Cathedral*. If the symmetrical rotation of scenes in a tropical setting and the use of a character who appears under different sobriquets in different narrative streams recalls the former novel, the theme of patriarchal tensions within the family that echo the larger power dynamics of a society ruled by a dictator, as well as the motif of political discussions in bars, appear to have been inspired by the latter work. Ramírez acknowledges this debt: "En aquel entonces, la influencia más determinante, en cuanto a la estructura, en mí era Vargas Llosa. *Conversación en La Catedral* y *La casa verde* tenían esa asombrosa capacidad para combinar los planos. Esa comienza a ser mi gran ambición, saber combinar planos y ir tejiendo varias historias al mismo tiempo" (Cherem 2004b: 111–12; "Back then, the most decisive influence on me, in terms of structure, was Vargas Llosa. *Conversation in The Cathedral* and *The Green House* had this amazing ability to combine planes. This became my great ambition: to be able to combine planes and weave together several stories at once").

The appearance of a Boom novel from a Nicaraguan writer in 1977 – a novel written in Europe, as were the novels of Cortázar, Vargas Llosa, and Donoso – risks evoking the prejudice that Central America suffers from a cultural time-lag by comparison with South America and Mexico. One way to resolve the contradiction between Ramírez's generational correspondence with the Post-Boom and his Boom aesthetics is to view *To Bury Our Fathers* as one of the late-Boom dictatorship novels that appeared in the mid-1970s and arguably brought the Boom to a close: a work contemporaneous with Augusto Roa Bastos's *Yo, el Supremo* (1974; *I, the Supreme*), Alejo Carpentier's *El recurso del método* (1974; *Reasons of State*), and García Márquez's *El otoño del patriarca* (1975; *The Autumn of the Patriarch*) (Martin 1989: 237–95). Ramírez's approach, however, differed from those of these writers; in Claudia Schaeffer's characterization, "en vez de presentar la psicología del dictador en la primera persona narrativa como eje central de la narración, o como un ser ya muerto y mitificado, Ramírez opta por presentar los efectos de una dictadura en la 'intrahistoria' del pueblo y en las 'voces' del pueblo mismo" (Schaeffer 1987: 148–9; "instead of presenting the psychology of the dictator in the first person narrative as the central narrative axis, or as a being already dead and mythologized, Ramirez opts to present the effects of a dictatorship in the 'inside story' of the people and in the 'voices' of the people themselves").

Yet, as Arturo Arias suggests, there were other reasons for the Boom's arrival in Central America just as the region's wars were beginning. Boom aesthetics provided a way of participating in "subaltern power" – the power of the marginalized, incarnated by predominantly expatriate writers from larger Spanish American countries – as a bulwark against colonization by US imperialism. This sort of identification enabled the writer – particularly the male writer who was taking on political responsibilities – to speak on behalf of the nation, bridging the gap between himself and "the people." This assertion, as Arias contends, "did not so much try to integrate Central America into modernity through literature as it used the modernity of literature to justify the revolutionary need for social and political transformations, thus creating an illusion of avant-garde writers as the equivalent of avant-garde revolutionaries" (Arias 2007: 13). In a symbolic sense, the fusion of the nineteenth-century novel of society inherited from Honoré de Balzac (who provides the epigraph to Vargas Llosa's *Conversation in The Cathedral*) with the Modernist legacy of William Faulkner and James Joyce – novelists who mythologized societies marginalized and colonized by linear Western progress – that lay at the heart of Boom aesthetics became a way of taking possession of the nation. In the Nicaraguan context, the Boom's "total novel" was a reappropriation of the nation. The abolition of national history by a regime that gained its legitimacy from being the prolongation of a US military occupation, and that presented Yankee modernization as the sole credible reality, claimed no previous Nicaraguan government or tradition as its forerunner, denied the possibility of a Nicaraguan culture, and effectively ceded representation of the nation to the Sandinista counter-culture. Having sputtered through the 1960s, this counter-culture had become more visible in the early 1970s in the poetry of Leonel Rugama and Ernesto Cardenal (after his conversion to socialism), the pamphlets of Carlos Fonseca, and the folk music of Carlos and Luis Mejía Godoy, as well as in Christian Base Communities inspired by liberation theology and student political organizations such as the Frente Estudiantil Revolucionario.

To Bury Our Fathers, then, provided a totalized vision of the counter-nation, to which the Somozas, by virtue of their subservience to Yankee cultural assumptions, could offer no competing version. No one had ever before provided a narrative of Nicaraguan national experience during the years leading up to, including, and following the regime of Anastasio Somoza García. In addition to its originality, Ramírez's rendition of events acquired authority because it participated in the Boom, the definitive cosmopolitan expression of Spanish American "subaltern power," and was too difficult for most Nicaraguans to read.

Concluding in a bar in Granada in 1961 that echoes the seedy Lima bar in which Santiago and Ambrosio reconstruct the eight years of the Peruvian dictatorship of General Manuel Odría in *Conversation in The Cathedral*, *To Bury Our Fathers* charts the origins, trajectory, and aftermath of the rule of the dictator who is known only as *el hombre* ("the man"). The events of the past thirty years are filtered through the consciousness of two guerrillas taking part in the 1959 uprising. Its chronology reaching back as far as 1930, the novel touches on the major watersheds in mid-twentieth-century Nicaraguan history: Sandino's guerrilla war, the annihilation of the Sandinista cooperative on the Coco River after his assassination, the tracking down and decapitation of Sandino's lieutenant Pedro Altamirano, the fraudulent elections contested by the Conservative leader Fernando Agüero, the 1954 April Rebellion, and the 1959 insurgency of Olama y los Mollejones that marked the final effort of the Conservative families to overthrow Somoza. The novel's action concludes with the suppression of the 1959 rebellion. All of the historical events are presented in distorted, fictionalized form. The only figures who retain their historical names are John F. Kennedy and Franklin D. Roosevelt, Augusto César Sandino and Pedro Altamirano, the Guatemalan dictator Carlos Castillo Armas and the martyr Rigoberto López Pérez (yet nothing in the novel divulges why López Pérez is a martyr). The reader deduces, from remarks made in conversation, that in the novel's narrative present *el hombre* is dead, though the dictatorship continues under the command of "*los hijos del hombre*" (*TDMS*, 53; "*el hombre*'s sons" [*TBF*, 34]). López Pérez's assassination of Somoza García in León in 1956 is not recounted, though early in the novel Indio Larios tells Catalino López that he is innocent of "la muerte de *el hombre*" (53; "the death of *el hombre* " [*TBF*, 34]). As the novel concludes, the opposition appears to have been quashed; the country's future has been kidnapped by the United States. Yet this sombre vision is alleviated by the epilogue's setting in 1961, the year the FSLN was founded.

The novel describes a series of vertical patriarchal relationships, some of which describe the mentorship of one man by another, or comradeship among small groups of men; many are characterized by authoritarianism, violence, and torture. The novel's narrative present is the 1959 guerrilla campaign and concentrates on two members of an insurgent group, Turco, a man from a rural lower-class family of Liberal allegiances who is a former National Guardsman, and Jilguero, who comes from a wealthy Conservative family and whose grandfather has been defrauded out of the presidency.

The guerrillas sit around a "fogata" (*TDMS*, 14; "campfire" [*TBF*, 1]), a word traditionally used to symbolize the presence of Sandino's example. Within a few lines, however, this present-tense narration has merged into recollections of past events that are described in the past tense. The transition occurs with an injunction in the subjunctive: "el Turco ... se queda de pie junto a la hoguera ya casi extinguida del campamento y le dice al Jilguero que se acuerde" (*TDMS*, 13; "Turco ... stops by the dying campfire and says to Jilguero, remember" [*TBF*, 1]). This unleashes recollections of events they have experienced together and acts as a catalyst to memories recounted by other narrators, both dramatized and non-dramatized, ultimately setting the stage for the novel's closing line, "Recuerdos te dejaron" (*TDMS*, 308; "they left you memories" [*TBF*, 249]).

The incident that Jilguero and Turco reconstruct together is how in 1957, in Guatemala, they and a long-exiled opposition member named Indio Larios kidnapped the National Guardsman Colonel Catalino López, took him to a brothel in the Guatemala City suburb of Mixco, and visited on him an unnamed punishment for his crimes committed as the dictator's henchman. This story, sectioned into episodes spaced at regular intervals throughout the first half of the novel, and interspersed with other scenes that follow different narrative threads, is narrated in a first-person plural voice that at times feels like a non-dramatized third-person narration. The polyphonic nature of this narrative thread becomes evident at points where one of the narrators identifies himself in the first person, or where the two narrators disagree. In the novel's opening scene, for example, the first-person plural narration, in the "nosotros" ("we") form, is interrupted by a paragraph, which a close reading identifies as being narrated by Jilguero, that starts: "Y yo, aturdido de aflicción ..." (*TDMS*, 18; "Terribly upset ... I explained ..." [*TBF*, 5]). In the next paragraph, Turco offers his rejoinder to Jilguero's protestations of the difficulties he experienced in manoeuvring the captured Colonel López across the floor of the brothel's crowded bar: "Pero lo lograste, Jilguero" (*TDMS*, 19; "But you did it, Jilguero" [*TBF*, 6]). In sequences later in the novel that continue the relation of these events, the men's amendments to one another's stories recur as corrections to the flow of the narrative of López's punishment. A description of the funeral that López has come to Guatemala to attend is succeeded by a paragraph that opens: "Pero el Jilguero no recuerda tanto como eso ..." (*TDMS*, 83; "But Jilguero cannot remember that much ..." [*TBF*, 59]). The competing versions of events (and the sheer difficulty, on a first reading, of understanding how this narrative thread is being generated) summon the "active reader" demanded by novelists of the Boom.

It is significant that the opening scene is set in Guatemala, a country that for a decade experienced the freedom that Nicaragua seeks, during the funeral of a tyrant. Colonel Castillo Armas, handpicked by the CIA to be dictator of Guatemala after the US overthrow of the democratic government of Jacobo Arbenz in 1954, was assassinated in the presidential palace on 27 July 1957 (Schlesinger and Kinzer 1982: 95–6, 235). His funeral stands in, in the novel's structure, for the suppressed assassination of *el hombre*; it introduces the Freudian theme of the killing of the despotic father-figure that is announced by the novel's epigraph from Aristophanes: "the skylark, ingenious of necessity, buried its father in its own head" (*TBF*, epigraph page); perhaps most significantly, by inaugurating the action in the region's most populous country, these scenes contextualize the novel's events within a pattern of Central American dictatorships.

While the opening scene is set in Guatemala, whose culture is one of the core preoccupations of "Balcanes y Volcanes," the second scene restores the story to Nicaragua, referring to the history described in "El muchacho de Niquinohomo" to flesh out the nation's distinctness within the concert of Central American dictatorships. As in Vargas Llosa's *La ciudad y los perros* (1962; *The Time of the Hero*), where the identity of the narrator of a crucial first-person monologue is revealed only more than three hundred pages into the novel, so here only a very alert reader will infer in the first half of the book that the anonymous good Samaritan who spares Sergeant Catalino López from a court martial after Pedro Altamirano wipes out his platoon and leaves López naked in the jungle, and who reorients his military career in a way that leads to a promotion, is Indio Larios. And as in Vargas Llosa's *The Green House*, where the same character appears as Bonifacia in one narrative stream and La Selvática in another, the second scene of *To Bury Our Fathers* introduces a young boy named Santiago Taleno who is travelling through the Atlantic Coast region in the company of his father, an itinerant labourer, and his brother Trinidad. Only more than one hundred pages into the novel will the most attentive reader grasp that Turco and Santiago Taleno are the same character.

Santiago's odyssey, beginning in the San Juan River that delineates the border between Nicaragua and Costa Rica, initiates the novel's sounding of national reality. The father and his two sons emerge from the mouth of the river into the Atlantic as though it is Nicaragua itself that is giving them birth. The motherless boy's origins in a liminal zone that is neither Nicaragua nor Costa Rica qualify him to explore the nation ruled by *el hombre* with the fresh eyes of someone who, although he has been told that this is his country, begins to experience it for the first time when his father points it out to him on the horizon: "y Taleno el padre les señala entonces que todo aquello azul en la lejanía es en verdad lo mismo: Nicaragua" (*TDMS*, 24; "Taleno's father points and says that all the distant outline is in fact the same: Nicaragua" [*TBF*, 10]). The narrative stresses the ambiguity of Santiago's birth in a passage that complicates Ramírez's use of intertextual echoes with earlier writers: "Porque nació a lo mejor en San Carlos y de allá venían, más arriba del río, pasando los raudales y entrando ya en aguas del lago, o acaso en El Castillo, o en Sábalo, en cualquier orilla del río San Juan" (*TDM*, 21; "Because he was born possibly in San Carlos and that is where they had come here from, further upstream, down through the rough water and into the calm waters of the lake; or perhaps in El Castillo, or in Sabalo, anywhere along the banks of the San Juan River" [*TBF*, 8]). Santiago's birth "anywhere along the banks" of the river – possibly in Nicaragua, possibly in Costa Rica, but by implication outside any firm national identity – emphasizes his status as someone who, since he comes from nowhere, is a neutral monitor of Nicaraguan experience. This motif's lineage bypasses the Latin American writers who were influencing Ramírez, plunging one step farther back to the influences' influence: William Faulkner.

Almost certainly the most crucial single literary ancestor of García Márquez and a very important figure for Vargas Llosa (*The Green House*, among other things, is a rewriting of *The Wild Palms* [1939]), Faulkner also played an important direct role in Ramírez's development. As he stated in an interview in Cuba: "De Faulkner aprendí que aproximándose a realidades parecidas – él, el sur, yo, mi país – se podrían encontrar muchos puntos en común" (*AO*, 303; "I learned from Faulkner that approaching similar realities – he, the South, me, my country – one could find a lot of similarities"). Faulkner employs the same motif of a character who, since he comes from outside recognized boundaries, provides an unbiased point of origin for his homeland's experience. In *Absalom, Absalom!* (1936), Faulkner's Modernist chronicle of the rise and fall of a great Mississippi family, Quentin, the inheritor of the family's decaying traditions, and his roommate Shreve reconstruct the history of Quentin's ancestor Colonel Sutpen: "Because he was born in West Virginia, in the mountains –" ("Not in West Virginia," Shreve said. "Because if he was twenty-five years old in Mississippi in 1833, he was born in 1808. And there wasn't any West Virginia in 1808 because –" "All right," Quentin said. "– West Virginia wasn't admitted –" "All right, all right," Quentin said. "– into the United States until –" "All right all right all right," Quentin said.)" – and he was born where what few other people he knew lived in log cabins boiling with children like the one he was born in – ..." (Faulkner 1936: 220–1).

Like Santiago, Colonel Sutpen can embody an essentialized form of identity because, in a novel riven by the divisive legacy of the Civil War between the Union and Confederate states, his origins are in a region that, having come late to statehood, is historically exempt from identification with either of the contending parties. Sutpen enters the South as neither a northerner nor a southerner, but a free agent. In a similar vein, Santiago is identified neither with Nicaraguan Liberals nor Conservatives, nor with any particular region: he is a tabula rasa who is undergoing induction into Nicaraguanness. Like the first Spanish conquistadors, he enters Nicaragua on the Atlantic Coast and will eventually come to know all regions of the country and all levels of society. Ramírez's intertextual adoption and reworking of this and other motifs from Faulkner has a variety of consequences. Where critical perceptions of intertextuality derive from Julia Kristeva's assertion that "tout texte est absorption et transformation d'un autre texte ... et le langage poétique se lit, au moins, comme *double*" (Kristeva 1978: 85; "every text is the absorption and transformation of another text ... and literary language is read, at least, as *double*"), in the Americas, this practice is strongly inflected by historical and political considerations that limit the utility of readings that concentrate solely on the transmission of aesthetic patterns. Lois Parkinson Zamora observes that "Faulkner, acknowledged master of García Márquez and admired contemporary of Borges, created synchronic structures not so much to suggest psychological processes (as European stream-of-consciousness writers did) as to encompass the diverse and discontinuous histories of his cultural community" (Zamora 1997: 152). This helps to explain why the elements of earlier texts that are absorbed by Latin American writers are often those, such as a character who is free to assess his own country because he is born outside its history, that throw into relief historical and political structures.

In the case of a writer such as Ramírez, whose Central Americanness and whose birth date relegate him to being an echo of the Boom rather than a member of either the Boom or the Post-Boom, borrowing and distorting Faulkner on his own terms (rather than merely absorbing the borrowings pioneered by García Márquez and Vargas Llosa) enables him to overcome his anxiety of influence with regard to these older writers and make a claim to standing in the Boom's front lines by establishing his own distinctive personal relationship with Faulkner. At the same time, given the dominance of the theme of US-sponsored tyranny in *To Bury Our Fathers*, the Faulknerian echoes have unmistakable political resonances. García Márquez's affinity with Faulkner stems from what the Colombian author himself has characterized as "analogías [que] son más geográficas que literarias ... Los pueblos ardientes y llenos de polvo, las gentes sin esperanza" (Mendoza 1982: 66; "analogies [that] are geographic rather than literary ... The scorched, dusty towns and the defeated people" [Mendoza 1983: 47]) – the kind of places and characters who populate both rural Mississippi and the Caribbean coast of Colombia; to which one might add the prevalence of plantation agriculture and the social structures it shapes, along with the problematic integration of, or failure to integrate, African-descended peoples and their cultures. Ramírez, who, like García Márquez, grew up in a rural zone of the tropics, but whose engagement is predominantly with the apparatus of the US security state rather than with the United Fruit Company, shares with Faulkner the experience of coming from a region subjugated by the US military. The presence of Faulkner within the pages and structures of *To Bury Our Fathers* undercuts the imperialist's claim to superiority by brandishing a pre-eminent asset of the oppressor's culture. Ramírez enlists into his cultural anti-imperialism a classic US writer who has turned opposition to the armies funded by US big business into US cultural myths. Shadows of the United States's own culture expose the consequences of US imperialism and consolidate a conception of Nicaraguan history that challenges imperialist suzerainty.

From the moment that Santiago and his family enter Nicaragua, he becomes aware of the country's identity as forged by cultural diversity, patriarchal authority, foreign occupation, random violence, and, epitomizing all of these strains, Sandino's insurgency against the US Marines and its suppression by *el hombre*. Patriarchy is Santiago's inheritance even before his odyssey through Nicaraguan society: "Taleno el padre les arrancaba a sus mujeres los hijos temprano para criarlos a su semejanza" (*TDMS*, 22; "Taleno took his children from his wives early on, to bring them up in his own way" [*TBF*, 8]). This habit of the father – whom the narrator always refers to as "Taleno el padre" ("Taleno the father"), condemning Santiago to perceive himself as an echo of his progenitor – reinforces the double-edged epigraph from Aristophanes that suggests that a man's attempt to bury his father is likely to end with his becoming his father. This insight, which perceives dictatorship not as a problem confined to the rule of a tyrannical individual with powerful foreign sponsors, but as a malaise that irradiates all social interactions, is central to the novel's depiction of Nicaraguan society.

Even though Ramírez's narrative universe is a masculine one of soldiers and guerrillas, in which women appear primarily as sexual objects, the structures within which he couches his depictions of masculinity imply a critique of patriarchy that coincides in a number of respects with the analyses of the confluence of patriarchy and dictatorship of his Post-Boom contemporaries, such as Luisa Valenzuela.[2] From the moment the Taleno family enters the Atlantic Coast, the father appears to be seeking not only a means of earning a living but also a model of Nicaraguan masculinity into which to induct his sons. The opening scene of this sequence, while it showcases the religious variety of the Atlantic Coast, which ranges from Franciscan brothers to Moravian pastors, culminates in references to Sandino's recent passage through the region summed up by a vision of the skeleton of a US Marine pilot hanging in a tree: "ven colgando de la rama de un espino un esqueleto movido por la brisa, flojo y cubierto de lama verde su uniforme de marino norteamericano, un mechón rubio de pelo reseco en el cráneo pelado y unos gusanos dorados y luminosos que reptan por sus extremidades para caer al suelo, y se transparentan también tras los anteojos de aviador puestos sobre las cuencas vacías" (*TDMS*, 27; "they spot a skeleton dangling from a hawthorn branch, swaying limply in the breeze, green slime obscuring the US Marine uniform, a tuft of withered blond hair still clinging to the skull. Some golden, luminous worms crawl out along the fleshless limbs and drop off to the ground; the same worms glitter behind the airman's goggles pulled over sightless sockets" [*TBF*, 12]). Turco's first sight of an American as a rotting, worm-covered corpse instills in his mind the reality that US power is not invincible.

This seed germinates only much later, however, because after his brother Trinidad is killed by a bull at a country fair, Santiago's father forms a relationship with a fortune teller named La Milagrosa (Miracle Woman), who encourages him to move the family to Managua, where she gives birth to his daughter. The arrival of a female child, whom he cannot bring up "in his image," obliges the father to seek elsewhere a model of Nicaraguan masculinity to serve as a model for his surviving son. He hoists Santiago onto his shoulders to glimpse Somoza at a public event: "Ese es pues el de los retratos, le dice severamente al volverlo al suelo, y se lo repite al oído como para que no vaya a olvidarlo, *el hombre de Nicaragua*, la misma Nicaragua que desde el remolcador le había señalado brumosa a lo lejos un día" (*TDMS*, 128; "It is the man in the portraits, he tells him sternly as he drops him to the floor one more, and whispers it in his ear a second time so that he will never forget: *el hombre de Nicaragua*, that same Nicaragua he had once pointed out to him from the boat, hazy in the distance" [*TBF*, 97]). The total identification of the dictator with the nation solves the riddle of Nicaraguanness posed by Santiago's first glimpse of the Nicaraguan shoreline. The patriarchy is inseparable from the patriarch. As Catalino López insists in a defensive tone after being captured: "*el hombre* fue un verdadero padre para todos" (*TDMS*, 153; "*El hombre* has been a true father to all of us" [*TBF*, 118]). The father enrolls his son as a National Guard cadet, an event that is celebrated by a photograph of the two of them with the dictator, "Taleno el padre y él protegidos bajo el abrazo de *el hombre*" (*TDMS*, 163; "el hombre with his arms around Taleno and his father's shoulders" [*TBF*, 125]), a photograph in which *el hombre*'s paternal hug makes explicit the vertical chain of authority from dictator to father to son. The upward extrapolation of this line appears in a newspaper clipping that shows *el hombre* with his master, Franklin Delano Roosevelt, beneath a banner that lauds the two presidents as "Campeones de la Democracia Continental" (163; "CHAMPIONS OF CONTINENTAL DEMOCRACY" [*TBF*, 125]).

The novel does not narrate Santiago's disillusionment with the dictatorship. Prior to the 1954 April Rebellion, Chepito reveals to Jilguero that he has seen Captain Santiago Taleno, known for his loyalty to *el hombre*, in the company of Jilguero's brother Carlos (*TDMS*, 36; *TBF*, 21), a prominent Conservative opponent of the regime. This passing reference, the first indication that Liberal and Conservative youth are collaborating in opposing the dictatorship, adumbrates the possibility of the unified nation that the novel seeks to imagine into existence. The tension between a Testimonio-influenced quest for the truth of the life of the people and avant-garde literary virtuosity (which threatens to dissolve defiant truths into a concert of subjectivities) that would be symptomatic of Ramírez's career is a salient feature of *To Bury Our Fathers*. As soon as the active reader deduces that the collaboration between Taleno/Turco and Jilguero, the Conservative presidential candidate's grandson, who will become the last two surviving guerrillas in their battalion, is reconciling the antagonistic binaries of Nicaraguan politics – Liberalism versus Conservatism, the lower classes versus the bourgeoisie – a fledgling new conception of nationhood is adumbrated that can be realized only through the guerrilla struggle. Claudia Schaeffer alludes to this apparent disjuncture: "hay por un lado el testimonio directo de la historia oral de la gente del pueblo nicaragüense, y por otro una crítica indirecta que toma la forma de monólogos internos, diálogos, recuerdos, sueños, flashbacks y cambios de punto de vista" (Schaeffer 1987: 149; "on the one hand there is direct testimony from the oral history of the Nicaraguan people, and on the other an indirect criticism that takes the form of internal monologues, dialogues, memories, dreams, flashbacks and changes in viewpoint").

Returning to Arias's point about Boom techniques recasting "avant-garde writers as the equivalent of avant-garde revolutionaries," it is precisely the integration of oral history into avant-garde literary techniques that promises to remake the nation in a form more flexible, polyphonic, and accommodating than that of the dictatorship's linear, authoritarian imagination. The novel's circularity and multiplicity are integral to its unravelling of patriarchal authortity. Tim Richards argues that "la narración cuestiona la capacidad de la voz autoritativa (¿autoridad literaria? ¿autoridad social?) de narrar legítimamente experiencias que le son netamente ajenas" (Richards 1994: 199; "the narrative questions the ability of the authoritative voice [literary authority? social authority?] to legitimately narrate experiences that are clearly foreign to it"). This is true, yet these experiences from diverse levels of society are drafted into the novel's oppositional regeneration of the Nicaraguan nation: in a challenge that would confront both literature and politics over the next two decades, the multiplicity of voices of those oppressed by the dictatorship must coalesce into a new conception of nationhood. It is in this sense that the epigraph from Aristophanes sees the skylark's father dying and being buried in its head at a time "when the earth did not yet exist" (*TBF*, epigraph page). Nicaragua having been wiped off the map by the Somozas' subservience to the United States, the novel's authoritarian fathers have been buried in the protagonists' heads prior to the "creation" of the country. As Salman Rushdie posits: "The Nicaraguan meaning of the

Aristophanes quote could only be that in those days the country *wasn't there*" (Rushdie 1987: 126).

The fact that a (new) nation is imagined before being engendered is underlined by the third of the three epiphanic glimpses of Nicaragua that mark Turco's life. The opening sight of the coastline, which begs a cultural definition, is supplanted by the fusion of Nicaragua and "*el hombre de Nicaragua.*" When, in 1954, Santiago revolts against this definition, and is denounced by his father as "un fugitivo de las leyes" (*TDMS*, 164; "an outlaw" [*TBF*, 127]), he requires a new definition of Nicaraguanness to motivate and define his guerrilla struggle. Since the action is set in the late 1950s, the Sandinista counter-culture developed by Carlos Fonseca and the students of the 1960s is not available to him. The passage of the guitar that belonged to Lázaro, the sublime musician stabbed to death in a meaningless barroom brawl, into the hands of opposition members in Honduras, where it literally nourishes them, enabling them to earn a living by playing Nicaraguan songs (ironically, in a bar owned by an American), symbolizes the central role that will be occupied by culture in reviving Nicaraguan nationhood.

If, as Jilguero complains of Nicaragua, "en este país no respetan lo que es el arte" (*TDMS*, 67; "in this country there's no respect for art" [*TBF*, 46]), Lázaro's name suggests that music (and by extension other artistic expressions of Nicaraguan identity) will rise from the dead in the post-dictatorship future. By singing about Nicaragua in Tegucigalpa bars, these young exiles (in contrast to Indio Larios, who fled the country more than a decade earlier) begin to create what Anderson would term the "imagined community" of their nation. Even though they regard "Managua Nicaragua," the song they are obliged to sing over and over, as a "musiquita tan pendeja" (*TDMS*, 212; "stupid little song" [*TBF*, 167]), when they play it in a bar that is being watched by the police it is transformed into a banner of insurgency sufficiently powerful that they are jailed and deported from Honduras to Guatemala. During their deportation, "se perdió la guitarra de Lázaro" (*TDMS*, 214; "they had lost Lazaro's guitar" [*TBF*, 169]), which is impounded by the Honduran police. It is because of this artistic input that, when Turco has his final epiphany of the Nicaraguan nation, as he crosses the border as a guerrilla to die for his homeland, he imagines that he already knows what Nicaragua will look like.

> Taleno a la vanguardia de la fila india se detuvo para señalar las lomas vecinas, los pinares oscuros en las crestas, desde las que les llegaba con el viento un suave olor a ocotes: "aquí es Nicaragua, muchachos". Y al avanzar y hundir las botas en el barro, tarde había repasado él que ese era ya el barro de Nicaragua, sorprendido entonces por la falta de

novedad porque cuando en las pensiones donde estuvieron escondidos en Tegucigalpa se hablaba de este precioso momento de trasponer la frontera, se imaginaba que los árboles, piedras, hasta el barro, iban a cambiar de substancia y de color, iban a lucirle distintos apenas le dijeran: aquí es ya Nicaragua. (*TDMS*, 231–2; Taleno, leading them in single file, stopped and pointed to the next range of hills, their tops covered with dark pine woods whose resin smell reached them on the breeze: 'We've reached Nicaragua, boys!' As he trudged on, his boots sank into the mud, and it was some time before it dawned on him that this was the mud of Nicaragua – and at once he was surprised that it was not more of a shock, for in the cheap boarding houses where they had been hidden in Tegucigalpa they had always talked of this very moment, when they would actually cross the frontier. They had imagined that the trees, flowers, even the mud itself, would somehow take on a different nature and colour; everything was bound to seem different as soon as they heard: we've reached Nicaragua. [*TBF*, 183])

Taleno views this final installment in his succession of Nicaraguan identities from his location in the "vanguard" ("la vanguardia"): this description in the Spanish original of his position in the line of men who are marching into Honduras is not innocent. By the 1960s, the "vanguard," by definition, was the FSLN. Even though these events take place two years prior to the FSLN's founding (also in Tegucigalpa), it is evident that Turco already possesses a vanguard mentality. He is capable of pointing out to his compañeros when they have reached Nicaragua. If his momentary failure to distinguish Nicaraguan jungle from Honduran jungle disappoints him, this is because, unlike the leaders of earlier insurgencies, he has developed an articulated idea of the constitution of Nicaraguan identity. He possesses the nation in a way that the dictator does not, and the other guerrillas have not yet learned to do.

Later, as the three surviving guerrillas try to escape the National Guard, they make a pilgrimage all the way across the country to the edge of the border with Costa Rica. When Chepito visits Raúl, the only survivor of this incursion, in prison, he points out to him that "según su declaración del periódico, se había atravesado a pie casi toda Nicaragua" (*TDMS*, 280; "according to his statement in the newspaper they had crossed nearly the whole of Nicaragua on foot" [*TBF*, 226]). Turco and Jilguero are captured and executed on the outskirts of San Carlos, Turco's possible birthplace: his life describes a circle through the homeland that begins in obliviousness and concludes in commitment.

Ramírez seizes on motifs from Nicaraguan history: scenes such as that where Turco is locked in a cage in the dictator's private zoo or where the

National Guardsmen dance with the daughters of US Marines memorialize idiosyncracies of the Somoza dictatorship. His fidelity, though, is to fiction, not to historical verisimilitude. For dramatic reasons related to the development of the character of Colonel Catalino López, for example, the tracking down and killing of Pedro Altamirano and the transportation of his head on a stick to be displayed in a Managua market is shifted from its historical location in 1939 to late 1934 or early 1935. Turco and Jilguero's 1959 invasion occupies the same chronological space as the Rebellion of Olama y los Mollejones, but nearly all of the details are different. The April Rebellion of 1954 here has support from active members of the military, which was not true of the original event, whose leader was a retired military officer. Embedded in this narrative of Nicaragua in the 1950s are discreet nods to events from the 1960s and 1970s. Turco and Jilguero sing the national anthem as they are executed, as did the guerrilla poet Leonel Rugama and two compañeros as they were being shot to death by the National Guard in January 1970 (Borge 1989: 300; 1992: 294). Jilguero is the grandson of the 1940s Conservative presidential candidate Dr Rosales; his name resembles that of Carlos Agüero, a Sandinista guerrilla of oligarchical lineage whose uncle, Fernando Agüero, was the Conservative presidential candidate in the 1940s.[3]

If the comradeship between Turco and Jilguero sketches a nascent conjunction between dissident strands of Liberalism and Conservativism, the first-person narration of Colonel Catalino López exemplifies the subservient mentality of the loyal lackey of the regime. Richards aptly describes López's narration as "una primera persona ingenua. El modo confesional que asume la voz personal revela el egoismo y las lealtades inconstantes que determinan su trayectoría en el seno del sistema socio-político" (*TDMS*, 195; "A naive first person. The confessional mode taken on by the personal voice reveals the selfishness and fickle loyalties that determine his trajectory through the socio-political system"). On the advice of the anonymous officer, who is later revealed to be Indio Larios, López shoots himself, the wound covering the incompetence and cowardice that led to his humiliation by Pedro Altamirano, and transforming probable court martial into a cause for promotion. López's slippery language justifies crimes such as the 1934 massacre of the members of the Sandinista cooperative on the Coco River by citing, in the verbiage of official propaganda, the necessity to "caer sobre los reductos de bandoleros que quedaban en las márgenes del río Coco" (*TDMS*, 245; "fall on the bandits' strongholds along the banks of the Coco River" [*TBF*, 195]).

López represents the debasement of a lineage of literary colonels that runs from Faulkner's Colonel Sutpen to García Márquez's Colonel Aureliano Buendía. Like Colonel Buendía, Catalino López is a Liberal; his close identification with Liberalism is underscored when he obtains his military commission by going to the author's birthplace, Masatepe, to visit the Liberal leader "mi padrino el Presidente Moncada" (*TDMS*, 143; "my godfather President Moncada" [*TBF*, 110]).[4] As his trajectory signals, in the Nicaraguan context, persisting in an adherence to Liberalism is inseparable from being complicit with the dictatorship. Polyphonic counterpoints that give the lie to López's account of Nicaraguan reality appear in events such as the election in which Dr Rosales is defrauded out of the presidency, and the recurrence of this event as farce in the Miss Nicaragua contest in which López's adopted daughter defeats Jilguero's sister by fraud. At the end of the novel, López's corruption merges with that of the dictatorship when he makes his adopted daughter into his concubine.

A theme that is introduced by *To Bury Our Fathers* and returns in Ramírez's later novels, particularly *Sombras nada más*, is the near-impossibility of tracing the moments of rupture when, in a society as small, tightly intermarried, and politically divided as that of Nicaragua, best friends or close relatives are drawn into opposing camps and become one another's enemies, torturers, or murderers. Catalino López may owe his military career and his induction into the Masonic order to Indio Larios, the two men may once have been "uña y carne" (*TDMS*, 65; "such a friend [one to the other]" [*TBF*, 43]), yet when Larios is jailed after turning against the dictator, López counsels *el hombre* to have Larios killed because, with so many allies in the National Guard, he is certain to escape. Larios, in turn, connives in capturing and, the reader assumes, torturing, López sixteen years later.

The novel lays the foundations of a narrative world to which Ramírez will return, establishing references such as the urn containing "un cerebro extraño y descomunal que era el de Rubén Darío (*TDMS*, 44; "the extraordinary, colossal brain of Ruben Dario" [*TBF*, 26]) and the "la Casa Prío [donde] los parroquianos escuchan, rodeando al capitán en su mesa" (*TDMS*, 263; "the Casa Prio [where] the regulars are huddled round El Capitán at his table" [*TBF*, 211]) as the favourite spot for discussion of local events in León; the former becomes a central image in *Margarita, How Beautiful the Sea*, while the latter appears in both this novel and *Castigo Divino*. López's adopted daughter, "la huérfana" ("the orphan"), and a builder "de nombre Campuzano" (*TDMS*, 158; "named Campuzano" [*TBF*, 122]) will reappear in *Sombras nada más*.

This sketching of a personal Yoknapatawpha County anchored in Nicaraguan history is buttressed by intertextual echoes of Faulkner's *As I Lay Dying* (1930). The rotating narrative voices of *To Bury Our Fathers*, even though not all of them are in the first-person singular, imitate the structure of this novel. The strongest parallel to Faulkner's novel arises in the scenes where Indio Larios's son, Bolívar, drives his father's body back to Nicaragua from Guatemala in a pick-up truck. The odyssey across Central America, from Guatemala, which once had a revolution, to Nicaragua, which aspires to have one, recapitulates the Bundren family's journey across the South on a horse-drawn cart to bury their mother's body in Jefferson.

Like the intertextual nod to *Absalom, Absalom!* in Turco's birth, the engagement with *As I Lay Dying* asserts Ramírez's position in the front lines of the Boom, and his credibility as a remaker of his nation, who wields the same burly cultural capital as writers from larger countries. In opposition to a dictatorship whose only ideology is Americanization, this sequence asserts a mastery of the high culture of the United States that undermines the regime's claim to cultural authority. Bolívar's journey opens and dominates the second part of the novel, yet it is not recounted in chronological order. By the end of the first scene, Bolívar Larios has reached the Nicaraguan border where he, the son of the dead exiled revolutionary, must petition the sons of the dead *el hombre* for the entry of his father's body into the country. Later scenes in this sequence consist of flashbacks to Bolívar's uncomfortable meeting with his father's second wife in Guatemala City, his assumption of responsibility for the coffin, and, crucially, the memorable episode where he discards his father's cherished revolutionary archive by tossing it page by page out the window of the truck as he drives across Honduras. This, the most enigmatic scene in the novel, may be read as the denouement.

The novel includes several pages of the archive compiled by Indio Larios, supposedly the exile most feared by *el hombre*, but in fact a man who had given up politics to sell *piñatas* in his second wife's business. This Guatemalan wife insists on the importance of this bequest from father to son: "Y la caja, que no fuera a dejarla por ningún moitivo" (*TDMS*, 241; "'He mustn't on any account forget [the archive]'" [*TBF*, 192]). When Bolívar opens the archive, he finds letters full of hortatory rhetoric: "amar a tu patria como a tí mismo: ten siempre presente que en el altar de la patria debe consumarse cualquier sacrificio ... " (*TDMS*, 264; "love your country as you do yourself; always bear in mind that its altar is worthy of the highest sacrifice" [*TBF*, 212]). The contrast between this language and Larios's passivity in exile is accentuated by the scrapbook-like trivia that the archive contains. Photos of Larios with his National Guard friends in the 1930s and his exile friends in the 1940s, acronyms of tiny, impotent opposition groups, and a feeble claim that, while still a National Guard member, Larios rigged the Miss Nicaragua contest not "por servilismo, sino para encubrir mis planes de rebelión"

(*TDMS*, 268; "out of servility, but to cover up my plans for rebellion" [*TBF*, 215]) lead to a naive telegram to US President John F. Kennedy asking him to establish democracy in Nicaragua. The telegram, the first item Bolívar allows to be carried away by the breeze, is the catalyst to his disposal of the archive and, symbolically, of his father's legacy. Unlike the other male characters, Bolívar refuses to bury his father in his head.

Though the reader is not privy to his thought-processes, it is clear that the path to the future is represented by Larios's mother, who remained in Nicaragua, bravely named her bakery La Opositora ("Woman of the Opposition"), and kept alive the memory of her husband's rebellion against *el hombre*, even as he himself lost interest in the struggle and betrayed her by having two children with his Guatemalan wife (about whom the family officially knew nothing). At Larios's funeral in León, which is attended by almost no one, Bolívar sees the orator's hand "reafirmando el peso de sus palabras con golpes de puño que da en el vacío" (*TDMS*, 271; "thumping the empty air with his fist to emphasize his words" [*TBF*, 217]). This image of futile gestures amounting to nothingness is nullified, however, by the example of Turco and Jilguero's self-sacrifice and the scene's setting in 1961, the year of the founding of the FSLN. The intertextual echoes with *As I Lay Dying*, in which the burial of Mrs Bundren is succeeded by the appearance of a second Mrs Bundren as the father marries a woman he meets while preparing for his wife's funeral – a scene that Faulkner portrays as positive: "It made him look a foot taller, kind of holding his head up" (Faulkner 1930: 249) – suggest the beginning of a new cycle. In Ramírez's case, this is a cycle of opposition activity that will have repercussions far greater than those of the ineffectual posturing of Indio Larios.

Renewal depends on the flourishing of a national culture. Chepito and Pastorita discuss the fate of the novel's principal characters in a bar and a barber shop after meeting at a baseball game in Granada in 1961. The balancing, late in the novel, of scenes set in León and in Granada hints at the convergence of Liberals and Conservatives in a united opposition. In this concluding scene, which is divided into two sections, the rise, tribulations, and dissolution of the musical group Los Caballeros (The Gentlemen), in which Lázaro, Jilguero, Raúl, and Pastorita played, emerges as the connecting thread of the novel's narration that runs across its six major narrative streams. The first half of their conversation, which concludes the last chapter and, by way of the novel's montage techniques, delivers the description of Turco and Jilguero's execution, takes place in a cheap bar. This conversation resumes, as the novel's final scene, in the second half of the epilogue. Pastorita invites Chepito to visit the barbershop he owns. The description of the wall next to the mirror includes the phrase: "Y en el tabique, colgada de un clavo, la guitarra con su moño azul y blanco de seda desvanecida ... " (*TDMS*, 305; "A guitar with a faded blue-and-white silk ribbon hangs from a nail on the wall ..." [*TBF*, 247]). Though nothing more is said about this, it is clear that Lázaro's guitar, lost to the Honduran police, has made its way back to Nicaragua. The mysterious return of the instrument that enabled Turco and Jilguero to begin the formulation of Nicaraguan identity plants in the text an emblem of potential renewal.

The conversation between Chepito and Pastorita concludes on a contradictory note. Pastorita is a lonely bachelor whose only love affair was a troubling incident when he abducted Alma Nubia, Turco's adolescent half-sister, and kept her locked in a bar for a week. In explaining his method of entertaining the girl, Pastorita confirms that the guitar on the wall is that which belonged to Lázaro: "esa guitarra allí colgada le había ayudado" (*TDMS*, 306; "that guitar over there had a lot to do with it" [*TBF*, 247]). As evening arrives, Pastorita receives bad news from his old friend concerning Alma Nubia: "escucha a Chepito invisible, responderle, una vez oyó decir cómo se había casado con un americano, y que se fue a vivir a San Francisco de California. Y delante de Chepito ausente, se duele de no haber conocido nunca, ni de cara, a aquel niño su hijo" (*TDMS*, 307; "[he] hears the invisible Chepito reply: he heard once she has married an American and had gone off to live in San Francisco, California. Pastorita complains to his vanishing friend that he had never seen the boy who was his son" [*TBF*, 249]).

This revelation complicates the image of the guitar and Los Caballeros, the group it held together. As Pastorita's machista actions indicate, the members of the group did not live up to their title as gentlemen. If he has lost his paternity to the United States, this imperialist domination is also the reflection of his own patriarchal domination of Alma Nubia. The guitar may provoke reflection about the homeland, but the ethos that will liberate Nicaragua from the patriarchal tyranny of US intervention, *el hombre*, the sons of *el hombre*, and all the men who replicate the despotic male behaviour of earlier generations by burying their fathers in their heads requires an evolution beyond that of this dissident 1950s folk group. As Pastorita observes the guitar he thinks: "pasaron a la historia Los Caballeros" (*TDMS*, 308; "Los Caballeros are a thing of the past" [*TBF*, 249]). This statement, like Chepito's response to it – "Recuerdos te dejaron" (*TDMS*, 308; "they left you memories" [*TBF*, 249]) – highlights that only a new era and a new way of thinking will permit the construction of the autonomous nation; in spite of the seeds they have sown, the struggles of the 1950s must be consigned to the past.

WORDS OF THE REVOLUTIONARY LEADER: SPEECHES AND ESSAYS, 1979–84

During the eleven years that separated *To Bury Our Fathers* from *Castigo Divino*, Ramírez became successively the leader of The Twelve (1977–79), a member of the governing junta of revolutionary Nicaragua (1979–84), and, after the November 1984 elections, vice-president. His next six books (seven if one includes the expanded edition of *El pensamiento vivo de Sandino* that appeared in 1984) were collections of essays, speeches, or reflections that often belonged more to the politician than to the writer.

In both capacities, Ramírez assessed the contours of the Nicaraguan nation. The early volumes continue the work of the novel: to draft the authority of Boom aesthetics and the Boom novelist's mastery of national history through technical audacity into channelling the "imagined community" of revolutionary Nicaragua. His closest ally in this endeavour would be Julio Cortázar, the Boom writer who made the most sustained commitment to Sandinista Nicaragua, visiting the country five times between 1979 and 1983 and writing a book about his impressions, whose rights he signed over to "el pueblo sandinista de Nicaragua" ("the Sandinista people").[5] After Cortázar's death in February 1984, and as the austerity and brutality of the Contra War restricted the latitude to reimagine the nation with optimism – and as the Boom itself lost influence to more populist forms of writing, from Testimonio to post-modern pastiches of genre fiction, whose references were often to transnational archetypes rather than national history – this model would enter a crisis that yielded the more provisional, ironic, even beleaguered vision of nationhood, and the masculinity that buttressed it, of *Castigo Divino*.

Theoretical models for the Nicaraguan nation that Ramírez was attempting to define are not easy to identify. The tendency of anglophone academics to gather disparate forms of sovereign self-assertion on the part of poor countries under the rubric of postcolonialism is of little help in theorizing Sandinismo. Homi K. Bhabha's notion of "DissemiNation," for example, studies the ways in which hybridity and the presence of migrants who are not susceptible to assimilation – at least not, it seems, according to Bhabha and in the United Kingdom – can delineate "the internal contradictions of the modern liberal nation" (Bhabha 1990a: 299). This concentration of much postcolonial theory on "the predicament of the postcolonial migrant in the Western metropolis" (Moore-Gilbert 1997: 121) distances it from the questions that were of greatest urgency for Nicaragua. Like postcolonial theory, Sandinismo draws inspiration from the work of Frantz Fanon, but it applies

Fanon's analysis of oppression, cultural alienation, and the drive towards nation building as a prescription for action in the present, as Ramírez does at the close of "Balcanes y volcanes." His endorsement of Fanon's Marxist-nationalist approach contrasts with postcolonial theory's interpretation of Marxism and nationalism as oppressive Western discourses. This academic approach estranges postcolonial theory from Fanon's intimate understanding of the legitimacy of revolutionary violence as a response to oppression. The Fanon with whom Sandinismo identifies is not the theorist of cultural alienation of *Peau noire, masques blancs* (1952; *Black Skin, White Masks*), but the Fanon who, in *Les damnés de la terre* (1961; *The Wretched of the Earth*) writes: "Castro siégant en tenue militaire à L'O.N.U. ne scandalise pas les pays sous-développés. Ce que montre Castro, c'est la conscience qu'il a du régime continué de la violence. L'étonnant c'est qu'il ne soit pas entré à L'O.N.U. avec sa mitraillette ..." (Fanon 1961: 110; "Castro sitting in military uniform at the United Nations Organization does not scandalize the underdeveloped countries. What Castro demonstrates is the consciousness he has of the continuing existence of the rule of violence. The astonishing thing is that he did not come into the UNO with a machine-gun ..." [*The Wretched of the Earth*, 78]).

In spite of Nicaragua's twentieth-century history as a near-protectorate of the United States, the Nicaraguan nation was both too old and too young to be adequately captured by the dynamics of postcolonial theory. Central American independence in 1821 was the particular legacy of more than three centuries of Spanish colonialism, whose mission was to evangelize rather than to civilize, and which was defined by violence, ruthless vertical structures, and, crucially, a culture of racial mixing that hastened the marginalization or extinction of the most widely spoken aboriginal languages. This legacy, as well as the history of warfare in the nineteenth century that started with anti-Mexican Central American separatism and led to regional wars and Liberal-Conservative strife, differentiated Nicaragua's experience from those of nations such as India or Ghana, which emerged from a predominantly non-racially hybrizing British colonialism by comparatively peaceful means (whatever may have happened after independence) to take up late nationhood in the mid-twentieth century.

Further distancing Nicaraguan experience from the models from which postcolonial theory was derived was the fact that, though Nicaragua suffered neo-colonial depredations at the hands of the linguistically, racially, and religiously distinct culture of the United States – "hombres de ojos sajones y alma bárbara" in Rubén Darío's summation (Darío 1905: 52; "men with Saxon eyes and barbarous souls" [Darío 2004: 87]) – it was not cast in the role of the "other" in the way that Edward Said perceived Middle Eastern cultures as being "orientalized" in his eponymous volume that popularized postcolonial theory among Western scholars (Said 1978: 1–28). Indeed, until 1979 Nicaragua was barely noticed by Westerners other than nineteenth-century would-be builders of trans-isthmian canals. Lacking Mayan pyramids, or similar attractions, Nicaragua was not exoticized, as Guatemala or Mexico may have been; it was overlooked. The fundamentally nationalist nature of the Nicaraguan Revolution located it outside the parameters established by postcolonial theory. As Neil Larsen observes: "The governing impulse of postcolonialism ... is clearly one of hostility to national*ism*, in implicit recognition of the betrayal of those who once saw in it the emancipatory alternative to colonialism and imperialism" (Larsen 2001: 39). The Nicaraguan Revolution, though it coincided with the rise of postcolonial theory, was committed to this emancipatory alternative.

Yet neither does the Nicaraguan Revolution fit, either in its antecedents or its chronology, into Larsen's own category of "Bandung Era" struggles that were simultaneously anti-colonialist and Marxist-nationalist, which he defines as running from Indian and Pakistani independence in 1947 to the revolutions in Angola and Mozambique in 1975. Larsen's characterization of the conditions of Bandung Era struggles does resonate in the Nicaraguan case: "To emancipate the nation ... is to attain national *sovereignty*, a *telos* in relation to which categories such as the *popular* and *culture* predominate over those of class, capital and labor" (ibid.: 14). The upsurge of a unifying national culture, rooted in the popular forms (the peasant Mass, folk music, hammock-weaving, primitivist painting, workshop poetry) of an assumed mestizo norm, but reaching into the redoubts of high culture in works such as *To Bury Our Fathers*, is one of the most marked traits of the Nicaraguan experience.

This presumption of national unity, however, also walls off Sandinista Nicaragua from the post-1990 world of accelerated globalization, where nations tend to be defined by cultural diversity. Antonio Cornejo Polar's essays on Andean heterogeneity, for example, which emphasize the nation's "desgarrada condición heteróclita" (Cornejo Polar 1994: 207; "fissured heterogenous condition"), or Walter D. Mignolo's assessment of the "global idea of 'Latin' America being employed by imperial states" as "a resource of cheap labor, full natural resources, exotic tourism, and fantastic Caribbean beaches waiting to be visited, invested in and exploited" (Mignolo 2005: 96), deconstructs not only First World imperialism but also the drive of national bourgeoisies, or bourgeois-peasant alliances, as in Sandinista Nicaragua, to deflect imperialism with nationalism. While Cornejo Polar interprets *mestizaje* as a fundamentally skewed nationalist ideology that claims to homogenize discrete social formations, Mignolo, an Argentine who works in the United States and studies the Renaissance and the Andean region, bypasses the particular dynamics of Central America. Where Mignolo is able to assert that the "Latin" component of Latin America is an artificial, arguably "orientalizing" construct imposed by Europe, Nicaraguan nationalism, particularly in the form expressed by Ramírez in his essays, is built on the bedrock of a common Central American identity. Unlike the idea of Latin America (or, as Mignolo would have it "Latin" America), the concept of a shared Mesoamerican identity predates European colonialism, US neocolonialism, or globalized consumerism, having been, in Arturo Arias's words, "first conceptualized as a region by Mayas over two thousand years ago" (Arias 2007: xvii–xviii). The assumption of this Mayan concept of a region of connected states by modern people of mixed racial heritage is an endogenous process that dates back to the sixteenth century. This is true even though a strict, Mayan-Náhuat definition of Mesoamerica, as understood by contemporary archeologists, would complicate Nicaraguan nationalism by excluding Nicaragua's Atlantic Coast, which lies outside this two-thousand-year-old cultural formation.

If Nicaraguan nationalism, as it emerged in the 1970s and 1980s, was too old to fit the paradigms of postcolonialism, or too rooted in Cold War struggles to be understood by way of contemporary globalization-inspired theories such as those of Mignolo, it was also too young to mesh with them. During the Revolution, the paired portraits of the turn-of-the-century poet Darío and the early twentieth-century guerrilla Sandino adorned the walls of the Rubén Darío Theatre in Managua, in an echo of Cuba's evocation of José Martí and Che Guevara; but it was the ghosts of the martyrs of the 1970s that urged Nicaraguans to work together to rebuild their country. "To understand the living in Nicaragua, I found, it was necessary to begin with the dead," wrote Salman Rushdie (1987: 7). Most of these martyrs had died in extreme youth; even at the time that the Sandinista Revolution came to an abrupt end in February 1990 many of them, had they lived, would have been less than forty years old. This sheen of youth and newness, of discovering a country that had been concealed from its own citizens, of inventing a nation almost from nothingness, was one of the most arresting traits of Nicaraguan nationalism.

For all of these reasons, the underpinnings of Ramírez's definitions of revolutionary Nicaragua knit together dependency theory, references to early twentieth-century Panamericanism, allusions to fraternal Latin American struggles, and the cult of Nicaragua's 1970s martyrs, over the frame of a high literary culture that runs from the *modernismo* of Rubén Darío to the Modernism of the Boom. The first of the books that Ramírez published between *To Bury Our Fathers* and *Castigo Divino* is co-written with a Boom author and takes as its title a quote from Darío. A slender volume consisting of the speech Cortázar gave after he was awarded the Order of Rubén Darío by the Sandinista Directorate in February 1983, with an introduction by Ramírez and the two writers listed as co-authors, in a decision that asserts the Nicaraguan's parity with the cosmopolitan, *La edad presente es de lucha* (1983; The Present Age Is One of Struggle) places culture at the core of the battle for national sovereignty. Cortázar states that "apenas se llega a Nicaragua ... la palabra *cultura* empieza a repiquetear en los oídos" (*EP*, 23; "barely had the word *culture* arrived in Nicaragua ... than it began to be repeated, to reverberate ..." [*Nicaraguan Sketches*, 129]); he goes on to argue that culture in Nicaragua is not "elitista" (23; "have ... connotations of ... elitism" [ibid.: 130]), as it is in countries where it is purely a concern of privileged people. He defends the Ministry of Culture and its poetry workshops (*EP*, 25–7), which at that time were being attacked by Rosario Murillo, whose life-partner, Daniel Ortega, would have to stretch to pin the Darío medal on the enormously tall Cortázar's chest at the end of this speech.

In his introduction to Cortázar's talk, Ramírez evokes the anti-imperialist imagery developed by Darío and his contemporaries, such as the Uruguayan essayist José Enrique Rodó (1877–1917), as a way of building a bridge between the high culture of the past and resistance to the Contra War in the present. Ramírez praises "el continente en lucha contra el mismo enemigo en aquella vuelta del siglo que atestiguó Darío; contra el mismo invasor, contra los mismos calibanes, búfalos de dientes de plata, los mismos bárbaros aborrecedores de la sangre latina en este último cuarto de siglo que atestigua Julio Cortázar" (*EP*, 5; "the continent that struggles against the same enemy in this turn of the century as was borne witness to by Darío; against the same invader, against the same Calibans, silver-toothed buffalos, the same haters of Latin blood, that in this turn of the century is witnessed by Julio Cortázar"). This sentence links the early-twentieth-century Pan-Americanist rhetoric of Darío and Rodó, with its emphasis on the racial otherness of the Yankee invader, with the contemporary anti-imperialism expressed in Cortázar's speech, using the anti-materialism common to both discourses as a connecting tissue. He extends this parallel by equating the Monroe Doctrine and the multiple US military interventions in the Caribbean and Central America during Darío's lifetime with US imperialist policies of the 1980s, exemplified by a quote from CIA Director William Casey. Finally, he cites with approval Darío's praise of the Russian writer Maxim Gorky

(1868–1936) as the voice of his people. In emphasizing Darío's positive view of Gorky, Ramírez was following the example of Carlos Fonseca, who drew attention to Darío's "elogioso comentario sobre Gorki" ("laudatory commentary on Gorky") in order to refute the notion that the founder of *modernismo* was a mere "poeta de cisnes y princesas" (*Obras*, 407; "poet of swans and princesses").

The tendency to cast the net wide in an effort to forge multiple allegiances is conspicuous in the next essay collection Ramírez published. The Sandinistas were acutely conscious of the need to nourish the international solidarity movements that pressured governments in the Americas to aid Nicaragua. Mexico, which had supported the FSLN at an official level since the 1970s, was of crucial importance. The demand for Sandinista texts among Mexican readers inspired Siglo Veintiuno Editores to launch a series entitled "Nicaragua en Siglo XXI" that included, in addition to Ramírez's title, books by Pilar Arias, Tomás Borge, Omar Cabezas, Ernesto Cardenal, Mayra Jiménez, Margaret Randall, and Jaime Wheelock Román. *El alba de oro: La historia viva de Nicaragua* (1983; The Golden Dawn: The Living History of Nicaragua) is a substantial volume that reprints "El muchacho de Niquinohomo" with twenty-five other essays, speeches, or interviews. It provides a panorama of the Nicaraguan Revolution directed at the solidarity audience, including speeches on controversial topics such a press freedom, and others that celebrate the launching of programs in education and literacy and the nationalization of natural resources.

The book opens by underlining that the revolution is "un proceso histórico crucial para la América Latina" (*AO*, 9; "a crucial historical process for Latin America") and closes by defining the two pillars that enable the revolution to withstand US aggression as the strength of the Nicaraguan people and "la solidaridad internacional" (*AO*, 306; "international solidarity"). The book's title is derived from a clever juxtaposition of a line by Rubén Darío with its rewriting by the revolutionary Cuban poet Nicolás Guillén (1902–89), who calls on the long-dead Darío to raise his voice "junto al claro pueblo mío / No más el yanqui sombrío /nos quita la patria y el decoro" (*AO*, 7; "along with my shining people / No longer will the lugubrious Yankee / take away our homeland and our respectability"). This yoking of the Cuban and Nicaraguan Revolutions as companions who had been seeking the same golden dawn since the beginning of the twentieth century was vital to securing the support of the pro-Cuban Latin American left. The book's dedication, "A Daniel" (*AO*, 8), certifies its status as an authentic expression of the Nicaraguan regime. While the earlier pieces, written in Berlin or during Ramírez's involvement with The Twelve, retain an essay-like form, as it progresses *El alba de oro* approaches the status of oral history. The imperative to identify with the people induces the writer of Boom fiction to adopt a Testimonio voice, as though asserting that by abolishing the hierarchies that bred this form as the outlet of the oppressed, the Revolution has made Testimonio a tool equally accessible and legitimate in the mouths of a guerrilla, a peasant woman, or an erudite member of the governing junta.[6]

The first of the post-revolutionary talks is a speech that Ramírez gave on 17 October 1979 to commemorate the guerrillas who died in the October 1977 offensive, particularly young men from Solentiname. Like the succeeding speeches, this one closes with the Sandinista sign-off slogan, "¡Patria Libre o Morir!" (*AO*, 91; "Free Homeland or Death!"). The second speech included in the book was given on 7 November 1979 when "more than one hundred thousand people packed the Plaza de la Revolución in Managua" (Zimmermann 2000: 1) to attend the reburial of the body of Carlos Fonseca in the centre of the capital. Though delivered in a popular idiom, this talk alludes to earlier revolutionary texts in the same way that *To Bury Our Fathers* affiliates itself with earlier literary texts. As the principal speaker for this pivotal, highly emotional event, Ramírez assumed a revolutionary prestige equivalent to that of guerrillas "from the catacombs" such as Tomás Borge and Daniel Ortega, both of whom served as Fonseca's pallbearers on this day. Ramírez's language reflects guerrilla concepts; the rhetorical repetition that Carlos Fonseca is present in each act of the Revolution (*AO*, 93) imitates Che Guevara's assertion that those who wished to see him after his death need only go to Cuba. His reference to "el ideario sandinista, el ideario de Carlos Fonseca" (95; "Sandinista ideology, the ideology of Carlos Fonseca") alludes to *Augusto César Sandino: Ideario político* (Augusto César Sandino: Political Ideology), the short book Fonseca wrote to summarize Sandino's ideology, which would be published in Nicaragua for the first time the next year and underlines the leadership's responsibilities as the inheritors of the tradition of Sandino and Fonseca. The denouement of this speech is to insist on the resolutely nationalist nature of the Nicaraguan Revolution. Rooted in a revolt against the nation's suppression and exploitation, over time, by metropolitan power centres, this expression of nationalism contains an implicit dependency-theory analysis that Ramírez would develop in more explicit form in his speeches to specialized groups. In the plaza, he proclaims: "Y decimos nuestra revolución, porque esta revolución no puede ser sino nicaragüense porque resulta del dolor de nuestra historia, de la lucha contra las intervenciones extranjeras, del reclamo sandinista por nuestra soberanía " (95; "And we say our revolution, because this revolution can only be Nicaraguan because it results from the pain of our history, from the struggle against foreign intervention, from the Sandinista demand for our sovereignty").

The powerful nationalism of the Revolution, its insistence on perceiving itself as a unique outgrowth of the suffering of Nicaraguan history, yet at the same time a transformative event for all of Latin America, presented a challenge to a writer who counted among his greatest pleasures reading avant-garde writers such as Lawrence Durrell in the original English (Rushdie 1987: 128). On 25 February 1980, in a speech entitled "Los intelectuales y el futuro revolucionario" ("The Intellectuals and the Revolutionary Future"), delivered at the first meeting of the Trabajadores de la Cultura (Cultural Workers), Ramírez proposed a definition of Nicaraguan culture that, as Larsen would predict, saw it as a collective, as well as individual, creation. This engagement with the popular emphasized the Revolution's quest for cultural authenticity.

At first glance, such a program nearly rules out the writing of cosmopolitan novels such as *To Bury Our Fathers*. Yet, though he engages in the statutory dismissal of the alienated intellectual who must "visitar un museo en París o Nueva York, para saber qué cosa iba a pintar aquí" (109; "visit a museum in Paris or New York to know what he was going to paint here"), Ramírez opens the final section of this speech by clamping firm limits on the value of a culture which, in the name of authenticity, walls itself off from the outside world. He tells the cultural workers: "no podemos pretender que nuestra forma de defensa frente a la penetración cultural imperialista y frente a la enajenación cultural que viene de fuera, sea encerrarnos dentro de nuestras fronteras, y creer que a través de lo vernáculo, de lo folklórico, vamos a resolver la autenticidad de nuestra cultura nacional" (108–9; "we cannot maintain that our defence against imperialist cultural penetration and against the cultural alienation that comes from outside, is to lock ourselves up within our borders and believe that through the vernacular, through folklore, we are going to resolve the authenticity of our national culture").

In this formulation, a novel such as *To Bury Our Fathers*, which employs international forms to illuminate national dilemmas, is legitimized within the ambit of a powerful nationalism. The sacrifice on which Ramírez insists is that which he himself is making: not a sacrifice of aesthetic values, but of time and commitment: "los escritores, los pintores, los escultores, los artistas, los intelectuales en general, fuera de su propia actividad creativa … deben tener en nuestra revolución una participación política que es una forma de estar conectados con la revolución" (110; "writers, painters, sculptors, artists, intellectuals in general, in addition to their own creative activity … must have in our revolution a political participation that is a means of being connected with the revolution"). This moral imperative of "being connected" with the Revolution, in their daily lives though not necessarily acting as mouthpieces for it in their art, was the most that Sandinista Nicaragua demanded of its artists, none of whom was censored or prevented from travelling in or out of the country, in striking contrast to the Cuban Revolution's decrees that art must reflect government ideology and the tight control Cuba exercised over its artists (Williamson 1992: 555).

Ramírez returns to the theme of culture in a talk given in Managua on 2 February 1982. By this time, the looser organization of the Cultural Workers had been consolidated into the Asociación Sandinista de Trabajadores de la Cultura (ASTC; Sandinista Association of Culture Workers), under the leadership of Rosario Murillo, who was fighting to wrest responsibility for cultural policy from Ernesto Cardenal's Ministry of Culture, which Murillo claimed was rigid and doctrinaire. The dispute opened with a series of articles in *Ventana*, the cultural supplement of the Sandinista daily newspaper *Barricada*, in March 1981, that attacked Cardenal's poetry workshops. On 4 October 1982, after the resignation of Daisy Zamora as deputy minister of culture, and in an attempt to impose peace, Daniel Ortega would ban all discussion of cultural policy, arguing that the Sandinista Revolution had no cultural policy (Wellinga 1994: 122–9).

In this context, Ramírez's talk to the ASTC in February 1982 is charged with tension. It is a less precise, telling speech than his address to this organization's forerunner in February 1980, clouded by a (probably deliberate) vagueness concerning the direction of cultural policy. Ramírez reviews the history of the *Ventana* literary movement and its role in generating the culture of the Revolution, apparently as a way of reminding the audience that he, not Murillo, is the true voice of *Ventana*. He tries to reconcile the warring factions by arguing for a renewed Ministry of Culture. At the same time, Ramírez cautions that, "si ahora revisamos lo que el Ministerio de la Cultura ha sido en estos primeros años, debemos decir que ha sido un Ministerio Popular de Cultura o un Ministerio de Cultura Popular" (*AO*, 283; "if we now revise what the Ministry of Culture has been in these years, we must say that it has been a People's Ministry of Culture or a Ministry of Popular Culture"). He underlines that he is stating this because "no pocas veces debemos enfrentarnos con el desdén, la incomprensión y a veces con la sorna con que se suele hablar de la labor cultural" (283–4; "not infrequently we face the scorn, misunderstanding and sometimes the sarcasm with which cultural labour is often spoken of"); this not-so-coded allusion to Murillo's attacks is the most partisan statement in the speech. Ramírez's strategy for reconciling the two sides is to argue that the Revolution has abolished the contradiction between high and low culture, which was particularly pronounced in Nicaragua owing to the absence of a strong bourgeoisie, leading to the contrast between the extreme aesthetism of the Vanguard and the Betrayed Generation, and the total illiteracy of more than half of the adult population. Murillo, raised in a Conservative intellectual milieu, perpetuated the positions of the Betrayed Generation within the Sandinista context, while the Ministry of Culture carried to revolutionary extremes the counter-arguments that had been made by the young Liberals of *Ventana* in the early 1960s, fused with the lessons of Cardenal's experiences with cultural production in Solentiname. The Revolution's resolution of society's contradictions annuls, at least in theory, the ground on which this conflict occurred.

To reassure those who may fear the imposition of a Cuban-style cultural policy, Ramírez states: "La revolución garantiza la plena elección de formas, la búsqueda permanente de modos de expresión, para que se pueda elevar constantemente la calidad y la diversidad de esas formas de expresión ... y para que, frente a las masas, nuestros creadores se coloquen siempre como vanguardia en el arte, y así se pueda comunicar a las masas una cultura siempre viva" (285; "The revolution ensures the full choice of artistic forms, a permanent quest for modes of expression, so that the quality and diversity of those forms of expression may be constantly raised ... and so that, before the masses, our creators always situate themselves in the role of an artistic vanguard and communicate to the masses a culture that is always alive"). Even though this ingenious verbal concoction of the vanguard face-to-face with the masses, put forward as a paradigm to harmonize elite with popular culture, did not lay to rest the fractiousness in the ranks, it illustrates the crucial importance of cultural policy to revolutionary unity and to the imaginative construction of the nation as a cohesive "imagined community." The debate itself highlights the persistence of Conservative and Liberal strains of thought within Sandinismo.

The most substantial contribution Ramírez makes to the understanding of his country in *El alba de oro* is his dependency-theory analysis of Nicaraguan history. In spite of the book's subtitle, Ramírez's portraits of the past surpass in incisiveness his observations on the present: the latter, given his position, are necessarily provisional and partisan. Many of the articles, though written in clear, vigorous language, simply tout the achievements of the Revolution, or list the contraventions of international law committed by the United States in its attacks on Nicaragua. Ramírez develops his analysis of Nicaraguan class formation in what is, after "El muchacho de Niquinohomo," the longest piece in the volume: a speech of twenty-five closely printed pages entitled "Sandino: Clase e Ideología" ("Sandino: Class and Ideology"), which must have lasted for well over an hour on 12 May 1980, when he delivered it to a training school for FSLN managers. Ramírez focuses on the weakness and servility of the Nicaraguan oligarchy and the lack of articulated middle sectors, whether working class or middle class. His scorn falls equally on Liberal and Conservative leaders:

> Tanto Adolfo Díaz, como Emiliano Chamorro, como Carlos Cuadra Pasos, así como más tarde José María Moncada estarían listos a saltar en defensa de la intervención en nombre de su clase y a ofrecer una melosa e impúdica complicidad con el disfraz ideológico del mecanismo de dominación: la intervención norteamericana es ensalzada como un hecho civilizador ... (119; Adolfo Diaz, just like Emiliano Chamorro, Carlos Cuadra Pasos, and later José María Moncada as well, were ready to jump to the defence of intervention on behalf of their class and offer a smarmy and shameless complicity in the ideological guise of the mechanism of domination: United States intervention is hailed as a civilizing fact ...)

Rather than employ the term "comprador bourgeoisie," developed by dependency theory,[7] which would imply the existence of a functioning bourgeoisie, albeit a sickly one, Ramírez speaks of "los grupos intermediarios dominantes" (119; "the dominant middleman groups"). In this way he adapts concepts derived by Raúl Prebisch and ECLA in the contexts of Argentina and Chile, where both national bourgeoisies and organized working classes were significant factors, to the very different social structures of Central America. Ramírez's use of "dominant middlemen" stresses that the Conservative oligarchy and the Liberal leadership shared the role of facilitating US intervention and suzerainty. Conforming to dependency theory's analysis of the shaping of peripheral societies as responses, over time, to the demands of the metropolis, Ramírez underlines that, though the collaborationist elites repeated the pretexts for US military interventions and occupations, they did not originate them: "no debemos olvidar que todas estas justificaciones ideológicas jamás se engendran en Nicaragua sino que vienen desde el centro metropolitano de dominación, se reflejan aquí y aquí reciben una reelaboración, un retoque criollo" (119–20; "we must not forget that all of these ideological justifications never originated in Nicaragua but rather came from the metropolitan centre of domination, were reflected here and here received a reworking, a local flavour"). The sardonic concluding phrase illustrates that the irony that characterizes Ramírez's short stories survives in flashes his transplantation to the political realm, even as the word "metropolitan" underlines the dependency-theory provenance of his analysis.

Yet Ramírez bends class analysis in creative ways that are both intellectually impressive and politically astute when he circumvents the dilemma of applying this tool to a nation that, in the early twentieth century, did not have an articulated social class structure. He tells the manager trainees: "La lucha de Sandino contra los yanquis no es la lucha de la burguesía nacional en contra de la ocupación militar norteamericana, sino la lucha del pueblo como clase, que asume en armas la defensa de la nación y de la nacionalidad" (*AO*, 126; "Sandino's struggle against the Yankees is not the struggle of the national bourgeoisie against the US military occupation, but rather the struggle of the people as a class, which takes up arms to defend the nation and nationality"). This ingenious sleight-of-hand enables Ramírez to restore to the FSLN's progenitor the credentials of class struggle – hence of a dialectical engagement with history, hence of an authentic revolutionary movement capable of inspiring support among young revolutionaries in Nicaragua and left-wing internationalists abroad – by claiming the entire Nicaraguan nation as a unified social class. Paradoxically, this manouevre cements Sandinismo's bourgeois nationalist appeal at the same time that it refutes any suspicion that Sandinismo might be *merely* bourgeois nationalism. Furthermore, by defining all Nicaraguans as a single social class, Ramírez has prepared the ground for the notion that deviation from revolutionary duty is treasonous. This assumption echoes one of Fidel Castro's basic principles, first articulated in his 1953 speech *La historia me absolverá* (History Will Absolve Me): "somos cubanos, y ser cubano implica un deber, no cumplirlo es crimen y es traición" (Castro 2004: 96; "We are Cubans and to be Cuban implies a duty, not fulfilling it is a crime and is treason").

It is both ironic and fitting that Ramírez's greatest ideological congruence should be with the Castro of the early 1950s, prior to the Cuban leader's conversion to socialism. The second half of Ramírez's talk to the trainee managers, entitled "el pensamiento sandinista" (*AO*, 128; "Sandinista thought"), propounds two lessons: that Sandinismo can be understood only as a prolonged struggle that "tiene una dinámica en el contexto contemporáneo" (128; "has a dynamic in the contemporary context"), never as an historical phenomenon confined to the 1920s and 1930s; and that Sandino's thought is not a theoretical proposition but rather the "praxis" of a "hombre de acción" ("man of action") whose writings should not be consulted in the search for answers to questions about "medios de producción, lucha de clases" (129; "means of production, class struggle"). While the word "praxis" is often associated with Marxism, the anti-generalizing charge that

Ramírez gives his reading of Sandino's texts mitigates against class-based analyses of social organization in favour of a broadly left-wing nationalism. He defines three fundamental characteristics of Sandino's thought: anti-imperialism, anti-oligarchism, and social justice.

After elaborating each of these precepts, Ramírez doubles back, in a somewhat contradictory manoeuvre, to warn against casting Sandino as simply a bourgeois nationalist. Sandino's revolutionary message, he insists in his conclusion, stems from the fact that the link between his anti-imperialism and his anti-oligarchism is "indissoluble" and that this is due to his frank admission of his class status as "obrero, artesano" (138; "worker, artisan"). It is noticeable that, in this post-revolutionary context, Ramírez cites the word "worker," not just the "artisan" that appears in "El muchacho de Niquinohomo"; yet, in spite of this nod to socialist language, his depiction of the Nicaraguan nation as a single social class promotes a broad-based movement towards national unity and national self-assertion, not unlike that which he orchestrated as leader of The Twelve, over the turmoil of ongoing class struggle. The emphasis on the nation as the primary unit of analysis reinforces the dependency-theory perspective that focuses on relations between centre and periphery. By employing dependency-theory concepts to delineate Nicaragua's predicament, Ramírez redoubles the assertion – crucial to securing the active participation of international solidarity communities – that the Nicaraguan Revolution is an event in which the entire hemisphere has an interest.

Yet it would be wrong to see the nationalism of *El alba de oro* as devoid of class content. The caustic portraits of the delusions of the alienated Somocista elite that characterize *De Tropeles y tropelías* and *Charles Atlas también muere* now populate talks such as "Los viejos socios" ("The Former Business Partners"). This speech, given on 27 December 1980, the sixth anniversary of the Sandinista raid on the Somocista Christmas Party, offers a savage account of the paradise for deluded millionaires created by Somocismo. Ridiculing the nostalgia for the 1960s expressed by the dictator's former cronies, such as the banker Eduardo Montealegre (the father of the early-twenty-first-century centre-right opposition leader of the same name), Ramírez evokes "aquellos días llenas de fotos, fiestas de rigoroso smoking negro o guayaberas de lino" ("those days filled with photos, parties of formal black tuxedos or cotton guayabera shirts"); he states that "ése es el paraíso que ellos perdieron y … que quieren recuperar, aliándose con la guardia genocida …, conspirando en Miami y Costa Rica con los tenebrosos coroneles" (*AO*, 187; "this is the paradise they lost and … they want to recover, allying themselves with the genocidal National Guard …, conspiring in Miami and Costa Rica with sinister colonels"). The novelist's eye is drafted into enlivening speeches that might otherwise be dreary recitations mandated by protocol.

Paradoxically, one of the few moments when Ramírez's role as a politician degrades his language is when he addresses the question of the creative life he is sacrificing by pouring his writing energy into political speeches. His discomfort is palpable when he concludes the book's introduction by writing:

> Para alguien que, como yo, añora su oficio de creador y añora el misterio de la página en blanco, aceptar que la revolución le quita su tiempo de escribir, sería lo más injusto. Por el contrario, es la revolución, mi pueblo intransigente y humilde, en armas y en sueños, lo que me permite seguir siendo escritor, en una forma y con una dimensión que son las únicas que harán posible mis libros futuros. (*AO*, 10; For someone like me who yearns for his creative vocation and the mystery of the blank page to accept that the revolution is taking away his writing time, would be the most unfair thing. On the contrary, it is the revolution, my humble, intransigent people, in arms and in dreams, who allow me to remain a writer, in a manner and with a dimension that are the only ones that will make my future books possible.)

Oddly, given its position in the introduction, this paragraph contains the most insincere language in the book. The phrase "my humble, intransigent people, in arms and in dreams" summons up every imaginable cliché of revolutionary romanticism. It also conveys an unsavoury sense of the leader's feeling of superiority to "my people" (though this sort of discourse was standard fare on the Latin American left at the time). The paragraph romanticizes both the poor subjects of the Revolution and the writer's imagination ("the mystery of the blank page").

The interview with the Cuban magazine *El caimán barbudo* (The Bearded Alligator) that concludes the book addresses the problem of a writer's immersion in a political whirlwind in language that is more frank and direct. Here Ramírez characterizes the Revolution as "la experiencia más importante de mi vida" ("the most important experience of my life") because it enables him to participate in a process "que tiene que ver no sólo con mi país sino con Centroamérica y América Latina. Cuando uno piensa que pudo no haber participado, la nostalgia es terrible" (*AO*, 302; "that has to do not only with my country but with Central America and Latin America. When you think you might not have participated, the regrets are terrible").

This open incredulity at having been swept up in a world-historical event rings far truer than the rhetoric of the introduction. In a similar vein, when asked by the Cuban interviewer Bernardo Marqués how he reconciles his government responsibilities with being a writer, Ramírez replies: "No los concilio. Es muy difícil. Ojalá tuviera la disciplina y la capacidad de trabajo para hacer una labor seria en el gobierno y escribir una hoja al día o dos" (304; "I don't reconcile them. It is very difficult. I wish I had the discipline and the capacity for work to do a serious job in government and write a page or two a day"). An artist, he states, referring to the eight hours a day that he worked on *To Bury Our Fathers* in Berlin, or the non-stop work habits of the painter Armando Morales, is a full-time creator; this is a question of "respeto profesional" (305; "professional respect"). In a sly writerly way, however, he admits that the Revolution is not only a duty but also provides material for his writing and that he hopes some day to be able to "aprovechar todo el material que tengo en notas y aquí, en mi cabeza" (305; "take advantage of all the material I have in notes and here, in my head").

This was not possible during the early years of the Revolution. The next book Ramírez published was *Balcanes y volcanes y otros ensayos y trabajos* (Balkans and Volcanoes and Other Essays and Works), which was brought out by Editorial Nueva Nicaragua in 1983. Though it also appeared in an Argentine edition in 1985, this collection is directed at a Central American audience. All of the pieces included address the problem of the Central American artist from the early days of independence to the first years of the Sandinista Revolution. In addition to the title essay (see chapter 4), which takes up more than half the book, the volume contains a talk entitled "Seis falsos golpes contra la literatura centroamericana" ("Six False Strikes against Central American Literature"), given in Costa Rica in 1975, essays on José Coronel Urtecho and the Salvadoran writer Salarrué, the two talks to the cultural workers that also appeared in *El alba de oro*, and the talk given to accompany Julio Cortázar's reception of the Rubén Darío Medal that had appeared in *La edad presente es de lucha*.

The publication of "Balcanes y volcanes" complemented Ramírez's dependency-theory analysis of Nicaraguan history with a compatible assessment of the context in which Central American literature was written. The fallacies about Central American literature outlined in the first of the shorter essays all refer to the supposed impossibility of writing novels in Central America, of capturing Central American reality in prose fiction, or of the irresponsibility of writing fiction whose purpose is not to protest social injustice. As in his later talks to the cultural workers, Ramírez defends the quest for new artistic forms. The essay closes by comparing the tedious protest novels of Miguel Ángel Asturias's *Trilogía bananera* (1950–60; The Banana Trilogy) with the striking results of Asturias's attempt to forge a new Central American literary idiom, inclusive of indigenous perceptions, in *Men of Maize*. The latter novel's innovations create "un lenguaje mágico y pleno de ecos y de símbolos [que] corre la oscura historia de una opresión secular, revelada sin ningún ánimo contaminante de furias retóricas" (*BV*, 128; "a magical language, full of echoes and symbols [that] runs through the dark history of a century-long oppression, revealed without any contaminating mood of rhetorical fury"). Not only does the search for new aesthetic forms produce better literature, it also conveys the kernel of oppression in more persuasive ways.

The essay on Coronel focuses on two long short stories written by the poet in the late 1930s as a way of returning to one of Ramírez's obsessive themes: the absence in Nicaragua of a credible bourgeoisie. Coronel's avant-garde elitism is portrayed as the consequence of a plantation-based oligarchy being obliged to stand in for this absent bourgeoisie. Ramírez concludes the essay by noting the contradiction that, in spite of its "ideología confesamente reaccionaria ... que se identificaría más tarde con el fascismo" (*BV*, 136; "unabashedly reactionary ideology ... that would later identify with fascism"), Coronel's avant-garde posture at least had the virtue of introducing new literary forms into a Central American writing that was dominated by naturalism.

The long introductory essay to the collected works of Salarrué – the pen name of Salvador Salazar Arrué (1899–1975) – is a discussion of the writer's vocation in Central America. Ramírez rescues Salarrué from the common reduction of his career to that of a quaint chronicler of local customs, influenced by *costumbrista* writers from Argentina and Uruguay, by illustrating the wide variety of forms the Salvadoran writer explored over the course of his career. He notes that (as in his own case) Salarrué was born in a region with a strong indigenous heritage; in contrast to Ramírez, who grew up in what had long been a mestizo culture, Salarrué witnessed the genocide of El Salvador's aboriginal people committed by the anti-Communist brigades of General Maximiliano Hernández Martínez in 1932. Ramírez cites the pro-genocide statements of prominent Salvadoran citizens in illustration of the social currents against which Salarrué's fiction was struggling. As in the case of Asturias, he argues that Salarrué's most politically telling work, the short story collection *Cuentos de barro* (1933; Tales of Clay), which commemorates indigenous life on the eve of the campaign that rendered aboriginal culture in El Salvador extinct by murdering 30,000 native people and obliging the survivors to abandon traditional dress and customs, also represents his highest artistic achievement. Storytelling itself becomes a form of resistance: "Y desde esa resistencia solitaria, su obra narrativa vindica el oficio de escritor en Centroamérica" (*BV*, 166; "And from that lonely resistance, his narrative creation vindicates the profession of writer in Central America").

Yet in the context of the Nicaraguan Revolution it is difficult to vindicate writing as a "profession"; the writer, particularly the male writer with revolutionary responsibilities, acquires legitimacy because he is the voice of his people. As Ileana Rodríguez has demonstrated, earlier revolutionary leaders such as Fidel Castro and Che Guevara (and certainly Augusto César Sandino) assumed this mantle as a natural role. In 1980s Central America, among both the Sandinistas and the FMLN guerrillas in El Salvador, the assumption that educated male revolutionaries could speak on behalf of women, peasants, and workers (and on behalf of a nation sometimes imagined as a female body) began to be called into question; after 1990 it became unsustainable (Rodríguez 1996: 62–90). Ramírez himself had explored some of the problems inherent in countering a violent patriarchal dictatorship with assertions of male bravado in *To Bury Our Fathers*. The writers of the Boom provided a model for shifting the roots of male authority from brute power to cultural continentalism.

The republication of "El profeta en su tierra" ("The Prophet in His Country"), the speech that Ramírez gave on the occasion of the awarding of the Rubén Darío Medal to Cortázar, as the closing essay in *Balcanes y volcanes y otros ensayos y trabajos* and again as the opening essay in his next book, *Seguimos de frente. Escritos sobre la Revolución* (Forward We Go: Writings on the Revolution), lends the piece a pivotal resonance in this process. Sketching the outlines of a continental unity that knits together such disparate Latin American locations as Buenos Aires, Argentina, and León, Nicaragua, Ramírez poses the journey of Rubén Darío to the Argentine metropolis in search of cultural nourishment against the journey of the *porteño* Cortázar to Sandinista Nicaragua in search of ideological and spiritual renewal. Underlying this counterpoint is the assumption that the male intellectual embodies his people and carries them with him. Ramírez stresses this point (while he also recognizes that it needs to be proved) by citing Augusto César Sandino's assertion of his insurgency as representative of the Nicaraguan nation: "Yo estoy representando con mi ejército el propio sentir de mis conciudadanos. La gran mayoría de nicaragüenses, aunque no estén empuñando el rifle en mi ejército, en espíritu están conmigo" (*BV*, 195; "I am representing with my army the intimate feelings of my fellow citizens. The vast majority of Nicaraguans, although they are not wielding a rifle in my army, are with me in spirit"). This culminates in the citation of Darío's assessment of Gorky: "es lengua del pueblo, y se hace oír con el aliento de todo un vasto pueblo" (*BV*, 202; "he is the tongue of the people, and makes himself heard with the breath of an entire vast people"). In applying this label of the tongue of the people to Darío, Gorky, and Cortázar, Ramírez implicitly claims it for himself as well, as the natural posture of a writer engaged with his people in building a revolutionary state.

Ramírez illustrates that Sandino cited Darío in his writings, integrating the poet's words into the action of a military campaign. The belief that the intellectual not only can speak for his nation, but, by describing it in a certain way, may effect changes in its social construction, is evident in *Seguimos de frente* (a punning title that can be read either as "Forward We Go" or "We're Still a Front"). Directed at a solidarity readership, like *El alba de oro*, this collection published in Venezuela in 1985 targets a South American readership. The decision to open the collection with the Cortázar talk boosts the Nicaraguan Revolution's credibility in a South American context, where Central American culture is sometimes regarded in dismissive terms, by affiliating it with the cultural capital of the Boom. Most of the speeches and interviews date from 1983 and 1984; although some are undated, internal references make clear that "El profeta en su tierra," delivered on 6 February 1983, is the earliest of them. The assertion of the writer's role in defining the nation reaches its zenith in the book's final installment, "La razón de mi vida es ser lengua de mi pueblo" ("The Meaning of My Life Is to Be the Tongue of My People"), which expresses in explicit form the assumptions that are latent in the Cortázar talk. In concert with the book's back cover, which offers an assertive presentation of Ramírez's revolutionary credentials ("En 1962 ingresa al Frente Estudiantil Revolucionario y se entrevista en León con Carlos Fonseca, clandestino"; "In 1962 he entered the Revolutionary Student Front and had an underground interview in León with Carlos Fonseca"), this speech, given in Quito, Ecuador, on 9 August 1984, on the reception of an honorary doctorate from the Universidad Central del Ecuador, represents Ramírez's most overt appropriation of the idea that the intellectual's words embody his nation's history and geography. The writer's vocation of representing his people is the speech's organizing principle. After opening his talk by telling his audience that he is receiving this doctorate on behalf of "mi pueblo sandinista" (*SF*, 349; "my Sandinista people"), he begins each paragraph by elaborating on this duty:

> Hablo aquí por los campesinos de mi patria, ocupada dos veces en este siglo por los interventores extranjeros, por los campesinos olvidados y analfabetos que se alzaron con el general Sandino …

Hablo aquí por los miles y miles de hombres y mujeres de mi patria, los de las montañas de Las Segovias y las riberas del río Coco en el norte, los de las selvas del Atlántico, indios y mestizos, miskitos, sumos y ramas, todos los nicaragüenses de los valles, las cañadas, los del río San Juan en el sur y las llanuras ardientes del Pacífico, los de los barrios humildes que no sabían ni poner su nombre en una planilla, que fueron expulsados por siglos de la cultura, expatriados de la educación …

Hablo aquí por los miles de niños que antes morían en Nicaragua de disintería y de poliomielitis …

Hablo aquí por los obreros mineros de Siuna y Bonanza …

Y hablo aquí por los miles de combatientes, campesinos, obreros, estudiantes, técnicos, profesionales; por nuestros soldados que hoy, mientras hablo aquí, combaten por detener y para derrotar a los mercenarios y agresores, a los antiguos guardias somocistas y a los nuevos traidores; que combaten por conquistar la paz que se nos niega, y que combaten por hacer posible en Nicaragua la democracia, la justicia y la paz … En nombre de todos ellos, soldados de la independencia de Nicaragua frente a la voluntad agresora de los Estados Unidos, recibo este doctorado *Honoris Causa*. (*SF*, 349–53; I speak here for the peasants of my country, occupied twice in this century by foreign interventionists, for the neglected and illiterate peasants who rose up with General Sandino …

I speak here for the thousands and thousands of men and women of my country, those in the Segovia Mountains and on the banks of the Coco River in the north, those in the jungles of the Atlantic Coast, indigenous people and mestizos, Miskitos, Sumos and Ramas, all Nicaraguans of the valleys, of the glens, of the San Juan River in the south and of the burning plains of the Pacific, those in the humble neighbourhoods that couldn't even write their name on a form, who were expelled for centuries from culture, expatriated from education …

I speak here for the thousands of children who used to die in Nicaragua of dysentery and polio …

I speak here for the miners of Siuna and Bonanza …

And I speak here for the thousands of soldiers, peasants, workers, students, technicians, professionals, for our soldiers that today, as I speak here, are fighting to stop and defeat the mercenaries and aggressors, the former Somocista Guardsmen and the new traitors; who are fighting to win the peace that we are denied, and who are fighting to make possible democracy in Nicaragua, justice and peace … On behalf of them all, soldiers of Nicaragua's independence against the aggressor's will of the United States, I receive this doctorate Honoris Causa.)

Rarely has a Spanish American writer provided such an exhaustive itemization of the meaning of being the voice of his people. Ramírez makes explicit the ethnic, geographic, and class diversity that his words must integrate and embody; he depicts the Revolution as ushering the deprived masses into the sphere of culture. This, in addition to the academic setting, helps to explain the prominence he gives elsewhere in the speech to the literacy campaign. Literacy is the key if the people of the Segovia Mountains and the diverse cultures of the Atlantic Coast are to overcome their marginalization and consider themselves "Nicaraguan"; in place of Benedict Anderson's literate bourgeoisie, Ramírez imagines literate peasants, children, indigenous peoples, and miners finding a source of cohesion in the "imagined community" of Nicaragua once they are taught how to read and write. At the core of this imagined community stands the writer, whose language becomes the medium that harmonizes the imaginative visions of different peoples, the touchstone that they share to become full citizens.

Ramírez closes the speech with the words, "La razón de mi vida es ser lengua de mi pueblo" (*SF*, 355; "the meaning of my life is to be the tongue of my people"). This phrasing, reflecting a long-standing conception of the male artist, had been an article of faith for Ramírez since his declaration in the *Ventana* manifesto in February 1960 that literature was the "voice" of the people. Yet being the tongue of the people also has specific Central American resonances. It is an obvious (and no doubt self-conscious) echo of Miguel Ángel Asturias's identification with the Guatemalan Revolution and the Mayan peoples, whose culture he claimed to voice as their "Gran Lengua" ("Great Tongue").[8] By using this term, Ramírez not only arrogates to himself the responsibility of speaking for the people, but also emphasizes that the people on whose behalf he is speaking are, like him, the inheritors of Mesoamerican indigenous culture, and that indigenous understandings of culture and community contribute to the authenticity of Nicaraguan mestizo nationalism. In Bloomian terms, he "creatively misreads" Asturias, bending his middle-class nationalism to more revolutionary ends.

The sequence of paragraphs beginning with "I speak ..." opens and closes with allusions to US military aggression against Nicaragua. It glorifies those who fought against the US Marines under Sandino and, particularly, those who fight against the Contras in the present. The provocative final line of this section, in which Ramírez accepts the honorary degree on behalf of those who fight against the "the agressor's will of the United States," makes evident a change in emphasis that has occurred in the two years since the publication of *El alba de oro*. Where the earlier book included optimistic speeches given on the occasion of the initiation of new programs by the revolutionary government, *Seguimos de frente* is dominated by the gruelling Contra War. In its attempt to consolidate international support for Nicaragua, it tries to persuade the South American reader that the US military threat does not stop at the shores of the Caribbean: "son los mismos Estados Unidos que se aliaron contra América Latina en la guerra de las Malvinas ... que intenta destruir el dique que significa Nicaragua para inundar Centroamérica y después todo el continente con programas de estabilización monetaria, bases militares, tropas asesoras y regimenes represivos y verdaderamente totalitarios" (*SF*, 119; "it is the same United States that was allied against Latin America in the Falklands War ... that seeks to destroy the dam represented by Nicaragua to flood Central America and then the entire continent with monetary stabilization programs, army bases, military advisers and truly totalitarian repressive regimes"). The reference to the Falklands War of 1982 (in which US troops did not participate, though the US supported Great Britain against Argentina) skirts the fact that in the Americas direct US military occupation has never occurred south of the northern coast of Venezuela (LaFeber 1983: 78–83). The sentence puts to South Americans the case that their sovereignty, too, will disappear should the Nicaraguan "dam" be breached. In fact, at this time, all of the countries in the southern cone of South America – Argentina, Chile, Uruguay, and Paraguay – were already ruled by brutal military dictatorships that were aided and advised by the United States. Ramírez's "dam" thesis constitutes an appeal to readers in the Andean region that was closer to Central America and where military government was being held at bay (Colombia, Venezuela), had just ended (Peru), or was just beginning (Ecuador).

Seguimos de frente continues Ramírez's exploration of Nicaragua's obsequious governing classes and the distortions wrought by an agrarian elite substituting for a national bourgeoisie. In "La educación: formar actores y no espectadores del cambio" ("Education: To Make Participants and Not Spectators of Change"), a talk given in Managua on 19 May 1983, he draws attention to the astonishing fact that it was impossible to study engineering, the quintessential middle-class profession, in Nicaragua until the 1960s and that only a handful of students ever graduated as members of this profession (*SF*, 88–9). The longest article in the book, the sixty-page "Sandino y los partidos políticos" ("Sandino and the Political Parties"), published here for the first time, opens with an extended analysis of the origins of the Liberal and Conservative parties in the nineteenth century. Ramírez traces how the conflict between the Liberals' capitalist modernizationist policies and the Conservatives' "proyecto oligárquico y reaccionario" (*SF*, 230; "reactionary, oligarchical project") was resolved by the two sides' shared compliance with the US takeover of 1910; "liberales y conservadores yanquistas ya unidos desde entonces" (232; "since then Liberals and Conservatives have been united as Yanquistas"). Mining history for telling quotes, he cites presidents such as the Conservative Diego Manuel Chamorro, who called in the Marines because his deepest concern was that US interests be protected, and the Liberal José María Moncada, who urged that "la Doctrina Monroe se extendiera al nuevo mundo ... que la debían aceptar sin recelo todas las repúblicas americanas" (227; "the Monroe Doctrine be extended to the New World ... that all the republics of the Americas should accept it without fear"), as examples of the quisling political traditions of the Nicaraguan elite. The Conservative opposition parties that submitted to the rigged elections of Somocismo are referred to as "los ideólogos del diálogo perpetuo y la componenda electorera que representó Fernando Agüero, y los sempiternos asiduos de la embajada americana" (*SF*, 263; "the ideologists of perpetual dialogue and shady electoral manoeuvring represented by Fernando Agüero, and the everlasting frequenters of the American Embassy"). Only Sandinismo is exempt from this denigration of the nation; only those who draw on Sandino's example understand Nicaraguan history; only their actions grow out of the needs and experiences of the Nicaraguan people. All roads to nation building, of necessity, obviate the political parties.

This analysis is then projected onto the present to highlight the internal opposition's lack of connection to the realities of most Nicaraguans. Ramírez illustrates the opposition's knee-jerk subservience to the United States with telling quotes. The purpose of this elaborate, learned, raptly executed argument is to deny the internal opposition (and even more so the leaders of the Contras) legitimacy as the voices of constituencies within Nicaragua. The revolutionary leader's authority to speak for the nation is enlarged because the leaders of the opposition are denationalized. The putative goal of this essay is to refute the US demand that the Sandinistas negotiate with the Contras and COSEP; but it has the subsidiary effect of confirming Ramírez's self-definition as a spokesman for his "people."

A parallel argument occurs in "Libertad de expresión, conquistada y defendida" (Freedom of Expression Won and Defended), a talk given on 25 June 1984 to the Second Conference of Journalists from Central America and the Caribbean. After describing the diverse media outlets and public fora through which Nicaraguans express themselves, Ramírez characterizes the opposition newspaper *La Prensa*, which the US government funded and the Sandinistas censored, and the censorship of which had become a central plank of the Reagan administration's anti-Sandinista propaganda, as a publication that, in the month of January 1984, "dedicó 605,8 columnas pulgadas para imprimir las opiniones oficiales de la Administración Reagan … y apenas 40,8 columnas pulgadas para referirse a los puntos de vista del Gobierno de Nicaragua … dedicó una sexta parte de sus informaciones a reproducir los criterios de una potencia militar que está agrediendo militarmente a Nicaragua, el país donde se imprime *La Prensa*" (323; "devoted 605.8 column inches to printing the official views of the Reagan administration … and just 40.8 column inches to refer to the views of the Government of Nicaragua … allotted a sixth of its information to repeat the criteria of a military power that is militarily attacking Nicaragua, the country where they print *La Prensa*").

This extrapolation of Ramírez's analysis of the Nicaraguan upper classes into the context of the Contra War is consistent with his earlier writing about the elite. The most unexpected feature of *Seguimos de frente*, and one that sets it apart from dozens of other Latin American denunciations of Yankee imperialism, is his attempt to understand the origins of the enemy's aggressive behaviour. With rare exceptions, such as the columns José Martí wrote from New York in the 1880s, Spanish American nationalist essays have tended to take the thirst for continental domination as an innate characteristic of the US population. Though he lacks Martí's prolonged experience of daily life in the United States, Ramírez makes a concerted effort to analyze the historical roots of US political culture. "La desestablización norteamericana en Nicaragua" ("US Destabilization in Nicaragua"), an interview with Carlos Rincón published in Germany in September 1983, follows familiar pathways, tracing the route from early-twentieth-century US interventions to the overthrow of Salvador Allende's government in Chile to Reagan's henchmen William Casey and John Negroponte. Returning to the Falklands War, Ramírez points out that US support for Great Britain abrogated the mutual-defence pact of the Organization of American States, the 1947 Rio de Janeiro Treaty, which pledges members to protect each other from aggression from outside the hemisphere.

By contrast, "Una Revolución propia y un modelo soberano" ("A Revolution of Our Own and a Sovereign Model"), given in Managua on 14 July 1983, at an international meeting of intellectuals to discuss the problems of Central America, attempts to grasp how the United States "cambió su proyecto original de libertad y democracia por el Destino Manifiesto" (171; "exchanged its original project of freedom and democracy for Manifest Destiny"). Responding to the Reaganite accusation that the Sandinistas are trying to export their Revolution, Ramírez makes the daring assertion that "las revoluciones siempre han sido exportables a lo largo de la historia" (172; "revolutions have always been exportable throughout history"). He charts the mutually dependent development of the eighteenth-century revolutions in France and the thirteen southernmost British colonies in North America through the transatlantic influences of Thomas Jefferson, Benjamin Franklin, French Enlightenment pamphlets, and the Marquis de Lafayette.

Concluding that "la revolución que dio origen a los Estados Unidos como nación, ha sido la revolución más exportada de la historia contemporánea" (173; "the revolution that led to the creation of the United States as a nation has been the most exported revolution in modern history"), Ramírez reminds his audience of the explosive impact of US ideas on early-nineteenth-century Central America, where, under the rule of the absolutist monarchy of Spain, "leer a James Madison en aquellos tiempos, era delito de lesa majestad, como leer a Marx en estos tiempos puede costar la vida en Guatemala o El Salvador" (174; "in those days reading James Madison was high treason, just as reading Marx these days can cost you your life in Guatemala or El Salvador"). The quest for justice in Central America, of which the wars that broke out in the 1970s are the long-term consequence, was ignited by the exportation of the Enlightenment-inspired revolution in the Thirteen Colonies. Even as Central America absorbed these ideas, the United States, Ramírez maintains, began to betray its revolutionary heritage: "James Madison, padre de la Constitución americana, ya se mostraba temoroso en 1829 de que la expansión perpetua de la nueva nación controlada por fabricantes y comerciantes, acabaría con el experimento del gobierno republicano" (178; "In 1829 James Madison, father of the American constitution, was already fearful that the new nation's perpetual expansion, controlled by manufacturers and merchants, would put an end to the experience of republican government"). The marginalization of egalitarian values under this expansionist drive reaches its climax in the repeated US military interventions in Central America and the Caribbean: "la dominación [de] nuestros países, en nombre de los banqueros y financieros cuyas garras no previeron ni Jefferson ni Madison" (185; "the domination [of] our countries, on behalf of bankers and financiers whose claws neither Jefferson nor Madison foresaw"). The attitudes developed during these occupations are the forerunners to the "desdén" (185; "disdain") with which the Reaganite New Right regards attempts by Central Americans to govern themselves.

While this capsule version of history would be rejected in many quarters in the United States, it does serve as an attempt to understand US history from without, in a way that conceives the country as an entity with a particular historical trajectory rather than a blind oppressive force. The most surprising omission from Ramírez's analysis is that of the all-pervasive influence of anti-Communist ideology, and how US politicians and the media projected anti-Communist paranoia onto events in Latin America. As "Dictado sobre el Dragón y los Paladines" ("Dictation on the Dragon and the Paladins"), an article published in the German magazine *L-8* on 29 May 1983, demonstrates, Ramírez understands anti-Communism in historical perspective, as merely the most recent expression of a fable that is as old as the United States and whose origins he attributes to John Quincy Adams, that there is a "dragón que quiere tragar a Estados Unidos" (103; "a dragon that wants to swallow the United States"). In this allegory, which adapts José Enrique Rodó's *Ariel* (1900) to the modern world, Ramírez inverts the fable of the knight in shining armour who slays the dragon, converting the dragon into the hero: "El dragón vencerá. Y no pasarán" (108; "The dragon will triumph. And they shall not pass").

In *Seguimos de frente*, Ramírez acts as an informant who, by virtue of coming from a country that for decades was reduced to a quasi-colony of the United States, possesses the authority to explain the workings of this imperial democracy. This fulfills his role as the "tongue" of his people. Yet the cultural capital that both Ramírez and the Nicaraguan Revolution gleaned from their fraternization with the Boom waned after Julio Cortázar's death. The pivotal importance of this event is evident in the fact that the only book that Ramírez published between his second and third novels that was conceived and written as a single volume was *Estás en Nicaragua* (1985; *Hatful of Tigers: Reflections on Art, Culture and Politics*), his memoir of Cortázar's solidarity journeys. This book represented the first step in Ramírez's return to his literary vocation.

THE VICE-PRESIDENT'S RETURN TO WRITING: *HATFUL OF TIGERS*

Between 1977 and 1984 Ramírez had written nothing but essays and speeches. After 4 November 1984, when his election as vice-president confirmed that he would remain in politics for at least five more years, he decided that he must find a way to combine his political duties with imaginative writing. *Hatful of Tigers*, written between March and June 1985, is not a novel, but it is conceived as a single volume, much of it more whimsical and literary than the books that precede it.

Intended as a companion piece to Cortázar's *Nicaragua tan violentemente dulce* (1984), and published by the same company, Muchnik Editores in Barcelona, in the same format as Cortázar's book, *Hatful of Tigers* represents Ramírez's most consistent depiction of Revolution as the product of the literary reimagining of the nation. The volume's short, sketch-like chapters and numerous black-and-white photographs give it the texture of a scrapbook. The structure is broadly contrapuntal. In the first half of the book, "Before," chapters that relate encounters with Cortázar or his writing in Europe or Costa Rica in the 1960s and 1970s, alternate with others that contain meditations on Central American history and culture, or brief portraits, called "Daguerreotypes" of 1970s Sandinista martyrs such as Luisa Amanda Espinosa and Eduardo Contreras. In the second half of the book, "After," the Central American context recedes as the focus closes in on the early years of the Nicaraguan Revolution, in which Cortázar is inextricably enmeshed. Literature and history, in *Hatful of Tigers*, and, by extension, literature and revolution, merge to become a single essence. This essence, of its nature, distances regional patterns: the nation becomes a unique experience. Yet, in spite of the fact that the title of the Spanish-language edition includes the word "Nicaragua," and the book is a proud advertisement for the Nicaraguan Revolution, the pre-revolutionary "Before" chapters survey the shared history of injustice and state violence, as well as the cultural and literary preoccupations, of the five original republics of the isthmus. Ramírez has little good to say about Honduras – standard practice in Central America during the 1980s, when the country had been reduced a US military base – but he offers committed, provocative insights into Guatemala, Costa Rica, and El Salvador. Though the volume is a homage to revolutionary heroes, Cortázar foremost among them, the real hero of the revolutionary spirit as it is presented here is literature itself.

The Spanish title comes from a piece of upbeat doggerel that Cortázar wrote as the epigraph of *Nicaraguan Sketches*. A twenty-four-line poem about arriving in Managua, it concludes: "No, no te equivocaste de aeropuerto:/entrá nomás, estás en Nicaragua" (Cortázar 1989: 7; "No, you're not at the wrong airport/Come on in, you're in Nicaragua").[9] Ramírez reprints the poem as the epigraph of his volume (*EN*, 9–10); the connotation of the phrase "you're in Nicaragua," however, has changed. Cortázar may no longer be found visiting the markets of Managua. The purpose of this volume is to tell Cortázar that he is present in Nicaragua after death because the Nicaraguan nation in its revolutionary incarnation is the long-range outcome of the audacious reimagining of Spanish American identity achieved by the Boom. Where in *El alba de oro*, Ramírez declared Carlos Fonseca to be visible in revolutionary Nicaragua, here the contours of the revolutionary nation are the product of literature.

The opening sketch recalls the apartment of the Salvadoran poet Roberto Armijo (1937–97) during the years before the outbreak of the wars in Central America. The apartment embodies the conjunction of the nation and literature in the view of "los cerros y los cielos de San Salvador" (*EN*, 11;

"the hills and skies of San Salvador" [*HFT*, 11]) that is visible from the balcony and the books "que desbordaban los estrechos dormitorios, el retrete, la salita, incluso la cocina" (*EN*, 11; "the overflow of books in the narrow bedrooms, the bathroom, the small living room, even the kitchen" [*HFT*, 11]). At the time Ramírez writes *Hatful of Tigers*, Armijo's family has joined the guerrillas: his wife has been "disappeared," one of his sons is dead and has gone to "los cielos" ("heaven"), and the surviving guerrilla son is in "los cerros" (*EN*, 12; "the hills" [*HFT*, 11]). The fate of the Armijo family establishes the motif of literature that melts into revolutionary activism to become the historically charged essence of the nation.

The opening description leads from Ramírez's discovery of Cortázar's short story collection *Bestiario* (1951; *Bestiary*) as a student in León to his purchase of *Rayuela* (1963; *Hopscotch*) in a bookstore in Costa Rica. After buying the novel, he signs the inside leaf with his name and the date, May 1965. This talismanic edition of the work that symbolized the emergence of the Spanish American Boom was "manoseado a lo largo de los años por tantos amigos, incluyendo a Carlos Fonseca" (*EN*, 20; "worn with handling by so many friends over the years – one was Carlos Fonseca" [*HFT*, 20]). Ramírez attributes his generation's discovery of a Spanish American literature of intense aesthetic achievement, and its ability to "distinguir entre lo vernáculo y Juan Rulfo" (*EN*, 21; "distinguish between the vernacular and Juan Rulfo" [*HFT*, 21]), to this dog-eared copy of *Hopscotch*. When, twenty years later, Cortázar spots this book on Ramírez's shelves in Managua, pulls it out, and signs his name below that of Ramirez "al pie de aquella fecha" (*EN*, 20; "under that date" [*HFT*, 20]), he inscribes Ramírez into the Boom; yet, since this is the copy that was read by Carlos Fonseca, Cortázar is also attesting to the indivisible unity of the Boom and the Nicaraguan Revolution.

Another short chapter returns to the subject of Fonseca's reading of Ramírez's copy of *Hopscotch* between July and October 1965, while the FSLN's founder was working on an essay on Rubén Darío in San José. Ramírez reports that the two men discussed "la nueva novela latinoamericana que empezaba a sonar" (*EN*, 24; "the new Latin American novel that was beginning to make waves" [*HFT*, 24]). Adopting Cortázar's distinction between cronopios and famas, in which people who are "famas" are obtuse squares (Cortázar 1962: 107–33), in a way that weaves Boom concepts into the foundations of the Nicaraguan Revolution, he credits the merged influences of Fonseca and Cortázar of curing him of the "riesgo de convertirme en fama" (*EN*, 24; "risk of turning into a company man" [*HFT*, 24]).

The generation of a cultural essence that is both literature and revolution, a development of the imagination that induces social and cultural transformation, continues in a chapter entitled "Octubre, 1967. León, Nicaragua"

(*EN*, 29; *HFT*, 28). The politically alert Latin American reader will be aware that October 1967 is the month when Che Guevara was killed in Bolivia. By describing concurrent events in "León, Nicaragua," Ramírez weaves Nicaragua into the net of continental revolution. Yet the event he describes is a short course on the literature of the Boom that he gave in this month at his alma mater, UNAN. The course coincides with the FSLN's unsuccessful Pancasán offensive: "Estamos explicando la novedad de la nueva narrativa en los días y en las noches de Pancasán" (*EN*, 29–30; "We are explaining the new trend and speaking of the new narrative during the days and nights of Pancasán" [*HFT*, 28]). The sentence suggests the interwoven nature of the activities of literature and revolution. The thirty students in the course have read *Hopscotch, The Death of Artemio Cruz, Pedro Páramo*, and *The Time of the Hero*. Among the students is Jaime Wheelock, with whom Ramírez has long conversations after the class on "novela compromiso escritor literatura revolución" (*EN*, 30; "novels, commitment, the writer, literature, revolution" [*HFT*, 29]); this indefinable, yet nearly palpable, substance coheres in the blending of the literary and the political that would give birth to revolutionary Nicaragua, almost as if to a novel that occupies the space of objective reality. The chapter closes by emphasizing the simultaneous events of Pancasán: "Y Pancasán la lumbre de las hogueras, el lejano clamor, la rayita de alba debajo de la puerta cerrada" (*EN*, 31; "And Pancasán, the glow of bonfires, the distant rumble, the first faint ray of dawn beneath the closed door" [*HFT*, 30]). As Ramírez writes at the end of the first of the chapters, in which he narrates his own discovery of Central America, after meeting writers in Guatemala and El Salvador who will be murdered in later years: "En serio que valía la pena ser escritor en Centroamérica y ésta era la gracia de lo lúdico, que el juego era en serio, es en serio, lejos de lo abstracto; la pasión de lo vivo y el rencor de lo real" (*EN*, 28; "It was definitely worthwhile being a writer in Central America, and that was the essence of the ludic: that the game was for keeps and is for keeps, far from abstract; the passion for the living and the rancor of the real" [*HFT*, 27]). In this sentence Ramírez struggles to define the imagination's incursions into the public sphere that make being a writer in Central America serious, dangerous, and a matter of the "real" world, not merely of the imagination.

The sections on Central American history are the most problematic element of *Hatful of Tigers*. In relating in semi-whimsical fashion episodes from the region's often grotesque past, Ramírez wades into the nineteenth-century debate between Liberals and Conservatives. This struggle plays out most clearly in Guatemala, the isthmus's most populous country, where he identifies Manuel Estrada Cabrera, the early-twentieth-century dictator on whom Miguel Ángel Asturias's novel *The President* is based, as having forged the initial link in a chain of oppressive tactics employed by the Central American right. Estrada Cabrera "fue quien inventó los cementerios clandestinos, otros inventaron después los escuadrones de la muerte, y otros aún después las aldeas estratégicas, y de mis amigos de la Universidad de San Carlos de aquellos años sesenta ya no queda nadie" (*EN*, 26; "was the one who invented clandestine cemeteries; later others invented the death squads, and still others the strategic villages [hamlets]; of my friends at the University of San Carlos in the sixties, not one is left" [*HFT*, 26]). The itemization of the different ways in which his intellectual friends were murdered delineates the culture to which "novels, commitment, the writer, literature, revolution" is opposed: a culture of death squads, disappearances, torture, and abject subservience to the US Embassy carried out "en nombre de Dios, la patria, la familia, la religión" (*EN*, 41; "in the name of God, the fatherland, the family, and religion" [*HFT*, 40]). Yet, in projecting backwards in time the causal chain that engendered this culture of violent dictatorship, Ramírez sets up a dichotomy between the crusading nineteenth-century Liberal Francisco Morazán, who is commemorated in a number of Central American cities as the region's first nation builder, and the mestizo *caudillo* Rafael Carrera, who ruled Guatemala from 1839 to 1865. Ramírez presents Carrera as the man who "inspiró" (*EN*, 41; "inspired" [*HFT*, 40]) later Guatemalan tyrants such as Cabrera and Jorge Ubico and served as the forerunner of the Somozas and other Central American dictators at the service of the US Embassy:

> "El mejor aliado de los yankis y enemigo acérrimo de Morazán, fue el general Carrera de Guatemala. Es cierto que aún los yankis no existían por aquí, pero como gran visionario que era, sabía que de todos modos iban a venir y fue así su más grande aliado ... Y cuántos Carrera no han sido engendrados a partir de entonces, sapos amamantados en leche de sacristía ..." (*EN*, 40; "The Yankees' best ally and sworn enemy of Morazán was General Carrera of Guatemala. It's true that the Yankees didn't yet exist in these parts, but, great visionary that he was, he knew they'd be coming, and he was their greatest ally ... And how many Carreras have been engendered since then: toads suckling on vestry milk ..." [*HFT*, 39–40])

This vision of Carrera as an illiterate who was allowed to retain the presidency because he acted as the strong right arm of a reactionary Catholic hierarchy was a common slur in Central American Liberal quarters from the nineteenth century until the 1960s. Ramírez's repetition of these prejudices is in contradiction not only with his own consistent support for the advancement of people of mixed-race heritage,[10] but also with the reassessment of Carrera's career that had begun more than a decade before he wrote *Hatful of Tigers*. This fresh appreciation of Carrera depicted him as a defender of indigenous rights, an enemy of corruption, a man who changed the tax system to create a more egalitarian society, broke the power of the white ruling class, ensured that indigenous people "participated directly in government" (Burns and Charlip 2002: 117), and resisted the phoney pseudo-European culture of the nineteenth-century elites that Ramírez criticized in "Balcanes y volcanes." Contemporary scholars see Carrera's regime as a nineteenth-century parallel to the Sandinista government or Guatemala's revolutionary government of 1944–54.[11] Ramírez's sarcastic denigration of a man who was coming to be seen, albeit in retrospect, as one of the early heroes of the Central American left is a puzzling contradiction. Asked about this passage twenty years later, Ramírez replied that Carrera "era un hijo de casa de los curas. Lo pusieron los curas. Entonces, no sé si Carrera fuera declaradamente un reaccionario por ideología sino porque él tenía una lealtad con la iglesia" (*UISR*; "was a son of the parish house. The priests put him in power. So I don't know whether Carrera was openly reactionary by ideology or rather because he was loyal to the Church"). This response makes clear that the key line in the passage from *Hatful of Tigers* cited above is "toads suckling on vestry milk." Ramírez's opposition to Carrera springs from an anticlericalism nurtured by his Liberal, half-Protestant background, reinforced by the transmutation of nineteenth-century Conservative religious discourse into the death-squad doctrine of "God, the fatherland, the family, and religion" that was invoked to justify the murder of tens of thousands of Central Americans in the 1970s and 1980s. Ramírez's animosity to Carrera is an ideological contradiction that is revealing of the constitution of Sandinismo. As insurgent peasants and workers, disaffected Conservative oligarchs, and rebellious Liberal professionals converged in the FSLN ranks, they brought with them, to an extent that perhaps has not been appreciated fully, the cargo of their respective ingrained approaches to history. In spite of the power and clarity with which Sandinista ideology was articulated by Augusto César Sandino, Carlos Fonseca, and their successors, residual strains of Liberalism and Conservatism remained latent and occasionally surfaced in the declarations of Sandinista leaders.

Subsequent sketches in the "Before" half of *Hatful of Tigers* allude to Ramírez's early encounters with Cortázar and his writing (including a failed first attempt at a rendezvous in East Berlin in 1974) and, in the historical sections, to the frustration of attempts to forge a Central American union. The final chapter in this section returns to a theme that Ramírez had developed in "Balcanes y volcanes": the difficulty of sustaining writing as a vocation in the impoverished Central American context, and how the phenomenon of the writer who has only a part-time commitment to his craft mitigates against formal innovation, creating a situation where "algún tipo de arte provinciano se llega a defender ... como clásico" (*EN*, 71; "a certain type of provincial art comes to be defended ... as classical" [*HFT*, 70]). The solution to this impasse is revolution, which brings artistic innovation to Nicaragua in the tangible form of Julio Cortázar.

The first installment of the "After" section itemizes Cortázar's five visits to Nicaragua during the Revolution, and his itinerary on each visit. The second sketch describes León, the first city in Nicaragua to be liberated from Somocismo, on the day of the triumph in 1979, when for the formal installation of the provisional government Ramírez and Jaime Wheelock, along with other Sandinista leaders, returned to the UNAN auditorium where the Boom literature course had taken place in 1967. In this way, the Revolution anoints the course's conjunction of the debates about "novels, commitment, the writer, literature, revolution" with the revolutionary ghosts of Che Guevara and Pancasán. The presence of Cortázar, Boom writer and ally of revolutionary regimes, incarnates the successful fusion of these traditions.

Subsequent chapters elaborate on Cortázar's commitment to Nicaragua as the Parisian-based writer's symbolic return to Latin America "por mucho que esté enterrado en Montparnasse" (*EN*, 99; "despite the fact that he is buried in Montparnasse" [*HFT*, 97]). Ramírez weaves an argument that *Hopscotch* is a deeply Latin American novel into more hard-nosed strategic assessments of the position of Nicaragua in a hemisphere dominated by the United States. He dismisses the Cold War as an imposition of European philosophical categories on Latin America, where the East-West dichotomy does not apply because the true struggle is between "lo viejo y lo nuevo, y como detonante de lo nuevo [uno] pone la posibilidad permanente de la revolución" (*EN*, 89; "the old and the new, and ... as a detonator of the new you have the permanent possibility of revolution" [*HFT*, 86]).

Cortázar's recognition of Latin America's search for newness is contrasted with the subservience to European categories and US imperialist rhetoric of the Mexican poet Octavio Paz. Telling audiences during his US speaking tours that "revolutionary movements now are linked to Soviet imperialism," Paz urged that the United States "cannot allow, as I understand it, Nicaragua to become a basis for active revolution" (Porter 1986: 86–7). Paz gained the lucrative patronage of US neo-conservatives by exaggerating conditions under Sandinismo. (His assertions were less popular at home, where students burned the poet in effigy in front of the US Embassy in Mexico City.) Ramírez does not mention Paz by name, but references to Paz's magazine *Vuelta* (Return) and to a well-known incident where Paz played a piano duet with Ronald Reagan make clear it is he to whom Ramírez is alluding: "Es una tragedia acabar tocando con Reagan el piano a cuatro manos y jurando que en Nicaragua la marea roja del comunismo internacional está ahogando bajo el más abyecto totalitarianismo bolchevique el ser latinoamericano" (*EN*, 100; "It is a tragedy to wind up playing four-hand piano duets with Reagan and swearing that in Nicaragua the red tide of international communism is suffocating the Latin American being, the individual, under the most vile Bolshevik totalitarianism" [*HFT*, 98]). By accepting Western categories and misreading Latin America through the univocal focus of the Reaganite caricature of freedom, Paz has become alienated from Latin American reality; he contributes to suppressing the free speech of those who are excluded by poverty from erudite debate. In a line that reflects his own experience of attending meetings in rural Nicaragua, Ramírez recommends to Paz that he "permitirles el derecho tan occidental de la palabra a miles de campesinos sin luz eléctrica, carretoneros, vivanderas, mozos de cuerda, maestros rurales que enseñan sin pizarras, milicianos que siembran con el rifle al hombre, y que bien podrían coger un micrófono y explicarte con una lucidez que te dejaría pasmado qué cosa es la libertad entre nosotros" (*EN*, 103; "allow the very Western right of freedom of speech to vegetable sellers, porters, rural teachers who teach without blackboards, militiamen who plow with rifles slung over their shoulders, who could easily pick up a microphone and explain to you with astonishing lucidity just what freedom means among us" [*HFT*, 101]).[12]

The treatment of Paz, when juxtaposed with that of Rafael Carrera, exposes an ideological contradiction in *Hatful of Tigers*: Western liberalism is denounced as an ideology alien to Latin America, yet nineteenth-century Central American Liberalism, which springs from the same historical soil in the eighteenth-century Enlightenment-inspired revolutions in France and the United States, persists to a sufficient extent to denounce Rafael Carrera, one of the pioneers of the Latin American left's critique of liberalism. This vestigial Liberalism is not evident elsewhere in the book, which shares with *El alba de oro* and *Seguimos de frente* the promotion of the Sandinista model for radical social transformation.

Once Cortázar becomes a frequent visitor to Nicaragua, he participates in events such as the nationalization of the mines, meetings with mothers of martyred Sandinistas, the distribution of agrarian reform titles to peasants, and the inauguration of rural schools. This volume's scrapbook form enables Ramírez to include documents such as the slips used by the mines to show that they had paid Anastasio Somoza Debayle his personal "Subsidy Tax of $10.00 for each kilo of gold shipped" (*EN*, 109). In spite, or perhaps because of, its literary subject matter, the book illustrates the motivation for Sandinista policies even more vividly than its two predecessors. The closing image of Cortázar's travels in the country is of him and Ramírez embracing the mothers of murdered Sandinista youths in the village of Belén: "mi imagen más constante y más precisa de la revolución, madres humildes, cordiales, severas, al abrazarlas tantas veces hemos abrazado la pobreza y hemos abrazado la dignidad y son tantas, cuántas veces no te sentís resucitar, sacar fuerzas de ese abrazo" (*EN*, 138; "my most constant and precise image of the revolution: the mothers, humble, cordial, stern; embracing them so many times, we have embraced poverty, embraced dignity, and there are so many times, and there are so many of them. How many times have you felt yourself reviving, drawing strength from that embrace" [*HFT*, 130]). This description of the two literary intellectuals' embrace of the poverty and suffering at the core of the Revolution, of the interpenetration of the erudite and the rural, consummates Cortázar's integration into revolutionary Nicaragua.

By way of a coda, Ramírez includes in the final "Daguerrotype" section a description of how he presumptuously wrote a statement of allegiance to the Revolution for the Spanish priest Gaspar García Laviana to sign, only to discover that García Laviana had written his own statement. Months later, on seeing the priest's dead body displayed on television by the Somoza government, "te has acordado que Gaspar también era escritor, que entre otras cosas te enseñó un día que también era escritor" (*EN*, 143; "you remembered that Gaspar also was a writer, that among other things he taught you one day that he also was a writer" [*HFT*, 133]). This reminder that being a writer is not the exclusive prerogative of the intellectual, that the Revolution is meant to disseminate the capacity for self-expression throughout the populace, may threaten to dethrone the male intellectual from his position of authority, yet it confirms his values, his perception of the revolutionary nation as the product and the vehicle of the diffusion of literary culture.

The concluding sketch, dated one year to the day after Cortázar's death, narrates Roberto Armijo's attempt to arrange for a photograph to be taken of Cortázar on his deathbed in Paris. Having opened with a vision of Armijo's family being absorbed into the Revolution by literature, the book closes with an image of Cortázar, the incarnation of literary authority, dying not as an Argentine exile in Paris but as a Central American. Like the characters in many of his short stories – middle-class urbanites who cannot help but metamorphose into salamanders or participants in ancient rituals – Cortázar himself leaves the world via a mysterious transformation: "Roberto Armijo ... anduvo peleando para lograr que le tomaran una foto a Julio yacente en su lecho del hospital, peleando para que se permitiera hacerle una mascarilla mortuoria, (tan centroamericano eso de las fotos de cuerpo presente y las mascarillas mortuorias)" (*EN*, 144; "Roberto Armijo ... had been fighting to get them to take a photograph of Julio lying in his hospital bed, fighting for permission to make a death mask (so Central American, this thing of photos of the body and death masks)" [*HFT*, 134]). As the photographer enters the hospital room, Ramírez evokes Michelangelo Antonioni's film *Blow-Up*, which was based on the short story "Las babas del diablo" ("Blow-Up"), from Cortázar's early collection *Las armas secretas* (1959; *Secret weapons*), and "Apocalipsis de Solentiname" ("Apocalypse in Solentiname"), the piece that Cortázar wrote about his clandestine visit to Ernesto Cardenal's community in 1976 and included as a short story in his collection *Alguien que anda por ahí* (1977; Somebody Walking Around), then later as a memoir in *Nicaraguan Sketches*. Both works describe photographs whose images prove to be volatile. In the latter story, photographs taken by Cortázar of primitivist landscape paintings in Solentiname transform, when the narrator develops his film in Paris, into images of Central American violence. Ramírez imagines the film of Armijo's photographer, once developed, yielding images not of the dying Cortázar but of the landscapes where he contributed to the Nicaraguan Revolution: "vas a revelar el rollo y te sale Siuna, Solentiname, Bismuna, las madres de Belén [...]" (*EN*, 145; "you develop the roll and ... you find Siuna, Solentiname, Bismuna, the mothers of Belén" [*HFT*, 135]). The last book that Cortázar read, the book on his bedside table in the hospital, was a volume by Rubén Darío. The Central Americanization of Cortázar enshrines him as someone who is "in" Nicaragua; he and his literary vision are now an enduring part of the Revolution, definitively fused with the poor, to whom Ramírez returns in the book's final sentence: "Me están esperando las madres de Belén" (*EN*, 145; "The mothers of Belén are waiting for me" [*HFT*, 135]). The struggle must continue in Cortázar's absence, yet he will always be part of the Revolution.

The most literary of the non-fiction works of the 1980s, *Hatful of Tigers* connects the essays and speeches of the immediate post-revolutionary years to *Castigo Divino* (1988). The final book of essays Ramírez published in the 1980s, *Las armas del futuro* (1987; The Weapons of the Future), is a large compilation of nearly four hundred closely printed pages, assembled by the Cuban journalist Reynaldo González, that opens with a thirty-six-page introduction to Ramírez's life and career and the context of the Nicaraguan

Revolution, apparently directed at a Cuban readership. However, *Las armas del futuro* was published in Managua; it made available to Nicaraguan readers many of the speeches in the foreign-published *El alba de oro*, *Seguimos de frente*, and *Hatful of Tigers*. The volume contains only one essay previously unpublished in book form, the concluding piece, "El fascismo sigue vivo como ideología y como sistema" ("Fascism Remains Alive as an Ideology and a System"), a speech that Ramírez delivered in Managua on 8 May 1985 to celebrate the fortieth anniversary of the end of the Second World War. The remainder of the contents consists of fifteen of the twenty-six essays in *El alba de oro*, five of the fifteen essays in *Seguimos de frente*, the entire contents of *Balcanes y volcanes y otros ensayos y trabajos*, and three short sections from *Hatful of Tigers*. No particular principle of inclusion appears to have guided the selection. Some of the pieces that were dropped were linked to events, such as the inauguration of the literacy campaign or early debates over cultural policy, which by 1987 belonged to the past. Both "La razón de mi vida es ser lengua de mi pueblo" and "Costa Rica y nosotros" ("Costa Rice and Us") from *Seguimos de frente* are quoted at length by González in his introductory essay (*AF*, x, xxiv), but are omitted from the book.

Las armas del futuro focuses on Nicaraguan history and literature as viewed in historical perspective. In this vein, the closing essay resumes Ramírez's attempt to understand the origins of US aggression. The warping of a quest for liberal democracy into an obsession with Manifest Destiny, developed in "Una revolución propia y un modelo soberano" from *Seguimos de frente* – which in *Las armas del futuro* serves as the title-essay for the second of the three sections into which the book is divided – becomes the central focus of the concluding essay. Most of the third section of the book is devoted to literary topics; the modulation back into political themes is achieved via the inclusion of the three short sections from *Hatful of Tigers*.

This return to the theme of the United States, deeper into the Contra War, finds Ramírez angrier and less forgiving. No longer willing to understand US imperialism as the abdication of the values of Thomas Jefferson and James Madison, he takes the measure of United States foreign policy in the twentieth century and finds it to be ideologically contiguous with that of Nazi Germany. Fascism, he argues, did not arise as the result of an historical aberration; rather, it was a concerted response on the part of wealthy industrialists to the creation of a workers' state, the Soviet Union, in 1917. The seeds of Fascism lie in Western nations' decision to "respaldar a la contrarevolución en Rusia" (*AF*, 382; "support the counter-revolution in Russia"). This interventionist policy foreshadows the creation of the Contras in response to the triumph of the Nicaraguan Revolution. Ramírez reminds his audience that in 1932 German industrialists asked Hindenburg to confer dictatorial powers on Adolf Hitler "porque los mecanismos parlamentarios ya no eran suficientes para salvaguardar sus intereses" (*AF*, 382; "because the parliamentary mechanisms were no longer sufficient to safeguard their interests"), an event that he portrays as an extension of the campaign to crush the Soviet Union. While this presentation omits the period of the Soviet-German truce of the Molotov-Ribbentrop Pact, it is sustainable as a depiction of the consistent long-term pursuit of a policy objective. A clear echo of Nicaragua's predicament is audible when Ramírez praises "el pueblo soviético" (382; "the Soviet people") for their resistance to the 1941 Nazi invasion and their defence of their homeland. This heroism, he maintains, obliged the United States to "colocarse en una línea de conducta justa" (383; "adopt a line of just conduct") and, rather than succumbing to the industrialists' imperative of supporting Fascism, to ensure that US soldiers sacrificed their lives alongside "soldados belgas, canadienses, británicos" (383; "Belgian, Canadian, British soldiers"). This apparent renewed commitment to democracy on the part of the United States broke down in the post-1945 era as colonial wars made "superioridad racial" (383; "racial superiority") key to the assertion of Western power. Within the United States, McCarthyism and the Truman Doctrine, which is often seen as marking the beginning of the Cold War, revived the Fascist notion of "espacio vital" (384; "living space"), which Nazism had framed as *Lebensraum*. Ramírez's rendering of US President Truman's assertion that "every nation must choose between alternative ways of life" ("Truman Doctrine") into a Spanish term that coincides with the translation of the Nazi slogan of *Lebensraum*, makes the language of Truman identical to that of Hitler. Ramírez quotes in translation Truman's original phrase, cited above, but he also, less fairly, encapsulates it as equivalent to *Lebensraum*; he notes that Reagan reprises Truman's habit of attributing the existence of governments opposed by the United States to "several thousand armed men" ("Truman Doctrine").

This leads into a sketch of US interventions in Latin America from the 1940s to the 1970s that evokes familiar touchstones. In response to Ronald Reagan's renewal of the Truman Doctrine in a 1983 speech in which he pledged to rid the Western Hemisphere of foreign ideologies, Ramírez retorts that "las ideas de los pobres siempre han sido exóticas para los poderosos" (*AF*, 387; "the ideas of the poor have always been exotic for the powerful"). He underlines the congruence of tactics and language between Hitler and Reagan, both of whom practised "el asesinato sistemático de trabajadores, dirigentes populares, sacerdotes, religiosas como forma de defender lo que también Hitler creía los valores de occidente, patria, raza, familia, religión" (387; "the systematic murder of workers, grassroots leaders, priests, nuns as a way of defending what Hitler also believed to be the values of the West: country, race, family, religion"). Between Hitler and Reagan there is "una consistencia, una muestra ideológica de continuidad histórica de una línea de pensamiento" ("a consistency, an ideological sample of historical continuity of a line of thought") that is responsible for the fact that in Nicaragua "nos alcanzan ... las llamas de aquel mismo holocausto" (388; "the flames of that same Holocaust ... reach us"). Commenting on United States plans to launch biological warfare and the notorious Reagan "Star Wars" plan to militarize space, Ramírez asks: "¿De dónde vienen estos sueños de exterminio? ¿Quién las ha inspirado? Estos sueños son viejos, los conocemos: Auschwitz, Buchenwald" (389; "Where do these dreams of extermination come from? Who inspired them? These dreams are old, we know them: Auschwitz, Buchenwald"). This analysis of Reaganism's Fascist lineage is rendered more credible by Ramírez's recognition that a large portion of the "pueblo norteamericano" (388; "United States population") retain their allegiance to the ideals of freedom, democracy, and justice. Yet, thanks to Reagan's policies, it is now Nicaragua's "espacio vital" (391; "living space") that is under threat.

This speech, while it bypasses the fact that Reaganism's impact on the US domestic population, however pernicious, was in no way comparable to the impact of Nazism on the diverse peoples of Germany, serves as a reminder that the understanding of Reaganite ideology from a Central American perspective was bound to contextualize US aggression within a global history of aggressive movements. The sum of Ramírez's talks from the first six years of the Revolution provides one of the most vivid records of the thoughts, hopes, and conceptions of nationhood that guided Nicaragua in the early Sandinista years. In "El fascismo sigue vivo," as in earlier essays, Ramírez speaks on behalf of the Nicaraguan people, whom he envisages as a unified social class, aligning nationalism and class analysis. This tactic, developed in "Sandino: clase e ideología," underlies most of these essays and speeches. Four months after delivering "El fascismo sigue vivo," in September 1985, Ramírez began to devote his writing energy to *Castigo Divino*. The speeches of the first half of the decade are instrumental to understanding the themes of the novel.

POISONING CIVIL SOCIETY: *CASTIGO DIVINO*

Ramírez's achievement in completing *Castigo Divino* in less than two years while serving as vice-president is unique in the history of modern literature. Yet he was not the only Sandinista who devoted more of his time to writing as the euphoria of the immediate post-1979 period yielded to the stalemate of the Contra War. The poet Gioconda Belli, having quit her government job, completed her first novel, *La mujer habitada* (*The Inhabited Woman*), which was also published in 1988, and which went on to become the Nicaraguan novel with the highest international sales. *The Inhabited Woman* was translated into a dozen languages; the German sales alone exceeded one million copies. The most successful Sandinista writer of the early 1980s, Comandante Omar Cabezas, whose oral history of his guerrilla education, *La montaña es algo más que una inmensa estepa verde* (1982; *Fire from the Mountain: The Making of a Sandinista*), had become the most popular book ever published in Nicaragua, selling more than 100,000 copies inside the country and many more in foreign editions and in translation, released a bloated, far less successful sequel entitled *Canción de amor para los hombres* (1988; Love Song for Mankind). In 1989 Minister of the Interior Tomás Borge published *La paciente impaciencia* (*The Patient Impatience*), a lyrical memoir that placed a surprisingly strong emphasis on his literary education. In the same year, Ernesto Cardenal published *Cosmic Canticle*.

Yet Borge and Cardenal had been working on their books for many years; both Cardenal and Belli left government service to become full-time writers. Ramírez, by contrast, was a full-time vice-president who wrote for two hours in the early morning, jogged, then devoted ten to twelve hours a day to his vice-presidential duties. His example was intended to inspire other Nicaraguan writers, who sometimes complained that their participation in the Revolution increased their ability to publish their works but placed severe limits on the time available to them to write. Wellinga argues that Ramírez's achievement may have intimidated other writers; he completed a very long novel "a pesar de su abrumador cargo de gobierno. Era como demostrarles a los escritores de que no tenían motivo para quejarse y que si querían podían hacerse el tiempo para escribir, hasta para escribir obras voluminosas" (Wellinga 1994: 144; "despite his overwhelming government duties. It was like proving to writers that they had no reason to complain and that if they wanted to, they could make the time to write, even write voluminous works").

Castigo Divino was not only long; it was a major literary achievement. Even though its international success was curtailed by the cancellation of the German and English editions during the 1991 recession,[13] in the Spanish-speaking world this novel remains Ramírez's most highly regarded, and most frequently reprinted, work. In terms of sheer literary brilliance, the only Spanish American novel of the 1980s that can match it is García Márquez's *El amor en los tiempos del cólera* (1985; *Love in the Time of Cholera*).

Even though writing and politics have often been soulmates, no parallel case exists of a writer who produced a major work of literature while holding high political office, particularly under the extraordinarily demanding conditions created by military assault by a superpower. Two writers from an earlier era in Spanish American history, the essayist Domingo Faustino Sarmiento, who served as president of Argentina from 1868 to 1874, and the novelist Rómulo Gallegos, who was president of Venezuela for a few months in 1948, did not produce substantial works while in office. Between the 1960s and the 1990s, politics in the Dominican Republic was divided between the followers of the poet Joaquín Balaguer and those of the short-story writer Juan Bosch, each of whom enjoyed terms as president; yet neither produced a work comparable to *Castigo Divino*. There is a venerable Spanish American tradition of appointing writers as ambassadors. Beneficiaries of this tradition have included Alfonso Reyes, Pablo Neruda, Octavio Paz, Carlos Fuentes, Antonio Skármeta, and numerous others. However, as Ramírez contends, "la tradición del embajador, yo no la veo muy política. Ésa es otra cosa. Yo estoy hablando del manejo, del uso, del poder" (*UISR*; "the tradition of the ambassador is one that I don't see as very political. That's a different thing. I'm talking about the handling, the use, of power").

Looking beyond Spanish America, the Victorian English novelist Anthony Trollope wrote novels from five to eight in the morning, and directed the British post office the rest of the day; but Trollope, like the nineteenth-century Brazilian novelist Machado de Assis, was not a politician but a high-ranking civil servant (Trollope's sole attempt at seeking elected office was a failure). In the modern era, politicians such as François Mitterand in France and Pierre Trudeau in Canada were accomplished political essayists prior to being elected leaders of their countries, and US President Barack Obama wrote an affecting memoir of his quest for identity before entering electoral politics; but none was a novelist. André Malraux's novels were long behind him when he became minister of culture in Charles de Gaulle's government in France in 1959. Václav Havel had ceased to be a dramatist by 1989, when he was elected the last president of united Czechoslovakia; only after stepping down as first president of the Czech Republic in 2003 did he attempt to write new works for the stage. The cases of Malraux and Havel exemplify cultural capital that has accrued from past literary achievement being brought to bear in the political realm. This is different from a working writer who is also a leader of the nation. It is also different from a leader who is an occasional writer. National leaders such as Mao Zedong in China, Saddam Hussein in Iraq, and Moammar Khaddafi in Libya took advantage of their dictatorial clout to publish poems, novels, and short stories respectively, but none of these figures had literary credibility. The closest parallels to Ramírez may be the 1970s African poet-presidents Léopold Sédar Senghor of Senegal and Agostinho Neto of Angola, who owed their elevation to high office to the anti-colonial struggle. Neto, like Ramírez, held office in a revolution under military siege by forces sponsored by the United States (and apartheid-era South Africa). Though he was a respectable poet, who emerged at a crucial juncture in Angola's history, Neto's literary output was limited to one book of poems; he never wrote a work of international stature such as *Castigo Divino*. Since the end of the Cold War and the onset of more pronounced forms of globalization, the attempts of writers to be elected to executive office, such as that of Mario Vargas Llosa in Peru in 1990 (or that of Ramírez himself in 1996), or that of the Canadian journalist, historian, and novelist Michael Ignatieff in 2011, have ended in defeat. During the post-1990 era, as Ramírez himself posits, the roles of writer and politician have been subjected to a "división de trabajo" (*UISR*; "division of labour").

If *To Bury Our Fathers* was a novel that reflected the aesthetics of the Boom, in *Castigo Divino* Ramírez joined his generational contemporaries in the adoption of a Post-Boom aesthetic of playfulness and humour combined with a satirical approach to the discourses of officialdom. Yet Ramírez's novel is less optimistic than those of Skármeta or Allende; its readability stems from the ominous inevitability with which the Somoza dictatorship encroaches on Nicaraguan society, from the ambiguity that surrounds the enigmatic figure of Oliverio Castañeda, and from the impossibility of being certain that Castañeda committed the murders that are attributed to him. The attitude of the narrator – who, late in the novel, is revealed to be the historical author, Sergio Ramírez – towards this material is rife with paradoxes. *Castigo Divino* is at once a savage, even didactic portrait of a certain Central American bourgeois life of the early 1930s, and a novel that at some points appears to insinuate that reality is ultimately unknowable.

The novel is a rewriting of the poisoning plot of a 1932 Hollywood movie, *Payment Deferred* – which is known in Spanish as *Castigo Divino* – that stars Charles Laughton and Maureen O'Sullivan, and of the historical case of the Guatemalan lawyer Oliverio Castañeda, who was charged with poisoning members of the middle-class Gurdián family in León, who are renamed Contreras in the novel.[14] The narrative strategies, which rely on the arsenal of postmodernism, include reworkings of popular cultural forms such as Hollywood movies and tabloid journalism, burlesques of official documents, contradictory testimonies, the anachronistic insertion of literary and political figures at times when they were not alive, juxtaposed with documentary references to other figures who are rigorously depicted as acting as they did in their historical context, the presentation of competing versions of the same event, and the intrusion of the historical author into the narrative. Through this postmodern stew, Ramírez brings to bear on the feeble, pretentious middle sectors of Nicaraguan society the same analysis that is developed in "Balcanes y volcanes," *El alba de oro*, *Seguimos de frente*, and *Hatful of Tigers*: the obsequious servility of the aspiring middle sectors as the point of origin of foreign domination and dictatorship, the paired trajectories of the Guatemalan and Nicaraguan progressive movements, and the breakdown of unity among the Central American middle classes under the weight of petty localisms.

The novel's action takes place between 18 July 1932 and 31 December 1933. This is the crucial interregnum when the US Marines left the country (on 1 January 1933) after a six-year military occupation, and the bourgeoisie failed to rally to the support of the constitutional norms embodied in the government of President Sacasa, allowing the nation to drift into the hands of the Somoza family. The enraged reaction that the publication of *Castigo Divino* provoked among the Nicaraguan bourgeoisie illustrates that they understood all too well the criticisms that Ramírez was making of their failure. Ramiro Gurdián, a descendant of the family depicted in the novel, who in 1992, as president of COSEP, would attempt to block the Nicaraguan broadcast of the television mini-series of *Castigo Divino*, complained after Ramírez's Managua book-launch party in 1988: "This book is aimed at showing that the traditional bourgeoisie has no moral authority and that the Sandinistas were justified in confiscating our properties and cutting us off from power" (Kinzer 1988).

In spite of its jaundiced tone, this howl of protest may be one of the most astute critical commentaries on the novel. Yet the roots of the book are complex and its many resonances open up multiple possible interpretations. The novel's origins lie deep in Ramírez's past, prior to his development of the social analysis that he expounded in his 1980s essays. The judge who tried the Gurdián poisoning case was Ramírez's mentor Mariano Fiallos Gil. Thirty years later, in the law classes that Ramírez took with Fiallos at UNAN, the Castañeda case was one of the subjects of study. Fiallos planned to write a novel about the case, but died before he could start this project. Ramírez first summarized the Gurdián-Castañeda poisoning case in his 1971 biography of his mentor:

> Castañeda era un guatemalteco que estudiaba Derecho en León, adonde llegó a residir con su esposa Marta. Gozaba de gran estima en la población y frecuentaba a las más importantes familias, con algunas de las

cuales llegó a intimar y a las que envolvió después en la tragedia. El 13 de febrero de 1933, murió misteriosamente su esposa y al quedar solo, la familia de Don Enrique Gurdián Castro lo convidó a vivir con ellos. El 3 de octubre del mismo año murió en circunstancias parecidas Ena Gurdián, hija única del matrimonio y seis días después, Don Enrique. Al ocurrir esta última muerte, Mariano Fiallos decretó el auto de detención de Castañeda por sospechas de asesinato …

Con esta lúgubre historia folletinesca, de envenenamientos misteriosos y truculentas historias de amor que salieron después a relucir en la trama del proceso, se sacudió por casi un año la modorra provincial de León, que tuvo oportunidad de vivir y presenciar lo que solo era antes objeto de las historietas por entrega de fines del siglo XIX. El héroe, como un truco legítimo del folletín, se convirtió de pronto en villano. (*BFM*, 49–50; Castañeda was a Guatemalan who studied law in León, where he came to reside with his wife Marta. He enjoyed high esteem among the population and frequented the most important families, with some of whom he became intimate and whom he later involved in the tragedy. On 13 February 1933, his wife died mysteriously and since he was alone, the family of Don Enrique Guardián Castro invited him to live with them. On 3 October of the same year, Ena Gurdián, the couple's only child, died in similar circumstances, as did Don Enrique six days later. When this last death occurred, Mariano Fiallos issued a warrant for Castañeda's arrest on suspicion of murder …

This gloomy melodramatic story, of mysterious poisonings and gruesome love stories that came to light after in the course of the trial, shook up the sleepy provincial society of León for nearly a year. The city had the opportunity to live and witness what was once only the object of serialized late-19th-century melodramas. The hero, as though in a melodramatic trick, suddenly became a villain.)

In taking over Fiallos's unrealized ambition, Ramírez must contend with the harsh verdict that the judge, a man of classical liberal principles, might have rendered on the Sandinista government led by many of his former students of the *Ventana* generation. As portrayed in the novel, Fiallos denounces the bourgeoisie's collaboration with the consolidation of the dictatorship, and the interference in due legal process by Captain Ortiz of the National Guard, yet in his interrogation of Oliverio Castañeda, the political radical and possible murderer, he maintains a strict distance from the suspect's political engagement. The novel depicts Fiallos with biographical accuracy, even recounting the birth of his first son in June 1933 (*BFM*, 51), and casts him as a pillar of procedural rectitude in a lax, corrupt milieu where civil society is withering before the swelling personalistic authority of Anastasio Somoza García.

Ortiz is also a historical character, who in July 1959 would give the order to open fire on Ramírez and the other UNAN student demonstrators; as with Fiallos, his views and actions are rendered with documentary precision. The same is true of Manolo Cuadra, a well-known pro-Somoza journalist of the period who had fought against Sandino, and whose comments on the Castañeda case provide an accurate reflection of his historical role. Captain Prío and his cronies at the Casa Prío bar, who make a preliminary appearance in *To Bury Our Fathers* and become central characters in *Margarita, How Beautiful the Sea*, are based on historical figures. The captain's real-life existence is underlined at the novel's conclusion, where the historical Sergio Ramírez returns to León in 1986 to interview him about the fate of the men who meet around the "mesa maldita" (*CD*, 16; "table of the damned") to try to disentangle truth from fantasy in nights of beer-fuelled conversation.[15] The two physicians who participate in these debates, staking out opposing positions concerning the scientific evidence presented by the poisoning case, the upper-class, British-descended Dr Juan de Dios Darbishire and his former student, the upwardly mobile mestizo Dr Atanasio Salmerón, represent the novel's mingling of documentary narrative and fiction. Salmerón appears to be fictitious. Darbishire is based on Dr Juan Dervishire, an "excéntrico, por no decir loco" (*VP*, 396; "eccentric, not to say insane") uncle of Ernesto Cardenal. Like the character in the novel, Dervishire was a graduate of the Sorbonne; unlike Ramírez's character, the bachelor Dervishire was alienated from the León bourgeoisie, who ceased consulting him because of his cobwebbed consulting room crammed with bizarre, threatening instruments. By contrast, in the novel the dog-loving, once-widowed, once-separated Darbishire becomes the unimpeachable spokesperson for the bourgeoisie's version of the truth and the leader of religious processions that pass through the streets to urge the citizens not to deviate from God's will.

It is evident from *Biografía Mariano Fiallos* that, from his first encounter with the Castañeda case, Ramírez was aware that it could be recounted only in the style of a "historia folletinesca" ("a melodramatic story"); yet in the novel this sensationalistic tale serves as an entertaining foreground, while in the background the ominous erosion of civil society coincides with a philosophical debate about the nature of truth. One may only speculate as to the origins of this thematic concern, but the ongoing battle being fought in the world's media over the nature of the Sandinista regime must have sharpened Ramírez's awareness of the way in which a single event in Nicaragua could be presented as having dramatically different significance by the *New York Times*, the Reagan White House, the Sandinista newspaper *Barricada*, and dozens of other commentators, each with their own agenda. Similarly, just as the novel's ironic use of the language of legal and administrative documents reflects Ramírez's experience in government, so the disquisition on the difficulty of defining truth almost certainly stems from the mediatization of the Nicaraguan Revolution, in which foreign reporters swarmed through the most remote areas of the country, and local people involved in even minor political incidents would be interviewed by an array of journalists, each pursuing different narratives of the Revolution.

Like *To Bury Our Fathers*, *Castigo Divino* combines a scrupulous respect for the chronology of Nicaraguan history with fictitious characters and names and details altered to suit the story: the historical Gurdián family had one daughter, the fictional Contrerases have two and a son named Carmen. Unlike *To Bury Our Fathers*, *Castigo Divino* disrupts its own literary structures with anachronistic and self-referential intrusions that oblige the reader to consider its artificiality. The most obvious of these intrusions is Ramírez's own appearance as an interviewer at the novel's conclusion. The revelation that the narrator is the historical author is made by stages. From the novel's opening pages it is clear that the reader is dealing with a narrator who draws attention to his own presence, employing turns of phrase such as "como ya vimos," "querido lector," and "de la cual vamos a ocuparnos más adelante" (*CD*, 35, 59, 176; "as we have seen," "dear reader," "with which we will deal later"). The first reference to the narrator's objective identity is oblique: "Tal como el juez Fiallos le confesaría al que esto escribe muchos años después ..." (*CD*, 709; "Just as Judge Fiallos would confess to this writer many years later ..."). The confluence of narrator and historical author is confirmed in the scene in which Captain Prío is interviewed. The narrator refers to "una grabación que el autor le hizo el 17 de octubre de 1986 ..." (*CD*, 735; "a recording that the author made of him on 17 October 1986 ..."). During the interview, Prío addresses the narrator as "hombre Sergio" (*CD*, 738; "My man Sergio"). The last mask drops when the narrator reminisces about his days working as Mariano Fiallos's secretary, when he used to question the rector about the Castañeda case "que me interesaba antes que nada porque el voluminoso expediente podía leerse como una novela, y porque él era el protagonista de esa novela" (*CD*, 740; "which interested me above all because the large file could be read as a novel, and because he was the protagonist of that novel").

This revelation that the fiction we are reading began life as a legal document that resembled a novel (and has now become a novel carpentered together from legal documents both real and invented) arrives during the work's denouement. Other postmodern traits are evident much earlier. The most jarring of these is Ramírez's penchant for naming minor characters after well-known figures, particularly Spanish American writers. The name of the Cuban writer Miguel Barnet (b. 1940) is given to a character – also Cuban – who befriends Oliverio Castañeda. This fictitious Barnet enlists Castañeda in his plan to create an annual encyclopedia that will provide vital statistics on each of the Central American republics. Castañeda is to write the chapter on Nicaragua. Unlike the other anachronistic personages, who appear only fleetingly, Barnet develops into a functioning character, even appearing as a dinner guest in a scene where Castañeda dines with the Contreras family (*CD*, 305). The reading of Castañeda as representative of the revolutionary forces in Central America (which will be explored below) would make this alliance with a Cuban, albeit a quarter-century prior to the Cuban Revolution, a logical connection.

Some of the other anachronisms are also discernible political allusions. After the bodies of Castañeda's wife, Marta Jerez, and Matilde Contreras are exhumed, the report that describes the autopsy procedures notes that "se hizo uso de las técnicas de demostración de J. Kirkpatrick, corregidas por su díscipulo Eagelburger" (*CD*, 453; "the demonstration techniques of J. Kirkpatrick were used, corrected by her disciple Eagelburger"). In the same vein, later techniques for the vivisection and analysis of human remains employ "el método de destilación de E. Abrams" and "los procedimientos de reacción orgánica de Secord y Allen" and "el método North-Singlaub" (*CD*, 471; "the distillation method of E. Abrams"; "the organic reaction procedures of Secord and Allen"; "the North-Singlaub method"). These references to the Reagan administration officials Jeane Kirkpatrick, Lawrence Eagleburger, Elliott Abrams, Richard V. Secord, Charles Allen, Oliver North, and John K. Singlaub, who supplied the ideological justifications and financial support for the Contra War, provide a caustic commentary on their "methods" for assessing the remains of a corpse. In this specific context, Ileana Rodríguez's contention that the bodies of the women killed by Castañeda represent the murdered revolutionary nation, conceived as a female body, has some resonance (Rodríguez 1996: 10–14), even though Rodríguez's analysis of the novel, as will be discussed below, is seriously flawed. The allusions to the Reagan officials also act as a reminder that, for all its ebullient playfulness, *Castigo Divino* is a deadly serious book in which the nation's survival is at stake. The dedication reads: "A los combatientes/ en todos los frentes de Guerra/que han hecho posible este libro" (*CD*, 11; "To the fighters/on all the fronts of the war/who have made this book possible"). Without military struggle, the nation would have already fallen to the enemy and both the imagining and the physical writing of this book would have been impossible.

While some anachronistic allusions may be deduced to have a thematic purpose, others appear gratuitous, or simply distracting. Allusions to Gustave Flaubert's novels *Bouvard et Pécuchet* (1881) (*CD*, 495) and *L'Éducation sentimentale* (1869; *The Sentimental Education*) (*CD*, 507) make some sense since the former is a satire of the bureaucratic mentality and the latter dismantles the conventions of the courtship novel. By contrast, the Guatemalan writer Hugo Cerezo Dardón (1920–2000) appears as Castañeda's probable first murder victim (*CD*, 87) at a period when the historical Cerezo Dardón was an infant; another of Castañeda's suspected victims is "el joven poeta masayés Julio Valle Castillo" (*CD*, 526; "the young poet from Masaya"), who is murdered by Castañeda in January 1930 and whose namesake, a well-known Nicaraguan writer, was born in 1952. Mentions of Ramírez's literary friends, such as the Costa Rican novelist Carmen Naranjo (*CD*, 212) and the Chilean Post-Boom writer Antonio Skármeta (who set his novel *La insurrección* (1982; *The Insurrection*) in León) (*CD*, 679), are simply clever winks. In Kozak Rovero's apt characterization, the sheer variety of styles, schools, and writers alluded to or parodied in the novel "despliega un vasto ejercicio de intertextualidad que asume su carácter distintivo en 'pastiche' de diversos géneros literarios" (Kozak Rovero 2001: 29; "unfurls a vast exercise in intertextuality that takes on its distinctive character in the 'pastiche' of various literary genres").

The notion of pastiche is central to the initial formulation of postmodernism in Jean-François Lyotard's description of the skepticism created by the post-Second World War reconstruction of Western Europe. The rebuilt Europe claimed to have the same history as that which had been reduced to rubble, yet it was a simulacrum, whose visible links to this history had been severed. For Lyotard, the primary consequence of this historical phenomenon was "l'incrédulité à l'égard des métarécits" (Lyotard 1979: 7; "incredulity toward metanarratives" [1984: xxiv]). These "metanarratives," often referred to as "grand narratives," – all-encompassing explanations of life, such as Christianity, Western civilization, or Marxism – lost their ability to explain the world or command unquestioning belief. In Lyotard's conception: "La fonction narrative perd ses foncteurs, le grand héros, les grands périls, les grands périples et le grand but. Elle se disperse en nuages d'éléments langagières" (1979: 7–8; "The narrative function is losing its functors, its great hero, its great dangers, its great voyages, its great goal. It is being dispersed in clouds of narrative language elements" [1984: xxiv]). Words deprived of their historical contexts could generate only pastiche, or art that was opaque and devoid of shared significance. Behind this prognosis lies an assumption of the universal relevance of European history.

Ramírez's postmodernism, by contrast, must be understood as an outgrowth of a Central American history that casts his pastiches as the wrecking ball of certain grand narratives (US Manifest Destiny, Somocista modernization, Nicaraguan bourgeois pretensions) yet, paradoxically, is also the pioneer and promoter of other narratives that offer all-encompassing historical explanations (Sandinismo, the writer's authority as the "Great Tongue" of his people). With reference to the latter point, Kozak Rovero argues that Ramírez incarnates "un escritor que unió las figuras del intelectual y del hombre de acción" ("a writer who unites the figures of intellectual and man of action") but who has witnessed "la caída de las grandes utopías que marcaron el ánimo de tantos intelectuales del continente" ("the fall of the great utopias that defined the outlook of many of the continent's intellectuals") and therefore can no longer aspire to the title of "Gran Lengua de su tribu" (Kozak Rovero 2001: 39; "the Great Tongue of his tribe") defined by Asturias. Though this is true of Ramírez in later years, it does not apply to the period 1985–87, when he was writing *Castigo Divino* and the Sandinista quest for utopia was still underway; even after 1990, as will be argued in chapter 10, Ramírez developed strategies to retain his authority as arbiter of the nation, albeit in more provisional forms.

By the mid-1980s, the Sandinista Revolution, though still promising, was starting to outgrow its first flush of optimism; immersing himself in the liberalism of his mentor, Mariano Fiallos, Ramírez confronted a powerful critique of the radical ideological course that he and his nation had chosen. In writing the novel Fiallos had hoped to write, rather than responding to a finished book by a writer of an older generation, Ramírez was far more aware that he was deliberately "misreading" the intentions of his "mighty, often antagonistic ghosts" than Harold Bloom's theory of influence would allow (Bloom 1973: 26). The resultant questioning may account for some of the subversive, anti-authoritarian elements in the text, where Ramírez appears to be straining against an authority of which he himself forms part.

Uriel Quesada, on the other hand, suggests that anti-authoritarianism is an ingrained characteristic: that, regardless of whether Ramírez has been in government or in opposition, his fiction has always been "un ejercicio constante de resistencia contra el saber oficial" (Quesada 2002: 17; "a constant exercise of resistance against official knowledge"). Yet Ramírez also drafts anachronism, pastiche, and fragmentation into the task of building the nation. The allusions to Miguel Barnet and the members of the Reagan administration are pointedly political; the nods to Naranjo and Skármeta may be read as reinforcing besieged Nicaragua's claims to solidarity on the part of other Central and South Americans. Techniques that in a European context would speak of subversion here become the building blocks of a coherent vision of Nicaraguan history. In a country whose bourgeoisie has not been dramatized to the point of exhaustion since the mid-nineteenth century – a country that, never having had its Honoré de Balzac, then spent the middle of the twentieth century under strict censorship – *Castigo Divino* must assume the challenges of both originality and imitation. The novel – the first in Nicaraguan history in which Somoza can be called by name – must both chart the bourgeoisie and subvert its pretensions. Ramírez's postmodern playfulness is the voice of a country rejoicing in being able to speak of itself with freedom. Peter Ross captures this when he writes:

> The writer can no longer write tragedy because the nation has been redeemed. The past is no longer the same. The bourgeoisie has lost, the dictator has fallen, and the people are in power. Even the writer's public has been transformed. Censorship is over and many more people have learned to read ... The novel set in the past must now take heed of the fact that the past has helped produce the revolution. The injustices of the past ... do not lie in the body politic as deadly cancers that must be excised, but rather exist as medical specimens in jars of formaldehyde on the shelves of history. (Ross 1991: 173)

Ross concentrates on Dr Darbishire's flasks of preserved specimens, and on the preservation of Don Carmen's organs after an autopsy is performed on his body, rather than on the debates between him and Dr Salmerón about the impact of toxins on the body. His suggestion that the Revolution has changed the perception of the past is crucial. *Castigo Divino* describes the onset of Somocismo, but it also foreshadows the dictatorship's overthrow by Sandinismo. Castañeda, the political radical, symbolically murders the bourgeoisie, then faces interrogation for his acts by Fiallos, the principled liberal opponent of dictatorship. This is the most personal, psychologically probing dimension of a novel that presents itself as a broad social canvas with scant autobiographical content.

By writing the novel that Fiallos intended to write, after having rejected Fiallos's liberal positions in favour of Sandinista radicalism, and having broken with the Liberal politics of his own father (who died three years before he began to write this novel), Ramírez is assuming the mantle of male authority, both as writer and revolutionary leader, in a posture that defies his own male mentors and their traditions. The novel's structure reflects his anxieties about assuming a revolutionary form of male authority that is unprecedented in his nation's history. The account of Fiallos's sifting of the evidence of Castañeda's crimes becomes Ramírez's way of interrogating his own radical political trajectory and, at a metatextual level, the anti-bourgeois allegory that he is forging by fictionalizing the Castañeda case.

Fiallos, had he lived, could have been expected to use this material to write a novel with a more centrist political analysis. As if to mitigate these anxieties, the judge is depicted as growing increasingly angry and frustrated with institutional structures as the novel progresses. His mounting disenchantment is calibrated by his three confrontations with Captain Ortiz at pivotal points of the novel. The first time they speak to each other is at the opening of chapter 27, whose title, "Un novel juez entra en acción" ("A Novel Judge Goes into Action"), reflects the judge's status as would-be novelist reduced to a fictional character. Here Ortiz waits for Fiallos at the train station as the latter returns to León in October 1933. The description of Ortiz's dress underlines the National Guard's function as the extension of the US occupation: "vestido de caqui, el sombrero Stetson de los marinos embutido hasta las orejas ... el capitán Ortiz tenía la catadura de las tropas de ocupación que sólo pocos meses atrás habían abandonado el país" (*CD*, 422; "dressed in khaki, the Stetson hat of the Marines pressed over his ears ... Captain Ortiz had the appearance of the occupation troops that had left the country just a few months earlier"). Ortiz's blond hair and blue eyes accentuate his gringoized aura. He invites Fiallos into a Ford convertible left behind by the US Marines, symbolically requesting the judge to join him in the vehicle of neo-colonial authority. Their cordial relationship breaks down as the National Guard interferes in the Castañeda case to skew the evidence and the outcome of the trial.

The judge and the National Guardsman remain on sufficiently good terms in chapter 40, for Ortiz to be "el primero en abrazarlo" (*CD*, 652; "the first to hug him"), when Fiallos celebrates his birthday. Yet in chapter 42, Fiallos turns against Ortiz, criticizing the illegal arrest of Dr Salmerón. Finally, in a scene in chapter 46 that serves as the novel's denouement, positioned between the narrator's flash-forward to the day in 1959 when Ortiz orders the National Guard to fire on the students and the climactic account of Castañeda's death on 24 December 1933, and that links together these two murderous acts for which Ortiz is responsible, Fiallos and Ortiz shout at each other from their respective Fords, which are idling side by side on the street. Both men are contained within the chassis of neo-colonial authority, but Fiallos is bristling against these limitations. Fiallos protests the break-in at his chambers in which the letters that are the case's most vital evidence were stolen; he denounces the subversion of legal norms. After Ortiz accuses Fiallos's assistant, the poet Alí Vanegas (also a historical figure), of being a "bolchevique" (*CD*, 756; "Bolshevik"), Fiallos despairs that the system no longer imposes legal restraints on the actions of the National Guard, who are free to kill Castañeda as they please: "¿Y quién jodido va a detener a esos salvajes si lo quieren matar?" (*CD*, 760; "And who the fuck is going to stop those savages if they want to kill him?"). The last words uttered by Fiallos in the novel, this sentence assuages the historical author's anxieties by implying that if the judge had lived to see the Nicaraguan Revolution, his outrage at Somocismo's disdain for legal norms might have led him to agree with his former students that a powerful extra-legal force was required to counteract the GN's violence; this line, however, offers a mere hint of a countervailing suggestion in a novel in which the preoccupation that the *Ventana* generation has abused the teachings of its mentor is a steady, if submerged, undercurrent.

The novel's pastiches of popular culture are integral to its structure and meaning. The forty-eight chapters are divided into four parts, each of which bears a title that gives instructions, in the imperative, on how to proceed in assembling a file on a criminal case: "Establézcase el cuerpo del delito," "Acumúlense las pruebas" (*CD*, 7, 8; "Establish the corpus delicti," "Accumulate the proofs"). By contrast with this legalistic diction, the language of the chapter titles imitates the tongue-in-cheek sensationalism of the tabloid press. The chapter narrating the death of Oliverio Castañeda's wife is entitled "Oli, Oli, ¿qué me has dado?" ("Oli, Oli, what have you given me?"); the opening chapter of the fourth part of the novel is called: "Escándalo de ribetes insospechados conmueve a la sociedad metropolitana" ("A Scandal with Unsuspected Touches Moves the Society of the Metropolis"). One of the central characters, Rosalío Usulutlán, whose Náhuatl surname announces his mestizo origins, is a tabloid journalist and an outsider in León society. Usulutlán's sensationalistic, pseudo-fictionalized explanation of the deaths of Marta Jerez de Castañeda, Matilde Contreras, and Don Carmen Contreras, which appears as chapter 38, is the catalyst that drives the action towards its conclusion by dividing León society along lines of class and ideology.

The language of official discourse and that of the popular press clash over the course of the narrative, just as the mingling of allusions to high and popular culture was prolonged in *Castigo Divino*'s critical reception: the novel was shortlisted for the Rómulo Gallegos Prize, Latin America's most prestigious literary award, and it won the Dashiell Hammett International Prize for the year's best detective novel. In employing a popular cultural vocabulary in lieu of the Boom-influenced literary allusions and demanding narrative techniques that characterize *To Bury Our Fathers*, Ramírez, as Kozak Rovero argues, rejoins his generational literary cohort: "Los escritores nacidos en la década de los cuarenta viven en medio del auge de la industria cultural de los medios de comunicación de masas y de la influencia norteamericana, razón por la cual las adjustas [*sic*] jerarquías entre baja y alta cultura no tienen para ellos mayor sentido" (38; "Writers born in the decade of the Forties lived amid the boom of mass media culture and United States influence, which is why the strict hierarchies between low and high culture don't have great meaning for them"). *Payment Deferred*, the Hollywood movie that supplies the title, serves as a key (misinterpreted by Usulutlán though understood by Salmerón) to unravelling the poisoning plot. George McMurray sees the film as "a kind of leitmotif referring to the fate of both the defendant Castañeda and the city of León" (McMurray 1990: 156). Yet, while defendant and city receive "divine punishment," the film's plot details, which the habitués of the "mesa maldita" comb through for clues to understanding the Castañeda case, may be more pertinent to the story than this reading allows.

The novel opens with a description, in pseudo-documentary language, of Rosalío Usulutlán leaving the Teatro González after seeing *Payment Deferred*. Rosalío never misses a movie at the González cinema, yet, as the novel is quick to demonstrate, in a Nicaraguan context the enjoyment of US popular culture is tainted by the fact that the country is under occupation by the Marines. When Oliverio Castañeda and his wife arrive in León, the reader is told that they do so "en plena ocupación del país por las tropas de la Marina de Guerra de los Estados Unidos" (*CD*, 19; "in the midst of the occupation of the country by troops of the US Marines"). The implicit criticism of the bourgeoisie for having allowed the public sphere to deteriorate to the point where rabid dogs roam the streets – inspiring the novel's first use of poison – veers into an awareness that the supreme civil authority is a foreign army. The request to allow the city's pharmacies to sell strychnine must be authorized by an American: "Se pide por lo tanto al jefe de Policía, capitán Edward Wayne USMC, que autorice, tal como ya los superiores de la Marina de Guerra lo han hecho loablemente en el pasado, la adquisición de venenos" (*CD*, 19; "A request is therefore made to the Chief of Police, Captain Edward Wayne USMC, to authorize, just as the Marine commanders have commendably done in the past, the acquisition of poisons"). The discreet "therefore" ("por lo tanto") emphasizes the naturalness with which the León bourgeoisie regards US rule, a subservience that prepares the way for their equally sanguine acceptance of the Somoza dictatorship.

The Somoza name appears for the first time when Usulutlán goes to the prison to interview Oliverio Castañeda, who protests the disruption of legal norms that has marked his arrest: "He estado detenido a la orden del señor jefe director de la Guardia Nacional, general Anastasio Somoza. Pero no es sino hasta hoy que se me ha notificado auto de detención por parte de la autoridad competente" (*CD*, 50; "I've been detained on the orders of the director of the National Guard, General Anastasio Somoza. But it was not until today that I was notified of the arrest warrant by the competent authority"). As long as the US Army is present, so are the troops of Augusto César Sandino, who are fighting the occupation. The inauguration of a new railway line is disrupted by "la incursión de una columna sandinista al mando del general Juan Pablo Umanzor" (*CD*, 100; "the incursion of a Sandinista column commanded by General Juan Pablo Umanzor"): a Sandinista leader who would be murdered with Sandino on 21 February 1934. Carmen Contreras Guardia, the Contreras family's son, testifies that Castañeda and his wife Marta first took refuge in the Contreras home because a GN official, who was residing in the same hotel, accused them of being "sospechosos de comunismo y sandinismo" (*CD*, 112; "suspected of Communism and Sandinismo").

Castañeda, the tall, dashing law student who has taken León society by storm, yet whose mien remains ominous since he always wears black mourning garb, suffers the sudden death of his wife, Marta. In an access of sympathy for his solitude, the Contrerases invite him to live with them. In quick succession, Matilde Contreras, the European-educated twenty-one-year-old daughter, and the family's father, Don Carmen Contreras, die of what may be either fever or poisoning. Usulutlán suspects (and will write in his tabloid account in chapter 38), that Castañeda was romantically involved with Matilde, her teenage sister María del Pilar, and their mother, Doña Flor de Contreras. The evidence of the film *Payment Deferred* suggests that this is a misinterpretation, yet the novel offers a cornucopia of contradictory evidence that rules out each thesis offering a solution to the crimes.

One of the novel's first postmodern gestures is an allusion to Ramírez's own fiction that surfaces in the background to the Contreras family: "descendientes remotos del Cid Campeador y emparentados con la Virgen María, según se establece en *Tiempo de fulgor*, se casaran solamente entre ellos" (*CD*, 174; "remote descendants of the Cid Campeador and related to the Virgin Mary, as stated in *Tiempo de fulgor*, they married only among themselves"). Ramírez cites his own first novel as though it were a valid historical source. The reference is contradictory since the Contreras clan is meant to have become extinct at that novel's conclusion. By giving the historical Gurdián family the name Contreras, when many other historical figures retain their real-life names, and insisting that they belong to the same Contreras family which, in his first novel, represents the Conservative quest for exclusivity, purity, and religious devotion, Ramírez resuscitates the Liberal-versus-Conservative sparring of the Nicaraguan past in a novel whose development charts the eclipse of these traditional fissures in the elite by the rift between Somocismo and Sandinismo that is destined to permeate all levels of society. This persistence of the Liberal critique of Conservatism – anachronistic in the post-1979 context – is highlighted by the dominant presence in the novel of Mariano Fiallos, the embodiment of liberal (and, in the 1930s, Liberal) values.

At the close of Ramírez's first novel, the Liberal and Conservative traditions blend in their decadence. In this sense, whether the Contreras family are Conservatives or Liberals is no longer a pressing question. The merged Liberal-Conservative identification inherited from the earlier novel enables the family to stand in for Ramírez's charge, developed in his speeches, that both wings of the elite represent a bourgeoisie that exists on the brink of moral and financial bankruptcy. When Doña Flor de Contreras appeals for Castañeda to be released from prison, she directs her appeal not to Judge Fiallos but to the "jefe director de la Guardia Nacional, general Anastasio Somoza" (*CD*, 117; "National Guard Director General Anastasio Somoza"). This choice illustrates the bourgeoisie's contempt for legal norms and its willingness to recognize the National Guard, rather than the nation's duly constituted institutions, as the supreme source of authority. While Ramírez acknowledges that the legal record strongly suggests that the historical Oliverio Castañeda was guilty of the poisoning charges (Kinzer 1988), he forges a plot that indicts the bourgeoisie for having failed to provide the nation with functioning institutions and a viable public sphere. Dr Darbishire, when considering the possibility that the three victims may have died of fever, says; "¿Quién no es palúdico en este botadero de basura?" (*CD*, 323; "Who doesn't have malaria in this garbage dump?"). Peter Ross provides a succinct summary of the León described by the novel:

> Disease in León is rife, and particularly virulent forms of malaria threaten even the bourgeoisie. Health authorities do little to prevent the spread of malaria. Pools of stagnant water are allowed to lie in the city, flooding is common, and sewage is discharged directly into the streets. Stray dogs roam freely and threaten the inhabitants even in their places of business and their homes. Plans to bring potable water to more people in the city are thwarted due to the rapaciousness of the elite, such as

> Carmen Contreras, who want to increase tariffs to a level which cannot be supported by most people. (Ross 1991: 171)

This disregard for the public sphere depends on a culture that rejects the lessons of the outside world and suffocates difference and debate. In spite of being lionized by the local bourgeoisie, who admire his height, good looks, prowess on the dance floor, erudition, and record of government and diplomatic service in his native Guatemala, Oliverio Castañeda is a threat because he challenges the city's throttled provincialism with a culture of enquiry. His request to Doña Flor de Contreras that she conceal banned books for him is a reminder that literary censorship in Nicaragua did not begin with Somoza but was enforced by the bourgeoisie and the Catholic Church prior to the dictator's rise to power. The fact that Castañeda must ask the Contreras family to hide not only a book by Josef Stalin and one about Sandino but also a tract on the early-twentieth-century fad of theosophy (*CD*, 154) – presumably because Sandino was a follower of this movement – illustrates this obscurantism. Castañeda's sympathy with the Contreras family originates in the fact that both he and Doña Flor are foreigners. Señora de Contreras has remained an outsider in León society for more than twenty-five years because her uninhibited behaviour reflects the more open culture of Costa Rica, where she was born and raised: "Comenzaron a llamarla, de manera despectiva, 'la tica,' y a lo largo de los años no dejaron nunca de verla como extranjera, pese a la alcurnia de sus apellidos" (*CD*, 174; "They began to call her, in a derogatory manner, 'la tica,' and over the years they never ceased to regard her as a foreigner, despite the lineage of her surnames"). By the same token, León society, which finds Castañeda fascinating, turns against him instantly once Usulutlán's article alleges that he has been sleeping with all three Contreras women. This reversal, the opposite of the protective treatment that would be granted to a local family, betrays the petty suspicion of "foreigners" that prevents the formation of the unified Central American identity that Ramírez associates with a progressive polity. Castañeda, a Guatemalan who has lived in Costa Rica and studied in Nicaragua, incarnates this integrated Central Americanness. For this reason, he also embodies the politics of the left; as the novel advances, and Somoza's grip on power tightens, he takes on traits of the Sandinista culture that will overthrow the dictatorship.

An opaque figure who mediates a variety of meanings over the course of the novel, Castañeda is viewed primarily through the stories told about him by others. He is seen directly by the reader only during the interview that he gives to Rosalío Usulutlán from his prison cell – strategically located near the novel's opening – and the official transcripts of his lucid self-defence during his interrogation by Judge Fiallos. He comes to Nicaragua fleeing the dictatorship of Jorge Ubico (1931–44), whose nephew he may have poisoned in Costa Rica. The overthrow of Ubico will usher in the October Revolution governments of 1944–54, whose cultural expression Ramírez analyzed in "Balcanes y volcanes" and with which the cultural flowering that occurred in Sandinista Nicaragua had strong parallels. Ubico's fall and the dethroning of the Somozas epitomize the paired destinies of Nicaragua and Guatemala. The proto-Sandinista identity that Castañeda assumes by the novel's conclusion harmonizes in a single character the differing struggles against the two dictators whose regimes will be replaced by revolutionary governments.

In the context of the 1980s, the name Oliverio Castañeda was politically charged, not only because of the 1930s poisoning case, but also because of the historical Castañeda's great-nephew, Oliverio Castañeda de León (1955–78), a galvanizing public speaker who was elected general secretary of the Guatemalan Asociación de Estudiantes Universitarios (AEU; University Students' Association). After his assassination by paramilitary forces while leaving a Guatemala City park where he had given a speech, this Oliverio Castañeda became one of most frequently evoked martyrs of the Central American left. Arturo Arias dedicated his 1979 book *Ideologías, literatura y sociedad durante la revolución guatemalteca, 1944–1954* "A la memoria del compañero/Oliverio Castañeda/asesinador por las fuerzas fascistas/el 20 de octubre de 1978" (7; "To the memory of compañero/Oliverio Castañeda/murdered by the Fascist forces/on 20 October 20, 1978"). Among the foreign delegations recognized by Ramírez in the speech he gave to formally close the Nicaraguan Literacy Crusade on 23 August 1980 was the Oliverio Castañeda International Brigade (*AO*, 166). The younger Castañeda's bespectacled face often appeared on revolutionary posters.

For Central American readers, then, the name of *Castigo Divino*'s protagonist is a synecdoche for the struggle of the regional left. The character's straddling of the two Central American resistance movements that will usher in decade-long radical nationalist governments is confirmed when, shortly after his arrival in León, this Guatemalan helps to organize a student demonstration against the US occupation of Nicaragua that passes through the streets beneath a banner that reads, "Aquí yace Nicaragua asesinada por la bayoneta yanqui" (*CD*, 154; "Here lies Nicaragua, assassinated by the Yankee bayonet").

The Central American revolutionary culture that Castañeda embodies is by definition one in which literature and activism are indistinguishable from one another and the nation is reconstructed in an emancipated form through writing. Not only does Castañeda read books that are considered politically dangerous, such as those that relate to Sandino and Stalin; he also promotes an adventurous sexual morality when he counsels Matilde, and later her friend Alicia Duquestrada, to read his manuscript copy of the nineteenth-century French illustrated pornographic novel *Gamiani*, whose authorship is attributed to Alfred de Musset.[16] Literature becomes his accomplice in breaking down bourgeois Catholic morality. Authority, in consequence, regards writing, particularly foreign writing, with suspicion: one of the central pieces of evidence against Castañeda in his trial is his ownership of a French treatise on toxicology called *Secretos de la naturaleza* (*CD*, 302; Secrets of Nature), which is suspected of having provided him with his education as a poisoner. Yet his status as a revolutionary is also dependent on the fact that he writes. Inevitably, Castañeda is a poet; above all, though, he plans to write (or rewrite) the contours of the Nicaraguan nation. As the author of the Nicaraguan chapter of a book that will define Central America, he threatens to counter the self-delusion of the bourgeoisie with an unvarnished empirical report on national reality. The title of the book is to be *Nicaragua 1934*, one that is resonant to a later reader since this is the year of Sandino's assassination. In order to write this book, Castañeda proposes to "recorrer las distintas poblaciones del país" (*CD*, 54; "travel through all the different towns of the country"), a plan that recalls Santiago Taleno's traversing and taking possession of the nation in *To Bury Our Fathers*. The fact that this book project is coordinated by a Cuban, Miguel Barnet, and that he and Castañeda "vimos lógico acometer la empresa a partir de [Nicaragua]" (*CD*, 246; "viewed it as logical to begin the project from [Nicaragua]"), may be read as a tongue-in-cheek allusion to the accusations of the Reagan administration that Nicaragua was the base for spreading Cuban-style revolution through Central America. Even though the bourgeoisie does not perceive this book as a menace –Dr Darbishire is aware of it only as "algo así sobre la geografía de Nicaragua" (*CD*, 278; "something about Nicaraguan geography") – literature remains a disruptive force, and the activity of writing is regarded as anti-social and subversive of the norms of respectability.

One of the strongest images in *Castigo Divino* is that of Castañeda writing obsessively during the death of Don Carmen, to the point where he fails to pay attention to what is happening behind his back. Here the act of writing is literally criminalized. The scene may display Castañeda's inhumanity, as some members of León society maintain, but it is also a commentary on the self-absorption implicit in the act of literary creation. The writer may reshape the nation in his work; yet, paradoxically, when he is writing he blots out the suffering of those nearest to him. As the Nicaraguan bourgeoisie, represented by the dim-witted, insular, financially inept, hypocritical, and dishonest Don Carmen, enters its death throes, Castañeda thinks only of the next words he will put on the page. This scene may be interpreted as a self-critical allusion to Ramírez's own decision to spend the morning hours writing a putatively frivolous, sensationalistic novel while the nation of which he is vice-president is being ravaged by the Contras. Castañeda's failure to go to the aid of Don Carmen outrages witnesses and raises the ire of Judge Fiallos, who cannot understand his indifference (hence demonstrating why Fiallos did not succeed in becoming a writer):

> JUEZ: ... Usted, a pocos pasos, continuó escribiendo a máquina, como si nada. Si eran tan amigos, estaba usted faltando a un deber elemental ...
> REO: Debo confesarle que no me di cuenta, tan embebido estaba en el trabajo de copiar los mensajes de pésame recibidos con motivo del deceso de Matilde. En esa tarea ponía tanto empeño y cariño que olvidaba por completo la atención de las demás cosas. (*CD*, 399–400;
> JUDGE: ... You, only a few steps away, continued typing, as if nothing were going on. If you were such good friends, you were remiss in a fundamental duty ...
> DEFENDANT: I must confess that I did not realize, so absorbed I was in the task of copying the messages of condolence received on the occasion of Matilde's death. In this task I put so much commitment and love that I completely forgot to pay attention to other things.)

Castañeda is typing the messages of sympathy received by the family in the wake of Matilde's death into the memorial album he is preparing, to which he himself has already contributed a poem (*CD*, 397). A careful reading of the novel's text suggests that, in addition to his literary commitment, Castañeda may fail to notice what is occurring behind him because he is devastated by Matilde's death, which has struck him as a total surprise.

Readings of *Castigo Divino* that perceive it as a postmodern disquisition on the impossibility of knowing anything – "una meditación sobre la imposibilidad de capturar esa realidad" (Quesada 2002: 23; "a meditation on the impossibility of capturing that reality") marked by "esa inestabilidad que impide la construcción de una verdad" (ibid.: 28; "that instability that prevents the construction of a truth") – take for granted that the thickets of conflicting evidence and Castañeda's own contradictory statements concerning the nature of his relations with the Contreras women render impossible any deciphering of the text. Yet the novel's momentum depends on a meticulously calibrated account of the shifts that occur in the public sphere – both in terms of how governmental institutions function and of the changes in ideological alignments – during the months after the withdrawal of the US Marines. In spite of its postmodern play, *Castigo Divino* is the work of a writer committed to narrating the development of his society. The mystery cannot be cleared up with the clarity of the puzzle-like novels of Agatha Christie and her imitators, and the infinite deferral of the revelation of what happened forms part of the novel's pastiche of the traditional courtroom drama; yet Ramírez provides consistent evidence to suggest the broad outline of events. Like the Boom-influenced *To Bury Our Fathers*, this novel demands an "active reader" who is capable of putting the pieces together.

One of the most important clues, paradoxically yet appropriately, is the film *Payment Deferred*, on which the novel's action is patterned. Ramírez takes historical liberties in order to insert this film into the text: the opening sentence states that Rosalío Usulutlán sees the film on 18 July 1932; in fact, it was not released until 7 November 1932 ("Payment Deferred"). The film's action revolves around William Marble, a London bank clerk played by Charles Laughton, who needs to settle an outstanding bill in order to avoid being fired from his job. When his rich nephew James (Ray Milland), who is visiting from Australia, refuses to lend him money, Marble poisons him, takes his cash, speculates on the stock market with the stolen money, and becomes wealthy. Marble's wife, Annie (Dorothy Peterson), realizes that something is wrong, so Marble sends her and their daughter Winnie (Maureen O'Sullivan) away on a vacation. During their absence, he stumbles into an affair with a woman who works at a local shop. Returning from her vacation a day early, Annie discovers the affair. The daughter, Winnie, begins to associate with wealthy people and runs away with a man. The woman who works at the shop, realizing that the family is now rich, blackmails Marble over their affair. Annie, distraught, commits suicide with the same poison that Marble used to dispatch his nephew. Marble is arrested for her "murder" and sentenced to death. On the day of his execution, he tells his daughter that he did not murder her mother, but that, having got away with murdering his nephew, he is paying a bill that has been deferred.[17]

This moralistic plot, which the film carries over intact from the novel of the same title by C.S. Forester, published in 1926, stems from a middle-class, early-twentieth-century British belief in the universality of cosmic justice. As part of its critique of bourgeois illusion, *Castigo Divino* inverts this ideology, producing a novel that condemns bourgeois collaboration in creating the Somocista society of universal injustice. Castañeda is the harbinger of tens of thousands of Nicaraguans who, over the next forty-five years, will face incarceration and death at the hands of the Somozas. He is lured to León by Flor de Contreras, whom he meets in Costa Rica. An attractive, outgoing woman in her early forties, described by the men of the "mesa maldita" as "más bella que sus dos hijas juntas" (*CD*, 259; "more beautiful than her two daughters put together"), she is bored with life in León, and with her husband, who is both a financial disappointment and her intellectual and cultural inferior (she reads poetry and goes to the theatre alone because "su marido no quería acompañarla" (*CD*, 174; "her husband didn't want to accompany her"). Though she is initially cool and formal in her response to Castañeda's ardour for her, as revealed by a letter that surfaces at the novel's conclusion, which states "una visita suya a nuestra casa, junto con su esposa, no sería incorrecta" (*CD*, 763; "a visit by you [*formal*] to our home, along with your wife, would not be improper"), they develop a complicity, even though they may not become lovers. To hold Castañeda's attention, either because she is his lover and fears this much younger man will stray, or, as the text suggests more strongly, as a substitute for her body because she decides to withhold her favours, Flor concedes Castañeda her teenage daughter María del Pilar, with whom the two of them travel back from Costa Rica, as a sexual conquest.[18]

María del Pilar's account of her outings with Castañeda in San José suggests that their relationship is too fervid to be innocent: "había ido con él a paseos al volcán Irazú y a fincas en Aserrí y en Curridabat; a fiestas en el Club Unión, y a funciones de gala el en Teatro Nacional" (*CD*, 249; "she had gone with him on field trips to the Irazú volcano and to farms in Aserrí and Curridabat, to parties at the Union Club, and gala performances at the National Theatre"). Her refusal to classify their relationship as a "jalencia" (249) – an archaic term for a courtship leading to marriage – even as she praises him to the skies may simply indicate that what has occurred between them does not conform to the chaste bourgeois conception of courtship. However, Castañeda's affair with María del Pilar becomes an encumbrance when, on settling in León, he meets her polished, cultured twenty-one-year-old elder sister, Matilde. Like her mother, Matilde is a sophisticated, independent woman who defies bourgeois convention. According to the rumour-mongers of the "mesa maldita," she has already had at least one lover: at night she "cogía camino para el Cementerio de Guadelupe, en compañía de Noel Robelo. Y si las tumbas conversaran, cuántas cosas te dirían" (*CD*, 129; "took the road to the Guadalupe Cemetery, accompanied by Noel Robelo. And if the tombs could speak, how many things they would tell you"). When she dies, a number of León's young swains rush to her bedside, raising further suspicions.

The first evidence of Castañeda's involvement with the Contreras women in the novel addresses his conundrum. A fragment of a letter from Matilde to Castañeda expresses her uncertainties about what appear to be Castañeda's claims that it is now she, not María del Pilar, whom he loves: "¿Desde cuándo me quiere usted? ¿Y por qué? Me aflige pensar que tal vez no lo pensó lo suficiente y vaya a arrepentirse pronto" (*CD*, 63; "Since when did you [*formal*] start to love me? And why? It pains me to think that perhaps you did not think about it enough and will soon repent"). Castañeda demonstrates his loyalty by poisoning his wife, Marta Jerez, in order to liberate himself – though it is possible that Marta dies of malaria, as originally declared, and is a victim of the bourgeoisie's neglect of the public sphere. Throughout most of the novel, it appears that Castañeda planned to take advantage of his liberty by marrying Matilde, less out of passion for her than out of intellectual companionship and because she is a good match, and, crucially, in order to seal his intimacy with her mother, Flor, with whom he is deeply in love. In his formal testimony, he states that "sostuve relaciones de carácter íntimo con Matilde Contreras, las cuales se iniciaron en diciembre de 1932" (*CD*, 698; "I had intimate relations with Matilde Contreras, which began in December 1932"); their affair, he claims, took place in the cemetery "donde cumplimos en repetidas ocasiones el acto amoroso" (*CD*, 699; "where we carried out on repeated occasions the act of love"). Ironically, this is where Matilde made love with her previous lover. Castañeda contradicts his testimony when he and Dr Salmerón become cell-mates, saying of Matilde that "nunca la toqué" (*CD*, 726; "I never touched her"). Yet the letter to him from Matilde, written in August 1933, which is one of the two letters that Castañeda gives to Dr Salmerón when they share a prison cell (*CD*, 729), and which appears at the novel's close, refutes this denial, as she speaks of a past time when "yo no te conocía ni había sentido el fuego de tu cuerpo" (*CD*, 796; "I did not know you nor had I felt the fire of your body"). These letters also reveal that the language Castañeda uses to address Matilde is far less passionate than that which she directs at him; while she slips into addressing him with the intimate "tú" – in contrast to her earlier letter to him – he uses the formal "usted" to write to her. He closes his letter with the words "Le besa castamente en la frente" ("I kiss you [*formal*] chastely on the forehead") and adds a P.S. where he sends his best wishes to her father (*CD*, 794). She, by contrast, refers to their kisses by writing: "Me hacen falta tus besos, desde que me besaste la primera vez fue mi perdición" (*CD*, 795; "I miss your kisses, since the first time you kissed me I've been a goner").

The catalyst for Matilde's death, whether it be suicide or murder, is Castañeda's dreadful decision to continue his purely physical affair with the teenage María del Pilar after Matilde falls in love with him. Even though he later rescinds his initial statement to the court that he was Matilde's lover, the evidence of her letter suggests that, like Dr Darbishire and the newspaper *El Cronista*, whose obituary describes Matilde's death as a "sueño virginal" (*CD*, 295; "virginal slumber"), he is dissimulating in order to protect her honour. At the same time, from December 1932 to October 1933, he makes regular assignations with María del Pilar. They drive in a black Packard to an abandoned farmhouse, where, after they enter the bedroom where María del Pilar's aunt died of tuberculosis, "chirriaron después los resortes del catre, un ruido como de chicharras" (*CD*, 664; "the springs of the cot would squeal, a noise like crickets"). The image of the youngest member of this respectable family having sex in a decaying house on a cot where her aunt died of a wasting disease conjures up images of bourgeois decay worthy of Thomas Mann.

The death of the most modern, open-minded, and promising member of the family occurs as a direct consequence of this decadence, either because Matilde kills herself, or because María del Pilar kills her sister. In the letter from August 1933, two months prior to her death, Matilde repeatedly tells Castañeda how badly he is hurting her, going so far as to say: "Máteme, sí, si de todos modos muero en vida y no hago más que rezarle a usted como si fuera un santo" (*CD*, 795–6; "Kill me, yes, if in any event I die in life and do no more than pray to you as if you were a saint"). Matilde opposes the family's decision to invite Castañeda to live with them after he becomes a widower on the grounds that "iban a darse muchas habladurías en León sobre las relaciones de Castañeda con su hermana, pues todo el mundo iba a pensar que como ya andaban juntos desde en Costa Rica, juntos volvían" (*CD*, 248; "there will be a lot of gossip in Leon about Castañeda's relations with her sister, since everyone would think that, as they had been together since they met in Costa Rica, they came back together"). It is clear that behind this pretext lies her more urgent concern of denying Castañeda, with whom she has fallen in love, easy access to María del Pilar's body. The night before her death she plays the song "El amor sólo aparece una vez en la vida" ("Love Only Happens Once in a Lifetime") for Castañeda, with unmistakable intent, while María del Pilar seats herself at a distance to observe the scene "con evidente enojo" (*CD*, 310; "with evident anger"). As the astute serving girl Leticia Osorio states in her testimony, on her death bed Matilde cries out: "Mamá, me muero, les pido perdón a las dos. Le pido perdón a usted. Y vos, hermanita, perdóname" (*CD*, 328; "Mama, I'm dying, I apologize to you both. I apologize to you. And you, little sister, forgive me"). The family members censor these lines from their testimony to avoid the scandal of suicide and preserve Matilde's right to be buried in consecrated ground. Even the poisoning thesis is discounted by Dr Darbishire, who claims that "he visto y tratado muchos casos de fiebres palúdicas que degeneran en esa clase de crisis, por lo general mortales. La muerte de mi propia esposa es un ejemplo cabal" (*CD*, 332; "I have seen and treated many cases of malarial fever which degenerate into that sort of crisis, usually fatal. The death of my own wife is a perfect example").

It is only after Don Carmen's death that Castañeda is arrested (over the protests of Doña Flor and María del Pilar). In imitation of the fate of William Marble in *Payment Deferred*, Castañeda is tried and executed for the one murder he certainly did not commit. While the novel leaves open the questions of whether Marta Jerez died of poisoning or fever, and whether Matilde commits suicide, like Annie Marble in the film, or whether María del Pilar kills her out of jealousy after realizing that she cannot compete with her older sister's sophistication, which enables her to engage Castañeda on levels beyond the purely physical, the death of Don Carmen is comparatively unambiguous. Doña Flor virtually incriminates María del Pilar during her testimony. Judge Fiallos, in a rare lapse in his impartiality, allows Flor to testify a second time, amending her original statements. Some of these changes are innocuous, such as her explanation that she tried to prevent the National Guard from arresting Castañeda, not out of love or loyalty, but "por el atropello que significaba llevar a efecto tal cosa en mi domicilio" (*CD*, 405; "for the outrage implicit in such a thing occurring in my home"). She claims that she opposed an autopsy on her husband's body after Castañeda gave her a gory account of what the procedure would entail. On the crucial question of who had access to the quinine pills that Don Carmen was taking for malaria, and which turn out to have been laced with strychnine, she initially says that the box containing the pills "se encontraba bajo llave en un aparador; y que cuando María del Pilar fue por la medicina ... le pidió las llaves, que sólo ella [Flor] guardaba" (*CD*, 401; "was locked in a cupboard, and when Maria del Pilar went for the medicine ... she asked for the keys, that only she [Flor] kept"). Her revised testimony exonerates María del Pilar and indicts Castañeda as having had easy access to the pills.

The text provides sufficient evidence for an "active reader" to discern the outlines of Castañeda's tragic relationship with the Contreras women. Never having recovered from the death of his mother when he was fourteen years old and continuing to wear mourning dress "como constante tributo de duelo por la muerte de su madre" (*CD*, 44; "in eternal tribute to the death of his mother") – even though malevolent whispers claim that his career as poisoner began when he ended her suffering from cancer in a poorly equipped hospital in Chiquimula, Guatemala, by giving her strychnine – he falls desperately in love with Doña Flor. Even when he is in prison and she has turned against him, his eyes appear to mist up when he speaks of her, obliging him to "mirar ... en dirección del piso" (*CD*, 726; "look ... in the direction of the floor"). His Oedipal attachment to this mother-substitute (a repetition of the Oedipal sexuality of Andrés Rosales in *Tiempo de fulgor*) is both highly sexual – his first letter to her contains Freudian puns such as "sueño que en el erecto término coloca usted una corona en que dos rosas frescas la púrpura detona" (*CD*, 762; "I dream that in the erect term you place a crown in which two fresh roses detonate into purple") – and is infused with the unique loyalty of a child to its mother: "El amor sólo aparece una vez en la vida. Tengo para usted, entre mis discos, una canción" (*CD*, 761; "Love only happens once in a lifetime. I have for you, among my records, a song"). María del Pilar's body becomes the bridge between the two lovers. Matilde, having fallen in love with Castañeda, tries to wean him from her younger sister by virtue of her artistic accomplishments; but she misfires with the song "El amor sólo aparece una vez en la vida," failing to realize that when she plays it on the piano to communicate her feelings for him, Castañeda receives it as a homage to his love for Doña Flor. Though Matilde is the best match for the handsome foreigner, she cannot inspire in him the unquestioning devotion he feels for her mother, nor can she prevent him from continuing to sleep with her little sister. Her desperation ends when she either commits suicide or is murdered out of jealousy by María del Pilar. (Castañeda cultivates Matilde's feelings for him, even though Doña Flor remains his true love, because of her "amor sincero" [*CD*, 729; "sincere love"]). The younger sister's determination to have Castañeda for herself, and to protect and defend him, leads her to poison her father. Like William Marble in *Payment Deferred*, Castañeda is being blackmailed as a result of an affair. During his testimony he says of Don Carmen, "cuando murió, en su caja fuerte conservaba trescientos pesos de mi propiedad, que por delicadeza no he reclamado a la familia" (*CD*, 399; "when he died he was keeping in his safe three hundred pesos of my property, which out of courtesy I have not asked the family to return to me"). By seducing a girl who is not of age, Castañeda has committed a crime. It is a measure of Don Carmen's corruption that he is willing to exploit his younger daughter's body in order to shore up his shaky financial position, allowing Castañeda to sleep with her as long as he pays for the privilege.

The reader of *Castigo Divino*, then, is not confronted by an absence of meaning, or an assertion that reality is unknowable, but rather by facts that are susceptible of being read and deciphered. In this environment, the reader must make choices. One may decide that Castañeda murdered his wife, Marta Jerez, or that she died of fever; that Matilde committed suicide, or that her sister poisoned her. These choices have political consequences, like the choices that the characters must make as the novel progresses. The novel's residual Boom faith that texts may be decoded, as Aureliano Babilonia decodes Melquíades's manuscripts at the conclusion of *One Hundred Years of Solitude*, or as an attentive reader may create a coherent chronology of the events of a labyrinthine novel such as Vargas Llosa's *Conversation in The Cathedral*, undergirds the postmodern hijinx.

As in *To Bury Our Fathers*, an Oedipal rage against patriarchy animates the action. Since the novel is set in Liberal León, the Conservative elite is present only through the newspaper *La Nueva Prensa* and the historical figures of the journalist Manolo Cuadra and the paper's editor, Pedro Joaquín Chamorro Zelaya; the focus is on a declining urban bourgeoisie. While Ramírez's speeches of the early 1980s, such as "Sandino: Clase e Ideología," argue that the Liberal and Conservative elites were identical in their self-abasement before occupation and dictatorship, *Castigo Divino* recognizes an implicit difference in its condemnation of the Liberals, who owed their status less to plantation agriculture than to the urban professions that traditionally institutionalize a society. The corrupt, ineffectual patriarchy embodied by Don Carmen is countered by his daughter Matilde. Born to a foreign mother and educated in Europe, she represents the potential for the bourgeoisie to overcome its debilitating provincialism, open itself to the world, and reform and strengthen Nicaraguan society. Matilde's death dooms hopes of reform, just as her father's death signals the end of the illusion of respectable bourgeois society and the recognition of the country's new face as a violent dictatorship. From this point on, the National Guard's increasing interference in the Castañeda trial drives the often ambiguous social relations of the first half of the novel towards a series of binary oppositions, such as those presented by the evidence that surrounds the deaths of Marta Jerez and Matilde Contreras. Characters must choose whether they are for or against the dictatorship; their views of Castañeda become the litmus test for these stances.

The death of Don Carmen, which prompts Castañeda's arrest and the entry of the National Guard into a bourgeois home, a transgression that signals the eclipse of bourgeois authority, is the pivot around which the novel turns. From this point on, the changes in Nicaraguan society accelerate. It is telling that, of the novel's victims, the only one whose corpse is described in detail is Don Carmen. The bodies of Marta and Matilde are exhumed and their remains subjected to scientific tests, yet physical description of their cadavers is displaced by the lengthy debates between Dr Darbishire and Dr Salmerón about whether vestigial strychnine may be detected after a body has been interred. The novel contains no physical description of the women's cadavers similar to that given by the forensic doctor of the patriarch with his body laid bare:

> Despojado por completo de sus ropas y colocado sobre la losa de disección de la morgue ... Se trata de una persona del sexo masculino, de la raza blanca, de una edad aproximada de cincuenta años. No presenta mutilaciones ...
>
> Llevando personalmente la cuchilla, inicié la disección del cadáver, para lo cual tracé una incisión desde la región torácica superior hasta la región abdominal inferior ...
>
> Exploré luego el bazo, comprobando su normalidad ... (*CD*, 431–2; Completely stripped of his clothes and placed on the dissection slab of the morgue ... This is a male, Caucasian, aged about fifty years. No mutilations ...
>
> Personally wielding the knife, I started the dissection of the cadaver, for which I made an incision from the upper thoracic region to the lower abdominal region ...
>
> I then explored the spleen, checking for its normality.)

The description of the vivisection of Don Carmen's corpse, which covers seven paragraphs, stresses his normative role as a white, male authority figure; it concludes with his vital organs being placed in flasks "sin agregárseles ninguna solución preservativa" (*CD*, 433; "without any preservative solution being added to them"). Don Carmen's legacy will rot: bourgeois respectability has no future; one must choose to be with the dictatorship or against it.

The two monitors of this shift in social alliances are the changing attitudes of the citizens of León to Castañeda during his imprisonment, and the debates between Dr Darbishire and Dr Salmerón concerning the nature of reality and the credibility of the actions that are attributed to the prisoner. These are supported by other alterations in patterns of social intercourse, such as the deterioration of the professional relationship between Judge Fiallos and Captain Ortiz, as outlined above. At the beginning of Castañeda's incarceration, he remains the darling of the bourgeoisie. In his interview with Usulutlán, Castañeda thanks Doña Flor because "Ella y María del Pilar han tratado de aligerar con sus atenciones las molestias de mi reclusión en esta celda" (*CD*, 57–8; "She and María del Pilar have tried to ease with their attentions the discomforts of my confinement in this cell"). This pattern is derived from the reaction of the León bourgeoisie to the imprisonment of the historical Oliverio Castañeda. As Abelardo Cuadra, who met Castañeda in jail after being imprisoned for having conspired against Anastasio Somoza, reports in *Hombre del Caribe*, which Ramírez edited, Castañeda "contaba con la simpatía de la alta sociedad de León; perfumes, pañuelos, licores finos había recibido en la prisión" (Cuadra 1977: 175; "had the sympathy of the upper class of León; in prison he received perfumes, scarves, fine liquors"). As the trial proceeds and Doña Flor realizes that she must incriminate Castañeda in order to spare María del Pilar from being convicted, she severs her ties with the prisoner, ceasing to send him food and gifts, and obliges María del Pilar to lie during her testimony. (Even so, María del Pilar's loyalty to Castañeda remains unwavering: at the novel's conclusion [*CD*, 805], it emerges that she has consented to cut her hair to make a false beard that Castañeda may use during his escape.)

At the beginning of the novel's fourth part, in which the nature of the regime that has taken over in the wake of the withdrawal of the US Marines becomes clear, the lines of allegiance alter. The publication of Rosalío Usulutlán's sensationalistic account of the case, in which he asserts that Castañeda was sleeping with all three Contreras women, casts the family into ill repute. Public opinion turns against Doña Flor and María del Pilar; demonstrators attack their house. Manolo Cuadra, of the Conservative newspaper *La Nueva Prensa*, reports of Castañeda that "no hay duda de que el público llano ha comenzado a ponerse abiertamente de su parte, resistiendo a dar crédito a los cargos que se le formulan, como puede verse por la crudeza de las manifestaciones callejeras" (*CD*, 581; "there is no doubt that the general public has begun to side with him, refusing to believe the charges made against him, as shown by the severity of the street demonstrations"). In Kozak Rovero's summation, "el proceso a Castañeda se convierte en un escenario de lucha entre los sectores sociales desfavorecidos … y los grupos influyentes de León" (Rovero 2001: 36; "Castañeda's trial becomes an arena of struggle between socially disadvantaged groups … and the influential groups of León"). While the medical team poisons and buries dogs in clumsy attempts to incriminate Castañeda, the streets of the city are for the first time placed under the control of the National Guard. Later, opponents of the National Guard will sing a pro-Castañeda song, "Ya Oliverio triunfó" (*CD*, 707; "Oliverio has already won"). The about-face of the "general public," which now supports Castañeda as a figure of resistance against the abuses committed by the oppressive new order, and disdains the bourgeoisie, represented by Doña Flor, as corrupt, is foreshadowed by the incremental changes in the debates between the two doctors. Both the novel's first and second parts conclude with discussions between Darbishire and Salmerón; initially about the nature of reality, these arguments become increasingly political.

At the close of Part One, Salmerón insists on the poisoning thesis; Dr Darbishire, in his role as the proponent of bourgeois respectability, rejects it. While their discussion has a toxicological dimension, it ultimately revolves around the difference between Darbishire's conventional perception of reality and the more iconoclastic outlook of his young protégé. Darbishire accuses Salmerón of having filled his head "de esos argumentos de cinematógrafo ... se ve que se contagió usted con el suspense de *Castigo Divino*. Pero la realidad es diferente, colega. En este pueblo nunca pasa nada" (*CD*, 240; "a film-maker's plots ... I can see that you got caught up in the suspense of *Payment Deferred*. But reality is different, my friend. Nothing ever happens in this town"). In a parallel scene that concludes Part Two, the discussion resumes, its philosophical tone shouldered aside by practical political concerns. Darbishire is shocked when Salmerón reveals that he has acted on his suspicions that the deaths are the result of poisoning by informing Captain Ortiz of crucial details and offering to assist the National Guard in its surveillance of the Contreras home. Demonstrating his bourgeois disdain for Guardsmen, and his desire not to taint the reputation of a respectable family, Darbishire reprimands his young colleague: "¿Cómo se le ocurre que va a evitar un crimen involucrando a la soldadesca? ... Y entonces, si ya está usted de acuerdo con la Guardia Nacional, ¿para qué necesita al juez?" (*CD*, 371; "How do you think that involving crude soldiers will prevent a crime? ... And then, if you are already in agreement with the National Guard, why do you need the judge?"). The first of these statements reflects an upper-class prejudice against the social origins of Captain Ortiz and the National Guard: one that Salmerón, as a dark-skinned man of modest background, does not share. The second point, ironically, is one that by the end of the novel will be the property of Darbishire's opponents: that an autonomous paramilitary force must not be allowed to subvert legal norms.

Darbishire's reiteration of the accusation that Salmerón's vision of reality has been distorted by the movies remains jocular, yet in Parts Three and Four of the novel, as the injustices that are being committed become more blatant, the relationship between mentor and protégé deteriorates. Darbishire and Salmerón become competitors, debating their divergent interpretations of the scientific evidence in private correspondence, then in the public forum of opinion articles published in the newspapers. This contest exposes Salmerón to greater and greater danger. As Cosme Manzo of the "mesa maldita" warns Salmerón, Dr Darbishire's statements will be regarded by León society as unimpeachable: "Todo lo que él declare, es carne" (*CD*, 483; "Whatever he says is the truth"). Darbishire, by this point, has adopted an "afán ... confrontativo" (*CD*, 506; "desire ... for confrontation") in his assertion of bourgeois normality; this provokes Salmerón, at the close of chapter 32, to challenge Darbishire in the newspapers (*CD*, 511) on his interpretation of the scientific evidence. The two doctors evolve into apostles of the proto-Somocista and proto-Sandinista tendencies respectively. Darbishire, in spite of his lofty despisal of the lower-class origins of National Guardsmen, aligns himself with them and against Castañeda. Salmerón, initially Castañeda's accuser, comes to realize that he and the alleged poisoner, now the prey of the emerging dictatorship, are on the same side. Once these alignments coalesce, Salmerón is destined to lose. The reversal of the two doctors' positions consolidates the dictatorship. In the chapter that follows that in which Salmerón resolves to debate Darbishire, Captain Ortiz responds to a demand from Judge Fiallos that he observe standard legal procedure with the words: "Yo cumplo órdenes de Managua ... Castañeda está a la orden del general Somoza, y quien decide es él" (*CD*, 515; "I obey orders from Managua ... Castañeda is under the authority of General Somoza, and it's he who decides"). This unvarnished assertion of the rule of the National Guard over the judiciary sets the stage for the concluding section.

It is only at the beginning of Part Four that the positions of Darbishire and Salmerón are transposed. In the wake of the scandal caused by Rosalío Usulutlán's article asserting that all three Contreras women have committed sexual improprieties with Castañeda, the upper class ceases to defend them; their house is defaced with a sign identifying it as a lodging of ill-repute and Doña Flor is reminded that she is a foreigner. Darbishire helps to lead a "Cruzada de Sanidad Moral" (*CD*, 583; "Crusade for Moral Health") through the city. As he does so, in a scene that is emblematic of their divergent fates, Salmerón is called to testify before Judge Fiallos and realizes for the first time that he is in danger. The threat to Salmerón delineates the collapse of the institutions of civil society. The first victim is the free press. The tabloid journalist Rosalío Usulutlán is fired from his job and must skulk around León disguised as a priest. Darbishire is granted the space to rebut Salmerón at length in the pages of *El Centroamericano*. His tone is more circumspect than before as he specifies that "no arguyo ante usted para favorecer a Oliverio Castañeda" (*CD*, 631; "I'm not arguing with you to favour Oliverio Castañeda"). In spite of the fact that he continues to downplay the possibility that poisoning took place in a respectable home, a position that might be taken as exonerating Castañeda, Darbishire bows to the obvious desire of the nation's new authority to see Castañeda condemned. Claiming that Salmerón and Castañeda resemble each other in their penchant for spreading calumnies, Darbishire warns in his article that: "Ya los llegaremos a ver juntos, comiendo en el mismo plato. No olvide el lector esta profecía" (*CD*, 631; "We will yet see them together, eating from the same plate. The reader should not forget this prophecy"). This first intimation that, under the new order, questioning individuals such as Castañeda and Salmerón are destined to share the same fate coincides with the interruption of public discourse.

Salmerón's arrest signifies the definitive breakdown of civil society. Only elite criticism of this event is tolerated. The Conservative opposition newspaper, *La Nueva Prensa*, based in Managua, is able to print a report that is critical of the National Guard: "El conocido galeno fue golpeado y ultrajado al momento de la detención" ("The well-known physician was beaten and insulted at the time of the arrest"); the report goes on to cite a witness who refers to the arrest as "un verdadero salvajismo" (*CD*, 670; "true savagery"). Yet the León papers refuse to publish Salmerón's latest riposte to Darbishire. The fact that Salmerón has been obliged to "hacerla imprimir en hoja suelta" (*CD*, 681; "have it printed on a piece of paper") and have it distributed in the streets indicates that there is no longer a public sphere in which all may participate; the event signals the symbolic birth of the culture of the underground writing that will go on to nurture modern Sandinismo. When Fiallos complains to Captain Ortiz about the unjustified arrest of Salmerón and is told that Ortiz is not available, he issues a statement proclaiming: "La reiterada interferencia de la Guardia Nacional en este proceso es no sólo a todas luces improcedente, sino también ilegal" (*CD*, 674; "The repeated interference of the National Guard in this trial is clearly not only unfair, but also illegal").

This statement, which brings the posture of Fiallos into implicit alignment with those of Usulutlán, Castañeda, and Salmerón, adumbrates the emergence of the concept of "nación como clase"("nation as a class") that is developed by Ramírez in his essays: the moment when all who define themselves as Nicaraguan are grouped in common opposition to an alien force. When Salmerón is obliged to sweep the city's streets as part of a work detail of ordinary convicts, those who profess to be shocked that such a humiliation could be inflicted on a medical doctor soon fall silent. Confirming the new social and political contours, which depend not on the prestige of the bourgeois professional but rather on allegiance or opposition to the National Guard, Dr Darbishire rebuffs entreaties that he appeal to Anastasio Somoza for his former student's release: "¿una petición mía al general Somoza? Ni loco" (*CD*, 684; "a plea from me to General Somoza? No way"). The culmination of this definitive realignment of society occurs when Salmerón, finding himself in a jail cell with a man he despises and regards as a seducer and poisoner of young women, realizes that the two of them are on the same side. When Salmerón speaks of Castañeda's victims, the accused murderer replies: "Las víctimas somos ahora usted y yo" (*CD*, 724; "Now it's you and I who are the victims"). Castañeda suggests that the medical fraternity will obtain Salmerón's freedom; the doctor rejects this prediction, decreeing: "Esos cabrones son los peores" (*CD*, 730; "Those bastards are the worst"). As class privileges lose their ability to protect, the "nation as a class" emerges in Castañeda's escape plan. It depends on a joint effort on the part of Dr Salmerón, the serving woman Salvadora Carvajal, and Castañeda himself, a member of the upper class of another Central America republic. Their alliance offers a distant foreshadowing of the confluence of forces that will unite to bring down Somoza.

The collapse of the institutions of civil society is confirmed by the latter stages of the trial. María del Pilar lies under oath; Leticia Osorio, the young servant who knows the truth, is intimidated and suborned; the Contreras women's love letters to Castañeda, which El Globo Oviedo turns over to the pertinent legal authority, disappear when the National Guard burgles Judge Fiallos's chambers; Oviedo himself is ordered into exile as the Nicaraguan consul in a provincial town in El Salvador; and, as a consequence of these and other disruptions, Captain Prío's "mesa maldita," which represents the essential function of gossip in a free society, is dispersed. By the end of Part Four, the only remaining authority is that of Anastasio Somoza García, as implemented by the National Guard; the only alternative to this power is underground activity, including writing. Any suggestion that bourgeois custom and decency might curb the dictator's power is revealed to be an illusion by Dr Darbishire's complicity, El Globo Oviedo's impotence, and the hypocrisy demonstrated by María del Pilar. As Ramírez wrote of this historical period in his introduction to Abelardo Cuadra's Testimonio, *Hombre del Caribe*: "el dominio personal de Anastasio Somoza García ... comienza por desmantelar las frágiles instituciones políticas tradicionales" (Cuadra 1977: 12; "the personal dominance of Anastasio Somoza García ... begins by dismantling the fragile traditional political institutions"). The bourgeoisie, Ramírez contends, adopting the language of dependency theory, was easy prey because of the way it had been conditioned by the long US military occupation: "su ideología se reduce a servir de cámara de resonancia a la tesis que desde la metrópoli bendicen la intervención como hecho de civilización y progreso" (ibid.: 13; "its ideology is reduced to serving as an echo chamber for the thesis that, from the perspective of the metropolis, blessed the intervention as an act of civilization and progress").

In consequence, postures other than collaboration with the dictatorship or subversive activity become untenable. The outsider stance that had been adopted by Doña Flor, for example, is no longer viable; the social space that Flor occupies at the novel's opening, of being a cosmopolitan foreigner, an independent woman who challenges insular local mores, no longer exists. By the novel's close, Flor is both reviled by the local bourgeoisie and, in self-defence, has fallen into line with bourgeois hypocrisy. Yet the most conspicuous victim of the drive towards a binary society that characterizes the novel's later sections is Judge Fiallos. His position of upholding liberal objectivity and the legal norms and usages of civil society is exposed as merely another form of bourgeois illusion. One may ascribe Bloomian "misreading" to this portrait. Taking over the novel Fiallos intended to write from his position as vice-president of a government in whose radicalism his mentor would have seen a violation of much that he had taught the *Ventana* generation, Ramírez is obliged to create a homage to Fiallos which, at the same time, proves that Fiallos's course of liberal-democratic reform of the dictatorship through the creation of autonomous spaces within society, such as UNAN, was not feasible. The rejection of Fiallos's positions by later radicals is presaged when Castañeda says of him: "es un timorato, igual que todos los demás, que se llaman entre ellos aristócratas" (*CD*, 723; "he's a coward, like all the others who call themselves aristocrats"). In his final, angry confrontation with Captain Ortiz, who twenty-five years later will murder the judge's students, Fiallos is shown as coming into conflict with the National Guard and condemning the force's destruction of civil society. He has no practical answer, however, to the GN's dominance. The principal concession made to him by the text is that he is granted the novel's final word on the moral repercussions of the Castañeda case. Unlike other members of the León bourgeoisie, he recognizes his own responsibility for the tragic events. As the city is drenched in volcanic dust expelled by an eruption of the nearby Cerro Negro (Black Summit) volcano, Fiallos refers to León as "la ciudad castigada por la providencia" (*CD*, 805; "the city punished by providence") and declares: "Llueve fuego y todos pagamos el precio del pecado. Castigo divino" (*CD*, 806; "It's raining fire and we're all paying the price of sin. Divine Punishment").

CASTAÑEDA AS SANDINO, CRITICISM OF *CASTIGO DIVINO*, AND GIOCONDA BELLI'S *THE INHABITED WOMAN*

The event that seals León's moral perdition is the murder of Oliverio Castañeda, shot while trying to escape. The narrator's reflection on his fate epitomizes the novel's persistent refusal to opt for a single truth in favour of obliging the reader to choose: a choice that is not arbitrary or innocent, but that, like the choices made by the novel's characters, has moral consequences: "¿Inocente, culpable? Dejamos estas preguntas al viento" (*CD*, 784; "Innocent? Guilty? We leave these questions to the wind"). This implication that the decision to kill Castañeda is the result of larger political machinations is present from the novel's opening. In his letter to his father, Castañeda attributes his imprisonment to his dissidence from the Ubico regime (*CD*, 79). Captain Ortiz confirms this later, when he confides to Fiallos that "Ubico le mandó un mensaje a Somoza, pidiéndole la cabeza de Castañeda. Le considera su enemigo político" (*CD*, 518–19; "Ubico sent a message to Somoza, asking him for the head of Castañeda. He considers him his political enemy").

The parallel between the two dictatorships whose overthrows will usher in revolutionary governments nourishes the growing association, in the novel's final chapters, of Castañeda with Augusto César Sandino. The extrajudicial murder of Castañeda presages the murder of Sandino, three months later, that will seal Somoza's grip on power. In the final pages, Castañeda's death becomes a quasi-mystical allegory of Sandino's death. During the final obstreperous discussion between Fiallos and Ortiz, the two figures' fates mingle. Fiallos complains of the National Guard: "Deciden exhumar cadáveres, me secuestran testigos, y ahora se roban pruebas del proceso. Ésta es la nueva ley que hay en Nicaragua. La que le van a aplicar a Sandino, de seguro" (*CD*, 755; "They decide to exhume corpses, kidnap witnesses, and now trial evidence has been stolen. This is the new law in Nicaragua. The one they're sure to apply to Sandino"). In the ensuing argument, the names of Castañeda and Sandino become almost interchangeable, to the point where Fiallos must clarify that "Y yo no he estado llevando ningún proceso contra Sandino. Estoy hablando del caso Castañeda" (*CD*, 756; "And I have not been conducting any trial against Sandino. I'm talking about the Castañeda case"). When Castañeda escapes from prison, only to be captured in the home of Salvadora Carvajal in the very moment in which the Christmas Eve religious procession enters the cathedral, he is "disfrazado de comarcano, con sombrero de palma aludo, calzón de manta china y sobrebotas" (*CD*, 774; "disguised as a country bumpkin, with a wide brimmed straw hat, breeches of Chinese cloth and overboots"), an appearance that replicates the rustic garb – particularly the breeches and hat – associated with Sandino. Ortiz later insists that it was necessary to take Castañeda to a "paraje desolado" (*CD*, 775; "isolated spot"). Sandino was murdered at an abandoned Managua airfield; Castañeda is shot at an isolated hippodrome. The sequence that narrates Castañeda's death is presented as an article by the Conservative journalist Manolo Cuadra, written in short, ironic dispatches, each one preceded by a tabloid-style headline. Cuadra's article reflects public skepticism concerning prisoners who are reported as having been "shot while trying to escape": "Medianoche. Cementerio. El prisionero corre. Conocemos esa historia. ¿Quién no la conoce en la desgraciada Nicaragua?" (*CD*, 778; "Midnight. Cemetery. The prisoner runs. We know that story. Who doesn't know it in wretched Nicaragua?"). As Castañeda is shot, sightings of Anastasio Somoza are reported in the city, symbolizing the consolidation of his power and the melding of Castañeda's death with that of Sandino. The lower classes, which have supported Castañeda during his trial, are intimidated: there are no protests and only Dr Salmerón attends Castañeda's burial.

At the burial, Salmerón vows to write a "folletín" (*CD*, 784; "melodrama") about the case. His choice of this popular form, which depends on sensationalism and thrives outside official cultural channels, reinforces the impossibility of expressing dissident views in the public sphere. The apocalyptic rain of volcanic dust that falls on New Year's Eve, predicting that 1934 will be a year of disaster, completes the dismantling of pre-dictatorship society by driving the major characters out of León. Fiallos retreats to his farm in the country; Rosalío Usulutlán, now unemployed and a pariah, "se iba de León, huyendo también de la catástrofe" (*CD*, 807; "left León, also fleeing the catastrophe"). All forms of civil-society organization having dissolved, and all means of dissent having been quashed, the nation and its history may be preserved only in writing. This is the single form of expression that lies not only beyond the control of the National Guard but also beyond the force's comprehension. As Judge Fiallos says of poetry: "de eso los guardias no entienden nada" (*CD*, 756; "the Guardsmen don't understand any of that").

Castigo Divino's multipurpose postmodernism derives from the fact that it must substitute for a variety of books that could not be written during decades of censorship. The author must draw eras together to fill the chasm left by more than four decades of oppression. *Castigo Divino* is simultaneously a version of the novel that Fiallos did not live to write, of Salmerón's unwritten "melodrama," and of the book describing conditions in Nicaragua in 1934 that Castañeda and Barnet are unable to complete; at the same time, it is a mid-1980s Sandinista leader's explication of the history that brought his government to power, presented in an ironic mode that allows doubts, as well as certainties, to filter through its pages. Yet the binary construction that undergirds its playful surface forges a world in which there is no choice but to support Somoza's victims over Somocismo, and, by extension, the Sandinista government over the Contras.[19]

The analysis of this novel that is most widely available in English is that of Ileana Rodríguez in her book *Women, Guerrillas and Love: Understanding War in Central America* (1996). While Rodríguez's larger themes, such as the decade-by-decade erosion of the male revolutionary leader's authority (which will be discussed in chapter 10), are important, her reading of *Castigo Divino*, which pivots on the contention that "dead women ... are available metaphors for the deconstruction of nation-states" (Rodríguez 1996: 5), is not sustainable. She asserts that Castañeda is "accused, prosecuted and condemned for the killing of several women" (ibid.: 10). Even though the text ultimately leaves in serious doubt whether the fictional Castañeda has killed anyone, if one were to take all the deaths that are attributed to him at different points, he is accused of having killed more men – Hugo Cerezo Dardón, Julio Valle Castillo, Rafael Ubico (the Guatemalan dictator's nephew), and Carmen Contreras – than women: Marta Jerez, Matilde Contreras, and possibly his mother. Rodríguez sees *Castigo Divino* and Tomás Borge's *The Patient Impatience* as works that "speak of the perverse 'de-eroticization' of woman, centered around the clinical investigation of her body," and asserts that "death of the state and death – murder or disappearance – of woman occur simultaneously" (ibid.: 4). But she suppresses the fact that the only body whose dissection is described in detail is that of a man, Carmen Contreras, whose innards, the reader infers, are destined to rot. Rodríguez is correct to note that there are references to a stench during the exhumation of the bodies of Marta Jerez and Matilde Contreras, yet her leap from this description to the generalization that "women are putrid" is tendentious and overshoots the available evidence. It is possible to argue that Ramírez's dramatization of the extinction of the weak bourgeoisie of the early 1930s may betray anxieties about the durability of the revolutionary order to which he belongs, yet it is troubling that in order to make this case Rodríguez erases the overwhelming bulk of the novel's action and its highly developed theme of the corruption of the old bourgeoisie. Her substantial chapter that analyzes *Castigo Divino* and Borge's memoir (ibid.: 3–18) does not mention Mariano Fiallos, the novel's central character.

Rodríguez's case that *Castigo Divino* is about the dissolution of the revolutionary state, expressed by converting the female body into an object of disgust, is made feasible only by basic errors in chronology. Her chapter opens with the sentence: "For more than seven years the Sandinistas had refused to talk to the contra leaders" (Rodríguez 1996: 3). She goes on to portray the first negotiations between the Sandinistas and the Contras in "Zapoa [*sic*], a small town in the middle of the Nicaraguan hinterland … the small town, lost in the wilderness" (ibid.: 3–4) as a quasi-perverse relinquishment of the revolutionary state: "the image of the fading agendas of the revolutionary state" (ibid.: 4). To accept their own apostasy, she suggests, Sandinista leaders had to deride the state in the form of woman. Rodríguez does not give the date of the negotiations with the Contras, but her allusion to "seven years" will lead readers familiar with the Nicaraguan Revolution to assume that the negotiations took place roughly seven years after the 1979 triumph, either in 1986 or 1987.

Her argument is based on a succession of misrepresentations. "Zapoa" is called Sapoá. Though small, it is far from "the Nicaraguan hinterland" and is not "in the wilderness," but rather sits on the Pan-American Highway, next to the shore of Lake Nicaragua (Eltringham 2004: 550). The village lies less than four kilometres from the Costa Rican border post at Peñas Blancas, on the Pacific Coast route between the two countries. Peace negotiations were held in Sapoá between 21 and 23 March 1988 (LeoGrande 1998: 536–42). Ramírez's novel, published in 1988 – not 1989, as Rodríguez insists – was written between September 1985 and August 1987; it cannot be a reaction to an event that occurred after it was completed. As the details of its characters and construction illustrate, *Castigo Divino* coheres around the combative Sandinista mentality of the mid-1980s, particularly the critique of the bourgeoisie that had collaborated with the dictatorship, rather than any putative perverse embrace of defeat. Even if the novel had been written after the negotiations, Rodríguez's attribution of a mentality of giving up on the nation to the talks at Sapoá would still be unconvincing since the Sandinistas initiated these talks in order to push the Contras' backs to the wall. As Dario Moreno writes of Sapoá: "The refusal of [the US] Congress to approve additional military aid to the contras created a diplomatic opportunity for the Sandinistas … The contras entered these negotiations in a very weak position. By 1988, after suffering a series of military defeats, they lacked the ability to conduct large-scale military operations. Political defeats had compounded the military losses. Esquipulas II … recognized the legitimacy of the Sandinista regime" (Moreno 1994: 101–2). Contrary to Rodríguez's erroneous characterization, at Sapoá the Sandinista vision of the nation was in a position of strength.

Rodríguez's analysis, which is supported by quotes from English translations of French theorists, notably Michel Foucault, Michel de Certeau, and Roland Barthes, whose translated Parisian assumptions she takes as being thoroughly compatible with Central American history and culture, typifies a cultural studies approach that places European theory at the core of criticism and pays insufficient attention to the work under discussion, or to local history. The crisis of revolutionary masculinity that Rodríguez traces in later chapters of her book is persuasive, but the artistic outcome of this crisis, which peaked in the years after 1990, is an ironic treatment of the male self that, in most cases, results in a softening of misogynist stereotypes rather than an accentuation of them. Rodríguez links the crisis of the male revolutionary's conception of his masculinity to the dilemma of whether he can really represent the peasant masses – what she terms "the collapsing [i.e., merging] of peasantry and the feminine" (Rodríguez 1996: 75). But this crisis of representation is not grounded in masculinity. Of the five ambitious books published by Sandinista leaders in the years 1988 and 1989, the one that clearly evinces a pronounced crisis in relating to the masses is that which was written by a woman.

In Gioconda Belli's novel *The Inhabited Woman*, Nicaragua is called Faguas, Anastasio Somoza Debayle is "El Gran General," his late father is referred to as the founder of the dynasty, and the elite's two social and political formations are known as "Verdes," who resemble Nicaraguan Conservatives, and "Azules," who resemble the Liberals. In spite of these fictionalizations, the context is recognizably that of Nicaragua in the early 1970s. There are references to the case of David Tejada, the Sandinista guerrilla who was supposedly thrown into an active volcano; the protagonist's guerrilla lover, Felipe, shares biographical traits with Eduardo Contreras, who was Belli's lover (though Felipe is the son of a stevedore, while Contreras's father was a wealthy bottler of Coca-Cola).[20] The novel culminates in a recreation of the 1974 Sandinista raid on the Somocista Christmas party. The protagonist, Lavinia, returns to her small country after completing architectural studies in Europe, where she also learned personal independence and sexual emancipation. In order not to be socially or sexually constrained by her assigned role as a debutante from a socialite family, she moves into her late aunt's house rather than live with her parents; she gets a job with an architecture firm. Her discovery of Faguan society, in tandem with her relationship with Felipe, leads her towards a commitment to the guerrillas. Much of the novel concentrates on her battles with revolutionary machismo and her struggle to be accepted by the liberation movement on her own terms, rather than as an adjunct to Felipe. At the same time, Lavinia's commitment stems from abstract ideals and residual Verde (Conservative) resentment of the fact that the rather lower-class Gran General has usurped the levers of power rather than from a tangible engagement with the poor. The extensive critical biography on this popular novel skirts what is arguably its central theme: the difficulty experienced by a member of the Conservative elite in accepting that to join the guerrillas is to exist for the poor.[21]

This lapse, like Rodríguez's unsustainable reading of *Castigo Divino*, is the product of a critical culture that places a high premium on questions of racial and gender identity yet too often ignores social class, a central concern of Belli's novel. Descended in part from upper-middle-class immigrants from northern Italy who arrived in Nicaragua in the early twentieth century, Belli is also the great-granddaughter of the sister of Conservative strongman General Emiliano Chamorro. The first experience that shapes Lavinia's political consciousness in the novel is her memory of a massacre that occurs after the Verde candidate is defrauded out of the presidency by the Gran General. Based on the events of 22 January 1967, when the defeated Conservative candidate Fernando Agüero called on the people to rise against the dictator, this scene concludes when "las radios anunciarion que el candidato Verde y sus colaboradores se habían refugiado en un hotel y solicitado la protección del embajador norteamericano" (Belli 1988: 22; "the radio stations announced that the Green candidate and his collaborators had taken refuge in a hotel and had requested protection of the United States ambassador" [Belli 1994: 23]). It is telling that the novel presents the thwarting of Conservative ambitions, rather than the oppression of the poor, as the motivation for the first conversions of young people to "la lucha armada" (Belli 1988: 23; "armed struggle" [Belli 1994: 23]).

The life of Lavinia's family revolves around "the Social Club," whose members guard their aristocratic lineages with ferocity:

> Ser admitido en el club era todo un procedimiento. No sólo se requería el dinero para pagar la cuantiosa suma de ingreso, era necesario pasar el escrutinio de la Directiva del Club. Se reunían y discutían largamente el pedegrí de los solicitantes. Votaban con bolas negras y bolas blancas. Ni siquiera los altos mandos del Gran General eran admitidos. La mayor parte de la aristocracia era Verde, El partido Azul del Gran General y sus miembros eran considerados "chusma", "guardias sin educación", "nuevos ricos". Al menos en la vida social, los Verdes conservaban el poder. (Belli 1988: 155; To be admitted into the club was a long procedure. Not only did you have to have the money to pay the high membership fee, you also had to pass the scrutiny of the club's board of directors. They met and discussed the "pedigrees" of the applicants at length. They voted with black and white balls. Not even upper echelons of the Great General were admitted. The majority of the aristocrats were "Green." The "Blue" party, which was the Great General's, and its

> members, were considered "low class," "uneducated policemen," "nouveau riche." At least on the social level, the "Greens" were still in control. [Belli 1994: 185])

Though the tone is droll, the feelings of Conservative social superiority are unmistakable. Later, the reader learns that, in the alternative social club established by the Gran General for members of his inner circle, the debutantes who are presented "no eran bonitos ... morenitas, pelito lacio, sin gracia" (Belli 1988: 215; "weren't really very pretty ... brown-skinned, straight hair, not very graceful" [Belli 1994: 257]). These words are spoken by the wife of one of the dictator's generals, yet, even as Lavinia establishes a mystical relationship with a tree in her garden that contains the spirit of a Náhuat warrior woman who died fighting against the Spanish conquistadors five hundred years earlier, her relationship with the brown-skinned poor who are the Náhuats' descendants and whom she aspires to represent after joining the liberation movement remains conflicted. When Lavinia accompanies her maid, who has had a life-threatening back-alley abortion, to a public hospital, she lavishes her attention on the difference between her own elegant white feet and the rough brown feet of the young woman opposite her: "Pies morenos. Ásperos. Las uñas exhibían un esmalte casi púrpura descascarado, viejo. Venas protuberantes" (Belli 1988: 149; "Brown feet. Rough. The nails had old, flaking polish, almost violet. The veins protruded" [Belli 1994: 178]). This confrontation with brownness, working-class taste in nail polish, and premature varicose veins provokes a crisis in Lavinia's sense of what Rodríguez terms "the ontologies and epistemologies of being and existing for the *campesino* masses" (Rodríguez 1996: 70). Lavinia's crisis is more acute than any described by Ramírez or Borge in part because, as a woman, she cannot deflect her doubts by immersing herself in an inherited masculine mythology of heroic guerrilla struggle. Yet the key factor in her greater discomfort with the masses is social class: where Borge and Ramírez grew up as brown-skinned men from modest rural backgrounds, Lavinia reflects the dilemma of her creator, a white, upper-class Conservative. Here the nation is not a woman – at least not a contemporary woman. The crisis Lavinia faces is that:

> Ella se había comprometido a luchar por los derechos de los pies toscos, pensó, a ser una de ellos, a sentir en carne propia las injusticias cometidas contra ellos. Esa gente era el *pueblo* del que hablaba el programa del Movimiento. Y, sin embargo, allí, junto a ellos en la sala de emergencia sucia y oscura del hospital, un abismo los separaba. La imagen de los

> pies no podía ser más elocuente. Sus miradas de desconfianza. Nunca la aceptarían, pensó Lavinia. (Belli 1988: 150; She had pledged she would fight for the owners of those rough feet, she thought. Join them. Be one of them. Feel the injustices committed against them in her own flesh. These were the "people" the Movement's program referred to. And yet here, being with them in the dark, dingy emergency room of the hospital, an abyss separated them. The image of their feet couldn't be more eloquent. And their distrustful glances. They'd never accept her, Lavinia thought. [Belli 1994: 178])

While the way in which the narrator draws attention to the "rough feet" as an "image" is overly obvious, the scene crystallizes Lavinia's predicament. She attempts to find common ground with less privileged women, but her efforts are not successful. Her moment of epiphany, when she resolves to commit herself to improving her country even if this means sacrificing her life, does not spring from a connection with living compatriots, but rather from her becoming "inhabited" by the spirit of the Náhuat warrior woman who has taken up residence in the tree in her garden. Hence her engagement is less with the problematic, untrusting masses, than with a landscape:

> Bien valía la pena morir por esa belleza, pensó. Morir tan sólo para tener este instante: el sueño del día en que aquel pasaje realmente les perteneciera a todos. Esa imagen resumía su noción de patria, fue con la que soñó cuando estuvo al otro lado del océano. Por este paisaje podía comprender los sueños descabellados del Movimiento. (Belli 1988: 294; It was well worth it to die for that beauty, she thought. To die just to have this instant, this dream of the day when that landscape would truly belong to everyone. This landscape was hers, her idea of homeland; this is what she had dreamed of when she found herself on the other side of the ocean. This landscape made the most outlandish dreams of the Movement understandable. [Belli 1994: 348–9])

The fact that the narration needs to resort to magic realist trickery – Lavinia absorbs the ancient warrior woman's spirit when she eats an orange from the tree – to inveigle the protagonist into aligning herself with the crazed dreams of the "Movement" –the novel's stand-in for the FSLN – confirms that identification with the masses is an intractable problem for a Conservative with minimal exposure to working-class or peasant life. Lavinia commits herself to a landscape, not a people.[22] Even more telling is the way in which Belli rewrites the outcome of the Christmas party raid.

Where the historical action was a successful collaboration between the upper-class Eduardo Contreras and Germán Pomares, who was from a poor rural family, in *The Inhabited Woman* the two upper-class guerrillas, Lavinia and Pablito, her childhood acquaintance from the Social Club, die, while the guerrillas from poor backgrounds survive. The clear implication is that the Verdes will not belong to the revolutionary nation. Belli's pessimism is at odds with the large number of Conservatives who were serving in the Sandinista government at the time she wrote this novel; yet it is also a reminder that revolutionary society depended on the integration of proletarian rebels, renegade Conservative aristocrats, and radicalized Liberals into a common national project. Official imagery rarely gendered the nation as either female (as in Rodríguez's view of *Castigo Divino*) or male (the stance that is implicit in Belli's decision to give Felipe, whose dead body opens the way for her to join the raid, a working-class background). Rather, in the vaguely Marxist vocabulary, influenced by dependency-theory notions of metropolis and periphery, that Ramírez had developed in his essays and speeches, the nation became a single social class. This integrationist vision, pitted against a consciousness of the weakness and subservience of earlier twentieth-century Nicaraguan bourgeoisies, is the consistent theme of the books Ramírez wrote during his years as vice-president. His response to the negotiations with the Contras in Sapoá in early 1988 was not to abandon the nation but to follow the completed *Castigo Divino* with a work of total commitment to the Revolution.

The final volume in which Ramírez was involved during these years, a Testimonio entitled *La marca del Zorro: hazañas del comandante Francisco Rivera Quintero contadas a Sergio Ramírez* (1989; The Mark of Zorro: Deeds of Comandante Francisco Rivera Quintero told to Sergio Ramírez), was based on seventeen hours of videotaped interviews with a Sandinista comandante of peasant extraction, undertaken in September 1988. In direct contrast to the double versions of events that characterize *Castigo Divino*, this work emphasized that "la veracidad de los hechos permanence intocada a lo largo de la narración porque se trata de un testimonio vivo, sin mácula de adornos o acomodos" (Ramírez 1989: 13; "the veracity of the facts remains untouched throughout the narrative because it is a living testimony, without a taint of ornaments or compromises"). Rivera and Ramírez were awarded the Carlos Fonseca Order by the Sandinista National Directorate for creating this book.

The pairing of *Castigo Divino* and *La marca del Zorro* expresses the duality between the cosmopolitan artist and the committed political activist that had been present since the beginning of Ramírez's career; yet the two books have more in common than at first may appear to be the case. The novel demolishes the old bourgeoisie; the Testimonio forges the unified revolutionary nation where people of different class backgrounds work together. Though *La marca del Zorro* did not enjoy the huge popularity of Omar Cabezas's *Fire from the Mountain*, it contains vivid and touching scenes. Perhaps the most moving of these concerns the revolutionary comradeship between Rivera, who grew up as one of ten children of a washerwoman on the destitute outskirts of Estelí, and Claudia Chamorro, a tall, blonde young guerrilla from the Conservative elite. Known to her comrades as La Yanka, due to her gringo physique, Chamorro is initially dismissed by Rivera as an alienated rich girl; yet, when they are separated from their *compañeros*, and must survive alone together in the bush while being pursued by the National Guard, Rivera comes to respect Chamorro's physical courage and ethic of self-sacrifice. On 9 January 1977 (Ramírez 1989: 129–31), Chamorro died covering Rivera's escape as the National Guard closed in on them. Like Lavinia in *The Inhabited Woman*, this upper-class young woman gave her life so that the peasantry could live. In the Testimonio, however, the abyss between the social classes that torments Belli is healed by the peasant guerrilla's respect for and acceptance of the upper-class woman who has shared his hardships and sacrificed for the cause. The concept of the nation as a unified social class depended on the development of shared experiences and belief systems among upper- and lower-class Nicaraguans. During the years of the Revolution, the creation of a harmonized vision of the cosmos capable of encompassing these disparate experiences of dictatorship and revolutionary struggle, and of expressing Nicaraguan culture's twin debts to indigenous and European sources, was the central focus of the poetry written by Ernesto Cardenal.

8

Cardenal: The Revolutionary Poet (1969–89)

HYBRIDIZING THE AMERICAS: THE INDIAN POEMS

Cardenal published the first version of *Homenaje a los indios americanos* (Homage to the American Indians), the product of a more than a decade's reflection, in 1969; expanded editions appeared in 1970 and 1972.[1] In the Gethsemani monastery in 1957 or 1958 he had begun reading "los primeros libros de espiritualidad indígena, facilitados por Merton, que los pedía prestados a algunas bibliotecas; libros algo especializados y de poca divulgación" (*VP*, 193; "the first books of indigenous spirituality, provided by Merton, that he borrowed from some libraries; books that were somewhat specialized and of limited circulation"). At this time, before the widespread rediscovery of indigenous American cultures of the 1960s and 1970s gave birth to an extensive popular literature on the subject, such interests were regarded as arcane. As Cardenal writes of Thomas Merton's decisive influence:

> Siendo él un norteamericano, un gringo, y yo un latinoamericano, fue él quien me descubrió el valor de los indios. Porque yo desconocía el valor de nuestras culturas indígenas, tal vez no tanto en teoría pero sí en la práctica. Y no sólo yo sino los demás escritores latinoamericanos. ¿Quién de ellos ha ido a buscar el contacto con las tribus indígenas, teniendo tantas en nuestra América? Una cosa es admirar los grandes monumentos arqueológicos, y otra considerar que esas son culturas vivas que aún pueden influenciarnos. La poesía, la cosmovisión, la sabiduría, el misticismo de nuestros indios eran ignorados por los escritores (no los investigadores indigenistas) tal vez sólo con la excepción del novelista José María Arguedas, que se crió entre los indios. (*VP* 192; He being an American, a gringo, and I a Latin American, it was he who

Ernesto Cardenal reads the New Testament to Sandinista guerrillas, rural Nicaragua, 1978 (courtesy of Pedro Meyer and Zone Zero)

revealed to me the value of the Indians. For I was unaware of the value of our indigenous cultures, perhaps not so much in theory but in practice. And not only I but all the other Latin American writers. Who among them went to seek contact with Indian tribes, of which there are so many in our America? It's one thing to admire the great archaeological monuments, and another to consider that these are living cultures that can still influence us. The poetry, the worldview, the wisdom, the mysticism of our Indians were ignored by writers (not by researchers of indigenous cultures) maybe with the sole exception of the novelist José María Arguedas, who grew up among the Indians.)

Cardenal's study of indigenous cultures coincided with, and informed, the years of his religious training: indigenous spirituality suffused his concept of divine harmony and nourished the mysticism of his later verse. His emphasis on the status of indigenous cultures as "living cultures" did not mean, though, that he concentrated primarily on the contemporary living conditions of indigenous people, but rather that he absorbed indigenous histories and mythologies into a hybridized conception of the history of the Americas. This focus is evident when he describes the continuation of his indigenous research after his move to the seminary in Colombia: "En las vacaciones del seminario me estuve yendo a Bogotá a sumergirme en la biblioteca del Museo Etnográfico, riquísimo en cuanto a indios, y la mayor parte de lo que he sabido de los indios, y que tanto me ha servido después para mi poesía, lo saqué de allí" (*IE*, 39; "During vacations at the Seminary, I went to Bogotá to immerse myself in the library of the Ethnographic Museum, which was very rich in Indian materials, and most of what I have learned about the Indians, and that has served me so much for my poetry since then, I took from there").

After following up this archival research with interviews with indigenous leaders and visits to communities in Colombia and Panama whose religious belief systems he had read about, Cardenal began publishing newspaper articles about indigenous cultures, concentrating on the harmony between their religious beliefs and the organization of their societies. Merton, to whom he sent clippings of these articles, replied: "Yo no me he olvidado de los indios y todo lo que significan para nosotros dos" (*IE*, 41; "I have not forgotten the Indians and all that they mean to the two of us"). Cardenal's engagement with indigenous cultures offered him a way of sustaining his relationship with Merton in the face of their physical separation. The connection to Merton also shaped his contextualization of indigenous cultures as a heritage shared by the two Americas: "La gran unión de las dos Américas no podrá darse si no es enraizada en lo indígena" (*IE*, 41; "The great union of the two Americas cannot take place if it is not rooted in indigenous culture").

In rewriting his newspaper articles as poems throughout the 1960s, Cardenal was forging a verse counterpart to what Ángel Rama, drawing on the work of the Cuban sociologist Fernando Ortiz, described as "transculturación narrativa" (Rama 1982: 209–29; "narrative transculturation"): the creation of Latin American myths through the incorporation of elements of indigenous, rural, or African-derived cultural formations into fiction written in styles influenced by the international avant-garde.[2] But where prose works such as Miguel Ángel Asturias's *Men of Maize* (1949), Arguedas's *Los ríos profundos* (1958; *Deep Rivers*), or Augusto Roa Bastos's *Hijo de hombre* (1960; *Son of Man*) drew on indigenous sources to poeticize an all-inclusive national mythology of Peru, Guatemala, or Paraguay, Cardenal's poems presented indigenous cultures in a bi-continental context as a prelapsarian common heritage of the fallen, materialistic world of a vast American territory (including that of the United States) twice conquered: by sixteenth-century European colonization and by twentieth-century commercial imperialism. The overt influence of US poetry, from Whitman to Pound to Merton, on Cardenal's art, which became occluded only as the Sandinista struggle intensified in the mid-1970s, contributes to this adoption of a pan-American, rather than a Nicaraguan, optic. Cardenal's long absence from Nicaragua during the years when he was beginning to write these poems also may have contributed to his omission of the indigenous cultures of Nicaragua's Atlantic Coast and northern highlands from *Homenaje a los indios americanos*. Even though he and Merton had considered establishing a religious retreat on the Corn Islands, Cardenal's heightened awareness of the indigenous predecessors of contemporary Americans did not naturally embrace the cultures of his own country: his education in indigenous matters having taken place abroad, his vision of Nicaragua remained that of a man from Granada.

Nicaragua receives only passing mention in *Homenaje a los indios americanos*, in a few scattered references to the Somoza dictatorship. Like *Marilyn Monroe and Other Poems*, *Homenaje* consists of an extended critique of modern materialism. It is a far more successful book than *Marilyn Monroe* because, rather than belabouring the problem, it unveils misunderstood cultural riches that offer a possible solution. The use of the indigenous world as a counterpoint makes Cardenal's critique of materialism concrete and highly effective. Young Latin American intellectuals received the book as a revelation. Roberto Bolaño recalled finding it "muy superior en algunos aspectos al *Canto general* de Neruda" (Bolaño 2004: 168; "much better in some respects than Neruda's *Canto General*"). According to Jeffrey Gould: "Ernesto Cardenal's poetry inspired a generation of progressive students and intellectuals, sensitizing them to the indigenous roots of the rural poor ... His Indian poems used pre-Columbian themes both to ennoble the indigenous roots of contemporary Latin American society and to adumbrate a more egalitarian and less materialistic society" (Gould 1998: 245–6).

Like the novelists of transculturation identified by Rama, Cardenal yokes autochthonous material to literary techniques influenced by the international avant-garde – particularly, in this case, Ezra Pound – to forge Panamerican myths. The kinship with the novelists of transculturation is enhanced by the poems' narrative texture. As in *Zero Hour* and *The Doubtful Strait*, the use of narrative enables Cardenal to assimilate a diversity of sources into an Exteriorist collage. The fact that relatively few writings survive from the pre-Columbian cultures results in textual surfaces that are more discreet imbrications than are the pages of *The Doubtful Strait*. Nevertheless, as Greg Dawes stresses, "in employing this narrative technique, which harks back to epic poetry, Cardenal is able to cite the conquistadors' chronicles as well as historical sources" (Dawes 1993: 77). The confluence of different sources creates a poetic voice of multiple resonances. In García-Antezana's pithy summary, Cardenal's voice, "es simultáneamente una *voz* individual, la *voz* del pueblo y la *voz* del profeta. En su identidad colectiva latinoamericana, se remonta al principio de la historia, denuncia el presente de *caos* social, económico y político, y profetiza el *orden* y la armonía, la invulnerabilidad de las culturas americanas" (García-Antezana 1995: 389; emphasis in original; "it is simultaneously an individual voice, the *voice* of the people and the *voice* of the prophet. In its Latin American collective identity, it dates back to the beginning of history, it denounces the present of social, economic and political *chaos*, and prophesies the *order* and harmony, the invulnerability of American cultures").

Opening in early-twentieth-century Panama, in indigenous resistance to the construction of the Panama Canal, the initial conduit of foreign imperialism in twentieth-century Central America, the collection delves into ancient Peru and Colombia. It places its greatest emphasis on the indigenous cultures of Mesoamerica and the territory of the present-day United States. The book's lengthy gestation over more than a decade, during which Cardenal's ideology underwent a dramatic transformation, means that, while all of the poems present indigenous cultures as a harmonious alternative to the disorder and materialism of the present, some are more overtly socialist than others.

The collection contains one of Cardenal's most widely anthologized poems: his evocation of the Inca Empire of the central Andes, "Economía de Tahuantinsuyu" ("Economy of the Tahuantinsuyu"), written in 1965. The opening lines – "No tuvieron dinero/el oro era para hacer la lagartija"

(*HIA*, 37; "They had no currency/gold was used to fashion the lizard" [*GOLD*, 375]) – establish the Utopian treatment of indigenous cultures as untainted by capitalism. The poem's 247 lines have a reiterative structure that describes the American Utopia and its destruction. Then, at the point where the poem might end, having dramatized the contrast between conditions before and after the European incursion, the narrator returns to the pre-Colombian Utopia to subject it to more thorough scrutiny, discovering some of its drawbacks as well as its advantages, before moving on to an all-out assault on the irrationality that characterizes a capitalist economy. The narrator's skeptical second look at the Inca Empire (Tahuantinsuyu, or "four horizons" in the Quechua language of the Andes) strengthens the case for the Utopian alternative and renders more convincing the condemnation of contemporary materialism. The title is ironic, since, by Western definitions, the Tahuantinsuyu had no economy; as this method of social organization is demonstrated to be superior to that of modern capitalism, the word "economy" acquires a scornful resonance, its mere use becoming evidence of materialist corruption. The opening itemization of the advantages of the Incas' cashless society culminates in the crucial issue of myth making: "Y se comía 2 veces por día en todo el Imperio/Y no fueron los financistas/ los creadores de sus mitos" (38; "And they ate twice a day throughout the Empire/Financiers were not/the creators of their myths" [*GOLD*, 377]). Wresting society's myth-making potential from the capitalist class is of equal importance to feeding the masses, even though the initial contrast adumbrated between the Inca Empire and its successor, the Peru that was a colony of Spain, is dramatized in economic terms, as the gold of the opening lines is reduced to ingots:

> Después fue saqueado el oro de los templos del Sol
> y puesto a circular en lingotes
>   con las iniciales de Pizarro
> La moneda trajo los impuestos
> y con la Colonia aparecieron los primeros mendigos
> (38; Later the gold was stolen from the temples of the Sun/and went into circulation in ingots/with Pizarro's initials/Money brought taxes/and the first beggars appeared with colonial times. [*GOLD*, 377])

The advent of a Western economy – even though the economy of the Spain that conquered the Andes was a composite of late feudal and early capitalist forms (Stein and Stein 1970: 3–27) – is inseparable from the appearance of beggars.

Not only does the Incas' intricate social organization unravel with colonization, but so, too, do their finely wrought works of engineering: "las carreteras están rotas/ las tierras secas como momias" (38; "the roads are broken up/lands as dry as mummies" [*GOLD*, 377]). The image of "mummies," which becomes a central axis of the poem's structure, appears first in this portrait of the collapse of Incan society. The mummies, which contain life in desiccated form, become a counterpoint to the Spaniards' ingots, which are barren. The introduction of this image serves the important role of initiating the poem's reconsideration of the Tahuantinsuyu, in its strengths and its drawbacks, through contrasts with contemporary forms of social organization. The repetition of the opening line "They had no currency" prefaces a detailed evocation of Incan full-employment policy: "trabajaban los cojos los mancos los ancianos / ni había ociosos desocupados / se daba de comer al que no podía trabajar" (39; "the lame the maimed the old worked / there were neither lazy nor idle men / whoever could not work would be fed" [*GOLD*, 379]). Cardenal contrasts the dignified industriousness and charitable generosity that characterized indigenous society during this Utopian past with the centuries since the conquest, during which the indigenous individual

> ... no ha hecho sino pensar ...
> indiferente a los rascacielos
> a la Alianza para el Progreso
> *¿Pensar?* Quién sabe
> El constructor de Macchu Picchu
> en casa de cartón
> y latas de Avena Quaker.
>
> (39; ... has done nothing but think ... / indifferent to skyscrapers / to the Alliance for Progress / To Think? Who knows? / The architect of Macchu Picchu / in houses of cardboard / and Quaker Oats boxes. [*GOLD*, 379])

Names of commercial brands and contemporary political organizations, their juxtaposition epitomizing modern economic and political power, emphasize the degrading treatment of people with a heritage of work and hard-earned achievement. These avatars of capitalist power are trivialized by the indigenous individual's indifference to them as his mind remains trained on the superior life of the past.

The indigenous person's immobile separation from contemporary activity, dismissed as indolence by the Latin American bourgeoisie, is construed by Cardenal as evidence of a panoptic vision. Repeated images of tourists photographing the miserable state to which Andean people have been reduced culminate in a description of an indigenous person who watches "al turista /

pegado a sus amos" (40; "at the tourist/close to its owners" [*GOLD*, 381]), underlining the confluence of local and foreign forces of domination. The stanza that follows opens with the repetition of "They did not have money" (*GOLD*, 381) and lists the many vices obviated by pre-Columbian Andean society as a consequence of the absence of money: there is no slavery, minimal environmental degradation thanks to prohibitions on mercury mining and harvesting pearls, land for all, festivals and corn beer at the opening of the planting season, legislation to protect llamas, vicuñas, and domestic animals; and the difficult terrain of the Andes is made accessible through a rigorously maintained network of roads and bridges. In an expression of patriarchy without materialism, each new Inca inherits his father's throne but not his material possessions. This summary leads the narrator to evaluate the Tahuantinsuyu as an expression of socialism in practice:

"EL IMPERIO SOCIALISTA DE LOS INCAS"
Neruda: no hubo libertad
        sino seguridad social
Y no todo fue perfecto en en "Paraíso Incaico"
Censuraron la historia por nudos
Moteles gratis en las carreteras
        sin la libertad de viajar
¿Y las purgas de Atahualpa?
        ¿El grito del exiliado
en la selva amazónica?
          El Inca era dios
  era Stalin
    (Ninguna oposición tolerada)
Los cantores sólo cantaron la historia oficial
Amaru Tupac fue borrado de la lista de los reyes.

(41–2; "THE SOCIALIST EMPIRE OF THE INCAS" /Neruda: there was no freedom/but social security/And not everything was perfect in the "Inca Paradise"/They censured history, as told by knots/Free motels on the roads/without freedom to travel/And the purges of Atahualpa?/The scream of the exile/in the Amazonian forest?/The Inca was god/was Stalin/(No opposition was tolerated)/Singers sang only the official history/Amaru Tupac was erased from the list of kings. [*GOLD*, 383])

This description challenges Pablo Neruda's evocation of Inca society in "Las Alturas de Macchu Picchu" ("The Heights of Macchu Picchu"). Neruda's concern is for the state of "man," by which he means, above all, the individual proletarian: "Piedra en la piedra, el hombre, dónde estuvo?" (Neruda 1950: 137; "Stone upon stone, and man, where was he?" [Neruda 1991: 38]). In contrast to Cardenal, Neruda views the Inca Empire not as an example of socialism but as a place whose undeniable grandeur and significance for modern Latin Americans was, nevertheless, built on the exploitation of the workers: "Macchu Picchu, pusiste/piedra en la piedra, y en la base, harapos?" (Neruda 1950: 138; "Macchu Picchu, did you put/stone upon stone and, at the base, tatters?" [Neruda 1991: 39]). The poem's soaring conclusion envisages a fusion of Latin American identity across the centuries through the conjoined prisms of cultural inheritance and proletarian solidarity: "Sube a nacer conmigo, hermano" (Neruda 1950: 140; "Rise up to be born with me, my brother" [Neruda 1991: 41]).

By contrast, Cardenal, who had not visited Peru at this point, and whose work is based on substantial research into Andean history (while Neruda's poem originated as a lyrical response to a 1943 visit to the then little-known ruins of Machu Picchu), concentrates on the political edifice of Incan society. The discrepancy is highly revealing, as it illustrates the origins of Cardenal's socialism in a concern for the organization of societies at a national or transnational level. Neruda's exploration of the treatment of the workers corresponds to Cardenal's denunciation of the lack of freedom of speech, the exile of political dissidents, and the distortion of national history by the regime in power. Compared to Neruda's themes, these preoccupations may seem almost bourgeois; yet they flow naturally from Cardenal's experiences of the Somoza dictatorship in Nicaragua, a country with more peasants than proletarians. Where Neruda, the ally of the Chilean miners and their Communist unions, seeks working men, Cardenal, the dissident descendant of a suppressed agrarian-based Catholic elite, approves of the fact that the peasants owned their land, and is astonished that the Inca Empire's "national" myths were not forged by businessmen or economists, and, crucially, that religion and politics were indistinguishable from one another:

> Pero sus mitos
>   no de economistas!
> La verdad religiosa
>   y la verdad política
> eran para el pueblo una misma verdad
> Una economía *con* religión
> (*HIA*, 42; But their myths/were not those of the economists!/Religious truth/and political truth/were one and the same to the people/ economics with religion. [*GOLD*, 383])

The privilege of living in a society whose myths are not dictated by economists, and where economic policy is an outgrowth of religious values, the poem suggests, may be worth the cost of some restrictions on individual liberty. Or, at least, it may provide a model of how to move towards a society that contains the virtues of the Inca Empire but not its faults.

The existence of this mythic past affects the present as both an inspiration and a reproof. The resonances of the Incan model surpass questions of social organization, exemplified by Cardenal's contrast of the Incas' "Imperio de *ayllus/ayllus* de familias trabajadoras" (42; "Empire of ayllus/ayllus of working families" [*GOLD*, 385]) with the feudal "latifundios" (42; "latifundia" [*GOLD*, 385]) of contemporary Latin America, positing a Utopian fusion of the political and spiritual realms that would become far more explicit in his poetry of the 1970s and 1980s: "el universo entero todo un gran *ayllu*" (42; "the entire universe one great Ayllu" [*GOLD*, 385]). An evocation of the Incas' sacred vision of the earth as "Madre de todos" (42; "Mother of all" [*GOLD*, 385]) foreshadows the poem's closing assault, much of it expressed in block capitals, on the irrationality of modern capitalism. In an Exteriorist vein, mock newspaper headlines describe a world where the stock market panics at bountiful harvests that threaten to drive down prices, linking such behaviour to an evocation of the sadness of the contemporary Andean landscape that displays a lyricism unusual in Cardenal's work. This landscape initiates a series of rhetorical questions about whether a return to the efficient infrastructure and greater social equality of the Inca Empire is possible: "¿Y el universo del indio volverá a ser un *ayllu*?" (*HIA*, 44; "And will the universe of the Indian become an Ayllu again?" [*GOLD*, 387]). Though the question is posed in terms of the well-being of indigenous peoples, the implications of this question involve all people in the Americas. The final stanza underlines the potential for rebirth: "en la vitrina del Museo/la momia aún aprieta en su mano seca/ su saquito de granos" (44; "in the glass case of the Museum/the mummy still squeezes her pouch of grain/in her dry hand" [*GOLD*, 387]). The seeds of rebirth – both specifically of indigenous cultures and of an American world that has strayed from its Utopian vocation – are contained in this manifestation of the indigenous past.

Other poems in the collection culminate in similar juxtapositions of ancient grandeur and modern technology in order to pose the question of the lost world's potential return. "Las ciudades perdidas" ("Lost Cities"), for example, which was the first of these poems written by Cardenal, in Cuernavaca in 1959 (Pring-Mill 1992: 57), concludes with: "y el avión de la Pan American vuela sobre la pirámide/¿Pero volverá algún día los pasados katunes?" (16; "and a plane of the Pan American Airlines flies over the pyramid./But will the past katuns ever come back?" [*GOLD*, 331]). The opening poem, "Nele de Kantule" ("Nele of Cantule"), which was the first indigenous poem Cardenal completed after his arrival in Colombia (Pring-Mill 1992: 60), concludes with an image of how the coastline of the Cuna people of Panama looks "si uno pasa por allí en avión" (*HIA*, 13; "if one flies by in a plane" [*GOLD*, 47]). In various poems the tension between indigenous and occidental conceptions of civilization are epitomized by the presence of a significant or sacred indigenous object in a modern museum. "Mayapán," the second-longest poem in the book, opens with a description of stelae from this post-classical alliance of Yucatán Mayan city-states on display in the Carnegie Institution. Like "Economy of the Tahuantinsuyu," "Mayapán" evokes an indigenous culture – in this case that of the classical and post-classical Maya – as a reproach to the present: the dictatorial politics and cultural poverty of the Maya in their post-classical decadence are equated with present-day dictatorships and the ersatz culture of "anuncios de gasolineras en una carretera de Texas" (*HIA*, 29; "gas-station signs on a Texas highway" [*GOLD*, 341]). This poem has aged less well than "Economy of the Tahuantinsuyu" owing to dramatic advances in Mayan archaeology. Following the now debunked theories of Sylvanus G. Morley and J. Eric S. Thompson (Coe 1999a: 123–44), Cardenal portrays Mayan ruins such as Copán, Yaxchilán, and Tikal as "no Commercial Centers/sino centros ceremoniales, Ceremonial Centers/las filas de estelas y estelas, no/neón, no anuncios comerciales" (27; "not Commercial Centers/but ceremonial centers, Ceremonial Centers/rows of stelae and stelae, not/neon, not commercial adds" [*GOLD*, 337]). We now know that these places were not "ceremonial centres" that lay vacant for most of the year, filling only on religious occasions, as mid-twentieth-century archaeologists believed, but rather bustling cities not unlike our own, with all the attendant problems of overcrowding, pollution, and commercialism. The stelae that serve as the central image of "Mayapán" were not "poemas en las piedras" (27; "poems on stones" [*GOLD*, 337]). Since the deciphering of Mayan script in the mid-1980s, it has become evident that these stelae vaunted the ruling monarch's power and recited his version of the city-state's history (Coe 1999b: 103).

The most complete exposition of Cardenal's engagement with indigenous cultures in order to refine the relationship between poetry, national history, and political commitment appears in "Netzahualcóyotl." The longest poem in *Homenaje a los indios americanos*, at 541 lines, it explores the life and policies of the Aztec poet-emperor (1402–72), who had already been alluded to in "Cantares mexicanos I" ("Mexican Songs I"). Belonging to the final group of poems that Cardenal wrote for the book, it was published in the Mexican journal *Comunidad* (Community) in June 1968 (Pring-Mill 1992: 65). The depiction of Netzahualcóyotl as an insurgent guerrilla-poet of pacifist leanings who concentrates opposition to a dictatorship in an alternative community, and whose ethos he succeeds in converting into that of the nation, echoes Cardenal's project in Solentiname. The style is less Exteriorist than usual in Cardenal's work, in part because of the paucity of surviving documents related to the subject's life; the imbricated texts are limited to quotes attributed to the emperor, and a few words in Náhuatl. Cardenal draws the contours of the biography in such a way as to elide discrepancies between his own position and that of the emperor – such as the fact that, unlike other Aztec emperors, Netzahualcóyotl was not ethnically Mexica, the dominant people of Mexico's Central Valley, but came from a minority culture. Netzahualcóyotl's opposition to the Aztec "dictatorship," which originated in tribal divisions (in his youth his home city had been razed by the Aztecs) is here portrayed as being primarily ideological: "Derrocó tiranos y juntas militares/Con los sacrificios humanos no. No/estaba de acuerdo./No era ésa su religión" (*HIA*, 67; "He overthrew tyrants and military juntas/As for human sacrifices, no. He/did not approve./That was not his religion" [*GOLD*, 217]).

Cardenal's allegiance to Gandhian principles of non-violence influences this depiction; yet his growing sympathy for armed struggle is evident in the characterization of the period of the emperor's life when the destruction of his home obliged him to flee as "sus años de guerrillero en las montañas" (66; "his guerrilla years in the mountains" [*GOLD*, 215]). Netzahualcóyotl recaptured his home at the head of a vast military alliance that fielded an army of more than one hundred thousand warriors, yet Cardenal consistently portrays him as a guerrilla, an underdog, and an outsider, and also as a "democrat," in phrases such as "Un Estadista-poeta, cuando había democracia en Texcoco" (*HIA*, 67; "A Poet-Statesman, when there was democracy in Texcoco" [*GOLD*, 217]). As Pring-Mill observes, such phrases are revealing of Cardenal's conception of democracy: "Cardenal has a somewhat 'two-tiered' view of an ideal world in which, while everyone should have the opportunity to realize his full potential (and the humblest campesino has unrecognized gifts), the upper tier consists of those who have already done so and now use their talents in the service of the *pueblo* in a mildly paternalistic way" (Pring-Mill 1992: 67). The extraordinary artistic vibrancy of the court in Texcoco founded by Netzahualcóyotl – particularly in the areas of architecture and poetry, of which the emperor himself was the most talented exponent – was matched by egalitarian gestures such as opening the granaries to the poor at times of food shortages and building durable aqueducts to channel water from the mountains for the use of ordinary people; yet this microcosmic city-state, whose ethos later expanded to encompass that of the entire Aztec Empire, was not a democracy. The emperor's distaste for human sacrifice (though not for the death penalty) and his devotion to literary enthusiasms, in contrast to the totalitarian tendencies that, prior to his ascent to power, reigned on the opposite shore of the lake, in the Aztec capital of Tenochititlán – "En Tenochititlán, Itzcóatl el títere de Tlacaélel / está quemando libros" (*HIA*, 75; "In Tenochititlan, Itzcóatl, puppet of Tlacaélel / is burning books" [*GOLD*, 231]) – were the product of an enlightened dictatorship. The poem suggests that Cardenal's experiences among the peasants of Solentiname have confirmed, rather than called into question, his Granada Conservative ideas about the civilizing role of a cultured elite. This elite, characterized by self-abnegating monastic devotion to the good of the populace, acts as a political and artistic vanguard.

Like Cardenal, Netzahualcóyotl abstains from marriage to serve art and the people: "Y a los 40 sin casarse / Coyote Hambriento sin muchacha en las noches" (*HIA*, 69; "And at 40 and unmarried / Hungry Coyote with no girl at night" [*GOLD*, 221]). Historical evidence suggests that Netzahualcóyotl and his circle preferred "homosexual rites" (Brotherston 1975: 12) to the company of young women. If Cardenal is aware of this fact, he is not comfortable evoking it, though he does describe the poet-emperor's circle as a zone of male camaraderie. His depiction of the emperor's life, acquaintances, and foes generates a litany of names in which not a single woman appears. In this way, Texcoco society resembles those of the Colegio Centroamericano, Gethsemani, Cuernavaca, and La Ceja, where Cardenal had lived entirely among men, and even Solentiname, where the majority of his young protégés were male. The overt homosexuality of Aztec warrior culture, however, clashes with the ritualized sublimation that governs the male communities of Catholicism. Cardenal's portrait of Netzahualcóyotl as the fifteenth-century equivalent of a modern priest-poet entails a stealthy "Catholicization" of the Aztec's life.

In certain details, the parallels between Texcoco and Solentiname cross the line into overt anachronism. The most widely discussed example is a description of the arrival of poets and artists at Netzahualcóyotl's palace, replete with a wealth of authentic period details, which is interrupted by the statement: "Y el Rey va de sala en sala vestido en blue-jean / inspeccionando las obras" (*HIA*, 71; "And the King goes from room to room wearing blue-jeans / inspecting the work" [*GOLD*, 223]). Borgeson views this reference to the fifteenth-century poet as "una manera de ligarlo simbólicamente, y desde su remota realidad temporal, a actividades y situaciones que hoy son tan vigentes como entonces" (Borgeson 1984: 174; "a way to symbolically link him, from his remote temporal reality, to activities and situations that are as valid today as they were then"). While the reference to the emperor wearing bluejeans claims Netzahualcóyotl for the people, and, as Borgeson suggests, for a cultural continuum in which the indigenous civilizations of the past merge with the artistic vanguard of the present, this reference, like that to the emperor's failure to marry, is also patently autobiographical. Having adopted bluejeans and the *cotona* as his uniform in Solentiname, Cardenal employs this device to posit himself and his community as the inheritors of Texcoco's artistically nourished egalitarianism. The allusion contains an element of prophecy, insinuating that Solentiname culture will expand to encompass that of Nicaragua, as the culture of Texcoco expanded to become the official culture of the Aztec Empire – and, by extension, that Cardenal himself may become the Netzahualcóyotl of the new Nicaragua. In an ironic vein, Pring-Mill notes that "except for that principle of Non-Violence (an ideal which Cardenal dropped about 1970), this Texcocan court-circle bears a quite remarkable resemblance to the Sandinista directorate of *comandante*-poets: men with a middle-class background and a good education, determined to give all citizens the right to come up to their level, within the framework of an egalitarian constitution" (Pring-Mill 1992: 67).

Pring-Mill's observation underscores Solentiname's importance in forging the Sandinista ethos: if Netzahualcóyotl, as described in the poem, is recognizable as a harbinger of the archetype of the poetry-loving Sandinista comandante, this attests to Cardenal's influence in forming the Sandinista ethos; in this sense, Sandinista Nicaragua of 1979–90 *did* represent an expansion of the Solentiname microcosm. Even in this poem, Cardenal portrays the society of poets as one characterized by the self-discipline necessary to effect social change, stressing of Netzahualcóyotl and his circle: "No bebían pulque ni comían hongos. No eran bohemios" (*HIA*, 73; "They neither drank pulque nor ate mushrooms./They were not bohemians" [*GOLD*, 227]). Poetry, like religion and politics, demands self-control. In a further anachronism, Cardenal ideologizes Texcoco culture by counterpointing its humanism with the bloodthirsty zeal for human sacrifices of "los nazi-aztecas" (*HIA*, 79; "the Nazi-Aztecs" [*GOLD*, 237]). Here Texcoco becomes the explicit opponent of a totalitarianism which is seen as stemming from the absence of cultural openness.[3] In a reference to Huitzilopochtli, the most bloodthirsty of Aztec gods, who demanded incessant human sacrifices, Cardenal alludes to "Los hijos-de-la-chingada huitzilopochtlistas" (*HIA*, 68; "The huitzillopochtlist sons of bitches" [*GOLD*, 219]). The adjectival phrase, a very vulgar colloquialism used by Mexicans to refer in a derogatory vein to their racial origins in the concubinage or rape of Náhuat women by Castilian men, belongs to modern Mexico. By attributing it to fifteenth-century followers of an unforgiving Aztec god, Cardenal suggests an equivalency between times and places in which violence springs from self-hatred and a failure to perceive "Las flores de las cosas" (69; "the flowers of things" [*GOLD*, 219]), an image that incarnates Netzahualcóyotl's appreciation of beauty and deity. The anachronistic reference to racial mixing has the effect of denying the fears of inferiority that are sometimes associated with *mestizaje*: if "hijos-de-la-chingada" existed prior to the Spaniards' arrival, then mixed blood is not the source of Spanish American political or economic "underdevelopment," as positivist discourses imply.

The image of a flowering tree that evokes Netzahualcóyotl's enlightenment and poetic vocation is the vehicle for a further intermingling of centuries. While the depiction of the emperor in bluejeans, with its provocative assertion of Netzahualcóyotl's contemporary relevance, has attracted much critical attention, the poem's structure has passed relatively unnoticed. In writing of Cardenal's effort to suffuse the present with the indigenous past, García-Antezana observes: "Las imágenes de la *resurreción* y de la *intemporalidad* son recurrentes en el mito americano evocado en su poesía" (García-Antezana 1995: 399; emphasis in original; "The images of the *resurrection* and *timelessness* recur in the American myth evoked in his poetry"). In "Netzahualcóyotl" the transit between past and present is anchored in the poem's architecture in an overt form by the voice of a first-person narrator from the modern world who returns to tour the emperor-poet's court. In contrast to the non-dramatized poetic speaker of "Economy of the Tahuantinsuyu" and other poems in the collection, this narrator realizes the desire to make the journey between the present and the indigenous past. His odyssey enables him to express openly – although not necessarily to greater emotional effect – a nostalgia that is merely implied, albeit very strongly, in the other poems.

"Netzahualcóyotl" uses a frame structure in which the opening and closing stanzas are spoken from the perspective of the modern world and the intervening fifteen pages constitute a journey through the past. The opening line speaks of rebirth: "El árbol está brotando flores/en *Tamoanchan*" (*HIA*, 66; "The Blossoming Tree is in bloom/in *Tamoanchan*" [*GOLD*, 215]). The italicized reference is to a mountain ridge in Mexico's Central Valley that is identified as the location of a "felled tree" (Brotherston 1992: 106). In Aztec mythology, this location was an important stopping-off point on the journey from Aztlan, the Aztecs' supposed place of origin in northwestern Mexico, to Tenochititlán, where they founded their empire. The budding of flowers in this spot defined by a tree that has been cut down promises rebirth while the reference to the "Blossoming Tree" that evokes Netzahualcóyotl and his community of poets represents a transcription of the Náhuatl term for poetry: *in xochitl in cuicatl*, or "flower song" (ibid.: 342). The poem's narrator seeks the community of fifteenth-century Texcoco poets: "Y digo: 'Aquí sin duda viven.' Y oigo su canto florido/como si estuviera dialogando la montaña" (*HIA*, 66; "And I say: 'They surely live here.' I hear the blossoming song/as if the mountain were talking" [*GOLD*, 215]). The rhythms of poetry, audible in the natural sounds of birds and wildlife, and the sight of vivid colours, alert the first-person narrator to the persistence, and enduring presence, of Netzahualcóyotl's legacy. A glimpse of a quetzal bird that is portrayed as the reincarnation of the emperor-poet "cantando cantos floridos en el Árbol Florido" (*HIA*, 66; "singing blossoming songs in the Blossoming Tree" [*GOLD*, 215]) serves as the vehicle of his return to the Texcoco court.

First-person verbs return at the poem's conclusion, where the narrator, who identifies himself as a poet, wrestles with the metaphysical dilemma of whether Netzahualcóyotl's return is possible: "Yo cantor lloro al recordar a Netzahualcóyotl/Oh Netzahualcóyotl/nadie vive 2 veces" (*HIA*, 81; "I, singer, cry when remembering Netzahualcóyotl/O Netzahualcóyotl/nobody lives twice" [*GOLD*, 241]). The emperor-poet, who ordered that his death be marked by extravagant parties rather than traditional mourning, responds by enquiring across the ages about the fate of his native region: "¿Cómo quedó la tierra de Acolhuacan?" (*HIA*, 81; "How is the land of Acolhuacan now?" [*GOLD*, 241]). The question confirms the narrator's supposition that he has located the spirits of the Texcoco poetry circle, causing him to repeat the statement made at the poem's opening: "aquí sin duda viven" (*HIA*, 81; "they live here, there is no doubt" [*GOLD*, 243]). The quetzal bird, and its accompanying "aves canoras" (*HIA*, 81; "musical birds" [*GOLD*, 243]), usher him into the Tierra Florida, an image that combines a vision of the wisdom of the indigenous civilizations of the Americas with an evocation of the realm of poetry. This leads to a moment of revelation: "Allí vi al fin las flores y los cantos" (*HIA*, 82; "There I finally saw the flowers and the songs" [*GOLD*, 243]). In this instant of contact with the past, the narrator hears once again Netzahualcóyotl's question, this time expressed through the use of a plural imperative that addresses the query not merely to the narrator but to all in the contemporary world who are able to listen: "díganme, cómo quedó la tierra de Acolhuacan?" (*HIA*, 82; "tell me how is the land of Acolhuacan now?" [*GOLD*, 243]). The narrator's response suggests the dire state of "Acolhuacan" – read here as a metonymic reference to the entire American world – when he urges the emperor-poet to return: "Ven otra vez a presidir junto al lago la reunion/entre flores y cantos, de Presidente-poetas" (*HIA*, 82; "Come once again to the lake to preside/at the meeting of President-Poets among flowers and songs" [*GOLD*, 243]). The shift from "king" to "President" insists on the importance of Netzahualcóyotl's ethos to the contemporary context of independent Spanish American republics, and the need for "President-Poets" who will govern with Netzahualcóyotl's wisdom.

The frame structure, although more common in fiction than poetry, is not unusual. Yet Cardenal's anachronistic mingling of centuries extends beyond his use of this device. In the scene that describes the meeting of Netzahualcóyotl's circle of poets, the narration slips into a first-person plural voice that appears to project the present-day narrator into the Aztec past, including him in the gathering of fifteenth-century poets at the point at which Netzahualcóyotl states that his poetry (like that of the author) stems from a spiritual yearning to understand life after death. The poet-emperor tells his fellow artists: "Estaremos en Texcoco poco tiempo/amigos míos/poco tiempo aquí en Texcoco. Donde se vive sin cuerpo, allí es mi casa" (*HIA*, 72; "We shall be in Texcoco for a short time/my friends/a short time here in Texcoco./My house is there, where one lives with no body" [*GOLD*, 225]). In light of this statement, the narrator's closing injunction that Netzahualcóyotl return to "preside at the meeting" should be interpreted, among other things, as a call for greater spiritual consciousness. By anchoring this plea in the context of Aztec spirituality, Cardenal diverges from orthodox Catholicism; at the same time, he adulterates the polytheistic Aztec religion with Christian monotheism. The result is to make "Netzahualcóyotl," like many of the poems in *Homenaje a los indios americanos*, a syncretic work that prophesies for Spanish American society a Utopian future in which the humanism of both Western Christianity and indigenous animism will shine forth in composite forms that suppress neither heritage.

Since the indigenous American world was not divided between the legacies of two different colonial traditions, as the contemporary Americas are split between northern (English-French) and southern (Spanish-Portuguese) branches, Cardenal includes the aboriginal cultures of the United States in his vision. He insists on the cultural unity – though by no means uniformity – that characterized the pre-1492 Americas as an enduring foundation that continues to defy, and to some extent mitigate, post-conquest political and cultural divisions. In an anachronistic reference in "La danza del espíritu" ("The Ghost Dance") that evokes the alliance of present-day bohemianisms of north and south, Cardenal speaks of nineteenth-century United States expansionism as a drive to annihilate "aquella grandiosa Confederación de tribus/pobres/harapientas, hippies/desde los Grandes Lagos hasta México" (*HIA*, 104; "that magnificent Confederacy of/poor/ragged, hippy tribes/from the Great Lakes to Mexico" [*GOLD*, 149]). His criticisms of the nineteenth-century genocide of aboriginal peoples in the United States, and of contemporary US imperialism in Latin American and Vietnam, are tempered by assertions of hemispheric connections among artists, priests, and indigenous people. In "Kayanerenhkowa" birds again bridge gaps, this time not between past and present, but between Nicaragua and the United States: "Las tanagras de Ohio/las tijeretas de Oklahoma y Texas/vienen a Nicaragua./El cormorán viene de Michigan/a Solentiname" (*HIA*, 48; "Tanagers from Ohio/forktail ducks from Oklahoma and Texas/come to Nicaragua./The cormorant comes from Michigan to Solentiname" [*GOLD*, 117]). This vision of the unity of the Americas is fortified by Cardenal's personal connections; the migrating birds are described as arriving, "De Kentucky./Como la carta de Merton el martes" (*HIA*, 55; "From Kentucky./Like Merton's letter last Tuesday" [*GOLD*, 129]).

"The Ghost Dance," which closes with Cardenal's encounter with an elderly aboriginal man in Taos, New Mexico, who wonders where the buffalo have gone, makes explicit the link between Cardenal's friendship with Thomas Merton and his devotion to the hemispheric condition of indigenous peoples. After the conversation about the buffalo, which closes the poem – Cardenal feels that the old man understands him when he suggests that the extinct animals have gone "to heaven" – Cardenal appends the parenthetical note, "(otoño 1965, mi viaje a usa a/ver a Merton y los indios)" (*HIA*, 114; "[fall 1965, my trip to the usa to see/Merton and the Indians]" [*GOLD*, 167]).

CHURCH, NATION, REVOLUTION: "NICARAGUAN CANTO," *ORACLE OVER MANAGUA, LA SANTIDAD DE LA REVOLUCIÓN*

The 1965 journey to Kentucky, followed by a bus trip to visit indigenous communities in the southwestern United States, was Cardenal's final meeting with Merton. By the time *Homenaje a los indios americanos* was published, Merton was dead, the guerrilla struggle in Nicaragua was intensifying, and Cardenal was preparing to travel to Cuba, where Thomas Merton would be supplanted as his male mentor by Fidel Castro. The United States ceased to be a fellow "American" territory of indigenous cultural roots, becoming the imperialist force that crushed Nicaragua's autonomy and identity. Literary allusions to US models, such as Whitman and Pound, faded. The title of Cardenal's next major work of poetry, "Canto Nacional"

("Nicaraguan Canto"), negotiates his passage from a pan-American position – one that draws on US influences – to Latin American revolutionary nationalism. The word "canto," which in the context of *Zero Hour* and *The Doubtful Strait* signalled an intertextual relationship with Pound, here regains its Spanish sense of "song"; in literary terms the word's point of reference is now Pablo Neruda's pan-Latin American, Marxist *Canto General*. Cardenal, however, differentiates his purpose from that of Neruda: he agitates for the rebirth of his nation. The myths of Mayas, Incas, Aztecs, and Pawnees, which belong to a common heritage, give way to the figure of Sandino, who epitomizes the struggle for Nicaraguan autonomy. The poem's dedication announces its purpose: "Al FSLN" (*AN*, 139; "To the FSLN" [*ZHOD*, 16]).

In the penultimate section of *Zero Hour*, describing the aftermath of the murder of Sandino, Cardenal had predicted the rebirth from the ashes of Nicaraguan nationalism with the May rains. The opening lines of "Nicaraguan Canto," written more than a decade and a half after *Zero Hour* and published in 1972, announce that the moment of rebirth has arrived: "En las mañanas de mayo, cuando empiezan las lluvias/canta el zenzontle" (*AN* 139; "During May the thrush sings in the morning/when the rains are starting" [*ZHOD*, 16]). The earlier poem responded to its intertextual jousting with English-language Modernism by bracketing off Nicaraguan seasons from the English trope of April showers. In "Nicaraguan Canto," the assertion of Nicaraguan difference has become superfluous: no longer writing for an imaginary elite readership, Cardenal follows the example of his hosts in Cuba by asserting the primacy of his national reality. The statement that the rains begin in May draws the reader into Nicaraguan patterns, as the evocation of the zenzontle insists on Nicaraguan language and wildlife. Birds, which in Cardenal's preceding work link Nicaragua and the United States, here assert Nicaraguan distinctness. In lines that read like a conscious renunciation of the inclusiveness of *Homenaje a los indios americanos*, the zenzontle, as though picking up the tune uttered by the birds that lament Sandino's death in the final section of *Zero Hour*, is depicted singing in freedom in the north of the country, where the Sandinista guerrillas are based. The parallel between the two instances of bird song seals Cardenal's acceptance, after a long ideological evolution, of the FSLN as the modern inheritors of the tradition of Sandino. Subsequent ornithological references make more explicit the birds' ideological cargo:

  canta su canto dulce el zenzontle
canta libre en el norte. Y el

zanate clarinero, *Cassidix nicaraguensis* (es un pájaro
nicaragüense) negroazulvioláceo vuela
en octubre o noviembre sobre los pueblos nicaragüenses
es un pájaro proletario – sin ningún adorno – anda siempre
entre pobres.
(*AN*, 139; the thrush sings sweetly and/in freedom, in the North. Later, the trumpeting zanate, Cassidix nicaragüensis/(a Nicaraguan bird) flies blueblackviolet/in October, or November, over Nicaraguan villages./ It is a proletarian bird: no glamor, always/found among the poor. [*ZHOD*, 16])

The reader identifies the poem's setting through an ornithological classification in Latin. This internationally recognized classification system certifies the authenticity of Nicaraguan nationhood. In light of the demeaning history of national humiliation narrated in the poem's second section, Cardenal must establish early the idea that Nicaraguan nationhood is a legitimate, objectively verified concept. No proof could be more devoid of political pleading than a scientific classification. The poem's two-page opening section eschews political commentary, narrating, through description interspersed with often capitalized onomatopoeia, the nesting habits and songs of a selection of Nicaraguan birds. These birds are depicted as engaging in activities that are either aesthetically pleasing (their song) or constructive (nesting, producing young). They are described as ranging over a large expanse of the Nicaraguan backlands, from Solentiname, close to the Pacific Coast, to Matagalpa, in the northern hills, where the FSLN established its first durable outpost inside Nicaraguan territory, to Bluefields on the Atlantic Coast, home of the hybridized indigenous Miskito people, who, in a trait that demonstrates the contribution of the research for *Homenaje a los indios americanos* to Cardenal's vision of Nicaragua, play an enlarged role in the country's cultural geography in "Nicaraguan Canto." The opening section concludes with a reference to the legendary quetzal bird in Ocotal, site of Augusto César Sandino's 1927 attack on a US airfield. The significance of the geographical references is not explained, yet by establishing these towns and villages as the salient points on the poem's map of Nicaragua, the opening section plots potential national rebirth to a network of revolutionary strongholds.

The second section of the poem, in an explicit reprise of the second section of *Zero Hour*, consists of a long, prosaic, anti-lyrical taxonomy of the sacking of the nation by foreign capitalism. In contrast to the earlier poem, Nicaragua's fate is presented not as one variation on a common Central American condition, but rather as a discrete national trajectory. The oppression recounted is not wreaked by banana companies distorting the agricultural framework of the entire isthmus, but by state-to-state violence: "Pero sucedió que otro país tenía necesidad de estas riquezas" (*AN*, 140; "But another country found it needed all these riches" [*ZHOD*, 17]). The description of how the Brown Brothers Bank's destruction of the Nicaraguan financial system in the years after 1911 (see chapter 2) set the stage for the US occupation is Marxist in its emphasis on the imperial power's drive to secure a safe investment climate in which to multiply its surplus capital: "expansión económica porque el capital no era suficientemente/reproductivo en los Estados Unidos" (*AN*, 142; "economic expansion because capital did not produce enough in the United States" [*ZHOD*, 19]). More striking, however, is the repeated reference to "Nicaragua" as the recipient of this violence. The nation is anthropomorphized into a quasi-human subject who suffers abuse and near-annihilation: "Nicaragua cedió sus aduanas" (*AN*, 140; "Nicaragua had to cede her customs rights" [*ZHOD*, 17]); "Los marinos .../se quedaron en Nicaragua por 13 años" (*AN*, 141; "The Marines .../ stayed in Nicaragua for 13 years" [*ZHOD*, 18]); "Nicaragua también vendió su territorio" (*AN*, 141; "Nicaragua sold her territory as well" [*ZHOD*, 18]); "Nicaragua se encontraba (cuando apareció Sandino) con/ una parte de su territorio enajenado" (*AN*, 143; "Thus Nicaragua (when Sandino appeared) found herself with/part of her territory alienated" [*ZHOD*, 20]). Having cited an international scientific source at the poem's outset to establish the Nicaraguan nation's distinct existence, Cardenal turns to another foreign authority to attest to the nation's disappearance: "a no ser que quiera jugarse con las palabras/– un profesor, por 1928, al *Daily News* en París –/nadie duda que la independencia de Nicaragua/no existe" (*AN*, 142; "Unless one simply plays with words/– a professor,/to the *Daily News*, in Paris, ca. 1928 –/'nobody doubts that Nicaragua's independence is nonexistent'" [*ZHOD*, 19]).

The poem extends the imagery of creatures in flight in its depiction of the oppressors of Nicaraguan nationhood; but rather than colourful birds, the Brown Brothers bankers, and the local politicians whom they suborn, such as Alfredo Díaz, are equated with black bats and vultures that urinate and defecate on the national territory.

> Corrupción, corrupción nacional fue el banquete de los banqueros
>   un banquete de zopilotes
> caballeros de negro frac en rueda como zopilotes.
> Y los políticos: como murciélagos ciegos que nos cagan
> colgados en lo oscuro cagándonos y orinándonos

cagadas y meadas de los murciélagos de color de tinieblas
negras alas revoloteando en el aire negro.
(*AN*, 141; Corruption, national corruption was the bankers' banquet/ a buzzards' banquet/a ring of buzzard-gentlemen in morning coats./ Politicians: like blind bats hanging over us/to shit upon us in the dark and piss on us/the shit and piss of bats as black as night/black wings beating black air. [*ZHOD*, 18])

The repetition of "black," boxing in the final line by standing at both its opening and its close, emphasizes the gloom in which Nicaragua is drenched by its subjugation. The poem concentrates rage in accessible, colloquially expressed insults that open up the possibility of a new order by deflating the authority of figures who appear invincible. It is notable that, unlike the US bankers, the Nicaraguan politicians are described as "blind," suggesting that they do not perceive their responsibilities as citizens; they collaborate in their own oppression. The bankers, however, soon yield their primacy to the US government, and particularly the State Department. The modulation from private to state oppression occurs because the bankers are "asociados con el Secretario de Estado de los Estados Unidos" (*AN*, 142; "in association with the US Secretary of State" [*ZHOD*, 18]). Subsequent references present the United States, also, as a quasi-anthropomorphized actor: "Los EE.UU. adquieren sin limitaciones una zona Canal" (*AN*, 142; "Whereby the United States acquired exclusive rights over a Canal Zone" [*ZHOD*, 19]); "le bastaba a EE.UU. dominar el país" (*AN*, 142; "domination satisfied the States" [*ZHOD*, 19]). The United States becomes less a national polity than the incarnation of a malevolent force: "el imperialismo como elemento perturbador desorganizador etc" (*AN*, 143; "imperialism as a disturbing and disrupting element etc." [*ZHOD*, 20]). Nicaragua, on the other hand, is reduced to a mere remnant of a nation: a row of squalid tropical huts epitomized by "un zopilote y un perro disputándose una tripa de pescado" (*AN*, 143; "a buzzard squabbling over fish guts with a dog" [*ZHOD*, 20]).

Having traced battered Nicaraguan nationhood to its nadir, Cardenal initiates the process of rebirth announced in the poem's opening line with a stanza that sketches for the first time the fusion of evolutionary cycles, cosmic love, and terrestrial Marxist political struggle that would become the core of his creative vision over the next twenty years. This stanza makes "Nicaraguan Canto" a crucial transitional work in Cardenal's trajectory, even though the poem's resolution is not as compellingly realized as that of *Zero Hour* or *Oráculo sobre Managua* (1973; *Oracle over Managua*), which succeeded it. In a dozen lines Cardenal creates an incantatory history of the world that begins with the first sound emitted by a living creature and proceeds inexorably to the birth of Augusto César Sandino, which brings the promise of national liberation. This conception of the cosmos, which would attain fully realized expression in *Cosmic Canticle*, insists on the inevitability of Sandinismo as a process mandated simultaneously by science and deity. The opening lines of the third stanza of "Nicaraguan Canto" present in outline a vision that Cardenal would later explore in infinitely greater depth:

> Decía que desovan las iguanas ... Es el proceso. Ellas
> (o las ranas) en el silencioso carbonífero
> emitieron el primer sonido
> la primera canción de amor sobre la tierra,
> la primera canción de amor bajo la luna
> es el proceso
> El proceso viene desde los astros.
> Nuevas relaciones de producción: eso
> también es el proceso. Opresión. Tras la opresión, la liberación.
> La Revolución empezó en las estrellas, a millones
> de años luz. El huevo de la vida
> es uno. Desde
> el primer huevo de gas, al huevo de iguana, al hombre nuevo.
> Sandino se gloriaba de haber nacido del "vientre de los oprimidos"
> (El de una indita de Niquinohomo).
> Del vientre de los oprimidos nacerá la Revolución
> Es el proceso.
> (*AN*, 143; I said iguanas lay their eggs ... It is the process. They/(or else the frogs) in the silence of the carboniferous age/made the first sound/sang the first love song here on earth/sang the first love song here beneath the moon/it is the process./The process started with the stars./New relations of production: that too/is part of the process. Oppression. After oppression, liberation./The Revolution started in the stars, millions/of light-years away. The egg of life/is one. From/the first bubble of gas, to the iguana's egg, to the New Man./Sandino was proud he had been born "from the womb of the/oppressed"/(that of an Indian girl from Niquinohomo)./From the womb of the oppressed the Revolution will be born./It is the process. [*ZHOD*, 20])

This stanza marks the first appearance in Cardenal's poetry of the capitalized word "Revolution." The Revolution is explicitly Marxist in its forging of "new relations of production"; yet it is also the culmination of an evolutionary process that "started in the stars," and combines a Darwinian interpretation of evolution with a Christian message of cosmic love. The stanza's irregular line breaks, incantatory repetitions and deliberately off-balance use of internal rhymes ("oppression ... liberación," "huevo ... hombre nuevo") lend it the authority of a prophecy that is also a prayer anchored in a faith of unimpeachable foundations. Cardenal buttresses revolutionary belief with the force of the Christian faith shared by almost all Nicaraguans, then bends this faith into an inevitable advance of Marxist precepts that is backed up by scientific rationalism. This fusion is rooted in a theory of history that is teleological: revolution is scientifically inevitable; the first croak of a frog has as its eventual outcome the birth of the selfless New Man who incarnates both the Marxist revolution's new relations of production and the infinite love of God and the cosmos. By emphasizing "the process," Cardenal evokes a movement –the FSLN – that may be joined in confidence of the inevitability of its eventual triumph. "The process," however, stresses that the blending of Christian love and Marxist self-sacrifice is the product of a journey through nature and history; that it is never a fixed, given point or dogma, but rather a perpetually unstable yet dynamic apprehension of consciousness reacting to experience. The fused Marxist-Christian perception of the cosmos becomes accessible to those who commit themselves to the rebirth of the nation through the struggle to change the "relations of production" that oppress the poor. While "the process" is cosmic in its reach, it is insistently national in both its appeal and its goals; it is the force of national rebirth that drives these pivotal lines of "Nicaraguan Canto."

This stanza represents the poem's ideological climax. The next section descends into an itemization of Nicaraguanness that borders on folkloric *costumbrismo*, reciting distinctively Nicaraguan place names ("Nindirí, Niquinohomo, Monimbó/Nandaime, Diriá, Diriomo" (*AN*, 144; *ZHOD*, 21), evoking typical national dishes ("los nacatamales, la sopa de mondongo con/su culantro y su chile congo" (*AN*, 144; "tamales, and tripe soup/with coriander and wild chili peppers" [*ZHOD*, 21]), and, alluding to Rubén Darío, the Managua-Granada train and the country's volcanoes. The reference to the volcano leads into a lengthy description of the beating and torture of a young man whose body is hurled into the Masaya volcano, merging the then-recent case of David Tejada with the indigenous myth, described in *The Doubtful Strait*, of an old woman god who lives in the volcano. Subsequent stanzas evoke an exile's nostalgia for Granada, nineteenth-century US plans to build a maritime route across Central America via Lake

Nicaragua, other examples of US imperialism, personal memories of rural areas, and, once again, instances of birdsong.

The poem offers a sense of a writer marshalling his materials and winnowing through them to find the most resonant images: for example, there is a fleeting reference to Leonel Rugama (*AN*, 157; *ZHOD*, 34), who will become the central figure of *Oracle over Managua*. Evidence of Cardenal's modified ideological perspective, in the aftermath of his trips to Cuba, is omnipresent, particularly in his treatment of the indigenous populations of the Atlantic Coast. One vignette depicts a Miskito "que oía Radio Habana en miskito" ("who listens to Radio Habana in Miskito") deciding that socialism is "bueno para Miskito/miskito no tener nada" (*AN*, 153; "good for Miskito/he not got anything" [*ZHOD*, 30]). Radio Habana's Miskito-language broadcast fulfills Sandino's prediction that "después sería internacional" (*AN*, 153; "It would be international one day" [*ZHOD*, 30]). The fractured Spanish may stake out the cultural difference of the populations of the Atlantic Coast, yet the national revolutionary project promises the harmonization of such differences in a Utopian future.

The poem, presaging policies implemented by the Sandinistas when they took power, interrupts a description of a battle between the original Sandinistas and the US Marines with the lines, "Vienen las grandes cooperativas campesinas/ya va a empezar la campaña de alfabetización" (*AN*, 155; "Soon: campesinos running great co-operatives/the campaign against illiteracy" [*ZHOD*, 32]). These sequences, which are excessively long and less well coordinated than analogous passages of *Zero Hour* or *Oracle over Managua*, conclude with an exhortation to all of Nicaraguan history to join the Revolution and a suggestion that a revolutionary triumph will resurrect in spirit those who have died for the nation: "Levántese todos, también los muertos" (*AN*, 157; "let all the people rise, even the dead" [*ZHOD*, 34]). The final page-and-a-half-long stanza opens with the summary: "Ésta es la tierra de mi canto" (*AN*, 157; "This is the land of which I sing" [*ZHOD*, 34]). The closing stanza returns to evocations of birds and imitations of their songs. In the absence of a resonant image, the poem concludes with nine lines of birdsong transcribed in block capitals. The final two lines – "CHE CHE/MARÍA YA ES DE DÍA/MARÍA YA ES DE DÍA" (*AN*, 159; "CHE CHE/MARY DAWN IS HERE/MARY DAWN IS HERE" [*ZHOD*, 36]) – combine a possible allusion to the revolutionary example of Che Guevara with an assertion that the land itself, through the birds' voices, is acclaiming the moment of rebirth.

Oracle over Managua, published a year later, responds to contemporary events with a prophecy of the capital's reconstruction after the 1972 earthquake. Cardenal correctly predicts that the earthquake's devastation will open the door to a revolutionary reimagining of the city's meaning. Dawes, characterizing the poem as "explosive," suggests that it makes "clear that Cardenal's ideology has steered towards a greater understanding of historical materialism and of scientific socialism" (Dawes 1993: 78). Yet, in contrast to "Nicaraguan Canto," *Oracle over Managua* does not explicate the mechanisms by which the nation has been subjugated to foreign imperialism; it contains no direct references to the United States, and only passing allusions to US corporations such as Chevron and City Bank. A revolutionary geology of the imaginative space of the capital, it counterpoints the flight of ancient people and animals, whose footprints have been preserved in the "estrato volcánico" (*AN*, 160; "volcanic layer" [*ZHOD*, 43]) in the lakefront district of Acahualinca, with the impossibility, for contemporary citizens, of flight from the dictatorship and the calamity of the earthquake; it proposes revolutionary self-sacrifice as the appropriate response to these oppressive conditions. A parenthetical interjection in the poem's opening evocation of a textile factory makes this setting clear: "(si ha quedado/la fábrica tras el terremoto)" (*AN*, 160; "(if there's anything left of the factory after the earthquake)" [*ZHOD*, 43]). Cardenal's greater immersion in science, which informs his depiction of revolution as the inexorable outcome of millennial processes, contributes to the poem's Utopian optimism. By excluding the United States from his imaginative framework, and presenting the evolution of the "city" – here understood as both an Aristotelian *polis* and an Augustinian "City of God" – as a process that is simultaneously local and universal in scope, the juxtaposition of recent events and geological processes, Cardenal makes a persuasive case for his prophecy of revolutionary transformation. His decision to erase the intervening horizons of medium- to long-term historical dynamics and global geopolitics, which pose the most daunting obstacles to this transformation, enables him to describe the self-sacrifice of Leonel Rugama, the young seminarian, poet, and guerrilla – an idealized form of revolutionary manhood – as a certifiable step towards revolution.

As imperialism is absent from this poem, so, too, significantly, is the figure of Augusto César Sandino, to whom there is only one passing reference. As a result of Cardenal's tight focus on current events and urban space (relegating the nation-space to a subordinate role), Sandino is supplanted by Rugama; the references to revolutionary models are all contemporary: Fidel Castro, Che Guevara, Mao Zedong. These figures provide a theoretical perspective on a concrete, local situation. Mao, for example, supplies his theory of the Great Leap Forward, suggesting that revolutionary transformations may skip over stages of social development or even planes of reality: "La evolución es por saltos dijo Mao / la evolución es la revolución / la revolución no es ilusión" (*AN*, 165; "Evolution comes in leaps, said Mao, / evolution is Revolution / Revolution is not illusion" [*ZHOD*, 48]). This disregard for formal Marxist analysis would become one of the defining traits of the Tercerista faction of the Sandinistas, which Cardenal would join in 1975.

By restricting the poem's focus to a space even smaller than the nation – the nation's capital and political cockpit – Cardenal heightens the urgency of his call to arms. A description of the dictator's palace occupying the Tiscapa Mound – itself the remnant of an ancient volcano – culminates in the realization of the impossibility of flight: "En las ruinas del volcán que hizo huir a los antepasados / el palacio con ametralladoras trincheras tanques cañones / como la erupción prehistórica aterrorizando al pueblo / ¿Ahora para dónde huir?" (*AN*, 162; "In the ruins of the volcano that made the ancestors flee / the palace with machine guns trenches tanks cannons / like the prehistoric eruption terrorizing the people. / Now which way do we run?" [*ZHOD*, 45]). The confined space, the absence of any possibility of escape, brings opposing forces into inexorable conflict. The poem's engagement with two different epochs of history forges a dialectical progression characterized by the juxtaposition of images of fossilized prehistoric life with descriptions of contemporary squalor, particularly the garbage that engulfs the homes of the poor, and the acts of torture committed in the dictator's palace. The tension between these two geological strata enables the narrative to overleap the intervening stratum of US imperialism, which has installed and maintained the dictatorship. The earthquake has reduced the capital to a field of rubble, severed from the world, where the forces of oppression and liberation confront each other in raw form, lending revolutionary self-sacrifice renewed urgency and meaning.

The footprints preserved in the volcanic soil are so persistently associated with the filth that permeates the lives of the inhabitants of the lakeside district of Acahualinca that Cardenal is able to evoke the fossilized tracks as a metonymic reference to the living conditions of the oppressed. The opening link between "basuras, bacinillas rotas" (*AN*, 160; "rubbish, broken chamber pots" [*ZHOD*, 43]) and "las huellas, impresas en estrato volcánico" (*AN*, 160; "the footprints, stamped in volcanic layer" [*ZHOD*, 4]) establishes this background. Cardenal relates the geological processes that created rocks which became "materiales de construcción de Managua" (*AN*, 160; "Managua building materials" [*ZHOD*, 43]). This opening reference to the city's construction prepares the ground for the concluding verse: "Dios ha dicho: 'He aquí que hago nuevas todas las cosas' / y ésa es la reconstrucción" (*AN*, 184; "God has said: 'Behold I make all things new' / and that is reconstruction" [*ZHOD*, 68]).

As Borgeson points out, reconstruction, in this context, is also spiritual rebirth (Borgeson 1984: 141). This rebirth is conceived within a Christian framework that is tinged with Cardenal's growing mysticism. One of the successes of *Oracle over Managua* is that Cardenal's seamless development of the poem's imagery fuses spiritual and social "reconstruction" so thoroughly that it becomes almost impossible for the reader to imagine one without the other. The Exteriorist imbrication of materials from disparate sources includes a powerful testimonial vein in which the poetic speaker recounts his observations during a visit to Acahualinca, well known as the site of the prehistoric footprints but more notorious as Managua's worst slum. The image of vultures quarrelling over garbage, which summarized the state of the nation in "Nicaraguan Canto," animates an extended description of the district's ugly poverty. When old women finally shoo away the vultures, the narrator sees

> Los rostros de la gente, sonrientes, pero cubiertos de moscas.
> Sobre techos de cartón y ripios un lago de tarjeta postal.
> Damnificados de un sismo permanente, no vendrán aviones
> trayendo alimentos enlatados a esta gente …
> (*AN*, 161; The faces of the people, smiling, but covered with flies./Above cardboard roofs and rubble a picture-postcard lake./Victims of a permanent tremor, these people will have/no planes bringing canned food … [*ZHOD*, 44])

The earthquake has brought no misery with which these people were not already familiar; they will not be recipients of international aid. Watching raw sewage flow towards the lake, the narrator witnesses "la corriente de mierda de Managua/y en ella huellas de pies desnudos/como los de aquellos que por allí fueron huyendo" (*AN*, 162; "the current of Managua shit/and in it prints of bare feet/like the feet of the people who went along there fleeing" [*ZHOD*, 45]). The depths of the slum-dwellers' misery, and the "lunar" (*AN*, 162; *ZHOD*, 45) landscape they inhabit, are counterpointed by snippets of dialogue from the Apollo 11 lunar expedition and the image of the dictator's palace "Allá arriba" (*AN*, 162; "Up there" [*ZHOD*, 45]). The description of Somoza's torture techniques in the poem's third stanza, developed through the incorporation of personal testimonies, emphasizes once again the impossibility of escape.

The past and present planes overlap in the poem's single-line fourth stanza: "Los seminaristas iban de paseo a Acahualinca" (*AN*, 163; "The seminary students used to take a walk to Acahualinca" [*ZHOD*, 46]). The compressed force of this line depends on Cardenal's restraint in not explaining that the seminary students, presumably having gone on an outing to see the ancient "footprints," encountered, also, the modern "prints of bare feet" in the sewage. The shock of the opening lines of the next stanza, is both surprising and inevitable: "Sucedió que te metiste a la clandestinidad/ y moriste en la guerrilla urbana" (*AN*, 163; "And so you went underground/and died in the urban guerrilla fighting" [*ZHOD*, 46]). This first reference to Leonel Rugama, the poem's model of revolutionary self-sacrifice, does not name the seminary student and poet who joined the Sandinistas and died at the age of twenty in a confrontation with the GN that enshrined him as a hero in the Sandinista pantheon of martyrs for having held out for a whole afternoon against dozens of National Guardsmen who had surrounded his safe house. Prior to naming Rugama, Cardenal invokes the cosmic context of his death. Revolutionary action is presented as a means of participating in the progression of history, which mimics the even more insistently dialectical movements of the cosmos:

> Aunque la muerte es tan antigua como el cosmos
> los antiprotones combaten a los protones
> los antineutrones combaten a los neutrones
> la antimateria combate a la materia
> Y ahora pretenden con bazukas
> detener la historia.
> (*AN*, 164; Although death is as ancient as the cosmos/the antiprotons fight the protons/the antineutrons fight the neutrons/antimatter fights matter./And now with bazookas they try/to stop history [*ZHOD*, 47])

The Somoza dictatorship's arms are puny by comparison with the intergalactic inevitability of revolution. The struggle of each force to merge with and annex its opposite assimilates mystical, Catholic, and scientific rationalist discourses into a prophetic voice armoured with the layered strength of disparate forms of knowledge. In this sense, *Oracle over Managua* represents a "great leap forward" in Cardenal's poetic technique. It is the first work in which Christian, Marxist, and scientific languages merge to form an integrated discursive fabric. Rugama's gun battle with the GN is the product of inevitable transitions mandated by these higher forms of knowledge. Rugama is depicted telling his friends in the Cafetería La India that "la revolución es la comunión con la especie" (*AN*, 164; "the Revolution/is communion with the species" [*ZHOD*, 47]). The fusion of discourses is evident in successions of lines such as: "Anunciad que el Reino de Dios está cerca./Como una célula seminal masculina penetra en el óvulo femenino./

Por eso peleaste toda la tarde en aquella casa" (*AN*, 164; "Announce that the kingdom of God is at hand./As a male sperm cell penetrates the female ovum …/That's why you fought all evening in that house" [*ZHOD*, 47]). In this optic, the disappearance of the dinosaurs ("los seres superiores del Jurásico" (*AN*, 165; "the superior beings of the Jurassic Age" [*ZHOD*, 48]), and the foretold disappearance of the dictatorial order with its attendant social vices, such as prostitution, become parallel events.

The depiction of revolution as inevitable enfolds, almost as a dialectical opposite, the assertion that injustice and highly stratified societies are against nature. The poem presents such societies as a very recent aberration in a cosmic history of harmonic motion: "Un millón de años sin propriedad privada/y sólo 7.000 con propiedad privada y/ricos y pobres" (*AN*, 172; "A million years without private property/and only 7000 with private property and/rich and poor" [*ZHOD*, 55]). This portrait of history is reinforced by a religious vision of "the city" that is both the physical city of Managua and "la Ciudad donde se nos revele la humanidad de Dios" (*AN*, 172; "the City where God's humanity will be revealed to us" [*ZHOD*, 55]), where the acceptance of divine love will liberate citizens from the oppression of class-based society. The reconstruction of the city becomes a spiritual and social enterprise in which the task of "Hacer de cada hombre un hombre" (*AN*, 172; "To make out of each man a man" [*ZHOD*, 56]) takes precedence even over the rebuilding of streets or houses, and is, in fact, the only way to ensure that such physical reconstruction is meaningful: "Conoceremos a Dios cuando no haya Acahualincas" (*AN*, 171; "We shall know God when there are no Acahualincas" [*ZHOD*, 55]). The method of attaining this higher form of reconstruction is through revolutionary self-sacrifice, such as that exemplified by Rugama. The narrator refers to "tu muerte, mejor dicho tu resurrección" (*AN*, 178; "your death, or rather your resurrection" [*ZHOD*, 62]). The phrase echoes the statement, made of Sandino at the conclusion of *Zero Hour*, that "the hero is born when he dies" (*ZHOD*, 15), yet in *Oracle over Managua* the emphasis on resurrection is both more religious and more insistently socialist. The narrator cites V.I. Lenin on the uncertainty of when paradise will be achieved and contrasts the fate of those who died by chance in the earthquake with Rugama's decision to choose death:

> pero la muerte nace con el cuerpo y *muere* con él
>   la muerte es la del individuo
>   "un matiz" de dolor
> para resucitar hay que morir
> (amaste el porvenir y moriste por él. Aceptaste

antes que éstos este matiz, murió tu muerte compañero).
(*AN*, 183; yet death is born with the body and it *dies* with it/death is the death of the individual/a "touch" of grief/to be reborn you must die/(you loved the future and you died for it. You accepted/this touch before these people, brother, your death is dead.) [*ZHOD*, 67])

Rugama appears as the prototype of the revolutionary who embraces death as a method of hastening the advent of the Utopian future in which he will be reborn into an eternal life that is both socialist and Christian as a ubiquitous presence among the people: "el pueblo nunca muere" (*AN*, 183; "the people never dies" [*ZHOD*, 67]). For the revolutionary, death is a "compañero" in the revolutionary struggle. The most resonant exemplar of this attitude, of course, is Che Guevara, who expressed impatience with life and the possibility of survival. *Oracle over Managua* makes a concerted effort to establish Rugama as a Nicaraguan Che Guevara and a model for the country's youth. His death is depicted as reprising that of Julio Buitrago, the first prominent urban guerrilla in the Sandinista movement, who also died in a lengthy gun battle with National Guardsmen who had surrounded his safe house. These two courageous deaths (both guerrillas greeted offers to surrender with scorn) dramatically increased support for the Sandinistas among the urban proletariat. The deaths of Buitrago and Rugama gain authority through the poem's association of their acts with those of Che Guevara. Cardenal writes in tones of sincere, impassioned homage; yet there is also an element of calculation, of creating a mythology that will inspire young people to overcome the fear of death that may make them hesitate to join the isolated and outnumbered FSLN. Building on the insight he expressed during his visit to Cuba, Cardenal associates the revolutionary movement with the Roman Catholic religion to which nearly all Nicaraguans are loyal. He stresses Rugama's background as a seminarian and depicts him drawing explicit connections between the Christian and socialist traditions:

Decías tomando café en La India o el Hotel Santa Cruz
que la revolución interior y la otra son la misma ...
decías que el revolucionario "es un santo militante."
Tambien hablando de: "la fuerza santificante del revolucionario."
Llamaste a la clandestinidad, cuando entraste, *catacumbas*.
Y el seminario fue también una especie de clandestinidad.
(*AN*, 169; Drinking coffee in the India or the Hotel Santa Cruz you used to say/that the inner revolution and the other are the same .../you said that the revolutionary "is a militant saint."/Also talking of "the

sanctifying force of the revolutionary."/You called the underground, when you entered it, catacombs./And the seminary was also a kind of underground. [*ZHOD*, 52])

The word "catacombs" establishes an explicit parallel between the small, underground Sandinista movement, which in the early 1970s numbered fewer than one hundred guerrillas, and the early Christian Church that existed in underground caverns on the outskirts of Rome. In part as a result of its use in *Oracle over Managua*, "catacumbas" later entered popular parlance in Nicaragua as a way of distinguishing guerrillas who had been Sandinistas since the movement's early days from leaders who had been in exile, or those who had become Sandinistas only during the final uprising against the dictatorship. The term's widespread adoption illustrates the extent to which FSLN members succeeded in presenting their revolution as a religious undertaking.

Cardenal's depiction of Rugama insists on this interpretation of his motivation, even though the historical Rugama may have perceived Christianity and Marxism as antagonistic, rather than complementary, forces. Omar Cabezas, a secondary school classmate of Rugama's who met him again as a university student, recalled that "Leonel era marxista-leninista y anticlerical" (Cabezas 1982: 24; "Leonel was Marxist-Leninist and anticlerical" [Cabezas 1985: 12]). Cardenal parses the tension inherent in Rugama's departure from the seminary and his adoption of materialism by asserting that the young revolutionary's anti-clericalism did not exclude a commitment to the God of his imagining: "hay muchos Dios/–el Dios de John D. Rockefeller./Vos buscabas la comunión, la/comunión con la especie" (*AN*, 171; "there are many Gods/the God of John D. Rockefeller .../You were looking for communion,/communion with the species" [*ZHOD*, 54]). Rugama's experiences doing volunteer work in an asylum are equated with the often humiliating reality of day-to-day life as a political insurgent: "También conoció esa lucha el Che/... Y cuando fuiste acólito en el manicomio: los locos cagados/y la misa oliendo a mierda" (*AN*, 169; "Che knew that struggle too./... And when you were an acolyte in the insane asylum: the madmen/covered with crap/and the Mass smelling of shit" [*ZHOD*, 52]).

As the account of Rugama's formative years continues, some details appear to be coded references to Cardenal's own life: "El celibato, una Sierra Maestra o la Larga Marcha./Por eso podías predicar después (Cafetería La India)/'la liberación es nuestra MUERTE pero con ella damos VIDA'" (*AN*, 170–1; "celibacy, a Sierra Maestra or the Long March./That's why afterward you could preach (India Coffee House)/'freedom is our DEATH but with it we give LIFE'" [*ZHOD*, 53]). If the views expressed in Rugama's "preaching" sound as if they might come from one of Cardenal's sermons in Solentiname, the characterization of celibacy as analogous to Fidel Castro's campaign in the Sierra Maestra or Mao Zedong's Long March are an even better fit with the poem's author than with its subject. Whatever youthful sexual frustrations Rugama may have experienced, his death at the age of twenty prevented this celibacy from becoming a "Long March"; the image is a far more apt summary of the life of the forty-eight-year-old priest who is writing the poem than of the young man whom the poem is about. Similarly, the description of seminary life as "a kind of underground" recalls the fraught atmosphere of Cardenal's studies at La Ceja.

The coded autobiographical elements in *Oracle over Managua* add an extra resonance to the focus on the theme of reconstruction: through his description of Rugama, Cardenal reconstructs his own masculinity. By arrogating to himself the privilege of articulating Rugama's self-sacrifice, he adds to his revolutionary self-image an association with armed struggle while reinforcing his distinctive amalgam of Marxism, Roman Catholicism, and cosmic evolutionary theory. His imaginative entry into the urban arena refutes contentions that Cardenal's ideas, the product of a remote, pastoral environment, apply only to peasants. In claiming the urban guerrilla struggle, also, as congruent with his vision, he extends his moral and political authority; in this, too, Rugama, who spent most of his life in León yet became a leader in the struggle of the Managua proletariat, serves a forerunner. Rugama even becomes a precursor of the poetry workshops that Cardenal would found in 1976: "Querías poemas para el camionero" (*AN*, 174; "You wanted poems for the truck driver" [*ZHOD*, 57]).

This enterprise of identification, however, is wracked by anxiety. For reasons of age, class background, international fame, artistic vocation, temperament, and other factors, Cardenal cannot become a clandestine guerrilla in the catacombs. He can live the life of active combat only vicariously, by encouraging others to follow it, and by writing poems about their heroism and self-sacrifice. His later decision to remove his library from Solentiname when the community's young men joined the Sandinistas, and to be out of the country when the assault on the San Carlos barracks took place in 1977, underlines his position as a revolutionary mentor one step removed from the front lines. As much as this separation may have been mandated by hierarchies of class and demographic cohort – Tomás Borge, five years younger than Cardenal, was probably the FSLN's oldest active guerrilla – the contradiction of urging young men and women to die for the people, while refraining from doing so himself, made a discernible impact on Cardenal's perception of both his own spiritual standing and his masculinity. The narrator places in Rugama's mouth the phrase, "El que conserve su vida la perderá" (*AN*, 169; "Whoever saves his life will lose it" [*ZHOD*, 52]), a quote from Luke 9: 24 that resonates through Cardenal's later career, almost as a form of survivor's guilt. Cardenal later made this self-questioning explicit in choosing the phrase as the epigraph of the first volume of his memoirs. The suggestion that his life is "lost" because he did not martyr himself for the people occurs within the context of a Sandinista culture in which undergoing torture or violent death becomes the supreme affirmation of masculinity. No matter how closely he may associate himself with Rugama's generation, Cardenal remains separated from these heroic youths, whether urban or rural, by a variety of factors, including his priestly celibacy. The more political successes the Sandinista guerrillas achieve, the more problematic Cardenal's masculine identity will become, even as his ideas earn justification and larger numbers of adherents.

Rugama, by contrast, as guerrilla, poet, martyr, and (ex-) seminarian, was the incarnation of Sandinista masculinity. Dawes wonders at Sandinista reverence for Rugama and his meagre, rather juvenile clutch of poems, which persisted for at least two decades after the young man's death (Dawes 1993: 92). The reason for this adulation, as *Oracle over Managua* makes clear, lies in Rugama's perfect fit with the ideal of the New Man. This concept of the selfless individual, both the maker and the product of revolutionary socialist society, is the ideological concept that Sandinismo borrowed most directly from the Cuban Revolution. In the Cuban context, the prototype of the New Man is Che Guevara, the restless revolutionary devoid of egotism, who cut sugar cane in the fields with the peasants, accepted only a worker's salary for his government service, always ensured that he suffered more and received less than his *compañeros*, and finally gave his life for the cause. The concept was first articulated by the Cuban poet, essayist, and political leader José Martí, who died a martyr's death in 1895 fighting for Cuba's independence from Spain. In his 1891 essay "Nuestra América" ("Our America"), Martí wrote: "En pie, con los ojos alegres de los trabajadores, se saludan, de un pueblo a otro, los hombres nuevos americanos" (Martí 2004: 165; "Erect, with the happy, sparkling eyes of workingmen, the new Americans salute one another from country to country" [Martí 1954: 148]).[4] From its initial articulation, the New Man is a Pan-American concept, implicitly transferrable across national boundaries.

Cardenal develops Rugama as a Nicaraguan representative of this tradition through a digression in a long stanza that directly precedes the narration of Rugama's death. From a discussion of the City of God, the narrator makes a filmic jump-cut into an incident where Che Guevara, escorting a visiting delegation around Cuba, berates his pilot to fly back to Havana in spite of bad weather: "y es que el Che no tenía para pagar el hotel/para él y sus invitados/(y el Che era presidente del Banco de Cuba)" (172; "and the fact was that Che didn't have the money to pay for hotel/rooms/for himself and his guests/(and Che was president of the Bank of Cuba)" [*ZHOD*, 55]). This example of incorruptibility, building on the earlier equation of Rugama's hardships in the asylum with Che's struggles in the mountains, sets the stage for Cardenal's concluding prophecy of Rugama's rebirth in the form of the New Man. Cabezas corroborates the historical Rugama's desire, during the late 1960s, to re-enact Guevara's life:

> La estrella de Leonel es en ese entonces el comandante Ernesto "Che" Guevara, que tiene apenas meses de muerto ... Recuerdo que entonces dijo al grupo de compañeros que estaban allí discutiendo con él, fruncido el ceño: "Hay que ser como el Che ... ser como el Che ... ser como el Che ..." ... Salí de la universidad con la frase repitiéndola interiormente como si fuese una cinta magnetofónica; aún recuerdo con nitidez los gestos y la expresión de la cara, la firmeza con que Leonel pronunció eso: "ser como el Che ... ser como el Che ..." (Cabezas 1982: 24; Leonel's guiding star at that time was Comandante Ernesto Che Guevara, who had been killed only a few months earlier ... I remember what he said to the group of compañeros that had gathered around to talk. He spoke with a frown: "We have to be like Che ... be like Che ... be like Che ..." ... I came away from the university with that phrase running over and over in my mind like a tape recording. I can still see Leonel's gestures, the expression on his face, the determined way he spoke those words. "To be like Che ... to be like Che ..." [Cabezas 1985: 11–12])

Cardenal's narration of Rugama's martyrdom, which stresses his desire to die for the poor people of the most oppressed neighbourhoods of Managua, includes the detail that, prior to dying, Rugama and his two *compañeros* sing the national anthem. This act, connecting the urban world to the nation, converts Managua, like Solentiname, into a microcosm of the revolutionary national society of the future. The first condition for the establishment of this Utopian future is the banishment of the urban-rural divide and pride in material wealth; in this sense, the earthquake has brought the city down to the level of peasant communities such as Solentiname, creating a common national experience of humility and deprivation that promises the possibility of unity among all Nicaraguans on the basis of Christian-Marxist principles. Cardenal describes the appearance of the levelled city, its symbols of oppression and foreign imperialism brought low, "desde el seminario" (*AN*, 179; "from the seminary" [*ZHOD*, 62]). This vision of the city in ruins succeeds the four-page account of Rugama's gun battle with the GN, as though claiming Rugama's self-sacrifice as the catalyst for this purifying catastrophe. From the vantage point of the seminary – a religious perspective replete with revolutionary connotations – the narrator can confirm that "todo el orgullo se fue a la mierda" (179; "all the pride was shit upon" [*ZHOD*, 62]). In the sole passage in the poem in which US imperialism receives detailed treatment, Cardenal revels in the humbling of the institutions that buttressed the oppressive order:

> el rascacielo del Banco de América era una antorcha en la noche
>   la Pepsi Cola en el suelo
> el Gran Hotel como bombardeado por las tanquetas Sherman
> la cárcel de La Aviación sin paredes ni presos ni guardianes
>   la embajada de USA en rodillas
> el Luis Somoza hueco tumbado en tierra hecho tucos
> como un cadáver más desenterrado de las ruinas.
> (*AN*, 179; the Bank of America skyscraper was a torch in the night/Pepsi Cola was flat on the ground/the Grand Hotel as if bombarded by Sherman tanks/the Air Force Prison without walls or prisoners or guards/the American Embassy on its knees/the Luis Somoza statue hollow toppled to the ground a stump/like one more corpse dug up from the ruins. [*ZHOD*, 63])

The image of the statue of the dictator's deceased brother as "one more corpse" becomes the climax of a rising crescendo of humbled imperialist symbols. Divine wrath, implicitly congruent with Rugama's self-sacrifice, has beggared the moneylenders who had taken over the temple. By obliterating the underpinnings of the Somoza regime, such as Pepsi Cola and the Bank of America, the earthquake demolishes the dynasty's authority. The itemization of the collapse of the institutions of foreign imperialism, which opens with the recurrent symbol of the vulture, this time wheeling not over the Nicaraguan nation, but over its oppressors – "zopilotes sobre el City Bank" (*AN*, 179; "buzzards over the City Bank" [*ZHOD*, 62]) – culminates in the image of Luis Somoza's tumbled statue, which in turn sets up an account of the destruction of the dictator's palace on the Tiscapa Mound, including its grounds and security facilities. The disintegration of the regime's security apparatus – "las salas de tortura resbalaron hacia el lago" (*AN*, 180; "the torture chambers slithered toward the lagoon" [*ZHOD*, 63]) – and the dispersal of its allies, such as the reclusive US multi-millionaire Howard Hughes, who fled from his penthouse refuge in the Hotel Intercontinental on the morning of the earthquake, have contributed to creating a city which, in both negative and positive senses, is "toda una gran Acahualinca" (*AN*, 180; "all a great Acahualinca" [*ZHOD*, 64]).

The evocation of the lakeside slum suggests an equality of poverty, but also a potential for revolutionary solidarity, in post-earthquake Managua. This creation of the necessary preconditions for revolution is depicted insistently as an act of divine intervention: "¿Puede haber una catástrofe en una ciudad/ que no la mande Yavé?" (*AN*, 180; "Can there be a catastrophe in a city/if Yahweh didn't order it?" [*ZHOD*, 64]). The biblical citation appears as a prophecy, confirming Cardenal's insistence that Nicaragua's future will re-enact biblical patterns, even if the dictatorship's continued monopoly on military force makes such a possibility appear remote. Cultivating an analogy with Jews in the Holy Land, who also lived under occupation, Cardenal responds to assertions of the revolutionary movement's beleaguered position by equating Somoza and his US advisers with the Egyptian king: "Para Faraón y sus técnicos eran sólo 'reveses económicos'/Y todavía nos dicen no profeticen/Estamos bajo Ley Marcial, no profeticen" (*AN*, 182; "For Pharaoh and his technicians they were only 'economic setbacks.'/And they still tell us not to prophesy./We're under Martial Law, don't prophesy" [*ZHOD*, 65]).

The poem's resolution employs a return to the testimonial voice that detailed the poverty of the Acahualinca district at the outset. The poetic speaker recalls his own intimate associations with buildings levelled by the earthquake. The tone of these recollections begins with the innocence of adolescent love ("Ésta fue mi ciudad/donde yo iba de tarde con Adelita de la mano" (*AN*, 182; "This was my city/where I'd go in the afternoon hand-in-hand with Adelita" [*ZHOD*, 66]), passes through memories of favourite eating spots that have been annihilated, then modulates into a darker tone with recollections of the narrator's own enmeshment in the corruption of Somocista society ("Nos fuimos donde la Manuela González/Aquí fueron burdeles" (*AN*, 182; "We've gone to Manuela/González's./Here there used to be whorehouses" [*ZHOD*, 66]) that set the stage for evocations of the victims of the earthquake and the cruelty of the social order whose foundations have been shaken by the catastrophe: "La diversión de unos guardias, hacer correr a la/gente tras los camiones de alimentos, lanzando/de vez en cuando unas cuantas latas al suelo" (*AN*, 183; "Some of the guards had a lot of fun getting people/to run after the food trucks and from time to time/tossing out a few cans" [*ZHOD*, 67]).

The poem's concluding verses, mingling Christian and Marxist-Leninist forms of prophecy, insist on the earthquake's failure to destroy the urban proletariat: "El pueblo está intacto" (*AN*, 183; "The people are untouched" [*ZHOD*, 67]); "Pero el pueblo es inmortal. Sale sonriente de la morgue" (*AN*, 184; "But the people are immortal. They come smiling out of the morgue" [*ZHOD*, 6])). The reappearance of newspaper vendors, itinerant bubblegum salesmen, and youths who look after parked cars on the streets of Managua in the days following the earthquake attest to the continued presence of "la *base*" (*AN*, 184; emphasis in original; "the foundation" [*ZHOD*, 67]), here conceived in the Marxist sense of the "base" as the productive forces whose interrelations will determine the "superstructure" of politics and legal norms (Eagleton 1976: 4–5). The vitality of the proletariat forecasts the inevitable creation of a socialist superstructure. To prophesy the coming of this new order, the narrator complains, is "nuestro delito" (*AN*, 184; "our crime" [*ZHOD*, 68]). In spite of the proliferation of Marxist phrasing, the poem's resolution stresses the Christian aspects of Cardenal's prophecy, particularly in the closing lines of the penultimate stanza:

> El Reino de Dios está cerca
> la Ciudad Definitiva compañeros
> Sólo los muertos resucitan
> Otra vez hay otras huellas: no ha terminado la peregrinación.
> (*AN*, 184; The Kingdom of God is at hand/the City of Communion, brothers./Only the dead are reborn./Once more there are more footprints: the pilgrimage has not ended. [*ZHOD*, 68])

Both Christian and Marxist teleologies, in Cardenal's reading, depend on dialectics – implicitly compatible – that reach a plateau where continuous evolution, achieved through the individual's self-sacrifice for the collective good, yields to a paradise that is eternal, though not static. The poem concludes with a Biblical quote: "'He aquí que hago nuevas todas las cosas'/y ésa es la reconstrucción" (*AN*, 184; "'Behold I make all things new'/and that is reconstruction" [*ZHOD*, 68]). The concluding emphasis on reconstruction reinforces the prophecy of a coming Christian-socialist order. By narrowing the focus from the nation to the city, Cardenal achieves a concentration of his theme of an integrated society struggling for justice in both the temporal and the spiritual realms. The "rebirth," based on natural images, of "Nicaraguan Canto," becomes a "reconstruction" in which the prehistoric footsteps serve as a point of departure for applying natural processes to urban life. In its implicit depiction of the earthquake as a divine response to the self-sacrifice of Leonel Rugama, Cardenal plants the revived Sandinista movement at the core of national, and even spiritual, history; at the same time, *Oracle over Managua* "reconstructs" Sandinista masculinity in the form of the self-sacrificing guerrilla strongly influenced by Christian and Marxist concepts and sensitive to poetry. Through his narration of this reconstruction, Cardenal reconstitutes his own masculinity, debilitated by priestly celibacy, in a more virile form. He appropriates acts of revolutionary bravado, and moves his own preoccupations of Christianity and poetry to the centre of the revolutionary agenda. The figure of Rugama acts as both a certification of Cardenal's revolutionary potency and a nationalized Che Guevara-like prototype capable of inspiring young Nicaraguans to give up their lives for the revolutionary project.

Oracle over Managua, a climactic statement both of Cardenal's mingling of the Exteriorist and testimonial currents in his verse, and of the refinement of his Christian Marxist ideology, was followed by a hiatus in his poetry. The two volumes of *The Gospel in Solentiname* (1975) would be his last full-length original book prior to the triumph of the Sandinista Revolution; as Nicaragua's civil war exploded, politics consumed most of Cardenal's time. Journeys to speak, read, and raise funds in Europe, Latin America, and the United States kept him constantly occupied. After the death of Pablo Neruda in 1973, Cardenal became Latin America's most famous revolutionary poet, and the demands on his time increased. In the mid-1970s he edited two anthologies that promoted his Exteriorist approach to verse, *Poesía nueva de Nicaragua* (1974; New Poetry of Nicaragua) and *Poesía cubana de la Revolución* (1976; Cuban Poetry of the Revolution). During this period, he published two widely reprinted poems, "Epístola a José Coronel Urtecho" ("Epistle to José Coronel Urtecho"), which relates the quest for a poetic language that he shared with his uncle and mentor, and "Epístola a monseñor Casaldáliga" ("Epistle to Monsignor Casaldáliga"), an open letter to a Brazilian prelate imprisoned for promoting revolution. In adopting the word "epistle," which is used for papal communiqués, Cardenal arrogates to himself the privilege of defining the theology of the liberationist wing of the Catholic Church. His epistles, like his psalms, establish an insurgent theology that offers Latin American Catholics a framework for entering revolutionary movements without relinquishing their faith. By adopting the letter form, Cardenal advances his Exteriorist assertion that poetic language is sufficiently ample and flexible to assimilate other forms of discourse. The epistolary structure, with its demand for direct communication, becomes a way of expressing Cardenal's aesthetic position, now sharpened by the open civil war in his country:

> No es tiempo ahora de crítica literaria.
> Ni de atacar a los gorilas con poemas surrealistas.
> ¿Y para qué metáforas si la esclavitud no es metáfora
> ni es metáfora la muerte en el Río das Mortes
> ni lo es el Escuadrón de la Muerte?
> (*SDR*, 103; It is not time now for literary criticism./Or to attack the gorillas with Surrealist poems./And why metaphors if slavery is not a metaphor/death in the River das Mortes is not a metaphor either/nor is the Death Squad?)

These two epistles, along with a third, less successful poem, "Condensaciones – y visión de San José de Costa Rica" ("Condensations – and a Vision of San José, Costa Rica") – a denunciation of materialism – two extended interviews, a portfolio of photographs of life in Solentiname with an introduction by Hermann Schulz, were collected in *La santidad de la revolución* (1976; The Sanctity of the Revolution), a slender volume of 103 pages that was Cardenal's only published book of the late 1970s. With the exception of the three new poems, most of the material had appeared previously in West Germany, the European country where Cardenal's readership was largest, in 1972. The cover, featuring Cardenal's face repeated in quadruplicate, exploited the growing prominence of his public image. His own intervention in public events became a theme of his poetry. The section of the book containing the three poems was entitled "Poemas de inspiración cristiano-marxista" ("Poems of Marxist-Christian Inspiration"). The epistle to Monseñor Casaldáliga opens:

> Monseñor:
> Leí que en un saqueo de la Policía Militar
> en la Prelatura de São Félix, se llevaron, entre
> otras cosas, la traducción portuguesa (no sabía
> que hubiera) de "Salmos" de Ernesto Cardenal. Y
> que a todos los detenidos han dado electrodos
> por Salmos que muchos tal vez no habían leído.
> (*SDR*, 93; Monsignor:/I read that in a sacking by the Military Police/in the Prelature of São Félix, they carried off, among/other things, the Portuguese translation (I didn't/ know there was one) of *Psalms* by

Ernesto Cardenal. And/that all those arrested were given electric shocks/for Psalms that many had perhaps not read. [*ZHOD*, 84])

The ambivalent sentiments, mingling omnipotence and guilt, attendant on being a public figure are evident. The poem expresses Cardenal's realization that his work and public image have slipped the leash of his control: he learns of the Portuguese translation of *Psalms*, of which he had no knowledge (and for which he presumably received no royalties), through a newspaper story; he finds his name in the article as an emblem of liberation theology; at the same time, he is plagued by the worry that he is no more than a symbol: that, his name having become shorthand for a position, his poems are no longer read. The proliferation of Cardenal's speaking engagements during this period of his life made him more conscious of this trivial aspect of being famous; as he says elsewhere in this book: "No me gustan las entrevistas" (*SDR*, 35; "I don't like interviews"). His recognition that innocent seminarians have been tortured in his name seems to be both mortifying and intoxicating; the phrasing verges on suggesting that the thought of their torture would be endurable had they at least read his poems.

These mixed emotions presage related anxieties that would become discernible at a later stage among all of the writers involved in the Sandinista movement. As the last revolution of the twentieth century, and one that occurred in a territory that had been a near-colony of the most powerful country on earth, the Nicaraguan Revolution was subjected to sustained international media scrutiny that almost certainly exceeded that concentrated on any country of its size at any point in history up to that time, with the debatable exception of Israel and Palestine. The youth, idealism, perceived ideological flexibility, and personal flamboyance of many of the Sandinista leaders, the commitment of well-known writers and elements of the Catholic Church to the revolutionary process, the widely covered literacy and land-reform campaigns, the brutality of the Contra war, the high-profile visits to revolutionary Nicaragua of famous intellectuals, as well as figures from the entertainment world, such as Susan Sarandon, Bianca Jagger, Richard Gere, Ed Harris, Carlos Saura, Chico Buarque de Holanda, Joan Baez, Bruce Cockburn, and many others (Cherem 2004b: 23; *RP*, 340), the Revolution's defiance of the two most powerful men on earth, US President Ronald Reagan and Pope John Paul II, all struck deep chords in Europe and Latin America. The debates over US congressional funding for the Contras resulted in incessant, nearly obsessive, news coverage in the United States.

This non-stop scrutiny was due in part to the exceptionally late stage of historical development at which the Revolution in Nicaragua occurred.

Attaining power on the brink of the 1980s and reaching its conclusion three months after the fall of the Berlin Wall, the Nicaraguan Revolution is the historical event that comes closest to straddling the gap between the Cold War era, marked by an acute consciousness of history, national boundaries, and divergences between ideologies, and the post-1990 period of accelerated globalization in which the allegiance commanded by political belief systems is usurped by the force of media-nourished personalities and absorption in the individual's self-image, dissolving history and the nation into an eternal present of instantly accessible entertainment and commerce and round-the-clock communication.

The transitional era in history in which the Revolution took place resulted in the inflation of certain of its participants, Cardenal among them, into media icons: forms of visual shorthand epitomizing, in a vastly oversimplified way, complex ideas such as the revolutionary priest (Cardenal) or the hard-line guerrilla (Borge). Such attention was deeply destabilizing to Sandinista ideology, as it cast the nation, and the project of national renewal, into the shadow of the individual media figure. As Cardenal would write in *Cosmic Canticle*, reflecting on a night when an astonishing thirteen hundred people showed up for his poetry reading in Hamburg, Germany: "ustedes saben: la publicidad/la celebridad ... y la causa de Nicaragua – " (*CANC*, 419; "you know: the publicity/fame ... and the Nicaraguan cause –" [*COSC*, 348]). He became skilled at deploying his image to strengthen international support for the Revolution, yet the palpable contradiction of making a commitment to submerge one's personality in the struggle to forge a just, independent nation, only to confront the disquieting irony that this personality epitomized the nation in the eyes of the international media, persisted. The first inklings of this tension are visible in "Epístola a monseñor Casaldáliga."

"Epístola a José Coronel Urtecho," written in celebration of his mentor's seventieth birthday in 1976, focuses on revolution as a process of disentangling language from its corruption by big business, advertising, and the media and restoring to words their original clarity, meaning, and power. The theme is related to that of the other epistle in its implicit assumption that to be absorbed by the media is to enter a realm of corruption. Behind Cardenal's warnings about the crimes that may be concealed by contaminated language – "Y cuando la defoliación en Vietnam/es Programa de Control de recursos/es también defoliación del lenguaje" (*SDR*, 90; "And the defoliation of Vietnam/is a Resource Control Program/it's also a defoliation of language" [*ZHOD*, 96]) – lies an anxiety that the project of rebuilding the nation according to a culture of Christian Marxism may be overwhelmed by the immersion of the Revolution's most salient protagonists in the deceitful language of the mass media. The roots of the corruption of language lie in the capitalist system of production and, particularly, in the institution of private property.

The poem opens with Cardenal reporting to Coronel that he has read the latter's "Conferencias a la Iniciativa Privada" ("Speeches to the Private Sector"). Structured around repeated motifs, such as the knowledge that the FSLN is advancing from the north and that private property still exists but may not exist much longer, and Mao Zedong's assertion that "el arte revolucionario sin valor artístico/ no tiene valor revolucionario" (*SDR*, 87; "revolutionary art without artistic value/has no revolutionary value" [*ZHOD*, 95]), the poem employs the Exteriorist style in its imitation of a letter, or a leisurely conversation between friends. Cardenal explicates his political position to Coronel, quoting Fidel Castro's line that the land will be as free as the air, and justifies his preoccupations to his mentor by stating that "Le han dicho que yo ya sólo hablo de política/No es de política sino de Revolución/ que para mí es lo mismo que reino de Dios" (*SDR*, 85; "They've told you I only talk about politics now./It's not about politics but about Revolution/ which for me is the same thing as the kingdom of God" [*ZHOD*, 93]). In spite of the two poets' very different uses of language – Coronel's poems have a jaunty, musical rhythm and often rhyme – they share the Granada Conservative heritage and the legacy of the Betrayed Generation's haughty rejection of materialism. The conversion, albeit tardy, to the Sandinista cause of the man who was the first and most enduring in Cardenal's succession of public father-figures – his model in poetry, as Merton was later his model in religion and Castro his model in politics – resolves an ideological contradiction between his early and his later mentors. Coronel's political conversion is the final essential step in grounding Cardenal's revolutionary masculinity by integrating it into his Granada Conservative heritage. It was Coronel who, in 1943, persuaded Cardenal's father to allow young Ernesto to study literature at university in Mexico City, rather than law, as his family was insisting (*AG*, 151).

The epistle draws attention to the fact that Coronel wrote his critical lectures on the private sector "en Granada, en la casita del lago" (*SDR*, 81; "in Granada, in your little/house on the lake" [*ZHOD*, 91]). Coronel's integration into the anti-Somocista ranks confirms that Sandinismo is the unavoidable home of a Granada Conservative in the 1970s:

Usted antes fue reaccionario
y ahora está "incómodo" en la izquierda
pero en la extrema izquierda,

sin haber cambiado nada en su interior:
la realidad a su alrededor ha cambiado.
(*SDR*, 87; You were a reactionary before/and now you are "uncomfortable" in the left/but in the extreme left,/without having changed anything inside you;/the reality around you had changed. [*ZHOD*, 95])

Cardenal's analysis of Coronel's experience (and, by implication, his own) is congruent with that proposed by Gobat in his study of the radicalization of the Granada elite: "The (largely unintended) 'democratizing' consequences of US imperial rule can fuel an even more intense rejection of the 'American way of life'" (Gobat 2005: 17). If indeed nothing has changed in Coronel's "interior," the same may be said of Cardenal. The latter's yearning to link their positions is evident in the poem's observation that Coronel's farm on the San Juan River is threatened by an oil pipeline planned by Aristotle Onassis, just as Cardenal's community on Solentiname is threatened by Howard Hughes's plan to build a casino there. The discussion of poetic language culminates in Cardenal's praise of Coronel's linguistic formulation of the tensions in Nicaraguan society: "la lengua del gobierno y la empresa privada/contra la lengua popular nicaragüense" (*SDR*, 90; "the language of the government and private enterprise/against the language of the Nicaraguan people" [*ZHOD*, 96]). Cardenal's characterization of Coronel's Conservatism echoes his equation of his own religious and political beliefs with those of ancient Christians: "Usted antes estuvo en la reacción. Pero su 'reacción'/no era tanto la vuelta a la Edad Media sino a la de Piedra" (*SDR*, 91; "You were with the reaction before. But your 'reaction'/was not so much the return to the Middle Ages as to the Stone Age" [*ZHOD*, 97]). In the contemporary context, the morality of agrarian values and primitive Christianity is expressed most clearly by Sandinismo. Cardenal defines Coronel's entry into the anti-Somocista ranks as part of the inexorable spread of revolutionary hope, a development he expresses by reprising the image of sprouting grass that appears at the conclusion of *Zero Hour*.[5] Here the natural "process" of grass growing, an accomplice of the revolutionary "process" evoked in "Nicaraguan Canto," inexorably splits the industrial façade of concrete.

La santidad de la revolución, with its provocative title, offers a distillation of the ideological position Cardenal had reached by the late 1970s, presenting his fused Christian Marxist vision shorn of some of the complexities that characterize his longer poems. It represents a refinement, not so much of his poetic language, as of his political discourse; the phrasing of the interviews that make up most of the book represents a compromise with the inevitable media inflation of his personality, and an attempt to speak through the screen of this image with a clarity that will make his position appear rational to Latin American Catholics. He explains his own evolution in terms of his engagement with the peasants of Solentiname: "Vine a esta isla buscando la soledad, el silencio, la meditación y, en último término, buscando a Dios. Dios me llevó a los demás hombres. La contemplación me llevó a la revolución" (*SDR*, 70; "I came to this island looking for solitude, silence, meditation and in the final instance, seeking God. God led me to other men. Contemplation led me to the revolution"). He invokes Leonel Rugama as the model of contemplation leading to action, presents Cuban socialism as "el único camino para salir del subdesarrollo" (*SDR*, 36; "the only way out of underdevelopment"), and yet insists that the true inspiration behind his revolutionary allegiances is religious, not ideological, in origin: "No fue la lectura de Marx lo que me llevó al marxismo, sino la lectura del evangelio" (*SDR*, 70; "It wasn't reading Marx that brought me to Marxism, but reading the gospel"). Cardenal's honing of these concise, easily repeatable dictums opens up the possibility of Latin American Catholicism becoming the basis for revolution.

THE REVOLUTIONARY NATION: *FLIGHTS OF VICTORY*

Cardenal's next book of poems, *Vuelos de victoria* (1984; *Flights of Victory*), deploys his newfound near-aphoristic accessibility to celebrate Sandinista Nicaragua. In contrast to epics such as *Zero Hour*, the longer works in *Homenaje a los indios americanos*, "Nicaraguan Canto," or *Oracle over Managua*, or even eight- or nine-page poems, such as the epistles, none of the poems in *Flights of Victory* exceeds three pages in length. While anchored in extremely concrete historical circumstances, this verse dispenses with the Exteriorist layerings of citations and imbricated texts that, in the earlier works, painstakingly assemble Cardenal's holy trinity of science, religion, and revolution. One of the literary banners of the Sandinista Revolution, *Flights of Victory* became Cardenal's most popular and widely read collection; individual poems were recited aloud, read on the radio,[6] reprinted, and translated as Cardenal travelled the world to drum up international support for Nicaragua. The poems' brevity, while a virtue, was a by-product of the relentless demands on Cardenal's time. As one of them, "Ocupados" ("Busy"), concludes: "la verdad es que estamos muy ocupados" (*VV*, 27; "the truth is that we're very busy" [*FV*, 59]). Another, "Reflexiones de un Ministro" ("Reflections of a Minister"), laments the narrator's obligation to attend a diplomatic reception when "Quisiera quedarme aquí/para observar mejor ese gato,/de qué color es" (*VV*, 66; "I'd like to stay here/to observe this cat all the more,/what his color is" [*FV*, 61]). Yet where Pablo Neruda's digression into making his language accessible to the workers in his three books of "odes"[7] hobbled the lyrical flare that was his greatest strength, Cardenal's verse acquired a heightened lyricism from the compression of the more popular mode. As prominent as they became during the 1980s, though, these poems have aged less well than some of Cardenal's other works.

Paradoxically, even though the poems in *Flights of Victory* belong to the five years after the Sandinista triumph, a period sometimes dubbed "the Reconstruction" (Beverley and Zimmerman 1990: 81–114), the new political context permits Cardenal to eschew the recapitulations of the humiliations of Nicaraguan nationhood that characterize *Zero Hour* and "Nicaraguan Canto." The history of the nation, which is fundamental to his ideology and poetic vision in opposition, becomes dispensable in victory. The growth of the shoots of grass that sprout through the ashes and concrete relieves him of the burden of the past. *Flights of Victory* contains numerous references to the Frente Sandinista and Sandinismo, but the historical figure of Augusto César Sandino appears in only two poems, "Luces " ("Lights"), where he is evoked as a quasi-mystical inspiration, and "Aterrizaje con epitafio" ("Landing With Epitaph"), where his name appears in a long list of Sandinista martyrs.

The book's table of contents is divided into two sections (a division that is not reflected within the text itself): the first, consisting of five poems, is called "Antes de la victoria" ("Before Victory"), and the second, which contains thirty-five poems, is "Después de la victoria" ("After Victory"). All of the poems in the first section, which describe events during the struggle against Somoza, have more optimistic sequels in the second section that confirm the realization of the revolutionary ideal: "La llegada" ("The Arrival") is completed by "Otra llegada" ("Another Arrival"), and "Las campesinas del Cuá" ("The Peasant Women from Cuá") by "Llegaron las del Cuá" ("The Women from Cuá Arrived"). The collection's lyricism arises in part from the absence of the intertextual freight of economic, scriptural, or scientific discourses.

Flights of Victory describes Utopia in the making. Its tone of joyous fulfilment is implicitly a form of divine praise, yet the religious element is noticeably more discreet than in "Nicaraguan Canto" or *Oracle over Managua*. In contrast to the earlier works, where religious prophecy serves as the basis for predictions of political change, here religion becomes simply one more component of the political panorama. "Recordando de pronto" ("Recalling

All of a Sudden") establishes a contrast between a young woman whom Cardenal remembers being attracted to many years ago on a beach ("Sus curvas como la curva de la costa" (*VV*, 41; "Her curves like the curve of the coast" [*FV*, 101]) –inevitably she is a cousin – and the same woman's current identity as an enemy of the Revolution: "en plena revolución nicaragüense/ es monja reaccionaria" (*VV*, 41; "in the full bloom of the Nicaraguan Revolution/she's a reactionary nun" [*FV*, 101]). The political division between the cousins trumps their common decision to subordinate the youthful pull of natural desires to a religious vocation. In a similar vein, "Misa ecuménica en Dusseldorf" ("Ecumenical Mass in Düsseldorf") parlays the union of diverse Christian faiths implicit in ecumenicalism into the campaign for world revolution. Cardenal's account of a mass he gave for two thousand young left-wing German Christians culminates in a citation that echoes Che Guevara's voluntaristic call to reproduce the Cuban Revolution in other countries: "'Que en el mundo haya muchas Nicaraguas'" (*VV*, 73; "'Let there be many Nicaraguas in the world'" [*FV*, 79)]). The religious event becomes an occasion for reiterating the political message, rather than being the moral foundation of that message, as is the case in the earlier poetry.

The book reflects Cardenal's delight in the FSLN's triumph, but the poems are also shaped significantly by his duties during these years as a globe-trotting salesman for Revolution who spent more than half of each year outside Nicaragua.[8] The best of Cardenal's post-revolutionary poems, including "Luces" ("Lights"), "Ante una foto" ("Before a Photo"), and "En la tumba del guerrillero" ("In the Tomb of the Guerrilla Fighter"), are compelling, involving advertisements for the Nicaraguan Revolution, and were read by students, writers, Christians, and activists in many countries. Yet there is no doubt that, in spite of its unprecedented audience, augmented by the global media's remorseless scrutiny of Nicaragua, *Flights of Victory* represents an attenuation of Cardenal's grappling with the ideological contradictions of constructing a national identity. His immersion in the transformations of the present dissolves the longer perspective in which national experience acquires form and meaning. Any contradictions between the needs of workers and peasants and the assertion of national sovereignty are subordinated by the lyrical moment and by his sheer wonder at the Revolution's triumph.

Critics such as Rosario Murillo and Bayardo Arce accused Cardenal of imposing his personal aesthetic on the Sandinista poetry workshops for workers and the newly literate. Yet there is much truth, also, in Beverley and Zimmerman's observation that "we may perceive the influence of workshop poetry on Cardenal's own work, his sense of wanting to produce a poetry useful to the new social sectors only recently brought to a level of minimal literacy, able to capture the everydayness of the revolution" (Beverley and Zimerman 1990: 103). In the workshops, young men and women wrote of watching their lovers depart for the front in combat fatigues; Cardenal responded by writing of his own revolutionary duties, or of the personal sacrifices of people he had met. An element of ideological uncertainty creeps in: now that the Revolution has enthroned the poor, Cardenal's status as a *letrado*, capable of explicating the nation's economic subjugation, understanding the theories of Ezra Pound, or citing Marx or Mao, counts for less; if the poor are in power, as the omnipresent Sandinista chant "*¡Poder popular!*" ("People Power!") insisted, his privileges as a foreign-educated priest from the Conservative oligarchy are in abeyance. To fulfill the Revolution's destiny, Cardenal must write like the poor people who are finding their voices.

The drawbacks of this stance are obvious in retrospect. Gonzalez and Treece, though they claim erroneously that the epistles to Coronel Urtecho and Monseñor Casaldáliga, published in 1976, were written "after the Nicaraguan Revolution of 1979" (Gonzalez and Treece 1992: 297), are correct to state that, in the workshop poetry, as in Cardenal's own verse of the immediate post-revolutionary period, the "very features of the shared public emotion concealed and suppressed the tension and conflict, the doubt and dilemma out of which growth and exploration was born" (ibid.: 298). Cardenal's own later assessment of *Flights of Victory* is made clear by the contents pages of his anthologies. His *Antología*, published in Managua in 1983 and intended for a Nicaraguan readership, contains, in addition to representative works from the rest of his career, more than twenty new poems that would be included the next year in *Flights of Victory*.[9] In *Antología nueva* (1996), *Flights of Victory* is subsumed into the section dedicated to *Cosmic Canticle*. Entitled "Vuelos de victoria (Fragmentos) (De *Cántico cósmico*)" (*AN*, 218; "Flights of Victory [Fragments] [From *Cosmic Canticle*]"), this section of what was presented as Cardenal's definitive anthology mingles stanzas from various of the poems in the 1984 collection, as though conceding a certain indistinguishable sameness among them. The only two poems that are set apart in their entirety (though untitled) are "Waslala" and "Nueva Ecología" ("New Ecology"), both of which stress the natural world, which, by definition, endures after the Revolution has been destroyed; the final line of this seven-page section of *Antología nueva* reads: "La revolución/es también de lagos, ríos, árboles, animales" (224; "The revolution is also one of lakes, rivers, trees, animals" [*FV*, 71]).

The original volume defines the nation in terms of the geography of the insurrectionary struggle and the martyrs who died to make the Revolution.

Flights of Victory opens with the line "Ya están cantando los gallos," (*VV*, 7; "Now the roosters are singing" [*FV*, 5]), a declaration that dawn is breaking at last. The contours of the nation revealed by the "dawn" of the final days of the insurrection and the broad daylight of the revolutionary state are charted through the poems' evocation of national geography as delineated by the struggle. Part of forging a "new Nicaragua" is the recasting of the significance of different features of the national geography in order to define the distinctive contours of the "patria socialista" (*VV*, 12; "socialist country" [*FV*, 7]) dreamed of by the narrator of "The Arrival." As suggested by the image of the roosters crowing in the book's opening line, and the closing declaration of "New Ecology" cited above, the natural world, too, is depicted as having been rejuvenated by the political transformation. "Another Arrival," which describes the Sandinista leadership's return flight to Nicaragua after attending Cuba's national celebrations on 26 July 1979, one week after the revolutionary triumph, describes "el Momotombo/libre por primera vez desde la época de los indios" (*VV*, 22; "Momotombo/free for the first time since the epoch of the Indians" [*FV*, 39]) and a conversation between Cardenal and Dora María Téllez in which they marvel at "Qué hermosa ahora nuestra naturaleza sin Somoza" (*VV*, 22; "How lovely our nature now without Somoza" [*FV*, 39]).

This reconceptualization of the natural world, however, is inseparable from the revolutionary recharting of the country's population centres. "Another Arrival" broaches the subject of the replacement of Somocista names with places' original, pre-Somoza designations, or with names reflective of Nicaraguan history as construed by the Revolution. "Ofensiva final" ("Final Offensive") compares the task of making the Revolution to the technical intricacy of a journey to the moon. In stressing the strategic coordination required to keep the various Sandinista comandantes supplied with munitions and rearguard support, the poem sketches a revolutionary geography in which the authentic Nicaragua is as foreign as the moon and the country's major cities are known by their revolutionary code names:

> "Aquí Taller" – "Aló Asunción" – "Aló Milpa."
> "Taller" era León, "Asunción" Masaya, "Milpa" Estelí.
> Y la voz calmada de la chavala Dora María desde "Taller" …
> Y la voz de Rubén en Estelí. La voz de Joaquín en "Oficina."
> "Oficina" era Managua.
> (*VV*, 23; "Workshop here" – "Come in, Assumption" – "Come in,
> Cornfield."/"Workshop" was León, "Assumption" Masaya, "Cornfield"

Estelí./And the calm voice of Dora María, the girl from "Workshop" .../ And the voice of Joaquín in "Office."/"Office" was Managua. [*FV*, 3])

Presaging the crucial importance of revolutionary martyrs to later poems in the collection, "Final Offensive" closes with a vow to "Leonel" (Rugama) that Nicaragua is beginning to belong to the poor. Subsequent poems extend the Sandinista renaming of the nation, which accords a changed historical significance to the places it touches. "Waslala" is portrayed as blessed by a renewal that mingles the vitality of natural and revolutionary essences – "Qué bello el verde de los campos y el verde de los compas" (*VV*, 29; "How beautiful the green of the field and the green of the soldiers" [*FV*, 67]) – and culminates in the radiation of undiluted happiness ("Qué alegre está Waslala" [*VV*, 29]; "How joyous Waslala is" [*FV*, 67]) through the mountains of what had been one of the most persistently brutalized regions of Nicaragua. The poem raises the question of the limited social reach of the voice of lyrical praise to accommodate ongoing social tensions. Beverley and Zimmerman comment that "all is too joyous in Waslala, in spite of the real difficulties of bringing the Miskito Indians into the revolution. The leap from insurrectional victory to the solution of the problems of a backward, struggling, multiethnic, fragmented country is too easily elided" (Beverley and Zimmerman 1990: 103).

Perhaps the most striking element of this critique arises from the word "multiethnic": in his depiction of a nation integrated by the common experience of the anti-Somoza struggle, the author of *Homenaje a los indios americanos*, who took care to refer to the Miskito in "Nicaraguan Canto," here paints a Nicaragua of implicit ethnic uniformity. In contrast to the adjustments made to Sandinista policies and ideology in the latter half of the 1980s to accommodate indigenous self-government, the first five years of the Revolution reinscribed the myth of "mestizo Nicaragua." Jeffrey Gould, in a study focusing not on the indigenous communities of the Atlantic Coast but rather on the "mestizo myth" that de-Indianized rural communities in western Nicaragua, praises "Cardenal's capacity to observe and powerfully evoke rural life in Nicaragua." He goes on to make the crucial observation that

> despite his fascination for and commitment to indigenous culture, his poetry lacks concrete references to contemporary indigenous communities in western Nicaragua. When he did write of indigenous areas such as Tuma, a coffee-growing region in Matagalpa, or Nindirí, the imagery was entirely about the natural world and lacked social references.

> This lack of specificity contrasted sharply with his poetry about non-Nicaraguan contemporary Indians, such as the Kuna of Panama, which exhibited a plethora of details about indigenous politics, society, and culture. (Gould 1998: 247)

Gould cites the examples of poems such as "The Peasant Women of Cuá" and "The Women from Cuá Arrived," which construct the women of an indigenous community terrorized by Somoza's National Guard as peasants ("*campesinas*"), victims of the dictatorship whose oppression is explicitly gendered, as mothers who protected their Sandinista sons and brothers in the face of threats and torture, but which do not acknowledge the women's identity as indigenous people. The assumption of a common mestizo heritage – an ideological relic from earlier Nicaraguan regimes, which under Sandinismo, at least during its first five years in power, was deployed to promote revolutionary unity – renders invisible the presence of Miskito, people in the Western highlands who still claim indigenous identities, and the Atlantic Coast Afro-Caribbean communities (even though some representatives of the latter group, such as the poets David McField and Carlos Rigby, held positions in the government [Beverley and Zimmerman 1990: 104]). Facing mounting US aggression, the Nicaraguan Revolution placed a high premium on what Cardenal characterized as "la unidad de todos/la unidad garantía de la Victoria" (*VV*, 35; "the unity of everyone,/unity the guarantee of Victory" [*FV*, 41)]. Paradoxically, this enforcement of an undifferentiated mestizo nationalism imposed "colouring" on the elite minority of Nicaraguans, such as Cardenal, who were of solely European ancestry. Enjoined to enter the ranks of a mixed-race proletarian norm, Cardenal purges his poems of learned discourses. The simplification of his diction, and his political vision, are essential to his claim to belong to the revolutionary, brown-skinned peasant nation in which no one is of either entirely European or entirely indigenous culture.

One of the most successful poems in *Flights of Victory*, "Lights," is an attempt to reconcile this identity, and the accessible, lyrical diction that accompanies it, with the trinity of revolutionary, religious, and scientific elements developed by Cardenal's poetry of the early 1970s. Like "Final Offensive," "Lights" is set during the last days of the insurrection; it, too, charts the geography of the coalescing sovereign nation that emerges as the Somoza dictatorship crumbles. The poem recounts the flight made on the night of 17–18 July 1979 by the Sandinista leadership, based in Costa Rica, to León, then recently captured by Sandinista forces led by Comandante Dora María Téllez. Here the Sandinistas would declare a provisional government and leave by road to enter Managua on 19 July. One of the few poems in the book that reflects, albeit in shorthand form, Cardenal's cosmic preoccupations, "Lights" opens with a vision of the Milky Way as seen out the window of the small plane that is carrying the comandantes: "masa blancuza y rutilante en la noche negra/con sus millones de procesos de evoluciones y revoluciones" (*VV*, 19; "a whitish and shimmering mass in the black night/with its millions of processes of evolutions and revolutions" [*FV*, 31]). The argument that the Sandinista Revolution is an inevitable natural process, first articulated in "Nicaraguan Canto," is scarcely necessary now that the Revolution is becoming a fact. "Lights" describes the transition from revolutionary hope, enshrined in a celestial realm conceived as both material and spiritual, to a revolution on the ground. The Utopian idealism that had to take refuge in the skies during the dictatorship becomes embedded in the geography of the emerging liberated nation. In "Lights" the repository of the revolutionary spirit is not so much the natural features of the Nicaraguan landscape – as in "Another Arrival," "New Ecology," or "Waslala" – but rather, as in "Final Offensive," the network of the country's cities, now defined in terms of their contributions to the crucial experience of making the Revolution. In the low-flying plane, the cities appear as historically charged clusters of lights in the darkness:

> Primero las luces de Rivas, tomada y retomada por los sandinistas,
> ahora a medias en poder de los sandinistas.
> Después otras luces: Granada, en poder de la Guardia
> (sería atacada esa noche).
> Masaya, totalmente liberada. Tantos cayeron allí.
> Más allá un resplandor: Managua. Lugar de tantos combates.
> (El Bunker.) Todavía el bastión de la Guardia.
> Diriamba, liberada. Jinotepe, con combates …
> La Vía Láctea arriba, y las luces de la revolución de Nicaragua.
> Me parece mirar más lejos, en el Norte, la fogata de Sandino.
> ("Aquella luz es Sandino.")
> (*VV*, 19; First the lights of Rivas, taken and retaken by the Sandinistas,/ now halfway in the Sandinistas' hands./Then other lights: Granada, in the hands of the guard/(it would be attacked that night)./Masaya, completely liberated. So many fell there./Further on, a glitter: Managua. The site of so many battles./(The Bunker – still the bastion of the guard)./Diriamba: liberated. Jinotepe, still fighting …/The Milky Way above, and the lights of Nicaragua's revolution./I seem to see further off, in the north, Sandino's campfire/("That light is Sandino.") [*FV*, 3]))

Cardenal's declarative testimonial voice shades into the quasi-mystical diction of "Nicaraguan Canto" and *Oracle over Managua* as he draws connections between the lights of the Sandinista Revolution, with its origins in Sandino's campfire in the hills and celestial forces. The history of the struggle, encapsulated by the cities' lights, becomes the terrestrial incarnation of the mystical elaboration of the evolutionary-revolutionary cycles that fuelled Cardenal's poetry when the Revolution was a longing rather than a fact. For the rest of the book, the revolutionary endeavour, in both its hope and, more sombrely, its legacy of martyrdom, becomes anchored in the Nicaraguan landscape and those who struggle to make revolutionary society. The light evoked in the references to the Milky Way becomes an all-pervasive essence bestowing a celestial blessing on the Sandinista project:

> … Pienso: todo es luz.
> El planeta viene del sol. Es luz hecha sólida.
> La electricidad de este avión es luz. El metal es luz. El calor
> de la vida viene del sol.
> "Hágase la luz."
> (*VV*, 19–20; … I think: everything is light./The planet comes from the sun. It is light made solid./This plane's electricity is light. The metal is light. Life's/warmth comes from the sun./"Let there be light." [*FV*, 31])

The transmission of this light, both sacred and material, into the landscape and protagonists of revolutionary Nicaragua is confirmed at the poem's conclusion when, after having landed in León, the comandantes embrace their revolutionary compañeros, who await them on the ground: "Sentimos sus cuerpos calientes, que también vienen del sol/que también son luz" (*VV*, 21; "We feel their warm bodies, which also come from the sun,/which are also light" [*FV*, 33]).

Strategically located at the opening of the book's second section, "After Victory," "Lights" sanctifies the land and those who give their lives to the Revolution. Many of the poems in *Flights of Victory* are narrated from a sitting position in an airplane, a location that symbolizes Cardenal's role as a revolutionary leader engaged in important business, but that also serves to bridge the natural/spiritual realm in the skies and the Nicaraguan earth, now saturated with sacred light from above. "Meditación en un DC-3" ("Meditation in a DC-3") articulates this link when Cardenal, flying "en el cielo de la patria liberada" (*VV*, 49; "in the sky of the liberated homeland" [*FV*, 35]), remembers a line from the German poet Novalis: "Tocar un cuerpo desnudo es tocar el cielo" (*VV*, 49; "Touching a naked body is touching heaven" [*FV*, 35]). The homeland's human and natural bodies have become "el cielo," in both senses of the word: sky and heaven. "Lights" states that "Es contra las tinieblas esta revolución" (*VV*, 21; "It's against the darkness this revolution" [*FV*, 33]); yet in the second half of the book the shadows gather as Cardenal commemorates those who died to make the Revolution.

The martyrdom of the tens of thousands of young people who gave their lives to the revolutionary struggle permeates the Nicaraguan earth. This theme is first broached in "Vuelo sobre la patria sin escala" ("Flight over the Homeland without Stopover"), the final poem in the book's opening, pre-revolutionary section. Here Cardenal, flying from Costa Rica to Lisbon for a meeting, thinks of the many deaths in the ongoing war in Nicaragua, remembering particularly his peasant protégé Elvis Chavarría: "Elvis y su guitarra. ¿A ellos dónde los enterró la guardia?" (*VV*, 17; "Elvis and his guitar. Where did the guardsmen bury them?" [*FV*, 19]). The fact that the Nicaraguan earth holds the bodies of the young men he mentored makes it for Cardenal, at this point living in exile, "La amada geografía para mí negada" (*VV*, 18; "The beloved geography denied to me" [*FV*, 19]). This identification with national geography becomes more powerful once the triumph of the Revolution has consecrated the sacrifice made by the young men of the Solentiname community and other young Nicaraguans.

"Meditation in a DC-3," which equates the nation with a human body, opens with an image of the plane's pilot, who "abría el mapa de la patria/para la niña morena de nueve años/(abajo la tierra nuestra)/su mano rozando su manita" (*VV*, 49; "opened the map of the homeland/for the dark-skinned girl of nine/(below, our land)/his hand touching her small hand" [*FV*, 35]). The "dark-skinned girl" acts as an archetype of the mestizo nation, while the touching of hands between her and the pilot extends the metaphor of the Nicaraguan earth as a human body. The remainder of the poem, revolving around the death in combat of Felipe Peña, a member of the Solentiname community ("Abajo Muy-Muy, ríos, Nueva Guinea donde cayó Felipe" (*VV*, 49; "Below was Muy-Muy, rivers, Nuevo Guinea where Felipe fell" [*FV*, 35]), insistently eroticizes the relationship with the beloved earth of the nation. Adopting the liberation theology trope of seeking the kingdom of heaven on earth, Cardenal portrays the national geography as "nuestra Tierra llena de humanos que se aman" (*VV*, 49; "our Earth full of humans who love each other" [*FV*, 35]) and states that this land "es el cielo/es el Reino de los cielos" (*VV*, 49; "is heaven/it's the Kingdom of Heaven" [*FV*, 35]). The poem depicts this divine love in profane terms, extending the series of encounters between flesh and flesh, from the pilot's hand touching that of the little girl, to the smooching ("besuquear") of a baby, to a couple caressing each other, to the assertion that "la unión de la piel humana con la piel humana" ("the union of human skin with human skin") is like touching "el Comunismo con el dedo compañeros" (*VV*, 49; "Communism with your finger compañeros" [*FV*, 35]). Yet *Flights of Victory* does not sustain this audacious, ecstatic tone; while, as critics have maintained, the book fails to capture the social contradictions of the immediate post-revolutionary period, it evokes with power the moral and spiritual imperatives of living in a state of independence that has been made possible by the deaths of idealistic youths.

In the second half of the collection, flights through the skies – realm of light and spiritual connection, symbol of revolutionary victory, vantage point on the exuberant natural world – are increasingly troubled and, symbolically, brought down to earth, by the moral claims of the dead revolutionaries who rest in that earth, and, as their bodies decay, suffuse it with their sacred martyrdom. The last two poems in the collection are the resonant "In the Tomb of the Guerrilla Fighter," which, more than any other poem in the book, finds a compact, accessible form in which to express Cardenal's cosmic mysticism, and, significantly, "Landing with Epitaph." In this final poem, a plane landing in Nicaragua becomes the occasion for a seven-line listing of the names of martyrs remembered by the narrator, who imagines the on-board personnel announcing: " … Señoras y Señores/la tierra que vamos a tocar es muy sagrada/… Las ruedas ya acaban de tocar, señores pasajeros, una gran tumba de mártires" (*VV*, 77; "… Ladies and Gentlemen/the ground we're about to touch is very sacred./… The wheels have just landed, passengers,/on a great tomb of martyrs" [*FV*, 37]). This sombre image, which closes the book, ultimately wins out over buoyancy, flight, and ecstacy.

Cardenal works his way towards this image through a series of increasingly explicit engagements with his, and the nation's, debt to the martyrs of the Revolution, particularly the peasant youths of Solentiname whom he converted to the Sandinista cause. These are the most personal, emotional poems in *Flights of Victory*, yet, perhaps for this reason, they are the least polished, and tend not to be studied by critics. Their most disarming feature is Cardenal's openness in depicting the youths of Solentiname as the offspring denied him by his vow of celibacy. This emotional charge leaves the unmistakable impression that Cardenal's insistence on the young men's revolutionary "sainthood" is validated less by Sandinista ideology than by personal grief and guilt. "A Donald y Elvis" ("To Donald and Elvis"), an unusually long poem for this collection, evokes the variety of ways in which Elvis Chavarría and Donald Guevara, the two young men to whom Cardenal was closest, remain present in the nation's life after the triumph. At the core of the multiple references to schools and boats named after the two teenagers who were mutilated by the National Guard, who cut off their hands and lashed them to their backs before torturing them to death, lies the poem's description of the exhumation of their bodies:

> Se distinguen las cuerdas del uno y las del otro
> porque un lazo es más estrecho y otro más ancho
> y Elvis tenía unas manotas más anchas.
> Cuando vi los huesos desenterrados de los dos
> te recordé Donald diciendo en la misa de Solentiname
> que la resurrección no eran las quirinas saliendo de las tumbas
> sino la supervivencia de la conciencia en los otros.
> (*VV*, 43; We can tell one set of strings from the other/because one is narrower and the other wider/and Elvis had the wider hands./When I saw the disinterred bones of the two of you/I remembered you Donald in the Solentiname Mass saying/that the Resurrection was not skeletons coming out of the tombs/but survival in the consciousness of others. [*FV*, 103])

As in "Meditation in a DC-3," the hands become the symbol of the fusion of the revolutionary's body with the soil of the homeland. "Nada más humano que una mano" (*VV*, 69; "Nothing more human than a hand" [*FV*, 45]), states "La mano" ("The Hand"), another poem in the collection. Yet, in spite of the poem's adherence to the Sandinista ideology of the dead living on in the consciousness of the citizens of the liberated homeland, the gruesomeness of this description makes the rest of the poem feel faint by comparison. The narrator's assertion that "ustedes ahora son santos" (*VV*, 44; "now you are saints" [*FV*, 105]), and the culminating image of the lake where the boys lived reflecting in "el cielo" (*VV*, 44; "the sky" [*FV*, 105]), projecting their sacrifice heavenwards, cannot disperse the awful fact of their mutilation and death.

A later poem, "Elvis," underscores Cardenal's attempt to reconcile himself to the young man's death by positing an equivalency that, ultimately, rings false. The narrator describes a dream in which Chavarría, who had already fathered a daughter with a girl on the island, brings Cardenal "un nuevo hijo tuyo" (*VV*, 70; "a new child of yours" [*FV*, 107]). This symbolic grandson provokes envy in Cardenal that Chavarría may do that which he cannot do "porque me lo he negado/yo" (*VV*, 70; "because I have denied it to myself" [*FV*, 107]). The contrast is revealing of the ways in which Cardenal finds in Elvis and the other young men vicarious vessels for the sexualized or bellicose traits that his religious vows, age, and social class have caused him to suppress. The need to identify with the peasantry in whose name the nation is ruled is visible here, also, as it is in the collection's aesthetics. The poem's resolution revolves around the establishment of an equivalency between Cardenal and his slain protégé on the grounds that both are dead in body but alive in spirit. Waking from his dream, the narrator remembers that "ya no podías tener ese nuevo hijito que se parecía a vos/como tampoco yo,/estabas muerto igual que yo/aunque estamos vivos los dos" (*VV*, 70; "now you couldn't have this new little child who looked like you/just as I couldn't,/you were dead just like me/although we're both pretty much alive" [*FV*, 107]).

While the intent of these lines is to assert that liberated Nicaragua is a celestial realm in which those who died for the Revolution are as present as the living,[10] an equally forceful impression arises of a certain specious insistence on Cardenal's part that his exclusion from sexual or military activity means that he is as dead as Elvis. This internalization of the crudest definitions of masculine virility, and of the author's anxieties at not being an equal participant in the sexually freewheeling society of revolutionary Nicaragua, where the eclipse of traditional forms of Catholic worship and the omnipresence of death contributed to an uninhibited sexual morality, underlines the moulding of Cardenal's outlook by "people power." This acceptance of his own status as less "alive" – in the sense of being less completely masculine – than the young revolutionaries who surround him combines with his desire to be reunited with his young charge, by sharing both his "death" and his "life."

The book's most overt expression of thwarted paternity appears in "Viaje muy jodido" ("A Very Screwed-Up Trip"). Cardenal, on an official visit to Trinidad, receives a telephone call informing him of the death of the last of his young protégés, Laureano Mairena, who died fighting the Contras after the triumph of the Revolution. As he flies "Trinidad-Barbados-Jamaica-Habana-Managua" (*VV*, 63), the sea outside the window of the plane growing steadily darker, he wrestles with the death of the foul-mouthed youth (also the father of two children) who served as his altar boy in Solentiname:

Su expresión más frecuente: ME VALE VERGA.
Hijo mío y hermano Laureano
  hijo indócil y cariñoso
como todo hijo con su padre
y como además yo no era tu verdadero padre
fuiste sobre todo mi hermano

hermano bastante menor en años
pero sobre todo compañero
¿esa palabra te gusta más, verdad?
(*VV*, 64; Your most frequent expression: I DON'T GIVE A FUCK./ My son and brother Laureano,/intractable and affectionate/like every son with his father/and since I was also not your real father/you were above all my brother/brother much the younger in years/but above all compañero/this word you like the most right? (*FV*, 111])

The confessional rawness of these lines reads more like the product of a Sandinista poetry workshop than the work of the author of *Oracle over Managua*. Cardenal renounces the egotism of asserting his symbolic paternity over his former altar boy in favour of a relationship defined by the Revolution: compañero. The narrator's insistent mockery of Mairena's coarse language preserves the mentor-protégé relationship at the same time that it delivers a symbolic one-finger salute to death. The poem concludes with Cardenal imagining himself joining Mairena in declaring from heaven that "me valió verga la muerte" (*VV*, 65; "I didn't give a fuck about/death" [*FV*, 115]). The realm of the dead from which Cardenal envisages himself making this declaration is inseparable from "lo que llamamos cielo" (*VV*, 65; "[what] we call heaven" [*FV*, 115]) – the Sandinista pantheon of martyrs. This heaven, which extends the boundaries of the conventional Christian realm, cannot be separated from the ever more imposing presence of the Nicaraguan earth saturated with the bodies of the martyrs.

The emotional denouement of *Flights of Victory*, capped by the coda of "Landing with Epitaph," is "In the Tomb of the Guerrilla Fighter," where Cardenal adapts his cosmic imagery to the culture of martyrs in a highly personal voice, uniting the strengths of his pre-revolutionary and post-revolutionary verse. As "Lights" establishes the metaphysical underpinning of the collection's high-flying first half, so this poem, which expresses Cardenal's vision of the sacredness of the soil of the revolutionary nation, provides a theology for the centrality of the experience of martyrdom. The poem opens with an evocation of the dead guerrilla's body: "tu cuerpo que se ha ido desbaratando bajo la tierra" (*VV*, 75; "your body that has been falling apart beneath the earth" [*FV*, 119]). The narrator appears to find a limited consolation in the fact that this fate is not unique to the anonymous young man to whom the poem is addressed, but rather is shared by "todos los demás humanos/que han existido o existirán en la bolita del mundo" (*VV*, 75; "all the other humans/who have existed or will exist on this small ball of the world" [*FV*, 119]). Uniting the dominant imagery of the book's two halves, the earth is described as resembling a "luminosa tumba/(tu tumba y la de todos)" (*VV*, 75; "luminous tomb/(your tomb and the tomb of everyone)" [*FV*, 119]). The narrator anticipates the day when, after the extinction of human life, the planet will be "todo tumba, silenciosa tumba" (*VV*, 75; "all tomb, silent tomb" [*FV*, 119]). This almost nihilistic vision is vitiated by a mysticism rooted in the struggle for national sovereignty, through which the narrator finds his way back to the vital image of light: the planet is humanized by its cargo of decaying bodies. This image becomes the vehicle for Cardenal's fusion of Christianity and Marxism, building on the depictions that recur, from "Nicaraguan Canto" onward, of the Nicaraguan Revolution as an indispensable stage in a cosmic evolutionary process. This eternal succession of expansions and contractions gives birth to a resurrection that is both material and spiritual:

> Y tal vez la materia es eterna hermano
> sin principio ni fin o tiene un fin y recomienza cada vez.
> Tu amor sí tuvo un comienzo pero no tiene final.
> Y tus átomos que estuvieron en el suelo de Nicaragua,
> tus átomos amorosos, que dieron la vida por amor,
> ya verás, serán luz ...
> (*VV*, 75; And perhaps matter is eternal, brother,/without beginning or end or it has an end and starts again each time./Your love surely had a beginning but has no end./And your atoms that were in the soil of Nicaragua,/your loving atoms, that gave their life for love,/you'll see, they'll be light ... [*FV*, 119])

By locating a form of Christian eternal life in the decaying body as it diffuses through the earth, Cardenal coordinates the forbidding image of Nicaragua as the tomb of thousands of young revolutionaries with the promise of divine light that opened the collection. The resurrection offered here is twofold: first, it is not that of a soul presumed to be conscious, as in traditional Christianity, but rather of the continuation and eventual cohering once again of the material substance of the cosmos, from which we are all formed; second, in a more mystical turn, this persistence of the atoms that constituted the young guerrilla's body projects the Sandinista triumph through eternity, extending the legacy of the nation far beyond the span of human life on earth: "me imagino tus partículas en la vastedad del cosmos como pancartas" (*VV*, 75; "I imagine your particles in the vastness of the cosmos like signs" [*FV*, 119]). The poem closes with the promise that the guerrilla's name will be shouted, with an accompanying cry of "¡Presente!"

(*VV*, 75; "Present!" [*FV*, 119]), for all eternity. In an assertion that is paradoxical in light of the imagery that has preceded it, which foresees the extinction of all life (and its eventual reconstitution in a different form in another region of the universe), the nation supplies the individual with a vessel in which to deposit his revolutionary love in order to sail through eternity.

The popular voice adopted by Cardenal in *Flights of Victory* makes these poems pivotal to his poetic evolution. The confessional mode promoted by workshop poetry induces him to grapple, in language that is affecting and accessible, with the debt owed by all Nicaraguans to those who died for the Revolution. The fate of the Nicaraguan earth is a particularly poignant theme because it is the repository of the bodies of Cardenal's symbolic descendants, the young men who were his protégés and surrogate sons, and for whose death his prosletyzing is to some degree responsible. The heightening of this mysticism will reach its most full-blown expression in *Cosmic Canticle*.

Both the lyrical and the mystical influences spilled over into Cardenal's return to poetry on indigenous subjects in the late 1980s. *Los Ovnis de oro. Poemas indios* (1988; *Golden UFOs. Indian Poems*), which collected his old and new indigenous poetry, contains shorter, more subjective poems, such as "La niña náhuatl" ("The Náhuatl Girl"), which narrates an Aztec girl's perceptions of the changing face of the moon, as well as involved, Poundian works similar to those he had collected previously in *Homenaje a los indios americanos*. The writing of these new indigenous poems coincided with the Sandinistas' successful reconciliation with the Miskito and other Atlantic Coast cultures. The poems focus on indigenous communities in Panama, Paraguay, Guatemala, Colombia, Peru, the United States, and, above all, Mexico. Their impulse is Panamerican, emphasizing the indigenous cultural substratum that unifies the hemisphere.

The most ambitious of Cardenal's indigenous poems of the 1980s, "Quetzalcóatl," depicts the Náhuatl heritage that western Nicaragua shares with Mexico as a source of Spanish American solidarity with the Nicaraguan Revolution. A forty-line stanza that begins by asserting the affiliation of a pre-Columbian settlement of Tola – now the town of Rivas – with places of similar names in the Central Valley of Mexico, concludes with the arrival of the Mexican presidential jet, named Quetzalcóatl, in Managua after the Sandinista triumph of 1979. The poem emphasizes the indigenous heritage as a common subsoil that forges connections between the nations of the Americas. The poor, dusty town of Rivas, near the shore of Lake Nicaragua, is paved, at a subterranean level, by pottery that makes this shared heritage clear: "Todo el subsuelo lleno de cerámica de colores/esplendor bajo la pobreza/En el ahora polvoriento pueblito de Tola" (*OO*, 66; "The entire subsoil packed with colored pottery,/splendor under poverty./In the now-dusty village of Tola" [*GOLD*, 301]). The Nicaraguan Revolution rights not simply forty-five years of dictatorship, but nearly five hundred years of colonialism: "Pero Quetzalcóatl también se fue de Tola, Rivas/Al llegar los españoles había sacrificios humanos,/hasta aquel 19 de julio" (*OO*, 67; "But Quetzalcóatl also left Tola, Rivas./When the Spaniards arrived there were human sacrifices,/until that July 19th" [*GOLD*, 301]). The stanza's final lines, linking Augusto César Sandino, whose name now adorns the Managua airport, with the plumed serpent god on the side of the Mexican presidential jet, converts Sandinismo into the contemporary expression of the Náhuat heritage that Nicaragua and Mexico share. At the same time, it depicts inter-American solidarity – vital to the Sandinistas in the mid-1980s – as an ancestral duty.

Unlike the poems in *Homenaje a los indios americanos*, though, the indigenous poems of the 1980s do not contain the Marxist economic analysis that appears in "Economy of the Tahuantinsuyu." In an extension of the themes of the second half of *Flights of Victory* and in anticipation of *Cosmic Canticle*, the focus of the new indigenous poems included in *Golden UFOs* is spiritual and mystical. As "El secreto de Machu-Picchu" ("The Secret of Macchu Picchu") concludes, "Los caminos de Machu-Picchu son interiores" (*OO*, 153; "The roads of Machu Pichu lead inward" [*GOLD*, 405]). The triumph of the Revolution and the establishment of the revolutionary nation on a foundation of mass martyrdom fuses the quest for cultural identity with a spiritual pilgrimage that Cardenal expresses through a scientific vocabulary in order to give it concrete, comprehensible form.

ATOMS OF THE DEAD: *COSMIC CANTICLE*

Cosmic Canticle, the most vast and daunting of Cardenal's works, and the most polyphonic in the multiplicity of discourses harnessed by his Exteriorism, was completed after the elimination of the Ministry of Culture during the 1988 "compression." The loss of his ministerial position liberated Cardenal not only in the practical sense of enabling him to retreat to Solentiname to write; it also freed him from the representative role in which he felt obliged to claim the left-wing Latin American Neruda rather than the right-wing gringo Pound as his major poetic influence. The poem advertises its status as Poundian cantos rather than Nerudaesque *canto* (song). A documentary film made about *Cosmic Canticle* in 1995, shortly after Cardenal had resigned from the FSLN, contradicts with startling bluntness the account of his poetic influences given in interviews from the 1980s. In the film, Cardenal says:

> Este libro no es un libro que yo crea que se puede ubicar en la literatura latinoamericana ni menos centroamericana. La influencia principal de mi poesía, mejor dicho, la única influencia de mi poesía, es la de la poesía norteamericana, desde Whitman hasta Ezra Pound, y después lo más nuevo … [Pound] me ha influído a mí, y yo parto de la lección que nos ha dejado Pound – parto hacia más adelante. Me refiero a la gran épica de los cantos. Pound no se metió en ese territorio. (*Ernesto Cardenal* 1995; This book is not a book that I believe can be situated in Latin American literature, much less in Central American literature. The main influence on my poetry, or rather, the only influence on my poetry, is US poetry from Whitman to Ezra Pound, and then the latest … [Pound] has influenced me, and I depart from the lesson that Pound has left us – I move ahead from there. I mean the great epic songs. Pound did not enter that territory.)

This astonishing claim to have abstracted himself from the tradition of Latin American literature can be interpreted in light of his 1995 rupture with the FSLN: his statements serve as a way of separating his creative work from its identification with an opportunistic populism that no longer reflects his ideals. Indeed, *Cosmic Canticle* employs the Exteriorist techniques that Cardenal had developed through his engagement with Pound. But, if the poem's subject is all of time, the content of that time remains fiercely Nicaraguan; some sections of *Cosmic Canticle* display Panamerican tendencies that resemble those of Neruda's *Canto General*. This is most evident in Cantiga 24, "Documental latinoamericano" ("Latin American Documentary"), whose often vignette-like tour of Latin American dictatorships also displays the influence of the work of Eduardo Galeano in *Las venas abiertas de América Latina* (1971; *The Open Veins of Latin America*) and *Memoria del fuego* (1982–86; *Memory of Fire*). The cantiga acknowledges this influence by supporting its opening statements with the line "(Está en Galeano)" (*CANC*, 269; "It's in Galeano" [*COSC*, 223]) and through later references to "Las venas abiertas" (*CANC*, 277; "The open veins" [*COSC*, 230]).

Yet the poem needs to be understood, too, in the context of the historical moment in which it was published, in November 1989, only three months prior to the Sandinista electoral defeat. Sergio Ramírez's novel *Castigo divino* (1988), Gioconda Belli's *The Inhabited Woman* (1988), Tomás Borge's *The*

Patient Impatience (1989), Omar Cabezas's *Canción de amor para los hombres* (1988), and *Cosmic Canticle* constitute a quintet of epics in which Sandinista leaders anchor in history the contours of the revolutionary nation precisely at the point where, as a consequence of the US proxy war, it is losing the ability to deliver on its promise of national sovereignty and social justice. These five works – a postmodern crime novel set during the 1930s, a feminist novel set among upper-class young people who join the guerrillas in the 1970s, two memoirs that blend the author's personal history with that of the Sandinista struggle, and an epic poem that uses science and materialism to create a mystical Christian vision of the trajectory of the life-force from the Big Bang to the end of time and presents the Nicaraguan Revolution as an integral part of this cosmic destiny – preserve the revolutionary nation in narrative just as the hardships of war make the realization of revolutionary ideals more elusive in daily life.

Cosmic Canticle was welcomed by the US avant-garde to whom Cardenal claims an aesthetic affinity. Allen Ginsberg and Robert Bly responded to the 1993 English translation by praising what Ginsberg called its "post-Poundian verse." At the same time, Ginsberg saw the poem as belonging to "the grand lineage of the Central American prophet Rubén Darío"; Bly, ironically, claimed that *Cosmic Canticle* "continues the tradition of Pablo Neruda" (*COSC*, back cover). While the poem's Exteriorism may constitute a prolonged homage to Pound, the references to Neruda are more overt and aesthetically charged; the mentions of Darío, by contrast, are more numerous and more direct in their claiming of a relationship with an illustrious ancestor.

The allusions to Neruda act to limit the influence, within the text, of the great left-wing Latin American poet of the generation that preceded Cardenal's. An incursion into autobiography in Cantiga 4 depicts a young man and a teenage girl – the couple is almost certainly Cardenal and his first love, Carmen Chamorro Benard – saying farewell forever on a Granada street: "y fue cuando él le recitó a Neruda:/'… los versos más tristes esta noche'/'La noche está estrellada/y tiritan azules los astros a lo lejos'" (*CANC*, 43; "and it was when he read Neruda to her:/'… the saddest verses this night.'/'The night is filled with stars/and blue, stars, in the distance, shiver'" [*COSC*, 37–8]). These citations from "Poem 20," one of the most melancholy poems in Neruda's most youthful, romantic and popular work, *Veinte poemas de amor y una canción desesperada* (1924; *Twenty Love Poems and a Song of Despair*), capture the Neruda whom Cardenal discovered as a young man. In the cantiga's final lines, Neruda's romantic conception of the stars prevails over Cardenal's customary scientific characterization of their movements. The two lovers who are parting at first appear to illustrate the divergence of galaxies in the cosmos ("Las dos direcciones cada vez más divergentes" [*CANC*, 43]; "The two directions ever more divergent" [*COSC*, 38]). Yet the cantiga's final lines are overwhelmed by a nostalgia – "He pensado otra vez en vos, porque la noche está estrellada" (*CANC*, 43; "I have thought of you again because the night is filled with stars" [*COSC*, 38]) – rare in Cardenal's verse: these sentiments are authorized and facilitated by this intertextual mingling with Neruda's effusive youthful work. The presence of the Chilean poet is implicit in *Cosmic Canticle*'s political commitment to a revolutionary Panamerican agenda, and even in the way in which this agenda ultimately proves to be secondary to the narrator's account of his own country.

As in *Canto General*, where the Panamericanism that dominates the first nine books of Neruda's epic yields in the final six books to a tighter focus on the narrator and his Chilean context, *Cosmic Canticle*'s international and intergalactic themes constantly circle back to the revolutionary struggle in Nicaragua. Cardenal accords a larger portion of his poem to his own nation (and a far smaller portion to his autobiography) than does Neruda. Nevertheless, *Canto General* provides a model for the balancing of national and Panamerican imperatives. No citations of Neruda's verse that are identified as such appear after Cantiga 4, but the ghost of Neruda's example and ambitions are omnipresent. The only other named reference to Neruda in the poem occurs in a passage that equates Cardenal's youthful adherence to a highly Conservative form of Catholicism with Neruda's disastrous adulation of Josef Stalin: "Pío XII fue para mí lo que Stalin para Neruda" (*CANC*, 149; "Pius XII was for me what Stalin was to Neruda" [*COSC*, 12]). This epigrammatic summation depicts Pope Pius XII, who reigned from 1939 to 1958 and was an anti-Communist known for intervening in Italian elections to support the political right, as the moral equivalent of a mass murderer. The line also contributes to the theme of Neruda as a poet of youth – of youthful political mistakes as well as of first love. This type of relationship between a poet and his main literary influences is characterized by Harold Bloom as *Tessera*, meaning that "[a] poet antithetically 'completes' his precursor, by so reading the parent-poem as to retain its terms but to mean them in another sense, as though the precursor had failed to go far enough" (Bloom 1973: 14). Cardenal's anxiety of influence underlines the limitations of the early Neruda, yet deflects direct engagement with the mature Neruda, in spite of the poem's obvious debt to the form and ambitions of the best-known work of Neruda's maturity.

The overt presence of Ezra Pound is even sparser, but, as seen in the film interview, Cardenal also suggests that Pound "did not go far enough" in the sense of not using the Canto form to write an epic as ambitious as *Cosmic Canticle*. Pound's name is mentioned only once. Perhaps significantly, this reference occurs in the final cantiga, only five pages from the poem's conclusion. Yet this appearance, in a section that evokes the darkness prior to the advent of a prophet, is not a homage to the poet whose aesthetic innovations inspired Cardenal, but rather a passing mention: "Jonás muy enraizado en la mente de los pueblos primitivos / dice Frobenius. / Otra vez Frobenius. Querido Pound. / El héroe vence al monstruo en el mito pigmeo ..." (*CANC*, 576; "Jonah, deeply rooted in the mind of primitive peoples / says Frobenius. / Once again Frobenius. Dear Pound. / The hero defeats the monster in the Pygmy myth" [*COSC*, 480]). The phrase "Dear Pound" alludes to the correspondence between the US poet and the German ethnographer Leo Frobenius (1873–1938), who studied, and made accessible to a Western readership, detailed knowledge of the cultures of West Africa. The "once again" recognizes that Frobenius is a recurring presence in *Cosmic Canticle*; in Cantiga 19, for example: "Y Frobenius, que desde las primeras migraciones de pueblos / comenzaron a fijarse en el cielo ..." (*CANC*, 218; "And Frobenius, that from the earliest migrations of peoples / they began to take note of the sky" [*COSC*, 182]). In fact, at the time Cardenal was polishing these words, the Nigerian writer Wole Soyinka had just denounced the German ethnographer's descriptions of the Yoruba as "[a] direct invitation to a free-for-all race for dispossession" in his 1986 Nobel Prize lecture (although Soyinka also acknowledged that Frobenius could "be profoundly stirred by an object of beauty, the product of the Yoruba mind and hand" [Soyinka, n.d.]). Cardenal views Frobenius as a groundbreaking presence in the incorporation of the insights and mythologies of indigenous cultures into the Occidental poetic tradition. The allusions to Frobenius demonstrate the degree to which Pound's outlook and references saturate the poem, even if he is only once referred to by name; it also identifies Pound, and not just Thomas Merton, as a source of Cardenal's interest in aboriginal cultures.

The text's allusions to Rubén Darío, by contrast, draft the earlier Nicaraguan poet into the unexpected role of supporting Cardenal's mystical vision of the cosmos. The preciousness of Darío's early *modernista* poetry, exemplified by *Azul* (1888; Blue), with its flight from Latin American reality into European mythologies, is the subject of frequent tangential allusions; yet the more politically engaged post-1898 Darío, who wrote the anti-imperialist poem "A Roosevelt" (1904; "To Roosevelt"), is far less present. Cardenal incorporates Darío into the poem as a mystic whose ideas support and intertwine with his own. In contrast to Neruda, a metaphorical father-figure from whose influence Cardenal distances himself in order to forge a distinctive poetic identity, Darío, who died before Cardenal was born, appears in the poem as part of the bedrock of Cardenal's cosmovision. A citation from Darío describing Nicaragua as "Tierra de lagos y volcanes" (*CANC*, 59; "Land of lakes and volcanoes" [*COSC*, 52]) is integrated into Cardenal's account of the salient features of the national landscape as "consecuencia demorada de la explosión de las estrellas" (*CANC*, 59; "consequences of the explosion of the stars" [*COSC*, 52]), making Darío an accomplice of Cardenal's mystical vision of the homeland as the product of cosmic processes. The pattern repeats in an account of a visit to the "Museo Geológico de South Kensington" (*CANC*, 85; "Geological Museum of South Kensington" [*COSC*, 72]) (which could be either the Natural History Museum or the adjacent Science Museum) where a quote from Darío – "Carne celeste" (*CANC*, 85; "Celestial flesh" [*COSC*, 72]) – is used to support the contention that "También somos hijos del sol" (*CANC*, 85; "We too are children of the sun" [*COSC*, 72]).

Similarly, a protracted discussion of consciousness as a defining feature of life concludes with a citation from Darío in which the poet envies a stone because it does not feel. An evocation of the birth of planet Earth from the cooling of gases contains an apparent allusion to the *modernista* poet in the line, "su luz es desnudez dice Rubén,/el que trajo de la sagrada selva la armonía" (*CANC*, 239; "Their light is nakedness says Rubén,/he who brought harmony from the sacred forest" [*COSC*, 199]). This citation alludes to the non-politically engaged *modernista* phase of Darío's career, finding the music of the spheres in the earlier poet's quest for aesthetic beauty. A notorious drunken conversation between Darío and the French symbolist poet Paul Verlaine, in which the latter denounced glory as "*merde*" (*CANC*, 448; *COSC*, 372), appears, idiosyncratically, as an illustration of chaos theory. Cantiga 39, which opens with references to the cultures of ancient Greece and Rome, evokes another element of Darío's early poetry, his predilection for Classical allusions, by incorporating the citation "hacia Belén la caravana pasa" (*CANC*, 488; "Bethlehem bound, the caravan passes" [*COSC*, 404]) into this clustering of historical, religious, and mythological references.

Only two allusions to Darío refer to the anti-imperialist stance of his later years. Cantiga 24, "Latin American Documentary," where the influences of Neruda and Galeano are prominent, notes in passing the abomination of General Rafael Trujillo, dictator of the Dominican Republic from 1930 to 1961, having been awarded the "orden Rubén Darío" (*CANC*, 288; "Rubén Darío order" [*COSC*, 240]) by Anastasio Somoza García. Cantiga 27 claims Darío as an ancestor of modern Sandinismo by remarking, in the midst of a long list of atrocities committed by the United States around the world, that

"... Darío/fue el primero en llamarles enemigos de la humanidad" (*CANC*, 319; "...Darío/was the first to call them enemies of humanity" [*COSC*, 265]), a reference to the Sandinista anthem, written by Carlos Mejía Godoy, which vows that "luchamos contra el yankee/el enemigo de la humanidad" ("Himno de la unidad"; "We fight against the Yankee/the enemy of humanity").

The most surprising feature of these references is the recourse to Darío as a source of authority in matters cosmic and aesthetic (particularly in light of the chasm that separates Darío's exquisitely lyrical language from Cardenal's quasi-oral vernacular), and the sparing references to the Panamerican, anti-imperialist Darío, who might be expected to play a central role in a poem such as *Cosmic Canticle*. In this sense, a parallel exists between the treatment of Neruda and that of Darío. While Neruda's politics receive cursory, disparaging attention, those of Darío, limited to a single reference, serve as a source of authority for the Sandinista vision of the Yankee as the enemy of humanity. The allusion provides this contentious line in the Sandinista anthem – dropped from the song for much of the 1990s – with an impeccable lineage in the work of an aesthetically oriented Nicaraguan intellectual who was the greatest Spanish-language poet of his day. The particulars of Darío's anti-imperialism, however, like those of Neruda's socialism, are absent from *Cosmic Canticle*. The reasons for the two omissions differ. Neruda is confined to a scant presence in order to enable Cardenal to unfurl an independent identity as a revolutionary poet. In the case of Darío, his Panamericanist anti-imperialism appears less important than his artistic example of how a poet from Nicaragua may become a voice heard across continents; his far more extensive presence in the poem reveals Cardenal's greater comfort with this more remote legacy, as well as his need to relate his international themes to Nicaraguan material. Allusions to Darío become a cultural banner to be brandished in the service of the Nicaraguan nation; yet the details of Darío's post-1898 Panamericanism, which depended on the glorification of the Peninsular heritage, and on a traditionalist form of Catholicism incompatible with Cardenal's liberation theology (and which did not prevent Darío from consorting with Central American dictators), paradoxically, offers little direct support either to Cardenal's socialist-influenced nationalism or his unorthodox Christianity.

The deployment of Darío as a source of support for Cardenal's mysticism is one of *Cosmic Canticle*'s many contradictions. Debate about the poem, which many critics agree is important but which has yet to be subjected to scrupulous study, has not probed the text in sufficient depth to reconcile such internal contradictions. The work's sheer length – approximately 17,700 lines – and its almost overwhelming breadth and intertextual complexity, have deterred critics from undertaking the detailed analysis it deserves.[11] Borgeson is correct when he states: "Ninguna escritura [de Cardenal] tiene semejante densidad de alusiones, tan amplia base de lecturas en materias diversas, tan variado manejo del lenguaje" (Borgeson 1994: 255; "No writing [of Cardenal] has such a density of allusions, such a broad base of readings in various subjects, such a varied use of language"). In *Cosmic Canticle* Cardenal brings to Exteriorism a heightened lyricism and directness that are the fruit of the experience of the Nicaraguan poetry workshops. The literal directness is more pronounced than in earlier Exteriorist works such as *Zero Hour* and *Oracle over Managua*, but so, too, is the lyricism that arises in the interstices of the declarative explanations of theories of astrophysics. The present study will focus on those elements that illuminate Cardenal's treatment of the revolutionary nation.

Even though he was able to devote himself full-time to the poem only in 1988, internal evidence suggests that Cardenal began concentrated work on *Cosmic Canticle* soon after the publication of *Flights of Victory*. An autobiographical anecdote in Cantiga 6 includes the phrase "Ahora tengo 61 años" (*CANC*, 58; "Now I'm 61"[(*COSC*, 51]), suggesting that it was written in 1986. Pope John Paul II's withdrawal of Cardenal's right to administer the sacraments in 1985 also may have contributed to the poem's imaginative framework by forcing him to emphasize the contemplative dimension of his religious vocation. The existence of a revolutionary government in Nicaragua relieved Cardenal of the burden of maintaining the "Christian-Marxist" stance of *Oracle over Managua* and *La santidad de la revolución*. *Cosmic Canticle* is unmistakably the work of a left-wing Christian; but Cardenal no longer needs to invoke God for the purpose of urging the masses to revolutionary action. The revolution has taken place; although Cardenal still imagined the Nicaraguan Revolution to be eternal, he had just lost an internal power struggle with Rosario Murillo and his focus had shifted to the (much) bigger picture. This is evident in the closing Cantigas, where the scientific vocabulary yields to that of religion. In Cardenal's own description: "El poema cada vez va teniendo más temática divina; las últimas cantigas son del amor divino. Termina con Dios ..." (*Ernesto Cardenal* 1995; "The theme of divinity becomes ever more important in the poem; the last cantigas are of divine love. It ends with God ...").

Christian Marxism was an authentic synthesis of initially antagonistic strains of Cardenal's belief system reached through his experiences in Colombia, Solentiname, and Cuba, but it was also a political posture he played up during the struggle against Somoza in order to render the Sandinista platform palatable to church-bred oligarchs of his own social class, the devout Nicaraguan masses, and the rest of Latin America. He continued to perceive the universe as God's creation, but his intellect was often most engaged by physics and theories of the evolution of the cosmos. In later years, when challenged, he would concede that his belief system might be compatible with the theory of Intelligent Design (Morrow 2010: 24). Yet Cardenal's hosts during his visits to universities in the United States were often surprised that, when he asked to visit local bookstores, he did not go to either the poetry or the theology section but rather purchased recent volumes by writers such as Richard Feynman, David Bohm, Carl Sagan, and James Lovelock: exponents of new theories of the earth and the universe.[12]

Cosmic Canticle narrates nothing less than the expansion of the universe from the Big Bang to the end of time. This temporal and spatial span, which in theory includes everything that has ever been or ever will be – as though he has found a way of solving the aesthetic conundrum that thwarted Carlos Argentino Daneri in Jorge Luis Borges's "The Aleph" – enables Cardenal to combine, adapt, and adulterate discourses from the realms of science, theology, history, anthropology, literature, and politics, blending these often imposing blocks of ideologies and specialized languages and information with autobiographical vignettes, newspaper headlines, and lyrical evocations of the cosmos. In its extension of poetry into a form capable of equalling the novel's ability to contain all varieties of human experience, *Cosmic Canticle* exceeds even the ambitions of Ezra Pound. The poem's structure is circular, in conformity with the conception expressed in "In the Tomb of the Guerrilla Fighter" that "la materia es eterna hermano/sin principio ni fin o tiene un fin y recomienza cada vez" (*VV*, 75; "matter is eternal, brother,/without beginning or end or it has an end and starts again each time" [*FV*, 119]). *Cosmic Canticle* opens with the lines

En el principio no había nada
  ni espacio
    ni tiempo
      El universo entero concentrado
en el espacio del núcleo de un átomo.
(*CANC*, 11; In the beginning there was nothing/neither space/ nor time./The entire universe concentrated/in the space of the nucleus of an atom. [*COSC*, 11])

Three lines later "fue el Big Bang" (*CANC*, 11; "that was the Big Bang" [*COSC*, 11]) and this concentrated world begins to diffuse, disperse, and separate. Cardenal establishes early on the crossover between discourses that nourish the poem as his narration of the creation of life oscillates between descriptions of the origins of the universe based in the vocabulary of physics ("su geometría imprecisa/con el principio de incertidumbre de la Mecánica Cuántica" (*CANC*, 11; "its geometry imprecise/with the uncertainty principle of Quantum Mechanics" [*COSC*, 11]) and those rooted in the accounts of this event given by indigenous peoples from around the world, in lines such as "... Primero era el gran huevo cósmico. Dentro del huevo/había caos. Y sobre el caos flotaba P'an Ku" (*CANC*, 14; "... First was the great cosmic egg. Within the egg/there was chaos. And P'an Ku floated above the chaos" [*COSC*, 13]). Cardenal attributes his inclusion of aboriginal explanations of the origins of life to aesthetic concerns: "Pero eso viendo yo que sería demasiado seco, árido, monótono si fuera solamente el relato científico, lo voy intercalando con mitos de muchas tribus indígenas o aborígenes del mundo sobre la Creación" (*Ernesto Cardenal* 1995; "But seeing that it would be too dry, arid, monotonous if it were solely the scientific account, I interspersed it with myths of many Native American tribes, or aboriginal peoples of the world, on Creation"). Yet, in an extension of Cardenal's earlier aboriginal poems, the indigenous discourses challenge the primacy of rationalist modes of enquiry.

The poem's attempt to go "beyond Pound," in both its unrivalled temporal ambition and its extension of the canto form to embrace an ever wider range of materials, suggests that the mingling of disparate discourses stems not merely from an effort to avoid "aridity," but from an impulse to achieve Pound's goal of enabling poetry to reclaim from prose narrative its central role as the great assimilator of language and event: "Y también usar muchas veces los temas que tradicionalmente eran propios de la prosa y no de la poesía, como, por ejemplo, hablar de la situación política actual o económica, o las noticias de los periódicos" (*Ernesto Cardenal* 1995; "And also to use often themes that traditionally belonged to prose, not poetry, for example, to talk about the current political or economic situation, or the news in the newspapers").

This quasi-novelistic, or chronicle-like, ambition coexists with a need to stake out a distinctive poetic identity. Cardenal's aesthetic inheritance from Pound distinguishes his *Cosmic Canticle* from Neruda's *Canto General*; yet his decision to call his cantos "cantigas" creates a distance from the United States tradition. Asked about the relation of his cantigas to Pound's cantos, Cardenal responds: "Yo uso una palabra que es del español antiguo de la Edad Media, es cantiga, que equivale lo mismo" (ibid.; "I use a word that is from old Spanish of the Middle Ages, it is cantiga, which amounts to the same thing"). The thirteenth-century Galician-Portuguese cantiga, which developed out of the Provençal troubadour tradition, was normally a lyrical love song (although some were also satirical or obscene); the tradition's popularity meant that "until about the 16th century, even Castilian poets used the Galician dialect in their *cantigas*, since it was the conventional medium of expression for lyric poetry" (Newmark 1956: 53). This tradition of working in a foreign idiom – in the case of the cantigas, the forerunner of modern Portuguese – reiterates Cardenal's paradoxical project of writing a great epic in the US poetic idiom. While his assertion that "cantiga" "amounts to the same thing" as "canto" may be disingenuous, this residual allegiance to an older Hispanic – but not Spanish American – tradition serves as a brake against absorption by either Latin American or US literature, and bolsters the poem's claim to cosmic sui generis. The declarations of loyalty to Pound repudiate claims of the far more threatening (in the sense of having the potential to overshadow or diminish his distinctive identity) possibility of being seen as simply another left-wing Latin American poet who follows in Neruda's footsteps. Yet, by dividing his "canticle" into "cantigas," Cardenal anchors his identity in the Iberian past, mitigating the potentially treasonous resonances of his fealty to the US fascist sympathizer Pound.

Cantiga 2, "La Palabra" ("The Word"), establishes the combined religious-aesthetic importance of language: "Las cosas existen en forma de palabra" (*CANC*, 25; "Things exist in the form of word" [*COSC*, 22]). The conception of language expressed by Cardenal is binary: words arise from dialogue, which also generates the overarching force of love, whether sacred or profane. Love saturates all things, as all things exist because they exist in language. The binary nature of both love and language, which Cardenal parlays into a brand of intergalactic erotics, persists in palpable contradiction to the poem's polyphonic cannibalization of discourses. The insistence on the binary suggests that the many discourses included in the poem in fact break down into two great streams: those that exalt and generate human freedom, and those that oppress the individual in his quest for selfless love in an autonomous community in harmony with God and the universe. The poem's momentum derives from this dialectical tension. The dialectic begins, in Cardenal's portrayal, with the residual static from the echoes of the Big Bang:

Y empezó la danza dialéctica celeste.
"El *yang* llama;
el *yin* responde."
Él es en el que toda cosa es.
Y en el que toda cosa goza.

Toda cosa coito.
  Todo el cosmos cópula.
Todas las cosas aman, y él es el amor con que aman.
(*CANC*, 28; And the celestial dialectical dance began./"The yang calls;/ the yin responds."/He is in that which each thing is./And in that which each thing enjoys./Each thing coitus./The entire cosmos copulation./ All things love, and he is the love with which they love. [*COSC*, 25])

The citations from external texts are sometimes identified, but in many cases, as with the "ying and yang" quote above, they are unattributed. This citation also illustrates the theologically impure blending of discourses – in this case, Christian with Taoist – characteristic of the poem's polyvalent spirituality. God, here, is not merely love, but rather "love in action"; deity is the essence with which each particle in an eternally copulating universe penetrates its counterpart.

The poem's forty-three cantigas fall into three parts: Cantigas 1 to 15, which emphasize the formation of the cosmos, give the strongest emphasis to a scientific vocabulary; Cantigas 16 to 33, which emphasize the secular, political world, particularly the struggle for independence in Nicaragua; and Cantigas 34 to 43, where discussions of deity, employing a religious vocabulary, come to the fore. All three strands of discourse – scientific, political, and religious – are present throughout the poem; each in turn becomes dominant for a number of cantigas while the other two slide into supporting roles.

The repetition of lines previously stated is employed to revive thematic strands that have slipped into the background. The poem's most salient structuring device is the repetition of the phrase "En el principio" ("In the beginning") at the opening of individual cantigas. The phrase emphasizes the poem's thematic circularity by presenting not only theological or scientific discourses, but also those narrating secular matters, as inextricably linked to questions of life's origins and meaning. In a more basic structural sense, the repetition of this phrase enables Cardenal to bring one line of narration to a close and open discussion of a fresh thematic strand, imposing a minimal degree of order on the poem. The cantigas that open with "In the beginning" tend to appear in clusters.[13] This grouping of successive cantigas that open with this leitmotif is used to ring changes on the perpetually readjusted equilibrium among the scientific, theological, and secular (political, autobiographical, and anthropological) threads of the poem's development.

To illustrate the uses of this technique, three consecutive cantigas late in the poem that open with variations on the opening line, "En el principio no había nada" ("In the beginning there was nothing"), will be examined.

Cantiga 36, "La tumba del guerrillero" ("The Grave of the Guerrilla"), begins: "En el principio .../A la pregunta qué había antes del principio/puede responderse que nada/pero que la nada es inestable" (*CANC*, 443; "In the beginning .../To the question what was there before the beginning/it may be replied that nothing/but that nothingness is unstable" [*COSC*, 368]). In spite of its politically engaged title, this cantiga deploys scientific theories to elucidate in religious terms the significance of the guerrilla's sacrifice for the nation. The cantiga's opening page repeats the "in the beginning" motif a second time, and on this occasion finds that at the beginning of time "el espíritu de Dios flotaba sobre la radiación./Dios dijo: ¡Hágase la luz!/y las partículas sub-atómicas empezaron a encenderse" (*CANC*, 443; "the spirit of God hovered over the radiation./God says: Let there be light!/and the sub-atomic particles began to light up" [*COSC*, 368]). The motif of burning suggested by the final verb (particularly in the original) is extended through an anthropological itemization of ritual uses of bonfires in traditional societies, notably in Europe, which culminates in a vision of humanity as clusters of burning particles, an image that equates those who have died for the nation with deity: "no vemos a los dioses pero creemos que son inmortales/por el culto que les damos y los favores que recibimos/y lo mismo sucede con los que han muerto por su pueblo" (*CANC*, 454; "we cannot see the gods yet believe them to be immortal/through the worship we give them and the favors we receive/and that the same goes for those who have died for their people" [*COSC*, 378]).

These lines are followed by the poem "En la tumba del guerrillero" (here translated as "At the Grave of the Guerrilla") in its entirety, which concludes this cantiga. Even though Cantiga 36 belongs to the section of the poem that Cardenal has presented as charting a transition towards the theme of God, the depiction of deity ultimately serves to amplify the cult of the guerrilla martyr. Similar ideological paradoxes crop up throughout the poem, complicating any attempt to rigorously classify its development. In the film, Cardenal identifies this avoidance of an excessively symmetrical structure, which mimics the universe's patterns of order underlying a surface chaos, as one of his goals: "El libro aparentemente es un gran revoltijo, es caótico, desordenado, aparentemente, pero tiene cierto orden, no excesivo, no muy rígido" (*Ernesto Cardenal* 1995; "The book appears to be a big mess, chaotic, with everything out of place – apparently, but it has a certain order, not excessive, not very rigid").

The tripartite division outlined above is rough and riven with inconsistencies, yet an inexorable circular movement persists. The repeated lines exist in a state of perpetual metamorphosis, similar to that of the protons and electrons whose union generates the different forms of life. Cantiga 37, "Cosmos como comunión" ("Cosmos as Communion"), repeats the "In the beginning" motif, but spins off it in a more theologically driven direction, consigning all of Cantiga 36 to the status of a digression within the concluding third of the poem's inexorable movement towards deity. The cantiga opens with, "En el principio fue el caos" (*CANC*, 457; "In the beginning was chaos" [*COSC*, 379]), and goes on to make a sustained argument that the movement of the universe favours communion among peoples. It refers back to the poem that concludes Cantiga 36 by evoking "los muchachos que murieron en la revolución de Irán/y los que están muriendo en la de Nicaragua. Vivirán eternamente" (*CANC*, 457; "the young people/who died in the Iranian revolution/and those who are dying in Nicaragua's./They will live forever" [*COSC*, 39]). The self-sacrifice of these young men, whether they live in Nicaragua or in Iran, becomes the motor that drives the quest for a vision of a unified cosmos. This unity is presented as innate to the micro-structure of life. Yet the understanding of the universe draws on the work of the physicist Richard Feynman:

> Leo que los electrones
> no se van indistintamente a derecha y a izquierda
> sino prefieren la izquierda
> Y (leo):
> "Yang y Lee tenían razón: el universo parece ser izquierdista."
> Hasta ahora hemos visto el fondo de la materia. ¡Y no sabíamos
> que la materia fuera de tanta belleza!
> (*CANC*, 466; I read that electrons/do not travel indiscriminately to the right and left/but prefer the left./And (I read)/"Yang and Lee were right: the universe would appear to be leftist."/Only now have we seen the depths of matter. And we never knew/matter would be so beautiful! [*COSC*, 387])

Cardenal's deliberately disingenuous reading of Feynman's observation that electrons tend towards the left as "leftism" in a political sense is an example of the poem's Exteriorist tactic of amassing all material within its (very extensive) reach as fodder for its layered vision of life that is presented both with priestly seriousness and in a conversational tone that includes a degree of humour and self-mockery. Cantiga 37 unfurls this ecumenicalism across galaxies and continents, positing that extraterrestrials may "tener su propio Crucificado" (*CANC*, 460; "have their own Crucified Man" [*COSC*, 382]) as it recounts the author's experiences among radicalized religious communities in the Amazon, Iran, and the United States, and mingles the beliefs of classical Greece with those of indigenous Guatemala.

Like the universe, the short poems of *Flights of Victory* undergo their own Big Bang in *Cosmic Canticle*, expanding to reveal the multiple resonances that are elided by the earlier volume's terseness. At a decade's distance from the revolutionary triumph, at a time when the poetry workshops have been abolished, Cardenal reinscribes these poems into the Poundian Exteriorist tradition by elaborating a layered "back story" that amalgamates multiple references and disparate texts. It is in this context that Cardenal's clearly overstated assertion that *Cosmic Canticle* does not belong to Latin American literature must be understood. It is as if *Flights of Victory* were a volume truncated by the political exigencies of the author's service as a highly visible cabinet minister in a government that had become a global symbol. Aside from three fragments from *Marilyn Monroe and Other Poems* that appear in Cantigas 3, 15, and 31, all of the poems cannibalized by Cardenal in *Cosmic Canticle* come from the final days of the insurrection against Somoza or his years as minister of culture (Borgeson 1994: 254). Having been released from this representative role, Cardenal is free to write these poems as he might have written them had he not been under the obligation to harness his work to a revolution made in the name of the semi-literate, or newly literate, poor. "Latin American literature," to which Cardenal does not see his epic as belonging, may be read as a particular strain of broadly accessible, politically committed literature.

And so, just as Cantiga 36 culminates in "At the Grave of the Guerrilla," the scientifically based depiction of a unified cosmos, supported by images of ecumenicalism, concludes with another poem from *Flights of Victory*, "Ecumenical Mass in Düsseldorf." The mass performed by Cardenal in Dusseldorf acquires broader resonances than are immediately evident in *Flights of Victory*, where, surrounded by other poems lauding the Sandinista Revolution, the poem turns on the axis of its closing line: "Que en el mundo haya muchas Nicaraguas" (*CANC*, 473; "May there be many Nicaraguas in the world" [*COSC*, 393]). In the more thoroughly prepared context of *Cosmic Canticle*, communion and connection across continents trump the immediacy of the revolutionary message; the reader's eye is more likely to linger on lines such as "Todos los rostros formaban juntos un sólo rostro de todos/y un sólo rostro de uno" (*CANC*, 472; "All the faces together formed a single face of all/and a single face of one" [*COSC*, 392]), which reflect the themes developed earlier in this cantiga. The shift in emphasis is evident in Cardenal's decision to write a new stanza to close the cantiga rather than to let the final line of the original poem stand as the conclusion. The additional stanza emphasizes the theme of communion across space. Cardenal, writing in Managua about Dusseldorf, receives a radio message from Solentiname. Contained within the crackle of the radio are all the sounds and sights of the natural world of the islands at night, each of which is presented as a reflection of a connected sound or image: "el lago color de luna bajo la luna/el latido repetido de la ola en la orilla/repetido repetido" (*CANC*, 473; "the lake color of moon under the moon/the repeated lapping of waves on the shore/over and over" [*COSC*, 393]). The "cambio" – "over" – of radio communication becomes an image of ecumenical-like connection between beings and belief systems. The extra verse shifts the poem's thematic direction, integrating it into the movement towards deity that dominates the final third of *Cosmic Canticle*.

The crossover between the political and the divine results in a pattern where each movement in the direction of either religion or politics is waylaid by the other theme. Where Cantiga 37 sets the account of the mass in Dusseldorf in a context that brings out the theme of religious communion rather than direct political statement, Cantiga 38 surrounds terrestrial revolutionary action with divine resonances. The cantiga's title, "Asaltos al cielo en la tierra" ("Assaults on Heaven from Earth"), comes from a line from Roque Dalton cited in the cantiga: "Nosotros desencadenamos el asalto a todos los cielos" (*CANC*, 479; "We have unleashed the assault on all heavens" [*COSC*, 398]). Like Cardenal, Dalton mingled the concepts of revolutionary and divine love in his verse; yet the central thrust of this cantiga is to express in Christian terms the actions of prominent revolutionaries not necessarily known for their religious devotion.

The crux of Cardenal's approach is to facilitate this encirclement of revolutionary actions with religious resonances by employing scientific knowledge to deconstruct the Book of Genesis. The line that "En el principio Dios creó los cielos y la tierra" (*CANC*, 475; "In the beginning God created the heavens and the earth" [*COSC*, 394]) is challenged by the statement that the earth came into existence five billion years after the heavens; this in turn leads to an investigation of the nature of communion on earth that broadens to include those forms of communion that grow out of revolutionary action. Cardenal draws attention to the similarities between revolutionary and religious forms of faith. Revolutionary actions are depicted as "assaults" on heaven in the sense of attempts to attain divine grace within a profane context. This is evident in the religious vocabulary often employed by those engaged in revolutionary activity. The second stanza opens with the lines: "Y fe también de los ateos. O así llamados./'Llevaré la fe que me inculcaste'/(carta del Che a Fidel)" (*CANC*, 475; "And the faith also of atheists.

Or so-called./'I will carry forth the faith you imbued in me'/(letter from el Che to Fidel)" [*COSC*, 394]). The quote from Guevara is repeated twice during the cantiga in order to break down a distinction between Christians and atheists that Cardenal portrays as artificial: "El padre Teilhard de Chardin no excluía de la Iglesia/a nadie que creyera en el Amor" (*CANC*, 476; "Father Teilhard de Chardin excluded no one/from the Church who believed in Love" [*COSC*, 395]). Those who demonstrate love by making revolutions that alleviate the suffering of the poor are Christian in the sense that their destiny is cosmic; by advancing human evolution, the revolutionary promotes the fusion of humanity with the cosmos. The "Heaven" to which the revolutionary lays siege is both a Christian paradise and "las profundidades del universo" (*CANC*, 477; "the depths of the universe" [*COSC*, 396]). Hence "La lucha para Sandino no era sólo terrestre:/También implicaba otros planetas" (*CANC*, 477–8; "To Sandino the struggle was not only of this earth: Other planets where also involved" [*COSC*, 396]).

In this sense, the Revolution becomes an imperative not merely of politics, or even of religious morality, but of human destiny as inscribed in the laws of physics and biology. Humans are motivated by "la necesidad biológica de la asociación" (*CANC*, 479; "The biological need for association" [*COSC*, 397]); the first humans huddled around the campfire, like the revolutionaries gathered around a campfire in the mountains, are exposed to the stars and the heavens and filled with faith in unseen forces: "Fe en lo invisible" (*CANC*, 476; "Faith in the invisible" [*COSC*, 395]). In this sense, the martyr who dies for the people is enacting in exemplary form the role of all humans, which is to die so that others may be born: to prepare the earth for those who follow. Cantiga 38 concludes with references to the Nicaraguan Revolution, now conceived as an event whose secular, cosmic, and devout resonances are inextricably entangled.[14]

Cantigas 36, 37, and 38 illustrate Cardenal's use of a pattern of repetition with variations in order to elaborate and interweave the poem's three principal thematic strands, using each in turn as a counterweight to the other two until they all merge into a rugged palimpsest within which the poem's themes cohere. Yet, even though scientific explanations of the cosmos, liberation theology-influenced explications of Catholic theology, and the promotion of revolutionary politics in Latin America constitute a kind of Holy Trinity of the poem's themes (dramatized, somewhat paradoxically, through a series of binary tensions), it is an inherent trait of the poem's encyclopaedic qualities that many other themes are also present. Some of these themes relate to contemporary secular life: what Cardenal characterizes as "the news in the newspapers." This includes events both within and outside Latin America, particularly in other regions where revolutionary governments had come to power, and where Cardenal travelled during the 1980s, such as Iran or Vietnam. Other themes, such as the frequent invocations of the mythologies or customs of indigenous peoples from around the world, combine the secular and sacred dimensions. *Cosmic Canticle* also contains many intertextual references to other works, particularly religious texts, as well as to Cardenal's own biography. The autobiographical elements eschew Neruda's flamboyant self-advertising, yet the romanticized Nerudian conception of the poet as impetuous lover and explorer of the world exercises a palpable pressure on Cardenal's self-portrait in the poem.

The tradition of an epic poem including references to the narrator's love life extends back at least as far as Dante's *Divine Comedy*, a work that offers a model for combining evocations of romantic travails with a profound religiosity. This tradition assists Cardenal in reconciling the conflicting pressures of the Casanova-like example of Neruda and his own vows of celibacy. The fact that one of the first overtly autobiographical moments, the vignette that concludes Cantiga 4, both depicts a scene from Cardenal's romantic life and includes citations from Neruda's *Twenty Love Poems and a Desperate Song* is expressive of this tension. *Cosmic Canticle*'s references to Cardenal's romantic autobiography includes encounters so tenuous that the decision to dramatize them reveals a touching naivety reflective of the outlook of a man whose experience of intimacy with the opposite sex is divided between idealized, chaste flirtations with upper-class girls not yet out of their teens in a Conservative, Catholic provincial milieu of the 1940s and early 1950s, and loveless sex with prostitutes in Mexico City, Madrid, and Managua (to which the poem does not refer). The pattern of mediating the emotional impact of memories of failed courtships by presenting them as illustrations of the theories of time and space that underlie the poem, adumbrated at the close of Cantiga 4, returns in more explicit form in later passages, such as these lines from Cantiga 7:

> Una materia muy activa, eso es la vida
> Por ejemplo Myriam en su cumpleaños de 15 años
> soplando 15 velitas
> (Avenida Bolívar, Managua pre-terremoto)
> una Myriam que (como lo analiza este poema)
> no se volverá a repetir.
> Esa característica del ser vivo
>   impredictibilidad.
>   ¡La tuviste tanto!
> (*CANC*, 78–9; Hyperactive matter, that's what life is./For example Myriam on her 15th birthday/blowing out fifteen candles/(Avenida

> Bolívar, Managua, pre-earthquake)/a Myriam who (as this poem maintains)/will never be repeated./That characteristic of human beings:/unpredictability./You had so much of that! [*COSC*, 67])

Not only the girl, but also the street where she lived, has been obliterated by the movements of time and the planet. By emphasizing the fifteen-year-old Myriam's "unpredictability," these verses both establish the existence of the narrator's romantic life and, by enshrining it in a scientific vocabulary, hold feeling and desire at a distance. This pattern persists even when the narrator confronts the emotionally artificial idealization of young women characteristic of his youth:

> Bellas eran muchas. Eran *las* otras.
> Ella era perfecta. Y aún más que eso,
> la única.
> Si por un descubrimiento científico
> sí, si por un descubrimento científico se pudiera
> escoger el sueño, yo soñaría siempre como la otra noche
> el largo sueño en que estuvimos juntos tanto tiempo …
> (*CANC*, 149; The beautiful were many. They were the others./She was perfect. And even more than that,/the only one./If through some scientific break-through,/yes, if through some scientific break-through it were possible/to choose one's dreams, I'd always dream like the other night/the long dream in which we were so long together … [*COSC*, 126])

The scientific vocabulary collaborates in the ironic treatment of the narrator's tendency to objectify women by converting them into unattainable ideals. Here the science is an almost whimsical conceit; yet at the stanza's conclusion this conceit turns out to be a self-conscious tactic for masking "aquel dolor que fue real una vez" (*CANC*, 150; "that pain which once was real" [*COSC*, 126]). The narrator's reflections on male desire for the female body in Cantiga 15, "Nostalgia del paraíso" ("Nostalgia For Paradise"), continue to emphasize objectification ("Algo onírico hay en la mujer, algo como nacido/del sueño del varón" (*CANC*, 150; "There's something oneiric in woman, something seemingly born/from the male dream" [*COSC*, 126]). At the same time, such thoughts are to some extent defused in their potency by scientific vocabulary that casts the woman's body as a "cosmos chiquito" (*CANC*, 150; "tiny cosmos" [*COSC*, 126]), parlaying the stereotype of the female as territory to be conquered into an image of the woman as an entire cosmos in compressed form.

In addition to perpetuating patriarchal objectification of women, these distancing techniques reflect the fact that for the mature Cardenal, even more than for most older men, romantic flirtations with women belong to a long-vanished youth prior to the watershed of his 1956 decision to adopt a religious life. The single account of romantic energy with the opposite sex after 1956, in Cantiga 34, is explicitly nostalgic in its references to the day of his surrender to God thirty years earlier. While giving a poetry reading in Germany during the 1980s, Cardenal spots in the audience a German girl who reminds him of Ileana, the young woman whose rejection triggered his decision to follow his religious vocation: "Una renuncia que fue dura/y aún dura, era de una vida entera" (*CANC*, 421; "A denial that was hard/and hard still, it was for a whole life" [*COSC*, 349]). The lines that follow extend the pun on "dura" – both "hard" and "it lasts" – that evokes the romantic disappointment that has converted him into the public figure of the revolutionary priest-poet who is on stage:

y ahora otra vez la renuncia
tan pasajera esta vez,
   pero aun así dura, dolorosa,
entre los aplausos de las sombras,
el dolor de que vos fueras ella otra vez
y a la vez, tal vez peor, el que no lo eras.
Muchacha alemana, supongo yo, que ignora todo esto
que lo sabe la otra que antes fuera como vos sos,
   mi niña entonces de 18 años
   (ella que sabe que estos versos son para ella)
en aquella lóbrega noche somocista …
(*CANC*, 421; and now once again the denial,/so fleeting this time,/but even so, hard, painful,/amid the applause from the shadows,/the pain that you were her again/and at the same time, maybe worse, the pain that you weren't./German girl, I presume, unaware of all this/known to the other who was as you are,/my girl then 18 years old/(she knows these lines are for her)/on that gloomy Somoza night … [*COSC*, 349–50])

Even though the cantiga's closing line subordinates the poet's personal pain to his success in raising "15.000 marcos para el pueblo de Nicaragua" (*CANC*, 422; "15,000 marks … for the Nicaraguan people" [*COSC*, 350]), the interspersing of memories of Ileana with the present of the public reading covers three pages. In its repetition of the assertion that losing Ileana, and with her a lifetime of marriage, love, and sex, is "even so, hard, painful," the second adjective defining the rendering of "dura" as "painful" rather than "lasting," this passage bolsters the narrator's image as a lover of women, fulfilling Nerudian expectations in spite of his vows of celibacy. At the same time, by ushering Cardenal's desire for women into the narrative present, obviating its confinement to a remote past, the passage acts as a brake against the homoerotic overtones that sometimes intrude when, during the revolutionary struggle, his idealizing energy shifts to the young people, primarily males in late adolescence, who become his protégés. Between 1956 and the mid-1970s, Cardenal relinquishes the love (or at least the idealization) of young women and undergoes his apprenticeship in the world of male faith, first religious and then revolutionary, as the acolyte of father figures such as Thomas Merton and Fidel Castro (in spite of the fact that Castro, born in 1927, was two years younger than the Nicaraguan). After the founding of Solentiname, Cardenal's role evolves: he becomes the father figure to the young men whom he introduces to the social gospel and inspires to give their lives for the Sandinista cause.

Cardenal's relationships with these young people, which are charged with feeling, produce some of the poem's most memorable passages. In contrast to his admiration of Myriam and Ileana, which takes place at an enthralled distance, his interactions with his young charges, such as Elvis Chavarría and Laureano Mairena, are earthy and richly textured. The clash of opposing personalities (in this case, that of the contemplative upper-class intellectual of European descent with those of the uninhibited, scantily educated peasants of indigenous background) characteristic of intimate relationships is a central feature in his descriptions of these figures. Passages incorporated or adapted from the short poems of *Flights of Victory* reiterate the propensity of Mairena, Cardenal's acolyte in the church in Solentiname, for using foul language even during Mass, and the fact of Elvis Chavarría, the protégé mentioned most frequently and affectionately, having fathered a child in his teens. Cardenal's willingness to make the sacrifices necessary to share his life with people of habits so different from his own displays love in a way that his idealized objectification of young women does not. José Coronel Urtecho compared *Cosmic Canticle*, in its identity as "a canto de Amor" (back cover; "a song of Love"), to Dante's *Divine Comedy*; yet what is missing from Cardenal's work is a Beatrice of sufficient presence to incarnate love in human form. None of the evanescent young women who appear in the anecdotes of Cardenal's youth becomes such a figure; however, the narrator's struggle to lend immortality to the youthful peasants who became guerrillas at his urging has the depth and poignancy of human feeling confronted by an intractable dilemma. The contradiction between his social norms and theirs comes to a head in Cantiga 35, "Como las olas" ("Like the Waves"), which addresses the young men's martyrdom. The sometimes coarse physicality of the young *campesinos* infiltrates the cloistered realm of the contemplative literary intellectual:

> Recuerdo Elvis la noche que llegaste borracho sin que lo notáramos
> y subiste a acostarte al tabanco del rancho
> y caía un líquido sobre la mesa donde yo escribía mi poesía:
> ahora para nosotros esa vomitada se volvió sagrada.
> Santa Teresita de Lisieaux a los trece años
> (entonces no se llamaba así)
> en Roma besó la arena del Coliseo.
> (*CANC*, 436–7; I remember Elvis the night you came back drunk unknown to us/and you went up to lie down in the hut loft/and a liquid was dripping onto the desk where I was writing my poetry:/now to us that vomit has become sacred./St. Theresa of Lisieux at the age of thirteen/(she wasn't called that then)/kissed the sands of the Coliseum in Rome. [*COSC*, 363])

The peasant's vomit spattering the oligarch's writing table lends an authentic essence to the narrator's poetry. (After the Revolution, Cardenal named a library after Elvis Chavarría.) The revolutionary triumph, redefining the nation as the property of the poor, renders this essence "sacred," as Santa Teresa of Lisieaux saw the sand of the Roman coliseum, where Christians had been slaughtered, as sacred. The saint's kiss becomes the cantiga's dominant image, a symbol of the sacraments which is not, however, entirely shorn of its erotic connotations.

Cardenal's impassioned description of these young men arises in part from the legitimacy that his association with them lends his poetry in the context of the revolutionary nation, and partly, one may hypothesize, from a sense of guilt or obligation towards his young companions whom he indoctrinated as future guerrillas in the knowledge that they would die. The relationship between the priest and the young men who shared his life, and even his living quarters, is so laden with erotic potential that the bodies of Elvis, Laureano, and the others may be contemplated only once they are dead and safely interred in the Nicaraguan earth. This is the source of poems such as "The Grave of the Guerrilla," which (minus the "at" used earlier in the translation) becomes the title poem and conclusion of Cantiga 36.

Most of the latter half of Cantiga 35 is also drawn from *Flights of Victory*. Poems such as "A Very Screwed-Up Trip," relating the death of Laureano Mairena, and "Donald and Elvis," about the two boats on Lake Nicaragua that bear the martyred young men's names, are included in the cantiga in their entirety. Like Cantiga 37, and in contrast to Cantiga 36, Cantiga 35 does not conclude with the original closing line from the poem in the earlier collection. A new concluding stanza takes up and extends the image of Santa Teresa's kiss:

> Si estoy en esta costa del lago
> las olas vienen para acá,
> si estás en la costa opuesta
> las olas van para allá …
> y el agua no se mueve sino sólo la ola
> que va igual hacia aquí o hacia allá
> y así toda ola encontrará su costa
> donde sola, sin ningún agua, la besará.
> (*CANC*, 441; If I'm on this shore of the lake/the waves come in this way/if you're on the opposite shore/the waves go that way./… and the water doesn't move but merely the wave/which runs equally this way or that way/and thus every wave will find its shore/where alone, without any water, it will kiss it. [*COSC*, 367])

The images refer back to the cantiga's opening stanza, which speaks of "ondas de radio" that "corren hacia la costa mas no el agua" (*CANC*, 423; "the waves of radio" that "run in towards the shore but not the water" [*COSC*, 351]). Ironically, this linking of "ondas" (radio-waves) with "olas" (waves in the water) is most evident to those who, like Cardenal, have a reading knowledge of English, in which both terms are translated by the same word. Seen in this light, the boats that cross Lake Nicaragua, bearing the names of the murdered young men, and the waves that run from the islands to the coast are symbolic of particles propelled through the cosmos in search of their equal and opposing particle: protons and neutrons, for example. The closing reference to a wave meeting its coast "without water" projects the waters of Lake Nicaragua, which represent the spirits of the young men, towards the cosmic union embodied by the "kiss" of the waterless wave on "its shore." The kiss here is sacred and related to holy communion, but it is also a form of the union of two opposites that appears in the poem from its opening lines and is particularly developed in the descriptions of "Toda cosa coito. Toda cosa cópula" (*CANC*, 28; "Each thing coitus./The entire cosmos copulation" [*COSC*, 25]) in Cantiga 2. This perpetual quest for union promises the young men eternal life as intergalactic particles (as well as, in the national context, as martyrs of the Revolution); at the same time, the repetition of the image of the kiss sustains the erotic connotations of this "communion," albeit couched in terms that do not transgress the boundaries of acceptable imaginings concerning reunions (or "unions") between a priest and his protégés. The intimacy of these relationships is authorized by a dominant assumption of a heterosexual, Catholic norm which ensures that it is the young men's spirits that Cardenal is contemplating, and that he observes their bodies only in the form of decaying cadavers that have become "huesos desenterrados" (*CANC*, 436; "disinterred bones" [*COSC*, 362]) or "suave tierra, humus otra vez" (*CANC*, 454; "soft earth, humus once again" [*COSC*, 378]).

The ineluctable presence of the decaying bodies of the martyrs, in fact, is in many ways the catalyst animating *Cosmic Canticle*'s entire vast, dense architecture. The circularity of creation, from the Big Bang to the final phase of expansion of the galaxies, succeeded by the condensation of the universe and a repetition of the Big Bang, provides a scientific illustration of the potential form of human immortality in the cosmos. Cardenal's description of the universe is literal and scientific and promises a physical resurrection in the form of particles of matter that will recombine with each other forever; yet, while this scientific account of creation is presented meticulously and at face value in the poem, it is, simultaneously, a metaphor. Cantiga 43 posits that the universe may be a "super-conciencia" (*CANC*, 580; "super-consciousness" [*COSC*, 483]) and questions whether the particles of our material being, which are destined to fly through space for eternity, might be "¿Átomos espirituales?" (*CANC*, 580; "Spiritual Atoms?" [*COSC*, 483]). Human destiny, at the poem's conclusion, is portrayed as "Ya todo confundido con el Todo, las personas con la Persona/en un Todo que es Persona/y Persona que es Amor" (*CANC*, 580; "Now all confused with the All, and persons with the Person/in an All that is Person/and Person that is Love" [*COSC*, 483–4]). The poem's opening words, "In the beginning ...," are also its closing words. The revolutionary martyr is the concrete form assumed by cosmic love. The martyr gives his or her life out of love for the people and the nation, who acknowledge the sacrifice by venerating him or her as a saint of the new revolutionary order.

Che Guevara is the protoype for this kind of New Man; but Cardenal concentrates on the Nicaraguan Revolution. Most of the stanzas that address the theme of Nicaraguan martyrs and martyrdom have already appeared in *Flights of Victory*, where the heaviness of the corpse-laden earth acts as a counterpoint to the ecstatic flights of revolutionary triumph. *Cosmic Canticle* achieves a synthesis of the earlier work's terrestrial and airborne dimensions. The epic's focus is made clear in Cantiga 18, "Vuelos de victoria" ("Flights of Victory"), which rearranges the material of the earlier book, running together most of its better-known poems, although others appear elsewhere, such as in Cantigas 35–37, or, in one case, "En Managua a media noche" ("In Managua at Midnight"), as the concluding stanza of Cantiga 11, "Gaia." The most striking section of Cantiga 18, however, and certainly one of the most striking of the entire epic, is a passage original to the longer poem that serves as the cantiga's denouement. Combining a rigorously symmetrical structure with vigorously colloquial Nicaraguan language, this section makes explicit the revolutionary leader's debt to the martyrs:

Cuando recibís el nombramiento, el premio, el ascenso,
pensá en los que murieron.
Cuando estás en la recepción, en la delegación, en la comisión,
pensá en los que murieron.
Cuando has ganado la votación, y el grupo te felicita,
pensá en los que murieron,
Cuando te aplauden al subir a la tribuna con los dirigentes
pensá en los que murieron ...
(*CANC*, 209; When you receive a nomination, a prize, a promotion,/ think of those who died./When you are at a reception,/on a delegation, in a commission/think of those who died./When you have been voted in, and the group congratulates you/think of those who died./When they applaud you as you mount the leaders' podium,/think of those who died ... [*COSC*, 176])

The use of the colloquial Central American *voseo* ("pensá"), rather than the conventional intimate "tú" or the formal "usted," contrasting with the official language associated with the world of public office ("nomination," "delegation," "commission"), adds a degree of intimacy to the repeated, prayer-like exhortation, which continues for four more couplets. The dead, however, are not a mere phantasmagoric memory: they are ugly, brutalized corpses. The symmetry of the lines urging the reader to remember the dead is broken by a more scrambled series of lines – "un revoltijo" ("a mess"), to use Cardenal's description in the film – that insist, in the imperative, that the dead be remembered not in the abstract terms of their honour, duty, or self-sacrifice, but rather as tortured, abused, discarded bodies:

Miralos sin camisa, arrastrados,
echando sangre, con capucha, reventados,
refundidos en las pilas, con la picana, el ojo sacado,

degollados, acribillados,
botados al borde de la carretera,
en hoyos que ellos cavaron,
en fosas comunes,
o simplemente sobre la tierra abono de plantas de monte:
Vos los representas a ellos.
Ellos delegaron en vos,
los que murieron.
(*CANC*, 209–10; Look at those without shirts, dragged along,/bleeding, hooded, broken,/plunged into tanks, suffering the electric prod, an eye torn out,/beheaded, shot to pieces,/dumped by the roadside,/in ditches they themselves dug,/in mass graves,/or simply on the land, fertilizer for wild plants:/You represent them./You have been delegated,/by those who died. [*COSC*, 176])

The final image of the bodies, in which they are mulch for the undergrowth of the jungle, sets up the stanza's concluding lesson by depicting the dead guerrilla as nourishing the Nicaraguan landscape from which he or she is inseparable. The contemporary individual who lives as a delegate of the dead is enjoined to recall always the physical details of the martyrs' deaths. In this way, an enormous, rough-edged epic that Cardenal claims does not belong to Latin American, and much less Central American, literature, and that is built around metaphysical images and scientific theories of the cosmos, reveals itself as an emanation of the soil of the nation and of Nicaraguan history.

9

Nicaraguan History after 1990

THE YEARS OF LIBERAL RULE

After the 1990 elections, thousands of Sandinistas looked ahead to the transition to Violeta Chamorro's government with foreboding. For more than ten years, these devoted servants of the Revolution had lived in housing assigned to them by the FSLN, eaten rations allotted to them by the government, and benefitted from free education and health care; these privileges enabled them to subsist on civil-service salaries that were as low as $3 per month. Having taken for granted that the Sandinista state would always look after them, they now faced the evaporation of their government jobs and the prospect of being tossed into an unforgiving market economy without cash, property, or even legal access to housing. Between 26 February and 25 April 1990, the FSLN granted property titles to thousands of low-level loyalists in order to prevent them from becoming homeless. According to Jaime Wheelock, 85 per cent of the property titles granted during these weeks were to beneficiaries of the land reform whose titles to their property had not been finalized at the time of the elections; 87 per cent of these allotments consisted of very small parcels (Castañeda 1993: 349).

This part of the operation was only responsible. Public attention, though, focused on the way in which the FSLN as a party seized assets that would provide it with future financing, and particularly on how certain Sandinista leaders, most notoriously Tomás Borge, Bayardo Arce, and Humberto Ortega, signed over the titles to cattle ranches, plantations, cooperatives, supermarkets, mansions, and beachfront homes to themselves, becoming overnight multi-millionaires. Even though other comandantes, notably Henry Ruíz – the legendary Comandante Modesto, who had fought for years in the country's northern mountains – left office with nothing to live in impoverished obscurity, the *Piñata*, as this flurry of legislation became known, tarnished the Sandinista ethos in the eyes of both Nicaraguans and international supporters. What most enraged the Sandinistas' political opponents about the *Piñata* was that it paralyzed the Chamorro government before it had taken office; the new property titles "froze the status quo" (Castañeda 1993: 349), meaning that any attempt to roll back the Sandinistas' land reforms would be predicated on an across-the-board rescinding of property titles that would set off devastating civil strife.

As a result of this act, Violeta Chamorro's coalition began to unravel almost before the votes were counted. Aware that stability depended on Humberto Ortega, who commanded the ninety-six-thousand battle-hardened troops of the EPS, Chamorro invited him to stay on as minister of defence and oversee the reduction of the army to peace-time levels; Ortega facilitated this decision by resigning from the Sandinista National Directorate. His appointment outraged Chamorro's right-wing supporters, who were straining to obliterate every vestige of the Sandinista state. They were outraged again when Chamorro's son-in-law, Antonio Lacayo, an old-style Conservative oligarch, emerged as the power behind the throne in the Chamorro regime, pushing aside the hardline Somocistas, ex-National Guardsmen, and their political representatives, such as Liberal Vice-President Virgilio Godoy.

Much of Chamorro's mandate was consumed by internal squabbles within her fractured coalition, most notably over the issue of property rights. The country experienced simmering instability as demobilized EPS soldiers and twenty-three thousand demobilized Contras tried to find land and sources of income in a ruined economy. In 1992 and 1993, these desperate, heavily armed men attacked towns, occupied the city of Estelí for three days, and kidnapped numerous politicians, including Vice-President Godoy (Close 1999: 98). The córdoba continued to be devalued, university funding was cut, and those who had jobs found their purchasing power reduced to below the levels of the war years. The policy that had the most pernicious long-term impact was Chamorro's decision to abolish public schooling, a move that denied hundreds of thousands of poor children access to primary and secondary education. Many other families faced "tremendous hardship" (White and Calderón 2009: 63) as they struggled to scrape together the money for tuition fees, uniforms, and books. The new minister of education, Humberto Belli (who was Gioconda Belli's brother), ordered all textbooks printed during the Sandinista years burned. Belli stocked the now fee-paying former public schools with textbooks funded by USAID that taught children to obey authority and loathe any deviation from Catholic dogma (Robinson 2003: 77).

Chamorro's supporters in both Nicaragua and the United States expected her to reverse the Sandinistas' land reforms and return property to former National Guardsmen and Somocistas who had sat out the Revolution in Miami. Her coalition partners identified one hundred thousand families who were living on land that "belonged" to right-wing supporters. Recognizing that dispossession of these families would ignite a civil war, Chamorro outlasted constitutional coups and walk-outs by large swathes of her coalition to push through compromise legislation that legalized Sandinista agrarian reforms as property titles and stipulated that only those living in houses with more than 100 square metres of floor space would be obliged to make extra payments to retain their titles (Close 1999: 168). This legislation cost her US aid. Many Somocistas had become US citizens while living in Miami, a fact that enabled the right-wing US Senator Jesse Helms to pass the Helms-Gonzales Amendment to the Foreign Assistance Act. This legislation required the US government to suspend aid to Nicaragua and vote against loans to the country by international organizations on the grounds that President Chamorro had "seized the property of US citizens" (ibid.: 167). The US aid bonanza that Chamorro had been promised by the administration of President George H.W. Bush was ruled illegal. No help came from Washington. Under President Bill Clinton, who was elected in 1992, US attention shifted to economic issues and problems in the Middle East and the Balkans. Latin America was forgotten – except by its enemies.

The very poor, who had elected Chamorro, suffered the most. The annual inflation rate declined from 13,000 per cent in 1990 to 12.4 per cent in 1994 (Anderson and Dodd 2005: 212) at the expense of heightening class divisions that had become muted under Sandinismo. The poor took to the streets in months of violent confrontations with authority. Chamorro's Liberal, Somocista coalition partners pushed for even more doctrinaire free-market reforms, the eradication of all vestiges of Sandinismo from public life, and the purging of Sandinistas from positions of authority. In the face of this intransigence, Chamorro began to depend on Sandinista votes to push through her policies. The patterns of the 1950s returned: the country was divided by the mutual loathing between Liberals and Conservatives (now trapped in the same government), while the latter engaged in surreptitious collaboration with the legacy of Sandino.

In 1994 and 1995 the dozens of state enterprises created by the Sandinistas were privatized, many of them sold at bargain-basement prices to entrepreneurs related to the intermarried Chamorro and Lacayo families. This orgy of patronage became known as *Piñata II*. President Chamorro, who had institutionalized bribery by placing over half of the members of the National

Assembly on the government payroll (Morris 2010: 175), appeared unaware of the damage the second *Piñata* had done to her image: "Though she held certain principles firmly – which judging by her record included a great respect for the Catholic Church, belief in the free market, and a desire for national unity – Chamorro was not an administrator" (Close 1999: 72). At the start of the 1996 election campaign, a poll showed that, by a two-to-one margin, Nicaraguans saw Chamorro as more corrupt than the Sandinistas; the Sandinistas were seen as more competent than Chamorro in every policy area except civil liberties (Anderson and Dodd 2005: 222). A significant democratizing force, however, was that during the Chamorro years, the National Assembly became an effective legislative check to the executive: "Two parliamentarians, Sergio Ramírez and Luis Humberto Guzmán, were instrumental both in shifting power toward the National Assembly and in spearheading reform of the constitution" (Close 1999: 72).

Chamorro came into conflict with the constitution when she tried to install her son-in-law, Lacayo, as her successor in 1996. Such nepotism was explicitly outlawed by the constitution, which, in order to prevent a recurrence of Somocismo, barred a president from being succeeded by a close relative. Nicaraguans had not seen their vote for peace in 1990 as approving the foundation of a new Conservative dynasty. Furthermore, Lacayo was enmeshed in corruption on a gargantuan scale. At the same time, the Sandinistas were in crisis. Daniel Ortega remained visible as a politician with a large constituency, but the mystique of Sandinismo as an all-encompassing world view – the only distinctively Nicaraguan philosophy, supported by its own history, poetry, music, religious tradition, and ideology – had weakened. The dramatic mural paintings of Latin American history with which the Sandinistas had emblazoned the streets of Managua were whitewashed by Liberal zealots during the early months of the Chamorro government. In 1994 Daniel Ortega orchestrated the dismissal of Carlos Fernando Chamorro as editor of *Barricada*. Tomás Borge, who was trying to reinvent himself as a journalist, took over, but "if the newspaper was his trophy, he seemed rarely around to polish it" (Jones 2002: 194). Borge's neglect resulted in the paper losing influence. By the time it ceased publication in January 1998, it had been supplanted as the public voice of the FSLN by the stridently downmarket Radio Ya.

By the mid-1990s Sandinista poetry and handicraft workshops were a thing of the past, and the *Barricada* literary supplement *Ventana* had ceased publication, as had the popular, mass-produced cultural magazine *Nicaráuac*. Editorial Nueva Nicaragua, the publishing house that had made more than three hundred affordable books, many of them by Sandinista authors, widely available, had gone out of business. Print-runs for literary works dropped from 10,000 copies in the 1980s to an average of 500 copies by the 1990s (White and Calderón 2008: 92). The final separation of Sandinismo from a national cultural agenda that had helped to define and distinguish it came in late 1994 and early 1995, when the FSLN split and most of the influential writers associated with the Frente, including Ernesto Cardenal, Sergio Ramírez, and Gioconda Belli, resigned.

The question of how to reformulate Sandinista ideology for the post-Cold War era had arisen as early as the October 1991 party congress, when the failure of Comandante Dora María Téllez to gain a seat on the National Directorate had exposed a residual revolutionary machismo and lingering hostility to policies seen as social-democratic "revisionism" (Randall 1992: 21–33; Hoyt 1997: 83–6). By the time of the May 1994 party congress, the National Directorate had been expanded to fifteen members and included five women (Hoyt 1997: 153). In September 1994 the National Directorate asked Daniel Ortega to take his seat in the National Assembly, displacing Sergio Ramírez, who had earned the loyalty of most of the Sandinista National Assembly members and attracted their support for his more social-democratic vision of Sandinismo. This loyalty had strengthened Ramírez's claim to become the Sandinista presidential candidate in 1996. *Barricada* began to attack Ramírez as a traitor. As the tension between "orthodox" and "renovation" tendencies increased, the resignations began. The split divided the FSLN along unfamiliar lines, with former members of the Marxist GPP walking out with the renovationists while Daniel Ortega and Tomás Borge, who had led opposing wings of the FSLN in the 1970s and 1980s, were united by their allegiance to what they perceived to be an unbroken tradition of revolutionary activism. In some cases (though Dora María Téllez, Henry Ruiz, and Luis Carrión were exceptions) the division was between renovationists who had not been front-line guerrillas in the 1970s and orthodox loyalists who had been. Even so, by the time of the 1996 elections, the National Directorate had dissolved, more than thirty of the thirty-nine FSLN members of the National Assembly had defected to Ramírez, and Ortega ruled his depleted party like an old-time *caudillo*, driving it in an increasingly populist direction.

In May 1995 Sergio Ramírez and his supporters founded the Movimiento Renovador Sandinista to launch his 1996 presidential bid. Yet the MRS's "Swedish" socialism failed to resonate in a country in crisis, where over three hundred people a year were dying in armed confrontations involving former members of the EPS and ex-Contras (Close 1999: 94). The economy remained moribund, Chamorro was discredited, the smaller conservative parties had broken with the governing coalition, and Liberal Vice-President

Godoy had been marginalized. A new Liberal leader, the former Somoza official Arnoldo Alemán – an obese, personalistic right-wing *caudillo* who as mayor of Managua earned the allegiance of the poor through the selective dispensation of favours, even as he removed the names of Sandinista martyrs from streets and neighbourhoods – became the country's dominant political figure. Alemán promised the poor that he would look after them, and he promised the wealthy that he would implement the radical anti-Sandinista policies that Chamorro had not dared to put into practice. His campaign faltered until it received a large injection of funds from Miami and endorsement from Archbishop Obando y Bravo, who intervened in the election to tell Catholics not to support the Sandinistas; on election day, two newspapers carried front-page photographs, of Obando y Bravo blessing Alemán (Pérez Baltodano 2012: 75).

Alemán defeated Daniel Ortega 51 per cent to 38 per cent, in an election, plagued with irregularities on both sides, that was conducted in a less transparent and professional manner than those of 1984 and 1990 (Close 1999: 175–7). The president's personal charisma exceeded that of his party, which won a bare plurality of seats in the National Assembly. This development obliged the hostile forces of Liberalism and Sandinismo to collaborate. Alemán's government, staffed by families with close links to the Somozas, ex-National Guardsmen, and former Contras, appeared to represent a return of the dictatorship. Foreign investment began to crowd out local entrepreneurs identified with either the old Conservative oligarchy or the new Sandinista elite. Though Alemán was ideologically allergic to enshrining support for the poor in social programs, he built some schools and health centres and successfully repaved the country's road network, shattered by years of war. However, he was unable to respond effectively to national emergencies, most notably Hurricane Mitch, in October 1998, judged by some to be the "most serious natural disaster in Nicaragua for centuries" (Plunkett 1999: 58) because of the long-term impact of its dispersal of the thin topsoil. Rather than addressing the environmental damage, Alemán focused on meeting agricultural production targets, then created a distraction by decreeing a national celebration of the reopening of the McDonald's restaurant franchise in Managua (Babb 2001: 61).

The Alemán years marked the suffocation of the multi-party democracy that had made a fledgling appearance in the 1980s and early 1990s. By the middle of Alemán's term, the leaders of Nicaragua's two largest political parties were both beleaguered. It was evident that Alemán and his associates were committing acts of corruption on a scale worthy of the Somozas; and in 1998 Daniel Ortega's stepdaughter, Zoilamérica Narváez Murillo, accused him of having sexually abused her throughout the years of Sandinista rule.[1] It was in the interests of both men to prevent parties that might try them for these alleged crimes from gaining a share of power. In 1999 the Liberals and the FSLN created an electoral pact. The twin brothers Ricardo and Manuel Coronel Kautz, sons of the poet José Coronel Urtecho, represented a nascent group of "big business Sandinistas"; they were instrumental in bringing the two parties together behind the scenes in a deal whose thirty-three provisions were unveiled to the public on 17 August 1999 and were passed by the National Assembly on 18 January 2000 (González 2011: 169–70). By setting high thresholds for electoral participation, the electoral pact made it impossible for smaller parties to participate in elections. Not even the Miskito Indians were able to meet the requirements necessary to run a Miskito rights party on the Atlantic Coast (McConnell 2012: 141). The two large parties divided government appointments between them. Benefits to individuals or communities flowed from the munificence of the two *caudillos*. This degradation of Nicaraguan democracy signalled the resurgence of an authoritarian strain that is embedded in the country's culture and history. As White and Calderón suggest:

> An important concept in the understanding of Nicaraguan culture and politics is *el caudillismo*, which is support for a *caudillo*, or political strongman. *El caudillismo* is the dark shadow that has been passed on to Nicaragua throughout its history, and may even have a parallel in the pre-Columbian indigenous rulers called *caciques*. It was established as the surest way to survive politically in a country where polarization spreads its effects and foreign intervention is constant. It represents the permanence of populist politics as an answer to the poorest, most vulnerable members of society, who are most in need of specific social programs of the so-called democratic governments. (White and Calderón 2008: 29)

Barred from succeeding himself in 2001, Alemán picked his vice-president, the septuagenarian Enrique Bolaños, as his successor, with the project of returning to power in five years' time. A visceral anti-Sandinista, whose property had been expropriated during the land reforms of the 1980s and who once had been jailed by the FSLN, Bolaños ran a polarizing campaign that prompted a huge turnout at the polls. Held on 4 November 2001, less than two months after the 11 September attacks in the United States, the election was skewed by destabilizing interventions on the part of the US ambassador, who suggested that the election of Daniel Ortega would result in Nicaragua being classified as a terrorist state. The election machinery was unable to handle the high volume of voters; again the results were in doubt.

Officially, Bolaños defeated Ortega by 56 per cent to 42 per cent. The Liberals won fifty-six National Assembly seats, the FSLN thirty-eight, and the Conservatives one. Smaller parties had been quashed; the institutionalized division of spoils between the two parties in the electoral pact politicized the judiciary in a way that impeded appeals of the election results (McConnell 2012: 141).

In this atmosphere of collusion, Nicaraguans were astonished when the newly elected President Bolaños, announcing that his government would follow an anti-corruption agenda, stripped his former boss of his parliamentary immunity (while preserving that of Daniel Ortega) and put Alemán on trial. The governing party retaliated by expelling the president from its ranks; he was obliged to form a makeshift new party. Yet Alemán's trial proceeded. Having been found to have siphoned at least $100 million in public money into his personal bank accounts (among other crimes), he was sentenced to twenty years' imprisonment. Alemán became the first president in Latin American history to be imprisoned for corruption (even though he served much of his sentence under house arrest on his lavish estate). Transparency International later named Alemán the ninth most corrupt president in the world since 1945.

The election of US President George W. Bush had resulted in the reappointment in Washington of many of the officials who had managed the Contra War. Still obsessed with crushing the Sandinistas, these officials intervened in Nicaragua's internal affairs in ways not seen since the 1980s. When Bolaños and the FSLN began to collaborate in prosecuting Alemán, US Secretary of State Colin Powell flew to Managua to order Bolaños to end all dealings with the Sandinistas (McConnell 2012: 144). Bolaños complied, prompting the Sandinistas to join a Liberal attempt to impeach him. The day after the 2004 municipal elections, in which Sandinista candidates won the mayoralties of twenty-five of the country's forty-two largest cities, US Defense Secretary Donald Rumsfeld flew to Managua to extract from Bolaños a promise that he would destroy Nicaragua's stockpile of surface-to-air missiles before they could fall into Sandinista hands. A few weeks later, when former FSLN Comandante Dora María Téllez, now an academic active in the MRS, was appointed Robert F. Kennedy Professor of Latin American Studies at Harvard University, the Bush Administration banned her from entering the United States. In the run-up to the 2006 election, Bush administration officials issued dark warnings that, if Nicaragua re-elected Daniel Ortega, it would face the same fate as Iraq.

Supported by his wife, the polyglot European-educated poet Rosario Murillo, who had stood by her husband in denying the allegations of sexual abuse directed at him by her daughter from an earlier relationship (who withdrew her legal action in March 2004, stating that she had been manipulated by enemies of the Sandinistas), Ortega softened his image. He and Murillo re-married in a religious ceremony presided over by their long-time foe Archbishop Obando y Bravo. Ortega adopted a policy that criminalized abortion even when failure to abort meant that the mother would die: this instantly gained him the support of the Catholic Church. He reached out to the private sector, changed the FSLN flag (at Murillo's behest), and met voters in small, intimate encounters rather than large rallies marked by aggressive rhetoric. He announced that the Somocista whose house he had appropriated and lived in would be his vice-presidential running mate (Morris 2010: 203).

A constitutional reform in 2005 had made it easier for parties to register for this election. The party pact had added a provision that, in the event that no candidate received 50 per cent of the vote, the leading candidate became president; a run-off election was required only if the leading candidate obtained less than 35 per cent of the vote and did not lead by at least 5 per cent. This amendment favoured Ortega since the Alemán-Bolaños split had divided the Liberals between Alemán's hardliners and a new centre-right movement founded by the Harvard-educated banker Eduardo Montealegre, who had served as Alemán's foreign minister and whose father, also named Eduardo Montealegre, had been a prominent banker under Somoza. The MRS promised to make its strongest showing yet under Herty Lewites, a personable Jewish Sandinista who had been a popular FSLN mayor of Managua. Early in the campaign, Lewites was polling ahead of Ortega. But the MRS's hopes were cut short by Lewites's sudden death from a heart attack in July 2006. Former Reagan administration officials such as Oliver North, whose plotting had led to the Iran-Contra Affair, arrived in Nicaragua to campaign against Ortega, who received his worst election result ever with 37.99 per cent of the vote. Yet, owing to the Liberal split, he became president. Montealegre came second with 28 per cent, José Rizo of the Alemán Liberals got 27 per cent, and the MRS, which had replaced Lewites with the uninspiring economist Edmundo Jarquín, polled 6 per cent of the vote.

ORTEGA'S RETURN

In January 2007 a re-elected Daniel Ortega began to consolidate his power. FSLN headquarters was moved into the Ortegas' home (Martí i Puig 2012: 37), where tactical decisions were taken by Rosario Murillo. No significant leaders or officials from the 1980s played roles in the new government. Among historic FSLN leaders, only Tomás Borge and Bayardo Arce remained active in the party; in 2006, 1980s turncoat Edén Pastora had also become a supporter. Until his death at the age of eighty-one on the eve of May Day 2012, Borge, who spent much of his time in Peru with his new wife, was wheeled out on occasions when the FSLN's heroic history and original revolutionary principles needed to be invoked. Arce, who during the *Piñata* had seized control of an unnerving proportion of Nicaragua's food-production capacity, as either administrator or outright owner, exercised his economic power from the shadows.

In contrast to the Sandinista governments of the 1980s, the new regime had a murky agenda, no youthful idealism or creativity, and few policy ambitions beyond tightening its grip on power. Adopting the strategy of the Mexican PRI, the most successful political organization in Latin American history, Ortega combined free-market policies at home with a left-wing foreign policy that satisfied the anti-imperialism of the traditional Sandinista vote. He aligned himself with the Bolivarian Revolution of President Hugo Chávez of Venezuela, whose massive aid to Nicaragua now constituted 7–8 per cent of the country's GDP ("The Survivor" 2011). Ortega expanded ties with Cuba and forged close links with Iran and Colonel Khaddafi's Libya. He supported the Free Trade Area of the Americas and other Bush administration economic initiatives, while he denounced Bush as an imperialist. Ortega's imposition of conservative Catholic policies in education and reproductive questions sustained the loyalty of Archbishop Obando y Bravo. Having defended Alemán's corruption in the late 1990s in a way that "was open and shameless," Obando y Bravo now declared himself "a good friend" of Hugo Chávez (Pérez Baltodano 2012: 86–7).

Ortega's first act as president was to re-establish public schooling, abolished by Violeta Chamorro in 1990. He announced the launch of a new, Venezuelan-managed national literacy campaign to serve those who had missed out on learning to read and write during the sixteen years when Nicaragua had no public schools (White and Calderón 2008: 63). As the economy improved, assisted by Venezuela and rising prices for Nicaragua's agricultural products, the country's growth rate surpassed that of every Central American nation except Panama. The proportion of Nicaraguan homes with access to electricity increased during Ortega's first term from 55 per cent to 70 per cent. In addition, the poor benefitted from heavily subsidized transportation and the Hambre Cero (Zero Hunger) program that donated livestock and seeds to more than seventy-five thousand hungry families (Kampwirth 2011: 14).

At the same time, Ortega succeeded where other Central American leaders failed by keeping the Mexican drug cartels out of his territory, paradoxically converting Nicaragua into the safest country in the region. In 2010 Honduras, El Salvador, Belize, and Guatemala were all among the world's seven most violent countries, and even better-off Panama and Costa Rica had skyrocketing murder rates. Under the leadership of the former guerrilla nun Aminta Granera, Nicaragua's police, ranked second in Latin America in trustworthiness and aversion to corruption, kept the murder rate constant at 13 per 100,000 people, about one-sixth that of neighbouring Honduras ("A Surprising Safe Haven" 2012).

Unlike the Mexican PRI, the FSLN did not renew itself by choosing a new leader every six years. Ortega's goal from the outset was to remain in power. During the 2008 municipal elections, which consolidated FSLN control, foreign election observers from the Carter Center and the European Union were denied entry to the country. Eduardo Montealegre, who ran a strong campaign for mayor of Managua, claimed that his FSLN opponent had won by fraud, setting off violent clashes between pro- and anti-FSLN gangs. Internal dissent, particularly from former Sandinistas, was met with retaliation: Ernesto Cardenal was prosecuted for libel, and a collection of the poetry of Carlos Martínez Rivas (1924–98) was prevented from being published on the grounds that the introduction was to be by Sergio Ramírez. But the international criticism and local protests stirred up by these incidents remained the concerns of a dissident elite, failing to take hold among students or the broader population as erudite protest literature had done during the 1960s and 1970s. This loss of power of the "lettered city," Jean Franco argues, is innate to Latin American societies during globalization: "In the market-driven neo-liberal states of the 1990s, the intelligentsia would find it difficult to reimagine forms of resistance for they could no longer assume a position as sharpshooter from the outside. The separation between inside and outside the state was now as obsolete as the simple binary alternatives of the Cold War itself" (Franco 2002: 13–14). In an ambiance of all-enveloping consumerism that erased their authority by absorbing them into an undifferentiated mass society, literary intellectuals found that their capacity to incarnate and imagine a potential alternate reality to that of the state had evaporated. Literature itself became marginalized: Metrocentro, the shopping mall built under Arnoldo Alemán as the new centre of Managua, contained dozens of shops, but no bookstore.[2] In Granada, which had nourished so many of the country's poets, the city's only serious bookstore closed.

In 2009, in a prolongation of the party pact, Ortega pardoned Alemán for his crimes. The former president's freedom appears to have been purchased by his agreeing to influence Liberal members of the National Assembly to collude in the Supreme Electoral Council's decision to change the law in order to permit Ortega to run for a second consecutive term in 2011. In October 2009, to consolidate Ortega's unique claim to Sandinista history, the FSLN opened the Museum of the Sandinista Victory, which rewrote the history of the revolutionary struggle. The museum portrays events such as the 1978 occupation of the National Palace and the 1979 Sandinista capture of León without mentioning Dora María Téllez, who commanded both operations. By contrast, photographs show Daniel Ortega and Tomás Borge commanding battle fronts where they were not present, often at times when they were outside the country or in jail. Photographs of Ortega are omnipresent, as though he had commanded all fronts of the revolutionary struggle simultaneously – the same claim, as former Comandante Luis Carrión noted, that was made by North Korean leader Kim Il-Sung. Commenting on the exclusion from the museum of Sandinistas who had left politics or joined the MRS, Dora María Téllez said: "Pronto Ortega, que es el único líder de su facción, será el único combatiente, el único revolucionario, el único gobernante, el único libertador, el indispensable" (Córdoba 2009; "Soon Ortega, who is the only leader of his faction, will be the only fighter, the only revolutionary, the only ruler, the only liberator, the indispensable man").

Ortega's cult of personality represented a reversal of the collective government of the 1980s, which had made a conscious effort to avoid replacing a right-wing strongman with a revolutionary strongman. Yet, in spite of the absence of many policies that could be described as revolutionary, Ortega had now appropriated the concept of "revolution" in an ahistorical void where the term became an article of allegiance or a social fashion statement rather than a cogent description of a program. The phrase's repetition convinced many of the president's youthful followers that they were participating in a revolution, even though what they were experiencing was a carefully engineered postmodern simulacrum of revolutionary transformation. Government press releases, for example, referred to Daniel Ortega as "el comandante-presidente," establishing an equivalency between his revolutionary and democratic sources of authority. During the 2008 riots, a young Sandinista supporter named Zeledón told *Time* magazine: "We are willing to give our lives for the triumph, for the nation, and to defend the revolution to the end" (Rogers 2008). The language of martyrdom – evident in the evocation of the national hero Benjamín Zeledón, who was shot by US Marines in 1912 – used by historic Sandinismo in its struggles against the National Guard and the Contras between 1961 and 1990 persisted, shorn of any concrete reference in objective reality. Unlike earlier Sandinistas, those of the twenty-first century were highly unlikely to go into armed combat or be obliged to sacrifice their lives for the cause – a cause that was nebulous and ill defined.

Ortega's neo-liberal economics was mixed with charity for the poor, but it built few sustainable social programs. Even during the chaos of the Chamorro regime, the remnants of Sandinista programs from the 1980s had ensured that Nicaragua performed better on the human-development index than any Central American country except Costa Rica (Close 1999: 121). But the implementation of full-blown neo-liberalism under Alemán had set off a race to the bottom that reduced Nicaragua to being the poorest country in the Americas after Haiti ("The Survivor" 2011). By 2006, when Ortega was re-elected, most of the gains of the Revolution had disintegrated. The illiteracy rate had crept back up to 34.3 per cent. In a population of 5.6 million, 800,000 children under the age of fifteen did not attend school and 1.6 million adults were unemployed (White and Calderón 2008: 2). The central initiatives of Ortega's first five years were: tightening FSLN control of the media through acts such as buying the television station that broadcast Carlos Fernando Chamorro's independent investigative program *Esta Semana*, then purging Chamorro from the station; and keeping the business elite and the Catholic Church loyal. By the time of the 2011 election, the majority of the Nicaraguan media, particularly radio and television (including two television stations run by Ortega's children), "cast him in a light that is benign, or at least innocuous" (Schmidt 2011). Buoyed by high world prices for Nicaraguan produce, Ortega oversaw a boom for the wealthy that led to a nascent merging of the Liberal and Sandinista elites; only the diminished Chamorros and their Conservative cousins remained hostile.

The Liberals' choice of a presidential candidate for 2011 reflected both the growing importance of the media and the business elite's lukewarm enthusiasm for defeating a president who was serving their economic interests. Fabio Gadea, an eighty-year-old former Contra who had worked for many years as the host of a crude right-wing radio program that attacked the FSLN and the MRS with equal venom, was a weak candidate. The faltering MRS, forced into an alliance with its Liberal enemies, contributed Edmundo Jarquín as Gadea's vice-presidential candidate. Yet an estimated 80 per cent of campaign contributions from business went to the FSLN. Ortega had the support not only of Fidel Castro and Hugo Chávez but also of the International Monetary Fund and the World Bank, which ranked him the Central American president who "best protects investors' rights" ("The Survivor" 2011). Foreign pressure was alleviated by the replacement of George W. Bush as US President by Barack Obama, a transition that purged the White House of Sandinista-haters from the Reagan years. In a country where

70 per cent of the population was under thirty and the voting age was set at 16,[3] 50 per cent of voters were under twenty-four. The astute management of the media by Rosario Murillo, and many of the eight Ortega-Murillo children,[4] ensured that youth continued to identify with the FSLN ("The Survivor" 2011; Schmidt 2011). This public-relations success obscured the fact that most Nicaraguan politicians were weathered veterans of the 1970s and 1980s who were unimaginably ancient by comparison with their youthful constituents; the intermediate generation that was in its forties and fifties was shut out of power.

Though the 2011 election results were marred by fraud, it was clear that Daniel Ortega had won his biggest election victory since 1984. Officially, Ortega received 63 per cent of the presidential vote; even his enemies conceded that he probably got 50 per cent (Rogers 2011). Making large gains over the 2006 elections, the FSLN won two-thirds of the seats in the National Assembly, a majority powerful enough to permit the party to rewrite the constitution in order to allow Ortega to run again in 2016. By the time of the November 2012 municipal elections, effective political opposition had virtually disappeared. The FSLN won 127 out of 153 municipalities; the mayor of Managua, Daysi Torres, was re-elected with more than 83 per cent of the vote. Though official turnout was 57 per cent, many opposition voters appeared to have boycotted the election (Williams 2012).

Viewed in historical perspective, the forty-year period between the urbanization of the guerrilla war in the early 1970s and Ortega's election to a third presidential term in 2011 charts Nicaragua's inexorable return to immemorial patterns of *caudillismo* and family dictatorship. As the *cacique* and his family ruled in the Chorotega, then the Náhuat culture, the Dávila-Contreras family during the colonial period, the Chamorros in the late nineteenth and early twentieth centuries, and the Somozas in the mid-twentieth century, so the Ortega-Murillo family dominated the new millennium. In spite of having enriched themselves in power, they showed some restraint; in the spirit of the new millennium, they concentrated on dominating the electronic media, leaving the old and new rich in peace to pursue their agricultural and industrial interests. The Ortega regime resorted to occasional bouts of intimidation, such as unleashing armed gangs onto the streets during elections, or making public-sector employment dependent on loyalty to the FSLN, but it did not murder or torture like the Somozas. In this, as in their adoption of a conservative version of Catholicism, the Ortegas resembled the Chamorros more than they did the Somozas or the Dávila-Contreras dynasty.

In Daniel Ortega's second and third governments, the Yankee modernizationist doctrine of the Somozas and the Marxist-tinted nationalism of the modern form of Sandinismo, formulated by Carlos Fonseca, were synthesized into a capitalism that legitimized itself with rhetoric stemming from the Sandinista revolutionary tradition: a capitalism that incorporated a paternalistic concern for the poor, provided that the poor could be helped without endangering increasingly globalized capitalist structures. The Ortegas were credible emissaries for this populist message because, unlike the white Chamorros or Yankified English-speaking Liberal strongmen such as the Somozas or Alemán, they were mestizos of modest background and impeccable proletarian lineage. Daniel Ortega's father had been a minor merchant and a supporter of Sandino; Rosario Murillo, though she came from a wealthy family, was a descendant, on her mother's side, of the Sandinos. Like the Somozas, the Ortegas promoted an imported model of development, although it was arguable that they did so in the interests of Nicaragua's poor. Where Anastasio Somoza Debayle had wished to turn Managua into 1960s Miami, the Ortegas tried to convert it into 1990s Caracas. As Sergio Ramírez said in an English-language interview given after the 2011 election: "According to Daniel's thinking, this project is just getting started. I think these next five years will focus on consolidating and institutionalizing his political project with profound changes to the constitution to create a new type of state based on citizen power or committees of citizen power" (Rogers 2011). The "Bolivarian" concept of a militarized consumer society, buttressed by socialist rhetoric, some socialist-influenced redistributive and welfare policies for the poorest of the poor, and apparently open elections which, nevertheless, only one side would be allowed to win, came to Nicaragua as an import. Ortega's imitation of Hugo Chávez's model is evident in his choice of the head of the armed forces during the Contra War, retired General Omar Halleslevens, as his 2011 running mate.

In the second decade of the twenty-first century, as in the 1970s, Nicaragua had a higher economic growth rate than other Central American republics yet the country was subjected to a foreign political model and an aging political class associated with a past time. This time, however, young people were not in rebellion. Their quiescence may have been due to the government's acknowledgment of, and attention to, the poor; but it also derived from the replacement of literary culture by visual culture as youth's primary means of expression. Young people of the past had been inspired by literature to dream of great deeds. The young Tomás Borge learned "la lealtad, la rectitud, la defensa de los humildes" (Borge 1989: 14; "Loyalty, rectitude, defense of the humble" [Borge 1992: 10]) from reading Karl May's Westerns in the 1940s. In the 1960s, young activists imagined new forms of freedom when they read the novels of the Latin American Boom.[5] Students of the 1970s promoted rebellion in the name of the solidarity with the nation's workers, or a church that struggled for the poor, after reading the poems of Pablo Neruda, Leonel Rugama, or Ernesto Cardenal. Middle-class young people in twenty-first-century Nicaragua were absorbed by Facebook, clothes, electronic gadgets, and pop idols; their concerns were personal rather than societal. The abundance of consumer goods sated wealthy and middle-class young people, diverting them from the sense of social duty that had driven 1960s Conservative youth to join the guerrillas. The regime's postmodern pastiche of "revolution," combined with some authentic gains for the poor, earned the allegiance of less privileged younger people.

In concert with Pierre Bourdieu and Jean-Claude Passeron's argument that one can understand "the maintenance of a system of power by means of the transmission of culture" (Bourdieu and Passeron 1990: xiv), a European process that came to Nicaragua with the accelerated globalization of the early twenty-first century, it is evident that Sandinismo, the only idea that constructed a credible, inclusive notion of Nicaraguan national identity in the twentieth century, has itself become a commodity, whose only convincing salesman is Daniel Ortega. As the sole surviving FSLN politician who can claim to have been a pivotal figure in the Revolution that forged an autonomous Nicaraguan nationhood (Bayardo Arce and Humberto Ortega both having retreated to the wings), he has become the literal proprietor of the national culture of revolutionary Sandinismo – in spite of – or, as Jean Franco might contend, *because of* – the fact that the cultural part of the Sandinista project has been sheared away. The Museum of the Sandinista Victory's exaggeration of Ortega's role as a front-line guerrilla illustrates the cultural imperative that the leader of Nicaragua be one of the makers of the Nicaraguan Revolution. After the 2011 election victory, Rosario Murillo baptized the new government "Gobierno de Reconciliación y Unidad Nacional" ("Government of National Unity and Reconciliation"), in a calculated echo of the post-1979 Governing Junta of National Reconstruction. Government publications, documents, and billboards were stamped with the slogan "Cristiana. Socialista. Solidaria" ("Christian. Socialist. In Solidarity"). The evocation of the fusion of Christianity and Marxism pioneered by Ernesto Cardenal and others during the 1970s obscured the fact that in twenty-first-century Nicaragua the dominant form of Christianity was orthodox and conservative; socialism permeated the government's rhetoric but was absent from its policies. "Socialism" and "Revolution" were nostalgic forms that the government must allude to on every occasion, but which it must never attempt to put into practice. The reference to "solidarity" was accompanied by photographs of Ortega in the company of Fidel Castro, Hugo Chávez, and Evo Morales, the left-wing president of Bolivia, as though to reassure Nicaraguans that the course their government was charting would not isolate them. Photographs of the young Ortega in combat fatigues became omnipresent. And, even though Ortega was not a long-term battlefield commander like Tomás Borge or Henry Ruíz, he did spend seven years of his youth being brutalized in Tipitapa, Somoza's most feared prison.

In retrospect, the 1980s fall into relief as an extraordinary period when young Nicaraguans took the measure of their country's history of authoritarianism and injustice, and made a conscious effort to break these patterns. Having plumbed their culture, they tried to forge original, creative secular and religious structures that corresponded to their nation's needs. Their heightened consciousness was nurtured by the country's literary culture: *El triunfo de la revolución es el triunfo de la poesía* ("The Triumph of the Revolution Is the Triumph of Poetry") read street graffiti in León in 1979 (Craven 2002: 117). In the early 1980s this became a slogan printed on banners. A poet had killed the first Somoza; the *Ventana* manifesto had proclaimed that poetry was the voice of the people; Carlos Fonseca, the most single-mindedly militant of all the Sandinistas, never travelled anywhere, not even in disguise, without a volume of the poems of Rubén Darío. Daniel Ortega and Rosario Murillo were products of this culture, whose origins go back at least as far as Darío. Ortega was once an avid reader, who finished difficult works such as Marcel Proust's *In Search of Lost Time* during his years in prison. He became an amateur poet (Morris 2010: 47–57). Rosario Murillo was the published author of eight books of poetry. Much as the red-and-black of Sandino yielded in the new millennium to less militant red-and-gold motifs and pastel colours in FSLN election posters, Ortega stopped reading serious literature in favour of the New Age authors such as Paulo Coelho preferred by his wife (Cherem 2004b: 163). Murillo wrote less poetry in order to produce the lyrics of FSLN campaign songs. She distributed these pro-Ortega songs from her website, entitled "Con Amor Nicaragua" (Morris 2010: 203); here she also offered downloads of her poetry collections, podcasts of interviews and speeches from Radio Ya, and, occasionally, new poems that she had written. The governing couple epitomized the trivialization of a politically charged, historically conscious literary culture.

After 1995, the split between the FSLN and the MRS took the form of a rift between dominant public-relations campaigns that emphasized visual images and nostalgic phrasing camouflaged as an engagement with the present, and a vision that derived from literary elaborations of national history. Both tendencies traced their construction of Nicaraguan identity to the life of Augusto César Sandino and the 1979 Revolution that he inspired, but in their respective interpretations of this heritage lay a great divergence.

10

Ramírez: The Politician as Writer after the Revolution (1990–2006)

WHAT NATION AFTER REVOLUTION?: *CONFESIÓN DE AMOR, CLAVE DE SOL, OFICIOS COMPARTIDOS*

Even before they took place, the 1990 elections destabilized the Sandinista concept of the nation. As Ramírez had argued during the 1980s, the Nicaraguan bourgeoisie had failed to create national institutions. The absence of a credible national bourgeoisie legitimized the FSLN as the only force capable of forging viable institutions, a coherent sense of nationhood, and the conditions for creating social justice. If Sandinismo was a necessary pre-condition to the idea of Nicaraguan nationhood, the assertion that elections were needed to sanction FSLN rule could be seen only as a contradiction. The first book Ramírez published after 1990, *Confesión de amor* (1992; Confession of Love), which collects essays and interviews from the years 1988 to 1991, illustrates that even before the elections produced the shocking result of a Sandinista defeat, the arguments that needed to be made to justify them, and to promise that they would conform to Western liberal-democratic standards, triggered a crisis in the integrated political and cultural conception of nationhood that defined Sandinismo.

Confesión de amor is a more political book than Ramírez's previous essay collections, in the sense that the reader detects the presence of a politician. Ramírez continues to speak as the explicator of the historical role of the FSLN; yet, at the same time that he searches for a way to assimilate the electoral defeat, and confront the emerging contours of post-1990 globalization, he also positions himself within the party. The introduction by Ernesto Cardenal identifies Ramírez as a figure who is capable of leading Sandinismo into the twenty-first century:

Sergio Ramírez, Managua, mid-1990s, with a portrait of Augusto César Sandino (courtesy of Jorge Colón Torres)

La compañía de Sergio me ha ayudado mucho antes y me sigue ayudando ahora a través de este libro: asimilar positivamente la derrota, ver lo que en realidad no fue derrota en la derrota; el que la revolución siempre sigue; sandinismo en el poder es no sólo en el gobierno sino también en la oposición, con el poder de los de abajo, el poder que tuvo por muchos años el sandinismo antes de tomar el gobierno ... (*CA*, 6; Sergio's company helped me a lot before and continues to help me now by way of this book: to assimilate the defeat in a positive frame of mind, to see what in reality was not a defeat in the defeat; that the revolution goes on; that Sandinismo in power is not only in government, but also in opposition, with the power of the underdogs, the power that Sandinismo had for many years before taking over the government ...)

Cardenal's summary echoes the response to the electoral defeat expressed by Daniel Ortega in his concession speech on the morning of 26 February 1990: "The Sandinista National Liberation Front, with the Nicaraguan people, will continue governing from below" (Morris 2010: 166). Yet there is a difference. While for Ortega "governing from below" meant using the power of Sandinista mass organizations, conceived as a truer reflection of the people's interests than any balloting, to thwart the efforts of Violeta Chamorro's government to implement neo-liberal policies, Cardenal, like Ramírez, claims that advancing liberal-democratic institutions was part of the Sandinista project from the beginning: "La alternabilidad en el poder es una de las características del modelo de revolución sandinista" (*CA*, 7; "alternation in power is one of the characteristics of Sandinista model of revolution"). Though this statement is not congruent with characterizations of the Revolution made during the 1980s, it is clear that in this introduction Cardenal is recognizing the democratic rules by which power will be won in Nicaragua and is identifying Ramírez as someone who promises to be one of the winners: "Es el libro de un dirigente, y es un sandinista escritor, que así como mucho me ha enseñado a mí igualmente enseñará a muchos otros" (*CA*, 7; "It is the book of a leader, of a Sandinista writer who, just as he has taught much to me, will also teach much to others").

This acceptance of the rules of the democratic game destabilizes Sandinista ideology, particularly the concept of the vanguard, and of national sovereignty. To accept liberal democracy is to espouse a universalist conception of how the nation should function, nullifying the Nicaraguan exceptionalism, based on the country's history of resistance to foreign intervention, that underlay Sandinismo. The end of the Cold War and the acceleration of globalization accentuated universalist pressures. In June 1991 the General Assembly of the Organization of American States, meeting in Santiago, Chile, would adopt documents recognizing "representative democracy" as the form of government of the Americas. Even though, as Brad Roth notes, this imperative was attenuated by the simultaneous adoption of resolutions that reinforced state autonomy (Roth 2011: 209–10), the existence of a transnational blueprint was undeniable.

The changed conditions of the post-1990 environment require Ramírez to demonstrate two contradictory propositions in *Confesión de amor*: that, as a leader and an intellectual, it is his natural role to show the people the path to the future; and that, as a democrat, he bows with good grace before the people's wisdom. The result is a book that contains moments of deeply felt writing – particularly in the fifty-page essay "Confesión de amor," which mingles the history of Nicaragua's struggle for autonomy with personal recollections of the author's involvement with Sandinismo between the mid-1970s and 1990 – yet also one in which the tenacious defence of a consistent ideological position begins to falter. The opening essay, "El naufragio de los sobrevivientes" ("The Survivors' Shipwreck"), a master class given to graduate students in Nicaraguan history at the Universidad Centroamericana in Managua on 7 March 1988, extends into the late Sandinista years the argument made by Ramírez during the early and mid-1980s, concerning the failure of the Nicaraguan bourgeoisie to assume its nation-building role. Here the disloyal bourgeoisie is captured in the image of survivors of the shipwreck: "Las enseñanzas de la historia se repiten bajo Taft, bajo Hoover, bajo Reagan. Siempre hubo en Nicaragua sobrevivientes en cada naufragio" (*CA*, 14; "The lessons of history are repeated under Taft, under Hoover, under Reagan. In Nicaragua there were always survivors of each shipwreck"). Ramírez employs this historical context to counter the claims of the 1980s bourgeoisie that the Sandinistas have marginalized and repressed them. The levers of economic decision making may have passed to new hands, but the bourgeoisie remains welcome to join the pluralist Sandinista project, with its mixed economy, provided that it contributes to the construction of the nation. Yet this, Ramírez maintains, is precisely what the bourgeoisie refuses to do. The result of this argument is to blur the distinction between the recusant internal opposition and the Contras: both become historical tools of US imperialism, united in "un mismo chantaje ... una misma amenaza" (22; "a single blackmail ... a single threat").

The decision to include this essay, which concludes with the resonant phrase, "vigilando el sueño de nuestros muertos y el resplandor de su sangre, entraremos en la próxima década y en el próximo siglo" (*CA*, 29; "standing watch over the sleep of our dead and the gleam of their blood, we shall enter the next decade and the next century"), in a book that aims to establish Ramírez as a central figure in the post-1990 FSLN, illustrates the extent to which, at this early stage of the post-Cold War era, a dual-track consciousness persisted. As in Cardenal's introduction, the belief that "the revolution goes on" coexists with the acceptance of democratic procedures. Ramírez, like others at this time, has failed to grasp that globalized liberal democracy abolishes the moral claims of a history of revolutionary martyrs, and thwarts the expression of diachronic conceptions of the nation. The extent to which post-1990 globalization projects the nation into an eternal present where its most cherished myths endure only as mediatized simulacra has not yet become evident; this phenomenon would be exploited by the post-2006 FSLN, reshaped by Rosario Murillo's public-relations techniques.

The book's second instalment, "Nación y soberanía: el orgullo de ser nicaragüense" ("Nation and Sovereignty: The Pride of Being Nicaraguan"), reprints the original Spanish text of an interview that served as an epilogue to the *Newsweek* journalist William Frank Gentile's 1989 book, *Nicaragua*. Ramírez recapitulates the foundations of Nicaraguan nationhood: the eternal struggle for sovereignty and, crucially, the roots of the country's identity as a mestizo culture. The interview begins with a discussion of Nicaraguan identity in which Ramírez rejects the contention that the protagonists of the anonymous seventeenth-century Nicaraguan theatrical monologues known as *El Güegüense*, one of the major literary works of the Americas in the colonial period, are indigenous: "Son mestizos" (30; "They're mestizos"). Ramírez's insistence on the primacy of a mixed racial and cultural heritage foreshadows later challenges to the notion of Nicaragua as a "mestizo nation." The most striking aspect of the interview is the contradiction between the concept of the revolutionary vanguard and the FSLN's commitment to liberal democracy:

> Nosotros como partido político que tomó el poder por fuerza de las armas, consideramos que para poder llevar adelante el proceso revolucionario, hay que asumir el papel de vanguardia porque éste es un proceso revolucionario que no murió a los pocos años de la revolución … sino que es un proceso profundo de cambios sociales, económicos, políticos, de independencia nacional. ¿Dentro de cuáles parámetros? Dentro de los que la Constitución establece: elecciones libres y el cambio de gobierno a quien las gane. (*CA*, 35; We, as a political party that took power by armed force, consider that in order to advance the revolutionary process, it is necessary to adopt the role of a vanguard because this is a revolutionary process that did not die a few years after the revolution … but rather it is a process of deep social, economic and political changes, of national independence. Within which parameters? Within those that the Constitution establishes: free elections and a change of government for the winning party.)

The contradiction between vanguard notions of national organization and liberal- democratic principles arises from the imperative to extend the Revolution. While this interview owes its inclusion in the book to the fact that it provides pre-1990 evidence of the FSLN's commitment to the democratic process, it reveals a competition between two discourses whose incompatibility would become one of the catalysts of the movement's 1995 split. The tangled nature of these assertions is revealed by declarations such as, "La vanguardia tiene que ser capaz de aceptar perder en unas elecciones, pero su verdadera capacidad debe demostrarla en conservar el poder habiendo aceptado y definido ella misma las reglas del pluralismo" (*CA*, 36; "The vanguard has to be able to accept losing elections, but it must demonstrate its real ability in retaining power, having itself accepted and defined the rules of pluralism"). The vanguard's strength, in other words, flows from its ability to set up a form of pluralism in which it will not lose. Even as it cedes to the universalist demand for democratic procedures, it does so on its own terms: "que una vanguardia revolucionaria pueda conducir al país en una sociedad abierta" (36; "that a revolutionary vanguard may led the country in an open society"). What Ramírez proposes may not be so much a flagrant contradiction as a restatement of the traditional tenets of Spanish American corporatism as exemplified by governing parties such as the Mexican PRI, which won elections, not all of them rigged, for more than seventy years in an open society driven by the heritage of revolutionary rhetoric. This is the sort of thinking targeted by Zimmermann in her contention that "in the course of the 1980s ... leaders of the FSLN mentioned Cuba less and less often, finally rewriting their own history by substituting a Swedish or Mexican model for Cuba" (Zimmermann 2000: 9).

Zimmermann, though, places too much emphasis on Carlos Fonseca, and not enough on Augusto César Sandino. The Mexican Revolution, as the strongest single influence on Sandino, is an important element of the Sandinista heritage. Ramírez's discrepancies with Fonseca, as discussed in chapter 4, stem from the former's insistence on Nicaraguan national identity as the creation of people of significant indigenous ancestry; this, too, is a legacy of the Mexican Revolution, that flourished in the mural paintings of Diego Rivera or José Vasconcelos's book *La raza cósmica*, where this philosopher and 1920s cabinet minister wrote: "Una mezcla de razas consumada de acuerdo con las leyes de la comodidad social, la simpatía y la belleza conduciría a la formación de un tipo infinitamente superior a todos los que han existido" (51; "A racial mixing consummated in accordance with the laws of social convenience, sympathy and beauty would lead to a human type infinitely superior to all of those who have existed").

In the essay that closes the cycle of Ramírez's 1980s writings on Nicaraguan nationhood, "Revolución, identidad nacional y cultura" ("Revolution, National Identity and Culture"), *mestizaje* assumes a renewed centrality.

This essay displays Ramírez's analysis at its most wide-ranging, arguably for the last time. The speech had to overcome the curious circumstance of being delivered to open a conference in Berlin in November 1989.[1] Ramírez refutes the neo-liberal discourse that claims "liberty" as a positive good and "liberation" as a dangerous fantasy by documenting the oppression of the Nicaraguan people that rendered a liberation movement essential to the creation of a viable national culture. A key factor in this movement, established in the opening paragraph, is the question of race. The essay begins with the Battle of San Jacinto, on 14 September 1856, where, according to tradition, a Nicaraguan national consciousness coalesced for the first time. The first sentence's subordinated third clause establishes that the Nicaraguan commander, General José Dolores Estrada, was "un mestizo de Nandaime" (*CA*, 49; "a mestizo from Nandaime"). Estrada fought against William Walker, who wished to establish "el predominio de la raza blanca" (*CA*, 49; "the dominance of the white race"). The story of Andrés Castro killing a Yankee filibuster by hurling a boulder at his head[2] morphs into an image of David and Goliath. Castro's boulder "ha viajado por más de un siglo a través de la noche de la historia de Nicaragua" (*CA*, 50; "has travelled for more than a century through the night of Nicaraguan history") until it comes to earth in the Revolution. This formulation enshrines the Revolution as the culmination of a mestizo heritage of resistance to white racist US imperialism, which in turn prolongs the history of indigenous resistance to Spanish colonialism.

Ramírez's decision to locate the roots of Sandinismo in indigenous and mestizo resistance obviates the waning appeal of socialism during the months when Eastern Europeans were rebelling against this doctrine and economic hardship in Nicaragua had called into question socialist forms of management. In spite of the Sandinistas' consistent espousal of an economic pluralism that left more than 60 per cent of the economy in private hands, and the obvious role of the Contra War in ruining the economy, the 1988 compression – dubbed by some "Sandinista Reaganomics" – represented a move away from socialist precepts. This required other sources of legitimacy to come to the fore. By relying on the centrality of indigenous identities, in both their original and hybridized forms, Ramírez also outflanks Pablo Antonio Cuadra, the only serious Nicaraguan intellectual who opposed the FSLN. Cuadra adopted the neo-liberal formula of "good liberty" versus "bad liberation"; alluding to the early high-art phase of Rubén Darío's *modernismo*, when the national poet aspired to the creation of an Athens in the Americas, Cuadra claimed that under the Sandinistas Nicaragua was becoming Sparta and planning to invade the rest of Central America. Ramírez refutes Cuadra's former contention by arguing that his advocacy of this atomized conception of liberty overlooks the concrete conditions of Nicaragua as a "país dominado y atrasado" ("backward, dominated nation"); drawing on dependency theory, Ramírez contends that Nicaragua's oppressed, peripheral position had inculcated such poverty that "es necesario afianzar la identidad nacional" (*CA*, 54; "it is necessary to consolidate national identity") in a project of national liberation. The struggle for a new culture *is* the struggle for social justice and better living conditions. This is arguably the last time that Ramírez will express this core concept of pre-1990 Sandinismo.

The centrality of literature to the project of national liberation is reiterated when Ramírez closes the essay by challenging the reading that Cuadra, who in his early years had been a promoter of Nicaragua's indigenous traditions, gives to Rubén Darío's poem "Tutecotzimi," which praises a pre-Columbian Náhuat ruler of Nicaragua. Ramírez maintains that the poem is not, as Cuadra asserts, a warning against becoming Sparta, but rather a hymn of praise to a king whose purpose is "no para invadir militarmente Centroamérica, sino para defender a su país de poetas y guerreros" (*CA*, 64; "not to invade Central America militarily, but rather to defend his nation of poets and warriors"). The essay concludes by citing Antonio Gramsci on the organic, political essence of culture and Bertolt Brecht on how the democratization of art is not achieved by the direction of the state, as a prelude to returning to the David and Goliath motif. The universal appeal of Nicaraguan art stems from the assertion of "nuestra identidad nacional" (*CA*, 70; "our national identity"); poetry is the boulder that enables David to slay Goliath, or Andrés Castro to slay the filibuster.

The fact that *Confesión de amor* contains short articles from the Sandinista newspaper *Barricada* that promote the party's platform in the 1990 elections suggests that Ramírez, like many Sandinistas, still believed at this early post-1990 stage that these issues and the revolutionary diction in which they were couched would retain their currency. The most discordant of these pieces is "Retrato de Daniel" ("Portrait of Daniel"), which evokes the biblical Book of Daniel to praise Daniel Ortega as "el único candidato a Presidente de Nicaragua que tendría en mí a un compañero de fórmula, y el mejor Presidente que ha conocido la historia de Nicaragua" (*CA*, 85; "the only candidate for President of Nicaragua whom I would accompany as a running mate and the best President that Nicaraguan history has known").

Similarly, a substantial essay published in the Madrid newspaper *El País* on 30 June 1990 serves as a reminder that, in the months that followed the fall of the Berlin Wall, the Latin American revolutionary project retained its viability as a platform from which to criticize the emergence of the United States as the world's only superpower. The essay presents the collapse of Soviet hegemony in Central and Eastern Europe as evidence of a progressive outlook on the part of Moscow that is absent in Washington: "Mientras la Unión Soviética abandona su concepto tradicional de fronteras estratégicas, y deja paso a insospechados cambios de sistema en los países bajo su antigua influencia, Estados Unidos no hace sino renovar este concepto arcaico, y reforzarlo" (*CA*, 86; "While the Soviet Union is abandoning its traditional concept of strategic borders, and allows unsuspected changes to its system, the United States is simply renewing and reinforcing this archaic concept"). Ramírez attacks neo-liberalism as an intensification of US hegemony, noting the uniformity of this pattern in Latin American nations such as Argentina, Brazil, and Guatemala. Ramírez depicts this continental imposition of market ideology not as a new, globalizing phenomenon – the way it was often greeted in English-language media – but as the perpetuation of the "estructuras arcaicas" ("archaic structures") and a "sistema ya agotado" (89; "exhausted system") of Yankee imperialism. At the same time, the essay recognizes that, in the new context of a single global superpower, the ability of Latin American countries to bring to fruition "proyectos nacionales" (89; "national projects") to alleviate poverty and social injustice will depend on the good will of the United States.

The primacy lent to the construction of a national identity is also a central theme of "Nicaragua: Identidad y Transformación" ("Nicaragua: Identity and Transformation"), a talk given in Madrid on 6 June 1990. Here Ramírez identifies the principal achievement of the Nicaraguan Revolution: "Se afirmó en Nicaragua la soberanía, rescatamos nuestra identidad nacional … ganamos para el siglo venidero un país propio, capaz de identificarse a sí mismo y de ser identificado" (*CA*, 93-94; "Nicaraguan sovereignty was affirmed, we rescued our national identity … we won back our own country for the next century, capable of identifying itself and being identified by others"). The relinquishment of power makes another boast possible: "Ganamos, al mismo tiempo, un país democrático" (*CA*, 95; "We won, at the same time, a democratic country"). In making this claim, Ramírez is speaking less of elections than of the Revolution's destruction of encrusted social hierarchies, its breaking down of walls between people who would not have spoken to each other, much less collaborated with one another, prior to 1979. The Nicaraguan future will be the "futuro que la revolución hizo posible" (*CA*, 100; "future that the revolution made possible"). Here electoral conventions are only a detail in the democratization of culture.

Even as Ramírez maintains a discourse developed amid Cold War conflict, the Revolution, along with its definitions of culture, sovereignty, self-sacrifice, and duty, begins to slide into the past. The volume's central essay, "Confesión de amor" ("Confesión of Love"), narrates the Revolution as history. Commissioned by the London magazine *Granta,* which published sections of it, the essay appeared in its entirety in the August 1990 issue of the Mexican magazine *NEXOS*. The epigraph, which consists of the opening lines of *A Tale of Two Cities*, Charles Dickens's novel about the French Revolution, treats the Sandinista Revolution with an ironic distance. Each of the declamatory clauses of Dickens's opening becomes the heading for one of the essay's sections.[3] "Confesión de amor" reprises the benchmarks of Nicaraguan history that appear in Ramírez's earlier essays; what is new is the obtrusion of the autobiographical "I": the self as vice-president. Making its first sustained appearance in Ramírez's post-revolutionary writing, the "I" figure is spontaneous and authentic, less stylized than it would become during its later iterations, particularly in the novel *Mil y una muertes* (2004; *A Thousand Deaths Plus One*). If the evaporation of a sense of historical chronology deprives the individual of a palpable engagement with history, throwing each of us back on the resources of a postmodern self that is at once mediatized and susceptible to incessant reinvention, then for Ramírez, in this essay, the self to whom the commitment to the nation begins to yield is that of "the Vice-President."

Writing of the return of Central American guerrilla comandantes to secular life in the early 1990s, Régis Debray argued that "le retour au monde profane paraît désintégrer le missionaire avec la même nécessité que la rentrée dans l'atmosphère pulvérise un corps de lanceur spatial" (Debray, 172; "the return to the profane world seems to make the missionary disintegrate with the same inevitability that the return to the earth's atmosphere pulverizes the body of a booster rocket"). As a writer with an established career, Ramírez had far better defences against this pulverization of the missionary-like revolutionary self, and far more latitude to construct a secular post-1990 identity, than did figures such as Tomás Borge, whose oscillating post-1990 identities (celebrity interviewer, newspaper editor, landowner, diplomat, new father, nostalgic relic of the revolutionary past) attest to the difficulty of finding a place for a lifelong guerrilla comandante in the world of globalization. In "Confesión de amor," the emotional reactions of the man who experienced the Revolution remain accessible, not yet displaced by the mediatized shadow of the vice-president. He recalls leaving his wife and children for the flight to Nicaragua on the night of 17–18 July 1979 and realizing that, if the plane is shot down, "no les dejaba sino mis libros … y el Volvo golpeado ya en múltiples viajes a la frontera para llevar armas" (*CA*, 103; "I left them nothing but my books … and the Volvo battered by multiple trips to the border to carry arms"). This man, who has always been reluctant to express his feelings, and whose public image is polished but opaque, comes as close here as anywhere to psychoanalyzing himself, hinting that revolutionary discipline suppressed his emotions. The one time in his life that he cries, his tears are for the death of the Revolution; yet this cathartic moment may also presage an escape from the impassive persona of the committed revolutionary, and a return to ordinary human interaction; an exit from a life that occurs in the public sphere into one in which private life has a place:

> Cuando mataron a Eduardo Contreras, cuando mataron a Camilo Ortega, a Israel Lewites, a tantos otros compañeros, nunca lloré, tragándome las lágrimas de desesperanza y frustración. Tampoco había llorado cuando murió mi padre, o mi hermana mayor, Luisa, aunque el dolor me inundara como una marea ciega que no encontraba salida en las lágrimas, tensas las mandíbulas. El llanto viejo y reprimido de toda mi vida rompía sus diques en aquella madrugada que juntaba desde atrás todas las horas de dolor y volvía la más triste de mi vida. (*CA*, 148; When they killed Eduardo Contreras, when they killed Camilo Ortega, Israel Lewites, and so many other *compañeros*, I never cried, swallowing my tears of desperation and frustration. Nor had I cried when my father died, or my older sister, Luisa, even though pain flooded me in a blind wave that found no outlet in tears as I clenched my fists. My whole life's old, repressed tears broke their dikes in that dawn that gathered together all the painful hours of my past and became the saddest of my life.)

Having subsumed all other aspects of life, the totalizing project of the Revolution – a combined social, political, economic, cultural, and personal project – provides an occasion for totalizing mourning. Private miseries, such as the death of a sister, find an outlet only in this public event. Once the Revolution is gone, all that remains is ordinary life, ordinary politics: actions bereft of transcendent significance. The essay delays the climactic description of election night to the final sequence, "El invierno de la desesperación" ("The Winter of Despair"). An earlier sequence, "Una temporada de fulgor" ("A Season of Light"), describes the work of the Bancada Sandinista in the post-1990 National Assembly, including its efforts to block the "desmantelmiento de todo lo que signifique conquistas populares de la revolución" (*CA*, 131; "the dismantling of all of the people's revolutionary attainments").

Written at the lower emotional temperature appropriate to a world in which dialectical struggle between conflicting concepts of history has yielded to tactical manoeuvring, this section includes genial portraits of the better-known Sandinista National Assembly members. The clash in tones between the different sections of "Confesión de amor," while foreshadowed by the clauses in apposition in the epigraph from Dickens, also hints that the ebullient experimentation with language that characterized the Nicaraguan Revolution may have ended: "Todos experimentábamos con la palabra, tras tantos siglos de silencio … Nuestros discursos en las plazas públicas eran interminables al final de los actos interminables … El verbo se hacía carne y habitaba entre nosotros" (*CA*, 122–3; "We all experimented with the word, after so many centuries of silence … Our speeches in the squares were interminable, at the close of interminable meetings … The verb became flesh and dwelt among us").

The Revolution forges the nation in language. It brings together Nicaraguans who would not have heard each other's voices under the old order, giving all levels of society the opportunity to hurl their language into the public sphere, and swirling together their accents, vocabularies, and social discourses into a polyphonic expression of the nation. The public square becomes a site where one hears not only the rhetoric of revolutionary comandantes and the refined tones of Conservative oligarchs who have converted to the Sandinista cause, but "campesinos de tierra adentro … que sostenían el sombrero en la mano mientras se acercaban con aprensión al pedestal del micrófono, y empezaban a confesarse en voz alta, con dejes y giros de lenguaje arcaicos que revelaban el aislamiento en que habían vivido" (*CA*, 122–3; "peasants from upcountry … who held their hats in their hands while they approached the pedestal or microphone with apprehension, and began to confess aloud, with the accents and turns of phrase of an archaic language that revealed the isolation in which they had lived").

The nation is at the core of Ramírez's first sustained post-election attempt to assess the Revolution; the love confessed by the essay, and the book, is love of the nation. Yet, as he evokes this entity, his language modulates from that of a writer fascinated by the expressive riches of Nicaraguan diversity into that of a politician declaring his allegiance to a population that he hopes will return him to power. The section entitled "Una época de fé" ("An Epoch of Belief"), which narrates the exhilaration of the early days of the triumph, concludes with a paragraph constructed around the repetition of the phrase "El país …" ("The nation …"):

> El país visto a través de una mira distinta, el país recuperado que recorrí tantas veces … El país que recorrí sin tregua en la campaña electoral de

> 1984, y que volví a recorrer con esa misma ansiedad de quien descubre a cada paso lo suyo, lo que le pertenece, en la campaña electoral última … El país que sigue allí, con su misma gente y sus mismas esperanzas de una vida distinta, complejo y diverso, al que a veces no alcanzamos a comprender, por mucho amor que pusiéramos de por medio, y al que ahora siento comprender mejor, porque los votos adversos me ayudan a desempañar el cristal de mi mira, para seguirlo viviendo en todo su esplendor. (*CA*, 124; The nation seen from a different point of view, the recovered nation that I crisscrossed so many times … The nation that I crisscrossed without a break in the 1984 electoral campaign, and that I crisscrossed again with that same anxiety of someone who discovers the world that is his, that which belongs to him, at each step, in the last election campaign … The nation that is still there, with its same people and their hopes of a different life, complex and diverse, which at times we do not succeed in understanding, for all the love that we may invest in it every day, and which I feel I now understand better, because the negative votes help me to wipe the mist from the glass I'm looking through in order to follow it in all its splendour.)

Here language yields to geography: the act of traversing the nation instills a consciousness of Nicaragua's intangible complexity. In spite of global political shifts, the nation "is still there," waiting to be reconquered; the people remain the same, as do their aspirations, which, like any defeated politician, Ramírez now claims to understand with greater clarity and humility. The transition in this section from the nation as a quasi-mystical integrated articulation of oral language to the nation as a constituency to be courted encapsulates the contradictions of the transitional era in which these essays were written.

Elsewhere in this piece, Ramírez doubts his ability, and that of the Revolution, to represent the peasantry. These passages, which call into question the ability of the male revolutionary leader to march onward into the post-1990 era in full possession of the authority staked out three decades earlier by Fidel Castro or Che Guevara, will be discussed later in this chapter. The most striking feature of this pivotal essay is its insistent allegiance to the Sandinista martyr culture. The moral authority of murdered revolutionaries held sway over the Sandinista conception of citizenship by instilling duty to the dead; this concept of duty stands in opposition to a liberal-democratic culture of rights and freedoms. Ramírez imagines a return to power within these same revolutionary coordinates; he claims that he expects this to happen "más temprano que tarde" (*CA*, 104; "earlier rather than later"). This citation from the radio broadcast given by Salvador Allende as the Chilean military stormed the presidential palace on 11 September 1973 emphasizes the extension of revolutionary diction into the future. (It also equates the 1990 elections with a military coup.) The core of this diction is the language of serving as the delegate of the martyrs. As an intellectual, Ramírez is able to stand outside this culture and analyze its origins: "La causa sandinista no deja de recoger tradiciones ancestrales; nuestros antepasados aborígenes celebraban a sus muertos y los convocaban en todos los actos de sus vidas ... y de la tradición cristiana imitamos el valor superior del martirio, la inmolación como prueba última de la fe" (*CA*, 137; "The Sandinista cause continues to gather in ancestral traditions; our aboriginal ancestors celebrated their dead and evoked them in all the ceremonies of their lives ... and from the Christian tradition we imitated the high value of martyrdom, self-immolation as the ultimate proof of faith"). In this formulation, martyr-worship, by combining indigenous and Christian traditions, becomes another proof of the mestizo essence of Nicaraguan culture, and of Sandinismo as an ideology rooted in this reality. It is striking that Ramírez concludes this essay, intended to serve as the foundation of his post-1990 career, not with a renewed assurance to the people that he has learned from the experience of electoral defeat, but rather with a lyrical evocation of the revolutionary martyrs as the point of origin of future Sandinista governments: "Y debajo de la tierra, en los surcos, la semilla de nuestros muertos, esperando otra vez ser fecundada. Ellos nos hablarán, otra vez, con sus voces de esperanza y con la alegría de los frutos nuevos" (*CA*, 150; "And beneath the earth, in the furrows, the seed of our dead lies waiting to be fertilized again. They will speak to us, once again, with their voices of hope and with the joy of new fruit").

Even as he positions himself as a repentant democrat within a liberal-democratic culture, Ramírez resorts to the mystical, indigenous-derived appeal of the martyrs as the force that will restore Sandinismo to power. An interview that was published in the Uruguayan magazine *Brecha* on 10 August 1990 under the title "El sandinismo condiciona una relación positiva con Washington" ("Sandinismo Depends on a Positive Relationship with Washington") appears in *Confesión de amor* under the more assertive title "La paz y la democracia son frutos de la revolución" ("Peace and Democracy Are Fruits of the Revolution") (*CA*, 151). Yet, even though Ramírez learned to move with dexterity within liberal-democratic culture, becoming a very effective leader of the Bancada Sandinista in the National Assembly between April 1990 and January 1995, his essays cleave to diachronic conceptions of history and assertions of national sovereignty that are linked to definitions of citizenship based on rights earned through the performance of duties. Ramírez's paradoxical personality, encapsulating both social-democratic and revolutionary strains, which is present in his public actions since his student days, is rarely more in evidence than during the early 1990s.

The lone essay in *Confesión de amor* that was not published previously, "El nacimiento de la utopía" ("The Birth of Utopia"), is a refutation of the idea that with the fall of the Berlin Wall, history had ended. On the US right, the neo-liberal form of this argument was made by Francis Fukuyama, who celebrated the onset of a purported liberal-democratic homogeneity as evidence that dialectical struggle had concluded with all parties agreeing on the single correct form of social organization. Both cultural differences and ceaseless change were supplanted by "the idea of a universal and directional history leading up to liberal democracy" (Fukuyama 1992: 338). On the European left, the French philosopher Jean Baudrillard argued that history had ceased to exist because major events were experienced as entertainment shorn of diachronic reference points. Baudrillard maintained, for example, that the 1991 Persian Gulf War had not occurred because the way in which it had been packaged and televised had removed it from history: "En fait, ce que nous vivons en temps réel, ce n'est pas l'événement, c'est ... le spectacle de la dégradation de l'événement et son évocation spectrale" (Baudrillard 1991: 46–7; "In fact, what we live in real time is not the event, but rather ... the spectacle of the degradation of the event and its spectral evocation" [Baudrillard 1995: 48]). The crux of this evaporation of history, in both cases, was the status of autochthonous cultures. Fukuyama's book, shockingly, closes with a laudatory image of the nineteenth-century US genocide of the aboriginal people of the western United States. He equates the nations of the world advancing towards US norms to wagons in a wagon-train moving across the prairies. Some of these countries "will be attacked by Indians" (Fukuyama 1992: 338), Fukuyama asserts, but most will eventually roll into town. Baudrillard, for his part, asserts that in the Gulf War "ce à quoi [les Américains] font la guerre, c'est à l'altérité de l'autre, et ce qu'ils veulent, c'est réduire cette altérité, la convertir, ou sinon l'anéantir si elle est irréductible (les Indiens)" (Baudrillard 1991: 30–1; "What they make war upon is the alterity of the other, and what they want is to reduce that alterity, to convert it or failing that to annihilate it if it proves irreducible (the Indians)" [Baudrillard 1995: 37]). Beneath the ideologically opposed visions of Fukuyama and Baudrillard lay a shared assumption that contemporary life unfolded outside the realm of a meaningful engagement with history, enshrined in indigenous cultures.

Ramírez, by contrast, needs to sustain the potency of a diachronic conception of nationhood. Without history, there is no distinct Nicaraguan identity, no nation, no demand for the implementation of a revolutionary program.

The point of origin of revolutionary programs is trampled nationhood. In 1953, when he was on trial for raiding the Moncada military barracks, Fidel Castro linked revolutionary citizenship predicated on duty (as opposed to the liberal version based on ideas of freedom) as having its point of origin in the nation. Castro evokes "una razón más poderosa que todas las demás: somos cubanos, y ser cubano implica un deber, no cumplirlo es crimen y es traición" (*La historia me absolverá*, 26; "a reason more powerful than the others: we are Cubans, and being Cuban implies a duty, not to fulfill it is a crime and is treason").

In his attempt to reinvigorate Utopian politics in the post-1990 context, Ramírez's target, though he does not deign to name him, is Fukuyama. Fifteen years later, when asked about Fukuyama's theory, he responded with disdain: "Es una boludez. Se cayó por su propio peso al poco tiempo. Yo no sé por qué una propuesta tan ingenua tuvo tanta resonancia. Eso me asombra mucho" (*UISR*; "It's idiotic. It fell from its own weight in no time. I don't know why such a naive theory had such a wide reception. That really astonishes me"). In "El nacimiento de la utopía," Ramírez analyzes Fukuyama's contention through a dependency prism, as part of the ideological cargo imposed on the periphery by the metropolis: "La trampa filosófica que proclama el fin de la historia proviene de nuevo de los centros metropolitanos de poder, como otras tantas artimañas que en el pasado han tratado de aturdir los sueños de justicia de los países marginales" (*CA*, 156; "The philosophical trap that proclaims the end of history issues once again from the metropolitan centres of power, like so many other tricks that in the past have attempted to bamboozle the dreams of justice of the countries on the margins"). By proclaiming that history is dead, US imperial power sweeps off the table the consciousness of injustice and national humiliation that fuels mass movements capable of implementing a more egalitarian order in the periphery; it enforces the economic status quo and delegitimizes the thinking that would be necessary to imagine a just social order.

To refute Fukuyama's underlying assumption that the collapse of the Soviet Union marks the end of left-wing authority everywhere in the world, Ramírez asserts that to Latin America the Soviet Union "ofrecía la abolición de la explotación, y el poder novedoso de los obreros y campesinos, capaz de encender por sí mismo el motor de la historia" (*CA*, 159; "offered the abolition of exploitation, and the novelty of workers and peasants in power, capable of igniting for themselves the motor of history"). The US, by contrast, offered only a continuation of the Big Stick policies of the early twentieth century. With regard to the Cold War, Ramírez insists that "en América Latina, aprendimos nuestra propia visión de esta confrontación" (*CA*, 159;

"in Latin America, we developed our own vision of this confrontation"). The Latin American reading of the Cold War underlines the fact that, although Soviet ideology was wrong about other matters, it was correct concerning the "fenómeno de la dominación impuesto por Estados Unidos sobre América Latina" (*CA*, 159; "phenomenon of domination imposed by the United States on Latin America"). This phenomenon, Ramírez stresses, predated the Cold War and, nourished by doctrines such as those of Fukuyama, promises to outlive it. In an echo of the late-nineteenth- and early-twentieth-century Panamericanist ideology of writers such as José Martí, José Enrique Rodó, and Rubén Darío, Ramírez argues that the only effective resistance to US hegemony and the poverty inflicted by structural adjustment programs lies in continental unity and cooperation. Reflecting on the dire poverty into which such programs have plunged Bolivia, Ramírez concludes that "no estamos llegando en América Latina al fin de la historia, a menos que se piense en el fin de los seres humanos que habitan el continente" (*CA*, 163; "in Latin America we are not reaching the end of history, unless one is thinking of the end of the human beings who inhabit the continent"). Latin America's quest for Utopia will be achieved by internal unity and economic engagement with non-imperialistic actors abroad, such as the European Union, which must be persuaded not to write off Latin America as part of the US sphere of influence. Utopia is not an idea that should be abandoned simply because the Cold War has ended: "el triunfo de una identidad continental" (*CA*, 164; "the triumph of continental unity") is within reach; the consolidation of such an identity will begin the work of abolishing poverty and injustice.

This defiance of the "end of history" paradigm elides the fact that the solution Ramírez proposes to the problem of US hegemony in a unipolar world does not depend on the nation. The recourse to continental unity, and even continental cultural identity, suggests a tacit acceptance of the aspect of globalization discourse that maintains that the nation can no longer stand on its own. This acceptance calls into question the language of the martyrs, and of national history, which fuels the earlier essays. After three short requiems for deceased foreigners – one Panamanian, one Mexican, one from the United States – who were Sandinista allies during the 1980s, Ramírez the practical politician looks forward. The final essay, "Los principios y la práctica" ("Principles and Practice"), compiled from shorter pieces published in his Managua weekly *El Semanario* in January 1991, begins the task of outlining a program for post-Cold War Sandinismo. Here, for the first time, the nascent tension between orthodox and renovationist tendencies that would divide the FSLN four years later, becomes discernible.

The essay's opening installment rebuts the assertion that, in the aftermath of the electoral defeat, Sandinistas must choose between principles (or orthodoxy) and practice (or renovationism). "Si estamos de acuerdo en los principios," Ramírez writes, "como consecuencia estaremos de acuerdo en su necesaria dimensión prágmatica" (*CA*, 177; "If we agree on principles, in consequence we will be in agreement on their necessary pragmatic dimension"). Arguing that the fruit of concerted action will be the continuation of the Revolution, he devotes the second section of the essay to outlining the policies on which all Sandinistas agree. The ordering of these priorities is telling. The first, "el legado principal de Sandino" (*CA*, 178; "Sandino's principal legacy"), is to make Nicaragua a sovereign, independent country; the second, is to end economic dependency and create a new economic order in the country, "favoreciendo en primer lugar a los sectores marginales y más pobres" (*CA*, 178; "giving first priority to the poorest and most marginalized sectors"); the third is to create "una verdadera democracia" ("a true democracy"), by which Ramírez understands not mere liberal-democratic balloting, but rather the act of "conquistando para el pueblo el poder real de decisión" (*CA*, 178; "conquering real decision-making power for the people").

While it is fair to say that these principles are shared by all FSLN members, and that the list of Somocista principles that Ramírez provides by way of contrast are abhorred by all, the concrete recommendations that appear in the third section of the essay are more divisive. Unlike Daniel Ortega or Tomás Borge, Ramírez now argues that the events of 25 February 1990 mark "el fin de una etapa para el sandinismo y la apertura de una nueva, distinta, que implica hoy la necesidad de un replantamiento de objetivos, metas y estrategias" (*CA*, 180; "the end of one stage of Sandinismo and the beginning of a new, different one, which implies the necessity, today, of rethinking objectives, goals and strategies"). In the more open society that will be forced on Nicaragua by the post-Cold War international order, the FSLN cannot succeed if it retains its guerrilla characteristics of secretiveness and strategic plans implemented by an all-powerful National Directorate: "Como cuerpo vivo, el sandinismo debe renovarse, y hacerse cargo de los elementos de modernidad que le son necesarios" (*CA*, 181; "Like a living body, Sandinismo must renew itself and take on board the elements of modernity that it requires"). This belief leads Ramírez to propose three goals for the FSLN at its 1991 party congress. While the expression of these goals is left vague, all three represent significant concessions to the ideology of liberal democracy. Whether Ramírez makes these proposals because he believes they are essential to the Sandinistas' electoral survival in 1996, because they provide a way to open up the question of who will be the party's presidential candidate, or out of an authentic conversion to liberal democracy, is impossible to ascertain. The three proposals are: to renew the party's "estructuras internas y darle al partido un carácter democrático" ("internal structures and give the party a democratic character"); to hold an open discussion about the FSLN's political program "para ganar consenso de los distintos y múltiples sectores de la población" ("to earn a consensus from the varied and multiple sectors of the population"); and to give the party "una nueva dinámica política" ("a new political dynamic") that will move it "hacia la renovación y la transformación" (*CA*, 182; "toward renewal and transformation").

In spite of Ramírez's use of "the people" in the essay's second section, his elaboration of his suggestions includes an atomization of the integrated, corporatist nation of Sandinismo, forged by a common history and a shared struggle, into a succession of discrete constituencies, each with its own interests. He argues that a renewed FSLN program will enable the party to "recuperar la base campesina de Muy Muy, Matiguás, Nueva Guinea, a los comerciantes y artesanos de Masaya, a los alfareros de San Juan de Oriente, a los ganaderos de Esquipulas y Camoapa" (*CA*, 183; "regain the peasant base of Muy Muy, Matiguás, Nueva Guinea, the shopkeepers and artisans of Masaya, the potters of San Juan de Oriente, the cattle ranchers of Esquipulas and Camoapa"). The extensive list of professions and cities that follows may be read by other Sandinistas as an abdication from the principle that the Nicaraguan people are one and indivisible. Though Ramírez assures his readers that "no habrá ninguna división, de eso puede estar segura la derecha" (*CA*, 184; "there will be no division, of that the right can be certain"), it is clear that this is the fear he must allay. Even as he counsels that debate strengthens one's position, this argument for liberal procedures yields to the pragmatic point that renewal will "ponernos en el camino seguro de la recuperación del poder" (*CA*, 184; "put us on the certain path to the recovery of power"). The appeal of the adoption of elements of the liberal-democratic package is that it will enable the FSLN to return to government.

Even if this is true, it is not compelling or inspiring. As the development of *Confesión de amor* illustrates, the nation, the entity to which Ramírez proclaims his allegiance in the title essay, slides out of focus in the second half of the book. It is displaced by the strategic goal of continental Latin American unity as a necessary bulwark against a re-imposition of US imperialism, or by the discrete, atomized identities of target constituencies within Nicaragua. Globalization elevates both the transnational paradigm and the personal or local preoccupation, sucking the nation into a crevice between these two levels. In this environment, it is no longer possible to write novels preoccupied with the national trajectory, such as *To Bury Our Fathers* or *Castigo Divino*. The nation, arguably, can no longer be dramatized in history as a literary protagonist because history, even though it may not have ended, is fast losing its rootedness and diachronic, integrative, culture-shaping authority. (This is the most obvious answer to the question of why Fukuyama's book, though biased, insular, and jejune, struck a chord among readers.) Ramírez's response, in the fiction he wrote immediately after 1990, is to abandon the nation for the *patria chica*, the local community of family and cultural distinctness of Hispanic tradition. With time, the other branch of globalized culture also became more visible in his work, as dramatizations of the self came to the fore.

Clave de sol (A-Major), rooted in family and community, initiates Ramírez's reconstruction of his identity in a post-Cold War order. In his recourse to localism, he anchors identity in popular cultural traditions: baseball, the lottery, and, above all, the music that permeated his upbringing. The first edition of *Clave de sol* features photographs of Ramírez's uncles, Carlos José Ramírez and Alejandro Ramírez, playing the flute and the clarinet respectively, on the front and back covers. The photographs were taken by Ramírez's younger brother Rogelio, to whom the book is dedicated, and who died suddenly three months prior to the volume's publication. The first two stories, which were written in 1984, reflect the anti-imperialism of the early Sandinista period in that each recounts the misadventures of a Latin American who is denied consecration by the mythology of Western popular culture. "Juego perfecto" ("Perfect Game"), which would become one of Ramírez's more widely anthologized stories, revolves around baseball. As Plunkett writes: "There is really only one sport that arouses people's passions in Nicaragua: baseball" (Plunkett 1999: 83).

The fatal tension that designates baseball as both Nicaragua's national pastime and a reminder of its multiple occupations by the US Marines saturates the story's language. A timid young man who has seen scant service as a relief pitcher is given a starting assignment and seems to be on his way to pitching a perfect game, allowing neither hits nor walks. The story's mythical dimension is accentuated by the fact that the game is between San Fernando and Bóer, two legendary teams in Nicaragua. According to Richard McGehee, the Managua team of Bóer was founded in 1905 and the Masaya team of San Fernando in 1915; in 1995 Bóer's defeat of San Fernando "was followed by a riot" (McGehee 1996: 121). From 1956 to 1966 the Nicaraguan leagues were professionalized as a Winter League, meaning that players from the US Major Leagues would play there in the off-season. This explains the fact that the Bóer team's clean-up hitter is "un yankote chele, importado" (*CS*, 20; "a blond, imported Yankee"). The other dangerous hitter on the Bóer team is an Afro-Cuban, "requeneto y musculoso" (*CS*, 34; "statuesque and muscular"). The nameless young pitcher, whose father watches him from the stands, is from Ramírez's home town of Masatepe. Though the story avoids an allegorical mapping of characters to fixed identities, it evokes the cultural tensions inherent in this confrontation of an anonymous young man from the region that Ramírez portrays as the cradle of Nicaraguan cultural identity with players from the US and Cuba (at this time, a pro-US dictatorship). A reference to Don Larsen's perfect game in the 1956 World Series as having occurred "hacía sólo dos años" (*CS*, 27; "only two years ago") sets the story in late 1958, immediately prior to the January 1959 Cuban Revolution.

A perfect game represents the ultimate accolade of the culture that has colonized Nicaragua. Don Larsen's example becomes "la hazaña a la cual este pitcher desconocido de Nicaragua parece acercarse ahora paso a paso, lanzamiento por lanzamiento" (*CS*, 27; "the feat that this unknown Nicaraguan pitcher was now closing in on, step by step, pitch by pitch"). In the eyes of one of the fans, "Juego perfecto significa la gloria" (*CS*, 28; "a perfect game means glory"). Yet this glory eludes the pitcher, who loses his perfect game to an infield error in the bottom of the ninth inning, then loses both his no-hitter and the game when a long drive to the outfield, compounded by a throwing error, becomes a two-run inside-the-park home run, giving Bóer a 2–1 victory over San Fernando. His failure to reach Yankee heaven is lent its emotional force by the story's language. The proliferation of anglicized baseball terminology creates a sporting Spanglish that illustrates linguistic inventiveness at the same time that it speaks of cultural colonization. English words like "strike," "hit," "pitcher," and "inning," and distortions of English terms, such as "dog-out" (from dugout), mingle with the syntactical anglicisms of verbs such as "batear" (to hit) or "ponchar" (to strike out a batter). The story conveys no sense, however, of a reappropriation of the conqueror's language as a defiant banner of national identity. The pitcher and his father are left to confront their failure and marginalization by another country's system of values. As the pitcher eats in disconsolate silence in the abandoned stadium, his baseball cap is blown off by the wind. The father chases down the cap and puts it back on the young man's head in a gesture that combines paternal love with the reaffirmation of the Yankee dominance symbolized by his uniform.

Just as the pitcher is marooned in the uniform of United States conventions, so the protagonist of "Heiliger Nikolaus" ("Saint Nicholas"), the second of the stories written in 1984, is trapped inside another of the monkey-suits of Western materialism: the Santa Claus costume. Sent by his father to study engineering in West Berlin, the Venezuelan protagonist has spent fifteen years pretending to be a student. The story's central theme is the way in which the long-term exile is deprived of his national identity without acquiring that of the host nation. One Christmas, in desperate need of money, the Venezuelan agrees to play Santa Claus at a wealthy couple's flat. The scene degenerates into drunken debauchery; the woman insists that this Santa Claus is from Spain, shouts "*¡Qué viva España!*" (*CS*, 63–5; "Long live Spain!"), and dances with the protagonist; the jealous drunken husband shoots at him, then orders him arrested for "violencia de un extranjero en hogar extraño" (*CS*, 66; "being a violent foreigner in a strange home"). The arrest leads to deportation; the protagonist knows that when he returns to Venezuela "le llamarán con sorna piadosa 'el alemán.' Ya para siempre" (*CS*, 66; "they will call him, with pious sarcasm, 'the German.' This time forever"). Like the pitcher, this ersatz Santa is condemned to eternal cultural inauthenticity. He lives his life in the chimera of identities that he does not possess: having been a "Spaniard" in Germany, he becomes a "German" in Venezuela. The common thread that unites "Juego perfecto" and "Heiliger Nikolaus" is that the solution to both protagonists' dilemmas lies in the promise of the nation. The pitcher is damaged by Nicaragua's cultural colonization, the Santa Claus by losing access to his Venezuelan identity without having acquired that of Germany.

The post-1990 stories, by contrast, bypass the nation, deriving meaning from local and family history, which often contains explicit autobiographical elements. Yet, even in this local world, many of the characters do not fit in. The first work of fiction Ramírez wrote after the 1990 elections, significantly entitled "Volver" ("Return"), is about a man who returns to Masatepe to find that he no longer has a home there. The date of his return, significantly, is 5 August 1942, the day of Ramírez's birth. He would return to this day and place for the setting of his first post-1990 novel, *Un baile de máscaras* (A Dance of Masks). The story may be read as Ramírez's own quest for a symbolic return to the culture of the village in the aftermath of the collapse of the national project of Sandinismo. The unnamed protagonist is an errant musician who fled Masatepe in youth after a tragedy: his father, having gambled away the family home, committed suicide. The young man left town with his guitar, from which he has made a good living, becoming a moderately well-known popular musician. The focus of identity in this story shrinks, from the town to the house to the balcony that is the house's most attractive feature, where Ibrahim Mahmud, the merchant to whom the father lost the residence, celebrated his acquisition by shaving in the mornings

(*CS*, 73–4). While the merchant is from a Middle Eastern immigrant family, the protagonist also lacks a local extended family in this provincial environment where life depends on such support networks; his parents were "forasteros que llegaron cuando se inauguró la luz eléctrica, el padre contratado como contador de la compañía" (*CS*, 74; "strangers who arrived with the advent of electric light, the father hired as the company accountant"). The protagonist has no obvious point of re-entry into the town; no relative with whom he can stay. He can only make his way to the darkened house and stare at it as he recalls the events that led to his father's suicide. The story's lack of a forward narrative illustrates what is lost when the nation ceases to be the touchstone of dramatic action: stripped of its central theme of the struggle for national self-assertion, Ramírez's fiction must find other stakes to prevent the retreat into the local from inducing narrative stasis. "Volver" is more of a sketch than a fully resolved story.

A second story that Ramírez composed at the same time – November 1990 – skirts this immobilized nostalgia by recounting a family anecdote. The family in "Ilusión perdida" ("Lost Illusion") is Ramírez's own: the characters are referred to by their real-life names. The central figures are Ramírez's paternal grandparents. The grandmother, Petrona Gutiérrez, fights a lifelong battle against jealousy as her husband, Lisandro Ramírez, falls in love with a succession of other women. Lisandro is a successful artist, the leader of the family band, "la Orquesta Ramírez, que se hizo famoso en Masatepe y los demás pueblos del sur" (*CS*, 95; "the Ramírez Band, which became famous in Masatepe and the rest of the southern towns"). Each new woman with whom Lisandro falls in love inspires fresh songs; his art is achieved at the cost of wounding his wife, the mother of his fourteen children. Late in life, Lisandro falls in love with Salomé Sabino, the only woman who fails to yield to his courting. His frustration produces "Ilusión perdida," his last successful song. In the aftermath of his failure as a seducer, he relapses into an embittered puritanism, condemning "libertinajes" (*CS*, 97; "liberal behaviour") and becoming the guardian of his daughters' virginity. In extreme old age, nearly blind, he is hauled out of his rocking chair by Petrona, who forces him to watch the huddled wreck that Salomé has become dragging herself down the street: "Allí va tu ilusión perdida" (*CS*, 99; "There goes your lost illusion"). Yet this is not a story of disillusionment: Salomé is not the music she inspired; yet that music has been created at a human cost, as the presence of an artist always exacts a cost on a family.

Though the nation fades from the front lines, political events remain present. They are understood in terms of their impact on an individual who may not grasp the broader picture. "La múcura que está en el suelo" ("The

Earthenware Pot on the Floor") takes place in León in 1959. Written in a lyrical first-person monologue by a young man who falls in love for the first time just before the July 1959 massacre, the story plumbs the role of art in creating the integrated cultural vision that emerged in opposition to the Somoza dictatorship. By inviting the narrator, a repressed young musician, to dance, Celina liberates him in both personal and political terms: "Celina de mi destino, Celina del desatino" (*CS*, 106; "Celina of my destiny, Celina of a missed opportunity"). The condition she imposes on their relationship is that "paso que dé yo adelante, paso que das vos" (*CS*, 107; "the step I take to lead is the step you follow"). A figure who seems to have been conjured up by the popular music of the era, Celina whirls the narrator into protests and student strikes; like Ramírez during his first weeks as a student, the narrator joins the opposition without reasoning why he is doing so. While Celina's family has a long tradition of activism against the dictatorship – "tu abuelo amarrado, asesinado, tirado dentro de un pozo, carceleado tu padre, culateados tus tíos, exiliados tus hermanos" (*CS*, 107; "your grandfather bound, murdered, thrown down a well, your father imprisoned, your uncles tortured, your brothers exiled") – his father is a Somocista poltician who, on seeing a newspaper photograph of the narrator participating in a demonstration, sends him a telegram ordering him to desist from political activity. The music they dance to conditions not only their daring relationship, and their political impetuosity, but also the story's language. Repeated riffs employing Celina's name – "Celina altanera, Celina retrechera" (*CS*, 111; "haughty Celina, seductive Celina") – serve as a refrain.

The story's denouement is the massacre of the students on 23 July 1959. The historical death of Erick Ramírez – a classmate of the author's, whom he was about to take to the hospital when he realized he was dead (Cherem 2004b: 78) – is integrated into the story. The narrator describes the dead student as "tu primo de alma, mi saxofonista" (*CS*, 110; "your beloved cousin, my saxophonist"). This death exposes the inadequacy of the couple's relationship by underscoring that music alone will not end the dictatorship. In the story's final scene, Somoza himself, on a visit to León, insists on dancing with Celina. The narrator's only response is "el honor es mío, general" (*CS*, 114; "The honour is mine, General"). His impotence signals the need to move beyond romantic and artistic ideas of revolution to a more committed program.[4] "Ilusión perdida" and "La múcura que está en el suelo" probe the relationship of art to family life and the public sphere respectively, revealing the concerns of a writer who is searching for the significance of his creative identity in the face of a continuing immersion in politics.

The lyricism of "La múcura que está en el suelo" recurs in "Pero no lloraré" ("But I Won't Cry"), one of the most surprising stories in the collection in that it is set during the years of Sandinista rule, a period that Ramírez (like Gioconda Belli) would explicitly avoid in his later fiction. The narrator is the kind of young woman it was easy to meet in provincial Nicaragua in the 1980s, who has had one or more of her early lovers die in battle against the Contras. The title, which comes from a popular song, confirms the collection's focus on the musical culture of rural Nicaragua. The lyrics, in which the singer promises not to cry "por ese amor que fue, una Aventura ..." (*CS*, 130; "for this love that was, a fling ...") find resonance in the young woman's one-night stand with a soldier on his way to the front, who reminds her of an earlier lover who died in battle: "Dos veces lo vi desnudo, pero la segunda vez fue en la morgue" (*CS*, 127; "I saw him naked twice, but the second time was in the morgue"). After the first soldier's death, she goes to meet his family, getting to know him, as often occurred in Sandinista Nicaragua, as a martyr. As she makes love with the second young man, she cries over the first one. While the story does not develop beyond the epiphany supplied by the association of the two young men, it remains an intriguing glimpse of the kind of fiction that might have been written about the years of the Nicaraguan Revolution, a period still nearly untouched in the nation's literature.

The emphasis on popular culture, particularly as transmitted by local radio stations, is perpetuated by "Kaliman el Magnífico y la Pérfida Mesalina" ("Kalimán the Magnificent and the Perfidious Mesalina"), in which a radio fortune-teller learns of his wife's serial infidelities, her plans to leave him, and the fact that he is not the biological father of most of his seven children, when she phones the radio station to convey this information to his on-air persona, Kalimán. Both of these stories, illustrating the entangling of private and public lives, betray the urge to construct meaning in a sheltered sphere where the public world does not intrude. The young woman's glimpse of the dead lover she barely knew in another young man attests to the difficulty of adequately commemorating those who sacrificed their lives for the nation. In a parallel vein, Kalimán's public triumph exposes (if only to him) the failure of his private life, which in turn demolishes his standing as a public figure; as a result of this moment of recognition, "me abandaron las voces" (*CS*, 152; "the voices abandoned me"). Having lost his job, he must retreat to a private life; yet, like the young woman in "Pero no lloraré," or the musician in "Volver," no private sphere awaits him. This anxiety is latent in nearly all of the post-1990 stories: will private life still be there if one decides to return to it?

The stories' temporal settings, ranging from 1942 in "Volver" to the present of 1992 in the final story, "La suerte es como el viento" ("Luck Is like the Wind"), spread this post-1990 quest for a viable private sphere across the historical span of Ramírez's life. The stories are not arranged in chronological order: the second baseball story, "Tarde de sol" ("Sunny Afternoon"), which, like "Juego perfecto," is set in 1958, is placed next to last. Like "Pero no lloraré" and "La suerte es como el viento," this story is told in the first person by a female narrator. The political references are more conspicuous than in "Juego pefecto": the Cuban pitcher, Silverio Pérez, whose prowess enables the Granada players to threaten to defeat Anastasio Somoza's private team, the Cinco Estrellas ("Five Stars"), stands in counterpoint to Domingo Vargas, the slugger who has been sent to Somoza as a gift by the Dominican dictator General Rafael Trujillo. When Pérez flees Nicaragua, still wearing his baseball uniform, he claims to have been the object of an attempted kidnapping by "los barbudos de Fidel Castro" (*CS*, 162; "the bearded men of Fidel Castro"). The story presents baseball as a spectacle as expressive of Nicaraguan culture as bullfighting is of that of Spain or Mexico. The title sounds a distant echo of Ernest Hemingway's *Death in the Afternoon* (1963), while the Cuban pitcher has the same name as a great Mexican bullfighter of the 1930s and 1940s, whose career, as McGehee points out, was "immortalized in the Spanish bullfighting march (*pasodoble*) 'Silverio Pérez,' written by Mexico's great composer (and bullfight fan) Augustín Lara in 1943" (McGehee 1996: 122).

The deliberate echo of the Mexican bullfighter's name draws out by contrast the difference between the "indigenous" sporting traditions of other Spanish-speaking nations and Nicaraguan baseball, whose history is unimaginable without the excitement induced by players imported from Cuba, the Dominican Republic, and the United States. The narrator of "Tarde de sol" states at the story's opening and conclusion (*CS*, 158, 178) that she is always willing to close her cantina in order to attend a game at the Granada stadium. Yet the tale of Silverio Pérez depicts baseball players as merchandise, and as agents of foreign exploitation. The narrator is the friend and lover of Chelú, a Cadillac-driving oligarch who owns the Granada team. Silverio Pérez is not threatened by Fidel Castro, as he maintains, but by Chelú, whose daughter, Michi, he has impregnated. The slugger flees before Chelú can kill him; but Michi, too, flees to San Francisco in pursuit of Silverio, who is trying to break in to the US major leagues. The narrator is left to contemplate the Granada baseball diamond in the vain hope that Silverio will spurn US glamour to restore to Nicaraguan baseball "aquel pasodoble ... con donaire de torero" (*CS*, 178; "that bullfighting march ... with his bullfighter's grace"). The underlying didacticism is leavened by nostalgia and musical references.

The final story, which feels even more didactic, is lightened by humour. The first-person narrator, a young girl in Ciudad Darío, a provincial town in north-central Nicaragua, watches her best friends, two sisters, dispute the ownership of a car they have won in a scratch-and-win contest. The sisters destroy their relationship in a succession of often humorous quarrels; their exasperated mother burns the scratch-and-win card before they can claim their prize. In the midst of the upheaval, the seemingly shy narrator absconds with the well-off young man who had been the boyfriend of one of the sisters. More than any other in *Clave de sol*, this story transmits a denunciation of the post-1990 culture of lottery capitalism. The narrator reads a story in *La Prensa* in which "comandante Dora María Téllez" warns against "las ilusiones peligrosas que provocan los juegos de azar en una situación de empobrecimiento y miseria como la que vive el pueblo de Nicaragua" (*CS*, 203; "the dangerous illusions caused by games of chance in a situation of impoverishment and misery such as that in which the Nicaraguan people live"). Written in May 1992, barely six months after the October 1991 party congress at which male comandantes had closed ranks to keep Téllez off the National Directorate, "La suerte es como el viento" is Ramírez's first creative expression of discord with FSLN policy. The dedication to Téllez underlines his support for her opposition to both retrograde attitudes within the FSLN and the destructive capitalism of Violeta Chamorro's Nicaragua.

A growing sense of a writer who is finding his post-revolutionary voice is evident in *Oficios compartidos* (1994; Shared Trades), a collection of articles and interviews from the years 1991 to 1993 that was published in Mexico. This book represents an extension of the approach emphasized in the second half of *Confesión de amor*: Ramírez attempts to reconcile the Sandinista experience with the liberal-democratic discourse that dominates the post-1990 world, going so far as to claim of the democratic process that "los sandinistas somos sus creadores, y somos parte de ella" (*OC*, 16; "we Sandinistas are its creators and we are part of it"). In contrast to his essay collections since *El alba de oro*, and most strikingly, to *Confesión de amor*, published only two years earlier, this book does not reprise the history of Nicaragua's subjugation by the United States, or the subservience of the Nicaraguan bourgeoisie. References to William Walker and Augusto César Sandino nearly vanish. The corpse in dispute is that of the Sandinista Revolution. The dual-track approach of *Confesión de amor*, riven by the conflicting discourses of revolutionary duty and liberal democracy, gives way to a more personal duality: that of the writer-politician. Ramírez's reassertion of his identity as a writer, announced in the book's title, is facilitated by his embrace of liberal-democratic discourse, which encourages the expression of obligations towards oneself, not merely towards a revolutionary society. As he writes in the title essay, "la obligación del que quiere ser escritor, es escribir, aunque también pretenda cambiar el mundo, de otra manera"

(*OC*, 77; "the obligation of one who wants to be a writer is to write, even though he may also presume to change the world in another way"). For the first time, writing becomes an obligation, on an equal and separate footing to service to the Nicaraguan people. In contrast to *El alba de oro* and *Seguimos de frente*, whose titles announced the priority of the revolutionary enterprise, *Oficios compartidos* asserts a moral parity between the claims of the collectivity and those of the individual.

Devoid of a strong diachronic dimension, *Oficios compartidos* contains no passage that evokes "the nation," as does *Confesión de amor.* This all-encompassing category, in which history, literature, music, art, religion, and politics fused to constitute a distinctive national identity, splinters into discrete concerns: the correct strategy for returning to power in 1996, how to manage future diplomatic relations with the United States, how to respond to neo-liberalism. When cultural questions are addressed, the focus is on the achievements of individual artists, such as Rubén Darío, Carlos Fuentes, Gabriel García Márquez, or the painter Armando Morales; speculations on identity concentrate, as in "El Nuevo Mundo" ("The New World") or "Modernidad y cambio en América Latina" ("Modernity and Change in Latin America"), on the continental context.

The sole essay whose approach resembles that of the earlier collections in its historical-structural development is about Managua rather than Nicaragua. The nation puts in a brief appearance in "Nicaragua, visión del paraíso" ("Nicaragua, a Vision of Paradise"), where one of the collection's two passing references to Sandino presents the nationalist hero as one wing of a Nicaraguan search for Utopia that is balanced between the personal and the collective, between art and politics, "una doble herencia que no se agota, una doble marca que no se borra" (*OC*, 111; "a double heritage that is not exhausted, a double brand that is not erased"). In the past these impulses would have been integrated into a single entity. Here they are divided, pursuing distinct ends by different means.

Among these polished pieces, "La novela, la política, la vida: una revolución permanente" ("Novel, Politics, Life: A Permanent Revolution") stands out for its rawness and its revealing glimpses of the ongoing changes in Ramírez's outlook. This interview, more than forty pages in length, was published in *Ventana* on 15 July 1991. It acquires a particular significance because of the identity of the interviewer: Rosario Murillo. The reader has the impression of eavesdropping on the Sandinista inner circle as it wrangles over how to position itself for a return to power; yet, as the interview progresses, the dawning rift between what will become the orthodox and renovationist tendencies becomes impossible to ignore. A disarming intimacy is on display as Ramírez confesses to Murillo the personal cost of the Revolution: "me doy cuenta ahora que no participé en la formación de mis hijos" (*OC*, 49; "I now realize that I didn't participate in my children's upbringing"). He presents the post-1990 period as a time to recapture the private life that was obscured during the 1980s by the expansion of the public sphere into every corner of existence: "Ahora trato de buscar un nuevo espacio de relación con mi familia ... trato de sentarme a hablar más con mi mujer" (*OC*, 50; "Now I'm trying to look for a new space in which to relate to my family ... I try to sit down and talk to my wife more often"). In light of earlier definitions of Sandinista masculinity in terms of total commitment to public life and the popular masses, to the exclusion of formalized marital relations or even fidelity to a single partner (a definition with which Ramírez's long, stable marriage was always in conflict), this confession represents a challenge to the dominant FSLN ethos.

At the time of the interview, Ramírez and René Núñez had been nominated as the first non-guerrilla candidates to join the National Directorate at the October 1991 party congress: "Y yo entro a la Dirección, y soy algo así como un *civil* ... porque yo no soy comandante ... He sido otro tipo de figura, objetivamente, dentro de la dirigencia de la revolución" (*OC*, 54–5; emphasis in original; "And I enter the Directorate and I'm something like a *civilian* ... because I'm not a comandante ... I've been a different type of figure, objectively speaking, within the revolutionary leadership"). This question of being a civilian, and of the prospects for generating civil society in Nicaragua, stakes out the fault lines between Ramírez and Murillo. His way of pursuing private life is through his writing: a paradoxical definition since writing, once published, becomes public. His biggest surprise of the post-1990 experience is that the chaotic political situation, in which "hay reunions ... a la hora menos pensada" (*OC*, 17; "there are meetings ... at the most unexpected times"), makes it impossible to establish the rigorous writing routine that he maintained as vice-president. Even as he responds to the post-Cold War era's promise of a fulfilling individuality, Ramírez reaffirms his commitment to the revolutionary Sandinista project, and particularly to its renewal in an effective post-1990 form that will enable civil society to thrive. He dismisses the notion that one may comfortably abandon political commitment in 1990s Nicaragua as an illusion that had a brief life

> después de la derrota. Pensamos que uno podía retomar su propio espacio individual, y que lo que ahora se llama "sociedad civil," florecería de manera autromática, y habría espacio político y humano para todo el mundo ... la realidad es que vivimos un drama, que somos

> actores en este drama ... Y en lo que a mí personalmente se refiere, voy a seguir haciendo lo posible por ser escritor, pero sin dejar de estar en la pantalla de la revolución. (*OC*, 18; after the defeat. We thought that one could take up again one's own individual space and that what's now called "civil society" would flower automatically. And that there would be human and political space for everyone ... the reality is that we are living through a drama, that we are actors in this drama ... And so far as I'm personally concerned, I'm going to continue doing everything possible to be a writer without ceasing to appear on the screen of the revolution.)

Having vowed not to depart from the public "screen," Ramírez is obliged to pursue his quest for individuality in this public forum rather than in his family, where, as he confesses to Murillo, in spite of his good intentions, he finds himself too busy to be "disfrutando la abuelitud" (*OC*, 50; "enjoying grandfatherhood") by spending time with his five-month-old first grandchild. Respect for the individual necessarily assumes the form of a liberal-democratic challenge to the Sandinista ethos of self-sacrifice, duty, and loyalty to the National Directorate. It is here that the discrepancies between Ramírez and Murillo fall into relief. Their disagreements foreshadow the split in the FSLN that will occur three and a half years later. Yet Ramírez's adherence to the idea of revolution, now stripped of the diachronic authority lent to this concept by the traditional touchstones of Nicaraguan history, is revealed to be precarious precisely because his adoption of a liberal-democratic discourse prevents him from evoking references that would bolster his revolutionary credibility. Even as he asserts his intention to remain a fixture on the screen of the Revolution, he clashes with Murillo over freedom of speech. The crux of this debate is the freedom to criticize the direction taken by the FSLN: "Insisto en que no debe asustarnos que la gente reclame su libertad dentro del partido" (*OC*, 38; "I insist that we shouldn't be afraid that people demand their liberty within the party"). When Murillo asks: "¿Impedimos la libre expresión de la gente?" ("Are we blocking people's freedom of speech?"), Ramírez replies: "Tenemos esa tendencia" (*OC*, 38; "We have that tendency"). He attributes the difficulty of fostering the development of a vigorous journalism in post-1990 Nicaragua to the fact that "se trató de educar al periodista en valores pseudorrevolucionarios (por retóricos) ... Porque aquí casi no se formó un periodista crítico, dialéctico" (*OC*, 39; "an attempt was made to educate the journalist in pseudo-revolutionary values (because they were rhetorical) ... Because we barely created a critical, dialectical journalism"). Murillo, for her part, criticizes Ramírez for serving on the editorial board of *El Semanario*, which publishes opinion columns by anti-Sandinista commentators. As they debate the future of the Sandinista newspaper *Barricada*, Murillo insists on "la diferencia entre el perfil editorial de una publicación … y las opiniones de sus editores, su director, sus periodistas y colaboradores" (*OC*, 37; "the difference between a publication's editorial outlook … and the opinions of its editors, journalists and contributors"). In this way, she claims, by promoting a version of FSLN policy modified to respond to a liberal critique, a publication may permit individual opinions to be expressed within an overarching uniformity of outlook. Murillo's views foreshadow the media landscape that she would create in Nicaragua after 2006.

Murillo and Ramírez disagree over internal procedures. Ramírez makes clear that he believes that people who are to be elected to a three-year term should serve "*por tres años*, y que dentro de tres años debería haber un recambio en la dirigencia del Frente Sandinista" (*OC*, 22; emphasis in original; "*for three years*, and that after three years there should be a complete change in the leadership of the Sandinista Front"). Later, he expresses discomfort with his own scheduled presentation to the October party congress as "un candidato oficial que viene a llenar un hueco predestinado. Eso me mortifica" (*OC*, 55; "an official candidate who's going to fill a predetermined spot. That torments me"). He states that he would prefer to have his candidacy subjected to a free vote and that all positions should be decided this way. The implication is obvious: that Daniel Ortega should not be the FSLN's 1996 presidential candidate unless he earns the support of the party; by repudiating his privileges, Ramírez opens a space in which it is possible to imagine that he, rather than Ortega, might be the candidate. In order to remain a contender for this position, Ramírez, must reiterate his primary allegiance to the permanence of the Nicaraguan Revolution, to which even his writing is subordinated. Yet the very concept of "revolution" is now recast in a liberal-democratic frame. The interview closes with Ramírez saying: "Mi mejor novela sería que aquí hubiera siempre revolución, en el sentido de que siempre aceptáramos que el mundo y todo mundo debe y puede cambiar … Creo que se llamaría *La revolución permanente*" (*OC*, 59; "My best novel would be to always have revolution here, in the sense that we should always accept that the world and everybody can and must change … I think it would be called *The Permanent Revolution*").

"Revolution," no longer annealing the historical scars of foreign intervention, disloyal elites, pervasive poverty, and cultural alienation, evolves into an injunction against the re-institutionalization of Sandinismo. Permanent change implies changes in leadership and orientation, a threatening notion to Sandinistas shattered by the 1990 defeat, who long to reconstruct the status quo ante. The most unexpected aspect of the debate between Ramírez and Murillo is the absence of references to Nicaraguan history or to the movement's revered martyrs. National history has been superceded by discussions about tactics. Ramírez laments that Sandinista doctrine estranged him from the syncretized, mestizo religious culture of Masatepe:

> Nunca me olvido que en los primeros años de la revolución estaba en mi casa de Masatepe a ver la pasada de la procesión del Señor de la Trinidad, que es un Cristo Negro, y al pasar la imagen, por la esquina, uno de los que iba cargando me dijo: "Ve, Sergio, vení … cargá al Señor"… Y no fui, por orgullo, por vergüenza de hacer el ridículo, aunque en mi intimidad estaba convencido de que debía hacerlo, pero no lo hice. (*OC*, 48; I'll never forget that in the first years of the revolution I was in my house in Masatepe to watch the procession of our Lord of the Trinity, which is a Black Christ, and as the image passed by the corner, one of those carrying it said to me: "Come on, Sergio … Carry the Lord"… And I didn't go, out of pride, out of shame of looking ridiculous, even though inside I was convinced that I should do it, but I didn't do it.)

The revalorization of a local culture of mixed-race symbols, exemplified by the Black Christ, plugs the gap left by the dwindling of the nation. Bereft of the high-stakes urgency that fed his earlier volumes, these essays betray a tone of indulgent affirmation that fails to carry difficult analyses to their conclusions. Even though the essay about the capital is entitled "Managua, la ultrajada" ("Managua the Abused"), the summary of the city's terrible history concludes in an avuncular tone: "Se maltrata de palabra lo que más se quiere. Yo, por lo menos, jamás la abandonaría" (*OC*, 119; "One verbally abuses what one loves most. I, at least, will never abandon her"). Similarly, "Modernidad y cambio en América Latina," a talk that Ramírez gave in half-a-dozen locations in Europe and the Americas, concludes a substantial overview of Latin American history with the anodyne statement that "el cambio" is "un factor indispensable" (*OC*, 105; "change … is an indispensable factor") to maintain democracy and modernity.

It is telling that a talk given to the policy elite at the Woodrow Wilson Institute in Washington, D.C., on 11 May 1993 under the title "Towards a Modern Relation between the United States and Nicaragua," and reprinted here as "Por una relación moderna entre Estados Unidos y Nicaragua," recovers the incisiveness of his talks of the previous decade. Ramírez reminds his audience of the pernicious pattern of US interventionism in his country, evident in the parallels between the Contra War of the 1980s, purportedly undertaken to stave off "Soviet influence," and the US military assault on the Liberal government of José Santos Zelaya at the beginning of the twentieth century because "se le acusaba de querer entregar la ruta del canal al Japón y Alemania" (*OC*, 160; "he was accused of wanting to hand over the canal route to Japan and Germany"). Referring to the way in which Senator Jesse Helms has blocked aid to the government of Violeta Chamorro, Ramírez advises that "Estados Unidos debe desideologizar sus relaciones con Nicaragua" (*OC*, 161; "the United States must de-ideologize its relations with Nicaragua"). If the Clinton administration is renewing the internal policies of the United States, it must also renew its foreign policy by ending its "visión paternalista, arcaica y primitiva" (*OC*, 161; "paternalistic, archaic and primitive vision") which denies Nicaraguan self-determination. The issues of the future, on which the two countries must collaborate, will be "pobreza y narcotráfico" (*OC*, 164; "poverty and drug-trafficking"). Confronting the United States nation-to-nation, in English, Ramírez expresses himself with a vigour that is lacking from other essays in *Oficios compartidos*.

A recurrent question is that of the Revolution's legacy. Here, too, the framework of the nation reappears, vitiated, however, by an anxiety to sustain the Sandinista inheritance against the depredations of Chamorro's neoliberalism. These speculations gain urgency from the realization that history has not ended, that time is passing and the 1979–90 period will inevitably recede into the past. The question of how the Sandinista Revolution will be remembered animates "Entre dos revoluciones" ("Between Two Revolutions"), Ramírez's commemoration of the centenary of Zelaya's Liberal revolution of 1893. Contending that future historians will see the revolutions of 1893 and 1979 respectively as the two defining moments of modern Nicaragua, Ramírez argues for the integration of Sandinismo into the trajectory of Nicaraguan history. His depiction of Sandino's insurgency as a legacy of Zelaya's reforms, which were designed to strengthen the national bourgeoisie, enfolds the Sandinista Revolution in the nationalist pageant. The difference between the two revolutions is that Zelaya's "proyecto nacional" (*OC*, 173–4; "national project") was overthrown by the United States, which "desmantelaron al estado nacional. Por el contrario, la revolución sandinista no fue desmantelada por el triunfo de las armas de la contrarrevolución militar que se repitió en términos muy similares" (*OC*, 174; "dismantled the national state. By contrast, the Sandinista revolution was not dismantled by an armed triumph of the military counterrevolution, which was repeated in similar terms"). Fatally, Zelaya's strong-arm Liberalism bequeathed the country a legacy of authoritarianism that paved the way for the dictatorial Liberalism of the Somozas; in Sandinismo, by contrast, "la marca es la transición democrática, y el cambio pacífico de gobierno" (174 "the key is the democratic transition and the peaceful change of government"). Though one bequeathed authoritarianism and the other democracy, the two revolutions have in common the fact that they are "irreversible" (174–5).

Throughout *Oficios compartidos*, Ramírez refers to a historical novel he is writing about Rubén Darío. He tells Murillo that he has taken notes on more than twenty books about Darío; in a presentation originally given in English at the South Bank Centre in London in 1991 and reprinted here as "El artista frente a su modelo" ("The Artist Confronts His Model"), Ramírez states of Darío: "Quiero contar su llegada a París en 1893, su primer encuentro con Verlaine … O sus encuentros con Oscar Wilde, también en París … Y la muerte de Rubén Darío en León, porque volvió a Nicaragua para morir en 1916" (*OC*, 144; "I want to relate his arrival in Paris in 1893, his first meeting with Verlaine … Or his meetings with Oscar Wilde, also in Paris … And the death of Rubén Darío in León, because he returned to Nicaragua to die in 1916"). Only the third of these events survived to take its place in *Margarita, How Beautiful the Sea*. Before Ramírez could relegate national history to the status of pastiche, however, he needed to find a firm purchase on which to stand as a replacement for the diachronic, integrative vision of the nation that he had promoted from the early 1970s until 1990. Like many people confronting globalization, Ramírez took refuge in a local culture, and in the self.

RETREAT TO THE MESTIZO VILLAGE: *UN BAILE DE MÁSCARAS*

By December 1992, Ramírez was writing a novel confined in its geographical and temporal scope to Masatepe during the twenty-four hours of the day of his own birth, 5 August 1942. As foreshadowed by *Clave de sol*, in the aftermath of the collapse of the national project, Ramírez returns to his *patria chica*. The immersion of *Un baile de máscaras* in a local culture whose customs and quaint characters are recounted with affection obscures the fact that the protagonists and their actions acquire significance by virtue of the baby who is born at the novel's conclusion. While staging a putative retreat from the post-Cold War world, the novel mythologizes the birth of the self who will dominate Ramírez's next three novels: *Margarita, How Beautiful the Sea*; *Sombras nada más* (2002; Only Shadows Remain); and *A Thousand Deaths Plus One*.

Ramírez spoke often of the Nicaraguan Revolution as a set of "reflectores" ("spotlights"). He told Rosario Murillo that, like other Sandinista writers, he owed the foreign publication of his books to these spotlights and that, after 1990, the "deslumbre publicitario de nuestra revolución va quedando atrás, y hemos entrado en otra etapa en que los escritores y los artistas tienen que presentarse lejos de la luz de estos reflectores, se está probando si vamos a sobrevivir o no" (*OC*, 29; "the publicity glare of our revolution falls away and we have entered a new stage in which writers and artists have to present themselves far away from these spotlights, we're testing the water to see whether we're going to survive"). Paradoxically, the most effective international literary passport for Sandinista writers in the post-1990 period – not only Ramírez, but also Ernesto Cardenal and Gioconda Belli – turned out to be the fact of their having been leaders of the Nicaraguan Revolution. All three writers were constituted as literary figures in the international marketplace by the twentieth century's last revolution; they endured into the post-1990 era as postmodern simulacra of the revolutionary artist. The fact that global developments in ideology, finance, the media, and international governance and security during this period virtually eliminated armed, left-wing revolution as a potential method of national transformation heightened the premium enjoyed by the very few writers who could still lay claim to having participated in this experience.

The dominant shadow with whom the Sergio Ramírez of the years 1990 to 2006 would have to contend was the bloated image of Vice-President Ramírez, which mediated a host of international discourses nostalgic for national history, meaningful social action, and lost idealism. In the three novels that follow *Un baile de máscaras*, Ramírez the post-1990 writer never quite throws off the image of Ramírez the pre-1990 Sandinista leader. Indeed, one can make the case, as does Arturo Arias, that this image is what these novels are about:

> Ultimately we have the posturing of the writer as a codified body image to defend the inviolability of the ontological field of the past revolutionary hero, reconfigured now as a wise *letrado* ... he occupies center stage, conveying the sense that he has chosen to memorialize himself and he has earned his spot as a subject of memorialization. The stories around which his last novels are woven ... are but background material ... his postwar novels are primarily parables of the exemplary hero making a self-reference so as to convert the narrated event into the regularization of the revolutionary *letrado*. The writer as reified iconic celebrity travels throughout the world – Miami, Poland, Majorca – to evidence his

> status and recapture the sensation of power he lost with the end of the revolutionary cycle. (Arias 2007: 20–1)

This summarizes eloquently the dilemma posed by these books, even though one of them, *Margarita, How Beautiful the Sea*, is a deft, highly readable, and popular novel and another, *Sombras nada más*, is one of Ramírez's most densely wrought creations and a major work. Arias does not mention *Un baile de máscaras*, Ramírez's first "postwar novel," which, literally, gives birth to the "codified body image" that will dominate the next three novels. The birth occurs in the pre-revolutionary past, in a town that is aware of world events yet clings to its customs of courtship, celebration, and religious observance. The novel's opening chapter notes the importance of the "día del patrono de Masatepe, el cristo negro de la Santísima Trinidad" (*BM*, 22; "day of Masatepe's patron saint, the Black Christ of the Very Holy Trinity"). This acknowledgment of the syncretized Black Christ marks the return to the husk of the sacred world that existed prior to the nation. Benedict Anderson, drawing on Eric Auerbach, stresses that under the sacred order an apprehension exists that he describes as "a simultaneity of past and future in an instantaneous present" (Anderson 1983: 24). Writing in the early 1980s, Anderson distinguishes this simultaneity from the notions of simultaneity that built the nation: people in different regions of a given territory sharing national myths and elaborating a common national project (as occurred during the Nicaraguan Revolution).

A post-1990 commentator would need to define a third phase of simultaneity, that of which Manuel Castells is thinking when he writes that "the timelessness of multimedia's hypertext is a decisive feature of our culture ... The whole ordering of meaningful events loses its internal, chronological rhythm" (Castells 1996: 492). *Un baile de máscaras* presents a simultaneity, incarnated in the novel's Aristotlean unities and compressed time frame, which purports to be that of the sacred order and immemorial custom yet slides inexorably into the annunciation of a time-defying mediatized image characteristic of the anti-diachronic third phase, that of a postmodern globalized world where national projects are no longer sustainable and the return to ethnic belonging coexists with an irresistible slippage into timeless imagery. Events in *Un baile de máscaras* are not, of course, literally simultaneous nor confined to a single twenty-four-hour period. The villagers' dialogues and memories relate many events that occurred prior to 5 August 1942, such as the courtship and marriage of the author's parents. These events, narrated in the past tense, weave in and out of the present-day (and sometimes present-tense) narration of the preparations for the masked ball and the birth of the Ramírez family's first male child. In fact, Ramírez adopted the day-in-the-life model as a means of bringing together events from disparate time frames:

> La estructura de la narración resolvía mi propuesta de escribir sobre la historia de mi familia: todas las múltiples historias de mis dos familias, por parte de mi padre y por parte de mi madre, que yo tenía en mi cabeza desde niño. Pero escogí la estructura de ponerlo todo en un día porque me resolvía el problema fundamental del libro, que es cómo contar muchas historias en vías diferentes. Me resultaba muy complejo de armar, pero si yo creaba el eje de un día y hacía girar todo alrededor de ese eje, entonces me facilitó mucho el problema. (*UISR;* The narrative structure solved my goal of writing about my family history: all of the multiple stories of my two families, on my father's side and on my mother's side, that I'd had in my head since childhood. But I chose the structure of putting it all in a single day because it resolved the book's fundamental problem, which is how to tell many stories on different tracks. It turned out to be very complex for me to assemble, but if I created a single day as an axis and made everything revolve around that axis, then it eased the problem a lot for me.)

Though references occur to historical figures, such as General Emiliano Chamorro and Anastasio Somoza García, no national problematic appears in the novel. Augusto César Sandino has been dead for only eight years, yet, though Masatepe lies a mere six kilometres from Sandino's birthplace of Niquinohomo, and both his native village, and his father, Gregorio Sandino, appear in the novel, he himself has been nearly forgotten. The only reference to Augusto César Sandino occurs when an unidentified figure dresses up as him for the masked ball: "lo iba a echar preso el teniente Sócrates Chocano y tuvo que huir por los solares" (*BM*, 161; "Lieutenant Sócrates Chocano was going to arrest him and he had to escape through the back yard").

A national consciousness coheres only in the novel's three opening pages, where newspaper accounts of international news are interspersed with advertisements from Nicaraguan businesses. Even though the novel's first word, "recapturan" (*BM*, 9; "they recapture"), hints at the Proustian enterprise of recapturing the past, the particular patchwork of international events, filtered through a local prism, forges the "imagined community" of national consciousness that Anderson traces to the eighteenth-century foundation of newspapers in the Americas, which facilitated "the refraction of 'world events' into a specific imagined world of vernacular readers" (Anderson

1983: 62). The novel's opening paragraph illustrates the construction of such an Andersonian national outlook:

> Recapturan los chinos la ciudad de Hunan obligando a los japoneses a retroceder en dirección sudoeste hasta Ling, mientras los aviones norteamericanos arrojan bombas de gran tamaño sobre Linchwan *Cuchillas* Durham Duplex *las que Ud. esperaba para complacer su barba se las ofrecen Carlos y Rodolfo Cardenal establecidos en Managua y Granada.* (*BM*, 9; The Chinese recapture the city of Hunan, obliging the Japanese to retreat in a southwesterly direction to Ling, while US planes drop large-scale bombs on Linchwan. *Durham Duplex razor blades, the ones that you were waiting for to please your beard, are offered to you by Carlos and Rodolfo Cardenal, established in Managua and Granada.*)

The conjunction of a particular article on the progress of the Second World War in Asia with publicity for US commercial products being marketed by Nicaraguan merchant families (Rodolfo Cardenal was Ernesto Cardenal's father), assembles the imagined community of the Nicaraguan nation. The newspaper makes accessible features of national history, such as the commercial prowess of the great families of Granada; sometimes national chronology becomes more pungent, as when the newspaper refers to a mother who lost five sons "en distintos combates" ("in different battles") during the 1926 uprising and who "ha sido favorecida con pensión vitalicia de veinticinco córdobas mensuales" (*BM*, 11; "has been favoured with a lifelong pension of twenty-five córdobas a month"). The echo of the suffering of mothers of the martyrs of the 1970s and 1980s is obvious. After three pages, the rhythm of blended news and advertising halts, and, after a space break, yields to a description, in a more elegiac voice, of the newspaper reader in whose consciousness this peculiarly Nicaraguan perception of reality is taking shape:

> Como todas las tardes, salvo los domingos que no hay periódico ni llega el tren, viene tu abuelo Teófilo leyendo *La Noticia* por la mediacalle, de regreso de la estación de ferrocarril que queda ahora atrás envuelta en el humo de la locomotora, aunque la estela de vapor se extiende rastrera más allá de las barandas y parece perseguirlo con bocanadas hambrientas. (*BM*, 12; As he does every afternoon, except on Sundays when there is no newspaper nor does the train arrive, your grandfather Teófilo comes down the middle of the street reading *La Noticia*, returning from the train station, which lies behind him now, wrapped in smoke

from the locomotive, though the trail of steam stretches out, creeping beyond the iron railings and seems to pursue him in hungry mouthfuls.)

The national consciousness that is being forged is that of Ramírez's maternal grandfather, Teófilo Mercado, the stern self-made man who attributed his work ethic and his rise from poverty to the discipline of his Baptist religion. All of the members of the Ramírez and Mercado families bear their original names in the novel; all are referred to in terms of their relationship to the baby who is about to be born, as though the narrator were telling the story to the fetus in the womb. The patriarchal cast of the local culture is evident in the younger Teófilo's telegram, in which he announces his upcoming plane trip to the Atlantic Coast on business: "*espero noticias feliz parto queridísima hermana Luisa coma dígale espero que sea varón*" (*BM*, 20; "*await news happy delivery much loved sister Luisa comma tell her I hope it's male*"). The Mercados' engagement with the outside world and the diverse regions of the nation contrasts with the immersion in village life of the Ramírez family, who are introduced in chapter 2, which opens with the words, "La tienda se sume en la oscuridad" (*BM*, 33; "The shop is plunged in darkness"). This darkness is both physical and intellectual. In contrast to Teófilo Mercado, the Ramírez family displays a naive understanding of the world that has not been mediated by the imagined community of the nation. The pride of Lisandro Ramírez's shop is a portrait of Winston Churchill, hung to celebrate the British prime minister's "defensa de la democracia" (*BM*, 82; "defence of democracy"); it is clear that the Liberal Ramírezes have not contemplated the fact that they themselves support a dictator. Their lack of political consciousness is reflected in the impartial, indulgent narrative voice, which reports that the coup in which Anastasio Somoza García formally took over the presidency in 1936 was the cause of two demonstrations in Masatepe, one in favour and one against. The narrator, who refrains from judging the merits of the two positions, reports political events at a village level. The nation, the tier where policies are implemented, lies beyond the scope of this vision.

The Masatepe of 1942 sees itself as a spectator of, not a protagonist in, the history of both the nation and the world. In this innocent environment in which the movers and shakers of great events are perceived as movie-star-like figures, and the consequences of their policies are obscured, it is possible for Domitilo Regidor, an admirer of German culture, to attend the masked ball dressed as Adolf Hitler; Teófilo Mercado plans to dress as Josef Stalin. The residents of Masatepe are able to regard the world with this levity because they are confident that the events that fill the newspapers do not touch them. As the Ramírez uncles say, "Qué saben en Inglaterra dónde queda Masatepe si aquí es el culo del mundo" (*BM*, 82; "What do they know in England about where Masatepe is, if this is the asshole of the world"). At the same time, the narrator assembles the information that would be required to construct an analysis of US imperial domination of Nicaragua, even though these facts, related in a droll tone, appear as discrete items rather than components of an integrated analysis (which is inhibited by the fact that the characters do not conceive of themselves on a national plane). The author's father, Pedro Ramírez, becomes the founder of the Masatepe Lions' Club "por mandato supremo que recibió de Chicago" (*BM*, 29; "by supreme orders received from Chicago"). General Macedonio Barquero, a Masatepe resident who serves a brief term as president of Nicaragua in the late 1920s, builds a highway down the slope of the Masaya volcano "empleando zapadores de los cuerpos de marina americanos, ocupantes por entonces del país" (*BM*, 68; "employing sappers of the US Marines, who were occupying the country at that time"). These details remain mere scattered references in the non-stop flow of village storytelling.

Like *Tiempo de fulgor* and some of the short stories of *Cuentos* and *Nuevos cuentos*, *Un baile de máscaras* contains echoes of the rural Modernist fiction of Juan Rulfo and Gabriel García Márquez. The most striking evolution between Ramírez's early works and *Baile de máscaras*, however, aside from the highly accomplished polyphonic prose and seamless structure of this novel, is the presence not only of settings or tones that are reminiscent of Rulfo or García Márquez, but also of magic realist events that defy rational logic. These events are rooted in the peculiarities of the culture of Ramírez's fictionalized Masatepe, as those in the work of the Mexican and the Colombian are in the fictitious towns of Comala and Macondo respectively. Where the political urgency of *To Bury Our Fathers* and *Castigo Divino* precluded extra-rational flourishes, here, redeeming himself for having refused to carry the Black Christ, Ramírez plants this symbol of syncretized mestizo culture at the heart of his novel. Other magic realist elements that appear also serve to emphasize that the vision of the village, with its myths and eccentric local belief systems, takes precedence over rationalist constructions of reality. Priscila Lira, being carried by train to Masaya for burial, is revived in her coffin by the wind flowing over the railway line. In a scene reminiscent of the arrival of the first gringos in Macondo in García Márquez's *One Hundred Years of Solitude*, the letter that Pedro Ramírez writes to Winston Churchill to request a signed portrait of the British prime minister results in "la imprevista aparición de dos ingleses feos, flacos, dientones y orejudos, pantalón corto y medias altas, con cascos de la jungle"

(*BM*, 82; "the sudden appearance of two ugly, skinny, toothy and big-eared Englishmen, in short pants and high socks, wearing pith helmets"). The appearance of these colonialists, who deliver the portrait that Pedro has requested, represents the ascendancy of the villagers' collective imagination over any reality compatible with the conditions of the Second World War. Such perceptions of reality descend from the animism of the indigenous cultures to which the villagers trace their ancestry. Aboriginal people continue to live among them, and influence their reception of Christian world views.

The novel's incorporation of magical realist elements is influenced by the work of Miguel Ángel Asturias, in whose *Men of Maize* events that defy Western rationality are lent credence by a mythologization of the Mayan cosmovision. Ramírez's characters are mestizos, yet they respect the power of indigenous culture. Like Asturias, Ramírez associates Mesoamerican indigenous civilization with the corn that was these cultures' dietary, economic, and symbolic staple. When the Ramírez brothers dig up the patio of their house in the hope of finding buried treasure, they discover, in Pedro's words, "maíz de los tiempos de los indios que ponían en las tumbas para que comieran los muertos"("corn from the days of the Indians, who put it in their tombs to be eaten by the dead"); he goes on to speculate that "a lo mejor, y quien quita, vivimos encima de la propia tumba del cacique Mazaltepelt" (*BM*, 66; "at best maybe we're even living on top of the tomb of Chief Mazaltepelt"). This image identifies the Ramírez family as the hybridized successors of the village's original inhabitants.

Mazaltepelt first appears in the opening chapter when Luisa Mercado imagines that he, rather than Josef Stalin, would be an appropriate costume for her husband to wear to the masked ball. The indigenous contribution to the local culture nourishes Masatepe's eccentricity and acts as a bulwark against assimilation into institutionalized discourses of church or nation. Even the village priest, Father Misael Lorenzano, agrees to bury a witch ("hechicera") "dentro de la iglesia" (*BM*, 87; "in the church"). The priest believes in "el cadejo," a shape-shifting nocturnal creature that originates in indigenous Mesoamerican belief systems.[5] In the indigenous-descended yet politically Liberal community of Masatepe, "el cadejo" is associated with the Conservative strongman General Emiliano Chamorro, to whom the gift of a shape-shifting is attributed. Avelino Guerrero and the priest, Father Misael Lorenzano, exchange accusations of having diluted the Catholic faith, the former by lighting candles to el cadejo in church, the latter by burying witches and other non-believers in the sanctified ground of the cemetery. Yet the priest, as the representative of officialdom, betrays his syncretic culture. He invites a specialist in sacred images from Catholic Granada, whom he puts to work on the Black Christ, "lijando la madera y dándole después el nuevo esmalte a la imagen" (*BM*, 107; "sanding the wood and then applying a new varnish to the image") until the sacred image is light skinned rather than dark. Pedro Ramírez demands that he restore the Christ to its original colour: "Ese cristo negro es el santo patrono de este pueblo" (*BM*, 108; "That Black Christ is the patron saint of this town"). Pedro warns the priest that the indigenous community will retaliate against him for changing the saint's identity: "Le van a echar en motín las hechiceras a toda esa indiada que ellas manejan a su gusto y antojo, y amarrado por las calles lo van a arrastrar" (*BM*, 108; "The witches are going to stir up that whole Indian rabble that they control at will and they're going to tie you up and drag you down the streets").

The Black Christ becomes the pivot of the struggle over the village's identity. Whitened, the Christ submits to the predominance of national discourses and the imposition on Masatepe of the norms of a putatively "white" national bourgeoisie. Yet the syncretic elements of the local culture prove capable of resisting the incursions of national politics. The novel's last two chapters are related through the perceptions of Pedro Ramírez, who is referred to as "el beduino" ("the bedouin"), as he moves around town dressed for the masked ball. As Pedro has predicted, the indigenous people revolt against the priest. In this act of retribution against a national ideology, both sides are portrayed as untrustworthy. The indigenous people from the Nimboja district appear as a drunken mob: "los alzados empuñaban rajas de ocote encendidas en el afán de pegarle fuego a la casa cural, y mecates gruesos de esos que sirven para apersogar reses ... todos andan tomados" (*BM*, 208; "the rioters gripped lighted spars of pine wood in their urge to set fire to the parish house, and thick twine of the sort that's used to hitch up cattle ... they were all drunk"). While the indigenous people threaten violence, the priest is a prejudiced man whose probity has been called into question by his fondness for using the parish house as a venue for "concursos de miembros viriles" (*BM*, 109; "contests of virile members") – which, scandalously, Pedro's brother Edelmiro has attended. When the priest goes into hiding disguised as the Virgin Mary, Pedro is left to confront the rebellious indigenous people who allege that Father Lorenzano is trying to "negociar la imagen sagrada con pastores protestantes de [Estados Unidos] que sólo la querían para hacerle leña porque no creen los protestantes en imágenes de crucificados ni en ninguna otra, menos en imágenes negras" (*BM*, 211; "sell off the sacred image to US Protestant ministers who only want it to make firewood because Protestants don't believe in images of the cross nor in any others, far less in black images").

It is striking that here, in contrast to the rest of Ramírez's work up to this point, evil designs on the part of Americans – even in a burlesque form – are attributed to Protestantism rather than to military or economic expansionism. The mestizo norm that Pedro represents, which obviates both the priest's "whitening" project and the indigenous people's pre-modern wrath, serves as a shared ground on which the village's opposing forces may reconcile their differences. *Mestizaje* also becomes a point at which the two wings of Ramírez's own family – the mercurial, artistic Catholic Ramírezes and the disciplined, ambitious, Protestant Mercados – meet. The priest tells the author's paternal grandmother, Petrona, that "estoy dispuesto a que el cristo vuelva a ser negro, que regrese a su color" (*BM*, 217; "I'm willing to let the Christ be black again, to return to his colour"). Pedro's father, Lisandro Ramírez, calms the mob by negotiating the transfer of the formerly Black Christ to the Nimboja district, where "mañana mismo se comenzaría el trabajo de volverlo a pintar" (*BM*, 225; "tomorrow the work of repainting him would begin"). By acting as mediators between the priest and the indigenous people, the Ramírez family confirm their position as emissaries of a local, anti-national culture that draws upon both Iberian and Náhuat heritages.

At the novel's conclusion, the indigenous people celebrate their victory. Ironically, this is not a triumph of Náhuat culture, but of local syncretism: the Black Christ, though cherished by indigenous people, is not a trait of indigenous culture, but rather a product of the mixing of the European Catholic and Mesoamerican animist religious systems. In a similar vein, the three "witches" who direct the mob allude to both the traditional role of the medicine woman in the Americas, and European traditions of witchcraft as expressed by figures such as the three witches in William Shakespeare's *Macbeth*. This mixed culture defines the *patria chica* that resists absorption into the nation. Pedro's penultimate line of dialogue in the novel is: "¡De aquí no salgo más!" (*BM*, 228; "I'm never leaving here again!").

The risks of embracing the nation are evident in the fates of other residents of Masatepe. The program of the masked ball, played by the Orquesta Ramírez, opens with a prelude to *Un Ballo de Maschera* by Giuseppe Verdi. Providing further evidence of their mixed culture, the Ramírezes, who may live atop the tomb of an indigenous chieftain, are well versed in European classical music. In an echo of the murder that occurs in Verdi's opera, the night of the ball is marred by a series of sudden deaths. Macabeo Regidor, the son of the Germanophile, commits suicide; another local resident, Amantina Flores, is burned to death after falling asleep with a cigarette in her hand. Two other deaths illustrate the perils of the national context. General Macedonio Barquero, the one-time president and current collaborator of the regime, who is regarded as "igual ... a Tacho Somoza en Managua" (*BM*, 191; "equal ... to Tacho Somoza in Managua"), orders his son Ulises to be locked up in Masatepe to save him from his alcoholism. This enforced cold turkey backfires when, unable to tolerate the deprivation, the son of Masatepe's most powerful representative on the national stage commits suicide in his prison cell. Finally, as Pedro Ramírez is on his way to meet his newborn son, he receives a telegram informing him that his wife's brother, Teófilo, has died in a plane crash on his way to the Atlantic Coast.

The values marshalled in *Un baile de máscaras* to substitute for the collapsed edifice of the nation are local, racially mixed, and culturally syncretic, yet they are also patriarchal. By retreating from the national context, where demands for equality of all kinds, including gender equality, are integral to the modernizing ethos of Sandinismo, to the folkloric traditionalism of the village, which is exempt from national and international politics, Ramírez enables a rehabilitation of masculinity that compensates for the loss of his authority caused by the 1990 electoral defeat. In defiance of the dictum that a novel should end with a birth and a death, *Un baile de máscaras* concludes with a single birth that must counterbalance a spate of deaths. The new baby is capable of taking on this role because he is male. While the characters' repeated expressions of the hope that the baby will be a boy are presented in an ironic tone, the presence of an underlying reaffirmation of unquestioned male authority as part of the comforting quaintness of the rural past is undeniable. By being born on the day that his young uncle, Teófilo, dies, the infant Sergio becomes not only the first male child on his father's side, but also the symbolic replacement son in the maternal family. The fact that he is named Sergio – a name with no prior history in the Ramírez family – indicates that, rather than languishing in the symbolic darkness of the Ramírezes' adherence to the circular time of the village, he will join the future-oriented telos incarnated by Grandfather Teófilo's forward-looking values. Pedro's decision not to mire the child in repetitive cycles of naming – such as those that breed multiple Aurelianos and José Arcadios in García Márquez's *One Hundred Years of Solitude* – becomes the occasion for Grandfather Teófilo's reconciliation with the son-in-law whose marriage to his daughter he opposed: "está muy bien pensado que no le pongás Pedro, como vos, a este niño que es tu primer varón, pues uno no debe repetir en los hijos su propio nombre porque después cualquier cosa pasa, alguna desgracia, y resulta doble el dolor" (*BM*, 225; "it's very well thought-out not to call this child who is your first son Pedro after you, for one shouldn't repeat one's own name in one's children because later anything can happen, some misfortune, and the pain is twice as bad"). This statement is bitterly prescient in light of the fact that Grandfather Teófilo is not yet aware of his son Teófilo's death; in spite of the obvious significance of the grandfather's words in healing the family rift and, at an emblematic level, reconciling progress with tradition, the fact that Ramírez himself named his own son Sergio, hence returning to the circularity of village time, makes it difficult to know how to read this injunction.[6] The most notable feature of this transmission of values is that the author's father is the novel's central character; his maternal grandfather represents access to the broader, riskier frame of national consciousness. In spite of the adult Ramírez's declarations that his mother was the defining influence on his childhood (Cherem 2004b: 63–4), the mother who is about to give birth, "Luisa la grávida" (*BM*, 33; "Luisa the expectant"), is a peripheral character in the novel. By contrast, patriarchal figures appear as benevolent. When Amantina Flores dies in the fire, for example, Averino Guerrero steps forward to admit that he is the father of her illegitimate son, and takes the boy into his home.

While the patriarchal values of male authority and the unbroken cycles of village traditions, from the worship of the Black Christ to the celebration of the masked ball, are reaffirmed in *Un baile de máscaras*, time remains a linear force that scatters cultural certainties. The prelude to Pedro's decision to give the baby a non-repetitive name is his recognition of the inevitability of temporal progression. This perception is expressed through his memories of a kaleidoscope that Father Lorenzano brought as a gift for Luisa: "a otra vuelta del tubo, se deshacen las imágenes entroncitos de colores, ruinas de espejismo, ensueños hechos trizas, fragmentos de ilusiones, perdida para siempre la perfecta simetría, la felicidad perfecta que apenas tuvo forma y nunca más se volverá a repetir" (*BM*, 194; "at a turn of the tube, the connected images disintegrate, the ruins of a mirage, dreams smashed to bits, fragments of illusions, their perfect symmetry lost forever, the perfect happiness that barely took shape and never will be repeated again"). In response to the verb "recapture," with which the novel opens, the narrator reiterates that the past is lost forever and the happiness of a newborn baby or an innocent rural culture cannot be repeated. Behind the smile that the child's parents exchange in the novel's final sentence lies the not-yet-divulged knowledge of the wife's brother's death in a distant region of the country, shrouding the family in the tragedy of national history, whose violence is destined to engulf the life of the newborn infant.

PATRIARCHY DISCREDITED: THE FSLN SPLIT AND "CATALINA Y CATALINA"

Un baile de máscaras, though an accomplished work, has received less critical attention than Ramírez's other novels. (By contrast, it is a popular text for final-year students in Nicaraguan private high schools.) The narrative technique, employing an art that conceals art, is less overtly innovative than that of any of the other novels except for *Tiempo de fulgor* and the detective novel *El cielo llora por mí* (2008; The Heavens Weep for Me). Yet it represents a crucial stage in Ramírez's reconstitution of his post-revolutionary identity.

Pursued as a new model, *Un baile de máscaras* would have been a dead end, relegating Ramírez to the status of a reactionary promoter of folkloric rural values. The most problematic of these values is an affirmation of patriarchal assumptions. This issue came to a head in Ramírez's public career during the time that *Un baile de máscaras* was in press. The split in the FSLN in December 1994 and January 1995, described in chapter 9, revolved around questions not only of democratic accountability but also of revolutionary machismo. Ramírez was prevented from prolonging his embrace of the patriarchal tradition, auditioned in *Un baile de máscaras* as the indulgent companion of rural mestizo culture, by machista attacks on himself and his family. The most notorious event of the FSLN rupture was a campaign during which the pro-Ortega Radio Ya broadcast reports that Ramírez's political ally Dora María Téllez, a thirty-nine-year-old single woman who would later speak at gay rallies (Babb 2001: 236–7), and his elder daughter, FSLN Member of National Congress María Ramírez, a twenty-seven-year-old married woman, were lesbian lovers. While in many societies such an accusation might be seen as trivial or laughable, in Nicaragua, where Violeta Chamorro's government had made homosexuality a punishable crime, liable to a sentence of one to three years' imprisonment, and adolescents who demonstrated "traits of homosexuality" (White and Calderón 2008: 61) might be expelled from school, Radio Ya's assertions constituted an aggressive attack.[7]

"Catalina y Catalina," the short story Ramírez worked on during these months, which would become the title story of his collection of the same name, published in 2001, provides a reconsideration of the dangers of rural patriarchal values. As in the events that were taking place at the time of the story's composition, machismo is expressed by an accusation of sexual scandal. The female narrator who, the reader deduces, is the second Catalina of the title – the daughter who has the same name as her mother yet, resisting the cycle created by repetitive naming, longs for a different destiny – reveals in the opening sentence that her mother has been accused of adultery and that she has never known whether to believe this accusation. Crucially, given the story's setting, like that of *Un baile de máscaras*, in a village in the Department of Masaya – this time in the 1970s – it is the narrator's father who is the accuser. At the end of the closing paragraph, the narrator confesses that "ya no tuve otra forma de verla en adelante que a la luz de aquella acusación terrible que me recordaba la historia sagrada, derribada a pedradas en el polvo Catalina, ensangrentada bajo una lluvia de piedras, hasta morir" (*CYC*, 215; "from this point on I had no way of seeing her other than in light of that terrible accusation that reminded me of the story from scripture, Catalina felled by stones in the dust, bloodied by a rain of stones until she died"). Patriarchal speech is the only extant conduit for understanding reality; in the village, no other voice carries authority. The vision of Catalina stoned to death evokes not only biblical punishments for adultery but also a millennial history of women unjustly accused of this transgression by husbands whose word, in patriarchal societies, decreed the contours of reality.

The father in "Catalina y Catalina" does not dominate the family by virtue of physical size – on the contrary, he is described as "menudo y nervioso" (*CYC*, 217; "slight and nervous") – but rather on the strength of his masculinity, which gives him the right to control what is said and believed within the home. The mother is complicit in this pattern. As she prepares to leave the house under the accusation of having committed adultery, "nos decía que no creyéramos nada malo de ella, que no era ninguna adúltera, eran cuentos y enredos de sus cuñadas que nunca la habían querido, pero que lo mejor era obedecer, que todos le debíamos obediencia a mi padre aunque estuviera equivocado" (*CYC*, 217; "she told us not to believe anything bad we heard about her, that she wasn't any adulteress, those were just stories and confusions started by her sisters-in-law, who had never liked her, but it was best to obey, we all had a duty to obey my father even if he was wrong"). Rather than denouncing the father's delusions, the mother blames them on other women, her sisters-in-law.

The father, a tractor mechanic, dresses like a cowboy and refuses to take off his hat indoors. Yet his "crudeza de carácter" ("severity of character") is epitomized for his daughter by his voice: "una voz de órdenes secas que no tenía matices, la voz que le ordenó a Catalina salir para siempre de la casa después de llamarla adúltera" (*CYC*, 219; "a voice of dry commands that had no shades of meaning, the voice that commanded Catalina to leave the house forever after calling her an adulteress"). The narrator insists that the father's voice remains without "shades of meaning" even when he sings boleros during the village's Saturday fiestas. Within the family, the father possesses culture yet is incapable of deploying it; he renders the boleros lifeless and keeps the house's few books on the window ledge without reading them. The two Catalinas, by contrast, have voices that are "ronca"

(*CYC*, 216; "hoarse"), a trait that indicates, in the case of the mother as in that of the daughter, that they lack the liberty to express themselves freely and are suspected of excessive sensuality. Suffering the immemorial predicament of women in a patriarchal society, mother and daughter are not permitted to speak with authority and are defined by their sex. The daughter, having reached the age of twenty-six – the age at which her mother was accused of adultery – says that she has "la voz ronca, una voz que, según me dicen, es de tono sensual; una voz de alcoba, me dijo alguien una vez" (*CYC*, 224; "a hoarse voice which, I'm told, has a sensual tone; a bedroom voice, somebody once told me"). In spite of having gone into exile as a Sandinista guerrilla and not as an adulterous wife, the daughter remains caught in the tensions of her childhood home.

The defining moment in the narrator's life takes place when she and her brother learn that their mother has left the country. They receive this news not from the father, who proves incapable of communicating, but from a man who does not fit the village's patriarchal definitions of masculinity, the mother's brother, who is described by one of their aunts as the "hermano alcahuete, Noelito, el escribiente del juzgado que no tenía dónde caer muerto" (*CYC*, 220; "gossipy brother Noelito, the court notary who doesn't have a cent to his name"). As a single man who does not work with his hands, a man who writes for a living and tries to console the children after their mother flees, Uncle Noelito transgresses patriarchal norms. The other men with whom the mother gets along well, including the two men whose friendship appears to have triggered the accusation of adultery, also defy patriarchal definitions of masculinity. Valentín, a waiter in a private club, insists that he must maintain an elegant appearance, even though, according to the narrator, he is "un hombre común y corriente" (*CYC*, 223; "an ordinary-looking man"). Peter, a banker, tells the mother jokes and, after each joke, "iniciaba un paseo por el cuarto, moviendo las caderas" (*CYC*, 224; "made a little stroll across the room, moving his thighs"). These admirers, whom the mother attracts in her job as an ironer of shirts who habitually works dressed in a bra and a slip, may in fact be homosexual. But the textual evidence is fleeting and the key point, in terms of the story's development, is that these men, by contrast with the father, enjoy conversing (not simply speaking) and sharing their feelings.

The patriarchal inheritance of a lack of communication is reinforced by the mother, who, following the dictates of the father, communicates little to her children when she leaves. It remains to Uncle Noelito to invent a consoling fantasy in which the children will visit their mother in Los Angeles, learn English, and become friends with the canine Disney character Lassie. The children's reaction to the news, however, is shaped by the norms imposed by the father: they struggle not to cry. Only Uncle Noelito is able to say: "No tiene nada malo que lloren por el recuerdo de su mamá" (*CYC*, 222; "There's nothing wrong with crying for your mother's memory"). The rule that boys do not show their feelings prevents the girl from crying, also. This scene illustrates how women's silence is a creation of the male subject's fear of communication. The two male characters in the immediate family – father and son – lack names, while mother and daughter have the same name. Men, being unable to share their feelings, are condemned to anonymity; women, who are unable to free themselves from male patterns, are condemned to repeat them.

The younger Catalina refrains from crying in order to spare her brother the indignity of tears. The father, terminating his emotional life, never brings another woman into the home. To expiate the mother's sins, the daughter is excluded from the supper table; father and son eat together in silence. When a few years later the brother disappears and joins the Sandinista guerrillas, the narrator comments of her father's lack of reaction to this event: "Él no dijo nada, ni preguntó nada, y en su aparente tranquilidad daba a entender que mi hermano lo había prevenido de su desaparición, sólo para no verse disminuido en su autoridad; algo muy falso, si costaba que los dos se pasaran palabra" (*CYC*, 226; "He said nothing and asked nothing, and in his apparent calm left the impression that my brother had warned him of his disappearance, just so that his authority would not be diminished; something very false, if it was that difficult for the two of them to exchange a word"). The daughter is also involved with the guerrillas. In her case, political commitment is linked to an attempt to escape from the feminine role as experienced by her mother. She has the same name and hair as her mother; but, rejecting traditional femininity, she cuts her hair short and remains single, refusing to define herself in terms of a man.

Patriarchal power, incarnated by both the father and the dictatorship, ebbs away. When the younger Catalina goes into exile in Costa Rica after the September 1978 offensive, her father comes to the airport to bid her farewell, a demonstration of affection that he never would have allowed himself with his wife.

> Subíamos al avión charter en fila de uno, lo vi desde lejos en el balcón de la terminal desierta ... No quitó un solo momento las manos de la barandilla, no hizo ningún ademán de saludo. Pero había venido a despedirme, por eso estaba allí bajo el sol; y desde lejos creía verlo masticar algo entre sus calzaduras metálicas, palabras que no salían

> de su boca cerrada, o acaso sólo masticaba sinsabores. (*CYC*, 227; We boarded the plane in single file, I saw him in the distance on the balcony of the deserted terminal ... His hands never left the handrail, he made no gesture of greeting. But he had come to say goodbye to me, that was why he was there beneath the sun; and in the distance I thought I saw him chewing something between his metallic dentures, words that wouldn't come out of his closed mouth, or maybe he was just chewing over his troubles.)

The father tries to communicate with his daughter, yet lacks the words. His metallic dentures symbolize the clamping-shut of potential communication. The balance of social forces shifts as the revolutionaries advance; the triumph of the revolution entails the destruction of the patriarchal order. Even the patriarch tries to adapt to the new rules. At the same time, the inheritance of the disintegrating patriarchal world, particularly its incapacity for dialogue, remains latent in the revolutionary forces. The story's climax occurs in 1979 with the brother's death in combat "en plena ofensiva final" (*CYC*, 227; "in the middle of the final offensive"). His death coincides with the collapse of the dictatorship; in this sense, he serves as the father's surrogate. The father, like the dictator, vanishes. The brother, who did not warn his family of his departure, perpetuates the patriarchal culture of silence, even as he is enshrined as a revolutionary martyr: "le pusieron su nombre a la columna revolucionaria" (*CYC*, 229; "they named his revolutionary column after him"). Ironically, this now-public name remains unknown to the reader. This paradoxical inheritance of a revolutionary struggle that shared many elements of the patriarchal culture against which it was rebelling would become of increasing importance to Ramírez after the 1995 FSLN split. It is evident in "Catalina y Catalina" in the portrait of the father who, combining Somocista and Sandinista traits, wears a hat like that of the first Somoza dictator yet has the fine-boned physique of Tomás Borge. Analysis of the nation is tempered, or even vitiated, by analysis of the dynamics of patriarchy.

Ramírez's renewed attentiveness to gender politics, enlightening in many respects, would nevertheless weaken the diachronic force of his focus on the nation since gender, though constructed in distinctive ways in particular places, is a transnational category, one that Ramírez would analyze in a continental context. His essay collection *Mentiras verdaderas* (2001; True Lies) illustrates the form taken by his thinking in the late 1990s. Ramírez describes the political legacy of the nineteenth century in Spanish America as "libertad y autoridad democrática, unidad y diversidad, como quiso Bolívar, pero encima sentaba el padre, *pater noster*, *pater familias*, patrón, padrote, patriarca, caudillo. Su rostro volvió de cuero y su mirada legañosa envejeció la modernidad que pronto se disolvió en ayer" (*MV*, 114; "freedom and democratic authority, unity and diversity as Bolívar wished, but above it all sat the father, pater noster, pater familias, boss, stepfather, patriarch, warlord. His face turned to leather and his bleary gaze aged modernity, which quickly dissolved into a yesterday"). The traditional *caudillo* travelled on horseback; Ramírez emphasizes this trait to demonstrate that *caudillismo* is also an ingrained tendency in the Liberal and revolutionary traditions: "A caballo San Martín, a caballo Bolívar, a caballo Morazán, a caballo Sandino, a caballo Zapata, a caballo el Che" (*MV*, 118; "On horseback San Martín, on horseback Bolívar, on horseback Morazán, on horseback Sandino, on horseback Zapata, on horseback Che").[8]

In "Catalina y Catalina," the father's disappearance and the son's death and transformation into a touchstone of martyrdom open the door to a dialogue between women. As soon as the brother dies, the older Catalina calls the younger from Los Angeles. Yet, still corralled by the norms of the father, the two women are unable to speak. The pain they feel is expressed by means of "una explosión lejana, un fulgor, un derrumbe, una polvareda de llanto" (*CYC*, 228; "a distant explosion, a flash of light, a collapse, an uproar of tears"). These tears, of course, are those that the mother forbade when the father expelled her from the house. The triumph of the Revolution opens the way to expression of their shared suffering yet the persistence of patriarchal structures prevents this suffering from being transmuted into a dialogue. Catalina and Catalina experience a meeting of two bursts of tears: "uno que venía y otro que se iba para encontrarse, rechazarse y volver a encontrarse otra vez" (*CYC*, 228; "one that came and the other that went, to meet and reject each other, and meet each other again"). They do not have a conversation. The daughter thinks of all the reproaches she could hurl at her mother for not having communicated with them in years, yet she remains silent. Her suppression of her feelings, and the persistence of her hoarse voice, epitomize the residual patriarchal repression that silences them both. When the mother breaks the silence that falls after they have finished crying by asking the daughter if she is still there, the daughter rejects her overture by hanging up the phone.

This ambiguous conclusion could mean that, thanks to her own efforts and the revolutionary triumph, the younger Catalina has freed herself from uncommunicative patriarchy. Having mourned her motherless childhood, she hangs up the phone to begin a new life. Yet the fact that she continues to share the mother's hoarse voice and cannot articulate her anger renders this reading unconvincing. By hanging up on her mother, Catalina does not transcend her childhood patterns; she reaffirms them. The patriarch – both father and dictator – is absent, yet the daughter, voice of the triumphant Revolution, perpetuates the tradition of silence. Both of her parents make belated attempts to open channels of communication; it is she who rejects these overtures, assuming the former discourse and customs of the father. Gioconda Belli, whose controversial form of feminism was discussed in chapter 7, wrote of her desires as a revolutionary woman: "Quería los privilegios masculinos: independencia, valerse por sí misma, tener vida pública, movilidad, amantes … Sin renunciar a ser mujer, creo que he logrado también ser hombre" (*El país*, 12; "I yearned for the privileges men enjoyed: independence, self-reliance, mobility, lovers … Without renouncing my femininity, I think I have also managed to live like a man" [Belli 2002: x]). The daughter's adoption of strands of patriarchal custom in "Catalina y Catalina" displays a similar tendency.

The incorporation of patriarchal patterns into revolutionary comportment, even that which seeks the liberation of women, and the sometimes fine line that divides the revolutionary from the reactionary, became crucial insights in Ramírez's subsequent fiction. The analysis of patriarchy, particularly for a male writer, entails the investigation of one's own patterns of behaviour; in this sense, such a focus promotes an individualistic, even narcissistic (to revert to Arias's "body image"), concentration on the self. General societal patterns may also play a part; yet the contours of the nation shrink from view. In Ramírez's case, these issues are complicated not only by his status as a former figure of revolutionary authority, but also by the reversal of stereotyped patterns with which he had grown up, with an austere Baptist mother who did not display her feelings and artistic, sentimental uncles who, like his father, were emotionally expressive. Thanks to his uncles, Ramírez did possess a model of male communication; yet, as *Un baile de máscaras* had illustrated, this model had little resonance beyond the village.

HISTORY AFTER HISTORY'S END: *MARGARITA, HOW BEAUTIFUL THE SEA*

The mid-1990s crisis of the nation, combined with the sudden prominence of the demise or survival of patriarchy, reoriented Ramírez's long-standing project of writing a historical novel about Rubén Darío. The trajectory of the poet's life, as a Nicaraguan encountering the world in South America and Europe, yielded to a narrower focus on the city of León: home of Darío, site of the assassination of the first Somoza, and scene of the author's education and politicization. The key date in Darío's relationship with his homeland is no longer 1916, when he came home to die, but 1907, when, on his previous trip to Nicaragua, he wrote a poem on the fan of a woman whose sister would marry Anastasio Somoza García. In *Margarita, How Beautiful the Sea*, the poet's life is subordinated to the central importance of the proto-macho who is the point of origin of the patriarchal impulses that the FSLN absorbed from Somocismo, even as it fought to overthrow the dictatorship. National history is no longer a diachronic development that will stake out the contours of the nation, as in *To Bury Our Fathers*, nor does it provide the material necessary to understand why the dictatorship came into existence, as in *Castigo Divino*. Like the latter novel, *Margarita, How Beautiful the Sea* employs postmodern narrative techniques; yet underlying the in-jokes, popular-culture references, and deliberate anachronisms that mark the narration of Oliverio Castañeda's trial and death is an assumption of a knowable truth that makes possible a politically charged analysis of the moral lapses of the Nicaraguan bourgeoisie.

When Ramírez returns to national history to complete *Margarita, How Beautiful the Sea* in 1997, the diachronic development of Nicaraguan nationhood is no longer a primary text. It is reduced to a series of picturesque personalities and scenes that can be shuffled at will, and whose significance may be better grasped in terms of individual, masculine identity rather than as an insurgent national chronology. This blunts the social criticism that is wielded so sharply in *Castigo Divino*. *Margarita, How Beautiful the Sea*, which by winning the 1998 Alfaguara Prize, made Ramírez "the best-known Central American novelist in the Spanish-speaking world since 1967 Nobel Prize winner Miguel Ángel Asturias," illustrates Arias's contention that, in the aftermath of the early 1990s, "Central American literary discourse has been disempowered politically while, paradoxically, being empowered as a commodity by globalizing trends" (Arias 2007: 4, 25).

Margarita, How Beautiful the Sea straddles the emerging chasm between historically grounded radical analysis and the challenging aesthetics of the Boom, and transnational cultural commercialism. In addition to winning the prize administered by Alfaguara, the conglomerate that dominated Spanish-language publishing in the era of globalized commerce, this novel was awarded the José María Arguedas Prize by the government of Cuba. The novel that globalized book marketing turned into an international best-seller was also the object of a separate Cuban edition and a book-launch party in Havana, hosted by Fidel Castro (Cherem 2004b: 175). This duality is not simply a peculiarity of the novel's editorial history, but is ingrained in the text itself, in which vestigial revolutionary and innovative impulses compete with the novel's best-seller format and underlying apoliticism. Arias offers a cutting summary of internationally marketed post-1990 Central American fiction, with *Margarita, How Beautiful the Sea* as the most salient example, describing it as "an exoticized commodity validated in the transnational or postnational space, even though, often enough, it is no more than a copy of its old self, a pastiche, a defanged placebo, ideal for consumption in metropolitan centers for its representation of a certain tropical frisson without the risk of genuine transgression" (Arias 2007: 25).

The analysis that follows, by contrast, argues that in spite of the undeniable tendencies that Arias articulates, a close reading of Ramírez's novel provides an opportunity to measure the extent to which writers in the Americas may reconstruct autochthonous cultures in the face of globalizing homogenization by continuing to narrate through the vehicle of their national histories without losing sight of the ways in which globalization and the collapse of traditional categories and ideologies have rendered the assumptions of national integrity increasingly problematic. This is not to deny the debilitation of the nation-state, nor is it an attempt to claim, as some critics do, that commercial fiction is redeemed by "subversive" messages. Rather, it is an argument that, in writing *Margarita, How Beautiful the Sea* after 1990, Ramírez faces a series of paradoxes, which he consciously manipulates in an effort to reconstruct some of the sense of shared national endeavour that has been dispersed by the end of the Cold War. At the same time, such an analysis must contend with the former revolutionary leader's grappling with the evaporation of his masculine authority, evident in the multiple mutilations of masculinity that are paraded by a novel in which nearly all of the male characters suffer from sexual malfunction or physical deformation.

The contradiction between national history and the neo-liberal assumptions of globalization is evident in the novel's simultaneous depiction of Sandinismo as a liberalizing force that bestowed democracy and open discussion on Nicaragua, and, at the same time, as a revolutionary doctrine that promoted self-abnegation, heroic death, class warfare, national liberation, and other Sandinista values that are not congruent with liberal democracy. In the epilogue, one discovers that after 1979 Captain Prío learns more about the 1956 assassination of Anastasio Somoza García, the novel's central event, by reading government reports that, thanks to the liberal facets of the Nicaraguan Revolution, are now available to the public. In counterpoint to this expression of liberal values, Ramírez enshrines the historical figure of Rigoberto López Pérez, the young poet who assassinates the first Somoza, as the prototype of the Sandinista cult of martyrdom. Rigoberto's farewell letter to his mother resounds with phrases that reflect a revolutionary ethos of duty, responsibility, and absolute values (as opposed to a liberal vocabulary of rights, freedoms, and relativism). Rigoberto's invocation of "mi más alto deber de nicaragüense" (*MLM*, 178; "my highest duty as a Nicaraguan" [*MBS*, 142]) foreshadows Sandinista rhetoric of the 1970s and 1980s. Rigoberto is a partisan of spreading revolution through both radical political action and literature. Though a figure of the 1950s, he incarnates the novel's nostalgia for the 1980s, when writing had the potency to shape nations.

Ramírez constructs a revolutionary genealogy that leads from Augusto César Sandino to Rigoberto's self-sacrifice to the FSLN guerrillas of the 1960s and 1970s. The parallel between Sandino and Rigoberto is made explicit in Ramírez's repeated assertion that both are castrated in death and buried separated from their testicles. (In Sandino's case, this procedure is necessitated by the fact that his testicles are unusually large.) Rigoberto is a poet and journalist; one of the portraits of Sandino that was most popular during the Revolution showed him carrying a pencil (*AM*, 289). In this sense, the two heroes' castration echoes the symbolic castration of Ramírez as a writer who has lost the power to sculpt political events and bring about the combined literary-political reinvention of the nation. Ramírez compensates for his loss of potency by positioning himself as the inheritor of the literary tradition of Rubén Darío. Diana Moro, drawing on Ramírez's essay "El artista frente a su modelo" in *Oficios compartidos*, argues that in *Margarita, How Beautiful the Sea* "su autofiguración como continuador de Rubén Darío es clara" (Moro 2008: 78; "his self-construction as the successor of Ruben Dario is clear"). Referring to his self-insertion into the Latin American Boom, discussed in chapter 7, which this study argues is more prominent in *To Bury Our Fathers* than in *Margarita, How Beautiful the Sea*, Moro concludes that, in the context of the 1990s, this gesture "es anacrónico ... Aquellos escritores con los que se identifica y se percibe como uno de sus continuadores ya no son hegemónicos en el sistema literario latinoamericano de las últimas décadas del siglo XX" (ibid.: 80; "is anachronistic ... Those writers with whom he identifies and whose successor he perceives himself as being are no longer hegemonic in the Latin American literary system of the last decades of the twentieth century").

The strongest evidence for Moro's position is that the Boom aesthetics borrowed by *Margarita, How Beautiful the Sea* are not those of the most challenging Boom novels, such as Vargas Llosa's *Conversation in The Cathedral*, which inform *To Bury Our Fathers*, but rather depend on a contrapuntal narrative structure. The novel is structured according to the alternation between two different types of chapters. The even-numbered chapters (though the chapters have no numbers, and all of them bear citations from Darío's poems as chapter headings) contain linear narration of twenty-four hours in 1956 leading up to the assassination of the dictator Anastasio Somoza García during his visit to León. The odd-numbered chapters begin in the third person, nearly all of them with the character of Captain Prío, convener of the "mesa maldita" ("table of the damned"), who makes a brief appearance in *To Bury Our Fathers* and is a pivotal character in *Castigo Divino*. From the vantage point of his café overlooking Plaza Jerez, León's central square, Prío becomes the sole character who is able to perceive the totality of the novel's events. Rather than a reliable arbiter, though, Prío exercises the more limited authority of a referee: the novel's opening sentence compares his appearance to that of a "referee de boxeo" (*MLM*, 15; "boxing referee" [*MBS*, 3]). He adjudicates and organizes the competing versions of events without rendering definitive judgments on them. From a description of Captain Prío's observations during the hours that precede the assassination, the action passes to a flashback that narrates, from one odd-numbered chapter to the next, the last two journeys made by Rubén Darío to his native land.

In the Latin American context, the contrapuntal structure was popularized by Mario Vargas Llosa in his novels of the 1970s and 1980s, when he relaxed his aesthetic quest for innovations that would make the reader work hard, and adopted a more populist idiom in novels such as *La tía Julia y el escribidor* (1977; *Aunt Julia and the Scriptwriter*) or *El hablador* (1987; *The Storyteller*). Taking over this structure in a self-conscious act of borrowing, Ramírez moves it in a postmodern direction. The role of the "mesa maldita" – whose members have changed since the 1930s setting of *Castigo Divino* – expands. Whereas in *Castigo Divino* the group of local journalists and gossips who gather in the Casa Prío provide irreverent commentary on the Castañeda murder trial, in *Margarita, How Beautiful the Sea* the young conspirators who are planning the assassination of Somoza García invent the details of Darío's last two visits to Nicaragua and his involvement with the Debayle family, on whose daughter Margarita's fan he would write one of his most famous poems.[9] Margarita's sister Salvadora would marry Somoza García and become the mother of the final Somoza tyrant, Anastasio Somoza Debayle. Recycling and questioning Ramírez's own scrupulous research for the historical novel about Darío that he made unsuccessful attempts to write, in 1985 and 1993, the flashbacks to the interactions between Darío and the Debayles are perceived by the conspirators as whimsical films. The group debates the verisimilitude of the novel's account of Darío's visits. The perception of these events not as prose but as a film underlines the novel's depiction of history as a fluid, ungraspable entity, and emphasizes the dissolution of the boundaries between elite and popular narrative forms that is associated with postmodernism.

One member of the "mesa maldita," Erwin, asks "¿Quién estaba allí filmando esa película?" ("Who was there to film those scenes?") and receives this response from Rigoberto: "Son reconstrucciones históricas ... No hay que dudar de ellas" (*MLM*, 69; "They're historical reconstructions ... There's no need to question them" [*MBS*, 49]). This ironic comment confirms the integration of post-1990 Central America into a globalized sphere where, as argued by Jean Baudrillard, history has been diminished to a video show. The members of the "mesa maldita" recognize the unreliable fluidity of the version of history that is being presented to them. Was Rubén Darío a drunk or wasn't he? Did the young soldier Somoza García ask for Salvadora Debayle's hand during Darío's funeral, or at a more discreet moment? By contrast with *Castigo Divino*, where doubts about the true course of events are charged with political and dramatic significance, in *Margarita, How Beautiful the Sea* reality becomes silly putty. In a depiction inimical to constructions of a national history forged by bold actions or dialectical struggle, the characters' destinies are portrayed as the random outcome of the knitting of lives by the fates. The penultimate chapter, for example, opens with the statement: "Se irá Somoza sin chaleco antibalas a la fiesta, así lo ha tramado una de las hermanas que se divierte con las sorpresas" (*MLM*, 330; "Somoza will attend the fiesta without his bulletproof vest, that's how it has been plotted by one of the sisters who likes to spring surprises" [*MBS*, 275]). These "sisters," who knit men's fates, animate a narrative voice that attributes events to happenstance, or "mala fortuna" (*MLM*, 320; "A bit of bad luck" [*MBS*, 266]).

One of the conspirators, Erwin, complains about the concept of narrative omniscience when he faults Rigoberto, who appears to be narrating the Darío scenes, by saying: "Ya llegamos a un punto en que Rigoberto sabe hasta lo que Darío estaba pensando" (*MLM*, 101; "You're trying to tell us Rigoberto even knows what Darío was thinking" [*MBS*, 76]). Erwin's point is clear: even when one succeeds in establishing an accepted chronology, the thoughts and motivations of historical actors remain enigmatic. This insight calls into question the contrary view of Rigoberto, who demonstrates supreme confidence in the correctness of his historical interpretations. As a revolutionary destined to carry out an assassination, Rigoberto cannot allow himself to fall prey to the doubts that saturate postmodern relativism. Past events are a sacred text that dictates the script for future actions; there is no room for multiple interpretations, differing points of view, or the intervention of luck. Rigoberto inhabits a world bounded by moral certainties that necessarily repose on an unambiguous interpretation of history. In a later discussion of the "films" of Darío's life, he claims not only to know what the poet is thinking but to be privy, also, to the thoughts of his physician, and Somoza García's father-in-law, Dr Debayle. Incarnating the Nicaraguan insurgent tradition, Rigoberto rids himself of doubts about the outlines of the past in order to be free to act decisively in the present. At the same time, in a contradiction that is typical of this novel, the Rubén Darío imagined by Rigoberto is a man skeptical of the authority of formal history. He invites his listeners: "Escuchen esta historia que no aparecerá nunca en mi autobiografía" (*MLM*, 133; "Listen to this story ... It's one that will never appear in my autobiography" [*MBS*, 104]). History's chronic incompleteness is part of the anguish that Rigoberto's seer-like reimagining of the past – like the Boom's total novel, or the totalizing explanations of revolutionary ideology– attempts, without success, to banish.

As the narrative advances, the arbitrary qualities of the odd-numbered chapters begin to contaminate the even-numbered chapters. The third-person narrator of the even-numbered chapters interrupts the story to address the reader, confessing the limitations of his omniscience. Describing the events of the afternoon prior to the assassination, the narrator of the even-numbered chapters states: "Rigoberto había hecho una estación en la casa de Rosaura ... no prevista para mí, y por eso hasta ahora puedo darles cuenta. Ya dije que no era fácil" [*MLM*, 224; "unbeknownst to me, that morning, Rigoberto had stopped by Rosaura's house in the San Juan neighborhood, which is why I haven't been able to give you an account of it until now. As I've already said, this wasn't an easy day" [*MBS*, 182]). As events fly out of control, whirling towards the closing image of chaos, the narrator grows more hortatory, enjoining the reader to contribute to his scrutiny of the action: "Vengan conmigo cuanto antes para situarnos ... Vean a *La Caimana* ... Quédense mejor todos donde están" (*MLM*, 267–8; "Come with me quickly now and stand ... See The Alligator Woman ... Better to stay where you are" [*MBS*, 222]). References to destiny as a capricious, uncontrollable force proliferate: "¡Oh, tristes costureras! ¡Con qué hilos equivocados se alistan a remendar la tela!" (*MLM*, 230; "Oh, sad seamstresses! What twisted threads you are readying to stitch your cloth!" [*MBS*, 188]) and "Fortuna, soberana de las veleidades" (*MLM*, 319; "Fortune, queen of capriciousness" [*MBS*, 265]).

Even as he mythologizes Nicaraguan history, Ramírez mocks historical chronology. Yet his narrative hews out a historical dimension within a post-modern, post-diachronic historical landscape. In fact, the postmodern hijinx are more restrained than those in *Castigo Divino*, which was written at a time that history, retaining its political potency and existential authenticity, was capable of outlasting such irreverence. The anachronistic insertion of famous names from other eras into the narrative, for example, is far more sparing than in the earlier novel. These narrative winks are confined to friends of the author, such as the Salvadoran novelist Manlío Argueta, whose name is given to a shopkeeper in 1950s San Salvador, and the playwright Harold Pinter, who appears as a "sabio victoriano" (*MLM*, 126; "learned Victorian" [*MBS*, 99]).

Some of the more playful details are private jokes, while others have a clear literary resonance. Ramírez nicknames Rubén Darío's widow La Maligna (*MLM*, 30–2; The Malevolent Woman), a name that is doubly wicked in light of the fact that the widow's birth name, by a coincidence of history, was identical to that of the woman who is accused of corrupting Sandinismo: Rosario Murillo. In other cases, however, apparently self-indulgent jokes contain a literary significance, gesturing towards the novel's intertextual pedigree. The dictator's Yankee security adviser is named Sartorius Van Wynckle. The surname, an obvious allusion to Rip Van Winkle, contains an implicit jab at the United States for remaining metaphorically "asleep" in its relations with Latin America. Van Wynckle, "habla un español perfecto, con acento argentino" (*MLM*, 259; "He speaks perfect Spanish, with an Argentine accent" [*MBS*, 214]). The Argentine accent is borrowed from William Bowdler, the Buenos Aires-raised US State Department official with whom Ramírez negotiated the 1979 transition agreement that paved the way for the Sandinistas' accession to power (*AM*, 100, 267). Van Wynckle's first name, a reference to William Faulkner's character Colonel Sartoris, extends the Faulknerian intertextual allusions broached in *To Bury Our Fathers*. The repetition of characters and histories from novel to novel, mythologizing the narrative ground of León, is one that Faulkner developed in his creation of Yoknapatawpha County; this procedure was adapted to rural Latin America in García Márquez's Macondo, and to urban Latin America in the Uruguayan writer Juan Carlos Onetti's Santa María novels.

Margarita, How Beautiful the Sea evokes characters from earlier novels in scenes such as that which describes the pedigree of the newspaper *El Cronista (The Chronicle)*: "Fue adquirido luego por el doctor Absalón Barreto, en la época de los crímenes del envenenador Oliverio Castañeda, cuando Rosalío Usulutlán trabajó allí" (*MLM*, 204; "It was acquired next by Dr. Absalón Barreto, during the period of the crimes of Oliverio Castañeda, the poisoner, when Rosalio Usulutlán worked there" [*MBS*, 165]). The reference to Usulutlán contributes to the elaboration of a mythical history of

León, while Dr Barreto's first name reinforces Ramírez's Faulknerian intent by echoing the title of Faulkner's novel *Absalom, Absalom!* The figure of Captain Prío, the eternal witness to the city's political convulsions, acquires mythical dimensions over the course of three novels. Some of the characters who are revisited in *Margarita, How Beautiful the Sea* have changed since their appearance in *Castigo Divino*, a fact that contributes to the sense of an organic, evolving history. Dr Anastasio Salmerón, the embittered opponent of the dictatorship who is ostracized by the medical establishment in the earlier novel, here becomes "miembro de la directiva de la Guardia de Honor, que nunca falla en sus diagnósticos" (*MLM*, 257; "his never-erring friend ... member of the Board of Directors of the Rubén Darío Honor Society" [*MBS*, 212]).

This intertextual tissue, both with Faulkner's Yoknapatawpha County novels and with Ramírez's three earlier novels set in León, generates a narrative universe in which, as Moro contends, "León representa metonímicamente Nicaragua" (Moro 2008: 79; "León is a metonymical representation of Nicaragua"). It is the persistence of this impulse to mythologize national history, in spite of a belief that the nation has ceased to be a relevant category and that history is an arbitrary sequence of random occurrences rather than a trajectory developed by like-minded individuals who work together, that constitutes this novel's central paradox.

The accumulation of gratuitous postmodern gamesmanship coexists with scenes, buttressed by different degrees of authority, that mythologize vital moments in Nicaraguan history. One scene that may be read as both postmodern pastiche and Modernist forging of the consciousness of the nation in the smithy of the novelist's Joycean soul describes the sage Debayle's extraction of Rubén Darío's brain after the poet's death. The character of Dr Debayle – who is claimed to be the grandson of the nineteenth-century French novelist Stendhal (Henri Beyle) and the grandfather of Anastasio Somoza Debayle – incarnates the blending of high and low, cultured and crude, details both resonant and trivial, on which the novel thrives: "¡La mierda revuelta con la gloria!" (*MLM*, 70; "Shit mixed with glory!" [*MBS*, 50]). Dr Debayle's extraction of Rubén Darío's brain – the source of Nicaragua's greatest claim to high culture – presages, in a farcical vein, the brutality that his grandson will inflict on the Nicaraguan body politic, tracing the origins of the ideology behind this violence to the positivism dominant in Latin American intellectual circles in the late nineteenth and early twentieth centuries. Debayle's elation on discovering that Darío's brain weighs more than that of Victor Hugo or Johann Schiller parodies both positivist pseudoscience and the Modernist myth of the artist as transcendent genius. Like Sandino and Rigoberto after him, Darío is buried with one part of his body separated from the rest.

The living link among the three mutilated bodies that describe the arc of Nicaraguan history during the first half of the twentieth century (four, if one counts Somoza García, as will be argued below) is the centaur-like Quirón. Moro contends that Quirón constitutes "una clara referencia" (Moro 2008: 77; "a clear reference") to the hunchbacked Quasimodo in Victor Hugo's *Notre-Dame de Paris* (1831; *The Hunchback of Notre Dame*). In tandem with allusions to writers such as Henrik Ibsen, this constitutes part of the novel's intertextual sparring with the literary tastes of the late nineteenth century. As a young man, Quirón steals the flask containing Darío's brain from Major Appleton, the commander of the US occupation forces; in late middle age, he steals Rigoberto's testicles from under the nose of Van Wynckle and the National Guard, creating the novel's nihilistic closing image of a madman clutching a flask careening "hacia la fuente de noche y de olvido, hacia la nada" (*MLM*, 369; "towards the fountain of darkness and oblivion, towards nothingness" [*MBS*, 309]). Quirón's birth is obscure. Though he is the illegitimate son of a local priest, the narrative suggests that he may have been engendered from the pages of Darío's mythologically rich poetry collection *Prosas profanas* (1896; Profane Prose), and that he "nació ... con el siglo" (*MLM*, 28–9; "was born ... with the century" [*MBS*, 14]), confirming his role as a paradigm of twentieth-century Nicaragua. In snatching back Darío's brain and Rigoberto's testicles, Quirón makes a blind attempt to reassemble Nicaraguan wholeness. In Nicasio Urbina's apt characterization, the centaur becomes "el salvador de los dos símbolos claves en esta representación de la historia de Nicaragua ... La inteligencia y el valor, la suave armonía de la palabra de Darío y la valentía del sacrificio ulterior de López Pérez" (Urbina 2004b: 367; "the saviour of the two key symbols in this representation of the history of Nicaragua ... Intelligence and courage, the smooth harmony of the words of Dario and the courage of the later sacrifice of López Pérez"). Quirón's gesture, however, indicates the futility of such acts when perceived from the post-1990 vantage point. The end of the Cold War re-installs the cycle of repetition and neo-colonial subjugation to which Nicaragua was condemned prior to the 1979 Revolution, guaranteeing that the cultural reconstruction that both Quirón and this novel undertake in different ways are doomed to end in "nothingness," the closing word of the narration.

Thwarted attempts to reconstruct the nation are expressed in pervasive images of masculine impotence and sexual dysfunction. The novel opens with a celebration of Somoza's machista dominance over Nicaragua. As the dictator arrives in León, a jubilant shout from the crowd greets him with the words: "¡Qué viva el perromacho, jodido!" (*MLM*, 16; "Long Live The Man, the best goddamn man there is!" [*MBS*, 4]). In his study of Nicaraguan machismo, Roger Lancaster emphasizes that machismo is "a means of structuring power between and among *men* ... a matter of constantly asserting one's masculinity by way of practices that show the self to be 'active,' not 'passive' ... Every gesture, every posture, every stance, every way of acting in the world is immediately seen as 'masculine' or 'feminine,' depending on whether it connotes activity or passivity" (Lancaster 1992: 236–7). In the structuring of power among Nicaraguan men, Somoza is, literally, the top dog ("perromacho," in the Spanish original). His violent machismo renders other men's gestures effeminate by inducing quiescence in any who might oppose him. Under the dictatorship, all other Nicaraguan men become "cochones" – passive participants in homosexual sodomy – who are metaphorically screwed by Somoza. The only characters who retain their virility are the disorganized young men who plot to assassinate the dictator and whose rather unprofessional assassination attempt succeeds through a stroke of sheer luck. Those on the sidelines, such as Captain Prío or Erwin of the "mesa maldita," are, literally, passive observers who fail to masculinize themselves through activity; neither character, tellingly, has a visible sex life. Quirón, the "centaur," who twice rouses himself to activity to commit theft, is masculine without being fully human. Even the national hero, Darío, a famous seducer on two continents, by the time of his return to Nicaragua, has been reduced by alcoholism to sexual impotence.

The plague of passivity is most evident in those who are closest to Somoza. One of his early business associates, with whom he ran a counterfeiting operation in his youth, is La Caimana (Alligator Woman), a transgendered individual who appears "marimacha" (*MLM*, 84; "butch" [*MBS*, 62]) to her acquaintances and whose lifelong dream is to "orinar ... de pie" (*MLM*, 324; "pee ... standing up" [*MBS*, 269]) like a man. Dr Debayle transplants a penis onto La Caimana, but it rots and must be removed. Born on the same day as Quirón, La Caimana is the opposite half of Nicaraguan identity during the twentieth century: not an outcast like her counterpart, but a being unable, like the nation she inhabits, to achieve the active state of masculinity. In the novel's postmodern spirit, La Caimana originates in literature. Her name, toughness, and profession as the owner of a brothel all signal her kinship with La Chunga, the hard-nosed owner of the second of the two brothels in Vargas Llosa's *The Green House*.

The treatment of La Caimana underlines the association of the overturning of the Sandinista state – the only government in history to endow Nicaragua with an active, "masculine" virility as a nation – with the crisis of masculinity. For members of the Sandinista government, the regime's collapse calls into question their masculine identities. Among other phenomena, this helps to explain the resurgence of machista attitudes within the National Directorate during the 1990s. In *Margarita, How Beautiful the Sea*, the crisis is evident in the fractured masculinities of the male characters. Even Somoza's violent masculinity conceals passivity and physical malfunction. As the leader of a nation that is not autonomous, but is a mere colony of the United States, Somoza secretly shares in the passivity of the "cochón." His manhood is suspect. During the governing couple's arrival in León, the First Lady, Doña Salvadora, is described as suffering during her public appearances, "atormentada por el corsé que reprimía sus carnes" (*MLM*, 16–17; "tortured by the corset that dug into her flesh" [*MBS*, 4]). The narrator employs a parallel structure to equate Somoza with his wife and the bullet-proof vest given to him by his friend, FBI Director J. Edgar Hoover (who was homosexual), with Doña Salvadora's corset. Rumours of the dictator's organic incompleteness run through the novel. After Rigoberto shoots him, the medical examination reveals that part of Somoza's anus is missing and that he defecates into a rubber bag attached to his waist. Seen in this light, Somoza's deathbed command that Rigoberto's corpse be castrated imposes his own physically neutered condition on other Nicaraguans. The National Guard inflicts the same punishment on those members of the "mesa maldita" who are captured alive. Erwin, Norberto, and Cordelio are judged not by Nicaraguan law but under the code of the US Marines; once imprisoned, they are executed, after being "castrados en vida" (*MLM*, 373; "castrated alive" [*MBS*, 313]).

TOWARDS THE MAN OF LETTERS: *ADIÓS MUCHACHOS*, *MENTIRAS VERDADERAS*, *CATALINA Y CATALINA*

Margarita, How Beautiful the Sea is set in 1956, but the crises of national and masculine identity it dramatizes belong to the 1990s. In a private letter to the Colombian critic Carlos Rincón on the subject of Somoza's assassination, on 18 March 1997, Ramírez wrote: "Por lo menos para mí, ahora que el somocismo tiende sus velos otra vez sobre Nicaragua, éste es un tema que recobra actualidad" (*SRP*, box 38, folder 9; "At least for me, now that Somocismo is spreading its veil over Nicaragua once more, this is a theme that again becomes current"). The shadow of Arnoldo Alemán's revived Somocismo reprised old crises of national and personal identity.

The most surprising feature of *Adiós muchachos: Una memoria de la revolución sandinista* (1999; *Adiós Muchachos: A Memoir of the Sandinista Revolution*) is that it addresses the crisis of individual masculine identity only in oblique fashion, postponing full-fledged confrontation with this theme to Ramírez's next two novels. The account Ramírez gives of the Revolution is noticeably less emotional and immediate than that found in "Confesión de amor." In a restrained, even reticent register, the memoir establishes the "I" figure that, in a more bloated incarnation, will obtrude on *Sombras nada más* and *A Thousand Deaths Plus One*. (It is telling that, in spite of the novel's self-referentiality, Ramírez keeps himself out of *Margarita, How Beautiful the Sea*; only his grandfather, Lisandro Ramírez, makes a cameo appearance as a violinist whom one of the characters has heard perform.)

In its popular reception, *Adiós muchachos* was bracketed with two other Sandinista memoirs that were published during the same period: *Vida perdida* (1999; Lost Life), the first volume of Ernesto Cardenal's memoirs, which will be discussed in chapter 11, and Gioconda Belli's *The Country under My Skin: A Memoir of Love and War* (2002). As Arias points out, all of these books received a mixed reception among Central American readers for being "more sentimental and nostalgic evocations of a lost youth and of lost power than they are historically significant reflections on the guerrilla period of 1960–90, about what went right, what went wrong, and what a renovated movement ought to do in the future" (Arias 2007: 221). Belli's memoir was by far the most popular of the three outside Central America, enjoying commercial success in English and German translation. Certainly the most readable of the three memoirs, it was, nevertheless, harshly criticized within the region.[10] In contradiction of the Sandinista Revolution's egalitarian goals, Cardenal, in the first volume of his memoirs (the second and third volumes expand their focus), and Belli concentrate on the forging of the self within an oligarchical Conservative environment and the question of belonging to what could be broadly construed as "masculine identity." This may seem paradoxical in Belli's case, since she is a heterosexual woman who defines herself as a feminist, yet her construction of herself in *The Country under My Skin* conforms to a striking degree to Lancaster's conclusion that in Nicaragua any active individual is masculine. When Belli, as cited earlier, writes that "I think I have also managed to live like a man" (Belli 2002: x), she confirms this definition of masculinity. Cardenal, in *Vida perdida*, is afflicted by more acute versions of similar anxieties in his struggle to balance masculinity with celibacy. Yet Ramírez, though his memoir shares the chronology and contrapuntal structure of Belli's book, shuttling between the anti-Somoza struggle in the late 1970s and the run-up to the 1990 election, is present in the volume as a public figure. Even though it concludes with a nostalgic affirmation of the value of the Sandinista struggle, of the three books, *Adiós Muchachos* comes closest to providing a meaningful reflection on power. It offers far more detail about the middle years of the Nicaraguan Revolution (rather than just the beginning and the end), and more information about the inner workings of the Sandinista government, than other memoirs. In spite of the author's acrimonious departure from the FSLN, figures from whom he is estranged, such as Daniel Ortega[11] and Father Miguel d'Escoto, are treated with impartiality and even lingering affection; only Pope John Paul II is savaged.

While much of the book's popular appeal lies in its anecdotes about intimate encounters with Omar Torrijos, Olof Palme, Bruno Kreisky, Jimmy Carter, Cyrus Vance, Boris Yeltsin, or Margaret Thatcher, Ramírez does make an attempt to assess "what went right, what went wrong." Unlike Belli's memoir and Cardenal's first volume, *Adiós Muchachos* is not about the construction of the author's identity, or decisions that he must make about his sexual choices. Ramírez enters the book as a fully formed adult, a writer and academic administrator who is married with three children and who longs to see the Somoza dictatorship overthrown. The first and last chapters evoke the impact of the Revolution on Ramírez's personal life, through his family. The bulk of the book concentrates on the course of the war against Somoza in the 1970s and the Contra War in the mid-1980s, and on alliances, fund-raising, power-structures, or negotiations with South American presidents, the US State Department, the bourgeoisie, or the Contras. Ramírez's assessment of the Sandinista record is dispassionate and in some areas, such as economic policy, unexpectedly harsh. He devotes the first chapter of this central section of the book to the evolution of the Sandinista ethos of self-sacrifice, claiming an intimate connection to the ideals of the "catacombs" through his younger brother Rogelio's friendship with Leonel Rugama, the archetype of Sandinista self-abnegation. Ramírez describes how this ethos earned the confidence of the Nicaraguan people, and how the *Piñata* betrayed these values – even though he defends the measures that were taken to provide property titles to "familias que … habían habitado [las viviendas] por años como inquilinos" (*AM*, 56; "families who had been living in [their homes] for years as tenants" [*AMM*, 32]). These central chapters, though highly informative for students of the Nicaraguan Revolution, display some of the dryness of a politician's memoirs in their focus on the composition of committees, and on who organized and who attended pivotal meetings.

The book's questioning of post-revolutionary masculine identity occurs at a one-step remove, in the author's tracing of his son Sergio Ramírez Guerrero's path from revolutionary soldier in the 1980s to body-building mature student in the late 1990s. This concentration on heredity, on the fate of the male line, is significant because it is unexpected. Except for passing references to his wife, Ramírez usually keeps his family off-stage in his essays. *Adiós Muchachos*, by contrast, opens and closes with Sergio, Jr, and his friends. The brief introduction contextualizes the Nicaraguan Revolution as the final chapter of 1960s Third World activism, and the most popular solidarity cause in global progressive circles since the Spanish Civil War. In an about-face from Ramírez's earlier writings, the democratic elections whose existence challenged the Sandinista construction of the nation become Sandinismo's benchmark achievement: "La revolución no trajo la justicia anhelada para los oprimidos, ni pudo crear riqueza y desarrollo; pero dejó como su mejor fruto la democracia, sellada en 1990 con el reconocimiento de la derrota electoral, y que como paradoja de la historia es su herencia más visible, aunque no su propuesta más entusiasta" (*AM*, 17; "The revolution did not bring justice for the oppressed as had been hoped; nor did it manage to create wealth and development. Instead, its greatest benefit was democracy, sealed in 1990 with the acknowledgement of electoral defeat. As a paradox of history, this is its most obvious legacy, although it was not its most passionate objective" [*AMM*, 4]).

By conceding this central role to the creation of democracy, a unifying value of the post-1990 globalized world, Ramírez abandons the construction of national autonomy, based on the distinctive experience of Nicaraguan history and conceived and fuelled by a combined political-literary imagining of the nation-space as a zone of rights and social responsibilities. The corollary of this approach is that, for the first time in his writing, the culture of sacred Sandinista martyrs is imperilled: "Y mientras escribo estos recuerdos me pregunto: ¿Quién fue Armando Joya, cuyo nombre llevó hasta hace poco la Biblioteca del Banco Central? ¿Quién César Augusto Silva, que así se llamó un día el antiguo Country Club, convertido después en el centro ceremonial del gobierno revolucionario y ahora en ruinas? ¿Y Lenín Fonseca, como se bautizó un hospital de Managua?" (*AM*, 44–5; "Now, as I write this memoir, I ask myself: Who was Armando Joya, whose name was on the Central Bank's library until recently? Who was César Augusto Silva, which is what the old Country Club was named one day, that later became the revolutionary government's ceremonial center, and that is now in ruins? What about Lenín Fonseca, the name that was given to baptize a hospital in Managua?" [*AMM*, 24]). Ramírez's rhetorical questions are disingenuous: he knows who these people were. But he realizes that the post-1990 erosion of revolutionary history ensures that they will be forgotten.

Near the book's conclusion, on the authority of the Conservative intellectual Emilio Álvarez Montalván, Ramírez claims a second achievement for the Revolution, to complement the institutionalization of democracy: "que el sandinismo había traído por primera vez a la cultura política nicaragüense la sensibilidad por los pobres" (*AM*, 225; "that Sandinismo had brought compassion for the poor to Nicaraguan political culture for the first time" [*AMM*, 159]). This "compassion" towards the poor is a watered-down, liberal-democratic residue of the project of a nation restructured in order to reverse the oppression of the poor. In a similar vein, the history of US intervention and domination, which Ramírez analyzed with vigour and originality in "El muchacho de Niquinohomo," *El alba de oro*, *Seguimos de frente*, and *Confesión de amor*, appears here in a cursory summary. The colonized subservience of the bourgeoisie, the central thread of Ramírez's historical analysis in earlier volumes, is absent. It is telling that, in the post-1990 context, this history of US occupation is explained not in terms of nation or class, but rather as a manifestation of racism, an ill for which liberal remedies are usually sufficient. The reader learns that the core of William Walker's ideology "era que la raza blanca – la mente – y la raza negra – el músculo – estaban destinadas por la Providencia a complementarse; pero los mestizos, indolentes y viciosos, lejos de ese esquema, no servían para nada" (*AM*, 137; "was that the white race – the mind – and the black race – muscle – were destined by Providence to complement one another. But the mixed-race mestizos, indolent and vice-ridden, were worthless and absent from that plan" [*AMM*, 93]). The Revolution becomes an act of mestizo self-assertion.

This consciousness of how individual and racial traits have surpassed the nation as the touchstones of identity is made explicit in the introduction. Ramírez emphasizes that these tendencies, which are generalized phenomena during the onset of accelerated globalization, were of particular gravity for Nicaragua: "El mundo cambiaba a final de los ochenta, se hundía todo el aparato de los ideales, eran destrozadas las quimeras. Pero en Nicaragua saltaba en pedazos el primer modelo real de cambio que el país había vivido nunca" (*AM*, 16; "The world changed at the end of the eighties. The entire framework of ideals broke down, and the illusions collapsed as well. Yet in Nicaragua, there were glimpses of the first real model for change that the country had ever experienced" [*AMM*, 3]).[12] In the aftermath of this shattering of core values and revolutionary hope, Ramírez is left to marvel at the extraordinary fact of his personal participation in a remarkable event in world history: "Yo estuve allí," the introduction's concluding paragraph begins (*AM*, 17; "I was there" [*AMM*, 4]). Yet the self as witness does not replicate the aesthetics of Central American Testimonio narratives: *Adiós Muchachos* is not about Ramírez as *Hombre del Caribe* is about Abelardo Cuadra or *La marca del Zorro* is about Francisco Rivera. These two memoirs that Ramírez edited narrate the formation of subjects who, in different ways, are subalterns. In *Adiós Muchachos*, the subject is not a subaltern and is already formed when the narrative begins. The book is an intimate history of the Revolution; it explains many details that only an insider could know: how Humberto Ortega became minister of defence, or how Fidel Castro advised the Sandinistas not to persist in trying to obtain Soviet MiGs (whose delivery Washington vowed to block), but rather to opt for the attack helicopters that would prove decisive in the Contra War. These revelations are of interest to historians; the personal dimension, and particularly the question of how identity is formed after the dissolution of the revolutionary state, is displaced from the author to the generation of his children and their friends. The question of who the author has become after the disappearance of the assertive, integrated, implicitly "masculine" revolutionary nation is both expressed and obscured by the lives of the next generation.

In the opening sentence of the first chapter, Ramírez states that all of his children were born in Costa Rica; he plumbs their identities as "hijos ... del exilio" (*AM*, 20; "children of exile" [*AMM*, 6]). Upon the family's return to Nicaragua, the children participate in the National Literacy Crusade and the coffee harvest and perform military service: their Nicaraguan identity is that of the Revolution, arguably the only existentially authentic Nicaraguanness that has ever existed. Yet the opening page hints at a preoccupation that this identification with a defeated Revolution may have emasculated Sergio, Jr. Unusually for a Nicaraguan man in his mid-thirties, Ramírez's son has not married: "Sigue soltero, aunque conozco sus entretelones sentimentales porque al fin, después de muchas vueltas y revueltas, somos buenos amigos" (*AM*, 19–20; "He is still single, although I know his private feelings because, in the end, after so many twists and turns, we are good friends" [*AMM*, 5]). The assertion that he has a good relationship with his son secures Ramírez's own masculinity by certifying that of his heir. In an ironic echo of "Charles Atlas Also Dies," Sergio, Jr, has responded to the absence of a strong national identity by becoming a body builder: "va todos los días al gimnasio Hércules, hace pesas, está suscrito a revistas de *body building* y es un hombrón de más de seis pies y cien kilos de peso" (*AM*, 24; "[he] goes everyday to Hercules Gym, lifts weights, and subscribes to bodybuilding magazines. He is a big guy, over six feet tall and weighing more than 220 pounds" [*AMM*, 9]). The conspicuous signs of his son's masculinity – his "private feelings" (the Spanish original suggests romantic involvements), his muscularity – shore up potential doubts about his own masculinity that might be inherent in Ramírez's loss of revolutionary power and relinquishment of his post-1990 political career to become purely an artist.

The assertion of sexual normality on the part of his children is discernible, also, when Ramírez states that the announcers of Radio Ya "ultrajaban" (*AM*, 34; "attacked" [*AMM*, 16]) his daughter María, yet withholds the nature of the calumnies made against her. This parental protectiveness acquires a gendered resonance in the context of Ramírez's departure from political office, which, to use Lancaster's terms, challenges him to display continued "activity" even as he ceases to be an "active" in public life. Ramírez's writing career, which began with his sitting at a typewriter with the secretaries at UNAN in León, mingles non-masculine identifications with a public dimension that is construed as masculine. Choosing to sit with the secretaries is balanced by the public recognition that came from fellow students who looked over his shoulder to see what he was writing. In spite of this, writing, associated with women, such as the secretaries and his mother, the high-school literature teacher who sent him to girls' schools, becomes suspect once the counterweight of political activity in the public sphere is no longer present. *Adiós Muchachos* illustrates Ramírez's attempt to negotiate the gender contours of a longed-for yet unsettling identity as "just a writer."

These concerns dovetail with the awareness that each generation is judged by that which succeeds it. The fulcrum of *Adiós Muchachos* is Claudia Miranda, a friend of Sergio, Jr, introduced in chapter 4, who presents herself as the daughter of Idania Fernández, a Sandinista with whom Ramírez was acquainted, who was raped and murdered by the National Guard in 1979. Claudia, an infant at the time of her mother's death, asks Ramírez to share with her his memories of Idania; their meeting, delayed until Ramírez is completing his book as a visiting professor at the University of Maryland, forms the memoir's denouement. Claudia's statement that she does not resent her mother's abandoning her for the Sandinista cause, but that, on the contrary, "Yo hubiera hecho lo mismo … Sobre todo … en este tiempo sin ideales" (*AM*, 295; "I would have done the same thing … Above all … in this age without ideals" [*AMM*, 210]), serves as a form of absolution and a closing validation of the sacrifices such as abandoning one's children (like Fernández) or bringing them up in foreign countries (like Ramírez) that were Sandinismo's defining characteristic.

Claudia's statement also emphasizes the vacuum that Ramírez enters with the disassociation of the two threads of the interpenetrated literary-political essence of Sandinismo. The only bulwark against this emptiness is literature, which must now suffice not only to give shape to private fantasies but also to substitute for the author's activity in the public sphere. Ramírez made this parallel explicit in a 1997 letter to the Uruguayan writer Mario Benedetti: "la revolución duerme en el polvo, sucia y herida … me siento contento como nunca, escritor full-time como otros por estos pagos se han vuelto pícaros exclusive-time" (*SRP*, box 36, folder 2; "the revolution sleeps in the dust, besmirched and wounded … I feel happy as never before, a full-time writer as others in this neck of the woods have become exclusive-time villains"). By releasing literature from complicity in a combined enterprise with politics, the globalization-driven disappearance of a dominant national chronology requires literary art to reconstruct history and society as purely fictive imaginings.

This impetus towards reconstruction, rather than "engagement" or "political compromise" with surrounding reality, is evident in *Margarita, How Beautiful the Sea*; it may also help account for the proliferation of historical novels in many literatures during the post-1990 period. In Ramírez's case, literature's promise of continued activity in the public sphere is made explicit in the scene in *Adiós Muchachos* where he resigns from the FSLN. During the January 1995 press conference where he announces his resignation, Ramírez sits beneath a portrait of Augusto César Sandino: "Era como si hubiera estado allí, otra vez, para despedirme. O para recibirme" (*AM*, 289; "It was as if he was there once again to bid me farewell, or to welcome me" [*AMM*, 205]). The message could hardly be clearer: Sandino is dispatching Ramírez back into private life to perform his revolutionary's duty through his writing. Ramírez notes that in the portrait Sandino brandishes "un juego de lapicero y estilográfica" (*AM*, 289; "a fountain pen and pencil set" [*AMM*, 205]). The guerrilla, adorned with an interlaced pencil and fountain pen, is also a writer, while Ramírez, the man who is leaving politics to become a writer (though first, against the advice of his family, he will launch his 1996 presidential campaign), preserves the ethos of the guerrillas from the catacombs. This scene cites the well-known Argentine tango, written and first popularized by Carlos Gardel, from which the book takes its title. Ramírez echoes one line of Gardel's song by reflecting that it is "los mismos compañeros de mi vida" (*AM*, 289; "my very own lifelong compañeros" [*AMM*, 205]) who hatch the plot to attack his daughter that drives him out of the FSLN (Gardel n.d.).

The absence of a national framework and the daunting shadow of the vice-president he used to be mould the two books that follow *Adiós Muchachos*: the essay collection *Mentiras verdaderas* (2000; True Lies) and the short-story collection *Catalina y Catalina* (2001). *Mentiras verdaderas*, which contains the texts of lecture courses given in Guadalajara, Mexico City, and Madrid in 1997 and 1998, when Ramírez was paying off his debts from his 1996 presidential campaign, is an elegant book, but it has less bite or originality than his earlier essay collections. Its tepid sensibility highlights a core dilemma of the post-1990 era: once the grievances of the past, the weight of national history that nourished national liberation movements, have been erased from the intellectual agenda, one is left only with general principles. These principles of the liberal globalized world, among which freedom of speech and imagination are foremost, are not compelling unless they are anchored in specific detail.

Though the title of Ramírez's book echoes that of Mario Vargas Llosa's collection of essays on his favourite novels, *La verdad de las mentiras* (1990; The Truth about Lies), its form and style are influenced by the essays and public lectures of Carlos Fuentes. Unlike Fuentes, however, and in spite of the close friendship that united the two men – Fuentes was instrumental in securing Ramírez's invitations to teach in Mexico – Ramírez is not a brilliant generalizer. The effectiveness of his essays of the 1980s, like that of his short stories, depends on mordant insights derived from meticulously observed detail. Nor, like Vargas Llosa, did Ramírez become an impassioned apostle of neo-liberal principles after his break with the official left. Following Fuentes, Ramírez remained on the centre-left, where his defences of freedom were tempered by a residual hostility towards the free-market right. One of the book's rare sparks of acid political commentary appears in a disparaging reference to "el neocaudillismo neoliberal" (*MV*, 126; roughly, "neo-liberal neo-tyrantism").

Mentiras verdaderas, which eschews direct reference to the Nicaraguan Revolution, presents the author as a writer. It opens with the declaration that "me propongo hablar sobre el oficio literario" (*MV*, 15; "I propose to discuss the literary profession"). This enquiry into what it means to be "just a writer" does not reach clear conclusions. Ramírez's lectures allude to Dante, Juan Rulfo, Cortázar, Shakespeare, Balzac, Flaubert, Raymond Queneau, Franz Kafka, Greek mythology, H.G. Wells, W. Somerset Maugham, Derek Walcott, Virginia Woolf, Eudora Welty, Superman comics, and many other works, quoting from most of them in the original languages; yet, in contrast to Fuentes's ransacking of literary traditions in books such as *Myself with Others* (1988) or *The Buried Mirror* (1992), these essays do not lead the reader to an understanding of the contours of the culture of a particular epoch. They are imbued with a palpable sense of the author bolstering his image as a man of letters in the public sphere to compensate for lost political authority. The quotes in foreign languages betray an anxiety to impose intellectual authority. The result is essays that, paradoxically, lack the caustic humour of those written in the heat of battle in the 1980s; the Greek column that adorns the cover reflects this portentous solemnity. The original perceptions that break through this veneer stem from observations about the world around him, rather than about particular works of literature, as, for example, when Ramírez ponders the implications of the increasing digitalization of literature: "Los signos electrónicos no son materiales y, por primera vez, la escritura deja de ser real. Lo real, lo palpable, lo indeleble, lo que se ve y se toca es lo que ahora está en juego" (*MV*, 107; "Electronic symbols are not material and, for the first time, writing ceases to be real. That which is real, palpable, indelible, that which is seen and touched, is what is now at risk"). Ramírez's point that an electronic text ceases to exist once the computer has been turned off, whereas a physical book is always present, is far more provocative than his summaries of masterpieces. The later essays develop these ideas in more detail: "Por la primera vez la palabra asume un riesgo metafísico que es el de no existir, y reaparecer bajo riesgo, sólo como efecto de una manipulación" (*MV*, 137; "For the first time the word assumes the metaphysical risk of not existing, and of reappearing in an imperiled state, as simply the effect of a manipulation"). The threat to the word posed by digitalization strikes at the heart of Ramírez's identity as a writer – his only remaining source of authority – just as dictatorship, imperialism, and the Contra War struck at his identity as a Nicaraguan and a Sandinista. As always, Ramírez's best writing springs from a sense of uncertainty and looming threats, not from entitlement.

In addition to the title story discussed above, *Catalina y Catalina* collects one story from the past, "Vallejo" (see chapter 4), some stories written in 1995, such as the title piece, and "La viuda Carlota" ("The Widow Carlota"), an earthy mystery story with a clever twist, and others that date from 1999 and 2000. A strong collection, *Catalina y Catalina* nevertheless occasionally struggles to portray Nicaragua without being overshadowed by the image of the vice-president that the author used to be. These tensions are embedded in one of the collection's most effective stories, "Perdón y olvido" ("Forgive and Forget"), which dates from 1999.

The narrator of this story, Ernesto, a member of a Conservative family that converted to Sandinismo, perceives himself as the product of a Nicaraguan culture of opposition to Somocismo. Named after his father, he was born in 1950, when Fernando Agüero's pact with Somoza permitted his parents to return from exile in Mexico. In the late 1990s, with the Revolution over, Ernesto continues to drive a Communist-red Russian Lada and to refer to his wife as "mi compañera ... como se estilaba decir en tiempos de la revolución" (*CYC*, 88; "my partner ... as we used to say in the days of the revolution"). His life-partner, Guadelupe, is a Mexican television journalist who was sent to Nicaragua to cover the 1979 final offensive and remained in the country because she and her crew were "encandilados con el sandinismo" (*CYC*, 77; "dazzled by Sandinismo"). Ernesto and Guadelupe, who met making Sandinista propaganda films, now survive by creating publicity spots for Nicaraguan television. Their livelihood has become precarious: "en estos tiempos de globalización, todavía pescamos algunos spots publicitarios de cigarillos y cerveza, aunque cada vez más los traen ya enlatados" (*CYC*, 88; "in these times of globalization, we still wangle a few spots for cigarette or beer commercials, although more and more they arrive here already in the can").

Ernesto is obsessed with 1940s Mexican films. His obsession stems in part from the fact that during their exile his parents acted as extras in these productions. In the last film in which they appeared, *Perdón y olvido*, which was completed just prior to their return to Nicaragua, his parents and another man and woman are visible having a discussion behind the main action. Curious as to the nature of the conversation, the narrator asks an acquaintance who works for "una asociación de padres de niños discapacitados fundada en los años de la revolución" (*CYC*, 86; "an association of parents of disabled children founded in the years of the revolution") to find someone to lip-read the conversation. As a result of this assistance from the revolutionary past, Ernesto learns that his mother had an affair and that his biological father is Mexican. These melodramatic events, as he comments to Guadelupe, are "como en tus películas mexicanas" (*CYC*, 97; "like in your Mexican films"). Having imagined himself as the staunch embodiment of revolutionary values and Nicaraguan autonomy, Ernesto discovers that his life is a mere fabrication of Mexican popular culture: he was conceived on a Mexican film set, his father is Mexican, his wife is Mexican, his popular culture is Mexican. Guadelupe's silence in the face of these revelations suggests that this Mexicanization of Ernesto's identity has rendered him less attractive to her.

The story illustrates the way in which, in the post-1990 era, the distinctive traits of smaller nations' identities become more vulnerable to assimilation by adjacent larger nations' popular cultures. It also displays the persistence of revolutionary traits, however anachronistic, as the enduring source of Nicaraguan national identity. That this poses a dilemma not only for Ernesto, but also for his creator, is evident in the narrator's recollection that he and Guadelupe met when she was "enviada por Juanita Bermúdez, la asistenta de Sergio Ramírez" (*CYC*, 78; "sent by Juanita Bermúdez, the assistant to Sergio Ramírez") to the Sandinista film unit that he was setting up. The impossibility of avoiding his own long shadow – or his insistence on this shadow's pervasiveness – bespeaks Ramírez's awareness that not only are the institutions of the Revolution the only viable touchstones of Nicaraguan identity, but that those who held power during the revolutionary period are enshrined in this national mythology; yet, as the story's conclusion makes clear, such avatars of national identity are being overwhelmed by the popular culture spread by globalization.

This theme recurs in other stories in *Catalina y Catalina*. In "Ya todo está en calma" ("Everything's Quiet Now"), which describes the funeral of Diana, Princess of Wales, as viewed from Managua by a single father, popular culture drenches every aspect of existence. Contaminated by television soap operas, the narrator suffers a fit of jealousy after finding his wife, also named Diana, having lunch with her boss. He finally loses his job as a result of missing too many days' work after staying up all night watching English-language television with his daughter. In a similar vein, the ambitious "Aparición en la fábrica de ladrillos" ("Apparition in the Brick Factory"), completed in February 2000, literally strips a Nicaraguan athlete bare to expose the emptiness of a life defined by a succession of alienating cultural identifications. Once a successful baseball player, the narrator is now an ill, overweight elderly man who awaits death confined to a wheelchair. This immobility in which his life culminates is the consequence of three moments of specious rebirth, at each of which he finds himself naked. The first occurs when he stumbles out of bed naked to urinate outdoors and senses the presence of legendary New York Yankees manager Casey Stengel behind him, "bañado por los focos de las torres del Yankee Stadium" (*CYC*, 65; "bathed by the spotlights of the towers of Yankee Stadium"). Stengel, who returns at key points in the narrator's life, tantalizes him with the American Dream, speaking of how baseball permitted him to overcome poverty (*CYC*, 71). The apparition inspires the narrator to become a baseball player. In 1972 he hits the home run that enables Nicaragua to defeat the invincible Cubans; later, as he lies naked and asleep in his hotel room, Anastasio Somoza Debayle bursts in with his bodyguards to have his photograph taken with the sporting hero. Somoza offers him a house as a reward for his services to the nation. The house never materializes and the narrator's services prove to be a liability when the national identity shifts: the photograph with Somoza condemns him to bad treatment under the Sandinistas. In impoverished late middle age, he experiences a third false rebirth as he is converted to evangelical Christianity by Protestant missionaries who operate out of a tiny church with "un altar con una cortina roja que fue una vez bandera de propaganda del Partido Liberal" (*CYC*, 74; "an altar with a red curtain that was once a Liberal Party propaganda flag"). The association of the missionaries, who baptize the narrator in a filthy river where he catches an infection, with Somoza's political party, now restored to power, emphasizes the persistence of the Somocista subservience to US popular culture. As the narrator contemplates his death, he imagines Casey Stengel leading him out of life and into the next world. His trajectory through the three key stages of twentieth-century Nicaraguan history – pre-revolutionary, revolutionary, and post-revolutionary – condemns globalization as the mere reimposition of Somocista self-abasement to the cultural discourses of larger nations.

FORGING THE NATION: *SOMBRAS NADA MÁS*

During the Alemán and Bolaños years, it became more difficult to make the case that the Revolution had left a positive residue in Nicaraguan society. Nicaragua entered the 2000s as a poorer country than it was in the 1960s. The fact that the narrator of "Aparición en la fábrica de ladrillos" does not experience any positive value from the Sandinista Revolution reflects Ramírez's own growing doubts about the revolutionary heritage and the intellectual's ability to communicate with and improve the lives of "the people." In the stories from the mid-1990s, such as "Catalina y Catalina," the Revolution remains a liberating event. Yet, from the glum vantage point of 2000, the 1990 electoral defeat is seen as the moment when the people rejected activists and intellectuals. This change in the relationship between the intellectual, who is construed as male even when she is an emancipated female, and the peasants and workers is made explicit in Gioconda Belli's description of the morning of 26 February 1990:

> Teníamos las espaldas encorvadas. En los ojos el desvelo, la tristeza, la incredulidad. Círculos hondos en los rostros cenizos. Cuando alcé la mirada para la ciudad distante, me impactó sentir en el verdor de las montañas una emanación hostil alzándose de mi propia tierra. El pueblo nos rechazaba. Nunca creí que me tocara vivir ese día. (*El País*, 395; We were hunched over, stunned, anyone could see the sadness in our bleary eyes and our sallow faces. When I looked out at the city beyond, I was disturbed to feel a hostile emanation rising from my own land. The people had rejected us. I never thought I would live to see this day. [Belli 2002: 356])

The shattering of the organic idea of nation that was implicit in the words of generations of Spanish American intellectuals when they spoke of "mi tierra" ("my land"), "mi patria" ("my homeland"), or "mi pueblo" ("my people") curtails the ability to generate the conglomerated political-artistic matter that was the stuff of the nation. The fact that Belli feels the people's rejection in a hostility emanating from the greenness of the mountains illustrates the inextricable links between the notions of "land" and "people."

Ramírez's next novel, *Sombras nada más*, which stands with *To Bury Our Fathers* and *Castigo Divino* as one of his major works, is a response to this cultural predicament, which Néstor García Canclini summarized in *Latinoamericanos buscando lugar en este siglo* (Latin Americans Looking for a Place in This Century), also published in 2002:

> ... perdieron convicción vanguardias artísticas y propuestas nacionalistas en la cultura. No han venido a sustituirlas otras teorías ni otros movimientos con consistencia e impulso equivalentes. La situación actual se caracteriza por una crisis de los modelos de modernización autónoma, el debilitamiento de las naciones y de la idea misma de nación, la fatiga de las vanguardias y de las alternativas populares. (García Canclini 2002: 38; ... artistic avant-garde movements lost conviction, as did nationalist policies in culture. They have not been substituted by other theories or movements with equivalent energy or coherence. The current situation is characterized by a crisis of models of autonomous modernization, the weakening of nations and of the very idea of the nation, the exhaustion of the avant-garde and of progressive political alternatives.)

Though they are present everywhere, these dilemmas do not take the same form in each Latin American country. García Canclini points out that the economic and spiritual deprivations associated with globalization are felt in Central America "de modo más severo que en otras regiones" (ibid.: 44; "in more severe form than in other regions").

This turn-of-the-millennium crisis was particularly acute in Nicaragua. The presidency of Arnoldo Alemán (1997–2002), devoted to eradicating the memory of Sandinismo, made the disappearance of the nation a deliberate policy and a tangible shared experience, particularly in the capital. As Florence Babb recounts in an analysis of the Alemán period:

> The changes brought about with neoliberalism in Nicaragua are most striking in the remaking of Managua as a city emulating developments in other urban centers ... Most revolutionary murals have been removed, while new monuments are being erected. Streets, plazas and barrios have been renamed in an effort to erase the memory of the previous decade, while grandiose traffic circles use precious water for fountains and make use of colored lights and music to hail the modern city

> under construction. Restaurants and shopping malls give Managua the appearance of a modernizing place in the social landscape and offer the urban elite safe destinations when they venture from closely guarded homes. All these changes in Nicaragua's capital signal efforts to construct a new national identity centered on consumption, for those who can afford it, in the market economy. (Babb 2001: 243)

By replacing history with consumption as the source of national identity, the city as redesigned by Alemán dethrones the intellectual from a position of authority. A writer such as Ramírez finds that his expertise in Nicaraguan history and culture is marginalized. This shaky ground is rendered even more uncertain by the globalization of publishing, which has led to the collapse of the Spanish American publishing industry, once based in Buenos Aires, Mexico City, and Caracas, and its removal to Spain; by 2002, 70 per cent of the books produced in Spain were exported to the Americas (García Canclini 2002: 50). Published by the Mexico City branch plant of Madrid-based Alfaguara, *Sombras nada más* had to be "exported" to Nicaragua. Many larger Spanish publishers will export books only to countries where they anticipate a market of three thousand copies or more. In smaller and poorer countries "national literature" exists under the threat that the works of the nation's writers will not be exported to their own country.

Like *Margarita, How Beautiful the Sea*, *Sombras nada más* is riven by the besieged, provisional nature of the nationhood it attempts to enshrine. The novel does not propose to reconstruct Nicaraguan history in the face of an awareness that history has lost its diachronic authority, being reduced to something light and diaphanous, as its predecessor does, but rather broods over the arbitrary nature of the course of historical events. The telling of the story depicts history as random and lacking a defined trajectory or purpose; yet that telling nevertheless simulates an entity that approximates the remains of the Nicaraguan nation and its history in an era in which only popular culture and the swelling contours of the individual self command authority. As Neil Larsen argues, in a refutation of the post-colonial theories of Homi Bhabha, which Larsen sees as anti-historical and part of the globalization problem rather than the solution: "'Nation' is not ultimately reducible to 'narration.' But narration, arguably, simulates nation in our globalized, interchangeable 'locations,' now off just about everyone's 'cognitive map,' and about which stories cannot really be told" (Larsen 2001: 31). The fragmented sense of location evoked by Larsen corresponds to García Canclini's account of the "place" of Latin American culture as pulverized and externalized by mass emigration and globalized commerce, which has centralized

Latin American publishing in Madrid and Barcelona, Latin American television and music production in Miami, and scattered the Latin Americans who consume this culture through East Los Angeles, Queens in New York, San Antonio, Texas, the Elephant and Castle district of London, England, the factory belt in Seoul, South Korea, and dozens of other foreign locations. García Canclini writes of Latin America: "Su imagen le llega de espejos diseminados en el archipiélago de las migraciones" (García Canclini 2002: 12; "Its image reaches it from mirrors disseminated through the archipelago of the migrations"). One of the paradoxes of globalization is that this is true even when the author lives in Managua.

Ramírez had stated that he would not write a novel about the Nicaraguan Revolution. Yet the Alemán government's suppression of the revolutionary heritage, compounded by the unravelling of the fusion between the literary avant-garde and popular nationalism, appears to have forced a reconsideration of this decision. Strictly speaking, Ramírez has kept his promise, since the temporal span of *Sombras nada más* does not include the years of Sandinista government. The novel's action takes place between the 21 and 23 June 1979, less a month before the triumph of 19 July. Ramírez has described the events that inspired the novel:

> Parto de una anécdota que escuché muchas veces en 1979, después de haber tomado el poblado de Tola en el sur de Nicaragua, un numeroso grupo de guerrilleros atacó la vecina hacienda San Martín, propiedad de Cornelio Hüeck Salomon, un viejo cacique somocista distanciado para entonces del régimen. Somoza se apiadó finalmente de él, dándole un contingente militar para defenderlo, y luego le mandó una lancha para que lo llevara a San Juan del Sur, desde donde lo trasladarían en helicóptero a Managua. Sin embargo, al cabo del combate, fue capturado mientras huía corriendo por la playa y sometido a un juicio popular en Tola, ante una multitud anardecida.
>
> Pocos días antes, en Belén, un pueblo vecino, había habido una masacre. Guardias nacionales entraron disfrazados de guerrillas … Mataron a más de cincuenta niños. Debido a ese hecho, la gente estaba aún más enardecida.[13]
>
> Los dirigentes guerrilleros le permitieron a Hüeck defenderse en una especie de juicio público, y le advirtieron que si al final recibía aplausos o hacía reír, se salvaría, y si no, que sería ejecutado, como finalmente ocurrió. A mí siempre me obsesiona esa imagen de Hüeck indefenso, tratando de salvarse con aplausos ante una multitud. (Cherem 2004b: 258–9; I proceed from an anecdote that I heard many times in 1979.

After having captured the village of Tola, in southern Nicaragua, a large group of guerrillas attacked the neighbouring San Martín hacienda, property of Cornelio Hüeck Salomon, an old Somocista chieftain who by then was estranged from the regime. Somoza finally took pity on him, giving him a military contingent to defend him and later he sent a speedboat to take him to San Juan del Sur, from where they would transfer him by helicopter to Managua. Nevertheless, he was captured in the course of the combat as he fled running down the beach and subjected to a people's trial in Tola, before an enraged multitude.

A few days earlier there had been a massacre in Belén, a nearby town. National Guards had entered the town disguised as guerrillas ... They killed more than fifty children and adolescents. Due to this fact, people were even more enraged.

The guerrilla leaders allowed Hüeck to defend himself in a sort of public judgment and they warned him that if at the end he received applause or laughter he would be spared, and if not he would be executed, as finally occurred. That vision of Hüeck defenceless, trying to save himself with applause before the multitude, always obsesses me.)

At first glance, Hüeck, the dictator's crony, might appear to be an unlikely figure to capture Ramírez's imagination. Yet, like Ramírez, Hüeck was a leader in a government to whose initial ideals he remained loyal but which had lost the support of the majority of the population. In the novel, Alirio Martinica, the character based on Hüeck, is depicted as having been the number two man in Somoza's regime, as Ramírez was the number two man in Daniel Ortega's government. Ernesto Cardenal maintains that Hüeck remained in his hacienda "en espera de la caída de Somoza y en espera que los yankis lo escogieran a él" (*RP*, 250; "waiting for the fall of Somoza and waiting for the Yankees to choose him") as Somoza's successor. The novel's title comes from a song by Javier Solis. The song's refrain is, "Sombras nada más entre tu vida y mi vida/ sombras nada más entre tu amor y mi amor" (Solis n.d.; "Only shadows between your life and my life/only shadows between your love and my love"). Ramírez's invocation of this lyric suggests that, ideology aside, only happenstance separates his destiny from that of Hüeck.

Extending the theme of the implacable role of a fickle fate in shaping history that he developed in *Margarita, How Beautiful the Sea*, Ramírez discovers in Hüeck's biography a life that might have been his. In contrast to the unbreachable doctrinal borders of the 1980s, from the perspective of the new millennium, ideological allegiances appear aleatory. In the ideological debates between modernization theorists and dependency theorists, Ramírez could have sided with the former group during his student years. He has stressed, for example, the efforts to modernize Nicaraguan society of the Hüeck/Martinica generation of entrepreneurs, known in Nicaragua as the "Minifaldas" ("Miniskirts") because their rise coincided with the popularity of this garment. Ramírez characterizes their ambitions as "un proyecto de desarrollo capitalista viciado por los vicios del sistema político somocista. Era un proyecto que si no hubiera tenido los vicios del sistema político somocista, pues, hubiera podido haber tenido resultados. No eran locuras lo que proponían" (*UISR*; "a capitalist development project gutted by the vices of the Somocista political system. It was a project that, had it not been for the vices of the Somocista political system, well, it could have had results. Their ideas weren't crazy.") In this vision, each man participated in a flawed attempt to modernize Nicaragua. Yet the theme of happenstance in *Sombras nada más* runs much deeper. This is Ramírez's last "Faulknerian" novel, in which characters who have appeared in *To Bury Our Fathers*, *Castigo Divino*, and *Margarita, How Beautiful the Sea* make return appearances. There are references to Dr Debayle (*SNM*, 154), Captain Prío (*SNM*, 155), and the Yankee security adviser Sartorius Van Wynckle, now an instructor at the notorious School of the Americas in Panama (*SNM*, 323); Lorena López, the orphan adopted by a Somoza crony who wins the rigged beauty contest in *To Bury Our Fathers*, becomes a central character. Other correspondences with earlier novels are more ambiguous. The name Campuzano becomes important in *Sombras nada más*, even though it is not clear whether these working-class Campuzanos from León are the same Campuzanos who throw a party for Somoza in their home in *Margarita, How Beautiful the Sea* (*MLM*, 110), or the Managua builder, "un maestro de nombre Campuzano" (*TDMS*, 158; "a builder named Campuzano" [*TBF*, 122]), from *To Bury Our Fathers*.

Sombras nada más is also Ramírez's most thorough attempt at the "total novel" practised by the writers of the Boom: here the web of characters drawn together by avant-garde literary techniques offers illumination not only of the society of León, as in the earlier novels, but also of Granada, Managua, and the rural Pacific Coast, in a desperate attempt to knit together a national unity that is dissolving under globalization and Alemán's assault on the Sandinista heritage. In a trait that is revealing of the post-2000 era, this is also the last time Ramírez will write a novel that purports to encompass national history but does not include the Atlantic Coast. Finally, the burly narrative structure, discussed below, represents Ramírez's final attempt at replicating the structural ambitions of a Boom novel.

The notion that individual fates diverge in imperceptible moments of decision is incarnated in the novel by the three university friends, Alirio Martinica, Jacinto Palacios, and Ignacio Corral. They were roommates at UNAN in the early 1960s, and their interwoven lives enact the evolution of Nicaraguan history during the two decades that lead up to the Revolution. Alirio's father, who had the same name as he, participated in the 1954 April Rebellion and was executed by Somoza in a torture chamber. Jacinto's father, Macario Palacios, is a powerful Liberal who has acquired land and money in return for his services to the dictatorship. Ignacio comes from an oligarchical Conservative family that lives on the emblematic Calle Atravesada in Granada, in a house that bears a plaque that celebrates an ancestor who was executed by William Walker in 1856 (*SNM*, 160).[14] Ignacio has status, but less money than Jacinto, who owns the "Chevrolet Impala aerodinámico, modelo 1962, verde" (*SNM*, 84; "green aerodynamic 1962 Chevrolet Impala") in which the three young men cruise between León and Managua. Lorena López recalls that, "de los tres amigos que siempre andaban juntos en sus tiempos universitarios" (*SNM*, 210; "of the three friends who always went around together in their university days"), it is Jacinto, who comes from her own Somocista milieu, who is her friend; yet she marries Alirio and has an extramarital affair with Ignacio. At university, Alirio is the radical. Like Ramírez himself, he is a charter member of the left-wing student group FER, and a friend of Francisco Buitrago and Jorge Navarro, two of the first Sandinistas killed in combat. Also like Ramírez, Alirio declines to play a combat role and calls Masatepe home, since his widowed mother has married a man from the town (*SNM*, 160). Ignacio, by contrast, is a Social Christian, a follower of the Conservative anti-Somocismo promoted by Pedro Joaquín Chamorro. By 1971, when Ignacio seeks refuge in Alirio's house (though his real goal may be to pursue Lorena, who is now Alirio's wife), he has become a fugitive FSLN guerrilla. After Ignacio is captured, his torturer hurls his body into a volcano: an act that leads Somoza, who even in his omnipotence remains terrified of the Granada oligarchy and "el apellido Corral" (*SNM*, 333; "the surname Corral"), to condemn his own security forces. In death, Ignacio lends his name to the Sandinista unit that carries out the 1974 raid on the Somocista Christmas Party.

By evoking recognized milestones in Nicaraguan history, such as the April Rebellion, the David Tejada case (see chapter 5), and the Christmas Party raid, Ramírez creates a postmodern simulacrum of Nicaraguan history. Rather than an inexorable march towards revolution, this version of history is the random product of a succession of coincidences and unforeseeable personal decisions in which any character could have ended up playing the role of any other. Ramírez unravels Sandinismo's heroic history even as he consecrates it as myth. The three men's fates come to a head during the Christmas Party raid, where Ignacio has passed into Sandinista mythology, Alirio is the government negotiator who speaks to the kidnappers over the phone, and Jacinto, one of the hostages, is murdered. All three men die violent deaths, yet two of the three die in circumstances that contradict their original political orientations.

The theme of interconnected fates and the arbitrary nature of destiny is not limited to the three protagonists. In the novel's forward action, Compañera Judith, one of Martinica's captors, identifies herself as the daughter of one of Alirio's father's co-conspirators during the April Rebellion; she is also the guerrilla who murdered Jacinto during the Christmas Party raid. Comandante Nicodemo, Martinica's interrogator and the incarnation of Sandinista doctrinal rectitude, turns out to be Ignacio's older brother, a Conservative Jesuit who was a graduate student in the United States until the news of his brother's murder brought him back to Nicaragua to join the FSLN. The guerrilla Manco-Cápac is the much younger brother of Erlinda Campuzano, a working-class girl who was one of Alirio's lovers during his student days. The phrase, "fuimos en un tiempo cuñados, cuñado," (*SNM*, 39, 406; "at one time we were brothers-in-law, brother-in-law"), uttered by Martinica at the novel's opening and by the young guerrilla at its close, seals the unexpected bonds that unite characters across lines of social class or political allegiance.

Early in the novel, Martinica overhears Manco-Cápac announcing his capture over the radio with the words "Caifás en mi poder" (*SNM*, 34; "Caiaphas in my power"). Martinica's identification with Caiaphas, head of the supreme tribunal of the Jews, who is powerless to sentence or save Jesus of Nazareth and can only pass him on to Pontius Pilate for judgment, stresses both his ultimate impotence and his culpability in the dictatorship's crimes. The contradictory role of Caiaphas raises the question of Ramírez's own association with Sandinista abuses such as the execution of Cornelio Hüeck.[15] The issue is framed in historical and ideological terms that dramatize the tension between the humanist and radical strains in Sandinista ideology that is played out through the actions of the guerrillas who capture Martinica. As the Sandinistas close in on his mansion, the reader learns that "por la Radio Sandino, la radio clandestina de los guerrilleros que él sintonizaba cada noche con miedo y curiosidad, siempre estaban repitiendo que ésta iba a ser una revolución humanista, sin paredón, y que se garantizaba la vida a todos los que se rindieran" (*SNM*, 19; "on Radio Sandino, the guerrillas' clandestine radio station, to which he tuned in every night with fear and curiosity, they were always repeating that this would be a humanist revolution, without firing squads, and that they guaranteed the lives of all those who turned themselves in"). The irony of this statement is evident in the fact that the novel closes with Martinica's execution by firing squad. Martinica himself, questioning Manco-Cápac about his fate, associates the image of the "firing squad" with revolutionary radicalism: "Sí, dijo él, paredón, como en Cuba" (*SNM*, 111; "'Yes,' he said, 'firing squads, like in Cuba'").

The novel presents the justification for allowing the crowd, or "la turba" ("the mob"), to decide a prisoner's fate as a means of conferring power on the masses. This empowerment is not couched in the language of liberal democracy that corresponds to a humanist agenda, but in more radical terms of citizenship conceived as an interplay between rights and responsibilities. Martinica asks his fellow prisoner El Niño Lobo (Wolf Child), the former president of the Association of Somocista Students, how his fate will be decided: "¿Una votación en urnas? Nada de urnas, el voto va a ser un aplauso" (*SNM*, 373; "A vote placed in an urn? No urns here, the vote will be an applause"). El Niño Lobo counsels Martinica to forget the guerrillas who have been interrogating him: "no fueron más que personajes secundarios en toda esta mojiganga, la verdadera función empieza ahora, en cuanto nos suban al tablado de los actos escolares" (*SNM*, 373; "they were only secondary characters in all of this farce, the real show starts now, when they take us up onto the stage of the school auditorium"). Sandinista and Somocista leaders share their powerlessness before the masses.

The image of leaders of the regime standing before the people to be judged by them resonates through the novel, evoking questions not only of revolutionary justice but also of the people as supreme yet untrustworthy arbiters of the nation's destiny. As Manco-Cápac states: "era de necesidad que el pueblo mismo asumiera desde ahora misma sus responsabilidades ... sangre era sangre, y al ser derramada no podía caer solamente sobre la cabeza de los jefes de la revolución" (*SNM*, 386–7; "it was necessary that the people themselves assume their own responsibilities ... blood was blood and when it was spilled it couldn't fall only on the heads of the revolutionary leaders"). If the people wish to complete their Revolution, they must get their hands bloody, earning their new citizenship rather than expecting the comandantes to take all the responsibility. The contradictions inherent in this outlook are incarnated in Manco-Cápac's name. He is both "manco" ("lame'), as symbolized by his ruined hand, and "capac," which recalls "capaz" ("capable"), a key word in the Sandinista lexicon of "capacitación": training people to exceed their former capabilities, a crucial step in engendering the revolutionary New Man.

Manco-Cápac's narrowness of vision and his politico-military adroitness contribute equally to his character. In a similar vein, his guerrilla training in Cuba and his Catholic education have become so entangled that both bear equal responsibility for his strengths and his limitations. He states: "No veo en qué puede oponerse la religión cristiana a la causa proletaria" (*SNM*, 114; "I do not see how the Christian religion and the proletarian cause can contradict each other"). Taking his name from an Inca emperor, Manco-Cápac is rooted in the soil of the Americas; he represents a tradition that can boast of being indigenous, unlike Martinica, who is a lackey of a dictatorship so subservient to the United States that the dictator prefers to conduct business in English. (As a Jew, Martinica's prototype, Cornelio Hüeck, was also distant from the ethnic origins of the vast majority of Nicaraguans.)[16] As Somoza says to Martinica: "Being fluent in english [*sic*] like hell es lo único que te falta para ser mi secretario perfecto" (*SNM*, 292; "is all you're missing to be my perfect secretary"). Yet the privileged Martinica and the humble Manco-Cápac cannot escape their intimate connection: the legacy of Erlinda Campuzano when she was a cleaning girl in León. The people, as embodied by Manco-Cápac, are aggrieved, temporarily empowered by the Revolution and limited in their understanding of their own circumstances.

The form to be taken by relations between government leaders, whether reactionary or revolutionary, and the population is the tension that propels the story and generates the novel's narrative structures. Like *Margarita, How Beautiful the Sea*, *Sombras nada más* employs a contrapuntal structure where alternating chapters present different threads of the narration. Both novels are charged by the interaction between Modernist and postmodern modes of narration, an overlapping that is representative of Ramírez's need to participate in the fluid, popular-culture-drenched post-1990 world, while at the same time consecrating national history through resonant images, as was done by the novelists of the Boom. While Vargas Llosa and Fuentes had by this time abandoned the extremely challenging narrative techniques whose decipherment required the engagement of an "active reader," Ramírez's fiction continued to exert these sorts of demands upon the reader. As in late Boom novels such as Vargas Llosa's *Conversation in The Cathedral* or José Donoso's *El obsceno pájaro de la noche* (1970; *The Obscene Bird of Night*), *Margarita, How Beautiful the Sea* and *Sombras nada más* employ labyrinthine temporal structures, passages where important speakers' names are withheld, sudden shifts of time or setting, the intercalation of past and present dialogue, characters with multiple names whose common identity becomes clear only after hundreds of pages, and the running together of dialogue and narration in the absence of dashes.

More revealing, however, is the point at which the two novels' techniques diverge. In *Margarita, How Beautiful the Sea* both sides of the contrapuntal narrative equation display daunting complexity; but in *Sombras nada más* the avant-garde techniques of the numbered chapters alternate with non-numbered chapters consisting of personal testimony, which is presented as having been culled by Ramírez, concerning the fate of Alirio Martinica. The literary suavity of the narrative voice alternates with many other voices; half of the novel appears not to have been written by the author. Some of the non-numbered chapters are raw and colloquial while others, made up of transcripts of interviews and interrogations, are formal and stilted. The novel concludes with an eleven-page section entitled "Sobre los documentos que auxilian a este libro" (*SNM*, 409–19; "On the Documents That Contribute to this Book"), where Ramírez describes how he located these testimonies. The anecdotes are presented in an affable manner and include, for example, a three-page description of a Miami book publicity tour, replete with accounts of bilingual conversations and lunch dates with glamorous personalities such as Álvaro Vargas Llosa. Ramírez identifies friends and members of his family as the sources for other documents, explaining how they helped him to locate transcripts or interview subjects. The non-numbered chapters have an unedited feel, with the interviewees giving Ramírez their opinions of his earlier novels or, in one case, berating him to reconcile himself with Daniel Ortega: "arréglese con Daniel, ¿cuándo van a arreglarse?" (*SNM*, 379; "make up with Daniel. When are you going to make up with him?"). In a lengthy e-mail, Martinica's widow Lorena, now living in a luxury condo in Miami, complains about having been referred to in *To Bury Our Fathers* as "la huérfana" ("the orphan"). In apparent mockery of her complaint, the next chapter opens, "La huérfana no lloraba su partida" (*SNM*, 225; "The orphan didn't cry when she left").

The clash here is not merely of tones, but of literary modes: the inheritance of an avant-garde tradition (if that paradox may be allowed) dominates the numbered chapters and the Testimonio tradition that became the most influential literary form in Central America during the 1980s occupies the non-numbered chapters. There is only one problem with this formulation, and that is that Ramírez's testimonies are forgeries. The eleven-page section at the end of the novel, with its seductive tone and apparent autobiographical intimacies, is designed to mislead the reader into believing that fiction is fact. Ramírez makes this clear in an interview with his long-time friend and literary agent, Hortensia Campanella:

> No creo que haya menos imaginación en esta última novela, pero la forma de presentarla varía, porque he tratado de convertir la invención en piezas de realidad, acercándome a lo que el lector puede llegar a creer literatura documental, y yo lo induzco a ello. Cada vez más trato de ser un realista absoluto, y utilizar la invención con ese propósito, por lo menos en esta novela, porque me pareció el recurso técnico más adecuado. (Campanella 2004: 52; I don't think there's any less imagination in this latest novel, but the means of presenting it alters, because I've tried to convert the invention into pieces of reality, approaching what the reader may come to believe is documentary literature, and I induce him to do so. More and more, I try to be an absolute realist and use invention with this purpose, at least in this novel where it seemed to me to be the most appropriate technical recourse.)

The most striking question raised by this admission is why going to such lengths to induce the reader to believe that invented documents and monologues are in fact "documentary literature" should be the "most appropriate technical recourse." This novel's roots in the rupture of the fusion of Spanish American high literary art and nationalistic impulses, in the fissuring of the left-wing intellectual's ability to speak for the people, help to illuminate this decision. By asserting the literary author's ability to fabricate oral testimonies, Ramírez is neutralizing, by subsuming into fiction, the Testimonio genre whose prominence during the 1980s coincided with both the decline in the literary novel's technical ambition and the shredding of the alliance between the literary intellectual and national-popular projects. At this point it is worth recalling John Beverley's definition of Testimonio as

> a novel or novella-length narrative in book or pamphlet (that is in graphemic as opposed to acoustic) form, told in the first person by a narrator who is also the real protagonist or witness of the events she or he recounts. The unit of narration is inevitably a "life" or a significant life experience (for example, the experience of being a prisoner). Since, in many cases, the narrator is someone who is either functionally illiterate or, if literate, not a professional writer, the production of a testimonio often involves the recording and then the transcription and editing

of an oral account by an interlocutor who is an intellectual, journalist or writer. (Beverley 1993: 70–1)

The popularity of Testimonio during the 1970s and 1980s was a response to the urgency of Latin American politics, particularly the armed conflicts in Central America and the dictatorships in the Southern Cone, which made some writers impatient with the ambiguities of magic realism. Elzbieta Sklodowska proposes that "muchos testimonios perciben su proyecto en términos de un contra-discurso con respecto a la escritura mágicorrealista y metaficticia del boom" (Sklodowska 1992: 99; "many Testimonios perceive their project in terms of a counter-discourse to the magic realist and metafictional writing of the Boom"). In response to the success of the best-known Testimonios, such as *Hasta verte, Jesús mío* (1969; *Here's to You, Jesusa!*) by Elena Poniatowska, *Los días de la selva* (1980; *Days of the Jungle: The Testimony of a Guatemalan Guerrillero, 1972–1976*) by Mario Payeras, *Fire from the Mountain* by Omar Cabezas, and *Me llamo Rigoberta Menchú y así me nació la conciencia* (1983; *I, Rigoberta Menchú*), edited by Elisabeth Burgos-Debray, major Boom writers attempted to integrate subaltern voices or documentary material into their fiction, in works such as García Márquez's *Crónica de una muerte anunciada* (1981; *Chronicle of a Death Foretold*) and Vargas Llosa's *The Real Life of Alejandro Mayta* (1984). In Central America, where Testimonio's influence was strongest, Ramírez's friend, the Salvadoran novelist Manlío Argueta, absorbed Testimonio-style influences into the novel in *Un día en la vida* (1982; *One Day of Life*).

During the 1980s, with the almost simultaneous publication of *Castigo Divino* and Francisco Rivera's Testimonio, *La marca del Zorro*, Ramírez contributed to both branches of the perceived tension between literary fiction and Testimonio. After 1990, however, the cognitive dissonance required to promote simultaneously the artifice of literary fiction and writing based on "la veracidad de los hechos" (*Zorro*, 13; "the veracity of the facts") lapsed. The relationship between revolutionary authorities and the masses was called into question. As suggested by Sklodowska, the means of literary expression associated with the two groups came into confrontation with each other. Writing at the beginning of the new millennium, after a decade's reflection on the electoral defeat of Sandinismo, Ramírez can no longer co-opt Testimonio into a dominant avant-garde novelistic tradition. As García Canclini points out, in the new context both "the avant-garde and progressive political alternatives" have exhausted their authority. The crisis faced by writers is particularly evident because of the loss of their intellectual and political centrality. Jean Franco, looking back on "the military regimes in the southern Cone, the civil wars and repression in Central America, the economic crisis of the 1980s in Venezuela, the election of Fujimori in Peru," argues that "the changes destabilized the literary intelligentsia, altering cultural institutions and the book industry and forcing a reassessment of the intellectual's relationship to the new order" (Franco 2002: 179).

From the perspective of life under President Alemán's society of historical amnesia and mass consumption, Testimonio's clamour of subaltern voices appears in retrospect as one of the early-warning signs of the disintegration of the Latin American literary intellectual's authority. Seen through this lens, the differences between Testimonio and "the mob" dwindle. "The mob," expressing itself in raw, colloquial language, disdains democracy, ultimately rejects the Sandinistas, who fight to improve the lives of the poor, and ends up succumbing to the tawdry populism of the neo-liberal (and criminal) Alemán, who wrenches the gulf between rich and poor wider than ever before. This optic makes Testimonio the accomplice of reactionary forces as, in the post-1990 environment, subaltern populism slides indistinguishably into the reactionary gospel of mass consumption. In a book inspired by the search for new paradigms in the aftermath of the defeat of Sandinismo, John Beverley makes this case in a more positive light, arguing that

> the commodification of cultural production through the operation of the market and the technologies of commercial mass culture can be a means of cultural democratization and redistribution of cultural use-values, allowing not only new modes of cultural consumption but also increased access to the means of cultural production by subaltern social subjects. By contrast, the cultural policies undertaken by both the Soviet model of state socialism and the various forms of populist nationalism in Latin America and elsewhere imply the perpetuation of a cultural ideology founded on the norms of literature and high culture – an ideology that maintains a close affinity with bourgeois humanism and, in the case of Latin America, with colonial and neocolonial castes. (Beverley 1999: 159)

This statement exemplifies the kind of academic cultural-studies argument that Ramírez pits himself against. By passing off fiction as Testimonio and incorporating his inventions into a work of high art, Ramírez is staging an intellectual counter-attack designed to subvert the forces that have subverted his cultural authority. In reappropriating the literary form that was the original protagonist of the "massification" of culture and melting it down into fiction, he reclaims the traditional authority of high art and the male intellectual in the turn-of-the-millennium vacuum.

When evaluating the argument for a democratic renaissance propelled by popular culture, it is worth noting that Beverley never explains how his "subaltern social subjects" gain their increased access to the means of cultural production under the market economy, when in fact the tendency is towards greater concentration of power in fewer hands. His casual conflation of "populist nationalism in Latin America" with "the Soviet model of state socialism" is exaggerated and unsupported. Beverley's assertion that "bourgeois humanism" is the hegemonic ideology of "neocolonial cultural castes" is at odds with the anti-humanist market positivism that animated turn-of-the-millennium Latin American neo-liberalism. Yet, in spite of these inconsistencies, Beverley's praise of Alemán-style commodification is useful because it illuminates the continuity between the putatively subaltern concerns of Testimonio and the pretensions of neo-liberal ideology to promote individual "freedom."

The patterning of Ramírez's counterpointing of the literary and pseudo-testimonial chapters is mimetic of the novel's anxieties about the erosion of the male leader's authority over the people. The first informant in the pseudo-testimonial chapters is a male professional, the medical doctor Edgard Morin. As the novel progresses, the informants become increasingly marginal to the power structures of patriarchal Spanish American society. Martinica's widow, the socially privileged Lorena López, is the first female informant; the second woman speaker, Compañera Cristina, is a rural schoolteacher who became a Sandinista guerrilla; the third, María del Socorro Bellorín, is a peasant woman from a poor rural area. The only male informant in the second half of the novel is a sixteen-year-old office boy who portrays himself as having been subjugated by the patriarchy in the most brutally literal fashion by alleging that he was sodomized by Alirio Martinica in the presidential palace. The contrast between literary and testimonial aspects progressively destabilizes patriarchal rhetoric as the novel advances. False accusations of sexual impropriety are one means of realizing this destabilization, as when, for example, the accusation of sodomy against Martinica turns out to have been fabricated by Somoza's mistress to avenge Martinica's spurning of her sexual advances (*SNM*, 367).

Critics such as Beverley need to find a solution to the dilemma posed by the defeat of the Sandinistas – "we need a new paradigm" (Beverley 1999: 5) – even if this means praising the market forces they used to oppose by trying to locate a subversive or liberating potential in mass consumption.

Ramírez, by contrast, resuscitates the historically conscious Nicaraguan nation invented by Sandinismo in full awareness of the artificial nature of this revival, while mordantly charting the erosion of his own capacity to bring his ideals to fruition. In *El alba de oro* (1983), written in the heat of the Revolution, he had praised "mi pueblo intransigente y humilde, en armas y en sueños" (*AO*, 10; "my humble, intransigent people, in arms and in dreams") as the source of his literary inspiration. His turn-of-the-millennium brooding culminates in the climactic image of *Sombras nada más*, where Martinica, the former number two man in the Nicaraguan government, stands before an uncomprehending mob that condemns him to death. The origins of this scene lie in an anecdote about a public event in October 1984 in which a peasant who had been fighting for the Contras was scheduled to climb on stage and hand Ramírez his rifle to signal his reintegration into revolutionary Nicaragua:

> Subió a la tarima un hombrecito desmedrado, pobremente vestido, que daba la impresión de un ave desplumada. Portaba un rifle Fal que a falta de correa llevaba una cuerda de los arneses …
>
> Los sueños de la revolución. Frente a aquel hombrecito humilde, miserable en su vestimenta, aturdido por el espectáculo en el que entraba a escena brevemente para hacer mutis tan silencioso como había llegado, dejándome su viejo fusil en las manos, me hice entonces una reflexión que no ha dejado de rondar mi cabeza a lo largo de estos años: ¿qué mundo había en su cabeza y qué mundo había en la mía? ¿Cuál era la conexión, el hilo perdido entre estos dos mundos, si es que existía alguno? …
>
> En mi proyecto, que era la organización de mi sueño, estaba férreamente establecido un nuevo sistema de vida para aquel campesino, para sus hijos y para todos los suyos …
>
> Pero mi sueño de justicia y modernidad para su vida, chocaba dramaticamente con el mundo que a él seguía rodeándolo, aislamiento, miseria, atraso, y con su propia percepción del mundo. Y el esfuerzo, lejano y disperso que para reorganizar su vida que se maquinaba desde los centros de poder de la revolución, y que los agentes de ese poder trataba de imponerle frente a su concepto de libertad como individuo, también chocaban directamente con él. (*CA*, 116–18; A shrivelled little man, poorly dressed, climbed onto the stage. He looked like a plucked chicken. He held a Fal rifle which, lacking a belt, he carried with a chord from a harness …

The dreams of the revolution. Facing this humble little man, miserably dressed, troubled by the spectacle in which he passed briefly across the stage to exit as silently as he had arrived, leaving me his old rifle in my hands, I asked myself a question that has not ceased to haunt my mind down the years: what world was in his head and what world was in mine? What was the connection, the lost thread between these two worlds, if one existed? …

In my project, which was the organizing principle of my dream, I had rigorously planned a new system of life for that peasant, for his children and for everyone in his life …

But my dream of justice and modernity for his life collided dramatically with the world that continued to surround him – isolation, misery, backwardness – and with his own perception of the world. And the distant, dispersed effort to reorganize his life that was plotted in the revolution's power centres, and that the agents of the revolution tried to impose on him in the face of his concept of his freedom as an individual, collided directly with him.)

The image of the leader on stage, conscious of his inability to communicate with the peasant masses, is consolidated by the change in the connotation of the word "humilde" ("humble"). In the 1983 citation this word comes across as a patronizing romanticization of the poor, while in this 1992 extract "humilde" expresses suffering, the pain of underdevelopment, and, ultimately, the peasant's inability to imagine the literary intellectual's dreams of social transformation. More ominously, this use of "humilde" adumbrates a social distance from the poor that would become a hallmark of Nicaragua under Alemán, whose policies included moving the poor to peripheral areas where they lived out of sight of well-off Nicaraguans (Babb 2001: 241–51). Ileana Rodríguez aptly situates Ramírez's insights in the passage above as the concluding stage in the inexorable erosion of the male Spanish American revolutionary tradition:

Che [Guevara] disregards the ideological reproductions of his speech. In him, in any event, it is neither the peasantry (*campesinado*) nor the agrarian societies, but rather the proud military ontology of the rebel that is in question. In [Roque] Dalton, by contrast, there is a quest, an inquiry, doubt, a search. By the time we reach Ramírez, the question has already become politically acute. The most pertinent questions of being and existing for the *campesino* masses, subjects of revolutionary

> transformations in agrarian societies, had come home to roost. The *campesino*'s relationship to economic changes, the politics of war, and the transition to productive and distributive justice must be grasped. (Rodríguez 1996: 69–70)

Yet it is precisely this understanding that remains elusive. *Confesión de amor*'s image of the leader standing on stage, unable to communicate his vision to the peasant masses before him, is also the image that closes *Sombras nada más*. In the novel, however, it is Martinica, rather than Ramírez, who is standing on stage. Convinced that the people will sympathize with him because of his ejection from the dictator's inner circle and his father's execution by Somoza in 1954, he is duped by El Niño Lobo, who precedes him. Having coaxed Martinica to tell him a story of how he was one of a group of Somocista officials who were standing in the presidential swimming pool when Somoza, who weighed three hundred pounds, defecated in the pool, El Niño Lobo relates this story to "the mob."[17] He uses the anecdote to deflect the crowd's anger towards Martinica. Prior to going on stage, El Niño Lobo speaks a cultivated Spanish, laced with citations from Rubén Darío (*SNM*, 365); once facing the masses, he switches to a populist Central American register:

> todo lo que estoy contando es la verdad, papito, y no me podés desmentir, vos estabas metido hasta el pescuezo dentro de esa piscina, no te atreviste a moverte una sola pulgada mientras aquello avanzaba y te llegaba al borde de la boca, imagínense, con todo lo que Somoza come ... ¡El somocismo no es más que pura mierda, y en esa mierda se bañan los serviles! (*SNM*, 394; everything I'm saying is true, buddy, and you can't deny it, you were up to your neck in that pool, you didn't dare move a single inch while that stuff floated right up to the edge of your mouth. Think about it! With all that Somoza eats ... Somocismo's pure shit, and bootlickers swim in that shit!)

In his use of colloquial language and his insistence that he is telling what really happened, El Niño Lobo reproduces the populist techniques of Testimonio. Like the discourse of contemporary neo-liberalism (and in contradiction to Beverley's assertions), this discourse benefits an agile reactionary. The first fissuring of organic society spares a cynical opportunist rather than liberating the poor who are oppressed by traditional power structures. Trapped in the older patriarchal tradition of the leader as authority figure, Martinica is unable to match El Niño Lobo's assumed voice. He tries to win over the crowd with jocular remarks about the ample sexual endowment of the town's men, only to be repudiated by shouts that he is showing disrespect for the Virgin Mary. By catering to patriarchal values, he has overlooked the important constituency of women, who used the opening of the Sandinista Revolution to demand a greater voice in society. In a clear prefiguration of post-1990 events, the nascent splintering of organic society into factions, each making its own demands, thwarts Martinica's ability to rule the crowd. Accustomed to giving orders, Martinica can try to win their applause only by commanding them to cheer him: "¡Vengan esos aplausos! ¡Arriba esas palmas!" (*SNM*, 397; "Bring on the applause! Raise those hands"). El Niño Lobo, who is astute enough to adapt to the peasants' Testimonio-style language, is spared in spite of his unrepentant Somocista past; the dissident Martinica is condemned to death.

The novel concludes with a little boy gazing up at the sky from near the spot where Martinica, seated in front of an adobe wall, awaits execution. As the boy stares at the sky, the narrative perspective inverts: the final sentence is narrated from the vantage point of the heavens:

> Y desde lo alto, más allá de los penachos de las palmeras, la multitud parecía girar en un remolino de cabezas, giraba la silla contra el muro de adobe, giraban los milicianos apuntando al prisionero sentado en la silla, y todo se cerraba en un torbellino irisado en el flotaban cada vez más minúsculas las cabezas, una masa gaseosa en la que crepitaban las banderas como las chispas rojas y negras de una fogata. (*SNM*, 407; And from high above, beyond the crests of the palm trees, the crowd seemed to spin in an eddy of heads, the chair in front of the adobe wall spun, the soldiers aiming at the prisoner spun, and everything condensed into a whirlwind shot through with light, in which the heads floated, looking ever smaller, a gaseous mass in which the flags waved like the red and black sparks of a bonfire.)

The "whirlwind," possibly a literary allusion to "el viento, tibio, incipiente, lleno de voces del pasado, de murmullos de geranios antiguos, de suspiros de desengaños anteriores a las nostalgias más tenaces" ("Then the wind began, warm, incipient, full of voices from the past, the murmurs of ancient geraniums, sighs of disenchantment that preceded the most tenacious nostalgia") that closes García Márquez's *One Hundred Years of Solitude* (491; 421 English ed.), evokes the literature of the Boom, whose techniques Ramírez reinscribes without wielding their original transformative assumptions. The wind sweeps away the patriarchal tradition that gave birth to both Somocismo and Sandinismo. Seen from this perspective, Sandinismo is not an ideology that succeeded in bringing to fruition its own ideals but rather, as Ramírez maintains in *Adiós Muchachos*, a force that ushered democratic procedures into Nicaraguan society, along with an attention to the poor (or at least the need to be seen to be acting on their behalf); with the convergence of postmodernity and democracy, comes the populist peril. The final words make clear that Sandinismo is at the root of these changes by describing the red-and-black FSLN flags as "the red and black sparks of a bonfire." In Nicaraguan discourse, the word "bonfire" ("fogata") is an established metonymic reference to Augusto César Sandino. As Omar Cabezas writes in his own Testimonio, *Fire from the Mountain*: "Entonces la fogata era síntonita de subversión, era símbolo de agitación política, de ideas revolucionarias llevadas por los estudiantes a los barrios" (Cabezas 1982: 60; "So the bonfire was a sign of subversion, a symbol of political agitation, of revolutionary ideas brought by the students into the barrios" [Cabezas 1985: 44–5]).

Sandino's campfire in the Segovia Mountains, the point of origin of the Nicaraguan Revolution, becomes the force that swirls all Nicaraguans towards a future they can neither control nor understand. The final sentence promotes this second meaning of the novel's title. Not only is Martinica a shadow of the dictatorship and a man who feels most comfortable in his leader's shadow, but, as the refrain of the Javier Solis song insists, there are "Only shadows between your life and my life." The image of the "whirlwind," complementing the fates of the novel's three central characters, Alirio, Ignacio, and Jacinto, establishes a vision of destiny as happenstance, even though other images in the novel contradict this assertion of arbitrariness. In one of Ramírez's provocative echoes of the language of the novel's Testimonio chapters, a section describing how Alirio Martinica, Sr, was shot dead by Anastasio Somoza García while he was handcuffed ("esposado") in a cell is juxtaposed with a chapter that opens with a description of Alirio Martinica, Jr, handcuffed by the Sandinistas in the mirror-lined bedroom of his mansion: "Esposado a uno de los barrotes del espaldar de la cama miraba su figura multiplicada a la luz del quinqué" (*SNM*, 109; "Handcuffed to one of the crosspieces of the headboard of the bed, he watched his image multiplied by the light of the oil lamp"). The multiplication of handcuffed men, the father executed by Somoza and the son executed by the Sandinistas, suggests that although history continues to proceed in a dialectical progression and has not ended, as Francis Fukuyama would maintain, individual fates have become arbitrary. Any sense of a telos, a diachronic logic, has broken down. Ramírez could have followed in the footsteps of his Liberal father and ended up on the wrong side of the Revolution; Martinica (or Hüeck) could have carried his expulsion from Somoza's inner circle to its logical conclusion and joined the Sandinistas. Fates are juggled by cyclical patterns, reflecting Ramírez's belief in "la dialéctica, no como una categoría filosófica perecedera, sino como un simple mecanismo capaz de animar la realidad" (*CA*, 156; "the dialectic, not merely as a perishable philosophical category, but rather as a simple mechanism capable of animating reality").

In his interview with Campanella, Ramírez echoes the Boom novelists' quest for the elusive "total novel": "Siempre me ha fascinado la novela ecuménica, de pretensión total, que quiere ser una copia del universo a la misma escala" (Campanella 2004: 49; "I've always been fascinated by the ecumenical novel, of totalizing ambitions, which wants to be a copy of the universe on the same scale"). In *Sombras nada más*, the narrative techniques of the Boom's total novel swallow and neutralize the Testimonio voices that fracture the nation's cohesion and impede the realization of the national-popular project. Yet the major novels of the 1960s and 1970s deployed their technical bravado to mythologize national identities. Ramírez's invented testimonies forge the nation in the sense of creating a simulacrum of national history; his use of avant-garde techniques generates a pastiche of the Boom novel which, even as it plays up the postmodern ironies of its condition through strategies such as measured echoes between Testimonio and non-Testimonio chapters, insists on its drive to rehabilitate a discourse of national autonomy and historical distinctness in spite of the author's despondent awareness that this enterprise will be fruitless. In the accelerated globalization of the new millennium, the retreat of national history as an organizing principle leaves in its wake the community-based identities of women, indigenous people, Miskito, or Afro-Caribbeans (and, less conspicuously, those of gays and lesbians); such identities promote a preoccupation with defining the self.

The shadow that looms largest as *Sombras nada más* approaches its conclusion is the shadow of the author himself. First addressed in his literary persona by Lorena López in her assessment of his novels, then in his political persona by María del Socorro Bellorín, who reprimands him for not making peace with Daniel Ortega, he reveals himself as the ringmaster and prestidigitator in the final section, which describes the origins of each of the Testimonio chapters. By insisting on the documentary reality of these Testimonios, Ramírez consolidates his own image as personality and ultimate arbiter of a narrative universe whose arbitrariness threatens his authority. The novel's appendix opens with the words: "Antes de partir hacia Berlín en abril de 2001, donde debía ocupar la Cátedra Samuel Fischer de

Literatura Comparada en la Universidad Libre ..." (*SNM*, 409; "Before leaving in April 2001 for Berlin, where I was due to occupy the Samuel Fischer Chair in Comparative Literature at the Free University ..."). From this assertion of authority in the "factual" world, certified by a visiting chair at a prestigious European university, the closing section culminates in a declaration of the writer's prerogative to manipulate reality to suit his own purposes. The final sentence, noting the chronological inconsistencies between historical events and the dates given in the novel, states that "yo he querido dejarlo así por razones de novelista" (*SNM*, 419; "I wished to leave it like that for a novelist's reasons"). The novel concludes with a statement that history is no longer a dialectical force with which the intellectual engages, but rather an infinitely malleable fiction that the celebrity-personality-as-author fashions as he wishes.

At first glance, *Sombras nada más*, one of Ramírez's most accomplished novels, appears to be marred only by the obtrusion of his own self-image; yet this bloated self-image, which blemishes the perfectly reproduced structures of the Boom novel, is inherent to the post-2000 context in which Ramírez writes. The self-image is an unavoidable element of an attempt to construct a Boom novel in the twenty-first century, when history is adulterated by projections of the self through a host of new media. Even though the achievement of *Sombras nada más* appears to augur well for continued historical engagement in the face of globalization's sapping of the credibility of national histories and revolutionary ideologies, it is what Arias terms "the posturing of the writer as a codified body image" (Arias 2007: 20) that will dominate his next novel, *A Thousand Deaths Plus One*.

THE SELF IN HISTORY: *EL VIEJO ARTE DE MENTIR* AND *A THOUSAND DEATHS PLUS ONE*

Between *Sombras nada más* and *A Thousand Deaths Plus One*, Ramírez completed *El viejo arte de mentir* (2004; The Old Art of Lying), lectures from a creative writing course given at the Technological Institute of Monterrey, Mexico, in 2002. A much more rewarding book than *Mentiras verdaderas*, *El viejo arte de mentir* skirts the pitfalls of glorifying the writer as authority figure and offers sound advice on the use of historical material in fiction, cogent discussions of the employment of point of view, and lucid summaries of the strengths of the modern novel in Latin America. The preoccupation with how to integrate history into fiction, whether in a work of reportage, such as Truman Capote's *In Cold Blood* (1966) or García Márquez's *Noticia de un secuestro* (1996; *News of a Kidnapping*), or in a novel that fictionalizes historical events, such as Daniel Defoe's *Journal of the Plague Year* (1722), or in books that fictionalize notorious murder cases, such as Theodore Dreiser's *An American Tragedy* (1925) or Stendhal's *Le Rouge et le Noir* (1830; *The Red and the Black*), dominates the early lectures. In contrast to *Mentiras verdaderas*, there are no self-aggrandizements of the figure of the author, no lengthy quotes in foreign languages, no murky generalizations.

Divided into short, focused sections, *El viejo arte de mentir* provides pithy advice from a craftsman on how to create persuasive fictions. Ramírez's fidelity to history is evident in his insistence that it is "el poder de los hechos ... que crea el universo de la novela" (*VAM*, 40; "the power of the facts ... that creates the universe of the novel"); but this same power that is inherent in stories that come from history, rather than from the author's imagination, also animates non-fiction reportage. The verisimilitude that is necessary to convince the reader of the story's credibility springs from creating the illusion of access to a reliable witness, which Ramírez refers to as "estuvo allí" (*VAM*, 41; "he or she was there"). This presentation perpetuates the enterprise of *Sombras nada más*: subsuming Testimonio-style accounts into an overarching literary force-field that is dominated by seductive lies, elaborated on a foundation of historical fact: "Y debajo de la Historia pública siempre estarán el amor, la locura, el deseo, la ambición, la pasión, el celos ..." (*VAM*, 70; "And beneath the public history there will always be love, madness, desire, ambition, passion, jealousy ..."). The novelist's terrain is the human residue of historical upheaval. Surpassing Vargas Llosa's description of the novelist as a "deicide" who wishes to "suplantar a Dios, rehacer la realidad" (Vargas Llosa 1971: 86; "supplant God, remake reality"), Ramírez portrays the novelist not as he who kills God by creating even bigger fictions, but rather as God himself within his own fictional universe: "Es Dios padre, que siempre resuelve sobre el destino de manera arbitraria y tantas veces dramática; Dios Flaubert, o Dios Tolstoi, que empuja a Ana Karenina delante del tren en marcha que va a destrozarla" (*VAM*, 50; "He is God the Father, who always resolves destinies in an arbitrary and so often dramatic manner: God Flaubert or God Tolstoy, who pushes Anna Karenina beneath the moving train that will destroy her").

The novel, says Ramírez, remains the last redoubt of patriarchal authority in a world levelled by commercialized mass culture; it shelters the random nature of fate at the same time that it lends lies credibility by anchoring them in facts. As Ramírez tells his students in a later lecture: "Yo prefiero el realismo que no sustituye siquiera los nombres de los personajes, cuando se trata de una historia real. Así me acerco más a esa ambición de fundir la

Historia pública, en su relieve de hecho real, con la historia privada, en su relieve de hecho imaginario" (*VAM*, 96; "I prefer a realism that does not even substitute the characters' names in the case of a true story. In this way I draw closer to that ambition of blending public History, in its importance as verifiable fact, with the private history, in its importance as the imaginary fact"). This dictum explains Ramírez's insertion of himself into *Sombras nada más* (and particularly *A Thousand Deaths Plus One*) as less an act of egotism or self-obsession, or even a postmodern gambit, than as a simple fidelity to the facts. Were he to obviate his own presence in national history (as Vargas Llosa would later do, for example, in *Las travesuras de la niña mala* [2006; *The Bad Girl*], where he arranges for the protagonist, Ricardo Somocurcio, a Peruvian who lives in Europe, to lose touch with his country's politics just at the point where Mario Vargas Llosa becomes a presidential candidate [Vargas Llosa 2006: 341]), Ramírez would be violating his fidelity to historical reality and his belief that this factual framework is the best trampoline for the lies of the imagination. He cannot decide to include in *Margarita, How Beautiful the Sea* the actual text of Rigoberto López Pérez's last letter to his mother – "decidí insertar íntegra la carta, sin ningún retoque" (*VAM*, 96; "I decided to insert the entire letter, without any revisions") – yet erase his own presence from Nicaraguan history.

The sections on point of view and the autobiographical account of Ramírez's own induction into the traditions of narrative through childhood reading and his employment at the Masatepe cinema at the age of fourteen are enlightening, but the most crucial insights in *El viejo arte de mentir* occur in the final chapter, "El ángel de la historia (Temas y motivos de la escritura narrativa en América Latina)" ("The Angel of History [Themes and Motives of Narrative Writing in Latin America]"). Here Ramírez moves beyond literary technique to the relationship between novel and society. Though many of his observations are generalizations, they are more telling than those in *Mentiras verdaderas*. His comments, which revolve around the novel's interweaving of public and private histories and identify the family as the point at which these two currents cross, reveal his shifting perception of the Nicaraguan nation. Though the course is geared to students in northern Mexico and many of Ramírez's examples come from Mexican literature, he notes that a prime concern for the early-twenty-first-century novelist is "la interrogante de nuestra identidad como mestizos atrapados entre el mundo indígena, el mundo negro y el mundo europeo" (*VAM*, 113; "the questioning of our identity as mestizos trapped between the indigenous world, the Black world and the European world"). What is striking about this statement, particularly in light of the fact that he makes it in Monterrey – arguably the "whitest" major city in Mesoamerica, where the indigenous component is less pronounced than it is farther south and the African component is non-existent – is precisely the inclusion of the "Black world" as one of the pillars of *mestizaje*. In this way Ramírez abandons his native Department of Masaya, with its strong indigenous element mixed with southern Spanish heritage, as the mestizo norm, ushering Africanness into mestizo identity. This announces a strategy that will be central to the novels *A Thousand Deaths Plus One* and *El cielo llora por mí*, as well as the book-length essay *Tambor olvidado* (2007; Forgotten Drum).

The shift in outlook remains discreet in *El viejo arte de mentir*. Ramírez identifies the likely themes of the twenty-first-century Spanish American novel as: drug trafficking, corruption, the collapse of the middle class, the social consequences of a deteriorating physical environment, the conflict between globalized culture and traditional cultures, massive clandestine emigration, the effects of globalization in eroding national sovereignty, and the threat of "big brother" (*VAM*, 126) technologies that will subject the citizen to perpetual surveillance. As this list confirms, Ramírez insists that the novel will retain a strong commitment to the public and political themes that compelled the great novelists of the nineteenth century. In a distinction that would prove vital to numerous literatures, and often would be misunderstood, he distinguishes between the crucial element of the novelist's engagement with history and the often potboilerish form of the historical novel, which would become one of the early twenty-first century's staple cultural products and whose rise would expose the evasion of a commitment to history on the part of many writers.[18]

> No estoy hablando de la novela histórica, que se ciñe a los acontecimientos y resulta tantas veces engorrosa, sino de la novela que se inserta, como aparato de ficciones, dentro del esplendor de la Historia y se funde con ella en disputa …
>
> Al despuntar el nuevo siglo XXI, lo que cambian son las variables de la Historia pública … La novela hispanoamericana seguirá apegada a esta tradición de reflejar lo extraordinario que viene de la propia Historia …
>
> Entre la marginación y la postmodernidad, entre el crecimiento de la pobreza y la globalización, surge una nueva Historia pública que contar y nuevas historias privadas que caen bajo su dominio. (*VAM*, 124; I'm not speaking of the historical novel, which takes on events and so often

> becomes tiresome, but rather of the novel that inserts itself, as a fictional apparatus, within the splendour of History and merges with it in a spirit of dispute …
>
> With the onset of the twenty-first century, what changes are the variables of public History … The Spanish American novel will remain inseparable from this tradition of reflecting upon the extraordinary events that come from History itself …
>
> Between marginalization and postmodernity, between the growth of poverty and globalization, a new public History presents itself to be told and new private stories take shape under its reign.)

This prediction, however, would prove difficult to realize, either for younger writers or for Ramírez; the former often turned to genre fiction, including formulaic historical novels with a thin literary veneer, or whose engagement with a capitalized History was so attenuated by postmodern ironies as to jeopardize its critical or emotional force: what Beatriz Cortez has called "la estética del cinismo" (Arias 2009: 145; "the aesthetic of cynicism"). As noted above, *Sombras nada más* is Ramírez's last "Faulknerian" novel in the sense of a work that mythologizes a place of origin through the elaboration of Modernist literary techniques. If, as Moro contends, León is a metonymical representation of Nicaragua, the extension of the web of repeating characters beyond León's borders in *Sombras nada más* signals a heightened anxiety to capture a nation that grows ever more diaphanous. Those narrative techniques often described as "Faulknerian" were evolved by Faulkner to mythologize a lost nation: that of the defeated Confederacy. Intercalations of contrapuntal or multiple narrative streams throw into relief and mythologize the vanished societal structures of the past, be their metonymic referent Yoknapatawpha County or León, and lend the society that has disappeared an authenticity equal to that of the present. Yet, with the onset of accelerated globalization, these techniques can also become stylized. Vargas Llosa writes *The Green House* (1965) by evoking the lush setting of the Amazon as Faulkner evokes the lushness of the US Deep South in *The Wild Palms* (1939), and by elaborating the parallel-stories model employed by Faulkner in this novel into a far more complex cycle of rotating narratives that dramatizes the interactions of a vast, intricate society. This movement reaches its maximum degree of complexity in Vargas Llosa's *Conversation in The Cathedral*. Between the late 1970s and the beginning of the twenty-first century, Vargas Llosa shrinks this model back to its original contrapuntal design, as was noted above, in works such as *Aunt Julia and the Scriptwriter* and *The Storyteller*. These novels, like *The Real Life of*

Alejandro Mayta, are marred by the intrusion of an affable, self-confident, even complacent, first-person narrator, who commands one of the two principal narrative streams and who shares the name, fame, biography, and family relations of Vargas Llosa himself.

It is this model – that of Vargas Llosa the globalized personality and suave entertainer rather than the 1960s Vargas Llosa of demonically ingenious narrative innovations – that Ramírez assumes in *A Thousand Deaths Plus One*. Each of the two parts of this novel opens with a pastiche of a text by an early-twentieth-century writer, the first by Rubén Darío, the second by the Colombian writer José María Vargas Vila; the remaining chapters alternate between two erudite first-person narrators whose voices are subtly differentiated: the globetrotting late-nineteenth-century Nicaraguan photographer Castellón, and the equally globetrotting late-twentieth-century Nicaraguan political and literary personality Sergio Ramírez, who traces his compatriot's footsteps from Warsaw to Paris to Nicaragua to Mallorca. Each narrator is afflicted by the anxiety of coming from "un país que no existe" (*MUM*, 57; "a country that does not exist" [*TDPO*, 43]): Castellón because his ancestry is divided between Nicaragua's mutually uncommunicative Pacific and Atlantic Coasts, and because his conception in 1855 coincides with William Walker's subjugation of the Nicaraguan nation; and Ramírez because he is wandering the world bereft of the vice-presidential privileges that he describes in his first narrated chapter, recounting his state visit to Poland, privileges whose disappearance mirrors the fate of his country, which has been erased from the front pages of the world's newspapers. The debt to Vargas Llosa's narrative voice, contrapuntal structure, and linking of nineteenth-century high-art European themes to Latin America is made explicit in *A Thousand Deaths Plus One* when the Peruvian novelist makes a cameo appearance as a guest in a French inn where Castellón's father dines

> en el comedor del hostal, apenas en la compañía de un criollo de Arequipa, meticuloso y taciturno, que comía sin desatender sus libros y cuadernos de apuntes, siempre ocupado en investigar los avatares de la vida de una anarquista cotérranea suya muerta años atrás y llamada a ser la abuela del pintor Gauguin ... (*MUM*, 124; in the hotel's dining room, hardly paying attention to the company of a native of Arequipa in Peru, meticulous and taciturn, who was eating without neglecting his books and collections of notes, tenaciously occupied in investigating the ups and downs in the life of a female anarchist from his country who had died some years before and was destined to be the grandmother of the painter Gauguin. [*TDPO*, 108])

Arequipa is Vargas Llosa's birthplace; the novel this character is researching is *El paraíso en la otra esquina* (2003; *The Way to Paradise*), which, like *A Thousand Deaths Plus One*, focuses on nineteenth-century European history and employs a contrapuntal structure (in this case to narrate the lives of the painter Paul Gauguin and his Peruvian grandmother, the socialist activist Flora Tristán).

Ramírez's assimilation of the nonchalantly self-absorbed first-person voice of Vargas Llosa's novels of the 1980s, and his paring-down of the more demanding contrapuntal structures of *Margarita, How Beautiful the Sea* and *Sombras nada más* into a simpler form, more reminiscent of *The Storyteller*, enhances the bloated self-image of which Arias is critical. This narrative voice is particularly unsettling in the first chapter, which follows the opening pastiche of an article by Rubén Darío, where Ramírez recalls with fondness his 1987 state visit to the Polish dictator General Wojciech Jaruzelski, replete with FSLN insider gossip, such as the fact that, "por eso de los anteojos oscuros, quienes gobernábamos solíamos llamarlo, en la intimidad de nuestras bromas, 'José Feliciano,' nombre del cantante ciego puertorriqueño entonces de moda" (*MUM*, 28; "because of his dark glasses, in Nicaragua those of us in the government used to refer to him, in the privacy of our jokes, as 'José Feliciano,' the name of the blind Puerto Rican singer who was all the rage then" [*TDPO*, 28]). The narrator recalls the Warsaw palace where he was lodged during this visit, as he does Jaruzelski's "afabilidad, atento como estuvo en aquella entrevista a mis historias de la lejana Nicaragua en guerra ..." (*MUM*, 28; "his affability, interested as he was during that interview in listening to my stories of the far-off Nicaragua at war ..." [*TDPO*, 24]). The past is recalled with warmth as a time when even a government leader in the corner of Europe farthest from the Americas is obliged to be "attentive" to Nicaragua's problems.

Chapter Two, "A Country That Does Not Exist," establishes the contrapuntal contrast between the revolutionary years and both the nineteenth century and the post-1990 era when, in the eyes of the world, Nicaragua vanishes. Among other reasons, Ramírez evokes his own past image as a statesman as a means of resuscitating a time when the word "Nicaragua" prompted recognition and attention. Paradoxically, in the case of a former national leader, this post-1990 indulgence of the self is complementary to, rather in contradiction with, the effort to perpetuate the nation that has disappeared with the fall of the Sandinista government. Against the grain of the 1980s Nicaraguan ethos of building the nation through self-sacrifice, after 1990 the self becomes the only route back to the nation, via the identity established by one's contribution to the Revolution, even as this inflation of the narrator's past image arises in response to an anguished awareness of the nation's disappearance. Arias, in an article published two years after his book, is at pains to emphasize that his criticism of the narrative voice is not a personal attack on Ramírez:

> Entendemos, desde luego, que esta no es una crítica al individuo llamado "Sergio Ramírez" quien se encuentra fuera del texto y lo precede … sino más bien a los mecanismos que delimitan las condiciones de posibilidad de cierto tipo de textos por encima de otros, o bien a los mecanismos editoriales que hacen que circulen ciertos modelos escriturales por encima de otros en espacios transnacionales. (Arias 2009: 137–8; We must understand, of course, that this is not a criticism of an individual named "Sergio Ramírez" who is outside the text and precedes it … but rather of the mechanisms that delimit the possibilities of certain types of texts over others, or, that is, of the publishing mechanisms that make certain models of writing circulate in transnational spaces in preference to others.)

Drawing on Roland Barthes's concept of "the death of the author" in *S/Z*, Arias argues that under the regime of globalization, "la función autoral queda limitado a designar un producto de consumo masivo, intercambiable con cualquier otro y como cualquier otro" (ibid.: 138; "the authorial function is restricted to that of designating a mass consumer product, interchangeable with and indistinguishable from any other"). As authorship is a form of branding, the presence of the author within the narrative enhances the book's marketability. Yet, according to *El viejo arte de mentir*, Barthes's pre-globalization European theory does not fit contemporary Latin American reality. Ramírez would contend that he inserts himself into the narrative to heighten its realism, augmenting the persuasiveness of his storytelling by leading the reader from known names to others of his invention as a way of imbuing his fiction with reality and so making it more persuasive. As he said in a 2006 interview: "I am a fictitious person who is real at the same time, because I go in with my own name and my own story, and that's how I prefer to include myself" (Cabrera 2006: 13).

At the same time, Ramírez recoups his depleted authority in *A Thousand Deaths Plus One* by completing his approach to Rubén Darío. Where Moro concludes that, in *Oficios compartidos* and *Margarita, How Beautiful the Sea*, Ramírez defines himself as Darío's successor, the opening sequence of *A Thousand Deaths Plus One* takes the final step and impersonates a text by Darío, providing a flawless imitation of the *modernista*'s decadent style that introduces the aristocratic Mallorca setting where Ramírez will later pursue the ghost of the photographer Castellón, whose existence he discovers after stumbling upon an exhibition of his works in Warsaw: a plot device that reproduces the opening of Vargas Llosa's *The Storyteller*, where a character named Mario Vargas Llosa wanders into an exhibition of Amazonian photographs in a gallery in Florence and glimpses an old friend's face in one of pictures. Though the opening section bears the explicit declaration "por Rubén Darío" (*MUM*, 15; "by Rubén Darío" [*TDPO*, 13]), the *modernista* prose that follows is that of Ramírez. He addresses this forgery in his interview with Enriqueta Cabrera in which he notes that the Mexican novelist Héctor Aguilar Camín advised him that he should have included a warning that "everything in the book is a product of the imagination ... Someone might think that I'm adding a ready-made piece to a work of fiction to get more mileage out of the story" (Cabrera 2006: 13).

The "mileage" that this novel offers stems from both political and artistic sources of authority. Ramírez claims to have gained access to the Vargas Vila excerpt that opens the novel's second part as a result of his service as secretary of the Betancur Commission on Iberoamerican Identity, convened in Madrid in 1992 under the chairmanship of former Colombian President Belisario Betancur (whose name the novel misspells). Betancur is presented as a friend of Ramírez from his days in power: "Cuando la guerra estaba encendida en Centroamérica, me tocó hacer constantes visitas confidenciales a Bogotá para conversar con don Belisario sobre la compleja urdimbre del proceso de paz" (*MUM*, 149; "While the war was going on in Central America, it had fallen to me to make numerous confidential visits to Bogotá to talk with Don Belisario about the complex schemes for the peace process" [*TDPO*, 130]). Betancur sends Ramírez a photocopy of an essay in which Vargas Vila describes Darío's drunkenness in Mallorca and how Castellón came to photograph the great poet wearing a monk's hood. Here, as in the opening sketch, Darío, Ramírez, and the fictitious Castellón are tied up in a knot of mutual interconnection that attempts to forge a system of diachronic reference capable of supplanting the defeated construct of the Sandinista nation.

Culture, in *A Thousand Deaths Plus One*, replaces nationality as a transnational texture capable of calibrating time and lending meaning to experience. The novel is larded with allusions to major figures of nineteenth-century European culture, such as Frederick Chopin (who, like Darío, was known as "the Swan"), George Sand, Gustave Flaubert, and Ivan Turgenev, whose destinies cross paths with that of Castellón. Like Ramírez, Castellón is closely affiliated with a regime that is overthrown: in this case the reactionary rule of Napoleon III, which brings him from Nicaragua to France at the age of fifteen as a reward for his father's having helped the emperor, at that time Prince Louis Napoleon, escape from prison in 1846. Castellón has barely arrived in Europe when Germany's victory in the Franco-Prussian War of 1870 destroys the Second Empire and replaces it with the Third Republic. Like Ramírez, this Nicaraguan finds himself identified with a vanished political formation and wandering the world as an itinerant artist. The triangular identification of Darío, Ramírez, and Castellón, like the triangle of male destinies depicted in *Sombras nada más*, becomes a way of asserting a continuity of experience across time and in defiance of historical change.

Yet the nineteenth-century chapters are replete with other triangles, these ones amorous. The most notable triangle is the well-known ménage-à-trois of the Russian novelist Ivan Turgenev, the soprano Pauline Viardot-García, and the singer's husband, Louis Viardot. Castellón's life, too, turns out to be defined by romantic triangles. Castellón's triangles are bisexual, or homosexual. When he comes to Mallorca, he begins a relationship with a handsome young Polish hussar who, like him, has been recruited into the service of the Archduke Luis Salvador in order to be the decadent nobleman's lover: "Si Wenceslao le atrajo [al Archiduque] por los rasgos clásicos de su belleza, tan helénica, en Castellón lo enamoraron más bien sus facciones salvajes 'príncipe de las selvas ignotas,' como lo llama en su diario" (*MUM*, 265–6; "If Wencelas attracted him with the classic features of his beauty, with Castellón instead it was his primitive characteristics he was enamored of – prince of jungles unknown, he calls him in his diary" [*TDPO*, 222]). The Polish hussar and Castellón later share a Mallorcan woman of Jewish descent, Catalina Segura, as a lover. It is unclear which of them fathers her child, Teresa Segura. As an adult, Teresa also becomes enmeshed in a romantic triangle, which clouds the identity of the father of her son, Rubén.

These tempestuous three-way relationships are echoed as postmodern pastiche in Ramírez's post-1990 travels in Europe in the company of both his wife, Gertrudis Guerrero, and his German translator and intimate friend of many years, Peter Schultze-Kraft, "otra vez con nosotros" (*MUM*, 213; "with us once again" [*TDPO*, 182]), as he notes when the three of them rent a house together in Mallorca. While Ramírez says of the triangle of Turgenev and the Viardots that since, "todos se llevaban bien ... me parece admirable" (*MUM*, 270; "everyone lived happily ever after ... How admirable" [*TDPO*, 227]), his own triangle is presented as sexually innocent.[19] This innocence underscores the condition of re-enacting, yet without the original vitality, the lives of the artistic models whose biographies and works the postmodern artist can only pay homage to as pastiche. The romantic triangle, as an alternative form of social organization, is characteristic of bohemian contexts and decadent societies; it is not compatible with nation building. The proliferation of triangular relationships in *A Thousand Deaths Plus One* arises in the aftermath of the collapse of nation-building projects: not only Sandinista Nicaragua and the French Second Empire, but also the Liberal attempt to unify Nicaragua in the nineteenth century by way of a trans-isthmian canal tying together the country's Pacific and Atlantic Coasts, a dream that was destroyed by Walker's invasion.

The prospect of extending the water course of the San Juan River and Lake Nicaragua into a passage from the Atlantic to the Pacific Ocean was the cause of great-power manipulation of Nicaragua in the nineteenth century (see chapter 2), yet it also represented the country's best hope to achieve national integration, prosperity, and international recognition. Castellón's uncle, the Miskito King Frederick, argues that, in a treacherous international environment, national unity must be consolidated prior to the canal's construction: "Era necesario un solo país, desde el Pacífico hasta el Caribe. Sólo un país así, fuerte y unido, sería respetado a la hora de la construcción del canal por Nicaragua" (*MUM*, 84–5; "A single country was necessary, from the Pacific to the Caribbean. Only a country like that, strong and united, would be respected at the time of constructing the canal through Nicaragua" [*TDPO*, 73]).

The debilitated nationhood characteristic of the post-1990 era of accelerated globalization raises the issue of integration with fresh urgency. As Ramírez has stated: "La fractura entre las dos costas es un asunto que sigue pendiente pero no sólo culturalmente, sino físicamente" (*UISR;* "The rupture between the two coasts is an issue that remains unresolved, but not only culturally, also physically"). Whether in the nineteenth century or the twenty-first, a geographically divided Nicaragua enters the global system condemned to weakness. When Castellón's father meets Prince Louis Napoleon in the Ham prison in 1846, the future emperor confuses Nicaragua with the isthmus of Panama, at that time part of Colombia. Indicating the possible future location of a canal in this area, Louis Napoleon tells Francisco Castellón: "¡Allí tiene a su país, llave del futuro de la humanidad!" (*MUM*, 132; "There is your country, the key to the future of humankind" [*TDPO*, 114]). This near-royal decree of obliviousness to his nation reiterates the themes of the first Castellón chapter, "A Country That Does Not Exist," in which historical figures such as Frederick Chatfield (see chapter 2) underline the ease with which a fragmented Nicaragua may be subjugated. By way of diagrams, Francisco demonstrates to Louis Napoleon the advantages of a canal through Nicaragua (though, in a geographically illogical flight of fancy, his proposed canal passes through León, strengthening the bastion of Liberalism). He finally wrings from the future emperor the promise that "El canal es suyo" (*MUM*, 134; "The canal is yours" [*TDPO*, 116]).

The photographer Castellón's birth is the fruit of a plot between his Liberal politician father[20] and his uncle, King Frederick of the Miskitos, to unify the country, in imitation of the European custom of kingdoms united by marriage alliances. The uncle imagines a day when the father will be president of Nicaragua: "Pues entonces firmaremos un tratado de incorporación de los dos territorios en uno solo, bajo tu mando ... Sólo entonces ofrecerás a los Estados Unidos los derechos territoriales al canal" (*MUM*, 88; "Then we will sign a treaty of incorporation of the two territories into a single one, under your command ... Only then you will offer to the United States the territorial rights to the canal" [*TDPO*, 76]). Offering to abdicate and abolish the position of Miskito king, Frederick proposes to seal the integration of Nicaragua's two halves through the marriage of his infant sister Catherine, once she comes of age, to Francisco Castellón. The photographer Castellón is born as the living embodiment of the hope of an integrated Nicaragua, and the potential creation of a bi-coastal bourgeoisie capable of guiding the country's destiny rather than merely acting as local proxies to foreign powers.

The divisions that Castellón's conception is intended to anneal are made evident when, at the age of sixteen, Catherine travels across the country to be married. All but two of her bodyguards are murdered, her serving ladies are kidnapped, and, of her original train of six wagons, only two arrive in León. The geographical and cultural separation of the two coasts is underlined by the fact that Catherine's family appears to have been unaware of the civil war raging in the western half of the country when they dispatched her. She arrives in a León devastated by cholera and under the occupation of William Walker. The union of the two Nicaraguas occurs in an atmosphere of violence and mutual incomprehension. Rather than celebrating a wedding, Francisco Castellón, the male principle and stronger partner, as the populous west of Nicaragua dominates the sparsely inhabited east, forces himself on the Miskito princess in act that approximates a rape: "la penetró con una violencia de la que él mismo se asustó, mientras ella daba un grito, el aullido de una pequeña bestia herida de muerte" (*MUM*, 212; "he came into her with such a degree of violence that even he himself was shocked, and she let out a scream, the howl of a small beast being wounded unto death" [*TDPO*, 181]). She has lost her honour, a "prometida cambiada de pronto en concubina en una noche" (*MUM*, 241; "a fiancée suddenly become a concubine for the night" [*TDPO*, 202]).[21] Francisco writes in his diary that he has lowered himself, in evident contradiction of his Liberal self-image as a man of culture, though, as his son notes, "sigo sin saber a qué se había rebajado, si al acto de estupro, o a buscar amores delictivos con una niña zamba de tan pobres atractivos físicos" (*MUM*, 242; "I still do not know what he thought he had lowered himself to, whether it was the act of rape or else the attempt at an illicit love relationship with a *zambo* girl whose physical attractions were poor indeed" [*TDPO*, 203]).

The novel links the nation-building impulse, epitomized in debased form by the events that lead to Castellón's conception, to nineteenth-century Liberalism. When King Frederick broaches the possibility that Francisco may have racial objections to marrying a *zamba*, Francisco responds with a Liberal credo: "He sido educado en ideas de igualdad y libertad" (*MUM*, 86; "I have grown up on ideas of equality and liberty" [*TDPO*, 74]). The Miskito king's declarations concerning the need to consolidate the nation prior to entering the international arena anticipates the ideology that would be put into practice forty years later by the positivist strongman Zelaya. When Francisco Castellón dies in the cholera epidemic that accompanies the civil war, his death, that of the country and of outward-looking Liberalism (suppressed by the onset of thirty years of Conservative rule) – here cast as a creed that might have permitted Nicaragua to engage with the nineteenth-century form of globalization on more favourable terms – combine into a single death. The promise of a national bourgeoisie is dashed; with the death of the Miskito king, the two halves of Castellón's family, and of the country, lose touch with each other.

Yet, at the same time that Castellón incarnates Nicaragua's failure to cohere as a nation, his heritage illustrates the post-2000 extension of the concept of *mestizaje* in Ramírez's work to embrace a triple, rather than a double, heritage. Just as his Monterrey lectures defined a mestizo as someone of mixed indigenous, European, and African ancestry, Castellón becomes Ramírez's first protagonist of partly African descent. His mother, Catherine, is lighter skinned than many of her Atlantic Coast compatriots, but, as her older brother, the Miskito king, explains: "Yo soy un zambo, descendiente de indios caribes y de esclavos negros, los negros que no se ahogaron cuando naufragó el barco en el que los transportaban como una partida de ganado" (*MUM*, 86; "I am a *zambo*, a descendent of Carib Indians and black slaves, the slaves who didn't drown when the ship wrecked that was transporting them like a herd of cattle" [*TDPO*, 74]). This extension of the mantle of *mestizaje* serves as a tactic for enfolding within the nation those who, through the assertion of particularistic identities, threaten to leave it. It is a tendency in Ramírez's work that, as will be discussed in chapter 12, becomes even more pronounced following the FSLN's re-election in 2006.

A Thousand Deaths Plus One is a novel about the power of writing to create history, identity, and nationhood. Yet it is also about writing's loss of authority in the new millennium, which coincides with and contributes to the fissuring of national identity. Each of the novel's Nicaraguan artists employs a form ill-suited to his time: Castellón, surrounded by great writers, is a photographer, while Ramírez, who inhabits an age that is defined by the transmission of images, is a writer. Their marginalization is also that of their country since Nicaragua is a nation ushered into existence through the written word, with the literary imagination supplanting a dysfunctional state, then creating the myths and models for the only institutionalized state the nation had known. The theme of photography threatens to erode the integrated historical-literary essence generated by revolutionary Sandinismo. The many full-page photographs that are interspersed with the text of the most widely available edition of *A Thousand Deaths Plus One* heighten this sense that, in spite of the richness of the novel's prose, and its elaboration of intertextual parallels with Darío, Vargas Vila, Vargas Llosa, Cortázar, Flaubert, Turgenev, and other writers, language is being dismissed as a deficient medium for the expression of history. There are photographs of historical figures such as Rubén Darío and William Walker, as well as of characters and events that are clearly fictitious. In this sense, the photograph, in *A Thousand Deaths Plus One*, does not merely document; it also assumes language's ability to invent and create.

This trait of the novel is itself a product of globalization. The inclusion of photographs did not form part of Ramírez's design for *A Thousand Deaths Plus One*, but was mandated from Madrid by the novel's European publisher (the Latin American edition, published in Mexico City, does not have photographs). As Ramírez recounts:

> La editora de Alfaguara, que está en España, se entusiasmó con la idea de que llevara fotografías … Una vez que estaba en México, me pasé un sábado entero en el mercado de La Lagunilla, viendo fotos antiguas … Para mí fue una experiencia muy singular: hacer una especie de "casting" de mis personajes. Enfocaba quién más parecía a la persona que yo había imaginado … Ya no es una cosa que está a mi cargo. (*UISR*; The Alfaguara publishing company, which is in Spain, got excited about the idea that the book should have photographs … One time when I was in Mexico City, I spent a whole Saturday at the La Lagunilla market

looking at old photographs … It was a very unusual experience for me: to do a kind of casting of my characters. I concentrated on who most resembled the character I had imagined … But it's no longer something that's within my control.)

The presence of the photographs adds an extra layer of problematization to the novel's Madrid edition, questioning the authority of literature and the written word. In the absence of the authority of literature, the construction of Nicaraguan nationhood evaporates. These anxieties are played out through the self-referentiality of the two principle narrative streams. The novel's postmodern qualities are accentuated as it approaches its conclusion. Castellón's narrative of his exile in Paris in the circle of Louis Napoleon during the weeks prior to the Franco-Prussian War smuggles into the text an anachronistic allusion to Julio Cortázar, the modern archetype of the Latin American exile in Paris. At the parties Castellón attends, "no faltaba un melancólico escritor emigrado de la República Argentina, de cejas encontradas y tan alto que no parecía dejar nunca de crecer" (*MUM*, 297; [the parties] "were never missed by one gloomy writer from the Argentine Republic, with eyebrows that met each other, and so tall that he never seemed to stop growing" [*TDPO*, 246]). This reference to features of Cortázar's physical appearance is matched by a literary allusion. Though Castellón's erudite relation appears for most of the novel to be a simple nineteenth-century document, he is aware from the outset that "alguien me anda buscando …" (*MUM*, 57; "there is someone who is on my trail …" [*TDPO*, 49]).

As Ramírez closes in on the story of Castellón in the present-day chapters, this nineteenth-century narrator addresses him directly, writing: "Aquel que me anda buscando habrá podido iluminar hasta ahora algunos meandros del mapa ciego que debe parecerle mi vida, y tal vez llegue a saber sobre mí lo suficiente como para satisfacer los ardores de su curiosidad" (*MUM*, 300; "That fellow who keeps searching for me will have probably been able to throw light on some of the meanders around the bizarre map that my life must appear to him, and perhaps he may manage to find out enough about me to satisfy the most burning needs of his curiosity" [*TDPO*, 250]). He goes on to state that his "perseguidor" (*MUM*, 301; "pursuer" [*TDPO*, 250]) may wonder why he has devoted energy to a country he left at the age of fifteen, rather than concentrate on his adult life in Europe. The word "perseguidor" or "pursuer" alludes to Cortázar's novella of the same title, originally published in *Las armas secretas* (1959; Secret Weapons), in which a jazz musician chases the ultimately ungraspable sources of his inspiration. Having defined (implicitly, political) ambition as "una enfermedad de la conciencia" (*MUM*, 300; "a sickness of one's conscious self" [*TDPO*, 250]), Castellón launches a criticism of Ramírez by boasting that "yo no jugué jamás a las cartas frente a un croupier tramposo, apostando al poder en un país más digno de misericordia que de ilusiones, como Nicaragua" (*MUM*, 301; "neither did I ever play my cards against a crooked croupier with the stakes being power in a country such as Nicaragua, that is more worthy of compassion than of dreams" [*TDPO*, 251]).

As Ramírez assesses the life of his subject, the subject delivers a metatextual reprimand to his creator's career. Castellón's implicit claim of having remained devoted to his art alone, in contrast to Ramírez, who has squandered his time on Nicaraguan politics, like the photographer's father and uncle, raises the issue of the artist's ability to shape his creations and the way in which people appear in his work. On his arrival in Mallorca, Ramírez reveals in an interview with the local newspaper that he is writing a novel set on the island. From this point on, his interview subjects respond to his questions by asking whether they will appear as characters. They even collude to complicate his route to Castellón's grandson Rubén, who claims to be the author of the chapters apparently narrated by Castellón, and who provides Ramírez with the final ambiguous pieces of the puzzle. As Rubén tells him when he complains about the other Mallorcans' obfuscations: "Quizás lo único que ellos querían era hacer tu búsqueda más interesante … fíjate qué cutre si te mandan directo aquí, y ya. No le convendría a tu novela" (*MUM*, 332; "Maybe the only thing they wanted was to make your search more interesting … Think how mean it would have been to send you directly here and that's it. It wouldn't have been good for your novel" [*TDPO*, 278]).

Rubén Segura emerges at the novel's conclusion to embody the debasement and dispersion of the literary-political tradition that, both in Castellón's parents' generation and in that of Ramírez, strove to imagine and integrate the Nicaraguan nation. Bearing the name of Rubén Darío, whose writing first created a credible certitude of Nicaraguanness in the international sphere, he denies this heritage. The novel's chronology opens and closes in Mallorca, moving from a great poet's night of drunkenness to the repudiation of high culture and Nicaraguan heritage on the part of a debased figure who shares Darío's name. Rubén is the inheritor not only of Nicaragua's travails but also, through the murder of his Jewish mother, of the Holocaust, the defining cataclysm of twentieth-century history. The photographs of the Warsaw ghetto and the Mathausen concentration camp, where, prior to his death from pneumonia in March 1944, the octogenarian Castellón was permitted by the Gestapo to take his final photographs – those upon which

Ramírez stumbles during his Warsaw state visit – represent the photographer's transit from national to international history. Rubén, the product of two consecutive generations of women who conceived their children in triangles that rendered paternity ambiguous, elects to deny any blood relationship with Castellón or Nicaragua, claiming that he is a Habsburg, the illegitimate grandchild of the Mallorcan Archduke Luis Salvador: "¿No me encuentras parecido al Archiduque?" (*MUM*, 328; "Don't you think I look like the Archduke somewhat?" [*TDPO*, 275]). In a shop in the Jewish neighbourhood of Palma, Mallorca, that he inherited from his maternal ancestors, Rubén sells New Age paraphernalia and runs a minor cult; he wears extravagant robes and paints his toenails. His hermaphroditism, like his devotion to pseudo-science that refutes both empiricist rationalism and humanist literary-historical engagement, embodies a form of paralysis: he is destined not to extend his line, in either a biological or an artistic sense.

Rubén's New Age allegiances, like Testimonio in *Sombras nada más*, unravel the patriarchal lineage of the novelist as arbiter of history and high art. In spite of this apparently antagonistic stance towards literary-historical culture, Rubén's desk is piled with the books that are sources for *A Thousand Deaths Plus One*, including titles invented by Ramírez, such as the nonexistent volumes in which the forged essays by Darío and Vargas Vila are purported to appear. Though he enters the novel as the arid endpoint of the Nicaraguan literary-historical enterprise, mired in the decadence and destruction of European history, and in cult-like mysticism, Rubén, against all odds, presents himself as a writer, claiming that his composition of the Castellón chapters has coincided with Ramírez's writing of the rest of the novel. His identity as a sort of spectral brother to Ramírez, a distorted reflection of his own image that the author longs to reject, is confirmed when the two men establish that Rubén, like Ramírez's late younger brother Rogelio, is a diabetic.

The most salient contradiction is that Rubén, though estranged from the Spanish American literary tradition, claims to be the author of a Latin American novel of his possible grandfather's origins in nineteenth-century Nicaragua. The consolation implicit in his achievement is that literature and the nation may outlast globalization, albeit by adopting fresh guises, in the manner suggested by Arias in his commentary on *A Thousand Deaths Plus One*: "Es una nueva manera de vivir imaginariamente la nación desde un espacio afectivo libre de patriotismo y nacionalidad, un no-espacio ubicuo donde el escritor postnacional reterritorializa su presente sin nativismos, pero con tropos territoriales de una comunidad fantasma cuya sustancia es la memoria y cuya materia es la riqueza del lenguaje" (Arias 2009: 14; "It is a new way of imaginarily living the nation from an affective space free of patriotism and nationality, a ubiquitous non-space where the post-national writer reterritorializes his present without localisms, but with the territorialized tropes of a ghost-community whose substance is memory and whose material is the richness of language").

The pre-condition for the literary aesthetic that Arias describes is the eradication of the nation as a source of hope. *A Thousand Deaths Plus One* concludes with two of Castellón's memories – one of Rubén Darío in Mallorca and the other of the death camps – followed by a vision. In the death-camp scene the photographer claims to have written the nineteenth-century chapters himself on the backs of sheets of photographic paper and to have arranged with a German soldier "que ... se las entregue a Rubén" (*MUM*, 349; [to] "hand them to Rubén" [*TDPO*, 293) after his death. This explanation appears to confirm Rubén's decadence and the extinction of a history of writing at the same time that it drafts the photographer into the community of writers.

The tension between national and international events reaches a climax in the dying Castellón's concluding vision, in which he imagines returning to León and finding not the bustling port he had hoped to engender by routing the trans-isthmian canal through the city, but a León of the end of the twentieth century that is about to be devastated by Hurricane Mitch (in 1998). This apocalyptic destruction of León by wind and water recalls the volcanic eruption at the conclusion of *Castigo Divino* that covers the city with dust. The earlier catastrophe signals the definitive marginalization of the national bourgeoisie at the onset of dictatorship; the hurricane heralds Castellón's rebirth, attended by the ghosts of his mother and stepfather, mingling this prognostication of disaster with residual memories from the Holocaust scenes. This hurricane symbolizes the definitive destruction of the nation and its relegation to the status of a memory. Images of pigs, which recur throughout the novel, return to symbolize the terminal elimination of national identity as a fertile, viable category. The final page of the novel contains a photograph of a pig approaching the corpse of a naked child. Where *Castigo Divino*'s closing pages condemns a given social class, the end of *A Thousand Deaths Plus One* submerges the Nicaraguan nation in its entirety beneath a "nueva avalancha de piedras, lodo, troncos descuajados que me arrastra a la oscuridad" (*MUM*, 351; "a new avalanche of rocks, mud, and broken tree trunks dragging me into the darkness" [*TDPO*, 295]). The parallels with the wind that closes *Sombras nada más*, and the intertextual references to the conclusion of García Márquez's *One Hundred Years of Solitude*, in which the apocalypse, embodied by a great wind, is announced by the birth of a child with a pig's tail, serve as benchmarks to indicate that the nation as constructed by the intermingling of history and literature will have no viable form in the twenty-first century.

THE LIMITATIONS OF LIBERALISM: *SEÑOR DE LOS TRISTES* AND *EL REINO ANIMAL*

A century that begins with the flattening of the nation by Hurricane Mitch struggles to exert claims of national duty or the call of a distinctive chronology. If, as noted at this chapter's outset, the Sandinista community of duty and self-sacrifice began to unravel when FSLN spokesmen such as Ramírez adopted the position that elections were necessary to justify continued rule (and, by implication, continued Nicaraguanness), by the middle of the first decade of the new millennium this atomistic liberal ideology had become the hegemonic force that shaped the attenuated nation-space that surrounded the post-national author.

After *A Thousand Deaths Plus One*, Ramírez published a substantial collection of his literary essays, prefaces, and introductions under the title *Señor de los tristes: sobre escritores y escritura* (2006; The Knight of the Sad Countenance: On Writers and Writing). Though broad in its reach, this is not one of Ramírez's more compelling essay collections. It attests above all to the large number of talks Ramírez had to produce during his years on the lecture circuit paying off the debts from his 1996 presidential bid; the collection suffers from the taste of recycling. The book is divided into two sections, "Oficios compartidos: Literatura y política" ("Shared Trades: Literature and Politics") and "Los verdaderos vicios se adquieren temprano: sobre escritores y escritura" ("True Vices Are Acquired Early: On Writers and Writing"). The best material in the first section is reprinted from *El viejo arte de mentir* and, to a lesser extent, *Oficios compartidos*. The second section, hobbled by Ramírez's obligation to praise the works he is discussing – most of these pieces started life as introductions – holds his critical intelligence in check.

The collection is softened by affable affirmations, chummy recollections of fellow writers, and vague liberal declarations of the importance of the freedom of speech. Only in a few of the introductions does Ramírez appear to be fully intellectually engaged. Two of the strongest essays present new editions of Graham Greene's *The Power and the Glory* (1940) and Miguel Ángel Asturias's *Mulata de tal* (1963; *Mulatta*). These novels raise issues with which his engagement is undiminished: the intervention of the Catholic Church in politics and the contradictions between sin and faith, and the sometimes murky lines separating indigenous, mulatto, and mestizo identities in Central America. The former themes look back at the struggles of the 1980s (Ramírez mentions John Paul II's canonization of the religious fanatic who assassinated Mexican President Álvaro Obregón in 1928), while the latter ones gaze forward to the issue of national unity in racially segmented societies, insisting that the Guatemala that appears in Asturias's novel is "arcaica en su globalidad, y eso incluye lo ladino" (*SLT*, 207; "archaic in its totality, and that includes the ladino elements"). Indigenous and non-indigenous Guatemalans are locked together in a single national condition. Even as the nation fades, it holds diverse cultures together.

Ramírez's final book of the period that culminated in the re-election of the FSLN in November 2006 balances the liberal value of empathy with the shattering of the nation. *El reino animal* (2006; The Animal Kingdom) fictionalizes incidents Ramírez collected from newspapers; the anecdotes revolve around either an animal or an individual who is given a nickname that associates him with a bird or animal. This practice has resonance in Central America owing to the indigenous belief that each individual has a *nahual*, or an animal who serves as a double, an alternate identity. The events that befall characters who have animal nicknames also befall their animal selves. This is particularly evident in a story such as "Miss Junie persigue a Miss Junie" ("Miss Junie Pursues Miss Junie"), in which a US biologist working to preserve tortoises on Nicaragua's Atlantic Coast places a tracking device on a tortoise that she names after herself. The narrative voice promotes the interpenetration of the identities of scientist and subject: "por las propias manos de Miss Junie, la bióloga marina, Miss Junie, la tortuga, fue llevada de regreso a la playa" (*RA*, 207; "Miss Junie, the marine biologist, carried Miss Junie, the tortoise, back to the beach with her own hands"). The animal and the individual merge. Ramírez's intention, as explained to Enriqueta Cabrera, is that the stories "be read as a great parable that has to do with our discomfort with the 'other,' with the person who is not like us ... What we don't understand, we push away. And it seems to me that the animal kingdom can be a parable" (Cabrera 2006: 12).

Indigenous belief systems, one of the resurgent particularistic identities of the post-1990 period that filled the gap left by the collapse of the nation, bolster the liberal project. As in *A Thousand Deaths Plus One*, this book contains photographs, suggesting a weakening of the autonomy of the written word in which the nation was inscribed. Each of the book's nineteen sections opens with the name and photograph of an animal or insect (in Spanish, insects also belong to "the animal kingdom"), and an encyclopedia-like definition of its size, shape, colouring, diet, and customs. Other photographs, interspersed with the text of the stories, depict their action or settings. "Sic transit gloria mundi," in which the narrator claims to be writing at Ramírez's request, contains a photograph of the author standing with a daguerreotype of one of the narrator's ancestors, Hungarian immigrants whose attempt to settle in Nicaragua in the nineteenth century was brought to a savage conclusion by fever and alligators. The photograph, which evokes the themes of *A Thousand Deaths Plus One*, is a reminder that one aspect of globalization-era liberal individualism is the inflation of the self into a mediatized image. The collusion of images in the sapping of the authority of the literary text as an autonomous entity is pushed a step farther in *El reino animal*. In one instance, having included a web address in the text of the story, the narrator says: "El lector que se muestra escéptico al leer el desenlace de esta historia deberá visitar el mencionado sitio" (*RA*, 206; "The reader who remains skeptical after reading this story's denouement should visit the site mentioned above").

Though the adulteration of print fiction with photographs and Internet links does not predominate in *El reino animal*, the book's liberal ideology militates against its immersion in Nicaraguan materials. Most of the twenty-four stories are very short; some of them are recounted in parodies of bureaucratic diction that recall *De Tropeles y tropelías*. Since there is no longer a dictator to be satirized, or a unique national predicament to focus social criticism, as in the earlier book, this lampooning of official language contributes to the transnational assertion of the rights of the atomized liberal individual against forms of institutionalized authority. As many of the stories are adapted from newspapers, they are often set in foreign countries, particularly the United States. The postmodern salad of their forms nullifies the assumptions of what Jean-François Lyotard terms "grand narratives," most notably nationalism. Paradoxically in an artistic realm defined by the indiscriminate mixing of forms, Ramírez maintains a clear distinction between the novel and the short story: "I've always thought that the short story and the novel are two totally different genres" (*RA*, 12). This limits the extent to which one can interpret his prognostications concerning the twenty-first-century novel in *El viejo arte de mentir* as pertaining, also, to the short story. However, these stories do not support the prediction that the novel will continue to address national subject matter.

The opening story, "La estrategia de la araña" ("The Spider's Strategy"), embodies the dynamics of globalization. Presenting itself as a retelling of a case analyzed in the *Journal of the United Medical Association*, the narrative traces, in mock-scientific diction, how a traveller returning from Indonesia inadvertently carries spiders' eggs from India to the toilets of a restaurant in

Jacksonville, Florida. The second, and longest, story, "Por qué cantan los pájaros" ("Why the Birds Sing"), takes place nowhere at all. Three young women, all of whom are foreign students and each of whom comes from a different country, promise upon graduating from an academy run by nuns to meet in a restaurant at regular intervals throughout their lives to recount to one another their adventures with men and marriage. Counterpointing images of singing birds who are unaware of their own mortality with the human consciousness of the passage of time, the story is an effective parable; no indication is given of where the action is set, or where any of the women come from. This at once heightens the story's universality and strips it of the pungent details that characterize Ramírez's best work. The prominence lent female perceptions of relationships between women and men coincides with the expression of other themes consistent with an ideology of liberal individualism.

A number of stories feature animals that act out twenty-first-century debates about the limits of individual autonomy. In "Terrible simetría" ("Terrible Symmetry"), a tiger and an alligator that have found freedom in a decaying Harlem apartment building carry out a suicide pact when they are threatened with captivity. "Tribulaciones de la señora Kuek" ("Tribulations of Mrs Kuek") recounts the frustrations of a German scientist whose efforts to breed Peruvian penguins are thwarted by her subjects' persistent assertions of their homosexuality. The narrator of "Treblinka," which is presented as a lecture given at a conference, equates the conditions in which chickens are raised in captivity to Nazi death camps. Here the animal rights agenda is overt: "Los animales no nos pertenecen, ni son inferiores ni están en este mundo para servirnos. Son seres vivos, como nosotros, que sufren y padecen cuando los torturamos, los explotamos o los matamos" (*RA*, 160; "Animals do not belong to us, nor are they inferior nor are they in this world to serve us. They are living beings like us, and they suffer and agonize when we torture them, exploit them or kill them"). In most of the other stories, the fusing of images of human and animal destiny creates an implicit confluence of fates and sympathies rather than a partisan polemic. The book asserts that, after the breakdown of the communal project of the nation, all who are subordinated to resurgent power structures, whether women, animals, the poor, or homosexuals, are equally deserving of empathy.

El reino animal makes clear that the origins of this position lie in the fissuring of national identity. It is the defection of the people from the national project that eliminates the nation as a category. In two key stories, this outlook is expressed in the fates of animals that are hacked to pieces by the masses. "Mañana de domingo" ("Sunday Morning"), the third story in the collection and the first to contain explicit Nicaraguan references, describes the beaching of a she-whale on a deserted stretch of Nicaragua's Pacific Coast. Figures who represent the authority of both national and international institutions, such as Richard, a delegate of an international maritime organization, Lucía, a reporter for a national television network, Dr Incer, a scientist, Dr Romero, an anthropologist, and Inspector Quijano of the national police, see in the beached whale an object of study, sympathy, fascination, and possible rescue, and a situation that demands an orderly response. The starved local inhabitants, by contrast, regard the whale as a source of food and arrive bearing "machetes, picas y hachas" (*RA*, 42; "machetes, lances and axes"). The police called in by Inspector Quijano are overwhelmed by the "marea humana" (*RA*, 50; "human tide") and flee the scene. The whale, still alive, is butchered by the masses, who, as in *Sombras nada más*, demolish the nation through their self-serving indifference. The point is stated by Dr Romero: "La ballena es como el país … Sólo quedan los despojos" (*RA*, 52; "The whale is like the nation … Only scraps remain"). As long as the poor, in their desperation, succumb to destructive behaviour – voting against the Sandinistas, supporting the neo-Somocistas Alemán and Bolaños, butchering the whale – the nation, with its attendant concepts of duty, responsibility, and self-sacrifice, is not viable.

A similar pessimism concerning the poor, this time inflected by the cultural difference of the Atlantic Coast, concludes "Miss Junie persigue a Miss Junie," in which the quest for the turtle reaches a similarly stymied conclusion when it emerges that a foul-mouthed born-again Christian Afro-Caribbean man has captured the creature, which his wife has made into soup: "Sorry, ma'am, she is in this world no more" (*RA*, 212). The well-meaning foreign scientist's desire to preserve Nicaraguanness – charted by both the country's distinctive fauna and the turtle's peregrinations across a digitalized national map – founders on the same obstacle as that of the national and international authorities in "Domingo de mañana": the masses, whose oppression and hunger have rendered them short-sighted and fickle. In "Miss Junie," the masses' disconnection from the national project – paradoxically promoted by a US citizen – is thwarted by the cultural differences of the Atlantic Coast.

The poor become the primary victims of the fissuring of national authority in which they are complicit. As the country is invaded by drug-dealing gangs and its imagination is bludgeoned by globalized popular culture, the poor bear the brunt of the ensuing hunger, violence, and cultural confusions. "Parque de las madres" ("Park of the Mothers") is a first-person monologue, imitative of Testimonio narratives of women whose children had died fighting Somoza or the Contras, in which a woman who sells candy floss in a park named in honour of what Lorraine Bayard de Volo terms the "traditional gender values that [FSLN] attention to mothers entailed" (Bayard de Volo 2001: 13) recounts the death of a homeless boy. Yet María Engracia Bracamonte is neither an authentic mother nor is the boy she watches over, Manuel de la Cruz, known in the park as "Gallinita de monte" ("little bush hen"), which is what Nicaraguans call a partridge, her son. Having come to Managua from Matagalpa alone in search of food, Gallinita de monte is shot by mistake in an adolescent gang war. The story is full of echoes of the Revolution: the wounded boy is taken to the Lenin Fonseca Hospital; the would-be mother's grief may be real, but, unlike that of the mothers of the revolutionary era, it is neither based on a biological relationship nor is it consecrated in social institutions. As María says of Gallinita de monte: "ya que sin familia alguna y no teniendo madre que se sepa, me constiuyo en madre adolorida como si yo verdaderamente lo hubiera parido" (*RA*, 104; "since he's without any kind of family, not having any known mother, I'm constituting myself as bereaved mother as if I'd really given birth to him"). In the wake of the dissolution of the revolutionary nation, even elemental emotions must be "constituted."

The capturing of the Nicaraguan imagination by foreign popular culture, by contrast, is made plain in "Shakira y la Mosca" ("Shakira and the Fly"), in which twelve-year-old Raymundo, obsessed with the glamorous Colombian singer, decides to walk from Estelí to Miami to meet her. Like "Gallinita de monte," this story is narrated from the point of view of the mother – this time a biological single mother – in a colloquial first-person monologue interspersed with excerpts from press clippings about the incident. Miraculously, everything turns out all right for Raymundo, who crosses international borders without mishap and has reached Mexico when he is apprehended and returned to Nicaragua better fed and better dressed than when he left, as a result of the clothes and food donated to him in the detention centre. The story establishes a clear distinction between the popular-culture enthusiasms of young people of earlier generations, which were ploughed back into the national culture in the way that Ramírez himself did, for example, by learning narrative tricks from Hollywood movies to write stories about Nicaragua, and Raymundo's conviction, instilled by the dynamics of globalization, that one may connect with culture only by abandoning the nation for Miami, the ultimate "non-space," to use Arias's terms, of commercialized Latin American expatriation. Though Raymundo draws a map of Colombia in his school notebook, with an arrow pointing towards Shakira's home city of Barranquilla, his allegiance to the singer is divorced from any consciousness of Latin American solidarity. The map could as easily be of an imaginary world. Raymundo's mother opens his notebook from history class and discovers, "bajo el título Gloriosa Batalla de San Jacinto y la pedrada de Andrés Castro, pegado con almidón un retrato de Shakira recortado de alguna revista" (*RA*, 144; "stuck to the page with starch beneath the title of 'Glorious Battle of San Jacinto and Andrés Castro's Boulder,' a portrait of Shakira cut out of some magazine"). Here the globalized image has literally blotted out, by being taped over the top of, Nicaraguan national history. Raymundo's act is diametrically opposed to that of Ramírez himself, who, at nearly the same age, wrote his first published article to celebrate the centenary of Andrés Castro's deed at San Jacinto (see chapter 4).

This lament for the nation illustrates the tension between Ramírez's advocacy of liberal individualism, which first entered his discourse during the run-up to the 1990 election, and his despair, albeit accompanied, as always, by a tinge of irony, at neo-liberal globalization's enforced evaporation of national chronology and culture. The poor, cast into even more appalling conditions than those in which they lived prior to 1979, are objects of sympathy when they are individuals, yet the authors of their own misfortune when they cohere into the untrustworthy masses who derailed the national project. The trajectory of Ramírez's writing from 1990 to 2006 describes a thinning arc whose roots lie in the rich soil of the Sandinista construction of the nation and whose endpoint fades away into self-absorption and disillusionment. This outlook would be dealt a blow by the re-election of the FSLN in November 2006, an event that would oblige Ramírez to find new ways of imagining the nation's diaphanous persistence in the hostile element of globalization against the backdrop of a chimerical revision of Sandinismo. Nor was Ramírez's engagement with the decade-and-a-half that followed the Sandinista defeat the only available pattern. As will be depicted in chapter 11, Ernesto Cardenal responded to the setback of 1990 with an immediate retreat into the self, then moved by stages towards a re-engagement with the world.

11

Cardenal: The Poet as Memoirist, the Nation as Relic (1990–2006)

"LIKE MALE AND FEMALE": "TELESCOPE IN THE DARK NIGHT" AND CARDENAL'S RESIGNATION FROM THE FSLN

No prominent Sandinista intellectual tied his personal identity, in both its private and public dimensions, to revolutionary forms of life as tightly as Ernesto Cardenal. Few suffered such a severe crisis as he in the aftermath of 25 February 1990. In the social transformations of the 1980s, Cardenal had found consolation for the deaths of his young protégés from Solentiname. In the renaming of places and institutions, in the new holidays, rituals, and forms of speech, and in the liberation theology worship of the people's churches and Christian Base Communities, he had encountered ways of integrating his private mourning into the structures of the nation. At the same time, his long-standing equation of celibacy with castration, dating back to the events of 1956 (see chapter 3), was salved and subdued by the active role he assumed as a minister in a militant revolutionary government. In light of Lancaster's analysis that in Nicaragua, "every posture, every stance, every way of acting in the world is immediately seen as 'masculine' or 'feminine,' depending on whether it connotes activity or passivity" (Lancaster 1992: 236–7), it is evident that one of the greatest gifts the Nicaraguan Revolution bestowed upon Cardenal – greater, in its way, than international media attention or an enlarged readership for his poetry – was a secure masculine identity. In spite of being a celibate, he was perceived, both nationally and internationally, as an active agent. Having apprenticed himself to a succession of powerful male mentors, he himself became a dominant male. The nation reflected his image, the microcosm of Solentiname having expanded, as he had dreamed in the early 1970s, to encompass all of Nicaragua.

Ernesto Cardenal reads his poetry at a rally in Masaya supporting Herty Lewites, Sandinista Renewal Movement candidate for president, 2005 (Courtesy of Chris Vail)

The 1990 election not only destroyed Cardenal's political ideals, it also demolished his sense of himself as a man. His writing of the post-1990 period addressed the task of reconstructing his personal identity. Once this had been shored up, he devoted himself to memorializing the history of the revolutionary nation; only after this process was complete, could his poetry venture in new directions. The shock administered to Cardenal's system of reference by the electoral defeat was all the greater because it had not occurred to him that Violeta Chamorro, the high-society widow of his cousin Pedro Joaquín Chamorro Cardenal, could defeat the Sandinistas. On election night he went to bed early, not bothering to stay up to see results that he regarded as a foregone conclusion. He slept through the overnight crisis of Sandinismo, and learned what had happened only the next morning. In a passage from his *Granta* article "Election Night in Nicaragua" that is omitted from the Spanish version, "Confesión de amor," Sergio Ramírez describes running into his neighbour at dawn on 26 February 1990: "An early riser, he had gone to bed the previous evening certain that we would win the elections. He could not believe what I told him. I had to assure him that it was true: it was all lost; there was nothing we could do. He sat down hard on the kerb, and when I left him he was still sitting there, with his head in his hands" (Ramírez 1991: 129). Cardenal himself describes the crisis he suffered:

> Esa madrugada tuve una "noche oscura," que fue la más oscura de mi vida, yo creo. Acostado en mi hamaca estaba sin poder entender la voluntad de Dios. ¿Cómo era posible que el pueblo se hubiera volteado contra nosotros, que hubieran rechazado la revolución? Sentía también que mi poesía se venía abajo. Por años me había dedicado a cantar la revolución; primero anunciándola, antes que aconteciera; después celebrando su triunfo en mi libro *Vuelos de victoria*. ¿En qué quedaba ahora toda esa poesía? El cielo para mí estaba cerrado. (*RP*, 654; That night I had a "dark night of the soul" that was the darkest of my life, I believe. Lying in my hammock, I was unable to understand God's will. How was it possible that the people had turned against us, that they had rejected the revolution? I felt also that my poetry had fallen to pieces. For years I had dedicated myself to singing the revolution: first announcing it before it had occurred; later celebrating its triumph in my book *Flights of Victory*. What did my poetry mean now? For me the heavens were closed.)

Cardenal felt better after listening to Daniel Ortega's speech on the morning of 26 February: "le doy crédito ... que nos levantó el ánimo, y nos hizo ver que la pérdida del gobierno no era la pérdida de la revolución" (*RP*, 654; "I give him credit ... he raised our spirits and made us see that the loss of government was not the loss of the revolution"). In spite of this, it is evident that, at both a personal and a political level, it took Cardenal many years to resolve the crisis triggered by the electoral defeat. Even his identity as a poet was thrown into doubt by the end of the Revolution that defined the nation in terms of poetry. As Margaret Randall explains: "Ernesto embodied the very essence of what it was to be a poet in a nation of poets ... the respect for poetry in Nicaragua ... preceded Cardenal by generations but during the years of Sandinista rule it was largely focused on his persona" (Randall 2009: 200). He continued making notes for new cantigas of *Cosmic Canticle*, a work he regarded as unfinished, and which he had published simply because José Coronel Urtecho "me aconsejó de que no siguiera escribiendo" (*UIEC*; "advised me not to keep writing"). Yet it was clear, to Cardenal's friends if not to the poet himself, that the notes he was taking on his "dark night of the soul" belonged to a fresh phase of his creative evolution: "Pensé que sería una cantiga más de *Cántico cósmico*. Algunas amistades, y especialmente Luce López-Baralt de Puerto Rico, me aconsejaron que no, que debería hacer una cosa aparte … Y por eso lo publiqué aparte" (*UIEC*; "I thought it would be one more cantiga of *Cosmic Canticle*. Some friends, and especially Luce López-Baralt from Puerto Rico, advised me that no, it should be a separate work … That's why I published it separately").

The title of *Telescopio en la noche oscura* (1993; "Telescope in the Dark Night") contains a reference to a scientific instrument, yet the book's clean, intimate verses are devoid of the intertextuality with scientific discourses that characterizes Cardenal's magnum opus. López-Baralt sees in the title's juxtaposition of "el instrumento moderno de exploración astral al antiguo término técnico de la noche de los sentidos, que prestigiaron primero los sufíes musulmanes y luego San Juan de la Cruz" (López-Baralt 2012: 76; "the modern instrument of astral exploration with the old technical term of a night of the senses, which was privileged first by Muslim Sufis and later by St. John of the Cross"), an updating of the age-old mystical symbol of the dark night of the soul. Cardenal's followers were enthusiastic about this book, one of his most approachable and audacious works, and the first in which he confessed the story of his conversion to religious life. On 11 October 1993 Robert Pring-Mill wrote to Sergio Ramírez that "Telescope in the Dark Night" was "even better than the final sections of *Cántico cósmico*" (*SRP*, box 49, folder 2a). Pring-Mill suggested launching a campaign – the first of several – to nominate Cardenal for the Nobel Prize for Literature. "Telescope in the Dark Night" falls far from the shadows of Ezra Pound; this mystical confession is a clear successor to the early Iberian traditions of Teresa of Ávila (1515–82) and St John of the Cross (1542–91). The echoes of St John's *Noche oscura del alma* (1579; *Dark Night of the Soul*) and *Cántico espiritual* (1582; *Spiritual Canticle*), in which the poet seeks ecstatic union with Jesus Christ, are clear.

The stated subject of "Telescope in the Dark Night" is the poet's love affair with God, a sacred experience that he narrates in secular terms; yet at a connotative level Cardenal's poem wrestles with the fraught question of the poet's gender identity, and with how to define himself in a realm beyond the Nicaraguan Revolution, and beyond history itself, in which he no longer enjoys the authority of an active male agent. Most of the autobiographical references are to Cardenal's life in the 1950s, rendering inadmissible allusions to the martyred youths of Solentiname. The God whom the poetic speaker adores, and who adores him, becomes a mirror before which the narrator must assume the role of a binary opposite. Definitions of the narrator's gender identity are channelled by a remorseless bipolarity that conceives of all matter in the universe as male or female, active or passive. In this respect, and in spite of his political clashes with these figures in the year after the poem's publication, Cardenal employs the same conceptual framework as Sandinista leaders such as Daniel Ortega and Tomás Borge, who responded to the loss of political power by reaffirming the machista heritage of the guerrilla struggle, alienating many of their social-democratic, bourgeois, Catholic, gay, or, particularly, female supporters. Nicaraguan women's definitions of gender became more multifaceted in the early 1990s. Lorraine Bayard de Volo, for example, argues that prior to 1990 the imperative of contributing to the war effort kept women locked into traditional roles, yet "once the Sandinistas lost the elections and the war was over, many Sandinista feminists were freed from the pressure they had previously felt to toe the party line … With greater autonomy to set their own agendas, they focused on issues of domestic violence, rape, incest, family planning, sexual orientation, and the feminization of poverty" (Bayard de Volo 2001: 241). Sandinista men, by contrast, exalted the guerrilla past as a time of male bravura, accentuating the traditional division between maleness and femaleness explored by Lancaster. This retrenchment of a reactionary masculinity became evident not only in the refusal to admit women to the National Directorate, but, at a mass level, in events such as the first anniversary of the Revolution after Zoilamérica Narváez Murillo's accusations of sexual harassment against Daniel Ortega: "when tens of thousands gathered to celebrate the July 19 anniversary of Somoza's overthrow, many of the young men in the crowd sported Daniel's image on T-shirts that read, 'Daniel, I am with you' (*Daniel, estoy con vos*)" (Kampwirth 2004: 73–4). Cardenal's heartfelt account of his love affair with God is both honed and limited by these gender constructions. While, as was argued in chapter 8, binary thought is also present in *Cosmic Canticle*, where it underlies yet contradicts the poem's multiplicity of discourses, in "Telescope in the Dark Night" the binary model becomes central to the poet's search to situate and define himself.

The opening stanza establishes this bipolarity by describing a couple who are preparing to go to bed: "Amado y amada. La amada/mira desde la alcoba la luna que asciende./Una motocicleta en la calle acelerándose./El amado sin prisa por ir a la cama" (*TNO*, 29; "Lover and beloved. The lover/gazes from her bedroom at the moon rising./A motorcycle accelerating in the street./The beloved in no hurry to come to bed" [*PL*, 222]). The opening phrase, "Amado y amada" (whose male-female gender binary is lost in English translation), sets the boundaries within which Cardenal pursues his quest for his identity through his scandalous love of deity. The second stanza introduces the poetic speaker: "Yo nací por un amor extremista" (*TNO*, 29; "I was born for an extremist love" [*PL*, 222]). Yet, if the poetic speaker is possessed by madness, his God is an inconstant lover: "te vas y volvés/

inconstante *gurrión*/y otra vez te vas" (*TNO*, 30; "You leave and come back,/inconstant *sparrowe*,/then once again you leave" [*PL*, 222]). Being fickle, he must be lured by the poetic speaker. This recalls the depiction of the believer's relationship with deity in *Abide in Love* where, as seen in chapter 5, "the soul becomes a little flirtatious, knowing that it is loved and conscious of its charms" (*VA*, 82). In "Telescope in the Dark Night," the poetic speaker's soul, which inspires God's passion, reflects the contours of his physical being: "¿cómo será la belleza que tú amas?/¿cómo serán mis ojos que tú ves?/¿la cara que te encanta?" (*TNO*, 32; "what must the beauty you love be like?/what must my eyes be like that you see?/the face that enchants you?" [*PL*, 223]). This love affair between the poetic speaker and God depends on the insistent gendering of each:

> Como macho y hembra. Pero
> *positivo* y *negativo* es una manera de hablar.
> Yo te amo como opuesto,
> y no es una manera de hablar
>
> El que todo en el universo es macho y hembra
> (aun lo homosexual lo es a su manera)
> el que todo es macho y hembra es para mí confirmación
> de que el celibato es matrimonio.
> (*TNO*, 32–3; Like male and female. But/*positive* and *negative* is a manner of speaking/I love you as opposite,/and it's not a manner of speaking/The fact that everything in the universe is male and female/(in homosexual relations too in their way)/the fact that everything is male and female, is for me confirmation/that celibacy is a marriage. [*PL*, 223])

In declaring celibacy to be a marriage, Cardenal recapitulates the Catholic tradition of depicting religious life as a betrothal to God. Yet, in lines such as "and it's not a manner of speaking," he invests this spiritual tradition with intimations of sensuality that a conventional theologian would find unsettling. The poetic speaker's contention that the entire universe is gendered as male or female poses the question, which the remainder of the poem answers by stages, as to which slot in this binary structure is occupied by the narrator and which by his celestial lover. The most striking feature of the language in which Cardenal explores this relationship is the absence of Exteriorist imbrication of discourses in contradiction with each other. In his search for a voice that is intimate, sensual, confessional, and as close to lyrical as Cardenal's colloquial diction permits, he erases dialectical conflict from his verse: the purging of scientific discourses is also the purging of Marxism. In the two decades prior to 1990, the idea of Ernesto Cardenal writing a book-length poem from which Marxism was absent would have been unthinkable; the crisis of personal identity, which banishes the nation, unveils polarities that are conceived in terms of male and female rather than oppressor and oppressed.

The central paradox of the poetic speaker's relationship with deity is that it is at once sensual and immaterial. The contours of their affair mimic physical lovemaking, yet physicality is absent. In one of the few references to a scene that is not from Cardenal's youth, he recalls a poetry reading:

> Le dijeron a Gioconda Belli en aquel bar
> que ella podría entrenarme en erotismo
> y dijo que me podría entrenar bastante
> Yo callé Hoy pensé
> que hay un erotismo sin los sentidos, para muy pocos,
> en el que soy experto.
> (*TNO*, 40; They said to Giaconda [*sic*] Belli in that bar/that she could train me in eroticism/and she said she could train me a great deal/I said nothing. Today I thought:/there's an eroticism free of the senses, for very few,/in which I'm an expert. [*PL*, 227])

The notion of an "eroticism free of the senses" lies at the core of "Telescope in the Dark Night." The fact that this pleasure is reserved for "very few" suggests a spiritual elitism that contains a residue of the social elitism of Cardenal's youth. His early experience of love in the aristocratic Conservative milieu of Granada, which he had struggled to evoke in *Carmen y otros poemas* and would later narrate in *Los años de Granada* (2004; The Years in Granada), becomes the primary point of comparison for assessing his rapturous affair with his creator. The allusion to Belli, known for her love affairs, suggests that "eroticism" is a female, rather than a male, art. In spite of Cardenal's suggestion that he is "expert" in an eroticism divorced from the body, an implicit parallel arises between his non-physical erotics and the physical variety for which Belli is known. This parallel reinforces the assumption that, in the poem's male-female binary, the poetic speaker identifies with the female socket. God is associated with the male principle when Cardenal writes, "Amado, los prados están en flor" (*TNO*, 38; "Beloved [*masculine form*], the meadows are in flower" [*PL*, 226]). Following the pattern sketched in the poem's opening line – "Amado y amada" – if God is the active, male principle, then the poetic speaker, no matter how attracted he may be by the chaste Catholic debutantes of Granada and Managua, must assume the passive, female role; otherwise, no amorous relationship is possible. This open identification with the role of passive correspondent and the object of love is developed by stages, reaching its denouement on the poem's penultimate page.

Cardenal insists on his love as a re-enactment of sexual intercourse that occurs in the spiritual realm: "Amor, el de los dos, sin sexo/pero que es como si fuera sexo" (*TNO*, 44; "Lover, between the two of us, with no sex/but which is as though it were sex" [*PL*, 228]). The outrageousness of the intimacies that the poetic speaker shares with the reader is sharpened by the unusually short lines and broadly spaced stanzas in which the poem is arranged, as though each scandalous admission were conveyed in a brief whispered burst. Like any true love, the course of Cardenal's affair with God does not run smooth; in an echo of his characterization in *Abide in Love*, of God as a tyrannical, demanding lover, he complains: "Ciertas veces te extralimitaste/en cuanto a mi libre albedrío" (*TNO*, 45; "Occasionally you overstepped the mark/with regard to my free will" [*PL*, 229]). What is striking about this statement is the employment, on the part of a writer whose conceptions of humanity have been rooted in duty – first traditionalist and Conservative, then radical and revolutionary – of a liberal vocabulary of freedom. This possible concession to the liberal post-1990 world, here applied to the couple, who are free to leave each other if they wish, elicits feelings of terror: "Libre albedrío en todas las galaxias/Terror del universo el libre albedrío./Poder perderte, amor mío, si yo quiero" (*TNO*, 47; "Free will throughout the galaxies/Terror of the universe free will./Capable of losing you, my love, should I so wish" [*PL*, 230]). Cast into a universe where obligation has dissolved – a less merchanistic universe than that of *Cosmic Canticle* – the poetic speaker finds the charm of his union with God augmented by the fact that neither party is obliged to participate in this relationship, whose result will be that "seré experto en amores/en tu cama, entre las sábanas/Sexo de Dios" (*TNO*, 48; "One day I'll be an expert lovemaker/in your bed, between the sheets./Sex of God" [*PL*, 230]).

In the latter half of the poem, the poetic speaker's quest for a loving union with deity acquires tangible form in allusions to the young women he courted in his youth, which build towards the climax – in every sense of the word – of his union with God while listening to the din of Ileana's wedding procession on Roosevelt Avenue on 2 June 1956. His submission to God is expressed in terms that suggest a physical encounter in which the poetic speaker plays the passive role: "lo que me hiciste aquel 2 de/junio" (*TNO*, 50; "what you did to me that 2nd of June" [*PL*, 231]). This phrase occurs twice within eight lines; the intensity of the inaugural tryst with God contrasts with the distance the poetic speaker feels between himself and his beloved at the time of writing. In an allusion to his epigrams, where, for the first time in Cardenal's verse, a cosmic metaphor is applied to the human condition in his characterization of his separation from Ileana (see chapter 3), he states that God is as far from him now – as intangible and as difficult to conjure up – as "Cuando Ileana estaba más lejos de mí en la calle/Candelaria/que la galaxia de Andromeda" (*TNO*, 50; "When Ileana on Candelaria Street was more distant from me/than the Andromeda Galaxy" [*PL*, 231]). This introduces the theme of the day of Cardenal's "conversion" to religious life – he was, of course, already a devout Catholic – that dominates the poem's final twenty pages.

These pages reprise themes that are common in religious writing: the struggle to sustain faith, the fear that God is distant or unreachable. This prompts speculation on the life that Cardenal gave up in order to devote himself to his celestial lover: that of a Conservative bachelor socialite, experiencing serial infatuations with teenage girls from wealthy families. When the young women of Granada are juxtaposed with the crazed loving God, the latter wins, in spite of the persistent fear that He may be absent; the nothingness of an absent deity is judged superior to the poetic speaker's former life: "Efímero era, superefímero/aquello que yo renuncié" (*TNO*, 53; "Ephemeral it was, super-ephemeral/that which I renounced" [*PL*, 232]). By yoking himself to God in this way, the poetic speaker imposes on himself the obligation of flaunting his charms in order to attract a force that may not exist: "Atrás quedaron los epigramas y las muchachas" (*TNO*, 56; "The epigrams and girls were left behind" [*PL*, 233]). The impact of his conversion resonates beyond the poetic speaker's faith and his gendering to his aesthetic practice. The restrained surface of "Telescope in the Dark Night" does not make this development explicit; only a reader familiar with Cardenal's literary trajectory will grasp the significance of his putting his epigrams behind him. The exploration of new poetic forms coincides with female gendering, as the poet flaunts his attractions to draw the attention of his errant "amado": "He aquí que tu amada está desnuda./¿Se pondrá la túnica otra vez?" (*TNO*, 61; "Behold your lover is naked./Will she put on her robe again?" [*PL*, 236]). Mimicking the monologue of a woman who has begun to undress for her lover, this line represents the first unequivocal association of the poetic speaker with female gendering. At the same time, as though to defuse this identification, the poem insists on the speaker's love affair with God as an event that occurs in an immaterial realm: "Mis deseos sexuales han sido y son/tan sólo analogías de mi amor a vos./Creo que te agradan mis deseos sexuales" (*TNO*, 63; "My sexual desires have been and are/merely analogies of my love for you./I believe my sexual desires please you" [*PL*, 237]). This analogy has the paradoxical effect of making less shocking the speaker's self-identification as an "amada" (feminine lover) by reminding the reader of his infatuations with young women at the same time that it relegates these women to mere metaphors of a much more consuming love. In the poem's daring climax, the moment of the poetic speaker's submission to God's love is described as a sexual encounter in which Cardenal assumes the role of a young girl, such as those whom he courted, in the moment in which she loses her virginity:

> Fue casi violación,
> pero consentida,
> no podía ser de otro modo,
> y aquella invasión del placer
> hasta casi morir,
> y decir ya no más
> que me matás
> Tanto placer que produce tanto dolor.
> Como una especie de penetración.
> (*TNO*, 68; It was almost rape,/but with consent,/how could it be otherwise,/and that invasion of pleasure/until almost dying,/and saying that's enough/you're killing me./So much pleasure that produces so much pain./Like a kind of penetration. [*PL*, 238–9])

This wedding night, which is "almost rape," is couched in colloquial Nicaraguan language that depicts God as possessed of the rough masculinity that many Sandinista men reclaimed after 1990. The lack of any alternative to these binary gender dynamics is asserted by the line, "how could it be otherwise." The poetic speaker's remonstrations as he is experiencing his "penetration" by God reproduce stereotypical characterizations of female utterances in these circumstances, such as might be recounted by men in a bar: "that's enough/you're killing me." The use of the *voseo* heightens both the local resonances and the borderline burlesque nature of this segment, which teeters between moving audacity and self-parody. The poem's final stanza shows where this "female" identification has led. In a reference to Thomas Merton's warning to Cardenal that the contemplative life is a moment of semi-ecstacy followed by "cuarenta años de aridez" (*TNO*, 67; "forty years of aridity" [*PL*, 238]), the concluding lines depict him in the narrative present in "árida oración" (*TNO*, 68; "arid prayer" [*PL*, 239]) in a New York City hotel room, praying to the God who gave him this moment of overwhelming pleasure in 1956, then disappeared in a cosmos of "nadas sobre nadas reflejando nadas" (*TNO*, 69; "nothings upon nothings reflecting nothings" [*PL*, 239]).

The image of nothingness with which "Telescope in the Dark Night" closes expresses a despair that borders on a nihilism uncharacteristic of Cardenal's verse. The universe that once pulsed with scientific phenomena, figures from indigenous creation stories, the crisscrossing discourses of faith, science and politics, and the undying hope of national liberation, resonates with an emptiness that hints that neither Sandinismo nor Christianity can provide the consolation that Cardenal seeks in the aftermath of the electoral defeat that dissolved the Nicaraguan nation. It is not surprising that a dozen years passed before he published another book of poetry.

The loss of the ability to project his Solentiname microcosm onto the contours of the nation saps Cardenal of the prerogative of masculine activity, condemning him to symbolic "femininity." For the first three years after the electoral defeat, the FSLN maintained the commemoration of the Solentiname attack of 13 October 1977 on the San Carlos barracks. One week after the commemoration was cancelled and candidates from Solentiname were excluded from Sandinista committees, on 24 October 1994, Cardenal resigned from the FSLN. He was the first major figure to leave. The discontinuation of the FSLN celebration of his martyrs released Cardenal from his moral obligation towards his protégés at the same time that it deprived him of masculine authority. His resignation speech, devoted in large part to Solentiname, deplores FSLN officials' refusal to maintain the celebration: "Una explicación que dio uno de ellos es que esa era 'una celebración de los muertos, y no hay por qué seguir recordándolos'" ("Es mi deber renunciar …," 11; "One of them gave the explanation that this was 'a celebration of the dead and there's no reason to keep remembering them'"). The official's statement dismisses the value of Cardenal's martyrs, who act as his political capital.[1] The words violate the very concept of martyr-worship, one of Sandinismo's central tenets; this custom has continued into the new millennium, even though the martyrs' pantheon has changed.[2] Cardenal closed his nationally broadcast radio address with an assertion of the enduring centrality of his vision to the nation: "Continuaré siendo sandinista, lo cual lo era desde mucho antes de entrar al partido, inspirado siempre por Sandino, cuya gesta yo canté desde joven. Cuya cultura realicé en silueta y se ve desde todo Managua en la loma donde estuvo el palacio del dictador" ("Es mi deber," 11; "I'll continue being a Sandinista, which I was long before entering the party, ever inspired by Sandino, whose heroic deed I sang even when I was young. Whose likeness I created in silhouette and which is visible from all over Managua on the summit where the dictator's palace stood"). In spite of this bold assertion that it is *his* depiction of Sandino that has supplanted the dictator's palace, Cardenal's departure from the FSLN confirmed his loss of masculine authority, necessitating a reconstruction of his identity in order to confront the era of globalization. Here Cardenal adopted the same strategy that he used in the early 1970s, when the changing world around him rendered obsolete his stance as a Conservative Catholic dissenter from a Liberal dictatorship: he turned to prose to elaborate a new identity.

SUBMISSION AND RECONSTRUCTION: *VIDA PERDIDA*

Cardenal's memoirs consist of three volumes, *Vida perdida* (1999; Lost Life), *Las ínsulas extrañas* (2002; The Strange Isles), and *La revolución perdida* (2004; The Lost Revolution), supplemented by a coda, *Los años de Granada* (2002; The Years in Granada), a sequel to the first volume that was published as the last two chapters of *Vida perdida* in later editions of that work. The entire sequence is more than fourteen hundred pages in length. Through the act of narrating his life, and the historical events he lived through, Cardenal employs the memoir form to reconstruct his masculinity.

By 1999, when *Vida perdida* appeared, Cardenal had faded from the front lines of Latin American cultural politics. Roberto Bolaño was surprised to find that "la voz de Ernesto Cardenal suena igual que en sus memorables poemas, pero todo ha cambiado, y lo que antes era esperanza ... ahora es más bien silencio y quietud, un silencio y una quietud que surgen de una provincia perdida en donde el poeta Cardenal aún vive y aún se mueve, pese a haber perdido tantas batallas" (Bolaño 2004: 168–9; "Ernesto Cardenal's voice sounds exactly as it does in his memorable poems, but everything has changed, and what before was hope ... is now rather silence and stillness, a silence and a stillness that emerge from a lost province where the poet Cardenal still lives and still moves, in spite of having lost so many battles").

In this first volume, which recounts his childhood and his years in New York, Kentucky, and Mexico, Cardenal is often directionless, passive, or, as in "Telescope in the Dark Night," affiliated with images of femininity; in the second volume, invigorated by the mentorship of Thomas Merton, he founds Solentiname and establishes a contemporary masculine identity as a figure of authority on the Latin American left; in the third volume, his masculine persona blends with that of the Revolution, his private life subsumed into the torrent of public history as he enshrines his personal version of the Nicaraguan Revolution in prose as a monument that will withstand the hostile rewritings put forward by the political right and the post-1995 FSLN. The memoirs chart Cardenal's trajectory from being less than a man, within his own terms of reference, to being a man who defines a nation. The memoirs are often fascinating, though in literary terms they are an inelegant, ungainly work. The temporal structure is capricious (though not, as will be argued, without an internal logic), the editing is sloppy, and Cardenal's growing use, as the narrative advances, of a pseudo-Testimonio voice, as though he were speaking to his readers, can sound hackneyed and folksy.

Unlike Ramírez's *Adiós Muchachos* or Belli's *The Country under My Skin*, Cardenal's memoirs recount much more than the Revolution. As Nicasio Urbina observes: "Ésta sí es en realidad una autobiografía, un texto donde Cardenal se ha propuesto contar su vida" (Urbina 2004a; "*This* is a real autobiography, a text in which Cardenal has set out to recount his life"). The conception of a life that the memoirs reveal includes material that a more purist definition of autobiography would exclude: a long chapter consisting of notebook jottings made in the Trappist monastery, innumerable digressions into historical events or the life-stories of individuals with whom he was barely acquainted, unorthodox theological speculations. Sylvia Molloy argues that features such as these, which may appear eccentric, lie at the core of Spanish American autobiography:

> A strong testimonial stance informs autobiographical writing in Spanish America. If not always perceiving themselves as historians ... autobiographers will continue to see themselves as witnesses. The fact that this testimony is often endowed with the aura of terminal visions – the autobiographer bearing witness to that which is no more – not only aggrandizes the author's individual persona but reflects the communal dimension sought for the autobiographical venture. Spanish American self-writing is an exercise in memory doubled by a ritual of commemoration, in which individual relics (in Benjamin's sense of the term) are secularized and re-presented as shared events. (Molloy 1991: 8–9)

Though Molloy's conclusions are based on a study of nineteenth-century autobiographies, the majority of them Argentine, her definition is a remarkably good fit for Cardenal's memoirs. Her contention that the recreation of a past that is no more – though true of the entirety of Cardenal's autobiography, this applies particularly well to *La revolución perdida* – "aggrandizes the author's individual persona" enables the reader to perceive the link between

Cardenal's narration of history and his need to shore up the personal identity that has been left in ruins by the electoral defeat. *Vida perdida*, and its extension, *Los años de Granada*, diverge from one of the traits listed by Molloy in giving extensive treatment to the poet's childhood and adolescence. This contradicts Molloy's characterization of Spanish American autobiography as a genre in which "the first years of an individual's life are given short shrift" (Molloy 1991: 7). Even so, Cardenal's attentive focus on childhood enhances the "communal dimension" to which Molloy refers: without his roots in the Catholic oligarchy of Granada, many of whose members accompany him through the entire course of his life, Cardenal's trajectory would not make sense. The microcosm of Granada precedes and renders feasible the microcosm of Solentiname, which in turn telescopes into the macrocosm of the revolutionary nation. Unlike some of the subjects of Molloy's study, Cardenal does not leave a rural area to make his career in the capital. Since Central American nations are small and their elites are tiny, Cardenal frequents the same circles for most of his Nicaraguan life; his childhood gains importance as his initiation into the milieu where he will make his career, rather than, as in the cases Molloy studies, a space of nostalgia far beyond that milieu.

Yet the first volume of Cardenal's autobiography relegates childhood to the end rather than placing it at the beginning. The volume opens with Cardenal's trip to the United States in 1957 to enter the Trappist monastery in Kentucky. Asked about this structure, Cardenal replies: "Quería poner primero lo que me pareció más importante en mi vida, que es ese viaje a entrar en el monasterio. Y después ir poniendo distintos capítulos sobre otras fases de mi vida. Me pareció que después de lo de Gethsemani tenía que poner lo de Cuernavaca … Y después, entonces, me pareció que podía empezar a narrar la infancia" (*UIEC*; "I wanted to place first what seemed to be most important in my life, which is that journey to enter the monastery. And later to put in different chapters on other phases of my life. It seemed to me that after Gethsemani I had to put what happened in Cuernavaca … And afterwards, then, it seemed to me that I could start to narrate my childhood").

Childhood is not given "short shrift" in these memoirs; it is dealt with at length, but only after the autobiographer's religious conversion – the single certain thread that remains after 1990 – has been established as the impulse that inspires his exile and leaves him "a solas con Dios" (*VP*, 11; "alone with God"), as the opening sentence concludes. Resonating behind this assertion of the narrator's identity as a contemplative is the distant presentment of future Latin American revolutionary movements. Changing planes in Cuba, he recalls that "una prima me había contado que en unas montañas se había levantado en armas un joven muy popular" (*VP*, 11; "a cousin had told me that in some mountains a very popular young man had taken up arms"). The deliberate vagueness with which this allusion to Fidel Castro is made, in contrast to the naming of Castro in the account of the same journey that opens *In Cuba* (see chapter 5), does not negate the fact of the revolutionary's presence on the first page of the memoirs, instilling, albeit in discreet form, the twin poles of religious and political allegiances that will guide the subject through the remainder of his development.

This statement also establishes the memoirs' ingenuous tone. The oral, pseudo-Testimonio voice contributes to an impression of an innocent narrator whose political and religious experiences impel him to act. The narrative voice lends a certain inevitability to the fragmented structure, a reflection of the post-1990 fragmentation of the nation whose memory Cardenal will enshrine in its revolutionary wholeness in the third volume. The conversational tone enables Cardenal to recast structural disjunctures as authenticity incarnated, by the meandering rhythms of "genuine" Nicaraguan conversation. Cardenal addresses his readers in the plural forms of "ustedes" and "les." He claims to have had no particular aesthetic goal in adopting this form: "Simplemente me gustó más" (*UIEC*; "I just liked it better"). Yet the text of *Vida perdida* suggests another reason for this choice. Cardenal associates an oral-derived prose with Teresa of Ávila, one of his models in the religious confessional form, particularly, as "Telescope in the Dark Night" makes clear, in the post-1990 realm of feminine identifications: "Santa Teresa no está escribiendo el español sino que lo habla, es un lenguaje oral" (*VP*, 56; "Saint Teresa is not writing Spanish but rather she speaks it, it is an oral language"). Cardenal's oral style is signalled by the repetition of key phrases, a device that recalls both poetry and prayer. He breaks the rules of Spanish grammar: "Y eso se los contaré más tarde" (*VP*, 393; "I shall recount these [not "this"] to you later"). This confusion of the direct with the indirect object pronoun is common in colloquial speech, but is considered crude in writing. The Seix Barral edition, published in Barcelona, includes a warning: "Nota del editor: Por deseo expreso del autor, esta edición respeta formas y expresiones del español hablado en Nicaragua" (*VP*, 6; "Editor's Note: By express desire of the author, this edition respects forms and expressions of the Spanish spoken in Nicaragua"). At the same time, the hand of an author who is primarily a poet is evident in the narrator's habit of supporting prose descriptions of key moments in his life with quotes from poems he wrote during the same period. This tendency dwindles in the second and third volumes, inducing the reader to see *Vida perdida* as the text in which Cardenal crosses the border between poetry and prose.

The memoir opens with a border crossing that throws into relief the murky boundaries of Nicaraguan identity. When Cardenal reaches Miami airport, he is astonished by the resemblance of the tropical vegetation to that with which he knows from Nicaragua: "Había rincones cerca del aeropuerto que a la luz de la luna parecía que uno no estuviera en los Estados Unidos sino en el río San Juan de Nicaragua o en lo que entonces era un territorio en litigio, casi despoblada, entre Nicaragua y Honduras" (*VP*, 12; "There were corners close to the airport where, by the light of the moon, it appeared that one was not in the United States but rather on the San Juan River or in what was then a territory in dispute, almost uninhabited, between Nicaragua and Honduras"). Cardenal twice mentions this "territory in dispute," a phrase that underlines the uncertainty and volatility of weak countries' national borders, and of his own wavering conception of nationhood. In a theme expressed by his poetry collection *Gethsemani, Ky.* (see chapter 3), the Cardenal who is living these experiences has been expelled from Nicaragua by a dictator who has condemned him to exile by robbing him of his fiancée and then, having been assassinated, occupying the Nicaraguan earth; the Cardenal who narrates the memoirs has also lost his nation, the revolutionary state. The image of a "territory in dispute" bridges these two Nicaraguan nations of which he has been deprived, illuminating the analogy between Cardenal's crisis in 1956–57 and the crisis of meaning he confronted after 1990. The narrator reaches the conclusion that the United States "es también un país del Caribe, y que no debía considerarlo ahora como tierra extraña ... sino como mi misma patria" (*VP*, 12; "is also a Caribbean country, and that now I shouldn't consider it as a strange land ... but rather as my own homeland"). He feels God's will welcoming him to the United States, "mi nueva patria" (*VP*, 13; "my new homeland"). This surprising declaration resonates in the circumstances of both 1957 and the 1990s. In the years after 1990, it seemed as though Nicaraguans, having lost the only state that had ever articulated a distinctive Nicaraguan nationality, had become, through the imposition of neo-liberal policies, subordinate citizens of the United States. These images of a Caribbean United States that will act as Cardenal's new homeland, both in the 1950s and in the new millennium, and that yet also imply a disappearance of Nicaraguan nationality – echoed as well in Ramírez's novel *A Thousand Deaths Plus One* (see chapter 10), are made concrete when, after his arrival at Gethsemani, he meets an Italian monk who asks him where he is from.

> No se cansaba de decirme: "Qué lindo es Nicaragua!" "Qué lindo es Nicaragua!" Como alguien que la estuviera viendo. Parecía que estuviera teniendo una visión, con una mirada puesta en el vacío. Y más me pareció lo de la visión cuando me preguntó dónde quedaba: y al decirle yo que en Centroamérica, me dijo: *I never heard of it.* (*VP*, 17; He couldn't stop telling me, "How pretty Nicaragua is! How pretty Nicaragua is!" Like someone who was looking at it. He seemed to be having a vision with his gaze fixed on the void. It struck me as even more like a vision when he asked me where it was, and when I told him in Central America, he told me: "I never heard of it.")

It is difficult for Cardenal to resist the notion that events such as his 1950s expulsion from Nicaragua and the Sandinista defeat are products of divine will. Nicasio Urbina points out that Cardenal's account of his life is drenched in the language of predestination: "El texto entero está permeado por la predestinación, por la seguridad de que Dios habla por medio de los hechos, a veces baladíes, pero que indefectiblemente contienen un mensaje inapelable del Señor Todopoderoso" (Urbina 2004a; "The entire text is permeated by predestination, by the certainty that God speaks through events, at times trivial ones, but which unfailingly contain an irrefutable message from the All-Powerful Lord"). A believer's sole response is to memorialize that which existed, and pray to God, as Cardenal does on the memoirs' final page, to restore this realm.

Vida perdida stages a tentative recuperation of Nicaraguan nationhood, threatened with disappearance, which is vitiated and problematized by the difficulty of restoring a viable masculine persona that is capable of acting as the agent of this reconstruction. Cardenal defines this masculine persona through his relationship to young women. Chapters 2, 3, and 4 recount the flourishing and withering of his romantic life. "Muchachas en flor" ("Girls in Bloom") speaks of his early girlfriends (omitting Carmen, who will be the subject of *Los años de Granada*); "Otras tierras, otros climas" ("Other Lands, Other Climates") describes Cardenal's university studies in Mexico City and New York and his travels in Spain, including his experiments with prostitutes; and "Mi hora cero" ("My Zero Hour") narrates the rise and fall of his courtship of Ileana, whose marriage to a Somocista official dispatched him to the monastery. Cardenal's accounts of these courtships appear ingenuous: he admires the girls' beauty yet sees them as remote, ethereal, and, not surprisingly given the difference in their ages, too young and sheltered to be his intellectual equals. His attractions, devoid of sexual energy, are dominated by a quest for ideals that correspond to divine, rather than human, relationships: "Y es que yo sentía una atracción irresistible a la unión conyugal; obsesión sería mejor decir. Al mismo tiempo sentía dentro de mí, no con atracción sino con repulsión más bien, un llamado irreprimible a una entrega total a Dios en la vida religiosa" (*VP*, 21; "The fact was that I felt an irresistible attraction to conjugal union; obsession would be a better term. At the same time, I felt within me not an attraction but rather a repulsion, an irrepressible call for a total submission to God in the religious life").

The uncertainties that plague Cardenal's quest for union are reflected in the title of the second chapter, with its echo of Marcel Proust's *A l'ombre des jeunes filles en fleurs* (1919; *Within a Budding Grove*), the second volume of *In Search of Lost Time*, in which the attraction of the adolescent narrator, Marcel, to Gilberte and Albertine is nearly as diaphanous as Cardenal's courtships, and is overshadowed by his awestruck admiration of the glamorous young Count Robert de Saint-Loup. The evocation of *Within a Budding Grove*, with its mingled intimations of heterosexual and homosexual attraction complicating a young man's pursuit of adolescent girls against a sunstruck background –the French Riviera, as opposed to Granada and Managua – promotes the "doubleness" to which Julia Kristeva refers in her study of intertextuality (Kristeva 1978: 85). The second chapter's Proustian title induces the reader to regard Cardenal's professions of attraction to these unattainable young women as only one of two possible readings of his predicament, further impugning his claims to heterosexual masculinity in the aftermath of the destruction of the revolutionary nation that lent these claims credibility.

Cardenal's summary of his courtships is that "Dios me perseguía a mí y yo perseguía a las muchachas" (*VP*, 57; "God was pursuing me and I was pursuing girls"). In this way, too, Cardenal is a "territory in dispute": two gender identities, like two nationalities, compete for his allegiance; his intermediate position is fraught with anxiety. Repeating the dynamics that were dramatized in "Telescope in the Dark Night," the narrator is incipiently masculine in his relations with young women, yet feminine in his true and lasting passion with deity (which he genders as male). The very act of taking solace in religion after being rejected in love is a feminine gesture, recalling female characters of nineteenth-century Romantic fiction, such as Teresa in Gertrudis Gómez de Avellaneda's novel *Sab* (1844), who locks herself in a convent after failing to win the man she loves. Once he is inside the walls of the Gethsemani monastery, Cardenal becomes passive, contemplative, and subordinate to men in positions of authority, such as the abbot and his tutor,

Thomas Merton; he dresses in a long white robe: "Nuestro hábito es blanco, como traje de novias. Cristo se describe como el Esposo que viene donde la Esposa. Aunque biológicamente masculinos somos la Esposa" (*VP*, 251; "Our habit is white, like a bride's gown. Christ describes himself as the Husband who comes to visit the Wife. Though biologically masculine, we are the Wife"). This self-definition as a bride of Christ, though cogent in theological terms, is the nadir of Cardenal's descent after failing to consolidate his masculinity by marrying Ileana.

During his earlier stay in the United States, when he studies at Columbia University, Nicaraguanness remains an obscure identity, yet one that may be divulged among those who are familiar with its codes. When Cardenal and his cousin Filadelfo Chamorro attend a graduation ceremony where Hope Portocarrero, who later married Anastasio Somoza Debayle, receives a diploma, Cardenal, recognizing her surname as Nicaraguan, approaches the young woman: "… yo le pregunté en español si era nicaragüense. Ella, desconfiada, no quería contestar. Le dijimos que éramos nicaragüenses y continuó desconfiada. Hasta que le dijimos nuestros apellidos, conocidos por ella, Cardenal y Chamorro, admitió ser nicaragüense" (*VP*, 60; "I asked her in Spanish if she were Nicaraguan. Suspicious, she didn't reply. We told her we were Nicaraguan and she remained suspicious. Only when we told her our surnames, Cardenal and Chamorro, which were known to her, did she admit to being Nicaraguan"). Here nation is equivalent to social class: Hope Portocarrero engages the two young strangers once they offer the passwords of elite surnames. In a way that will become much more obvious in *Los años de Granada*, Cardenal's infatuations with young women are undergirded by a quasi-incestuous yearning to mate within his own social circle, sealing the unity of the wounded, marginalized aristocracy. He is at least as attracted by girls' surnames and fathers as by their personalities or good looks. His description of his relationship with Conchita Mantecón, the daughter of a Spanish Republican exile "admirado por todos" (*VP*, 47; "admired by all"), devotes as much attention to the qualities of the girl's father as it does to Conchita. At the age of thirty, Cardenal courts the fourteen-year-old daughter of Pablo Leal, who will die in the April Rebellion and "al cual yo hubiera querido tener por suegro" (*VP*, 36; "whom I would have liked to have for a father-in-law"). This reference highlights another striking feature of *Vida perdida*: the virtual absence from its pages of political activity; even references to the Somoza dictatorship, or Cardenal's activism in the April Rebellion or UNAP, are sparse. The crisis of masculinity that absorbs *Vida perdida* rules out the narration of political events because, as long as he is gendered as feminine, Cardenal cannot be a political player. Only after recovering his masculinity does he impinge on the political realm, a public space in which men deploy their influence.

To be feminine, or less than masculine, is to be passive and subordinate. All subordinations, whether unjust or just, forced or joyously voluntary, converge. This is evident in the scene in which Cardenal describes his submission to God as Ileana's wedding procession passes. Referring to the din made by the wedding party, he writes:

> Aquellas estruendosas sirenas sonaron en mis oídos como clarines de triunfo. Un triunfo sobre mí. Por extraño que parezca, rápido como un flash mi mente percibió una superposición de Dios y el dictador como si fueran uno solo; uno solo que había triunfado sobre mí. Pensé preguntarle al P. Elizondo (un jesuita que iría a visitar para consultarle sobre mi vocación) si en Somoza debíamos ver a Dios, según aquella frase enigmática de San Pablo de que todo poder viene de Dios. El hecho es que me sentí abatido hasta el fondo del abatimiento … Entonces me rendí a Dios. (*VP*, 88–9; Those deafening sirens sounded in my ears like triumphant clarions. A triumph over me. As strange as it may seem, as rapidly as a flash, my mind perceived the superimposition of God and the dictator as though they were a single being; a single being that had triumphed over me. I thought of asking Father Elizondo (a Jesuit whom I was going to visit to consult him on my vocation) if in Somoza we should see God, according to that enigmatic statement of St. Paul that all power comes from God. The fact is that I felt depressed to the depths of depression … Then I surrendered to God.)

Cardenal's sense of the duty to submit to the ruling power, bred into him by Conservative doctrine, blends all submissions into a single undifferentiated surrender to masculine authority. In submitting to God, he is also submitting to Somoza; his failure to overthrow Somoza two years earlier in 1954 makes this admission of defeat inevitable, and even a relief. To devote himself to God is to concede the Nicaraguan nation to Somocismo: converting a tyrannical, threatening authority into one that, if not benign, has ceased to be in conflict with him because he has been beaten down into a neutered self that is no longer impelled by masculinity to engage in the equally futile activities of pursuing young women and fighting against the dictatorship. The submission to God and the relinquishment of a masculine identity merge in his abandonment of active political and sexual roles.

The passage continues for another page, focusing, in terms similar to those used in "Telescope in the Dark Night," on the pleasure Cardenal experienced in this moment: a pleasure he censored, for reasons of theological orthodoxy, from *Abide in Love*. The description confirms his enjoyment of the passive role in an interaction with a force greater than himself. Once he has defined himself in such "feminine" terms, Cardenal loses both the ability to write the nation – as he had already done in the first draft of *Zero Hour*, completed prior to his conversion – and the presumption that it should be his role to do so. Unable to contest the dictatorship's stranglehold on Nicaragua, he must leave the country: "Cuando me decidí por ser trapense había renunciado a mi país" (*VP*, 215; "When I made up my mind to be a Trappist, I had renounced my country"). As long as his feminine identification persists, he cannot return to his country. His religious conversion instills in him "una total pasividad del alma" (*VP*, 205; "a total passivity of the soul"). Only if he reconstructs his masculinity, in a form that converts him into a recognized figure of authority, will such a return become possible.

The agent of his reconstruction is Thomas Merton. It is Merton who, in a proto-liberation theology vein, enables Cardenal to conceive of a submission to God that will at the same time entail an advocacy for his nation. The thin end of this wedge is Merton's fascination with indigenous American civilizations. By persuading Cardenal that the religious commune which, he claims, they are going to found together in Nicaragua must include a strong aboriginal component, Merton opens the door to the aristocratic Cardenal's identification with the Nicaraguan poor, who will invest him with the authority to challenge the Somoza regime with the microcosmic proto-nation of Solentiname. Merton's identity as a "Yankee" is crucial to his ability to effect this transformation. Having accepted the United States as his new homeland, in Gethsemani Cardenal is formally submitted to the authority of a famous American who is a monk and a poet, and who decries as poisoned materialism the Americanization promoted by Somocismo. The ambiguity of the transformation in Cardenal's outlook is evident in the two chapters he devotes to the monastery: the first, the longest chapter in the book, a recollection written in the 1990s, in which his evolution is clear; and the second, consisting of notebook entries made at the time and omitted from *Abide in Love*, in which doubt is visible. In addition to crediting Merton with sparking his interest in the aboriginal peoples of the Americas (see chapter 8), Cardenal learned from him that even US citizens could challenge United States beliefs and institutions. He depicts Merton telling him that "no podíamos creer en el *Time* porque era reaccionario!" (*VP*, 191; "we couldn't believe *Time* magazine because it was reactionary!"). He notes: "Merton era muy antiyanqui. Exageradamente antiyanqui algunas veces" (*VP*, 199; "Merton was very anti-Yankee. Exaggeratedly anti-Yankee at times"). Merton challenged Cardenal's admiration of US poets such as Whitman, Pound, and Eliot, claiming that Latin American poetry was superior. Having defined himself since childhood as a reactionary, Cardenal confronted a tutor invested with the authority of the United States, the Catholic Church, and literary success – three crucial touchstones – who urged him to oppose reactionaries. The foundation of Solentiname, the memoir makes clear, originated with Merton.

Even more important than Merton's advice that Cardenal return to Nicaragua was his willingness to conceive of Cardenal as a leader, a man capable of founding a community and exercising authority over it. This assumption re-energizes Cardenal's masculinity, even though his initial expectation is that they will create the community together and that Merton will be in charge: "me dijo que esperara su llegada en el monasterio de Cuernavaca. Si no le permitían salir, yo debía hacer la fundación" (*VP*, 216; "he told me to await his arrival in the monastery in Cuernavaca. If they didn't let him leave, I should found the community"). Cardenal recovers his agency by acting as Merton's agent. Yet Merton provides Cardenal with a clear route to authority within Nicaraguan society when he tells him that he must seek ordination. The suggestion that he return to Nicaragua as a priest – a role that commands authority and is consistent with Cardenal's Conservative heritage – resolves the question of how he will define himself, ruling out any return to the nebulous disputed territory of flirting with debutantes while God flirts with him. Though his politics remain Conservative, his mature identity has been decided.

This identity is inextricably linked to the nation, and to the concept – novel to someone such as Cardenal, who was raised to submit to authority – that it is possible, as citizens of the United States believe, to have God on one's side:

> Me dijo Merton que nuestra voluntad y la de Dios no siempre tenían que ser opuestas. A veces nuestra voluntad y la de Dios podían coincidir. Él veía más lógico que yo llevara una vida contemplativa en Nicaragua, y no tenía por qué ir a buscar esa vida en otro país. Allí es donde yo podía hacer más bien, y tener más influencia. (*VP*, 216; Merton told me that our will and that of God don't always have to be opposed. At times our will and that of God could coincide. He thought it was more logical for me to live a contemplative life in Nicaragua; I didn't have to look for

that life in another country. That was where I could do the most good and have the most influence.)

This counsel on Merton's part reverses the renunciation of the homeland that Cardenal had believed to be implicit in his surrender to God. The notebook entries elaborate Cardenal's struggle with conflicting yet converging forms of male authority. In one of his dreams he sees: "En la Casa Presidencial, en un sitio alto, Luis Somoza con su cara regordeta en la que estaban superpuestas las caras de mi padre y de Merton, y abajo yo con un gran número de periodistas tomando notas, todos de blanco como novicios" (*VP*, 291; "In a high spot in the presidential palace, Luis Somoza with his chubby face in which were superimposed the faces of my father and Merton, and beneath him I with a great number of journalists taking notes, all dressed in white like novices"). In the merging of God and the dictator that possessed Cardenal during his moment of religious ecstacy, God has yielded to Merton and his father. The replacement of a stern deity who invades him with pleasure yet symbolizes his moral defeat with an authority figure who urges him to secure his own authority by becoming a priest is a crucial step in the recovery of masculine activity. It was Merton himself who interpreted Cardenal's moment of ecstacy on 2 June 1956 as an Eros-and-Thanatos union with the dictator: "Merton escribió en su diario sobre *Hora 0*, diciendo … que la hora había sido mía y de Somoza. Somoza asesinado y yo muerto para el mundo" (*VP*, 201; "Merton wrote in his diary about *Zero Hour*, saying … that the hour had been mine and that of Somoza. Somoza assassinated and I dead to the world"). Cardenal's own explanation of why his recovery and the fall of the Somozas were delayed is skewed by his penchant for predestination: he claims (*VP*, 202) that the delay was necessary to fulfill God's design of creating the Nicaraguan Revolution. Yet the superimposed faces of the new Somoza dictator, the poet's father (who would soon go bankrupt, cutting off Cardenal's possibility of a cushioned return to secular life), and Merton chart a modulation from a dictatorial to a benign and instructive form of authority (on whose teachings he and others must take notes).

After Cardenal leaves Gethsemani, Merton, whom he would meet in person only one more time, displaces the hybridized God-Somoza authority figure; unseen yet commanding authority, Merton becomes God's emissary in Cardenal's life, opening up the possibility of interpretations of religion that do not require dutiful submission to terrestrial rulers on the grounds that their governments are manifestations of God's design. During his years in Cuernavaca, Cardenal continued to write to Merton denouncing Cuba as "un país soviético" (*VP*, 358; "a Soviet country"); yet his transition from passivity to activity, from subject of authoritarian dictates to active agent and incipient authority figure who believed, as Merton had taught him, that God could be on his side, became clear. In Mexico, he supported his cousin Pedro Joaquín Chamorro's Christian insurgency of Olama y los Mollejones, and published his first two books of poetry. The forward action of *Vida perdida* concludes with Cardenal taking the initiative to study for ordination in Colombia and found his community in Nicaragua.

This crisis of masculinity having been resolved, Cardenal may now narrate his childhood. Molloy comments on the absence of psychological reflection in Spanish American autobiographies, arguing that the "combination of the personal and the communal restricts the scrutiny of self so frequently associated with autobiography" (Molloy 1991: 9). In a compatible vein, the Cuernavaca chapter ends with Merton's dismay on learning that Dom Gregorio, Cardenal's Mexican mentor, has abandoned religion for psychoanalysis and broken his vows by marrying a young woman. Cardenal flees this indulgence of the self and intrusion of the feminine (the two tendencies appear as linked) for a return to a faith of communal and social commitment in the male preserve of a Colombian seminary. The next chapter opens with an evocation of Cardenal's childhood that situates him as a male Granada Conservative. His first memory, he recounts, is of the Calle Atravesada: the emblematic street of the Conservative elite: "Y mi recuerdo consiste en que otra mujer en la acera le pregunta [a mi niñera] si yo soy niño o niña. Y ella contesta que soy varón. No recuerdo si la respuesta despertó interés en mí, o la recibí indiferente como una simple información" (*VP*, 363; "And my memory consists in that another woman on the sidewalk asks [my nanny] if I'm a little boy or a little girl. And she says that I am male. I don't remember whether this reply awoke any interest in me, or if I received it with indifference, as simply information"). This untroubled assimilation of masculine gender identity confirms the resolution of his crisis of identity. It signals the end of the zigzagging narrative chronology: from this point on, with one exception, the memoirs are linear, leaving gaps only for portions of Cardenal's life that have already been narrated.

The childhood Cardenal narrates, as Molloy would posit, substitutes for analysis of the self the task of "generating a reflection on the fluctuating place of the subject within its community" (Molloy 1991: 9). Yet the book's catharsis belongs not only to the years after Cardenal's religious conversion in 1956, but, even more crucially, to post-1990 globalization, the period when the memoir is written. In order to anchor the image of the Sandinista Revolution that he wishes to enshrine, he must root these events in the overlapping histories of Nicaragua and his family. This process dates back to the monastery, when one of his notebook jottings broaches a reappraisal of his relationship with the Somozas, laying the foundation for the final chapter of *Vida perdida*, which he will write many years later:

> Dios le dijo a Abraham: "Deja tu patria y tu parentela." Mi parentela son los Somoza. Bernabé Somoza, el bandolero, abuelo del dictador, era mi tío tatarabuelo. El hijo de don Bernabé fue un Anastasio Somoza, y el hijo de éste, Anastasio Somoza el dictador, y un hijo de éste, otro Anastasio Somoza. No debo olvidar este parentesco. Ni olvidar que Dios me llamó a la libertad haciéndome renunciar a Nicaragua y a todo lo que hay en ella, incluyendo esta parentela lejana pero real. (*VP*, 302; God said to Abraham: "Leave your country and your relations." My relations are the Somozas. Bernabé Somoza, the bandit, grandfather of the dictator, was my great-great-great-uncle. Don Bernabé's son was an Anastasio Somoza, and his son, Anastasio Somoza the dictator, and his son, another Anastasio Somoza. I must not forget this kinship tie. Nor forget that God called me to freedom by making me renounce Nicaragua and all its works, including this distant but real kinship.)

In tiny Nicaragua, even the white, upper-class, Conservative Cardenals and the mestizo, lower-middle-class, Liberal Somozas are distantly related (by marriage, as it turns out). In the 1950s, when Cardenal is in the monastery, this fact becomes one more reason to renounce Nicaragua; but from the perspective of the 1990s, when the nation has become diaphanous and demands to be recovered, Cardenal's interpretation of Bernabé Somoza as an element of the history that laid the groundwork for his childhood changes. Just as the dictator's stern face, which formerly blended with that of God, is now mediated by associations with Rodolfo Cardenal and Thomas Merton, so the meaning of being a Somoza receives fresh scrutiny. In a notebook entry from the 1950s, Cardenal accuses himself of bearing the taint of Somoza kinship, whose violent tendencies enter Nicaraguan history with a nineteenth-century bandit. As a Nicaraguan of European descent, Cardenal cannot resort to the unifying glue of mestizo heritage that becomes a fall-back position in Ramírez's later work. He must establish continuity by way of ideology, incorporating a lineage of revolutionary activity into his Conservative heritage. The principal vehicle for this recasting of the communal context in which the self takes root is through the rehabilitation of Bernabé Somoza.

Bernabé was the brother of the wife of Cardenal's immigrant ancestor Johannes Jakob Teufel, who changed his name to Jacobo Martínez. More importantly, as Cardenal investigates history with the assistance of his grandmother Trinidad, he comes to the conclusion that this early Somoza was mislabelled a bandit. He turns out to be a role model for a man from a wealthy family who allies himself with the poor. Cardenal quotes a US historian who describes Bernabé Somoza as "temido de cierta clase, pero apreciado por las masas" (*VP*, 419; "feared by a certain class, but appreciated by the masses"). In an obvious parallel with his own situation, he notes: "Don Bernabé Somoza, aunque de una familia acomodada de provincia, estaba, tal vez por sus lecturas, con los calandracas [los pobres]" (*VP*, 420; "Don Bernabé Somoza, though from a well-off provincial family was, perhaps due to his reading, on the side of the *calandracas* [the poor]"). Don Bernabé was a Liberal, as were his descendants, the Somoza dictators; but he was an idealistic early-ninteenth-century Liberal who sided with Francisco Morazán in his attempt to build a progressive, unified Central America. His historical notoriety is attributed to a condition he shares with Cardenal: he was defeated. "Asesinatos y robos tendría. Es decir, tuvo. Pero no fue esa su principal motivación, sino la lucha por la libertad. Y su principal culpa histórica es que fue derrotado" (*VP*, 424; "He must have had murders and robberies. That to say, he did have them. But that was not his principal motivation, but rather the struggle for freedom. And his main historical fault was that he was defeated"). Cardenal's account of Bernabé Somoza's defeat ties together two strands of nineteenth-century Nicaraguan history, injecting the struggle for justice into the history of the Chamorro family. After his defeat, Bernabé Somoza surrenders to Fruto Chamorro, later the first Chamorro to become president, on the understanding that his life will be spared.[3] Overruled by a superior, who executes Somoza, "don Fruto Chamorro estuvo haciendo guardia de honor ante la cadáver" (*VP*, 425; "Don Fruto stood as a guard of honour next to the body").

The image that concludes Cardenal's extensive account of this distant ancestor's life depicts a Conservative oligarch paying his respects to a man who struggled on behalf of the poor. The union of Bernabé Somoza and Fruto Chamorro integrates Cardenal's beliefs with his heritage; it anchors the tradition of rebellion and fighting for justice in his Conservative lineage, where, at first glance, it would appear to be antithetical.[4] At the same time, the example of Bernabé Somoza warns that history, written by the winners, unjustly disparages those who commit themselves to the poor and lose; this insight anticipates and refutes post-1990 attacks on the Nicaraguan Revolution as the propaganda of globalization's winners. In the aftermath of the *Piñata*, dismissals of the entire revolutionary experience became commonplace, with the FSLN's enemies on the right popularizing the term "robolución" ("robbery-olution"). Cardenal's memoirs, particularly *La revolución perdida*, are a response to this slander, an effort to enshrine in literature the sacrifices and selfless acts that made the Revolution possible and characterized its reforms, in order to counteract globalization's erasure of this history.

The portrait of Bernabé Somoza at the end of *Vida perdida* brings full circle a memoir that opened with an anonymous reference to Fidel Castro in the Sierra Maestra. In spite of his refined upbringing, Cardenal asserts, this insurgent tradition is his legacy. Sandino, to whom the Conservative families of Granada lent their discreet support during the years of Cardenal's early childhood, was also betrayed and murdered after he had surrendered, and was also derided as a bandit. The implicit chain of alliances across class lines that runs from Bernabé Somoza and Fruto Chamorro to Sandino and the Conservative families that fought to erase references to him as a bandit from the legislative record, to the young FSLN guerrillas of Solentiname and Cardenal, spreading out internationally to embrace Fidel Castro and Thomas Merton, harmonizes a history of rebellion with a Conservative culture.

The future author's awareness of Nicaragua's political vicissitudes was accentuated by his childhood as part of a Conservative minority in Liberal León, where his father had been sent to run one of the Cardenal family's shops. León gave Cardenal a vision of the nation that was broader than that he would have formed in Granada. Living close to the house of Rubén Darío helped the young boy, who carried a notebook to write down all that he learned about Nicaraguan history, to feel in close contact with his country's poetic tradition. Yet his idea of nation was consolidated in the Colegio Centroamericano, on the shores of Lake Nicaragua, in the suburbs of Granada, where from the ages of twelve to eighteen Cardenal lived and studied in an institution where many of the students were his cousins. The resolution of the crisis of masculinity may lend him a voice in which to narrate his childhood and adolescence, before his difficulties in courting young women provoked the crisis of 2 June 1956; yet the structure of *Vida perdida* does not allow room for his schooldays. In a brief envoi, in which he reiterates his belief that the course of his life represents the fulfilment of a plan designed by the deity he addresses as "vos, Amor" (*VP*, 457; "you, Love"), Cardenal notes that "muchas cosas quedan aún por contar, pero estos relatos ya se han hecho grandes" (*VP*, 457; "many things are left to tell, but these tales have already become long"). Having already committed the second volume to Colombia and Solentiname, he has no place for his adolescence.

This is the origin of *Los años de Granada*, an intriguing ideological supplement that confirms his male, Conservative identification, in which Conservatism includes a paradoxical heritage of struggling for the poor and for national autonomy. Subsequent international editions of Cardenal's memoirs omit the final page cited above, and add *Los años de Granada* as two lengthy concluding chapters in *Vida perdida*; in Nicaragua, this "continuation" of the first volume was published as a separate book. The material covered by *Los años de Granada*, which Cardenal can neither include nor omit, recounts the deeply reactionary, yet dissident, culture in which he was raised. It narrates his first courtship, which dethrones his torments over Ileana from their position of uniqueness by revealing that such upheavals were a pattern in the young Cardenal's life. This pattern can be broached only once his masculinity is secure; it cannot, therefore, be included in *Vida perdida*, even though, in chronological terms, that is where it belongs. In later years Cardenal would maintain: "En realidad, es con el primer amor que termina el libro" (*UIEC*; "It's really with the first love that the first volume concludes"). Yet it is the composition of *Vida perdida* that makes the inclusion of this event possible.

COUSINS IN LOVE: *LOS AÑOS DE GRANADA*

As Cardenal reaches "la edad más perfecta del hombre, que son los doce años" (*AG*, 9; "the most perfect age of man, which is twelve years old"), his father's business affairs require the family to move to Managua. Young Ernesto is sent to boarding school at the Colegio Centroamericano. His discovery of his school, his original microcosm, the forerunner to Solentiname, Gethsemani, and Sandinista Nicaragua, is presented as a discovery of the nation: "En una historia juvenil del descubrimiento de Nicaragua, por Gil González, el protagonista era un niño de doce años" (*AG*, 9; "In a child's history of the discovery of Nicaragua, by Gil González, the protagonist was a twelve-year-old boy"). The Colegio Centroamericano community that the twelve-year-old explorer discovers shares national reference points that are reinforced by the boys' lessons. In a foreshadowing of the community of Solentiname, which included a married couple, notions of family and nation merge. The nation that young Ernesto discovers is populated by Cardenals: "Nosotros éramos como siete primos Cardenal de casi la misma edad, además de Pedro que era como cuatro años mayor por lo que era el líder del grupo" (*AG*, 25; "There were seven of us Cardenal cousins of almost exactly the same age, as well as Pedro who was about four years older and was the group's leader").[5] In a scene that is revealing because it illustrates that, even prior to meeting Merton, Cardenal possessed a latent conception of indigenous cultures as the ancestral core of the nation, and that even prior to entering Gethsemani, he linked the notions of celibacy and castration, the centre of the Colegio Centroamericano is a place known as the "Patio de los

Ídolos." Here the Jesuit fathers assembled a collection of statues from local indigenous cultures: "Las figuras eran masculinas y femeninas. A las masculinas, los jesuitas les habían cortado los genitales" (*AG*, 57; "The figures were masculine and feminine. The Jesuits had cut off the masculine figures' genitals"). *Los años de Granada* contains a photograph of the young Cardenal sitting on an indigenous statue reading a book. As a pupil at the school, he delves into national history through the excavation of "pedazos de cerámica indígena" (*AG*, 58; "shards of indigenous ceramics").

The narrator's sounding of the nation's contours occurs in part through his interactions with his Jesuit teachers. In this devout environment, all of the boys see the fathers as role models and dream of being priests; yet, as sons of the oligarchy, they are also aware that they will have "figuración en el país" (*AG*, 63; "influence in the country"). This presumption of an inheritance of political, economic, or cultural power, within the framework of the nation, is thwarted by the dictatorship of Anastasio Somoza García, which all of the boys oppose, not because of the dictator's abuses, but because he is a Liberal and the tool of US domination. Their revolt against the three-year-old dictatorship is splintered by contradictions. The cousins' favourite reading material is the work of anti-Fascist poets such as Federico García Lorca, Pablo Neruda, and Rafael Alberti, yet they found a Fascist club in the school, wear black shirts, and memorize Fascist anthems from the Spanish Civil War. When the Second World War breaks out, Cardenal, in spite of his Jewish ancestry, declares himself an admirer of Adolf Hitler. The twisted logic that underlies this startling allegiance stems from Franklin D. Roosevelt's support for the Somoza dictatorship. The boys belong to a generation whose childhood was scarred by US military occupation. Young Ernesto confronts a priest from Spain: "Una vez en la clase del Padre Aldaz yo escribí en enormes letras en el pizarrón MUERAN LOS YANKYS. Y él se enfureció porque era vasco y los vascos estaban contra Franco y Franco estaba con Hitler y los Yankys estaban contra Hitler y entonces él era yankyista" (*AG*, 113; "Once in Father Aldaz's class I wrote in enormous letters on the blackboard DEATH TO THE YANKEES. And he became furious because he was a Basque, and the Basques were against Franco and Franco was with Hitler and the Yankees were against Hitler and so he was a Yankeesta").

Cardenal shares his political enthusiasms with his uncle, José Coronel Urtecho, his adult cousin, Pablo Antonio Cuadra Cardenal, and his coeval cousin, Pedro Joaquín Chamorro Cardenal. Their debates revolve around subjects such as whether General Francisco Franco is better than Adolf Hitler because he is a Catholic (they seem to be unaware that Hitler, too, was raised a Catholic). The accord to which these debates lead, when the young men are on the verge of graduating from secondary school, surpasses the obscurantist thought of the era, moving beyond reproduction of their families' Conservative values to a wider vision of national renewal:

> Fundamos un partido político en el campo de futbol. O más bien planeamos un partido, para cuando saliéramos del colegio, y que iba a cambiar Nicaragua. Nuestra principal idea política, o tal vez la única era ser antiyankys. Los Estados Unidos nos tenían colonizados, igual que al resto de América Latina, y debíamos liberarnos todos juntos; y también acabar con los partidos liberal y conservador que no servían para nada, solamente para dividir al país ... Todo esto fue como preanuncios de lo que más tarde iba a venir, la Revolución Sandinista, 40 años más tarde de aquella primera reunión. (*AG*, 116–17; We founded a political party on the soccer field. Or rather we planned a party for when we graduated from high school, and it was going to change Nicaragua. Our main political idea, or perhaps the only one, was to be anti-Yankees. The United States had us colonized, just like the rest of Latin America, and we all had to free ourselves together; and also to do away with the Liberal and Conservative parties, which served no purpose, and only divided the country.)

This glorification, from beyond the defeat of 1990, of the reactionary culture of the past as the germ of a united nation, recalls Molloy's contention that much Spanish American autobiographical writing is concerned with constructing Benjaminesque "relics." What Walter Benjamin meant by this term, sketched in his essay, "Paris, Capital of the Nineteenth Century," is "the resolute effort to distance oneself from all that is antiquated – which includes, however, the recent past. These tendencies deflect the imagination (which is given impetus by the new) back upon the primal past ... the latter appears wedded to elements of primal history, '*Urgeschichte*' – that is, to elements of a classless society" (Benjamin 1999: 4). This idea was especially attractive in Western Europe, the first region to become industrialized; yet it resonates, also, in Latin America, where countless intellectuals have rejected the strife of the recent past in order to idealize the more distant past of the Aztecs, Mayas, Incas, or other indigenous civilizations. Cardenal rejects the recent past of the first decade of intensified globalization, between 1990 and 2000, in order to praise the Conservative oligarchy of the more distant past – seen here as natural and eternal – as the source of the "classless society" of the Revolution. The stunning class snobberies of Granada Conservatism are exonerated by the struggle against Somocismo and obviated by the fact that the poor do not appear in *Los años de Granada*. This provides the illusion that the unity of the boys on the soccer field is that of a society free of class differences. Later in Cardenal's memoirs, however, most notably in *La revolución perdida*, this pattern breaks down, as the revolutionary years themselves – the era that immediately precedes the globalized present – slip into the slot of the primal, egalitarian "relic." This pattern is more typical of backward glances taken during the first two decades of accelerated globalization in many parts of the world. Contrary to the pattern suggested by Benjamin, narrators now express longing for the articulated national entities that globalization has sluiced away, for the immediate past of the nation, which remains within living memory, rather than for a romanticized *Urgeschichte*.

The reactionary, family-based nationalism that the boys inherit from their parents has been converted, by the end of their secondary-school careers, into a broader, more integrative impulse, albeit one that still lacks a formal structure or a popular dimension. This constitutes what Benedict Anderson defines as "official nationalism." This is not the nationalism of a literate bourgeoisie that enables an "imagined community" to cohere. Rather, the cousins' nationalism is that of a Conservative local elite within an empire. Anderson writes: "In almost every case, official nationalism concealed a discrepancy between nation and dynastic realm ... The reason for this was ... the fact that at the core of empires nations too were emerging" (Anderson 1983: 110–11). He gives the example of Hungarian nationalism, defined by what he calls *Burgosozialismus* (ibid.: 107) or "court socialism." This is the socialism promoted by a conservative local elite within the Austro-Hungarian Empire around the year 1900. The debates among the Cardenal cousins, united by class and Conservative heritage, and motivated by bruised national feeling, constitute an analogous reaction, in the late 1930s, to the US policies of the "Big Stick" and the "Good Neighbour," which extended and enforced the empire of the United States in the Caribbean Basin (LaFeber 1980: 28–83). Sandino's insurgency or the Guatemalan Revolution of 1944–54 offer obvious examples of the emergence of nationalisms within this empire, yet the Conservative nationalism of the Cardenals, as Gobat argues (Gobat 2005: 175–201), is a distinct phenomenon because it lauds an abandonment of entrepreneurial capitalism in favour of more old-fashioned agrarian modes of production. While the Conservative families of Granada were not hereditary royalty, they were an aristocracy who saw the country as having been theirs to run until it was engulfed by US expansionism. In this context, revolts against the dictatorship, which was the prolongation by other means of the US military occupation, were "patriotic" (ibid.: 248).

The two long chapters of *Los años de Granada* provide an indispensable bridge between the recovery of the nineteenth-century history of Conservative support for the poor and later Sandinismo. The boys on the soccer field of the country's most elite private school lack a means by which to transmit their nationalistic vision to the rest of the nation, particularly the peasant majority. Yet the fact that Cardenal traces the germ of the Sandinista Revolution to this coming-together of Yankee-hating young aristocrats is telling. The key to diffusing this feeling through the rest of the Nicaraguan nation, as he later preaches in Solentiname, is love: love of country and love of one's neighbour. This is the message he implanted in his religious community and tried to implant in the nation. The message remained long after the original Sandinista state had collapsed. In 2012, for example, a *New York Times* reporter met an eighteen-year-old boy in Solentiname: "'If you have 30 tomatoes and a neighbor needs 2 tomatoes, you should give him 2 tomatoes,' he said. 'This is community. This is what Ernesto Cardenal taught'" (Bailey 2012). This love of the other, which is the glue of a community, and by extrapolation of a nation, provides a strategy for including within the hub of national feeling those who do not belong to the elite. While Cardenal would later usher the peasants of Solentiname into the imagined community of the nation by making them literate and encouraging them to write, the conditions of what Anderson terms *Burgosozialismus* require that an isolated, oppressed elite, in a country where extreme poverty rules out the forging of a national bourgeoisie as a possibility in the short or medium term, find another means of enlisting the mass of people into their project.

The second half of *Los años de Granada* illustrates love, the solution to this riddle, expanding from the all-consuming, egotistical emotional adventure of a young man who falls in love with a young woman for the first time, into a love of neighbour, community, and nation. The girl with whom the eighteen-year-old Cardenal falls in love belongs to the city of Granada and, by extension, to the Colegio Centroamericano, where her brothers study. This enhances the ingrown, incestuous nature of Cardenal's anxieties – romantic, artistic, and political – during this period. His initial solution to the national problem is to fortify the elite by planting himself more deeply in its core. The Freudian implications of this form of desire attenuated the ethereal – one might almost say unreal – texture of his longing.

As a representative of the city of Granada, with which the young Conservative who has spent his childhood in ideological exile in León longs to consolidate his relationship, fourteen-year-old Carmen Chamorro Benard represents the promise of integration into national history:

> Pero por qué callarlo: el primer apellido de ella era el más importante en la historia de Nicaragua … hay los Chamorros ricos que son los del poder económico, y los no ricos que han sido los del poder político.

> Hay Chamorros plutócratas, y Chamorros oligárquicos. Y en cuanto al segundo apellido de ella, Benard … ha sido de plutócratas y no oligárquicos pero sí aristócratas. (*AG*, 187; But why not come out and say it: her paternal surname was the most important in the history of Nicaragua … there are the rich Chamorros who have economic power and the non-rich ones who have held political power. There are plutocratic Chamorros and oligarchical Chamorros. And as for her maternal surname, Benard … it has belonged to plutocrats who were non-oligarchical, but were aristocratic.)

Carmen's pedigree is explicated with more enthusiasm than her personality, or even her physical charms. The prospect of their union offers the possibility of the renewal of the Conservative nation. This is what Doris Sommer identifies as "national romance" when she writes that, in nineteenth- and early-twentieth-century Spanish American fiction, "Eros and Polis are the effects of each other's performance … the lovers 'naturally' desire the kind of state that would unite them" (Sommer 1991: 47). Sommer's examples are predominantly South American and Liberal; Nicaragua's long history of neo-colonial domination delays by several decades the date at which "national romance" emerges and makes this a Conservative prerogative. In this context, falling in love with a Chamorro is inseparable from standing on the soccer field with a group of young oligarchs (and plutocrats) and planning the government that will supplant the dictatorship. It is the extension of this goal by other means, and, at the same time, the reproduction of the values of their parents' generation, dethroned by Somocismo. Cardenal is aware, when he gives his beloved a gift inscribed with the words "Ernesto y Carmen," that these are also her parents' first names.

Though Carmen boasts a film-star beauty, leading José Coronel Urtecho to criticize Cardenal's bourgeois romantic taste, *Los años de Granada* transmits no sense of an eighteen-year-old's breathless physical desire. Cardenal concedes that he succeeded only once in giving a Carmen a kiss on the hand "con mucha rapidez" (*AG*, 185; "very quickly"), and that he never kissed her on the mouth. What Carmen inspires in Cardenal is not desire but love, a titanic force that he commands. Shortly after meeting Carmen, he must leave for Mexico to attend UNAM. Though he longs to stay near her, to renounce university studies will render him ineligible to be her suitor: one does not marry a Chamorro without a foreign university degree. Yet his departure converts his love into a solitary obsession and a force without an object: "En el caso mío era amar solo, sin el objeto amado. Amar en el vacío" (*AG*, 164; "In my case it was loving alone, without the love-object. Loving in the void"). In the pensions where he stays in Mexico City, he keeps two photographs of Carmen, which he refers to as "iconos" (*AG*, 165; "icons"); he writes his thoughts about her in a notebook given to him by the poet Ernesto Mejía Sánchez, which he entitles *Cuaderno de Carmen* (Carmen's Notebook). The parallels with religious devotion, with the quest for union with an unseen deity, are obvious. Cardenal vaunts his extraordinary capacity for love, which he claims is greater than that of any man of his generation, yet the love he deploys is not that of a woman but of an image. Like an icon of the Virgin or an indigenous idol, Carmen protects him when he discovers that "era cierto lo que en Granada me habían dicho que se decía de muchos, de bastantes escritores de México" (*AG*, 169; "what I had been told in Granada about many, about quite a few, Mexican writers, was true"). Whether frequenting the sexually ambiguous Octavio Paz, or the flamboyantly homosexual Xavier Villarrutia and Salvador Novo, he is able to raise the banner of Carmen to preserve a safe distance between him and them.

To a reader of more conventional experiences, Cardenal's love appears to have been pulled inside-out: rather than being rooted in the complicity of the couple and shyly announced to the world, his love is public property, discussed at length with his fellow poets, analyzed, written and rewritten in his notebooks and his poetry, converted into a quasi-religious faith, complete with icons, and mulled over during his months in tiny student rooms in Mexico City; his reticence is reserved for his rare meetings with his beloved. Cardenal's attempts to characterize the feelings that his encounter with Carmen unleashes in him adulterate romantic passion with religious ecstacy. He describes his love of Carmen as "muy parecido a lo que sentí aquel 2 de junio cuando me enamoré de Dios. Yo diría que es igual, aunque uno sea el amor a una muchacha y el otro sea el amor a Dios" (*AG*, 141; "very similar to what I felt on that 2nd of June when I fell in love with God. I would say that it's the same, even if one is love of a girl and the other is the love of God"). The certification of Cardenal's love comes not from the girl saying that she loves him, too, but from the authorization of older male intellectuals: "Pablo Antonio Cuadra decía que nunca había visto un enamoramiento igual" (*AG*, 191; "used to say he had never seen anyone fall in love like that"), and "[Cuadra] y José Coronel Urtecho habían temido que me suicidara" (*AG*, 205; "had been afraid that I would commit suicide").

As in the Colegio Centroamericano, or later in the Gethsemani monastery or the seminary in Colombia, Cardenal's emotions are authenticated through their recognition by a community of male authority figures. In both Granada and Mexico City, where he asked Paz to critique his Carmen poems and where "La ciudad deshabitada" ("The Abandoned City"), his evocation of a

Granada from which Carmen is absent, would give him his first literary success, these figures are older male poets. Later in life, as his love levitates from the moorings of its attachment to young debutantes and becomes a cosmic force, the transformation begins from romantic love to divine love to "amor revolucionario," a phrase that had been used in the early years of the Cuban Revolution but into which Cardenal would breathe his own compelling theology in *Flights of Victory* and *Cosmic Canticle*.

His obsession with Carmen having ended in the usual way – she married Francisco Pellas Chamorro, scion of possibly the wealthiest family in Nicaragua after the rapacious Somozas – Cardenal consoles himself with the thought that "otro amor tuve en mi madurez, y éste sí fue correspondido" (*AG*, 197; "as a mature man I had another love and this one was requited"). He is referring, of course, to his affair with God. Yet, at a one-step remove, Cardenal also achieves union with Carmen Chamorro. The beautiful young girl is transformed into a young man at a point in Cardenal's life when he has transmuted his love into worldly authority by becoming famous as the founder of Solentiname. The adult Carmen visits Cardenal on his island, becomes one of the first purchasers of a Solentiname painting, then sends her son to him for counselling. While sexual union with a woman who is his social equal is beyond Cardenal's desires, intense tutelage bonds between older and younger men, with he himself now occupying the role of tutor, are his specialty. *Los años de Granada* concludes with the consummation of his union with Carmen in displaced form: "Un tiempo después me llegó a visitar su hijo como de 18 años, quien entonces no sabía, me dijo, si hacerse guerrillero, o hacerse sacerdote, o ser empresario y luchar al interior del sistema capitalista" (*AG*, 227; "A while later I received a visit from her son, who was about 18 years old and didn't know, he told me, if he should become a guerrilla or a priest, or be a businessman and fight from within the capitalist system"). The boy's arrival confirms the melting of the "official nationalism" that drew Cardenal to the boy's mother by "revolutionary love" and the first steps towards an imagined community, albeit one that is characterized more by rural classes exposed to literate culture than by Anderson's literate bourgeoisie.

DUTY TO GOD AND THE REVOLUTION: *LAS ÍNSULAS EXTRAÑAS* AND *LA REVOLUCIÓN PERDIDA*

Cardenal narrates the transformation of religious love and official nationalism into revolutionary love and an imagined community for the Nicaraguan nation in the second volume of his memoirs, *Las ínsulas extrañas*. This volume recounts his own transformation from apprentice to tutor; the book reaches its denouement when he attains the authority to send young people into battle. The first paragraph makes clear with whom Cardenal sees his autonomy and authority originating:

> Thomas Merton me había dicho que si a él no le permitían salir del monasterio y fundar la comunidad que habíamos planeado, yo debía estudiar para el sacerdocio en un seminario y realizar esa fundación. Así lo hice, y la fundación fue en una isla del Lago de Nicaragua, en el archipiélago de Solentiname. (*IE*, 13; Thomas Merton had told me that if they didn't allow him to leave the monastery and found the community that we had planned, I must study in a seminary to become a priest and bring this foundation to fruition. This I did, and the community was in Lake Nicaragua in the Solentiname Archipelago.)

In contrast to the chronologies of *Vida perdida* and *Los años de Granada*, scrambled by Cardenal's wrestling with conflicts of faith and passion, *Las ínsulas extrañas* proceeds in a teleogical arc from the community's foundation in February 1966 to the preparations for its self-immolation in the attack on the San Carlos barracks in October 1977. The final page announces the coming revolution; the last two paragraphs consist of two anecdotes. The first concerns a Sandinista who recognizes that his duty lies not in accompanying his wife to the United States for medical treatment (even though she may have cancer) but in undertaking a revolutionary mission: "él debía cumplir su deber" (*IE*, 483; "he had to fulfill his duty"). In the concluding anecdote, Cardenal writes "Amanecer" ("Dawn"), the opening poem of *Flights of Victory*, in which he announces the advent of the Revolution. The Conservative concept of doing your duty, redrafted to fit a Marxist ethos, has given birth to the revolutionary dawn.

The most readable volume of the memoirs, *Las ínsulas extranas* recounts Cardenal's long march from pastoral pacificism to active patronage of revolutionary violence. The book is divided into thirteen long chapters. The first six recount events in Colombia, Managua, and Solentiname prior to Cardenal's conversion to socialism in Cuba in 1970; the seventh chapter, which condenses and recycles many passages from *In Cuba*, narrates Cardenal's socialist conversion. In the final six chapters, the reader witnesses Cardenal putting into practice his hybridized Christian-Marxist beliefs. The Christian-Marxist cocktail that Cardenal developed by slow stages in Solentiname would become a crucial element of the Sandinista nation once the FSLN took power. Donald C. Hodges, in a comparison that is apt yet unexpected, equates this portmanteau faith with Augusto César Sandino's theosophy. Ignored or suppressed in works by Carlos Fonseca and Sergio Ramírez (see chapter 7), theosophy, Hodges maintains, nevertheless provided the original Sandinistas with a common spiritual outlook that strengthened their unity. Cardenal's reworking of liberation theology would play an analogous role in the Nicaraguan state invented by modern Sandinismo. As Hodges posits: "The FSLN's National Directorate became Sandino's political heir, and Ernesto Cardenal has become Sandino's religious heir as the spiritual father to Nicaragua's Marxist Christians. Cardenal's theology of liberation is hardly less exotic or bizarre than Sandino's ... its hybrid of Marxism and Christianity serves the singular purpose of breaking down the barriers that have traditionally separated Marxists from Christians" (Hodges 1986: 290–1).

To what extent Cardenal developed this philosophy as a political strategy to alleviate the isolation of the boys on the Colegio Centroamericano soccer field from the devout peasant masses who constituted their nation, as Hodges appears to suggest, and to what extent this hybrid faith arose organically from Cardenal's interaction with the peasants of Solentiname, is a question to which *Las ínsulas extrañas* does not give a clear answer. Cardenal presents the process as an organic one, arguing that "el contacto con la pobreza" ("contact with poverty") and "la realidad nacional cada vez peor" ("ever worsening national reality") contributed to the fact that "yo y nuestra pequeña comunidad nos fuéramos politizando y radicalizando" (*IE*, 206; "I and our small community became politiczed and radicalized"). Yet, after the 1968 Medellín Conference, the Catholic Church's "preferential option for the poor" provided an obvious constituency to priests who adopted this approach.

As Molloy would anticipate, Cardenal's autobiography transforms the subject's life into a succession of public events. His political radicalization, insinuated as a possibility by Merton's tutelage, fermented in the atmosphere of the La Ceja seminary and was inspired by the Colombian priest Camilo Torres's decision to join the ELN guerrillas. Yet the foundation of Solentiname was an upper-class affair that extended the terrain controlled by the recusant Conservative elite within Liberal Nicaragua: "mi firma estaba respaldada por firmas formidables de amigos empresariales, o de gran figuración política como Pedro Joaquín Chamorro, o millonarios como los gemelos Mántica, dueños de supermercados – todos los cuales se habían ofrecido como benefactores" (*IE*, 98; "my signature was guaranteed by the formidable signatures of friends who were businessmen or figures of great political influence such as Pedro Joaquín Chamorro, or millionaires like the

Mántica twins, owners of supermarkets – all of whom had offered to be benefactors"). The support Cardenal received from the elite confirms that, in spite of the ferment he had experienced in Colombia, in Nicaragua he remained identified with his religiously conventional social class. As late as 1967, he would refuse to speak in public on politics on the grounds that he was a priest (*IE*, 141).

Only Thomas Merton, Cardenal maintains, understood Solentiname's eventual significance and purpose. Cardenal depicts Merton as having received from God foreknowledge of the role Cardenal would play after his tutor's death. In a letter to Cardenal written shortly after the foundation of Solentiname, Merton predicted that the community would play an important role in creating a freedom that was not only spiritual but also temporal: "Fue hasta en los días de la revolución que yo reparé en esa mención profética de la libertad en lo temporal, que cuando lo escribió aún no estaba a la vista, y entonces parecía rara y fuera de lugar" (*IE*, 110; "It was only in the days of the revolution that I noticed this prophetic mention of temporal freedom, which was not within sight when he wrote it, and seemed out of place then"). In a similar vein, Merton knows, before scientific surveys have confirmed it, that the archipelago's soil is volcanic. Reinforcing the theme of predestination, in which the Nicaraguan Revolution occurs as part of God's design, Merton serves as a divine messenger. His support is integral not only to Cardenal's accumulation of a male authority that reverses the "castration" of celibacy, but, in a related vein, to the expansion of the Solentiname ethos of poverty, community, and revolutionary social change into that of the nation. Cardenal identifies with recently castrated horses he encounters in a community on a remote river: "Como esos caballos estaba yo ... Peor que eunucos, porque ésos ya no tienen ningún deseo, y los del Reino es con los órganos enteros" (*IE*, 170; "I was like those horses ... We're worse than eunuchs because they no longer have desires and those of the Kingdom have their organs intact"). Yet, at the same time that he feels less than other men, he is brimming with self-confidence that God has selected him for a special mission: "Desde épocas geológicas remotas Dios hizo este Solentiname pensando en mí. No sólo en mí, pero yo hablo de lo que a mí toca" (*IE*, 172; "since remote geological epochs God made this Solentiname thinking of me. Not only of me but also of my obligations").

This confidence in God's selection of him, to the point of creating the archipelago as the site for his project, is made possible by his belief in Merton's ubiquitous presence in the islands as the anointed spiritual father not only of the community but of Cardenal himself: "Aunque Merton tenía sólo diez años más que yo, para mí era como mi padre, y su muerte fue el mayor dolor que yo había tenido" (*IE*, 236; "Though Merton was only ten years older than I, for me he was my father and his death was the greatest pain I had suffered"). His growing confidence that "Merton estuvo todo el tiempo en Solentiname" (*IE*, 239; "Merton was in Solentiname the whole time") liberates him to radicalize the community. In spite of his early disagreements with Carlos Fonseca and Tomás Borge, he moves beyond Merton's pacificism by committing the young men and women under his influence to the FSLN.

The structure of *Las ínsulas extrañas*, which places the trip to Cuba at the book's centre, perpetuates the legend of the second conversion to Marxism and a new fealty to Fidel, two years after Merton's death, as the heart of this radicalization. Yet, as the text itself reveals, Cardenal did not fully embrace Marxism until he met other priests who were doing the same; in fact, even in his own country, he was not part of the first wave. By the time Cardenal travelled to Cuba in 1970, nearly a year had passed since a Pastoral Encounter in Managua on the theme of liberation theology had attracted the attendance of several hundred Nicaraguan Catholics (Reed 2008: 278–9). The watershed that changed Solentiname was not Cardenal's trip to Cuba but his 1971 journey to the Chile of President Salvador Allende and to Peru, ruled at that time by the "military radicals" of General Juan Velasco Alvarado. In Chile, as he would later recount to Fidel Castro (*EC*, 360), Cardenal met priests like Father Cortés, who told him that "decimos que un cristiano para ser auténticamente cristiano *debe* ser marxista" (*IE*, 305; "we say that a Christian, in order to be authentically Christian, *must* be a Marxist"). Cardenal's descriptions of these priests and their scriptural justifications of revolutionary violence –passages that he would recite in his sermons in Solentiname – extend over several pages.

Nourished by this encounter with revolutionary priests who are remaking a nation, Cardenal fuses what he has learned in Cuba with what he has learned in Chile. It is after his trip to Chile, rather than his trip to Cuba, that he writes: "En Solentiname entramos a otra etapa. Y el país entero estaba entrando a otra etapa. Por todas partes surgían grupos cristianos que se iban haciendo revolucionarios" (*IE*, 311; "In Solentiname we entered a new stage. And the whole country was entering a new stage. Everywhere Christian groups sprang up and became revolutionary"). Only once a mass community of radicalized Christians arises, both elsewhere in Latin America and in his own country, does Cardenal lead Solentiname in this direction.

Raised in the bosom of a religious marginalized elite, where everyone opposed the ruling temporal power, Cardenal finds an analogous devout consensus against tyranny in the Christian Base Communities of the 1970s.

The difference is that this time Cardenal's community includes the poor who make up the vast majority of Nicaragua's population, opening the possibility of not merely opposing power but of supplanting it with his alternate version of the nation. After the trip to Chile and Peru, Cardenal encourages his community to put into practice their earlier readings "de Fidel, de Allende, el Che, Mao ... No dejaba de ser eso prolongación de la Biblia" (*IE*, 213; "from Fidel, from Allende, Che, Mao ... This never ceased to be a prolongation of the Bible"). While this transformation feels organic, it is not exempt from political expediency. Praising the Nicaraguan Revolution as the first in the world to integrate Christianity into its revolutionary project, Cardenal writes: "Y éste fue uno de los grandes aciertos del Frente Sandinista: su reconocimiento de que el pueblo nicaragüense era en su mayoría cristiano, y que una revolución marxista para ser popular debía hacerse también con los cristianos" (*IE*, 337; "And that was one of the great wise moves of the Sandinista Front: its recognition that the Nicaraguan people were in their majority Christian, and that a Marxist revolution, in order to be popular, must also be on the side of the Christians").

To an even greater extent than *Vida perdida*, *Las ínsulas extrañas* and *La revolución perdida* are written in the oral voice of Testimonio. Though he wrote the memoirs by hand, Cardenal addresses his readers in the second-person plural "ustedes," playing up the tone of an old man – the second volume of his memoirs was published when he was seventy-seven and the third when he was seventy-nine – who is recounting tales to a younger audience that may become restive. The narrative is laced with phrases, such as "¿Y saben qué pasó? Ahora sí que no me van a creer" (*IE*, 216; "And do you know what happened? Now you really won't believe me"), that draw the reader into the deliberately naive narration as a participant. Cardenal claimed to have no particular stylistic goal in adopting this voice: "Me pareció interesante hacerlo así – más que el estilo escrito, con el estilo oral" (*UIEC*; "It struck me as interesting to do it that way – more than with the written style, with the oral style"). The Testimonio genre, like the foundation of Solentiname, allows Cardenal to bridge class divides by employing the literary mode associated with the bearing witness of the poor. This tactic snatches back revolutionary authority from the jaws of the 1990 defeat. Revolutionary authority no longer implies active command in a movement of radical social upheaval. Rather, strategies such as the adoption of the Testimonio voice provide Cardenal with a means of perpetuating the postmodern image of the revolutionary – the beret, the beard, the mien of a prophet, and the enduring faith in Marxism – which, in the post-1990 environment, become signs of anachronism yet, at the same time, markers of a distinctive individuality that remains uniquely recognizable and is an effective means of publicizing the author and his works to globalized literary markets. As Nicasio Urbina concludes in his survey of the memoirs of Cardenal, Ramírez, and Belli: "La escritura autobiográfica se puede ver como el acto más descarnado del capitalismo intelectual, por medio del cual el autor le saca la última gota de plusvalía a su capital cultural" (Urbina 2004a; "Autobiographical writing can be seen as the most blatant act of intellectual capitalism, by means of which the author sucks the last drop of surplus value from his cultural capital").

The ideological origins of these symbols, however, may not be consistent with public perceptions. Cardenal's revolutionary beret, so often interpreted as a visual salute to Che Guevara, was in fact adopted in imitation of his mentor in poetry and Conservative thought, José Coronel Urtecho. Describing his decision to grow his hair in the late 1960s, Cardenal notes that in Solentiname he often wore a headband,

> pero me parecía que en la ciudad luciría demasiado extravagante – demasiado hippie – y para presentarme en público opté por la boina, que no llama la atención; imitando en eso a Coronel, que tenía años de usarla. Por eso en las fotos aparezco casi siempre con boina. Después del Che la boina ha tenido una connotación revolucionaria, pero no es por eso que la escogí. (*IE*, 183; but it seemed to me that in the city it would look too extravagant – too hippieish – and to appear in public I chose the beret, which didn't attract attention, imitating Coronel, who had been wearing one for years. That's why in photos I almost always appear in a beret. After Che the beret had a revolutionary connotation, but that's not why I chose it.)

The Conservative roots of Cardenal's revolutionary stances are reiterated at the beginning of the final volume of the memoirs, *La revolución perdida*. This volume opens with the sole rupture that mars the linear chronology that is initiated at the beginning of the second volume. Like *Las ínsulas extrañas*, *La revolución perdida* consists of an odd number of chapters, with the middle chapter dominated by the volume's pivotal event. The first eight chapters relate the war against Somoza; in the ninth chapter, "El triunfo" ("The Triumph"), the guerrillas take power; the last eight chapters narrate the institutionalization, achievements, and eventual collapse of Sandinista Nicaragua.

The first chapter does not follow on from the final chapter of *Las ínsulas extrañas*, in which the young people of Solentiname decide to pick up guns, but rather leaps back into Cardenal's youth to insert the history of his early anti-Somoza militancy that is suppressed in *Vida perdida*. Here he speaks of his activism against Somocista Liberalism as a member of the nationalistic Conservative political party UNAP, his participation in the 1954 April Rebellion, and the fate of the Rebellion of Olama y los Mollejones led by his cousins Pedro Joaquín Chamorro and Luis Cardenal. The effect of this structural decision is to present the events of the years 1977 to 1979, which dominate the second through the ninth chapters, as though they were a prolongation, by other means and with new, heavily armed peasant allies, of the Conservative dissident project. Though UNAP's membership consisted of the boys from the Colegio Centroamericano soccer field, who accepted the precept that their Catholicism forbade them from being Communists,

> éramos revolucionarios y teníamos un lema que era: "Más a la izquierda que el comunismo." Éramos nacionalistas al ejemplo de Sandino, o sea antiimperialistas; propugnábamos la repartición de la propiedad, el apoyo al campesino mediante cooperativas, la defensa de las clases populares, la democracia." (*RP*, 10; we were revolutionaries and we had a motto: "Further left than Communism." We were nationalists who followed Sandino's example, in other words anti-imperialists; we campaigned for the distribution of property, the support of peasants through cooperatives, the defence of the working classes, democracy.)

In this way, the FSLN platform is presented as having originated in the 1950s in the tiny, marginalized, elitist UNAP. Whether or not this is historically accurate, it establishes the revolutionary retooling of the nation to which *La revolución perdida* is dedicated as a long-term extrapolation of the imagined community of renegade 1940s and 1950s Conservative youth.

As it proceeds, Cardenal's autobiographical trilogy opens out like a funnel: *Vida perdida* narrates a spiritual quest, *Las ínsulas extrañas* describes the life of a community, and in *La revolución perdida* the protagonist is the revolutionary nation. The tone of the third volume is often that of an historian. Cardenal reconstructs events by quoting both oral testimony, some of which he recorded at the time, and books and articles written after the fact. He claimed that he was not conscious of this widening focus when he was writing the memoirs: "Simplemente, el tema del que yo iba hablando me iba imponiendo esa diferencia. Es que, en gran parte yo no tuve participación. Pero quería hacer la historia de la revolución. No sólo contarlo aquello en lo que yo había participado" (*UIEC*; "Simply, the theme about which I was speaking imposed this difference on me. I did not participate in the majority of it. But I wanted to write the history of the revolution. Not just relate that part in which I had participated"). The story of the Revolution is Cardenal's autobiography. His being, as constructed in the post-1990 period, is inseparable from the Sandinistas' rise and seizure of power and the revolutionary state that forged an autonomous Nicaraguan nation.

Molloy's insights that "if not always perceiving themselves as historians ... autobiographers will continue to see themselves as witnesses" and that the subject of Spanish American autobiography is often "terminal visions – the autobiographer bearing witness to that which is no more" (Molloy 1991: 7) are germane to this discussion. As noted above, in contradiction of Benjamin's notion of the relic, *La revolución perdida* finds its moment of primal equality in the recent past, though it is a more distant, relic-like past of nineteenth-century Conservative suzerainty and 1950s elite nationalist agitation that the Revolution vindicates. Revolutionary Nicaragua, in Cardenal's depiction, represents the extrapolation, transformation, and diffusion of Conservative nationalist values into 1980s leftism; it is the non-revolutionary present of globalization that the narrative rejects. At the same time, the historian's lofty perspective, accentuated by Cardenal's belief that all that occurs is predestined by God, gives the narrative voice a chilly quality. In Daniel Gamper's characterization:

> Parece a veces despiadado, frío, cuando contempla los sacrificios del pasado, las muertes en ambos bandos de la guerra civil. Parece como si lo hiciera desde la eternidad. No con la frialdad del político profesional o del revolucionario ensorbebecido, sino con el hábito sacerdotal, esto es, con la costumbre de ver los asuntos humanos en toda su pequeñez y caducidad. (Gamper 2005: 251; At times he seems heartless, cold, when he contemplates the sacrifices of the past, the deaths in both camps in the civil war. It seems as though he's writing from eternity. Not with the coldness of the professional politician or the haughty revolutionary, but rather with the priestly custom of seeing human affairs in all their smallness and ephemerality.)

In fact, Cardenal is commemorating these "insignificant" individuals; his association of Sandinismo with primitive Christianity obliges him to record the sacrifices of the martyrs. Yet, as Gamper suggests, the tone is one of almost unseemly rejoicing at each young person who gives his or her life for the cause. For example, Cardenal tells the story of his nephew, Gabriel Cardenal, a wealthy, handsome young playboy educated in the United States, who incarnates the emptiness of modern life: "era marihuanero, se acostaba libremente con cualquier muchacha, estaba embullado con el rock: pero sentía un vacío interior" (*RP*, 271; "he was a pothead, he went to bed with any girl he met, he was obsessed with rock and roll: yet he felt a void inside him"). Persuaded by his brother to remain in Nicaragua during a vacation there in the late 1970s, Gabriel joins a Christian Base Community in a poor neighbourhood of Managua and undergoes "proletarianización" (*RP*, 273; "proletarianization") as he sheds his class privileges and lives among the poor. By the time of the final offensive, he is an urban guerrilla. Captured by the National Guard, he makes a morale-boosting speech to twenty-five other prisoners as he is taken away to be shot. One of the survivors recalls: "tenía el aspecto de un Nazareno, de uno de esos Cristos martirizados de las iglesias" (*RP*, 278; "he had the appearance of a Nazarene, of one of those martyred Christs in the churches"). Allegorical accounts such as this, in which each martyr becomes a Christ figure, reinforce the claim that the Nicaraguan Revolution is the work of a divine hand. The almost fable-like tone in which Cardenal narrates these martyrdoms may seem to condone the human cost, particularly when the martyr is young, a protégé or a close relative. The satisfaction that emanates from a narrative voice that takes pleasure in each shred of evidence of the fulfilment of God's design gives the impression that it devalues humanity at the same time that it exalts the individual act of self-sacrifice.

Even God's contribution to the Revolution is subordinated to the primacy of national self-assertion. *La revolución perdida* is a rough-edged book, marred by digressions, contradictions, and small factual errors, that feels as though it needed tighter editing. While the layout of the chapters is logical and sequential, the internal organization of some of these chapters is jumbled. The most controversial topics receive the clearest, most carefully documented treatment. The eleventh chapter, "Convirtiendo la oscurana en claridad" ("Converting the Shadows into Light"), is devoted to the literacy campaign's merging of social classes that did not know each other into a united nation in which "los jóvenes alfabetizadores eran llamados 'hijo' o 'hija' por los campesinos en cuyas casas vivían" (*RP*, 386; "the young literacy teachers were called 'son' or 'daughter' by the peasants in whose houses they lived"); the twelfth, "Gracias a Dios y a la Revolución" ("Thanks to God and the Revolution"), provides a meticulous excoriation of Pope John Paul II's manipulative arrogance during his 1983 visit to Nicaragua, concluding that "el pueblo le faltó respeto al Papa, es verdad, pero es que antes el Papa le había faltado respeto al pueblo" (*RP*, 429; "the people failed to show the Pope respect, it's true, but before that the Pope had failed to respect the people"); the sixteenth, "El Yanqui enemigo de la humanidad"

("The Yankee, Enemy of Humanity"), documents the Contra War and shows that even those who served the United States, such as Cardenal's cousin, the Contra leader Edgar Chamorro, were treated by the Americans with dishonesty. In chapters such as these, Cardenal recedes from autobiographer to historian in a way that makes his personal history indistinguishable from that of the nation.

Personal confessions sit uneasily in this context, and when they creep into the text, they are disconcerting. Speaking of his countless trips abroad to promote the Revolution, Cardenal mentions in passing that once, on his way back from Buenos Aires, "rompí en el avión los papeles que tenía de una muchacha, y hasta su dirección, porque ella me amaba y yo estaba a punto de enamorarme; era de 17 años y lindísima pero yo preferí quedarme con el amor de Dios que ya tenía" (*RP*, 491; "in the plane I tore up the papers I'd received from a girl, and even her address, because she was in love with me and I was on the point of falling in love; she was seventeen years old and very pretty, but I preferred to stick with the love of God that I had already"). These are the only details that he provides of this challenge to his vows of celibacy. The extremely naive tone reinforces the sense that the sixty-year-old priest who is experiencing this event (like the man in his late seventies who is narrating it) has a view of male-female relations that has not grown in subtlety since 1943, when he fell in love with fourteen-year-old Carmen Chamorro.

The Revolution is a vital, compelling experience because it induces the Nicaraguan nation to cohere for the first time in its history. This constitution of the nation is confirmed by both the internal articulation of a distinct culture and by the use of analogy to rank Nicaragua with other nations that have asserted their identities. Gamper claims that "Cardenal recibe el discurso romántico según el cual el espíritu del pueblo se expresa eminentemente en las formas artísticas reforzándose así la unidad nacional, requisito imprescindible para una revolución" (Gamper 2005: 255; "Cardenal accepts the Romantic discourse according to which the spirit of the people is eminently expressed through artistic forms, reinforcing national unity, an indispensable condition for a revolution"). This statement is accurate as a generalization, but it overlooks the Revolution's historical circumstances: both its inheritance of nationalist cultural discourses from the Mexican Revolution in the 1920s and the Guatemalan Revolution in the 1940s; and the crushing cultural alienation that prevailed in Nicaragua prior to 1979.

The concept of the "alma nacional" ("national soul") developed by José Vasconcelos, Mexican minister of education in the 1920s, adapted to Central America by the Guatemalan Revolution and absorbed, albeit less explicitly, by the Nicaraguan Revolution, was more nuanced than the Romanticism that Gamper mentions. The integration of indigenous elements into a mongrelized national culture was crucial to forging the hybridized "national soul" (Taracena Arriola 1988: 685): an expression that Cardenal does not employ, though his policies as minister of culture reflected its assumptions. The resurgence of traditional handicrafts is depicted as a spontaneous self-expression on the part of rural people, adopted by Nicaraguans of all classes:

> Los muebles de la gente rica, que también antes se pedían en Miami, ahora fueron nicaragüenses. La artesanía había decaído muchísimo, y creíamos que estaba perdida para siempre, y de pronto empezó a resurgir en todo el país. Se trabajaba el oro, el nácar y el coral negro en la costa del Caribe y los miskitos tallaban la madera; se labraba la piedra en San Juan de Limay y después en Camoapa, donde se descubrió una piedra igualmente buena. (*RP*, 346; Rich people's furniture, which used to be ordered in Miami, was now Nicaraguan. Traditional handicrafts had declined greatly, and we thought they were lost forever, and then they suddenly started to re-emerge all over the country. On the Caribbean Coast people worked in gold, mother-of-pearl and black coral and the Miskito carved wood; stone was sculpted in San Juan de Limay and later in Camoapa, where an equally good stone was discovered.)

This recuperation of despised or forgotten cultures in the most remote corners of the country was lent urgency and legitimacy by the cultural alienation instilled by fifty years of Yankee-worshipping dictatorship. Cardenal's Ministry of Culture, based in a house that had been built by Hope Portocarrero de Somoza, the last dictator's wife, was a replica of a Miami mansion: "Como los planos decían que los techos eran de *Spanish tiles*, los *Spanish tiles* fueron llevados en avión a Managua, para descubrir después que eran las vulgares tejas de barro del pueblo nicaragüense" (*RP*, 467; "Since the plans said that the roofs would be made of 'Spanish tiles,' the 'Spanish tiles' were brought by plane to Managua, only to have it discovered that they were the vulgar clay shingles of the Nicaraguan people"). Cardenal depicts the culture of the Nicaraguan Revolution as an unpremeditated reaction against this subservience: "Con el triunfo aparecieron Casas de Cultura dondequiera, creadas espontáneamente por el pueblo antes que hubiéramos tiempo de organizarlas nosotros" (*RP*, 472; "With the triumph, Houses of Culture appeared everywhere, created spontaneously by the people before we had time to organize them ourselves").

Much of Cardenal's account of his tenure as minister of culture focuses on the turf war conducted against him by Rosario Murillo, whose opposition to the poetry workshops and other initiatives he depicts as motivated not by verifiable ideological differences but by simple jealousy that he had been named to the post that she coveted. [6] Cast by Murillo in the role of Stalinist ideologue to her promotion of professional artists who pursued aesthetic values, he decries the inundation of Nicaragua with boring socialist tracts sent by Warsaw Pact countries (*RP*, 475) and denies that the poetry workshops were instilling "socialist realism," as Murillo claimed. Cardenal accuses Murillo of perpetuating the elite Conservative poetry incarnated by the Betrayed Generation: "Yo encontré que era necesario enseñar a nuestro pueblo, que era tan amante de la poesía, las técnicas de la buena poesía moderna" (*RP*, 498–9; "I found it was necessary to teach our people, who were such lovers of poetry, the techniques of good modern poetry"). If Cardenal's reference to "our people" sounds paternalistic, Murillo's policies, which would keep literature confined to the elite who had always practised it, were aristocratic.

Seeking the integration of indigenous culture into the national mainstream, Cardenal established his first two poetry workshops in indigenous neighbourhoods, Monimbó in Masaya and Subtiava in León. Refuting Murillo's claim that he was uninterested in high art, Cardenal points out that the first book published in Nicaragua after the Revolution was a mass-market edition of the poems of Rubén Darío. *La revolución perdida* devotes excessive space to the tactics employed by Murillo to discredit each policy promoted by the Ministry of Culture. Cardenal reiterates that "la revolución fue una cultura nueva. Esto es, una cultura nuestra" (*RP*, 535; "the revolution was a new culture. That's to say, our culture"). Hardship consolidated this allegiance to tradition: when the Reagan Administration cut off Nicaragua's access to wheat – even though Canada, Sweden, the Soviet Union, and Bulgaria found ways to break the US embargo – many Nicaraguans returned to the Mesoamerican tradition of baking with corn. The description of the revival of corn cults (*RP*, 538–40) extends the link with the Guatemalan Revolution, which produced, among other works, Miguel Ángel Asturias's *Men of Maize*.

The act of defining the nation is dual: the imagined community that, in the absence of a pre-existing literate bourgeoisie, depends on peasants who have passed through the literacy campaign, militia training, and poetry workshops, is echoed by bonds in the world beyond Latin America with nations whose predicaments are analogous to that of Nicaragua. Foremost among these, for Cardenal, is Iran. It is striking that the seventh chapter of *La revolución perrdida*, which immediately precedes the chapters on the final offensive and the triumph, is devoted to Cardenal's relationship with revolutionary Iran. In April 1979, shortly after the triumph of the Iranian Revolution, Cardenal became the second foreign dignitary received by the Ayatollah Khomeini (the first was Palestine Liberation Organization leader Yasser Arafat); he was granted a second audience with Khomeini a few weeks before the latter's death in 1989, at a time when Khomeini had refused to receive foreign visitors for more than two years.[7] Nicaragua and Iran had both been victimized by dictatorships imposed by US intervention, both revolutions triumphed in 1979, each mingled a religious revival with nationalist anger, and, crucially for Cardenal, Rubén Darío had written about ancient Persia. As Cardenal recalled, "en un exótico país que antes se llamó Persia y fue soñado por Rubén Darío, yo había soñado el triunfo de la revolución de Nicaragua" (*RP*, 233; "in an exotic country that used to be called Persia and was dreamed by Rubén Darío, I had dreamed the triumph of the Nicaraguan Revolution"). Darío's imaginings materialize in Iranian reality: a revolution in this country signals that revolution will also come to Nicaragua.

Cardenal arrives in Iran in search of a model of the imagined community of the revolutionary nation. He observes parallels between the two countries' respective experiences of subjugation by US foreign policy, learning that Anastasio Somoza Debayle's bosom buddy, Senator Jack Murphy (who would later appear as a character in Sergio Ramírez's *Sombras nada más*), also worked on behalf of the shah of Iran. When Cardenal meets Khomeini, the ayatollah's first words to the revolutionary priest are that "por ser yo de Nicaragua podía entender el sufrimiento de ellos, que había sido por 50 años" (*RP*, 223; "since I was from Nicaragua I could understand their suffering, which had lasted for fifty years"). Just as Cardenal will soon inherit a house built by the dictator's wife as his Ministry of Culture, Tehran, too, is full of mansions with unsavoury histories. Cardenal is lodged in the abandoned palace of Shapur Bakhtiar, the shah's final puppet prime minister:

> Siento en la cama una sensación de desagrado … Estas sábanas pueden haber sido las de Bakhtiar. Pero luego pienso: este palacio ahora es del pueblo, de los muchachos con sus ametralladoras; y que también me están cuidando a mí, no por mi persona sino por una revolución hermana. El que yo esté alojado aquí es un homenaje a los sandinistas nicaragüenses de parte de los "sandinistas" persas. (*RP*, 204; In bed, I feel a sensation of displeasure … These sheets could have been Bakhtiar's. But then I think: this palace belongs to the people now, to the boys with their machine guns; and they are looking after me, too, not for who I am, but because of a fraternal revolution. The fact that

I'm lodged here is a homage to the Nicaraguan Sandinistas from the "Persian Sandinistas.")

In dubbing the young Iranian revolutionaries "Persian Sandinistas," Cardenal makes explicit the sense of community shared by the two revolutionary cohorts. When he meets the revolution's deputy prime ministers, he is told that the Iranians regard Nicaragua in a similar light, as a "fraternal revolution":

> Les mostré fotos de la lucha de Nicaragua: los muchachos con sus pañuelos rojinegros en el rostro, los mitines a la luz de fogatas hechas con llantas, etc. Me dicen que al final se usó aquí lo de las fogatas con llantas. También usaron un poco lo de los pañuelos y las fogatas (y pienso que las dos cosas fueron tomadas de Nicaragua). Me dice el Dr. Yazdi que las dos revoluciones se parecían mucho, aunque la de Nicaragua era con más sufrimiento. Me dice también que ellos habían aprendido de la revolución de Nicaragua. Cuando nuestra insurrección de septiembre [1978], él se reunía todos los días en París con Khomeini para analizar las noticias de Nicaragua. (*RP*, 207–8; I showed them photographs of the Nicaraguan struggle: the boys with their red-and-black bandannas over their faces, the meetings by the light of bonfires lighted from tires. They also used the bandannas and the bonfires (and I think both traits were taken from Nicaragua). Dr. Yazdi tells me that the two revolutions resembled each other a lot, although Nicaragua's involved more suffering. He also tells me that they had learned from the Nicaraguan Revolution. During our September [1978] offensive, he met every day in Paris with Khomeini to analyze the news from Nicaragua.)

Sharing the custom of holding meetings around a bonfire may appear to be a tangential correspondence, yet this Iranian borrowing of a ritual central to the imagery of Sandino's struggle cements the two revolutions' fraternal connection. Like Nicaragua, Iran is discovering itself. Cardenal's travel companion Abdollah Ghasgai tells him: "Por primera vez en 2,500 años, Irán es una república" (*RP*, 209; "For the first time in 2500 years, Iran is a republic"). In spite of this enthusiastic discovery of the nation suppressed by US neo-colonialism, Cardenal's experiences in Iran provide an early warning of the ruptures that attend the revolutionary experience. Abdollah later revolts against Khomeini, and either dies in battle or is poisoned; when his sister arrives in Nicaragua to speak with Cardenal, he turns her away: "la mayor ayuda financiera que recibía Nicaragua era de Irán. Ella lo sabía; y ni ella ni yo podíamos hablar con franqueza. Lo lamento" (*RP*, 212; "Nicaragua's largest source of financial aid was Iran. She knew it; and neither she nor I could speak openly. I regret it"). These examples of post-triumph strife nevertheless complete the exchange between the two revolutions by informing Nicaragua's decision not to execute National Guardsmen as Iran executes the thugs and torturers of the Shah's regime: "Los fusilamientos me parece que fueron justos, pero a nivel internacional hicieron mucho daño a la revolución de Irán" (*RP*, 234; "The executions struck me as just, but at an international level they did the Iranian Revolution a lot of damage").

Beyond the inspiration of its anti-imperialist example, and the financial aid it provides, Iran offers Nicaragua a model of the integration of religious belief into revolutionary discourse. In both countries, the revolution is made possible by the fusion of nationalism and religious morality. Cardenal finds a kindred spirit in the revolutionary cleric Ayatollah Madari, who, like him, understands the potent force of religious belief at the service of an anti-imperialist struggle: "Esa fuerza no la pueden medir las computadoras. Y la usamos contra ellos y ganamos … Y eso deben hacer ustedes en América Latina con la fuerza religiosa de sus pueblos" (*RP*, 227; "This force can't be measured by computers. And we used it against them and we won … And that's what you in Latin America should do with your peoples' religious strength"). Ayatollah Taleghani goes further, claiming that Islam arose as a response to Christianity's abandonment of its original mission of defending the poor: "Si la hubiera cumplido no hubiera necesidad de Islam, ellos hubieran seguido siendo cristianos" (*RP*, 229; "If it had fulfilled it, Islam would not have been necessary, they could have remained Christians"). Primitive Christianity acts as a common text, an Andersonian shared newspaper, that unites literate religious leaders from Iran and Nicaragua in a transnational imagined community (even though other aspects of these situations do not match Anderson's model). This common ancestor of liberation theology and radical Islam becomes a point of origin for both revolutionary nations. Ayatollah Khomeini tells Cardenal: "Todos los pueblos del mundo les cortarán las manos a los extranjeros que les roban sus riquezas" (*RP*, 223; "All the peoples of the world will cut off the hands of the foreigners who rob them of their riches"). The internationalist vocation of the Iranian Revolution reposes on a foundation of shared religious belief that supports a notion of justice that is translatable across national, cultural, and ideological boundaries. The two deputy prime ministers emphasize that the slogan *Ahá o akhbar!* ("God is great!") was employed across the political spectrum: "Lo gritaban los religiosos y los no religiosos, incluso los comunistas" (*RP*, 209; "It was shouted by religious and non-religious people, including Communists").

The invocation of Communists shouting religious slogans has obvious resonance for the FSLN. Anderson's theories, rooted in distinctions between the sacred and secular orders, in which the secularization of print-capitalism creates the conditions for the articulation of the imagined community, do not explain this strain of nationalism. Nor does the arousal of fellow feeling between the FSLN and the Iranian Revolution – which has remained solid for more than thirty years – fit Anderson's model, in which nationalism is invented in Europe and imitated in or exported to the rest of the world. The conditions of nations such Iran or Nicaragua, which for much of the twentieth century, though formally independent, were ruled by tyrannical cliques at the behest of the United States, reducing the two countries to a reality not fully known, a conglomeration of a lost past, Utopian dreams of the future, and religious faith, demand a different paradigm. Here Walter Mignolo's concept of "border thinking," of a history imagined from the periphery, is illuminating. Rejecting the idea of the nation as a model exported by Europe, Mignolo provides a reminder that "the nation-state was not something already constituted in Europe but something that was being made both in Europe and in Latin America" (Mignolo 2000: 337). And, he might add, in Asia. Once the chronology that conceives the nation as a European invention has been broken – an outlook that is evident in Abdollah Ghasgai's words – one may view the nation as a concept that is incessantly renewed, one that feeds upon a wide variety of sources over the course of its history. It is a concept that Iran and Nicaragua reinvent in similar ways in 1979.

In the final analysis, though, and in contradiction of any fixed ideology, be it of internationalist solidarity or triumphalist globalization, each nation is alone with its history. By the time Cardenal returned to Iran in 1989, dreams of world revolution had retreated before the grinding reality of surviving counter-revolutionary aggression. This time there was no talk of common ancestors of radical Islam and liberation theology; in the urgent context of the final months of the Cold War, the Benjaminian relic of a primitive Christian *Urgeschichte* prior to distinctions of social class or neocolonialism is a luxury that no one can afford. The dying Khomeini's exceptional gesture of granting Cardenal an interview does not change the fact that each besieged revolution is on its own. Desperate to obtain shipments of oil to keep the Nicaraguan war machine in motion against the Contras, Cardenal recounts that:

> Yo le hablé [a Khomeini] de la conveniencia de una unión del cristianismo revolucionario y del Islam revolucionario. Me parece que indirectamente rebatió esa idea cuando, entre otras frases piadosas,

recomendó que cada uno se mantuviera fiel a su fe. Cuando le hablé de la guerra que nos estaba haciendo el Gran Satán ... me dijo que compadecía nuestros sufrimientos, pero que nosotros sólo teníamos ese enemigo, mientras que ellos tenían también a Irak, a Russia y al sionismo. (*RP*, 224–5; I spoke [to Khomeini] of the advisability of a union of revolutionary Christianity and revolutionary Islam. It seems to me that he indirectly rebuffed this idea when, amid other pious phrases, he recommended that each of us remain faithful to his own faith. When I spoke to him of the war that the Great Satan was making on us .... he told me that he sympathized with our suffering but that we had only that enemy, while they also had Iraq, Russia and Zionism.)

Like Cardenal, Khomeini, the author of more than forty books, has written his nation into existence and initiated his people into reading the nation from his text. The imagined community of the nation trumps international solidarity or border thinking-inspired analogies between peripheral nations in different corners of the globe; it fends off solidarity's grim post-1990 shadow, neo-liberal globalization. Yet, if Cardenal's ties with Iran prove ephemeral, and Khomeini, in his enviable position as a religious man who commands a revolutionary nation, ultimately fails to join Coronel, Merton, and Castro in Cardenal's pantheon of male mentors, the opportunities to address him as an equal nevertheless attest to the international stature of the Nicaraguan Revolution during the 1980s. Cardenal's account of his relationship with Khomeini's Iran confirms his own agency, certifying, in Lancaster's terms, his "activity," and the manhood he wielded prior to 1990. Like *La revolución perdida* in its entirety, the Iranian chapter consecrates revolutionary Nicaragua's role in world history, its validity as a relic that attracts attention even in the bleak post-1990 landscape.

Cardenal adheres to his religious faith, as Khomeini advised, and to the heritage of the Revolution. Having completed his autobiographical trilogy, he has consolidated his identity as a man of religion and revolution. However anachronistic this identity may appear after 1990, the fact of having preserved in prose the record of his role as community leader and government minister, and the dramatic achievements and worldwide attention that characterized the version of the Nicaraguan nation that he served, consolidates a bulwark against the depletion of his authority and masculinity that he had confronted in "Telescope in the Dark Night" and *Vida perdida*. As he told the Mexican newspaper *La Jornada*: "era indispensable recordar hechos ya olvidados" (Güemes 2003; "it was essential to remember facts that had already been forgotten"). Uninterested in reaching accommodation with the neo-liberal thought of accelerated globalization, he is content to remain swaddled by the past that he has now delineated on his own terms, aware that his period of political activity has ended but confident that God's design is destined to bring the revolutionary cycle back to earth. It is as a liberation theology priest that Cardenal concludes his memoirs:

> Creemos que el Reino de los Cielos es en esta tierra pero también en el cielo. Basta mirar arriba de noche y lo estamos viendo. Son esos millones y millones de estrellas con planetas habitados, con evoluciones y revoluciones como en el nuestro ... Toda revolución nos acerca a ese Reino, aun una revolución perdida. Habrá más revoluciones. Pidamos a Dios que se haga su revolución en la tierra como en el cielo. (*RP*, 666; We believe that the Kingdom of Heaven is on earth but also in the heavens. It's enough to look up at night to see it. There are millions and millions of stars with inhabited planets, with their evolutions and revolutions, like ours ... Every revolution brings us close to that Kingdom, even a lost revolution. There will be more revolutions. We pray to God that he make his revolution on earth as in heaven.)

By finishing this massive work with a prayer, Cardenal suggests his relative indifference to the present. Though he continued to participate in Nicaraguan politics, campaigning for MRS candidates, making political statements during poetry readings, and, in 2008, acquiring dissident status (see chapter 3), he regarded his own development as having concluded in 1990. He said of his memoirs: "Llego hasta el fin de la revolución. Contar lo que pasó después ya no me interesa" (Güemes 2003; "I reach the end of the revolution. Recounting what happened afterwards doesn't interest me").

Cardenal's aloofness from the present spares him from having to compromise with the liberal discourse of globalization. He continues to traffic in moral absolutes, in concepts of duty and justice. Though he supported democratic procedures, he would identify himself emphatically as a socialist, resisting any slide into social democracy. In a comment on Spanish politics in *La revolución perdida*, he laments the dilution of the anti-Franco socialism of the early 1970s by an electorally successful social democracy: "Lástima que el socialismo auténtico que era el de Tierno Galván sucumbiera ante el partido de Felipe González" (*RP*, 63; "What a shame that the authentic socialism of Tierno Galván should have succumbed before the party of Felipe González"). This point of contrast with Sergio Ramírez, who was comfortable with social democracy to the point of being endorsed by González during his 1996 presidential campaign, reaffirms Cardenal's separation from contemporary discourses.

After 1990, Conservatives who had become Sandinistas were able to evoke their ideals only by alluding to a revolutionary past festooned with Conservative references. This is clear in a work such as Gioconda Belli's novel *Waslala* (1996). Though much less artistically successful than *The Inhabited Woman*, *Waslala* is revealing of the conundrum that faced Conservative Sandinistas after 1990. The novel sketches in simple, dramatic terms the outlook shared by Cardenal, Belli, and others. The subtitle, "Memorial del futuro" ("Memoir of the Future"), encapsulates the paradox of waiting for the future to reactivate the past. The novel is set at a time when nations have been formally dissolved, English is the only language, and poor regions of the earth have been abandoned as lawless nature preserves whose leaders enrich themselves by exporting oxygen to wealthy regions. Books have been replaced by screens and virtual travel makes physical journeys unnecessary. Officially, Faguas – Belli's fictional term for Nicaragua – no longer exists. Yet, as the characters insist, the concept of the nation persists and provides the only hope for the future; the young protagonist Melisandra states, "Al no haber causa, ni concepto de nación, no hay reglas" (Belli 1996: 173; "If one doesn't have a cause, or a concept of nation, there are no rules"). Faguas has degenerated into an amorphous terrain defined by endless warfare between rival bands in which the most powerful figures are two moustached brothers, blatantly reminiscent of Daniel and Humberto Ortega, who still see themselves as revolutionaries even though they are devoted to suborning oxygen revenues and trafficking in a potent new drug. Melisandra is brought up on a riverside farm by her wise grandfather, who is over one hundred years old and who represents the only hope for the future. The grandfather and the farm are obvious portraits, as Belli confirms in an author's note, of José Coronel Urtecho and his retreat on the San Juan River. The contradiction at the heart of the novel, and of the position of intellectuals such as Belli and Cardenal, is that Coronel Urtecho, regarded by a Conservative such as Arturo J. Cruz, Jr, as "the most influential Nicaraguan mind of the twentieth century" (Cruz, Jr 2002: 4), becomes the point of origin of the reactionary/revolutionary past and the inspiration for the potential revolutionary future.

The novel's title is also that of a poem from Cardenal's *Flights of Victory* about an indigenous community enjoying its first flush of revolutionary radiance (see chapter 8). In Belli's novel the word "Waslala" refers to a paradisal community – a conflation of Sandino's commune of Wiwilí,

Solentiname, and revolutionary Nicaragua in its entirety – that was founded by Melisandra's grandfather and other poets, most notably, "Ernesto, un poeta callado, sabio, con profundos conocimientos de la física y del cosmos" (Belli 1996: 52; "Ernesto, a quiet, wise poet with a deep knowledge of physics and the cosmos"). The novel's action consists of a quest to discover whether this nationalist, egalitarian Utopia still exists. Revolutionary mythology endures: Waslala is believed to be in the north of the country, redoubt of the insurgencies of Sandino and Fonseca; enemies of the nation are haunted by ghosts from Wiwilí, even though the memory of Sandino has vanished and the massacre of his followers has become confused in the popular imagination with the Siege of Troy. Engracia, the family servant, who connects the elite protagonists to the ordinary people and the post-national present to the revolutionary past, creates the novel's denouement by taking up the revolutionary act of writing on paper to attest to the marvels of the lost society of Waslala: "fue lo más hermoso que me sucedió en la vida. No puedo imaginar que hubiera sido de mí sin esa experiencia" (*Waslala*, 286; "it was the most beautiful thing that happened to me in my life. I can't imagine what my life would have been without that experience"). Melisandra discovers that she is able to return to Waslala through a fold in time; there she finds her mother, who gives her a legacy of printed books and typed manuscripts that will enable her to rebuild Waslala on the scale of Faguas: to parlay the revolutionary microcosm, undergirded by Conservative thought, into the literary culture that will animate the rebirth of the nation.

Like Cardenal in the closing scene of *Los años de Granada* and the opening chapter of *La revolución perdida*, Belli traces the inspiration behind modern Sandinismo and the creed's pure, unsullied essence to the writings and ideas of intellectuals from Conservative backgrounds.[8] Allergic to liberal relativism, schooled in concepts of absolute value, duty, and unbending morality, Conservative Sandinistas made uncomfortable converts to the post-1990 liberal world order of individual freedom, consumerism, free markets, women's equality, gay liberation, and the inflation of the self through the media. This is true, paradoxically, even though Belli's own life exemplified female sexual emancipation and *Waslala* includes a positive portrayal of a lesbian couple.

Belli reiterates a long-standing Sandinista precept that the nation is forged through literature, exists in literature, and may be rediscovered and revived there. By the same token, continuing to write became Cardenal's way of perpetuating the 1980s Sandinismo that he incarnated in his views, values, and personal appearance. Yet, as his return to poetry after concluding his memoirs would illustrate, the dialectical discourse of his revolutionary verse, from "Nicaraguan Canto" to *Cosmic Canticle*, was no longer feasible in the twenty-first century. Even when revolutionary touchstones were evoked, they were alluded to as relics, as discrete elements of a Utopian past that might eventually come around again, rather than as components of a potentially liberating synthesis. The structures of his verse no longer embodied radical reconfigurations of social organization.

"EVOLUTION IS REVOLUTIONS": *VERSOS DEL PLURIVERSO*

Versos del pluriverso (2005; Verses from the Pluriverse), Cardenal's first volume of poetry after his memoirs, sections off concerns that overlapped in the poetry of the 1980s into discrete topics that are addressed in separate poems. The collection consists of six long poems, ranging from seven to fifteen pages in length. The verse oscillates between the cosmic and personal levels; in the interstices of this shuttling between vastness and intimacy, the reader is confided glimpses of the nation in conserved form. Revolutionary and nationalist symbolism, when it appears, is often a kind of fondly recalled emblem of a primal era of equality prior to the social divisions that have been accentuated by accelerated globalization. This is particularly evident in "Con Martí mirando las estrellas" ("Gazing at the Stars with Martí"), where Cardenal's scientific characterizations of the cosmos culminate in the testimony of a ninety-year-old man in Cuba – taped by Cardenal's friend, the Catholic Cuban poet Cintio Vitier – who as a twelve-year-old boy spent part of an evening sitting next to José Martí and watching the stars. This poem ties cosmic evolutions most closely to terrestrial revolutions; in other poems, the nation is a more fleeting presence, a mere flicker of past glory unleashed by the swirling of the universe.

The opening poem, "Pluriverso" ("Pluriverse"), challenges the predestination that ordered Cardenal's memoirs with theories from contemporary physics. This work by an eighty-year-old poet conveys a sense of a very old, very lucid, man, steeped in the infinite yet ductile time of the cosmos, contemplating his own mortality: "Nuestra vida pasa a la velocidad de la luz/que es lo único absoluto de la Relatividad,/de la luz que no se atrasa no vuelve para atrás./Nunca para atrás. Astrofísica triste" (*VPL*, 10; "Our lives elapse at the speed of light/which is Relativity's only absolute,/of light that never slows down nor ever turns back./Never turns back. Sad astrophysics" [*PL*, 200]). The only consolation offered by quantum theory, which Cardenal reads as the expression of the complexity of the universe created by God, lies in the parallel existence of worlds in which events have turned out in different ways: "hay un mundo en que Napoleón venció en Waterloo./Y un mundo en que ella aceptó mi amor en Granada./Pero esos mundos y el nuestro no se juntarán jamás" (*VPL*, 11; "there's a world in which Napoleon won at Waterloo./And a world in which she accepted my love in Granada./ But those worlds and ours will never come together" [*PL*, 201]). Physics posits that a world may exist in which Cardenal and Carmen Chamorro lived happily ever after, or in which the Sandinistas won the 1990 elections. A meagre consolation arises from imagining such worlds, as they are inaccessible. Most of the poem's human references are to the girls Cardenal courted in his youth; this reconceptualization of the cosmos for a post-revolutionary era refuses to extrapolate the predestination of the memoirs into an assertion that God intended the Sandinistas to lose in 1990. While Solentiname, the revolution and Cardenal's role in it are portrayed in the memoirs as expressions of God's design, *Versos del pluriverso* rejects the assumption that the Cold War could not have ended otherwise than it did: "Tampoco Dios diciendo:/'Perdimos. Ya no hay campo socialista./Perdimos tambien las elecciones sandinistas'" (*VPL*, 18; "Nor God saying:/'We lost. The socialist camp is no more./We lost the Sandinista elections'" [*PL*, 207]). This, Cardenal asserts, supporting his vision with quotes from physicists, would be a Fascist universe. In reality, "El mal es porque Dios nos hizo libres" (*VPL*, 18; "Evil is because God made man free" [*PL*, 207]).

At the same time, Cardenal stages an assault on the notion of a fixed reality, depicting perception as dependent on the observer's perspective and location, creating a plural universe in which Schrödinger's cat may be alive in one dimension and dead in the other, emphasizing that our bodies are mainly liquid, that the electrons of which we are composed do not exist but rather "tienen tendencia a existir" (*VPL*, 20; "have a tendency to exist" [*PL*, 209]): that the objects described by physics may not, in the end, have a physical dimension. The citations from quantum theory lead to the poem's conclusion that we are essentially beings of spirit, not matter. While Cardenal retains his allegiance to binary structures – "Cada encuentro de dos unifica el universo" (*VPL*, 23; "every meeting of two unites the universe" [*PL*, 212]) – he asserts a plurality of universes. The poem closes with the label "pluriverse," spoken to him by a German physicist; yet Cardenal's vision of multiplicity is not founded on liberal give-and-take, or a celebration of postmodern "diversity," but rather on unions of opposites that are still implicitly dialectical in that neither component yields its essence, however fluid and ungraspable this may be, in order to merge with another.

In most of the poems, this process, falling somewhere between dialecticism and syncretism, operates on a limited, personal scale. At the same time, Cardenal's immersion in quantum theory renders him impervious to the exchange of opinions ranked as equal in validity until they are put to the test of debate that is promoted by manifestations of the post-1990 liberal world order, such as the June 1991 Santiago recognition of "representative democracy" as the form of government of the Americas (see chapter 10). His intellectual tradition remains Conservative rather than Liberal, Marxist rather than liberal. John Stuart Mill, the intellectual ancestor of modern liberal ideas, argued that an individual "is capable of rectifying his mistakes by discussion and experience. Not by experience alone. There must be discussion to show how experience is to be interpreted. Wrong opinions and practices gradually yield to fact and argument" (Mill 1972: 82). By contrast, Cardenal, in "El universo en 3 libras" ("3-Pound Universe"), the third poem in *Versos del pluriverso*, argues for the virtual impossibility of an exchange of perspectives.

His reading of physics insists that individual perspective is an illusion, but above all an illusion that is not accessible to others: we are each immured in our own three-pound brain. These thoughts are stimulated by a dinner in the Alps in the company of a female friend: "Y si te miro a ti como afuera/(hablando ahora en este restaurante)/te miro sólo en mi pupila./Y tocarte, si es que te tocara,/no sería que tocara tu piel/sino la mía, sus vibraciones en mi cerebro./No es que no existas, afuera, verdadera/amiga mía/pero tu realidad dentro de mi es ilusión" (*VPL*, 37; "And if I look at you as though outside/(talking now in this restaurant)/I see you only in my pupil./And touching you, were I to touch you,/wouldn't be touching your skin/but mine, the vibrations in my brain./It's not that you don't exist outside/dear friend, that you're not real/but your reality within me is an illusion" [*PL*, 213]). The poem cycles through a series of theoretical propositions by Richard Feynman, David Bohm, and Werner Heisenberg in search of the answer to the question: "¿Lo que llamamos el mundo real es mental?" (*VPL*, 38; "Is what we call the real world mental?" [*PL*, 21]). At first glance, ideas such as this would appear to be consistent with liberal cautions about the need for debate with those who hold opposing views prior to taking action: if we do not know the nature of the world beyond our senses, how can we act to change it? This poses severe restraints to revolutionary enthusiasms, almost necessitating that they come from the beyond, as part of an evolution in the cosmos, since the individual possesses no objective perception of his conditions. However, having hewed out a space for liberty in the opening poem, Cardenal requires a way around this impasse, without which there can be no criticism, no social progress, much less revolutionary action or a resuscitation of the nation.

Cardenal finds the solution to his metaphysical conundrum in his faith in the binary, the union of two in one that creates a synthesis that engenders a new reality. Even if their perceptions coincide only for a short time, or in a way that proves to be illusory, their union may still yield transformative change. After calling into question the materiality of life down to the level of the subatomic particle and of time, the poem concludes with an affirmative image of the consequences of Adam and Eve's congruent perceptions of the apple in the Garden of Eden, in spite of the differences between their neurons: "¿Es la manzana roja la misma para ti que para mí?/La misma fue para Adán que para Eva/… Las manzanas se pudren y las neuronas/ pero algo que no muere sale como mariposa …/del universo de 3 libras" (*VPL*, 46; "Is the red apple the same for you as for me?/It was the same for Adam as for Eve/… Apples rot and so do neurons/but something that doesn't die emerges like a butterfly …/from our 3-pound universe" [*PL*, 221]). A blind faith in union, whether this takes the form of interpersonal relationships or commitment to political action, redeems the human from the state of being sequestered in an impregnable palisade of untrustworthy perceptions. It is here that the hope for the revival of the nation, and particularly the revolutionary nation, slips through the cosmic grillwork.

The enshrinement of the revolutionary nation that emerges from the core of the universe and its genesis, and always accompanies us, is depicted in the second poem, "Gazing at the Stars with Martí." Revolving around the image of Martí, the father of Cuban independence and the forerunner of the twentieth-century Latin American literate revolutionary, observing the stars with a little boy and asking him whether he does not think that "¿habrá algo más grande que nosotros?" (*VPL*, 35; "that there has to be something greater than us?" [*OS*, 107]), this poem synthesizes Cardenal's cosmic and revolutionary preoccupations; the third plank of his 1980s triumvirate, radical Catholic theology, is addressed by a later poem, "Hoyos blancos" ("White Holes"). This synthesis of the cosmic and the revolutionary, as illustrated in the most striking stanza of "Gazing at the Stars with Martí," gives birth to the nation. Tracing the geological history of a mass of magma that begins to cool and solidify, the stanza follows this inanimate lump through time:

  al fin quedó quieto en un llano
reduciéndose poco a poco su tamaño
por la lluvia, el sol y el viento
puliéndose y haciéndose casi redonda
  cada vez más pequeño su tamaño
hasta que una mañana mojada de septiembre
cuando los filibusteros atacaban a San Jacinto
Andrés Castro la levantó del suelo
y con ella mató un yanki.

(*VPL*, 29; finally coming to rest on a plain/being worn down gradually/by the rain, the sun and the wind/making it smooth and almost round/increasingly smaller in size/until one wet September morning/when the filibusters were attacking San Jacinto/Andrés Castro picked it up from the ground/and killed a Yankee with it. [*OS*, 101–2])

The birth of the Nicaraguan nation in a humble man's killing of a well-equipped invader is the long-range outcome of cosmic processes: of the cycles of the heavens and individual effort, which intersect to create the diachronic time of history. Here Cardenal drafts David Bohm's ideas about the unity of all creation into an implicit endorsement of revolutionary action on behalf of a suppressed national entity: "El pecado es ir contra la evolución./La irrupción del futuro en el presente es la evolución./… La evolución son las revoluciones" (*VPL*, 33; "Sin is going against evolution./The irruption of the future in the present/that's evolution … Evolution is revolutions" [*OS*, 105]). This intertwining of the evolutionary process and the dialectical accretion of history, building towards revolution, first appeared in "Nicaraguan Canto" (see chapter 8). The connection endures in *Versos del pluriverso*, even though the language is leaner, more purified of discordant vocabularies, and less dialectical.

Near the poem's close, returning to the authority of physicists, Cardenal reiterates: "No hay partículas separadas/dice Bohm" (*VPL*, 35; "There are no separate particles/says Bohm" [*OS*, 107]). In this way, he salvages the revolutionary nation, at least in retrospective form, from the liberal relativism of accelerated globalization. The conclusion that to oppose the revolutionary impulse is a "sin" reinscribes the society of revolutionary duties in a context in which market individualisms have eroded the possibility of enunciating such moral imperatives. The verdict of "sin" no longer wields much potency once the society of duties and responsibilities, whether reactionary or revolutionary, has been dispersed by relativism; yet this framework persists as a potent relic of a past that the poet maintains will eventually return.

The absence of overlapping discourses that clash, such as the economic and the political with the scientific, the personal, or the religious, gives the merged languages of physics and theology the opportunity to blend in a register that is more lyrical than that of many of Cardenal's revolutionary-era poems. In spite of his allusions to revolutionary tropes, and his rejection of the globalized present, his focus is more concentrated on problems of the self than in his earlier work. "White Holes" exemplifies these changes. Opening with a pastoral description of the campus of the University of

British Columbia in Vancouver on the first day of classes, the poem recalls the UNAM campus more than forty-five years earlier to evoke the memory of the Mexican writer Rosario Castellanos, a contemporary and classmate of Cardenal's, who died in an accident in Israel in 1974. Castellanos's death becomes the point of departure for a consideration of where we go when we die. Over several pages, Cardenal develops the notion of death as part of a cycle that allows individuals to stimulate the progress of cosmic evolution by making way for their successors. While the references to people who have died are to revolutionaries, such as the young men of Solentiname, Che Guevara, and Camilo Torres, the speculations have the appearance of being strictly metaphysical in nature. Yet repeated references to evolutions and processes make clear that, among other things, the death of the individual ushers in the next generation of revolutionaries: "La muerte/por tanto necesaria. Alejandro, Laureano,/habrá otros ustedes que surgirán después./ Vendrán otros Camilos, dijo Fidel" (*VPL*, 55; "Death/therefore necessary. Alejandro, Laureano,/there'll be other yous who will come after./There'll be other Camilos, said Fidel" [*OS*, 78]).

The poem's title, inverting the nihilistic image of the black hole, argues for an immanence beyond death. The black hole is the absence of matter; the white hole, by contrast, represents the acquisition of a glowing materiality by those who have died. While we die as individuals, we are resurrected, Cardenal asserts, as part of a collectivity. The poem traces a movement from the loneliness of death to the comradeship of resurrection. Even in the act of dying, the individual is touched by the divine: "Morir es entrar en Dios./ Cuando Dios ya no es un Otro sino vos./Vos sos Dios./Es la unión con Dios ya sin religión" (*VPL*, 49; "To die is to enter into God./When God is no longer Another but you./You are God./It is union with God now free of religion" [*OS*, 72]). This union with God is "free of religion" in the sense that religion is no longer necessary to serve as a mediating force because after death one becomes part of God's presence. Simultaneously, the poem conceives death in terms of physics; the underlying revolutionary precepts – and the echoes of revolutionary slogans – even become a source of cosmic humour: "'Venceremos la Segunda Ley de la Termodinámica?'/es el grito de todos los muertos de la tierra" (*VPL*, 51; "'We will defeat [literally: we shall overcome] the Second Law of Thermodynamics?'/ is the cry of all the earth's dead" [*OS*, 75]). While "overcoming" the Second Law of Thermodynamics as one might an oppressive dictatorship – the context in which "venceremos" was often uttered in Cental America – is beyond human capability, the theory that white holes will create "muertos ... con dimensión otra vez" (*VPL*, 57; "The dead will recover their dimension" [*OS*, 80]) dovetails with

Cardenal's faith in Christ and his belief in the unity of revolutionary martyrs after death to conclude the poem with a vision of collective resurrection that assuages the fear of death:

> en el siglo primero de nuestra era
> cristiana que es o era nuestra era
> Dios destruyó la imagen religiosa de Dios.
> Comió y bebió con nosotros, cagó y orinó.
> Lutero aclaró que a la diestra de Dios es en todas partes
> Por lo que hay la Transcendencia de Nicaragua o de Nigeria.
> La resurreción no es individual sino colectiva.
> (*VPL*, 57; in the first century of our Christian/era which is or was our era/God destroyed the religious image of God./He ate and drank with us, shat and pissed./Luther clarified that God's right hand is everywhere./Which is why there's the Transcendence of Nicaragua and Nigeria. [*OS*, 80])

The pun on "era" – in Spanish the word means both "era" and "was" – obscures Cardenal's calling into question whether we still inhabit the "Christian Era" in which he was raised (or whether, presumably, globalization has propelled us into a new era). His theology is ecumenical in the sense that it embraces not only physics and revolution but also Martin Luther, the founder of Protestantism. It interprets the advent of Jesus among humans as radically iconoclastic. The poem's denouement insists that the "collective" resurrection is not merely of an undifferentiated mass of humanity – though Cardenal explicitly includes extraterrestrials among those who will be resurrected – but rather may include the transcendence of "Nicaragua or Nigeria": that we may be resurrected in nations – a possibility that suggests that this category, too, can revive from its moribund state in the post-Christian Era. In this light, it is striking that Cardenal repeats, almost unchanged, an image he first used in the early 1970s: "En la Revolución final los muertos/estarán todos resucitados" (*VPL*, 55; "In the final Revolution the dead/will all be resurrected" [*OS*, 78]). Though "Revolution" may be read here as a metonymic reference to the Christian resurrection, the phrasing repeats that of Cardenal's blended prophecy of resurrection and revolution at the close of *The Gospel in Solentiname* (see chapter 5). This clarion call to pick up arms, echoed in the anti-revolutionary twenty-first century, endures more as relic of a time when egalitarianism seemed to be within grasp than as an engagement with the present.

The prophetic tone of these poems, couched in a voice that radiates terrestrial and cosmic authority, contrasts with the wounded passivity of

"Telescope in the Dark Night" and *Vida perdida*. In this sense, *Versos del pluriverso* represents the culmination of the reconstruction of the masculine identity for the post-1990 era that Cardenal undertook in *Las ínsulas extrañas* and *La revolución perdida*. The robust voice in which he recounts his journeys around the world makes this evident. His command of theoretical physics comes to the fore, to a point where it both substitutes for the exhausted discourses of liberation theology and revolutionary Marxism, and acts as a vehicle to smuggle them across the boundary-line of 1990 into the era of accelerated globalization. Like the afterglow of the autonomous, revolutionary Nicaraguan nation, these discourses are relics of a past time; no longer at the centre of debate, they retain a forceful appeal as avatars and images of a more primitive epoch of greater equality. Above all, and contrary to what appeared to be the case in the first flush of post-1990 globalization, they do not disappear.

The endurance of such discourses – and even of Cardenal himself as a poet who maintains an evolving, contemporary vision and a large readership as he enters his ninth decade – raises questions about the nature of the human being and the lifespan of art. These are addressed in the book's final two poems, "*Ecce Homo*" ("Ecce Homo") and "Las cavernas" ("The Caves"). The former is the shortest and least compelling of the poems in *Versos del pluriverso*. It clusters facts and images about the human being around a reconciliation of Christian scripture and Darwinian theory: "*el Génesis* no contradice el *Origen de las Especies*/ pues el paraíso/no es origen sino meta./Meta original, digamos" (*VPL*, 59; "*Genesis* does not contradict *The Origin of Species*/since paradise/is not origin but goal./Original goal, let's say" [*OS*, 92]). The question of why humans wear clothes, addressed in a variety of contexts, from the nakedness of Adam and Eve to a glimpse of hedonistic nude sunbathers in southern Sweden, leads to other unique human features: manipulating fire, contemplating one's death, crying during birth. No particularly striking conclusion, beyond an appreciation of the features particular to humanity, emerges from this itemization.

The final poem, whose uncluttered style verges on that of conventional lyricism, is an affecting account of the paintings in the Lascaux caves in the south of France. It marvels at an art that outlasts the passage of centuries and epochs: "Y el pintor ha perdurado 30.000 años" (*VPL*, 65; "And the painter has endured 30,000 years" [*OS*, 81]). The paintings survive, even though many of the animals depicted in them are extinct in Europe. In these images, Cardenal discovers a "antiguo diálogo con la eternidad./Y con lo cotidiano" (*VPL*, 69; "That age-old dialogue with eternity./And with the day-to-day" [*OS*, 85]). He marvels at the mystical conception of life harboured by the people who made the paintings, at how different they were from us, even though, in biological terms, they were identical to modern humans. Their preoccupation with fertility rites, displayed in paintings of coupling bisons in caves which themselves were associated with maternal images – "la caverna era la Madre" (*VPL*, 73; "the cave was the Mother" [*OS*, 88]) – recalls Cardenal's praise elsewhere of binary relationships as the unifying glue of the cosmos.

Yet the poem does not levitate into the cosmic realm, remaining concentrated on a "mundo de fantasía bajo la tierra" (*VPL*, 75; "a fantasy world under the earth" [*OS*, 90]). Unlike contemporary humans, Cardenal maintains, the people who made the paintings were not ravaged by the ceaseless change ushered in by linear history: "Parece que vivían sin pasado ni futuro./Sin tiempo. Solamente vivían" (*VPL*, 71; "It appears that they lived without past or future,/Without time. They just lived" [*OS*, 86–7]). The condition that exempted them from the burden of a history of wars, battles, and shifting power structures was the absence of inequality. Though Cardenal stresses at the poem's conclusion that we will never know the religious beliefs that inspired the paintings, excavations of the neolithic period have revealed a "completa ausencia de armas./Y en las pinturas de las cavernas no hay combates" (*VPL*, 74; "complete absence of weapons./And in the cave paintings there are no battles" [*OS*, 88]). His praise of the thousands of years of peace of the neolithic age and the Stone Age concludes in the origins of politics: "Las espadas aparecen con el bronce/y ya no ha habido paz hasta hoy./El poder almacenar creó la desigualdad./Lo que no hemos podido suprimir todavía" (*VPL*, 74; "Swords appeared with bronze/and ever since there has been no peace./The ability to store created inequality./What we have still been unable to suppress" [*OS*, 88]). As the poem concludes with a pastoral image of the playing children who rediscovered the caves in 1895, the plain-spoken oral style, purged of political, scientific, or even Christian discourses, bespeaks a reconciliation with the crazed zigzags of human history, an understanding of where centuries of political strife have come from. This understanding signals that the spiritual damage Cardenal suffered as a result of the 1990 elections has been superseded by the reassertion of a patriarchal authority nourished by revolutionary tropes whose protective force flows from the lure of the anachronistic world that they represent.

In 2006, the year after the publication of *Versos del pluriverso*, a new FSLN government reappropriated these symbols, requiring Cardenal's literary strategies to shift again.

12

Ortega's Nation: Two Dissident Writers Face Globalization (2007–12)

NICARAGUAN NATIONAL SOVEREIGNTY UNDER GLOBALIZATION

The weak, diaphanous nation of globalization resists Modernist elaboration. In the twenty-first century, Boom-style novels that mythologize the nation by engaging its history through avant-garde literary techniques yield to historical novels that turn both the writer's gaze and those of readers away from the challenges of the present, recapitulating, in painless, often romanticized form, conflicts that the past has already laid to rest. Poetry turns inward and addresses personal conundrums, or global public dilemmas such as the media or the environment. All literary forms have a reduced impact on public debate. In Nicaragua, as noted in chapter 9, the centrality of literature as an indispensable component of the re-imagination of the homeland, wanes during this period. Like other artistic forms – arguably like the fiction of the nation itself – literature can create only a ghost or pastiche of engagement with dilemmas of national identity, as the nation itself may make only gestures towards alleviating social or economic cleavages that are global in scale.[1] "Imagined communities" proliferate, but they are no longer the print-capitalist Andersonian community of the nation; in the twenty-first century, communities are based on shared ethnic, regional, gender, or class identifications, or on identities that cluster around online nodes or popular cultural phenomena. In William I. Robinson's formulation, the nation is now "National in Appearance, Transnational in Essence" (Robinson 2003: 24).

This transnationalization renders almost meaningless the notions of "metropolis" and "periphery" that underlay dependency theory, the intellectual foundation of pre-1990 nationalist activism in Latin America and elsewhere in what was then known as the "Third World." Imperialism itself becomes an empty slogan when the sources of oppression are no longer US Marines storming ashore to violate national sovereignty, but rather financial structures whose only certifiable location is in the digital ether and whose collaborators are diffuse, denationalized investors whose money retains no national label, shifting at the press of button to a corner of the world with a "more favourable investment climate." The expropriation and redistribution of the goods of this system's local cronies is no longer a viable solution to economic inequality, since instantaneous capital flight will reduce nations that attempt to implement such measures to pauperdom, and the transnational system will rapidly recruit new on-the-spot collaborators to replace those who have been dispossessed or even physically eliminated. The ideological murkiness of the post-2006 FSLN government in Nicaragua, particularly the way it derives its legitimacy from being a simulacrum of a past revolutionary regime whose radical social transformations it alludes to but cannot replicate, is a product of such transnational trends. In a work published prior to Daniel Ortega's return to power, Robinson observes:

> The disciplinary power of global capitalism shifts actual policymaking power within national states to the global capitalist bloc, which is represented by local groups tied to the global economy. In countries where states have been captured by popular classes or by national fractions of local dominant groups, such as Haiti, Nicaragua, South Africa, Venezuela and elsewhere from the 1970s into the twenty-first century, the transnational elite has been able to use the structural power of the global economy to instill discipline and undermine policies contrary to globalization. (Robinson 2003: 41–2)

Ortega's return to power, under a purportedly revolutionary banner, accompanied by a rhetoric still sufficiently potent to alienate a moderate US administration such as that of President Barack Obama (Morris 2010: ix–xv), collaborates with transnational capital yet, by promoting a rhetoric of national self-assertion, fosters the illusion that it is revolting against it. The principal illusion, of course, is that a revolution of the sort defined by Samuel Huntington in the 1960s – "the rapid and violent destruction of existing political institutions, the mobilization of new groups into politics, and the creation of new political institutions" (Huntington 1968: 266) – remains possible in the twenty-first century. While young proletarian supporters who act as FSLN enforcers during municipal elections, most of whom were not born when the revolutionary Sandinista government of the 1980s was in power, may believe that they are participating in a "revolution" (see chapter 9), members of the bourgeoisie and the elite, whose professional lives (including the lives of professional artists) are sustained by transnational structures (particularly in light of the collapse of readership within Nicaragua), perceive this to be an illusion. This may be why neither resuscitated post-2006 Sandinismo nor the Bolivarian "revolution" initiated by Hugo Chávez in Venezuela in 1999 has produced an emblematic "novelist of the revolution," the role embodied by Alejo Carpentier in revolutionary Cuba and by Sergio Ramírez in revolutionary Nicaragua.[2]

At the same time, the Nicaraguan and Venezuelan regimes, though often paired in public commentary after 2006, have different histories. Until his death in March 2013, Chávez arrogated to himself a transnational vocation, as though leading a national revolution no longer commanded verifiable authority in the twenty-first century, by invoking Simón Bolívar, who fought for the freedom of five Spanish American republics. His interventions in other countries – including his supplying of Cuba and Nicaragua with oil and financial aid – are an innate feature of his "revolutionary" identity: both the fulfillment of his Bolivarian vocation, and the reason why Washington saw him as a hemispheric menace. Yet Chávez's revolution did not come to power, as past Spanish American revolutions did, via the "rapid and violent destruction," in Huntington's phrase, of existing institutions, but rather by the liberal-democratic route of the ballot box. Chávez, like Ortega, held his subsequent elections in circumstances where some citizens felt coerced into voting for him out of fear of losing government jobs or contracts, yet, in its ostensible conformity with liberal procedures, his government obeyed the ground-rules of globalization. Likewise, Chávez's revolution did not enjoin Venezuelans to engage in self-abnegation, monastic deprivation, or rationing to promote the common good; rather than preaching socialist anti-materialism, it tried to satisfy the hunger for consumer goods. "*That*'s a socialism for the 21st century!" were words spoken in envy about Venezuelan society by a family whom the author of this study visited in Cuba in late 2009. The Cuban family extolled the state-of-the-art refrigerators, flat-screen televisions, microwave ovens, and cars made available by Venezuelan "socialism."

All of these features underline important differences between the FSLN's return to power and other post-2000 resurgences of the Latin American left. The Chávez-inspired populisms of Evo Morales in Bolivia and Rafael Correa in Ecuador also came to power via the ballot box. The social-democratic governments that have ruled Chile, Uruguay, Paraguay, Argentina, Brazil, and later Peru were conspicuous for adhering to transnational norms. The FMLN government of Mauricio Funes, elected in El Salvador in 2009, like the FSLN, represented the conversion of a guerrilla organization into a successful populist political party; yet these were guerrillas who had never taken power or imposed their stamp on the nation, and whose most radical historic leaders had died or faded into the background by the time the party was elected. The FMLN government created a more socially conscious variation on the existing neo-liberal state rather than promising a "revolution."

The Zapatista uprising in Chiapas that rebelled against an international trade pact, NAFTA, represented a distinctive post-1990 insurgency, whose goal was not to capture and reshape the nation but to alter a regional culture's relationship with international capital. The movement's most visible leader, Subcomandante Marcos, followed, and even parodied, the Latin American tradition of the literate guerrilla, producing essays that critiqued globalization, gnomic pieces of pseudo-New Age wisdom, poems, and even children's stories; yet his writing tried to dissect transnational power, just as his movement attempted to persuade the national government in Mexico City to strike a better deal with international finance for the indigenous communities of Chiapas. Marcos's goal was not the re-institutionalization of the Mexican nation.[3]

The return to power of the FSLN in 2006 stands out as a unique event. The peculiarity of this event was signalled by Sergio Ramírez six months before it occurred, when he noted that "los que están ahora militando siempre con Daniel Ortega en el Frente Sandinista ven a la revolución como un bloque, que no tiene fisuras" (*UISR*; "Those who are still campaigning today with Daniel Ortega in the Sandinista Front see the revolution as a block, without ruptures"). This refusal to recognize any discontinuity between the 1980s and the twenty-first century became the defining trait of the new government. Though Rosario Murillo had softened the movement's most contentious symbols, the party of Marxist-influenced nationalist revolution returned to power in the twenty-first century, with the revolutionary president, and two legendary guerrillas, Tomás Borge and Edén Pastora, recruited to evoke the armed struggle (and sometimes flank Ortega, the "comandante-presidente," on stage during speeches). Ortega alluded to the Cold War past by establishing friendly relations with Moscow, even though Moscow was no longer socialist. Not only did the regime's symbolism promise the egalitarian fruits of a violent upending of the social order, but, crucially, its purported frame for action was that of the integrated, pre-1990 nation.

This differentiated the post-2006 FSLN from its ideological fellow travellers in Venezuela, Ecuador, and Bolivia, all of which exploited the post-1990 articulation of regional and ethnic identities, against national assumptions, traditions, and institutions, to consolidate their power. Chávez, of mixed indigenous and Afro-Venezuelan background, owed much of his appeal among the Venezuelan masses to the fact that, in a country where modern presidents had come from the white elite, he was the first national leader in decades who looked and sounded like the majority of his constituents, even as his "Bolivarian" project blurred the nation's importance by aspiring to influence a transnational oppressed class, a "greater Venezuela" whose contours were delineated by his transnational television network, TeleSur, a CNN or Fox News clone for Latin American leftists. Morales was the first modern indigenous president in a country whose indigenous majority had been excluded from power. Correa, in Ecuador, became a champion of indigenous rights, gaining support by hewing out autonomous spaces for indigenous people within the weakened hull of the nation. Ortega, by contrast, invoked the same nation of *mestizaje* that had made the Nicaraguan Revolution, the country characterized by Jeffrey Gould as the inheritor of the "Indohispanismo" promoted by Augusto César Sandino, in which "any questioning of the primordial value of mestizaje threatened that racial unity in the face of Anglo Saxon imperialism" (Gould 1998: 160).

This peculiarity means that theories of cultural dynamics under globalization do not fit the Nicaraguan case. Walter Mignolo's influential development of the idea of "border thinking," a transnational successor, as Mignolo himself concedes (Mignolo 2000: 49), to dependency theory, elides the nation. Where dependency theory, while aggregating many nations into the oppressed "periphery," employed an historical-structural approach that emphasized the distinctness of each peripheral nation's formative experiences, over time, before the particular exigencies inflicted on it by the metropolis, "border thinking" is constructed against the idea of firm national boundaries. Mignolo describes it as "*thinking from dichotomous concepts rather than ordering the world in dichotomies*. Border thinking, in other words, is, logically, a dichotomous locus of enunciation and, historically, is located at the borders (interiors or exteriors) of the modern/colonial world system" (ibid.: 85; emphasis in original). Drawing on the aspects of post-colonial theory that focus on the experiences of migrants, and on "subaltern studies," Mignolo's ideas respond to the dynamics described by Robinson, in which "local groups tied to the global economy" belong to the international financial system rather than to their nations. Mignolo shifts emphasis from the nation to a succession of opposing forces that straddle national boundaries. While "border thinking" is consistent with the Bolivarian Revolution, it does not address the world of tightly locked national autonomy that the FSLN purports to be building.

Nor do many theories of globalization confront the fact that, in the era of Facebook, national self-assertion is inextricably tethered to an individual personality. The nine comandantes who constituted the Sandinista National

Directorate during the 1980s eschewed the glorification of revolutionary strongmen. An essential element of the Revolution's mission was to break the tradition of the personalistic *caudillo*, whether right-wing like Somoza or left-wing like Castro. Daniel Ortega emerged gradually as first among equals for a variety of reasons, among which his introversion and relative lack of charisma played a prominent part, in opposition to Tomás Borge, who was a threat to this mission because he had the charismatic authoritarianism of a potential Nicaraguan Castro. The 1980s National Directorate presented itself as mere agents of the historical legacy bequeathed by Sandino himself, and by Carlos Fonseca Amador: the historical martyrs had ultimate authority, and all Sandinistas participated in perpetuating their example. By contrast, the post-2006 government revolved around the "comandante-presidente," who ruled because he had fought in the Revolution of which this government was supposedly the uninterrupted extension. While Sandino and Fonseca remained important touchstones, and Borge and Pastora served as reminders of the sources of Ortega's authority in revolutionary combat, the new martyr cult developed by Rosario Murillo that surrounded the memory of Camilo Ortega highlighted the comandante-presidente's individual suffering, giving priority to this personal story over the historical analyses of trampled Nicaraguan nationhood that had been written by Sandino, Fonseca, Ramírez, Wheelock, or other Sandinista thinkers. The consolidation of national dignity was embodied in the image of an individual.

In spite of their estrangement, in the early stages of the Sandinista return to power, Sergio Ramírez and Daniel Ortega continued to share the imperative to buttress the integrity of the nation against the transnational system. The assault on the nation came not only from globalizing economic forces but also from activists who took advantage of the country's weakened post-1990 condition to enlarge the space for cultural recognition and autonomous action on the part of ethnic minority cultures. It was reflected in anthropological research such as that of Gould, who argued that certain rural communities in western Nicaragua had not undergone the transition from indigenous to mestizo that supposedly was completed during the late-nineteenth-century coffee boom, or from literary critics, such as Antonio Cornejo Polar, whose studies of Andean literature challenged the socially integrative structures and transculturating assumptions of Boom fiction by concluding that "pierde sentido la problemática de la 'integración nacional,' o de la nación como cuerpo social uniformemente homogéneo, y adquiere en cambio la opción de imaginarla en términos de convivencia justa y articulada entre lo plural y lo distinto" (Cornejo Polar 1994: 238; "the problematic of 'national integration' or of the nation as a uniformly homogenous social body ceases to have meaning, and, by contrast, the option of imagining the nation in terms of the just and openly articulated coexistence between entities that are plural and distinct gains strength"). Yet, in the context of accelerated globalization, re-imaginings of the nation such as that of Cornejo Polar's assertion of "heterogeneity" might appear simply to participate in its dissolution. The desire to sustain the imaginative framework of the autonomous nation – in spite of the reality of "revolutionary" post-2006 Nicaragua's total compliance with the requirements of foreign investors (see chapter 9) – demands a unified field of reference capable of welding together into a single entity the disparate manifestations of national "heterogeneity" that have grown more pronounced in the post-1990 era.

In Nicaragua, the most salient cultural difference remains that of the Atlantic Coast. The linguistic and cultural divergence of this region amplifies the dissenting posture of other groups – women, gays, fundamentalist Protestants, indigenous people in western Nicaragua – from the perceived norms of a traditionally patriarchal, Spanish-speaking, Catholic Latin American society. Ironically, it was the Sandinistas themselves who, in their efforts to resolve the debacle that engulfed the Miskito Indians in the early years of revolutionary government (see chapter 6), first granted autonomy to the Atlantic Coast in 1984; this led to the approval of two regional councils in 1987, and the initial round of elections for membership of these councils in 1990. Residents of the Atlantic Coast saw the creation of the councils as redressing an historic wrong that they traced to the formal incorporation of the coast into Nicaragua by the Liberal government of Zelaya in 1894 (see chapter 2). This perception makes their vision antagonistic to that of mestizos in western Nicaragua, for whom Zelaya's administration represents the first authentic assertion of national dignity and autonomy after the invasions and great-power manipulations of the mid-nineteenth century. In 1993 Ramírez had greeted the hundredth anniversary of Zelaya's revolution by suggesting that this Liberal revolution and that of the Sandinistas in 1979 were the two key, complementary moments in the creation of modern Nicaragua (see chapter 10).

The implementation of regional autonomy on the Atlantic Coast challenges the nationalist narrative – whether Liberal, Conservative, or Sandinista – of the struggle for national integration and the securing of Nicaragua's borders against the invasions and threatened dismemberments that have characterized its history. This development grants the Miskito, the Sumu, the Rama, the Garifuna, and Jamaican-descended Afro-Caribbeans, all of whom are either Protestants or profess animist religious beliefs, the right to imagine themselves as separate, self-defining communities on whom

Spanish-speaking, mestizo, Catholic, "Nicaragua" impinges less and less. One Atlantic Coast intellectual wrote that regional autonomy "has created laws and institutions that established their own autochthonous model of public administration ... [based on] the recognition and respect of the identity and cultures of each group and ethnic community from a pluricultural vision" (Castro Jo 2011: 2). This adoption of pluriculturalism as the basis for administrative procedures stands in opposition to Ortega's orchestrated illusion of the resuscitation of the integrated "revolutionary" nation, or indeed to the vision of the nation held by nearly all members of the generations that fought against Somocismo. As a result, ongoing tension with the national government, particularly over the interrelated issues of the granting of titles for ancestral land to Miskito and African-descended inhabitants and the presence on the coast of increasing numbers of mestizo settlers (referred to by residents of the region as "Spaniards"), has been a consistent feature of post-2006 government. Similarly, conflicts have arisen over ownership of natural resources, particularly the region's virgin forests, and the central government's decision to delay regional elections in 2008, allegedly because the infrastructure was still in disarray from Hurricane Felix the previous year (Morris 2010: 225). For all of these reasons, Atlantic Coast difference has become a central node around which anxieties about national integration have clustered.

DEFINING THE TRIPLE MESTIZO: *TAMBOR OLVIDADO*

Ramírez's response to the assertion of Atlantic Coast difference became discernible, as seen in chapter 10, in his Monterrey lecture series, when he included African racial and cultural heritage within the definition of *mestizaje*. In *A Thousand Deaths Plus One*, the photographer Castellón becomes the first mestizo character in Ramírez's fiction whose heritage includes an African-descended, Atlantic Coast component. *El reino animal*, though it reflects a twenty-first-century liberal ideology, depicts the cultural difference of the Atlantic Coast as a discordant element in Nicaraguan nationhood as it laments the dissolution of the integrated pre-1990 nation.

By the time this short-story collection was published, Ramírez was immersed in a novel about post-revolutionary Nicaraguan society. In 2005 he stated: "Me atraería escribir unas historias sobre los noventa" (*UISR*; "I'd like to write some stories about the 1990s"). In fact, he had already started *El cielo llora por mí* (2008; The Heavens Cry for Me), his detective novel set in Nicaragua in the year 2000; he suspended this project in order to complete the book-length essay *Tambor olvidado* (2007; Forgotten Drum).

This is a crucial milestone in Ramírez's career, and one of his most accomplished works of non-fiction. Though published in Costa Rica and little distributed outside Central America, *Tambor olvidado* appears likely to make a significant long-term impact on Spanish American debates about racial identity. In spite of the fact that it is essentially a rearguard action that attempts to outflank the fragmented identities of globalization, herding them together again into a revived unified national essence, this essay pioneers a provocative new concept, that of the "triple mestizo." The integrative capacity of *mestizaje* having been diminished by the institutionalization of African-descended identities (since not only Afro-Caribbeans but also the Miskito and Garifuna claim African descent), Ramírez responds by extending the mestizo tent and welcoming Africans inside. Yet this is not a whimsical or merely polemical essay: the documentation is intimidating, Ramírez's knowledge of the different African cultures from which slave, servant, and labouring populations were drawn is detailed and accurate, and his familiarity with Nicaraguan cooking, customs, and language, as one would expect, is encyclopedic.

The case he makes may be directed at assuaging early-twenty-first-century anxieties, but it is also persuasive. Where his essays of the 1970s and 1980s concentrated on Nicaraguan and Central American history from the mid-nineteenth century to the present, *Tambor olvidado* provides an original interpretation of Nicaraguan history prior to the nineteenth century, explaining who the Nicaraguan people were in racial and cultural terms. The crux of his argument is that the perceived ethnic division between an African-descended Atlantic Coast and an "Indohispano" Pacific Coast is a false dichotomy, that all Nicaraguans have significant African heritage, and that Nicaraguan culture, like the cultures of Cuba or Brazil, cannot be understood unless one recognizes this pervasive African contribution. By the end of the eighteenth century, Ramírez argues, shattering the national mythology, mulattos were the largest ethnic group on Nicaragua's Pacific Coast. The universal denial of this basic fact leads to another contention that Ramírez had been making in interviews for a few years prior to the publication of *Tambor olvidado* and that becomes one of the book's central threads. Since Africanness was seen as socially intolerable or scandalous, it must be hidden and for that reason "todo aquello que proviene de la herencia africana, es disfrazado como indígena" (*TO*, 11; "all that which stems from the African heritage is disguised as being indigenous"). In this way, he suggests, Nicaraguan discourse confined Africanness to the Atlantic Coast where it was seen as "nuestra en términos territoriales, pero ... al mismo tiempo nos es tan ajena que podemos contemplarla desde lejos" (*TO*, 11; "ours in territorial terms but … at the same time it is so alien to us that we may regard it from a distance").

Proceeding from the assumption that the African inheritance is part of daily life for all Nicaraguans, Ramírez dismantles national myths. The first among these, surprisingly, is the mythologization of Rubén Darío as the inventor of Nicaragua's Indohispano identity. Ramírez debunks this depiction, as it was developed by Pablo Antonio Cuadra, on the grounds that, "bajo esta propuesta, la cultura de la costa del Caribe que tiene origen o participación africana, no pertenece a los elementos de la identidad nicaragüense, restringida a lo hispano y a lo indohispano" (*TO*, 16; "according to this reading, the culture of the Caribbean coast that has African origins or an African contribution does not belong to the elements of Nicaraguan identity, which is restricted to that which is Hispanic or Indohispano"). Darío, for all his genius, cannot explain Nicaraguan identity in its entirety. And where in the 1980s Ramírez's Darío was an anti-imperialist, the Darío of globalization becomes an emblematic tri-racial figure who represents the integration of potentially disruptive Africanness into the fabric of a renewed, more flexible *mestizaje*.

Ramírez problematizes received Nicaraguan wisdom: Nicaragua is a product not only of Spanish, but also of British, colonialism; the term "Atlantic Coast" (rather than the more accurate "Caribbean") is indicative of the attempt to distance Africanness; yet, though this coast is viewed as alien because it is English and African, it is the only part of Nicaragua that was visited by Christopher Columbus, through whom Nicaragua traces its connection to Spain. Not even Darío himself is exempt: though he never admitted it, this exemplary cosmopolitan, light-skinned mestizo from León was himself "fruto de la cultura del silencio, que niega cauce al tercer río que viene a dar a las aguas revueltas del gran mestizaje triple" (*TO*, 19; "fruit of the culture of silence that denies passage to the third river that flows into the rough waters of the great triple *mestizaje*"). Ramírez produces evidence that at least two of Darío's grandparents were classified on their marriage documents as "mulatos" (*TO*, 19). Contextualizing this reticence within nineteenth-century Spanish American debates about culture, Ramírez surveys the sparse, contradictory references to Africanness in Darío's work. The poet's evasiveness appears troubled, or even dishonest, in light of the second chapter of *Tambor olvidado*, which details the different African cultures that were transported to Nicaragua, and the diverse cultural influences exercised by, for example, Wolof from Cameroon, Kimbundu from Angola, Kikongo from Angola and the Congo, Ashanti from Ghana, Yoruba from Nigeria, Africans who had already been slaves in Spain and arrived in

Nicaragua as bearers of a mixed African-European culture, and African-descended peoples from the French Caribbean.

The documentation that Ramírez cites to illustrate who these Africans were and where in western Nicaragua they settled between the sixteenth and the late eighteenth centuries renders even more hypocritical the silence that surrounds the contribution of African-descended people to the national stew. Ramírez's contention that "indigenous" was often a code-word for "African" is reinforced by the evidence he produces of early African settlement in marginal neighbourhoods of provincial Nicaraguan cities that today have a reputation for having a strong "indigenous" element, such as Sutiaba in León. His insistence on *mestizaje* as a national norm, however, becomes visible in one of the distinctions between the Pacific and Atlantic Coasts that he allows to stand: the recognition of the survival of indigenous languages on the Atlantic Coast, in contrast to the Pacific regions, where these languages had "desaparecidas bien pronto como sistemas lingüísticos bajo el peso de la colonización" (*TO*, 59; "disappeared very quickly as linguistic systems beneath the weight of colonization"). The confusion over origins grew deeper as the result of pervasive illiteracy: the Catholic tradition did not require people to read in order to be evangelized; they had only to listen to the priest. Here, perhaps thinking of how conversion to Protestantism had contributed to his maternal grandfather's escape from illiteracy, Ramírez stresses an important difference between the two coasts: "religión y educación se presentaron de manera conjunta en la costa del Caribe ... Una catequización alentaba la lectura de la Biblia, y la otra la prohibía" (*TO*, 60; "Religion and education went together on the Caribbean coast ... one conversion nourished the reading of the Bible, and the other forbade it").

The Catholic and Protestant heritages establish important distinctions between the two coasts (even if today this dichotomy is adulterated by an influx of Spanish-speaking Catholics into the Atlantic Coast and the conversion of some Pacific Coast residents to fundamentalist Protestantism by US missionaries). Just as these religious traditions coexist in Ramírez himself, so they coexist in the united body politic of the Nicaraguan nation. The African heritage is not a distinguishing feature of an isolated region, but rather one that, like the indigenous and Spanish inheritances, unifies the nation by being spread over both coasts. Ramírez attributes the suppression of this reality to the positivism that animated Zelaya's 1893 Liberal revolution. The revolution's quest for progress and differentiation of the upwardly mobile commercial classes from the masses they were now ruling created the category that Ramírez refers to as "mestizos ladinos" (*TO*, 64). This term, echoing the use of "ladino" in Guatemala (where the word "mestizo" is not in general use) to ascribe European identities to those who promote Western technological culture, regardless of their origins, buried the reality of the "triple mestizo." By referring to themselves as "ladinos," ambitious Liberals obscured their indigenous heritage and denied any connection with Africa.[4]

As Ramírez, Gould, and others have shown, this false consciousness was arrested only when Sandino began to refer to Nicaraguans as "Indohispano"; yet Sandino did not rescue the obscured African heritage of people from western Nicaragua. Ramírez devotes a chapter to demonstrating that the Pacific Coast-bred protagonists of the 1893 revolution, for all that they might rename themselves "ladinos," were not lacking in "sangre africana" (*TO*, 64; "African blood"). Furthermore, in the first decades of the colony, liaisons between Spanish or Náhuat people and Africans were not necessarily frowned upon. An anonymous rhyming dialogue from sixteenth-century Masaya depicts an African servant persuading his white mistress to become his mistress in a physical sense by arguing that "lo negro luce/al pie de la mejor dama" (*TO*, 70; "blackness shines/at the foot of the finest lady"). Revelling in the incredibly rich vocabulary that evolved to capture the many different mixtures of racial heritage that were present in colonial Nicaragua, Ramírez emphasizes that nearly all Nicaraguans belonged to one of the nearly twenty recognized racial categories that signalled some sort of African heritage: "Y si a finales del siglo diecesiete los mestizos triples, en los que no faltaba la sangre africana, formaban ya la mayoría de la población, en 1820, un año antes de la independencia, representaban un abrumador 85%" (*TO*, 74; "And if at the end of the seventeenth century triple mestizos, who had no lack of African blood, already formed a majority of the population, in 1820, one year prior to independence, they represented an overwhelming 85%").[5]

Just as Rubén Darío, the swan of Nicaraguan Liberal cosmopolitanism, and the guiding spirit for Ramírez's own artistic vocation, mutates in *Tambor olvidado* into a man of partly African descent, so, astonishingly, do the pillars of the white Conservative oligarchy, the Chamorros. Ramírez points out that in wealthy families where the father had both light-skinned children born within matrimony and darker skinned illegitimate children, circumstances sometimes led to the illegitimate children becoming

> los jefes de familia, como ocurrió con Fruto Chamorro, figura principal de la oligarquía conservadora de Granada a mitad del siglo diecinueve, y el primer presidente con tal título que hubo en el país. Su padre, Pedro José Chamorro, estudiaba en Guatemala cuando preñó a Josefa Pérez,

> una muchacha que se ganaba la vida como lavandera. Al volver se casó en Granada con una mujer de su clase, quien, al quedar viuda, envió por Fruto para que se hiciera cargo de administrar el patrimonio, y lo hizo tomar el apellido Chamorro. (*TO*, 76; the heads of household, as happened with Fruto Chamorro, a leading figure of the Conservative oligarchy of Granada in the middle of the nineteenth century, and the first president with that title that existed in the country. His father, Pedro José Chamorro, was studying in Guatemala when he impregnated Josefa Pérez, a girl who earned her living as a washerwoman. On his return he married a woman of his social class who, when she was left a widow, sent for Fruto so that he could take on the chore of administering the family's wealth, and she made him take the surname Chamorro.)

Nicaragua's first real president was a mulatto, or possibly a triple mestizo; his younger, whiter half-brother, Pedro Joaquín Chamorro Alfaro, may have become the emblematic Conservative president, identified with the prosperity of the late-nineteenth-century coffee boom, but it was the brown older sibling who paved the way for later Chamorro presidents. Such events were a natural extension of the colonial period, when multiple edicts issued from Madrid had regulated the relations between the different racial groups yet the colonial authorities ignored the laws whenever their economic interests were served by, for example, the promotion of people of colour beyond their assigned stations in life; furthermore, as Ramírez notes, "aquellos mandamientos se disolvieron en las camas" (*TO*, 121; "those edicts dissolved in bed").

Tambor olvidado explores the concealed, unacknowledged triple culture bequeathed to modern Nicaragua by three centuries of tri-racial mixing during the colonial period. In the final chapter of Part One, Ramírez attributes the absence of recognition, in part, to the fact that the African component in the society of western Nicaragua was not replenished in the nineteenth century, as occurred in Brazil and the Caribbean (including Nicaragua's Atlantic Coast). Analyzing the classic seventeenth-century Nicaraguan play *El Güegüense*, a multilingual comedy about the survival of a clever mestizo who "makes his way, carrying his own mixed race heritage, creating a space for himself and his racial identity" (White and Calderón 2008: 114), Ramírez extends its reach beyond the Spanish and Náhuatl languages in which the majority of the text is delivered (there is also some Basque); instead, he sees it as a work "que expresa el triple mestizaje cultural madurado a través de los siglos" (*TO*, 130; "that expresses triple cultural *mestizaje* matured over the centuries"). The anonymous author, though he has a magisterial command of both Spanish and Náhuatl, to the point of being able to pun in both languages, and is clearly well versed in the classical theatre of Golden Age Spain, adopts the outlook of a fused Náhuat-African rural community that has begun to thrive by running small local businesses (*TO*, 135–6).

Refuting the interpretations of *El Güegüense* made by Darío and Cuadra, who see in the work the fusion of the Spanish and Náhuat cultures, Ramírez insists on its importance as the first expression of the upward mobility of those who would later lead the Liberal revolution: "Los mestizos triples habían entrado de lleno en la competencia por el poder, y serían los actores principales de la revolución liberal de1893" (*TO*, 142; "Triple mestizos had entered into full competition for power, and would be the leading figures in the Liberal revolution of 1893"). This is not merely a way of reprimanding the bourgeoisie for a hypocritical denial of its racial origins; to an even greater extent, Ramírez's target is the multiplicity of identities that are claimed in the post-1990 period by those who would campaign for their apartness from the ever more evanescent nation on the basis of an assumed immemorial racial and cultural identity. In opposition to the assertion of indigenous identities in western Nicaragua, or other forms of local essentialism, Ramírez posits a folkloric presentation of what are really triple mestizos. He underlines that this does not deny the validity of the land titles which were granted to some of these communities during the colonial era, and which they continue to struggle to have respected; but these communities are not ancestral indigenous homelands. Where Gould, for example, sees in Sutiaba an indigenous community that in the mid-twentieth century "was able to resist the advances of mestizaje and agrarian capitalism and thus survive as an indigenous community" (Gould 1998: 103), Ramírez depicts it as typical of districts that grew up during the colony out of the plantations and mining camps where African, mestizo, and Náhuat workers lived together for decades until they fused into a single group:

> El indio que los conquistadores españoles encontraron en Nicaragua en el siglo dieciséis dejó de exisitir – reducido primero por el exterminio, y disuelto luego en sucesivos mestizajes – pero sobrevive como imagen, y en algunos rasgos de identidad cultural, y de identidad social. Los indios de Sutiaba y los indios de Monimbó se reconocen e identifican como tales, aunque son verdaderos mestizos triples, y viven congregados en barrios tradicionales, lo mismo que los de Matagalpa, o Monzonte … y se les convierte en fuente de tradición folclórica, muchas veces impostada. (*TO*, 144–5; The Indian that the Spanish conquistadors met in Nicaragua in the sixteenth century ceased to exist – first reduced by

extermination, and later dissolved in successive *mestizajes* – but he survives as an image, and in some traits of cultural identity and racial identity. The Indians of Sutiaba and the Indians of Monimbó recognize and identify themselves as such, even though they are true triple mestizos, and live together in traditional neighbourhoods, just like those in Matagalpa or Monzonte ... they are converted into a source of folkloric tradition, often falsified.)

These communities may have retained local governance structures, but neither in racial nor cultural nor linguistic terms are they indigenous. In response to Gould's study of Sutiaba's resistance to *mestizaje* between 1900 and 1960, Ramírez asserts that triple *mestizaje*, in which the African strain was more pronounced than the indigenous, was already complete by the eighteenth century.[6] For Ramírez, over-statements of the indigenous component in the Nicaraguan national fabric, whether in order to promote a homogenous mestizo norm or to assert the existence of the kind of "national heterogeneity" that Cornejo Polar finds in Peru, is rooted in shame of the African ancestry of modern Nicaraguans, the refrain that "no existen, no se ven, nunca existieron. No existimos en ellos, no existen en nosotros" (*TO*, 151; "they don't exist, are not seen, never existed. We do not exist in them, they do not exist in us"). The word "mandinga," the name of one of the African ethnicities transported to Nicaragua to serve as slaves, "pasó a significar el diablo" (*TO*, 173; "came to mean the devil").

Ramírez devotes the latter half of *Tambor olvidado* to a virtual encyclopedia of African influence in Nicaragua. A chapter that sifts the anthropological evidence for the origins of the Black Christs found in some Central American churches concludes that this tradition developed in Guatemala, where the Christ's blackness was a syncretic transmutation of the colours associated with Ek-chuah, the Mayan god of merchants, and Ek-Balaam Chat, the black jaguar of the rain, yet that upon its arrival in Nicaragua, where Mayan deities were not known, the Black Christ changed to reflect the local majority population: "no se trata de un Cristo de facciones indias, ni del color de la piel de los indios, sino de un Cristo negro de facciones europeas, es decir, un Cristo mulato" (*TO*, 170; "it's not a Christ with Indian features, nor with the skin colour of the Indians, but rather a Black Christ with European features, in other words, a mulatto Christ").

A chapter that concentrates on Nicaraguan Spanish notes the presence of multiple loan-words from Kimbundu, a language still widely spoken in the area around Luanda, Angola, and Kikongo, spoken in present-day northern Angola and southern Congo. This is the significance of the book's title: "tambor," the Spanish word for drum, comes from the Ashanti *bombaa* or the Kimbundu *mbomba*; though this borrowing did not take place in Nicaragua, it is indicative of the "forgetting" of African culture. Ramírez reviews the well-known case of the marimba, often presented as the "traditional instrument" of indigenous communities throughout Central America, but which in fact was brought to the region by African slaves.[7] He picks apart Nicaraguan Spanish to determine what came from Spain, what from West Africa, what from Náhuatl, and what few shards remain from the Mangue language of the Mayan-related Chorotega whom the Mexican Náhuat subjugated and assimilated in the eleventh and twelfth centuries. He cites the popular *sopa de mondongo* – an African-derived soup made from a cow's stomach – as a prominent legacy of the habit of employing people of African descent as cooks on plantations and building crews, and unmasks "indigenous" storytelling traditions of the coyote and the rabbit as being largely of West African provenance though here, as everywhere, he stresses the "huellas cruzadas" (*TO*, 255; "crossed tracks") that define all of Nicaraguan culture.

This book, which concludes with a twenty-page dictionary of African words that appear in Nicaraguan Spanish, is a rehabilitation of *mestizaje*. It reinvigorates Ramírez's engagement with the Nicaraguan nation, liberating him from the combined reactionary stance and neo-liberal loss of faith in the nation to which his nostalgia for a unified Nicaragua appeared to be confining him in *El reino animal*; it enables him to recover his iconoclastic radicalism. Where the onset of accelerated globalization has neutralized his long-standing critique of the bourgeoisie for failing to assume its nation-building mission (since it is doubtful whether any sort of coherent state may be constructed under transnational norms), in a new millennium obsessed with the politics of identity, he discovers a fresh angle of attack by drubbing the bourgeoisie that descends from the 1893 revolution for failing to acknowledge its true racial composition. This renews the foundations of national unity, sapping the legitimacy of ethnic movements that would claim difference from national norms by finding in the African heritage a common glue that unites them. In a Nicaragua whose integration is challenged by creeping Atlantic Coast separatism and reassertions of indigenous identity in the west, Ramírez champions Africans on the Pacific Coast – a group that it is safe to laud since they do not exist; yet his convincing demonstrations of the pervasiveness of African cultural traits weaken dissident ethnic groups' claims to essentialist uniqueness.

In contrast to essay collections that lacked the bite of his best polemical work of the 1970s and 1980s, either because they were too broadly generalizing to pull the nation into focus, such as *Mentiras verdaderas*, or because they consisted of rather safe literary criticism, such as *Señor de los tristes*, *Tambor olvidado* reclaims Ramírez's role as a writer who defines the nation, partaking of the combined literary-political essence that had consolidated Nicaragua's imagined community under Sandinismo. This shores up the fraying edges of his identity as a masculine authority figure within the public sphere. These professional motives for the composition of *Tambor olvidado* coincide with more obscure personal motives about which a reader may only speculate; yet it seems clear that in this essay Ramírez is sounding out the unknowable pre-history of his own rural, Pacific Coast heritage. In many parts of provincial Spanish America, families that are tall are suspected of having African "blood"; his grandfather Teófilo Mercado's identity as an "indigenous" person from a poor, marginal neighbourhood such as those where triple mestizos were bred, and a believer in the ideals of the 1893 revolution, resonates in the background of this book.

THE LAST SANDINISTA MICROCOSM: *EL CIELO LLORA POR MÍ*

The persistence of the unified nation – which, in Nicaragua, means the nation of Sandinismo, the only force that has created an integrated Nicaraguan state – is the central theme in Ramírez's detective novel, *El cielo llora por mí*, on which he resumed work after the publication of *Tambor olvidado*. Here the nation that persists is that of the Sandinista ethos of self-sacrifice, justice, and national unity, which triumphs at the novel's conclusion to safeguard the country's integrity in an environment degraded by President Alemán's corruption, the tawdry Americanization of transnational economic forces, and the chaotic protests against this order of a buffoonish opposition led by Daniel Ortega. *El cielo llora por mí* is a classic example of the postmodern recycling of a popular cultural form, the detective story, to facilitate commentary on an otherwise difficult-to-grasp present by filtering it through genre-based conventions and bathing it in corrosive irony. Written in a prose less dense than that of Ramírez's earlier novels, *El cielo llora por mí* is an unpretentious romp through a society in crisis. As though conforming to the tastes of the character of Inspector Palacios, who states that "no me gustan las novelas tipo *Rayuela*, a ver cuándo me la cuentan en orden" (*CLM*, 240; "I don't like novels like *Hopscotch*, let's see if you can tell me things in order"), this is the only novel of Ramírez's career in which the action is linear; it is his only post-1990 novel other than *Margarita, How Beautiful the Sea* in which he himself does not appear as a character. In tone, the Nicaraguan novel that *El cielo llora por mí* most resembles is Gioconda Belli's *The Inhabited Woman*; like that novel, its tight focus on the society of a small country (this time in the year 2000 rather than during the 1970s) converts it, almost inevitably, into a *roman à clef* in which Nicaraguan public figures are instantly recognizable.

Like detective novels of the Anglo-American vein that were popular in the early and mid-twentieth century, *El cielo llora por mí* is a conservative book that depicts the preservation of traditional values and the restoration of a pre-established order as the paramount concern of the forces of good. These values are characterized by Julian Symons as "those of a class in society that felt it had everything to lose by social change ... what crime literature offered ... was a reassuring world in which those who tried to disturb the established order were always discovered and punished" (Symons 1974: 16). In a turn-of-the-millennium Nicaraguan society whose bourgeoisie has been sucked away into the transnational networks described by Robinson, and most of whose public institutions are rotten with corruption or neoliberal bias, the police, paradoxically, become society's only reliable institution, securing Nicaragua a far lower crime rate than most of its Central American neighbours (see chapter 9). They achieve this by sustaining the Sandinista values of self-sacrifice, social justice, and fighting for national sovereignty around which the Nicaraguan state cohered after 1979. The police become, oddly, the last redoubt of authentic Sandinismo.

Here fiction mirrors real life. Aminta Granera Sacasa, a former nun from a wealthy Liberal family in León, who became a Sandinista guerrilla in the late 1970s, worked under Tomás Borge in the Ministry of the Interior during the 1980s, and has been the country's national chief of police for most of the years since 1990, is a virtual virgin-warrior mother of the post-Sandinista nation (an image that persisted even after she married and had children). One of Daniel Ortega's first acts on being elected to his third term as president in 2011 was to reappoint Granera until 2016. In a blog post that appeared three months prior to the publication of *El cielo llora por mí*, Ramírez marvels that, under Granera's leadership, Nicaraguan police officers who earn salaries of $120 a month and often cannot fill their clapped-out police cruisers with gas consistently resist the temptation to give themselves a cut of the hundreds of thousands of dollars' worth of cocaine that they impound. Abandoning the skeptical eye with which he customarily tracks events in his society, he lauds the mystical Sandinista combination of ethical behaviour and service to the nation that, though it has disappeared nearly everywhere else, survives in the national police force:

> ... detrás de esa pobreza, hay mística, extraña cualidad en los tiempos que corren para un cuerpo policial. La directora general de la policia, la comisionada Aminta Granera, es el personaje más popular de Nicaragua,

extraño también para un jefe policial, porque la población ve en ella honradez y sinceridad, y le tiene confianza, y ella refleja esa conducta moral inspirada en la vieja ética guerrillera: los altos mandos de la policía son aún los viejos combatientes contra la dictadura de Somoza, y Aminta representa a quienes no se han dejado contaminar por la ambición del dinero fácil ("Mística, incongruencia aún mayor"; … behind that poverty, there is mysticism, a strange quality for a police force in the present era. The Director General of the police, Commissioner Aminta Granera, is Nicaragua's most popular personality, which is also strange for a police chief, because the population sees in her honesty and frankness and has confidence in her, and she reflects that moral conduct inspired by the former guerrilla ethos: the upper echelons of the police remain staffed by former combatants against the Somoza dictatorship, and Aminta represents those who have not allowed themselves to be contaminated by the lure of easy money.)

The unusually exalted tone of this passage suggests that, in the moral morass of the post-nation, debased by Alemán's greed and Ortega's amoral expediency, Ramírez has discovered a microcosm where the Sandinista nation survives. His evocation of the police recalls "Living like the Saints," the second chapter of *Adiós Muchachos*, where he sets out the high moral standards that the Sandinistas established for themselves early in the anti-Somoza struggle (and which were betrayed by *La Piñata*). The obverse side of the "autonomous" UNAN of the early 1960s, a microcosm that promised to expand into a civil-society nation, the twenty-first-century police force is a post-revolutionary microcosm that preserves the defeated nation of Sandinismo, inspiring hope that it may some day become dominant once again. Aminta Granera's background as both a nun and a guerrilla, as someone who declined the luxury offered by her wealthy family and refuses the access to illicit funds that accompanies public office, recapitulates the armed and unformed Christian-Marxist nationalism of pre-*Piñata* Sandinismo. The fact that the Nicaraguan people respond, in an almost instinctual way, to this figure of an armed nun in a police uniform illustrates their enduring attachment to Sandinista values. The masses, depicted in *Sombras nada más* as having betrayed the Revolution, are rehabilitated in *El cielo llora por mí*. As will be argued below, the representative of the Nicaraguan people, in whom Ramírez's faith appears to have increased, thwarts the plot at the heart of this detective story, safeguarding the integrity of the nation.

The novel's putative detective anti-hero embodies the troubled state into which the Sandinista ethos has lapsed in the twenty-first century. Inspector Dolores Morales (literally "Moral Pains") is a collection of the best and worst traits of revolutionary Sandinismo (though he is free of the corruption that attends the post-1990 variety). The T-shirts he wears beneath his uniform tunic are olive-green, the colour that was worn by Sandinista guerrillas, symbolizing the Sandinista "skin" that persists underneath the contemporary uniform. Morales drives a superannuated Soviet Lada; his close friends address him as "Artemio," which was his guerrilla pseudonym (and which recalls, by contrast, the central character of Carlos Fuentes's *The Death of Artemio Cruz*, a novel about a former revolutionary who has betrayed his ideals). Having lost most of one leg on the Southern Front during the struggle against Somoza, Inspector Morales is a limping hero who walks with a prosthesis. Known to his colleagues as "Placeres Físicos" ("Physical Pleasures"), a satiric inversion of Dolores Morales, he suffers from the male Sandinista vice of preferring multiple "free unions" to a committed relationship. An early marriage, performed in the bush by the Spanish guerrilla priest Gaspar García Lavinia, having broken up due to his numerous infidelities – his wife fled Nicaragua to join the Contras – the middle-aged Morales now specializes in seducing married women. In spite of this failing, Morales is incorruptible and committed to preserving the unity and order of the nation. He contributes to the integrated nation of Sandinismo through his close professional relationship with his Atlantic Coast opposite number, Sub-Inspector Bert Dixon.

While Morales is a brown-skinned mestizo who grew up in Granada and lives in Managua, Dixon is an English-speaking Afro-Caribbean man from Bluefields. Significantly (though, in historical terms, somewhat improbably), Dixon shares the Sandinista heritage of having been a guerrilla: he and Morales met underground in 1971 in a safe house "en el barrio Sutiaba de León" (*CLM*, 36; "in the Sutiaba neighbourhood of León"); this fortuitous encounter in a neighbourhood that Ramírez identifies in *Tambor olvidado* as one of the key melting pots of triple *mestizaje* lends their union a nation-building significance. In an ironic yet telling mode, Dixon concludes a lengthy message to Morales with the words, "¡Patria Libre o Morir!, ¡Dirección Nacional, ordene! Besitos, by by" (*CLM*, 77; "Free Homeland or Death! National Directorate, give us our orders! Little kisses, bye-bye"). The tongue-in-cheek reiteration of archaic revolutionary slogans attests to their loyalty to the values of Sandinismo in its untainted, pre-1990 form. The "little kisses" are also ironic, yet they evoke an underlying current of unease that envelopes the two men's relationship. When Dixon visits Managua on business, he stays at Morales's house, after first enquiring, in a nervous way, whether Morales will be inviting in a lover. Dixon's lack of a discernible emotional or sexual life is rendered more suspect by the existence in the novel of a parallel Pacific-Atlantic male couple who are both openly gay and portrayed in a negative light.

The murder victim's cousin, Juan Bosco Cabistán, is a decadent Granada oligarch with a fake law degree who acts as the attorney for a fishing company that is a front for drug trafficking. Known as Giggo, Cabistán has been embroiled in notorious gay scandals from the Colegio Centroamericano in Granada to Belgium to Egypt that his mother has spent much of her family's depleted fortune trying to keep out of the newspapers. Cabistán's lover is a muscular Afro-Caribbean bodyguard from Bluefields known as Black Bull. If the companionship between Morales and Dixon depicts bonds between the Atlantic and the Pacific as the sinew of the nation and a re-enactment of the triple *mestizaje* that unites all Nicaraguans, the relationship between Cabistán and Black Bull presents this linkage as perverse and, in a profound sense, unnatural. (Cabistán is expelled from the Colegio Centroamericano for "actos contra natura" (*CLM*, 184; "acts against nature").

Yet Dixon, too, is framed as an object of desire, as the narrative insists that he and Morales form an enduring if enigmatic couple. The threatening former Sandinista Caupolicán (see below), recalling their days together as youthful guerrillas, tells Dixon: "Siempre te quise coger, negra divina" ("I always wanted to fuck you, divine black girl"); Dixon does not reply, but Morales says, "Yo no soy celoso" (*CLM*, 228; "I'm not jealous"). Though this may be mere brutal jesting, it raises again the image of the two cops as a couple and asks what kind of couple they are. When the drug dealers open fire on them, Morales jokes that if they had been killed together, the newspaper headlines would have read "Juntos hasta en la muerte" (*CLM*, 247; "Together even in death"). The pairing of the novel's two male Atlantic-Pacific couples betrays a discomfort with intimate ties with the Africanness of the Atlantic Coast, even as these are advanced as essential to the nation's maintenance of its integrity. At the same time, the queasy counterpointing of Morales's compulsive womanizing and Dixon's sexual ambiguity, and of this combined political, professional, and personal bond with the frankly sexual liaison between Cabistán and Black Bull (whose brother claims that he isn't really gay and only had sex with Cabistán for money), illustrates the merging of anxieties about the disappearance of the nation with the erosion of male authority and virility. In both couples, in a reprisal of the dynamics of the photographer Castellón's parentage in *A Thousand Deaths Plus One*, it is the Pacific Coast partner, whether the white Granada oligarch or the brown Managua mestizo, who plays the active role and the Black Atlantic Coast partner who is present as the exotic object of desire. Yet, even as the Pacific Coast partner's desire glues together the nation, it renders his masculinity suspect. At a thematic level, the mystery that Morales needs to solve is how to promote national unity without debilitating or rendering suspect his masculine identity.

In spite of his years of experience, revolutionary convictions, and rank of inspector, Morales is not an effective investigator. He drives around Managua conducting interviews and talks to Dixon on the phone, yet, owing to his personal failings, he damages the investigation more than he advances it. He violates protocol by having sex with the murder victim's mother; at one point a police cruiser in which he and other officers are riding is attacked by an enraged man wielding a fake pistol, who turns out to be the vengeance-seeking husband of Morales's current lover. The guerrilla machismo of the 1980s is no longer acceptable or efficacious in the twenty-first century. A parallel is perceptible between Morales's stumbling leadership of the investigation and striking hospital workers who try in vain to make their demands heard by blocking the highway, as they curse neoliberalism and vow that "en la próxima vuelve Daniel" (*CLM*, 51; "next time Daniel's coming back").

The real detective work in the novel is done by Doña Sofía, the police force's cleaning lady. As Emilian Coello Gutiérrez observes: "La novela plantea la paradoja de que cuanto más se sube en la escala jerárquica de la Policía, más disminuye en proporción la capacidad investigativa, de modo que los altos funcionarios nacionales y norteamericanos se limitan a aprovechar los aportes geniales de la limpiadora" (Coello Gutiérrez 2010: 8; "The novel poses the paradox that the higher one rises in the police hierarchy, the more investigative capacity diminishes, so that the high-ranking officials, both Nicaraguan and US, do nothing more than take advantage of the inspired contributions of the cleaning lady").

Doña Sofía's competence dethrones Morales's masculine authority; it suggests that the society of accelerated globalization is more responsive to female intelligence than was that of the 1980s, yet it is also confirms that the Nicaraguan people remain the repository of the nation's history and the most reliable guarantors of its survival. Like the modern Nicaraguan nation itself, Doña Sofía is the product of the proletariat's encounter with US intervention: her father was a US Marine and her mother was a seamstress who sewed for the Marines' wives. A fervent Sandinista, whose son died in the Revolution, she has reacted to the new era by taking refugee in evangelical Christianity: "era una dura mezcla de dos devociones" (*CLM*, 13; "she was a severe blend of two devotions"). Doña Sofía complains about the Catholic religious procession that is described by the novel's opening scene. She reprimands Morales each time he strays from the strict moral standards of revolutionary Sandinismo. Significantly, she has kept alive not only the memory of national history and Sandinista ethics, but also the literary culture that served as the medium around which Sandinista visions of the nation cohered. In concert with the times, she – like the novel itself – has adapted to the populist literary tastes of genre fiction, and rents formulaic novels from stalls in the Eastern Market.

As the only reader among the characters, Doña Sofía – whose name evokes the quest for knowledge – is the most direct inheritor of El Apóstol ("The Apostle"), the novel's somewhat burlesque stand-in for the memory of Carlos Fonseca. El Apóstol, "igual que los predicadores evangélicos obstinados en entrometer en cualquier conversación los textos de la Biblia, él lo hacía con los textos de Lenin que estudiaba con un gozo desaforado en el encierro clandestino, cerrando de un golpe a cada trecho de la lectura el tomo de turno de la editorial Progreso empastado en tela ... para quedarse reflexionando con sonrisa beatífica" (*CLM*, 38; "just like evangelical pastors determined to interject biblical texts into any conversation, he did the same with the texts of Lenin that he studied with uncontrolled delight in his clandestine hideout, slamming shut every now and then the cloth-bound volume from Progress Publishers ... to sit there contemplating with a beatific smile").

The Sandinista skill with texts and concern with literacy and literary interpretation that forms part of Fonseca's erudite legacy enables Doña Sofía to take the first step in the murder investigation by showing Morales and Commissioner Selva, the head of the narcotics detachment, how to interpret the evidence of the novel that the as-yet-unknown murder victim was reading when she was killed.[8] Her initiative relegates Morales, in spite of his heterosexual ardour, to the passive role in a country where, as Lancaster argues, passivity throws doubt on the male subject's masculinity. While Morales's surname suggests that he continues to adhere, however uneasily, to the moral purity of early Sandinismo, his first name, Dolores, is one that is normally given to a woman. The status of criminal investigation as a man's world is under siege: Morales notes, for example, that among the journalists who cover these crimes, "cada vez había más mujeres" (*CLM*, 56; "there were more and more women"). Furthermore, he must concede his loss of authority, as both inspector and man, before Doña Sofía's investigative prowess; he is surprised to hear Commissioner Selva cite Sofía at him as an authority:

> – Nada tiene que ver con ella, son conclusiones mías – dijo el inspector Morales, en un tartamudeo.
>
> – ¿A quién quieres engañar? De lejos se nota su mano en el informe – dijo el comisionado Selva –. No es la primera vez. (*CLM*, 96; "It has

nothing to do with her, these are my conclusions," Inspector Morales stuttered. "Who are you trying to fool? From the first glance her influence is evident in the report," Commissioner Selva said. "It's not the first time.")

If Doña Sofía dethrones Morales's male authority, she does so in pursuit of the goal of re-establishing the Sandinista nation. In addition to being a literal product of the US occupation, she is also, by virtue of her fallen son, a mother of a martyr and "siempre había subido a las tarimas ... con las otras madres de héroes y mártires, todas enlutadas cargando en el regazo el retrato enmarcado de sus hijos" (*CLM*, 13; "had always gone up onto the stages ... with other mothers of heroes and martyrs, all dressed in mourning, holding in their laps the framed portraits of their children"). In this sense she preserves the definition of motherhood of 1980s Sandinismo, in which, as Bayard de Volo observes, the mothers of Sandinista martyrs gained the authority "to take an active part in the construction of a new society and enter traditionally male activities such as grassroots politics, productive work outside the home, and the predraft military" (Bayard de Volo 2001: 101). Doña Sofía's activity as an investigator (even though this is not her professional role) reincarnates the Sandinista nation of the 1980s; it does not make her masculine, as one could understand from Lancaster's paradigm, but rather invests her with the aura of a militant Sandinista woman who builds her nation to honour the memory of her fallen offspring.

Coello Gutiérrez comments that in this novel "se escarnece todo lo que tenga que ver con alguna clase de devoción, venga esta de donde venga" (Coello Gutiérrez 2010: 16; "all that which has anything to do with any type of devotion, wherever it may come from, is savaged"); yet it is the Catholic faith that is condemned, while Protestant evangelicalism is subjected only to half-admiring mockery. Doña Sofía's Protestant fervour – the novel opens with her protesting the inclusion of an image of the Virgin of Fátima in the annual police procession – becomes a conduit for holding at bay a transnationalized anti-culture in which the Catholic Church is no longer the home of liberation theology, but simply one more transnational corporation that colludes in the commercialized invasion of the nation. One may read in this pattern a return to Ramírez's Protestant roots; but, above all, it forms part of his critique of transnational structures and his effort to marshal a counter-attack against these forces.

It is established early in the novel that Nicaragua is under the rule of the "obeso presidente" (*CLM*, 23; "obese President"). Alemán puts in cameo appearances, always on television, where he demonstrates his subservience to transnational capital by inaugurating Esso gas stations or pandering to the transnationalized elite in ways that explicitly recall the Somoza dictatorship. (Alemán arrives at one event on horseback, evoking the equestrian statue of Somoza that stood in the centre of Managua in the 1970s.) The Catholic religion is complicit in this alienation: at the festival of Santo Domingo, the elite guests receive "collares de flores traídos de Miami en un avión refrigerado" (*CLM*, 188; "collars of flowers brought from Miami in a refrigerated plane"). This gesture worthy of the Somoza years links the transnational elite to Miami, the ultimate non-place, where national Spanish American identities melt in a commercial glare. The Catholic Church, as a collaborator with the imposition of transnational dominance, has been gutted of nation-building potential. The hideous, out-of-the-way new Managua cathedral, with its "múltiples cúpulas en forma de tetas parecía una mezquita en medio del oasis. Había sido donada por Glenn Müller, el magnate mundial de las pizzas Dominó" (*CLM*, 189; "multiple cupolas in the form of udders, looked like a mosque in the middle of the oasis. It had been donated by Glenn Müller, the global magnate of Domino's Pizzas"). The governing couple's ceremonies to welcome transnational capital or celebrate its local collaborators are invariably attended by an obsequious Archbishop Obando y Bravo. This sycophantic, greed-induced expression of Catholicism stands in contrast to the authentic self-sacrifice of the Sandinista years. The Carlos Fonseca-like El Apóstol, though he is also recalled in a somewhat ironic vein, is described as having been "un monje ateo" (*CLM*, 37; "an atheist monk") whose implicit successor in the globalized present is La Monja, a character based on Aminta Granera, who appears in the novel as the incorruptible deputy commissioner of the Narcotics Division and "seguía siendo monja aun sin el hábito, y lo seguiría siendo hasta el fin de sus días" (*CLM*, 196; "continued to be a nun even without her habit, and would be one until the end of her days"). This promise of eternal self-abnegation illustrates her authority as the bearer of the Sandinista ethos. Though the biographies of both Fonseca and Granera are altered in the novel, the transition from one to the other – from "monje" to "monja" – demonstrates how, by relinquishing guerrilla masculinity and merging with the feminine, Sandinismo may survive globalizing structures and preserve the nation in the face of the transnational commercial assault.[9]

This invasive English-speaking commercialism debases Nicaraguan culture. The gas stations that Alemán inaugurates also contain stores "de esos que ahora llamaban *conveniences* en la jerga en inglés que invadía el país como una calamidad bíblica" (*CLM*, 118; " which people now called 'conveniences' in the English slang that was invading the country like a biblical calamity"). The simile suggests the misdirection of religious language inherent in the gaudy, ostentatious devotion exemplified by the new cathedral. Similarly, the women's names of the revolutionary era, drawn from guerrilla heroines or mountain villages where battles took place, have yielded to "nombres de personajes de telenovelas, Marisela, Estefanía, Marcela, o de marcas comerciales … O raras combinaciones de sílabas que resultaban difíciles de escribir y pronunciar, Maydelyn, Johanndery, o Glendilys" (*CLM*, 160; "names of characters in soap operas, Marisela, Estefanía, Marcela, or of commercial brand names … Or bizarre combinations of syllables that were difficult to write and pronounce"). The application of brand names to little girls, like the use of weird inventions that illustrate the ways in which English names transmitted by the media are half-understood by the Nicaraguans who hear and adopt them in an attempt to project their children into the glow of transnational modernity, reinforces the subjugation of the nation.

Yet, on the cusp of the twenty-first century, it is no longer clear that the United States remains an imperial force from which sovereignty must be wrested. Commissioner Canda, the corrupt head of the National Police, who siphons off half of the money impounded by Morales and Dixon, misses the investigation because he is literally trapped in Disney World, attending the fifteenth-birthday celebrations of a millionaire's daughter named Glendilys. Yet Florida and Miami are no longer staging-points for imperialist incursions into Nicaraguan territory; they are simply other locations swamped by commercialized mass culture. The US Drug Enforcement Agency (DEA) office in Managua, a shrivelled parody of earlier Yankee occupations, is staffed by an amiable but not particularly diligent agent known as Chuck Norris, who is "siempre en sandalias … [v]estía una guayabera típica … los faldones demasiado largos" (*CLM*, 254; "always in sandals … he wore a typical Panama hat … the brim too large"). Named after an aging star of ultra-violent films, Chuck Norris embodies declining US military power to dictate events in other countries; he waits for the Nicaraguans to set up the sting to get the drug dealers, then simply approves it, in concert with La Monja. Other powers are encroaching on this traditional US "sphere of influence." The new Foreign Ministry building is "una donación del gobierno del Japón" (*CLM*, 105; "a donation of the government of Japan"), while the casinos on the edge of the capital are full of "capataces taiwaneses de las maquiladoras de ropa de la zona franca y comerciantes palestinos de las vecinidades del mercado Oriental" (*CLM*, 283–4; "Taiwanese foremen from the sweatshop industries in the tax-free zone and Palestinian merchants from the area around the Eastern Market"). While the latter group belong to a community that has existed in Nicaragua for generations, and are based in Managua's most traditional market, the former are interlopers brought to the country by the kinds of practices – sweatshop labour, tax-free zones – that typify the ways in which, under accelerated globalization, marginal countries must compete in a "race to the bottom" to offer favourable conditions to attract restless transnational capital. Yet, as disheartening as the impact of these forces may be, none of them constitutes a deliberate threat to Nicaraguan sovereignty; rather, they are contributing factors to the generalized erosion of the nation as a category.

While plot is not really central to this detective novel, it opens with an abandoned yacht being discovered near Bluefields. A bloodstain suggests that a murder has taken place. The murder victim turns out to be Sheila Marenco, a young woman from the Managua area who became an accomplice of drug cartels, then made the mistake of double-crossing them by pocketing $100,000 of drug money. The death of a Nicaraguan from the Pacific Coast on the Atlantic Coast, also portrayed as the unintegrated nation's soft underbelly, through which drug cartels enter the country, establishes the anxieties that drive the story. Yet, insofar as the twenty-first-century debilitation of national sovereignty can be attributed to threats posed by other nations, the culprits are not the faltering United States or the new economic tigers of Asia, but Colombia and Mexico. Mimicking the paradox that globalization makes smaller nations more dependent on their larger neighbours,[10] *El cielo llora por mí* materializes the threat to the nation in a plot, which the Sheila Marenco murder reveals, to convert Nicaragua into the location for a strategic meeting between the Cali and the Sonora cartels, and a future theatre of operations for these groups. The days when Colombia and Mexico were Nicaragua's supporters in the Contadora process (see chapter 6) are long gone. The threat to Nicaragua, though, does not stem from the Colombian and Mexican states, but from the shadow-states of organized crime (which are interpenetrated at certain points with the weakened official states through webs of corruption).

The plans for a meeting of the two cartels are discovered by Doña Sofía during a freelance infiltration of a casino run by organized crime. Behind the back of the corrupt commissioner, who is still in Florida, and other high-ranking officials of dubious moral standards, an agreement is reached to raid the meeting and arrest the Mexican and Colombian drug lords.[11] Former Sandinistas – Doña Sofía, La Monja, Morales, and Dixon – save a margin of the Nicaraguan state's autonomy by working on equal terms with a weakened United States, in the form of Chuck Norris. By definition, that which may be preserved of the nation is Sandinista in essence. The tension that cuts deeper is what kind of Sandinismo, and particularly what kind of male Sandinismo, will survive, perhaps to rule another day. The point of origin of the Sandinista nation, in both its striving for justice and ethical purity, and its triple mestizo consciousness, is the safe house in Sutiaba in 1971, where Morales and Dixon met when they were in hiding there with El Apóstol and a fourth Sandinista known as Caupolicán. While El Apóstol is dead – he does not die for the cause like his prototype Carlos Fonseca, but in a meaningless boating accident after the Revolution – Morales, Dixon, and Caupolicán live on to wrestle with accelerated globalization.

For better and worse, Morales and Dixon continue to act like Sandinista men of the 1980s; Caupolicán represents those Sandinistas who were corrupted during *La Piñata*. His name first appears early in the murder investigation when a suspicious charter flight turns out to have been contracted by "Engels Paladino, un viejo compañero de la clandestinidad, tanto del inspector Morales como de Lord Dixon, quién tras el triunfo de la revolución había servido por años como jefe de Inteligencia en la Dirección General de Seguridad del Estado, la DGSE" (*CLM*, 34; "Engels Paladino, an old underground compañero of both Inspector Morales and Lord Dixon, who after the triumph of the revolution had served for years as intelligence chief of the Department of State Security, the DGSE"). Engels Paladino is based on Lenin Cerna, a cellmate of Daniel Ortega in the Tipitapa Prison from 1967 to 1974, "the toughest member of the Sandinistas' inner circle" (Morris 2010: 179) and head of the DGSE from 1979 until Violeta Chamorro abolished the organization. Cerna was a fanatical Ortega loyalist from the 1995 split in the FSLN until he was removed from his administrative positions in 2011, after losing a power struggle with Rosario Murillo. In the novel, the nickname Caupolicán comes from a poem by Rubén Darío that compares an indigenous chieftain in Chile to an American Hercules. Morales, however, rejects the power and wealth that have accrued to Caupolicán in the post-1990 period: "Si se trata de esas alturas, prefiero el suelo" (*CLM*, 55; "I prefer the floor to those kinds of heights"). Caupolicán turns out to have been one of the murder victim Sheila Marenco's lovers, and the father of her child.

While it is true, as Coello Gutiérrez argues, that Caupolicán shows a concern for his son that is at odds with the rest of his personality, what is more striking is his tacit complicity in Sheila's execution. Fearful of being implicated by the investigation being conducted by Morales and Dixon, Caupolicán sets up a hit on his two former compañeros. This violation of the Sandinista ethos of unity is the novel's denouement. Dixon is fatally wounded in the ambush, and dies a few hours later. His death unravels the couple who have incarnated the nation as the outgrowth of a triple *mestizaje* whose origins lie in marginal communities such as Sutiaba. The novel's pastiche of popular conventions reinforces this event: Dixon is blown away much as the white hero's ethnic sidekick is shot in the closing battles of Hollywood B movies. Both Pacific-Atlantic couples having been dissolved by the death of the Afro-Caribbean Atlantic Coast partner, the Nicaragua that remains is restricted to Pacific Coast mestizos. La Monja, Doña Sofía, and Morales have remained true to the Sandinista creed, while Caupolicán represents the Sandinismo corrupted by *La Piñata*.

In the novel's closing scenes, Morales avenges his partner by conveying to the cartels falsified "proofs" that Caupolicán, not Sheila, stole the money. Having condemned his former compañero to death, he bids farewell to the unsuspecting Caupolicán with the words, "Nos vemos en el infierno" (*CLM*, 286; "I'll see you in hell"). He is not sure where this phrase comes from, though he believes he heard it in "una película" (*CLM*, 286; "a movie"), a source emblematic of the intractable grip of popular culture even on the imagination of two former revolutionaries who used to speak to each other on the phone by exchanging quotes from Rubén Darío. Morales's recognition of his responsibility for the murder that is going to occur nevertheless entails a recovery of his masculine identity. Doña Sofía solves the mystery and La Monja coordinates the arrest of the drug lords, but only Morales, the former guerrilla, can purge the rotten heart of Sandinismo and return the movement to its original purity and virility.

Even the act of avenging Dixon, though, is tainted by the suspicion that arises from the fact that the only enduring relationship in Morales's life is with another man. The novel's closing image – a memory of Dixon flirting with a black woman who later appears at his funeral – tardily certifies his late partner's heterosexuality, sparing the partners from recapitulating the relationship between Cabistán and Black Bull. The woman's blackness confines Dixon's assumed desires to his own region of the country, eliminating the last possibility of an egalitarian Pacific-Atlantic couple. The metaphors that surround this image include that of a cage "donde se agitaba, como si peleara con su sombra, un gallo color de llamarada" (*CLM*, 290; "where a flame-coloured fighting cock danced about as though battling with its shadow"). The "flame-coloured fighting cock" combines the flames of bonfires associated with images of Sandino with the counter-productive identity of "El gallo ennavajado" (*AM*, 276; "The Fighting Gamecock"), selected for Daniel Ortega by his 1990 campaign managers; it suggests both the shadow-boxing between the FSLN and the MRS, and the dwindling of Atlantic Coast Nicaraguan culture into a "shadow," in which the shared African heritage is more evident, to the dominant culture of Pacific Coast Nicaragua.

In spite of his success in avenging his partner and cleansing their relationship of unwanted homoerotic connotations, Inspector Dolores Morales, as his name suggests, is morally compromised as an agent of the future Sandinista struggle to secure national sovereignty against flows of transnational capital. His womanizing and his tricking of the cartels into killing Caupolicán make him a relic of the past, while the superior investigative skills of La Monja and Doña Sofía attest to the transition from a machista society to one managed by women according to female principles. The novel closes, as it opens, with a religious procession, this time a funeral march that accompanies Dixon's body to the airport, where it will be flown to Bluefields. Significantly, La Monja is absent, leaving Doña Sofía, the representative of the Nicaraguan people, as the dominant Sandinista figure at the funeral. In contrast to the procession in the novel's opening scene, this one is politicized by a vigorous cultural syncretism that elevates Doña Sofía, the embodiment of the nation's history, to a representative position. As Morales's lover Fanny tells him, "Doña Sofía tiene ahora vara alta" (*CLM*, 289; "Now Doña Sofía has the upper hand"). The people, it is suggested, conserve their mestizo national identity as a bulwark against the transnational commercial invasion: "la multitud de bailantes enardecidos no era más que una demostración de la rebeldía ancestral indígena en contra la dominación del colonizador español, que ahora se expresaba en contra del sistema de explotación capitalista y del imperialismo" (*CLM*, 288; "the crowd of frenetic dancers was nothing more than a demonstration of ancestral indigenous rebelliousness against the domination of the Spanish colonizer, which now expressed itself against the capitalist and imperialist system of exploitation"). The indigenous traditions of rebellion remain viable, the narrator asserts, even though "imperialism" no longer emanates from a national state. Dixon's funeral procession may appear to be a manifestation of a dual "Indohispano" identity, yet the man it is celebrating and incorporating into a traditional manifestation of the national culture is of Afro-Caribbean heritage. This heritage, too, has contributed to "Indohispano" identity, where it is visible in elements such as "cofrades uniformados de cotonas amarillas" (*CLM*, 289; "members of traditional brotherhoods wearing the uniform of the yellow peasant tunic"), which Ramírez associates in *Tambor olvidado* with the unacknowledged African contribution to what Nicaraguans perceive as "indigenous" traditions.

El cielo llora por mí both skirts the full fusion with the African that might appear to be promised by *Tambor olvidado*, and insists on African culture's persistence as one thread subsumed into a heritage of resistance, national sovereignty, and self-sacrifice. Nation-building Sandinismo will survive, Ramírez suggests, as long as it retains its moral probity and its connection to Nicaragua's cultural history; to do this, it needs to allow the feminine to predominate over the masculine (even though this relinquishment of authority provokes a crisis in male Sandinista identity). At the novel's close, Morales is left beneath the sway of the nun-like figures of the maternal proletarian Protestant Doña Sofía and the pure, once-upper-class Catholic La Monja, the novel's two most authentic emissaries of Sandino's example. Nevertheless, *El cielo llora por mí* is the last major work by either Ramírez or Cardenal to attempt to claim an alternate Sandinista identity for the Nicaraguan nation. Sandinismo may remain present in latent form, promoted by those who have stayed faithful to its moral precepts, yet unlike the 1960s and 1970s, when this counter-culture was a nation-in-waiting, however oppressed and marginalized, the Sandinista ethos now faces systemic obstacles, inherent to the transnational system, that nullify its prospects for expanding into any kind of "national" ideology (if autonomous national cultures are still feasible). Like the Nicaragua portrayed by Cardenal in his memoirs, particularly in *La revolución perdida*, vestigial Sandinismo in *El cielo llora por mí* is a Benjaminesque relic, an idealized, egalitarian, classless society, which, contrary to Benjamin's predictions in the European context in an earlier historical period, emanates from the recent past and is enshrined in the form of the unrecoverable autonomous nation.

THE REGIONALIZATION OF IDENTITY: *PASAJERO DE TRÁNSITO, LA FUGITIVA, TATA VASCO*

As Daniel Ortega consolidated his power after 2006, Sandinismo itself became a commercial product, shaped by Rosario Murillo's public-relations dexterity. While portraits of Sandino and Carlos Fonseca remained visible in public spaces and FSLN propaganda, the energies of the increasingly centralized governing structures converged on the "comandante-presidente," Daniel Ortega. Institutions such as the Museum of the Sandinista Victory (see chapter 9) presented the nation as the unique creation of Ortega's personal struggle. No longer a proving ground for higher moralities, the nation is now indescribable as a diachronic entity because it has been reduced to the expression of one man's image, impervious to chronology.

In the final three books discussed in this study, the quest for idealized spaces moves beyond the nation's borders. No longer nourished by the drive for national autonomy, or even by attempts to reclaim such autonomy in a post-1990 context, the work of both authors diminishes in vividness and intensity. The references in these works grow increasingly regional, absorbing Nicaraguan literature into a Mesoamerican area of financial and cultural commerce that is dominated by Mexico. Cardenal's *Pasajero de tránsito* (2009; Passenger in Transit) and *Tata Vasco* (2011), and Ramírez's *La Fugitiva* (2011; The Fugitive) all refer to a globalized environment in which Nicaraguan references no longer command their former authority, and Mexico, a player in the globalized world through its membership in NAFTA, becomes the backdrop that lends events credibility.[12]

These ambiguous developments raise the question of whether the novelist or epic poet can write the transnational nation. *Pasajero de tránsito* pulls Nicaraguan history from the early 1970s to the present inside-out: where the Cardenal of the 1970s and 1980s complained that his incessant travelling bored him because it took him away from the evolving revolutionary nation, the object of his political commitment and the subject of his verse, this new collection portrays the years of revolutionary struggle through vignettes and diaries of journeys around the world. It is the reverse-image of the 1970s and 1980s, imbued in a left-wing Christian ideology but drained of the nation and national history. Nicaragua is present only in references to Cardenal's status as the master of Solentiname or the minister of culture: the foreground is occupied by New York, Santo Domingo, Lapland, Greece, Vietnam, Cambodia, Japan, India, Malta, Chile, Armenia, Germany, and other locales. The collection of journeys continues uninterrupted into the new millennium in trips to destinations such as Chiapas, Baja California, and the Amazon; in contrast to Cardenal's Nicaraguan-focused work, this transnational narrative of his perceptions flows undisturbed by the rupture of 1990. The cosmic nostalgia for the revolutionary past that saturated *Versos del pluriverso* is absent.

Pasajero de tránsito contains thirty-three poems, most them little more than a page in length; some are new, some are older. A few have complicated publication histories. "Viaje a Nueva York" ("Trip to New York"), a fifteen-page diary-as-poem that dates from the early 1970s, recounts a week's socializing with the religious left of the US East Coast during the era of President Richard Nixon and the Vietnam War. Omitted from the militant *La santidad de la revolución*, presumably because it says little about Nicaragua and showcases a Cardenal who is well connected in the United States, "Trip to New York" first appeared in book form in English in *Zero*

Hour and Other Documentary Poems (1980). The poem's freshness survives in this first book publication in Spanish in the twenty-first century, even though the attention Cardenal focuses on mid-twentieth-century US counter-culture figures such as Dorothy Day and Father Daniel Berrigan, whom only elderly US readers will recall, is bound to puzzle most readers of Spanish. Like Cardenal's admiration of Ezra Pound, this poem had to be dissimulated during the revolutionary years.

Likewise, though for different reasons, "Concentración en Grenada" ("Rally in Grenada"), first published in an anthology of Cardenal's works issued by Editorial Nueva Nicaragua in 1983 but dropped from *Flights of Victory* after the revolutionary government of Grenada was overthrown by an internal coup that opened the door to a US military invasion, may appear in an international edition now that the Cold War belongs to the past. Yet, the assumptions of the Cold War having dissolved, Cardenal must change the poem's closing lines. In the Nueva Nicaragua edition, the poem is titled "Concentración en St. George" (*AT*, 292); the 2009 version replaces the name of the capital with that of the country. Where the first published version concludes with the encapsulation of Grenada as "una isla solita en el océano desafiando al imperialismo" (*AT*, 293; "a little island alone in the ocean defying imperialism"), in *Pasajero de tránsito* the conclusion reads, "una islita sola en mitad del océano/ desafiando a Estados Unidos" (*PT*, 16; "a tiny island in the middle of the ocean/standing up to the United States" [*OS*, 126]). The replacement of "alone," which might inadvertently suggest that Grenada was abandoned by its friends in Cuba and Nicaragua, by "middle" is less significant than the need to specify the United States as the malevolent force that threatened Grenada. In the Cold War context, "imperialismo," by definition, meant the United States; the passage of time has obscured this identification, as the internal power struggles that precipitated the end of the Grenadian regime have enlarged the cast of characters who might be alluded to as "imperialist" (Payne, Sutton, and Thorndike 1984: 117–45).

By contrast, two poems from Cardenal's travels as a government minister, "Hidrofoil en el Mar Egeo" ("Hydrofoil on the Aegean Sea") and "Horror en Cambodia" ("Horror in Cambodia"), are plucked from Cantos 12 and 33 respectively of *Cosmic Canticle*. The Aegean Sea poem describes a hydrofoil trip with Melina Mercuri, the Greek actress whose tenure as minister of culture in a left-wing government coincided with Cardenal's period in the same portfolio in Nicaragua. While this poem's inclusion is logical, that of "Horror in Cambodia" is startling. Reprinted without changes, this stanza of a little more than a page, written in Cardenal's concrete style, itemizes a visit to a museum in Cambodia that commemorates the victims of Pol Pot's slaughter. The poem's opening line is: "Con el Comandante Daniel Ortega en un museo" (*PT*, 73; "With Comandante Daniel Ortega in a museum"). At first glance it may appear incomprehensible that Cardenal would reprint this respectful reference to a man who had connived for him to be condemned for libel and had his bank accounts frozen during the months when the poet was preparing this book. Yet, as a standard revolutionary locution at the time of its inclusion in *Cosmic Canticle*, this line becomes a reproof when it is reprinted in 2009: a reminder of the more righteous, revolutionary identity of "Comandante Daniel Ortega" from which the duplicitous "comandante-presidente" has strayed. Ortega's apostasy is not only political but also represents an abandonment of the revolutionary manhood that took him and Cardenal to Cambodia together. This is evident in the description Cardenal gave of Rosario Murillo in 2005: "Ella sigue interviniendo en política cada vez más. Domina a su marido Daniel Ortega. Ahora ella es la persona que manda en la campaña de Daniel Ortega" (*UIEC*; "She keeps intervening more and more in politics. She rules her husband Daniel Ortega. Now she's the person who gives orders in Daniel Ortega's campaign"). In this context, the poem's opening line becomes a reminder of the ethical male guild in which Ortega has resigned his membership. After building up a gruesome picture of the horrors of Pol Pot's Cambodia, the poem concludes: "Y EE.UU. ahora apoya a Pol Pot" (*PT*, 74; "And now the US supports Pol Pot"). While this statement is no longer true in 2009, when Pol Pot is dead, Cardenal's words evoke the ideological purity that Ortega has abandoned in his unscrupulous pursuit of a return to high office.

The other poems that refer to the Cold War years, whether they were written and published at that time, or whether they are new poems about the past, express the same revolutionary ideology; in those that refer to more recent experiences, Cardenal's ideology shifts to more pliant forms less channelled by revolutionary nationalism. The sudden appearance of detailed poems about events that are many years in the past – the most dramatic case being "La Diosa Blanca" ("The White Goddess"), a poem of more than 360 lines describing a visit to the poet Robert Graves at his home in Mallorca in 1950 – are almost certainly based on notes taken at the time the experiences occurred. Even Cardenal's most personal and mystical poems, such as "Telescope in the Dark Night," are reworkings in verse of notes taken in prose (*UIEC*); this is the likely genesis of recent evocations of past journeys such as "Pasajero de Tránsito en Santo Domingo" ("Passenger in Transit in Santo Domingo"), "En Chile cuando Allende" ("In Allende's Chile"), and "Con los lapones" ("With the Lapps"). Though "Misa ecuménica en Dusseldorf" ("Ecumenical Mass in Dusseldorf") had appeared in different forms in both *Flights of Victory* and *Cosmic Canticle* (see chapter 8), only one poem, "La llegada" ("The Arrival"), which also appeared in *Flights of Victory*, is an individual work reprinted unchanged from an earlier collection; like much of the book in which it first appeared, it was also integrated into *Cosmic Canticle*.

By displaying the obverse side of his participation in the Nicaraguan Revolution –his identity as globe-trotting minister and poet – Cardenal recaptures the masculine identity that the nation can no longer offer him. While Ramírez engages in ironic play with fissuring concepts of traditional masculinity in *El cielo llora por mí*, Cardenal, a generation older and motivated by a need to compensate for the "castration" of his celibacy, reacts against postmodern ambiguities. The opening poem, "Pasajero de Tránsito en Santo Domingo," evinces a sardonic disdain of ministerial privileges that combines an acceptance of first-class travel as his due, in a "avión donde me darán champaña espumoso con color/ de orines y sabor a espuma de jabón" (*PT*, 9; "plane where they will give me frothy champagne the colour/of urine and with the taste of soap suds"), with an ethical loner's disdain for the trappings of high office. These poems remind the reader simultaneously that Cardenal once held high office and that, unlike Ortega, he has not compromised his ethical probity to claw it back. The Nicaraguan nation remains nearly invisible in *Pasajero de tránsito*, appearing only in "The White Goddess," set decades before the Revolution, where Graves shows his sons where the unexpected visitor to his retreat comes from:

> El buscó el mapamundi de la sala y le dio
> vueltas hasta poner el dedo en Nicaragua y
> llamó a los niños para que vieran el sitio
> de donde llegaba yo: "Aquí estamos nosotros …
> Y aquí Nicaragua." Y los niños se inclinaron para mirar.
> El diminuto sitio del Mediterráneo donde estaban
> ellos, y el otro lugar también pequeño, admirados
> de que fuera tan lejos. "¡Aaaaaala …!"
> (*PT*, 81; He fetched the globe in the living room and spun it/round until placing his finger on Nicaragua and/he called the children so they could see where/I was from: "Here we are …/And here is Nicaragua." And the children bent over to see/the tiny Mediterranean spot where they were,/and the other equally tiny spot, amazed/that it was so far away. "Wow!" [*OS*, 46])

The linking of small places presages later bonds between Solentiname and Cuba, or Nicaragua and Grenada, yet the Cardenal who visited Graves was two decades away from becoming a revolutionary. He tells the poet of Náhuat myths that resemble the archetype of the white goddess; this is the only information about Nicaragua that appears in *Pasajero de tránsito*. The nation is present as a tiny, remote entity, barely visible on the globe and confined to the world of 1950: the globe, not the nation, is the book's theme. The post-1990 nation is invisible; the revolutionary nation may be descried by implication, in the restless journeys of its globe-trotting minister of culture.

The recurrence of what might be dubbed "international solidarity thought" acts as a unifying thread that links these generally short, precisely observed yet non-lyrical poems, exemplifying a consistent ethical stance in favour of social justice and the self-determination of peoples. The Exteriorism of discourses in dialectical opposition is not transferrable to the short poem, yet an emphasis on the concrete is central to these accounts of places visited and people encountered. As Cardenal writes at the conclusion of "With the Lapps": "Decir con las cosas no con ideas/decía William C. Williams./Del viaje a aquel día sin noche/son estas cosas" (*PT*, 70; "No ideas but in things/William C. Williams used to say./From the trip to that day without night/these are the things" [*OS*, 54]). As Pound is Cardenal's model for the long poem, William Carlos Williams provides aesthetic counsel on achieving precision and presence in the short poem.

As a gringo like Pound, Williams is an influence who may be owned up to more easily once the Revolution is over. Cardenal, however, bends Williams's aesthetic to his own ideological ends. These short poems build through an accumulation of "things" to an idea that many of them sum up in statements of allegiance to local struggles or defiance of imperialist designs. "En Malta" ("In Malta"), for example, proceeds from physical description of a small island through its history of foreign occupation to the installation of its "nuevo gobierno socialista" ("new socialist government'); the parallels with Cuba and Nicaragua become explicit when Cardenal thinks of a tree he planted there many years ago, which by now will have matured and will be waving "sus ramas verdes de uniforme verde-olivo/en protesta contra/ los misiles gringos" (*PT*, 67; "its green branches of an olive-green uniform/in protest against/the gringo missiles"). The "olive-green uniform," a metonymic trope for Sandinista guerrillas, confers a militant Sandinista identity on the Maltese government's anti-nuclear stance. Here, as in "Horror in Cambodia," the anti-imperialist statement concentrates on a specific political issue.

Other poems build towards realizations that are political in a broader sense. "El Ultra-Rápido" ("The High-Speed Train"), in which the narrator reflects on the centralized Japanese political system during a journey from

Tokyo to Nagoya, culminates in a condemnation of the historical amnesia instilled by US mass culture: "Y muchos jóvenes japoneses no saben quién bombardeó Hiroshima/ pero conocen perfectamente todo cantante norteamericano" (*PT*, 52; "And many Japanese young people don't know who bombarded Hiroshima / but they have a perfect knowledge of every US singer"). The miraculous technology of the train appears to share responsibility for this lapse.

Though the pattern is not rigorous, the poems in which the nation is veiled by a militant internationalism tend to fall in the middle of *Pasajero de tránsito*. Contrasting with the assiduous opposition to US policies expressed by these poems, three consecutive poems near the beginning of the book illustrate a strikingly apolitical approach to the United States during the prerevolutionary period; the book concludes with four poems that refer to post-1990 experiences "beyond the nation." The earlier vignettes "El Águila" ("The Eagle"), "Viajando en bus por Estados Unidos" ("Travelling by Bus in the United States"), and "A orillas del río Ohio, en Kentucky" ("On the Banks of the Ohio River, in Kentucky") are notable for their sanguine framing of images from US life: a girl painting a porch while her sister picks apples in an orchard, a glimpse of a bald eagle in Oregon that is shorn of any reference to the symbol of United States power, an evocation of the Ohio River as the border of the paradise sought by US woodsman Daniel Boone. These pastoral images evoke (and were written during) the period between the late 1950s and the late 1960s, when Cardenal's vision of the United States as an imperialist oppressor, instilled by his childhood under US military occupation and his youth under the Somocista extension of the occupation, and which revived during the Sandinista struggle, was suspended by his friendship with Thomas Merton (see chapter 8). In the twenty-first century, when the Nicaraguan nation is no longer available to Cardenal as a communal, diachronic entity and interventionist US politico-military policies have nearly ceased to be a threat to Latin America, the problematic of the nation recedes.

Pasajero de tránsito concludes with four new poems that echo the contours of the world forged by accelerated globalization, seeking Utopian affirmation within the boundaries delineated by configurations of power that not only make the nation and its present-day predicament nearly impossible to consolidate and articulate, but also represent the economic and cultural absorption of smaller nations into regional configurations dominated by emerging middle powers. Tellingly, two of these poems are set in Mexico, one in the Brazilian Amazon and one in the Peruvian Amazon, close to the Brazilian border. The regional powers of Mexico and Brazil frame contemporary debates, defined in terms of issues such as environmentalism, which cut across national boundaries (paradoxically undermining these countries' authority as nations just as their power begins to grow). No longer a government minister who is whisked away on excursions by political celebrities, Cardenal's travels now follow the routes laid out by the globalized industry of eco-tourism, which, Robinson argues, "has provided a convenient 'green' cover for practices that result in further degradation both of fragile ecosystems and of the conditions of poor and marginalized human communities" (Robinson 2003: 200).

"Zoológico de Iquitos" ("Iquitos Zoo"), "En el mar de Cortés" ("In the Sea of Cortez"), and ""Reflexiones en el río Grijalva" ("Reflections on the River Grijalva") all describe eco-tourism expeditions; the final poem, "Manaus resucitado" ("Manaus Resurrected"), grows out of an invitation to a literary festival in the Amazon's largest city. The fact that the intellectual's journeys are no longer unique diminishes his authority to pronounce upon public issues; his participation in the same day-trips that are frequented by well-off tourists from around the world assimilates his perceptions into those of the mass culture of an undifferentiated transnational class. Robinson warns against interpreting contemporary tourism in terms of state-to-state relations or the colonialism of one nation over another, preferring to approach it as evidence of the conquest of "some social groups in global society by others, but not some nations by others" (Robinson 2003: 197). At the same time that the intellectual's knowledge of national history and literature is relegated to the status of a peripheral attribute, depriving him of his role as arbiter and projecting him into a globalized sphere where his experiences will reproduce those of thousands of other tourists, the almost inescapable pervasiveness of this way of travelling makes the intellectual as complicit in the negative impacts of practices such as eco-tourism as anyone else, calling into question his command of ethical authority, exalted emotional states, or utterly original insights. Much of this taint was absent from Cardenal's earlier travels in locations such as Cuba, the Soviet Union, or Cold War-era Vietnam, not only because his journeys pursued a revolutionary political agenda whose goal was to enfranchise and better the living conditions of oppressed national social classes, but also because the "'social tourism' that predominated in the former Soviet-bloc countries ... was not a commodified activity" (ibid.: 203). Where his earlier travels were distinguished by their radical political goals, travel in the new millennium becomes uniform in the range of experiences, insights, and moral claims that may attach to it.

The most ambitious and provocative of these four concluding poems is "Reflections on the River Grijalva." Both "Iquitous Zoo" and "In the Sea of

Cortez" – an account of a whale-watching tour off Baja California – are evocations of nature that gesture in very mild ways in the direction of deeper links among species. "Reflections on the River Grijalva," in a vein more reminiscent of *Versos del pluriverso*, tracks down the cosmic implications of the journey described. In contrast to the poems in Cardenal's previous collection, this piece is not haunted by the ghosts of the revolutionary nation. The setting is firmly fixed in the transnational early twenty-first century. The nation has been eclipsed, giving way to the dualism of globalization, in which the individual's cultural frame is either a recalcitrant clinging to regionalism or a transnational context created by movements of capital.

The experience that acts as a catalyst for Cardenal's "reflections" is a popular boat trip down a spectacular canyon in Chiapas.[13] The poem opens with an anecdote about a regionalist Mexican poet who professes his dislike for the Grijalva canyon because it is located in the state of Chiapas rather than his native Tabasco: "es que el río pasa por Tabasco/*su* Tabasco/después de Chiapas" (*PT*, 89, emphasis in original; "because the river actually winds through Tabasco/*his* Tabasco/after Chiapas" [*OS*, 33]). This poet's chauvinism illustrates the comic rusticity to which those who cling to a defined identity are consigned by transnational dynamics. Cardenal's allegiance to the revolutionary left is evident only in a single tongue-in-cheek line, when he describes the forests on either side of the canyon as "el hábitat del quetzal y de los zapatistas" (*PT*, 90; "the habitat of the quetzal and the Zapatistas" [*OS*, 34]). Even this guerrilla movement, though, is postmodern, regionalist, and ethnic-based; it is not, in spite of its title, a national liberation movement.

The political consciousness evoked by the narrator derives from the contemporary transnational counter-ideology of environmentalism. Cardenal's awareness of the area's geological history, particularly the great age of its rock formations, and his recounting of the history of the local indigenous people are accompanied by his ironic eye for the way in which the animal and bird species are confined within a "parque ecoturístico/con miradores y lugares de picnic" (*PT*, 90; "the ecotourist park/with observation decks and picnic spots" [*OS*, 34]). The journey down river, by contrast, evinces a close attention to the system by which the river's water flows from Chiapas to the Gulf of Mexico, and to the despoilment of this natural pattern by human carelessness. A single block stanza of six lines lists all of the types of bottles, containers, toys, and dead pets that make up the notorious "alfombra fétida" (*PT*, 91; "fetid carpet" [*OS*, 35]) that floats in the middle of the river, marring this ecotourism experience. This "cadáver de un Super" (*PT*, 91; "corpse of a supermarket" [*OS*, 35]), as Cardenal describes the huge raft of garbage in the middle of the river, is held back before one reaches the hydroelectric dam that backs up the water and makes the boat tours possible. The description of the garbage consists of a discordant jangle of brand names and English words that jolts the appreciative rhythms – Cardenal's closest approach to lyricism – of his descriptions of the canyon's natural beauty. The transnational frame of the poem's setting is confirmed by the observation that the dam is part of the hydroelectric project "que da luz a México y Centroamérica" (*PT*, 91; "that provides power to Mexico and Central America" [*OS*, 35]). With this observation on contemporary structures that amalgamate Nicaragua into Central America, itself subordinated to the Mexican-dominated Mesoamerican region, Cardenal's boat trip ends and his reflections begin.

The erasure of the nation as the frame for Cardenal's speculations opens the door to thoughts that have not been expressed before in his work. As long as he engaged with Nicaraguan history, he did so, ineluctably, as a Granada Conservative, a priest, and a Sandinista; the disappearance of these identifications from a poem such as "Reflections on the River Grijalva" means that all bets are off: not even the existence of God can be taken for granted. This rupture illuminates the extent to which Cardenal's Catholic religious devotion was an inherent element of his construction of his identity as a Nicaraguan. Speculating as part of a transnational tourist class, he moves from ecological distress to an outright questioning of the existence of a higher intelligence. This seeming heresy is provoked by the urge to make the present matter in a context beyond the protective walls of national history. The disappearance of national history obliterates Cardenal's theological projection of life beyond death.

From *Oracle over Managua* to *Cosmic Canticle*, and in a vestigial way on to *Versos del pluriverso*, with the exception of "Telescope in the Dark Night," Cardenal found transcendental solace, in the face of death and within the vast temporal movements of the cosmos, in the individual's immortality as atoms of light specific to his nation. The promise of the resurrection offered consolation because it was not merely a resurrection of the soul but also, as dictated by his blending of the discourses of Catholic theology, quantum physics, and Marxism, a resurrection that contained a material dimension. This materiality carried within it a national charge: the individual's atoms, borne through eternity, would be differentiated by national experience; the committed individual would live on in the memory of the revolutionary nation. In "Reflections on the River Grijalva," this theology is no longer viable. A key trait that characterizes the progressive individual under globalized capitalism is concern for the environment, in part because effective environmental legislation would constrain the power of the fluid transnational capital whose capricious movements excavate gulfs of injustice as they sculpt human society. Yet, where the revolutionary nation offered a Utopian hope of creating a future paradise, environmentalism, in the twenty-first-century context, must face the question of whether the individual can reach beyond the boundaries of an inflated self and the temptations of consumerism to make environmental damage matter: "compremos y compremos en los Supers/alma mía que mañana moriremos" (*PT*, 92; "let us buy and buy in the Supermarkets/because tomorrow dear heart we die" [*OS*, 36]). Egotism such as this makes the natural world – God's world, if God exists – a hostile force since it is nature that dictates that we must die. The lure of nature-hating consumerism combines with the passage of time in this work by a poet in his eighties to make religious faith more fragile than ever before. Never in Cardenal's verse has death felt so near nor has it posed such an implacable conundrum. The unchallenged dominance of the atheism implicit in transnational forms of economic organization makes even a one-time revolutionary priest doubt "si hay un propósito o no/ en el universo" (*PT*, 92; "whether there's a purpose or not/in the universe" [*OS*, 36]).

The case for meaninglessness for "un cosmos que no es nuestra casa" (*PT*, 93; "a cosmos that is not our home" [*OS*, 37]) has never been made so strongly in his work. If, in the end, he succeeds in wresting hope and faith from despair and unbelief, the victory is earned by a thread; the only argument Cardenal can muster in support of faith is that it is necessary to ward off despair. The crux of the poem's philosophical argument lies in whether concern for the environment does not anchor the individual so firmly in the transnational present that he becomes incapable of perceiving spiritual connections. The poem's goal, therefore, must be to establish "la relación/entre nuestra visión ecológica/y nuestra cosmovisión" (*PT*, 94; "the relationship/between our ecological vision/and our cosmovision" [*OS*, 38]). Once this link has been made, nature ceases to be hostile – though it remains "severa" (*PT*, 94; "severe" [*OS*, 38]), insisting that we die to make way for succeeding generations – and the resurrection, which of necessity, in Cardenal's vision, must include a material dimension, once again becomes possible even if its precise form remains mysterious. Yet this tenuous faith in the resurrection emerges as the only sustainable option simply because the alternative is far worse: "porque si no/como San Pablo dijo/estamos jodidos" (*PT*, 94; "because if not/as Saint Paul said/we're fucked" [*OS*, 39]).

"Reflections on the River Grijalva," the most significant poem written by Cardenal during this period, is a troubled rebuttal of the challenges posed to his "cosmovision" by accelerated globalization. The coda of *Pasajero de tránsito*, "Manaus Resurrected," is a joyous affirmation of resurrection that rides roughshod over the contemporary world's disregard for spirituality, nationalism, and Marxism. Here, too, metaphysical speculation occurs in language that eschews the scientific discourses of *Cosmic Canticle*; economic decline is charted in light strokes that allude to Marxist economic analysis without reproducing its burly discourse. Invited to a literary festival in the Amazonian metropolis, Cardenal arrives with preconceptions formed by the history of the early-twentieth-century rubber boom that made the city a place of extravagant luxury, then, when rubber prices dropped, led to its precipitous decline into a jungle backwater. The opening stanza recounts this history: rather than giving a thorough economic explanation of Manaus's fall, as he would have done when Marxist analysis remained the language of revolutionary movements, Cardenal concludes a page-long list of the marvels that characterized Manaus at its zenith with the brief line: "la Bolsa de Londres acabó todo" (*PT*, 97; "the London Stock Market ended it all" [*OS*, 14]). The second stanza details the city's decline, while the third announces its resurrection.

This pattern, delineating the Utopian hope that underlies Cardenal's most uncompromising accounts of misery and oppression, collides in the poem with the structures of globalization. Manaus, it appears, owes its resurrection to the establishment of a free-trade zone. Drawn into an ideological contradiction in order to praise the vivid life he finds in the metropolis's streets, Cardenal must exclude from the poem the pernicious features of free-trade zones: low wages, long hours, minimal protection for workers, corruption, gambling, tawdry commercialism – vices denounced by Ramírez in his description of a similar zone in *El cielo llora por mí*. In a world in which no alternative exists to free-market economics, all praise of success and happiness is an implicit celebration of transnational capital. The religious metaphors that in past works were used to imagine a world beyond the avarice of the "free market" now apply to the results of this system:

> Pero ahora está hecha Zona Franca
> para todo el comercio del Amazonas
> Un Edén industrial digamos
> lujuriante selva de electrodomésticos
>   y rascacielos de vidrio
> y vi para mi sorpresa una urbe viva
> las colegialas bajando de buses ...
> (*PT*, 97; But now it has become a Free Zone/for all commerce in Amazonia/an industrial Eden we could say/luxurious forest of domestic appliances/and glass skyscrapers/and to my surprise I saw a lively metropolis/schoolgirls getting off buses ... [*OS*, 14])

References to "an industrial Eden" and a "luxurious forest of domestic appliances" reverse not only Cardenal's socialism of the 1970s and 1980s, but even the Mertonian critique of materialism that preceded it in the 1960s. The celebration of economic abundance and human life that occupies the rest of the stanza is sincerely felt, yet a Marxist analysis would classify the urban boom described by the poetic speaker as a mere superstructure erected on a base of exploitive labour and the principles by which comparative advantage economics irrationally allocates the construction of washing machines for the Latin American market to the Amazon. Cardenal, arguably, overlooks this dimension of his presentation of Manaus, in part because there is now almost no way to avoid implicit praise of capitalism, and in part because the poem is an epistle addressed to Milton Thiago de Mello, the famous Brazilian zoologist and proponent of biodiversity preservation, who invites Cardenal first to the literary festival, then to his house twenty-four hours upriver from Manaus. This invitation, also, represents a resurrection for Cardenal. During the trip upriver, he recovers quasi-ministerial privileges: "yo fui en el camarote del gobernador" (*PT*, 98; "I traveled in the governor's cabin" [*OS*, 15]). The poem concludes not only with the assurance that "tu Manaus Thiago ha resucitado" (*PT*, 100; "your Manaus Thiago has risen from the dead" [*OS*, 17]), but also with Cardenal's being named "poeta amazónico honorífico" (*PT*, 99; "an honorary Amazonian poet" [*OS*, 16]) and being inducted into the "Amazonian Academy." Forms of regionalized, cross-national belonging such as these displace those stemming from citizenship; as the nation dissolves, Cardenal revives his faith in the resurrection as a material phenomenon in a context in which all material objects are manifestations of transnational capital.

As Nicaragua exists only by implication in *Pasajero de tránsito*, so Sergio Ramírez's novel *La Fugitiva* (2011; The Fugitive) describes the nation in terms of what it is not. This reconstruction of the life of a female Costa Rican writer unfurls within a regional Mesoamerican frame in which most of the action occurs in Costa Rica, Guatemala, and Mexico. It promotes a transnational ideology, that of liberal feminism, yet lavishes inordinate attention on the history of Costa Rica. In a very real sense, the Costa Rican nation, rather than the unconventional, sexually liberated writer Amanda Solano, who is based on the historical figure of Yolanda Oreamuno (1916–56), is the novel's central character. Costa Rica's stability and repeated avoidance of the pitfall of violent upheaval act as an ongoing, if mostly unspoken, reproof to Nicaragua's history of wars and dictatorships. The unnamed Nicaraguan narrator, who has written a novel called *Tiempo de fulgor*, interviews three women who knew Amanda Solano. Two of the interviews take place in San José, the third in Mexico City. Each interview is roughly a hundred pages in length; once his subjects begin to speak, the interviewer does not intervene. Asked about Amanda, the interviewees provide lengthy summaries of decisive phases in the history of Costa Rica and, to a lesser extent, Guatemala and Mexico. Though presented as a figure who asserts her independence, as a woman and an artist, Amanda becomes a shuttlecock, buffeted about by these national histories, which, from the vantage point of the post-national present, are evoked in a nostalgic vein. Doubt is cast on her vocation as a writer: she produces little and even her friends and supporters remain uncertain whether she is actually writing, or merely talking about being a writer. Amanda never comes into focus as a character. As the Costa Rican reviewer Juan Murillo commented, "se echa de menos en esta novela, considerando la licencia artística que asume Ramírez, que no se escuche la propia voz de Yolanda Oreamuno, o más aún, su interioridad … Tampoco se explora su faceta de escritora que es, finalmente, el mérito en el que debería descansar su fama" (Murillo 2011; "One regrets in this novel, given the artistic licence that Ramírez assumes, that the voice of Yolanda Oreamuno herself is not heard, or, beyond that, her intimate thoughts … Nor is her writer's side explored, which, after all, is the merit on which her fame should rest").

The emphasis on Costa Rican history attracted adverse commentary. Defending this trait of the novel in an interview in Madrid with the Ecuadorean newspaper *El Universo*, Ramírez stated: "El lector debe disponer de elementos fundamentales de la historia de Costa Rica. No es un paisaje abstracto" (Villaruel 2011; "The reader must have at hand the fundamental elements of Costa Rican history. It is not an abstract landscape"). Yet, where in novels such as *To Bury Our Fathers* and *Sombras nada más* the history of Nicaragua is dramatized and mythologized through the characters' actions, Ramírez presents Costa Rican history in inert blocks, in the voice of an immensely knowledgeable but not entirely engaged outsider. Even the criticisms of the small-mindedness with which Costa Rican society responds to Amanda's freewheeling life occur at a one-step remove from the action. This concatenation of three sprawling monologues is Ramírez's least compelling and most loosely knit novel since *Tiempo de fulgor*. It is true that in much of Mexico and Central America – the "homeland" staked out here – even a liberal feminism of equal pay and equal sexual freedoms is not yet a mainstream ideology. In an interview in Mexico, Ramírez lamented the "grandes rezagos derivados de esa sociedad machista" ("Sergio Ramírez presenta novela" 2011; "the huge gulfs of backwardness stemming from this machista society"). But a more progressive consensus among readers of fiction situates this book in the position too often occupied by the contemporary historical novel: that of moving a social stance widely accepted in the present to the past, where it acquires a radical tint that, nevertheless, few readers will find challenging. Amanda's shocking condition is that of being divorced in a society where "si la mujer perdió al marido porque se divorció, pues es un ser que no se reconstruye ya más. ¡La divorciada!" (*LF*, 167; "if the woman lost her husband because she got divorced, well, she's a being who can't be put back together again. The divorcée!").

The relationship between history and fiction in *La Fugitiva* is problematic. A note at the conclusion states, "Esta novela es una obra de ficción. Todos los personajes y situaciones han sido inventados y se deben a la imaginación del autor" (*LF*, 311; "This novel is a work of fiction. All of the characters and situations have been invented and are creations of the author's imagination"). The protagonist's life is so tightly modelled on that of her historical prototype, Yolanda Oreamuno, that her two known novels have the same titles as those written by Oreamuno. Likewise, the third interview subject, Manuela Torres, a very famous Mexican lesbian singer of Costa Rican background, is a transparent transcription of the life of Chavela Vargas (1919–2012).[14] By contrast, the writers and politicians with whom Amanda mingles, including many of the central figures of Costa Rican, Guatemalan, and Mexican public life, are called by their real names, even when the actions ascribed to them may be invented. The criteria for deciding which characters' names are preserved and which are changed appear arbitrary. In opposition to the precisely coordinated analyses of Nicaraguan history that animate Ramírez's earlier novels, in *La Fugitiva* nationality loses its diachronic edge. The nation seems to be little more than the aggregate of the famous personalities who proceed from within its borders; image, rather than history, defines its nature. This focus on personalities blurs even the novel's sharpest line of division, that between Nicaragua and Costa Rica. At the same time, like all of Ramírez's novels, this one develops an intertextual relationship with past literature. The central point of reference is Marcel Proust. Yolanda Oreamuno's *La ruta de su evasión* (1948; His Escape Route), considered the first Central American novel to employ stream-of-consciousness techniques, which won a contest in Guatemala but was then forgotten, was dredged up by Ramírez, who published it with EDUCA in 1970.[15]

The theme of flight dominates *La Fugitiva*. As the second narrator says of Amanda: "Busca huir pero no la dejan las rejas, no la deja la puerta cerrada, y entonces, fugitiva, huye hacia su interior más profundo" (*LF*, 214; "She tries to flee, but the bars won't let her, the closed door won't let her, and so, a fugitive, she flees deep inside herself"). Oreamuno was obsessed with Proust to the point of never outgrowing his literary influence. The title of

Ramírez's novel, *La Fugitiva*, alludes to *La ruta de su evasión*; it is also a translation of the alternate title of volume six of Proust's novel *In Search of Lost Time*. Originally called *Albertine disparue* (1925; *The Sweet Cheat Gone*), this novel was included in the three-volume Pléiade edition of Proust's novel as *La Fugitive*. The novel opens with the disappearance of Albertine, Marcel's live-in lover, from his Paris apartment. She hides out in the countryside. Before they can patch up their relationship by correspondence, Albertine is killed in a riding accident. Marcel spends the rest of this volume purging his grief by investigating Albertine's past. He discovers that many of the women Albertine knew were also her lovers, and that she was betraying him with these women during the time when they were living together. In spite of its liberal-feminist promotion of a woman's right to sexual freedom, *La Fugitiva* "straightens" Proust's queer text by rewriting the lesbian Albertine as the heterosexual Amanda Solano. Where *To Bury Our Fathers* absorbs Faulknerian structures and motifs from its intertextual affinities to *Absalom, Absalom!* and *As I Lay Dying*, in *La Fugitiva* the evocations of the stream-of-consciousness techniques of *In Search of Lost Time* and *La ruta de su evasión* do not translate into similarly ambitious narrative devices: the three monologues are rambling and lack the precise coordination of motif and image that characterizes Modernist elaborations of stream-of-consciousness.

The entry into the novel of the Chavela Vargas character, Manuela Torres, compensates to some degree for the excision of Proust's Sapphic themes by introducing a sympathetic, if crusty, lesbian. Torres falls in love with Amanda and accompanies her on a disastrous train journey across the United States with one of Amanda's least promising lovers, a US con man named Dick de Palma. Manuela does not exclude the possibility that Amanda may have had other lesbian admirers: "Una belleza como la suya tenía que deslumbrar por igual a hombres y mujeres, y más de alguna la habría pretendido antes, desde los días del colegio, eso lo daba yo por seguro" (*LF*, 279; "A beauty like hers would have dazzled men and women equally, and more than one woman would have approached her before, ever since her high school days, of that I was certain"). Since Amanda and Manuela do not become lovers, the novel's hetero-normative ethos prevails; Amanda's divorcée's rebellion against prudish Costa Rican society confirms mainstream values of the present, even though it may outrage those of the 1940s. Her Proustian fixation dwindles to an affectation of cultural style. This strain undercuts the reading that would suggest that Amanda was in fact a gifted artist who was crushed by her abusive stepfather and her unfeeling husbands, the first a Chilean diplomat who may have infected her with syphilis, the second a humourless

Costa Rican Communist Party organizer, who gains custody of their son, then leaves for Guatemala to work for the Revolution.

As in *To Bury Our Fathers* and *Castigo Divino*, Guatemalan activism appears as a counterpoint to events farther south. Though Guatemala's revolutionary culture serves as an instructive example in the other two novels (and in "Balcanes y volcanes"), in *La Fugitiva*, where the primary point of comparison is democratic Costa Rica, the Guatemalan revolutionary experience appears in a more dubious light. When Amanda moves to Guatemala to try to regain custody of her son, the regime closes ranks to protect her ex-husband. Not even Amanda's flirtation with the diplomat, academic sociologist, and successful novelist Mario Monteforte Toledo – who played a role in 1944–54 Guatemala in some ways analogous to that played by Ramírez in 1979–90 Nicaragua – can prevent her from being deported.

Mexico, where Amanda spends the final years of her life, appears as the inevitable, dominant, fallback setting, the regional metropolis whose identity is recognizable around the globe; yet the most evocative moments of *La Fugitiva* occur when Ramírez describes the Nicaraguans who cross Amanda's path. This is the secret thread that runs through the book, unveiling the ideological obsession that underlies the surface statement of liberal feminism. The nation having disappeared with Daniel Ortega's return to power at the head of a postmodern simulacrum of historical Sandinismo, Nicaragua may be descried and assessed only in the human flotsam that are adrift in the remainder of the enlarged Mesoamerican homeland of accelerated globalization. This Mesoamerica, though, is a mere vestige of the Central America whose unity-through-diversity Ramírez promoted from the 1960s to the 1990s; in place of the discrete yet mutually supportive histories of Nicaragua, Guatemala, El Salvador, Honduras, and Costa Rica, in the new millennium one discovers an undifferentiated blur of personalities, absorbed by economic and cultural dependency into the dominant entity of Mexico.

La Fugitiva concentrates on Nicaraguans in both Costa Rica and Mexico; but, while the latter country is an unavoidable landscape through which all Central Americans of a certain social level must pass, and by whose music, movies, and television all are influenced, tiny Costa Rica's relative integration and economic and political success deliver a sharp reproof to Nicaraguan backwardness. The novel contains no mention of modern Sandinismo, in either its 1979–90 or its post-2006 incarnations; Sandino himself appears fleetingly, in Costa Rican references to Nicaragua as a place where wars and violence are rife. One of the first issues that the novel addresses is the status of Nicaraguans in Costa Rica, where, like Mexicans and Central Americans in the United States, they form a labour pool that completes menial chores and is considered to be physically recognizable as different or "other" owing to their darker skin and stronger indigenous inheritance.[16] When the narrator visits his first interview subject, a well-off elderly San José widow, he is struck by the appearance of the caregiver who answers the door:

> Una mujer madura, cuyo uniforme de enfermera cruje con el almidón al paso de sus zapatos imitación de Adidas, viene a abrirme. Me conozco esos rasgos, los anchos pómulos, la piel morena, el pelo lacio tan negro. Nicaragüense. Sólo lo había visto en la tele, me dice con intencionado acento costarricense, mientras su boca, en la que hay reflejos de calzadura de oro, enseña una entusiasta sonrisa cómplice que luego esconde tras el dorso de la mano (*TF*, 20; A mature woman, whose nurse's uniform crackles with starch at the steps of her imitation Adidas shoes, comes to open the door for me. I know those features, the broad cheekbones, the brown skin, the straight hair so black. Nicaraguan. I'd only ever seen you on television, she tells me with a deliberate Costa Rican accent, while her mouth, in which there are flashes of goldwork, shows me an enthusiastic smile of complicity that she then hides behind the back of her hand.)

The complicity between these two Nicaraguans who belong to opposite sides of the social gulf cleaved by transnational capital relegates Nicaraguan nationality to the status of a secret code. The woman with knock-off Adidas and gold teeth who changes her accent in a futile attempt to fit in, and who has been transnationalized as cheap labour, and the famous man who appears on television and has been transnationalized as a cultural celebrity, share a husk of a national identity that they can admit to each other but that is no longer viable in the public sphere and is looked down upon by their Costa Rican hosts.

By the same token, the narrator's consecration by television as an authority figure relieves him of the need to retail his past position as a revolutionary leader; his transnational celebrity as a writer reinscribes his masculine identity within the cultural contours of the new millennium. For this reason, the narrator is discreet and self-effacing by comparison with that of *A Thousand Deaths Plus One*, the last novel in which Ramírez used a semi-autobiographical narrator. The sharp observation evident in this encounter with the nurse is rarely matched in the narrative-summary scenes that narrate Amanda's life. Nicaraguan workers are ubiquitous bit players in the Costa Rican scenes. The widow introduces a minor character from the past as "ese viejillo Nicolás, que para variar era nica" (*LF*, 59; "that old-timer Nicolás, who, just for a change, was a Nica"). Nicolás the Nica had lost an eye in a battle against the US Marines "pero cuál batalla fue ésa, ni cuándo, no lo sé" (*LF*, 59; "but what battle that was, or when, I don't know"). Peace-loving Costa Ricans adopt an uncomprehending air with regard to Nicaragua's history of violence. In fact, the two countries share a nineteenth-century history of collaboration in securing national autonomy. The first interview subject refers with pride to an ancestor who "estuvo presente en la batalla de Rivas contra los filibusteros de William Walker" (*LF*, 65; "was present at the battle of Rivas against William Walker's filibusters").

The puzzle the novel addresses is how, from this history of common struggle, the two countries have become so different. While the putative goal of the regurgitation of blocks of Costa Rican history is to establish the background against which Amanda Solano's independent life was deemed scandalous, the unannounced but more piercing aim, as in *Castigo Divino* and other earlier works, is to shame the feeble Nicaraguan bourgeoisie, whose failure to harmonize competing interests into a successful national project is responsible for the country's history of authoritarianism. The historical patterns that have culminated in the return to power of a debased version of the FSLN are suggested by opposition, through the counter-example of Costa Rica. Like Nicaragua, Costa Rica suffered the disadvantages of small size, foreign imposition of backward economic structures such as banana plantations, US political interference, extreme left-wing reactions to social injustice, and even a short-lived civil war. But, in contrast to Nicaragua, the divergent progressive tendencies within the Costa Rican bourgeoisie overcame their differences for the benefit of the nation, forging a democratic welfare state in a landscape that might have been more propitious to an endless cycle of violence and dictatorship. In one of a number of references to this theme, the politically astute María Carmona, the second of Amanda's lifelong friends interviewed by the narrator, states:

> Las reformas sociales profundas del gobierno del doctor Calderón Guardia sólo fueron posibles gracias al respaldo de monseñor Sanabria, némesis de la oligarquía furibunda, y gracias también al respaldo del Partido Comunista. Una triple alianza, y mire qué alianza: Calderón Guardia, el médico de los pobres; monseñor Sanabria, el obispo socialista; Manuel Mora, el líder comunista. Y como resultado, el seguro social, el código del trabajo, la derogación de las leyes de la economía liberal decimonónica … (*LF*, 152; The deep social reforms of Dr Calderón Guardia's government were only possible thanks to the

> backing of Monsignor Sanabria, nemesis of the retrograde oligarchy and thanks also to the Communist Party. A triple alliance, and look at what an alliance: Calderón Guardia, the doctor of the poor; Monsignor Sanabria, the socialist bishop; Manuel Mora, the Communist leader. And as a result, social security, the labour code, the rescinding of the laws of the nineteenth-century liberal economy ...)

This "triple alliance" echoes the triple alliance of the FSLN's three tendencies that unified Nicaragua against Somoza in 1975 and brought the country deep, progressive social change. Even the 1944–54 government of Guatemala is depicted as imitating Costa Rica: the narrator's first informant claims: "Arévalo quiere un seguro social y unas leyes del trabajo como en Costa Rica" (*LF*, 107; "Arévalo wants social security and a labour code as in Costa Rica"). The splintering of progressive bourgeois alliances is responsible for the stagnation of change in Guatemala and Nicaragua.

Under the regime of accelerated globalization, contemporary Nicaragua is invisible. Like Cardenal's *Pasajero de tránsito*, *La Fugitiva* turns the nation inside out: only those Nicaraguans who participate in the transnational world are in evidence. Even though the novel's action takes place long before 1990, its perceptions are guided by post-1990 dynamics, in which social classes are yoked together across national borders and smaller countries are roped more tightly into the economic and cultural structures of the regional powers that mediate global capital flows. The evocation of Chavela Vargas, a Central American who became famous by moving to the dominant regional power, Mexico, and incarnating one of its traditional cultural forms, the ranchera, which is diffused through Central America on radio and television, underlines these themes (as does the colloquial Mexican Spanish in which her monologue is written). In the latter half of the novel, Nicaraguans who have become prominent in Mexico, such as Rogelio de la Selva, who rose to become the personal adviser of Mexican President Miguel Alemán (in office from 1946 to 1952) – "el mandamás de ese gobierno, aun siendo extranjero" (*LF*, 225; "that government's bigwig, even though he was a foreigner") – are granted generous attention.

The consummation of the affair between Costa Rica and Nicaragua, when it occurs, takes place in Mexico. Amanda meets Rogelio's brother Salomón de la Selva in Costa Rica when she is an adolescent, and either there, or later, in Mexico City, becomes his lover. This event raises the issue of the novel's mingling of fact and fiction. Salomón de la Selva (1893–1959) is an historical figure: a flamboyant mid-twentieth-century avant-garde Nicaraguan poet, whose life anticipated that of twenty-first-century transnationalization. De la Selva graduated from Williams College in Massachusetts on a personal scholarship from President Zelaya, fought as a US soldier in the First World War, published books in both English and Spanish, and was a friend of US literary and political figures, a drinking buddy of Pope John XXIII (before his election), a controversial pro-Sandino journalist in Costa Rica, a PRI official in Mexico, and, at the time of his death, Luis Somoza Debayle's ambassador to Paris. In the novel, Salomón lives with Amanda in her declining years and pays for her funeral. The historical Salomón de la Selva did not have an affair with the historical Yolanda Oreamuno (though, by most accounts, he was romantically involved with, among other prominent women, the best-selling American poet Edna St Vincent Millay).[17]

In *La Fugitiva*, history becomes mush: a palimpsest of personalities to be manipulated for the reader's titillation.[18] This falsification of history differs in kind from the mythologization of a national chronology epitomized by the rewriting of the 1959 Rebellion of Olama y los Mojellones in *To Bury Our Fathers* or the reimagining of the 1974 Christmas party raid in *Sombras nada más*, or the fantasy version of the 1956 assassination of Somoza García in *Margarita, How Beautiful the Sea*, all of which invest national chronology with resonant images. The diachronic progression of history, like the hope for autonomy and social justice that this vision inspired, has evaporated. A provisional wholeness, paradoxically, can be found only in Mexico, the territory elevated by accelerated globalization to the status of the regional centre that concentrates both Mesoamerica's capital and its cultural identity. Here Central Americans may be referred to derisively as "chuscos" (*LF*, 261; "mongrels"), but in meeting each other they are able to stage a spectral re-enactment of their evaporated national identities, and the common isthmian identity that they share.

Amanda's death in Salomon de la Selva's Mexico City apartment confirms all that Costa Rica and Nicaragua need from each other because of their differences. The 1954 anti-imperialist rally in Mexico City that protests the US overthrow of the elected government of Guatemala, assembling most of the key figures of the Mexican section of the novel and preceding the account of Amanda's decline and death, also brings Central America to the heart of the Mesoamerican capital. The rally makes a political statement that is striking for belonging to a past when injustices had an identifiable culprit. It is this era, whose ideological lines Amanda tangles by writing articles against the US overthrow, then later returning to Guatemala, where she may become the lover of the US-installed puppet dictator, Colonel Castillo Armas, that is buried with her.

La Fugitiva smears this past of firm nationalities and ideologies with the nebulousness of the transnational present. Though the novel opens with the return, in 1961, of Amanda's remains to Costa Rica, where she is buried in an unmarked grave, it closes with Salomón de la Selva finding a spot for her in Mexican soil in 1956. Manuela Torres recalls: "No sé tampoco cómo Salomón consiguió el lote en el cementerio, ni los permisos, que en México todo trámite de ésos es cuesta arriba. Sería con puras mordidas" (*LF*, 306; "Nor do I know how Salomón got the cemetery lot, or the permissions, in Mexico paperwork like that is an uphill battle. He must have just paid a lot of bribes"). Manuela Torres's monologue concludes with a digression into the career of Chavela Vargas, on whom she is modelled, and a list of artistic and show business celebrities, such as Elizabeth Taylor and Debbie Reynolds, with whom she has had friendships or affairs. Manuela is confident that, unlike Amanda, she will be remembered: "Van a ser recordadas mis canciones, lo que fui, lo que sufrí" (*LF*, 306; "My songs will be remembered, and what I was, and what I suffered"). Whether Amanda's failure to be remembered as an artist is the fault of her insular, patriarchal milieu, or her own responsibility for not having disciplined herself and, above all, for not having integrated into the dominant culture of Mexico as Manuela did, remains ambiguous, though a strong suggestion persists that future Central American artists who hope to establish themselves will need to do so under the rubric of being "Mexicans." This theme dominates the final pages, displacing the liberal-feminist claims of a woman's right to independence that are *La Fugitiva*'s announced ideology but are not, in the end, what the novel is about.

Under accelerated globalization, nation-like communities thrive only outside the Nicaraguan nation-space. Ernesto Cardenal's poem *Tata Vasco* (2011; Grandfather Vasco),[19] a twenty-first-century reimagining of a Solentiname-style microcosm, is set in sixteenth-century Mexico. The Utopia of an agrarian-based community of justice and tranquillity assembled beneath a wise patriarch, which at different stages in Cardenal's life and literature had been incarnated by the Granada of the Chamorros, Thomas Merton's tutelage in the Gethsemani monastery, Netzahualcóyotl's Texcoco, Fray Bartolomé de Las Casas's colonial Antigua Guatemala, his own Solentiname, Fidel Castro's Cuba, and revolutionary Nicaragua, among other iterations, receives what may be its culminating expression in this poem. Where earlier constructions of microcosmic Utopias that lay outside the borders of the Nicaraguan nation-space brimmed with the hope that the ideal order could serve as a model for Nicaragua, *Tata Vasco* is barren of references or coy allusions that would connect the community described to national experience. In an explicit way, Cardenal now imagines his Utopia outside the nation. As the dynamics of accelerated globalization would predict, he himself persists as an individual with a particular biography; but references to Nicaragua are absent.

The poem mingles discourses in a mild way, employing citations from sixteenth-century authorities to document the achievements of the community founded by Vasco de Quiroga (1470–1565) in Michoacán, yet the diction, though colloquial, is smooth and undisturbed by ideological contradictions. It is an appealing poem, though it suffers from excessive repetition of key lines and lacks the narrative dimension of Cardenal's best work in the long poem. Preserving the Testimonio voice that Cardenal refined in his memoirs, *Tata Vasco* suggests in the opening line that this work by an eighty-six-year-old author is an exemplary, spoken tale of the past that not only certifies the feasibility of Utopian communities but insinuates the author's enduring faith that revolutionary Cuba remains the contemporary manifestation of this impulse. The poem begins: "Por si no lo saben/la isla Utopia de Sir Thomas Moro/era Cuba" (*TV*, 7; "In case you didn't know/ Sir Thomas More's island Utopia/was Cuba" [*OS*, 55]). Subsequent lines first clarify that the reference is to Cuba's shape as it appears on a sixteenth-century map, then draw the link between past and present: "La isla de Colón y de Pedro Mártir y Fidel Castro" (*TV*, 8; "The island of Columbus and Pedro Mártir and Fidel Castro" [*OS*, 55]). The inclusion of Pedro Mártir (1457–1526), an Italian-born priest and official of the Spanish crown with responsibility for the New World, who wrote a history of the Americas in Latin and was named bishop of Jamaica even though he never crossed the Atlantic, illustrates the latitude granted by the poem to Utopian bonds with communities that lie beyond one's homeland or experience.

The community Cardenal evokes transcends boundaries of time and place, and is joined by similarities of perception or belief; in this sense it owes more to pre-1990 progressive internationalism than it does to the post-1990 transnationalized roping together of social classes across national borders described by Robinson. This is evident in the inclusion of a reference in homage to one of Cardenal's pivotal internationalist connections, the Catholic Cuban poet Cintio Vitier (1921–2009), who persuaded Cardenal that the Cuban Revolution was compatible with Catholicism (see chapter 5). Cardenal suggests that the Americas' quest for identity, which was a guiding impulse of the struggles of Spanish America's revolutionary period between 1959 and 1990, remains unresolved. Alluding to the naming of the Western Hemisphere after Amerigo Vespucci, he writes: "Le dieron el nombre de Vespucio/ porque era sin nombre/y aún lo es" (*TV*, 10; "They gave it Vespucci's name/Because it had no name/and still has none" [*OS*, 55]).

History has not ended; it has barely begun. The making of history proceeds from texts, from the reading of texts by those who are already enlightened and can induce the structures imagined by texts to materialize in the objective world. This is a rigorously Catholic vision of priestly direction; it recapitulates the Sandinista assumption that literature is the foundation and substance of the nation. Vasco de Quiroga's achievement is depicted as noteworthy precisely because he transforms a literary fantasy into a tangible social reality:

> llegado a México como Oidor (magistrado)
> de su Majestad el Emperador Carlos V
> apenas diez años después de la caída de Tenochtitlán
>   – y más tarde obispo de Michoacán –
> leyó en México la *Utopia* de Moro, y la tomó en serio
> ¡y la realizó!
> Doscientos años después aún existía su obra
> y todavía lo recuerdan los indios como *Tata Vasco.*
> (*TV*, 13; came to Mexico as Judge (magistrate)/of his Majesty the Emperor Carlos V/barely ten years after the fall of Tenochtitlán/– and later bishop of Michoacán –/read More's *Utopia*, in Mexico, and took it seriously/and implemented it!/Two hundred years later his work still existed/and the Indians still remember him as *Tata Vasco*. [*OS*, 56])

The emphasis on reading Sir Thomas More "in Mexico" highlights the patriarchal authority figure's vital role as middleman between the discourses of dominant cultures and autochthonous American realities. It is the equivalent to Cardenal's adaptation of the imagery of Chaucer and T.S. Eliot "in Nicaragua" in *Zero Hour* (see chapter 3). The "Tata," or grandfather, ensures that foreign discourses are implemented in the homeland in a way that is both faithful to their textual essence and respectful of the interests of indigenous American people. Tata Vasco's triumph is to introduce foreign wisdom in a form that not only promotes social justice but also forges a strong local identity. This, in the poem's construction of the dynamics of power, stands in direct opposition to Western projects that lay waste to local cultures, such as Hernán Cortés's conquest of Mexico that leaves Michoacán in ruins. Vasco de Quiroga's resuscitation of the region's indigenous communities is a success not only because the political order that he implements endures for two centuries, but, even more important, because it is absorbed into indigenous lore *as part of the local culture*: "and the Indians still remember him today." The enlightened non-indigenous man's success is ratified when the ethos he implants ceases to be foreign and becomes indigenous.

If this process may be construed as a form of hybridization, it is a hybridization "from above" that diverges from the assumed *mestizaje* of post-revolutionary constructions of the origins of modern Mexico. The degree to which Cardenal "Nicaraguanizes" – or "Solentinamizes" – Mexico is evident if one compares his account of Vasco de Quiroga with that given by Carlos Fuentes in his keynote address at the 1966 international congress of the literary human rights organization PEN (Poets Essayists Novelists) in New York:

> In effect, the happiest community of the New World flowered for a time in the missions of Michoacán, where the friar Vasco de Quiroga, an avid reader of [Tommaso Campanella's] *The City of the Sun*, perfectly blended the teachings of Utopia with the Mexican Indian's tradition of communal life, universal sacrality, respect for the fabrication of objects both useful and singular, and consecration of the body as the living center of civilization. So, in one privileged moment, the best of the Indian values – the values that, in fact, had been suppressed by the fascist Aztec theocracy – and the best of the European values came together and flourished. (Fuentes 1977:142–3)

Like the earlier Cardenal of "Netzahualcóyotl," Fuentes labels the imperial reign of the Aztecs as "fascist," seeking a more authentic seam of indigenous values beneath the trappings of satrapy. Unlike Cardenal, Fuentes presents "the best of the Indian values" as having contributed as active agents to Quiroga's American Utopia. Perpetuating the mestizo ideology of the Mexican Revolution, Fuentes portrays this "happiest community of the New World" as the product of the mixing of two cultures. While mestizo ideology was also present in the Nicaraguan Revolution, particularly, as this study has argued, in the work of Sergio Ramírez, Cardenal's approach descends from a different tradition, best captured by Robert Pring-Mill's conclusion, based not only on the study of Cardenal's poems but on two substantial residences in Solentiname, that in Cardenal's ideal world enlightened people "use their talents in the service of the *pueblo* in a mildly paternalistic way" (Pring-Mill 1992: 67). Quiroga's position as a lawyer and a priest makes him ideally suited to guide his proto-nation. In an allusion to Plato, the narrator lauds "el plan de una República/para todos los indios del Nuevo Mundo" (*TV*, 15; "the plan of a Republic/for all the Indians of the New World"). These assumptions are evident in flashes in the poem's language. Quiroga's achievement, the reader learns, is "que concibió/ajustar la vida de los indios al esquema de Moro./Elevar a los indios/a un nivel más alto que el europeo/¡Todavía en plena conquista!" (*TV*, 22; "who conceived of/adjusting the lives of the Indians to More's scheme./To elevate the Indians/to a higher level than the European/Still in the thick of conquest!" [*OS*, 58]).

It is not that Cardenal sees the indigenous people as incapable of attaining a better life than that of the European, but rather that European standards are the benchmark by which success and happiness are measured. The written European text – "More's scheme" – is the germ of social justice. The assumption that the text's purpose is "to elevate the Indians," however, differs starkly from Fuentes's mestizo vision of two cultures that blend their wisdom on a nearly equal footing. To some extent, the depiction of these dynamics in *Tata Vasco* may be attributed to the pronounced awareness that, like Cardenal founding Solentiname under the Somoza dictatorship, Quiroga implements his Utopian design "in the thick of conquest." To achieve high living standards for indigenous people at a time when they are being brutally oppressed by colonialism is an even greater achievement than to do so at other times. While the initiative comes from Quiroga, "quitándoles lo malo y dejándoles lo bueno" (*TV*, 28; "taking away the bad from them and leaving the good with them" [*OS*, 60]), the religious reformer's goal must be to infuse indigenous communities with a self-generating dynamic of social improvement: "No el hacer las cosas por los indios/sino hacer que los indios las hicieran" (*TV*, 31; "Not the doing of things for the Indians/but making the Indians do them" [*OS*, 60]).

The oppressed people's discovery of self-consciousness and the ability to articulate and realize their desires for a better world depends on literature. Like Cardenal planning his poetry workshops, Quiroga observes "los niños en el lodo, panzones/A los que él va a enseñar latín, etc." (*TV*, 31; "the children in the mud, bellies swollen/Those to whom he is going to teach Latin, etc." [*OS*, 60]). The spread of Latin – "algunos hablándolo como los clérigos" (*TV*, 43; "some speaking it like clerics" [*OS*, 63]) – certifies his achievement.

Destruction is a pre-condition for the creative reimagining of society. When, in an allusion to Fray Bartolomé de Las Casas's pamphlet of the same title (see chapter 1), Cardenal emphasizes that "the destruction of the Indies" provides the opportunity for Quiroga to build his Utopia, he is drawing both on his own experience of the Nicaraguan Revolution and on Christian patterns of an annihilation that opens the path to redemption, such as he developed in *The Doubtful Strait*. Quiroga arrives in Michoacán at a time when the conquistadors of Cortés have destroyed the indigenous people's settlements and driven them away. He entices them back with land, then implements his program for their improvement directly from sagacious European texts: "Como en la *Utopia* y en *La República* de Platón/la tierra de todos y no de los individuos" (*TV*, 38; "As in *Utopia* and in Plato's *Republic*/the land belonging to all and not to individuals" [*OS*, 62]). The abolition of money, the six-hour workday, and similar policies derive directly from More's science fiction; yet Quiroga, in the real world, produces results that are superior to those imagined by More.

This result confirms Cardenal's belief in Utopianism – even if, in the post-1990 era, Utopias must be imagined outside the temporal and geographical boundaries of the nation. They may exist in Cuba or in sixteenth-century Mexico; they also existed, Cardenal insists, in an obdurate persistence of Cold War socialist faith, in the Soviet Union: "Cada familia con su casa y su parcela como en la URSS/Unidad básica la familia como en Moro" (*TV*, 39; "Each family with its house and plot of land as in the USSR/ Basic unit the family as in More" [*OS*, 62]). The wisdom of texts is socialist wisdom: "Moro y Quiroga, socialistas" (*TV*, 42; "More and Quiroga, socialists" [*OS*, 62]). The Utopian community is notable not only for peace and equality but also for artistic abundance. It is the production of art that lends such communities, whether in Solentiname or Michoacán, their immortality in the material world. Quiroga not only becomes a father or grandfather to the indigenous people but actually attains immortality: "(*Tata*, padre, también aplicado a Dios)" (*TV*, 46; "*Tata*, father, also applied to God" [*OS*, 63]). Like Cardenal, Quiroga plays a central role in reviving fading handicraft traditions, becoming the father not only of the community but also of its artistic forms: "Y Tata Vasco el padre de la artesanía mexicana./No solo perfeccionó las de los indios/sino introdujo nuevas" (*TV*, 47; "And Tata Vasco the father of Mexican handicrafts./He not only perfected the Indians' crafts/but introduced new ones" [*OS*, 63]).

No concern for essentialist "authenticity" plagues this account of an indigenous Utopia; art must evolve and, by definition, may be improved by contact with foreign masters. The socialist doctrine of the New Man wins out over Romantic portrayals of Noble Savages; Michoacán art has value not because "así fue siempre sino/porque hace 400 años/lo planeó Quiroga" (*TV*, 47; "it was always that way but/because 400 years ago/Quiroga planned it" [*OS*, 64]). Tata Vasco nourishes local creativity by bringing in masters from elsewhere in New Spain, as Cardenal imported Guatemalan artisans to improve the handicrafts of Nicaragua. It is telling that Pátzcuaro, the Quirogan community that is devoted to handicrafts, like Solentiname, is on an island in a lake. The revolutionary resonances are stoked up when the narrator identifies the members of Quiroga's community as imitating "la manera de vivir de los primeros cristianos" (*TV*, 41; "the way of life of the first Christians" [*OS*, 62]). The reference recalls Cardenal's equations of socialism with primitive Christianity in his earlier works, particularly *Oracle over Managua*.

Tata Vasco is immortal because the indigenous people still remember him four hundred years later; within Michoacán, his name makes him a benign approximation of God the Father. The parallels with Cardenal's role in Solentiname, and with the 1970s and 1980s image of the liberation-theology priest as master of the community that incubates socialist revolution, are obvious; yet art is Quiroga's most enduring legacy. *Tata Vasco* closes with ten pages of photographs of gorgeous Michoacán art that provide visual evidence of Quiroga's material legacy. Just as Solentiname naive landscapes and other handicrafts developed under Cardenal's guidance have been assimilated as "traditional Nicaraguan handicrafts," so the artistic forms Quiroga invents create an enduring Michoacán style: "colores de *ajes* mochacados en aceite que no se marchitan nunca" (*TV*, 51; "colors of *ajes* crushed in oil which never fade" [*OS*, 65]).

Having opened in the Testimonio voice, *Tata Vasco* closes with the essential act of the narrator authenticating all he has recounted by asserting that he himself is witness to this reality: "Bello lago de Pátzcuaro que yo vi/color cielo/el pescador en su pequeña canoa" (*TV*, 53; "Beautiful lake of Pátzcuaro that I saw/sky color/the fisherman in his small canoe" [*OS*, 66]). According to the Testimonio tradition, the "I saw" certifies Cardenal's claims for the community created by Quiroga. The narrator corroborates Quiroga's survival through art: "Todavía ves a Don Vasco en el mercado de Pátzcuaro/con la cerámica policromada y toda clase de lacas" (*TV*, 56; "You can still see Don Vasco in the market of Pátzcuaro/with the polychrome ceramics and all kinds of lacquer ware" [*OS*, 66]). The poem concludes with the repetition of an injunction that Quiroga's footprint not be erased; that his community's art survive forever.

While the parallels between Quiroga's position in Pátzcuaro and that of Cardenal in Solentiname are left implicit, the narrator does appear in the poem. Two brief autobiographical interjections prepare the ground for the concluding confirmation of the narrator's visit to Michoacán. In contrast to the autobiographical commentary in *Cosmic Canticle*, or even *Versos del pluriverso*, these rapid asides do not refer to courtships in Granada, the experience of the Nicaraguan Revolution, or other events that would identify the narrator as a Nicaraguan. The first is a response to the fact that Quiroga's initial attempt to purchase land on behalf of indigenous people took place in the district of Tacubaya: "(ahora es la misma Ciudad de México/y allí fue mi pensión de estudiante)" (*TV*, 37; (now it is part of Mexico City/and my student lodgings were there)" [*OS*, 61]). This reference to the district housing the Mascarones campus of UNAM – site of humanities courses prior to the construction of the vast main campus in the 1950s – establishes Cardenal as Mexican by undergraduate education. The image is reinforced when he refers to a Mexican Communist leader of the 1940s as "espanto de católicos en mis días de estudiante en México" (*TV*, 45; "the dismay of Catholics in my student days in Mexico" [*OS*, 63]). The neutrality of the latter line leaves open the possibility that the narrator was a foreign student, but does not make his identity explicit. Moving one step beyond the community of Mexico City "chuscos" depicted by Ramírez, Cardenal does not even intuit the nation's existence through the regional identities that surround the absent nation-space. The substantive and symbolic superstructure of Nicaraguan nationality having been garnisheed by Daniel Ortega's postmodern simulacrum of a revolutionary movement, Cardenal remains the proprietor of the Utopian model of the base. This model may be fitted onto a variety of times and places, but at no point do its contours and those of the nation coincide.

CONCLUSIONS

This study has analyzed the works of two of the major Spanish American writers of the final stages of the Cold War and the early years of post-1990 globalization. The writings of Ernesto Cardenal and Sergio Ramírez gained increased international exposure beneath the media spotlights of the Nicaraguan Revolution. Yet this exposure also distorted the public perception of each writer's creative trajectory by according foreign publication and critical attention to works that lent themselves to interpretation as manifestations of "revolution" and overlooking works that did not match this label. This book, therefore, has given the central place to literature and history to produce close readings of understudied major works such as Cardenal's *The Doubtful Strait* and *Cosmic Canticle*, Ramírez's *To Bury Our Fathers* and *Castigo Divino*, and both writers' abundant post-1990 production.

One purpose of the present work has been to reevaluate the two writers' careers as a succession of responses to the experience of Nicaraguan nationality during the three key periods of modern history: the Somoza dictatorship, the Nicaraguan Revolution, and the post-1990 onset of accelerated globalization. Above all, the readings explicated here have striven to remain attentive to the respective strata of Nicaraguan society from which the two writers emerged: European-descended, Conservative, Catholic, and upper-class in the former case, mestizo, Liberal, Protestant-Catholic-agnostic, and rural middle class in the latter. In so doing, the author hopes to have moved beyond simply providing a picture of how these two important writers evolved in response to their times.

By combining readings of Nicaragua's most important Conservative and Liberal writers respectively, during the period of their migration to a common participation in Sandinismo, with a narrative of Nicaraguan history during this period, this study has suggested that one of the best ways to understand a nation's deep historical evolution is through close readings of engaged literary texts. My argument in favour of this approach is not a plea for a return to New Criticism, but rather an attempt to employ theory in a way that keeps the attention of readers and critics focused on the construction of the literary text, and on the history that produced it. In order to illuminate these readings, other cultural configurations have been assessed. Foremost among these are: the existence of Central America as a region where common historical patterns are segmented by national particularities; the dynamics of masculinity under a dictatorship, a revolution, and accelerated globalization, as perceived in light of the erosion of Spanish American patriarchy; and literary evolution from the Modernism of the Boom to postmodernism, from politically committed poetry to Testimonio. The readings of the book's final three chapters interrogate the meaning of literary creation at a time when the traditional literary framework of the nation may no longer be taken for granted.

The core of this book, like many others, is the Nicaraguan Revolution of 1979–90, an event whose unexpectedness, idealism, great deeds, contradictions, and disasters defy reductionist explanation, in spite of merciless journalistic scrutiny during its course and intense academic research over subsequent decades. One of the paradoxes advanced by this study is that a meticulous reading of the works of Cardenal and Ramírez illuminates key elements of the origins of the Nicaraguan Revolution that were not previously visible, particularly by revealing the conjunction of a disillusioned young Liberalism and a renegade Conservatism with rising peasant and proletarian forces in forging the alliances that made the Revolution possible. In this respect, it is vital never to lose sight of the fact that the Nicaraguan Revolution is a crucial event because it offered, however unsuccessfully in the final analysis, the hope of material progress, spiritual and artistic sustenance, and increased self-respect and autonomy to some of the poorest, most oppressed people in the Western Hemisphere. This spark of possibility is what attracted the attention of observers around the world to a forgotten Central American backwater. It is important to guard against revisionist accounts that would deny the idealistic, liberating qualities of this experience; any study of literature produced in Nicaragua before, during, or after the Revolution is also an act of homage to an ethos of idealism, self-sacrifice, and unity across chasm-like barriers of social class.

In this light, just as this book began with the Nicaraguan-born Bianca Jagger, so, curiously, it must end with her. In a work published twenty-five years after his trip to Nicaragua, Salman Rushdie – whose *The Jaguar Smile* was the freshest and most attentive of the memoirs written by first-time visitors to the country during the revolution – marvels at the political and cultural influence writers still wielded in the 1980s, when it was possible "to see literature as a lofty, transnational, transcultural force … Twenty years later, in a dumbed-down and frightened world, it would be harder to make such exalted claims for mere wordsmiths. Harder, but no less necessary, perhaps" (Rushdie 2012: 78). The attention the present book concentrates on the work of two major writers takes up this challenge. Yet, in doing so, it insists on the Nicaraguan Revolution as a phenomenon that absorbed all of Nicaraguan society.

In this regard, Rushdie's account (referring to himself in the third person) of his radio interview with Bianca Jagger after the publication of *The Jaguar Smile* should be read as a warning: "Whenever he mentioned a prominent Nicaraguan, whether left- or right-wing, Bianca would reply, vaguely, neutrally, 'Oh, yes, I used to date him once.' This was the truth about Nicaragua. It was a small country with a very small elite class. The warring combatants had all gone to school together, were all members of that elite and knew one another's families, or even, in the case of the divided Chamorro dynasty, came from the same family, and they had all dated one another" (ibid.: 79). Droll though this may be, it is too glib.[20] The divisions within the elite – both among Conservatives such as the Chamorros, Cuadras, and Cardenals, and between Conservatives and Liberals – were significant. Conservatives and Liberals often did not go to school together, and the masses who made the Revolution often did not go to school at all. It was these divisions that inspired Sandinismo, a force that connected elite to non-elite Nicaraguans, and brought to prominence people who never had been heard from before: leaders with non-elite surnames such as Ortega, Borge, and Cabezas. In hamlets, towns, and cities across Nicaragua, thousands of marginalized individuals took up the microphone and sculpted Nicaragua in words, while hundreds of others came to writing or painting in local workshops; the country's professional writers became its leaders in the national activity of inscribing the nation's experience in literature. In a world that has been dumbed down and frightened away from understanding experience in historical context, this moment still resonates. The Nicaraguan Revolution reminds transnationalized readers that "mere wordsmiths" supply our best defence against cynical revisionism, and are one of our most resilient hopes for cultivating the attention to chronology, context, and collaboration across social classes that invests experience with meaning.

Notes

CHAPTER ONE

1 The sanctions imposed by John Paul II and Cardinal Ratzinger on priests involved in politics were blatantly ideologically selective. Commenting on the Drinan case in his essay "The State of the Nation: 1980," Gore Vidal wrote: "Drinan will presently give up his seat in the house at the order of the Polish pope, who says he does not want his minions in politics, which is nonsense. A neo-fascist priest sits as a deputy in the Italian Parliament, just across the Tiber from the Vatican. Father Drinan, alas, is liberal" (Vidal 2004: 114). Conor Cruise O'Brien reported that "through Ratzinger, John Paul II was addressing a magisterial '*Silencio*!' to the worshippers of *el Dios de los pobres* in Latin America" (O'Brien 1988: 107). "Silencio," of course, is the word that John Paul II shouted several times at Nicaraguan worshippers in March 1983, when refusing a request that he say Mass for young Nicaraguans killed by the Contras (see chapter 6).

CHAPTER TWO

1 Gioconda Belli writes of Contreras: "Su estrategia insurreccional … fue llevada a la práctica por la tercera tendencia del FSLN. Como suele suceder, los vivos se quedaron con el mérito" (*País*, 200; "His idea of an insurrectional strategy … was carried on by what became the third faction within the FSLN, the Insurrectional tendency, the Terceristas. As it usually happens, however, others took all the credit" [*The Country under My Skin*, 148]). In Belli's novel *La mujer habitada* (1988), the character Felipe, who appears to be partly based on Contreras, echoes his belief in the importance of urban guerrilla activity: "Estamos creciendo, empezando a operar en las ciudades. No nos van a poder

detener" (61; "We're growing and now we are beginning to operate in the cities. They won't be able to stop us" [*The Inhabited Woman*, 69]).

CHAPTER THREE

1 The seven rules were: 1. Poetry doesn't have to rhyme; if one line ends with "Sandino," the next one doesn't have to end with "destino"; 2. Use concrete terms rather than general ones; call trees by their names rather than saying "the tree"; 3. Use proper names of rivers, towns, and people; 4. Use the senses rather than ideas; the most important imagery is visual; 5. Use natural speech; don't invert word order to sound poetic; 6. Avoid clichés; find new ways to say phrases such as "heroic combatants"; 7. Condense language; omit the unnecessary. (This list is adapted from Pallier 1988: 123–4, and *RP*, 499.)

2 Dependency theory, developed by the Argentine economist Raúl Prebisch, posited that the societies of the world's "periphery" were conditioned, over time, by the demands of the nations of the "metropolis." See chapter 4.

3 Pound wrote: "In the spring or early summer of 1912, 'H.D.', Richard Aldington and myself decided that we were agreed upon the three principles following: 1. Direct treatment of the 'thing' whether subjective or objective. 2. To use absolutely no word that does not contribute to the presentation. 3. As regarding rhythm: to compose in the sequence of the musical phrase, not in sequence of a metronome" (Pound 1934: 3).

4 The motif of April as a time of death and political commitment is adopted by Gioconda Belli in her novel *La mujer habitada* (1988; *The Inhabited Woman*). The pivotal chapter, in which the heroine, who is an architect from a Conservative Nicaraguan family, decides to join the guerrillas, opens with the sentence: "Lavinia levantó los ojos del plano y miró el paisaje al atardecer, el cielo enrojecido por las quemas de abril" (Belli, *La mujer*, 92; "Lavinia raised her eyes from the blueprint and saw the landscape at dusk, reddened by the April burn-offs" [*The Inhabited Woman*, 108]). For a discussion of *The Inhabited Woman*, see chapter 7.

5 Tomás Borge writes of the FSLN's decision to communicate with Cardenal: "Se nos ocurrió contactarlo a finales de 1967" (*impaciencia*, 267; "It occurred to us to contact him at the end of 1967" [*The Patient Impatience*, 263]). Cardenal's own account of his meetings with Fonseca (*IE*, 222–6) summarizes a range of conversations in a way that makes it difficult to establish a chronology. Cardenal and the FSLN leader appear to have had a number of meetings in safe houses in Managua in 1968. They met again in Cuba in 1970 and had a final round of discussions in 1975, when Fonseca made his clandestine return to the Managua area prior to travelling to the Segovia mountains to fight and die as a

guerrilla. Ironically, Fonseca and Cardenal had met before, in 1953 (*RP*, 10). Under interrogation by the GN after an early arrest in 1957 for the crime of travelling in socialist countries, Fonseca stated: "Cuando todavía tenía 17 años, tuve simpatía por UNAP, y tuve relaciones con algunos dirigentes de dicha organización como Reynaldo Antonio Téfel y Ernesto Cardenal; pero mis inquietudes democráticas no fueron satisfechas por UNAP ... Yo pensé ... 'Téfel no es el dirigente con que yo había pensado tanto,' y lo mismo Ernesto Cardenal, pero estos señores me hablaban muy mal del marxismo, todo lo cual me llevó a pensar que a lo mejor había algo bueno en el marxismo" (*Obras*, 166; "When I was still 17 years old, I sympathized with UNAP, and had interactions with some leaders of that organization such as Reynaldo Antonio Téfel and Ernesto Cardenal; but my democratic yearnings were not satisfied by UNAP ... I thought ...'Téfel is not the leader that I had thought so much about' and the same was true of Ernesto Cardenal, but these gentlemen spoke very badly of Marxism, all of which led me to think that perhaps there was something good in Marxism").

6 For detailed discussion of this passage and the debate surrounding it, see Arias, ed., *The Rigoberta Menchú Controversy*.

7 These lines were later engraved on Fonseca's tomb when, after the Revolution, he was reburied in Plaza de la República in the centre of Managua. After his death in 2012, Borge, at his own prior request, was buried in the same square.

8 See, for example, Gonzalez and Treece's conclusion: "Out of 'Hora Cero' arose the development of Cardenal's poetry and his political development through the subsequent two decades" (Gonzalez and Treece 1992: 295).

9 Contemporary archeologists have established that most of the ruins are, in fact, on dry land; those that have been excavated have been opened to tourists.

10 In the summary of Burns and Charlip: "Juan Ginés de Sepúlveda ... relied heavily on Aristotelian theory for his arguments. Because of the intellectual superiority of the Europeans, Sepúlveda reasoned, the Indians should be subjected to them in a kind of natural servitude, which would permit the Indians to improve themselves by observing a better example of virtue, devotion and industry" (Burns and Charlip 1992: 34).

11 See Martin, *Journeys through the Labyrinth*, 171–235, and my "Two Paths to the Boom: Carpentier, Asturias and the Performative Split."

CHAPTER FOUR

1 In addition to other sources cited, the details of Ramírez's childhood included in this section are gleaned from Silvia Cherem, *Una vida por la palabra: Entrevista con Sergio Ramírez* (A Life by the Word: Interview with Sergio

Ramírez), and Silvia Cherem, "Presentacón" ("Introduction") in Sergio Ramírez, *El viejo arte de mentir* (The Old Art of Lying), 11–18.

2 At this time, UNAN was Nicaragua's only public university. In the early 1960s wealthy business people contracted the Jesuit Order to found the Universidad Centroamericana in Managua (Booth 1982: 81). The Somozas supported this initiative in the belief that a Jesuit institution would act as a pro-establishment counterweight to the rebellious students of UNAN. The strategy backfired: many Jesuits were from Conservative, anti-Somoza families. When Fernando Cardenal began to work as a professor at UCA in 1970, he became embroiled in an occupation of the campus and learned that the main question debated by students was "la lucha armada o no" (*Junto*, 39; "whether or not to join the armed struggle"). Among the UCA students who had chosen the armed option was Daniel Ortega.

3 Sandinista leaders such as Daniel and Humberto Ortega, Ernesto Cardenal, and Gioconda Belli also lived in Costa Rica in the late 1970s. Other Sandinista leaders, such as UN Ambassador Nora Astorga and guerrilla Comandante Mónica Baltodano, had studied in Europe; but none spent as long in democratic countries as Ramírez.

4 The Random House edition, which was to be published by Doubleday, was cancelled in a peculiarly abrupt manner, being pulled less than three months before the book was due to be released, on 27 January 1991. In 1993, again as a result of economic uncertainty, the Bulgarian publication of *Castigo Divino* was also cancelled after the translation had been completed (*SRP*, box 41, folders 4, 11–12).

5 Aside from Daniel Ortega's partner Rosario Murillo, the only salient exception to this female defection from the FSLN was the historic guerrilla and activist Doris Tijerino.

6 In fact, seven other men held this position between 1990 and 2008. No subsequent Nicaraguan vice-president has had as much power over national policy as Ramírez, who was the ultimate authority in most areas except foreign policy and the conduct of the Contra War, where Daniel Ortega's views took precedence.

7 For example, when the first issue of *Ventana* appeared in 1960, Ramírez, feeling that the aesthetics of Pablo Antonio Cuadra's *Prensa Literaria* and the tutelage he himself had received from Mariano Fiallos Gil "no eran antagónicos, pero sí diferentes" (*SLT*, 230; "were not antagonistic but were different"), travelled to Managua to introduce himself and his new magazine to Cuadra, whose creative stance *Ventana* criticized. Even writers associated with Liberal or socialist movements regarded the acceptance of their poems or stories by Cuadra's publications to be a question "de vida o muerte" (*SLT*, 230; "of life or death") in the development of their literary careers.

8 Baseball themes recur in *Clave de sol* (1992; A-Major), which is discussed in chapter 10. Nicaragua shares a passion for baseball with Panama, Cuba, Venezuela, and the Dominican Republic. During the 1980s, the "baseball theory of revolution" maintained that only those countries that had been occupied by the US Marines long enough for baseball to have supplanted football (soccer) as the national sport harboured sufficient nationalist rage to fuel successful revolutions. This theory predicted, correctly, that in spite of their military advances, the revolutionary movements in El Salvador, Guatemala, and Colombia would fail to take power because those countries played soccer.

9 In referring to Rulfo and García Márquez as Modernists, this discussion follows the argument made by Raymond Leslie Williams in *A Companion to Gabriel García Márquez*, 1–31, namely that these writers adapted European Modernism, albeit first absorbed through the work of William Faulkner, to the mythologization of Spanish American realities.

10 The classic formulation of this conception of the nation is that of Octavio Paz in *El laberinto de la soledad*: "El símbolo de la entrega es doña Malinche, la amante de Cortés. Es verdad que ella se da voluntariamente al Conquistador, pero éste, apenas deja de serle útil, la olvida ... Y del mismo modo que el niño no perdona a su madre que lo abandone para ir en busca del padre, el pueblo mexicano no perdona su traición a la Malinche" (77–8; "The symbol of this violation is doña Malinche, the mistress of Cortés. It is true that she gave herself voluntarily to the conquistador, but he forgot her as soon as her usefulness was over ... And as a small boy will not forgive his mother if she abandons him to search for his father, the Mexican people have not forgiven La Malinche for her betrayal" [*The Labyrinth of Solitude*, 65]). No equivalent figure exists in the history of the Spanish conquest of Nicaragua; this absence of a traitorous mother contributes to recurrent portraits of the nation as either ravaged or invisible yet eternally promising consolation and identity.

11 Monterroso would remain an exile until his death in 2003.

12 See my "No History to Absolve Them" (2004), 516.

13 This amicable attitude stands in contrast to Fonseca's loathing of the adoption of Sandino as a nationalist icon by Conservative opponents of Somoza such as Pedro Joaquín Chamorro. In Fonseca's eyes, Chamorro's benign view of the United States deprived him of the right to hang a Sandino portrait on his office wall (Zimmermann 2000: 145).

14 The writings of Fonseca, who had been a PSN member for a brief period in his youth, often included anti-PSN polemics, even though the PSN was not a significant force in Nicaraguan politics (Zimmermann 2000: 66–8).

15 It is probable that by "indígenas zambos" Ramírez means the Garifuna people, who are the descendants of racial mixing between Carib Indians from the island

of St Vincent and African slaves. They were deported to the Atlantic Coast of Central America by the British at the beginning of the nineteenth century. Garifunas, who "physically resemble blacks [but have] a number of cultural and linguistic features characteristic of the Indians who lived in the Lesser Antilles" (Vilas 1989: 5), form substantial communities in Belize and coastal Honduras and are also present on the Atlantic coasts of Nicaragua and Guatemala.

16 Another writer who made a point of attributing to aboriginal peoples a fundamental role in the history of Nicaraguan anti-imperialism was the Sandinista leader with whom Carlos Fonseca had the most conflicted personal and intellectual relationship: Jaime Wheelock Román (Cherem 2004b: 121; Zimmermann 2000: 168). Wheelock's doctrinaire Marxism, though it angered Fonseca, who may have seen in Wheelock's stance a shadow of the PSN, did not prevent this young intellectual from appreciating, in a book published in 1974, the achievements of an indigenous population that he believed had been devalorized by "una imagen increíblemente falsa acerca de su 'atraso cultural'" (Wheelock 1974: 4; "an incredibly false image about its 'cultural backwardness'"). According indigenous people some of the credit for Nicaraguan independence at the beginning of the nineteenth century, Wheelock wrote: "La independencia en Nicaragua estuvo precedida por tres siglos de resistencia indígena contra el poder español" (ibid.: 86; "Nicaraguan independence was preceded by three centuries of indigenous resistance to Spanish power").

17 See my *Assuming the Light* (1999), 28–55.

18 Allende's final words, broadcast over the radio as the military was storming the presidential palace, were: "Sigan ustedes sabiendo que, mucho más temprano que tarde, de nuevo se abrirán las grandes alamedas por donde pase el hombre libre, para construir una sociedad mejor" (Gómez 2006: 11A; "Continue to know that, much sooner than later, the great boulevards will open again, where free men can walk, to build a better society"). The error suggests that this section of "Vallejo" was written in the 1990s, not in the 1970s, when the quote, then common currency, would have been fresh in Ramírez's mind.

19 Ramírez had a personal connection to the Chilean coup: his younger brother, Rogelio, a graduate student in Santiago, was imprisoned by the Chilean military for two days after the coup but was fortunate to be released and allowed to return to Central America. On 5 October 1973 Rogelio wrote to tell Sergio that his two best friends at university had been murdered in the coup (*SRP*, box 40, folder 5).

20 It is possible to argue that the techniques of *The President*, though incubated in 1920s Paris, are not Surrealist. See my *Assuming the Light*, 148–93.

21 The impact of Ramírez's essay on younger intellectuals from the region is evident in a book such as Arturo Arias's *Ideologías, literatura y sociedad*

durante la revolución guatemalteca (Ideologies, Literature and Society during the Guatemalan Revolution), which won the Casa de las Américas Prize in 1979 and which both cites Ramírez (176–7) and shares his dependency-theory-based analysis of Central American culture.

CHAPTER FIVE

1 The English translation, *Abide in Love*, which was published by Maryknoll priests, omits certain passages, particularly those that use highly sensual imagery to describe spiritual relationships. This passage is one of those omitted. Translations from omitted passages are by the author; other translations are from *Abide in Love*.

2 Cardenal writes of his youth: "En México, en España, en Nicaragua yo no era uno que fuera mucho a burdeles; tampoco uno que fuera muy poco. Por lo general iba menos que muchos otros" (*VP*, 73; "In Mexico, in Spain, in Nicaragua, I was not one of those who would go to brothels often; neither was I one of those who seldom went. Generally, I went less than many others"). His relations with the young women of his own social class whom he courted, such as Carmen, Claudia, and Ileana, were chaste, occurring in the context of a Catholic elite where all parties adhered to a double standard that accepted that young men gained sexual experience with prostitutes while young women married as virgins.

3 A decade later, in early 1984, the author of this study was present at a talk by an official of the United States State Department, who argued that it was imperative to convert Latin America to Protestantism in order to "prevent the spread of Communism." According to this official, Protestant individualism would innoculate Latin Americans against Communism; Catholicism, because of its emphasis on community, created a predisposition towards Communist thought and must therefore be suppressed. The official's views, however misguided, nevertheless illustrate the success of the fusion between Catholicism and revolutionary ideology initiated by figures such as Camilo Torres and extended by others, such as Cardenal.

4 "This new … phase in the evolution of Cuba's revolutionary ideology and foreign policy began after Havana, surprisingly, had supported the Soviet invasion of Czechoslovakia in August 1968 … Havana's reaction to the invasion was a clear turning point in policy" (Duncan 1981: 444).

5 See my "No History to Absolve Them: Spanish-American Revolutionary Discourse after 1990" (2004). Having joined Che Guevara's band of revolutionaries in Bolivia, Debray was in prison in La Paz at the time of Cardenal's visit to Cuba.

6 A mistranslation. This should be, "I'll drop in on you one day at your island."
7 The English edition, published between 1976 and 1982, consists of four volumes.

CHAPTER SIX

1 The total death toll from the Contra War between 1980 and 1990 is now believed to be approximately fifty-eight thousand (Vilas 1995: 138).

CHAPTER SEVEN

1 On 6 January 1975 Ramírez wrote to DAAD official Karl Ruhrberg: "Schließlich ist der Entwurf meines Romans 'Lucky Seven' (ungefähr 450 S.) schon fertig; das Manuscript [*sic*] wird einem Verlag vor März übergeben" ("At last the draft of my novel 'Lucky Seven' [i.e., *To Bury Our Fathers*] (approximately 450 pages) is almost ready; the manuscript will be submitted to a publisher before March") (*SRP*, box 43, folder 13).
2 See in particular Valenzuela's *Cambio de armas* (1982; *Other Weapons*) and *Cola de lagartija* (1983; *The Lizard's Tail*).
3 At the time that Ramírez was writing the novel, Agüero, who had secured the release from jail in Costa Rica of Carlos Fonseca and Humberto Ortega by hijacking an airliner, was in exile in Cuba. In a case of life imitating art, Carlos Agüero would die in combat in northern Nicaragua in April 1977 (Zimmermann 2000: 205), just before *To Bury Our Fathers* was published.
4 Since "godfather" was sometimes a codeword for the biological father of an illegitimate child, there is a suggestion here that Moncada is López's father, as he was rumoured to be the biological father of Anastasio Somoza García.
5 *Nicaragua tan violentamente dulce*, 70; *Nicaraguan Sketches*, 128. Among Boom writers, Carlos Fuentes and Gabriel García Márquez also supported the Sandinista Revolution. Fuentes visited the country twice, once with the US novelist William Styron; in a show of symbolic support, the two writers escorted Daniel Ortega to the opening of a session of Central American peace negotiations. Teaching at Ivy League universities for much of the 1980s, Fuentes campaigned tirelessly against US intervention in Central America, most notably in his televised, widely reported 1983 Harvard University Commencement address, where he asked: "Why is the United States so impatient with four years of Sandinismo when it was so tolerant of forty-five years of Somocismo? Why is it so worried about free elections in Nicaragua, but so indifferent to free elections in Chile? ... How can we live and grow together on the basis of such hypocrisy?" (Fuentes 1988: 211).

Gabriel García Márquez, who had met Tomás Borge in Cuba in the mid-1970s, supported the Sandinistas from an early stage and wrote a journalistic account of the 1978 kidnapping of the National Assembly that was published by the Mexican newspaper *Excelsior*. He visited Nicaragua during the Sandinista years, but, as his biographer, Gerald Martin, writes: "García Márquez would always take an interest in the Nicaraguan revolution and would give it considerable support but he never showed the enthusiasm for it that he had shown for Cuba. For one thing he never had the same familiarity with Nicaragua as he had with Castro, nor at that time did he have the intimate relationship with any one member of the leading group that he enjoyed with Fidel. For another thing he always had a certain inevitable scepticism, as he had also shown towards the Chilean experiment: unless a country took the same ruthless military and political measures adopted by the Cubans, there was little chance that the USA would tolerate any kind of left-leaning regime" (Martin 2008: 402).

By contrast, Mario Vargas Llosa, who also visited Nicaragua during the 1980s on journalistic assignments, though he maintained a nuanced posture, was more critical than supportive (though he criticized the opposition even more harshly than he did the Sandinistas). Identified by many with the right, Vargas Llosa nevertheless excoriated right-wingers in the Reagan administration who exaggerated conditions in Nicaragua. Speaking of accusations of "totalitarianism," he wrote: "Esta tesis es exagerada y ... quienes la propagan y actúan como si fuera cierta – me refiero a los gobiernos democráticos – están haciendo un daño enorme a la causa de la libertad en ese país" (Vargas Llosa 1990b: 433–4; "This thesis is exaggerated and ... those who propagate it and act as though it were true – I'm referring to democratic governments – are doing enormous damage to the cause of freedom in that country").

6 For a more extended discussion of Testimonio, see chapter 10.

7 In a study based on the case of Chile, Andre Gunder Frank, one of the most influential dependency theorists of the 1960s and 1970s, wrote that the Latin American bourgeoisie continued "to become increasingly dependent on the world capitalist metropolis for finance, commercialization, capital goods, technology, design, patents, trade marks, licenses" (Frank 1969: 117); this dependency also engulfed the cultural sphere.

8 Asturias wrote: "Para mí, escritor significa hablar por los que no hablan. Entre los indígenas maya-quichés de Guatemala existe lo que se llama el Gran Lengua. El Gran Lengua es un personaje muy importante en las comunidades indígenas, en las cofradías, porque éste es el que lleva las peticiones, las quejas, las reclamaciones del conjunto de indígenas que forman su pueblo, que forman su barrio" (González 1999: 11; "For me, a writer means someone who speaks

for those who do not speak. Among the Quiché Maya of Guatemala there is what is known as the Great Tongue. The Great Tongue is a very important personage in indigenous communities, in the brotherhood associations of indigenous men, because he is the one who presents the petitions, complaints, and demands of all of the indigenous people who make up his village, who make up his neighbourhood").

9 This poem does not appear in the English translation. As the translator, Darwin Flakoll, notes, "The text is based on the Nicaraguan edition of *Nicaragua, tan violentemente dulce*, with the omission of Cortázar's introductory poem" (Cortázar 1989: 1).

10 Contrary to most contemporary scholars, Ramírez says of Carrera that "más que un indio era un mulato ... porque aquí, lo de indio y mulato se llegaba a confundir mucho" (*UISR*; "more than an Indian he was a mulatto ... because here, Indian and mulatto are confused a lot").

11 This analysis of Carrera's rule receives its definitive treatment in Ralph Lee Woodward, Jr.'s massive *Rafael Carrera and the Emergence of the Republic of Guatemala, 1821–1871* (1993), in which, on the basis of meticulous research, Woodward argues (56–101) that, like the Sandinistas, Carrera reached the presidency as the result of an uprising, known as the Battle of the Mountain, and had to keep fighting to hold onto power. Greg Grandin's *The Blood of Guatemala* (2000) equates Carrera's government with Guatemala's other great moment of radical reform, the October Revolution governments of 1944–54 (18–19).

12 In 1990 Ramírez participated in a panel in Mexico City, organized by Conaculta, Mexico's national arts council. During the debate, he pointed out that while on tour in Germany, Paz had read a Ronald Reagan speech that denounced Nicaragua, claiming it as his own work. When challenged, Ramírez produced a copy of the speech and read it to the Mexican audience. Paz, who was not present, was so furious that he demanded an audience with Mexican President Carlos Salinas de Gortari and arranged for the director of Conaculta, Víctor Flores Olea, to be fired (Cherem 2004b: 217–20). In 1998 Ramírez wrote of Paz in a letter to the Peruvian journalist Carlos Meneses, "como emperador usa su poder" (*SRP*, box 37, folder 20; "he uses his power like an emperor").

13 In early 2013 Ramírez announced that the English translation would be published by the small New York State publisher McPherson and Company.

14 In the first draft of *Castigo Divino*, Ramírez called the family Gurdián; the change to Contreras was introduced in the second draft (*SRP*, box 1, folder 10).

15 The historical Captain Prío was still serving at the bar as late as February 2006, when the author of this study bought a soft drink from him. According to an

article in *La Prensa*, dated 16 October 2005, Agustín Prío Largaespada, at that time ninety-one years old, retained clear memories of the historical Oliverio Castañeda (Espinosa 2005).

16 Ramírez describes his own discovery of this book at the age of fourteen as "una iniciación no sólo en el rito de la lectura, sino también en el de la sensualidad" (*SLT*, 215; "an initiation not only in the rites of reading, but also in those of sensuality").

17 Ramírez was unable to obtain a video copy of *Payment Deferred* and was told by the Agendas International Agency in New York that he would not be granted the right to read the script. Yet, by unknown means, he did acquire a photocopy of the script; this is almost certainly the source of his knowledge of the film's action (*SRP*, box 1, folder 7).

18 This pattern mimics that of a contemporary case of which Ramírez must have been aware. At the time that he was writing this novel, the knowledge that Rosario Murillo, the life-partner of Daniel Ortega, who had met the future Nicaraguan president in Costa Rica, had gained leverage over unwarranted areas of government policy in return for offering Ortega sexual access to her daughter, Zoilamérica Narváez Murillo, was a simmering, unspoken source of tension within the Sandinista inner circle (Morris 2010: 89–94; Kampwirth 2004: 213). See also chapter 9.

19 Ironically, the novel first appeared in the archaic form of the serialized melodrama, extending its postmodern pastiche to the re-enactment of past publishing procedures. On 7 April 1988 the newspaper *El Nuevo Amanecer Cultural* (New Dawn Cultural Supplement) announced: "*El Nuevo Amanecer Cultural* comenzará a publicar a partir del proximo sábado, por entregas, la última novela de Sergio Ramírez, *Castigo Divino*, de manera íntegra. De esta forma, nuestro suplemento literario recoge la vieja tradición del folletín, ofreciendo cada vez un capítulo hasta completar los cuarentisiete de que consta la obra, tal como en el pasado se recogieron, antes de aparecer en forma de libro, las más importantes novelas en los periódicos de Europa y América" (*SRP*, box 3, folder 5; "Starting next Saturday, *El Nuevo Amanecer Cultural* will begin to publish by installments, in its entirety, the latest novel of Sergio Ramírez, *Castigo Divino*. In this way, our literary supplement will recover the old tradition of the melodrama, offering one chapter at a time until we have completed the forty-seven of which the work consists, just as in the past the most important novels were serialized in the newspapers of Europe and the Americas before appearing in book form").

20 Belli's personal and political relationship with Contreras is the subject of her poetry collection *Línea de fuego* (1978; Firing Line), which won the Casa de las Américas Prize.

21 For example, Laura Barbas-Rhoden, in *Writing Women in Central America: Gender and Fictionalization of History* (2003), Linda J. Craft in *Novels of Testimony and Resistance from Central America* (1997), and Rudyard Alcocer in "The Ghost of La Malinche: Trees and Treason in *La mujer habitada*" (2010) all concentrate on themes of feminism and indigenous heritage and bypass questions of social class.

22 The upper-class feminism of Belli and Rosario Murillo, which concentrated on sexual liberation and was accused of paying insufficient attention to the concerns of women with fewer economic privileges, has been criticized by scholars such as White and Calderón (2008), who write that this brand of feminism "was nothing more than the feminine liberation to have many different sexual partners. Certain women poets, for example, published books of erotic poetry, and the literary success of these opportunistic women writers was celebrated in official luxurious parties. These authors, who were often from well-to-do families displaced by the 1979 revolution, lined up to take advantage of the Sandinista's [*sic*] access to power and privilege. Other women, seeking an honest place and not a bed, were dismissed by males in power as being resentful" (59). This harsh view should not be allowed to diminish any assessment of the undeniable literary value of Belli's poems.

CHAPTER EIGHT

1 According to Robert Pring-Mill, who spent the summer of 1972 in Solentiname studying the sources and order of composition of the poems, the first edition of fifteen poems was published in 1969, a Chilean edition of seventeen poems appeared in 1970, and a definitive edition of nineteen poems in 1972. The book was later absorbed into Cardenal's collected indigenous poems, *Los ovnis de oro* (1988; *Golden UFOs*), which contained thirty poems on these themes. Nine of the nineteen poems in the 1972 edition were written between 1959 and 1968 and reflect a variety of ideological tones as Cardenal's ideas evolved; the last ten were the result of a more concentrated effort in 1968 and 1969, but, according to Pring-Mill, these poems "merely continue lines of thought and modes of treatment which had all made their appearance by the end of 1967" (Pring-Mill 1992: 57).

2 Earlier prose fiction devoted to the indigenous question in Spanish America had been dominated by either positivist portrayals of indigenous peoples as inhabiting "decayed" or "decadent" cultures, such as Clorinda Matto de Turner's *Aves sin nido* (1889; *Torn from the Nest*) or Alcides Arguedas's *Raza de bronce* (1919; Race of Bronze), or works of socialist naturalism, such as Jorge Icaza's *Huasipungo* (1934), in which the indigenous people are oppressed

rural proletarians whose cultural differences from their white or mestizo masters are not appreciated.

3 This depiction has led some later scholars to claim that Cardenal is "complicit in the very colonialism that he so much abhors" (Lee 2008: 239), on the grounds that his negative view of Aztec centralism, it is asserted, provides a justification for the oppression of Aztec culture by Spanish colonialism. This view overlooks the negative characterizations of post-Conquest Spanish colonialism that appear throughout *Homenaje a los indios americanos*.

4 The phrase "los hombres nuevos americanos" could be translated literally as "American new men."

5 In December 1975, FSLN leader Carlos Fonseca mailed a copy of this poem to Sergio Ramírez, instructing him: "Te adjuntamos un ejemplar del inédito poema de Ernesto Cardenal 'Epistolas [*sic*] a Jose [*sic*] Coronel Urtecho.' Tiene mención destacada del FSLN. Urge su inmediata difusión de esa, preferible en páginas culturales de diarios" (*SRP*, box 37, folder 6; "I'm enclosing for you a copy of Ernesto Cardenal's unpublished poem, 'Epistolas [*sic*] a Jose [*sic*] Coronel Urtecho.' It makes prominent mention of the FSLN. Its immediate circulation, preferably in the cultural pages of newspapers, is an urgent priority."). Three decades later, in February 2006, Cardenal read "Epístola a José Coronel Urtecho" at the Granada Poetry Festival, during the ceremony commemorating the 150th anniversary of William Walker's burning of Granada and the centenary of the birth of Coronel Urtecho, to whom the 2006 festival was dedicated. The mayor of Granada, Álvaro Chamorro Mora – a cousin of Coronel – introduced Cardenal with a speech in which he argued angrily against the notion of political poetry. Cardenal's reading divided the crowd, provoking both shouts of "*¡Viva!*" and Somocista chants (See my "Verse and Versatility" [2007]).

6 For example, the author heard poems from *Flights of Victory* read on US National Public Radio during this time.

7 *Odas elementales* (1954; *Elementary Odes*), *Nuevas odas elementales* (1956; *New Elementary Odes*), and *Tercer libro de las odas* (1957; *Third Book of Odes*).

8 "Una vez mi asistente Luz Marina [Acosta] estuvo señalando en el calendario todos los días que [yo] andaba fuera y resultaron ser más de la mitad del año. Viajes que me aburrieron bastante" (*RP*, 344; "Once my assistant Luz Marina [Acosta] was noting in the calendar every day that [I] was away and it turned out to be more than half of the year. Trips that I found quite boring").

9 Cardenal's desire to maintain the collection's optimistic tone is evident in his exclusion from the Spanish-language edition of *Flights of Victory* of one new poem that appeared in the 1983 *Antología*. "Concentración en St. George" ("Mass Rally in St. George"), a hymn of praise to Maurice Bishop's

revolutionary government in Grenada that vaunts the uniforms supplied to the Grenadian militia by Nicaragua, was dropped after the split in the Grenadian regime and the US invasion in October 1983 that resulted in Bishop's overthrow and murder. It was reinstated for the English translation. See also chapter 12.

10 As an example of this culture of martyrdom, Cardenal recalls a 19 July anniversary of the revolution: "Ese día Tomás Borge pronunció un discurso estremecedor en el que empezó a enumerar nombres y nombres y nombres gloriosos de los caídos en la revolución, y a cada nombre de un caído el pueblo estallaba en un aplauso. Más tarde Vargas Llosa [que estuvo presente en la plaza] me preguntó por qué Tomás había callado el nombre del comandante Cero Edén Pastora (era cuando Edén Pastora se había volteado contra la revolución y la atacaba desde Costa Rica) y es que Vargas Llosa creía que aquellos aplausos habían sido para personalidades vivas. Lo que me hizo ver hasta qué punto Vargas Llosa no entendía la revolución" (*RP*, 403; "That day Tomás Borge gave a blood-curdling speech in which he began to list names and names and glorious names of those who had fallen in the revolution, and at every name of a fallen hero the people burst into applause. Later Vargas Llosa [who was present in the square] asked me why Tomás had omitted the name of Comandante Zero, Edén Pastora (it was when Edén Pastora had turned against the revolution and was attacking it from Costa Rica), and it turned out that Vargas Llosa thought the applause had been for living personalities. Which made me see to what extent Vargas Llosa did not understand the revolution").

11 Greg Dawes is refreshingly frank when he evokes the pressure to complete his book as his reason for giving short shrift to *Cosmic Canticle*: "I decided to devote my time to rewriting the manuscript, thinking that a reading of *Cántico cósmico* would set back completion of my study" (Dawes 1993: xix).

12 Aurora Camacho de Schmidt, presentation at the Undécimo Congreso Internacional de Literatura Centroamericana (Eleventh International Conference on Central American Literature), San José, Costa Rica, March 2003.

13 Cantigas 1, 2, 3, 9, 11, 12, 13, 19, 20, 22, 25, 30, 32, 33, 34, 36, 37, 38, 40, and 41 open with this phrase.

14 The poem's insistent political themes make it difficult to agree with Arias when he criticizes *Cosmic Canticle* for being "nonpolitical" (Arias 2007: 230n7).

CHAPTER NINE

1 In spite of various twists and turns, Narváez has not withdrawn the substance of these accusations, and the evidence suggests that they are founded. The

international debate the allegations provoke elicits contradictory positions. Morris, whose overall assessment of Ortega's career is positive, believes the abuse did occur (Morris 2010: 89–94). By contrast, Florence Babb interviewed members of a Managua women's collective who thought that Ortega was innocent and Narváez was being manipulated (Babb 2001: 238).

2 See my "Verse and Versatility" (2007), 44.

3 The voting age in Nicaragua was lowered to sixteen for the 1984 elections. This measure was not intended to be permanent, but rather designed to reflect the extraordinary responsibilities assumed by young people during the first years of the Nicaraguan Revolution. As Fernando Cardenal, then the minister responsible for youth, explained at the time: "El Frente Sandinista de Liberación Nacional no dice ... que los jóvenes nicaragüenses siempre van a tener el derecho que tienen estos jóvenes ... Estos jóvenes se han ganado el derecho y han probado que tienen madurez en la práctica. ¿Quién les va a negar el derecho al voto si nosotros les hemos pedido que pongan su vida por la patria a los quince o los dieciseis años?" (Cardenal, "Unpublished interview"; "The Sandinista National Liberation Front is not saying ... that Nicaraguan youth will always have the right that these young people have ... These young people have earned the right to vote and have proved through practice that they have maturity. Who will deny them the right to vote if we have asked them to put their lives on the line for their country at the age of fifteen or sixteen?").

4 This figure includes the four children Daniel Ortega and Rosario Murillo had together, the son fathered by Ortega with his mid-1970s girlfriend, the Moscow-educated guerrilla comandante, and later National Assembly member and diplomat Leticia Herrera, and the three surviving children born to Murillo from two earlier relationships (another of Murillo's children died as an infant in the 1972 earthquake). According to some sources, in 2009 Ortega fathered another child with the daughter of one of his security guards (Morris 2010: 198). The older children contribute to the promotion of Daniel Ortega's presidency. Zoilamérica Narváez Murillo was popularly believed to have been reintegrated into the clan after withdrawing her legal action for sexual abuse against her stepfather in 2004. In May 2013, however, she gave an interview in which she insisted that she had neither personal contacts nor business dealings with Rosario Murillo and Daniel Ortega, and that she stood by her accusations of extended sexual abuse against Daniel Ortega (Medina 2013).

5 Tomás Borge notes of a Sandinista safe house in 1969, where Julio Cortázar's *Rayuela* [*Hopscotch*] was also popular: "En esa casa ya se había hablado del coronel Aureliano Buendía, acribillado por la soledad. Gran parte de los clandestinos devoraron *La ciudad y los perros* de Mario Vargas Llosa. Obras de Carlos Fuentes y Mario Benedetti afinaron las cuerdas de nuestros violines. En

círculos más estrechos se leía a Juan Carlos Onetti ... Nadie leía a Borges, a pesar de que es el mejor" (Borge 1989; "In that house Colonel Aureliano Buendia, who was riddled with solitude, had already been talked about. Most of the underground militants devoured Mario Vargas Llosa's *The City and the Dogs* [*The Time of the Hero*]. We also tuned our violin strings to works by Carlos Fuentes and Mario Benedetti. Juan Carlos Onetti was read in narrower circles ... Nobody read Borges, despite the fact that he is the best" [Borge 1992: 285]). Cortázar was particularly popular reading material among guerrillas. The young martyr whose name was given to the Sandinista women's organization, Asociación de Mujeres Nicaragüenses Luisa Amanda Espinosa (AMNLAE; Luisa Amanda Espinosa Association of Nicaraguan Women), was famously found to have a copy of *Hopscotch* among her scarce possessions after she was shot dead by the National Guard on the street in León in April 1970 (*EN*, 32).

CHAPTER TEN

1 It is unclear whether the Berlin Wall had fallen on the day that Ramírez gave this talk, since, unlike the other pieces in the book, "Revolución, identidad nacional y cultura" is dated only by month and year, rather than by day, month, and year.

2 After Daniel Ortega's re-election in 2006, a portrait of this event, depicting Castro as brown-skinned and the US mercenary as white-skinned, was hung in many government buildings (Morris 2010: image after 126) and also appeared intermittently on Rosario Murillo's website.

3 *A Tale of Two Cities* begins: "It was the best of times, it was the worst of times, it was the age of wisdom, it was the age of foolishness, it was the epoch of belief, it was the epoch of incredulity, it was the season of Light, it was the season of Darkness, it was the spring of hope, it was the winter of despair" (Dickens 1859: 1).

4 In *Margarita, How Beautiful the Sea* this scene recurs, again to the lyrics of "El mucura que está en el suelo," with the variation that in the novel the student protagonist, Rigoberto López Pérez, shoots the dictator (*MLM*, 340).

5 The figure of "el cadejo" appears in "Leyenda del Cadejo" ("Legend of the Cadejo"), a short story from Miguel Ángel Asturias's collection *Leyendas de Guatemala* (1930; Legends of Guatemala). After a seventeenth-century nun cuts off her braid, it comes to life as a fantastical creature that the devil "arrastró al infierno" (Asturias 1930: 109; "hauled down to hell"). Ramírez defines "el cadejo" as: "un perro nocturno de doble identidad: uno blanco, que acompaña a los hombres bien portados hasta la puerta de sus casas; y uno negro que persigue a los amantes adúlteros que se aventuran por los caminos en sus andanzas

clandestinas" (*MV*, 88–9; "a nocturnal dog of double identity, one aspect white, which accompanies well-behaved men to the doors of their houses; and the other aspect black, which pursues adulterous lovers who wander the roads in their clandestine adventures").

6 Ramírez's elder daughter was also named after her mother, Gertrudis. As a child, she was known in the family as "Trudis"; after she became a Sandinista Youth leader in her teens she adopted her baptismal name, calling herself María Ramírez (*SRP*, box 40, folder 3).

7 Téllez responded by accusing the director of Radio Ya, Carlos Guadamuz, of being "sick" ("Nicaragua: More FSLN Resignations" 1995). In spite of the predominant environment of censure, since the late 1990s, public expressions of gay identity have been possible in Nicaragua. Florence Babb traces the history of this opening: "The mass mobilization of the population brought about by the Nicaraguan Revolution provided an opportunity for young women and men to explore and redefine their sexuality. During their years in power, the Sandinistas began to provide a space for more open discussion of gender and sexual relations and of personal life and politics, though they were ambivalent about the new desires expressed as a result of those spaces" (Babb 2004: 30). In response to Chamorro's criminalization of homosexuality in 1992, nascent gay-rights organizations announced a series of educational seminars; according to one foreign report, the only elected politicians who agreed to attend these seminars were "Sandinista deputies María Ramírez and Comandante Dora María Téllez" (Beecham 1992). The recourse to homophobic slurs in 1995 formed part of the retrenchment that attempted to preserve the "virile" guerrilla ethos in the post-1990 context; but this did not prevent the opening created in the late 1980s from growing and developing, albeit cautiously.

8 The tradition of travelling on horseback was extended into the 1990s by Subcomandante Marcos of the Ejército Zapatista de Liberación Nacional (EZLN; Zapatista National Liberation Front) in his meetings with journalists in Chiapas (*A Place Called Chiapas* 1998).

9 According to the historical Agustín Prío, the young Rubén Darío often spent nights in the Casa Prío during the period when it was owned by Prío's father: "Pero debo decirle que Darío vivió en la Casa Prío. Ahí tenía una cama y su mesa de noche. Todo hace suponer que por su vida bohemia en su propia casa no reconocían sus méritos, entonces él le pidió a mi papá que le dejara donde quedarse en la casa en la noche" (Espinosa 2005; "But I must tell you that Darío lived in the Casa Prío. He had a bed there, and his bedside table. One assumes that due to his bohemian lifestyle his family didn't recognize his merits, so he asked my dad to leave him a place in the house where he could spend the night.").

10 In 2003 the author was present at a panel discussion in San José, Costa Rica, where three female Central American intellectuals spoke in vitriolic terms of the class assumptions that underlay Belli's portrait of the Sandinista years in *The Country under My Skin.*

11 The book's most puzzling omission is Ramírez's failure to address the allegations that Daniel Ortega abused his stepdaughter for eleven years, which were breaking as Ramírez was writing his memoir. Ramírez has always remained silent on this issue.

12 The final sentence of this translation is inaccurate and misleading. A more faithful version would be: "Yet in Nicaragua the first real model for change that the country had ever experienced was shattered."

13 Ramírez also narrates these events in *Estás en Nicaragua* (135–6), dating them to 13 July 1979. The chronology of the massacre, and the timing of the death of the local guerrilla comandante, Ezequial, is altered in *Sombras nada más*, occurring a full month prior to the revolutionary triumph, rather than only a week before.

14 Ernesto Cardenal dramatizes Walker's execution of Ponciano Corral in "With Walker in Nicaragua" (see chapter 3).

15 After 19 July 1979 the FSLN abolished the death penalty, though, as Ramírez reports (*AM*, 228–9), this measure did not end all executions.

16 Ernesto Cardenal, being partly of German-Jewish ancestry, grew up in the same circles as Hüeck: "Durante mi juventud fuimos algo amigos, cuando [Hüeck] no era canalla como lo fue después, y también éramos un poco parientes por judíos" (*RP*, 290; "During my youth we were friends in a way, when [Hüeck] wasn't a bastard as he was later, and also, as Jews, we were distantly related").

17 This anecdote, attributed in the novel to Somoza, originates in the lore that surrounds the presidency of Arnoldo Alemán. According to legend, Alemán, who took slimming medicines, suffered intestinal incontinence in a swimming pool in the Dominican Republic where he was surrounded by his advisers: "Cuentan que nadie se atrevió a salirse. Usé este episodio atribuyendo el percance a Somoza" (Cherem 2004b: 262; "They say that nobody dared to get out. I used this episode, attributing the mishap to Somoza").

18 See, for example, my *When Words Deny the World: The Reshaping of Canadian Writing* (2002: 133–57).

19 Though not devoid of sexual themes and confidences. On 9 December 1993, Schultze-Kraft, having separated from his wife, wrote Ramírez a letter detailing his sex life as a single man (*SRP*, box 42, folder 7).

20 Francisco Castellón (1815–55) was briefly director general of Nicaragua prior to his death in a cholera epidemic. He led Liberal forces from León to besiege Granada; when the siege was unsuccessful, he invited William Walker into

the country. The other actions attributed to Francisco Castellón in the novel are fictitious.

21 This translation is imprecise: it should be "become a concubine in a single night."

CHAPTER ELEVEN

1 It would be a mistake to discount the long-term benefits, both material and spiritual, that Cardenal's community brought to those who continued to live in the Solentiname Archipelago. In 2012 the *New York Times* noted the egalitarian ethos and distinctive artistic style that prevailed among the islands' inhabitants. The article reported that, under the Sandinista government, "Father Cardenal … formed the Solentiname Development Association to create the tidy communities that visitors see today" (Bailey 2012).

2 After the FSLN's re-election in 2006, Rosario Murillo developed a cult around the memory of Camilo Ortega, Daniel and Humberto's younger brother, who died in combat in 1978, to replace the worship of martyrs associated with figures who had resigned from the FSLN.

3 In fact, Fruto Chamorro was the first Nicaraguan leader to receive the title of president; his predecessors were called directors general.

4 The Conservative historian Arturo J. Cruz, Jr, concurs with Cardenal's assessment of Fruto Chamorro's radicalism, though he criticizes it for having created political instability that later Conservatives had to quell: "His ideal constitution was based on the il-fated project of 1848" (Cruz, Jr, 2002: 35).

5 Ernesto Cardenal's grandfather, Salvador Cardenal, had thirteen children and more than 100 grandchildren (Christian 1985: 173).

6 The original designate for this post was Pablo Antonio Cuadra, who refused the nomination (*AM*, 260).

7 In spite of the long-standing alliance between Nicaragua and Iran, which revived after the 2006 elections, Salman Rushdie reports that "Daniel Ortega … vociferously opposed the death threat of the 1989 Khomeini fatwa against my novel, *The Satanic Verses*" (Rushdie 1987: xvii).

8 No Sandinista of Conservative background was implicated in the *Piñata* – perhaps because, unlike their proletarian comrades, they had sources of income other than their government salaries. By contrast, Conservative anti-Sandinistas were the main culprits for the corruption of the Chamorro years, particularly *Piñata II*.

CHAPTER TWELVE

1 This point is argued in detail in my *A Report on the Afterlife of Culture* (2008), 29–43.

2 The bridge between these two figures is Carlos Fuentes, who, as Carpentier's protégé, wrote much of *The Death of Artemio Cruz* in Havana, and, as Ramírez's mentor in the internationalization of his literary career, lent the symbolic capital of the Mexican Revolution to the two smaller countries even as he used his immersion in these two newly minted revolutions to distance himself from the corrupt, authoritarian legacy of what the Mexican Revolution and its political standard-bearer, the PRI, had become.

3 See Subcomandante Marcos 1999, *Desde las montañas del sureste mexicano*, and my "No History to Absolve Them" (2004).

4 Justin Wolfe argues in persuasive detail that many of the Liberal leaders of the 1840s and 1850s were "Afromestizos," and that, in fact, León became a Liberal city because upwardly mobile men from this background embraced egalitarian Liberal ideology in response to their experiences of racial discrimination. Since these men articulated their point of connection as being their origin in the neighbourhood of San Felipe and their education at what was then the Universidad de León, "rather than race, it appears that place ... served to nurture their political, social and economic networks" (Wolfe 2010: 182). This, combined with the embrace of "ladino" status on the part of the next generation of Liberals around 1870, complicates pinning down the origins of individual Liberal politicians. Wolfe points out (200) that much more is known about the Conservative Fruto Chamorro than about his Liberal counterpart, Francisco Castellón. In *A Thousand Deaths Plus One,* Ramírez portrays Castellón as white in appearance and self-identification. In *Tambor olvidado*, he states: "Son un criollo venido a menos, don Francisco Castellón, y un ladino mulato, el general Máximo Jerez, quienes hicieron venir a la falange filibustera" (*TO*, 150; "It was a criollo down on his luck, Don Francisco Castellón, and a mulatto ladino, General Máximo Jerez, who brought in the Fascist filibusters"). Yet for Wolfe, as for other contributors to his edited volume, Castellón, in spite of his blue eyes and white skin, was not a Spanish-descended criollo, but rather one of the "Afro-Nicaraguans" (185) – whatever his DNA may have been – by virtue of coming from the San Felipe neighbourhood. It is surprising that none of the contributors to Gudmundson and Wolfe's heavily researched book, *Blacks and Blackness in Central America* (2010), which quotes numerous Nicaraguan intellectuals, references *Tambor olvidado*.

5 It is not clear where the 85 per cent figure comes from. Wolfe, citing a late-eighteenth-century census, reports that "people of African descent ... accounted for 51 percent of the province's inhabitants" (Wolfe 2010: 178). Since this figure apparently refers to those of solely African descent, it is not incompatible with that cited by Ramírez for triple mestizos.

6 In response, Gould would argue – as he did when the author put these points to him – that his study concentrates on the maintenance of an indigenous culture in districts such as Subtiava, "whatever the DNA" of the people who identify with this culture. In this respect, Gould and Ramírez may agree on most of the history, though they interpret it from divergent angles.

7 In July 2005, during a visit to the National Museum of Anthropology in Luanda, Angola, the author of this study was startled to encounter two men on an upstairs balcony who were playing a marimba that was similar to those that had been presented to him two years earlier, in the Quiché Department of Guatemala, as "ancestral" Mayan instruments.

8 The novel is *El cantor de tangos* (*The Tango Singer*) by the Argentine writer Tomás Eloy Martínez. It is difficult to see any resonance between this dense, allusive work about a man who travels to Buenos Aires to engage with Argentine high culture and Ramírez's Managua detective story. The inclusion of Martínez's novel is also anachronistic, since it was published in 2004 and the action of *El cielo llora por mí* takes place in the year 2000.

9 One could argue that this is a summary of the goals of Ramírez's post-1995 political party, the MRS (see chapters 4 and 9).

10 This point is argued in detail in my *When Words Deny the World* (2002), 99–106.

11 Coello Gutiérrez demonstrates that these drug lords are based on historical members of the Cali and Sonora cartels (Coello Gutiérrez 2010: 7–9).

12 Ernesto Cardenal's collection of theological essays, *Este mundo y otro* (This World and Another) (Madrid: Editorial Trotta 2011), and Sergio Ramírez's short-story collection *Flores oscuras* (Dark Flowers) (Madrid: Alfaguara, 2013) appeared too late to be included in this study.

13 As an indication of the uniformity of twenty-first-century travel experiences, it may be worth noting that the author of this study took the same boat excursion during his visit to Chiapas.

14 An icon of Mexican ranchera music, Vargas is best known to international audiences for her appearances in films such as Pedro Almodóvar's *The Flower of My Secret* (1995) and Julie Taymor's Frida Kahlo biopic *Frida* (2002).

15 Discussing the paucity of women writers in mid-century Central America, Arias notes that "the only significant female antecedent to [Claribel] Alegría was Costa Rican Yolanda Oreamuno (1916–56). However, residing in Mexico, she remained largely unknown in Central America itself until she was rediscovered by Sergio Ramírez" (Arias 2007: 232n28).

16 On the importance of "whiteness" to Costa Rica's self-construction as a nation, see Colby 2011: 63–6.

17 In contrast to many Nicaraguan intellectuals of his generation, Ramírez has been a defender of Salomón de la Selva. In the early 1970s, in an introduction to an anthology of Nicaraguan poetry, Ernesto Cardenal identified de la Selva as a Somocista collaborator. At the request of the academic Stefan Baciu, Ramírez sent Cardenal a letter, dated 14 September 1974, asking that he either withdraw the criticism or identify all of the poets in the anthology who had at some point collaborated with the Somozas: "Son cuarenta años de contaminación que no han pasado en vano y la lista sería demasiado largo" (*SRP*, box 36, folder 19; "It's been forty years of contamination that have not passed in vain, and the list would be much too long"). In the 1980s Ramírez exhumed the manuscript of an unpublished pro-Sandino novel that de la Selva had written in 1935 and published it: *La guerra de Sandino, o el pueblo desnudo* (Sandino's War, or the People Naked) (Managua: Editorial Nueva Nicaragua 1985).

18 As in *Castigo Divino* and *Margarita, How Beautiful the Sea*, the cast of characters draws on the names of personal acquaintances. The doctor who operates on Amanda in a Washington, D.C., hospital in the early 1950s is named Carlo Castaldi (*LF*, 281). This is also the name of Gioconda Belli's third husband.

19 In many indigenous American languages, "tata" means "father." Informants from the region where Cardenal's poem is set have told the author that in Michoacán "tata" often means "grandfather." It has not been possible to document this translation.

20 This scene also fails to reflect Bianca Jagger's distinguished career as a hardworking advocate for human rights.

Bibliography

WORKS BY ERNESTO CARDENAL

Books

Gethsemani, Ky. 1960. México: Ecuador.

Salmos. 1964. Rpt. Buenos Aires: Ediciones Carlos Lohlé 1969.

Oración por Marilyn Monroe y otros poemas. 1965. Rpt. Lima: Serie Textual 1972.

The Doubtful Strait/El estrecho dudoso. 1966. Rpt. Ed. Tamara R. Williams. Trans. John Lyons. Bloomington and Indianapolis: Indiana University Press 1995.

Vida en el amor. 1970. Buenos Aires: Ediciones Carlos Lohlé.

En Cuba. 1972. Buenos Aires: Ediciones Carlos Lohlé 1972.

Homenaje a los indios americanos. 1972. Rpt. Barcelona: Editorial Laia 1979.

In Cuba. 1974. Trans. Donald D. Walsh. New York: New Directions.

El evangelio en Solentiname. 1975. Rpt. San José, Costa Rica/Managua, Nicaragua: Departamento Eucuménico de Investigaciones/Ministerio de Cultura de Nicaragua, 1979. 2 vols.

Marilyn Monroe and Other Poems. 1975. Ed. and trans. Robert Pring-Mill. London: Search Press.

The Gospel in Solentiname, Volume I. 1976. Trans. Donald D. Walsh. Maryknoll, NY: Orbis Books 1976.

La santidad de la revolución. 1976. Salamanca: Ediciones Sígueme.

Apocalypse and Other Poems. 1977. Eds. Robert Pring-Mill and Donald D. Walsh. Trans. Thomas Merton, Kenneth Rexroth, and Mireya Jaimes-Freyre and the editors. New York: New Directions.

The Gospel in Solentiname, Volume II. 1978. Trans. Donald D. Walsh. Maryknoll, NY: Orbis Books.
The Gospel in Solentiname, Volume III. 1979. Trans. Donald D. Walsh. Maryknoll, NY: Orbis Books.
Zero Hour and Other Documentary Poems. 1980. Trans. Paul W. Borgeson, Jr, Jonathan Cohen, Robert Pring-Mill, and Donald D. Walsh. New York: New Directions.
Psalms. 1981. Trans. Thomas Blackburn et al. New York: Crossroad Publishing Company.
The Gospel in Solentiname, Volume IV. 1982. Trans. Donald D. Walsh. Maryknoll, NY: Orbis Books.
Antología. 1983. Managua: Editorial Nueva Nicaragua.
Vuelos de victoria. 1984. Madrid: Visor Libros.
With Walker in Nicaragua and Other Early Poems, 1949–1954. 1984. Trans. Jonathan Cohen. Middletown, CT: Wesleyan University Press.
Flights of Victory. 1985. Ed. and trans. Marc Zimmerman. Maryknoll, NY: Orbis Books.
Los ovnis de oro. Poemas indios. 1988. Rpt. Managua: Ediciones Nicarao 1991.
Cántico Cósmico. 1989. Managua: Editorial Nueva Nicaragua.
Los ovnis de oro. Poemas indios/Golden UFOs. The Indian Poems. 1992. Trans. Carlos and Monique Altschul. Ed. with an Introduction by Russell O. Salmon. Bloomington and Indianapolis: Indiana University Press.
Cosmic Canticle. 1993. Trans. John Lyons. Wilmartic, CT: Curbstone Press.
Abide in Love. 1995. Trans. Dinah Livingstone. Maryknoll, NY: Orbis Books.
Antología nueva. 1996. Madrid: Editorial Trotta.
Vida perdida. Memorias 1. 1999. Barcelona: Seix Barral.
(With Luz Marina Acosta). 2000. *La obra primogénita de Ernesto Cardenal (Carmen y otros poemas)*. Managua: Anamá Ediciones.
Los años de Granada. Continuación de Vida perdida. 2002. Rpt. Managua: Anamá Ediciones 2004.
Las ínsulas extrañas. Memorias 2. 2002. Madrid: Editorial Trotta.
La revolución perdida. Memorias 3. 2004. Madrid: Editorial Trotta.
Versos del pluriverso. 2005. Madrid: Editorial Trotta.
Pasajero de tránsito. 2009. Madrid: Editorial Trotta.
Pluriverse: New and Selected Poems. 2009. Ed. Jonathan Cohen. Foreword by Lawrence Ferlinghetti. New York: New Directions.
The Origin of Species and Other Poems. 2011. Trans. John Lyons. Foreword by Anne Waldman. Lubbock: Texas Tech University Press.
Tata Vasco. Un poema. 2011. Madrid: San Pedro Garza García; Nuevo León: Vaso Roto Ediciones.

Uncollected Articles

"Un contemplativo debe estar siempre comprometido con su pueblo." 1991. *Nuevo Texto Crítico*, vol. 4, no. 8: 45–54.

"Prólogo." 1992. In Sergio Ramírez, *Confesión de amor.* Madrid: Talasa Ediciones. 5–10.

"Es mi deber renunciar a este FSLN." 1994. *El Semanario*, no. 208 (27 october–3 November): 11.

Interviews

Press Conferences, Managua, 1981 and New York, 30 November 1983. Pacifica News. Broadcast 30 November 1983.

Unpublished interview with the author. Managua. 13 February 2006.

Film

Ernesto Cardenal. Cántico cósmico. 1995. Prod. Claudia Fermín. Films for the Humanities and Sciences.

WORKS BY SERGIO RAMÍREZ

Books

La problemática del derecho constitucional nicaragüense. 1964. León: Universidad Nacional de Nicaragua.

Nuevos Cuentos. 1969. León: Universidad Nacional Autónoma de Nicaragua.

Lección inaugural del curso 1969–1970: La juventud y la nueva Nicaragua. León: UNAN.

Tiempo de fulgor. 1970. Rpt. Managua: Ediciones Distribuidora Cultural 2003.

Mariano Fiallos, Biografía. 1971. Rpt. León: Editorial Universitaria, UNAN-León 1997.

De Tropeles y tropelías. 1973. Rpt. Managua: Ediciones Distribuidora Cultural 2004.

El pensamiento vivo de Sandino. 1974. San José: EDUCA.

Charles Atlas también muere. 1976. Rpt. Managua: Editorial Nueva Nicaragua 1982.

Abelardo Cuadra, *Hombre del Caribe. Memorias presentadas y pasadas en limpio por Sergio Ramírez.* 1977. San José: EDUCA.

¿Te dio miedo la sangre? 1977. Rpt. La Habana: Casa de las Américas 1982.

El alba de oro. La historia viva de Nicaragua. 1983. México, D.F.: Siglo Veintiuno Editores.

Balcanes y volcanes y otros ensayos y trabajos. 1983. Managua: Editorial Nueva Nicaragua.

(With Julio Cortázar). 1983. *La edad presente es de lucha*. Managua: Dirección General de Divulgación y Prensa de la J.G.R.N.

To Bury Our Fathers: A Novel of Nicaragua. 1984. Trans. Nick Caistor. London and New York: Readers International.

Estás en Nicaragua. 1985. Barcelona: Muchnik Editores 1985.

Seguimos de frente. Escritos sobre la Revolución. 1985. Caracas: Ediciones Centauro.

Stories. 1986. Trans. Nick Caistor. London and New York: Readers International.

Las armas del futuro. 1987. Selección y prólogo de Reynaldo González. Managua: Editorial Nueva Nicaragua.

Castigo Divino. 1988. Rpt. México: Punto de lectura 2002.

La marca del zorro: hazañas del comandante Francisco Rivera Quintero contadas a Sergio Ramírez. 1989. Managua: Editorial Nueva Nicaragua.

Clave de sol. 1992. Managua: Editorial Nueva Nicaragua.

Confesión de amor. 1992. Prólogo de Ernesto Cardenal. Madrid: Talasa Ediciones.

Oficios compartidos. 1994. México: Siglo Veintiuno Editores.

Un baile de máscaras. 1995. México: Alfaguara.

Hatful of Tigers: Reflections on Art, Culture and Politics. 1995. Trans. D.J. Flakoll. Willimantic, CT: Curbstone Press.

Cuentos completos. 1997. México: Alfaguara.

Margarita, está linda la mar. 1998. Madrid: Alfaguara.

Adiós muchachos: Una memoria de la revolución sandinista. 1999. México: Aguilar.

Mentiras verdaderas. 2000. México: Alfaguara.

Catalina y Catalina. 2001. México: Alfaguara.

Sombras nada más. 2002. México: Alfaguara.

El viejo arte de mentir. 2004. Monterrey, Mexico: Instituto Technológico de Monterrey/Fondo de Cultura Económica.

Mil y una muertes. 2004. Mexico: Alfaguara.

El reino animal. 2006. Madrid: Alfaguara.

Señor de los tristes. Sobre escritores y escritura. 2006. San Juan: La Editorial, Universidad de Puerto Rico.

Tambor olvidado. 2007. San José: Aguilar.

El cielo llora por mí. 2008. Mexico: Alfaguara.

Margarita, How Beautiful the Sea. 2008. Trans. Michael B. Miller. Willimantic, CT: Curbstone Press.

A Thousand Deaths Plus One. 2009. Trans. Leland H. Chambers. Kingston, NY: McPherson and Company.

La fugitiva. 2011. Madrid: Alfaguara.

Adiós Muchachos: A Memoir of the Sandinista Revolution. 2012. Trans. Stacey Alba D. Skar. Durham, NC, and London: Duke University Press.

Uncollected Articles

"Election Night in Nicaragua." 1991. Trans. Nick Caistor. *Granta: A Paperback Magazine of New Writing*, no. 36 (summer): 109–30.

"Mística, incongruencia aún mayor." 2012. *El boomeran(g): Blog literario en español*. 8 August 2008. www.elboomeran.com (accessed 4 November 2012).

Interview

Unpublished interview with the author. Managua. 14 February 2006.

Archives

Sergio Ramírez Papers, 1916–2005 (Bulk 1963–2002). C1123, Manuscripts Division, Department of Rare Books and Special Collections, Princeton University Library.

Uncollected Short Story

"El Estudiante." 1960. *Ventana*, vol. 1, no. 1: 3–4.

CRITICAL WORKS AND OTHER SECONDARY SOURCES

Alcocer, Rudyard. 2010. "The Ghost of La Malinche: Trees and Treason in Gioconda Belli's *La mujer habitada*." *Isle: Interdisciplinary Studies in Literature and Environment*, vol. 17, no. 4: 735–53.

Anderson, Benedict. 1983. *Imagined Communities: Reflections on the Origin and Spread of Nationalism. Revised Edition*. Rpt. London and New York: Verso 1991.

Anderson, Leslie E., and Lawrence C. Dodd. 2005. *Learning Democracy: Citizen Engagement and Electoral Choice in Nicaragua, 1990–2001*. Chicago and London: University of Chicago Press.

Arellano, Jorge Eduardo. 1974. "Ernesto Cardenal: De Granada a Gethsemany." *Cuadernos Hispanoamericanos: Revista Mensual de Cultura Hispánica*, no. 289/19: 163–83.

Argueta, Manlio. 1980. *Un día en la vida*. Rpt. San José: EDUCA 1987.

Arias, Arturo. 1979. *Ideologías, literatura y sociedad durante la revolución guatemalteca, 1944–1954*. La Habana: Ediciones Casa de las Américas.

– ed. 2001. *The Rigoberta Menchú Controversy*. Minneapolis: University of Minnesota Press.

– 2007. *Taking Their Word: Literature and the Signs of Central America*. Minneapolis: University of Minnesota Press.

– 2009. "Post-Identidades Post-Nacionales: Transformaciones en la constitución de las subjetividades globalizadas." *Revista de Crítica Literaria Latinoamericana*, vol. 35, no. 69: 135–52.

Asturias, Miguel Ángel. 1930. *Leyendas de Guatemala*. Ed. Alejandro Lanoël. Rpt. Madrid: Cátedra 1995.

– *El señor presidente*. 1946. Ed. Alejandro Lanoël-d'Aussenac. Rpt. Madrid: Cátedra 1997.

– *Hombres de maíz*. 1949. Rpt. Madrid: Alianza Editorial 1972.

– *Mulata de tal*. 1963. Buenos Aires: Editorial Losada.

– *Paris 1924–1933: Periodismo y creación literaria*. 1988. Ed. Amos Segala. Nanterre: Centre de Recherches Latinoaméricaines.

– 1997. *The President*. Trans. Frances Partridge. Long Grove, IL: Waveland Press.

Babb, Florence E. 2001. *After Revolution: Mapping Gender and Cultural Politics in Neoliberal Nicaragua*. Austin: University of Texas Press.

– 2004. "Out in Public: Gay and Lesbian Activism in Nicaragua." *NACLA Report on the Americas*, vol. 37, no. 6 (May/June): 27–30.

Bailey, Steve. 2012. "In Lush Nicaragua, the Legacy of a Priest." *New York Times*. 2 March. www.nytimes.com (accessed 4 March 2012).

Baracco, Luciano, ed. 2007. *National Integration and Contested Autonomy: The Caribbean Coast of Nicaragua*. New York: Algora Publishing.

Barbas-Rhoden, Laura. 2003. *Writing Women in Central America: Gender and the Fictionalization of History*. Athens: Ohio University Research in International Studies, Latin American Series No. 41, Ohio University Press.

Barthes, Roland. 1970. *S/Z*. Paris: Éditions du Seuil.

Baudrillard, Jean. 1991. *La guerre du golfe n'a pas eu lieu*. Paris: Éditions Galilée.

– 1995. *The Gulf War Did Not Take Place*. Trans. Paul Patton. Bloomington: Indiana University Press.

Bayard de Volo, Lorraine. 2001. *Mothers of Heroes and Martyrs: Gender Identity Politics in Nicaragua, 1979–1999*. Baltimore: Johns Hopkins University Press.

Beecham, Carolyn. 1992. "Petition on Nicaraguan Sodomy Law." *Green Left Weekly* 72 (23 September). www.greenleft.org.au (accessed 12 June 2013).

Belli, Gioconda. 1978. *Línea de fuego*. La Habana: Ediciones Casa de las Américas.

– 1988. *La mujer habitada*. Rpt. Buenos Aires: Seix Barral 2006.

– 1994. *The Inhabited Woman*. Trans. Kathleen N. March. Willimantic, CT: Curbstone Press.

– 1996. *Waslala: memorial del futuro*. Rpt. Barcelona: Seix Barral 2006.

– 2001. *El país bajo mi piel. Memorias de amor y guerra*. Barcelona: Plaza y Janés.

– 2002. *The Country under My Skin: A Memoir of Love and War.* Trans. Kristina Cordero with the author. New York: Alfred A. Knopf.

Benjamin, Walter. *The Arcades Project*. 1999. Trans. Howard Eiland and Kevin McLaughlin. Cambridge, MA, and London: Belknap Press of Harvard University Press.

Beverley, John. 1993. *Against Literature*. Minneapolis and London: University of Minnesota Press.

– 1999. *Subalternity and Representation: Arguments in Cultural Theory*. Durham, NC, and London: Duke University Press.

Beverley, John, and Marc Zimmerman. 1990. *Literature and Politics in the Central American Revolutions*. Austin: University of Texas Press.

Bhabha, Homi K. 1990a. "DissemiNation: Time, Narrative and the Margins of the Modern Nation." In Bhabha, ed., *Nation and Narration*. London and New York: Routledge. 291–322.

– ed. 1990b. *Nation and Narration*. London and New York: Routledge.

La Biblia. Latinoamérica. 1972. Madrid/Navarra: San Pablo/Editorial Verbo Divino.

Blachman, Morris J., William M. LeoGrande, and Kenneth Sharpe, eds. 1986. *Confronting Revolution: Security through Diplomacy in Central America*. New York: Pantheon.

Black, George. 1983. "The 1972 Earthquake and After: Somocismo in Crisis." In Peter Rosset and John Vandermeer, eds. *The Nicaragua Reader: Documents of a Revolution under Fire*. New York: Grove Press. 147–51.

Bloom, Harold. 1973. *The Anxiety of Influence: A Theory of Poetry.* New York: Oxford University Press.

Bolaño, Roberto. 2004. *Entre paréntesis. Ensayos, artículos y discursos (1998–2003)*. Edición de Ignacio Echevarría. Barcelona: Editorial Anagrama.

– 2010. *Los perros románticos. Poemas 1980–1998*. Presentación de Pere Gimferrer. Barcelona: Acantilado.

Booth, John A. 1982. *The End and the Beginning: The Nicaraguan Revolution*. Boulder, CO: Westview Press.

Borge, Tomás. 1982. *Carlos, el amanecer ya no es una tentación*. Managua: Editorial Nueva Nicaragua.

– 1984. *Carlos, the Dawn Is No Longer beyond Our Reach: The Prison Journals of Tomás Borge Remembering Carlos Fonseca, Founder of the FSLN*. Trans. Margaret Randall. Vancouver: New Star Books.

– 1989. *La paciente impaciencia*. La Habana: Casa de las Américas.

– 1992. *The Patient Impatience: From Boyhood to Guerrilla: A Personal Narrative of Nicaragua's Struggle for Liberation*. Trans. Russell Bartley, Darwin Flakoll, and Sylvia Yoneda. Willimantic, CT: Curbstone Press.

Borges, Jorge Luis. 1980. *Prosa completa. Volumen 2*. Barcelona: Bruguera.

Borgeson, Jr., Paul W. 1984. *Hacia el hombre nuevo: poesía y pensamiento de Ernesto Cardenal*. London: Tamesis Books.

– 1994. "Nueva poesía de Ernesto Cardenal. *Poemas indios* y *Cántico cósmico*." In Jorge Román-Lagunas, ed., *La literatura centroamericana. Visiones y revisiones*. Lewiston, NY: Edwin Mellen. 251–64.

Bourdieu, Pierre, and Jean-Claude Passeron. 1990. *Reproduction in Education, Society and Culture*. Trans. Richard Nice. London, Newbury Park, CA, and New Delhi: Sage Publications.

Brand, Dionne. 1983. *Winter Epigrams & Epigrams to Ernesto Cardenal in Defense of Claudia*. Toronto: Williams-Wallace.

Brotherston, Gordon. 1975. *Latin American Poetry: Origins and Presence*. Cambridge: Cambridge University Press.

– 1992. *Book of the Fourth World: Reading the Native Americas through Their Literature*. Cambridge: Cambridge University Press.

Burgos-Debray, Elisabeth, ed. 1982. *Me llamo Rigoberta Menchú y así me nació la conciencia*. Rpt. México: Siglo Veintiuno 2007.

Burns, E. Bradford, and Julie A. Charlip. 2002. *Latin America. A Concise Interpretative History*. 7th ed. Upper Saddle River, NJ: Prentice Hall.

Cabezas, Omar. 1982. *La montaña es algo más que una inmensa estepa verde*. Managua: Editorial Nueva Nicaragua.

– 1985. *Fire from the Mountain: The Making of a Sandinista*. Trans. Kathleen Weaver. Foreword by Carlos Fuentes. Afterword by Walter LaFeber. New York: Crown Publishers.

– 1988. *Canción de amor para los hombres*. Managua: Editorial Nueva Nicaragua.

Cabrera, Enriqueta. 2006. "Sergio Ramírez: Between Reality and Fiction." *Américas*, vol. 58, no. 5 (September/October): 11–15.

Campanella, Hortensia. 2004. "Entrevista con Sergio Ramírez." *Cuadernos Hispanoamericanos*, no. 648 (June): 45–52.

Capote, Truman. 1966. *In Cold Blood*. New York: Random House.

Cardenal, Fernando. 1984. Unpublished interview with the author. Managua. 11 March.

– 2009. *Junto a mi pueblo, con su revolución. Memorias*. Prólogo de Sergio Ramírez. Madrid: Editorial Trotta.

Carpentier, Alejo. 1974. *El recurso del método*. Rpt. México: Siglo Veintiuno 1988.

Castañeda, Jorge G. 1993. *Utopia Unarmed: The Latin American Left after the Cold War.* New York: Alfred A. Knopf.

Castells, Manuel. 1996. *The Rise of Network Society*. Malden, UK: Blackwell Publishing.

Castro Ruz, Fidel. 2004. *La historia me absolverá*. La Habana: Editorial de Ciencias Sociales.

– "Lula (Part 1)." 2008. *Reflections of Fidel* [Blog]. 23 January. www.monthlyreview.org (accessed 2 May 2012).

Castro Jo, Gustavo Adolfo. 2011. "Preface." In Luciano Baracco, ed., *National Integration and Contested Autonomy: The Caribbean Coast of Nicaragua*. New York: Algora Publishing. 1–2.

Chaucer, Geoffrey. 1963. *Chaucer's Major Poetry*. Ed. Albert C. Baugh. Englewood Cliff, NJ: Prentice-Hall.

Chávez Alfaro, Lizandro. 1969. *Trágame tierra*. México: Editorial Diógenes.

Cherem, Silvia. 2004a. "Presentacón." In Sergio Ramírez, *El viejo arte de mentir*. México, D.F.: Instituto Tecnológico y de Estudios Superiores de Monterrey/ Fondo de Cultura Económica. 11–18.

– 2004b. *Una vida por la palabra. Entrevista con Sergio Ramírez*. México: Fondo de Cultura Económica.

Christian, Shirley. 1985. *Nicaragua. Revolution in the Family*. New York: Random House.

Close, David. 1999. *Nicaragua: The Chamorro Years*. Boulder, CO, and London: Lynne Rienner Publishers.

Close, David, Salvador Martí i Puig, and Shelley A. McConnell. 2012. *The Sandinistas and Nicaragua since 1979*. Boulder, CO, and London: Lynne Rienner Publishers.

Coe, Michael D. 1999a. *Breaking the Maya Code*. Rev. ed. New York: Thames and Hudson.

– 1999b. *The Maya*. 6th ed. New York: Thames and Hudson.

Coello Gutiérrez, Emilian. 2010. "*El cielo llora por mí* (2008) de Sergio Ramírez: una simbiosis de géneros policiales." *Istmo: Revista Virtual de Estudios Literarios y Culturales Centroamericanos*, no. 20 (January-June): 1–19.

Cohen, Henry. 1991. "*Tiempo de fulgor*, Sergio Ramírez's 'historia privada' of León." *Revista Hispánica de Cultura y Literatura*, vol. 6, no. 2 (spring): 45–59.

Colby, Jason M. 2011. *The Business of Empire: United Fruit, Race and US Expansion in Central America*. Ithaca, NY, and London: Cornell University Press.

Córdoba, Matilde. 2009. "'Es un museo a lo Kim Il Sung,' dice Luis Carrión." *El Nuevo Diario*, 9 October. www.impreso.elnuevodiario.com.ni (accessed 18 December 2011).

Cornejo Polar, Antonio. 1994. *Escribir en el aire. Ensayo sobre la heterogeneidad socio-cultural en las literaturas andinas*. Lima: Editorial Horizonte.

Cortázar, Julio. 1959. *Las armas secretas*. Rpt. Buenos Aires: Editorial Sudamericana 1974.

– 1962. *Historias de cronopios y famas*. Buenos Aires: Editorial Sudamericana.

– 1977. *Alguien que anda por ahí*. Rpt. Barcelona: Editorial Bruguera 1981.

– 1980. *A Change of Light and Other Stories*. Trans. Gregory Rabassa. New York: Alfred A. Knopf.

– 1984. *Nicaragua tan violentemente dulce*. Barcelona: Muchnik Editores.

– 1989. *Nicaraguan Sketches*. Trans. Kathleen Weaver. New York. London: W.W. Norton.

– 2009. *Papeles inesperados*. Ed. Aurora Bernárdez and Carlos Álvarez Garriga. Madrid: Alfaguara.

Craft, Linda J. 1997. *Novels of Testimony and Resistance from Central America*. Gainesville, FL: University of Florida Press.

Craven, David. 2002. *Art and Revolution in Latin America. 1910–1990*. New Haven, CT, and London: Yale University Press.

Cruz, Jr., Arturo J. 2002. *Nicaragua's Conservative Republic, 1853–93*. Houndmills, UK, and New York: Palgrave Macmillan.

Darío, Rubén. 1905. *Cantos de vida y esperanza*. Ed. Antonio Oliver Belmas. Rpt. Salamanca: Ediciones Anaya 1968.

– 2004. *Songs of Life and Hope/Cantos de Vida y Esperanza: A Bilingual Edition*. Trans. Will Derusha. Durham, NC: Duke University Press.

Dawes, Greg. 1993. *Aesthetics and Revolution: Nicaraguan Poetry, 1979–1990*. Minneapolis and London: University of Minnesota Press.

Debray, Régis. 1996. *Loués soient nos seigneurs. Une éducation politique*. Paris: Gallimard.

Defoe, Daniel. 1722. *Journal of the Plague Year*. Rpt. New York: Oxford University Press 2010.

De la Selva, Salomón. 1985. *La guerra de Sandino, o el pueblo desnudo*. Managua: Editorial Nueva Nicaragua 1985.

Dickens, Charles. 1859. *A Tale of Two Cities*. Rpt. London: Oxford University Press 1962.

Donnelly, Thomas, Margaret Roth, and Caleb Baker. 1991. *Operation Just Cause: The Storming of Panama*. New York: Lexington Books.

Donoso, José. 1970. *El obsceno pájaro de la noche*. Rpt. Barcelona: Argos Vergara 1979.

Dore, Elizabeth. 2006. *Myths of Modernity: Peonage and Patriarchy in Nicaragua*. Durham, NC, and London: Duke University Press.

"Downfall of a Dictator: Somoza Resigns, and a Rebel Regime Takes Control." 1979. *Time*. 30 July. 34–36.

Dreiser, Theodore. 1925. *An American Tragedy*. Rpt. Cleveland: World Publishing 1962.

Duncan, W. Raymond. 1981. "Problems of Cuban Foreign Policy." In Irving Louis Horowitz, ed., *Cuban Communism*, 4th ed. New Brunswick, NJ, and London, UK: Transaction Books. 429–57.

Dunkerley, James. 1988. *Power in the Isthmus: A Political History of Modern Central America*. London and New York: Verso.

Eagleton, Terry. 1976. *Marxism and Literary Criticism*. Berkeley and Los Angeles: University of California Press.

Eliot, T.S. 1922. *The Waste Land*. Rpt. and ed. Michael North. New York: W.W. Norton and Company 2001.

Eltringham, Peter, et al. 2004. *The Rough Guide to Central America*. 3rd ed. New York, London, and Delhi: Rough Guides.

Espinosa, Mario Fulvio. 2005. "Oliverio Castañeda y otros más en los recuerdos del 'Capi' Prío." *La Prensa*. 16 October. www.laprensa.com.ni (accessed 17 April 2012).

Fanon, Frantz. 1952. *Peau noire, masques blancs*. Rpt. Paris: Éditions du Seuil 1995.

– 1961. *Les damnés de la terre*. Rpt. Paris: Éditions Gallimard 1991.

– 1968. *The Wretched of the Earth*. Preface by Jean-Paul Sartre. Trans. Constance Farrington. New York: Grove Press.

Faulkner, William. 1929. *The Sound and the Fury*. Rpt. New York: Vintage Books 1954.

– 1930. *As I Lay Dying*. Rpt. New York: Modern Library 1967.

– 1936. *Absalom, Absalom!* Rpt. New York: Vintage Books 1972.

– 1939. *The Wild Palms*. Rpt. New York: Vintage International 1995.

Ferlinghetti, Lawrence. 1984. *Seven Days in Nicaragua Libre*. San Francisco, CA: City Lights Books.

Fiallos Gil, Mariano. 1961. *Los estados y la emancipación hispanoamericana*. León: Editorial Hospicio.

Floyd, Troy S. 1967. *The Anglo-Spanish Struggle for Mosquitia*. Albuquerque: University of New Mexico Press.

Fonseca Amador, Carlos. 1982. *Obras. Tomo 1. Bajo la bandera del sandinismo*. Managua: Editorial Nueva Nicaragua.

– 1984. *Augusto César Sandino: Ideario político*. Managua: Instituto Nicaragüense de Energía.

Fox, Arturo A. 2007. *Latinoamérica. Presente y pasado*. 3rd ed. Upper Saddle River, NJ: Pearson/Prentice Hall.

Franco, Jean. 2002. *The Decline and Fall of the Lettered City: Latin America in the Cold War.* Cambridge, MA, and London: Harvard University Press.

Frank, Andre Gunder. 1969. *Capitalism and Underdevelopment in Latin America: Historical Studies of Chile and Brazil.* New York and London: Monthly Review Press.

Fremantle, Anne, ed. 1977. *Latin-American Literature Today*. New York: Mentor/New American Library.

Fuentes, Carlos. 1962. *Aura*. México: Ediciones Er.

– 1967. *Cambio de piel*. México: Joaquín Moritz.

– 1977. "Central and Eccentric Writing." In Anne Fremantle, ed., *Latin-American Literature Today*. New York: Mentor/New American Library. 130–45.

– 1988. *Myself with Others: Selected Essays*. Rpt. London: Picador 1989.

– 1992. *The Buried Mirror: Reflections on Spain and the New World*. New York: Houghton Mifflin.

– 2004. "Prólogo." In Silvia Cherem, *Una vida por la palabra*. México: Fondo de Cultural Económica. 11–17.

Fukuyama, Francis. 1992. *The End of History and the Last Man*. New York: Free Press.

Galeano, Eduardo. 1971. *Las venas abiertas de América Latina*. Rpt. México: Siglo Veintiuno Editores 1980.

– 1982, 1984, 1986. *Memoria del fuego*. 3 vols. México: Siglo Veintiuno.

Gamper, Daniel. 2005. "La revolución perdida. Memorias 3." *Guaraguao*, vol. 9, no. 21: 251–4.

García Canclini, Néstor. 2002. *Latinoamericanos buscando lugar en este siglo*. Buenos Aires, Barcelona, and México: Paidós.

García-Antezana, Jorge. 1995. "Del mito a la revolución en *Homenaje a los indios americanos* de Ernesto Cardenal." *Alba de América: Revista Literaria*, vols. 24–25, no. 13. 387–400.

García Márquez, Gabriel. 1967. *Cien años de soledad*. Ed. Jacques Joset. Rpt. Madrid: Cátedra 1994.

– 1975. *El otoño del patriarca*. Buenos Aires: Editorial Sudamericano.

– 1981. *Crónica de una muerte anunciada*. Bogotá: Editorial La Oveja Negra.

– 1985. *El amor en los tiempos del cólera*. Bogotá: Editorial La Oveja Negra.

– 1996. *Noticia de un secuestro*. Barcelona: Mondadori.

Gardel, Carlos. n.d. "Adios muchachos." www.musica.com (acccessed 10 August 2012).

Gilbert, Dennis. 1988. *Sandinistas: The Party and the Revolution*. New York and Oxford: Basil Blackwell.

Gobat, Michel. 2005. *Confronting the American Dream: Nicaragua under US Imperial Rule*. Durham, NC, and London: Duke University Press.

Gómez, Gerardo. 2006. "El otro 11 de septiembre." *La Opinión* (Los Angeles). 13 September. 11A.

Gómez de Avellaneda, Gertrudis. 1844. *Sab*. Rpt. (ed. José Servera) Madrid: Cátedra 1997.

González, Marta Leonor. 2012a. "La Misa campesina 30 años después." *La Prensa*. 25 January. www.laprensa.com (accessed 28 January 2012).

– 2012b. "Tendrá premio con su nombre." *La Prensa*. 24 January. www.laprensa.com.ni (accessed 25 January 2012).

González, Miguel. 2011. "El Gigante que Despierta (The Awakening Giant): Parties and Elections in the Life of the Autonomous Regional Councils." In Luciano Baracco, ed., *National Integration and Contested Autonomy: The Caribbean Coast of Nicaragua*. New York: Algora Publishing. 147–90.

González, Miguel. 2012. "Ortega da plantón a la cumbre de Cádiz por un premio de poesía a Cardenal." *El País*. 16 November. www.internacional.elpais.com (accessed 19 November 2012).

Gonzalez, Mike, and David Treece. 1992. *The Gathering of Voices: The Twentieth-Century Poetry of Latin America*. London and New York: Verso.

González, Otto-Raúl. 1999. *Miguel Ángel Asturias el gran lengua. La voz más clara de Guatemala*. Guatemala: Ministerio de Cultura y Deportes, Editorial Cultura.

González-Balado, José Luis. 1978. *Ernesto Cardenal. Poeta Revolucionario Monje*. Salamanca: Ediciones Sígueme.

Gould, Jeffrey L. 1998. *To Die in This Way: Nicaraguan Indians and the Myth of Mestizaje, 1880–1965*. Durham, NC, and London: Duke University Press.

Goytisolo, Juan. 1985. *Coto vedado*. Barcelona: Seix Barral.

– 1989. *Forbidden Territory*. Trans. Peter Bush. San Francisco, CA: North Point Press.

Grandin, Greg. 2000. *The Blood of Guatemala: A History of Race and Nation*. Durham, NC, and London: Duke University Press.

Greene, Graham. 1940. *The Power and the Glory*. Rpt. London: Heinemann 1960.

– 1984. *Getting to Know the General: The Story of an Involvement*. London: Bodley Head.

Gudmundson, Lowell, and Justin Wolfe, eds. 2010. *Blacks and Blackness in Central America: Between Race and Place*. Durham, NC, and London: Duke University Press.

Guedea, Virginia. 2000. "The Old Colonialism Ends, the New Colonialism Begins." In Michael C. Meyer and William H. Beezley, eds., *The Oxford History of Mexico*. Oxford and New York: Oxford University Press. 277–99.

Güemes, César. 2003. "Ernesto Cardenal termina sus memorias y vuelve a la poesía." *La Jornada*. 29 October. www.rebelion.org (accessed 5 April 2005).

Guillermoprieto, Alma. 1994. *The Heart That Bleeds: Latin America Now.* New York: Random House.

"Half-Step to Democracy: Nicaragua's Loaded Election Is Not Necessarily a False Start." 1984. *The Economist.* 10 November. 13.

Hemingway, Ernest. 1963. *Death in the Afternoon.* New York: Charles Scribner's and Sons.

Henighan, Stephen. 1999a. *Assuming the Light: The Parisian Literary Apprenticeship of Miguel Ángel Asturias.* Oxford: Legenda.

– 1999b. "Two Paths to the Boom: Carpentier, Asturias and the Performative Split." *Modern Language Review*, vol. 94, no. 4 (October): 1009–24.

– 2002. *When Words Deny the World: The Reshaping of Canadian Writing.* Erin, ON: Porcupine's Quill.

– 2004. "No History to Absolve Them: Spanish-American Revolutionary Discourse after 1990." *Bulletin of Hispanic Studies*, vol. 81, no. 4 (October): 511–20.

– 2007. "Verse and Versatility: Central America's Poets Confront the Era of Globalization." *The Walrus*, vol. 4, no. 5 (June): 42–5.

– 2008. *A Report on the Afterlife of Culture.* Emeryville, ON: Biblioasis.

Hobsbawm, E.J. 1994. *Age of Extremes: The Short Twentieth Century, 1914–1991.* London: Michael Joseph.

Hodges, Donald. 1986. *Intellectual Foundations of the Nicaraguan Revolution.* Austin: University of Texas Press.

Holy Bible. 1911. Toronto: Copp Clark.

Horowitz, Irving Louis, ed. 1998. *Cuban Communism*, 4th ed. New Brunswick, NJ, and London: Transaction Books.

Hoyt, Katherine. 1997. *The Many Faces of Sandinista Democracy.* Athens: Ohio University Center for International Studies, Latin American Series No. 27, Ohio University Press.

Huntington, Samuel P. 1968. *Political Order in Changing Societies.* New Haven, CT, and London: Yale University Press.

Hylton, Forrest. 2006. *Evil Hour in Colombia.* London and New York: Verso.

Jones, Adam. 2002. *Beyond the Barricades: Nicaragua and the Struggle for the Sandinista Press, 1979–1998.* Athens: Ohio University Center for International Studies, Latin American Series No. 37, Ohio University Press.

Kampwirth, Karen. 2004. *Feminism and the Legacy of Revolution: Nicaragua, El Salvador, Chiapas.* Athens: Ohio University Research in Latin American Studies, Latin American Series No. 43, Ohio University Press.

– 2011. *Latin America's New Left and the Politics of Gender: Lessons from Nicaragua* New York: Springer Briefs in Political Science/Springer.

Kinzer, Stephen. 1988. "Leon Journal: A Tale of Lust and Death, Undimmed by 50 Years." *New York Times*. 16 September. www.nytimes.com (accessed 21 January 2012).

– 1991. *Blood of Brothers: Life and War in Nicaragua*. New York: G.P. Putnam's Sons.

– 2008. "Ortega's Last Straw in Nicaragua." *New York Times*. 3 September. www.nytimes.com (accessed 21 January 2012).

Kozak Rovero, Gisela. 2001. "*Castigo divino*, de Sergio Ramírez: novela polícial, folletinesca, satírica y autorreflexiva." *Iberoamericana: América Latina – España – Portugal*, vol. 1, no. 2 (June): 27–41.

Kristeva, Julia. 1978. *Sémeiotiké: Recherches pour une sémanalyse*. Paris: Éditions du Seuil.

LaFeber, Walter. 1980. *America, Russia and the Cold War: 1945–1980*. 4th ed. New York: John Wiley and Sons.

– 1983. *Inevitable Revolutions: The United States in Central America*. Rpt. New York: W.W. Norton 1984.

Lancaster, Roger N. 1992. *Life Is Hard: Machismo, Danger and the Intimacy of Power in Nicaragua*. Berkeley, Los Angeles, and Oxford: University of California Press.

Larsen, Neil. 2001. *Determinations: Essays on Theory, Narrative and Nation in the Americas*. London and New York: Verso.

Las Casas, Bartolomé de. 1974. *The Devastation of the Indies: A Brief Account*. Trans. Herma Briffault. Introduction by Hans Magnus Enzensberger. New York: Seabury Press.

– 1994. *Brevísima relación de la destrucción de las Indias*. Ed. José María Reyes Cano. Barcelona: Editorial Planeta.

Lee, Jongsoo. 2008. *The Allure of Nezahualcoyotl: Pre-Hispanic History, Religion and Nahua Poetics*. Albuquerque: University of New Mexico Press.

LeoGrande, William M. 1998. *Our Own Backyard: The United States in Central America, 1977–1992*. Chapel Hill, NC, and London: University of North Carolina Press.

Lernoux, Penny. 1980. *Cry of the People: United States Involvement in the Rise of Fascism, Torture, and Murder and the Persecution of the Catholic Church in Latin America*. Garden City, NY: Doubleday and Company.

Letson, D.R. 1990. "Foundations for Renewal: An Analysis of the Shared Reflections of Thomas Merton and Ernesto Cardenal." *The Merton Annual: Studies in Culture, Sprituality and Social Concern*, vol. 3: 93–106.

López-Baralt, Luce. 2012. *El cántico místico de Ernesto Cardenal*. Madrid: Editorial Trotta.

Lyotard, Jean-François. 1979. *La condition postmoderne: rapport sur le savoir.* Paris: Les Éditions de Minuit.

– 1984. *The Postmodern Condition: A Report on Knowledge.* Trans. Geoff Bennington and Brian Massumi. Foreword by Fredric Jameson. Minneapolis: University of Minnesota Press.

Macaulay, Neill. 1967. *The Sandino Affair.* Chicago: Quadrangle Books.

Martí, José. 1954. *The America of José Martí: Selected Writings of José Martí.* Trans. Juan de Onís. Introduction by Federico de Onís. New York: Funk and Wagnalls.

– 2004. *Ensayos y crónicas.* Ed. José Olivio Jiménez. Madrid: Cátedra.

Martin, Gerald. 1989. *Journeys through the Labyrinth: Latin American Fiction in the Twentieth Century.* London and New York: Verso.

– 2008. *Gabriel García Márquez. A Life.* London: Penguin.

Martí i Puig, Salvador. 2102. "The FSLN and Sandinismo." In David Close, Salvador Martí i Puig, and Shelley A. McConnell, *The Sandinistas and Nicaragua since 1979.* Boulder, CO, and London: Lynne Rienner Publishers. 21–44.

Matthews, Herbert. 1975. *Revolution in Cuba: An Essay in Understanding.* New York: Charles Scribner's Sons.

McConnell, Shelley A. 2012. "The Uncertain Evolution of the Electoral System." In David Close, Salvador Martí i Puig, and Shelley A. McConnell, *The Sandinistas and Nicaragua since 1979.* Boulder, CO, and London: Lynne Rienner Publishers. 121–59.

McFarlane, Peter. 1989. *Northern Shadows: Canadians and Central America.* Toronto: Between the Lines.

McGehee, Richard V. 1996. "Sergio Ramírez's 'Juego Perfecto' and 'Tarde de Sol.'" *Aethlon: The Journal of Sport Literature*, vol. 13, no. 2 (spring): 121–3.

McMurray, George R. 1990. "Sergio Ramírez's *Castigo Divino* as Documentary Novel." *Confluencia*, vol. 5, no. 2: 155–9.

Medina, Fabián. 2013. "Mi verdad está intacta." *La Prensa*, 12 May. www.laprensa.com.ni (accessed 10 June 2013).

Mejía Godoy, Carlos. n.d. "Himno de la unidad sandinista." www.revolucionentv.wordpress.com.

Mendoza, Plinio Apuleyo. 1982. *Gabriel García Márquez. El olor de la guayaba.* Barcelona: Editorial Bruguera.

– 1983. *The Fragrance of Guava.* Trans. Ann Wright. London: Verso.

Merton, Thomas. 1981. *The Literary Essays of Thomas Merton.* Ed. Patrick Hart. New York: New Directions.

– 1995. "Foreword." In Ernesto Cardenal, *Abide in Love.* Trans. Dinah Livingstone. Maryknoll, NY: Orbis Books. vii–xxv.

Meyer, Michael C., and William H. Beezley, eds. 2000. *The Oxford History of Mexico.* Oxford and New York: Oxford University Press.

Mignolo, Walter D. 2000. *Local Histories/Global Designs: Coloniality, Subaltern Knowledges and Border Thinking*. Princeton, NJ: Princeton University Press.

– 2005. *The Idea of Latin America*. Oxford: Blackwell Publishing.

Mill, J.S. 1972. *Utilitarianism, On Liberty and Considerations on Representative Government*. Ed. H.R. Acton. London: J.M. Dent and Sons.

Miranda, Roger, and William Ratliff. 1993. *The Civil War in Nicaragua*. New Brunswick, NJ, and London: Transaction Publishers.

Molloy, Sylvia. 1991. *At Face Value: Autobiographical Writing in Spanish America*. Cambridge: Cambridge University Press.

Monterroso, Augusto. 1959. *Obras completas (y otros cuentos)*. Rpt. México: Ediciones Era 1990.

– 1995. *Complete Works & Other Stories*. Trans. Edith Grossman. Introduction Will H. Corral. Austin: University of Texas.

Moore-Gilbert, Bart. 1997. *Postcolonial Theory. Contexts, Practices, Politics*. London and New York: Verso.

Morales, Miguel. 2012. "Ernesto Cardenal, consagrado." *El País*. 15 November. www.cultura.elpais.com (accessed 19 November 2012).

Moreno, Dario. 1994. *The Struggle for Peace in Central America*. Gainesville, FL: University Press of Florida.

Moro, Diana. 2008. "Mito, historia y autofiguración en *Margarita, está linda la mar* de Sergio Ramírez." *Canadian Journal of Latin American & Caribbean Studies*, vol. 33, no. 68: 65–88.

Morris, Kenneth E. 2010. *Unfinished Revolution: Daniel Ortega and Nicaragua's Struggle for Liberation*. Chicago: Lawrence Hill Books.

Morrow, John Andrew. 2010. *Amerindian Elements in the Poetry of Ernesto Cardenal: Mythic Foundations of the Colloquial Narrative*. Lewiston, NY, Queenston, ON, and Lampeter, UK: Edwin Mellen Press.

Murillo, Juan. 2011. "Lo que le debemos a Yolanda." *La Nación* (San José). 22 November. www.nacion.com (accessed 22 November 2012).

Neruda, Pablo. 1950. *Canto general*. Edición de Enrico Mario Santí. Rpt. Madrid: Cátedra 1998.

– 1957. *Antología*. Santiago, Chile: Nascimento.

– 1971a. *Nuevas odas elementales*. Buenos Aires: Editorial Losada.

– 1971b. *Odas elementales*. Buenos Aires: Editorial Losada.

– 1972. *Tercer libro de las odas*. Buenos Aires: Editorial Losada.

– 1991. *Canto General*. Trans. Jack Schmitt. Berkeley, Los Angeles, and Oxford: University of California Press 1991.

– 2004. *Twenty Love Poems and a Song of Despair*. Trans. W.S. Merwin. New York. London: Penguin.

Newmark, Maxim. 1956. *Dictionary of Spanish Literature*. Totowa, NJ: Littlefield, Adams and Company.

"Nicaragua: More FSLN Resignations." 1995. *Weekly News Update of the Americas*. Issue # 260 (22 January). www.tulane.edu (accessed 31 July 2012).

O'Brien, Conor Cruise. 1988. *Passion and Cunning and Other Essays*. London: Weidenfield and Nicholson.

Otis, John. 1992. "Novel, TV – and Court – Relive Nicaraguan Scandal." *Washington Times*. 7 November. www.bloom-picayune.mit.edu (accessed 16 April 2012).

Pallier, Claire. 1988. *Études de poésie contemporaine d'Amérique centrale*. Toulouse, France: Presses Universitaires du Mirail.

Pavón, Alfredo. 1977. "Charles Atlas y la enajenación de la sociedad nicaragüense." *La palabra y el hombre*, no. 21 (February-March): 84–6.

Payeras, Mario. 1980. *Los días de la selva. Relatos sobre la implantación de las guerrillas populares en el norte del Quiché, 1972–1976*. La Habana: Casa de las Américas.

"Payment Deferred." n.d. Internet Movie Database. www.imdb.com (accessed 20 April 2012).

Payne, Anthony, Paul Sutton, and Tony Thorndike. 1984. *Grenada: Revolution and Invasion*. New York: St Martin's Press.

Paz, Octavio. *El laberinto de la soledad*. 1950. Rpt. México, D.F.: Fondo de Cultura Económica 1972.

– 1961. *The Labyrinth of Solitude: Life and Thought in Mexico*. Trans. Lysander Kemp. New York: Grove Press.

Pérez Baltodano, Andrés. 2012. "Political Culture." In David Close, Salvador Martí i Puig, and Shelley A. McConnell, *The Sandinistas and Nicaragua since 1979*. Boulder, CO, and London: Lynne Rienner Publishers. 65–90.

Perri, Brad. 1999. "Disappearing Regions: Charles Atlas, the United States and Nicaraguan Identity." *Aethlon: The Journal of Sport Literature*, vol. 16, no. 2: 35–46.

Plato. 1979. *The Republic*. Trans. and ed. Raymond Larson. Arlington Heights, IL: AHM Publishing Corporation.

Plunkett, Hazel. 1999. *Nicaragua: A Guide to the People, Politics and Culture*. New York and London: Interlink Books/Latin American Bureau.

Poniatowska, Elena. 1969. *Hasta no verte, Jesus mío*. México: Ediciones Era.

– 1971. *La noche de Tlatelolco: testimonios de historia oral*. México: Ediciones Era.

Porter, Melinda Chamber. 1986. "An Interview with Octavio Paz." *Partisan Review*, vol. 53, nos. 1–2: 76–87.

Pound, Ezra. 1934. *The Literary Essays of Ezra Pound*. Norfolk, CT: New Directions.

– 1967. *Selected Cantos of Ezra Pound*. London: Faber and Faber.

Prebisch, Raúl. 1967. *Hacia una dinámica del desarrollo latinoamericano*. Montevideo: Ediciones de la Banda Oriental.

Pring-Mill, Robert. "Introduction." 1975. In Ernesto Cardenal, *Marilyn Monroe and Other Poems*. Trans. Robert Pring-Mill. London: Search Press. 7–32.

– 1992. "Cardenal's Treatment of Amerindian Cultures in *Homenaje a los indios americanos*." *Renaissance and Modern Studies*, vol. 35: 52–74.

Promis Ojeda, José. 1975. "Espíritu y Materia. Los "Salmos" de Ernesto Cardenal." In *Ernesto Cardenal, poeta de la liberación latinoamericana*. Buenos Aires: Fernando García Cambeiro. 15–38.

Proust, Marcel. *A la recherche du temps perdu*. 1927, Rpt. Paris: Éditions Gallimard 1954. 3 vols.

Quesada, Uriel. 2002. "La verdad, el poder y la ficción policíaca: el caso de *Castigo Divino* de Sergio Ramírez." *Mester*, vol. 31: 17–31.

Rama, Ángel. 1982. *La novela en América Latina: Panoramas 1920–1980*. Bogotá: Instituto Colombiano de Cultura.

Randall, Margaret. 1992. *Gathering Rage: The Failure of Twentieth Century Revolutions to Develop a Feminist Agenda*. New York: Monthly Review Press.

– 2009. *To Change the World: My Years in Cuba*. New Brunswick, NJ, and London: Rutgers University Press.

Rausse, Andrea. 1995. *Sergio Ramírez als Erzähler. Erzählstrukturen und gesellschaftlicher Kontext im narrativen Werk des nicaraguanischen Schriftstellers*. Hamburg, Germany: Lit Verlag.

Reed, Jean-Pierre. 2008. "Religious Dialogue in the Nicaraguan Revolution." *Politics and Religion*, vol. 1, no. 2: 270–99.

"El Reina Sofía de poesía para un agitador social y de la lectura." 2012. *El País*. 3 May. www.elpais.com (accessed 9 May 2012).

Richards, Tim. 1994. "Estrategia e ideología en *¿Te dio miedo la sangre?*" In Jorge Román-Lagunas, ed., *La literatura centroamericana. Visiones y revisiones*. Lewiston, NY: Edwin Mellen 1994. 193–201.

Ríos, María del Pilar. 2012. "No aspiro a ser un best seller, sino un long seller." *La Gaceta* (Tucumán, Argentina). 25 March. www.lagaceta.com.ar (accessed 25 March 2012.

Roa Bastos, Augusto. 1974. *Yo, el Supremo*. Buenos Aires: Siglo Veintiuno Argentina.

Robinson, William I. 2003. *Transnational Conflicts: Central America, Change and Globalization*. London and New York: Verso.

Rodríguez, Ileana. 1996. *Women, Guerrillas & Love: Understanding War in Central America*. Minneapolis and London: University of Minnesota Press.

Rodríguez Moya, Daniel. 2009. "Sergio Ramírez: 'Los sueños de revolución en Nicaragua fueron muy caros.'" *Cuadernos hispanoamericanos*, no. 703 (January): 117–27.

Rogers, Tim. 2008. "Why Nicaragua's Capital Is in Flames." *Time*. 14 November. www.time.com (accessed 18 December 2011).

– 2011. "Ramírez: Ortega Government 'Illegitimate but Strong.'" *Nicaragua Dispatch*. 13 December. www.nicaraguadispatch.com (accessed 13 December 2011).

Román-Lagunas, Jorge, ed. 1994. *La literatura centroamericana. Visiones y revisiones*. Lewiston, NY: Edwin Mellen.

Ross, Peter. 1991. "The Politician as Novelist: Sergio Ramírez's *Castigo Divino*." *Antípodas: Journal of Hispanic Studies of the University of Auckland and LaTrobe University*, vol. 3: 165–75.

Rosset, Peter, and John Vandermeer, eds. 1983. *The Nicaragua Reader: Documents of a Revolution under Fire*. New York: Grove Press.

Roth, Brad R. 1999. *Governmental Illegitimacy in International Law*. Oxford: Oxford University Press.

– 2011. *Sovereign Equality and Moral Disagreement: Premises of a Pluralist International Legal Order*. Oxford: Oxford University Press.

Rulfo, Juan. 1955. *Pedro Páramo*. Ed. José Carlos González Boixo. Rpt. Madrid: Cátedra.

Rushdie, Salman. 1987, rpt. 2000. *The Jaguar Smile: A Nicaraguan Journey, with a New Preface by the Author*. London: Vintage.

– 2012. *Joseph Anton: A Memoir*. London: Jonathan Cape.

Said, Edward W. 1978. *Orientalism*. New York: Random House.

Saldaña-Portillo, María Josefina. 2003. *The Revolutionary Imagination in the Americas and the Age of Development*. Durham, NC, and London: Duke University Press.

Schaefer, Claudia. 1987. "La recuperación del realismo: *¿Te dio miedo la sangre?* de Sergio Ramírez." *Texto Crítico*, vol. 13, nos. 36–37: 146–52.

Schlesinger, Stephen, and Stephen Kinzer. 1982. *Bitter Fruit: The Untold Story of the American Coup in Guatemala*. Garden City, NY: Doubleday and Company.

Schmidt, Blake. 2011. "Nicaragua's President Rules Airwaves to Control Image." *New York Times*. 28 November. www.nytimes.com (accessed 18 December 2011).

Schulz, Hermann. 1978. *Ein Land wie Pulver und Honig: Ernesto Cardenals Bruder, Verzweifelte u. Hoffende*. Gütersloh, Germany: Gütersloher Verlaghaus.

"Sergio Ramírez presenta novela inspirada en la autora Yolanda Oreamuno." 2011. *El Informador*, 1 June. www.informador.com.mx (accessed 19 November 2012).

Shaw, Donald L. "Sobre la técnica de Cardenal en 'Hora 0'." 1993. *La Torre: Revista de la Universidad de Puerto Rico*, vol. 26, no. 7 (April-June): 171–88.

Shaw, Donald W. 1994. *Antonio Skármeta and the Post-Boom*. Hanover, NH: Ediciones del Norte.

Skármeta, Antonio. 1982. *La insurreción*. Hanover, NH: Ediciones del Norte.

Sklodowska, Elzbieta. 1992. *Testimonio hispano-americano: historia, teoría, poética*. New York: Peter Lang.

Smith, Hazel. 1993. *Nicaragua: Self-determination and Survival*. London and Boulder, CO: Pluto Press.

Solis, Javier. n.d. "Sombras nada más." www.puroparty.com (accessed 14 August 2004).

Sommer, Doris. 1991. *Foundational Fictions: The National Romances of Latin America*. Berkeley: University of California Press.

Sorensen, Diana. 2007. *A Turbulent Decade Remembered: Scenes from the Latin American Sixties*. Stanford, CA: Stanford University Press.

Soyinka, Wole. n.d. Nobel Prize lectures. Literature laureates. www.nobelprize.org (accessed 4 November 2011).

Stein, Stanley J., and Barbara H. Stein. 1970. *The Colonial Heritage of Latin America: Essays on Economic Development in Comparative Perspective*. New York: Oxford University Press.

Stendhal. 1830. *Le Rouge et le Noir*. Paris: Garnier-Flammarion 1964.

Subcomandante Marcos. 1999. *Desde las montañas del sureste mexicano. (Cuentos, leyendas y otras posdatas del Sup Marcos)*. México: Plaza y Janés.

"A Surprising Safe Haven: How Central America's Poorest Country Became One of Its Safest." 2012. *The Economist*, 28 January. www.economist.com (accessed 31 May 2012).

"The Survivor: Buoyed by a Growing Economy and Venezuelan Cash, the Sandinista Leader Who Toppled a Dictator Is Set to Win an Unconstitutional Third Term." 2011. *The Economist*, 5 November. www.economist.com (accessed 18 December 2011).

Symons, Julian. 1974. *Bloody Murder: From the Detective Story to the Crime Novel: A History*. Harmondsworth, UK: Penguin.

Taracena Arriola, Arturo. 1988. "Miguel Ángel Asturias y la búsqueda del 'alma nacional' guatemalteca. Itinerario político, 1920–1933." In Miguel Ángel Asturias, *Paris 1924–1933: Periodismo y creación literaria*. Ed. Amos Segala. Nanterre: Centre de Recherches Latinoaméricaines. 679–708.

"Truman Doctrine. President Harry S. Truman's Address before a Joint Session of Congress, March 12, 1947." 1947. Lillian Goldman Law Library, Yale University. Avalon Project: Documents in Law, History and Diplomacy. www.avalon.law.yale.edu (accessed 7 April 2012).

Urbina, Nicasio. 2004a. "Las memorias y las autobiografías como bienes culturales de consumo." *Istmo: Revista Virtual de Estudios Literarios y Culturales Centroamericanos*, no. 8 (January-June). No pagination.

– 2004b. "Violencia y estructura en *Margarita, está linda la mar* de Sergio Ramírez." *Revista Iberoamericana*, nos. 206/207 (January-June): 359–69.

Valenzuela, Luisa. 1982 *Cambio de armas*. Hanover, NH: Ediciones del Norte.

– 1983. *Cola de lagartija*. Buenos Aires: Bruguera.

Vargas Llosa, Mario. 1962. *La ciudad y los perros*. Barcelona: Seix Barral.

– 1965. *La casa verde*. Barcelona: Seix Barral.

– 1969. *Conversación en La Catedral*. Rpt. Barcelona: Seix Barral 1981.

– 1971. *García Márquez: historia de un deicidio*. Barcelona: Seix Barral.

– 1977. *La tía Julia y el escribidor*. Barcelona: Seix Barral.

– 1983. *Contra viento y marea (1962–1982)*. Barcelona: Seix Barral.

– 1984. *Historia de Mayta*. Barcelona: Seix Barral.

– 1986. *The Real Life of Alejandro Mayta*. Trans. Alfred Mac Adam. New York: Farrar Straus and Giroux.

– 1987. *El hablador*. Barcelona: Seix Barral.

– 1990a. *La verdad de las mentiras: ensayos sobre literatura*. Barcelona: Seix Barral.

– 1990b. *Contra viento y marea, III (1964–1988)*. Barcelona: Seix Barral.

– 2003. *El paraíso en la otra esquina*. Madrid: Alfaguara.

– 2006. *Las travesuras de la niña mala*. Madrid: Alfaguara.

Vasconcelos, José. 1925. *La raza cósmica: Misión de la raza iberoamericana*. Rpt. Madrid: Aguilar 1967.

Veiravé, Alfredo. 1975. "Ernesto Cardenal: El Exteriorismo, Poesía de un Nuevo Mundo." In Veiravé, ed., *Ernesto Cardenal, poeta de la liberación latinoamericana*. Buenos Aires: Fernando García Cambeiro. 61–106.

Vidal, Gore. 2004. *Imperial America: Reflections on the United States of Amnesia*. Forest Row, East Sussex, UK: Clairview Books.

Vilas, Carlos M. 1989. *State, Class & Ethnicity in Nicaragua: Capitalist Modernization and Revolutionary Change on the Atlantic Coast*. Boulder, CO, and London: Lynne Rienner Publishers.

– 1992. "Family Affairs: Class, Lineage and Politics in Contemporary Nicaragua." *Journal of Latin American Studies*, vol. 24 (May): 309–41.

– 1995. *Between Earthquakes and Volcanoes: Market, State and the Revolutions in Central America*. New York: Monthly Review Press.

Villaruel, Patricia. 2011. "Sergio Ramírez: '*La Fugitiva* es la historia de muchos en una sola.'" *El Universo*. 24 April. www.eluniverso.com (accessed 14 November 2012).

Wallace, Scott. 1986. "The Real Miskito Coast: The Sandinistas Win Some Hearts and Minds." *Newsweek*. 15 December: 50.

Wellinga, Klaas S. 1994. *Entre la poesía y la pared. Política cultural sandinista 1979–1990*. San José-Amsterdam: FLACSO/Thela Publishers.

Wheelock Román, Jaime. 1974. *Raíces indígenas de la lucha anticolonialista en Nicaragua: de Gil González a Joaquín Zavala (1523 a 1881)*. México, D.F., Madrid, and Buenos Aires: Siglo Veintiuno.

White, Steven F. 1993. *Modern Nicaraguan Poetry: Dialogues with France and the United States*. Lewisburg, PA: Bucknell University Press.

White, Steven F., and and Esthela Calderón. 2008. *Culture and Customs of Nicaragua*. Westport, CA, and London: Greenwood Press.

Williams, Adam. 2012. "US Says Irregularities Marred Nicaraguan Municipal Elections." *Bloomberg*. 5 November. www.bloomberg.com (accessed 12 November 2012).

Williams, Raymond Leslie. 2010. *A Companion to Gabriel García Márquez*. Woodbridge, UK: Tamesis.

Williams, Tamara R. 1995. "Introduction." In Ernesto Cardenal, *The Doubtful Strait/El estrecho dudoso*. Trans. John Lyons. Bloomington and Indianapolis, IN: Indiana University Press. vii–xxxiii.

Williamson, Edwin. 1992. *The Penguin History of Latin America*. Harmondsworth, UK: Penguin.

Wolfe, Justin. 2010. "The Cruel Whip: Race and Place in Nineteenth-Century Nicaragua." In Lowell Gudmundson and Justin Wolfe, eds., *Blacks and Blackness in Central America: Between Race and Place*. Durham, NC, and London: Duke University Press. 177–208.

Woodward, Jr, Ralph Lee. 1993. *Rafael Carrera and the Emergence of the Republic of Guatemala, 1821–1871*. Athens, GA, and London: University of Georgia Press.

Zamora, Lois Parkinson. 1997. *The Usable Past: The Imagination of History in Recent Fiction of the Americas*. Cambridge: Cambridge University Press.

Zimmermann, Matilde. 2000. *Sandinista: Carlos Fonseca and the Nicaraguan Revolution*. Durham, NC, and London: Duke University Press.

Films

Walker. 1987. Prod. Edward R. Pressman. Edward R. Pressman Productions/Incine.

A Place Called Chiapas. 1998. Prod. Nettie Wild. Zeitgeist Films.

XXV – 19. Revolución Sandinista. 2004. Prod. Juan Carlos Ample. Esta Semana.

Index

Abrams, Elliott, 303
Acosta, Luz Marina, 701n8
Adams, John, 70
Adams, John Quincy, 282
Agudelo, William, 213
Agüero, Carlos, 253, 696n3
Agüero, Fernando, contests fraudulent elections, 38, 39, 243, 253, 280, 335, 514
Aguilar Camín, Héctor, 546
Alberti, Rafael, 591
Alberto, Eliseo, 135
Alcocer, Rudyard, 700n21
Aldington, Richard, 690n3
Alegría, Claribel, 709n15
Alemán, Arnoldo, 134, 431, 434; corruption of, 432–3, 435–6; presidency as revival of Somocismo, 505, 516–19, 530–1, 533, 643, 650–1, 706n17
Alemán, Miguel, 161, 676
Alfaguara publishing company, 134–5, 138, 495
Algeria, 130
Allen, Charles, 303
Allende, Isabel, 241, 298
Allende, Salvador, overthrow and death of, 182–3, 281, 455–6; as president, 53, 601–2, 660, 694n18
Almodóvar, Pedro, 709n14
Altamirano, Pedro, murder, 243, 254; resistance to Somoza, 179
Alvarado, Pedro de, 97–9, 104–5; death, 106–7
Álvarez Montalván, Emilio, 508
Amador, Fausto, 37
Amaru, Tupac, 347
Anderson, Benedict, *Burgosozialismus*, 593–4, 597; theory of nationalism, 6–7, 168, 216–17, 224, 252, 278, 478–80, 612
Anderson, Jack, 128
Angola, 205, 261, 298, 636, 641, 709n7
Antigua, 91
Antigua Guatemala (Santiago de Guatemala), 10, 110, 677; foundation, 104–8
April Rebellion, 36, 49, 243, 250, 254, 523–4, 604; EC's involvement in, 76–8, 581
Aquino, Corazon, 235
Arafat, Yasser, 610

Arbenz, Jacobo, 36, 166, 245
Arce, Bayardo, 226, 386, 441; corruption of, 426, 434–5
Arévalo, Juan José, 158, 676
Argentina, 165, 214–15, 274–5, 297, 629; Falklands War, 279, 281; national bourgeoisie, 16, 184, 187, 451
Arguedas, Alcides, *Raza de bronce*, 700n2
Arguedas, José María, 340, 342; *Deep Rivers*, 343; prize named after, 135, 495
Argüello, Leonardo, 35
Argueta, Manlío, 501, *One Day of Life*, 529
Arias, Arturo, 313, 709n15; on Central American literature, 7, 66, 72, 98, 242, 251, 262, 495–6, 506, 561, 691n6, 694–5n21; on EC, 702n14; on SRM, 477–8, 494, 506, 538, 544–5, 554–5
Arias, Óscar, 234
Arias, Pilar, 264
Arias de Ávila, Pedro. *See* Dávila, Pedrarias
Aristide, Jean-Bertrand, 12
Aristophanes, 245; Rushdie's interpretation of, 251–2
Aristotle, 365, 478, 691n10
Armenia, 658
Armijo, Roberto, 284–5, 291–2
Ashanti, 636, 642
Assis, Machado de, 297
ASTC (Sandinista Cultural Workers' Association), 54–6, 267
Astorga, Nora, 692n3
Asturias, Miguel Ángel, 126, 495, 691n11; death of, 240; as Great Tongue, 305, 697–8n8; influence on SRM, 151, 182, 192, 278; *Leyendas de Guatemala*, 704–5n5; *Men of Maize*, 189, 274, 343, 483, 609; *Mulatta*, 556–7; *The President*, 151, 189, 287, 694n20; *Trilogía bananera*, 274
Auerbach, Eric, 478
Augustine, St, 365
Austria, 127
Autonomy Generation, 122, 139, 158–9
Aztec, 21, 350–6, 358, 592; as tyranny, 353, 681, 701n3

Babb, Florence, 518–19, 702–3n1, 705n7
Baciu, Stefan, 710n17
Bacon, Francis, 167
Baez, Joan, 380
Báez Bone, Adolfo, 36, 49, 76–9, 83
Bakhtiar, Shapur, 610
Balaguer, Joaquín, 297
Balboa, Vasco Núñez de, 97–9, 104, 110, 114; decapitation of, 100
Baltodano, Mónica, 692n3
Balzac, Honoré de, 306, 513
Barbas-Rhoden, Laura, 700n21
Barnet, Miguel, 132, 303, 305, 314, 331
Barricada, 231, 302, 430, 450, 473; closure of, 429
Barthes, Roland, 333, 545
Batista, Fulgencio, 203, 207
Baudrillard, Jean, 457, 499
Bayard de Volo, Lorraine, 560, 567, 650
Beethoven, Ludwig van, 89
Belgium, 294
Belize, 24, 436, 694n15
Belli, Gioconda, 3, 56, 125, 427, 467, 477, 569, 692n3, 710n18; *The*

Country under My Skin, 506–7, 575, 603, 689n1, 706n10; on 1990 election, 236–7, 517; feminism of, 494, 506, 617, 700n22; *The Inhabited Woman*, 296, 334–8, 401, 643, 689–90n1, 690n4; *Línea de fuego*, 699n20; resignation from FSLN, 429; *Waslala*, 616–17
Belli, Humberto, 427
Bello, Andrés, 16
Benedetti, Mario, 57, 135, 511, 703–4n5
Benedict XVI, Pope (Josef Ratzinger), opposition to liberation theology, 13, 689n1
Benjamin, Walter, concept of relic, 592, 613, 657
Berkeley, George (Bishop), 167
Bermúdez, Juanita, 515
Berrigan, Daniel, 659
Berryman, John, 47
Betancur, Belisario, 546
Betrayed Generation, anti-materialist elitism of, 122, 139, 162, 188, 268, 382, 609
Beverley, John, 44, 77, 386, 389, 528–32, 534
Beyle, Henri. *See* Stendhal
Bhabha, Homi K., 259, 519
Bishop, Maurice, 701–2n9
Black Christ, as mestizo symbol, 474, 478, 482, 484, 487; as mulatto symbol, 641
Bloom, Harold, theory of anxiety of influence, 192, 278, 305, 329, 403
Bluefields, 359; in *El cielo llora por mí*, 646–7, 653, 656; history, 23, 28, 30
Bly, Robert, 402
Boff, Leonardo, 12, 13
Bohm, David, 408, 620, 622
Bolaño, Roberto, on EC, 14, 343, 574
Bolaños, Enrique, presidency of, 432–3, 517
Bolívar, Simón, 492–3
Bolivia, 214–15, 459; Che Guevara in, 37, 172, 216–17, 286, 695n5; under Evo Morales, 441, 629, 631
Böll, Heinrich, 128
Boom. *See* Latin American Literary Boom
Borge Martínez, Tomás, 3, 17; corruption of, 426; as editor of *Barricada*, 429; as FSLN founder, 37–8, 265; imprisonment and torture of, 36–7, 43, 80, 226; leader of GPP, 41, 161, 180, 226, 372, 381, 442, 601, 690n5, 697n5; as minister of the interior, 226, 296, 644, 702n10; origins of, 8, 336, 687; post-1990 political career, 430, 434–5, 437, 452, 460, 492, 567, 630, 632, 691n7; writing career, 38, 130, 264, 296, 332, 336, 401–2, 440, 703–4n5
Borges, Jorge Luis, 248, 408, 703–4n5; influence on SRM, 167–8
Borgeson, Paul, on EC, 48, 70, 97, 116, 353, 366, 407
Borneo, 139
Bosch, Juan, 297
Bourdieu, Pierre, 441
Bowdler, William, 43, 129, 501
Brand, Dionne, 63
Brazil, 132, 136, 215, 451, 629, 663, 669; African heritage in, 635, 639; liberation theology in, 12, 203, 378
Brecht, Bertolt, 450
British Honduras. *See* Belize
Buarque de Holanda, Chico, 132, 380
Buitrago, Francisco, 124, 523
Buitrago, Julio, 370

Buitrago, Pablo, 25
Bulgaria, 609
Bunke, Tamara, 37
Burgos-Debray, Elisabeth, 529
Burns, E. Bradford, 161, 691n10
Bush, George H.W., and 1990 Nicaraguan election, 234–5, 428
Bush, George W., 435, reappointment of Reagan officials, 433, 438
Bustamente, José, 161

Cabal, Antidio, 219
Cabezas, Omar, 130, 264, 402; *Fire from the Mountain*, 73, 296, 339, 371, 374, 529, 536
Cabrera, Enriqueta, 546, 557
El caiman barbudo, 272
Calderón, Esthela, 191, 700n22
Calderón Guardia, Rafael Ángel, 675–6
California Gold Rush, 25, 45
Camacho de Schmidt, Aurora, 702n12
Cambodia, 139, 658, 659, 660, 662
Cameroon, 636
Campanella, Hortensia, 528, 537
Campanella, Thommaso, 681
Canada, 294, 297; aid to FSLN, 232, 609
Capote, Truman, 538
Cardenal, Carlos, 480
Cardenal, Gabriel, 605–6
Cardenal, Isabel, 32
Cardenal, Lorenzo, 45
Cardenal, Luis, 36, 80, 604
Cardenal, Pedro (EC's great-grandfather), 45
Cardenal, Pedro (EC's cousin), 590
Cardenal, Rodolfo, 46, 480, 585, 587
Cardenal, Salvador, 32, 707n5
Cardenal Martínez, Ernesto, 3, 6, 126–7, 130, 140, 179, 264, 267, 292, 443, 446, 521, 562, 710n17; *Abide in Love*, 52, 117, 194–9, 568, 570, 583, 695n1; *Los años de Granada*, 71, 569, 574, 576, 579, 581, 589–98, 617; apprentice poems, 58–61, 569; biography of, 45–58, 118; conclusions, 685–8; *Cosmic Canticle*, 20, 56, 62, 80, 94, 199, 218, 296, 362, 381, 387, 399–425, 565–7, 570, 597, 618, 659–61, 666, 668, 684, 685, 702n11, 702n14; *In Cuba*, 199–210, 577, 598; *The Doubtful Strait*, 19, 52, 95–117, 200, 344, 358, 363, 682, 685; *Epigramas*, 50, 61–3; *Este mundo y otro*, 709n12; estrangement from FSLN, 429, 436, 573–4; *Flights of Victory*, 19, 55, 384–400, 407, 414, 420–1, 423, 565, 597, 598, 616, 659, 661, 701n6, 701–2n9; *Gethsemani, Ky.*, 50, 81–5, 194, 578; *The Gospel in Solentiname*, 52, 117, 212–22, 378, 624; *Homenaje a los indios americanos*, 53, 114, 340–59, 384, 389, 399–400, 701n3; how perceived, 13–15, 17, 222, 242, 381, 477, 617, 691n5; *Las ínsulas extrañas*, 56, 574, 597–604, 625; and liberation theology, 11, 144, 441; literary criticism on, 19–20, 30, 32, 42; *Marilyn Monroe and Other Poems*, 52, 83, 89–95, 116, 343, 414; milieu of upbringing, 8, 187, 193, 301, 480, 586–7, 695n2, 706n16; "Nicaraguan Canto," 53, 80, 357–65, 367, 378, 383–5, 389, 391–2, 398, 618, 622; *Oracle over Managua*, 53, 80, 361, 364–78, 384–5, 392, 397, 407, 666, 684; *Los Ovnis de oro*, 55, 399–400, 700n1; *Pasajero de tránsito*, 57, 658–69, 676; *Psalms*, 51, 83, 85–91, 222,

379–80; *La revolución perdida*, 56, 574–5, 588–9, 593, 602–17, 625, 657; *La santidad de la revolución*, 379–84, 407, 658; statue of Sandino, 56, 238; *Tata Vasco*, 57, 658, 678–85; "Telescope in the Dark Night," 56, 566–74, 577, 580, 583, 614, 625, 660, 666; *Versos del pluriverso*, 56, 618–26, 658, 665–6, 684; *Vida perdida*, 56, 203, 506, 574–90, 598, 602, 604, 614, 625; "With Walker in Nicaragua," 63–6, 706n14; *Zero Hour*, 19, 50, 64, 65–82, 85, 89, 92–3, 96–8, 110, 114, 116, 200, 344, 358–9, 361, 364, 369, 383–5, 407, 583, 658–9, 680

Cardenal Martínez, Fernando, 8, 13, 41, 692n2; Jesuit Order, 12; minister of education, 226, 702n3; visits Solentiname, 213, 220

Cárdenas, Lázaro, 161

Cardoza y Aragón, Luis, 189

Carías Andino, Tiburcio, 68

Carlos V, Emperor, 680

Carpentier, Alejo, 117, 242, 629, 691n11, 708n2

Carrera, Rafael, debate over significance of, 287–8, 698nn10–11

Carrión, Luis, 134, 225–6, 229, 430, 437

Carter, Jimmy, defeat of, 228; as election observer, 236, 436; relations with FSLN, 227, 507; relations with Somoza dictatorship, 41–3, 129

Casey, William, 263, 281

Castaldi, Carlo, 710n18

Castañeda, Jorge G., 15, 16, 185, 233

Castañeda, Oliverio, 239, 311, 313, 699n15, as character in *Castigo Divino*, 300–31; as image of Sandino, 330–1

Castañeda de León, Oliverio, assassination of, 313

Castellanos, Rosario, 47, 623

Castellón, Francisco, 548, 706–7n20, 708n4

Castillo Armas, Carlos, 244–5, 677

Castro, Andrés, 26, 137, 449, 562, 621–2, 704n2

Castro Ruz, Fidel, 15, 52, 70, 121, 171, 275, 365, 415–16, 438, 441, 455, 468, 632, 697n5; advice to FSLN, 235, 510; Catholic Church, political role of priests, 9–12; EC's admiration of, 48, 200–11, 222–3, 357, 381, 420, 576, 589, 601, 602, 614, 623, 678; EC's criticism of, 81, 94, 585–6; as guerrilla leader, 78, 260, 372; *La historia me absolverá*, 31, 270, 458; and liberation theology, 12–13; SRM's friendship with, 132, 135, 495

Centeno, Bosco, 216

Central America, cultural distinctiveness, 6–7, 20, 66–7, 72, 151, 180, 184–93, 557; history, 22, 95–116, 142, 159, 284, 304, 529; post-1990 subordination to Mexico, 658, 663, 666, 676

El Centroamericano, 326

Cerezo Dardón, Hugo, as character in SRM's fiction, 304, 332

Cerna, Lenin, 654

Certeau, Michel de, 333

Chamorro family, 29, 35, 36, 49, 65, 439, 581, 594–5, 638, 678, 687

Chamorro, Claudia, 339

Chamorro, Diego Manuel, 30, 280

Chamorro, Edgar, 607

Chamorro, Emiliano, 28–30, 34, 269, 335, 479, 483

Chamorro, Filadelfo, 581

Chamorro, Fruto, 588–9; as president, 25, 707n3, 707n4, 708n4; racial origins of, 638–9
Chamorro, Pedro José, 638–9
Chamorro, Violeta Barrios de, 3, 36, 231; and JGRN, 225, 228; presidency of, 426–31, 435, 438, 444, 469, 475, 488, 705n7; presidential campaign, 235–8, 564
Chamorro Alfaro, Pedro Joaquín, 27, 639
Chamorro Barrios, Carlos Fernando, as editor of *Barricada*, 231, 429; investigative journalism of, 438
Chamorro Benard, Carmen, in EC's memoirs, 594–7, 607; EC's poetry about, 59–60, 65, 402–3, 619
Chamorro Cardenal, Javier, 231
Chamorro Cardenal, Pedro Joaquín, 30, 45, 54, 225, 231, 523, 564, 591, 599; assassination of, 42; Rebellion of Olama y los Mollejones, 36, 50, 78, 80–1, 586, 604
Chamorro Cardenal, Xavier, 231
Chamorro Mora, Álvaro, 701n5
Chamorro Zelaya, Pedro Joaquín, 322
Chamorro-Bryan Treaty, 29–30, 34
Chardin, Teilhard de, 416
Charlip, Julie, 161, 691n10
Chatfield, Frederick, 25, 548
Chaucer, Geoffrey, 76, 680
Chavarría, Elvis (Elbis), 220, 420–1; torture and murder of, 393–6
Chávez, Hugo, 435, 438, 629–31
Chávez Alfaro, Lizandro, 191–2
Cherem, Silvia, 691–2n1
Chibcha, 22
Childers, James Saxon, 74
Chile, 16, 49, 57, 161, 348, 403, 445, 629, 654; under Allende, 53, 209, 601–2, 658, 660; military coup in, 182, 214–15, 279, 281, 694n19, 696n5; national bourgeoisie in, 16, 184, 197, 269, 697n7
China, 32, 297
Chomsky, Noam, 132
Chopin, Frederick, 546
Chorotega, 21, 23, 179, 439, 642
Christian, Shirley, 17
Christie, Agatha, 316
Churchill, Winston, 481
CIA (Central Intelligence Agency), 35, 41, 159; attacks on Nicaragua, 232, 263; in Guatemala, 245
Clayton-Bulwer Treaty, 25
Clinton, Bill, 428, 475
Cockburn, Bruce, 380
Coelho, Paulo, 442
Coello Gutiérrez, Emilian, 648, 650, 654, 709n11
Cohen, Henry, 154
Colby, Jason M., 709n16
Cole, Byron, 25
Colegio Centroamericano, 47, 352, 589, 590, 594, 596, 599, 604, 647
Colombia, 28, 136, 203, 215, 279, 399, 561; Contadora Group, 232, 546, 653; drug cartels, 653; EC's studies in, 50–1, 81, 89, 95, 342, 350, 407, 589, 596, 598–600; Liberalism and Conservatism in, 160
Colón, Cristóbal. *See* Columbus, Christopher
Columbia University, 47–8, 581
Columbus, Christopher, 22, 97, 636, 679
Congo, 636, 641
Conrad, Robert Edgar, 173
Conservatives, 7, 8, 9, 15–16, 24, 25, 352, 523, 584; anti-Americanism of,

26–9, 32–3, 210, 591–3, 633; decline of, 30, 39, 42, 160, 237, 279–80, 311; opposition to Somozas, 34, 35, 36, 47, 76–80, 253–4, 256, 335–7, 574, 604, 692n2; origins of, 99–102; in Sandinista government, 44, 210, 226, 268–9, 524; split in allegiances, 44, 210–11
Contras, origins of, 228–9, 258, 315, 646; Contra War, 232–4, 279, 281, 293, 380, 440, 449, 507, 510, 514, 560, 607, 689n1, 692n6, 696n1; post-1990 influence of, 427–8, 431, 437, 438 funding, 230, 233; Iran-Contra scandal, 234; military failure, 230
Contreras, Hernando, 113–14; decapitation of, 115
Contreras, Pedro, 113
Contreras, Rodrigo de, 22, 96, 112, 113
Contreras Escobar, Eduardo, death and martyr status of, 41, 227, 284, 453; insurrectional strategy of, 40–1, 128, 180; in Gioconda Belli's writing, 334, 338, 689–90n1, 699n20
Córdoba Rivas, Rafael, 228
Corn Islands, 29, 343
Cornejo Polar, Antonio, 261, 632–3, 641
Coronel Kautz, Manuel, 432
Coronel Kautz, Ricardo, 432
Coronel Urtecho, José, 45, 59, 71, 95, 273–4, 420, 432; as EC's mentor, 565, 595–6, 603, 614, 701n5; supports FSLN, 221, 378, 382–3, 616
Correa, Rafael, 629, 631
Cortázar, Julio, 18, 167, 241, 513, 551, 552; *Alguien que anda por ahí*, 292; *Las armas secretas* 292, 552; *Bestiary*, 285; *Blow-Up*, 292; death, 283, 292; friendship with SRM, 129, 131–2, 285; *Hopscotch*, 285–6, 289, 643, 703–4n5; *Nicaraguan Sketches*, 283–4, 292; receives Rubén Darío Medal, 263, 273; visits to Nicaragua, 213–14, 216, 258, 275, 283–92
Cortés, Hernán, 97, 104, 680
Cortez, Beatriz, 542
COSEP (High Council of Private Enterprise), 228, 280, 299
Costa Rica, 7, 35, 36, 39, 54, 66, 190, 229, 234, 272–3, 284, 438, 673; conflict with William Walker, 26–7; democratic values of, 188, 233, 312, 317, 436, 670–2, 675; Nicaraguans in, 390, 392, 673–4, 692n3, 702n10; radicalism in, 224; relations with Nicaragua, 293, 669, 677; setting for SRM's fiction, 146; SRM's residence in, 125, 128, 161, 283
Cox, Alex, 232
Craft, Linda J., 700n21
Crimean War, 25
El Cronista, 319, 501
Cruz, Arturo J., 3, 228, 233
Cruz, San Juan de la, 566
Cruz, Jr, Arturo J., 616, 707n4
CSUCA (Governing Council of Central American Universities), 125–6
Cuadra, Abelardo, 129, 323, 328, 509
Cuadra, Manolo, 301, 322, 324, 331
Cuadra Cardenal, Pablo Antonio, 45, 47, 126, 191, 596, 636, 640; Fascist sympathies of, 48, 71, 591; as mentor, 120, 122, 692n7; opposes FSLN, 238, 449–50, 707n6
Cuadra Downing, Orlando, 47
Cuadra Pasos, Carlos, 269
Cuba, 73, 314, 388; African heritage in, 209, 463, 635; baseball prowess of,

468, 516; EC's travels in, 199–212, 214, 358, 407, 664; as inspiration, 160, 175, 182–3, 215–16, 231, 303, 384, 597, 621, 662, 678, 679; as place of exile, 172, 690n5; relations with Nicaragua, 30, 37, 40, 50, 52, 56, 78, 121, 132, 135, 145, 159, 172, 175, 207, 232, 238, 262, 264, 267, 293, 314, 373, 386, 435, 448, 525–6, 661; relations with Venezuela, 629
Cuna. *See* Kuna
CUSO (Canadian University Services Overseas), 125
Czechoslovakia, Soviet invasion of, 205–6; Czech Republic, 297

DAAD (German Academic Foreign Exchange Service), 127
Dalton, Roque, 415, 533
Dante Alighieri, 417, 420, 513
Darío, Rubén, 126, 187–8, 292, 534, 609, 705n9; anti-imperialism of, 260–4; brain of, 255, 502–3; Fonseca's interest in, 172, 285, 442; influence on EC, 47, 58, 65, 69, 363, 402, 404–6, 589, 610; *Prosas profanas*, 503; in SRM's writing, 139, 263–4, 275–6, 470, 476, 494–505, 543–7, 550–1, 553–5, 636, 640, 654–5; as "triple mestizo," 636, 638
Da Silva, Luís Ignácio (Lula), 132
Dávila, Pedrarias, 22, 96, 105, 114; death of, 103; first dictator, 98–102, 114–16, 439
Dawes, Greg, 344, 365, 373, 702n11
Day, Dorothy, 659
DEA (Drug Enforcement Agency), 652
Debray, Régis, 207, 219, 452, 695n5
Defoe, Daniel, 539
De Gaulle, Charles, 297
dependency theory, 71–2, 184–5, 262, 268, 271, 450
Dervishire, Juan, 301
d'Escoto Brockmann, Miguel, 13, 41, 128, 507; as foreign minister, 226
de la Selva, Rogelio, 676
de la Selva, Salomón, 676–8, 710n17
Diana, Princess of Wales, 516
Díaz, Adolfo, 28–9, 31, 269, 360
Díaz del Castillo, Bernal, 110–11
Dickens, Charles, 452, 453, 703n4
Dominican Republic, 9
Donoso, José, 136, 152, 241; *The Obscene Bird of Night*, 526
Doolittle, Hilda (H.D.), 690n3
Dore, Elizabeth, 7, 23, 27
Dreiser, Theodore, 539
Drinan, Robert, 12, 689n1
Dumas, Alexandre, 120
Durrell, Lawrence, 266

Eagleburger, Lawrence, 303
Echeverría, Esteban, 15
Echeverría, José Antonio, 207
The Economist, 233
Ecuador, 12, 276, 279, 629–30
EDUCA (Central American University Press), 126, 128, 172, 173
Eisenhower, Dwight, President, 36; support for dictators, 158, 161, 189
Eliot, Thomas Stearns, 48, 76, 584, 680
ELN (National Liberation Army, 11, 85, 599
El Salvador, 5, 7, 26, 66, 188, 215, 227, 436, 673; civil war, 240, 282, 284–5; genocide of indigenous people, 274–5; post-2009 government, 629–30
England. *See* Great Britain
Espinosa, Luisa Amanda, 284, 703–4n5

Estelí, 43, 226, 339, 388, 427
Estrada, José Dolores, 449
Estrada, Juan, 28
Estrada Cabrera, Manuel, 28, 286–7
EU (European Union), 6
EZLN (Zapatista National Liberation Army), 10, 630, 705n8

Fagoth, Steadman, 229
Fanon, Frantz, 144, 191, influence on Sandinismo, 259–60
Faulkner, William, 32, 157, 247–8, 501, 693n9; *Absalom, Absalom!* 247, 254, 502, 672; *As I Lay Dying*, 255–7, 672; *The Wild Palms*, 247, 542
Feliciano, José, 544
FER (Revolutionary Student Front), 124, 243, 276, 523
Ferlinghetti, Lawrence, 14
Fernández, Idania, 511
Fernández de Oviedo, Gonzalo, 109–11
Feynman, Richard, 408, 413, 620
Fiallos Gil, Mariano, 119; and Casteñeda case, 300–2, 306–8, 311, 327–30; death of, 125; SRM's biography of, 157–61; SRM's mentor, 124–5, 172, 299, 304, 307, 692n7; university autonomy, 121–2, 143–5
Flakoll, Darwin, 698n9
Flaubert, Gustave, 304, 513, 539, 546, 551
Flores Olea, Víctor, 698n12
FMLN (Farabundo Martí National Liberation Front), 227, 275; in power, 629–30
Fonseca Amador, Carlos, 3; *Augusto César Sandino, ideario politico*, 265; death in combat of, 41, 53, 78, 80, 691n7; friendship with SRM, 124, 127, 172, 276, 285, 701n5; as FSLN founder and leader, 37–9, 41, 120, 193, 226–7, 238, 243, 252, 264, 442, 448, 599, 601, 617, 690–1n5, 693n14, 696n3; mythologization of, 265, 284, 632, 649, 651, 654, 657, 691n7; physical appearance of, 179; *Sandino, guerrillero proletario*, 172–80, 243, 632
Ford Foundation, 125, 127
Forester, C.S., 316
Foucault, Michel, 333
Fox, James, 50
France, 23, 24, 48, 132, 134, 160, 297, 547; influence on US independence, 282, 290
Franco, Francisco, 48, 71, 591
Franco, Jean, 436, 441, 530
Frank, Andre Gunder, 697n7
Franklin, Benjamin, 70, 282
Fraser, Lady Antonia, 132
Free University of Berlin, 134
Frobenius, Leo, 404
FSLN (Sandinista National Liberation Front), 8, 20, 78, 269, 449, 613; assumption of power, 129, 225–38, 384–6, 598, 603; Christmas party raid, 40, 523–4; as definition of Nicaraguan identity, 44, 237–8, 253, 295, 327, 359, 385, 443, 453, 633, 643–57, 662; and democratic procedures, 444, 446–7, 472, 557; divisions in, 133–4, 400–1, 442, 459, 461, 488, 573, 656, 676; early tactics, 38–9, 286–7, 370–1; 1984 election, 231; 1990 election, 235–6, 619; foundation of, 37; growth of, 42, 193, 214, 220–1, 589; post-2006 government, 439, 551, 562, 626, 628–30, 675

Fuentes, Carlos, 53, 117, 241, 297, 470, 681, 682, 703–4n5; *Aura*, 156; *The Buried Mirror*, 513; *The Death of Artemio Cruz*, 286, 646, 708n2; *Myself with Others*, 513; SRM's friendship with, 18, 132, 135, 513; support for Sandinista Nicaragua, 696n5
Fujimori, Alberto, 530
Fukuyama, Francis, 6; "end of history" theory, 457–9, 462
Funes, Mauricio, 629

Gabuardi, Luis, 79
Gadea, Fabio, 438
Galeano, Eduardo, 57, 401, 405
Gallegos, Rómulo, 297
Galván, Tierno, 615
Gamper, Daniel, 605, 607–8
Gandhi, Mahatma, 53, 101
García-Antezana, Jorge, 344
García Canclini, Néstor, 518–20, 529
García Lavinia, Gaspar, 227, 646; personal statement, 291
García Lorca, Federico, 120, 591
García Márquez, Gabriel, 117, 241, 248, 470, 501, 697n5; *The Autumn of the Patriarch*, 242; *Chronicle of a Death Foretold*, 529; friendship with SRM, 129, 132; influence on SRM's fiction, 150, 152–3, 192, 254, 693n9; *Love in the Time of Cholera*, 296; *News of a Kidnapping*, 538; *One Hundred Years of Solitude*, 152, 154, 156, 206, 241, 322, 482, 486, 535, 555, 703–4n5
Gardel, Carlos, 512
Garifuna, 633, 635, 693–4n15
Garrison, Cornelius, 25, 27
Gauguin, Paul, 543–4
Gentile, William Frank, 447
Gere, Richard, 380
Germany, 24, 28, 131, 135, 153, 296, 392, 463, 475, 506, 555, 658; EC's readership in, 379, 381; SRM's residence in, 125, 127–8, 696n1b
Gethsemani Monastery, 14, 49, 51, 81–5, 203, 340, 576–85, 590, 678
Ghana, 260, 636
Ghasgai, Abdollah, 611–14
Ginés de Sepúlveda, 108, 691n10
Ginsberg, Allen, 47, 402
GN (National Guard), formation of, 31, 33–4; 39, 120, 142, 612; looting by, 40–2, 49; post-1990 influence of, 428, 431, 437; in *Psalms*, 85–7; in SRM's fiction, 148–9, 253–5, 300, 307, 319, 320, 322, 325–6, 328–9; violence of, 339, 368, 391, 393–5, 505, 520–1, 606, 703–4n5
Gobat, Michel, 8, 72, 78, 210, 593
Godoy, Virgilio, 231, 427, 430–1
Gómez de Avellaneda, Gertrudis, *Sab*, 580
González, Felipe, 134, 615–16
González, Gil, 590
Gonzalez, Mike, 69, 387, 691n8
González, Reynaldo, 292–3
González-Balado, José Luis, 222
Gordillo, Fernando, death of, 124, 157; SRM's collaborator, 122, 172
Gorky, Maxim, 263–4, 276
Gould, Jeffrey L., 7, 343–4, 389–90, 631–2, 638, 640–1, 709n6
Goytisolo, Juan, 48
GPP (Prolonged People's War), 41
Gramsci, Antonio, 450
Granada, 59, 118, 363, 391, 422, 701n5; attempted burning of, 27; closure of bookstore, 436; as Conservative bastion, 8, 24–5, 27, 32–3, 45, 382–3, 483, 523, 570–1,

579–80, 596, 647, 678; foundation, 100; occupation by Walker, 64–5
Grandin, Greg, 698n11
Granera Sacasa, Aminta, 436, 644–5, 651
Granta, 452, 564
Grass, Günter, 132
Graves, Robert, 48, 660–1
Great Britain, 23, 294, 297, 520; and Atlantic Coast, 24–6, 28
Greece, 658
Greene, Graham, 14; *The Power and the Glory*, 556
Grenada, 659, 661, 701–2n9
Greytown, 25
Guadamuz, Carlos, 705n7
Guatemala, 66, 72, 261, 436, 451; civil war, 79, 214–15, 240, 282, 284, 694n15; as colony, 104–8, 638–9, 641; 1954 coup, 36, 160, 166, 245, 677; after independence, 698n11; indigenous population of, 7, 10, 21–2, 27–8, 187, 343, 399, 683, 697n8, 709n7; during October Revolution years, 158, 161, 188–9, 299, 313, 607, 609, 669–73, 676
El Güegüense, 447, 639
Guerrero, Gertrudis, marriage to SRM, 124–5, 172, 547
Guerrero, José, 25
Guevara, Donald, torture and murder of, 394–5
Guevara, Ernesto Che, 30, 37, 48, 53, 603; death of, 286; ethos of self-sacrifice, 163, 178, 182–3, 215–16, 222–3, 262, 265, 364–5, 370, 373–4, 378, 423, 623; and patriarchy, 171, 275, 455, 533; voluntarism, 172, 177, 386, 415–16
Guido, Clemente, 231
Guillén, Nicolás, 264
Guillermoprieto, Alma, 237
Gurdián, Ena, 300
Gurdián, Ramiro, 299
Gurdián Castro, Enrique, 300
Gutiérrez, Gustavo, 12
Gutiérrez, Petrona, 465, 485
Guzmán, Luis Humberto, 429

Haiti, 9, 135, 438, 628
Halleslevens, Omar, 440
Hanna, Matthew, 33
Harris, Ed, 380
Harvard University, 136, 433, 434, 696n5
Hasenfus, Eugene, 234
Hassan, Moisés, 225, 228
Haya de la Torre, Víctor Raúl, 31
H.D. *See* Doolittle, Hilda
Heisenberg, Werner, 620
Helms, Jesse, 428, 475
Hemingway, Ernest, 468
Hernández de Córdoba, Francisco, 60, 100; decapitation of, 101
Hernández Martínez, Maximiliano, 274
Herrera, Antonio de, 102
Herrera, Leticia, 703n4
Hidalgo, Miguel, 10–11
Hindenburg, Paul von, 294
Hitler, Adolf, 293–5, 591
Hobsbawm, E.J., 3
Hodges, Donald C., 598–9
Holland, 23
Holocaust, the, 87–8, 294–5, 553–5, 559
Honduras, 37, 39, 66, 68, 72, 188, 436, 578; indigenous heritage, 7, 21, 108, 694n15; in nineteenth century, 26–8, 64; in SRM's fiction, 252–3, 256; as US military base, 229–31, 284
Hoover, Herbert, 32, 446
Hoover, J. Edgar, 505

Hüeck Salomon, Cornelio, 42, 520–2, 524, 537, 706n16
Huembes, Roberto, 41
Hughes, Howard, 376, 383
Hugo, Victor, 120, 502; *The Hunchback of Notre Dame*, 503
Huntington, Samuel, 628–9
Hussein, Saddam, 297
Huxley, Aldous, 187

Icaza, Jorge, *Huasipungo*, 700–1n2
Ignatieff, Michael, 298
Incas, 182, 344–9, 358, 526, 592
India, 260–1, 558, 658
Iran, 130, 435, 707n7; EC in, 610–14; Iran-Contra scandal, 234, 434; revolution in, 413–41
Iraq, 130, 297, 433, 614
Israel, 380, 614, 623; aid to Contras, 233; arms shipments to Somoza, 42–3; religious significance, 215, 376
Italy, 48

Jagger, Bianca, 3, 380, 687, 710n18
Jamaica, 679; links to Central America, 24, 396
Japan, 28, 56, 139, 475, 652, 658, 662–3
Jarquín, Edmundo, 57, 434, 438
Jaruzelski, Wojciech, 544
Jefferson, Thomas, 70, 282, 293
Jenks, Jeremiah, 30
Jerez, Máximo, 708n4
JGRN (Governing Junta for National Reconstruction), 225; post-2006 allusion to, 441
Jiménez, Mayra, 219; departure from Nicaragua, 55; poetry workshops, 53, 54, 217, 264
Jinotega, 31
Joan of Arc, 197
John XXIII, Pope, 677
John Paul II, Pope, 380, 557; confrontation with EC, 55, 407; response to liberation theology, 12–13, 689n1; visit to Nicaragua, 230, 507, 606
La Jornada, 614
Joyce, James, 502

Kafka, Franz, 513
Kahlo, Frida, 709n14
Kellogg, Frank B., 32
Kennedy, John F., 38, 190, 244, 256
Khaddafi, Moammar, 297, 435
Khomeini, Ayatollah Ruhollah, 610–14, 707n7
Kikongo, 636, 641
Kimbundu, 636, 641
Kim Il-Sung, 437
Kirkpatrick, Jeane, 303
Knox, Philander, 28–9
Kozak Rivero, Gisela, 304–5, 309
Kreisky, Bruno, 507
Kristeva, Julia, 247, 580
Kuna, 350, 390

Lacayo, Antonio, 427–8
Lacayo, Francisco, 55
Lafayette, Marquis de, 282
Lancaster, Roger, on Nicaraguan masculinity, 7, 149, 504, 506, 511, 563, 614
Lane, Henry, 70
Lara, Agustín, 468
Larsen, Don, 463
Larsen, Neil, 261, 519
Las Casas, Bartolomé de, 9, 13, 16, 22, 79, 97, 114, 678; *The Devastation of the Indies*, 10, 682; Just War doctrine, 11–12; relations with Maya, 108–9, 111–12

Latimer, Julian L., 30
Latin American Literary Boom, as cultural capital in Central America, 117, 152–4, 239–43, 248, 251, 256, 259, 263, 265, 275–6, 283–6, 289, 298, 309, 316, 322, 440, 495, 497, 500, 522, 526, 529, 535, 537–8, 627, 632, 686
Laughton, Charles, 298, 316
Leal, Pablo, 77, 79, 581
Lempira, rebellion, 108
Lenin, Vladimir I., 369
León, 8, 24, 36, 43, 64, 158, 187, 372, 609, 644; as Darío's home, 275, 636; EC's residence in 46–7; foundation of, 100, 103; FSLN activity in, 37, 124, 388, 442; origins of Liberalism in African settlement of, 549, 550, 637, 646, 708n4; as provisional capital, 44, 288, 390–2; as scene of Castañeda case, 299–301, 308–9, 314, 317, 323, 324, 329, 498; in SRM's fiction, 138, 151–7, 494–505, 522, 523, 526; as symbol of Nicaragua, 502
Lewites, Herty, 434, 567
Lewites, Israel, 453
Lezama Lima, José, 205
Liberals, 7, 8, 9, 15–16, 24, 27; divisions in, 29–30, 175–6; 33; as ideology of exiles, 44 252–4; origins, 99–116; in nineteenth century, 28, 143, 151–7, 185–6, 548, 550, 633, 637, 706–7n20, 708n4; under Somozas, 35, 36, 40, 158–9, 254–6, 268–9, 476, 516–17, 523, 591, 604, 644; SRM's family as, 118–19, 137, 288; subservience to US, 279–80, 311; in twentieth-century Spanish America, 160–3, 288–90
Libya, 130, 297, 435
Life, 91
Lohlé, Carlos, 222
López-Baralt, Luce, 565–6
López Pérez, Rigoberto, assassination of Somoza García, 36, 244, 499, 503, 505, 540, 704n4; as example of self-sacrifice, 496–7
Lovelock, James, 408
Lugo, Fernando, 12, 57
Luther, Martin, 624
Lyotard, Jean-François, 304, 558

Madari (Shariat-Madari), Ayatollah Kazem, 612
Madison, James, 282, 293
Madriz, José, 28
Maimonides, Moses, 167
Mairena, Laureano, 420–1; death in combat, 396–8, 623
Malraux, André, 297
Malta, 658, 662
Managua, 8, 24, 27, 41, 50, 56, 57, 83, 158, 165, 231, 250, 254, 363, 480, 570, 573, 580; under Alemán, 518, 561; 1972 earthquake, 221, 364–78; under FSLN, 399–400, 415; in nineteenth century, 187; under Somoza, 417–18, 520–3, 598; SRM's essay on, 470, 474; uprising in, 388–9, 391
Mangue language, 21, 642
Manifest Destiny, 25, 27
Mann, Thomas, 319
Mántica, Carlos, 599–600
Mántica, Felipe, 599–600
Mao Zedong, 53, 297, 365–6, 372, 381, 387, 602
Marcos, Subcomandante, 630, 705n8, 708n3

Marines, US, occupations, 28–30, 40, 73, 78, 299, 307, 309, 316, 364, 482, 628, 675, 693n8; application of US law in Nicaragua, 505; withdrawal of, 324
Marqués, Bernardo, 273
Martí, Farabundo, 31
Martí, José, 175, 262, 618, 621; analysis of US, 281; concept of New Man, 373; influence on Fidel Castro, 205–6; statue of, 238
Martin, Gerald, 201, 691n11, 697n5
Martínez, Tomás Eloy, 709n8
Martínez Rivas, Carlos, 48, 137, 436
Mártir, Pedro, 679
Marx, Karl, 12, 205, 282, 384, 387
Masatepe, 118, 123, 464, 474, 476–87, 523, 540
Masaya, 24, 41, 54, 609, 638; Department of, 177, 179, 488; uprising in, 42, 43 388, 391
Matagalpa, 39, 179, 359, 389, 561, 640, 641
Matto de Turner, Clorinda, *Torn from the Nest*, 700n2
Maugham, W. Somerset, 513
May, Karl, 38, 440
Maya, 7, 592; Classical civilization, 21, 261–2, 358, 483, 642; colonial era, 105–6, 109, 187, 709n7; Great Tongue, 278
Mayorga, Silvio, 37, 39
McField, David, 390
McMurray, George, 309
Mebarak Ripoll, Shakira. *See* Shakira
Mejía Godoy, Carlos, 57, 213, 243, 406
Mejía Godoy, Luis, 57, 243
Mejía Sánchez, Ernesto, 47, 50, 596
Mena, Luis, 29
Menchú, Rigoberta, 79, 529
Meneses, Carlos, 698n12
Mercado, Luisa, 118, 487; death, 134; influence on SRM's education, 120
Mercado, Teófilo (SRM's grandfather), 119, 151, 480–1, 486–7, 643
Mercado, Teófilo (SRM's uncle), 481, 486–7
Mercuri, Melina, 659
Mérida, Carlos, 189
Merton, Thomas, 14, 47; death of, 52; EC's correspondence with, 81, 89, 196, 342, 357, 600; tutorship of, influence on EC, 49–51, 83, 87, 194–5, 210, 213, 340, 43, 382, 420, 572, 574, 583–5, 587, 590, 598, 599, 614, 662, 669, 678
Mexico, 10–11, 16, 25, 28, 32, 35, 41, 57, 128, 136, 156, 165, 187, 261, 538; Central Americans in, 561, 677, 709n15; conquest of, 104; Contadora Group, 232, 653; drug cartels, 436, 653; EC's studies in, 47, 50, 59–61, 66, 71, 72, 80–1, 95, 574, 585–6, 595–6; elections in, 233; indigenous heritage, 21, 27, 350–6, 399–400, 681; Mexican Revolution's influence on Central America, 98, 160, 162, 166, 178–9, 448, 515, 607, 708n2; as place of exile, 189; as post-1990 regional power, 658, 663, 666, 669–70, 673, 676, 678; support for FSLN, 264, 399–400, 459; Zapatista insurgency, 630, 665
Mignolo, Walter D., 261–2, 613, 631
Mill, John Stuart, 620
Milland, Ray, 316
Millay, Edna St Vincent, 677
Miranda, Claudia, 511
Miskito, 359, 364; alliance with British, 25, 28; under FSLN government, 229,

389–90, 399, 608; in nineteenth century, 547–50; origins of, 23, 635; post-1990, 432, 537, 633–4
Mistral, Gabriela, 32
Mitterand, François, 297
Molloy, Sylvia, theory of Latin American autobiography, 575–6, 586, 592, 605
Moncada, Jose María, 30–2, 70, 176, 255, 269, 280
Monroe, Marilyn, EC's poem about, 89–91
Monroe Doctrine, 25, 280
Montealegre, Eduardo (father), 271, 434
Montealegre, Eduardo (son), 271, 434, 436
Monteforte Toledo, Mario, 189, 673
Monterrey Technological Institute, 134
Monterroso, Augusto, 47, 126, 166, 189, 693n11
Montesinos, Antonio de, 10
Mora, Juan Rafael, 26
Mora, Manuel, 675–6
Morales, Armando, 273, 470
Morales, Evo, 441, 629, 631
Morazán, Francisco, 287, 493, 588
More, Thomas, *Utopia*, 679, 680–3
Morelos, José María, 11
Morgan, Charles, 25, 27
Morley, Sylvanus G., 350
Moro, Diana, 497, 502, 503, 542, 545
Morris, Kenneth E., 702–3n1
Mozambique, 130, 261
MRS (Sandinista Renewal Movement), 2006 campaign, 434–5; decline, 438, 442; foundation, 8–9, 134, 430, 656
Müller, Glenn, 651
Mulroney, Brian, Prime Minister, aid to FSLN, 232
Murillo, Juan, 670
Murillo, Rosario (married to Daniel Ortega), 501; literary career, 54, 442, 700n22; opposition to Ministry of Culture, 55–6, 263, 267–8, 386, 609; and Ortega sexual-abuse scandal, 433–4, 699n18, 703n4; reshaping of FSLN, 434, 439, 440, 441, 470–4, 476, 477, 630, 632, 654, 657, 660, 692n5, 704n2, 707n2
Murphy, Jack, 610
Musset, Alfred de, 314
Mussolini, Benito, 70–1

NAFTA (North American Free Trade Agreement), 6, 630; promotion of Mexico as regional centre, 658
Náhuat, cultural heritage, 7, 9, 23, 179, 187, 215, 336–7, 354, 399, 439, 450, 485, 638, 662; language, 21, 142, 308, 639–40, 642
Napoleon III (Louis Napoleon), 547, 548, 552
Naranjo, Carmen, 304, 306
Narváez Murillo, Zoilamérica, accusations of sexual abuse by Daniel Ortega, 431–2, 433–4, 567, 699n18, 702–3n1, 703n4
NATO (North Atlantic Treaty Organization), 5–6
Navarro, Jorge, 124, 523
Negroponte, John, 281
Neruda, Pablo, 65, 120, 297, 385, 441; *Canto General*, 343, 347–8, 358, 401, 403, 408, 417, 420; death, 378; influence on EC, 59–61, 400, 402, 405, 591; *Odes*, 701n5
Neto, Agostinho, 298, 302
Netzahualcóyotl, 350–6, 678
Newsweek, 447

New York Times, 3, 17, 594
Nicaragua, 3, 4; Atlantic Coast, 146, 170, 180, 229–30, 262, 364, 390, 549–50, 560, 633–4, 638–9; baseball in, 148–9, 462–3, 468, 516–17, 693n8; conception of nationhood, 174–5, 230, 259–65, 338–9, 392–4, 399, 402, 411, 425, 450–1, 453–5, 607–14, 630–1, 647, 673; history to 1855, 21–5, 635–42; history to 1934, 25–34; public safety, 435–6; relations with Venezuela, 629; Sandinista Revolution, 225–36, 602–16, 686–8; Somoza dictatorship and Sandinista Revolution, 3–4, 34–44
Nigeria, 404, 624, 636
Nixon, Richard, 658
North, Oliver, 303, 434
North Korea, 130
Novalis, 392
Novo, Salvador, 596
El Nuevo Diario, 231
La Nueva Prensa, 322, 324, 327
Núñez, Carlos, 225
Núñez, René, 471

OAS (Organization of American States), 168
Obama, Barack, President, 297, 438, 629
Obando y Bravo, Miguel, 231, 431, 434–5, 651
Obregón, Álvaro, 557
O'Brien, Conor Cruise, 221, 689n1
Ocotal, 31, 41
Odría, Manuel, 243
Olama y los Mollejones, Rebellion of, 36, 50, 120, 138, 243, 254, 586, 604, 677
Onassis, Aristotle, 383
Onassis, Jacqueline Kennedy, 165–6
Onetti, Juan Carlos, 501, 703–4n5
Oreamuno, Yolanda, 669, 670, 677, 709n15; *La ruta de su evasion*, 671–2
Orozco, José Clemente, 11
Ortega Saavedra, Camilo, 41; death, 42, 453, 632, 707n2
Ortega Saavedra, Daniel, 3, 8, 17, 39, 44, 54–5, 265, 654, 692n2, 692n3; allegations of sexual abuse, 433–4, 699n18, 702–3n1, 703n4, 706n11; career under Liberal governments, 429–31, 460, 473, 567, 643, 648; collaboration with SRM, 130, 132–3; conflicts with SRM, 137, 488, 507; persecution of EC, 57–8; post-2006 presidency, 20, 435–42, 616, 629, 631, 644, 657, 660–1, 673, 685, 704n2; as president, 134, 231, 235, 263, 444, 565, 655, 692n6, 696n5; release from prison, 40
Ortega Saavedra, Humberto, 41, 53, 128, 441, 692n3; corruption of, 426, 616; as minister of defence, 225–7, 427, 510; negotiations with Contras, 234–5; release from prison, 172, 696n3
Ortiz, Anastasio (Captain), 300–1, 306, 325, 329–31
Ortiz, Fernando, 343
O'Sullivan, Maureen, 298, 316

Padilla, Heberto, 52, 205
El País, 58, 135, 450
Pakistan, 261
Palestine, 380
Pallier, Claire, 690n1
Palme, Olof, 507
Panama, 36, 115, 435, 436, 459, 522; Contadora Group, 232; indigenous

cultures, 342, 344, 399; origins of, 28; 1989 US invasion of, 235
Pancasán, Battle of, 39, 52
Paraguay, 214, 228, 279, 343, 399, 629
Parrales, Edgardo, 13
Pasos, Joaquín, 62
Passeron, Jean-Claude, 441
Pastora, Edén, 3, 127; post-2006 support for Ortega, 435, 630, 632; raid on National Palace, 43, 129, 226; split with FSLN, 229, 702n10
patriarchy, association with national self-assertion, erosion of, 6–7, 9, 79, 150, 153–4, 224, 249–50, 322, 492–4, 686
Paul, St, 582
Paul VI, Pope, 51
Pawnees, 358
Payeras, Mario, 529
Payment Deferred, 298, 309–10, 316, 320–1, 699n17
Paz, Octavio, 47, 71, 297, 596; *The Labyrinth of Solitude*, 693n10; as Reagan propagandist, 289–90, 698n12
Peck, Gregory, 140
Pellas Chamorro, Francisco, 597
Peña, Felipe, 393
Peñalosa, María de, 114
Pérez, Carlos Andrés, 134
Peri Rossi, Cristina, 241
Perri, Brad, 163
Peru, 16, 49, 435, 530, 629, 663; indigenous heritage, 343–9, 399, 641; military radicals, 53, 182, 279, 601–2
Peterson, Dorothy, 316
Philippines, 235
Pierce, Harold Clifton, 31
Pinter, Harold, 132, 501
Pius XII, Pope, 403
Pizarro, Francisco, 97, 345
Plato, 681, *The Republic*, 218, 682–3
Poes Libre, 54
Poland, 45, 477, 547
Pol Pot, 660
Pomares, Germán, 40, 227, 338
Poniatowska, Elena, *Here's to You, Jesusa!*, 200–1, 529
Popol Vuh, 181
Portocarrero de Somoza, Hope, 581, 608
Portuguese language, 129, 379–80, 409–10
Pound, Ezra, 45, 48; influence on EC, 61, 66–76, 96–7, 116, 200, 343–4, 357–8, 387, 400–4, 408, 410, 414, 584, 659, 662, 690n3
Powell, Colin, 433
Prebisch, Raúl, dependency theory, 184–5, 269, 690n2
La Prensa, 36, 40, 42, 49, 54, 119, 120, 137, 159, 699n15; censorship of, 230; influence of literary section, 692n7; as propaganda organ, 280–1
Pressman, Edward, 232
PRI (Party of Revolutionary Institutions), 161, 233, 435, 448, 677
Primo de Rivera, José Antonio, 48
Pring-Mill, Robert, 351, 353, 566; in Solentiname, 51–2, 213, 681, 700n1
Prío Largaespada, Agustín (Captain Prío), 301–2, 328, 496, 498, 502, 504, 522, 698–9n15, 705n9
Proust, Marcel, 442, 671; *The Sweet Cheat Gone*, 672; *Within a Budding Grove*, 580
PSN (Nicaraguan Socialist Party), 177, 693n14, 694n16

Quechua language, 345
Queneau, Raymond, 513
Quiroga, Vasco de, 679–85

Radio Ya, 429, 442, 488, 705n7
Rama, 23, 229, 277, 633
Rama, Ángel, 342–4
Ramírez, Alejandro, 462
Ramírez, Carlos José, 462
Ramírez, Erick, death of, 465
Ramírez, Lisandro, 465, 481, 485, 506
Ramírez, Pedro, 118, 453, 481–6
Ramírez Guerrero, Dorel, 127
Ramírez Guerrero, María, 127, 131; political career, 133–4, 488, 511, 705n6, 705n7
Ramírez Guerrero, Sergio, 127, 131, 507–8, 510–11
Ramírez Mercado, Luisa, death of, 132, 453
Ramírez Mercado, Rogelio, 462, 507, 554, 694n19, death of, 132
Ramírez Mercado, Sergio, 3, 6, 7, 8, 564–6, 587, 603, 629, 681, 698n12, 701n5, 709n15, 710n17; *Adiós Muchachos: A Memoir of the Sandinista Revolution*, 135, 505–12, 536, 575, 645; *El alba de oro*, 264–73, 532; apprentice works, 137–8; *Las armas del futuro*, 131, 292–5; *Un baile de máscaras*, 134, 464, 476–88, 494; "Balcanes y volcanes," 128, 184–92, 245, 260, 288–9, 299, 313, 673; *Balcanes y volcanes y otros ensayos y trabajos*, 131, 293, 273–5; *Biografía Mariano Fiallos*, 126, 157–61, 189, 301; biography, 118–37; *To Bury Our Fathers*, 18–19, 128–9, 132, 145, 148, 181, 189, 192, 240–59, 261, 263, 265–6, 273, 275, 298, 301–2, 309, 314, 316, 322, 462, 482, 495, 497–8, 501, 518, 522, 527, 670, 672–3, 677, 685, 696n1, 696n3; *Castigo Divino*, 20, 132–3, 239, 255, 259, 263, 292, 295–335, 338, 401, 462, 482, 495, 498–9, 501, 502, 518, 522, 529, 555, 673, 675, 685, 692n4, 698n13, 698n14, 699n17, 699n19, 710n18; "Catalina y Catalina," 488–94; *Catalina y Catalina*, 135, 181, 512, 514–17; "Charles Atlas Also Dies," 19, 162–5, 510; *El cielo llora por mí*, 136, 488, 541, 634, 643–57, 661, 668, 709n8; *Clave de sol*, 133, 462–9, 476, 693n8; conclusions, 685–8; *Confesión de amor*, 133, 443, 445–62, 469, 470, 509, 534; *Cuentos*, 124, 138–43; *La edad presente es de lucha*, 131, 263–4, 273; *Flores oscuras*, 709n12; *La Fugitiva*, 136, 658, 669–78; *Hatful of Tigers*, 131, 283–93, 299, 706n13; how perceived, 17–18; "To Jackie with All Our Heart," 165–6, 239; joins FSLN, 239–40; *Lección inaugural del curso, 1969–1970*, 144–5; literary criticism on, 19–20; *La marca del Zorro*, 131, 338–9, 509, 529; *Margarita, How Beautiful the Sea*, 135, 139, 255, 301, 476, 478, 494–506, 512, 519, 521–2, 526–7, 540, 544–5, 643, 677, 704n4, 710n18; *Mentiras verdaderas*, 135, 492, 512–14, 538–40, 556, 642; *Nuevos Cuentos*, 126, 145–50; *Oficios compartidos*, 133, 469–76, 497, 545, 556; as organic intellectual, 15–17; *El pensamiento vivo de Sandino*, 127–8, 173–80, 191, 259, 632; post-1990 political career,

429–30, 436, 440, 615; in power, 225–6, 231, 235, 692n6; *La problemática del derecho constitucional nicaragüense*, 143; *El reino animal*, 136, 557–62, 634, 642; relationship with Daniel Ortega, 130–1, 133, 264, 450, 527, 537, 630, 706n11; resignation from FSLN, 429, 488; *Tiempo de fulgor*, 19, 126, 145, 150–7, 161–2, 170, 185, 192, 241, 310, 321, 482, 488, 669–70; *De Tropeles y tropelías*, 126, 166–72, 271, 558; *Seguimos de frente. Escritos sobre la revolución*, 131, 275–83, 290, 293, 299, 470, 509; *Señor de los tristes*, 136, 556–7, 643; *Sombras nada más*, 20, 135, 255, 476, 478, 506, 517–40, 542, 544, 547, 554–5, 560, 610, 645, 670, 677, 706n13; *Tambor olvidado*, 136, 541, 634–43, 646, 656–7, 708n4; *A Thousand Deaths Plus One*, 20, 136, 452, 476, 506, 538, 540–1, 544–58, 578, 634, 647, 674, 708n4; the Twelve, 41–2, 129; "Vallejo," 181–4, 514, 694n18; *El viejo arte de mentir*, 136, 538–43, 545, 556, 558, 692n1; visits Solentiname, 213, 215
Randall, Margaret, 15, 50, 179, 264, 565
Ratzinger, Josef. *See* Benedict XVI
Rausse, Andrea, 145
Reagan, Ronald, President 164, 380, 438, 446; and Contras, 228–9, 302–3; as Fascist, 293–5; piano duet with Octavio Paz, 290; propaganda of, 280, 306, 314, 434, 697n5, 698n12; violations of international law, 231–4, 268, 281
Restrepo, Laura, 57
Revista Conservadora, 49
Reyes, Alfonso, 297
Reynolds, Debbie, 678
Richards, Tim, 251
Rigby, Carlos, 390
Rincón, Carlos, 181, 281, 505
Rivas, 26, 33, 64, 391, 399
Rivas, Patricio, 26
Rivera, Brooklyn, 229
Rivera, Diego, 448
Rivera Quintero, Francisco, 131, 338–9, 509, 529
Rizo, José, 434
Roa, Raúl, 202–3, 212
Roa Bastos, Augusto, 242; *Son of Man*, 343
Robelo, Alfonso, 225, 228
Robinson, William I., 627–8, 631, 644, 664, 679
Robles, Alfonso, 122
Rockefeller, John D., 371
Rockefeller Foundation, 136
Rodó, José Enrique, 263, 282
Rodríguez, Ileana, 275, 303, 332–6, 338, 533
Román, José, 191
Romania, 212
Román y Reyes, Víctor, 35
Roosevelt, Franklin D., 244; support for dictators, 34, 159, 250, 591
Roosevelt, Theodore, 28
Ross, Peter, 306, 311
Roth, Brad, 232, 444
Rugama, Leonel, 53, 243, 254, 441, 507; in EC's poems, 364, 368–75, 378, 384, 389
Ruíz, Henry, 134, 161, 226, 426, 430, 442
Rulfo, Juan, influence on SRM's fiction, 150, 155–6, 192, 285, 482, 513, 693n9; *Pedro Páramo*, 155, 286

Rumsfeld, Donald, 433
Rushdie, Salman, 14, 131–2, 251–2, 262, 707n7; *The Jaguar Smile*, 687

Sacasa, Juan Bautista, 30, 33, 34, 299
Sagan, Carl, 408
Sàinz, Gustavo, 241
Salarrué (Salvador Salázar Arrué), 126, 187, 273–5
Salinas de Gortari, Carlos, 698n12
Salvador, Luis, 547, 554
Sanabría, Víctor Manuel, 675–6
San Carlos, attack on barracks, 41, 53, 219–20, 372, 573, 598; in SRM's fiction, 246
San Cristóbal de Las Casas, 10
Sand, George, 546
Sandburg, Carl, 61
Sandino, Augusto César, as Christ figure, 9, 53, 215; EC's sculpture of, 56, 238, 573; film images of, 44; and "indohispano" heritage, 638; influenced by Darío, 276; insurgency against US occupation, 29–33, 162, 244, 309, 359–60, 536, 589, 632; murder of, 34, 236, 330–1, 497, 617; origins of, 118; SRM and Fonseca's essays about, 172–80, 599; as symbol of national identity, 3, 66, 70, 93, 114, 205, 217, 237, 244, 270–1, 275, 312, 314, 362, 365, 385, 391, 400, 442, 448, 460, 469, 479, 493, 503, 512, 604, 632, 657, 673, 677, 693n13; in *Zero Hour*, 72–8
Sandino, Gregorio, 479
San Jacinto, Battle of, 26, 137, 449, 562, 621–2
San Juan del Norte, 25
San Martín, José de, 493
Santa Teresa, 421–2
Santo Domingo, 10
Saramago, José, 57
Sarandon, Susan, 380
Sardiñas, Guillermo, 209
Sarmiento, Domingo Faustino, 16, 297
Saudi Arabia, aid to Contras, 233
Saura, Carlos, 380
Schaeffer, Claudia, 242, 250
Schick, René, 38
Schiller, Johann, 502
School of the Americas, 36, 522
Schultz, George, 232
Schultze-Kraft, Peter, 547, 706n19
Schulz, Hermann, 128, 379
Secord, Richard V., 303
El Semanario, 132, 459, 473
Seminary of Christ the Priest, 50
Senghor, Léopold Sédar, 298
Shakespeare, William, 485, 513
Shakira (Shakira Mebarak Ripoll), 561–2
Shaw, Donald, 69
Shelton, Turner, 39, 40
Silva, Fernando, 191
Singlaub, John K., 303
Skármeta, Antonio, 181, 241, 297, 298, 306; *The Insurrection*, 304
Sklodowska, Elzbieta, 529
Solentiname, 56, 400, 415, 589; after 1990, 707n1; destruction of, 224; foundation, 51, 95, 117, 351–2, 407, 597–601, 682; influence, 144, 210–22, 292, 353, 374, 384, 392–3, 396, 563, 574, 589, 590, 594, 601, 623, 658, 661; workshops, 53–4, 268, 683
Solis, Javier, 521, 536
Solórzano, Carlos, 30
Sommer, Doris, 595
Somoza, Bernabé, 45, 587–9

Somoza Debayle, Anastasio, 3, 35, 36, 39, 40, 41, 42, 113, 123, 210, 217, 407, 440, 516, 534, 560, 587, 610, 645; assassination of, 228; brutality, 114, 197, 367, 439, 441; control of economy, 169, 291; flight, 44, 388; marriage of, 581; preference for English, 526
Somoza Debayle, Luis, 36, 83, 113, 119, 122, 585, 677; statue of, 375; and UNAN, 158
Somoza García, Anastasio, 45, 48–9, 62, 63, 70, 95, 119, 140, 145, 158, 405, 476, 478, 492, 514, 582, 587, 590; assassination of, 82–3, 100, 113, 135, 466, 496, 498, 499, 503, 505, 677; control of economy, 35, 38, 128, 155, 597; marriage of, 495, 498–500; murder of Sandino, 74–5, 79–80; origins of, 30, 33, 35, 118, 176, 405, 476, 478, 492, 514, 582, 587, 590, 696n4; repressive violence of, 34, 36, 170–1, 523, 536; seizure of presidency, 34, 301, 309, 311, 327, 481, 486; in SRM's fiction, 243, 495–505; as symbol of machismo, 148–9, 504–5
Somoza Portocarrero, Anastasio, 42
Sorensen, Diana, 154
South Africa, 298, 628
South Korea, 132, 520
Soviet Union, 5, 205–6, 614, 664; Fascism as a response to, 293–4; Latin American perceptions of, 451, 458, 530–1, 683; relations with FSLN, 231, 609
Soyinka, Wole, 404
Spain, 45, 110, 137, 160, 508, 579; colonialism, 21–4, 142, 185, 345, 640, 679; publishing industry, 519, 551; Spanish Civil War, 591
Spinoza, Baruch, 167
Stalin, Josef, 312, 314, 347, 403, 481
Stanford University, 127
Stendhal, 502, 539
Stengel, Casey, 516
Stimson, Henry L., 31, 32, 33
St Lucia, 91
Styron, William, 696n5
Suárez, Ignacio, 29
Sumu, 21–2, 229, 633
Swayze, Patrick, 232
Sweden, 609, 625
Switzerland, 48
Symons, Julian, 644

Taft, William Howard, 29, 446
Taleghani, Ayatollah Mahmoud, 612
Taylor, Elizabeth, 678
Taymor, Julie, 709n14
Téfel, Reynaldo Antonio, 49, 81, 691n5
Tejada, David, thrown into volcano, 217, 334, 363, 523
Téllez, Dora María, and capture of León, 390; as minister of health, 226, 388–9; post-1990 career, 430, 433, 437, 469, 488, 705n7; raid on National Palace, 43, 129
Terán, María Haydée, 172
Terceristas, 42, 53, 689–90n1; collaboration with private sector, 41, 43, 131; SRM's support of, 129
Teresa of Ávila, St, 566, 576
Teresa of Lisieux, St, 421
Testimonio writing, in EC's early work, 78–9, 111–12, 200–1; in EC's memoirs, 575–7, 602; in *Sombras nada más*, 527–31, 534–7, 539; SRM's responses to, 126, 129, 131, 239, 250–1, 258–9, 265, 328, 338–9, 509, 560; *Tata Vasco*, 679, 684, 686

Teufel, Johannes Jakob, 45, 49, 587
Thatcher, Margaret, 507
Thiago de Mello, Milton, 669
Thompson, J. Eric S., 350
Tiffer, América, 172, 177
Tijerino, Doris, 692n5
Time, 17, 129, 166, 437, 583–4
Tirado, Víctor, 41, 225
Tobago, 91
Tolstoy, Leo, 539
TP (Proletarian Tendency), 41
Torres, Camilo, 11, 50, 85, 213–14, 599, 623, 695m3
Torres, Daysi, 439
Torres Jiménez, Hugo, 43
Torrijos, Omar, 129, 507
Toscanelli, Paolo dal Pozzo, 97
Treece, David, 69, 387, 691n8
Trilling, Lionel, 47
Tristán, Flora, 544
Trollope, Anthony, 297
Trudeau, Pierre, 297
Trujillo, Rafael, 405, 468
Truman, Harry, as forerunner to Reagan, 293–5
Tünnermann Bernheim, Carlos, 125, 128
Turgenev, Ivan, 546, 547, 551

Ubico, Jorge, 161, 287, 313, 330
UCA (Central American University), 124, 221, 446, 692n2
Umanzor, Juan Pablo, 310
UNAM (National Autonomous University of Mexico), 47, 133, 595, 623, 685
UNAN (National Autonomous University of Nicaragua), 119, 120, 143–4, 522, 523, 645; course given by SRM, 286–92; Press, 126, 145, 177; SRM as student leader, 121, 124–5, 299, 301, 329, 692n2
UNAP (National Union for People's Action), 49, 581, 604, 691n5
Unión Nacional de Acción Popular. *See* National Union for People's Action
United Fruit Company, 67–8, 172, 248
United States, 1, 28, 57, 70, 290, 399, 459; economic influence, 159–60; EC's studies in 47–9, 81–2, 414, 576–85, 658, 663, 677; interventions and imperialism of, 1, 31–2, 35, 36, 42–4, 64, 76, 92, 147–8, 169, 173, 179–80, 189–93, 228–35, 243, 258–9, 263–6, 276–7, 279, 281–2, 293–5, 298, 301, 307, 309, 356–7, 360–1, 365–6, 375, 405–6, 446, 451, 457–9, 482, 591, 592, 593, 595, 606–7, 610–14, 631, 650–1, 659, 696n5; and transisthmian canal, 24–5, 29
USAID (United States Agency for International Development), 125
Université Laval, 124
University of British Columbia, 622–3
University of Kansas, 126
University of Maryland, 134, 511
Urbina, Nicasio, 503, 575, 579, 603
Uruguay, 274, 279, 456, 629
USAID (United States Agency for International Development), 190

Valdivieso, Antonio de, 112–14
Valenzuela, Luisa, 241, 249, 696n2
Valle-Castillo, Julio, 54, 55; as character in SRM's fiction, 304, 332
Vallejo, César, 181
Vance, Cyrus, 507
Vanderbilt, Cornelius, 25–7
Van Doren, Mark, 47

Vanegas, Alí, 308
Vargas, Chavela, 671, 676, 678, 709n14
Vargas Llosa, Álvaro, 527
Vargas Llosa, Mario, 53, 57–8, 132, 241, 248, 539, 543–4, 550; *Aunt Julia and the Scriptwriter*, 498, 542; *The Bad Girl*, 540; *Conversation in The Cathedral*, 241–3, 322, 497, 526; on EC, 14–15; *The Green House*, 241–2, 246–7, 504, 542; on SRM, 18; influence on SRM's fiction, 152–3, 241–2; in Nicaragua, 697n5, 702n10; presidential campaign, 16, 298; *The Real Life of Alejandro Mayta*, 14–15, 529, 542–3; *The Storyteller*, 498, 542, 544, 546; *The Time of the Hero*, 246, 286, 703–4n5; *La verdad de las mentiras*, 513; *The Way to Paradise*, 544
Vargas Vila, José María, 543, 546, 550, 554
Vasconcelos, José, 31–2, 607; *La raza cósmica*, 448
Vega-Bolaños, Andrés, 102
Veiravé, Alfredo, 70, 222
Velasco Alvarado, Juan, 53, 182–3, 601
Venezuela, 16, 51, 126, 219, 279, 464, 530; aid to Ortega, 435; Bolivarian Revolution, 628–31; Contadora Group, 232
Ventana, 8, 137, 180, 278; closure of, 429; foundation, 122–4, 692n7; generation associated with, 123, 151, 300, 308, 329, 442; under Murillo's editorship, 54, 55, 267, 470
Verdi, Giuseppe, 485
Verlaine, Paul, 405, 476
Vespucci, Amerigo, 679
Viardot, Louis, 547
Viardot-García, Pauline, 547
Vidal, Gore, 689n1
Vietnam, 41, 52, 206, 207, 357, 381, 417, 658, 664
Vilas, Carlos M., 123, 151
Villarrutia, Xavier, 596
Virgin of Guadelupe, 11
Vitier, Cintio, friendship with EC, 50, 52, 200, 204, 207, 212, 618, 679
Vogue, 91
Voltaire, 121, 145
Vuelta, 290

Walcott, Derek, 513
Walker, William, in EC poems, 63–5, 75; feature film about, 233; invasion of Nicaragua, 25–7; 45, 449, 469, 509, 523, 548–9, 551, 675, 701n5, 706–7n20
Warsaw Pact, 5, 609
Wellinga, Klaas, 296
Wells, H.G., 513
Welty, Eudora, 513
Wheelock Román, Jaime, 41, 175, 193, 264, 286, 289, 426, 632, 694n16; as minister of agriculture, 225–6
Whelan, Thomas E., 79
White, Steven, 70, 72, 74, 97, 191, 700n22
Whitman, Walt, influence on EC, 48, 61, 343, 357, 401, 584
Wilde, Oscar, 476
Williams, Raymond Leslie, 693n9
Williams, Tamara R., 96, 102
Williams, William Carlos, 48, 662
Williamson, Edwin, 10–11, 15, 160
Wolfe, Justin, 708n4, 708n5
Wolof, 636
Woodward, Ralph Lee, 698n11
Woolf, Virginia, 513

Yeltsin, Boris, 507
Yoruba, 404, 636
Yugoslavia, 130, 206

Zamora, Daisy, 54, resignation of, 55, 267
Zamora, Lois Parkinson, 248
Zapata, Emiliano, 493
Zelaya, José Santos, presidency of, 27–9, 143, 147, 151, 175, 475–6, 633, 637, 677
Zeledón, Benjamín, 29, 437
Zemurray, Sam, 68
Zimmerman, Marc, 44, 77, 386, 389
Zimmermann, Matilde, 175, 448